sociology

sociology

James Fulcher
and John Scott

OXFORD
UNIVERSITY PRESS

OXFORD

UNIVERSITY PRESS

Great Clarendon Street, Oxford OX2 6DP

Oxford University Press is a department of the University of Oxford.
It furthers the University's objective of excellence in research, scholarship,
and education by publishing worldwide in

Oxford New York

Athens Auckland Bangkok Bogotá Buenos Aires Calcutta
Cape Town Chennai Dar es Salaam Delhi Florence Hong Kong Istanbul
Karachi Kuala Lumpur Madrid Melbourne Mexico City Mumbai
Nairobi Paris São Paulo Singapore Taipei Tokyo Toronto Warsaw

and associated companies in Berlin Ibadan

Oxford is a registered trade mark of Oxford University Press
in the UK and in certain other countries

British Library Cataloguing in Publication Data

Data available

Library of Congress Cataloging in Publication Data

Fulcher, James.
Sociology / James Fulcher and John Scott.
Includes bibliographical references and index.
1. Sociology. I. Scott, John, 1949– . II. Title.
HM51.F885 1999 301—dc21 98-35146

ISBN 0-19-878102-4

10 9 8 7 6 5 4 3 2 1

Typeset by Best-set Typesetter Ltd., Hong Kong.
Printed on acid-free paper by
Book Print, F.L. Barcelona, Spain.

019293

Contents

Contents

Detailed Contents

3 Methods and Research   70

Part Two

4 Socialization, Self, and Identity   118

5 Deviant and Conformist Identities   150

6 Body, Health, and Population   188

8 Communication and the Media   272

9 Religion, Belief, and Meaning   316

---

10   Family and Household   352

---

11   City and Community   398

---

12   Nation and World   448

14 Inequality, Poverty, and Wealth   550

15 Stratification, Class, and Status   598

18 The State, Social Policy, and Welfare 724

Guide to the Book

A Different Textbook for a Different World

We have enjoyed writing this book, and we hope that you will enjoy reading it. Our aim has been to write a book which is comprehensive and interesting, but also easy to read and easy for you to find your way around. We have put in many **special features** to help you find your way through what is a complex subject, and we list some of these below.

We wanted to write a textbook that particularly reflects the society in which we (and you) live and the changes that are transforming that society. This textbook aims to give you a clear picture of these changes and the varying ways in which they have been interpreted by sociologists. You will find that we discuss many current and much-debated issues, such as transsexualism, drug culture, teleworking, media violence, single-parent families, new religious cults, and the effects of globalization. These issues are placed in the context of the social changes that are currently affecting the world.

Sociology is an interesting subject to study. It can also be quite a demanding subject. One of the things that makes it so interesting, exciting, and rewarding is its concern with many of the most fundamental issues of human life. This does mean that it raises large theoretical questions. We have, however, designed this book so that the discussion of theoretical questions is related to concrete matters and contemporary issues. We look at new theoretical ideas in relation to the work of the sociologists who are investigating changes in the real world, and we show how this work both extends and challenges the ideas of earlier sociologists.

We are keen to hear your ideas about the book. Visit our website on **www.oup.co.uk/best.textbooks/sociology** or e-mail us at **sociology@oup.co.uk** and let us know what you think of it.

Focus of the Book

This book, like most examination syllabuses and courses, is mainly concerned with contemporary British society. This is the society that most of you will be familiar with and we aim to broaden your understanding of the society in which you live. The information and evidence that we give, unless we say otherwise, relates to Britain.

It is important, however, to take a broader view of many issues, and you will find that we often discuss particular questions from a comparative or historical perspective. You will find, for example, that we make comparisons with the United States and Germany when we discuss recent changes in the British welfare state in Chapter 18. We refer to Japan when we examine changes in work organization and work relationships in Chapter 13. And we look at changes in the pattern of political power in Russia when we explore elite theories in Chapter 17. We also set our analysis of contemporary social change in the context of the longer-term development of society, as in our chapter on the family (Chapter 10), where we examine the historical development of relationships between husbands and wives, parents and children.

We have tried to show that it is no longer sensible to separate one society sharply from another. We live in a world where what happens in one society is often very closely related to what happens in another. Indeed, some would say that we now live in a 'global society', where the boundaries between countries no longer matter. The issues raised by globalization are discussed at many points in the book but we particularly address them in Chapter 12, where we examine such topics as the rise of transnational corporations, global tourism, the global population explosion, and world government.

THE STRUCTURE OF THE BOOK

Sociology is concerned with the study of whole societies and the ways in which their various parts are connected together, though most examination syllabuses and courses allow students to concentrate on certain areas of the subject and to give less attention to others. We recognize that it is unlikely that you will read the book from beginning to end and that you will want to focus on the topics that particularly interest you. However, no area of social life can really be understood in isolation from others. So, while this book is divided into chapters that focus on particular areas, we draw your attention to the many connections between different topics and ideas through cross-references and 'hint boxes' (see 'Special Features' below).

This book is divided into two parts:

Part One is concerned with the broad areas of **Theories and Methods**. Chapter 1 gives you a brief introduction to the nature of sociology, while Chapters 2 and 3 cover theoretical perspectives and research methods. These chapters provide a general discussion of many of the theories and methods that you will come across within the Part Two chapters on specific topics. You may find it useful to treat these Part One chapters as reference sources to turn to when you are looking at chapters in Part Two and wish to explore a theoretical question further or to consider the issues raised by the use of a particular method. You do not have to read the Part One chapters first and you should certainly not feel that you have to understand everything in Part One before you go on to Part Two.

Part Two deals with the various substantive topics that make up the sociological syllabus: family and household, the mass media, crime and deviance, health, stratification, and so on. Most syllabuses allow you to choose which of these topics to study, and the order in which you study them. In most cases, you will find that there is a whole chapter, or a part of a chapter, on each of the topics that you are studying. You will find that we do not have separate chapters on gender or ethnicity. This is partly because they are not usually treated as separate topics in examination syllabuses. It also reflects our belief that gender and ethnicity are dimensions that run through the whole of sociology. Few aspects of contemporary social life can be understood without reference to gender and ethnicity, and you will find that we refer to them throughout the book.

The Part Two chapters have a common structure. Each begins with an '**Understanding ...**' section, in which we review the principal theoretical debates and the main concepts that are relevant to the subject of the chapter. The later sections look in more detail at the studies and research carried out and how they relate to the theoretical debates. We look at **long-term tendencies**, often going back into the nineteenth century or earlier, but we concentrate in the later sections of each chapter on analysing **recent developments** and **contemporary issues**. We show how the fundamental social changes seen in Britain and elsewhere during the last few decades can be seen in a larger context.

SPECIAL FEATURES OF THE BOOK

The book contains many special features which should help you in your study:

▶ Boxes and Figures. The chapters contain a variety of boxes and figures, often with questions to stimulate your thinking or help you explore material and relate it to the text. Some boxes give you extra material and different viewpoints on matters considered in the main text. In other cases they draw out definitions of key concepts or summarize debates. We have listed as numbered 'Figures' the charts, diagrams, and tables that we refer you to in the text. Some readers may be a little worried by tables and charts, feeling that they are 'no good at maths'. You do not, however, need any particular mathematical skills to understand our various figures, though it is very important to develop the skill of extracting information from tables. To help you do this, we have written a section on 'Reading a table' in Chapter 3.

▶ Cross-referencing and Hint Boxes. To help you to understand the connections between the different parts of the subject, we have included a number of cross-references from one chapter or one section of a chapter to another. Where the cross-references are particularly important we have put them into hint boxes, which are indicated by a ☞ symbol. We often refer you to particular pages but occasionally we refer to whole sections or even chapters, when we simply want you to be aware of the general connections between two areas. We hope that you will follow up these cross-references and dip into chapters that cover topics that you are not studying in depth.

▶ Key Concepts. The key ideas of sociology are expressed in its concepts and it is very important that you understand their meaning and the ways in which sociologists have used them. We consider that formal definitions of concepts are not always very helpful and we have, therefore, discussed their meaning in the text instead of defining them separately in a glossary. We have, however, made it easy for you to find the place where they are discussed. The numbers in **orange** in the index indicate the page where you can find the main discussions of an important sociological concept. You can also easily identify the place on the page where it is discussed, for the concept is highlighted in **bold** in the main text or discussed in a separate box. You may sometimes find it useful to consult a good sociological dictionary, such as the Concise Oxford Dictionary of Sociology, as this will give you further background on particular concepts and ideas. You will also find that a good general dictionary, such as the Concise Oxford Dictionary of Current English (Ninth edition), comes in handy.

▶ Summary Points. At the end of each main section of a chapter, you will find a list of 'Summary points'. These are the key points only and are not a full summary of the chapter. They are intended to jog your memory about what we have covered, and they will be most useful if you have already read the section.

▶ Revision and Exercises. At the end of each chapter, you will find a 'Revision and Exercises' section. The exercises are not examination questions but are intended to help you to consolidate your work and think about the ideas and issues discussed in the chapter. These exercises have been organized around themes that cut across the sections in the chapter, in order to help you link up these sections and understand the connections between them.

▶ Further Reading and Bibliography. At the end of each chapter, you will also find a section on 'Further Reading'. This lists key books which will give further insight into the topics covered in each chapter and we have provided a brief description of the coverage and content of each of the books listed. Books are generally listed in order of their complexity, but they have also been grouped by their subject matter and how this relates to the content of the chapter. In the text itself, references to books and articles have been kept to a minimum, though you may not think this when you look at the length of the bibliography at the end of the book. We have tried to refer you to the key sources and the major studies used in our chapters but we do not refer you to every single study on which we have drawn. We hope, however, that you will use the bibliography to do some further reading and that you will treat it as a resource for future use.

part one

Part One of the book is concerned with matters of Theory
and Method in sociology. Chapter 1 gives a brief overview of
the nature of the subject, while the other chapters look at
this in more detail. Chapter 2 examines both the history of
sociological thought and the contemporary theoretical issues
that engage sociologists. Chapter 3 focuses on how to
assess critically the evidence used in sociological studies,
and it gives you some guidance on doing your own
sociological research.

These chapters raise issues that you will come across in
other parts of the book. Although they cover topics that are
important in their own right, you will also find it useful to
refer to them when you come across issues of theory and
method while studying particular areas in Part Two.

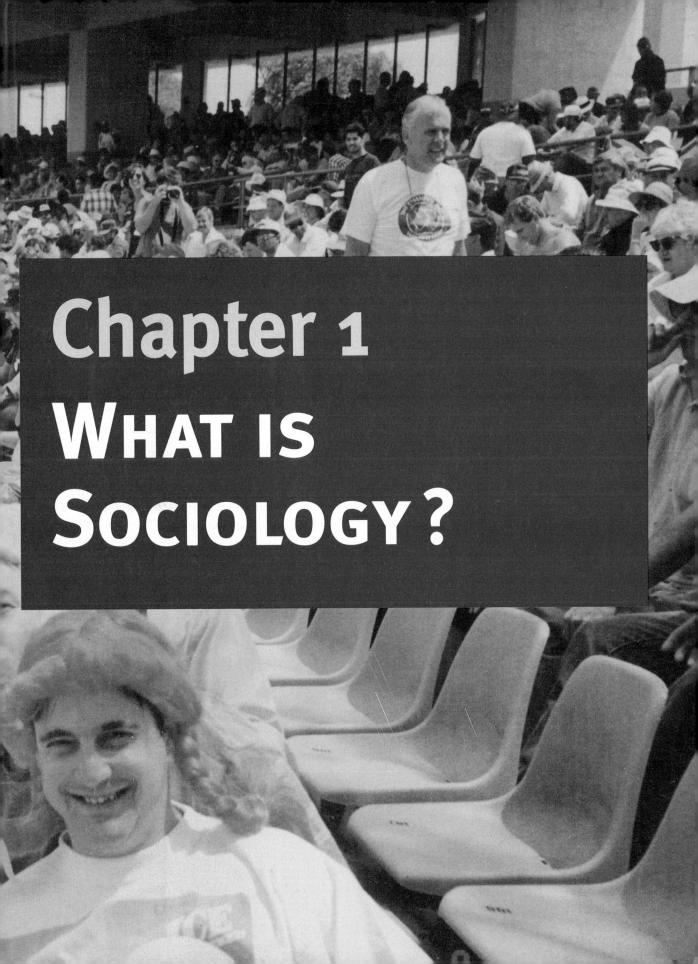

Chapter 1
WHAT IS SOCIOLOGY?

You get an ology, you're a scientist

BEATTIE. Hello Anthony, congratulations on your exam results.

ANTHONY. Grandma, I failed.

BEATTIE. You failed? What do you mean you failed?

ANTHONY. I mean I failed Maths, English, Physics, Geography, German, Woodwork, Art. I failed.

BEATTIE. You didn't pass anything?

ANTHONY. Pottery.

BEATTIE. Pottery, very useful Anthony, people will always need plates! Anything else?

ANTHONY. And Sociology.

BEATTIE. An ology. He gets an ology and he says he's failed. You get an ology, you're a scientist.

Source: from a BT television advert, repr. in Lipman and Phillips (1989).

SOCIOLOGY is the study of societies and the way that they shape people's behaviour, beliefs, and identity. Societies consist of the groups that people form, such as families, communities, classes, and nations. They also consist of institutions, which are the established ways of organizing the various activities, such as education, health care, politics, and religion, that make up social life. They also have shared beliefs, ideas, and customs, which sociologists refer to as their culture.

As this brief statement suggests, sociology is a wide-ranging subject dealing with all aspects of life. It operates at many different levels, from analysing the face-to-face interactions of daily life to examining the relationships between nation states. Though it is in practice mainly concerned with explaining and understanding the social life of contemporary societies, its subject matter in principle includes all societies that have ever existed. A proper understanding of contemporary societies anyway requires the sociologist to place them in historical context and examine the processes of social change that have created them and continue to transform them.

In this introductory chapter we take up a number of general issues relating to the subject as a whole. We begin by discussing why sociology should be studied and what you can get out of studying it. We then examine the relationship between individual and social behaviour, before considering in more detail what is meant by society. Lastly, we discuss whether sociology should be considered a science. One of the best ways to find out about sociology is, however, to plunge in and read about the sociology of any aspect of society that particularly interests you.

WHY STUDY SOCIOLOGY?

Probably the most important thing about sociology is that it enables us to make sense of the rapidly changing world that we live in. Some of the main changes that we have seen recently in Britain have been:

▶ an economic transformation, as old industries have declined and service occupations have rapidly expanded;

▶ the decentralization of cities as superstores, hospitals, hotels, and leisure complexes have moved from the centre to the edge of the city;

▶ changes in family life as more people have begun to live on their own, more women have found employment in paid work, and divorce rates have continued to rise;

▶ the transformation of work by information technology and the spread of more flexible and less secure forms of part-time and temporary work;

▶ advances in communications that make it possible to transfer large quantities of information and money instantly across the world;

▶ increasing inequality as more people have experienced poverty and exclusion, and the gap has widened between the rich and the poor.

You will find that we discuss all these changes and many others in this book. Each may seem to be quite distinctive in character, but they have many processes in common and are interconnected in various ways. It is sociology which has the concepts that enable us to grasp and comprehend these processes and the connections between them.

Sociology enables us to understand our place within this world. This is not just a matter of where we live, important as this is, but of where we are located within social structures. Sociologists use the term **social structure** to refer to any relatively stable pattern of relationships between people. Any group or organization, such as the family or the school, has a social structure. There are also the wider structures of class, gender, or ethnicity that stretch across a whole society. Some organizations, such as those of transnational corporations, cross national boundaries, and national societies themselves exist within a global structure of international relationships. By identifying such structures, sociology provides us with a map of society within which we can place ourselves and begin to understand the social forces that act upon us.

This view of sociology was put forward by C. Wright Mills in his well-known book *The Sociological Imagination* (1959). Mills distinguished between what he called *personal troubles* and *public issues*. He argued that people have many personal troubles—they may be unemployed, divorced, a victim of war or of crime. They tend to see these problems in individual terms and fail to realize that they are also public issues, because they are rooted in the institutional structures of the wider society. Thus, unemployment is a personal trouble for someone out of work but it is a public issue when large numbers of people are unemployed because of recession or structural changes in the economy.

According to Mills it was the capacity to link the personal to the structural which lay at the heart of the sociological imagination. As he put it: 'The sociological imagination enables its possessor to understand the larger historical scene in terms of its meaning for the inner life and the external career of a variety of individuals' (Mills 1959: 5).

Perhaps most fundamentally of all, sociology enables us to understand ourselves. The way that we think, behave, and feel, indeed our very sense of identity, is socially produced. People often speak of human nature as though deep within us there lies some reservoir of natural impulses that determine the way that we behave. There is, however, no such thing as human nature, for the way that we think, behave, and feel is shaped by what sociologists call the process of socialization. This provides us with language, gives us our values and beliefs, establishes our identity, and so turns us into members of society.

In creating a greater understanding of the way that society shapes people, sociology can also help them to liberate themselves. In his *Invitation to Sociology* (1963), Peter Berger argues that sociology can help people to take charge of their lives by making them aware of their situation in society and the forces acting upon them. Instead of seeing the way they live as natural or inevitable, they learn that it is socially constructed. By discovering the workings of society, they gain an understanding of how this process takes place.

People have, for example, often thought that patterns of behaviour are biologically determined when they are not. It is widely believed that the different roles performed by men and women are biologically prescribed. This can lead to the false idea that for biological reasons men cannot be, say, nurses or women cannot be, say, pilots. In Britain, beliefs of this sort became established in the nineteenth century as men sought to exclude women from many occupations and confine them to domestic and caring roles. Knowledge of the way this idea became established and the socializing processes that maintain it enable people to understand that gender role differences are socially constructed. This awareness makes it possible to challenge them and change them.

Most sociologists have been drawn to sociology because of its capacity to illuminate the workings of society and enable us to gain a better understanding of the world and our place within it. Sociology can be a purely intellectual exercise of this kind, but it can also serve practical purposes. Sociological knowledge has important applications in the world of work. This is not to say that it is a vocational subject, for it will not train you for a particular occupation. It is, none the less, highly relevant to a wide variety of occupations.

Sociology has made important contributions to the study of social problems and the work of those who seek to deal with them. Thus, sociologists have, for example, carried out research into drug use, crime, violence, industrial disputes, family problems, and mental illness. They have not, however, just been concerned with explaining why some people behave in ways that are considered problematic. They are also concerned

Are people puppets?

'We see the puppets dancing on their miniature stage, moving up and down as the strings pull them around, following the prescribed course of their various little parts. We learn to understand the logic of this theatre and we find ourselves in its motions. We locate ourselves in society and thus recognize our own position as we hang from its subtle strings. For a moment we see ourselves as puppets indeed. But then we grasp a decisive difference between the puppet theatre and our own drama. Unlike the puppets, we have the possibility of stopping in our movements, looking up and perceiving the machinery by which we have been moved. In this act lies the first step towards freedom.'

Source: Berger (1963: 199).

with the sources of such behaviour in, say, the patterns of family relationships, the structure of organizations, or the social distribution of resources. They are concerned, too, with the processes that lead to the treatment of certain actions as deviant behaviour. Why, for example, is the consumption of alcohol considered socially acceptable but the smoking of cannabis treated as a criminal act?

Sociology has also made a central contribution to the study of the management of people and the training of managers. One aspect of this is the development of structures that enable organizations to function productively and efficiently. This might seem a relatively straightforward matter but sociologists have shown that rationally designed organizations are commonly disrupted by internal conflicts and the unintended consequences of their rules and regulations. Sociologists have not, however, just been concerned with issues of organizational efficiency. They have also been concerned with the perspective of those facing increasing managerial control over their work and seeking to find ways of protecting and defending themselves against managerial interference and the degradation of work by technological change.

More generally, the collection, analysis, and interpretation of information about people is one of the central tasks of sociology. Information about people has become ever more important to a wide range of expanding occupations, such as those concerned with marketing, public relations, opinion formation, the media, education, research, and social policy.

Sociology can then enable you to understand and explain the world you live in and your situation in it. It

Challenging gender stereotypes

What careers do sociologists follow?

'The traditional occupation for sociology graduates has been social work or some other form of public sector welfare work, such as the probation service. However, in practice sociology graduates go into a much wider range of jobs. In industry, for instance, human resource management (or personnel as it used to be called) is one application close to welfare but, additionally, aspects of marketing draw upon sociological skills. Virtually all sociology courses include methods of social research and these can have an enlightening effect upon market research. Some of the large retail firms, from Laura Ashley through Marks and Spencer to Tesco, recognize that their chief concern is with people and consequently have taken sociology graduates into their management training schemes. In fact the range has tended to broaden in both the public and private sectors. For example, in recent returns graduate entry into the police force is a noticeable addition to the former and journalism to the latter. Many sociology graduates go into teaching. This embraces school teaching, further education, and the option to stay in higher education.'

Source: British Sociological Association (1997: 12).

Copies of this leaflet are available from BSA, Units 3F/G, Mountjoy Research Centre, Stockton Road, Durham DH1 3UR. The BSA homepage on the World Wide Web is: http://dspace.dial.pipex.com/britsoc/

can help you to understand any social situation in which you find yourself, and an understanding of what is going on is the first step to dealing successfully with any situation. Although it does not provide a training for any particular occupation, sociology is highly relevant to any occupation that deals with people, from management to social work or teaching, from health care to policing or the armed forces. It is, indeed, hard to think of any occupation that does not involve dealing with people in some way or other.

INDIVIDUAL AND SOCIAL BEHAVIOUR

We began by stating that sociologists study the way that society shapes people's behaviour, beliefs, and sense of identity. People have, however, a strong sense that they are individuals. They consider that they have their own reasons for doing things and see their thoughts and actions as those of an individual. They have a sense of free will, feel that they are responsible for their actions, and blame themselves, at least partly anyway, if things go wrong. When they do try to explain their actions, they tend to look for psychological explanations that see human behaviour as originating within the individual person.

This raises the general issue of the relationship between the individual and society, which has been much discussed in sociology. We first explore this question through Durkheim's study of the social factors that influence suicide. We then go on to discuss the process of socialization, which turns people into individual members of society.

THE SOCIOLOGICAL EXPLANATION OF SUICIDE

It was Émile Durkheim who first established sociology as a scientific discipline during the later years of the nineteenth century. In his study of *Suicide* (1897), he demonstrated that the taking of one's own life, apparently the most individual and personal of acts, was socially patterned. He showed that social forces existing outside the individual shaped the likelihood that a person would commit suicide. Suicide rates were therefore *social facts* (see our discussion of this concept in Chapter 2, pp. 35–7).

He demonstrated this by showing how suicide rates varied from one group to another and one social situation to another. Some of the main variations that he identified were as follows:

▶ *Religion*. Protestants were more likely to commit suicide than Catholics. The suicide rate was much higher in Protestant than Catholic countries. Similar differences could also be found between Protestant and Catholic areas within the same country.

▶ *Family relationships*. Those who were married were less likely to commit suicide than those who were single, widowed, or divorced. Whether people had children or not was also very important. Indeed, the suicide rate for married women was lower than that for single women only if they had children.

▶ *War and peace*. The suicide rate dropped in time of war, not only in victorious but also in defeated countries. Thus, Germany defeated France in the war of 1870 but the suicide rate fell in both countries.

▶ *Economic crisis*. Suicide rates rose at times of economic crisis. It might be expected that a recession that caused bankruptcies, unemployment, and increasing poverty would send up the suicide rate. Suicide rates also rose, however, when economies boomed. It was not worsening economic conditions but sudden *changes* in them that caused suicide rates to rise.

This demonstration of systematic variations in the suicide rate showed that suicide cannot be explained solely in terms of the psychology of the individual. Even the taking of one's own life is social behaviour and therefore requires sociological explanation. In order to provide an explanation, Durkheim put forward a sociological theory of suicide that would account for these variations.

> ☞ Sociology is not only concerned with the collection of information about social behaviour. It is also concerned with its explanation, which always involves theory. Indeed, as we shall see on pp. 15–16, science in general involves both theory and observation.

Durkheim's theory of suicide was based on the idea that it was the degree of social solidarity that explained variations in suicide rates. By **social solidarity** he meant the bonds that hold individuals together in society. If these bonds were too loose, a person was weakly connected to society and more likely to commit suicide. But if these bonds were too tight, this too could lead to a higher suicide rate, for people in this situation could lose their sense of self-preservation.

His theory went further than this, however, for he distinguished between two kinds of social bonds, those of *integration* and *regulation*. Integration refers to the strength of the individual's attachment to social groups. Regulation refers to the control of individual desires and aspirations by norms, which are rules of behaviour (see p. 40).

This distinction led him to identify four types of suicide, which corresponded to low and high states of integration and regulation:

▶ egoistic suicide;

▶ anomic suicide;

▶ altruistic suicide;

▶ fatalistic suicide.

Egoistic suicide. This resulted from the weak integration of the individual. The higher suicide rate of Protestants was one example of it. Protestantism was a less integrative religion than Catholicism, for it placed less emphasis on collective rituals and emphasized the individual's direct relationship with god. Those who were single or widowed or childless were also weakly integrated and therefore more prone to suicide. War, on the other hand, tended to integrate people into society and therefore reduced the suicide rate. This form of suicide was called egoistic because low integration led to the isolation of the individual, who became excessively focused on the self or ego.

Anomic suicide. This resulted from a lack of regulation. Durkheim believed that people would only be content if their needs and passions were regulated and controlled, for this would keep their desires and their circumstances in balance with each other. Changes in their situation, such as those brought about by economic change or divorce, could upset this balance. The normal regulation of a person's life then broke down and they found themselves in a state of *anomie*, which essentially means normlessness—that is, lacking regulation by norms.

Altruistic suicide. This was the opposite of egoistic suicide. In this case, it was not that social bonds were too weak but rather that they were too strong. People set little value on themselves as individuals or obediently sacrificed themselves to the requirements of the group. Durkheim saw this form of suicide as characteristic of primitive societies, though it was also found

Durkheim's types of suicide	Type	Degree of solidarity	Social situation	Psychological state	Examples
	Egoistic	Low	Lack of integration	Apathy, depression	Suicides of Protestants and single people
	Anomic	Low	Lack of regulation	Irritation, frustration	Suicides during economic crisis or after divorce
	Altruistic	High	Excessive integration	Energy and passion	Suicides in primitive societies; military suicides
	Fatalistic	High	Excessive regulation	Acceptance and resignation	The suicide of slaves

amongst the military, where it still existed as a kind of survival from earlier times. He used the term altruistic to convey the idea that the individual self is totally subordinated to others.

Fatalistic suicide. This was the opposite of anomic suicide and resulted from an excessively high regulation that oppressed the individual. Durkheim gives as an example the suicide of slaves, but he considered this type to be of little contemporary significance and discussed it in a footnote only.

Durkheim recognized that egoism and anomie were often found together, as, for example, when divorce occurred. This both isolated people and left their lives in an unregulated state. He was, however, careful to distinguish not only between the social processes involved in egoism and anomie but also between the states of mind which each produced. One of the notable features of Durkheim's theory of suicide, and one that is often overlooked, is that he does show the consequences of social situation for the individual's psychological state. He demonstrated not only that the behaviour of the individual was social but also that the individual's internal world of feelings and mental states was socially produced.

Thus, he argued that the social isolation characteristic of *egoistic suicide* resulted in apathy or depression. *Anomic* suicide was associated with a much more restless condition of irritation, disappointment, or frustration. When lack of regulation meant that desires or ambitions got out of control, people became upset and frustrated by their inability to achieve them. *Altruistic* suicide was generally accompanied by an energy and passion quite opposite to the apathy of egoism. Durkheim did not discuss the psychological state characteristic of *fatalistic* suicide but it would seem to involve a mood of acceptance and resignation.

Since Durkheim, the study of suicide has moved on and later sociologists have pointed out problems with the methods that he used. The main problem was that the suicide rates on which he based his study were calculated from official statistics. These depended on coroners' decisions on the classification of deaths as suicides and it has been shown that their practices vary (Douglas 1967; J. M. Atkinson 1978). For a death to be suicide, it must be intentional, and the assessment of intention is difficult, particularly if no suicide note is left. This leaves a lot of room for interpretation and considerable scope for others, such as friends and relatives of the dead person, to influence coroners' decisions. The existence of social variations in suicide rates cannot, however, be denied, and Durkheim's fundamental point, that the apparently most individual of acts requires sociological explanation, stands.

 We discuss general problems with the use of official statistics in Chapter 3, pp. 107–11.

SOCIALIZATION

Sociologists reject the idea that human behaviour can be explained *solely* in terms of individual actions or personal choice or free will. Everything that people do is based on ways of thinking and acting that they have learned as they have grown up. This learning occurs through what sociologists call socialization, and we examine this important process in detail in Chapter 4, pp. 120–47.

Sociologists do not, however, argue that behaviour is *determined* by the process of socialization. People think about what they do and have reasons for their actions. They may be strongly influenced to act in a certain way in a particular situation but, after thinking about it, they may resist this influence and act differently. We know that people are creative and inventive and are able to think of things that no one has ever thought of before. There is something unique about individuals which is expressed in their thoughts and actions. In which case, you may say, how can it be argued that they are socialized into particular ways of thinking and acting?

This issue can best be approached by considering the example of language. People are not born with a knowledge of language. It has to be learned through socialization. It is acquired through family life, through the interaction between children, through education, through the media. While the early stages of socialization are crucial in the learning of language, it never really stops. Indeed, languages are themselves dynamic, for new words and new ways of using existing words are constantly coming into a language.

Language shapes the way that people think, feel, and act. When people become cross about the way that others are behaving and say that they are not acting in a democratic or civilized or adult or male way, they can only have this thought because they have grown up in a society where a word exists to express it, which they have learned through the process of socialization. Societies vary in the range of words that they have and therefore the range of ideas that can be expressed.

Language acquisition is not just a matter of the society that one is born into. It is a selective process, for no one in a society knows all its words or all the different ways of using them. The particular words and usages that we acquire reflect the social context of socialization. It has, for example, been demonstrated that language use is linked to class background, and we discuss this in connection with education in Chapter 7, pp. 233–5. The way that people use language and the way that they think does then depend on both the society they have grown up in and their position in that society.

But while language enables people to think in a certain way, it does not determine what they think or how they use words. Indeed, people combine words to express their thoughts and feelings in individual ways that are quite unique to them. The ultimate example of this is poetry, which involves the creative use of language to express an intensely personal experience or feeling. This is not just special to poetry, however, for the creative use of language is part of everyday life as people comment on, reflect upon, and think about their experiences. The words used in this paragraph are common words that everyone who speaks English knows, but even this paragraph is unique and has never been written before.

The remarkable thing about this is that, while the use of language is quite unique to the person and situation, it is also understood by other people. When we open a book of poems or listen to a song, we can ourselves experience at second hand the experience expressed in the original work, because we possess a shared language through a common process of socialization.

Thus, socialization provides people with a language which enables them to think and communicate in certain ways. The importance of socialization processes in doing this is undeniable and fundamental. Socialization does not, however, determine the way that people think or speak or write, for it is perfectly consistent with the uniqueness and creativity of individuals.

WHAT IS SOCIETY?

Socialization turns the individual into a member of society but what do we mean by **society**? We discussed this briefly at the beginning of the chapter, but it is not really possible to give a short definition of something as complex as a society. The easiest way to get a sense of what society means is to examine its main aspects in turn. These are also the main lines of enquiry along which sociology has developed.

A COMPLEX OF INSTITUTIONS

Institutions are the established practices that regulate the various activities that make up social life. Examples of institutions are marriages, markets, school examinations, religious rituals, and laws. As societies developed, institutions became increasingly specialized and organized. In contemporary societies there are, for example, specialized institutions and their associated organizations concerned with the educational, economic, political, military, and religious activities of society. Indeed, the term institution is often used for the organizations themselves, as when schools or universities are described as educational institutions.

We speak of a complex of institutions because of their interrelationships. Let us, for example, consider educational institutions and their organizations. In Britain, public-sector schools, colleges, and universities

are dependent on political institutions for their funding. It is ultimately the government that decides how much money to distribute to them. Governments are themselves dependent on the economy. The amount of money that the government has to spend on education depends on how much it can raise in taxes. While this is partly a political question, it also depends on the state of the economy. This itself depends, however, on education, for it is education that supplies the economy with skilled labour. This has been an important issue in Britain since the 1970s, for it has been argued that education has not been giving people the skills that the economy needs, an issue that we take up in Chapter 7, pp. 257–60.

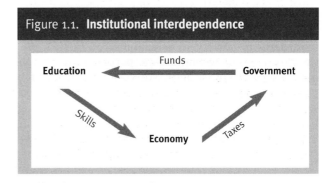

Figure 1.1. **Institutional interdependence**

These interrelationships mean that institutions should not be studied in isolation from each other. Sociologists cannot, of course, study everything simultaneously and they tend to specialize in the study of particular areas, such as the family or religion or the media. This book is divided into chapters that specialize in distinct areas of this sort. To achieve a complete understanding of what is going on in any one of these areas, you must always, however, bear in mind its links with others. In this book we have indicated what we see as the more important links through cross-references and hints.

It is one of the distinctive features of sociology that it is concerned with whole societies. It is, therefore, concerned with the complete set of institutions in a society. It is, indeed, the only subject that sees societies as 'wholes' in this way. This distinctive perspective means that sociology overlaps with many other fields of specialized enquiry. Economics and politics, for example, are subjects in their own right, which explore in detail the workings of the areas concerned and the issues

Education and politics

specific to them. Economic and political institutions are, however, crucial to the functioning of any society and there is also, therefore, a Sociology of Economic Life and a Sociology of Politics. These particularly address the relationships between these areas and the wider society.

Sociology's concern with whole societies and all activities that occur within them means that any aspect of social life can become a field within sociology. Indeed, one of the exciting and dynamic things about sociology is the way that new specialities are constantly opening up within it as sociologists begin to explore new areas of activity that have not been studied before or have newly emerged through social change. Examples of new fields are the Sociology of Fashion, the Sociology of Sport, the Sociology of Tourism, and the Sociology of the Body.

LEVELS OF SOCIETY

In discussing society as a complex of institutions we have been operating at one particular level, the national level, of society. We have discussed, for example, the relationship between British educational institutions, the economy, and the state. People do commonly see themselves as members of national societies. If someone asks you which society you live in, you will probably reply that you live in, say, British or American or Indian society. If you live in Britain, you might of course prefer to say that you live in Scottish or Welsh society, for nationality is a contentious matter, which we discuss in Chapter 12, pp. 451–3. The point that we are making, here, however, is that the national level is one level of society but only one level.

Most people live in family or household units consisting of a small number of closely related people. They have a sense of obligation to each other which is greater than that to those outside the group, and they see themselves as members of a family. They often speak of themselves as living 'in a family'. In thinly populated rural areas where people practise a self-sufficient form of agriculture one family may have very little contact with another and society may consist almost entirely of other members of the immediate family group. This is a rare situation, however, particularly nowadays, and the vast majority of people are involved on a daily basis with much larger social units.

One such unit is the community. Two centuries or so

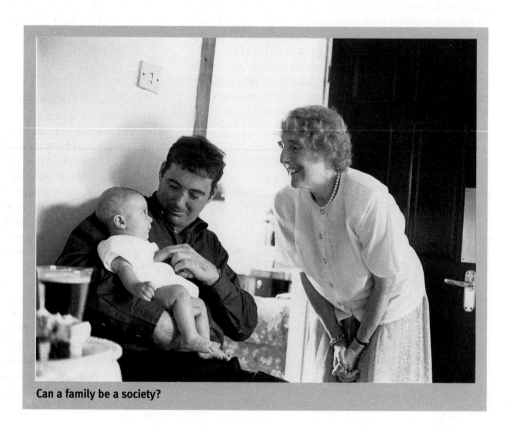

Can a family be a society?

ago most people lived in small, relatively self-sufficient and self-contained communities based on the rural village or the small town, where everyone knew everyone else. Industrialization and urbanization disrupted communities of this sort and brought large numbers of people who did not know each other together. As we show in Chapter 11, pp. 414–16, communities have, however, established themselves within cities. Many people still feel that they are members of a community of one kind or another.

Whether or not people feel that they are members of a community, they are members of a larger social unit, the nation state, which during the nineteenth and twentieth centuries has become steadily more important in people's lives. With the development of the nation state, national institutions emerged. At its centre is the state apparatus itself, but there are also national educational systems, national economic institutions, national health services, national armies, and national churches, to name some of the more obvious examples. People became members of a nation state, with the rights and responsibilities of citizens of that state and a sense of national identity. We examine the development of nations and nation states in Chapter 12, pp. 459–61.

Although people tend to see themselves as members of independent national societies, national units are not self-sufficient. They are interlinked with each other and dependent on each other in complex ways. These links developed particularly strongly with industrialization, which made national economies highly dependent on one another through an international division of labour. The industrial societies specialized in producing manufactured goods for the world as a whole, while other parts of the world specialized in producing food for the workers and raw materials for the factories of the industrial societies.

National societies have become ever more integrated with each other through a process known as globalization, which we also discuss in Chapter 12, pp. 456–9. The world—the globe—has become a 'smaller' place. Improvements in communication mean that one can travel to most places in the world within a day or so, while information can be transmitted instantly to any part of it. Nowadays many companies are global corporations operating in large numbers of countries on every continent. There are also global political organizations, such as the United Nations, and global movements such as Greenpeace. As well as being members of national societies, people are also members of a global society. Indeed, the term 'the global village' is sometimes used to express the idea that people have become closely linked with each other across the globe.

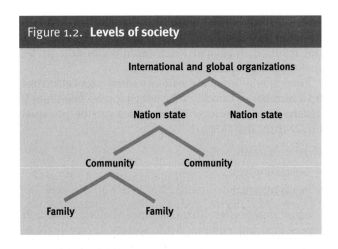

Figure 1.2. **Levels of society**

As society has developed, social units have become steadily larger in their scale. Communities became part of national societies and national societies have become part of a global society. At one time or another it has been argued that the family, the community, and the nation have all been in decline as social units have become larger. Smaller-scale units have, however, not so much disappeared as changed, as society has become multi-level in character. There are many important issues here for sociologists as they examine the relationships between the overlapping units that make up society.

INEQUALITY AND DOMINATION

In our discussion of society as a complex of institutions, we emphasized the way in which each organized a particular activity for society as a whole. Societies are also, however, divided by inequality. Some groups benefit more from these activities than others and seek to maintain or increase their advantages. Structures of inequality and domination stretch right across societies, as, for example, a particular group tries to gain control of all areas of activity and secure benefits in all aspects of life. We address the issues raised by inequality in particular in Chapters 14 and 15, but you will find them cropping up throughout the book.

There are various dimensions of inequality within national societies. There are class inequalities between, say, aristocracies and commoners or employers and workers. There are ethnic inequalities between, say, whites, Asians, and African-Caribbeans. There are gender inequalities between men and women. In some societies, religion or nationality have become major lines of division. There are also inequalities between national societies, for increasing global integration has not resulted in greater international equality, as we show in Chapter 12, p. 473.

The study of inequality and its consequences brings up a number of important issues that have been much discussed in sociology. These issues can be grouped under three headings:

▶ social stratification;

▶ social control;

▶ social conflict.

Social stratification. This examines the way in which layers, or strata, emerge within society. Typically there is a top layer of the rich and powerful, a bottom layer of the poor and powerless, and various other layers in between. Important questions that are raised are the number of layers that exist in a society, where the boundaries between them should be drawn, the ease with which people can move between them (social mobility), and the way in which the layers persist and change from one generation to the next.

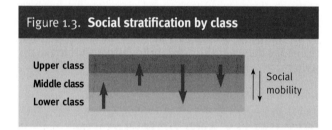

Figure 1.3. **Social stratification by class**

Social control. This raises the question of how inequality is maintained. How does the 'top layer' control those below it and maintain its various advantages? One way is through control of the use of force—that is, control of the military and police forces of a society. Sociologists generally emphasize, however, that there are various more subtle means of control that operate by influencing the way that people think. Thus, it has been argued, for example, that people are controlled through education, religion, the mass media, or social policy, and we discuss these arguments in the chapters on these areas.

Social conflict. Here the issue is whether and under what conditions inequality generates conflict. Do the mechanisms of social control break down? Do those in the lower layers organize themselves to improve their situation and challenge the domination of society by those with wealth and power? Under what conditions, for example, can workers organize themselves collect-

ively to demand higher wages and challenge the power of the employer? Under what conditions do women organize themselves through feminist movements to challenge male domination?

The study of inequality is linked to the study of institutions and their interrelationships, for the rich and powerful largely maintain their wealth and power by controlling the institutions of society. Similarly, those who challenge their position have to contest their control of these institutions. Thus, the study of this aspect of society is closely related to the issues we raised in our discussion of institutions.

STRUCTURE AND CULTURE

Sociologists distinguish between the *social structure* of a society and its *culture*. As we explained earlier (see p. 5), by social structure they mean a relatively stable pattern of relationships between social groups or organizations. By **culture** sociologists mean the beliefs of the society and their symbolic representation through its creative activities. A symbol is simply a representation, such as a word or a gesture or a painting, which communicates an idea or feeling. Culture can best be discussed by distinguishing between beliefs, which are the content of the culture, and creative activities, which express this content in actions or objects.

Beliefs are concerned with both ideas about the way things *are* and ideas about how they *ought* to be. Ideas about how things are include beliefs about the nature of things—the physical world, human nature, and the character of society. Ideas about how things ought to be are embodied in values and norms:

▶ **Values** establish what is considered to be good or bad, what is desirable or undesirable. Thus, the belief that people should accumulate wealth or the belief that they should live in harmony with the natural environment are both values, though rather different ones.

▶ **Norms** are rules of behaviour that regulate how people achieve the things they value. A typical norm, for example, is the rule that people should not accumulate wealth by stealing from each other. Such norms are often embodied in laws.

These different kinds of belief are commonly linked together by religion and politics. Thus, Christianity contains ideas about God's creation of the world and the belief that human beings are naturally sinful. Christianity also emphasizes certain values, such as love and charity, and provides a set of norms, such as the prohibition of sexual behaviour outside marriage. Political beliefs, such as socialism or liberalism, similarly link together ideas about the nature of society and ideas about what a society should be like. Thus, socialists have seen society as made up of classes in conflict with each other and seek to bring about a classless society. Liberals, on the other hand, have argued that society consists of individuals and seek to maximize freedom of choice.

Culture also takes the form of creative activities that express ideas and feelings. The term culture is often used to refer to the *high* culture of a society, its collections of paintings, its opera houses, and great works of literature. But there is also its *popular* culture, and this has become an area of growing interest in sociology, which we discuss in Chapter 8, pp. 279–80. Cinema, popular music, magazines, and soap operas are part of our culture in this sense. Activities as various as gardening, craftwork, dressing, cooking, and talking are all creative activities that can be considered part of popular culture.

Indeed, the term culture is often used in a very broad way to refer to the general customs and way of life of a society or a group within it, as in references to working-class culture or Asian culture. Culture in this sense includes the way that people meet and greet each other, the way they behave towards each other at work and at leisure, their sporting and religious activities, and so on. All social activity has a cultural aspect, for all social actions express people's ideas and feelings, and therefore communicate their culture.

The question then arises of the relationship between structure and culture, an issue that has been much discussed in sociology. One example of this is the relationship between structures of inequality and culture. As we pointed out above, one way in which those at the top of society dominate those at the bottom is through their control of education, religion, and the mass media. This enables them to influence people's beliefs and shape the way that they think and behave. Culture can, therefore, reinforce the existing structure of society, though subordinate groups can also challenge this structure by developing alternative ideas and beliefs, as shown, for example, by the growth of oppositional socialist and feminist cultures.

IS SOCIOLOGY A SCIENCE?

In the previous section we discussed what sociologists mean by society. Here we take up issues raised by the way in which they study it. The question of whether sociology should be considered a science has been hotly debated both inside and outside the subject. It is an interesting and important question that enables us to explore the nature of the subject, its distinctiveness, and its relationships with other subjects. Before discussing it, we must, however, first consider what is meant by science.

WHAT IS A SCIENCE?

It is first very important to clear away certain misconceptions about science. It is popularly associated with two things, the use of the experimental method and the collection of facts. Some scientists certainly do carry out experiments and collect facts but science involves considerably more than this.

The experiment is an important and powerful method but not the only one used by science. It is a powerful method because it enables the isolation and measurement of the effect of one variable. Thus, for example, the effect of an antibiotic can be established by preparing two identical dishes of bacteria, adding the antibiotic to one only, and then comparing the results after a suitable period of time. There are, however, various fields of investigation, commonly regarded as sciences, that cannot make much use of the experimental method. Astronomy, geology, and meteorology are obvious examples. They have to rely largely on other kinds of observational method for the collection of data. Important as the laboratory experiment undoubtedly is to the natural sciences, the use of this method is not a defining characteristic of science.

If experimental methods are not the only method used by scientists, surely, you might say, there can be no doubt that sciences are concerned with the collection of facts by one means or another. The first problem this raises is that facts are not simply collected. Scientists do not just look around to see what facts they can discover, for scientific enquiry is directed by the theoretical concerns of scientists. Scientific ideas lie behind the design of experiments or the search for data of a particular kind. Astronomers are, for example, discovering the 'dark matter' of the universe because the currently dominant theory of its origins suggests that there must be far more matter in the universe than can be accounted for by its visible material.

Secondly, the conventional idea of a fact is of something existing 'out there' waiting to be discovered. What actually happens is that scientists make observations, which then have to be interpreted and made sense of *before* they can become facts. Interpretation always involves explanatory ideas and this returns us again to the importance of theories. The existence of 'black holes' is now an accepted fact in astronomy. This fact is certainly based on observations of the behaviour of stars but it depends also upon a theory of what happens when matter becomes so highly concentrated that nothing can escape its gravitational pull. Without this theory, we could not have the idea of a black hole and therefore could not be aware of their existence.

Science is both an *empirical* and a *theoretical* enterprise. In saying that it is empirical we mean that it is based on observations. The word *empirical* is derived from the Greek word for experience and is commonly used to refer to observational work which provides us with experience of the world. In saying that science is theoretical we mean that it also involves systematic thought about the world. A *theory* is a logically connected set of ideas. Theories guide empirical work and are used to interpret and explain its observations, which may or may not fit the existing theory. If they do not fit it, the theory needs at least to be revised and may have to be abandoned. Science advances through the constant interplay of theoretical and empirical work.

While it is important to be clear about the logic of scientific activity, it is also important to bear in mind the scientific spirit. By this we mean the set of ideals which motivate and guide scientific work. Science is both *rational* and *critical*. It is rational in that it rejects explanations of the world that are based on religious beliefs or mysterious forces, rather than reasoned thought. It is critical, since it questions received ideas and accepted beliefs. It is concerned with establishing the truth about how the world is and how things actually work, rather than how they ought to be or how they are supposed to be.

This does not mean that scientists lack values and beliefs. Like anyone else, they hold values and beliefs, which may well influence what they do. For example, scientists concerned about the state of the natural environment might well carry out research into global warming. Values and beliefs should not, however, influence the scientist's investigation or interpretation of observations. Thus, however concerned such a scientist might be about pollution, if the observations did

When science goes wrong

'Just how far scientists will go to back up their preconceptions was recently revealed by an astonishing study of doctors working on drugs trials. The time-honoured method of testing a new drug is the so-called "double-blind" experiment, where patients are randomly and secretly selected to receive either the new wonder-drug, the old drug, or a placebo.* This method is designed to stop doctors giving the wonder-drug only to patients who are most likely to benefit, and to protect patients from giving up the fight because they know they have been given a sugar pill.

'So much for the theory. The practice, according to Dr Kenneth Schulz of the Centre for Disease Control and Prevention in Atlanta, Georgia, is quite different. In confidential interviews with 400 medical researchers over eight years, Schulz found that more than half had made efforts to subvert the clinical trial.

'Doctors admitted to rifling through desks in search of the secret lists of patients, sometimes using James Bond-style spying techniques to read the contents of sealed envelopes and break codes. This allowed them to interfere with the allocation of the patients, with dramatic consequences for the apparent efficacy of the drug.'

Source: Robert Matthews, 'Doctoring the Evidence', *Sunday Telegraph*, 23 Nov. 1997.

* A *placebo* is a substance that looks exactly the same as a drug but has no medical properties.

not support the theory of global warming, the scientist would be expected to say so.

We have in some ways presented an idealized picture of science. Most scientific enquiry is driven by the requirements of industry or government rather than the pursuit of knowledge. Scientists sometimes suppress results which do not fit their theories or which might damage their careers, because they conflict with their employer's interest in a particular policy or product. Research results are faked by some researchers who are more concerned to achieve publications and advance their careers than advance knowledge. At the heart of science there is, none the less, an ideal of disinterested enquiry into the nature of things and it is against this ideal that the work of scientists is judged.

IS SOCIOLOGY A NATURAL SCIENCE?

The first sciences to develop were the natural sciences and they therefore became the model for scientific activity. Some sociologists adopted this model and tried to develop a natural science of human behaviour. Most contemporary sociologists would, however, argue that society cannot be studied in the way that the natural world is studied. Social behaviour is in important respects quite different from natural behaviour.

Human behaviour is meaningful behaviour, for whatever human beings do means something to them. It is a characteristic of human beings that they act in the context of beliefs and purposes that give their actions meaning and shape the way that they behave. If sociologists are to understand and explain human behaviour, they have to take account of the meanings that people give to their actions. This makes the analysis of human behaviour quite different from the analysis of animal behaviour, for, in order to explain human behaviour, sociologists have to understand what it means. They cannot just observe human behaviour but have to 'get inside the heads' of those whose behaviour they are studying.

 Weber particularly emphasized the importance to sociological explanation of understanding the meaning of human action. See Chapter 2, pp. 40–2.

No universal statements can be made about human behaviour, for the same behaviour means different things in different societies. Let us take eating practices as a simple example. The eating of roast beef has been traditional in England and regarded as one of the distinctive features of English life. In India, however, cows are considered sacred and may not be killed, let alone eaten. On the other hand, while the eating of dogs in the Far East is commonplace, it is quite abhorrent to most British people. Behaviour considered quite normal in one society is quite unacceptable in another. This means that no general statements can be made about human eating behaviour in the way that they can about the eating behaviour of animals.

Human behaviour is also different because people think about what they are doing. They are at least partly aware of the forces acting upon them and can resist these forces and act differently. Thus, while the eating of snails and frogs' legs is not a normal feature of the British diet and is generally viewed in Britain with some disgust, some British people may consider that there is no good reason for rejecting these foods. They may decide that it must be possible to enjoy them, if the French eat them with relish, and may then try them out. Similarly vegetarians may reject traditional British eating practices. Behaviour is not entirely culture bound because individuals can break out from their culture and, indeed, change their culture.

None the less, it clearly remains the case that there are broad differences of culture between, say, British people and French people that result in different eating habits. Furthermore, those who do break away from established patterns will themselves be distinctive in certain ways. They may, for example, be educated to a higher level. Thus, we are not arguing that what people do is a matter simply of choice but rather that the patterning of social behaviour is much more complex than the patterning of natural behaviour.

IS SOCIOLOGY A SCIENCE AT ALL?

Given these differences between nature and society, can there be a science of society? Are the sociologist's explanations of behaviour any different from those given by the ordinary person in the street? Is sociology in the end any different from common sense?

The answer to all these questions is a resounding yes.

In their everyday lives people are too involved in what is going on around them to have any detachment from it. They are immersed in their own situations, their own families, their own work relationships, and their own friendship and leisure patterns. These colour their view of the world. Their knowledge of the world is limited to the situations that they have experienced. They generally interpret their own and other people's behaviour in terms of preconceived ideas and beliefs. In doing so they make little distinction between the way the world is and the way they think it ought to be. Their experience is fitted into these ideas and beliefs, which are important to their sense of identity, and they are therefore usually very reluctant to alter them.

The sociologist's knowledge of the world is very different. Sociology builds up a knowledge of society which is not based upon the experience of one individual but accumulated from the research of large numbers of sociologists. This is knowledge of many different aspects of many different societies at many different times. It is a cumulative knowledge which is constantly being added to by further research. This bank of knowledge means that the experience of large numbers of people in many very different situations and from very different cultures is available to the sociologist.

Sociologists are trained to develop their ideas in a logical, disciplined, and explicit way by constructing theories, which are quite unlike the everyday beliefs of common sense. They are explicit, because their assumptions have been brought into the open, thought about, and justified. Logical connections are made between the various ideas that make up a theory so that its train

of thought can be followed. Theories are also subject to the scrutiny of other sociologists, who will critically examine their assumptions and check the logic of their arguments.

Sociologists then test out their theories in an objective and systematic way. They do not assume that they know the answers or that their theory is right. They demonstrate the truth or falsity of their ideas by collecting appropriate information, using a wide variety of methods to do this. These range from large-scale surveys to the small-scale, in-depth, participant observation of particular situations. Sociologists draw on many different sources of material, from documents to census data or interview responses. As we show in Chapter 3, pp. 73–6, different methods are appropriate to different issues and different situations but can also be used to complement and check upon each other. As with their theories, their methods and the way that they interpret their data are open to the scrutiny of other sociologists.

Sociology is then a science. It has explicit theories and ways of collecting data in an objective and systematic way in order to check those theories and revise them if they are found wanting. It is not a natural science because there are important differences between the social and natural worlds as objects of study. It is a social science, not a natural science, but a science none the less.

SUMMARY POINTS

In this chapter we have discussed a number of general issues raised by the subject of sociology:

▶ We used Durkheim's study of suicide to explore the relationship between the individual and society.

▶ Durkheim demonstrated that the taking of one's life, apparently the act of an isolated individual, was socially patterned.

▶ We argued that socialization is a key process in this patterning but does not *determine* how people behave, as the example of language shows.

▶ Without language we cannot think or express our thoughts, but language does not determine the way that we think or the way that we express ourselves.

We then moved on to consider what sociologists mean by society, by examining the main features of societies:

▶ Societies consist of a complex of interdependent institutions.

▶ Societies are, however, organized at a number of different levels, from the family, through the community and the nation state, to the global level.

▶ Societies also consist of structures of inequality and domination.

▶ There is a cultural dimension to society which consists of beliefs and their symbolic representation in actions and objects.

Lastly, we discussed whether sociology should be considered a science:

▶ Science involves systematic observation and the development of theories to explain observations.

▶ Sociology is not a natural science because social behaviour is different from natural behaviour.

▶ The explanation of social behaviour requires the understanding of the meaning of actions.

▶ Sociology is, none the less, a social science that is based on systematic observational methods and the construction of explicit theories.

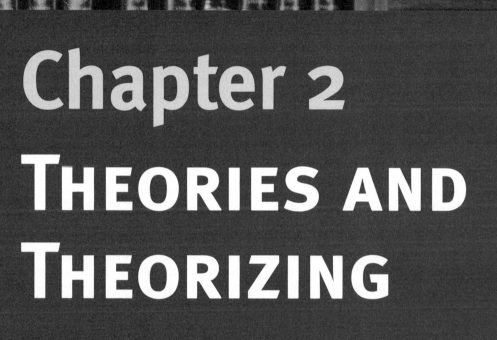

Chapter 2
THEORIES AND THEORIZING

Theory and science

'There are two types of scientist: the ones who build from evidence and painstakingly construct theories which can be proved—evolution, the link between smoking and lung cancer—and those who are basically campaigners, who decide the theory first, wave it like a banner, and then claim that every new fact, however contradictory, supports it.'

Source: Simon Hoggart, 'Simon Hoggart's Week', Guardian, 30 Aug. 1997.

CLAIMS such as this underpin much of the popular view of theory. Real scientists, it is held, develop firm and proven theories, while ideological charlatans simply give voice to their prejudices in the name of theory. The unspoken claim—though often made perfectly clear—is that real scientists are natural scientists and that so-called social scientists cannot hope to match their achievements. It is the social scientists and, above all, the sociologists who propagate ideology in the name of theory.

This often goes hand in hand with the assertion that sociological theory is, in any case, mere jargon: commonplace ideas dressed up in scientific mumbo-jumbo language. Theory consists of spinning out long but essentially meaningless words. The jargon serves as a mere smokescreen for ignorance or platitudes. The implication is clear: sociological theorizing is not the kind of thing that any self-respecting person need concern him or herself with.

It is undoubtedly true that sociologists can be as susceptible to prejudice and jargon as anybody else. Perhaps they have sometimes adopted cumbersome terminology in a misguided attempt to justify their claims to a scientific status in the face of exactly these kinds of objections. However, any scientific activity must employ technical terms in its theories, and these terms will not always be comprehensible to the person in the street. Many sociological terms come from everyday language, and they have to be given precise technical meanings if they are not to be misunderstood.

Theory lies at the heart of sociology. Theories enable us to understand and explain the nature of the social world. Many of these theories are concerned with specific social phenomena or with explaining particular social processes. They concern such things as crime, health, education, or politics, or they concern deviance, socialization, or stratification. You will encounter many such theories in the various chapters of this book. These theories are, however, connected into larger theoretical frame-

☞ Theory can be difficult and demanding. You will not necessarily understand all that we say in this chapter the first time that you read it. However, you should not worry about this. It is not your fault. The problem lies with the complexity of the theories and—it has to be said—with the failure of certain theorists to present their ideas clearly. You will find it best to skim through the chapter as a whole, not worrying too much about the detail. You can spend more time on the parts that you find easiest to handle. Treat the whole chapter as a reference source, as something to come back to as and when you read the 'Understanding' sections of the book. Theory is best handled in context.

works that grasp the most general features of social life as a whole. It is these theories that we will look at in this chapter. We will outline the key ideas of the main theorists, and we will show how these ideas are related to the issues that we raise in the other chapters of the book.

There is no single theory to which all sociologists subscribe. There are, instead, a number of different theories, each of which has its advocates and its detractors. These theories are sometimes presented as mutually opposed to each other and as defining rival positions from which sociologists must choose. It is sometimes assumed that adherents of one theory have nothing to learn from considering any others. Some textbooks, for example, present their readers with three (or perhaps four or five) different theoretical positions on each topic and imply that all are equally valid. It is as if you enter the sociological supermarket and see, laid out on the shelves in front of you, 'Marxism', 'functionalism', 'feminism', 'interactionism', and so on. You walk down the aisles, picking up those theories that appeal to you or that have the best packaging. Having made your choice, you return home to use your new theories.

Theoretical choice is not like this. The choice between theories is not made on the basis of individual preference ('I just don't like functionalism') or political standpoint ('I'm working class, so I'm a Marxist'). Preferences and politics do, of course, enter into sociology, but they do not determine the merits of particular theories. The choices that we must make among theoretical positions are shaped, above all, by empirical considerations. When judging a theory, what really matters is its capacity to explain what is happening in the real world. Theories must always be tested through empirical research. As we show in this and the next chapter, the 'facts' are not quite as straightforward as this statement suggests. However, the point still remains. Theories are attempts to describe and explain the social world. Their merits and limitations depend, ultimately, on their ability to cope with what we know about that world.

We will show that the leading theorists of the sociological tradition have attempted, in their different ways, to understand the modern world. They have each, however, concentrated on particular aspects of that world. None has given a full and complete picture. The least satisfactory theorists are, in fact, those who have tried to move, prematurely, towards that comprehensive picture. The most powerful theories are those that have emphasized particular aspects of the social world and have concentrated their attention on understanding that aspect. In doing so, they neglect or put to one side the very processes that other theories take as their particular concern.

If it is possible to produce a comprehensive understanding of the social world, this is likely to result from the slow synthesis of these partial viewpoints. In so far as the social world is constantly changing, it is undoubtedly true that any such synthesis would not last long before it, too, was in need of reformulation. Theoretical change and the development of new theories is a constant feature of scientific activity. Even in such a well-developed field as physics, there are numerous partial theories that have not yet been synthesized into a larger and more comprehensive theory.

For the present, then, different theories must be seen, in principle, as complementary to one another. We must emphasize that we are not proposing that all theories are of equal value, or that they can simply be hashed together in some unwieldy mixture. Some theories are bad theories that have received no support from empirical research. Even the useful theories have their particular strengths and, of course, their particular weaknesses. Each theory must be assessed against the facts that are relevant to its particular concerns, not against those that are more relevant to some other theory. By the end of this chapter you should have some appreciation of how the various sociological theories do, indeed, complement one another. You should begin to see how, collectively, they provide a picture of the social world that is far better than any of them can provide alone.

In this chapter we place great emphasis on the historical development of sociological theory. Theories constructed over 100 years ago are, of course, likely to have been superseded, in many respects, by more recent theories. Many of them, however, still have a great deal of relevance for us today, and most contemporary theories have developed out of the ideas of the nineteenth-century theorists. It is possible to gain a better understanding of them if these lines of development are traced.

We begin with an overview of the earliest attempts to establish a science of sociology, and we go on to show how these attempts were the basis of the classical statements of sociology produced around the turn of the twentieth century. The section on 'Sociology Comes of Age' looks at the three main theoretical traditions of the twentieth century: structural-functionalist theories, interaction theories, and conflict theories. We conclude the chapter with a sketch of the criticisms raised by the feminist and post-modernist theorists whose arguments we consider at greater length in the various chapters of Part Two. In this chapter and throughout the book you will find that we consider both classic and contemporary theorists, treating them as participants in the same great intellectual enterprise that is sociology.

PIONEERS OF SOCIAL THEORY

For as long as people have lived in societies, they have tried to understand them and to construct theories about them. So far as we know, people have always lived in societies, and so social theory has a long history. For much of this history, however, these attempts at understanding have shown little resemblance to what we currently mean by the word sociology. Early attempts at social understanding had a greater similarity to myths or to poetry than they did to science, and many of these attempts were religious or highly speculative in character. The creation of a distinctively scientific approach to social understanding is, in fact, a very recent thing. Only since the seventeenth century, and then mainly in Europe, has there been anything that could truly be called a science of society.

The origins of a *scientific* perspective on social life can be traced to the European Enlightenment of the seventeenth and eighteenth centuries. The Enlightenment marked a sea change in the whole cultural outlook of European intellectuals. In one field after another, rational and critical methods were adopted and religious viewpoints were replaced by scientific ones. It was in this period that the very idea of science first emerged.

The greatest of the early achievements of the Enlightenment were the philosophy of Descartes and the physics of Newton. Writing in the middle decades of the sixteenth century, Descartes set out a view of intellectual enquiry as the attempt to achieve absolutely certain knowledge of the world, using only the rational and critical faculties of the mind. From this point of view, science was the attempt to construct theories that could be assessed against the evidence of the human senses. Observation and direct experience of the world provided the raw materials for scientific work. The rational and critical faculties of the scientist guided the way that these were accounted for. In Newton's physics, this method led to the construction of elegant mathematical theories that saw the behaviour of physical objects in relation to their mass, volume, and density, and to the forces of gravity and magnetism.

During the eighteenth century, the scope of scientific knowledge in physics was enlarged, and the same scientific method led to advances in chemistry, biology, and many other specialist fields. Progress in the construction of a scientific sociology was much slower. At first, social life was understood in almost exclusively individual terms. Those who explored social life tried to explain it as resulting from the behaviour of rational, calculating individuals who sought only to increase their own happiness and satisfaction. They were aware that individuals lived in societies, but they saw societies only as collections of individuals. They had not grasped what most people now take for granted: that individuals cannot be understood in isolation from the social relations into which they are born and without which their lives have no meaning.

In Britain and France, and later in Germany, a more properly *social* perspective was gradually developed. British theorists were particularly concerned with economic activities and economic relations and have often been described as taking a **materialist** view of social life. For them, the central features of social life were the struggle over economic resources and the inequalities and social divisions to which this gave rise. French and German writers, on the other hand, highlighted the part played by moral values and ideas, and they have been described as **idealist** theorists. These theorists saw societies as possessing a cultural spirit that formed the foundation of their customs and practices.

SOCIAL DEVELOPMENT AND EVOLUTION

The first systematic theories of social life were those of Hegel and Comte. Hegel built on the work of his German predecessors to construct a comprehensive idealist theory of society and history. Similar concerns are apparent in the work of Comte, though he was a more self-consciously scientific writer who owed a great deal to the economic analyses of the earlier materialists. Where Hegel remained satisfied with a very general account of the nature of the distinctive social element in human life, Comte tried to analyse this into its constituent elements. These were, he said, aspects of the *structure* of social systems. Both writers identified long-term processes of social change that they described as processes of social development. Spencer, writing later in the nineteenth century, carried all these themes forward. He saw society as a social organism that developed over time through a process of social evolution.

Hegel: Society as spirit

The stimulus behind Georg Hegel's ideas was the philosophy of Immanuel Kant, the next great landmark in philosophical thought after Descartes. Kant's central argument was that scientific knowledge was an active and creative production of the human mind. All obser-

vations, Kant argued, depended upon the particular ways in which experiences were interpreted in relation to current cultural concerns. Hegel's key concept was that of spirit. According to Hegel, the interpretation of experience reflects the spirit of the culture. This term, taken from Montesquieu (1748), referred to the general principles and underlying ideas that lay behind particular customs and practices. The spirit of a culture shaped the subjective ideas and meanings on which individuals acted, and so Hegel saw individuals as the mere embodiments of the cultural spirit. There was, then, a one-to-one relationship between cultural spirit, social institutions, and social actions. Hegel saw actions and institutions as simply the means through which cultural ideas and values were formed into a social reality.

 Hegel's ideas are complex and his works are difficult to read. At this stage, you should not try to track down his books. If you ever do feel able to tackle him, you should start with his *Philosophy of Right* (Hegel 1821). Do not expect an easy ride!

Hegel saw history as involving a gradual shift from local to more global social institutions. In the earliest stages, family and kinship defined the basic social pattern. People's lives were contained within localized communities that were tied tightly together through bonds of kinship and family obligations. The family spirit prevailed. These communal forms of social life were followed in Europe and in certain of the great civilizations of the world, by societies in which the division of labour and market relations tied local communities into larger societies. Hegel saw these societies as marked by deep divisions into unequal social classes and as animated by the commercial spirit of property-owners and merchants.

In his own time, Hegel identified the beginnings of a new stage of social development. The nation state was becoming the key social institution. In contemporary societies, he held, the state embodied the spirit of the people as a whole and not just the spirit of a particular class or kinship group. This was what he called the *world spirit*, a universal and all-embracing cultural spirit that marked the end point of historical development.

Hegel's work, while pioneering, was not yet sociology. He saw history as the automatic and inevitable expression of an abstract spirit into the world. Spirit itself was seen as the active, moving force in social life. Yet spirit was an unsatisfactory idea and was not analysed in a scientific way. Hegel personified spirit, seeing it as some kind of active and creative force. Furthermore, when Hegel looked to what it is that drives the human spirit itself, he discovered God. The holy spirit lies behind the human spirit, and social development is seen as the progressive realization of God's will.

Hegel's work drew together many of the insights of the French idealists and put them into a comprehensive general framework. Its religious character, however, meant that he had few direct followers. Some aspects of his thought were taken ahead, in a very different direction, by Marx, as we will shortly show. Idealism had its greatest impact on the development of sociology in France. The key writer here was Auguste Comte, who was the first to set out a comprehensive, if flawed, account of a theoretical science of society.

Comte and Saint-Simon

It is thanks to Comte that the science of society is called 'sociology', as it was he who invented the word in 1839 to describe the system of ideas that he had developed. Comte, however, was carrying forward and enlarging some of the ideas that he had learned from his teacher and first employer, Saint-Simon. Comte's intellectual and personal relationship to Saint-Simon was very close, but a disagreement between the two men led Comte to deny the importance of Saint-Simon and to exaggerate the originality of his own work. Despite this, it is undoubtedly Comte's efforts at systematizing and unifying the science of society that made possible its later professionalization as an academic discipline.

Saint-Simon was a radical, but eccentric aristocrat who popularized the idea of what he called *positive science*. The term positive means definite and unquestionable, and Saint-Simon used it to describe the precise or exact sciences based on observation and mathematics that he saw emerging in one intellectual field after another. This led him to advocate the building of a positive 'science of man', a psychological and social science of the human mind. Once this science had been achieved, he held, we would be well on the way to possessing a complete knowledge of everything that exists. At this point, the various positive sciences could be unified into a single 'positive philosophy'.

The work of Saint-Simon was confused and unsystematic, and he recognized that he needed a collaborator. Comte, who had been convinced by the work of Montesquieu and Condorcet that there was a pressing need for a social science, took on this task and worked closely with Saint-Simon from 1817 to 1824. It was this period of intellectual apprenticeship that gave Comte the confidence to begin to construct the outlines of the positive philosophy and its positive science of society.

A positive science of society

Comte's importance in the history of sociology is due to the particular method that he proposed and his general view of the subject matter of sociology. The method that Comte proposed for sociology was that of positive science. He held that sociology could advance human understanding only if it emulated the other positive sciences in its approach. Comte was not saying that sociology had slavishly to follow the natural sciences. On the contrary, he was very concerned to emphasize that each of the major disciplines had its own distinctive subject matter, which had to be studied in its own right and could not be reduced to the subject matter of any other science. His point was simply that there was only one way of being scientific, whatever the subject matter of the science.

Comte's **positivism** presented science as the study of observable phenomena. The scientist must make direct observations of those things that are of interest, examining their similarities and differences, and investigating the order in which they occurred. These observations had then to be explained by theoretical laws, or logical connections. These laws stated causal relationships between observed events, so allowing the scientist to predict the occurrence of events. If, for example, we have a law that states that intellectual unrest is a cause of political instability, then the observation of intellectual unrest would lead us to predict a period of political instability. The task of the scientist is to produce theories that are able to arrive at just these kinds of laws.

 For Comte, the positivist approach in science simply involves an emphasis on rational, critical thought and the use of evidence. In many contemporary discussions, however, it is presented as a much narrower and more restricted idea. 'Positivist' is often used almost as a term of abuse, and is applied to those who use mathematics or social surveys. This kind of distortion is not helpful. You will find it much easier to handle sociological debates if you avoid trying to label people as positivists and non-positivists. If you must use the word, try to use it as Comte intended. Bear in mind, however, that Comte tied positive science to positive politics and his religion of humanity.

Auguste Comte

Isidore Auguste Marie François Xavier Comte (1798–1857) was born in Montpellier. After an unspectacular education, during which his political interests led him into conflict with the authorities, he settled in Paris. He was a dogmatic and self-important individual, whose arrogance made it difficult for him to establish secure relationships. His intellectual relationship to Saint-Simon was stormy, and ended a year before the death of Saint-Simon in 1825. His personal life was equally unstable. His early life was marked by periods of depression and paranoia, and his marriage broke down because of his extreme jealousy.

Comte decided on the plan for his life work while still working for Saint-Simon. He planned a *Course in Positive Philosophy*, which he delivered in public lectures and published in serial form between 1830 and 1842. The *Course* eventually ran to six volumes, covering the whole of what he took to be established knowledge in mathematics, astronomy, physics, chemistry, biology, and sociology. The part on sociology (which he originally called 'social physics') was its centrepiece and took up three of the six volumes.

Having completed this task, Comte went on to write what he considered to be even more important, the *System of Positive Politics*. This, too, was a multi-volume work and was completed in 1854, just three years before his death. The *System* set out a summary of his position and his programme for the social reconstruction of European society. This reconstruction involved the establishment of a 'Religion of Humanity', a religion that abandoned dogma and faith and was itself constructed on a scientific basis.

Auguste Comte: inventor of the word 'sociology'.

Sociology was to be the core of this religion, with sociologists replacing priests as the expert teachers and policy-makers.

Comte's works are difficult to get hold of in English editions, but you might like to scan some of the extracts reprinted in K. Thompson (1976).

While many of the details of Comte's sociology are no longer accepted by sociologists, his main principles have largely been accepted and they now form a part of the mainstream of the subject. His key insight was that societies had to be understood as complex *systems*. They are organic wholes with a unity similar to that of biological organisms. The human body, for example, is a biological system of parts that are connected together into a living whole. Similarly, a society may be seen as a cohesive and integrated whole. The parts of a society are not simply individuals, but social institutions. A society consists of family and kinship institutions, political institutions, economic institutions, religious institutions, and so on. These do not exist in isolation but are interdependent parts of the whole social system. Change in any one institution is likely to have consequences for the other institutions to which it is connected.

Comte identified two broad branches of sociology, corresponding to two ways in which social systems could be studied:

▶ *social statics*: the study of the coexistence of institutions in a system, their structures and their functions;

▶ *social dynamics*: the study of change in institutions and systems over time, their development and progress.

The study of social statics is similar to the study of organization or anatomy in biology. It looks at the **structure** of a social system, at the way in which the institutions that make up the system are actually connected to each other. Comte argues that the aim of social statics is to produce *laws of coexistence*, principles concerning the interdependence of social institutions.

The main elements of a society, according to Comte, are its division of labour, its language, and its religion. It is through their division of labour that people organize production and satisfy their material needs. Through their language they communicate with each other and can pass on the knowledge and values that they have learned. Through their religion, they can achieve a sense of common purpose and of working towards a common goal. These elements are all cemented together into the overall social structure.

The connections between the parts of a social system are studied by identifying their **functions**. We will come back to this idea in a later part of the chapter. In general terms, however, Comte used the term function to refer to the contribution that particular institutions or practices make to the rest of the society, the part that they played in reproducing or maintaining it in existence by contributing to its solidarity or coherence. Comte saw a coherent society as a 'healthy' society. Those systems that show a high level of solidarity, consensus, or coherence work more smoothly and are more likely to persist than those with only a low level of coherence. Such societies are in a healthy state of balance or equilibrium, with all their parts working well together. In some situations, however, societies, like other organisms, may be in a 'pathological' condition of imminent breakdown or collapse. If their parts are not functioning correctly, they will not have the kind of coherence that they need to survive.

The study of social dynamics is concerned with the flow of energy and information around a social system and, therefore, with the ways in which societies change their structures in certain ways. Structural change is what Comte calls development or progress. The aim of social dynamics is to produce *laws of succession* that specify the various stages of development through which a particular social system is expected to move.

Comte saw the emergence of positive science itself as something that could be explained by the most important law of succession that sociologists possess. This was what he called the law of the three stages. According to this law, the religious ideas produced by the human mind pass through three successive stages, and particular types of social institutions correspond to each of them. These three stages are the theological, the metaphysical, and the positive. In the theological stage, people think in exclusively supernatural terms, seeing human affairs as resulting from the actions of gods and other supernatural beings. In the metaphysical stage, theological ideas are abandoned and people begin to think in terms of more abstract spiritual forces such as 'Nature'. Finally, the positive stage is one in which these abstractions give way to scientific observation and the construction of empirical laws.

Comte saw the theological stage as having lasted in Europe until the fourteenth century. This period involved a vast range of human societies from the simplest tribal societies to more complex kingdoms. The metaphysical stage lasted from the fourteenth century until about 1800, and Comte saw its development as having been closely linked with the rise of Protestantism. Societies in the metaphysical stage were militaristic and feudal societies that depended on a vast agricultural base. The positive stage began early in the nineteenth century and corresponds to what Comte called **industrial society**. This term, now so taken for granted, was first used by Saint-Simon and was taken up by Comte to describe the type of society that was gradually maturing in the Europe of his day. The term industrial was initially contrasted with earlier 'militaristic' types of society, and was intended to suggest that social life had become organized around the peaceful pursuit of economic welfare rather than the preparation for war. More specifically, an industrial society is one organized around the achievement of material well-being through an expanding division of labour and a new technology of production. This kind of society is headed by the entrepreneurs, directors, and managers who are the technical experts of the new industrial technology.

As it developed, however, industrial society created great inequalities of income. The resentment that the poor felt towards the wealthy was responsible for a pathological state of unrest and social crisis. The only long-term solution to this, Comte argued, was for a renewed moral regulation of society through the establishment of a new, rational system of religion and education. This would establish the moral consensus that would encourage people to accept the inevitable inequalities of industrialism.

Comte's political aspirations were unfulfilled, and his religion of humanity inspired only small and eccentric groups of thinkers. His view of the need for a critical and empirical science of society, however, was massively influential and secured the claims of his sociology to a central place in intellectual discussions. His particular view of the development of modern industrial society rested on a rather inadequate historical understanding of pre-modern societies, but he accurately identified many of its most important characteristics. His concept of the industrial society has continued to inform debates about the future development of modern societies.

Spencer and social evolution

The materialist tradition in Britain had its major impact on the growth of economic theory (usually termed political economy), where a long line of theo-

Herbert Spencer

Herbert Spencer (1820–1903) was born in Derby and was privately educated in mathematics and physics. He started work in the new railway industry, and became a successful railway engineer. His intellectual interests in geology and biology, and his interest in political issues, led him to publish a number of articles, and in 1848 he decided to move into journalism. His first book was *Social Statics*. This and a series of papers on population and evolution were followed by a major work that was to take the whole of the rest of his life to complete. Like Comte, he aimed at an encyclopaedic summary of human knowledge; a 'synthetic philosophy'. He published this work in his *Principles of Biology*, *Principles of Psychology*, *Principles of Sociology*, and *Principles of Ethics*.

Spencer's sociological works are difficult to get hold of and it is probably better to approach him through the extracts reprinted in Andreski (1976).

rists attempted to uncover the way in which the production of goods was shaped by the forces of supply and demand. In the work of Herbert Spencer this was combined with ideas drawn from the work of Comte to form a broader sociological theory. Spencer was seen by many people as the direct heir to Comte, though this was certainly not how he saw himself. Although he gave far less attention to religious and intellectual factors than did Comte, there is, nevertheless, a great similarity in their views. It is also true to say, however, that Spencer remained very close to the British tradition in giving a great emphasis to individual action. Spencer took forward Comte's idea that societies were organic systems, but he also emphasized that they must be seen in terms of individuals and their actions.

Spencer adopted Comte's distinction between social statics and social dynamics as the two main branches of his sociology. His social statics stressed the idea of society as an organism. Each part in a society was specialized around a particular function and so made its own distinctive contribution to the whole. A society was an integrated and regulated system of interdependent parts. Much of Spencer's work in sociology consisted of the attempt to describe these interdependencies in general terms and as they are found in actual societies.

His most distinctive contribution to sociology, however, was his emphasis on the principle of **evolution** in his social dynamics. Evolutionary ideas

achieved a great popularity in Victorian Britain following the publication of Darwin's *Origin of the Species* in 1859. The debate over Darwin's work made widely known the idea that biological species evolve through a constant struggle for existence in which only the fittest can survive. Those species that are best adapted to the biological conditions under which they live are more likely to survive than those that are only weakly adapted or not adapted at all. In fact, the phrase 'survival of the fittest' had been introduced by Spencer some years before Darwin published his work, and both Darwin and Spencer acknowledged that the idea of a struggle for existence came from Malthus's (1798) work on population.

Spencer's great contribution to the debate over evolution, however, was his advocacy of the principle of *social* evolution. This consisted of two processes:

▶ structural differentiation;
▶ functional adaptation.

Structural differentiation was a process through which simple societies developed into more complex ones. This idea was modelled on the biological process through which, as Spencer saw it, advanced organisms had more differentiated and specialized parts than less advanced ones. In all spheres of existence, he held, there is an evolution from the simple to the complex. In the social world, structural differentiation involved the proliferation of specialized social institutions.

Spencer saw simple societies as organized around family and kinship relations, and as achieving their material needs through hunting and gathering. Few aspects of social life are specialized, and everything is, ultimately, organized through kinship. Gradually, however, separate governmental and economic institutions are formed and systems of communication are established. Many activities previously organized through the family come to be organized through these specialized institutions. As a result, the family loses some of its functions, which have been 'differentiated' into the specialized institutions. Over time, the specialized institutions are themselves subject to structural differentiation. Governmental institutions, for example, become differentiated into separate political and military institutions.

The reason why structural differentiation occurs, Spencer held, is that it allows societies to cope with the problems and difficulties that they face in their material environment (physical conditions, climate, natural resources) and from other societies. This process of coping with the environment is what Spencer called *functional adaptation*. Structural differentiation allows societies to become better adapted, and so a changing environment is associated with an increasing level of structural differentiation.

The nineteenth century, according to Spencer, was a period in which industrial societies were beginning to evolve. These societies were well adapted to the conditions under which people then lived. They were highly differentiated social systems with only a very loose degree of overall regulation. Individuals had a great degree of autonomy in an industrial society, and further evolution depended on the maintenance of their intellectual, economic, and political freedoms. Spencer tried to explore what he saw as the balance between individual freedom and collective welfare in industrial societies. Adam Smith had argued that the economic market operated as a 'hidden hand' to ensure that the greatest level of economic happiness resulted from individually selfish behaviour. Spencer extended this argument and held that all the structurally differentiated institutions of contemporary societies could be seen as working, generally in unintended ways, to produce the greatest collective advantages. There was a natural harmony or coherence that resulted only from the rational, self-interested actions of free individuals. Spencer was, therefore, opposed to state intervention of any kind, whether in the sphere of education, health, or the economy. Individuals had to be left to struggle for existence with each other. The fittest would survive, and this was, he argued, in the best interest of society as a whole.

KARL MARX

We have looked at two writers who were engaged in a common intellectual exercise. Despite the differences in their views, Comte and Spencer both produced pioneering versions of a science of sociology. Karl Marx too aspired to build a science of society, but he was very much on the margins of the intellectual world and he did not describe himself as a sociologist. To the extent that he took any account of the work of the sociologists, he was critical of it. This failure of Marx to identify himself as a sociologist reflects the fact that the word was still very new and, for many people, it still described only the specific doctrines of Comte and Spencer. As we will see in 'The Classic Period of Sociology', pp. 35–44, it was only in the next generation of social theorists that Marx's ideas began to receive any proper recognition as a part of the same *sociological* enterprise as the works of Comte and Spencer.

The inspiration for Marx's work was the growth of the European labour movement and of socialist ideas. He tried to tie his philosophical and scientific interests to the needs of this labour movement. Marx was trained in the tradition of Hegel's philosophy, studying at Berlin just a few years after Hegel's death, but he was also influenced by the British materialist tradition. He saw the work of writers such as Ferguson and Millar as providing the basis for an understanding of the power and significance of the labour movement, but only if combined with the historical perspective of Hegel.

Marx's model of society

The central idea in Marx's early work was **alienation**. This described the way in which the economic relations under which people work can change their labour from a creative act into a distorted and dehumanized activity. As a result, people do not enjoy their work or find satisfaction in it. They treat it as a mere means to ensuring their survival (by providing themselves with a wage) and therefore their ability to turn up the next week to work once more. In this way, work and its products become separate or 'alien' things that dominate and oppress people.

Marx accounted for alienation in terms of property relations and the division of labour. The economy, he held, was central to the understanding of human life. He argued that the existence of private property divides people into **social classes**. These are categories of people with a specific position in the division of labour, a particular standard of living, and a distinct way of life. The basic class division was that between property-owners and propertyless workers. The existence of classes and of social inequality was first highlighted by the British materialists, and Marx saw his own contribution as showing how and why these classes were inevitably drawn into conflict with each other. This he did in his later work for *Capital*. Classes, he argued, were involved in relations of exploitation. The property-owning class benefits at the expense of the propertyless, and this leads the classes to struggle over the distribution of economic resources.

Marx saw societies as social systems that could be divided into two quite distinct parts: the **base** and the **superstructure**. The economy and class relations comprised what he called the material base or substructure of society. The base always involves a particular **mode of production**. By this term, Marx referred to the technical and human resources of production and the specific property relations and division of labour under which they are used. This economic base is the foundation upon which a superstructure of political, legal, and customary social institutions is built. It is also the

Karl Marx and Friedrich Engels

Karl Marx (1818–83) was born in Trier, Germany. He studied law at Bonn and Berlin. His radical political views led him into a journalistic career, but this was cut short by the suppression of the various journals for which he wrote. He fled to Paris in 1843, to Brussels in 1845, and, finally, to London in 1848. It was in London that he spent the rest of his life. His massive tomb can still be seen in Highgate cemetery.

Marx began to work on a series of philosophical and economic books while in Paris, and he spent the rest of his

Karl Marx: highlighted the importance of class conflict in social change.

life studying, engaging in radical politics, and writing articles for newspapers and periodicals. He was able to use his time in this way only because of the financial support from his friend and collaborator Engels.

Friedrich Engels (1820–95) was the son of a wealthy cotton manufacturer. Like Marx, he was involved in radical politics and intellectual work, but he was sent to Manchester by his father to manage the English branch of the family firm. This gave him the financial independence to support both himself and Marx. Engels wrote an important study of poverty, *The Condition of the Working Class in England in 1844* (Engels 1845), and he collaborated with Marx in a number of works, including *The Communist Manifesto* (Marx and Engels 1848).

Marx found it difficult to complete books. A number of his most important studies were published long after his death, thanks to the editorial work of Engels and others. The most important of his early works, where he set out a theory of 'alienation', was the *Economic and Philosophical Manuscripts* (Marx 1844), published only in 1932. After *The Communist Manifesto*, he went on to produce a series of massive drafts for *Capital*, a critical study of economic theory and the economic basis of society. Only volume i (Marx 1867) was published in his lifetime.

The details of Marx's work are discussed in various parts of this book. You will find them in the following chapters:

▶ alienation and the nature of work   Chapter 13
▶ poverty   Chapter 14
▶ class relations and class polarization   Chapter 15
▶ labour organization, ruling class
   politics, and the state   Chapters 17, 18
▶ religion and ideology   Chapter 9

Useful discussions of Marx's ideas can be found in Giddens (1971) and Craib (1997). There is more detail in McLellan (1971), which contains some extracts from Marx's own work. A good biography is McLellan's *Karl Marx: His Life and Thought* (McLellan 1973). If you want to try to understand Marx's economic theory, you should try Mandel's *The Formation of the Economic Thought of Karl Marx* (Mandel 1967).

basis of various forms of consciousness and knowledge. The ideas that people form, Marx said, are shaped by the material conditions under which they live. They must be regarded as what he called **ideologies**.

There has been much controversy as to how Marx's division of the social system into a base and a super-structure is to be interpreted. In its most general sense,

it is simply a claim that only those societies that are able to ensure their material survival, through an efficiently organized system of production, will be able to sustain any other social activities. People must eat and have adequate clothing and shelter before they can stand for parliament, write poetry, or engage in sociology. The economic system acquires a compulsive power

Young Marx and old Marx

There is some controversy about the relationship between the works of the older, mature Marx of the 1860s and those of the youthful Marx of the 1840s. For some commentators, the early works on alienation were immature exercises that he later abandoned. For others, however, exploitation and alienation are closely related ideas. A close reading of Marx's texts shows that there is a great deal of continuity and that the so-called *Grundrisse* (Marx 1858) is a key link between the two phases of his work.

that shapes all other social activities because of the priority that has to be given to meeting basic economic needs.

Some of Marx's followers, along with his critics, have claimed, however, that he was setting out a form of economic determinism that allowed no autonomy at all for politics and culture. According to this view, political institutions and cultural ideas simply reflected economic divisions and struggles. While Marx did sometimes seem to suggest that the economy should be seen in this way, he was too sophisticated to accept such a deterministic position. Indeed, the claims for his work made by some of his followers led him to make the famous remark 'I am not a Marxist'.

Comte and Spencer saw social systems, in their normal states, as characterized by harmony and cohesion. Marx's view, on the other hand, recognized conflict and division as normal features of all societies. There are divisions not only within the economic base (between classes), but also between base and superstructure. While a superstructure normally reinforces and supports the economic base, it can frequently come into contradiction with it. By this, Marx meant that the form taken by the superstructure obstructs the further development of the mode of production. If production is to expand any further, the superstructure must be transformed to re-establish a closer correspondence with the economic base.

Historical materialism

Social systems develop over time as a result of the contradictions that develop within their economies. Marx's materialism, then, was a specifically **historical materialism**, the name by which Marxism is often known. Historical materialism is a theory of the transition from one mode of production to another.

Marx distinguished a number of modes of produc-

tion that he used to chart the sequences of historical development that resulted from increases in the level and scale of production. The simplest, least-developed forms of society were those in which the mode of production could be described as *primitive communism*. In this type of society, property is owned by the community as a whole, and the community itself is organized around bonds of kinship.

Marx argued that, as technology develops and production expands, so the property relations must change. If they do not, societies will not be able to continue to expand their powers of production. Out of the simple form of primitive communism, then, systems with private property and more complex divisions of labour evolve. In these societies, there are distinct political institutions and, in many cases, centralized states.

Marx often suggests that the evolutionary line in Western Europe led from the primitive communism of the Germanic and Celtic tribes, through the slave-owning systems of ancient Greece and Rome, and on to the feudal states of the medieval period. Feudal societies centred on the division between landowners and unfree labourers, who must work for the landlord as well as for themselves. Eastern Europe and the near East followed a similar progression, but passed through an 'Asiatic' stage instead of a feudal one. It is to feudalism that Marx traced the emergence of the capitalist societies to which he gave his greatest attention.

The form of society that was emerging in Western Europe at the time that Marx was writing was not simply an industrial society (as Comte had argued) but a specifically **capitalist society**. Beginning in the towns and commercial centres of the feudal world, a class of private property-owners had become the most important economic force. Since at least the sixteenth century, these capitalists had built plants, workshops, and factories in which they employed large numbers of workers. Capitalist entrepreneurs generated profits for themselves through a system of market exchange and the employment of wage labour. Marx held that these capitalists eventually became the **ruling classes** of their societies. They displaced the old feudal landowners, often through violent revolutions such as that in France from 1789 to 1799. They were responsible for the alienation, exploitation, and oppression of the workers who actually produced the goods that provided them with their profits.

As capitalist societies developed, Marx argued, exploitation grew and their superstructures no longer encouraged economic growth. If production was to continue to expand, property relations and the whole superstructure had to be swept away in a revolution. This time, however, it would be a revolution of the

Modes of production

Marx recognized six main modes of production, each defined by a particular type of property ownership and labour:

- ▶ primitive communism—relatively egalitarian, communal property;
- ▶ ancient—slave-owning systems;
- ▶ Asiatic—despotic and bureaucratic control;
- ▶ feudalism—serfdom, combined with urban commercial centres;
- ▶ capitalism—wage labour and private property;
- ▶ advanced communism—re-establishes communal property.

In each of these modes of production, the productive forces are developed to a different level. Before the stage of advanced communism they are also marked by growing levels of exploitation and alienation.

  Do not worry about the details of this scheme. We will introduce some of these, where relevant, in other chapters. You might like to compare Marx's scheme with the stages of development identified by Hegel, Comte, and Spencer.

workers, who would displace the capitalist ruling class. Workers, Marx held, would become conscious of their alienation and of the need to change the conditions that produced it. They would join together in radical political parties and, in due course, would overthrow the capitalist system. A workers' revolution, Marx rather optimistically thought, would abolish alienation, exploitation, and oppression, and it would establish a new and more advanced form of communist production.

A theory of knowledge

Marx derived a distinct philosophical position from his social theory. He accepted that the natural sciences might produce absolute and certain knowledge about the physical world, as Descartes and Kant had argued, but he held that this was not possible for the social sciences. The social world could not be known objectively, but only ever from particular standpoints. These standpoints were those provided by the class backgrounds of the observers. Members of a dominant class did, quite literally, see the social world differently from those who stood below them in the class hierarchy.

All social knowledge, then, is relative or ideological. It is historically determined by the class position of the knower. There is no standpoint outside the class structure, and so there can be no impartial or completely objective knowledge of the social world. For Marx, commitment is unavoidable. Social knowledge—and therefore social science—reflects a political commitment to one side or another in the struggle of classes.

Marx accepted the logical conclusion that his own theories were relative. They were relative, not to the standpoint of his own class, but to that of his adopted class. This was the **proletariat**, the subordinate class of the capitalist system. He believed that theorists who adopted the standpoint of this subordinate class, the oppressed and exploited class, were able to achieve a deeper and more adequate understanding of their society than those who were tied to the standpoint of the ruling class. It was for this reason that he did not hesitate to present his core ideas in a political manifesto for the communist movement (Marx and Engels 1848).

By contrast, he saw the ideas of almost all other social theorists as adopting the standpoint of the ruling, capitalist class. Classical economics and the sociologies of Comte and Spencer were, for Marx, uncritical expressions of the capitalist or **bourgeois** world-view. Their ideas could serve the labour movement only if they were subjected to rigorous criticism. Hence, he subtitled his major work on economics (1867) 'A Critique of Political Economy'. Unless bourgeois thought was subjected to criticism from the standpoint of the proletariat, it would remain simply an intellectual defence of the existing social order.

Marx's work provides a powerful challenge to the ideas of Comte. Where Comte emphasized that modern societies were *industrial societies* ruled by benign industrialists, Marx saw them as *capitalist societies* ruled by an oppressive capitalist class. Marx also differed from Comte in his stress on the importance of conflict and struggle in human history and in his emphasis on the

Marx saw all social knowledge as relative to the class standpoint of the observer. What social divisions, other than class, could he have seen as providing distinctive standpoints on the social world? Do you agree with his rejection of the possibility of 'objectivity'? Come back and consider this question again when you have read our discussions of Max Weber and of feminist theories.

economic basis of social life. Marx's claim to have produced a complete and comprehensive social theory cannot be upheld, but it is undoubtedly true that he highlighted many factors that had been minimized or ignored by Comte and Spencer.

SUMMARY POINTS

This section has traced the early stages of scientific sociology from the Enlightenment thinkers through to the pioneering statements of Comte, Spencer, and Marx. Although you are not expected to understand or recall everything that we have written about them, you should try to make sure that you have some familiarity with their key ideas.

▶ The idea of a *science* of society was a product of the European Enlightenment of the seventeenth and eighteenth centuries.

▶ Only gradually was an understanding of the distinctively *social* features of human life separated from an understanding of *individuals*.

▶ Social thought is diverse, each theoretical framework emphasizing particular aspects of social life. We looked at the way in which early social thought tended to follow distinct materialist and idealist traditions.

The pioneering statements of a specifically sociological approach are found in the works of Comte and Spencer. An alternative approach, that of Marx, broadened out this emerging form of social thought.

Comte established the idea of sociology as a *positive science* that explained empirical observations through causal laws.

▶ Both Comte and Spencer used a distinction between social statics and social dynamics. Social statics is concerned with the structure and functioning of social systems. Social dynamics is concerned with their development over time.

▶ The contrast between contemporary *industrial* societies and earlier *militaristic* societies was important for both Comte and Spencer.

▶ Spencer saw social development as a process of structural differentiation, shaped by functional adaptation.

While Marx also saw societies as systems that could be studied in terms of their structures and development over time, he placed more emphasis on the part played by conflict and struggle in social development.

▶ Marx saw economic activity as fundamental to social life. Work, property, and the division of labour form the economic *base* of society, its mode of production.

▶ Work and property ownership are the basis of class divisions that result in the alienation and exploitation of labour.

▶ Social development has followed a sequence of modes of production from primitive communism through feudalism to contemporary capitalist societies.

▶ Political and legal institutions, together with cultural values and ideologies form the superstructure of society and are shaped by the economic base.

▶ Revolutionary change, resulting from class conflict, will transform the base and the superstructure of capitalist society and will introduce a new system of communist production.

THE CLASSIC PERIOD OF SOCIOLOGY

The period from the 1880s to the 1920s was one in which sociology began to be established as a scientific discipline in the universities of Europe and North America. Increasing numbers of professors began to call themselves sociologists or to take sociological ideas seriously. Both Spencer and Marx had their heirs and followers. In Britain, Spencer's ideas were developed in a more flexible way by Leonard Hobhouse, the first person to hold a sociology professorship in a British university. In the United States, William Sumner developed versions of Spencer's ideas that had a considerable influence, and Lester Ward developed a sociology that owed rather more to Comte.

Marx's ideas were taken up in the leading Communist parties of Europe and, even before his death, they began to be codified into 'Marxism'. Those who regarded themselves as Marxists shared his identification with the proletariat. Marxism was seen not simply as a theoretical framework but as the basis for the political programme of the labour movement. The country in which Marxism had the greatest impact was Russia, where the revolution of 1917 led to the dominance of the Communist Party and the enshrinement of Marxism as the official ideology of the Soviet Union. The political content of Marxism limited its influence in academic sociology. While there was some attempt to grapple with his ideas—especially in Germany—Marxism was a neglected tradition of thought until the 1960s.

Sociology thrived most strongly in France and Germany, where a number of important theorists began to construct more disciplined and focused theoretical frameworks that could be used in detailed empirical investigations. In France, there was the work of Le Play, Tarde, and, above all, Durkheim. In Germany, the leading theorists were Tönnies, Simmel, and Weber. In terms of their impact on the later development of sociology, it is Durkheim and Weber who must be seen as the key figures.

ÉMILE DURKHEIM

Émile Durkheim saw one of his principal academic tasks as the construction of a philosophical basis for a *science* of sociology. He wanted to show that sociology could be a rigorous scientific discipline that was worthy of a place in the university system. An understanding of Durkheim's thought, then, must begin with this philosophy of science and his attempt to produce a distinctive view of the nature of sociology.

The nature of social facts

According to Durkheim, the subject matter of sociology is a distinctive set of **social facts**. These are not just any facts that happen to concern people's lives in societies. They are quite specific phenomena that can be sharply distinguished from the facts studied by other scientists. They are, in particular, distinct from the facts of individual consciousness studied by psychology and the organic facts of individual bodies studied by biology. They are the things that define the specific intellectual concerns of sociology.

Durkheim characterizes social facts as ways of acting, thinking, or feeling that are collective, rather than individual, in origin. Social facts have a reality *sui generis*. This is a Latin phrase that Durkheim uses to mean 'of its own type' or 'distinctive to itself'. Because this was a difficult idea for others to understand—and it is still not completely understood by many critics of sociology—he set out his views at some length.

Durkheim gives as an example of a social fact what later writers would call a role. There are, he says, certain established ways of acting, thinking, or feeling as a brother, a husband, a citizen, and so on. They are, in the most general sense, expected, required, or imposed ways of acting, thinking, or feeling for those who occupy these positions. They are conventional ways of behaving that are expected by others and that are established in custom and law.

Social facts are collective ways of acting, thinking, or feeling. They are not unique to particular individuals, but originate outside the consciousness of the individuals who act, think, or feel in this way. They most often involve a sense of obligation. Even when people feel that they are acting through choice or free will, they are likely to be following a pattern that is more general in their society and that they have acquired through learning and training. We learn what is expected of us quite early in life, and these expectations become part of our own personality.

Social facts, then, are *external* to the individual. They do not, of course, actually exist outside individual

Émile Durkheim

Émile Durkheim (1858–1917) was born in Épinal, France. He studied social and political philosophy at the École Normale Supérieure in Paris, reading deeply into the works of Montesquieu and Rousseau. He studied for a year in Germany. He taught educational theory at Bordeaux from 1887 to 1902, after which he moved to a professorship at the Sorbonne in Paris. He made a close, but critical study of the work of Comte, and he produced a number of exemplary sociological studies. In 1913, only four years before has death, he was allowed to call himself Professor of Sociology.

Durkheim's key works appeared regularly and became the basis of a distinctive school of sociology. His major writings were *The Division of Labour in Society* (1893), *The Rules of the Sociological Method* (1895), *Suicide: A Study in Sociology* (1897), and *The Elementary Forms of the Religious Life* (1912). He founded a journal that became a focus for his work. One of his principal followers was his nephew, Marcel Mauss, who produced some important work (Durkheim and Mauss 1903; Mauss 1925).

You will find more detailed discussions of Durkheim's principal ideas in various parts of this book:

▶ suicide — Chapter 1
▶ religion — Chapter 9
▶ education — Chapter 7
▶ anomie and the division of labour — Chapter 13

Émile Durkheim: saw sociology as the study of social facts.

The texts by Giddens (1971) and Craib (1997) give useful discussions of Durkheim. More detail and a biographical account can be found in Lukes (1973). A good brief introduction is K. Thompson (1982).

minds, but they do originate outside the mind of any particular individual. They are not created anew as each individual chooses what to do. They are passed from generation to generation and are received by particular individuals in a more or less complete form. Individuals are, of course, able to influence them and contribute to their development, but they do so only in association with other individuals. It is in this sense that social facts are the collective products of a society as a whole or of particular social groups.

Because they are matters of expectation, obligation, or deep commitment, social facts also have a 'compelling and coercive power', which Durkheim summarizes by the term *constraint*. This constraint may be expressed in punishment, disapproval, rejection, or simply the failure of an action to achieve its goal. Thus, someone who breaks the law by killing another person is likely to face arrest, trial, and imprisonment or execution. On the other hand, someone who misuses lan-

Social facts

Social facts 'consist of manners of acting, thinking and feeling external to the individual, which are vested with a coercive power by virtue of which they exercise control over him' (Durkheim 1895: 52). Social facts are characterized by

▶ externality;
▶ constraint.

Some social facts are institutions. These are beliefs and modes of behaviour that are long established in a society or social group. Others are collective representations: shared ways of thinking about a group and its relations to the things that affect it. Examples of collective representations are myths, legends, and religious ideas.

guage is simply likely to be misunderstood. Durkheim remarks, for example, that he is not forced to speak French, nor is he punished if he does not, but he will be understood by his compatriots only if he does in fact use the rules and conventions of French vocabulary and grammar.

Durkheim emphasizes that social facts are very difficult to observe. Indeed, they are often observable only through their effects. We cannot, for example, observe the role of husband, but only particular individuals acting as husbands. Similarly, we cannot observe the grammar of a language, but only the speech of particular individuals. Social facts are, in general, invisible and intangible and their properties have to be discovered indirectly. By observing the actions of large numbers of people who act in similar ways, for example, we may be able to infer the existence of the role of husband. By observing a large number of conversations, we may be able to infer the existence of particular rules of grammar.

In some cases, however, social facts may appear to be more visible. They may, for example, be codified in laws, summarized in proverbs, set down in religious texts, or laid down in books of grammar. Durkheim makes clear, however, that these laws, proverbs, texts, and books are not themselves the social facts. Social facts are mental, not physical, and what we have are simply the attempts that individuals have made to bring these social facts to consciousness and to make them explicit. These explicit formulations can, nevertheless, be useful sources of evidence about social facts and can be employed alongside the direct observation of actions in any investigation into social facts.

Studying social facts

Durkheim's approach to the study of social facts owes a great deal to Comte's positivism. It was set out as a set of rules or principles that Durkheim thought should guide the scientific sociologist. The first of these directly reflected Comte's contrast between metaphysical thought and positive science, though Durkheim cast it in a more convincing form. The first rule simply says 'consider social facts as things'.

What Durkheim meant by this was that it was necessary to abandon all preconceived ideas and to study things as they really are. He held that all sciences must do this if they are to be objective and of any practical value. The transformation of alchemy into chemistry and of astrology into astronomy occurred because the practitioners of the new sciences abandoned the common-sense preconceptions that they relied on in their everyday lives. Instead, they made direct observa-

tions of natural phenomena and constructed theories that could explain them. Sociology, Durkheim argued, must move in the same direction. It must treat its objects—social facts—as 'things'.

Our natural, everyday attitudes towards social facts tend to be shaped by religious and political preconceptions and by personal prejudices. We use a whole range of everyday concepts such as the state, the family, work, crime, and so on, and we tend to assume (with little or no evidence) that these are universal features of human life. We assume, for example, that all families in all societies are more or less the same as the families that we are familiar with in our own social circle. Such ideas, as Marx recognized, are ideological. They reflect our particular social position. While Marx simply accepted that all thought was ideological, Durkheim saw a fundamental distinction between ideology and science. Those who adopt the scientific attitude, he said, must abandon all the accepted ideas of their social group and attempt to construct new concepts that directly grasp the real nature of things. Preconceived ideas come from outside science; scientific concepts are generated from within scientific practice itself.

Durkheim's claim that we need to study things, rather than rely on preconceptions, is, perhaps, too simple. While he correctly identified the need to avoid the prejudice and distortion that often results from preconceived ideas, he was mistaken in his belief that it was possible to observe things independently of *all* concepts. Marx's philosophy, for all its problems, recognized that the things that exist in the world can be known only through concepts. As we will see, Max Weber, too, recognized this and produced a rather better account of scientific knowledge than did Durkheim.

Nevertheless, the core of what Durkheim was trying to establish remains as a valuable insight. He stressed that, if sociology is to be a science, it must engage in research that collects evidence through the direct observation of social facts. This must be done through the adoption of an attitude of mind that is as open as possible to the evidence of the senses. We cannot substitute prejudice and ideology for scientific knowledge.

Durkheim's approach to the study of social facts makes a distinction between two complementary aspects of sociological explanation. These are **causal explanation** and **functional analysis**. Of the two, causal explanation is the more fundamental. In a causal explanation, the origins of a social fact are accounted for in relation to the other social facts that brought it into being. The punishment attached to a crime, for example, may express an intense collective sentiment of disapproval. The collective sentiment, then, is the cause of the punishment. If the sentiment did not exist, the punishment would not occur.

> ☞ Showing causal relationships is not quite as straightforward as Durkheim implies. The fact that variations in *A* are followed by variations in *B* may not indicate that *B* is caused by *A*. The variations could indicate that both *A* and *B* are caused by some other, as yet unknown, third factor. We look at this problem in Chapter 14, pp. 576–7, where we consider it in relation to occupational achievement.

Functional analysis is concerned with the *effects* of a social fact, not with its causes. It involves looking at the part that a social fact plays in relation to the *needs* of a society or social group. The term 'need' refers simply to those things that must be done if a society is to survive. More generally, the function of something is the part that it plays in relation to the adaptation of a society to changing circumstances.

The nature of functional analysis is shown in Figure 2.1. This model simplifies Durkheim's account of the function of religion in a society. Durkheim argued that religion helps to meet a society's need for social solidarity. High levels of religious observance tie people together and so increase the level of social solidarity;

low levels of religious observance, on the other hand, reduce the level of social solidarity. This is matched by the effects that social solidarity have on religion. If the level of social solidarity is too low, then individualistic impulses may threaten the survival of the society. Stability can be maintained only if religious observance increases and a higher level of social solidarity is re-established. If, on the other hand, the level of social solidarity becomes too high, individual creativity may be stifled, and a reduction in the level of religious observance may be required. Religion and social solidarity are, then, interdependent.

There is much in this view of functional analysis that remains unclear. In particular, it does not show what mechanisms actually ensure that increases or reductions in religious observance take place. Durkheim minimizes this problem by equating need with 'goal' or 'purpose'. That is, he assumes that people consciously and deliberately act to meet social needs. Most later writers have rejected this view and have tried to show that the meeting of needs is often an unintended and unrecognized consequence of social action.

Social differentiation and social solidarity

Durkheim applied his scientific method in his great book on the development of modern society (Durkheim 1893). This book, the first that he wrote, was an attempt

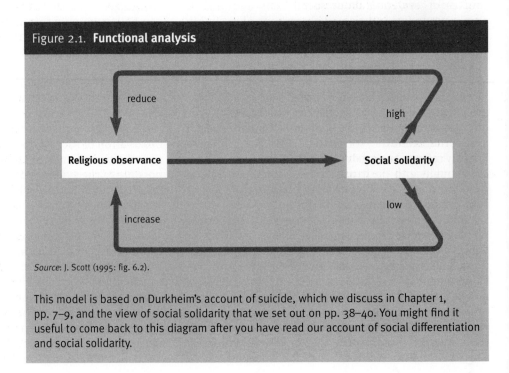

Figure 2.1. **Functional analysis**

reduce

high

Religious observance　　　　　**Social solidarity**

increase

low

Source: J. Scott (1995: fig. 6.2).

This model is based on Durkheim's account of suicide, which we discuss in Chapter 1, pp. 7–9, and the view of social solidarity that we set out on pp. 38–40. You might find it useful to come back to this diagram after you have read our account of social differentiation and social solidarity.

Rules of the sociological method

Durkheim (1895) set out a number of rules or principles. We have considered only the most important of these. A simplified and slightly shortened version of his list is:

▶ consider social facts as things;

▶ cause and function must be investigated separately;

▶ a particular effect always follows from the same cause;

▶ a full explanation of a social fact involves looking at its development through all the stages of its history;

▶ social facts must be classified according to their degree of organization;

▶ a social fact is normal for a given type of society when it is found in the average example of the type;

▶ a social fact is normal when it is related to the general conditions of collective life in a type of society.

Reread the discussion of Durkheim's philosophy and identify the paragraphs in which we discuss each of these rules.

In the title of his book, *Rules of the Sociological Method*, Durkheim uses the word method in the sense of a philosophy of science or 'methodology' of science. He is not talking about the specific research methods that we discuss in Chapter 3.

to examine **social differentiation**, the specialization of activities into a complex structure of occupations. Durkheim labelled this the **division of labour**, using this term to refer not only to the differentiation of economic activities, but also to the specialization of political, administrative, legal, scientific, and other tasks. The division of labour was a principal topic of investigation for economists, but Durkheim wanted to show that their understanding of it was limited. The division of labour, which had achieved an unprecedented scale in modern society, was not simply an economic matter. It was central to the very cohesion and integration of modern societies.

Durkheim's book is divided into two parts: the first is concerned with the causal explanation of the division of labour and the second with its functional analysis. Durkheim's discussion of the causes of the division of labour is the shorter part of the book and can be dealt with briefly. He argued that the division of labour can occur only when communal societies give way to more organized societies. Communal societies are divided into 'segments' (families, clans, local villages) and have little or no division of labour. Each segment is self-sufficient. As segments break down, however, individuals are brought into greater and more intimate contact with those in other parts of their society. This expansion in the scale of social interaction depends on increasing population density and on the emergence of cities and commercial centres. These all bring about an increase in what Durkheim called **dynamic density**. This refers to an increase in the number of social relationships and therefore of the amount of communication and interaction between the members of a society.

A growing population density leads to more and more people carrying out the same activities. This results in growing competition and an ever-increasing struggle to survive. The only way that this competition can be reduced is by people becoming more specialized in their activities. Self-sufficient households may, for example, become specialized in farming, milling, brewing, weaving, and other tasks. They begin to form a division of labour. The division of labour, Durkheim argues, develops in direct proportion to the dynamic density. As the dynamic density of a society increases, so the division of labour becomes more marked. Hence, growth in the scale of societies over time produces ever more complex and differentiated societies.

Far more attention has been given to Durkheim's functional analysis of the division of labour. In this part of the book, he looks at the consequences that the division of labour has for the wider society. In a division of labour, he argues, people's actions are complementary and interdependent. The division of labour creates not simply exchange relationships in a market system, but a feeling of **solidarity** that becomes an essential factor in the integration of the society as a whole.

Social solidarity consists of the *integration* of individuals into social groups and their *regulation* by shared norms. As a social fact, solidarity cannot be observed directly, but only through its external indicators. Durkheim argued that the most important external indicator of social solidarity is the system of law. In societies with an extensive division of labour, he argued, the law tends to be restitutive rather than repressive. Legal procedures attempt to restore things to the way that they were before a crime occurred. Punishment for its own sake is less important. This, Durkheim says, indicates a sense of solidarity that is tied to cooperation and reciprocity. Durkheim calls this **organic solidarity**. People are tied together through relations of trust and reciprocity that correspond to their economic interdependence, and each sphere of activity is regulated through specific types of norms.

The organized, organic solidarity that is produced by the division of labour is contrasted with the **mechanical solidarity** of traditional, communal societies. In these undifferentiated societies that are characteristic of the pre-modern, pre-industrial world, social solidarity revolves around a sense of similarity and a consciousness of unity and community. Conformity in such a society is maintained through the repressive force of a strong system of shared beliefs.

Organic solidarity is a normal or integral feature of modern society, but it may fail to develop in some. In the early stages of the transition from pre-industrial to industrial society, Durkheim argued, there is a particular danger that abnormal forms of the division of labour will develop. The normal condition of organic solidarity encourages a high level of individual freedom, controlling this through the normative systems that Durkheim called moral individualism. The abnormal forms of the division of labour, however, lack this moral framework, and individual actions are left uncontrolled. The two abnormal situations that he describes are egoism and anomie.

Egoism is that situation where individuals are not properly integrated into the social groups of which they are members. Anomie is the situation where individual actions are not properly regulated by shared norms. Durkheim saw anomie and egoism as responsible for the economic crises, extremes of social inequality, and class conflict of his day. As we show in Chapter 1, he also saw them as responsible for high rates of suicide. All of these problems, he held, would be reduced when the division of labour was properly established and organic solidarity instituted in its normal form.

MAX WEBER

Max Weber worked as an economic historian and a lawyer, but he also worked along with other social scientists in Germany to develop a distinctively sociological perspective on these issues. His approach to sociology, however, was very different from that of Durkheim. Weber argued that sociology had to start out not from *structures* but from people's *actions*. This contrast between a sociology of structure and a sociology of action, two complementary perspectives on social life, was to mark the whole of the subsequent development of sociology.

We will begin by discussing Weber's general approach to social science, and we will then look at his application of this approach in his investigations into the development of European societies.

Concepts, values, and science

Durkheim said that the sociologist must consider social facts as things, disregarding all preconceptions. Weber set out a more complex position, arguing that observation was impossible without concepts of some kind. In his principal essay on this subject (Max Weber 1904), he set out to show that this was perfectly compatible with the production of objective scientific knowledge.

Taking his lead from Kant, Weber argued that there can be no knowledge of things as they actually exist, independently of thought. To have knowledge is to give meaning to the world and to interpret it in some way. The world does not simply present itself to our senses already interpreted. It must be interpreted in the light of what is significant to the observer. An area of land, for example, may be of interest as a place for physical exercise, an environment for flora and fauna, an enjoyable aesthetic experience, the site of a historical ruin, and so on. The particular interest that we bring to our observation leads us to focus on different aspects of the world and to use different concepts to interpret it. All observers, scientists included, carve out particular aspects of reality to give them meaning and significance.

The concepts that are used to give this meaning to the world, Weber argued, derive from cultural **values**. It is our values that tell us which aspects of reality are significant and which are insignificant. All concepts are 'value relevant'. They are relative to particular cultural values. Those who hold on to feminist values, for example, are likely to focus on the relationships between men and women and to develop such concepts

Max Weber

Max Weber (1864–1920) was born in Erfurt, Germany, but spent most of his early life in Berlin. He studied law at the University of Heidelberg—his father was a lawyer—and did further academic work at Berlin and Göttingen. He was particularly interested in Roman law and agrarian relations, and he undertook a number of studies in economic history. He became Professor of Economics at Freiburg in 1893, and in 1896 he moved to Heidelberg. Following a dispute with his father, he suffered a mental breakdown and gave up his teaching post the following year. Although he was later able to continue with research and writing, he did not fully return to university teaching until 1917, when he was appointed to a professorship at Munich. Weber was actively involved in liberal politics, and he was a member of the German delegation to the Versailles peace treaty after the First World War.

Much of Weber's work appeared as essays in journals, appearing in book form only later in his life or after his death. His most influential work was his study of Protestantism and the rise of capitalism (Max Weber 1904–5), and he produced related studies of religion in China (1915) and India (1916). His key works on economic and political sociology were not completed in his lifetime and were brought together for publication after his death (Max Weber 1914, 1920).

You will find detailed discussions of Weber's main ideas in the following chapters:

▶ religion and rationality   Chapter 9
▶ social stratification   Chapter 15
▶ bureaucracy   Chapter 16
▶ authority and the state   Chapter 18

Giddens (1971) and Craib (1997) both provide very useful accounts of Weber's work. The standard biography is that written by his wife (Marianne Weber 1926). Parkin (1982) gives a good, brief introduction

Max Weber: saw sociology as the study of social action.

as patriarchy to describe the domination of women by men. Those who hold on to communist values, on the other hand, are likely to focus on the relationships between workers and property owners and to develop such concepts as exploitation to describe these relationships. Values differ considerably from one social group to another, and they change over time. There are no universally valid values, and so there can be no universally valid scientific concepts. There are a large number of possible value standpoints, and reality can only ever be known from particular value-relevant points of view.

This does not mean, however, that all knowledge is simply arbitrary or merely subjective. Scientific knowledge can be objective, despite being value relevant. This is possible if sociologists adopt strict and disciplined methods of investigation. They must be critical in their use of concepts and evidence, and they must follow strict logical principles in their reasoning. It must be possible for any other sociologist to replicate the research and test the results. On this basis, a feminist and a communist may disagree over which concepts are most useful for studying the modern world, but they should each be able to see whether the other has been honest, rational, and critical in carrying out his or her research.

In this way, Weber also distinguishes quite clearly between *factual judgements* and *value judgements*. Sociologists, like all scientists, come to objective factual judgements about what is happening in the world. They may also make subjective value judgements about those things in the world of which they approve or disapprove. These value judgements, however, are no part of science. That someone disapproves of inequality has no

Weber's argument is very difficult to follow, so do not worry if you have problems with it at first. It is probably one of the most difficult things that you will come across in sociology: it is not even fully understood by some professional sociologists! The important point is that Weber rejected the idea that we all experience the world in exactly the same way. He concluded that there can be a number of equally legitimate ways of doing sociology. Come back to Weber's argument after you have completed the rest of this chapter.

bearing upon the question of how great the level of inequality might be in any particular society. The latter is a purely empirical matter, a matter of fact. When a scientist makes a value judgement, he or she is making an ethical or political statement, not a scientific statement. Weber went to great lengths to show that those who allowed their value judgements to interfere with scientific activities were abandoning the principles of science and the pursuit of objective knowledge.

The final plank in Weber's scientific method is the **ideal type**. The principal concepts used by social scientists are constructions for specific scientific purposes. They are logical, ideal constructions from one-sided, value-relevant standpoints. From our particular perspective, we pull together those aspects of reality that are of interest to us and forge them into an idealized model. They can, therefore, be seen as idealizations in the sense that they do not actually exist in reality. These are 'ideal' because they are analytical or conceptual, not because they are desirable or perfect. Ideal types are conceptual models that help us to understand the real world. Such ideal types as capitalism, the nation state, and bureaucracy are not themselves realities. They are analytical devices that are constructed by social scientists in order to understand the more complex reality that actually exists.

This is also true, in many respects, for the natural sciences. The concept of H_2O, for example, is an idealization that does not exist in reality. Actual samples of water contain impurities and additives of all kinds, and it is only under highly artificial, laboratory conditions that it is possible to isolate pure H_2O. In the social sciences, laboratory experimentation is not usually possible and so sociologists are never likely to observe things that correspond precisely to their ideal types. Class and gender relations, for example, only ever exist in combination and alongside many other factors.

Understanding social actions

The most important types for sociology are, according to Weber, ideal types of social action. The more complex ideal types are nothing more than intricate patterns of action, so a typology of action can provide the building blocks for sociological investigations. Weber's emphasis on action marks another area where he differs from Durkheim. Social structures are not seen as external to or independent of individuals. All social structures must be seen as complex, interweaving patterns of action. They have a reality as social facts only when individuals define them as things with a separate existence. Sociologists can describe political activity in terms of the concept of the state only if particular forms of administration and decision-making have been reified—defined as things—by the people involved in them.

Weber identified four ideal types of action as the fundamental building blocks for sociology:

▶ instrumentally rational action;
▶ value-rational action;
▶ traditional action;
▶ affectual action.

Action is *instrumentally rational* when people adopt purely technical means for the attainment of their goals. The action involves a clear goal or purpose, and means are chosen as the best or most efficient ways of achieving it. The capitalist entrepreneur calculates the most efficient and economic means for attaining the maximum profit from a particular line of business. The party leader calculates the particular combination of policy proposals that will maximize the party's vote in forthcoming elections. Weber argues that much of the economic, political, and scientific action that involves rational choice and decision-making approximates to this type of action.

Value-rational action, on the other hand, is action that is rational in relation to some irrational or arbitrarily chosen value. The religious believer who prays and gives alms to the poor may be acting in a value-rational way. He or she is acting this way for its own sake and as an absolute duty, and no account at all is taken of instrumental considerations. In this type of action, there is no discrete or easily observable goal, even if a believer hopes that his or her actions might lead to salvation. In the case of value-rational action, there is no suggestion that actions are technically appropriate in cause–effect terms. They are, however, rational in the methods that they adopt for expressing particular values.

Traditional action is that kind of action that is unreflective and habitual. It barely involves any degree of rationality at all. Traditional action is carried out as a matter of routine, with little or no conscious deliberation. People simply act in the way that they always have done in that situation in the past. Many everyday actions have this traditional, habitual character. Finally, *affectual* action is that which directly expresses an emotion, taking no account of its connection to any specific goals or values. Angry outbursts of violence, for example, would be seen as affectual in nature.

Because these four types of action are ideal types, they do not exist in reality. All concrete patterns of action are likely to be interpretable in terms of more than one type. For example, the actions of a manager in a large business enterprise faced with the need to set a wage level for its employees may involve aspects of all four types of action. The manager may instrumentally calculate the financial consequences of different rates of pay, but may also rule out extremely low pay and certain forms of coercion as contrary to his or her values. The manager may also respond unreflectively to the wage negotiations, seeing them in the way that he or she has done in the past, and making knee-jerk reactions to trade-union proposals. Finally, a breakdown of negotiations may involve angry recriminations as one side or the other walks away from the bargaining table and storms out in the street.

In order to decide how closely a particular course of action corresponds to these and other ideal types, it is necessary to use a technique that Weber sees as central to sociology. This is the technique of **understanding** (*Verstehen* in German). The aim of a social science, says Weber, is to use ideal types as a way of understanding the meanings that people give to their actions. These meanings include their intentions and motives, their expectations about the behaviour of others, and their perceptions of the situations in which they find themselves. Sociologists must infer these meanings from their observations of people's actions, thereby aiming at an interpretative understanding of them. This involves *empathizing* with those that they study, though it does not mean *sympathizing* with them.

We may not approve of serial murder, for example, but we can hope to explain it only if we get close enough to serial murderers to begin to see the world as they see it. We must exercise empathy by trying to identify with them up to the point at which we can comprehend *why* they acted as they did. We do not, however, sympathize with them or condone their actions. To go beyond empathy to sympathy is to make the same mistake as those who go beyond factual judgements to value judgements.

Traditionalism and rationality

Weber's philosophy of science led him to reject deterministic systems of explanation. The causal explanations that sociologists produce must always be rooted in an interpretative understanding of the subjective meanings that individuals give to their actions. Any study of social development must recognize the part played by individual action, and Weber stressed that individuals have free will. Individuals have the power to act freely and not simply as the occupants of class positions or social roles. The future is open and undetermined, it cannot be predicted. The explanations of modern industrial capitalism and the predictions of its future given by Marx and Durkheim would be unacceptable to Weber.

The transition from feudal, pre-industrial societies to modern industrial capitalism is seen by Weber in terms of a shift in the typical meanings that individuals give to their actions. Europe, he argued, had undergone a process of **rationalization**. This involves a shift from value-rational actions to instrumentally rational actions. In medieval societies, people's actions were oriented to absolute religious and political values, while in modern societies they engage in a rational calculation of the likely effects of different courses of action. Political authority in modern society, for example, is based on formal, legal procedures, rather than ultimate religious values such as the divine right of kings.

In medieval societies, furthermore, a great deal of everyday action was not rational at all. It was traditional in character. Indeed, tradition itself was treated as an absolute value in many situations. In modern societies, on the other hand, more and more areas of social life have been opened up to rational, reflective considerations. Thus, economic actions have come to be based on market calculations and contractual relations, rather than on fixed ways of living rooted in traditional styles of life.

Much everyday action in modern societies, of course, remains traditional in character. It continues unreflectively and in routine ways with little direct concern for immediate ends or ultimate values. Traditional forms of action may even acquire a new importance in modern societies. This is clear from Weber's consideration of contemporary economic actions. He holds that religious values motivated the actions of those who became the first generations of calculating capitalist entrepreneurs, but later generations of individuals were more likely to continue with their business activities simply because they had become a matter of routine. As they become mere cogs in huge bureaucratic machines, their work becomes a 'dull compulsion' about which they have no real choice. Ultimately they may remain free, but in practice they are constrained.

 You will understand more about Weber's views on rational economic action when you have read our discussion of *The Protestant Ethic and the Spirit of Capitalism* in Chapter 9, pp. 323–4. You may like to read that discussion now.

SUMMARY POINTS

In this section we have looked at the two leading figures of the classical period of sociology, Durkheim and Weber. Durkheim was the principal French sociologist and founder of an approach that emphasized social structure as the fundamental social facts. He set this out in an account of the basic principles of sociology.

▶ Social facts are ways of acting, thinking, or feeling that are both external and constraining. They are collective products, and individuals experience them as coercive or obligatory.

▶ Social facts are to be studied as things, through observation rather than on the basis of prejudice and preconception. Although they cannot always be observed directly, social facts can be observed indirectly through their effects on individual actions.

▶ Durkheim recognized two aspects of sociological explanation: causal explanation and functional analysis. In causal explanation, social facts are accounted for in terms of the other social facts that brought them into being. In functional analysis, social facts are examined in relation to the part that they play in relation to the survival or adaptation of other social facts.

Durkheim applied this sociological approach in a number of substantive studies of the division of labour, suicide, education, and religion. We discuss a number of these studies in other chapters. These were seen as aspects of a general account of social development.

▶ Social development is a process of social differentiation in which the forms of solidarity change.

▶ Social solidarity comprises the integration of individuals into social groups and their regulation by shared norms. Durkheim contrasted the mechanical solidarity of traditional societies with the organic solidarity of modern societies.

▶ One of the central problems of contemporary society was the pathological state of individualism that Durkheim described as involving egoism and anomie.

Weber, as one of a number of important German sociologists, tried to build a sociology of social action that was sensitive to the meanings and motives that shaped people's behaviour.

▶ Social reality can only ever be studied through the use of concepts that reflect cultural values. Knowledge of social reality is objective only if it results from the rational and critical use of these concepts in a scientifically disciplined way.

▶ While all concepts are value relevant, Weber emphasizes the need to distinguish clearly factual judgements from value judgements.

▶ Sociological concepts are ideal types and do not correspond to things that actually exist in reality. They grasp particular aspects of reality.

▶ Ideal types of social action are the basic building blocks of sociological analysis. Weber identifies instrumentally rational action, value-rational action, traditional action, and affectual action.

▶ Actions are structured through a process of understanding that involves empathizing with those who are studied.

Weber rejected all forms of structural determinism, emphasizing the open-ended character of social life. He did, however, undertake a number of studies of social development, including the important study of religion that we look at in Chapter 9.

▶ Western societies had experienced a process of rationalization. This was a growth in the significance of rational motivations and a shift from value-rational to instrumentally rational considerations.

▶ In modern, capitalist societies, market calculation and contractual relations have achieved a central significance.

▶ Although capitalist economic actions originated in religiously motivated actions, they had come to be a mere matter of routine and dull compulsion.

SOCIOLOGY COMES OF AGE

In the hands of Durkheim, Weber, and their contemporaries, sociology finally became, by the first decade of the twentieth century, established as a legitimate science with a place in the system of university teaching and research. Although there were still few professors of sociology—and sociology was barely taught in schools—a sociological perspective had been established in the study of history, law, politics, education, religion, and many other areas of specialization. Figure 2.2 summarizes the origins of their ideas and the main lines of development in sociology into the first half of the twentieth century.

There were, of course, great differences in the theoretical positions that were put forward by those who called themselves 'sociologists'. Durkheim and his followers stressed the importance of structure in social life, seeing societies as systems of structured relationships. The German sociologists, such as Weber, tended to emphasize action as the central concept, showing that all social structures were, ultimately, to be explained as the outcome of human actions.

These positions must not be seen as stark alternatives to one another. In the early days of academic sociology it was easy for Durkheim and Weber each to believe that his particular theory was uniquely appropriate for the study of social life. Indeed, some writers today still suggest that there is a great gulf between structure and action perspectives and that only one of them can be correct. As soon as one tries to do any sociological work, however, it becomes clear that the two approaches are complementary.

Durkheim and Weber were emphasizing different aspects of a highly complex reality. Social life involves *both* structure and action. Some sociologists have tried to combine both aspects in the same theory, but these attempts have not been particularly successful. There may one day be a single, all-encompassing theory, but it is probably a long way from completion (but see Giddens 1976). The point is that sociologists need to develop a theoretical understanding of both the structural aspects of social life and their shaping by social actions. Distinct theoretical traditions may continue to exist, but they must cooperate in studies of particular phenomena.

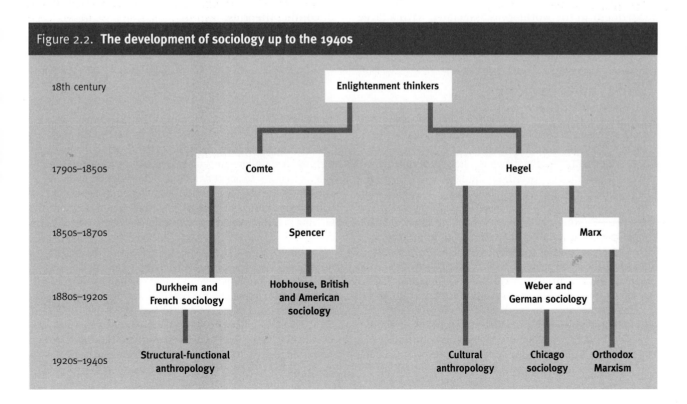

Figure 2.2. **The development of sociology up to the 1940s**

In the generation that followed Durkheim and Weber, their leading ideas were consolidated and further developed, though there were no major advances for some time. The mainstream of academic sociology in Europe and America owed most to the ideas of Durkheim. Sociology and intellectual life generally were suppressed in Germany during the 1930s and 1940s, and this limited the wider impact of the ideas of Weber and his contemporaries.

In Britain and the United States, Durkheim's ideas were welded into a theoretical framework that came to be described as 'structural functionalism', or simply as 'functionalism'. Much of this theoretical work was undertaken in the study of small-scale, tribal societies of the kind that Durkheim had studied for his own investigations into religion (1912), and many functionalists called themselves anthropologists rather than sociologists.

Much of the sociological research that was undertaken in the first thirty years or so of the twentieth century ignored theoretical issues. Work by Booth, Rowntree, and others in localities and communities across Britain, for example, investigated poverty and inequality with little concern for how these could be explained in terms of the overall structure of British societies. The principal exception to this neglect of theory was to be found in the United States, where the new Department of Sociology at Chicago—the first full department in the world—was associated with a large number of local studies that drew explicitly on European traditions of theory.

Like the anthropologists, the Chicago sociologists made a major contribution to fieldwork methods, but they did so from very different theoretical traditions. In their work, they paid little attention to Durkheim, finding their main inspiration in German sociology. The main influence was not Weber but his friend Georg Simmel. The Chicago sociologists took up, in particular, the German writers' emphasis on action and interaction, combining this with an awareness of the part played by group conflict in social life. Their main studies were concerned with the city of Chicago itself (Park and Burgess 1925), and they began to develop theoretical ideas that would achieve their fullest recognition only after the Second World War.

Figure 2.2 shows how these various strands of thought relate to the wider development of sociological theory. From the 1940s, and for at least a generation, sociological theorists continued to build on these foundations. By the 1950s, when sociology had begun to break through its old national boundaries, the theoretical landscape had been transformed. Theoretical debates crystallized into a smaller number of separate positions, each of which had a far more international character than before. Three principal traditions of thought dominated sociological debate: structural functionalism, symbolic interactionism, and a number of conflict theories.

Social anthropology

Social anthropology is the term often used to describe the work of those sociologists who specialize in the study of small-scale, pre-industrial societies.

Most influential among the early followers of Durkheim was Arthur Radcliffe-Brown, a Cambridge-trained anthropologist who carried out fieldwork in Australia and in the Andaman Islands of the Indian Ocean. His books (Radcliffe-Brown 1922, 1930) reported on religious ritual and kinship in tribal societies, and he drew out some general conclusions in a series of essays (Radcliffe-Brown 1952). Radcliffe-Brown inspired the work of Lloyd Warner, an American who undertook investigations in Australian tribal societies and small American towns during the 1930s and 1940s (Warner and Lunt 1941). Radcliffe-Brown added little to Durkheim's own ideas, but he popularized the idea that theories had to be applied in detailed fieldwork studies.

Bronislaw Malinowski developed this fieldwork tradition in Britain. He carried out some early research on native Australian kinship, but his most important work was undertaken in the Trobriand Islands of the Pacific. His main books (Malinowski 1922, 1929, 1935) emphasized the need to study all social phenomena in terms of their functions in relation to other social phenomena and in relation to the structure of the society as a whole. He further emphasized that this kind of research could most easily be undertaken by living in a society and trying to grasp its whole way of life.

Franz Boas carried forward a similar fieldwork method in the United States, though his work owed a great deal to Hegel as well as to Durkheim. Boas (1911) emphasized the importance of culture and the need to grasp the inner spirit of the culture as a whole. He and his many students carried out a series of studies of native American tribes and small communities in the Pacific. While Malinowski saw functional analysis in relation to material and environmental factors, Boas set out a more cultural or idealist theory.

STRUCTURAL-FUNCTIONALIST THEORIES

Post-war structural functionalism had its roots in the sociology of Durkheim and the social anthropology of the inter-war years. However, its leading figure came from a very different background. Talcott Parsons, who was to dominate sociology for more than two decades, was trained in economics, spending periods of time in Britain and Germany. He began, in the 1930s, to explore the relationship between economics and sociology and to build a novel philosophical basis for sociology. After this, and influenced by some early work by Robert Merton (1936, 1949), Parsons began to set out his own version of structural-functionalist theory. It was this theory that was to exercise such an influence on the development of sociology.

The action frame of reference

In *The Structure of Social Action* (Parsons 1937), Parsons set out to synthesize the insights of Durkheim and Weber. Durkheim, it will be recalled, had stressed the need to consider social facts as things and to abandon all theoretical preconceptions. Weber, on the other hand, said that observation was impossible without concepts and that all concepts were value-relevant. Parsons would not go along with either of these positions, though he recognized that each writer had glimpsed a part of the truth.

Parsons called his synthesis of the two positions **analytical realism**. It was analytical in that, like Weber, he recognized that all observations were dependent on concepts. But it was also realist in that, like Durkheim, he saw these observations telling us something about what the world was actually like (Scott 1995). He argued that we must use concepts to make observations, but we must check our observations against evidence.

 If you are interested in these philosophical issues, you should look back at our discussion of Durkheim on social facts and Weber on value relevance before continuing. We do not intend to go very far into these issues. You may prefer to look further at them when you have studied more sociology. Once you have tackled a few substantive topics, you may find it easier to struggle with some philosophy! For those who do want to read further, some good discussions are Keat and Urry (1975) and Williams and May (1996).

The particular concepts needed in sociology, Parsons said, comprise an **action frame of reference**. This is a set of concepts that allow sociologists to talk about social action rather than about physical events or biological behaviour. This frame of reference had begun to emerge in the work of the classical sociologists. Each started from his own distinctive theoretical position,

Talcott Parsons

Talcott Parsons (1902–79) was the son of a clergyman. He studied economics at Amherst, and then undertook postgraduate research at the London School of Economics and at Heidelberg. He taught economics from 1926 to 1931, when he switched to sociology at Harvard University. His early works were concerned with the relationship between economics and sociology, as this had been seen by Weber, Pareto, and the British economist Alfred Marshall. Under the influence of the biologist L. J. Henderson, Parsons began to take Durkheim's work more seriously and in 1937 he produced his first book, *The Structure of Social Action*. Parsons remained at Harvard throughout his academic career.

Parsons has a reputation for his impenetrable prose style and the large number of new, long words that he invented. His work is certainly difficult. Do try to read Parsons's work, but do not expect to understand it all at a first reading.

After his first book, his most important works were the massive *Social System* (1951), a book on the family (Parsons and Bales 1956), one on the economy (Parsons and Smelser 1956), and two shorter volumes on social development (Parsons 1966, 1971). Some of his more accessible work has been reprinted in a collection of essays (Parsons 1954). A valuable and brief introduction to his work is Hamilton (1983).

You will find more detailed discussions of Parsons's work in the following chapters:

▶ socialization and social roles   Chapter 4
▶ family and kinship   Chapter 10
▶ health and illness   Chapter 6
▶ social stratification   Chapter 15

but they had gradually and unconsciously begun to move towards a similar theoretical approach to social life. This approach was the action frame of reference.

According to the action frame of reference, any action involves five basic elements:

▶ *actors*: the people who actually carry out the actions;

▶ *ends*: the goals that these people pursue;

▶ *means*: the resources that are available to achieve these ends;

▶ *conditions*: the particular circumstances in which actions are carried out;

▶ *norms*: the standards in relation to which people choose their ends and means.

Parsons holds that sociologists must construct models of action using these elements. To do this, they must try to understand things and events as they appear to the actors. The various ideal types and general concepts that are used in sociological explanations, according to Parsons, must be compatible with these basic principles of the action frame of reference. You will probably recognize how much Parsons owed to Weber here.

This action frame of reference became the basis of the structural functionalism built by Parsons, Merton, and others from the 1940s. In undertaking this task, they drew heavily on the ideas of Durkheim. They built a set of concepts that could describe the *structural* features of social life, but that were grounded in the *action* frame of reference. Societies, and social groups of all kinds, were seen as *social systems* that consisted of mutually dependent parts, such as roles, institutions, and organizations. These parts together formed the social structure. The task of sociological analysis was to identify these parts and to show the functions that they fulfil in the system as a whole.

Social structure

Structural functionalists see the structure of a society as a normative framework. It consists of the norms that define the expectations and obligations that govern people's actions and so shape their social relations. At the heart of this normative framework are definitions of the various social positions that are linked together into a complex social division of labour. There may be, for example, family positions such as husband, wife, and child, economic and professional positions such as teacher, miller, doctor, and banker, and such other positions as student, priest, politician, and so on.

Those who occupy social positions are expected to behave in certain ways. These expectations define the social **roles** that are attached to the positions. A role is a cluster of normative expectations that set out a script for social actors in particular social positions. It defines standards of appropriate and inappropriate behaviour, telling people what is 'normal' or expected behaviour in particular situations. A teacher, for example, knows how he or she ought to behave in relation to pupils, parents, head teachers, governors, and others who play their parts in the same school and in the wider educational system (Merton 1957, Gross *et al.* 1958).

Many norms are quite specific and concern just one role. Others, however, may be very general in their scope. These generalized norms, rooted in widely shared cultural values, are termed social institutions by structural functionalists. Institutions, then, are established and solidified sets of norms that cross cut social roles and help to tie them together. The institutions of property, contract, and the market, for example, help to define a large number of economic and occupational roles. Similarly, the institutions of kinship and marriage regulate a range of family roles, and the institutions of bureaucratic administration and democratic leadership regulate political roles. Structural functionalists recognize a tendency for positions, roles, and institutions to cluster together into more or less distinct subsystems. A society may, for example, consist of an economic system, a political system, an educational system, a system of social stratification, and so on. At its most general, then, the structure of a social system might be described in terms of the connections between such subsystems. A simplified structural functionalist model is shown in Figure 2.3.

The key to the stability and cohesion of a social structure, argue structural functionalists, is **socialization**. In their infancy and childhood, as well as in their later

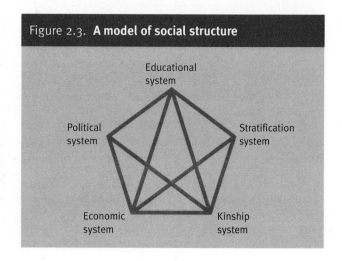

Figure 2.3. **A model of social structure**

life, individuals learn the norms of their society. They come to learn what is expected of them and of those with whom they are likely to come into contact. They learn, in short, how to be an acceptable member of their society. The cultural values and social norms that people learn are, according to many structural functionalists, widely shared in the society. That is to say, they assume the existence of a social consensus, an agreement over the basic principles that will regulate social life. All members of a society, for example, are seen as sharing a broad commitment to the same values, beliefs, and ideas. Merton (1938b), however, has recognized that this consensus may be far from perfect. Individuals may be commited to some aspects of their culture, while rejecting or remaining neutral about others. He used this insight to develop a very important theory of **anomie**.

> 👉 Merton's concept of anomie is not exactly the same as Durkheim's, although they are closely related. Whenever you come across the word 'anomie', make sure that you know how it is being used.
>
> In Chapter 4, pp. 129–31, you will find a full discussion of the structural-functionalist view of socialization on which Merton relies.

The starting point for this theory is Merton's discussion of culture. The culture of a society, he holds, specifies the *ends* or goals that people should pursue and the *means* that they are expected to follow in achieving them. People's goals include such things as promotion at work, pleasing a husband or wife, learning to drive a car, writing a book, and so on. Means are those things that help to achieve these goals: working hard, money, physical skills, power, etc. Where people are fully socialized into their culture, they will be committed to the ends and the means that are held out to them. They will be conformists who follow only culturally approved goals and use only culturally approved means. Someone may, for example, desire a pleasant and well-decorated home and will work hard to earn the money required. The conformist would not even consider stealing the money from others. If, however, a culture emphasizes the ends much more than the means, leaving the means only loosely regulated, people's commitment to the approved means—and therefore their conformity to social norms—may be eroded. This is especially likely where the material structure of opportunities available to people makes it difficult for them to achieve the approved ends. The

conditions under which they must act may mean, for example, that they lack the resources that are needed for the means to which they are supposed to be committed. It is the rift between culturally approved ends and means that Merton calls anomie. In a situation of anomie, conformity is far from automatic.

Merton suggests that his model is particularly applicable to a modern society such as the United States, where financial success in an occupation is a central social value. Contemporary culture, he says, places great emphasis on the need to maximize income. It also requires that individuals should pursue this end through occupational achievement: they should work diligently and efficiently in order to be promoted to a higher salary. The distribution of resources, however, makes it difficult for people to compete on an equal basis in this race for financial success. Not all people have the same opportunities to enter well-paid employment, for example. Divisions of class, gender, and ethnicity set limits on the chances that they are able to enjoy. In this situation, their commitment to the prescribed means may be weakened, especially if they are given less cultural emphasis than the overriding goal of success.

Merton argues that there are four possible responses to this anomie, as shown in Figure 2.4. The first possible response is what he calls *innovation*. The innovator is someone who responds to these cultural strains by

Figure 2.4. Conformity and responses to anomie

	Ends	Means
Conformity	+	+
Innovation	+	−
Ritualism	−	+
Retreatism	−	−
Rebellion	±	±

+   acceptance.
−   rejection.
±   rejection of dominant values and acceptance of alternative values.

Robert Merton was born in 1910 and studied under Talcott Parsons. He has published important papers on roles, anomie, and functional analysis. You will find applications of his model of anomie to the rise of new religions in Chapter 9, pp. 341–2, and to drug use in Chapter 5, pp. 174–7. A useful introduction to his thought is Crothers (1987).

rejecting the legitimate means and employing illegitimate ones. Criminal activities aimed at financial gain are typical innovative acts. This is particularly likely to occur, Merton argues, among the poorest members of society who have fewest opportunities. Merton recognizes this also as the response of those who are relatively successful, but who are willing to 'bend the rules' and engage in fraud and embezzlement to increase their income.

Ritualism is the second possible response to anomie. Here, people decide that they have little chance of attaining any significant success and so reject this as a goal. They remain, however, loosely committed to the conventional means. They simply go through the motions in a ritualistic way, with little or no commitment to the approved goal. The time-serving bureaucrat who rigidly follows rules and procedures, regardless of the consequences, is a typical ritualist. Such a person, if challenged about the consequences of his or her actions, is likely to respond that 'I'm only doing my job'. Ritualistic bureaucrats are likely to be fatalistic, resigned to their lot. They feel that they have no control over their lives.

The third response to anomie is *retreatism*. The retreatist decides to reject both the means and the ends prescribed by the culture. This is the response of the drop-out, of whom Merton sees the hobo or vagrant as the typical example. Others have suggested that persistent deviant drug use may also be the action of a retreatist. Merton's analysis of retreatism, however, fails to recognize that many of those who drop out of conventional society establish new conventions for themselves in deviant subcultures. This is the case for many drug users and vagrants.

The retreatist response, therefore, is difficult to distinguish from *rebellion*, where the legitimate ends and means are rejected but are replaced by alternative ends and means that may challenge conventional values. Radical political action, aimed at altering the distribution of resources or the political system, is, for Merton, the typical response of the rebel. This claim can be seen as Merton's reformulation of Durkheim's idea that organized class conflict can be seen as a consequence of anomie.

Functional analysis

Structural functionalists have developed and clarified the method of functional analysis outlined by Durkheim, making it the centrepiece of their work. Both Spencer and Durkheim, like many of their contemporaries, had seen parallels between societies and biological organisms. For Spencer, societies were to be seen as 'social organisms' that could be studied by the same scientific methods as biological organisms. The most important part of any scientific investigation, he held, is to uncover the functions carried out by the various structures of the organism. The function of the heart in the human body, for example, is to maintain the circulation of the blood. In sociology, Spencer suggested, we must investigate such things as the functions of government and ritual. In Durkheim's work, functional analysis was drawn out more clearly and set alongside causal explanation at the heart of sociological explanation.

The functional method has been much misunderstood. Some critics of structural functionalism have claimed that it involves the idea that societies literally are the same as biological organisms, or that social facts can be reduced to biological facts. These misunderstandings are, in part, the result of the misleading language used by many functionalists. Nevertheless, functional analysis is an important aspect of any sociological investigation into how societies work, and its core ideas are quite straightforward. The functionalist method sees any system as having *needs* or requirements. If a system is to survive and to continue in more or less its current form, then these needs must be met in some way. The function of a structure is the contribution that it makes to meeting a need, and a functional analysis consists in identifying the processes through which these needs are met.

The idea of a need is quite simple. A human body needs food if it is to survive; it will die without this food. However, it is important to recognize that there is nothing automatic about the meeting of needs. The need for food does not, in itself, cause food to become available. Many people across the world do, in fact, starve to death. It is for this reason that Durkheim tried to separate cause from function.

How, then, can functional analysis be used in the study of societies? The first step is to identify the needs of the society. A society is assumed to be a relatively self-contained unit that can be treated as a well-bounded system. As such, it has many internal needs. These include the biological and psychological needs of its members (for example, their needs for food and company) and the need to maintain its boundaries and identity. Some of these needs can be met, in whole or in part, from its own internal resources. The need to socialize infants, for example, can be met through the educational efforts of its already socialized members, such as the infant's parents.

However, many needs can be met only if the society

draws on resources from its external environment. This external environment comprises the natural world that surrounds the society, together with the other societies and social groups with which it has contacts. A society must adapt itself to its external environment, and the environment must be adapted to its needs. For example, if a large society is to feed its members, then crops must be planted and harvested, soil must be improved and irrigated, commodities must be imported, minerals must be mined and converted into ploughs and tractors, and so on. To achieve this kind of environmental adaptation, a society needs to restructure itself by establishing processes to handle its external relations and, perhaps, altering its own boundaries.

The initial internal needs, then, lead to external needs. As a result of its restructuring, the society may face new internal needs. If, for example, a system of food production is established, a society will then need to ensure that the pace and level of production are, in some degree, coordinated with its actual food requirements and that the resources given over to this production do not prevent it from meeting any of its other needs. Social systems, then, are dynamic systems, constantly altering their structures as the ways in which they meet, or fail to meet, their needs change.

It is important to emphasize again that needs will not be inevitably or automatically met, though some functionalists have tended to assume that they will. The needs of a social system are simply the conditions that are necessary for its survival in its current form. These conditions will actually be met only if, for whatever reason, people carry out the actions that meet them. The need does not itself cause the action that meets it.

A number of theorists have attempted to compile lists of the needs or functional requirements of a social system (Aberle *et al.* 1950; Levy 1966). The most influential was that of Parsons himself, though it was not without its critics. Parsons arrived at a classification of functional needs by looking at two aspects or dimensions of them:

▶ whether they are *internal* or *external* to the system;
▶ whether they involve the *ends* or the *means* of action.

As we have already shown, some needs are internal to the system itself, while others are external to it. Parsons defines internal needs as those that concern the integrity and cohesion of a social system. External needs, on the other hand, concern the facilities and resources that must be generated from its environment. Whether they are internal or external, needs may be relevant to either the means or the ends of action.

In the former case, they are concerned with the production and accumulation of human and physical resources for use in the future, while in the latter they involve the immediate use and consumption of resources in current actions.

According to Parsons—who followed Spencer on this—the gradual differentiation of social activities into structurally distinct roles, institutions, and subsystems is a response to attempts to meet functional needs. He held that a model of a social system can be constructed by cross-classifying the two dimensions that he identified, as shown in Figure 2.5. According to this model, any social system has four functional needs, and its structures can be classified according to which of the four functions they are mainly concerned with. This model lies at the heart of Parsons's work, and versions of it can be found throughout his books. It has come to be known as the Parsonian boxes.

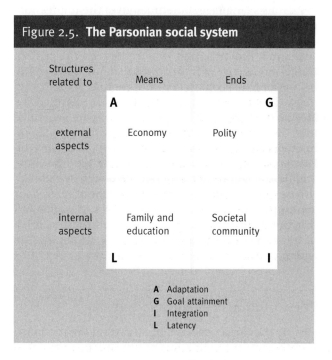

Figure 2.5. **The Parsonian social system**

Structures related to

	Means	Ends
A		**G**
external aspects	Economy	Polity
internal aspects	Family and education	Societal community
L		**I**

A Adaptation
G Goal attainment
I   Integration
L Latency

The four functions shown in Figure 2.5 are adaptation, goal attainment, integration, and latency. **Adaptation** is the need to accumulate and control resources from the environment so that they are available for future actions. Parsons said that this need is met through the economic structures of production, distribution, and exchange. **Goal attainment** is the need to mobilize existing resources in relation to individual and collective goals. This, he said, can be met through the political structures of decision-making and executive control.

Integration is the need to ensure the cohesion and solidarity of the social system itself. Parsons introduced the term societal community to designate the structures concerned with this function. The term refers not only to localized community structures of kinship and neighbourhood, but also to the larger bonds of national and ethnic community and of social stratification. Finally, **Latency** (or 'pattern maintenance') is the need to build up a store of motivation and commitment that can be used, when required, for all the various activities of the society. Institutions such as the family and education, where people are socialized into the values and norms of their society, are the main structures concerned with this need. These structures are much less likely to become differentiated than are other structures, and they remain closely tied to the structures of the societal community.

Parsons's language sometimes gives the impression that needs are automatically met. Perhaps Parsons did, on occasion, believe this. He maintained, however, that structural functionalism was rooted in the action frame of reference, which showed that functions would be met only if people acted in ways that actually did meet these needs. This point has been clarified by Merton (1949), who shows that functions are generally met, if at all, as the unintended consequences of human action. One of the strongest criticisms of Parsons has been that he failed to analyse action as thoroughly as structure and function. Although he claimed to base his arguments on the action frame of reference, action played a minor part in his work. A structural functionalist model that focuses on the structural level of analysis must be complemented by an analysis of action.

The evolution of modern society

One of the main concerns of structural-functionalist theorists was to use this idea to build an account of the development of modern society. They tried to show that the need to adapt to changing functional needs drove societies in a definite direction. Though no one intended it to occur, traditional agricultural societies underwent a process of *modernization* that brought into being the new social institutions that comprise modernity. Modern societies, then, are the results of long processes of structural differentiation that were shaped by the need to adapt to their changing environments and the unintended consequences of the responses made to these needs. This argument has been most clearly stated by Parsons, who places it in the context of a larger theory of social evolution.

The baseline for studying social evolution, according to Parsons, is provided by the 'primitive' hunting and gathering societies (Parsons 1966). In these relatively undifferentiated societies, the societal community is formed from a network of kinship relations that extend across the whole society and there are no functionally specialized structures. Each society is integrated through its shared religious beliefs, which provide an all-embracing cultural framework for people's actions. As these societies increase in size and become more involved in settled agriculture, so structures of private property and social stratification begin to develop to organize the new systems of production. When societies achieve this level of complexity, they may require systems of chiefhood or kingship to coordinate them.

Across the world, tribes and chiefdoms prevailed for thousands of years. In certain circumstances, however, development to even more complex forms of social organization occurred. In Egypt and Mesopotamia there were more complex forms of agriculture that were associated with the building of large systems of irrigation. Social stratification became sharper, religion came under the control of a specialized priesthood, and political control became stronger. By the third millennium BC, these societies had evolved into *advanced intermediate* societies that had both a historic religion and an imperial political system. Similar developments occurred somewhat later in China, India, and the Roman world. Following Comte, Parsons sees their religions becoming more philosophical and metaphysical in character.

The breakthrough to modern forms of society, Parsons said, occurred in medieval Europe in the centuries following the collapse of the Roman Empire and the gradual rebuilding of royal structures. Political and scientific spheres of action were differentiated from the previously all-encompassing religious structures, and a separate sphere of economic action also appeared. Private property, the market, and the division of labour expanded, forming specialized elements in the economies of the European societies. From the eighteenth century, industrialism and democracy transformed the ways in which the adaptation and goal-attainment functions were met, and more fully modern societies were formed. Nation states and industrial technologies were the characteristic institutions of these modern societies, which were characterized by the spread of bureaucracy and market relations. Modern social institutions developed especially rapidly in the United States, where pre-modern survivals were very much weaker, and it became the characteristically modern society of the twentieth century.

INTERACTION THEORIES

Structural functionalism provided the mainstream of sociological thought from the 1940s until at least the 1970s, and it remains an important part of contemporary sociology. With its roots in Comte, Spencer, and Durkheim, it is at the heart of the sociological tradition. However, it was never unchallenged. Many critics pointed out that, despite its advocacy of an action frame of reference, it did not really take sufficient account of action. In providing a comprehensive theory of social structures and their functions, it minimized the active and creative part played by social action. This concern for social action has a long history, and we have shown how it was central to the work of Weber and his contemporaries in Germany. However, it was a subordinate trend within sociology, and it has achieved a wider impact only since the 1960s. Writers critical of structural functionalism returned to the founding statements of Weber and, above all, the early Chicago sociologists in an attempt to construct a full-blown sociology of action. In this section, we will look at two related theories of interaction: the symbolic interactionism of the Chicago school and the phenomenological theories developed from a reconsideration of Weber's typology of action.

Symbolic interactionism

Symbolic interactionism was nurtured in the Department of Sociology at Chicago from the 1920s to the 1950s. However, it originated outside Chicago and it has, since the 1950s, spread far beyond it. The core of the sociological work carried out at Chicago was a series of empirical studies in the city of Chicago itself. The theoretical framework used to organize these studies and to explain some of their results stressed the struggle of social groups for resources and their competition over the use of the space in the city. When they wished to explain what was going on within each of these groups and how individuals responded to their situations, they drew on the ideas that later came to be called symbolic interactionism.

This was a theory of action that originated in the philosophical and psychological studies of William James, carried out at Harvard towards the end of the nineteenth century. William James, brother of the novelist Henry James, was not a particularly sophisticated philosopher. He had a number of insightful ideas, but he expressed these in a rather homespun and oversimple way. He did, however, nurture the brilliant work of the eccentric Charles Peirce. The works of James and Peirce together laid the foundations of the philosophical position of pragmatism, and it was this approach to knowledge and meaning that was transformed into symbolic interactionism.

Pragmatism holds that ideas are produced and used in practical situations. The knowledge that people acquire is not like a photograph. It is not a mental copy of things that actually exist in reality. It is, rather, an attempt to understand the world well enough to make practical sense of it and to act effectively. James summarized this point of view in the claim that truth consists simply of those ideas that happen to work. Knowledge is true if it helps us to get by in our practical actions. It is this practical *pragmatic* test that gave the philosophical position its name. Peirce's work added much subtlety to this basic argument. In particular, he presented pragmatism as a theory of *meaning*, rather than simply a theory of truth. What Peirce argued was that the meaning of a concept is given by the way in which that concept is used. What we mean by a chair is something to sit on when we wish to relax, and many different physical objects can meet this need. Similarly, one of the things that we mean by a mother is someone who looks after children. There can be no abstract definitions of these concepts that identify essential characteristics of what chairs or mothers 'really' are. They simply mean whatever they are used to refer to in practical everyday situations.

These arguments were developed—and made much clearer—in the works of John Dewey, Charles Cooley, William Thomas, and George Mead. It was Thomas and Mead, after they joined the staff at Chicago, who began to convert pragmatist ideas into a sociological theory of action. Mead was by far the more sophisticated writer of the two. He had undertaken his postgraduate studies in Germany, and he found many congenial ideas in the German philosophical and sociological tradition. Weber was, of course, an influence on him, but the most important of the German theorists in the shaping of Mead's position was Georg Simmel. Work by Simmel was translated and published in the *American Journal of Sociology*, the journal of the Chicago Department, and through these translations Simmel had a major impact on the new theory.

Mead argued that individuals give meaning to the world by defining and interpreting it in certain ways. The world is never experienced directly, but always through the ideas that we hold about it. The meaning of reality is, in a fundamental sense, the meaning that we

Georg Simmel

Georg Simmel (1858–1917) was born in Berlin, Germany. He spent most of his academic career at the University of Berlin. He studied philosophy, but he taught and wrote on both philosophy and sociology. During his lifetime he was probably better known than Weber among other sociologists.

Simmel stressed the need to study the *forms* of social relationships, rather than their content. He explored such things as the relations of insiders to outsiders, relations of domination and subordination, relations of conflict, and the significance of the size of groups. His ideas were developed in a book called *Sociology* (Simmel 1908), most of which has been translated in Wolff (1950). Simmel was particularly concerned with uncovering the distinctive features of contemporary urban life, and he set out these ideas in an essay on the metropolis and a book called *The Philosophy of Money* (Simmel 1900).

choose to give to it. Thomas summarized this point of view in the statement that 'When men define situations as real, they are real in their consequences'. What he meant by this is that the actions of men (and women) depend far more on how they define a situation than on the situation itself. People define situations and act upon those definitions. As a pragmatist, however, Thomas stressed that these definitions were not simply arbitrary and artificial constructions. Only those definitions that are useful in practical actions are likely to persist in use for any time.

This becomes clearer if we consider the example of a bus. A bus exists as a purely physical object, an assemblage of metal, plastic, rubber, fabric, and so on. Its meaning for us, however, depends on how we choose to define it. In calling it a bus, we define it as something that will follow a particular route, stop at particular places, and pick up people who pay to take a journey. Redundant buses, however, have been defined and used as social centres, caravans, chicken coops, and works of art. Each of these definitions—and many others—is compatible with the particular physical object that, in other circumstances, we define as a bus. What makes its definition as a bus appropriate is our practical success in being able to use it to travel to our destination. What is true of the bus is true of all social objects. It is possible to define things in any of a number of different ways, and the effective definition is simply the one that works when people come to act on their definitions.

These definitions cannot be unique to particular

individuals, or they will not work. The concept of a bus, for example, is one that is useful only because it is widely shared. It is a concept shared by all those interested in its operations: passengers, drivers, conductors, inspectors, traffic police, ministers of transport, and so on. Many of these people acquire their identities from the idea of the bus. It is, for example, impossible to have bus drivers unless we have the concept of a bus. It is usually possible to rely on a bus service because there are widely shared definitions and conventions concerning timetabling, queuing, and fare-paying. A widely shared meaning, communicated to us by others, has a greater reality to us than does an idiosyncratic one, and it is more likely to be useful in practical situations.

The definitions that people use are constructed from the *symbols* (the names and labels for objects) that are available to them in their culture. Spoken and written words, together with pictures, images, and other conventional signs, convey information and are used by people to give meaning to the situations in which they find themselves. These symbols are learned and communicated through interaction with others. This is why the theoretical position has come to be called **symbolic interactionism**.

This name was coined by Herbert Blumer (1966), who also did much to popularize it and to mark out its distinctiveness from mainstream structural-functionalist sociology. According to Blumer, societies were not fixed and objective structures. What we call 'society' is the fluid and flexible networks of interaction within which we act. To describe these overlapping networks of interaction as structures, Blumer held, is to reify them and to distort the part that individuals play in creating and altering them through action. This led Blumer to reject

Social construction

The case of a bus—discussed in the text—is typical of all social definitions, which is why we have discussed it at such length. Whenever we employ words to refer to objects in our social world, we are, quite literally, *constructing* them as meaningful social objects that we can take account of in our actions. Try to think about the implications of attempting to redefine some common social objects. What would happen if you defined a table as a chair? What consequences would follow if you defined newly washed curtains as paint covers (don't try this one at home!)? When you have considered these relatively simple cases, you might think about the consequences of defining an unmarried man as a homosexual rather than a bachelor.

all talk of structures, systems, and functional needs. There are simply actions, interactions, and their consequences for individuals.

Others in the symbolic interactionist tradition have been less extreme in their opposition to mainstream sociology. They have seen symbolic interactionism as concerned merely with those aspects of action and interaction that have not given their due attention in structural functionalism. This is, for example, the case with Erving Goffman, whose work owes as much to Durkheim as it does to Mead (Collins 1994: 218).

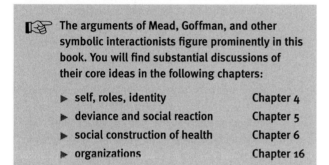

The arguments of Mead, Goffman, and other symbolic interactionists figure prominently in this book. You will find substantial discussions of their core ideas in the following chapters:

▶ self, roles, identity   Chapter 4
▶ deviance and social reaction   Chapter 5
▶ social construction of health   Chapter 6
▶ organizations   Chapter 16

Goffman's work, undertaken between the 1950s and the 1970s, gave particular attention to face-to-face interaction and small-scale social contexts. He called his approach *dramaturgical* (Goffman 1959). By this he meant that it was a theory of action that uses the metaphor of drama in a theatre to examine people's abilities to present particular images of themselves in their interactions with others. Goffman used such terms as actor, audience, and, of course, role in his theory. Actors play their parts in interaction, and they attempt to give their audiences convincing performances.

In their interactions, Goffman said, people aim to create a particular impression or image of themselves in the eyes of others. Goffman calls this image the **self**. People present this image through using techniques of impression management that help them to control the performances that they give. The image that they present will vary according to the expectations of the audience. The self that is presented to friends at a club on a Friday night is likely to be very different from that presented to a bank manager in an interview about an overdrawn account. The self that is presented to parents at home is likely to be different again. Whenever we wish others to think of us as a particular kind of person, we try to present exactly that image to them.

Goffman has emphasized the ability that people have to manipulate the images that they present to others. However, symbolic interactionism also shows that images and conceptions of self can be imposed on people by their audiences. The social process is an interplay of action and reaction, an interplay in which each actor interprets and responds to all others. Interaction involves a reciprocal and continuous negotiation over how situations are to be defined. A definition of the situation is the joint construction of the participants in interaction. Consensus exists only when this definition has been established and agreed by all involved. Though often implicit, this negotiation is necessary because any definition can be contested by others. What we call reality is constructed through social interaction; it is a socially constructed reality. Where there is disagreement, and dissension, the individual or group that is most powerful may be able to impose a definition of the situation on all others. They have the power to ensure that their views prevail.

This point of view became the cornerstone of the trends in the sociology of deviance that powerfully enlarged symbolic interactionism during the 1960s and 1970s (Becker 1963). This work stressed the way in which the *labels* used to define behaviour by those with the power to enforce them could influence the actions of those who were labelled. The use of such labels as 'criminal', 'junkie', 'queer', and so on defines behaviour as deviant by identifying it as a departure from social norms and attributing certain characteristics to the person labelled. Through their reactions to a person's behaviour, then, an audience of labellers may cause her or him to take on the image that is held out.

Phenomenological approaches to interaction

While symbolic interactionism mounted an increasingly successful challenge to the excessive claims made by some structural functionalists, it, too, was challenged in the 1960s by what claimed to be a more radical perspective on interaction. This was the approach of **phenomenology** that originated in the philosophy of Edmund Husserl. During the 1920s and 1930s, Husserl began to produce what he saw as the fundamental basis for knowledge. The aim of his philosophy was to describe the contents of people's experiences of their world. Husserl's work inspired a number of diverse approaches to sociology. The most influential has, perhaps, been that of Alfred Schütz, who saw his task as that of uncovering the content and form of everyday interpersonal experiences of the social world. Schütz took as his fundamental question, how is Weber's typology of action possible? That is, he asked how the types of action could be justified, on philosophical grounds, as the necessary basis for sociological research.

The work of Husserl and Schütz appeared rather idiosyncratic, and it was not until the 1960s that it really began to inspire specific approaches to sociology. In the works of Berger and Luckman (1966) and Douglas (1967), phenomenological ideas were used in order to investigate the taken-for-granted reality that people construct in the face of the reactions of others. These writers have stressed the way in which the everyday world comes to be seen as natural, inevitable, and taken for granted. People are born into a prestructured meaningful world, and they rarely question it in later life. This taken-for-granted reality has the character of a Durkheimian social fact. As well as being objective, however, they are also subjective.

The everyday world is seen as the product of human subjectivity. It is a product of human action that is *reified*—made into a thing—whenever people forget that it is a human product and begin to take it for granted. The language that we use is the principal means through which we reify social reality. An example might be the very use of the terms symbolic interactionism and phenomenological sociology as names for loose and diverse collections of writers. Use of these particular labels gives the impression that these approaches have more unity and reality than is, in fact, the case. Repetition of the words in textbooks, essays, and examination questions reinforces the taken-for-granted assumption that they exist as sharply defined schools of thought. When we give a name to something, we make it appear as something that is separate from us, external to us, and that is solid and substantial. Berger and Luckman show how this creates the apparent solidity of 'the family', while Douglas argues that suicide is a similarly reified term.

These phenomenological approaches began to rediscover some of the themes raised in classical German sociology and to translate them into contemporary concerns. They stressed, as Weber had done, that all social realities have to be studied from the standpoint of the subjective meanings given to them by individual actors. As they were being developed, however, yet another phenomenological approach was being developed from Schütz's work. This was the ethnomethodology of Harold Garfinkel and Aaron Cicourel. Ethnomethodology originated in Garfinkel's papers of the 1950s (see the essays collected in Garfinkel 1967), and it was taken up by others in the 1960s and 1970s.

Garfinkel criticizes Parsons and other structural functionalists for treating people as what he calls *cultural dopes*. Structural functionalists assumed that people were simply socialized into a cultural consensus and so had no real freedom of action. They acted in their roles as if they were puppets, controlled by the social system. In place of this point of view, Garfinkel stresses individual autonomy. He holds that the objective reality of everyday life is something that people struggle to achieve in their practical actions: it is, he says, a 'practical accomplishment'.

☞ Sociology is often criticized for using too many big words and phrases. Our use of phenomenology and ethnomethodology might have convinced you that these critics are right. Don't panic! Many professional sociologists still find it difficult to pronounce the words, let alone spell them. Concentrate on the ideas and do not get caught up on the words themselves. To help you along, however, the word 'ethnomethodology' has two elements in it: *ethno*, meaning 'people', and *methodology*, meaning 'how things are done'. So ethnomethodology simply means 'how people do things'.

In accounting for their actions and for the actions of others, people continually create and recreate their social world. Their accounts, however, are never complete but always leave something implicit or taken for granted. People rely on their audiences sharing a background of assumptions that allow them to fill in the gaps for themselves and so to understand what is being said. Organizational accounts, such as police records, medical records, and personnel files, for example, contain gaps and incomplete information that can be filled in by their readers. They are descriptions of actions and interactions that are seen as meaningful by those involved and that provide a satisfactory basis for action. They are not, however, so easily readable by non-participants, who are less likely to share the background knowledge and assumptions employed by those in the organization.

An important part of this taken-for-granted background is a sense of social structure that people use to interpret and account for the actions of others. People explain actions by showing that they are exactly the kinds of things that people in that situation would do. They see it as a part of their role, for example. These processes are not normally visible, and ethnomethodology assigns itself the special task of uncovering them in order to demonstrate what is really going on in the routine activities of everyday life. They believe that this

Action and system

The opposition between structural functionalist theories and interactionist theories can be usefully seen in terms of their central concepts of system and action. Where the concept of action points to issues of *agency* and will, the concept of system points to issues of *structure* and determinism. The contrast should not be taken too far, but it highlights a real difference in focus.

Action

- ▶ The actions of individuals are the basic elements in social life. They are the building blocks of sociology.
- ▶ Individuals define situations and construct social reality.
- ▶ Sociologists must understand actions in terms of their subjective meanings.

- ▶ Individuals improvise and create their own roles on the basis of what they learn during their socialization.

System

- ▶ Social structures are the basic elements in social life. They have a reality over and above individuals.
- ▶ Social reality is external to individuals and constrains their actions.
- ▶ Sociologists must look at the functional connections among the structural parts of social systems.
- ▶ Individuals conform to the role expectations that they learn during their socialization.

can be achieved through experimental interventions in social life. Taken-for-granted realities have to be disrupted or challenged so that people are forced to reflect on what they are doing. Only in this way can the ethnomethodologist obtain any proper knowledge about these processes. Garfinkel suggested, for example, that his students should react to their parents as they would if they were merely a lodger. This forced parents to bring out into the open the normally taken-for-granted assumptions about how children ought to behave in relation to their parents.

Theories of action prospered because of the failure of structural functionalists to pay serious attention to action and interaction. They promised a sociology that properly considered the creative element that human beings bring to their social relations. Symbolic interactionists, phenomenologists, and ethnomethodologists, in their various ways, aimed to uncover the processes of communication and interaction that allowed people to make sense of their social worlds and to construct the structures that structural functionalists treated simply as social facts. Many advocates of these theories, however, claimed that the matters that concerned structural functionalists could safely be forgotten. In saying this, they overstated their case. Action and structure are not alternative explanatory principles but complementary ones.

CONFLICT THEORIES

The analysis of conflict has a long history, yet structural functionalism developed as an approach that placed far more emphasis on consensus and cohesion. This was one of the reasons why Marx—who saw conflict as playing a central part in social life—refused to identify himself as a sociologist. While some sociologists, like Marx, recognized the importance of conflict, they had little impact on the mainstream of academic sociology. Marxism was, of course, a major influence on the work of Weber and other German sociologists, but this tradition itself was of secondary importance until after the Second World War. The growing dissatisfaction with structural functionalism as a complete and all-embracing theory of social life was associated not only with a growing interest in theories of interaction but also with attempts to recover an awareness of conflict.

Those who saw structural functionalism as paying too much attention to consensus looked to conflict theories for an expansion of the intellectual tools available to them. They highlighted, instead, the part played by divisions, power, force, and struggle. They looked at the ways in which groups came to be organized for collective action, entered into conflict with one another, and established relations of domination and control. No single theory of conflict has dominated the field, but a great many views of conflict have been put forward. We will look at three of the most influential arguments—those of Ralf Dahrendorf, John Rex, and Jürgen Habermas.

Authority, resources, and conflict

In the section on 'Interaction Theories' we showed that Weber had an important influence on some of the American symbolic interactionists. His major impact, however, has been on conflict theorists. Weber's discussion of social structure has been a particularly fruitful source of ideas, and the most important writers to develop this into conflict theories were Ralf Dahrendorf (1957) and John Rex (1961). Dahrendorf argues that structural functionalists presented, in effect, a consensus theory. They looked at only one side of reality, ignoring the existence of conflict and division. The theory of consensus, then, needed to be complemented by a theory of conflict. Dahrendorf wanted to use ideas from Weber and Marx to build a theory of conflict. He did not, however, see any need to bring consensus and conflict theories together into a new synthesis. Each theory had something separate to offer. Consensus theory illuminated some aspects of reality, while a conflict theory would be better able to illuminate others.

At the heart of Dahrendorf's theory of conflict is **authority**. In all organizations, he argues, there is an unequal distribution of authority that creates a division between the dominant and the subordinate, between those who rule and those who are ruled. In a business organization, for example, there is a division between managers and workers, in a state there is a division between the elite and the mass of citizens, and in a church there is a division between clergy and laity.

Where consensus theorists focus on the normative expectations attached to social positions, Dahrendorf looks at their **interests**. Those in ruling positions have an interest in the structure of authority as it is and so will act to maintain it. Those they rule, on the other hand, have an interest in altering the distribution of authority and will try to change it in order to improve their positions. Because of these differences in interest and outlook, rulers and ruled will tend to be formed into what Dahrendorf calls social classes. These are the base from which trade unions, political parties, and other associations are recruited. These **interest groups** come into conflict with one another and are the actual driving forces in social change.

Rex focuses on social divisions that originate in the distribution of economic, political, and cultural resources, rather than the distribution of authority. He

sees economic resources as fundamental, and he draws on a number of ideas from Marx to explore the conflicts that result from the unequal distribution of economic resources. He shows that classes are formed around differences of property and market situation and that they struggle with each other over this distribution. Agricultural land, company shares, factories, and houses, for example, are sources of power for their owners, who tend to come into conflict with those who lack these resources and seek to alter their distribution. Similar divisions are produced around political and cultural resources, and there is a close correspondence between the various distributions. Whole societies tend to be divided into sharply defined classes and these become organized for conflict through the kinds of interest groups described by Dahrendorf.

 Both Dahrendorf and Rex talk about the division of societies into conflicting classes. However, they mean different things by this. For Dahrendorf, classes are defined by authority relations, while Rex sees them as defined by economic and other resources. You will find a discussion of these issues in 'Class and Status', Chapter 15, pp. 604–12, and 'Elitist Theories', Chapter 17, pp. 691–3.

Collective action by conflict groups establishes what Rex calls a *balance of power*. In some situations, a powerful group may be able to impose its ideas and values on others, establishing a dominant ideology. In other situations, however, the conflicting groups may be more equally balanced and so the institutions of the society will reflect a compromise between the values of the two groups. Occasionally, the members of a subordinate group may be able to carry through revolutionary actions aimed at transforming their society.

 This might be a useful point at which to review Marx's main ideas, as you will find they help you to understand the following section on 'Critical Theory'. Look back at our whole discussion of Marx on pp. 30–4.

Critical theory

Rex and Dahrendorf made use of ideas from Marx and Weber. Marx's recognition of conflict, however, was kept alive even more strongly in Marxist political parties and in the works of a number of Marxist theorists. Of most importance in developing Marx's ideas were the so-called critical theorists. They have suggested that a renewed understanding of Marx's ideas will allow sociologists to advance beyond its conventional concerns and, indeed, beyond Marxism itself.

The idea of critique was, in many ways, a part of the Marxist tradition from its beginnings. This was certainly the way that Marx saw his own work. In the Marxism of the Russian, German, and other European Communist parties, however, Marx's thought was transformed into an uncritical and dogmatic system of theory. This began to change in the 1920s, when a number of independent thinkers started to develop a critique of established Marxism. Gramsci in Italy and Korsch and Lukács in Germany were the pioneers in developing a form of Marxism that broke with dogmatic styles of thought and also took the political and cultural spheres more seriously than earlier Marxists (see Lukács 1923). Although their ideas had little impact outside Marxist circles, they helped to change the direction of Marxist thought, and their ideas were taken up by radical writers in the 1960s and 1970s. Prominent among these has been Jürgen Habermas.

Some of Habermas's most important work has concerned issues of scientific method, where he has tried to clarify the nature of a truly critical theory. All knowledge, he argues, develops in relation to what he calls the **cognitive interests** of social groups. These are the particular social interests that shape people's needs for knowledge. There are three of these cognitive interests, each of which is associated with a particular kind of knowledge:

▶ an interest in technical control;

▶ an interest in practical understanding;

▶ an interest in emancipation.

An interest in *technical control*, argues Habermas, is inherent in the whole way in which human labour is organized for productive purposes. Labour involves an

---

Jürgen Habermas

Jürgen Habermas (1929–) studied under Adorno, a leading figure in critical theory, at Frankfurt. It is here that he has spent most of his academic career. He produced a number of essays on philosophy and scientific method in the 1960s (Habermas 1967, 1968), and he began to engage with the radical student movement. His initial attempt to construct a sociological account of this new movement (Habermas 1968–9) owed as much to Weber as it did to Marx.

Habermas set out the basis of a critical theory of modern society, along with a research programme to study it, in *Legitimation Crisis* (1973). Through the 1970s he worked on the more general theoretical principles underlying this, publishing the results in his *Theory of Communicative Action* (1981*a*, *b*). Since completing this, he has concentrated rather more on philosophical issues and on engaging with his political and philosophical critics.

You can find more on the applications of Habermas's theory in other parts of this book:

▶ state and crisis   Chapter 18
▶ social movements   Chapter 15

Critical theorists' views on the mass media are discussed in Chapter 8.

A good account of Habermas's early work can be found in McCarthy (1978), and a brief overview of his whole output can be found in Pusey (1987). The best accounts of the wider context of critical theory are Jay (1973) and Held (1980).

attempt to use and to transform the resources provided by the natural environment, and it stimulates people to acquire the kind of knowledge that will help them to control the natural world. The natural sciences and industrial technology are based on what he calls empirical–analytical knowledge of the kind produced in the positive sciences. This knowledge, he says, provides the kind of objective information that can be used to make explanations and predictions that will help to ensure the technical success of our actions.

An interest in *practical understanding*, on the other hand, is fundamental to human communication and interaction in everyday settings. In their interactions, people need to attain some kind of understanding of one another. They must build up a degree of consensus and shared understanding if their actions are not to collapse into mutual incomprehension and conflict. The cultural disciplines, concerned with understanding texts are based on what he calls historical–hermeneutic knowledge. You need not worry about the precise meaning of all the long words that Habermas uses. This knowledge provides the interpretations and meanings that make practical understanding possible.

Habermas sees approaches to the social world as having tended towards one or the other of these two types of knowledge. The positivism of Comte, Durkheim, and structural functionalism more generally has followed the natural-science model and has aimed at producing empirical–analytical knowledge for a positive science of society. The interpretative work of Weber and the interactionist theorists, on the other hand, has been closer to the cultural studies and has aimed at producing historical–hermeneutic knowledge.

Both forms of knowledge have their uses, but Habermas sees neither of them as giving a satisfactory base for social theory. Both the main traditions of sociological thought are partial and one-sided. They are limited and distorted by the underlying cognitive interests around which they are organized. Only an emancipatory interest, he holds, can produce the kind of knowledge that can synthesize these two partial perspectives.

An interest in *emancipation* is what is required if distorted forms of knowledge and action are to be overcome. Habermas holds that people can be liberated from ideology and error only through what he calls critical–dialectical thought. Once liberated, they can go on to achieve the kind of autonomy and self-determination that Marx saw as the ultimate goal of human history. An interest in emancipation develops along with the evolution of human society, and Marx was the first to construct a properly critical theory appropriate to this interest.

This is how Habermas locates his own work, along with that of the earlier critical theorists. An interest in human emancipation, he argues, requires that all knowledge is subjected to criticism. To be true to the interest that motivated Marx's work, it is necessary to go beyond it and to reconstruct it continually in the light of changing circumstances. Societies have changed since Marx's death, and a critical theory must reflect these changes. In contemporary societies there are new sources of division, unforeseen by Marx. It is no longer possible to see the working class as the sole agents of revolutionary change. A challenge to the system may come from any of its many oppressed social groups. For some time, critical theorists saw the radical student movement as the group most likely to initiate social change, but they now recognize a great variety of groups from the women's movement to environmental and anti-militarist movements.

Habermas's critical theory, then, is critical of contemporary social theories for their distorted views of social reality, but it is also self-critical. Critical theory must continually reassess its own foundations and the specific theories that it builds on them. Habermas's own major work (1981*a*, *b*) was cast in exactly this spirit. It was an attempt at a comprehensive reconstruction of Marx's social theory, but it made this reconstruction by critically reconsidering also the work of structural functionalists and interaction theorists. All of these strands are synthesized by Habermas.

With structural functionalism, Habermas emphasizes the importance of systems and structures, seeing these concepts as especially applicable to the economic and political systems of modern societies. However, he builds an awareness of conflict and social division into his account of these social systems. With interaction theories, on the other hand, he recognizes the importance of communication and meaning, which he sees as essential for understanding face-to-face encounters in everyday life. These face-to-face situations comprise what he calls the *lifeworld* through which people experience human communities.

These two traditions of theory, Habermas says, highlight different aspects of social reality. Modern societies, for example, are organized around the separation of systems of economic and political relations from a communal lifeworld of interpersonal interactions. The systems are concerned with the integration of actions and relations into more or less coherent and coordinated wholes. They are studied by tracing the functional connections among the structures and the parts that they play in the maintenance of the system as a whole. Habermas, like Marx, stresses that it is important to look at contradictions within these systems as

Consensus and conflict

While the opposition between consensus and conflict perspectives can be exaggerated, there are real differences that it is important to recognize. The approaches can be contrasted in terms of their main concepts and themes.

Consensus

- ▶ Norms and values are the basic elements of social life. There is a consensus over them.
- ▶ People conform because they are committed to their societies and their rules.
- ▶ Social life depends on cohesion and solidarity
- ▶ People tend to cooperate with one another.

Conflict

- ▶ Interests are the basic elements of social life. They are the sources of conflict.
- ▶ People react to one another on the basis of inducement and coercion.
- ▶ Social life involves division and exclusion.
- ▶ People tend to struggle with one another.

Source: adapted from Craib (1984: 60).

- ▶ **You might like to consider whether Habermas adequately combines consensus and conflict themes in his work.**

well as at their coherence. The lifeworld is concerned with the harmonization of the meanings given to actions in the communal life of social groups. It is studied by examining the shared ideas and values that form the taken-for-granted cultural framework for interaction.

SUMMARY POINTS

In this section we have identified three broad approaches to sociological theory, and have argued that they have to be seen as grasping different aspects of a complex reality. They are, therefore, complementary rather than alternative approaches. These three approaches are structural-functionalist theories, inter-action theories, and conflict theories.

The main source of inspiration for structural-functionalist theories was the work of Durkheim, who laid its foundations in the classical period. You might like to remind yourself about his key ideas.

- ▶ The key figure in the construction of structural-functionalist ideas was Talcott Parsons, who saw his task as that of synthesizing the ideas inherited from the classical writers. He set out the basis for this in his action frame of reference.
- ▶ The basic elements in the action frame of reference are actors, ends, means, conditions, and norms.

- ▶ The structure of a society is the normative frame-work that defines its social positions and their social relations in a division of labour. The normative expectations attached to social positions define the roles to be played by their occupants.
- ▶ Dislocations between culturally approved ends and structurally available means establish conditions of anomie. Individuals respond to anomie through innovation, ritualism, retreatism, or rebellion.
- ▶ The function of any structure is its contribution to meeting the needs of the system of which it is a part. At the most general level, needs include the internal needs of the system and its adaptation to its external environment.
- ▶ Parsons recognized four fundamental needs: adaptation, goal attainment, integration, and latency.

A diverse range of interaction theories have attempted to provide the analysis of action that tends to get lost in the work of the structural functionalists. We considered symbolic interactionism, phenomeno-logical approaches, and ethnomethodology.

- ▶ Symbolic interactionism originated in pragmatist philosophy, which held that the truth of theories and concepts depends on their value in practical actions.
- ▶ Central to symbolic interactionism is the idea of the definition of the situation. By acting in terms of their definition of the situation, people construct

and make meaningful the objects of their social world.

▶ Definitions are built in interaction through processes of self-presentation, labelling, and negotiation.

▶ Phenomenological approaches focus their attention on the taken-for-granted contents of everyday consciousness. When reified, these ideas form the external, constraining realities that constitute society.

▶ Ethnomethodology, originating in the work of Garfinkel, takes this one step further and examines the processes through which people sustain a taken-for-granted sense of reality in their everyday encounters.

The works of Weber and Marx inspired a number of theories that put conflict at the centre of their attention. These theorists criticized the structural-functionalist mainstream for its overemphasis on consensus.

▶ Dahrendorf saw conflict as originating in the distribution of authority.

▶ Rex saw conflict as originating in the distribution of resources.

▶ Both writers saw interest groups as recruited from classes and as engaged in a struggle. Classes, engaged in collective action, are the agents of social change.

▶ Critical theory aimed at a reconstruction of Marxism so as to combine its recognition of social divisions and social conflict with an awareness of how societies had changed since the death of Marx.

▶ Habermas placed his analysis of conflict and collective action in the context of a theory of the relationship between economic and political systems, on the one hand, and a communal lifeworld, on the other.

▶ The claims of critical theory depend on a particular account of the relationship between knowledge and interests in science.

RECENT TRENDS IN SOCIOLOGICAL THEORY

Structural-functionalist, interactionist, and conflict theories continue to provide the theoretical core of contemporary sociology, but they have not gone unchallenged. The rise of a strong and powerful women's movement in the 1970s led many women to challenge not only male domination of senior positions in sociology but also the intellectual content of sociology itself. A number of influential *feminist theories* challenged what they saw as the male bias in all the leading traditions of social theory. These have, they argued, ignored women and the part played by gender divisions. While feminists found much of value in existing social theory, they suggested that nothing less than its whole-scale reconstruction was needed if this bias was to be overcome.

A different challenge to the mainstream has come from the *theorists of the post-modern*. They have argued that contemporary societies have undergone a transformation that cannot be grasped by our existing intellectual tools. All existing forms of theory, including most feminist theories, are seen as too closely tied to the structures of modern societies. They must be replaced by new forms of theorizing that are better fitted to the *post-modern* condition that we have entered.

We will look at these two theoretical approaches in turn. You will find that our discussions of particular topics in Part Two of this book draw on these theories as well as the mainstream theories. Indeed, the suggested shift from modern forms of regulated, centralized, and organized social life to post-modern flexible and pluralistic forms is one of the principal ideas that we explore. While you will see that we are critical of the idea of post-modern society, you will find that each of the chapters in the second part of the book looks at contemporary changes in relation to the issues raised by theorists of the post-modern condition.

FEMINIST THEORIES

Feminist writers have posed a fundamental and comprehensive challenge to all existing social theories and to their attempts to inform and interpret empirical research. They have attempted nothing less than a long-overdue reformulation of the way in which sociologists—and other social scientists—have tried to understand modern societies. This transformation of theories and research is still under way, and it has not gone unchallenged by those who cling to existing styles of work. We look at the impact of these arguments in the various chapters that follow, and particularly in Chapter 4, where we look at the central issue of gender divisions, gender identities, and socialization. In this chapter we will concentrate on the philosophical questions that they have raised about the status of knowledge in sociology.

We showed on pp. 33–4 that Marx saw all social knowledge as related to the class position of the observer or theorist. This view was echoed by Lukács, an early influence on critical theory. Lukács held that the standpoint of the proletariat—the working class—was the only one that allowed its occupants to grasp the real nature of their society as a whole. In Habermas's formulation of critical theory, knowledge was related to deeper and more general cognitive interests. For Habermas, it was the standpoint corresponding to the emancipatory interest that allowed people a broader and deeper perspective on social reality than knowledge built from the standpoint of technical and practical interests.

One of the most significant and far-reaching features of contemporary sociology has been the way in which these kinds of arguments have been taken up and extended by feminist writers. The main thrust of feminist thought has been the claim that knowledge is related to divisions of sex and gender. Put simply, men and women have different experiences and so have different standpoints from which they construct their knowledge.

At one level there is an agreement among Marxists, critical theorists, and feminists, all of whom see aspects of social position and social action as determining what people can know about their world. Conventional, mainstream theories are seen, variously, as based on bourgeois, technical and practical, or male standpoints. Those who occupy these dominant and privileged positions in society are tied closely to the system from which they benefit; their ideas can do little but legitimate and reinforce existing social relations. Conventional science is neither objective nor neutral. Liberating and critical theories, on the other hand, are built from proletarian, emancipatory, or female standpoints. Those who occupy subordinate or oppressed social positions are uniquely able to challenge the social order and to produce knowledge that is critical of it.

Feminists, then, suggest that mainstream theory must be seen as *malestream* theory. It is rooted in patriarchal relations that embody male power over women and that establish the male standpoint on knowledge.

The technical character of scientific knowledge and its emphasis on objectivity reflects a male way of seeing the world. This **gendering** of knowledge is denied, ignored, or unacknowledged by mainstream theorists, virtually all of whom are male. Women, it is claimed, are invisible in social theory and in social research. Studies of people are, in reality, studies of men. This gendered knowledge, feminists argue, must be challenged by theorizing and research conducted from a female or feminist standpoint.

☞ Gender differences are those differences of masculine and feminine identity that are linked to biological differences of sex. We discuss these issues at length in 'Sex and Gender', Chapter 4, pp. 139–43, where various strands in feminist thought are identified.

Knowledge is said to be gendered when its content and its structure express specifically masculine or feminine characteristics. Look back over this chapter and see how few female theorists have been mentioned: can you find any? Is this simply bias on the part of two male authors, or is something deeper involved? When you have read more widely into sociological theory, you might like to see if you can find any female theorists who could have been mentioned in our sections on 'Pioneers of Social Theory' and 'The Classic Period of Sociology'.

A feminist standpoint is held to yield knowledge that is radically different from malestream knowledge (Hartsock 1983; Harding 1986; Smith 1987). The human mind, feminists argue, does not acquire knowledge in abstraction and detachment from the world. It is only through the senses and through bodily involvement in real situations that knowledge is possible. Differences of sex and gender, it is held, lead men and women to have quite different patterns of bodily involvement and experience, and so knowledge is necessarily *embodied*. Women have primary responsibility for childbirth, mothering, and domestic labour, and they learn to behave in distinctly female ways. They have quite different ways of being and acting in the world, and their lives are characterized by a much greater intensity of feeling and emotion than is typical for men.

Knowledge acquired from a feminist standpoint, then, is deeply marked by this subjectivity. Feminists do not, of course, see this as a failing, though this is how subjectivity has often been seen in mainstream theory.

Knowledge and standpoints

There are many different feminist approaches, and not all accept this particularly strong version of the argument for the feminist standpoint. There is, however, a broad agreement about the features that are supposed to characterize malestream and feminist knowledge. These are set out below. While malestream writers place a positive value on the things listed on the left-hand list, feminists see these in a negative light and stress the importance of things on the right-hand list.

Malestream	Feminist
▶ rationality	▶ emotion
▶ facts	▶ experiences
▶ objectivity	▶ subjectivity
▶ neutral	▶ personal
▶ detachment	▶ embodied
▶ public	▶ private
▶ culture	▶ nature

You might have noticed an interesting ambiguity in these arguments. It is the distinctive standpoint of women that has been identified, yet the theory describes itself as a 'feminist-standpoint' theory rather than a female-standpoint or feminine-standpoint theory. Is it valid to equate a female standpoint with a specifically feminist consciousness?

According to feminists, their standpoint gives women distinct advantages in the pursuit of knowledge. They have access to whole areas of social life that are inaccessible or unavailable to men.

Feminist writers have raised crucial issues about the gendered character of scientific methodology and empirical research. They have also suggested that sociological theory itself is gendered. Their argument suggests that such concepts as structure, system, and action may themselves be part of the malestream world-view. This is a difficult position to uphold, as feminists have developed their criticisms by drawing on precisely these concepts. There are, for example, structural feminists, interactionist feminists, and feminists who draw on Marxist ideas about conflict. It seems that the most general concepts of sociological theory are not intrinsically gendered, although they have often been *used* in gendered ways. That is, arguments about structure, action, and conflict are not, in themselves, malestream discussions. They become part of the malestream when they are discussed exclusively in terms of the world of male experience and involvement.

Feminist critics of the malestream have correctly identified, in particular, the gaps and the absences that have characterized substantive sociological work. This substantive work has, for example, tended to emphasize class as the overriding social division. Until femi-

nist critics raised the problem, little or no attention was given to the significance of gender divisions or to the theorization of the body and the emotions (Shilling 1993; B. Turner 1996).

However, in showing that knowledge is gendered and in promoting the claims of the feminist standpoint over malestream knowledge, feminist writers tend to accept many of the characteristics and consequences of contemporary gender differences. They argue that women have a distinctive standpoint because of their oppression, and they go on to advocate the cultivation of this standpoint. A truly critical and radical position would challenge this very differentiation of male and female and would try to overcome the oppression that it produces.

Feminist standpoint theorists have, of course, realized this problem, and they have made some attempts to overcome it. Harding (1986), for example, has tried to explore the ways in which feminist knowledge can be enlarged into knowledge that is not gendered at all. Current feminist standpoints are seen as transitional and as destined to be transformed in the future into a broader form of knowledge that is neither male nor female in character.

The possibility of achieving this kind of knowledge has been thrown into question by some very recent developments in feminist thought. The original formulations of feminist standpoint theories were based on the idea that the specific experiences of women were common to *all* women. A number of writers have reminded us, however, that women's experiences are shaped, also, by ethnicity and sexual orientation, as well as by such factors as class, age, and disability. Black feminist writers, for example, have challenged mainstream white feminists, on the grounds that they ignore the distinct experiences of women of colour (Hill Collins 1990).

These divisions are important for two reasons. First, they are factors that also divide men. Middle-class women and middle-class men, for example, may have more in common with each other than do middle-class women and working-class women. Secondly, and more importantly, these divisions cross-cut each other and prevent the construction of any single female standpoint. There is no single category of 'woman': there are black middle-class women, Asian working-class women, white gay women, and so on.

The feminist criticism of sociological thought has opened up possibilities for other critiques of the mainstream: black and anti-racist perspectives, 'queer theories', post-colonial theories, and many others have all been proposed. The end result of the critique of the mainstream seems to be a proliferation of competing perspectives. This proliferation has been encouraged and welcomed by the contemporary theoretical approach that we consider in the next section.

POST-MODERNISM AND THEORY

Throughout the 1960s there was a growing recognition that conventional science did not live up to the image of positive science presented in the philosophy textbooks. The focus of these discussions was not the social sciences but the natural sciences.

The leading figure in reconstructing the image of science was Thomas Kuhn, who stressed that science did not deal with *given* facts but *created* its facts. Scientists, he argued, worked within communities of theorists and researchers who shared certain basic concepts and methods. Without these shared preconceptions, no factual knowledge was possible. Scientists employ what Kuhn called *paradigms* of knowledge that tell them what to look for in their experiments and that help them to explain away observations that did not fit their preconceived theories (Kuhn 1962).

Eventually, Kuhn said, the sheer bulk of the observations that had been ignored would become so great that support for a paradigm might begin to crumble. Younger scientists might begin to use a new one that

was better able to handle these observations. The history of science, then, is a sequence of theoretical revolutions in which paradigms replace one another periodically. It is impossible, said Kuhn, to describe this in terms of scientific *progress* or the *advance* of knowledge, as there is no way of comparing the results produced by scientists using different paradigms. Each paradigm creates its own facts, and there are no theory-neutral facts that we can use to decide among them. The paradigm that survives is one that is able to attract the largest number of new recruits and the highest levels of research funding. As so often in the political world, might makes right. Theoretical approaches are, therefore, *different* from each other, but it is much more difficult to say whether any one is *better* or more truthful than another.

Kuhn's ideas were enthusiastically taken up in sociology, as his argument suggested that the differences between the natural sciences and the social sciences were not so great as many people assumed. Sociologists needed to have no feelings of inferiority about the theoretical disputes that ran through the discipline. As in physics, chemistry, biology, and astronomy, the clash of fundamental and irreconcilable theoretical positions was a sign of a healthy pluralism (Friedrichs 1970).

Kuhn was not as radical as many of his more enthusiastic supporters. His belief that a paradigm would collapse when a large number of problematic observations had accumulated implied that observations were not simply creations of the paradigm itself. If facts really were nothing other than the products of preconceived ideas, then no problematic observations would ever be made. Many of his followers conveniently ignored this point and saw Kuhn as justifying the proliferation of irreconcilable theoretical positions. Sociologists merely had to *choose* a theoretical position that appealed to them. In the world of science, they held, anything goes. There can be as many alternative positions as our imaginations can produce.

These arguments were echoed and elaborated in the works of two French writers, Foucault (1971) and Lyotard (1979). Both highlighted the plurality and diversity of scientific knowledge, and Lyotard argued that this reflected the *post-modern condition* that contemporary societies were entering. It was simply no longer possible to use such terms as truth and objectivity. In post-modern conditions, all thought has to be seen as relative, partial, and limited. No standpoint is fixed or absolute.

Lyotard's argument concerned the nature of science and technical knowledge, but he pointed to a wider cultural phenomenon. Cultural activities of all kinds are

Post-structuralism and post-modernism

Foucault's work is often described as 'post-structuralist', as he developed it in response to certain structuralist writers in the Marxist tradition (see Althusser 1965) We discuss his extremely important ideas at many places in this book, but particularly in Chapter 4. Foucault's work is often linked with that of Lyotard, though they differ in many ways. What they have in common is their rejection of the idea that there are overarching structures in social life, and their recognition of fragmentation and diversity in cultural and social life. Lyotard saw himself as setting out a theory of the post-modern condition, and he is generally seen as a 'post-modernist'. This position has been most forcibly developed by Baudrillard (1977).

You will find that some writers use a hyphen in post-modernism, but others prefer it without. In fact, the dictionary definition of 'postmodernism' (without a hyphen) refers to a movement of thought in art and architecture. This idea inspired contemporary writings, but the term has now acquired a different meaning. It is used in its hyphenated form to show this difference in meaning: a post-modern condition is one that goes beyond the modern condition.

seen as having become more important in the second half of the twentieth century. In modern societies, cultural institutions coexisted with other social institutions that shaped people's cultural activities. Marx's model of the economic base and the cultural and political superstructure was simply the most extreme formulation of this. As these modern societies have entered the post-modern condition, however, the autonomy of the cultural sphere has grown and it has become the most important aspect of social life.

Some theorists of the post-modern condition have seen this as resulting from changes in economic and political structures themselves. These changes are seen as leading from modern industrial capitalism to late capitalism (Jameson 1984), late modernity (Giddens 1990), or even post-industrialism and post-capitalism (Bell 1979). These writers point to such things as the development towards more flexible and globalized systems of production in which marketing, advertising, and consumerism play a more central part. The cultural sphere becomes extended and enlarged, and through the mass media it comes to stress diversity and choice in all matters. We discuss this further in Chapter 8, pp. 302–3. In the post-modern condition, the idea of absolute and universal standards loses its meaning (see also Lash and Urry 1987).

These writers have remained tied to Marxist or structural-functionalist theories and have, to a greater or lesser extent, been critical of the intellectual consequences of the post-modern condition. A more radical group of writers—epitomized by Lyotard—have

embraced the post-modern condition. These are post-modern theorists, rather than simply theorists of the post-modern. They argue that it is no longer valid to search for economic and political realities beyond our cultural images of them. According to Baudrillard, for example, the post-modern condition is one in which there is nothing for us to do except produce and consume cultural images. He argues that the cultural products of the mass media define reality for people, reflected in a growing intellectual interest in cultural studies and in the need to abandon the idea of building scientific theories to explain the world. Sociology, for Baudrillard, is no different from any other cultural activity: there is no real difference between building a theory, writing a poem, or composing an advertising jingle. Post-modern theorists enthusiastically accept the complete relativity of knowledge and the abandonment of the Enlightenment idea of scientific knowledge.

These ideas have had a massive impact on recent work, not only in sociology but also in literature, cultural studies, and many other disciplines. There are signs that some of the excessive claims made by post-modernists have begun to wane, and a more reasoned consideration of diversity and difference is beginning to take place. It is too early yet to say what the final outcome of this will be. We hope that your engagement with some of the implications of their work while you read the rest of this book will stimulate you to make your own contribution to this debate over the future of sociology and science.

SUMMARY POINTS

In this section we have sketched out the contemporary criticisms of the mainstream theories that we looked at in 'Sociology Comes of Age'. These criticisms are explored at greater length in our discussions of particular topics in Part Two.

▶ Feminist writers have criticized mainstream sociology for its malestream characteristics. They argue that the concern for rationality and objectivity can often mask the adoption of a male standpoint.

▶ A feminist standpoint is seen as offering a different and more adequate basis for knowledge. This standpoint reflects the distinct position and experiences of women. Knowledge is gendered.

▶ Black feminists and others have pointed to the need to abandon the category of woman and to recognize the diversity of female experiences.

▶ Post-modern theorists embrace a complete relativism in knowledge and reject the very ideas of rationality, objectivity, and scientific certainty.

When discussing post-modern theorists, we showed that their ideas were part of a wider movement of thought that suggested fundamental changes in the structure of modern societies.

▶ The modern structures of industrialism and capitalism, described by structural functionalists and Marxists, have developed into more flexible and fragmented structures that create the post-modern condition.

▶ In the post-modern condition, cultural activities of all kinds acquire a greater autonomy and significance in social life.

We stressed, however, that the claims made by the more radical post-modern theorists have themselves been challenged and that there is a need to explore the implications of their work in relation to specific substantive topics.

REVISION AND EXERCISES

Look back over the Summary Points at the end of each section of this chapter and make sure that you understand the points that have been highlighted:

▶ **Make sure that you understand the use of the following terms: materialist, idealist, positivist; standpoint, gendered knowledge.**

▶ **In what sense can it be said that sociological theory is malestream theory?**

▶ **What intellectual problems, if any, can you identify in the post-modern theorists' defence of relativism?**

THEORIES OF STRUCTURE

We looked at the origins of structural functionalism in the works of Comte and Spencer, its enlargement by Durkheim, and its consolidation by Parsons:

▶ **Make sure that you are familiar with the biographical details concerning: Comte, Spencer, Durkheim, Parsons, Merton.**

▶ **What is meant by the following terms: structure, function, structural differentiation, functional adaptation; social fact, dynamic density, social solidarity, role, socialization?**

▶ **How would you distinguish between social statics and social dynamics?**

▶ **Briefly outline the distinction between mechanical solidarity and organic solidarity.**

▶ **How did Durkheim distinguish between causal explanation and functional analysis?**

▶ How did Merton's concept of anomie differ from that of Durkheim? What were the responses to anomie that Merton identified?

▶ Define the following terms used by Parsons: adaptation, goal attainment, integration, latency.

Towards the end of the chapter, we looked at the debate over industrialism and post-industrialism that took place in the 1980s and 1990s:

▶ What did Comte and Spencer mean by industrial society. How did this differ from the way in which the term was used by Parsons?

▶ How useful is it to describe contemporary societies as having entered a post-industrial or post-modern condition?

THEORIES OF INTERACTION

We looked at a range of theories that emphasized the investigation of action and interaction. In particular we looked at symbolic interactionism, phenomenology, and ethnomethodology:

▶ Make sure that you are familiar with the biographical details concerning Weber and Simmel. Look at the biographical box on Goffman (Chapter 4, p. 133).

▶ What is meant by the following terms: value relevance, value judgements, ideal types, understanding; definition of the situation, social construction, dramaturgical?

▶ What are the types of action identified by Weber? Give a one-line definition of each of them.

▶ What did Garfinkel mean by the term 'cultural dope'?

▶ What does it mean to describe a theory of action as phenomenological?

▶ Do you remember what the word 'ethnomethodology' means?

▶ Why is it appropriate to consider Weber under the headings of both 'Interaction Theories' and 'Conflict Theories'?

THEORIES OF CONFLICT

Conflict theories have their origins in the works of Marx and Weber, but they have been extended by a number of later writers:

▶ Make sure that you are familiar with the biographical details concerning: Marx, Engels, Weber, Habermas.

▶ What is meant by historical materialism? Can it be seen as a form of economic determinism?

▶ What is meant by the following: alienation, exploitation, social classes; ideology, mode of production; base, superstructure; authority, interest groups?

▶ On what basis did Marx define the six main modes of production?

▶ Has the break-up of the Soviet Union and the other Communist states of East and Central Europe finally undermined the intellectual claims of Marxism?

▶ What did Weber mean by rationalization?

▶ How would you summarize the main differences between the theories of Dahrendorf and Rex.

We included Habermas as a theorist of conflict, although his theory is much broader in scope than this label might imply:

▶ What did Habermas mean by: technical control, practical understanding, emancipation? Which of these does he associate with the development of a critical theory?

▶ How did Habermas distinguish between system and lifeworld?

Do not worry if your answers to these questions are still a little vague. You will come across discussions of many of these ideas later in the book. You might like to return to these questions periodically to test how your understanding has developed.

FURTHER READING

Useful overviews of the main trends in sociological theory can be found in:

Craib, I. (1997), *Classical Social Theory* (Oxford: Oxford University Press). An excellent and very readable introduction to the ideas of Marx, Weber, Durkheim, and Simmel.
Giddens, A. (1971), *Capitalism and Modern Social Theory* (Cambridge: Cambridge University Press). Gives an excellent account of Marx, Weber, and Durkheim, but also puts them into the historical context of the development of European society.
Scott, J. (1995), *Sociological Theory: Contemporary Debates* (Cheltenham: Edward Elgar). Looks in detail at Parsons and at the various strands of theory that developed in relation to his work, including interaction theories and conflict theories.

More detailed discussions can be found in:

Berger, P. L., and Luckmann, T. (1966), *The Social Construction of Reality* (Harmondsworth: Allen Lane, 1971). An important and influential statement of the phenomenological point of view.
Dahrendorf, R. (1957), *Class and Class Conflict in an Industrial Society* (London: Routledge & Kegan Paul, 1959). A readable statement of the need for a conflict perspective that goes beyond the ideas of Marx.
Goffman, E. (1959), *The Presentation of Self in Everyday Life* (Harmondsworth: Penguin). Gives a powerful extension of the symbolic interactionist position. We look at his work in more detail in Chapter 6, pp. 133–4.

You should try to read at least one of the works of each of the leading classical theorists. The best starting points might be:

Marx, K., and Engels, F. (1848), *The Communist Manifesto* (Harmondsworth: Penguin, 1967).
Durkheim, E. (1897), *Suicide: A Study in Sociology* (London: Routledge & Kegan Paul, 1952).
Weber, Max (1904–5), *The Protestant Ethic and the Spirit of Capitalism* (London: George Allen & Unwin, 1930).

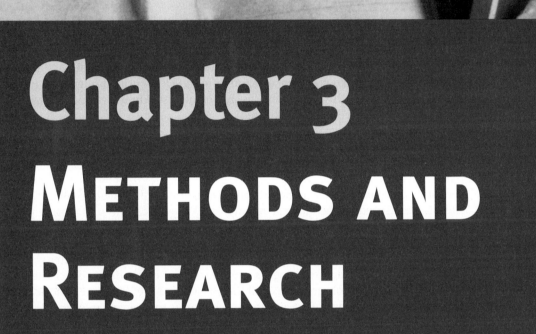

Chapter 3
METHODS AND
RESEARCH

How to lie with statistics

'The secret language of statistics, so appealing in a fact-minded culture, is employed to sensationalize, inflate, confuse, and oversimplify. Statistical methods and statistical terms are necessary in reporting the mass data of social and economic trends, business conditions, "opinion" polls, the census. But without writers who use the words with honesty and understanding and readers who know what they mean, the results can only be semantic nonsense.'

Source: Huff (1954: 8).

SOCIOLOGISTS are often told that 'you can prove anything with statistics'. The famous quotation about there being 'lies, damned lies, and statistics' is often produced as further evidence of the unfounded scientific pretensions of sociologists. How valid is this judgement? Is the sociologist simply a scientific charlatan whose methods leave much to be desired?

We have already shown in Chapter 1, pp. 15–18, that a scientific method is essential in scientific research. Any scientist must be careful and critical of the evidence that is used to build and to test theories. Handled properly, statistical sources are an essential part of the sociological enterprise. It is their *misuse*, not their *use*, that can mislead people. In this chapter we will look at the ways in which this kind of evidence can be collected and used in sociological research and how it can help to inform public debates.

Not all sociological evidence is statistical, however. The image of the sociologist as a survey researcher processing large numbers of statistics with a computer is only a part of the truth. In fact, sociologists use a variety of methods to collect their evidence. They carry out observations and interviews, and they examine historical and contemporary documents. Our aim in this chapter is to give you an overview of the range of sociological methods and the kinds of evidence that can be used in sociological work. In the section on 'Research Methods and Research Strategies' we look at the principal styles of sociological research and the ways in which they complement one another in the sociological toolbox. The section on 'Classifying, Displaying, and Using Data' helps you to read the tables and charts produced by other researchers and gives you some guidance on how to produce your own. Finally, 'The Ethics of Social Research' looks at the effects of research on the people studied and on the sociologist him or herself. It asks 'what are the ethical responsibilities of the sociologist'.

RESEARCH METHODS AND RESEARCH STRATEGIES

The studies that you will come across in this book and in your wider reading have used a great variety of research methods to collect their information. If you are to approach these studies critically, you need to know something about the advantages and disadvantages of the various methods that have been used. Our aim in this section is to give you some of the basic ideas about research methods that will enable you to do this.

Some of you may be carrying out a small project of your own as a part of your studies and we hope that this section will give enough information for you to make an informed choice about the kinds of research methods that you want to use. When you begin your research, you will find that you need to go beyond what we tell you and consult some of the many specialist books that give detailed guidance on the techniques and skills of sociological research (see O'Connel Davidson and Layder 1994; May 1997). Our discussion will, we hope, convey the flavour of social research, but it cannot provide you with the full recipe!

RESEARCH DESIGN

Research does not simply happen. It has to be planned in advance. This planning is called **research design**. Designing a research project involves translating general ideas and concerns into specific and researchable topics. You may start out with a general interest in, say, deviance, work, or health, but this must be made more specific before you can start to design a project. In this way, the focus of interest is narrowed down to something that can actually be investigated in an empirical study. Instead of a general wish to investigate deviance, a researcher might finally decide to look at violent street crime in urban areas, especially as this affects women. This topic is specific enough to suggest particular theoretical questions and practical issues to examine and therefore will point to the kinds of research methods that might be used.

Varieties of research

Research design involves decisions about many different aspects of the research process. We will highlight four of these. The researcher must be clear about the *purposes* of the research, the *methods* that will be used, the ways in which these methods are combined into a particular *style* of research, and the *strategy* through which these will be tied together into a coherent project.

There are many *purposes* for which research might be carried out. A researcher may be trying to please an employer, complete a Ph.D., advance the sum of human knowledge, and so on. We are focusing here, however, on the scientific purposes of a project. Robson (1993: 42) has usefully suggested that three broad scientific purposes can be identified:

▶ exploration;

▶ description;

▶ explanation.

A project concerned with *exploration* is one in which the researcher seeks to find out something in a new or under-researched area. The project seeks to map out the area in order to generate ideas and further questions to examine. An exploratory study asks 'what is going on here?'. A researcher may, for example, try to find out how many families are living in poverty in a particular city, or where the main areas of urban deprivation are to be found.

A project with a *descriptive* purpose, on the other hand, is one where the researcher tries to construct a clearer and more comprehensive picture of something in relation to the theoretical questions from which the research began. The research will build on existing bodies of knowledge and fill in further details in order to arrive at a rounded picture of the extent or significance of something. A descriptive project might try to show how poverty, health, and diet are related together as aspects of working-class life in a particular city. Both explanation and description are concerned with reporting the facts, and they are distinguished from one another only in terms of how well defined an area is already.

When a project has an *explanatory* purpose, it seeks to go beyond reporting the facts to seek out the causes and influences that are at work. It asks 'why is this happening?' or 'what is the most important factor in producing this?'. The theory that the researcher uses will suggest certain factors to study, or these may be drawn from previous exploratory and descriptive research. An explanatory study might try to see whether low pay, unemployment, or bad housekeeping is the most important cause of poverty.

When the most important causal factors have been identified, they may be combined into a **model** of the causal influences. A model is a simplified picture of a situation or process that tries to show how its various elements are connected to each other. A model may often be suggested by the particular theory that informs the research. Projects informed by structural-functionalist theories, for example, are likely to construct models of the functional connections among the things studied. A model may suggest one or more hypotheses that can be examined in further research. A **hypothesis** is a suggested relationship between two or more factors that can be tested against evidence. A model that links poverty to low pay, for example, may suggest the hypothesis that the introduction of a minimum rate of pay will reduce the level of poverty. A researcher whose model links poverty to unemployment, however, may draw the hypothesis that a minimum rate of pay, by increasing business costs, would increase the level of unemployment and, therefore, the level of poverty.

Once the purpose of the research has been clarified, it is possible for a researcher to choose the particular *methods* to use. A research method is a particular technique for collecting or analysing evidence, and the kinds of research methods that sociologists use include questionnaires, participant observation, interviewing, the interpretation of documents, content analysis, and many others. We will look at a number of these methods in this chapter and in other parts of this book. It is important that the methods chosen relate closely to the purposes of the research and the topics that are being examined. An attempt to explain the causes of poverty in contemporary Britain, for example, might seem to require a standardized method, such as a questionnaire that can easily be administered to a large number of people. An exploratory study of the consequences of poverty for lone-parent households, on the other hand, might seem to require more informal interview techniques.

It is rarely the case that a project will use one single method. Far more typically, methods are combined so that the strengths of one can compensate for the weaknesses of another. This combination of methods is called **triangulation**. The term 'triangulation' comes from geographical surveying, where it refers to a geometrical technique for working out unknown measures from two known measures. In social research, however, it refers to the use of two (or more) separate methods to illuminate different aspects of what is being studied. Quantitative and qualitative methods might be combined, official statistics might be supplemented by information from a questionnaire, and so on. This simple idea is shown in Figure 3.1.

The particular methods that are chosen and combined by a researcher will often be associated with a distinctive *style* of research. A style of research comprises methods that fit well together and that tend to be associated with particular theoretical approaches and philosophical assumptions. In this chapter, we will discuss three principal styles of research:

▶ survey research;

▶ ethnographic research;

▶ documentary research.

Survey research involves formal and standardized methods for asking questions that, it is hoped, those being studied will answer. Survey research is often, though not always, a quantitative form of research. In *ethnographic research*, on the other hand, observational and conversational methods are used, as these help to highlight the qualitative aspects of the social world. Finally, *documentary research* involves the use of written texts of all kinds, from government reports to mass-media broadcasts. This is often, though not always, concerned with historical investigations.

Survey research has often been linked with structural-functionalist theories, while ethnographic research has been seen as more closely linked with interaction theories. These links are, however, far from rigid, and there are many exceptions. Symbolic interactionists, for example, have used questionnaires, while structural functionalists have used participant observation. Similarly, it is not only Marxists and other conflict theorists who have relied on documentary research: documentary methods have been used by both structural functionalists and interactionists, and conflict theorists have undertaken both surveys and ethnographies.

It is not possible, then, to draw a rigid connection between particular theories and methods. More typically, researchers choose the particular style of research that seems appropriate for their purposes and which they feel match their particular skills. Many researchers, for example, do not feel comfortable with ethnographic methods, because they feel that they do not have the particular interpersonal skills that are required. Others are unhappy about the more mathematical aspects of much survey research. Each researcher has particular skills and personal characteristics that make them more likely to choose, and to successfully use, a particular style of research. This personal element is an important feature of all social research.

Nevertheless, many researchers will feel able to combine methods drawn from different styles of

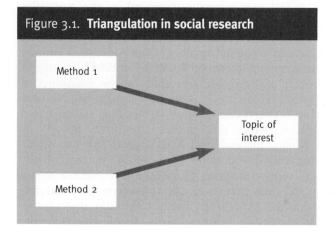

Figure 3.1. **Triangulation in social research**

Method 1

Method 2

Topic of interest

research. This form of triangulation is important in many projects. It is particularly likely to occur in team-based projects, where specialists in survey research, ethnographic research, and documentary research can be brought together in a scientific division of labour. A team can often investigate a problem more effectively than can a lone researcher.

The final decisions about research design that we have highlighted are those concerning the research *strategy* that ties together the various methods that have been chosen. A research strategy defines a logic of investigation or enquiry that specifies the way in which the researcher uses his or her subject matter. In formulating a research strategy, two decisions must be made. First, a decision must be made between a *case-study* and a *comparative* strategy. Secondly, it is necessary to choose between a *longitudinal* and a *cross-sectional* strategy.

In a *case-study strategy*, the researcher looks in detail at one particular case. This may be one individual, one organization, or one society. The aim is to carry out a detailed exploration or description of that case or to explain how things work in that case. Street violence, for example, might be examined in one particular inner-city district in order to produce the maximum amount of detailed knowledge. A case to study must be chosen with care if generalizations are to be made to some larger category. The researcher must know, for example, in what respects it is valid to generalize from the situation in, say, Bristol to that in other large British cities.

In a *comparative strategy*, on the other hand, a researcher chooses two or more cases to investigate in order to examine their similarities and differences. This is particularly helpful when testing hypotheses or producing classifications. Durkheim's (1897) research on suicide, for example, compared rates of suicide in different countries and among different social groups in order to uncover the factors responsible for high and low levels of suicide. He did this by classifying suicides into a number of different types.

A *longitudinal strategy* investigates changes over time. This may involve taking a historical approach to a society, a biographical or life-history approach to an individual, or it may involve following a particular group of individuals over a period. Longitudinal research can be combined with either a case-study or a comparative strategy. A longitudinal case study, for example, was undertaken by Max Weber (1904–5) when he looked at the historical relationship between Protestant religion and capitalist economic activity in Western Europe. However, Weber went on later in his career to combine this with comparative investigations into the development of religion and economic activity in China and India.

In a *cross-sectional strategy*, the researcher ignores time and produces a single picture of how things are at one particular date. Durkheim's study of suicide consisted mainly of cross-sectional comparisons, though he did make some use of longitudinal evidence. The cross-sectional case study is, perhaps, one of the most widely used research strategies. Many social surveys, for example, aim to collect information about a population

---

Issues of research design

Research design involves making decisions in relation to each of four issues: research purposes, research methods, research styles, and research strategies. These can be summarized as follows:

Research purposes	Research methods	Research styles	Strategies
▶ exploration	▶ questionnaires	▶ survey research	▶ case study or comparative
▶ description	▶ observation	▶ ethnographic research	▶ longitudinal or cross-sectional
▶ explanation	▶ interviews	▶ documentary research	
	▶ documents		
	▶ etc.		

Researchers must make decisions under each of the four headings, though their projects will often involve the triangulation of different forms of research

at a particular date. A survey may, for example, collect information about poverty in Britain in 1966, or domestic violence in the United States in 1922.

Whatever research design is used, research will, if properly carried out, be a difficult but rewarding process. This is something that you will discover if you undertake a project of your own. In the next three sections, we will try to illustrate some of the issues that arise in research practice by considering the three styles of research that we have identified. We will look first at survey research, then at ethnographic research, and finally at documentary research. You should remember, however, that these are often combined in particular studies.

SURVEY RESEARCH

Most people nowadays are familiar with surveys. The person with the clipboard is almost a fixed feature in high streets across the country. Thanks to opinion polls and market research, almost everyone is likely to have been stopped in the street or approached at home and asked if they can 'spare a few minutes to answer a few questions'. These surveys ask about such things as voting intentions, coffee preferences, purchases of washing powder, and television-viewing. Survey research in sociology has much in common with these commercial surveys and polls.

To survey something is to carry out a systematic overview in order to produce a comprehensive general report on it. The term came into sociology from geography, where it refers to the mapping of the boundaries and landscape of an area. Early urban sociologists extended this idea to the study of social areas and promoted social surveys of living conditions in town and country. The term soon came to mean the systematic collection of standardized information about a population through the use of comprehensive lists of questions. Although this kind of research had a much longer history, the idea of the social survey helped to fix it as a distinct style of sociological research.

Many social surveys are purely exploratory or descriptive. They collect information on such things as the extent of poverty, the level of divorce, experiences of crime, and so on. Of great importance in this kind of research is the collection of data on attitudes rather than simply on behaviour. There have, for example, been many studies of attitudes towards political parties and their leaders, work and employment, churches and religious beliefs, and so on. Other surveys are explanatory, going beyond description to search for the factors

The social survey: a familiar scene in any high street.

that might account for attitudes and behaviour. This involves the more explicit incorporation of theoretical ideas into the design of the survey, and surveys often attempt to test which of two or more rival theories is better able to explain what is being studied.

The growth of survey research was closely linked to the development of new techniques of statistical sampling that allowed conclusions to be drawn about large populations from investigations of relatively small numbers of people. These techniques developed rapidly during the first three decades of the twentieth century. A little later, ways of asking questions were themselves given more precision, and survey practice became far more rigorous.

Many commercial surveys have been designed and carried out with great technical sophistication. Indeed, it is probably true to say that many sociological surveys have been unable to match this level of sophistication. The reason for this difference between commercial and sociological research is their funding. Commercial

Data

Data are the items of information produced through research. In survey research, the data are the answers given to particular questions by each individual. The word comes from the Latin for 'given'. It is a plural word (an individual item of information is a *datum*), and this means that you should only ever say 'The data show . . .', and not 'The data shows . . .'.

surveys are funded by television companies, newspapers, political parties, and business enterprises. Their resources are generally far in excess of those available for sociological research, which usually relies on public funding. Commercial surveys can hire and train large numbers of interviewers, they can question large numbers of people, and they can employ the staff needed to analyse the results.

There are, of course, exceptions to this generalization. There are large private-sector research organizations that carry out excellent sociological research, and there are a number of public-sector research organizations (in government departments and in universities) that have carried out sophisticated large-scale survey research. It is undoubtedly the case, however, that far more good-quality survey research could be undertaken by sociologists if improved levels of funding were available.

The common element in all social surveys is the asking of questions in a more or less formal and standardized way. Information is sought on a number of matters through asking the same questions to large numbers of people and then collating the answers in order to produce a general picture. The printed list of questions used in a survey is called a **questionnaire**; the person who responds to the questions is called the **respondent**. Surveys differ in terms of the kind of questionnaire used and the way that respondents are approached. Three types of social survey are in common use:

▶ The *interview survey*. This is a door-to-door or street-based survey where a trained interviewer asks questions and records the answers. A questionnaire used by an interviewer is often called a schedule.

▶ The *postal survey*. This involves sending a questionnaire through the post to chosen addresses. This is said to be a self-administered or self-completion questionnaire, as respondents write in the answers themselves.

▶ The *telephone survey*. This is quite a recent variation on the interview survey, the interview being carried out over the telephone, rather than face to face.

In the following sections, we will look at the two main ways in which social surveys, of whatever type, differ. We will first look at the design and construction of questionnaires, and we will then look at the principles of sampling used in surveys.

Asking questions and getting answers

The design of a questionnaire is not easy, though people often think that it is. Deciding on the topics and themes to be covered can be quite straightforward, but converting these into precise and unambiguous questions that can be used to produce sociological data involves a number of steps. Unless a question is carefully worded, there will be scope for ambiguity and misunderstanding on the part of the respondents. As a result, the answers that they give may be difficult to interpret. To deal with this problem, professional questionnaires go through a long and complicated process of drafting and evaluation before they are used in an actual survey. Even the small-scale questionnaires used in student project work need to be carefully worked out. A model of the whole process of questionnaire design in shown in Figure 3.2.

The initial stage, of course, is to decide on the specific topics that are to be explored in the survey. This will often have been decided, in general terms, in the initial phases of research design, but it is important that they be clarified before any attempt is made to draw up specific questions. This is usually done by building a checklist of topics that can be broken down and combined until they form a reasonably coherent and manageable list. This list is usually kept as short as possible. A questionnaire takes time to complete, and if unnecessary topics are covered, there will be less time for the respondents to provide the more important information. This means, in practice, that information that is easily available elsewhere (for example, from other surveys or from published sources) should not usually be sought.

Once a brief and workable checklist of topics has been completed, it is possible to begin to turn these topics into specific questions. When all topics have been converted into questions, a questionnaire has been produced. The most important considerations are to make the wording of the various questions as clear as possible and to decide on the order in which they should be asked. We will look at these matters in some detail later in the section. In the initial phase of questionnaire

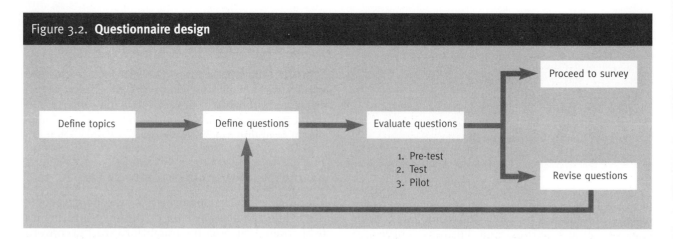

Figure 3.2. Questionnaire design

design, the aim is to produce fairly good, workable questions, but not the final, polished questions that will actually be used in the survey. Many alterations will later need to be made to the questions, and detailed polishing of grammar and vocabulary would be a waste of time in the early phases.

The draft questions must go through a process of evaluation. In the first phase of questionnaire design this is often called a *pre-test*. This involves an initial assessment of the questions by asking friends and colleagues to have a look at them and see if they can identify any obvious problems. Even experienced groups of professional survey researchers find it useful to get the opinions of professional colleagues. It is all too easy to miss problems in your own questions. Written comments on the questions, including suggestions for improvement, are usually obtained in the pre-test.

The draft questionnaire must be revised at the end of the pre-test to take account of the suggestions received. This involves reconsidering many of the same issues that arose in the first phase of question definition. In some cases, where the subject matter is complex or sensitive, this reconstruction may be quite substantial. Even if the outcome of the pre-test is positive and the draft questions all seem acceptable, it will be necessary to begin producing instructions for the interviewers or written instructions for the respondents. A questionnaire will, for example, need to have instructions added to it that tell the respondent 'Please tick the appropriate box', or 'Please go to question 8'.

Similarly, an interviewer needs written instructions about exactly how much further information to give the respondent when asking a question. An interviewer may, for example, need to probe further in relation to a respondent's answer by saying 'What exactly do you mean by . . .?', 'Could you say a little more about . . . ?',

or even just remaining silent until the respondent offers more information. If the questionnaire is to be standardized, it is essential that all interviewers respond in similar ways to each respondent. The written instructions are an attempt to ensure that this happens. Some questions may require that a number of *prompts* be given to the respondent. A list of possible answers may need to be read out to them in a particular order, or they may have to be shown to the respondent on prompt cards. All these matters need to be set down as a part of the questionnaire in order to ensure that each response is as standardized as possible.

Once the questionnaire has been reviewed, it must again be evaluated. In the second phase of questionnaire design this is often called a *test*. In a test there will be a trial of the full questionnaire under near-normal survey conditions. This may involve a small number of respondents who are similar to those who will eventually be approached in the full survey, but far less attention is usually given to the details of who is and who is not selected for interview. The test will seek comments on the questionnaire from interviewers and, very often, from respondents. These comments will, again, feed into the next revision of the questionnaire. In some small surveys, a pre-test and test will be sufficient to resolve most problems and to allow the survey to proceed. With very large surveys, however, a third evaluation may be carried out in a *pilot* survey. This is, in effect, a full dress rehearsal for the actual survey, but using a much smaller sample. Following the test or pilot survey, the final version of the questionnaire will be produced and, if interviewers are to be used, they can be trained to carry it out.

In practice, of course, questionnaire design is rarely as clear-cut as this discussion implies. The distinction between a test and a pilot survey, as we have noted, is not always drawn, and some poorly thought-out surveys may dispense with formal testing altogether. In good surveys, however, proper testing of the questionnaire will be of great importance, and full attention will be given to all the issues that we have discussed, even if some of the stages are compressed into one another. Similarly, it must not be assumed that there will be a neat arrangement of the various phases over time. Training of interviewers, for example, begins at an early stage in the planning of the survey. In some surveys that use people who have not previously worked as interviewers on sociological projects, the test and pilot surveys may be used as means of training. Similarly, the writing of instructions for interviewers and respondents will be undertaken in parallel with the defining of the questions.

We have, so far, talked about the drafting and redrafting of questions in very general terms. It is now necessary to look at this in a little more detail. The most important consideration is to make the individual questions as short, clear, and unambiguous as possible. It is important, for example, that the terms that are used in questions should be meaningful to the respondents. Questions that ask 'Have you ever experienced anomie?' or 'Do you occupy a contradictory class location?' are unlikely to get meaningful answers from respondents, unless they happen to be sociology graduates. Similarly, questions that ask about eligibility rules for social-security entitlements will be misunderstood by all except the most knowledgeable respondents.

Even if obscure and technical terms are avoided, the actual wording of the questions may be ambiguous. A question that asks 'How often have you been to the cinema?' is not likely to produce useful information as it does not make it clear what is meant by 'often' and what time period is to be considered. It is far more useful to ask 'How often have you visited the cinema to see a film in the last year?' and then to offer a choice of, say, 'once a month', 'once every two months', 'once every three months', 'less than once every three months', and 'not at all'.

This example also illustrates the difference between 'open-ended' and 'fixed-choice' questions. In a fixed-choice question, the respondent must choose one of the alternative answers provided on the questionnaire. This has the advantage that the results of the survey can easily be totalled up. Where the respondents are allowed to reply in their own words, they have more flexibility about how they answer. In these circumstances, however, the researcher may find it more difficult to quantify the results.

One of the most important considerations in wording a question is to avoid what have been called leading questions. These are questions that lead the respondent to a particular kind of response because of the way in which they have been worded. An example of a leading question is 'Why do you think Tony Blair makes a good prime minister?' This question makes it difficult for people to reply that they do not think that he is a good prime minister. They may simply follow the lead of the interviewer and give a reason, particularly if they are offered a fixed number of choices.

The things to consider when drawing up topics and forming them into questions are numerous, and many complex issues arise. The most useful discussions of these can be found in Moser and Kalton (1979), A. N. Oppenheim (1966), and de Vaus (1991). From these and other sources we have constructed a checklist of major issues. There are ten key points to remember when constructing a questionnaire.

The first key point involves making the whole task as easy as possible for the respondent. The questions on a questionnaire must always be kept as easy and as straightforward as possible, but it is sometimes necessary to include complex questions or even questions that may appear threatening or upsetting. Many people, for example, do not like to tell strangers details about their income, and most people would feel uneasy answering questions about their involvement in criminal activities. For this reason, it is generally a good idea to begin the questionnaire with the relatively easy and non-threatening questions that respondents will be happiest to answer. If a questionnaire begins with difficult and threatening questions, respondents are less likely to cooperate or to complete it.

For the same reason, it is always a good idea to have lengthy questions that require a lot of writing towards the end of the questionnaire. If a respondent must, from the beginning, write long responses on the questionnaire, she or he is far less likely to complete the task. Where an interviewer is asking the questions, the amount of writing should, in any case, be kept to an absolute minimum. If the interviewer has to write down a great deal, mistakes may occur and the respondent is left to sit idly while the interviewer writes.

Funnelling is a useful principle in questionnaire design. It involves starting out with the more general questions on a topic and gradually making them more specific. If the amount of detail required at the beginning of a questionnaire is too great, the cooperation of the respondents is put under great strain. Respondents are more likely to give the details required if they have been led on to them by more general questions.

Using the respondent's biography to organize questions is something that, where it can be done, gives a logic and coherence to a questionnaire. If the purpose

A checklist for questionnaire construction: Ten key points

1. *Easy*: start with straightforward and non-threatening questions.
2. *Writing*: put questions that require a lot of writing towards the end.
3. *Funnel*: questions should move from the more general to the more specific.
4. *Biography*: use the respondent's own biography to organize the questions.
5. *Transition*: when switching topics, make this as smooth as possible.
6. *Variety*: try to include a wide range of question types.
7. *Short*: keep the questionnaire as brief as possible.
8. *Attractive*: make the questionnaire as neat and well designed as possible.
9. *Code*: classify responses in advance, wherever possible.
10. *Confidentiality*: offer and maintain promises of confidentiality and anonymity wherever appropriate.

of a questionnaire is to explore work careers, then it will usually be sensible to begin with questions about the first job and then to follow through any job changes in sequence. Similarly, it is sensible to put any questions about education before those on work. Using this kind of chronological or biographical framework makes it far easier for people to organize their responses and makes it less likely that they will forget important events and information.

The first four of our key points suggest that, in general, a questionnaire should begin with easy, brief, and general questions and move gradually towards more difficult, lengthy, and specific questions. If appropriate, it should also have a biographical structure. For short questionnaires, these principles can usually be applied quite consistently. In larger questionnaires, however, a number of separate topics may be covered and a more modular approach will be needed. If a questionnaire covers, for example, both work career and political activities, then these would usually be treated as separate sections or modules of the questionnaire. Each module might be structured in terms of the principles that we have discussed, but the overall structure of the questionnaire will be more complex.

Our next key point concerns the transition from one part of a questionnaire to another. Where there are two or more sections, the transition from one to another must be as smooth as possible. It is important to avoid a sudden switch of topic that leaves the respondent confused. When changing topic, the interviewer might say something like 'I would now like to ask you a few questions about . . .'. In a postal questionnaire, such phrases can be printed before each batch of questions begins.

The next three key points in questionnaire construction relate rather more to the appearance and feel of the questionnaire than to its content. While the subject matter or purpose of a survey may often help to ensure that respondents cooperate, this is not always the case. A subject that is of great interest to the researcher may appear unimportant or baffling to the respondent. In these circumstances, the actual appearance of the questionnaire or the manner of its implementation may be critical.

Having a variety of question formats will help to retain the interest of respondents and prevent them from getting too bored. A mixture of open-ended and fixed-choice questions, for example, prevents the responses from becoming too mechanical. If the questionnaire is kept as short as possible, this will also help to retain the cooperation of the respondent. Survey researchers need to remember that respondents are giving up their time, and it is important that this is kept to a minimum. In postal surveys an attractively presented questionnaire can help to ensure that people complete it, especially if it is quite long. A questionnaire that is simply a dense list of single-spaced questions is unlikely to show a good response. Major surveys employ professional designers and specialist software packages to produce neat and attractive questions.

The coding of a questionnaire—the ninth key point on the checklist—is something that is of particular relevance to the person analysing the results. Coding is the process through which individual responses are converted into categories and classifications for use in the research. Sex, for example, may be coded as 'female' or 'male', and occupations may be coded into one of a set of class categories. In order to process the data more effectively, by computer, these categories are given numbers. This may be 1 for female and 2 for male, or classes numbered from 1 to 7. These numbers are generally quite arbitrary and are used simply as labels that a computer can handle more easily.

Where fixed-choice questions are used, it is very easy to *pre-code* the responses by printing the numbers beneath them or down the side of the questionnaire. Similarly, the scale points used in attitude scaling can be used as codes. Wherever pre-coding is possible, it can save a great deal of time. If pre-coding is not possible, as in the case of open-ended questions, the researcher has to look at a selection of responses after the survey has been completed and try to distinguish different types of answer. Only then is it possible to use these as codes to be applied to all completed questionnaires.

The final key point on our checklist relates to matters that we will discuss more fully in 'The Ethics of Social Research', pp. 112–14. In order to gain the cooperation of respondents, it will often be necessary to guarantee the privacy of their responses. They must feel that no one except those on the research team will read the questionnaires. This guarantee is usually given in a covering letter sent with the postal questionnaire or verbally by the interviewer, right at the beginning of the interview. It should go without saying, of course, that a researcher should give only those guarantees that can actually be kept. If the questionnaires are to be stored in an archive or made available to other researchers, full confidentiality may not be possible. A related issue concerns the privacy of the interview itself. If a person is interviewed in the presence of other people who can overhear what is said, this may affect her or his willingness to be completely open in answering the questions.

Selection and sampling

Unless a very small social group is being surveyed, it is not usually possible to include a whole population in the survey. There are practical limits to the number of people who can be interviewed, telephoned, or sent postal questionnaires. It may be possible to interview a few thousand people, but it is simply not possible to interview all the hundreds of thousands who live in even a small city. The only large-scale surveys that do cover a whole population today are the national censuses. These are carried out in Britain just once every ten years and use a very short postal questionnaire. Even this limited task is possible only because the government employs large numbers of full-time and temporary staff to collect and process the data.

Attitude scaling

Many surveys ask people for their attitudes and opinions. You will find that these kinds of questions tend to have a particular format. Surveys sometimes ask attitude questions in a normal question format: 'Do you agree with the view that the monarchy is out of touch with ordinary people?' More typically, however, they involve an attempt to measure—or *scale*—the strength of an attitude.

The most common way of doing this uses a so-called *Likert scale*, named after its originator. People are given a phrase and are asked to circle a number from 1 to 5, labelled to show the strength and direction of their attitude. For example:

Some people say that the unemployed should help themselves and not become dependent on welfare benefits. Do you

1	2	3	4	5
strongly agree	agree	neither agree nor disagree	disagree	strongly disagree

If items are labelled consistently across questions, it is possible to add up scores and get an assessment of the overall strength of a person's attitudes on a particular set of issues.

This method is similar to the way that magazine quizzes claim to measure such things as 'How sexy are you' from scored responses to questions. This was not exactly what Likert intended the method to be used for.

We discuss the development of the census and government surveys in Chapter 4, pp. 195–6. You may find it useful to return to this discussion of sampling after you have read that chapter.

In almost all surveys, then, it is necessary to use a **sample**. A sample is a selection drawn from the population that is being studied. The intention behind sampling is to draw a sample that will allow the researcher to generalize about the population as a whole. Sampling is a relatively recent innovation that resulted from mathematical advances made early in the twentieth century. You do not need to understand very much of the mathematics in order to understand the general principles of sampling.

Sampling rests on a particular branch of statistics called the theory of probability. Mathematical theories of probability concern the calculation of such things as the probability that a tossed coin will come up 'heads' and the probability that you will win the national lottery. Sampling is possible if we can calculate the probability that any sample will be *representative* of the population as a whole. If the probability of drawing a representative sample is the same as the probability of winning the lottery (about one in 140 million), then sampling would not be a very good idea. Fortunately,

there are ways of ensuring that the probability of a representative sample is quite high. There will always be a slight chance that the particular sample drawn will give inaccurate results, but it is possible to calculate the likelihood of this and to try and keep it as low as possible.

That is almost all that you need to know about the mathematics of probability theory. All the basic principles of sampling follow from these points. The basic principle is that getting a representative sample depends on whether it is possible to calculate the probabilities involved. When this is possible, the method of sampling is called **probability sampling**. When these kinds of calculation are not possible, other methods of sampling can be used, but these cannot be relied on to the same extent as a probability sample. They may produce perfectly valid results, but it is always difficult to know how confident we can be in them. We will try to explain these ideas a little further.

The simplest form of probability sample is the *simple random* sample. In this, respondents are drawn at random from a complete list of all those in the population. Technically, the list is called a *sampling frame*, and it might be an electoral register, a telephone book, an attendance list, and so on. The basic requirement is that it must be a complete list. A telephone directory would be an acceptable sampling frame for a survey of telephone subscribers, but it would be little use for a survey

Advantages and disadvantages of using questionnaires

Advantages

▶ Information is standardized and can easily be processed. This is especially useful for quantitative data.

▶ It is possible to collect information on a large number of people and so allow more valid generalizations to be made.

▶ Reliability is high: all respondents answer exactly the same questions in near identical situations. Differences in response can be assumed to reflect real differences among the respondents.

▶ Postal questionnaires are often the easiest and most efficient way of reaching large numbers of people.

▶ Postal questionnaires give great anonymity to respondents, encouraging honesty and openness.

Disadvantages

▶ Respondents may misrepresent or distort their views.

▶ Respondents may not remember relevant information.

▶ Large surveys can be very costly.

▶ Interviewers may antagonize respondents or cause biased responses if they are not properly trained.

▶ People may refuse to be interviewed or to complete a postal questionnaire, creating a non-response problem.

▶ Postal questionnaires may not be completed by the person they are addressed to, and they may not be taken seriously.

Sampling

There are two types of sampling: probability sampling (where the mathematical properties of the population are known) and non-probability sampling (where these mathematical properties are unknown). The population referred to is a technical term that refers to all the units that are of interest, not just the population of a country. The population may be a collection of organizations or countries, or any sub-group within a country. Statisticians sometimes refer to the population as the *universe*. The main types of sampling that you will encounter are listed below. They are discussed briefly in the text.

Probability samples
- simple random
- systematic random
- stratified random
- cluster
- multi-stage

Non-probability samples
- convenience
- purposive
- snowball
- quota

of the poor (who tend not to have telephones). In many surveys today, the official postcode address file is used to generate samples of addresses.

The word random does not mean haphazard, though many non-statisticians use it this way. A sample is drawn at random when every member of the population has an equal chance of being selected. This is the same principle that is involved in drawing a playing card from a well-shuffled deck: if the deck is complete (containing 52 cards) and has been properly shuffled, then every card has a one in 52 chance of being selected. Similarly, the selection of winning numbers in the lottery is a random process, as every numbered ball has the same chance of being drawn. Simple random samples are often drawn for sociological surveys by using printed tables of random numbers. These are generated by computer and are printed in books of statistical tables. If each person in the population is assigned a number, then the lists of random numbers allow the researcher to draw a simple random sample of people.

A variation on simple random sampling occurs where it is not possible or is impractical to number people or to use random numbers. The so-called *systematic random* sample involves making *one* random choice of starting point in the list and then selecting people on a systematic basis: say, every 10th, 50th, or 100th person. If the population contains 10,000 people, a sample of 100 could be drawn by choosing every 100th person on the list. It is crucial that the list itself should not be organized in any way that is relevant to the topic of the research. An alphabetical list, for example, would be useful for most purposes.

A more complex form of probability sample is the *stratified random* sample. This term is a little confusing,

as it has nothing at all to do with the social stratification that we discuss in Chapter 15. In sampling theory, a stratum is simply a group or category that has particular characteristics in common. A population may be stratified into its male and female members, into age groups, or, of course, into social classes. Whatever criterion is used, a stratified random sample involves drawing separate random samples from each of the categories into which the population has been divided. The sampling method is usually devised so that the numbers in each category are reflected in the sample. For example, if there are equal numbers of men and women in the population, there should also be equal numbers in the sample. In some cases, however, extra numbers may be drawn from very small categories. This is most likely if the number that would otherwise appear in the sample is too small to allow any reliable conclusions to be drawn. In general, however, stratified random samples are used to ensure that the sample matches the population in all crucial respects.

In some surveys, practical needs lead researchers to adapt these strict procedures. A sample of engineering workers, for example, might be drawn by making a random sample of engineering factories and then choosing all the workers in those factories. This would ensure that the sample is not too geographically dispersed, but it does involve a departure from strict probability principles. The technical term for such a method is *cluster* sampling. When this method is further adapted (for example, by taking a random sample of workers in each factory), the sampling is said to be *multi-stage* sampling.

In many research situations, there is no obvious

sampling frame that can be used or compiled. This means that it is not possible to draw random samples. In these circumstances, sociologists must resort to non-probability sampling. In these types of survey, the researcher tries to produce a representative sample but cannot be certain how representative it really is.

One of the most commonly used and, unfortunately, least useful non-probability sampling methods in smaller surveys is to build a *convenience* sample. This involves building a sample almost by accident from those who are most conveniently to hand. Interviewing friends and neighbours or standing on a street corner and stopping passers-by are examples. This method leaves the researcher open to all sorts of bias in the selection of respondents. It is, for example, all too easy to stop only those people who look as if they might be helpful or cooperative, and there is no likelihood that they will be at all representative of the population as a whole. This is, in general, a method to avoid.

A great improvement is the adoption of *purposive* sampling. Here the researcher deliberately seeks out those who meet the needs of the project. An investigation into student attitudes may involve seeking out students in areas where they are known to live in large numbers. This kind of sampling is often associated with so-called *snowballing* techniques, in which those in an initial sample are asked to name others who might be willing to be approached. The full sample grows with each round of interviews. This type of sampling has been used in studies of deviant or closed groups, where the names of members can be discovered only from those who might help in making contact.

Figure 3.3. **A grid for a quota sample**

Neither purposive nor snowball samples are useful in most large-scale surveys, and a method that tries to approximate to random sampling is most often used. This is the method of the *quota* sample. This is superficially similar to stratified random sampling, but it does not involve any statistically random procedures. In quota sampling the population is divided into categories that are known to be important and for which it is possible to get some basic information. A population might be divided by age and sex, for example, making it possible to construct a grid, as shown in Figure 3.3.

Using data from a census or a similar source, it is possible to work out how the whole population is distributed across the cells in the grid. In 1994, for example, males under 16 comprised 10.8 per cent of the population of the United Kingdom, while females under 16 comprised 10.2 per cent. A researcher seeking a representative sample would try to ensure that 10.8 per cent of the sample were young men and 10.2 per cent were young women. If a sample of 5,000 was to be drawn, it would need to contain 540 young men and 510 young women. These target numbers are the quotas that need to be filled, and the total quota is divided up into separate quotas for each interviewer. In such a survey, interviewers are given strict instructions that they must stop people in the street or call at houses until they achieve their particular quota.

The method of quota sampling is very widely used in large-scale surveys, as it is an economical and efficient way of achieving a sample that matches the broad and known features of a population. The actual individuals chosen, however, are not randomly selected and so it is not strictly legitimate to apply certain statistical measures to the results.

The aim of any method of sampling is to achieve a representative sample. It may fail to achieve this for two reasons. First, the sample itself may not be drawn at random. This is termed *sampling bias*. Secondly, a random sample may differ, by chance, from a truly representative sample. This is termed *sampling error*. This distinction is very important. Sampling error falls as the size of a sample increases, but this is not true of sampling bias. No matter how large a sample may be, if it has not been drawn at random it may be biased. The advantage of using a probability sample is that, if properly random methods are used, bias can be ignored and its representativeness can accurately be measured by the sampling error alone. These calculations are quite complex, and are purely technical. As a general rule, it has been found that increases in sample size above about 2,500 have little effect on the sampling error, regardless of the size of the population. For this reason, even national population samples rarely need to go above this level.

Statistics defines the ideal qualities that a sample should possess. In practice, it is difficult to meet these criteria. In actual research projects, corners have to be

Opinion polls and sampling error

In advance of each general election, and regularly through each parliament, the newspapers and the television report the results of opinion polls that claim to show the state of public support for various political parties and their leaders. These polls, like any survey, are subject to sampling error. In a survey using a random sample of about 1,000, the error is about ±3 per cent. That is, if a poll reports that Labour support in its sample stands at 47 per cent, the actual figure in the population as a whole is likely to be between 44 per cent and 50 per cent. This is as accurate as polls of this kind can be. The party lead is difficult to estimate when party support is fairly closely matched. If 44 per cent of the sample supported the Conservatives, the actual range of Conservative support would be 41 per cent to 47 per cent. So, it is just as likely that the Conservatives lead Labour by 47 per cent to 44 per cent as it is that Labour leads the Conservatives by 50 per cent to 41 per cent.

This problem with sampling error explains why polls differ from one another and why some newspapers feel that an average 'poll of polls' gives a more reliable picture. The problem is made worse if the polls are treated as predictions of the election result: questions ask about voting intentions, and, even if people tell the truth, their intentions may change between the date of the poll and the date of the election.

The calculation of the error that we have used is often used as a guideline in reporting poll results, though it is not strictly valid for non-random samples. Most polls have used quota samples with face-to-face interviews. In an attempt to increase the reliability of their results, some polling organizations now use random sampling methods with telephone interviews. Computerized telephone directories can be used as a sampling frame of electors, over 90 per cent of whom live in households with telephones. Random sampling helps to minimize bias and to give a precise calculation of error.

Types of sampling in the 1997 General Election polls:

Quota: Harris (*Independent*), MORI (*The Times*), NOP (*Sunday Times*).

Random: Gallup (*Daily Telegraph*), ICM (*Guardian*).

Marx and the social survey

In 1880 Karl Marx drew up a questionnaire that was to be distributed to readers of the *Revue Socialiste*, and to workers' societies, socialist societies, and anyone else who requested a copy. The purpose of the questionnaire was to explore the condition of the working class. Twenty-five thousand copies of the questionnaire were distributed, but very few replies were received. No results were ever published.

▶ **What do you think went wrong with Marx's research design? Would he have produced useful results if he had used a different sampling method? Why did he not do this?**

▶ **The questionnaire contained 101 questions. Have a look at some of these, shown below, and see if you can identify any problems with the ways that they are worded. Which questions do you think might have worked?**

1. *What is your occupation?*
3. *State the number of persons employed in your workshop?*
12. *Is your work done by hand or with the aid of machinery?*
13. *Give details of the division of labour in your industry.*
56. *If you are paid piece rates, how are the rates fixed? If you are employed in an industry in which the work performed is measured by quality or weight, as is the case in the mines, does your employer or his representative resort to trickery in order to defraud you of a part of your earnings?*

cut and *ad hoc* adjustments need to be made if any research at all is to be possible. Statistical purism would make research impossible. For this reason, it is important to be suspicious whenever a great battery of statistical tests and measures is reported. In some cases these may be precise reports on surveys using probability sampling, but in many other cases they are, at best, a rough-and-ready guide to how much reliance can be placed on the data. Many large-scale quota surveys, for example, cite measures of sampling error that should not, strictly, be taken seriously.

The basic problem with any sampling procedure is the problem of non-response. As we have shown, a sample is **biased** if it is not truly representative of the population. The aim of probability sampling, and of quota sampling, is to minimize the bias in the sample. This assumes, however, that all those who are drawn in the sample will actually cooperate. In fact, a great many of those who are selected refuse to cooperate with the survey. The proportion of the sample who do not respond is called the **response rate**. Non-response can result from direct refusals and because people are away from home or cannot be contacted.

A certain level of non-response is acceptable and need not mean that the remaining sample will be biased. In practice, it is very difficult to achieve more than a 75 per cent response rate, meaning that virtually all surveys will involve a degree of bias. If the response rate falls below 60 per cent (i.e. more than 40 per cent of the sample are non-responders), the results cannot usually be relied on with any certainty.

ETHNOGRAPHIC RESEARCH

Ethnography simply means 'writing about people', but it has come to be used in a more specific sense to describe forms of research that try to get close to how people actually feel and experience social life. Ethnographic methods, then, are oriented towards understanding the meanings that people give to their actions. Ethnography is a form of research in which the researcher actually participates in some way in the situation being studied. This kind of research may involve observation of what people are doing, engaging them in conversations and informal interviews, or some mixture of the two. It is easiest in small-scale, face-to-face settings, though ethnographies of large organizations and communities have been carried out.

Ethnographic participation may be overt or covert. In **overt research**, researchers are open about the fact that research is being undertaken and that they are trying to obtain relevant information. In **covert research**, on the

Quality and quantity

The distinction between qualitative and quantitative data should not be drawn too sharply. Quantitative data are those that involve the use of numbers to measure the extent of social characteristics and their trends over time. Qualitative data, on the other hand, are those that refer far more directly to the meanings that actions have for people. The distinction is related to that between Durkheim's emphasis on *social facts* and Weber's emphasis on *social actions*, but both writers were more subtle than this implies and tried to combine quantitative and qualitative approaches in their work. These are complementary, not alternative, forms of data.

other hand, researchers keep the research a secret and try to appear to others as just an ordinary participant.

Some see ethnography as including only participant observation and informal conversations, but this is rather restrictive. Long, informal interviews, for example, have played an important part in ethno-

E. E. Evans-Pritchard with a group of Azande, *c.* 1928: ethnographic researchers can sometimes find it difficult to be unobtrusive.

graphic studies. While these have some similarities with the questionnaire-based interviews of the survey method, they have far more in common with participant observation. This kind of interviewing has often been combined with observation and the use of personal documents. The advantage of taking this rather broader view of ethnography is that it highlights its most distinctive feature, which is to explore the *qualitative* and more intimate aspects of social life. While survey research is not exclusively *quantitative*, it is far more suited to the production of quantitative data.

Ethnographic methods were developed in the fieldwork techniques of the structural-functionalist anthropologists that we discuss in Chapter 2. Anthropologists such as Malinowski went and lived among the peoples that they studied, learning their language and trying to understand their cultures. This research was, out of necessity, overt research, as there was no way in which a white anthropologist could simply pass as a member of the black societies being studied. The purposes of the research were not, of course, fully disclosed to the subjects, who had little or no conception of what research was and probably identified the anthropologist with the colonial authorities.

Similar techniques were developed in the work of the Chicago sociologists, though these involved far more covert research. This is easier when the subjects of the research are ethnically similar to the researcher. The research carried out in Chicago combined observation and conversation with more systematic interviewing and the collection of personal data. In such classic studies as those of the hobo (N. Anderson 1923), the gang (Thrasher 1927), and the jack roller (Shaw 1930), powerful techniques of ethnographic investigation were developed.

> ☞ We briefly discuss the background to the Chicago school of sociology in Chapter 2, p. 53, and you might find it useful to look at that now. Goffman's work is an important example of ethnographic research that draws on this tradition. You will find a discussion of the use of life-history interviews by the Chicago sociologists in Chapter 5, p. 163, where we look at Sutherland's work on the professional thief.

Making observations

Observation is, of course, one of the principal ways in which sociologists can collect their data. In any of the situations that we enter, we can watch people to see what they do, and we can listen to what they say and who they speak to. However, sociological observation involves more than this. It is necessary to decide when and where to observe, how to ensure observation of exactly those things that are of interest, and how to make sociological use of the observations. The ways in which these issues are handled depend upon the particular research role that is taken. Sociological observers have typically chosen one of three research roles:

▶ the complete participant;

▶ the participant-as-observer;

▶ the complete observer (Schwartz and Schwartz 1955; Gold 1958).

In the case of the *complete participant*, observers take a highly active and involved stance towards those being observed. They aim to become a member of a group or to enter an organization in order to appear to others as an ordinary participant. The researcher may, for example, take employment in a factory or hospital in order to observe fellow workers. This kind of research is covert, as those being studied do not know that they are being observed for research purposes. This role has often been adopted in social research. In his study of a secretive religious group, Wallis (1976) joined in its activities as if he were an ordinary recruit. Another example is a study of homosexual activities in toilets, where Humphreys (1970) got to know the men and acted as a voyeur and look-out. Through participation, a researcher can observe people in many off-guard situations that would not really be open to an outsider. So long as entry to the group or organization is possible, this kind of research can be highly effective and allows the sociologist to understand activities from the standpoint of the actors concerned.

A major practical difficulty in complete participant observation is that it is difficult to ask questions or raise issues that would make it obvious that the researcher is not merely a participant. The researcher must always act in role and cannot step outside it. This may lead to such involvement in the life of the group or organization that it is impossible to maintain the distance that the research requires. A particular problem is the difficulty of recording observations. A complete participant may observe a great deal, but may not have the opportunity to write this down without arousing suspicion. In their study of a religious group, Festinger and his colleagues (1956) found that they had to make frequent trips to the lavatory in order to write up their field notes in secret. If this kind of subterfuge is not possible, observations will have to be written down many hours, and perhaps days, later, making errors and omissions very likely.

The role of the *participant-as-observer* resolves some of these problems. In this role, the researcher's purposes are overt and the actors know that research is being undertaken. This gives a researcher access to the situation to be studied, but it also allows questions to be asked and notes to be made. Research by Hargreaves (1967) and Lacey (1970) on schools used this method, as does much anthropological fieldwork. The main disadvantage of this research role is that it may be more difficult to gain entry to a group when its members know that they are going to be observed. Even if access is gained, people may be more guarded in what they say and do in the presence of the researcher.

The third observation role is that of the *complete observer* who engages in no interaction with those who are being studied. The thinking behind this is that any involvement through participation will affect the very situation that is being studied. The participant observer cannot help but affect what is happening. By avoiding any interaction, the complete observer hopes to avoid any influence on what is being observed. R. King (1978), in his study of classroom behaviour, adopted this role. He sat at the back of a classroom and refused to be involved in any way, even if spoken to.

It can be argued, of course, that the very presence of an observer—particularly an impassive and mute observer—will have just as much influence on people's actions as a participant-as-observer. In a famous set of experiments carried out at the Hawthorne electrical works in Chicago, researchers observed the behaviour of workers who were wiring electrical components (Roethlisberger and Dickson 1939). It was found that the mere presence of an observer affected the productivity of the workers. This effect of the observer on the observed has, since then, been called the *Hawthorne effect*.

 You will find a discussion of the Hawthorne researches in Chapter 16, p. 667.

The only way in which the complete observer can truly avoid having any influence is by staying out of sight and becoming a covert observer. This is very difficult to arrange in real life situations. The nearest approximations are the observations made by Bales (1950) of small-group behaviour. By using a one-way mirror, Bales was able to observe without being observed, albeit in a rather artificial laboratory setting.

The question of the influence that the observer has on the observed is a critical matter in ethnographic research. It is, of course, true that survey interviewers can influence the responses of their respondents if they do not behave in a standardized way. There is also some evidence that female interviewers generally achieve a better rapport, and therefore better results, than do male interviewers. The possibility of such influence in participant observation, however, is far greater. It is clear, of course, that women would make more obtrusive observers than men in a study of male gang delinquency. Women are likely to find it especially hard to gain any kind of access to such a gang and could certainly not undertake covert research as a gang member. However, things are not always this clear-cut. Warren and Rasmussen (1977) report that in an observation study of a nude beach in California a male researcher experienced difficulties studying men, while a female researcher had difficulties with women. Warren, the female researcher, also found that she had certain advantages when studying gay men. Similarly, Alexander (1996) has claimed that her study of black male youths was enhanced by the fact that she was a young

The observer and the observed

▶ We have suggested that the personal characteristics of researchers can influence their ability to carry out the research. Try to think how the gender of the researcher might affect each of the following participant observation projects:

▶ a study of a male street-corner gang;

▶ a study of domestic work in a convent;

▶ a study of classroom interaction in a mixed-sex secondary school.

How might the age, class, and ethnicity of the researcher have an effect in each of these projects?

woman and by the fact that she, too, was from an ethnic minority.

Using conversations

Conversation is an essential part of ethnographic research. Even when a researcher adopts the role of the complete observer, he or she is able to hear the conversations of others. The participant observer has the opportunity of engaging the subjects of research in a dialogue, of asking questions that will help in understanding how they see their world and the meanings that they give to their actions. This can be taken even further if it is possible for the ethnographer to interview the subjects. Collecting natural conversations as they occur and continuing conversations in the form of interviews are fundamental forms of data collection in social research.

Systematic collections of natural conversations can uncover the accounts that people produce to explain and justify their actions. Conversations are fundamental to the building of a sense of social order, as it is through their talk that people persuade each other of the reality of their social world. Many sociologists have investigated this using techniques of **conversational analysis**. This involves examining the structure of natural conversations in order to investigate such things as the rules and procedures used in turn-taking, interrupting, and accounting for actions (Sacks 1965–72).

Interviews involve a more deliberate use of conversation. The Webbs described the interview as 'conversation with a purpose' (Webb and Webb 1932). They were referring to what are now called **semi-structured interviews**, and not to the more formal, questionnaire-based interviews that we looked at in the section on 'Survey Research'. In a semi-structured interview, the interviewer has a checklist of topics and questions to be explored, but the way in which they are approached and the order in which they are asked depends upon the flow of the conversation with each individual. The interviewer can, therefore, take conversational opportunities as they arise in order to explore matters more fully or to pursue relevant issues that were not explicitly covered in the checklist.

This does not mean that the interviewer simply responds to the lines along which the subject takes the conversation. An effective interviewer must steer the conversation in those directions that are most relevant to the research. This requires great conversational skills. The interviewer must know when to keep silent, when to nod or smile, when to intervene, and even when to argue with the interviewee. The aim is always to establish the kind of rapport that will allow the research to be carried out as effectively and as efficiently as possible.

Research may often be carried out on subjects with whom the interviewer has little personal sympathy, but these personal feelings must not be allowed to interfere with the research process. A sociologist who interviews rapists or serial killers must establish the same kind of rapport and shared understanding as the sociologist who interviews nuns or nurses. This does not mean that their behaviour must be condoned or given implicit approval. Researchers must, however, put their personal feelings to one side and concentrate on trying to understand the way that their subjects actually see the world. Difficult as this may be, an understanding of why people engage in serial killing may do more to help reduce the murder rate than any amount of moral condemnation.

On the other hand, interviewers must avoid too close an identification with their subjects. Some research concerns intimate and highly personal matters that are of great significance to the subject, and a sympathetic and encouraging researcher runs the risk of becoming, in effect, a therapist. Most sociologists are not trained for this role. Furthermore, the overly sympathetic interviewer, like the observer who identifies with the observed, is unlikely to achieve the detachment that is necessary for effective research.

The topics covered in a semi-structured interview can range across all the areas covered in surveys. They are generally used, however, to get more detailed, in-depth information. This may be information on attitudes and values or on the knowledge that people have. A particularly common format is for the interview to follow a biographical pattern, building up a person's **life history** in so far as it is relevant to the research. The aim of such an interview is to uncover the development of a person's values and knowledge and to explore the causative influences on them, in so far as they are perceived and interpreted by the subject him or herself. In some cases, particular individuals have been taken as exemplary illustrations of specific social types and whole projects have been organized around them. Classic examples of this are the famous Chicago studies of a juvenile delinquent (Shaw 1930) and a professional thief (Sutherland 1937).

Another important style of interviewing is the **oral history** interview in which the aim is to uncover people's knowledge about the events through which they have lived and to construct a picture of their shared memories of the past (P. Thompson 1978). In some cases, this type of research involves an attempt to recapture the past from contemporary memories, while in other cases the focus is on the memories themselves. In the latter case, researchers are interested in the ways in which memories, whether real or false, become myths that justify and legitimate actions in the present.

Observational and conversational data are often supplemented by data from personal documents. We will consider the whole question of documentary research on pp. 91–4, but these particular types of document are so widely used in ethnographic research that they need to be mentioned here. Personal documents include such things as letters and diaries produced by people in their everyday lives, but which may be made available to researchers. A classic study by Thomas and Znaniecki (1918–19) used letters written by Polish migrants to supplement life-history data obtained from interviews with a particular individual. (See Plummer 1983 for a discussion of this use of personal documents).

The most important use of documents in ethnographic research, however, is where a document is produced explicitly for the researcher. An ethnographer may, for example, ask people to write accounts of their life or to keep a diary for a particular period. In these cases, the researcher does not rely on existing documents but gives detailed and explicit instructions to subjects about how they are to write them. Such diaries will often have to be kept in special booklets, issued by the researcher, so as to ensure a degree of standardization. This kind of diary can be considered as, in effect, a series of open-ended questions that are to be used in an observational or interview study. These documents can provide important information for the researcher and may later be used as the basis of an interview (Burgess 1984: ch. 6).

In survey research the interviewer can record responses on the questionnaire for analysis later on. In ethnographic research, observations and conversations have to be recorded in less formal ways. It may sometimes be possible to use pen and paper to note down what is said, but this is a very slow process, and it is difficult to produce complete, verbatim reports on what is said. It is crucial that interview notes remain as close to the actual words of the subject as possible. It is generally much easier to use a tape recorder, though some subjects may object to this or may be inhibited by it. Where conversations are tape-recorded, they must later be transcribed, converting them into a written text. This is a lengthy and time-consuming process, but if undertaken by the researcher it can be a useful way of consolidating the information collected.

Transcriptions can be analysed in the same way as

any other text. They may often be used alongside written records of observations and, perhaps, together with diaries and other personal documents produced by the subjects. Some of this textual analysis can be automated through specialized software packages that allow text to be indexed, sorted, and retrieved. There is, however, no substitute for reading and rereading ethnographic field notes. Only in this way can the researcher gain the level of familiarity needed for a proper interpretation of the data.

Ethnographic researchers must ensure that the situation and people that are chosen for study are appropriate for the purposes for which the research was designed (Burgess 1984). Sampling, then, is a matter for ethnographers as well as for survey researchers. In many cases, a representative group will be sought. A researcher studying teacher behaviour in classrooms, for example, might wish to investigate representative teachers in representative schools, so that the research has something to say about the educational system as a whole. In other situations, however, the researcher may deliberately search out places of research that are unrepresentative. A study of industrial change, for example, might choose to look at workers in workplaces that are at the forefront of technical advance. These are situations that may be untypical now, but are expected to be representative of work in the future.

Techniques of sampling in ethnography are not so straightforward and well defined as those that are used in survey research. Most ethnography might be said to use methods of non-probability sampling. Much of this kind of research relies on purposive or snowball sampling, and most studies make only impressionistic judgements about the appropriateness of the sample (see, for example, Becker 1953; Polsby 1969). Margaret Mead (1953) noted that the representativeness of an ethnographic sample depends not simply on the number of subjects but on whether the human properties of the subjects are representative of the wider social category with which the research is concerned. Thus, the life history of a professional thief may be treated as representative of professional thieves in general.

In some cases, of course, probability sampling may be possible, especially where interviews are carried out. A random sample of individuals for interview can be drawn in exactly the same way as in survey research, with the individuals being given semi-structured interviews rather than questionnaire-based interviews. The length of a typical semi-structured interview, however, means that the total sample size will usually need to be much smaller than in a survey.

DOCUMENTARY RESEARCH

The third type of research that we have distinguished is documentary research, where the sources of data are published and unpublished documents. A **document**, in its broadest sense, is an object that contains a text. A handwritten or printed text on paper, such as a letter or a government report, is the clearest example of a document, but there are many others. A text can be inscribed on clay, stone, parchment, film, or a cathode ray tube, and it can be produced with a pen, a pencil, a chisel, a printing machine, or a computer. Documents that can be used by sociologists include newspapers, diaries, stamps, directories, handbills, maps, photographs, paintings, gravestones, television broadcasts, and computer files.

Documents are often seen as the particular concern of the historian, but they have a wide relevance across the social sciences. Each of the three leading sociologists of the classical period made far greater use of documentary sources than any other research method. Marx's *Capital* (1867) rested on his heavy use of official publications produced by the factory inspectors and other government agencies. Max Weber's *Protestant Ethic and the Spirit of Capitalism* (1904–5) used religious tracts and pamphlets to explore seventeenth and eighteenth century beliefs and practices. Durkheim's *Suicide* (1897), perhaps the best known of all sociological studies, drew on a variety of official statistics on rates of suicide in European countries.

Classifying documents

The range of documents available to sociologists is immense, and it is important to have some understanding of the types of documents that can be used in research. Documents differ from one another in terms of their *origins* and the conditions under which researchers can have *access* to them. An important distinction is that between the personal and the official. Personal documents, as we showed in the section on 'Ethnographic Research', originate in households, being produced mainly for domestic purposes. Official or public documents, on the other hand, are produced in administrative situations. Some are produced in state bureaucracies and others in private bureaucracies, such as business enterprises and churches.

The issue of access concerns whether documents are made available to people other than their authors. Access ranges from completely closed access, where they are available only to a very limited group of people, to completely open access through publication.

Between these two extremes of closed and open access are the restricted documents that are available quite widely, but under tight and limited conditions.

Figure 3.4 classifies documents by origins and access to produce a typology of twelve different kinds. Closed personal documents (type 1) include letters, diaries, household account books, and other domestic items. These kinds of documents are normally available only to the individuals who own them or to their immediate households. Sometimes they may become available more widely through storage in public records offices (type 3) or through publication (type 4). Diaries, for example, are normally closed documents, although they are often produced with the intention that they should eventually be made available to a wider readership. This is the case with the diaries of many politicians. The records of many landed and wealthy families originate in the personal sphere, but may be deposited in public archives and so become more easily accessible to researchers. Many personal documents remain in private hands and can be seen only if their owners give specific permission (type 2).

Official documents are produced by businesses, schools, hospitals, the Church, and other private-sector organizations. Confidential organizational documents (type 5) include medical records, school records, and company personnel files. These can usually be seen only by those who have an administrative or professional responsibility within the organization. Documents of type 6 include share registers and lists of borrowers that are held by businesses and made available only to specified researchers when they are no longer of any current relevance to the business. Some of these, however, are periodically deposited in public archives, becoming documents of type 7. Share registers of

Figure 3.4. **Types of documents**

Access	Origins		
	Personal	Official	
		Private	State
Closed	1	5	9
Restricted	2	6	10
Open archival	3	7	11
Open published	4	8	12

companies in England and Wales, for example, have to be sent to the Companies Registration Office, where there is public access to them. Documents of type 8 include timetables, directories, newspapers, and the various other products of the mass media.

Official documents of local and national governments are, probably, the single biggest type of document available to social researchers. Those that are subject to closed access (type 9) include criminal records and security reports, local-authority housing records, and current taxation records. Many of these documents are covered by official secrecy laws that prevent unauthorized disclosure of them to people outside the department responsible for them. Some secret documents remain closed permanently, but some are made available on restricted access (type 10), while others are eventually made available in public archives (type 11). State documents are often put into public archives only when they are no longer seen as confidential or sensitive. For example, Cabinet papers are made available for consultation after thirty years and census returns after 100 years. Many state documents are produced explicitly for publication (type 12). This includes Acts of Parliament, Reports of Royal Commissions, statistical reports, and research reports. These state publications are among the most important sources of information for sociological research.

Using documents

It might seem as if documents are very straightforward sources of data that can be read and the data simply extracted. However, many texts are extremely difficult to understand. It is also necessary to consider many of the same issues of sampling and representativeness that we looked at when considering survey and ethnographic research. It has been suggested (J. Scott 1990) that, if a document is to be used in sociology, it must be assessed in terms of four criteria:

▶ *authenticity*: is it genuine?
▶ *credibility*: is it true?
▶ *representativeness*: is it typical?
▶ *meaning*: is it comprehensible?

The question of *authenticity* concerns the soundness and authorship of documents. A sound document is an original or a reliable copy, and a first step in assessing a document must be to find out whether it is an original or a copy. The process of copying, whether by hand writing, by re-typesetting, by filming, or by photocopying, can result in missing or unreadable text. Even originals can be incomplete if they have deteriorated over

the years. An 'unsound' document is one that is not close enough to its original form because it has been corrupted in some way. Researchers must try to reconstruct sound versions of their documents by trying to discover what is missing. The more corrupted a document has become, the more difficult this will be. In extreme cases, it may not be possible to reconstruct a sound version at all, and research may be impossible.

A genuine document is not only sound, but also of known authorship. Even when authorship seems straightforward, the possibility of forgery or fraud must be considered. It is important to know, for example, whether diaries attributed to particular individuals were actually written by them. In many cases the authorship of a document may not be clear. Official documents, even when issued in the name of a particular Minister, are produced by a complex administrative apparatus. In the same way, books and newspapers are the products of a division of labour in which the work of named writers is processed and reprocessed by copy editors, sub-editors, and editors. In these cases, it might be quite inappropriate to see a particular named individual as the author of a document.

Assessing the *credibility* of a document involves looking at its sincerity and accuracy. All documents are, to a greater or lesser extent, selective or distorted, as it is impossible to construct accounts that are independent of particular points of view. Nevertheless, they can be more or less credible as accounts, depending on whether an observer is sincere in the choice of a point of view from which to write and whether the account gives an accurate report from that starting point.

The sincerity of authors is related to their motives. Some people may be motivated to report on events with as much objectivity as possible. Others, however, may write to justify their own actions, to make propaganda, to deceive others, or for financial gain. The motivation is not always clear. Official documents may present themselves as factual information, but they may actually be attempts to persuade people towards a particular position or course of action. More obviously, newspapers are produced by journalists who are paid to write marketable material and who may be subject to political pressure from a proprietor.

 At this point you might like to consider some of the issues that we look at in Chapter 8, 'Communication and the Media'. Look, in particular, at 'Ownership and Control', pp. 306–8, and 'The Commercialization of the Media', pp. 309–11.

Primary and secondary sources

A distinction is often made between primary and secondary sources, though there is some confusion over this. For most historians, a primary source is a first-hand account produced by a participant. It involves little or no intervention by the historian. Diaries, autobiographies, letters, and many administrative documents are primary sources. Secondary sources, on the other hand, are those that have been produced by historians or others, using primary sources, and which are therefore second-hand accounts. When a historian relies on the work of other historians or commentators, instead of going to new primary sources, he or she is said to be using secondary sources.

Some sociologists have defined primary sources as consisting of data collected by researchers themselves, and secondary sources as comprising data that already exist. This means that the fieldwork data of a participant observer is correctly recognized as a primary source, but it is rather misleading to see letters and diaries as 'secondary' sources. This confusion seems to result from different concerns: historians are generally concerned with whether accounts are first hand (participant) or second hand; sociologists are more concerned with whether accounts are produced by a professional sociologist or by people in their everyday lives. Both points of view are important, but you may conclude that the attempt to see them in terms of a distinction between primary and secondary sources should be abandoned.

Even when an author has acted sincerely, the credibility of a document is affected by its accuracy. The accuracy of a report depends on the conditions under which it was compiled and how close the author was to the events reported. Historians have generally preferred to use what they call primary sources. These are first-hand accounts of events, and it is felt that they minimize any loss of accuracy due to lapses of memory and inadequate records. However, even first-hand observers may have difficulties in recording their observations in such a way that they can be used to construct accurate reports. As we noted in connection with interviews and observations, it is generally very difficult to record what is seen and heard with complete accuracy. Shorthand was invented only in the seventeenth century, and tape recorders were not available until well into the twentieth century. Accuracy of recall is, therefore, a problem even with primary sources.

The *representativeness* of a document is determined by its survival and availability. A representative sample of relevant documents will not always be needed, but it is important to know whether the chosen documents are, in fact, representative. Most documents are produced some time before they are used in research, and their users will need to know what proportion of the relevant documents have actually survived and whether they are all available for research purposes.

If documents are to survive, they must be stored in some way. This may simply involve dumping them in a cardboard box, as happens with many personal documents, or it may involve storage in a proper archive. Many public and private documents are destroyed soon after their production, while others are stored for a period and destroyed at a later date. Household receipts and many letters, for example, are often not retained at all. Because of the massive number of documents produced by modern bureaucratic organizations, it is impossible for them to retain more than a small portion. These official documents are stored while in current use and may then be 'weeded' for destruction before the remainder are transferred to an archive. In many private organizations, however, there is no archive and all non-current documents are destroyed.

Even when documents are stored, the number that survive may decrease over time through deterioration and decay or through periodic clear-outs. The introduction of computer technology has resolved some of the problems of paper storage, as large amounts of data can

Official statistics

The statistics produced by governments are one of the most important sources of data available to sociologists. They cover population, crime, health, employment, and a whole range of other issues. You will find a full discussion of them in 'Using Official Statistics', pp. 107–11. You might want to look at that discussion when you have finished this section. Try to apply the criteria of authenticity, credibility, representativeness, and meaning while you read what we say about crime and other statistics.

To get some idea of the kinds of statistics produced in Britain, look at a recent issue of *Social Trends*.

What does a content analysis of magazines tells us about attitudes towards women? See our discussion of this in Chapter 8, pp. 294–5.

Not all documents that survive will be available for research purposes. Considerations of confidentiality and official secrecy limit access to state documents, and access to private documents may be even more difficult. State documents often enter the public sphere after a particular period of time has lapsed, this period ranging from thirty years to 150 years, but some documents may be permanently closed. Problems can be even greater in the private sphere. Researchers will often be refused access to household documents such as diaries and letters, for obvious reasons. Unless they are stored in family archives—which is unusual, except among very wealthy families—personal documents tend to be neither available nor catalogued.

The final consideration is the *meaning* of the documents that the researcher wishes to use. This involves both the literal meaning of the document and its interpretation. The literal meaning of a document is its surface or word-for-word meaning. To produce this, the researcher must be able to read the language in which it is written, know the accepted definitions of the words that are used, and be able to understand any dating systems or shorthand conventions. In the case of handwritten documents, of course, the handwriting must be legible if it is to be read at all.

Once a literal reading has been produced, the researcher can go on to the far more complex task of interpretation. This is achieved by grasping the underlying selective point of view from which the individual concepts in a text acquire their meaning. Methods of interpretation are considered more fully in other parts of this book (see especially 'Methods of Media Research', Chapter 8, pp. 281–4). The two principle methods are quantitative **content analysis** and qualitative **textual analysis**. Content analysis involves counting the number of times that particular words or images appear, while textual analysis concentrates on grasping the qualitative significance of these words and images.

be stored on a single computer disk. However, computerized records are continually updated by over-writing existing files, which means that historical records may be lost. The survival of computerized records is further threatened by the rapid pace of change in software and hardware, which can make files unreadable.

Some classic studies and their methods

Survey research

▶ Young and Willmott (1957)
▶ Goldthorpe *et al.* (1969)
▶ Townsend (1979)
▶ Wellings *et al.* (1994)

Ethnographic research

▶ Hargreaves (1967)
▶ Wallis (1976)
▶ Festinger *et al.* (1956)
▶ Humphreys (1970)

Documentary research

▶ Durkheim (1897)
▶ Weber (1904–5)
▶ McRobbie (1991)
▶ Glasgow University Media Group (1976)

SUMMARY POINTS

In this section we have looked at a number of aspects of research design, and in detail at survey research, ethnographic research, and documentary research.

▶ Research design is the whole process of planning a project that relates to theoretical concerns and is easily researchable. It involves issues relating to purposes, methods, styles, and strategies of research.

▶ Triangulation is a fundamental feature of social research. It involves combining different methods so that the strengths of one complement the weaknesses of another.

Survey research involves the use of a questionnaire to study the behaviour, attitudes, or opinions of a sample of respondents.

Distinctions can be made between interview surveys, postal surveys, and telephone surveys.

▶ Questionnaire design involves a complex process of evaluation in which questions are drafted and modified in the light of practical tests.

▶ Good survey research needs to follow ten key points of questionnaire construction. (See the checklist on p. 80.)

▶ A sample is drawn from a larger population, of which it is supposed to be representative. The most important distinction is that between probability and non-probability sampling methods.

Ethnographic research involves observations and conversations aimed at understanding the meanings of social actions and social situations.

▶ Ethnographic observation may be overt or covert.

▶ Observers can take one of three research roles: complete participant, participant-as-observer, and complete observer.

▶ Ethnographic interviewing is semi-structured, rather than questionnaire based. Effective interviewing relies on good interpersonal skills.

Documentary research involves the use of written texts of all kinds.

▶ Documents may be personal or public documents, and the researcher may be granted varying degrees of access.

▶ Documents must be assessed in relation to the criteria of authenticity, credibility, representativeness, and meaning.

CLASSIFYING, DISPLAYING, AND USING DATA

We have shown that research design involves constructing a researchable project from theoretical ideas. Theories are systems of concepts that are connected together through logical reasoning and that may be translatable into models and hypotheses. If models and hypotheses are to guide empirical research, the concepts must be converted into *variables*. That is, a concept must be turned into something that is measurable. This is generally seen as a process of **operationalization**, of specifying the operations needed to produce evidence relevant to the concept. A concept that is successfully operationalized, then, is specified in terms of a number of quite specific empirical indicators and measures.

Anomie, for example, was a central concept for both Durkheim and Merton. But how do we know when we have observed a situation of anomie? Unless specific indicators of anomie are set out, we cannot do so. It was for this reason that Durkheim defined anomie as an absence of normative regulation, but took such things as a lack of religious affiliation and being unmarried as indicators of this.

When a concept has been defined in terms of a set of indicators that can be used in empirical research, it is said to have been transformed into a variable. A variable consists of a concept and its indicator(s). The concept is the idea, and the indicator is the item or items on which relevant empirical data can be collected. An example of this, which we look at more fully in 'Technology and the Meaning of Work', Chapter 13, pp. 512–15, is the Marxist concept of alienation. Seeman (1959) took Marx's ideas about alienation and developed them into a set of measurable indicators that Blauner (1964) went on to explore in his study of work relations (see the criticism of this in Lukes 1967).

The two fundamental issues that arise in the operationalization of concepts are validity and reliability.

When an indicator has been devised that gives a theoretically acceptable measure of a concept, the indicator is said to be *valid*. When the indicator can be used to generate reproducible results, it is said to be *reliable*. Blauner (1964) claimed to have produced a reliable indicator of alienation, but his Marxist critics claimed that he had failed to produce a valid one. No matter how reliable an indicator may be, if it does not relate properly to the concept that it is supposed to measure it will be of little use. Blauner produced some valuable information about work satisfaction and work attitudes, but he did not really address the theoretical issues that Marx referred to in his discussion of alienation.

Operationalization has led to the construction of relatively uncontentious indicators of such things as urban and rural contexts, employment and self-employment, church membership, voting intention, and many other concrete concepts. It is far more difficult, however, to operationalize the more basic sociological concepts. Lukes (1974) has suggested that it is difficult to arrive at an operationalization of a concept such as power, because there are so many different views of what power is. Similar problems arise with such concepts as class, patriarchy, and ethnicity. As we show in Chapter 6, even such concepts as health, illness, and mental health are difficult to define in uncontentious ways.

The difficulty in producing valid and reliable indicators of sociological concepts has been taken by some philosophers as a sign that sociology is not scientific. If Marx's concepts, for example, cannot be given operational definitions, then Marxism cannot be a scientific theory (Popper 1959). Countering this view, Marxists and others have decried what they have called the positivist view of science. By this, they mean an approach that seeks to reduce all theoretical and conceptual issues to measurable and, perhaps, quantifiable indicators (Adorno *et al.* 1969).

However, a positive science—in the sense in which this term was used by Comte and Durkheim—need not be as narrowly quantitative as this implies. It is important to recognize that conceptual differences are an essential feature of social life. This is true for all the concepts and variables that we use. Much research, for example, makes use of the concept of sex. We show in Chapter 4 that there are important theoretical issues surrounding the study of sex. The use of categories of ethnic origin, even if they are not presented as 'racial' categories, involve many similar issues (Burgess 1986). Even the category of age—used almost as widely in official statistics as sex—is far from straightforward, as chronologically defined categories rarely correspond to socially constructed concepts of age (Pilcher 1995).

One of the most problematic, and most widely discussed, concepts is social class. This has been used in official statistics as a routine way of summarizing occupational and employment data so that their effects on fertility, mortality, and health can be assessed. It has also been used as a fundamental concept in sociological studies on education, religion, family relations, crime, media viewing, language, and so on. The official categories of social class, though frequently used in sociological work, do not correspond in any straightforward way to any of the theoretically sophisticated concepts of social class that are current in sociology. This raises important questions about their validity and about the operationalization of sociological concepts in general. We will illustrate this through a detailed consideration of the operationalization of class and its use as a key variable in the analysis of sociological data. We will then go on to look at some of the practicalities of using sociological classifications and presenting sociological data. Finally, we will consider how, in the light of all this, it is possible to make use of official statistics.

CLASSIFICATION BY SOCIAL CLASS

Class has been a central concept for almost all sociologists. While they have differed in exactly what they mean by class, there has been a common recognition of the need for a concept of class that grasps economically generated differences in opportunities and ways of living. Empirical research has, therefore, had to make class into a measurable variable.

 You may prefer to glance quickly through our discussion, not worrying too much about the details. You will find it easier to understand some of the points that we make after you have read Chapter 15. Until you have worked through that chapter, you will find it most useful to treat this section for reference purposes. Whenever you come across a reference to class in the other chapters of this book and in your other reading, refer back to this section and find the figure that displays the particular class scheme used.

The most widely used indicator of class has been occupation. This has been seen as a useful indicator of the differences in working and living conditions that are associated with the inequalities and differences in lifestyle that sociologists have referred to as class differences. Questions on occupation have been a standard feature of most social surveys. Occupations have been grouped into categories with similar economic circumstances and lifestyles, and these occupational categories are taken as empirical measures of class differences. An individual person, therefore, can be allocated to a social class so long as we know his or her occupation.

A number of different class schemes have been proposed, each giving a slightly different picture of the class structure. Most of these schemes claim a high degree of reliability in the allocation of individuals to classes. The question of validity is more complex. An indicator of class is valid if it corresponds to the concept of class. However, it is unclear whether any of the available class schemes give a completely valid definition of class (Nichols 1979). This is not to say that we must reject them all. It is, however, important to be aware of their limitations. In this section we will look at the main social-class classifications that have been used in Britain.

The official view of class

The classification of social classes that has been used in many official statistics is the Registrar General's Classification. This is generally regarded as being the nearest that there is to an official listing of social classes for Britain as a whole. Because it has been so widely used in government statistics, it has also been used in a wide range of commercial and academic social surveys.

This was developed as a way of classifying data from the population censuses. Drawing on some pioneering work by Charles Booth (1886), government statisticians in the office of the Registrar General devised a classification of the population into five principal 'social grades' or 'social classes' (Szreter 1984). It has, for many years, been the standard social-class classification in social research, and a revised version is still in use.

 You might like to refer to our discussion of the rise of the census and the registration of population in 'Surveillance of Populations', Chapter 6, pp. 194–6. That discussion looks at the major government surveys and series of official statistics.

The Registrar General's view was that social classes described economic divisions of industry and employment. They are clusters of family households that have similar residential and working conditions and that enjoy a similar social standing, culture, and lifestyle. The Registrar General's Classification was not, then, supposed to be a simple income or asset classification. It was intended to be a more general classification of social advantage and disadvantage.

A related scheme was introduced in 1951. David Glass, who was carrying out his important study of occupational mobility (Glass 1954), helped the Registrar General to establish an industrial classification of occupations that divided them into seventeen so-called socio-economic groups (SEGs). These have been used in a number of publications, including those from the General Household Survey. The seventeen SEGs can be reduced to a shorter set of six occupational categories that are sometimes referred to as 'economic classes'. The SEGs and economic classes are widely used in government statistics, but they have not been used in many non-official surveys. You will find that some government statistics use the economic classes, while others use the social classes of the Registrar General's Classification.

The Registrar General's Classification revolves around three basic social classes—the upper and middle classes, skilled workers, and unskilled labourers—to which are added two 'intermediate' categories to cover those who do not fit neatly into the three principal social classes. The resulting five social classes are numbered in Roman figures from I to V. They have also been given an official label and description that makes it possible to use them simply by classifying individuals and family heads according to the description. However, this is not a very reliable or precise method. The correct procedure, used in all official studies, is to allocate individuals to a detailed occupational category, of which there are currently over 500 listed in the official *Classification of Occupations*. The correct social class for each occupational category is shown in the same publication.

Since 1971 the Registrar General's Classification has incorporated a distinction between manual and non-manual forms of skilled work, a distinction that had already been used in some unofficial versions of the schema. As a result, the current version has six social classes, which are shown in Figure 3.5. The incorporation of this manual/non-manual division makes it relatively easy to collapse the whole scheme into a rough and ready distinction between manual (IIIM, IV, V) and non-manual (I, II, and IIIN) social classes. These have often been referred to loosely as the working class and the middle class.

Claiming that Britain had become a 'classless' society, the Conservative government in 1987 argued

Figure 3.5. The Registrar General's Classification

Social class	Official description	Examples
I	Professional, etc., occupations	Exclusively non-manual: accountant, doctor, lawyer, university teacher
II	Intermediate occupations	Predominantly non-manual: aircraft pilot, farmer, nurse, police officer, schoolteacher
III (N)	Skilled non-manual occupations	Exclusively non-manual: clerk, shop assistant, secretary, waiter
III (M)	Skilled manual occupations	Exclusively manual: bus driver, carpenter, cook, miner, electrician
IV	Partly skilled occupations	Predominantly manual: farm worker, bus conducter, bar worker, postman, telephone operator
V	Unskilled occupations	Exclusively manual: labourer, office cleaner, kitchen hand, window cleaner

that it was time to abandon the practice of presenting official data in outmoded class terms. It suggested that there was no longer any need for an official classification of social classes. Although the Registrar General's Classification continues in use, it has been under review since then, and in 1994 a full academic review of the classification was set up. The initial report of the review group recommended that an official social-class classification should be retained and that it should combine the Registrar General's Classification with the SEGs. The aim of this change was to focus the whole classification more explicitly around employment differences.

Non-official social-class schemes

The first unofficial social class scheme to achieve any widespread popularity among researchers in Britain was that compiled by John Hall and David Caradog Jones in the 1930s and 1940s. This was used in the famous study of social mobility by Glass (1954). The so-called Hall–Jones Classification is slightly more complex than the Registrar General's Classification, and it contains seven social classes. These are usually numbered in Arabic from 1 to 7, and they are shown in Figure 3.6. Like the Registrar General's Classification, this scheme is based on a classification of individuals into occupational categories that have been combined into social classes by the researchers who produced the classification.

This Hall–Jones Classification, like the Registrar General's Classification, has been widely used in social

research, and a number of well-known studies have used it, or modified versions of it, to present their findings. The first attempt to completely rethink the approach taken in the Registrar General's Classification and the Hall–Jones Classification was undertaken by John Goldthorpe and his colleagues when planning the Oxford Mobility Study (Goldthorpe 1980). In order to make comparisons possible with the Glass study of social mobility, Goldthorpe devised a broader classification. He began from a detailed list of occupational categories, taken from official sources, and organized these into seven social classes that were numbered in Roman from I to VII. For some purposes he adds an extra

Figure 3.6. The Hall–Jones Classification

Social class	Description
1	Professional and high administrative
2	Managerial and executive
3	Inspectional, supervisory, and other non-manual, higher grade
4	Inspectional, supervisory, and other non-manual, lower grade
5	Skilled manual and routine grades of non-manual
6	Semi-skilled manual
7	Unskilled manual

social class of property-holders that he calls the 'elite'. The number of property-holders appearing in any sample survey, however, is so small that Goldthorpe relegates this social class to a footnote. It is not used as a category in the Oxford Mobility Study.

These social classes, Goldthorpe claims, are differentiated by their resources and their opportunities. Although he says that the social classes do not form a strict hierarchy, he does recognize that social classes I and II (together forming a service class) enjoy superior conditions to classes V, VI, and VII (together forming a working class). Social classes III and IV are often referred to as 'intermediate' classes, though Gold-

thorpe does not see them as being in the middle of a neat social hierarchy. The seven social classes are generally listed in the order shown in Figure 3.7. For all its problems, the Goldthorpe Classification is probably the best that is currently available. Until a more adequate class scheme is constructed, it is probably the most valid and reliable that we have for use in social research.

The classifications that we have looked at have been devised for use in studies of British society, and they cannot necessarily be used in studies of other societies or in comparative research. It cannot be assumed that the number of social classes and the boundaries

---

Figure 3.7. The Goldthorpe Classification

Social class	Description	
I	Higher professional and administrative; large managers and proprietors	Service class
II	Lower professional and administrative; small managers and proprietors	
III	Routine non-manual	Intermediate class
IV	Small employers, proprietors and self-employed	
V	Lower technical and manual supervisory workers	Working class
VI	Skilled manual workers	
VII	Semi- and unskilled manual workers	

Note: an 'elite' of property-holders is sometimes added as an additional social class at the top of the scheme.

Property and occupation

All of the classifications that we have looked at have used occupation as an indicator of class. If you have read our discussion of Marx in Chapter 2 (or more fully in Chapter 15), you will know that he placed particular emphasis on property ownership as the basis of class division. This is not well handled by a focus on occupations. Goldthorpe did not properly separate out large property-owners from small ones, and the Hall–Jones classification included property-holders and employers in all of the top four social classes. The Registrar General's Classification has even more problems. As Nichols remarks, in the 1951 Census 'the "capitalist", the "business speculator", the "fund holder" and the "landowner" were lumped together into the same residual category as the "expert (undefined)" and the "lunatic (trade not specified)"' (Nichols 1979: 71). In 1961, 'capitalist' was dropped as a Census category altogether.

▶ **When you have read Chapter 15, see if you can think how these classifications might be improved.**

between them will be the same in, say, the United States or Japan as they are in Britain.

Goldthorpe has gone some way towards recognizing this problem, and he has tried to modify his classification for use in comparative research. The main changes that he made involved attempts to take account of the fact that agricultural work was more significant in many societies than it was in Britain. He has divided a number of his social classes to handle the farmers and farm workers of France, Italy, and other societies with large agrarian sectors (Erikson and Goldthorpe 1993). So far, however, these changes have been rather arbitrary and *ad hoc*, and the classification has only a limited value in comparative work.

A final social-class classification must be mentioned. Although it has not been very widely used in sociological research, the classification produced by the Institute of Practitioners in Advertising for a consortium of market-research organizations is often used in commercial and mass-media reports. This consists of six social classes that are labelled from A to E—you will often hear journalists talking about politicians seeking to attract the 'C1 voters'. This is not a rigorously worked-out social-class classification, and only five of the categories are positively defined. For the sake of completion, however, we show this in Figure 3.8, together with summaries of the various other classifications. Although we have tried to indicate the broad equivalencies that exist among the various classifications, these are only very approximate and there are no direct translations from one to another.

Evaluating the class schemes

These social-class classifications provide useful ways of organizing sociological data, so long as their limitations are understood. Many of these are limitations that are common to them all. The most important are:

▶ they depend on detailed occupational information, which may not be available;

▶ they have difficulties with those who have no current employment;

▶ they have not properly handled the class assignment of women.

In order to use any of these classifications, it is necessary to have detailed information about the work and employment relations of the people being studied. An occupational title alone is not enough, as occupations can be carried out under a wide range of work and employment conditions. An electrician, for example, could be in employment or self-employed. An engineer may be a professionally qualified chartered engineer who works as a self-employed consultant, a technically qualified manager in a large or small firm, or a skilled mechanic working in a car-repair workshop. The occupational listing that is used for both the Registrar General's Classification and the Goldthorpe Classification can be used only if the researcher has quite a substantial amount of information about the nature of the work that people do (Marsh 1986). This became even more important in 1980, when the official listing of occupational categories was directly linked to a more detailed listing produced by the then Department of Employment.

When this kind of detailed information is not available, it is not possible to classify people with complete reliability. Many researchers simply turn to the basic listings of social classes, as shown in Figures 3.5, 3.6, and 3.7, and allocate people to whichever class seems appropriate. An electrician, for example, might simply be classified as a skilled worker (social class IIIM, 5, or VI, depending on the scheme used). Many uses of the classifications, then, are less precise and less accurate than might be thought. This does not necessarily make the results invalid, but it does show the need to treat them with great care.

Particularly difficult problems arise when people who are not employed have to be allocated to a social class. If occupation is the basis for allocation to a class, then how is it possible to decide the class situations of students, the unemployed, the retired, and women working at home? The unemployed and the retired have often been classified on the basis of their last major occupation. This can often be appropriate, unless someone has been unemployed for a very long time. This is possible, however, only so long as a survey has included a question about it. If 'unemployed' or 'retired' is written down and no further questions are asked, it is impossible to assign the person to a social class.

The young unemployed cannot be handled so easily, as they have often had no previous employment. If they have been students, they can, like current students, be classified according to the occupation for which they trained. This, however, is not straightforward, as some of those who train for particular occupations may never enter them. Equally, not all courses of education lead to a specific occupation: training as a doctor may do so, but training as a sociologist or a historian is less likely to.

None of the classifications has treated women properly. Men and unmarried women have usually been allocated to occupational positions on the basis of their own employment, but married women—even if they are

Classic studies and social class

To help you find your way around the major studies that are central to sociology, we have shown below some of those that use the social-class schemes discussed in this section.

Study	Reference	Class scheme used
Social Mobility in Britain	Glass 1954	HJ
The Affluent Worker	Goldthorpe *et al.* (1969)	HJ modified
Poverty in the United Kingdom	Townsend (1979)	HJ modified
Social Mobility and Class Structure	Goldthorpe (1980)	G
British General Election Study	Heath (1985)	G
The Constant Flux	Erikson and Goldthorpe (1993)	G modified
Relative Deprivation and Social Justice	Runciman (1966)	IPA

Note: abbreviations in column 3 correspond to those shown in Figure 3.8.

Figure 3.8. Social-class classifications

IPA	RG	HJ	G.	Manual/non-manual
A	I	1, 2	I	
B	II	3	II, IV	Non-manual
C1	III (N)	4, 5	III	
C2	III (M)	5	V, VI	Manual
D	IV, V	6, 7	VII	
E residual (including pensioners)				

Notes:
IPA Institute of Practitioners in Advertising
RG Registrar-General's Classification
HJ Hall–Jones Classification
G. Goldthorpe Classification

in employment—have generally been allocated to the occupational categories of their husbands. Married women working at home as full-time houseworkers have, then, been treated as mere dependants of their husbands or male partners. This has often been criticized on the grounds that it is unfair to classify women by their husbands' occupations. The real problem, however, is a theoretical and empirical one.

Classifying women on the basis of their male partners' occupations can be justified when they are full-time domestic houseworkers who are not in employment and have been out of the labour market for some time. In these circumstances, research has shown that their own previous occupations may be poor indicators of their current resources and opportunities (Goldthorpe 1983). For these women, it has been suggested, partners' occupations, where these are full-time, are far more appropriate as indicators of the actual opportunities and constraints that they face. Where a married woman has a current, full-time employment, this may be a more useful indicator than the employment of her partner.

There are, however, problems in using any of the existing social-class classifications for women in employment. These classifications were devised when the bulk of employees were male, and so they are geared towards men's work. As we show later in the book, there is a high degree of *occupational segregation* by gender (see Chapter 13, pp. 539–41). That is to say, women tend to find employment in occupations that are regarded as 'women's work' or that men tend not to enter. Employed women are concentrated in the lower professions, and in clerical, sales, and personal service work. Women working part-time are concentrated in shop work, cleaning, and catering. Women are therefore concentrated in certain specific occupations, and the existing occupational classifications give far less attention to those occupations. Almost a quarter of all employed women in 1971 were officially classified into just one of the 223 occupational categories then used for census data: that for clerks and cashiers. Over a half of employed women were assigned to just five of these categories.

Clerical and cashier work is not all of a type. It is carried out under a vast range of employment and working conditions and includes receptionists, proof readers, library assistants, stock-control clerks, postal clerks, meter readers, and so on (Arber *et al.* 1986). Existing classifications give far less attention to variations in women's work than they do to variations in men's work. This has led to a suggestion that separate occupational classifications for women should be devised, or that the existing classifications should be broadened to cover areas of women's employment more adequately. These issues are among the most pressing tasks facing sociology today.

PRESENTING DATA

Through the conversion of concepts into variables, sociologists are able to collect the data that they need for their research. Once these data have been collected, however, they must be organized and presented in ways that highlight their relevance for the theoretical interests that inform the research design. We are not able to look at the many specialist techniques that are available to sociologists for doing this. We can, however, look

at some of the procedures that will be most relevant to you when you try to understand the results of sociological research. We will look, in particular, at the ways in which data can be presented in tables and in charts, two different ways of trying to summarize sociological data. We will also, but very briefly, consider some of the statistical measures that you may come across.

Reading a table

The best way to approach the question of how to construct a table is to consider how to read one. Tables can be quite daunting, as many people are—quite unnecessarily—frightened by numbers. There is no need for this. A table can be read in exactly the same way as a piece of prose. You simply need to know where to start.

Look at Figure 3.9 for a few moments. Where did you look first? The chances are that you glanced down the left-hand side and then across some of the numbers. This is the wrong thing to do. The first thing that you should do when reading any table is to *read the title*. This is obvious when you think about it, but people tend to ignore the obvious when it comes to tables.

The title of this table is 'A table to read', but under this you will see the original title as it appeared in *Social Trends*. This tells you that it concerns 'AIDS cases' and 'HIV-1 infected persons' and that it looks at these in relation to 'probable exposure' and 'gender'. It also tells you that the data refer to 1995. We already know quite a lot about the table, just from its title. If you are not familiar with any of the terms used in a title, you should check back through the text or consult other sources to check them out. For example, in this case you would need to know, in general terms, what AIDS is, what HIV is, and how exposure and gender are likely to be relevant. In most cases, this will be obvious to you from the content of the book or article that you are reading. In the case of this example table, of course, this may not be the case, as we have introduced it out of its original context.

The next things that you should do is look for any notes about the table. These are usually underneath it. In this case, you will see that one of the notes relates specifically to the title. This note clarifies something about the date to which the information relates. A second note merely clarifies one of the headings in the table, so we do not need to worry about this for the moment. The final note is one that gives the original source of the data (ignore our own 'Source' reference to *Social Trends* 1996). This is often a very useful piece of information. The original source information in this table tells you that the data were produced by a centre that monitors 'communicable diseases', another term

Figure 3.9. **A table to read**

AIDS cases and related deaths and reports of HIV-1 infected persons: by probable exposure category and gender, to end June 1995[1]

United Kingdom	Numbers					
	AIDS				Reports of HIV-1 infected persons[2]	
	Cases		Related deaths			
	Males	Females	Males	Females	Males	Females
Probable HIV exposure category						
Sexual intercourse						
Between men	8,101	.	5,725	.	15,001	.
Between men and women	782	627	433	333	2,000	2,280
Injecting drug use (IDU)	449	202	292	118	1,885	859
Blood						
Blood factor (e.g. haemophilia)	493	6	424	5	1,218	11
Blood/tissue transfer (e.g. transfusion)	39	71	26	48	77	85
Mother to child	81	82	42	40	152	149
Other/undetermined	100	18	76	9	621	115
All categories	10,045	1,006	7,018	553	20,954	3,499

[1] Cumulative reported cases and deaths up to the end of June 1995.
[2] Includes 49 reports where the gender was not stated; also includes those individuals who progressed to AIDS.

Source: **PHLS Communicable Disease Surveillance Centre.**

Source: *Social Trends* (1996: table 7.10).

that you will need to understand. (PHLS is the Public Health Laboratory Service, though the table does not actually tell you this.) In many cases, these notes will give you some useful definitions or may give you details of any sampling method.

You can now turn to the main body of the table: but do not look at any numbers yet. Look at the headings along the top and down the left-hand side of the table. Immediately under the title you are told that the data relate to the 'United Kingdom' (not England, not Scotland, not even Great Britain, but the United Kingdom as a whole). You are also told that they are 'numbers'. It might seem obvious that the data are numbers, but this is stated in order to make it clear that you are being given the actual numbers and not percentage figures.

Along the top is given a breakdown of the columns showing the AIDS and HIV-1 categories mentioned in the title. The AIDS category is broken down into 'cases' and 'related deaths', while the HIV-1 category refers only to 'infected persons'. Each of these is further subdivided into 'males' and 'females', something else that you were told about in the title. On the left-hand side of the table there is a general heading referring to 'exposure category'. So far, then, the title has given you a very good idea about the whole structure of the table. It is going to compare AIDS cases, AIDS-related deaths, and HIV-1 infection in men and women, and it is going to

Columns and rows

Tables are divided into columns and rows. People are sometimes confused about this, but columns run *down* the page and rows run *across* it. Think of the columns in a Roman or Greek temple, which run from the top to the bottom of the building.

look at the causes of their exposure to the virus. To find out more about the table, you need to look at the row headings down the left-hand side.

The headings down the left-hand side show five main categories, followed by a total for 'All categories'. The categories are 'exposure categories': sex, drugs, blood, mother to child (during pregnancy), and 'other/ undetermined'. Two of these categories are subdivided: 'Sexual intercourse' is subdivided by type of sex, while 'Blood' is subdivided by the type of blood exposure.

By now you should have a very clear idea about the kinds of things that the table is trying to show you, even before you have looked at a single number. By far the best approach to the actual numbers in a table is to use the method called eyeballing. Simply cast your eyes down and across the table, looking for the biggest numbers. In this table, the columns are the important things, as all the numbers are totalled at the bottom. (Do you remember that the 'All categories' heading is down there?) Do not worry about the details of the numbers at this stage. If there are any decimal figures, just ignore them and concentrate on the very broad patterns.

This table shows that the biggest numbers are in the column for males and that the category for sexual intercourse between men is the largest. Ignoring the odd hundreds, there were 8,000 cases, 5,000 related deaths, and 15,000 infected persons. These are the most striking results in the table. Only under 'infected persons', where the total numbers are much bigger, did any other figure approach these levels.

Eyeballing is a very useful technique for summarizing a table. Ignoring numbers after a decimal point, ignoring odd hundreds, and so on allow you to scan the table and immediately identify its most significant features. The largest and smallest figures stand out from all the others. Can you see where the smallest figures are in the table?

In many cases, this is all that you will need to do. You may want to go on to conclude that 'nearly all' cases of AIDS in males were due to exposure in homosexual intercourse or that 'about three-quarters' of all reports of infected persons involved exposure to the same risk, but you will not often need to be more precise than this. If you do need greater precision for any reason, then you should by now have enough knowledge and confidence about the table to extract these without any difficulty.

Constructing a table

Once you have mastered the techniques for reading a table, you should be able to make critical assessments of other people's data. You will be able to do this more effectively, however, if you know a little more about how to construct tables. This is also useful knowledge for whenever you come to present data of your own in essays or research projects. Many of the skills necessary to construct a table are, of course, simply the opposite of those involved in reading one, but they are worth looking at in a little more detail. When you come to read tables (including some in this book), you will find that people often break the rules of table construction and make the tables unnecessarily complex.

The most useful overview of this whole question is an official handbook called *Plain Figures* (Chapman 1986), which gives an introduction to the dos and don'ts of table construction. The author distinguishes between tables for demonstration and tables for reference. The former are tables that aim to communicate a message and to show relationships, while the latter are the more comprehensive compilations that are found in many reports on official statistics. For many purposes, demonstration tables are quite sufficient, and they are what you will usually come across in books and newspapers. A good understanding of them will allow you to tackle more complex tables at a later stage in your career.

Chapman gives seven rules for the construction of demonstration tables:

▶ round all numbers to two effective digits wherever possible;

▶ put the numbers to be most often compared with each other in columns rather than rows;

▶ arrange columns and rows in some natural order or in size order;

▶ where possible, put big numbers at the top of the table;

▶ give column and row averages or totals as a focus;

▶ use layout to guide the eye;

▶ give a verbal summary of the main points in the table (Chapman 1986: 39).

Effective digits are those that vary and have the greatest significance. In a sequence of three-digit numbers, for example, it is usually the first two digits (the hundreds and the tens) that are the most significant, as the third digit (the units) is a very small part of the overall total. Rounding numbers to two effective digits simplifies matters by concentrating on the most important things. So, the sequence of numbers 152, 271, 384, 623, can usefully be simplified into the sequence 150, 270, 380, 620. This conveys the broad pattern more clearly, without any serious loss in detail.

The purpose of this rounding is to make it easier for people to eyeball the resulting table. Although there are many exceptions, and the rule must be used with care, it is generally a very effective technique to use. Whenever the data are to be used for reference purposes, however, the full numbers are likely to be important and rounding will not be appropriate.

The second rule that Chapman gives is to put the numbers to be compared in columns, not rows. It is far easier to eyeball a column than a row, especially when you need to do some arithmetic. It may be necessary, for example, to subtract a number from the overall total or to add up entries to produce a subtotal. We all learn to do our sums at school in columns, and it remains the most efficient way to do mental arithmetic for most people. In constructing a table, then, the researcher must decide which is the most important set of figures to compare and must use these as the columns.

The next two rules concern the order of the columns and rows. Nothing is more confusing than to have them listed in haphazard order. Chapman suggests that, if there is a natural order of size, then this should be used and that the largest should be put at the top of the column. This, again, makes the data very easy to inspect. Where data are organized by date (as in, for example, a year-by-year table), it is usually best to put the data for the earliest date at the top or at the left of the table so that the information appears to run logically down or across the table.

All columns and rows should, where appropriate, have average or total figures as a focus. These appear in the margins of the table (at the bottom and the right), and they are often referred to as the *marginals*. This can save the reader a lot of work and can, again, bring out any patterns that the data show.

Chapman's rule that the layout should be a guide to the eye is really a summary of all the previous rules. It should be obvious to the reader what the table is trying to show, even before the detailed numbers are considered. One aspect of this rule is to give proper headings to all columns and rows and to title the table appropriately. You should give as much attention to the construction of the table as you do to the grammar of your text. A reader can read your table, as described in the previous section, if you follow the rules of layout when you construct it.

The final rule is simply that you should never just insert a table without any comment. In some situations it may be useful to provide people with illustrative tables, but it is generally important to tie them into your text in some way. If they are to func-

tion as *evidence*, rather than illustrations, there must be some kind of verbal summary of the key points and their significance. It is not necessary to summarize everything in the table, as that would make the table unnecessary, but the main points should be covered. This normally means highlighting patterns or trends.

Chapman adds a final point that charts are often more useful when data are to be displayed for demonstration only, and we will look at the use of charts in the following section.

Drawing charts

If the actual numbers are not important and you simply wish to convey the broad patterns and trends, a chart is often useful. You will find a number of examples of charts in this book. These include maps and diagrams of various kinds, as well as graphs of numerical data. It is graphs that we will look at in this section. It is not necessary that you understand all the mathematics behind the graphs. You simply need to have some idea about how they are constructed. The three types of graph that we will consider (shown in Figure 3.10) are:

▶ line charts;
▶ bar charts;
▶ pie charts.

The **line chart** or line graph is especially useful for showing trends and patterns over time. If time is shown along the bottom of the graph, the particular variable that is of interest can be shown along the left-hand axis. This might be the percentage of the population that is unemployed, the percentage committing suicide, and so on. The percentage level for each time period is marked with a diamond, a cross, or some other symbol, and the points can be connected with a line that shows the trend. If there are separate data for men and women, for different age groups, or for different social classes, then these can each be plotted separately and a line drawn for each group. This kind of line chart allows the trends for the different groups to be compared.

Care must be taken in drawing a line graph, as the vertical scale (the scale for the variable along the left hand side) can exaggerate a trend. If we represent a change of 5 per cent in the crime rate by 5 centimetres on a graph, then this will look far more significant than if it is represented by 5 millimetres. This gives great scope for misleading people, as it allows the unscrupulous researcher or politician to produce the gee-whiz graph (Huff 1954: 60). An example of this is shown in Figure 3.11.

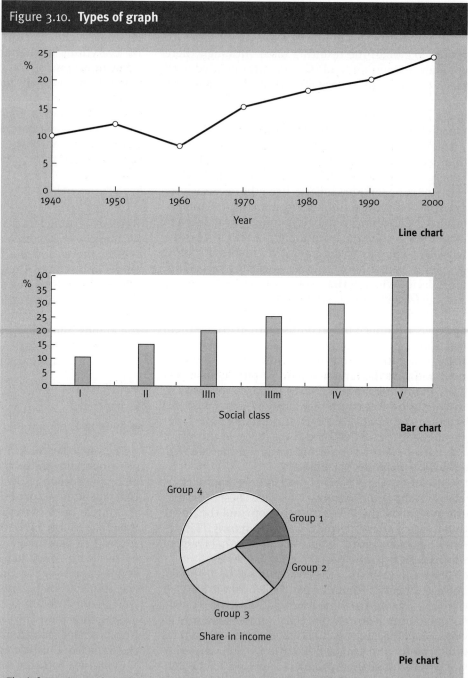

Figure 3.10. **Types of graph**

The information in these figures is artificial and is used simply to illustrate the three types of graph. For this reason, we have not included all the titles and labels that you would find on an actual graph.

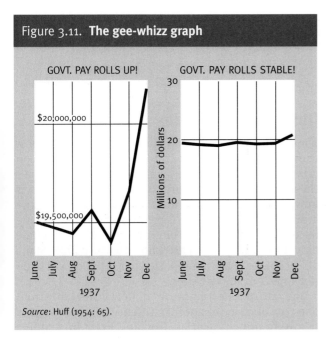

Figure 3.11. **The gee-whizz graph**

GOVT. PAY ROLLS UP!

$20,000,000

$19,500,000

June July Aug Sept Oct Nov Dec

1937

GOVT. PAY ROLLS STABLE!

Millions of dollars

30

20

10

June July Aug Sept Oct Nov Dec

1937

Source: Huff (1954: 65).

effect, the circumference of the circle. The chart is constructed by making the overall total of the variable measured equal to the 360 degrees that define the circle. A group that has, say, 25 per cent of the total would be represented by a slice that describes an angle of 90 degrees (a quarter of 360 degrees).

Certain skills are needed to construct charts by hand, but this is not always necessary. Many word-processing programs now contain built-in routines for producing tables and for converting them, instantly, to line charts, bar charts, and pie charts. Researchers who use survey analysis and statistical packages will have even more facilities available to them. So long as the general principles are understood, the computer takes care of the details.

What is true for charts is also true for the various statistics that sociologists formerly calculated by hand. If you can handle basic addition and subtraction, and if you can use a pocket calculator when necessary, you will be able to read and produce most basic tables. With just a few more skills, charts and diagrams can be produced, and with access to a computer numerous advanced statistical procedures are at hand.

 In other parts of this book you will find discussions of how to calculate and use averages, correlation coefficients, and various other statistical measures. You are unlikely, at this stage in your career, to need much more. If you want to learn about significance tests, standard deviations, variance, and chi-squared, you should look at a text such as Hinton (1995). The use of computers to produce these statistics is covered in Rose and Sullivan (1993). You should not try to learn any of these measures, but you might want to refer to the books if you come across research reports that use them.

A **bar chart** represents variables as horizontal or vertical bars. The lengths of the bars correspond to the totals shown in the columns or rows of a table. Separate bars can, then, be drawn for each social group or category in the original table. We might, for example, draw bars for each social class in the population, the length of each bar showing the percentage that go to church, the percentage convicted of offences, the percentage with substantial savings, and so on. When a bar chart is drawn with data that are measured in terms of a continuous variable (such as age or income) it is technically termed a *histogram*. Although this has certain distinct statistical properties, it is not necessary for you to worry about this.

The final type of chart that we will look at is the **pie chart**. This is a circular graph that, like a pie, can be divided into separate slices. If the area of the whole circle is made to represent a total figure, then the area of each slice represents the share of the total belonging to a particular social group or category. A population divided into six social classes, for example, could be represented as six slices of the overall circle, the size of each slice representing, say, their share in total national income.

A pie chart is a very useful visual representation of some kinds of data, but it requires just a little more skill to draw it. These skills are those of school geometry. While a line or bar chart has a vertical scale running along the left-hand side, the scale of a pie chart is, in

USING OFFICIAL STATISTICS

Official statistics are among the most important sources of data available to sociologists. They have been produced for administrative and political purposes and reflect the needs and concerns of politicians and civil servants rather than those of academic sociologists. They remain, however, a fundamental source of information on most of the topics with which sociologists deal and they are essential to the overall picture that sociologists try to construct. Official statistics are a relatively cheap and plentiful source of data. They are constructed in ways that, in general, make it possible to assess their reliability and validity, and they are often available on a regular basis over long periods of time. For all of these reasons, sociologists have made a great deal of use of them.

There has, however, been much discussion of the very serious problems that they involve. Criminal statistics, for example, are held to underestimate the real level of crime, unemployment statistics to underestimate the actual number of people who are out of work, and so on. For some, these problems are so great that the whole idea of using statistics to study real social processes has been rejected. Indeed, some interactionists and ethnomethodologists claim that there is no such thing as a real rate of crime, unemployment, or suicide, for all rates depend on definitions that are socially constructed. If this is so, the idea of using official statistics to measure them cannot make sense (Cicourel 1964; Douglas 1967; from a different theoretical perspective, see the similar point made in Hindess 1973).

These critics undoubtedly have some important arguments on their side. Suicide statistics, for example, depend on the ways in which coroners, police, and others classify deaths. This does not, however, mean that rates cannot be constructed or used. What it does mean is that whenever we use such a rate it is vital to be clear about the definitions that have been used in its construction. Differences in rates still require explanation, and the different definitions that have been used may provide a part of that explanation. It is also possible to control, at least in part, for differences of definition. This is how Durkheim examined not only differences between countries but also differences between areas within countries.

Important questions still arise, however, about how these rates might be explained. We might ask, for example, whether Durkheim's (1897) particular conclusions were valid, but the reality of suicide cannot seriously be questioned (J. M. Atkinson 1978).

Despite the problems involved in the use of official statistics, we will try to show that they remain an essential part of the sociological toolbox. So long as we are *aware* of their limitations, we can try to overcome them or, at least, be honest about the limits on the conclusions that we draw from the statistics. The problems of official statistics are, in fact, no greater than the problems of using participant observation or historical documents. One of the most valuable things that a sociologist can do is to *combine* various types of data in a single piece of research. The limitations of any one source would, wherever possible, be compensated by the advantages of another.

 If the word 'triangulation' did not spring to your mind at this point, read our discussion of combining research methods on pp. 74–5.

Official statistics of crime

The limitations of official statistics have been most comprehensively explored in relation to statistics on crime. It does make sense to talk about rates of crime—the numbers of rapes, murders, or burglaries—and it is important to try to measure these rates. However, the available criminal statistics provide wholly inadequate measures of these rates. The criminal statistics include only those offences that are 'known to the police'. Many offences are simply not reported to the police and so do not appear in the statistics.

The rate of reporting varies quite considerably from one type of crime to another. Offences that are seen as relatively minor, such as dropping litter in a public place, may be regarded as annoying, but they are not seen as worth reporting to the police. Most murders, on the other hand, are likely to be reported, as it is an offence that is generally regarded as serious, and, in any case, it is difficult to conceal a dead body for any period of time. Rape is far less likely to be reported. While it is undoubtedly regarded as a serious crime, many women victims of rape prefer not to face police questioning. The prospect of an interrogation in court, particularly when the likelihood of a successful prosecution is seen as fairly low, discourages many from reporting their rapes.

These remarks bring out the fact that victims and others make assessments of the likely consequences of reporting crimes. They try to judge whether the police will take the report seriously, or will simply file it away and get on with other business. Similarly, they try to assess the chances that the police will solve the crime and bring the offender to book. Detection rates for many crimes are very low, and victims may simply not think it worth reporting them. Burglaries, for example, have a low detection rate, and it is largely due to pressure from insurance companies that householders report burglaries. Insurance companies will not consider a claim for any burglary that has not been reported, and so those who wish to claim on their policy must report it, no matter how unlikely they think it is that the offender will be apprehended. Where householders have not insured their property, reporting rates for burglary are low.

Victims and others also take account of whether detected offenders are likely to be charged, rather than given a warning, and, if charged, whether they are likely to be convicted in court. Where these probabilities are seen to be low, as they are for many kinds of crime, reporting is also likely to be low.

Considerations such as these lead many people to talk about the 'hidden figure' or **dark figure** of crime. Crimes known to the police are merely the tip of an iceberg (see Figure 3.12), and there is an unknown amount of unreported crime that remains invisible in official statistics. The size of the dark figure varies from one kind of crime to another. In the case of murder, for example, it is likely to be very small, while in the case of traffic speeding it is likely to be very high. One of the major problems in research on crime is the unknown size of the dark figure. It is also very difficult to assess whether those crimes that are reported to the police are a representative sample of all crimes. If they are, then it is possible to discover some important characteristics of crime and criminals from the criminal statistics. If we do not know whether they are a representative sample, then any conclusions drawn from the criminal statistics may be unfounded.

One of the ways in which this problem has been addressed in the sociology of crime is through self-report and victim studies. In self-report studies, people are asked whether they have ever committed particular offences. In victim studies, they are asked whether they have ever been the victims of particular kinds of crime. Such studies have helped to quantify the dark figure and to show how crime statistics can be used. Recent research has suggested that, overall, only 47 per cent of all offences are reported to the police, and only 27 per cent are recorded by them. Just 2 per cent of all offences result in the conviction of an offender. However, the broad *trends* in crime rates are, for the most part, accurately reflected in the statistics.

On this basis, Lea and Young have concluded that criminal statistics 'have to be interpreted with extreme caution. It is not that they are meaningless; they do reflect public, police and court definitions of crime, the disposal of limited resources and the extent of infractions thus defined; but what they do not do is tell about an independent entity called "crime"' (Lea and Young 1984: 15). If the limitations of the criminal statistics are fully recognized, this helps us to make a proper and sensitive use of them (Maguire 1994).

Statistics of employment and health

What holds for criminal statistics also holds for other types of official statistics. For example, the newspapers and television regularly report the current unemployment rate. This is a figure that is calculated and published by the Department for Education and Employment. Since 1982, the department has regarded someone as 'unemployed' if he or she is registered for unemployment benefit. These are the people who are officially seen as both available for work and actively seeking employment. The official rate of unemployment is simply the number of those claiming welfare benefits on the grounds of unemployment (Jobseeker's

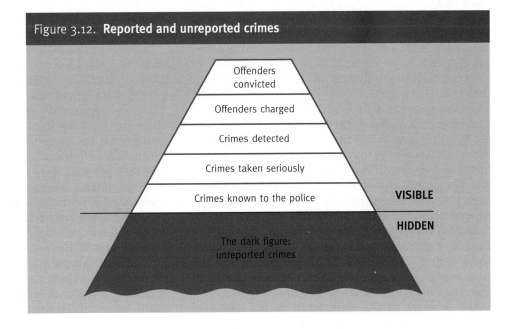

Figure 3.12. Reported and unreported crimes

Offenders convicted

Offenders charged

Crimes detected

Crimes taken seriously

Crimes known to the police

VISIBLE

HIDDEN

The dark figure: unreported crimes

Allowance, Unemployment Benefit, Income Support, and all their predecessors).

At first sight, this might seem a plausible measure of unemployment. This is the way that it has been treated by governments and the mass media. However, things are not that simple. Not everyone who would like to be employed is entitled to receive benefit. Many married women, for example, do not have a record of national-insurance contributions that would entitle them to a benefit. These people are not counted as unemployed in the official statistics.

Greater problems arise if trends over time are examined. Prior to 1982, welfare entitlement and registration as unemployed were not so closely tied. The official rate of unemployment was a measure of those on the register, whether or not they were entitled to benefit. The administrative change to a count of benefit claimants removed 200,000 people from the unemployed count almost overnight. Over the course of the recession of the 1980s and 1990s, Conservative governments sought to contain the welfare bill by changing criteria of eligibility for various benefits and so taking people off the registers. In all, thirty different changes were made to the rules for registration as unemployed between 1979 and 1989. In 1998 the Labour Government moved back to a measure closer to that used before 1979. The rate of 'unemployment' can alter purely because of administrative changes, and not because there has been a change in the real rate of employment (Levitas 1996). There is, then, a 'dark figure' of hidden unemployment.

Attempts to arrive at a more accurate measure of unemployment, avoiding the problem of the dark figure, have been made using data from the Labour Force Survey (LFS). As this is a sample survey, it is not affected by administrative changes to eligibility rules, but it does have problems of its own. The LFS uses an internationally agreed definition of unemployment that is far from perfect. Those who do *any* part-time work, no matter how little and how low paid, are not counted as unemployed. The numbers lost in this way are more or less balanced by the numbers of non-claimants counted as unemployed. As a result, the LFS measure does not differ significantly from the official rate. The nearest that we have to a measure that avoids these problems is one that comes from the 1991 Census, when people were asked (for the first time in a census) to identify themselves as employed or unemployed. The figure of 2,485,000 found in the April 1991 Census compares with a figure of 2,302,000 recorded by the LFS (just over 8 per cent of the labour force) in the same month (Levitas 1996: 58; see also Figure 3.13).

The problem of the dark figure is far less of a difficulty for the main demographic statistics pro-duced from the Census and the registration of births, deaths, and marriages. Because compliance with the Census and registration is a legal requirement, they are generally regarded as being complete and, therefore, very accurate. Nevertheless, concern over the possible use of census data to register people for the so-called poll tax (the Community Charge) led many people to boycott the 1991 Census. It has been estimated that there may have been an under-count of as many as two million people. Subsequent survey findings, on which this estimate is based, suggest that the 'hidden popula-tion' consisted mainly of young males living in inner-city areas who were not listed on the electoral register and did not complete census forms.

More significant problems have always existed for health statistics derived from general practitioners and hospitals (H. Roberts 1990). Not all illnesses are reported to doctors, especially when people believe that there is nothing that doctors can do to help them and when no medical certificate is required for absence from work. Colds, influenza, and other minor ailments may, there-fore, be significantly under-represented in the official statistics. The real rates of such illnesses are unknown (Stacey 1987: 213–14). Serious illnesses, on the other hand, are much more likely to be reported, as this is the only way in which it is possible to get medical treat-ment. Self-report studies—asking people about their ill-nesses—can help to resolve the problems of the dark figure of illness, but people cannot always recall all of the minor ailments that they have had during the survey period. In addition, they may not always be aware of the fact that they have had certain diseases if they have had them in a particularly mild form. It is, for example, possible to have very mild and virtually symp-tomless forms of such diseases as rubella.

Just as the users of the criminal statistics must know what is meant, in legal discourse, by 'summary offence', 'theft', and 'notifiable offence', so the user of mortality statistics must have some understanding of 'malignant neoplasm', 'respiratory disease', and so on. These problems are, in some respects, purely technical matters that can be resolved by checking the appropri-ate medical definition. We show in Chapter 6, however, that medical diagnoses are socially constructed and that, therefore, diagnostic categories cannot be regarded as technically neutral devices.

Demographic statistics from official sources, like crime statistics, emerged with the transformation of nation states in the eighteenth and nineteenth cen-turies. They continue to show the signs not only of their historical origin, but also of the contemporary admin-istrative purposes to which they are geared. They involve many technical and conceptual problems (J. Scott 1990: ch. 5). They are, however, the only sources

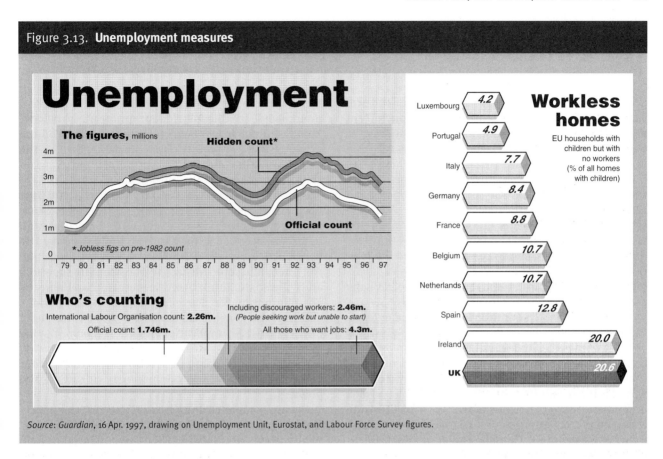

Figure 3.13. **Unemployment measures**

Source: *Guardian*, 16 Apr. 1997, drawing on Unemployment Unit, Eurostat, and Labour Force Survey figures.

that we have on many matters, and a proper understanding of their construction allows us to overcome many of their limitations. If they cannot be accepted at face value, they can, nevertheless, be used, with care, for a great many sociological purposes. They are an invaluable tool of sociological analysis.

SUMMARY POINTS

In this section we have looked at the way in which concepts can be converted into variables by constructing indicators. This involves issues of validity and reliability. We considered these issues in relation to the classification of social class and the use of official statistics.

▶ A number of social-class schemes have been used in sociological research. These include the Registrar General, the Hall–Jones, and the Goldthorpe classifications. Even the most reliable have problems of validity.

▶ Proper use of the classifications depends on the researcher having detailed occupational information.

▶ All the available schemes find it difficult to handle those who are not currently in employment.

▶ The class assignment of women has not been properly dealt with in any of the schemes.

▶ Official statistics are to be treated critically and with care, though they are essential sources of information in many areas of sociology.

▶ The problem of the dark figure in official statistics can be partly overcome through the use of such sources as victim surveys, self-report surveys, and other types of survey data.

This section has also been concerned with the principles involved in constructing and reading tables and charts.

▶ When reading a table, begin with the title, notes, and headings. Finally, eyeball the table to uncover its broad patterns.

▶ When constructing a table, follow the seven rules set out in Chapman (1986) (see above, p. 104).

▶ The most important charts for sociologists to use and to understand are line charts, bar charts, and pie charts.

THE ETHICS OF SOCIAL RESEARCH

Social research is not undertaken in a moral or political vacuum. Questions of confidentiality and anonymity in all styles of research are fundamental to the ways in which the research is undertaken and the uses to which the results are put. Once research results have been published, they can have unforeseen consequences for the groups studied, and the sociologist cannot stand aside from these consequences. In many cases, the ethical and political issues that need to be considered are the general questions of human responsibility for other human beings. These are, of course, massive questions, on which there are no easy answers. As sociologists, we cannot avoid them, but nor do we have any particular right to pontificate on them.

The detailed implementation of certain research procedures, however, does raise quite specific questions about how these general considerations are to be translated into specific rules of research practice. While these ethical issues cannot be resolved in any clear-cut way, it is important that they be aired and that various alternative answers be considered. We will illustrate these issues from ethnographic research involving participant observation, though similar issues arise in other forms of social research.

We first of all look at how these have been raised in debates around particular observational studies. We then go on to look at the response of the British Sociological Association (BSA), the professional body for sociologists in Britain, to see the guidance that it gives to its members. We reprint, by permission, the whole of the BSA's Statement of Ethical Practice towards the back of the book, and we suggest that you read this before you undertake any research of your own.

ETHICS OF COVERT RESEARCH

Covert observation is the research method of the hidden observer or the complete participant. In these situations, people are not aware that they are being observed for research purposes. They believe that they are merely going about their ordinary lives.

The main objection to covert participant observation is that it is unethical for sociologists to misrepresent their identity just in order to undertake research. To do this is to make an unwarranted intrusion into people's lives. Covert participant observation involves lies,

fraud, and deceit on the part of the sociologist and many people see this as an inappropriate way to behave. This is often justified by sociologists, however, on the grounds that any harm done is outweighed by the benefits of the research. These claims and counterclaims can be seen in a number of actual cases.

Simon Holdaway (1983) conducted covert participant observation on the British police during the 1970s. Holdaway had been a police officer for many years and had been seconded to university to study sociology. He decided to undertake a sociological research project on the force, but kept this fact secret from his superiors and colleagues. He felt that overt research would not be possible or would lead people to modify their behaviour and that the benefits that would flow from his study outweighed the implications of the secrecy that he adopted about the research. While he was apparently working as an ordinary police officer, he actually spent two years studying the occupational culture of the police.

Having completed the research and left the police, Holdaway faced the further ethical problem of whether to publish his results, which had been undertaken for a Ph.D. His own professional interests as a sociologist and his desire to make his work known had to be balanced against the rights of his subjects and the fact that publication would bring his deception into the open. To protect particular individuals from any recriminations, Holdaway changed their names and obscured the places where the research had been carried out, aiming to give people a degree of anonymity. His justification for the research and its publication was that his concern was with the *structure* of policing and the ways in which it constrains individuals. He was not trying to blame particular individuals for their actions (Holdaway 1982).

Similar issues arose in Nigel Fielding's (1981) study of the National Front, a racist political party of which he was not a member and of which he strongly disapproved. To begin the research he had to approach a party branch as a potential member, and this involved him claiming to have racist views to which he did not actually subscribe. By appearing to be sympathetic, he was able to obtain access to party situations and could observe meetings and talk to people freely. The ethical problem for Fielding was that he was not only *concealing* his intentions, he was actually *lying* and so misleading those he was studying.

Fielding's research also involved some overt interviewing, in different situations, and the research developed as a mixture of covert and overt methods. When it was completed, Fielding published his book but decided to retain the original names of all those that he had studied. He felt no obligation to protect the identities of his subjects, but he engaged a lawyer to read through the book to search for anything that might have left him open to legal action. Fielding faced fewer problems than Holdaway, because of his lack of sympathy with the National Front, but he still had to protect his own personal and professional situation (Fielding 1982).

It could be argued that, in these cases, the ends justified the means. Disclosing the causes of racism, for example, whether in the police or the National Front, might be seen as something that justifies any deception of the subjects. Not all would accept this justification, however; some would never see this kind of deception as acceptable. Before we can consider this view, however, it is worth considering another case where the justification was used. This is a famous study by Humphreys (1970) where the benefit claimed was that to the subjects themselves.

Humphreys studied male homosexual activities in public toilets. One of the accepted activities in these settings is that of the 'watch queen', who gets a voyeuristic excitement from watching homosexual sex but also acts as a look-out for any police activity in the area. It was this role that Humphreys adopted, and it allowed him to gain a great deal of information about the men that he studied.

Humphreys was able to use information on car number plates to get addresses from the police computer, pretending to the police that he was doing market research. He then approached the men and requested interviews. This was, of course, a further invasion of their privacy, but Humphreys argues that it could be justified if it led to a better understanding of homosexuality and, therefore, to an improvement in the social situation of the gay men that he studied.

Some sociologists have gone even further than Holdaway, Fielding, and Humphreys, claiming that no justification is necessary for deception. Lies, fraud, and deceit are part and parcel of everyday life in any case, it has been argued, and there is no reason to expect sociological research to be any different. We all keep things secret in our interactions with others (Goffman 1959). If we are constantly manipulating and misleading one another, why should the sociologist not do the same thing? Complete openness is, in any case, impossible to achieve in any social relationship. The very distinction between covert and overt observation cannot be drawn

so sharply as some discussions imply. The overt researcher, for example, will rarely give a full explanation of the nature of the research, and most people who agree to be studied would not be interested in the full account. A simple statement about 'doing research' or 'writing a book' is generally enough to persuade people to cooperate, and any further explanation of the research is kept as simple as possible in order to avoid technical language and to avoid having too much influence on what the researcher hopes to observe.

We live in a world in which there are few moral certainties, and there can be no clear-cut ethical standards. Bulmer has suggested, however, that the principle of *informed consent*, now accepted as the basis of medical experimentation, should be observed whenever possible. People have a right, in all circumstances, to be fully informed about those things that affect them, and they must freely consent to their involvement in any course of action. Medical doctors testing new drugs must inform patients that they will be part of a medical trial, and the patients must have the right to refuse and to continue with conventional treatment. In the same way, Bulmer argues, people must be informed that they may be involved in sociological research, and they must have the right to refuse any involvement. While it may be impossible to give people full knowledge of the nature and purpose of the research, he argues, the kind of deception involved in covert participant observation is clearly a denial of individual rights to informed consent. Even if there are great public benefits from a piece of research, these can never override individual rights to privacy. (There is a useful discussion in Homan and Bulmer 1982).

Decisions about the ethics of particular research methods will always involve balancing competing

☞ You might like to discuss some of these ethical issues with other people before reading much further. Imagine that you are going to carry out research into drug-trafficking in an inner-city district. Would it be justifiable to use covert-participant observation to study those involved? Would any study be possible if you did *not* use covert participant observation? When you have considered these issues, you should read the BSA guidelines that we reprint in the Appendix. pp. 766–70.

ethical demands and moral principles. To help in handling these issues, professional bodies of sociologists in the United States and Britain have set up guidelines on ethical practice that set out the things that researchers must take into account in coming to their decisions.

SUMMARY POINTS

Ethical issues are fundamental to social research. Like ethical problems in general, they cannot be resolved in any clear-cut or consensual way. No abstract principles can be applied under all circumstances.

▶ Covert research has often been justified in terms of the benefits of the research to the wider society or to the subjects themselves.

▶ This use of deception has to be offset against the need to ensure the informed consent of those who are the subjects of research.

▶ Professional associations have established guidelines that social researchers are expected to follow in their projects.

REVISION AND EXERCISES

Look back over the Summary Points at the end of each section and make sure that you appreciate the general issues raised:

▶ **How would you distinguish between exploration, description, and explanation?**

▶ **What is meant by the following: triangulation, model, hypothesis?**

▶ **Make sure that you understand what is meant by: a case study, a comparative study, a longitudinal study, a cross-sectional study.**

SURVEY RESEARCH, SAMPLING, AND STATISTICS

▶ **Make sure that you understand the following terms: questionnaire, open-ended question, fixed-choice question, coding; pre-test, pilot; sampling frame, representative sample, sampling bias, sampling error, response rate; validity, reliability; columns, rows.**

▶ **How would you distinguish between an interview survey, a postal survey, and a telephone survey? List the advantages and disadvantages of each of these.**

▶ **What is meant by attitude scaling?**

▶ **Write two or three sentences to distinguish between probability and non-probability sampling.**

▶ **What is meant by a stratified random sample? How does it differ from a quota sample?**

▶ **Using the data in Figure 3.9, draw a pie chart to show the various exposure categories for AIDS cases among males.**

ETHNOGRAPHIC RESEARCH AND RESEARCH ETHICS

▶ **Make sure that you understand the following terms: overt research, covert research; complete participant, participant-as-observer, complete observer, Hawthorne effect; semi-structured interview, conversation analysis, life history, oral history.**

▶ **How important is it that ethnographers study representative samples?**

▶ We have discussed the studies carried out by Holdaway, Fielding, and Humphreys. Using this book and any other sources available to you, identify any two other studies that have used covert observation methods. Find out as much as you can about these studies.

▶ Draw up a list showing the advantages and disadvantages of covert participant observation.

▶ What is meant by the principle of informed consent? Can it be consistently applied in social research?

DOCUMENTARY RESEARCH AND OFFICIAL SOURCES

▶ Make sure that you understand the following terms: open access, closed access, personal documents; authenticity, credibility, representativeness, literal meaning, interpretation; social classes, economic classes, socio-economic groups; dark figure.

▶ Choose any one document that is familiar to you and discuss its authenticity, credibility, representativeness, and meaning.

▶ How useful is it to distinguish between primary and secondary sources?

▶ Look at our list of sociological studies on p. 101. Add other studies to the list, showing which social-class scheme each used.

▶ Discuss possible ways in which the social-class position of women could better be handled in the available class schemes.

FURTHER READING

You will find a comprehensive coverage of many of the issues covered in this chapter in:
May, T. (1997), *Social Research: Issues, Methods and Processes* (2nd edn., Buckingham: Open University Press).
O'Connell Davidson, J., and Layder, D. (1994), *Methods, Sex and Madness* (London: Routledge).

Basic styles of research and handling data are covered in:

de Vaus, G. (1991), *Surveys in Social Research* (London: UCL Press). A useful compilation of principles and issues for survey research.
Burgess, R. G. (1984), *In the Field: An Introduction to Field Research* (London: George Allen & Unwin). Gives a comprehensive coverage of issues of ethnographic research.
Scott, J. (1990), *A Matter of Record: Documentary Sources in Social Research* (Cambridge: Polity Press). A systematic overview of the history and use of official and administrative documents, together with a discussion of the principles of documentary research.
Chapman, M. (1986), *Plain Figures* (London: HMSO). An excellent set of guidelines for the construction and use of tables and charts.

Issues of research methodology are taken further in:

Burgess, R. G. (1986) (ed.), *Key Variables in Social Research* (London: Routledge & Kegan Paul). A collection of discussions that cover the construction of basic sociological variables.
Levitas, R., and Guy, W. (1996) (eds.), *Interpreting Official Statistics* (London: Routledge). A useful collection that discusses the use of a wide range of official statistics.
Huff, D. (1954), *How to Lie with Statistics* (London: Victor Gollancz). A classic, if a little dated, example of how statistics can mislead the unwary reader.
Hinton, P. R. (1995), *Statistics Explained* (London: Routledge). A good introduction to statistical measures. One of many similar books.
Moser, C., and Kalton, G. (1979), *Survey Methods in Social Investigation* (London: Heinemann Educational Books). Probably the standard source on all aspects of sampling, questionnaire design, and interviewing.
Oppenheim, A. N. (1966), *Questionnaire Design and Attitude Measurement* (London: Heinemann Educational Books). A more detailed consideration of issues covered in Moser and Kalton.

part two

These chapters cover all the main substantive areas of the subject. You will usually be studying only some of the topics that we cover, but we hope that you will want to read as widely as possible. You will often be told which sections to study by a lecturer or teacher, and you should follow this advice, making use of our cross-references and hints as appropriate. The hint boxes and other cross-references that we make in these chapters are intended to help you to develop a broad overview of the subject.

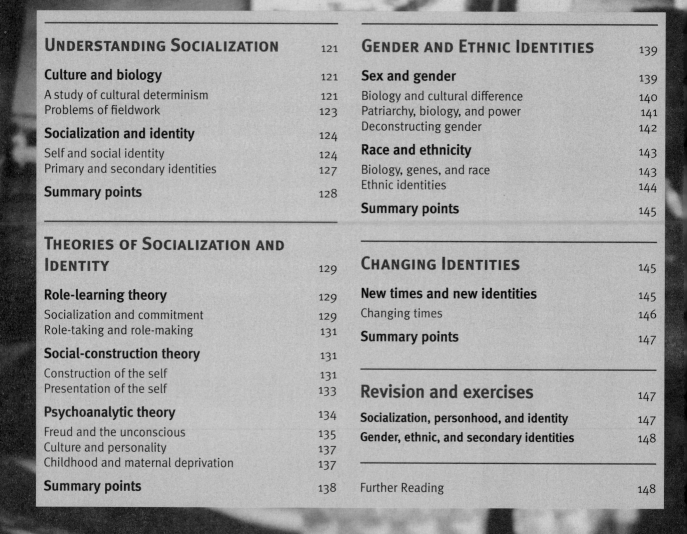

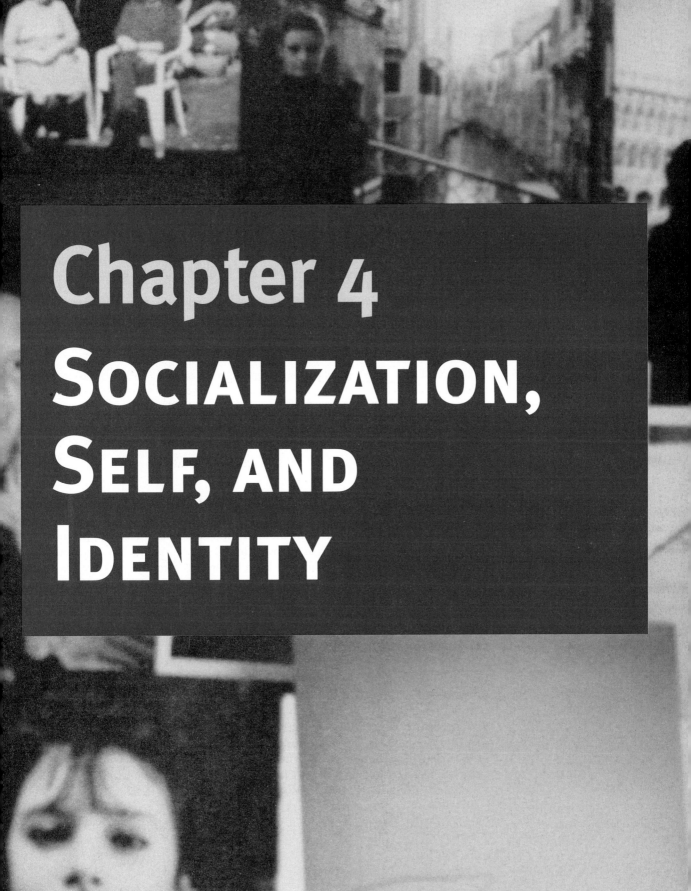

Chapter 4
Socialization, Self, and Identity

Questions of identity

'Helen Mather did not suspect she was any different from other women of her age. But two factors worried her. At 19, she'd never had a period. And penetrative sex had always been impossible. . . . Mather went for tests. . . . it was discovered that she did not have a vagina, or uterus, Fallopian tubes or ovaries. She was told that she had a rare genetic condition called Androgen Insensitivity Syndrome. . . . Tests showed that she was biologically male and had XY chromosomes, but in every outward way, she appeared female.

'"It would be grotesque to suggest I'm anything other than female," says Mather, now 46. "I wouldn't know how to be a man."

'Mather underwent reconstructive surgery to create a vagina. . . . In her mid-twenties, she married Wesley and they spent a very happy 11 years together, until his death from cancer. "My condition made no difference to him. It was only how I felt about myself that affected us."

'Naomi Walters . . . had been registered male at birth, as she was born with male genitalia. . . . From three years old, she underwent many surgical operations to augment her "maleness". . . . She was never comfortable as a boy. . . . Her confusion about her gender was exacerbated in her teens by the non-appearance of male sexual characteristics.

'It wasn't until her mid-twenties that Walters found the courage to live as a woman. . . . Switching gender roles was no problem for her—she'd always been mistaken for a female anyway. . . . She is currently taking time out . . . "to discover who I really am. . . . I have the stigma of having male on my birth certificate."'

Source: Beverley D'Silva, 'A Case of Mistaken Identity', *Guardian*, 29 Aug. 1996.

ARE Helen and Naomi really women, or are they men? What is it that determines who or what we 'really' are? For many people, biology is basic. Helen and Naomi both have male chromosomes, yet their biology is not that straightforward. They both had many external female characteristics, and they lacked many male characteristics. For both Helen and Naomi, how they saw themselves and how they were seen by others were more important for their sense of identity than were their chromosomes. Each found it easier to live as a woman than as a man—indeed, Helen had always lived as a woman and 'wouldn't know how to be a man'. Our identities as men and women, it would appear, are things that we learn, not things that are fixed by our biology.

In this chapter we will explore a number of issues about the relationship between biological factors, on the one hand, and cultural ideas and social relations, on the other. In the first section on 'Understanding Socialization' we will consider the nature of social learning and how people come to be social individuals with a conscious sense of their self. We then discuss the principal theories of socialization and identity. These issues are then illustrated through a consideration of gender and ethnic identities, where arguments in favour of biological explanation have had their greatest impact. A final section on 'Changing Identities' looks at some contemporary trends and raises matters that are looked at in greater depth in later chapters.

UNDERSTANDING SOCIALIZATION

One of the most striking things about human behaviour is that it is almost exclusively learned. While much that an animal does is determined by its biology, very little human behaviour is instinctive or fixed in this way. Children come into the world as helpless infants, and they develop into slightly less helpless adults only because they learn from their parents and from other adults how to speak, study, work, marry, vote, pray, steal, and do all the many other things with which people fill their time. All of these activities must be learned.

Animals also learn much of their behaviour. Birds, for example, must learn how to fly. Many animals can even be trained by human beings to do things that are not 'natural' to them—dogs can not only be house trained, but they can also be taught to sit up and beg for food. The dependence of human beings on learned behaviour, however, is fundamentally different from anything else that is found in the animal kingdom. While some aspects of human behaviour have similarities with animal behaviour—particularly with that of monkeys and the higher primates—the greater part of human behaviour is qualitatively distinct from all other animal behaviour. Human beings learn to be conscious agents, capable of reflecting upon their own behaviour and of modifying it in the light of their experiences. It is this conscious, subjective element in human conduct that makes it more appropriate to describe it as 'action' than as mere 'behaviour'. Action is behaviour to which a subjective meaning has been attached and which is, therefore, capable of reflexive monitoring by a human actor. To be a person is to *act*, not simply to behave.

This point is not always fully appreciated, and many non-sociologists have held that human behaviour can be explained in purely biological terms. As a result, the relative merits of biology and sociology have been hotly debated, though often with considerable misunderstanding on each side of the argument.

CULTURE AND BIOLOGY

The precise relationship between biology and culture has been hotly debated, with advocates of the most extreme positions tending to dominate the debates. For much of the nineteenth century and well into the twentieth century, the advocates of **biological determinism** held sway. Biological determinists hold that all aspects of human behaviour can be explained in terms of the universal and innate characteristics that people have as human beings. These claims have been further developed in recent years by advances in the understanding of genetics. Biological determinism has once more been forcefully promoted, most notably in the new scientific specialisms of sociobiology and evolutionary psychology.

Cultural determinism was promoted as a counter-doctrine to biological determinism in the early years of the century, and for a long time it held sway in the social sciences. The central figure in the promotion of cultural determinism was Margaret Mead, an anthropologist. Mead undertook a series of studies that seemed to show the infinite variability of human behaviour from one culture to another and which were therefore taken as firmly establishing the claims of cultural determinism. Recently, however, some of the key elements in Mead's account have been questioned. The way has been opened for a more sophisticated understanding of the interdependence of culture and biology, an understanding that avoids the extreme deterministic theories that have been advocated on both sides of the debate.

A study of cultural determinism

In the 1920s a study was launched that it was hoped would confirm the claims of cultural determinism. Franz Boas, the leading American anthropologist of the time, was a firm advocate of cultural explanations of social phenomena. His idea was to send a young graduate student, Margaret Mead, to the Pacific territory of Samoa, where she was to study adolescent behaviour. Boas expected her to discover a completely different approach to adolescence from that which prevailed in the United States and Europe. He reasoned that if people of the same physiological age could behave in radically different ways, then the problems faced by youth in the United States had to be explained in relation to its culture. They could not be explained in terms of the biological aspects of adolescence.

Mead's Samoan study (1928) was undertaken in the small island of Ta'u, part of the Samoan group of islands. Samoa was an American colony and naval

Margaret Mead

Margaret Mead (1901–78) — no relation to George Mead — studied anthropology at Columbia University. She used her Samoan fieldwork to write the book that was to make her name and that became the most influential anthropological work of all time: *Coming of Age in Samoa* (1928). A few years later, she carried out related work into adolescence in the Admiralty Islands, producing *Growing Up in New Guinea* (1930). Pursuing her interest in cultural determinism, she later carried out work, also in the Pacific, on sex and gender roles for *Sex and Temperament in Three Primitive Societies* (1935) and *Male and Female* (1950). She felt marginal to the male academic world and followed a career as Curator of the American Museum of Natural History in New York. Her work on cultural determinism was closely related to the ideas of Ruth Benedict on native Americans (1934) and on Japan (1946).

base. Ta'u itself was heavily dependent on its trading relations with the United States navy, and its chiefs were highly Westernized. During her fieldwork Mead lived in a house belonging to the only white family on the island. She concentrated her attention on a sample of twenty-five local girls, who ranged in age from 14 to 20. Working from the house, and using the school building during the holidays, Mead talked with the girls and began to collect a range of information about their lives. She claimed that, by contrast with those in the United States, adolescent girls in Samoa had a very easy and stress-free life. This, she thought, reflected the overall balance and moderation of Samoan culture.

Life in Samoa, Mead held, was 'easy' and relaxed, with little or no conflict. Its inhabitants lacked any deep feelings, and they had no strong passions. As they did not get worked up about day-to-day matters, they were rarely drawn into stressful or hostile relationships. Children grew up in large extended families and developed no strong attachment to their individual parents. They were, instead, embedded in diffuse, warm relationships with a large number of adults. They learned, early on, not to act impulsively. Samoa was a harmonious society. Its people, Mead claimed, were happy and well adjusted.

In this idyllic society, adolescence was the age of maximum ease and freedom. When they entered adolescence, Samoans were free to engage in sexual activity promiscuously. Mead felt that this reflected the adult view of sex: it was an enjoyable and playful activity that should not be taken too seriously.

The girls that Mead studied grew up with a great deal of sexual knowledge. This was unavoidable when large extended families lived in single-room houses with little or no privacy. They began to masturbate in early

childhood, generally at 6 or 7, and homosexual relationships were not uncommon during puberty. Adolescence was a time for erotic dancing and singing, and playful heterosexual relations emerged naturally out of this sexual experimentation.

As a result of this, Mead argues,

'adolescence represented no period of crisis or stress, it was instead an orderly developing of a set of slowly maturing interests and activities. The girls' minds were perplexed by no conflicts, troubled by no philosophical queries, beset by no remote ambitions. To live as a girl with many lovers as long as possible and then to marry in one's own village, near one's own relatives, and to have many children, these were uniform and satisfying ambitions.' (M. Mead 1928: 129)

Mead contrasted this with the typical adolescent experience in the United States. Adolescence there was widely seen as a period of great emotional turmoil. Because the ease and balance of Samoan adolescence could be related to the central features of Samoan culture, Mead argued that adolescence in the United States must be seen as reflecting the peculiarities of its culture. The biological universals of puberty and biological maturation, she claimed, have little or no direct impact on people's actions and relationships. Behaviour is shaped, above all else, by the culture into which people are born and socialized.

Mead's study became widely accepted as an exemplary proof of cultural determinism and as a final repudiation of biological determinism. By the 1960s it had become the most widely read of any anthropology book and it was a popular best-seller. Mead's reputation was confirmed by her studies in New Guinea (1930, 1935), where she explored the extent of cultural variation in gender relations. The three societies that she studied — those of the Arapesh, the Mundugumor, and the

Tchambuli—appeared to show all possible permutations of masculinity and femininity. Taken together, they further reinforced the claims of cultural determinism.

In Arapesh society, both men and women were gentle, caring, and passive, while in Mundugumor society both were assertive and sexually aggressive. By contrast with the United States and other Western societies, then, neither of these societies showed any significant gender differentiation. They varied considerably, however, in the type of personality that they valued most highly. Arapesh personality was similar to Western femininity, while Mundugumor personality was similar to Western masculinity. In the third society that she studied, the Tchambuli, Mead identified a sharp differentiation of gender roles, and she claimed that these varied in the opposite direction to the United States. Tchambuli men decorated themselves and gossiped with each other, while Tchambuli women were assertive and competent in practical affairs.

Problems of fieldwork

Mead believed that she had conclusively refuted the thesis of biological determinism. The single study of Samoa seemed sufficient to show that there were no universal biological stages of social development. The New Guinea studies simply added more weight to her argument for cultural determinism. Her conclusions have, however, been questioned. It has been shown that her understanding of Samoan society was seriously flawed and that, therefore, her defence of cultural determinism cannot be upheld. Freeman's (1984) systematic re-examination of Mead's work shows that she had been seriously misled in her Samoan studies. She had undertaken only very limited fieldwork, and she had a rather poor understanding of the language. In fact, she had got it all wrong.

Drawing on a wide range of less-well-known anthropological studies and his own period of more than five years of detailed fieldwork, Freeman conveys a very different picture of Samoa and of its adolescents. Samoan society, he says, is highly competitive and beset by conflict. Far from being the stable, peaceful, and cohesive society that Mead had claimed, it has much aggression, violence, and rape. Child-rearing is far from being the open and flexible system that Mead had described. It centres on firm parental authority and harsh discipline.

Above all, however, Freeman rejects Mead's account of adolescent sexual behaviour. He shows that virginity at marriage is held in extremely high esteem. A central aspect of marriage ceremonies throughout Western Polynesia is the ritual deflowering of the young bride in public by her husband-to-be. Through this violent and humiliating ritual assault, the girl's virginity is publicly demonstrated by a flow of blood. Mead had reported such things, but she had claimed them to be mere empty rituals that could easily be avoided. In fact, they were central to Samoan culture. Given the great importance that is attached to virginity, it is unlikely that adolescent promiscuity would be at all widespread. Young girls were always, in fact, tightly controlled by their parents and by others. They would themselves ensure that they maintain their purity—whether out of moral commitment or fear of public shame—until their marriages.

How, then, could Mead have got things so wrong? When she began to speak to the girls about their sexual behaviour, her lack of fluency in the language meant that she was unaware of the subtle nuances of speech and the emotional state of her interviewees. Freeman met one of the girls in 1987, by which time she was a rather elderly lady. She told him that she and the other girls had been so embarrassed by the questions that Mead had asked them that they had playfully lied to her. They created a picture of promiscuity and sexual freedom that accorded so well with what Mead had hoped to discover that she had not questioned its truth. As soon as she had completed the interviews, she wrote up her results and reported to Boas that her research was complete.

Mead's difficulties highlight important methodological problems in participant observation. The usual method in anthropological fieldwork is for the researcher to live as a participant in the society that is being studied for a period of one or more years. The fieldworker must learn the language and talk to the locals in order to try to understand their culture from within. Margaret Mead spent only two months studying the Samoan language, and she completed her fieldwork in just five months. In this time, she lived with a white, American family, not with a Samoan family, and she relied on rather formal and uncomfortable interviews. She reports very few of her own observations in the book. Instead of a close ethnographic encounter, Mead relied upon hearsay and on observation at a distance. In these circumstances, she had little or no way of checking the accounts of the girls with whom she spoke.

 Look at 'Ethnographic Research', Chapter 3, pp. 86–90. What lessons do you think that other ethnographers can learn from Mead's study?

Some of Mead's views have been supported by other evidence, and her fieldwork on gender roles in New Guinea may be more reliable than the Samoan research. However, the view that she had established the claims of cultural determinism beyond all question simply cannot be sustained. It is undoubtedly the case that cultural differences play a major part in shaping the ways that people respond to biological conditions. It is not the case, however, that biology can simply be ignored. Biological determinism—as we will show—certainly overstates its own case, but this does not justify the making of equally exaggerated claims for cultural determinism. Culture and biology interact in complex ways under specific social conditions, and it is impossible to generalize about the ultimate or absolute determining role of one or the other.

SOCIALIZATION AND IDENTITY

Human beings are social animals, and the process through which someone learns how to be a member of a particular society is termed **socialization**. It is through socialization that people learn specific skills and abilities and what kind of people they are.

People continue to learn throughout their lives, but the first few years of life are critical. Through their interactions with others, infants gradually become aware of themselves as 'individuals'. They come to see themselves as conscious and reflective entities—agents or subjects—capable of independent and autonomous action. Central to this growing awareness is a child's conception of him or herself as a person. Without close social relationships with other people during these early years, children will fail to learn how to interact and to communicate. For ethical reasons, it is impossible to deprive human infants of social experience in an experiment to produce direct evidence for this claim. Nevertheless, evidence from observations of those children who have, for one reason or another, been brought up in isolation from normal human contact shows this to be the case. Such children may, in later life, learn basic table manners and toilet behaviour, but they have no real ability to use or to understand normal language, and they have only a very limited ability to engage in normal social interaction.

A distinction can be made between primary socialization and secondary socialization. **Primary socialization** is that which takes place in infancy and childhood, typically within a family or a small household of carers. This early socialization provides the foundation for all later learning. Through their interaction with parents

Wild children

Kamala (about 8 years old) and Amala (about $1\frac{1}{2}$) were discovered in India in 1920, living as part of a pack of wolves. After their rescue they were seen to walk on all fours, to eat and drink with their mouths, directly from the plate, and at night they howled. No one knows how they came to live with wolves rather than in a human group. Amala did not survive the discovery for long. She died within a year. Kamala, however, lived to be 18. By the time that he died, he had learned to walk upright and to wear clothes, but he had learned to speak only a few words.

A boy called Ramu, also discovered living with wolves, was taken to an orphanage run by Mother Theresa. He continued to hunt chickens at night but, although he learned to dress, he never learned to speak before he died, aged 10, in 1985.

Source: Gleiman (1995: 73–80).

or carers, children are able to learn a great deal about what it is to be a member of their particular society. They also learn such specific skills as the ability to speak their own language and to interact and communicate with others.

Secondary socialization begins in later childhood, when children begin to interact more frequently outside the household and with people other than their parents. Interacting with other children and with teachers at school, they begin to learn a broader range of social skills and to acquire a more detailed knowledge of roles outside the family. As they get older, much of this interaction takes place beyond the direct control of their parents. During adolescence, the peer group of other adolescents becomes a particularly important agency of socialization. Secondary socialization runs parallel with formal education in contemporary societies, but much socialization takes place outside the school—for example, in clubs and on the street corner—and it continues into adult life. In a very real sense, human beings are still being socialized into their society, learning new things about it, until the very moment of their death.

Self and social identity

It is through socialization that a person acquires a sense of social identity and an image of his or herself. These are closely linked concepts that cannot easily be separated from each other, but it is important to try to distinguish them.

People attribute personality characteristics of all sorts to themselves, and the others with whom they come into contact also define their characters and their actions in various ways. When someone is defined as a specific *type* of person, it can be said that a **social identity** has been attributed to him or her. A social identity, then, is a particular label that has been applied in order to indicate the type of person someone is. As a result of the label, that person comes to feel that he or she *is* that kind of person.

Social identities do not refer to specific, discrete personality characteristics (such as cleverness, honesty, or reliability), though any of these may be involved in an identity. They are, rather, clusters of personality characteristics and attributes that are linked to particular social roles, categories, or groups. Examples of commonly employed social identities in contemporary societies include woman, child, father, Asian, Jew, doctor, teacher, clerk, mechanic, homosexual, drug-taker, and so on. Some of these identities are based around clearly defined occupational roles, some relate to more general social positions, and others correspond more to stereotypes than to actual roles. Nevertheless, each designates a particular type of real or imagined person, to whom particular moral characteristics and social abilities are imputed, and with whom people may identify themselves or be identified by others.

Someone identifies with a particular social type—or is identified in this way by others—when there is a feeling that the type adequately describes certain enduring features of his or her life. A social identity is regarded as being somehow fundamental to a person's whole way of being: it is what the person *is*, above all else. It should not be assumed, however, that people can identify themselves in only one way. In contemporary societies, in particular, people are likely to identify themselves in a number of ways. They can be said to have multiple identities. Because of the various roles or positions that she has, for example, a woman may see herself as a woman, an Asian, *and* a doctor. Multiple identification has become more common. Instead of identifying exclusively with one particular type of person—a worker, for example—people are now more likely to identify with a variety of social types. They may shift from one identity to another according to the situation or context in which they are acting and the roles that they take on. A man may, for example, regard himself as being a teacher when he is at work, a father when he is at home, and a Labour activist when he is involved in local politics.

We will often refer to social identity simply as iden-

tity, but this is a little ambiguous. The word identity is widely used to refer both to what we call social identity and to the related idea of personal identity. A social identity marks people out as, in certain respects, *the same as* others. A **personal identity** marks someone out as a *unique* and quite distinct individual. Central to a personal identity is a personal name. Personal names are attempts to individualize and so distinguish from all other people with whom a person may share one or more social identity. It is, for most people, the most immediate and important marker of personal identity. There may be many footballers, but there is—in the words of the terrace chant—only one Kevin Keegan.

Having a personal name marks out our individuality as a unique person. In fact, of course, few names are actually unique, as even a cursory examination of any telephone directory will show. Nevertheless, even those with quite common names regard them as being their personal property, and they can be quite disconcerted to come across other people with the same name. A name is closely tied to markers of individuality: signature, fingerprints, photograph, address, birth certificate, and various official identification numbers (R. Jenkins 1996: ch. 7). Where names are shared within a family or group, pet names or nicknames are often used to differentiate people and to emphasize their individuality.

Personal identity is the link between the concepts of social identity and self. Social identities are, in principle, *shared* with others. There are, for example, large numbers of people who might identify themselves as men, as English, or as engineers. The word **self**, on the other hand, is used to distinguish a person's sense of her or his own uniqueness or individuality. A sense of self is built up when people reflect on their personal history and construct a biography of how they came to be the people that they are. They grasp their various social identities and characteristics and unify them into a conception of what is particular or peculiar about them as an individual (Strauss 1959: 144–7). Only in very extreme situations where a person has a single, all-encompassing identity might a social identity and a sense of self coincide.

The sense of individuality that is central to the idea of the self is obvious from the importance that is attached to markers of personal identity in modern societies. This highlights a very significant social change. In many pre-modern societies, identities were collective and corporate. People had little sense of their own individuality. They had *public* social identities—as citizens, peasants, and lords, for example—but they had no real sense of a *private self* that was separate from

Identity and self

Social identity is a person's sense of the type of person that he or she is: man, woman, black, white, tinker, tailor, soldier, sailor. Personal identity, on the other hand, is a person's sense of his or her own individuality and uniqueness and is marked by a name, personal appearance, identification numbers, and so on. A sense of self is the particular image that is associated with a personal identity, the defining characteristic of individuality. It is how people see themselves and how they are seen by others.

What do people's clothes and appearance tell you about how they see themselves and who they identify with?

these social identities. Their whole existence was tied up in the collective life that they shared with others around them.

As societies have become more complex and diversified, so a greater sense of individuality has emerged. Durkheim (1893) saw this growth of individualism as a central feature of the spread of modernity. In societies with a growing sense of individuality, there is a greater tendency to use the idea of the self. Personal names become more important as ways of distinguishing among different individuals. The development of individual names, then, is a comparatively recent feature of human history. In England, for example, it was not until the twelfth or thirteenth centuries that surnames came into use for the majority of the population.

Primary and secondary identities

The moment of birth is, in contemporary societies, the point at which social identities are first ascribed to individuals. The period of preparation for birth may, of course, involve some anticipation of the child's identity: bedrooms may be decorated, clothes bought, and so on. Not until birth, however, can a true identity be given to the child. A newborn infant is immediately identified as being a boy or a girl and, soon afterwards, is given a name. The baby's sex and name, together with the names of his or her parents, are officially recorded by a government official, and they are often announced and affirmed in a religious service. Infants are not, of course, in a position to respond to these imputed social and personal identities—certainly not in any conscious or reflexive way—and will have little choice about them. Both the given identity and the official record are likely to remain with them throughout their life. A woman who marries and adopts her husband's name does so only by convention and custom, and only her 'maiden name' is shown on the marriage certificate.

Through the period of primary socialization, in infancy and childhood, the core social identities are added to. Children gradually take a more active part in the construction of their social identities. It is through these processes of primary socialization that **primary identities** of personhood, gender, and, perhaps, ethnicity are built up (R. Jenkins 1996: 62).

Personhood is a sense of selfhood and human-ness. It is something that develops quite early in infancy, but it does so only very gradually. The newborn child's first active role in determining its own identity comes as it develops a conception of its own personhood. An infant only gradually learns that it exists as something separate from its surroundings. Similarly, it slowly learns

that it is capable of making things happen, that it is capable of being an agent. This involves learning a sense of difference.

The child learns that it is different from its cot and its toys, and that it is different from its parents. It also learns, however, that it shares certain characteristics with its parents. These shared characteristics separate them not only from inanimate objects but also from the family pet and from other animals. In these ways, the infant begins to learn an initial sense of self and of its own human status: it learns that it is a person. This begins to develop prior to the acquisition of any language, and it seems to be a crucial precondition for developing a linguistic competence. It is, however, massively extended once a language is acquired. The sense of personhood develops rapidly as a child's language abilities expand in the second year of its life.

When a child becomes aware that it is a person, its parents or carers can begin to solidify those other social identities that they have made and recorded. These identities are those which the parents regard as being important defining characteristics of their own identities and circumstances. Most important among these is a gender identity—being masculine or feminine. This gender identity shapes the ways in which the parents act towards their child. Clothes, toys, and the use of language, for example, are all differentiated by gender from the very earliest hours of a child's life. In due course, gender also shapes the way that the child will act him or herself.

Closely linked to gender identity is a child's identity within its family or household. When learning that it is a boy or a girl, it typically learns that it is a child and, moreover, that it is the child of a particular mother and father. Through its parents, it may learn that it is the sibling of its brothers and sisters, that it is a grandchild, a nephew, and so on. All of these aspects of its gendered kinship identity define it genealogically within a particular family.

An ethnic identity—membership in a particular cultural group that is defined by 'race', religion, or language—is likely to be ascribed to a child in its early years whenever ethnicity is salient to its parents and those with whom they interact. In contemporary Britain, for example, being black is highly salient for most people of African or African-Caribbean background. It is something that their children learn very early on. Being white, on the other hand, is not so salient to members of the majority ethnic group. It is not widely employed by them as a personal marker, and many white children do not learn to see themselves as being white. Where ethnicity is salient, an ethnic identity is learned as an integral part of a gendered family identity. In these

Identity as a social fact

'Identities entered into early in life are encountered as more authoritative than those acquired subsequently. At most, a child can only muster a weak response of internal definition to modify or customise them. Taken on during the most foundational learning period, they become part of the individual's axiomatic cognitive furniture, "the way things are". Very young children lack the competence to counter successfully their external identification by others. They have limited reserves of experience and culture with which to question or resist, even were they disposed to. And they may not: during and before the process of language acquisition the human learning predisposition leaves the individual open to forceful and consequential definition by others.'

Source: R. Jenkins (1996: 62).

circumstances, it might be said, ethnicity is an aspect of genealogy.

Primary identities are far more stable than those that are acquired later in life. As the child grows up, it usually comes to think of its primary, ascribed identities as being fixed and all but unalterable. Some aspects of personal identity can be altered: given names may be shortened or modified into nicknames, and people have a certain degree of freedom to modify their name in relation to what they perceive to be its image or connotation. A man may, for example, prefer to be known as James rather than Jim, or Mick rather than Michael. This freedom rarely stretches to a complete change of name, though the law generally permits this. Sex and parenthood, however, are much more likely to be treated as permanent and unchangeable. They are seen as natural and normal features of the way the world is. Changes in these matters are likely to be seen as unthinkable or as extremely difficult, if not impossible. Only a very few individuals ever reconsider their gender identity, and few of these go so far as to seek medical treatment to change or correct their sexual characteristics. Those who do, often experience great difficulties in convincing others of their new social identity, and they may face very great difficulties in altering some aspects of their personal identity. In very few countries, for example, are they able to change the details that are recorded on their birth certificates. John Smith who has sex-correction surgery and becomes Joan Smith remains, as far as the official records are concerned, a male, no matter how female she may feel or appear. She

is likely to encounter resistance from others who refuse to accept that she is really female.

Secondary identities, acquired during secondary socialization, are built onto a foundation provided by the primary identities. The most important secondary identity that most people acquire in modern societies is an occupational identity. Through entering the labour market and a particular type of work, they come to see themselves as the type of person who fills that occupational role. They describe themselves and are described by others as an engineer, a baker, or a doctor. Other secondary identities are also important, and some of these have gradually become more important than occupational identity. Leisure- and consumption-related identities, for example, have become particularly important. People may define themselves as antiques collectors, football fans, opera buffs, horse enthusiasts, and so on.

A sense of national identity has also been sharpened for many people. In Britain and the United States, for example, nationality is an important secondary identity for many members of the white majority populations. For members of their ethnic minorities, on the other hand, their primary identities as black or Asian remain highly salient and these identities are reinforced by the actions of those who exclude and oppress them. The persistence of these ethnic identities may often run counter to governmental attempts to foster a common sense of national citizenship. We will return to secondary identities later in the chapter. We discuss them more fully in various parts of this book.

In the rest of this chapter, we will review the main theoretical perspectives on socialization and the formation of social identity. We will show how these theories illuminate the questions of gender and ethnicity. A principal theme of the whole chapter will be the interplay between biology and culture. We will critically review arguments that seek to explain primary identities in terms of the natural biological characteristics that people have, and we will show that human biology is far more flexible than is often assumed.

SUMMARY POINTS

In this section we have discussed the relationship between cultural and biological factors in socialization and identity. We have shown that:

▶ Human behaviour, unlike most animal behaviour, is learned.

▶ Neither biological determinism nor cultural determinism gives an adequate picture of social behaviour.

▶ Human learning involves processes of primary socialization and secondary socialization.

▶ People acquire social identities through their socialization. People today have multiple identities.

▶ Primary identities develop during primary socialization. These primary identities are those of personhood, gender, and ethnicity.

THEORIES OF SOCIALIZATION AND IDENTITY

Three major theoretical approaches to socialization and social identity can be considered. These are role-learning theory, social-construction theory, and psychoanalytic theory. Although they are often seen as rival theories, they actually contribute different components to an understanding of socialization. There are, of course, many points on which they disagree, but their central insights are complementary viewpoints on a highly complex phenomenon.

The first approach that we will consider is role-learning theory. This stresses the importance of role behaviour in social life and, therefore, of the need to learn role expectations. This theory sees people as learning about various social roles and then reproducing what they have learned in their own behaviour. Social-construction theory, on the other hand, gives more attention to the formation of the self through social interaction. It sees role-playing as a *creative* process, not simply as the replaying of things learned during socialization. Psychoanalytic theory, the third theory that we will look at, gives particular attention to the unconscious aspects of the mind and to the ways in which emotional forces drive people towards particular patterns of action throughout their lives. The sense of self that is built up during socialization is seen as reflecting the ways in which people come to terms with these unconscious emotional forces.

ROLE-LEARNING THEORY

Role-learning theory has been developed mainly by writers associated with the functionalist approach to sociology, though it is not only functionalists who have used it. It is a much broader approach towards the learning of social behaviour. The theory rejects the idea that human infants are born with inbuilt social responses that are ready to be put into play in their social relationships. The biological attributes with which they are born give only the *potential* for social action. These are capacities that have to be developed through processes of socialization. It is through their socialization that individuals learn the contents of their culture and, in particular, the normative expectations that define their social roles. People become social by learning social roles.

The theory starts out from the assumption that social roles must be seen as *social facts*: they are institutionalized social relationships that are—to all intents and purposes—matters of constraint rather than of choice. People are not free to renegotiate what it is to be a doctor, a teacher, or a mother. They must largely accept the ways in which these have come to be defined within their culture. Someone employed as a teacher, for example, is seen as having very little freedom of choice about how to act when carrying out that role. He or she must follow the specific requirements and obligations that define the role. Social roles are blueprints or templates for action. They provide people with examples or illustrations of how to behave in particular roles, and these can be directly copied in their own behaviour (H. M. Johnson 1961: 135–6). Socialization is, above all, the process through which individuals learn how to perform social roles.

Socialization and commitment

Conformity to role expectations is seen, in part, as something that results from external social pressure. This occurs because of the rewards and punishments that people apply to each other's behaviour. Role partners reward conformity and punish deviation, so bringing role performance into line with their expectations. A child seen as naughty, for example, may be smacked or offered an inducement—perhaps sweets or an extra hour of television-viewing—if he or she will behave as the parents expect. In the same way, a teacher thought of as poor may suffer the rejection or disapproval of children, parents, and other teachers, and may be denied promotion opportunities by his or her head teacher. A teacher who is felt to be good, on the other hand, may be awarded a higher salary, popularity from pupils, and high status from colleagues. In these ways, role performance and role expectations are kept in line.

Role-learning theory holds, however, that this kind of external coercion and constraint is insufficient on its own. If conformity to role expectations is to continue, there must be a process of **internalization**. People must internalize their roles, making them a part of their self, and so become committed to them (Parsons 1951; Parson and Bales 1956). They must not only learn the expectations that define particular roles; they must also come to see these as requirements. They must become integral elements in their own personality and motivation. People must *want* to act in the way that they are expected to act. These ways of acting must come to seem natural or normal to them because they are morally committed to them.

According to this point of view, a good mother does not remain good because of public approval or financial inducement—although these are, of course, seen as important. Rather, the good mother is committed to doing the best for her children simply because she loves them and knows no other way of being a mother. Ideas about what makes a good mother may vary quite widely from one culture to another, and the good mother is someone who has internalized the particular expectations of her own culture. Socially approved patterns of behaviour are so deeply ingrained in her personality that she no longer recognizes that they have their origin outside her in cultural expectations. She has truly internalized them.

Role-learning theory sees primary socialization within the family as laying the foundation for all later social learning. It is from their parents that children learn their culture and the basic roles of their society. Children internalize a large number of common social roles during their primary socialization. As well as learning the roles that become part of their own social identity, they build up an image of the basic roles of their society. They construct a mental map of its many social positions.

At the same time, people build up emotional attitudes towards these internalized representations. They can be recalled to memory and so become the objects of thought and of sentiments of approval or disapproval, desire or aversion. Children can, for example, imagine particular social positions and the roles associated with

them, and they can think and feel what it would be like to be that kind of person.

 Some proponents of role-learning theory write as if everybody is born into the same kind of family—the conventional nuclear family that we discuss in Chapter 10. The theory is, however, quite compatible with a recognition of a much wider range of family and household patterns. The key point is that primary socialization is seen as occurring in small social groups that are organized around face-to-face interaction, and that variations in the type and composition of this social group will result in variant patterns of socialization. Role-learning theory sees the potential for 'failures' of socialization to occur wherever this kind of small-group interaction does not exist or is weakened.

For most people today, this social group remains the two-parent or lone-parent family household. If you want to pursue this further, look at our discussion of family and household in Chapter 10.

The first roles that children are likely to learn are the immediate family roles of mother, father, brother, and sister, and their own role as a child. They may also learn wider family and friendship roles (aunt, uncle, cousin, friend) and, through their play, some basic occupational roles (train driver, postman, teacher, and so on). Secondary socialization begins when children enter schools and other groups and organizations to learn specific skills. Schools, for example, are more formal means of training and instruction into specific skills and bodies of knowledge, but they also deepen and enlarge a knowledge of social roles. Indeed, socialization is a lifelong process, as individuals continue to acquire role-specific knowledge through their interactions with others in the local community, at work, and in the political sphere. In all these ways, socialization gives people a knowledge of the particular cluster of roles that define them as an individual and that give them their identities.

While stressing the process of socialization, role-learning theory itself offers no specific theory of the actual mechanisms of learning that are involved. Its major contribution has been to emphasize the link between roles and socialization. The accounts offered of how socialization actually takes place tend to draw on one or other of the two theories that we will consider later in this chapter—interactionism and psychoanalysis.

Role-taking and role-making

Role-learning theory emphasizes a process of **role-taking**. It sees people as taking on culturally given roles and acting them out in a rather mechanical way. People's actions are seen as almost completely determined by the cultural definitions and expectations that they have learned during their socialization. This deterministic view of social behaviour has been criticized for its 'over-socialized' view of action (Wrong 1961). From this point of view, individuals are rather misleadingly seen as the mere puppets of their culture, as having no real freedom of action.

R. Turner (1962) has shown that individuals do, in fact, have considerable freedom in almost all situations to decide how they will act out their roles. Social roles are not tightly specified and compulsory blueprints for action, but are loose frameworks within which people must *improvise* their actions. Roles invariably allow people a degree of latitude in deciding how to conform and whether to disregard or to bend certain of the expectations that are placed upon them. This is especially true where—as is typically the case—people have to play two or more conflicting roles at the same time. A woman who is in paid employment as a teacher, but who also has childcare responsibilities as a mother, will often have to juggle the expectations that are attached to the two roles of teacher and mother. She must construct a course of action that will, she hopes, meet at least the more pressing demands of both work and home. This is likely to involve her disregarding many other expectations and acting in ways that have not been explicitly scripted in the cultural definition of the role.

It is important to recognize, then, that people create and modify the roles that they play. Socialization does not programme people in the same way that a computer can be programmed to behave in certain ways (Giddens 1976: 160–1). People are active, not passive: they *make* roles, rather than simply *take* them. In order to develop this point of view, it is necessary to draw on the work of George Mead and the symbolic interactionists.

SOCIAL-CONSTRUCTION THEORY

Social-construction theory is a part of the wider framework of symbolic interactionism that we discuss in Chapter 2. The key figures in the development of this approach were George Mead and Erving Goffman. It was Mead's ideas on the social construction of the self that were later developed by Goffman (1959) and extended into a theory of the social *presentation* of the self.

Construction of the self

Mead held that sociological analysis must always start out from the meanings that objects have for individuals. These meanings are not 'given' in the nature of the objects themselves. A meaning is a **social construction**. It is a definition that is decided through communication and negotiation and in relation to shared interests and concerns. The social construction of meaning is a process that depends upon the communication of meanings within and between social groups.

 Originating in the social psychology of William James, and developed in the early work of Cooley and Dewey, symbolic interactionism received its classic formulation by George Mead at the University of Chicago. The key ideas were set out in an influential set of lectures (1927). If you are unclear about the general framework of symbolic interactionism, reread the discussion of this in Chapter 2, pp. 53–5.

The social process is a complex pattern of socially constructed meanings. A man identifies other people with whom he interacts as, for example, wife, boss, bus driver, friend, and so on. These people, in turn, define him as husband, subordinate, passenger, and friend. The various objects that we use in our interactions—houses, offices, buses, pubs, beds, desks, coins, and glasses—are also socially constructed. They have no intrinsic meaning as physical objects. In many parts of India, for example, Hindu culture defines the cow as a sacred object that is to be protected. In Europe and America, on the other hand, it is culturally defined as a source of meat. The cow itself has no intrinsic social meaning independent of the ways in which it is seen in different cultures. Similarly, what it is to be a husband or a bus driver is a culturally relative social construction.

Social interaction is a process in which these constructions and definitions are used and built up. Mead argued that the creation and use of meanings depends upon individuals consciously monitoring their own actions. It is only when they have developed a sense of their own self that this is possible. A self is constructed through a process of socialization in which children, and adults, must continually come to terms with the reactions of others to their actions.

Mead saw play activities as the means through which young children initially develop into social beings. In their games, children imitate what they have seen their mothers, fathers, and other adults doing. By playing 'house' or 'mothers and fathers', for example, they gradually begin to learn how it might feel to *be* a mother or father. Mead called this process taking the role of the other. The role of the mother, for example, is taken on and explored by a young girl in her games, as the mother is typically the most salient person in her life. She is a **significant other**, an interaction partner who is especially important in an emotional sense. In her play, however, the child does not simply copy her own particular mother, but improvises motherly behaviour from her rudimentary understanding of the role expectations that are attached to motherhood. As the child's play becomes more complex, particularly through play with siblings and other children, so her understanding of these role expectations becomes gradually more refined.

By acting out the role of a parent towards a child,

Mead argued, the child also comes to acquire a conception of self, an idea of 'me' as someone who can be the object of other people's attention. In Mead's terminology, there are two aspects to the self: the 'I' and the 'me'. The I is the source of action, but other people observe and react towards the me. The me is the social self, constructed through interactions with others and reflecting the attitudes that they adopt. The me has been termed the 'reflected' or 'looking-glass self' (Cooley 1902) because it is a reflection of the attitudes of others.

The social self is seen as having developed by about the age of 4 or 5. At about 8 or 9, children's play activities become more detached from the roles of particular others (their mother or their father) and they begin to take on the attitude of what Mead calls the **generalized other**. They begin to infer the common or widely held values of their society by generalizing from particular adults to society in general. They begin to consider how other people in general within their society might react to particular kinds of actions, and they may also begin to objectify these attitudes as norms and standards of conduct that have a *moral* authority. The attitudes of the generalized other become the voice of their moral conscience.

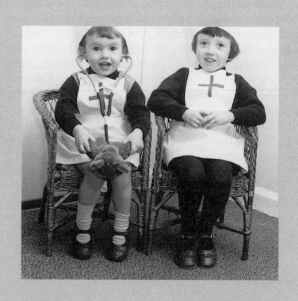

Play activities are important ways for children to learn about social roles and build a sense of identity.

Through constructing a sense of self and moral conscience, children become properly socialized members of their society, and they can begin to broaden their experience of the world through their secondary socialization.

Presentation of the self

Play involves pretending to be something other than what one really is: the child pretends to be a mummy or a teacher. Goffman (1959) has argued that, in important respects, people continue to play with one another when they interact in adult life. When they take on a particular role, they must interpret it creatively in their actions. As we have seen, roles are not fixed blueprints, but loose guides to action. People must play their social roles in the same way that professional actors play theatrical roles. Goffman holds that people are like actors on the stage, they employ props and scenery in their interactions in order to try to convince others that they really are what they claim to be. Their aim is to give a convincing dramatic performance in front of their audience.

A man who is employed as a hospital doctor, for example, might typically wear a white coat or hang a stethoscope around his neck in order to symbolize his medical competence. The scenery with which the doctor acts will typically include a couch, screen, sink, table, cabinets, and the particular coloured paintwork that define the room as a surgery rather than a kitchen, bedroom, or office. Many of the props and much of the scenery, of course, have a technical purpose, but Goffman argues that they also have a symbolic purpose that allows the doctor to persuade his patients that it really is all right to take their clothes off, swallow a pill, or allow him to insert a scalpel into their bodies. Without these props, patients may find it difficult to accept the man as a doctor. To sustain this acceptance, the doctor must also give a convincing performance through his actions: he must try to convey an air of competence, even if he must secretly resort to a textbook or ask the advice of nurses (Emerson 1970).

Goffman's argument, then, is that social interaction is a process of **self-presentation**. We are always presenting ourselves for others to observe, and we have a considerable amount of discretion as to exactly *how* we present ourselves. People cannot usually check out all the claims that are made by those with whom they interact, and much must be taken on trust. This is why it is so easy for the confidence trickster and the fraudster to gain at others' expense. More generally, however, we are all engaged in a more or less cynical manipulation of the others with whom we interact. We constantly try to present ourselves in the best possible light by 'bending' the truth, obscuring conflicting evidence, and employing the appropriate props.

Theatre actors can retreat backstage and avoid the gaze of their audience, and Goffman argues that social actors also rely on **back regions**. Much social interaction occurs in front regions, where people are on stage and acting out their roles in public. Offices, hospitals, factories, and schools are all, for most of their participants, public front regions. The back regions are those places to which people can withdraw and relax, abandoning some of the pressures of public performance. In the back regions, people can say and do things that are

Erving Goffman

Erving Goffman (1922–82) was born in Alberta, Canada. After graduating from the University of Toronto in 1945 he began his graduate work in sociology and social anthropology at the University of Chicago. Although he cannot be unambiguously regarded as a symbolic interactionist—he owed at least as much to structural functionalism—he was firmly grounded in the traditions of Chicago ethnography. He undertook fieldwork in the Shetland Islands for his Ph.D., producing the data on social interactions that became the basis of his famous book on *The Presentation of Self in Everyday Life* (1959). In the middle of the 1950s he carried out participant observation in mental hospitals that he later published in *Asylums* (1961b). His first teaching post, in 1957, was at the University of California, Berkeley, where Herbert Blumer—the systematizer of symbolic interactionism—also taught. During the 1960s and 1970s Goffman undertook a long series of studies in such areas as disability, advertising, and gambling. His best-known books include *Relations in Public* (1963a), *Stigma* (1963b), and *Gender Advertisements* (1979).

Self presentation involves the use of appropriate props and scenery. What does the scenery in this picture tell you about this doctor's attitudes?

incompatible with the self-image that they are trying to present in public. The front region of the hospital ward, for example, may have its back-region kitchen, where nurses can get away from their patients. Similarly, the school has its staff room and common rooms, the office block has its private office areas, and so on.

For many people, their home is the ultimate back region, a private haven for relaxation away from the public world. The distinction between back region and front region is maintained within the home, however. The hall and lounge, for example, may be treated as front regions where visitors can be entertained, while the kitchen and back sitting room may be a back region which only the family can enter. Even in private, family settings, however, people must still present a self to other family members. Members of the family may, therefore, defend their own bedrooms as back regions to which they can escape from the rest of the family and 'really be themselves'.

Our ability to act out multiple identities—and therefore to present different selves—is made possible by the segregation of different types of activity. We can behave as one kind of person at work, another at home, and yet another at a party because we interact with different people in each of these settings. In each setting, we present a self that conforms to the expectations of the particular audience and of which we think the audience will approve. By segregating activities in this way, we can try to ensure that those who see us in one situation will not see us in any other. Problems of self-presentation arise, however, if there is any seepage between different settings. When parents turn up at school on an open evening, for example, a child may not only find the parents' behaviour excruciatingly embarrassing, but will also experience a conflict between acting in the way that they usually act with friends at school and acting in the way that they usually act at home.

PSYCHOANALYTIC THEORY

The psychological theory that has come to be called psychoanalysis was founded by Sigmund Freud. Where interactionism has focused on cognitive meanings, psychoanalysis focuses more closely on *emotional* meanings. At the heart of this theory is the idea that human behaviour can be explained in terms of the relationship between the conscious and **unconscious** elements of the mind. People are seen as being motivated by unconscious drives. These are emotions of which they are unaware or that they experience only in a distorted form. Their conscious lives are dominated by the attempt to control the expression of these drives. Psychoanalysis, then, looks at the relationship between the surface structure of consciousness and the deeper structure of the unconscious.

According to psychoanalysis, it is early socialization that holds the key to adult emotional development. The theory looks closely at the ways in which young children learn to express or to withhold their emotions. For the satisfaction of most of their needs, they are dependent on an adult who will care for them. In most cases this adult will be the mother, whose pregnancy—so it is argued—will normally have led her to develop feelings of affection towards her baby and a willingness to provide for it.

The relationship between a baby and its adult carer is the critical factor in the development of its personality. The baby comes to perceive the carer as the source of its pleasure, as it is only through the carer's actions that its needs can be satisfied. Bonds of attachment are made with a person who can satisfy the baby's needs and bring it pleasure. Adult carers, however, can also be a source of frustration if they do not satisfy its needs immediately. As a result, the baby attempts to discover how to achieve satisfaction rather than frustration. It learns, for example, that a particular behaviour, such as

a sound (a cry or, later, a word), is likely to be an effective way of influencing the carer.

The reaction of the carer, then, becomes critical to the infant, who becomes greatly concerned with the carer's actual or anticipated approval or disapproval. This is the source of the key emotions identified by psychoanalysis. Adult responses are uncertain, and infants develop a sense of *anxiety* about the reactions of their carers. Later on, they develop a sense of *guilt* about those behaviours that meet with disapproval. It is the handling of anxiety and guilt, and their consequences, that psychoanalysts have seen as the critical element in personality development.

Much early psychoanalytical theory has emphasized the biological basis of the emotions and, therefore, the ways in which people learn to try to control their 'natural' tendencies and drives. A failure to successfully control the unconscious is seen as the source of mental disorder and of mental illness. Later psychoanalysts have broadened this out and have recognized the cultural formation of these unconscious drives.

Freud and the unconscious

The main theorist of unconscious mental processes was Freud, who saw them as rooted in the biological drives that motivate people. The conscious mind—which Freud called the 'ego'—had to come to terms with these forces. Freud (1900, 1901, 1915–17) held that the biology of the human body generated unconscious

---

Freud and psychoanalysis

Sigmund Freud (1856–1939) was born in Vienna and trained in medicine, specializing in nervous disorders and the use of hypnosis. From his clinical conversations with his patients, he developed his method of interpreting dreams and conscious processes in terms of deeper unconscious forces. Freud is, perhaps, best known for his emphasis on the centrality of sex in human life. As a Jew, he was forced to leave Austria when the Nazis seized power, and he spent the rest of his life in London. His key ideas were developed by his daughter, Anna Freud, and, above all, by Melanie Klein (1882–1960).

Later psychoanalysts, who built a firm awareness of cultural diversity into Freudian theory and who departed from some of the ideas of the Freudian orthodoxy, were Alfred Adler (1870–1937), Karen Horney (1885–1962), and Harry Stack Sullivan (1892–1949).

A number of writers attempted to synthesize aspects of psychoanalysis with Marxism, most notably Erich Fromm (1900–80) and Herbert Marcuse (1898–1979). More radical and controversial forms of psychoanalysis were produced by Carl Gustav Jung (1875–1961), who formulated theories of inherited unconscious symbolism, and Wilhelm Reich (1897–1957), who developed theories of the orgasm and authoritarianism.

Freud and Mead

The relationships between the psychoanalytic categories of id, ego, and superego, on the one hand, and the interactionist categories of I, me, and generalized other, on the other hand, are interesting, but far from straightforward. Mead had no real understanding of the unconscious, while Freud gave little attention to the situational presentation of self. The two approaches are, however, complementary.

The ego is the term that Freud used for the conscious mind in its broadest sense. It is similar to Mead's self, of which the I and the me are aspects. It is the interplay of the id and the ego that produces the impulsive, but reflexive, driving force that Mead termed the I. The me, on the other hand, is the 'looking-glass self', the image of how I appear to others. Where Freud gave greatest attention to the interplay of the id and the ego, Mead gave greatest attention to the 'internal conversation'—within the conscious ego—between the I and the me.

The generalized other and the superego have, perhaps, the most direct relationship to each other. They are terms for the internalized responses of others that are constructed into a supervising and controlling conscience.

drives and desires, in particular the drive for pleasurable experiences that satisfy bodily needs. Freud recognized many sources of bodily pleasure that could motivate people in diverse ways—the pleasures of eating, drinking, urination, and defecation, for example, all play an important part in human motivation. It is, for example, pleasurable to eat food that satisfies a feeling of hunger.

These pleasures are experienced through the senses, and Freud saw sensual pleasure as culminating in the pleasures of genital sex. For this reason, Freud virtually equated the sensual with the sexual, and he described all childhood pleasure-seeking as having a sexual character (Freud 1905). It is undoubtedly true that he seriously overstated the significance of sexuality, and also that he tended to see this in deterministic, biological terms (Webster 1995). Nevertheless, the broader implications of his thought, as explored by later writers, concern the need to explore human bodily pleasures in the broadest sense.

In his later work, Freud added an account of a drive towards aggression that operated alongside the drive towards pleasure, although he never properly spelled out the basis of this aggressive drive. As we will show, later psychoanalysts have explained this drive in cultural terms, just as they have also given greater attention to the cultural shaping of the drive towards pleasure.

The conscious ego is seen by Freud as responding to these emotional drives on a practical, rational basis. It must learn to control the ways in which they are expressed, forming them into habitual, recurrent patterns of behaviour that can be undertaken with little or no conscious deliberation. This control may involve deferring desires until they can be safely and properly expressed, and they may often be denied expression altogether. Those emotions that are denied are pushed back to form the unconscious part of the mind that Freud called the 'id'.

The id was seen as a seething mass of motivating forces formed from biological drives and their repression by the conscious mind. When denied and repressed, these drives could, however, return to consciousness in distorted forms. Repressed sexual desires, for example, can make themselves felt as slips of the tongue—so-called Freudian slips. They may also appear in a disguised form while dreaming, or as anxiety, hysteria, and more serious forms of mental disorder. It was this dynamic relationship between the conscious and the unconscious that Freud saw as being both a creative force and a destructive or pathological force in human action. Repression not only produced the energy that made social life possible, it also produced forms of mental illness.

Freud argued that the core elements of the personality are formed during childhood. It is through interaction with their parents and other members of their immediate family household that infants' drives are satisfied or frustrated. It is through their experiences of satisfaction and frustration that infants gradually become aware of themselves as individuals with a capacity for self-reflection and conscious thought. The conscious ego, like the unconscious id, is a product of the social interactions through which children learn how to respond to satisfaction and frustration. It is in the first few years of life that this sense of self and of conscious orientation to the world develops.

It is at this same time that a sense of morality develops. Parents place prohibitions upon a child's behaviour by punishing it and saying such things as 'don't do that, it's not right'. These parental prohibitions are gradually internalized by the child as its own sense of right and wrong, as a conscience. They become that part of the child's conscious mind that Freud called the **superego**. It is the superego that provides the standards in relation to which the demands of the id are assessed by the ego (Freud 1923). Particular kinds of sexual experience, for example, come to be judged as bad, and therefore as things that cannot be expressed in action. Mental illness results from states of anxiety or guilt that are caused by the conflict between the moral demands of the superego and the unconscious, urges of the id.

Culture and personality

Freud stressed the biological basis of people's unconscious desires, but he gradually came to give more attention to the cultural desires that they derived from their social experiences. This broadened understanding of the relationship between the biological and the cultural was taken further by a number of later psychoanalytical writers, who also moved away from Freud's overemphasis on childhood sexuality. Alfred Adler (1928), for example, held that people are motivated by a striving for power and for recognition or a sense of belonging or acceptance. They seek to be superior to others in these respects and to avoid any experience of inferiority. Feelings of inferiority are, however, inescapable, as superiority and inferiority are necessary consequences of social inequality. Adler, therefore, saw people as developing a sense of their self in relation to their perceived successes and failures. It was when people consistently felt inferior that they showed symptoms of the mental disorder that he called an **inferiority complex**.

Karen Horney (1937, 1946) opened up psychoanalysis even more. She argued that what is regarded as 'normal' varies from one culture to another, and that what is normal in one society may be regarded as neurotic in another (see also Fromm 1942; Riessman 1961). Nevertheless, Horney did still recognize that particular forms of socialization were essential for the formation of a coherent sense of self. Children who do not receive warmth or affection from their parents, Horney argued, will grow up with a deep-seated and generalized sense of anxiety. They will be unable to achieve a mental balance. Horney saw neurotic behaviours as the results of attempts to escape this 'basic anxiety'.

This move towards a proper recognition of cultural variability in socialization, and so towards a fully sociological form of psychoanalysis, culminated in the work of Harry Stack Sullivan (1939), according to whom anxiety results from a failure to realize biological and socialized needs in culturally appropriate ways. His understanding of this process has striking parallels with interactionist theories. While accepting that a drive for recognition and a sense of acceptance or of belonging was of fundamental importance in human life, Sullivan held that people are motivated to seek this from others by sustaining a particular image or *self-conception* that they believe will be valued by others. In Sullivan, then, the Freudian analysis of the unconscious—the hallmark of psychoanalysis—is united with an interactionist view of the self and self-presentation.

Childhood and maternal deprivation

One of the most contentious areas in psychoanalytic theory has been its association with the idea of maternal deprivation. This argument involves the claim that the mother is central to primary socialization and that, therefore, children who are deprived of the close and sustained attention of their mother will be inadequately socialized. They will experience serious psychological problems in later life. The chief advocate of this view is Bowlby, who has said that what is 'essential for mental health is that an infant and young child should experience a warm, intimate and continuous relationship with his mother' (Bowlby 1965: 13; see also Winnicott 1965).

This relationship is partially absent when the child is looked after by a childminder, and is completely absent when the mother has died or has rejected the baby, and where it is, therefore, brought up in residential care, an orphanage, or a hospital. Between these two situations, Bowlby suggests, is found the experience of children in so-called broken homes. Most controversially, Bowlby's conclusions have been extended by some commentators to the cases of children whose mothers are in full-time paid employment. In all of these situations, it is held, the child is deprived of close and continuing maternal care.

Bowlby produced evidence to show that maternal deprivation in early life results in anxiety, which is expressed in depression and withdrawal. Deprivation can produce serious physical, intellectual, and social problems in a child's later life, and it can result in physical or mental illness. The effects of protracted early separation continue into adult life and they are difficult to reverse or to overcome.

The crucial period, Bowlby held, is when an infant is aged between six months and one year. Separation before this time has little effect, so long as maternal care is re-established by six months of age. After the first year, the effects are, again, less stark, though serious problems continue to occur as a result of any separation in the first three years of life. After age 3, problems become less marked, and after 5 there are few significant problems.

A great deal of empirical evidence was produced by Bowlby to sustain his case—though he had no direct evidence on lone parents or on mothers in paid employment. Nevertheless, his research has been criticized for appearing to put all the responsibility for children's problems on their mothers. In fact, Bowlby did not do this. Although he held that, in contemporary Britain, the nuclear family provided the usual context for primary socialization and that in most families women take the main responsibility for childcare, he felt that 'mothering' could be provided by what he called a 'permanent mother-substitute'. It is the activity of mothering that is important. A 'mother-substitute' could, in fact, be a paid nanny. As a Kleinian psychoanalyst, Bowlby saw the gender of the carer as being important, but others have suggested that a male carer, such as the father, could provide the mothering that the child needs. The crucial thing highlighted by Bowlby was the establishment of a close, intimate, and enduring relationship in the critical period of infancy and early childhood. Thus, there is nothing in the broader thesis of maternal deprivation that requires that the principal carer should be a woman (Rutter 1972).

 We will look at the issue of gender identities on pp. 139–43. Think about Bowlby's argument and consider whether fathers can 'mother' a child.

The three theories that we have considered in this section have been used, separately and together, to build understandings of the development of social identities. Whatever insights have been generated by each theory, however, we hope that it will be clear by the end of this book that a more powerful understanding can be achieved if they are used as complementary approaches to socialization.

SUMMARY POINTS

In this section we have reviewed the three major theories of socialization and identity, and we have argued that they must be seen as complementary rather than competing theories. We first of all looked at role-learning theory.

▶ Role-learning theory stresses the importance of learning role expectations. Roles are social facts that constrain people.

▶ Conformity to role expectations depends upon commitment as well as rewards and punishments.

▶ Role-learning theory tends to have a rather over-socialized view of action. People make roles rather than simply take them.

Next we examined the social-construction theory associated with wider ideas drawn from symbolic interactionism.

▶ Social-construction theory stresses the construction of the self in social interaction.

▶ The self is a looking-glass self that reflects the attitudes of others.

▶ Social actors, like theatrical actors, play roles and act out their parts in public performances. This is how people 'present' their self to others.

The last theoretical framework that we looked at was that of Freudian psychoanalysis.

▶ Psychoanalytic theory places great emphasis on the role of unconscious emotional factors in primary socialization.

▶ Freud stressed the role of sexuality and, more generally, sensual factors in socialization.

▶ Later psychoanalysts have placed more emphasis on cultural factors in the formation of personality.

GENDER AND ETHNIC IDENTITIES

People derive their identities from their roles and from the reactions of others to their actions. We have shown that primary socialization results in the formation of primary identities that endure into later life. Gender is the most important of these primary identities, while ethnicity is also important under many circumstances. Being a man or a woman, and being black or white, are among the most important ways in which people can describe themselves to one another. These identities structure many aspects of people's lives and are major sources of social division and social inequality.

For many people, these primary identities are not seen as a matter of choice or as things that can be altered. They are treated as given features of human existence that reflect fundamental biological differences. These views are reflected in such statements as: 'That's just like a girl', 'Black people are so good at sport', 'Act like a man', and so on. Sociologists have rightly been critical of such stereotyped and prejudiced statements, particularly when they lead on to statements about the relative intelligence or morality of gender and ethnic groups. While the exact relationship between biological and social factors in gender and ethnic identities remains a very confused area, informed scientific opinion now rejects biological determinism and any attempt to reduce social behaviour to biological differences.

SEX AND GENDER

The discussion of sexual identity has tended to rest on ideas about the assumed universal biological

Ethnic identity is a matter of culture, not biology, but many people see it as fixed and unchangeable. What aspects of ethnic identity are a matter of choice?

characteristics of men and women. Much debate since the 1960s, however, has tended to view these matters in purely social terms, minimizing the significance of biology. These arguments have drawn on a distinction between sex and gender. This was first spelled out in criticisms of biological determinism by advocates of a conception of gender roles. Where sex has often been seen as a purely biological designation, referring to bodily differences between males and females that are associated with differences in their reproductive organs, **gender** differences are seen as social phenomena that define specifically masculine and feminine roles and identities (Oakley 1972).

According to this position, the cultural constructions that are placed upon sexual differences create gender identities that can vary considerably from one society to another. The work of Margaret Mead (1935), for example, suggested that universal sex differences could be given highly variable cultural definitions: in some societies women were expected to be subordinate, gentle, and submissive, while in others they were expected to be aggressive and competitive. In modern societies, it was argued, the distinctive 'masculine' and 'feminine' gender identities that have been formed cannot be seen as natural or necessary expressions of biological differences between the sexes.

The distinction between sex and gender allowed the construction of powerful accounts of gender roles and gender divisions. The roles of men and women were seen as culturally defined and as learned through socialization. They are general, overarching roles that define fundamental personality characteristics and that are the basis for recruitment to other social roles: domestic, occupational, political, and so on. Gender roles shape the ways in which these other roles are played. Role expectations are gendered. Men have found it easier to enter into the public worlds of paid employment and politics, while women have been confined to domestic roles or have been able to enter only certain forms of paid employment.

Even where men and women have entered the same occupation, they face different opportunities and are expected to act in different ways. A female doctor, for example, is expected to behave differently from a male doctor, and many women patients prefer to be treated by another woman, especially where reproductive or gynaecological matters are concerned. Critics of women's subordination have been able to argue for changes in these role relations because they have seen them as matters of culture and socialization alone. Gendered roles and their associated conceptions of masculinity and femininity can be disconnected completely from biological differences of sex.

Biology and cultural difference

Advances in the understanding of both biological and cultural processes have made this distinction between sex and gender untenable. In biological terms, sex may not be such an unproblematic term as it has sometimes been thought. Biological sex is determined by a particular pair of chromosomes in each cell of the body. Simplifying considerably, a female is simply someone with two X chromosomes, while a male is someone with one X and one Y chromosome. Despite the existence of very occasional chromosomal abnormalities, this provides an unambiguous biological distinction. Cells either do or do not have the Y chromosome. It is these differences in chromosomes that are responsible for the kind of internal reproductive organs (testes or ovaries) that will develop in a particular individual and, therefore, the particular hormones that will circulate around their body. These hormones, in turn, shape the outward form taken by the reproductive organs (a penis or a vagina).

Chromosomal differences, however, are not perfectly reflected in these primary sexual characteristics (as is clear from our discussion of Androgen Insensitivity Syndrome on p. 120). They are even less well reflected in secondary sexual characteristics such as body size, the distribution of body hair, pitch of voice, and so on. These observable differences in sexual attributes are rarely distributed as a simple dichotomy of male and female characteristics. They tend, rather, to show a continuous distribution in which sex differences are apparent only on the average. The distribution of female heights in contemporary Britain, for example, has a lower average than does the distribution of male heights, but this does not mean that all women are shorter than all men. The two distributions overlap: many men are shorter than many women, and many women are taller than many men.

The absence of a direct one-to-one relationship between chromosome differences and observable sexual characteristics is reinforced by the effect of social factors on bodily form. Secondary sexual characteristics are directly shaped by socialization patterns and by living conditions. Weight and body shape, for example, are significantly affected by patterns of work, by the adoption of regimes of exercise and slimming, and by practices geared to improving health. Cosmetic surgery and surgical interventions for sex correction can alter not only the secondary but also the primary sexual characteristics. The human body is not fixed and immutable, but is subject to social and cultural processes that construct and reconstruct it in various ways.

The social construction of biological sex cannot be separated from the social construction of gender identities. These identities are *embodied*—tied to people with particular bodies—and so are closely involved with differences of sex. Gender identities draw on culturally perceived sexual differences *and* they enter into the shaping of these sexual differences. A cultural conception of femininity (gender) as requiring an attractive body and specific forms of caring behaviour, for example, is likely to lead to the widespread adoption of physical regimes that overemphasize some female (sex) characteristics and underemphasize others. These arguments have been developed in radical feminist arguments about understanding sex differences.

Patriarchy, biology, and power

The founding figures in radical feminism were Kate Millett (1970) and Shulamith Firestone (1971). According to these writers, structures of male domination—generally referred to as structures of *patriarchy*—pervade all known societies. They create a pattern of sexual politics in which men and women comprise 'sex classes'. Men, as the dominant sex class, oppress women and ensure that the distribution of valued goods and services is biased in their own favour.

The roots of this oppression are seen in the power relations that surround human reproduction, and so it has its clearest expression in the intimate personal relationships of love, sex, and marriage. These relationships are subject to the constant threat of male violence—manifested in the potential for sexual relationships to degenerate into rape and pornography—and they are the templates for wider social and political oppression. Delphy (1977) argued that this oppression is particularly tightly structured around domestic labour, with men exploiting the unpaid labour of their wives or partners in family households. In contemporary societies, she argues, this is associated with a wider sexual division of labour. Women who enter the labour market are forced into low-paid, part-time, and insecure employment. For this reason, radical feminists argue, political activity cannot be confined to the conventional male issues emphasized in liberal and socialist party politics and trade-unionism. The economic and political oppression of women in public arenas is firmly tied to their oppression in the private, personal sphere of the household (Walby 1990). 'The personal is the political' was the slogan that highlighted the distinctiveness of feminist politics.

The biological basis of human reproduction, then, makes sex a unique form of human difference. It ensures that the social relations that surround sexual

Feminisms

A so-called first wave of feminist political programmes occurred between the 1890s and the 1920s, a period that included the struggles of the Suffragettes for the right to vote. Debate in this period was shaped by the pioneering ideas of Mary Wollstonecraft (1759–97) and the wider liberal tradition of John Stuart Mill (1806–73), the main issues being those of equality of opportunity and the extension of individual rights. A 'second wave' occurred in the 1960s and 1970s, when two main strands of thought emerged, each of which combined a deeper feminist political programme with a specific sociological position.

Socialist feminism shared the Marxist critique of capitalism and its liberal politics, seeing patriarchal relations as being inextricably tied to capitalist relations of production. Sociologically, attention was given to domestic labour and female waged labour, the role of the family in the reproduction of male wage labour, and the role of the state in the reproduction of the family. Key figures were Michèle Barrett and Heidi Hartmann.

Radical feminism rejected the liberal programme of legislative reform and engaged in direct action and political opposition aimed at challenging the basis of the social and political order. Sociologically, gender divisions were seen as being fundamental in all societies. Particular attention was given to love, sex, and reproduction, which were seen as closely linked to male domination and violence towards women. These processes were explained in terms of power relations. Key figures were Kate Millett and Shulamith Firestone.

These approaches never exhausted the full range of feminist thought, and many subsequent writers cannot be unambiguously assigned to either of them. Attempts to theorize similarities and differences among women now include those who combine feminist politics with psychoanalysis (Juliet Mitchell), symbolic interactionism (Liz Stanley and Sue Wise), and post-modernism.

reproduction are the key to all other social divisions. But most radical feminists have rejected any form of biological determinism. It is not the existence of any natural differences in feeling, thought, or physique that matter, but the social construction of reproduction and child-rearing by relations of power. It is power, not the biology of sex itself, which explains female oppression. This argument is, however, incomplete. If biological determinism is rejected, why is it that all known societies have been organized around male power, and what is the basis of this power?

The most compelling answers to this question have pointed to the particular relations of dependence that lie at the heart of reproduction. Women are dependent on their biology to a much greater extent than men, as it is only women who can become pregnant or breast-feed children. A human infant is completely dependent on others for its survival, and, at least in the early stages of its life, its mother is likely to be its carer. These dependencies have been organized through marriage and family relations of various kinds, and it is through marriage and the family that women become dependent upon men for their material needs while they are involved in child-rearing. The origins of male power, then, are to be found in the institutions of marriage and the family.

> ☞ **You might like to look now at our discussion of the family and marriage in Chapter 10, pp. 359 and 374–8. Do you think that a feminist political position involves the rejection of all forms of family relationship?**

Chodorow (1978) sees the power structure of marriage as establishing and reinforcing particular patterns of childhood socialization within modern family households. All infants, Chodorow argues, have a close attachment to their mothers. Because mothers have the main responsibility for child-rearing, children tend to identify with their mothers. Soon, however, they come to conform to the gendered expectations that are conveyed to them. Boys and girls are dressed differently, spoken to in different ways, given different kinds of toys, and accorded different amounts of attention and encouragement.

Boys, Chodorow argues, achieve their distinct 'masculine' identity by being encouraged to break their close attachment to their mothers and to avoid 'feminine' characteristics and attributes in their own behaviour. They grow up with a commitment to inde-

pendence and achievement, and they find it more difficult to express their emotions in close relationships. Girls, on the other hand, are encouraged to retain a strong identification with their mothers and to emulate their behaviour. By retaining this strong attachment, they grow up with a more emotional and sensitive outlook. Distinct masculine and feminine personalities are established in the first two or three years of life, and these are later reinforced in school, in the mass media, and at work. Through these socialization processes, a pattern of rigid masculinity, femininity, and heterosexuality is established. These personality characteristics tightly constrain the range of emotional expression in interpersonal relations (Rich 1980).

Radical feminists, then, have plausibly shown that sex is not merely a matter of biology. Gender cannot be sharply distinguished from sex. The relations between men and women are, at root, relations of power that express the pattern of interdependencies surrounding human reproduction. Relations between men and women—whether they be sexual relations, work and employment relations, or political relations—are patriarchal structures of collective male power rooted in the conditions of human reproduction. Gender identities cannot be separated from the nature of sex and the power relations that this involves. We cannot really speak of sex and gender, but only of **sex–gender** identities and relations (Rubin 1975).

Deconstructing gender

While the early radical feminists have uncovered the fundamental issues of power that surround the social construction of sex–gender, they have tended to assume a uniformity of female experience and identity across all cultures and periods. They have tended to minimize differences among women by emphasizing their common reproductive experiences and, therefore, their common fate and destiny. This emphasis has been one of the cornerstones of feminist politics, involving as it does the idea that there is a specifically female way of seeing and feeling, a distinctive 'standpoint' from which women view the world. This standpoint has been seen as the basis of a feminist consciousness that can be nurtured in the autonomous organizations and practices of the women's movement.

Many recent feminist writers, however, have rejected what they see as the essentialism of this position. They criticize the idea that there is some essential female experience—a shared standpoint and identity—that is (actually or potentially) possessed by *all* women and that divides them from *all* men. These critics point to the diversity of female experiences and, by implication, of male experiences. Black feminists, for example, have argued that feminism is simply the outlook of white, middle-class women and that it fails to recognize the distinctiveness of the black experience of racism or of black women's experiences *as* women. Conventional feminism is accused of assuming an essentialist view of what it is to be a women and of failing to recognize the diversity of their experiences. This has opened up a wider debate about the intersection of ethnicity and sex–gender (Anthias and Yuval-Davis 1993). 'Woman' cannot be used as a comprehensive and all-embracing category indicating a single standpoint; there are multiple voices of women (Stanley and Wise 1983).

What has been emphasized by these writers is an awareness of the varying cultural forms through which the categories 'male' and 'female' are constructed. While an emphasis on cultural variation might seem to hark back to ideas of gender roles, writers associated with post-structuralist and postmodernist theories have taken the argument in a new direction. Sharing with radical feminism an awareness that sex–gender itself is a social construction, these writers focus on the varying systems of ideas around which sexual differences are built (Foucault 1976). In many such theories, the radical feminist emphasis on power is in danger of being lost, but they have undoubtedly opened up once more the issues of cultural variation. Writers such as J. Butler (1993) have shown that discourses of sex and sexual difference underpin the construction of male and female identities which, in turn, legitimate manipulations of the body in order to

bring them into line with these identities. Slimming, cosmetic surgery, and eating disorders, for example, can all be seen as attempts to influence body shape and size in relation to culturally defined ideals.

RACE AND ETHNICITY

The issues of biology and culture that run through debates about sex and gender reappear in a similar form in discussions of race and ethnic differences. It has long been held that there are genetic differences, other than those in the sex chromosomes, that divide human beings into distinct racial categories marked by differences in skin colour, hair type, body form, blood group, and so on. Those who have accepted the reality of such racial differences have often taken the further step of attributing the existence of cultural diversity to them. Just as the personality differences between men and women have been seen as expressing biological sex differences, so the cultural differences between blacks and whites have been seen as expressing racial differences. A critical consideration of this view must begin with an examination of the idea of racial difference.

Biology, genes, and race

The concept of race in its contemporary sense originated in the eighteenth and nineteenth centuries. Biological scientists tried to come to terms with the human differences that had been uncovered by European colonial expansion and by the widespread adoption of slavery in the 'new world' of the Americas. Observable physical variations between social groups (most particularly differences in skin colour and facial characteristics) were linked to cultural differences, and both the physical and the cultural differences were seen as necessary consequences of their racial characteristics. The origins of these racial differences were seen in the genes. Genetic differences are inherited and, therefore, it was held that a person's racial characteristics must be inescapable.

Most contemporary biologists reject the concept of race and any idea that there ever were separate and distinct human lineages. Although advances in genetics have led scientists to recognize the important causal effect that genes can have on human behaviour, biology has also shown that separate human populations do not have the degree of genetic uniformity that would

Sex and gender

In the other chapters of this book, we will not always employ the cumbersome term 'sex–gender'. For convenience, we will normally use the word 'gender' to refer to all differences in identity, attitude, and action that relate to conceptions of masculinity and femininity. We will, however, use the word 'sex' wherever the reference is specifically to the ways in which the body is defined in relation to biological reproduction and associated 'sexual' behaviour.

Races

The main races that were identified by nineteenth-century biology were the *Caucasoid* (white Europeans and those of European descent), the *Mongoloid* (so-called red or yellow native Americans and Asians), and the *Negroid* or Ethiopian (black Africans and African-Americans). Although finer distinctions were sometimes made—Mongoloids were sometimes divided into American, Malay, and other subcategories—the basic threefold division into Caucasoid, Mongoloid, and Negroid was widely accepted. These races were seen in an evolutionary framework, with the Caucasoid being regarded as the highest, most evolved, and most civilized race, and the Negroid as the least advanced race.

warrant a scientific description of them as races. The observable characteristics that have been linked to the use of the term race (skin colour, hair type, facial form, and so on) are the outcome of a whole cluster of genetic and other biological factors that operate under particular environmental conditions.

Skin colour, for example, is not determined by any major genetic differences, but by relatively minor ones. These genetic differences are, in any case, the results of differences in climate and other environmental factors operating over the generations. These differences in colour are also not directly associated with any of the vastly more extensive genetic differences that produce other physical differences, such as those of blood groups. While certain natural clusterings of genetic differences can be found in different human populations, these are the results of normal reproduction within those populations as they have developed over time. These patterns of biological difference change as the boundaries of the populations change. They do not correspond to any lines of racial division.

Most importantly, *individual* differences in genetic characteristics (so-called within-group differences) are much greater than these *population* differences (between-group differences) and they vastly outweigh any differences among conventionally defined skin-colour categories. Two randomly chosen English men, for example, may differ far more from one another in genetic terms than do a typical English and Nigerian man. Similarly, the 'Black' and the 'White' populations in the United States are both internally quite diverse in their genes. Compared with other animal species, human beings are, overall, extremely homogeneous

in genetic terms. There are no identifiable subspecies. There is no scientific basis for any conception of biological races in human populations.

In the case of race, then, there is not even the degree of biological differentiation that is found in the case of sex. Race cannot be regarded as a serious scientific concept. Despite this scientific rejection of race as a useful biological category, it remains a current term in political debate. It is a central term in those political beliefs that draw on now discredited biological ideas to *racialize* social differences and so justify the oppression and exclusion of those deemed to be naturally inferior. Much prejudice and discrimination against ethnic minorities continues to be justified in racial terms.

The use of the term 'race', then, rests upon beliefs in the significance of supposed biological differences that are seen as determining social differences. **Racialization** occurs when the ideas that shape social identities are focused around these assumed or attributed racial characteristics. Race, then, is a purely social construct based on the observed physical and cultural characteristics of individuals and on discredited racial theories (Banton 1987).

Ethnic identities

Racial ideas are a common basis of ethnic classification. **Ethnic differences** are those social differences that are seen as reflecting the differing origins of social groups and that give each of them a shared sense of identity as an 'imagined community' (B. Anderson 1983; A. Smith 1986). The common origin that is held to be shared by members of an ethnic group might involve a shared history or culture, a common geographical origin, a common language or religion, and so on. Such labels as Asian, Black, Muslim, Scottish, Jewish, Basque, Kurd, and British are among those used as ethnic identifiers. Ethnic groups may construct a common identity and sense of community for themselves, despite the fact that they are widely dispersed. Ethnic relations are racialized whenever biological characteristics are used to define and construct social collectivities (Miles 1989). The supposed racial traits are often, but not always, seen as marked by differences of skin colour or of other physical features (Anthias and Yuval-Davis 1993). Nationalism is a form of ethnic identity based on attachment to a particular territory and to claims for a political sovereign state to promote and defend national interests. While they always have an ethnic basis, nations may or may not be defined in racial terms (A. Smith 1991).

> 👉 Issues of nationhood and nationalism are discussed at greater length in 'Nations, Nation States and Nationalism', in Chapter 12, pp. 451–3.

Use of the language of race divides populations from one another on the basis of their assumed *essential* biological differences, as reflected in their 'stock' or their collective inheritance of biological traits. As such, racial language makes absolute ethnic differences which are, in reality, in constant flux. It creates separate and distinct social groups from permeable and overlapping human differences (Gilroy 1987). Just as the construction of sexual identities is highly variable, reflecting cultural variation in ideas and concepts of sex, so variations in ideas of race will result in varying racial identities. The colonial and post-colonial experience, for example, has shaped and transformed ethnic and racial identities in both the former imperial powers and their ex-colonies.

Race, then, is not a scientific concept but a social construct that is employed in everyday definitions and discussions. While the term tends to be used mainly by dominant groups to reinforce their dominance, it can also be taken over by subordinate groups to construct an identity that enhances their resistance to exclusion and subordination. The emergence of a Black Power movement in the United States during the 1960s and its promotion of the slogan 'Black is Beautiful', for example, involved a positive assertion of collective identity by African-Americans.

SUMMARY POINTS

In this section we have looked at the relationship between cultural and biological factors in the formation of sex–gender and ethnic identities. We reviewed the various strands of feminist theory and we showed that:

▶ The social construction of sex cannot be separated from the social construction of gender identities. The term sex–gender should be used to describe these human differences.

▶ Gender refers to differences in identity, attitude, and action that relate to conceptions of masculinity and femininity. Sex refers to relations rooted in biological reproduction.

▶ Radical feminism shows the way in which sex–gender differences are rooted in patriarchal power relations.

▶ Recent feminist debates have stressed the importance of recognizing differences among women.

Our discussion of race and ethnicity showed that:

▶ There is no scientific basis to the biological concept of race.

▶ The use of the term 'race' in political debates involves a racialization of ethnic differences that hardens and sharpens them.

CHANGING IDENTITIES

All the remaining chapters in this book are concerned, in different ways, with the relationship between primary and secondary identities. Sex–gender and ethnicity are fundamental to many other forms of social difference. Secondary identities, such as those of work, politics, and religion, are organized around established differences in primary identities. Their gendered and racialized characters constrain people's choices and legitimate patterns of exclusion and inequality. While these relations will be explored more fully in later

chapters, we will give here a brief overview of how social identities are changing.

NEW TIMES AND NEW IDENTITIES

We suggest in Chapter 2 that contemporary societies are undergoing a transformation from the regulated and organized forms that they took in the past. Over the second half of the twentieth century the social structures of the advanced industrial societies have become more pluralistic and flexible. The process of production and the structure of organized politics have become less significant for most people, and new structures centred in culture and consumption have acquired a greater significance. In these new times, social identities take a different form as people come to see themselves and to define their situations in radically different ways. In particular, it is possible to trace a declining significance of class identity and an enhanced significance for consumer identities and for sex–gender and ethnic identities.

CHANGING TIMES

Many aspects of social life have been work based in modern societies. Until well into the twentieth century, people's identities and interests were tied to their work and employment conditions through the structure of the labour market and through the work-based communities in which they lived. Consumption and leisure, politics and education, religion and belief were all closely embedded in diffuse work and employment-based conditions. These conditions gave rise to the characteristic cultural patterns of class-based communities. The mining town, the fishing village, the shipbuilding town, and the cotton district, for example, were characteristic working-class communities.

> ☞ You will find a full discussion of class-based communities and their wider significance in Chapters 11 and 15. In various other chapters we look at their impact on education, work, religion, and voting, and at the ways in which they have been reflected in the mass media. Do not worry too much, at this stage, if you do not follow all that we are saying. Our aim is merely to sensitize you to issues that are taken up at greater length in the rest of the book. You may prefer to glance over this discussion and then return to it when you have studied some of the later chapters.

The most important secondary identity for most people was their occupation. Work roles dominated people's lives, providing them with their most important sense of social identity. They saw themselves, and were seen by others, as a coal miner, a farm labourer, a fisherman, a steel worker, a clerk, a cotton spinner, and so on. Other secondary identities were largely articulated in relation to the occupational structure through their dependence on work and employment relations.

Primary identities of gender and ethnicity were also structured in this way. Women, for example, saw themselves in occupational roles or as 'housewives', dependent on the family wage earned by the male breadwinner and head of household. As a result, *class identity* and class consciousness had a high salience. Virtually all other aspects of social life were subordinate to this. Gender differences, for example, could not be understood except in relation to the class situations of men and women. People therefore tended to give primacy to class over gender in defining their identity and sense of self. Working-class women and middle-class women, for example, were so divided by class that their common primary identity as women was submerged in their differences of class (Skeggs 1997; see also Sharpe 1976).

In the second half of the century, this class basis of social life has been transformed. Changes in the economy have helped to bring about what Lash and Urry (1987) have called a *decentring* of class identity. As more and more women have entered the labour force, it has become far more diverse. There is a division between a core of secure workers and a periphery of part-time, casual, and insecure workers with few prospects for promotion. It is women, members of ethnic minorities, and the young who are most likely to be recruited to peripheral jobs. At the same time, the more traditional jobs in manufacturing have declined, and manual workers are now as likely to be found in service work as in manufacturing work. The economic basis for class solidarity and cohesion is thereby much weakened. The taken-for-granted supports of class identity have been undermined.

At the same time, societies have come to be more organized around consumption than production. While production is still an essential precondition for most other activities—those things that are consumed must first have been produced—the pattern of production is now shaped, through advertising and media-led demand, by people's desires to consume particular kinds of goods. These consumer desires are tied to their pursuit of particular lifestyles that are promoted in the media and made available for people to choose. As a result, people are now more likely to identify themselves as a particular type of consumer than as a particular type of producer. The bases of secondary identity have been detached from their foundations in work and employment.

Work itself has come to be seen as instrumental, as a means to the enjoyment of leisure and consumer goods. Styles of life are no longer tied so directly to the relations of work and employment, but may be defined by advertising and media images. Something may well be bought because it has some material significance—as food or clothing, for example—but it also has a symbolic significance for consumers. People feel it important to buy the particular *kind* of food and clothes that accord with the lifestyle that they want to enjoy. The label is, for many people, more important than the product itself.

The once all-embracing class identity has fragmented into numerous separate and quite distinct identities. Social identities have become more diverse and pluralistic, and people exercise more choice about the kind of person that they will be. The weakening of class as a basis of identity has also freed gender and ethnicity from their close connection with class relations. They have become more and more important in their own right as enduring bases of social identity. Traditional ideas of all kinds are losing their compelling power over individuals, who can now choose and construct their identities from the diverse possibilities open to them. Politics itself has become less a politics of class and more a 'politics of difference'.

This is not to say that class relations have disappeared—far from it. Class divisions remain a fundamental feature of contemporary societies. Nor have economic and political constraints on action disappeared. The choices that people exercise remain constrained choices. Nevertheless, class is no longer so salient as a source of identity. Old identities have been freed from their dependence on class identity, and new identities have emerged as new ways of life have developed.

SUMMARY POINTS

This section has sketched out some features of changing social identities that are examined more thoroughly in later chapters. You are not expected to follow the details of the argument until you have read some of these chapters. When you have done this, however, you should understand that:

▶ Identities in the past tended to be based in work and employment conditions. This meant that people tended to adopt a class identity.

▶ Work and production have become less salient to people's identities in the second half of the twentieth century. They are less likely to identify themselves in class terms.

▶ Gender and ethnicity have been freed from their close association with class identity and have become much more important as sources of identity.

▶ Consumer identities have also achieved a greater significance in many people's lives.

REVISION AND EXERCISES

Look back over the Summary Points at the end of each section of this chapter and make sure that you understand the points that have been highlighted.

SOCIALIZATION, PERSONHOOD, AND IDENTITY

In 'Understanding Socialization' and 'Theories of Socialization and Identity' we considered a number of conceptual and theoretical ideas in learning a sense of self and social identity:

▶ **What do you understand by the following terms: socialization, self, social identity, personal identity; role-taking, role-making; social construction, self-presentation, back region; the unconscious, maternal deprivation?**

▶ How would you distinguish between (*a*) primary socialization and secondary socialization; (*b*) primary identities and secondary identities?

▶ Make sure that you understand the principal ideas of the following writers: Margaret Mead, George Mead, Goffman, Freud, Horney, Bowlby.

We compared and contrasted the main concepts used by Mead and by Freud to explore the social formation of personalities. (If you do not know which Mead we are referring to, go back and check!):

▶ How do social constructionists use the following concepts: self, I, me, significant other, generalized other?

▶ How do psychoanalysts use the following concepts: id, ego, superego, sexuality, guilt?

GENDER, ETHNIC, AND SECONDARY IDENTITIES

In 'Gender and Ethnic Identities' and 'Changing Identities' we looked at the nature of gender and ethnicity, and we contrasted these primary identities with secondary identities:

▶ How would you define each of the following terms: sex, gender; ethnicity, race; patriarchy, sexual politics?

▶ What is meant by the racialization of social roles? Can you think of examples?

▶ What do you think it might mean to describe social roles as being gendered?

▶ By what criteria would you distinguish (*a*) masculine from feminine, (*b*) male from female?

▶ Make sure that you are familiar with the major claims made by the following writers: Delphy, Chodorow, Gilroy.

▶ Although you may not yet have a full understanding of secondary identities, what do you think is meant by the terms 'class identity' and 'consumer identity'? (Come back to this after you have read later chapters.)

FURTHER READING

Good general reading on the issues discussed in this chapter can be found in:

Goffman, E. (1959), *Presentation of Self in Everyday Life* (Harmondsworth: Penguin). A highly readable and illuminating account of everyday interaction. A sociological classic.

Jenkins, R. (1996), *Social Identities* (London: Routledge). A useful overview of debates in the area.

Oakley, A. (1972), *Sex, Gender and Society* (London: Temple Smith). A very influential, but now somewhat superseded, text that covers a remarkably wide range of issues.

These and other issues are taken further in:

Anthias, F., and Yuval-Davis, N. (1993), *Racialised Boundaries: Race, Nation, Gender, Colour and Classes and the Anti-Racist Struggle* (London: Routledge). A comprehensive, if sometimes controversial, discussion of the intersection of a number of sources of identity.

Stanley, L., and Wise, S. (1983), *Breaking Out* (London: Routledge). An enormously important summary and statement of the arguments concerning feminist methodology and feminist theory.

Gilroy, P. (1987), *There Aint No Black in the Union Jack* (London: Hutchinson). An important but difficult account of the black experience in Britain.

Strauss, A. L. (1959), *Mirrors and Masks: The Search for Identity* (London: Martin Robertson, 1977), A useful and well-written statement of the social-constructionist position.

Parsons, T., and Bales, R. (1956), *Family, Socialization and Interaction Process* (London: Routledge & Kegan Paul). A useful and badly written statement of role-learning theory that tries to integrate it with psychoanalytic ideas.

Chapter 5
DEVIANT AND CONFORMIST IDENTITIES

False identities

'Witness protection is a growth industry in the UK. In recent years four police forces . . . have set up units with a formalised procedure to help vulnerable witnesses, possibly moving them and giving them new identities.

'Police provide a new name, passport, driving licence, national insurance number, and qualifications. "We would help them to find a home and bring the home up to the standard they would have left." . . . As far as employment goes, if they are working for a nationwide organisation—British Rail, for example—the police can assist them in transferring to a new area.

'In 1983, Joe Bennett . . . an IRA supergrass . . . was responsible for a group of friends being sentenced to a total of 200 years in jail for murders and bombings.

'Unsurprisingly, he didn't stay humble Joe Bennett of Belfast for much longer. He quickly became John Graham of Chaddesdon, Derby. Thanks to the Royal Ulster Constabulary and the intelligence services, he was given a completely new identity and received a monthly cheque to keep him off the streets. To put hit squads off the trail, British security even leaked a story claiming that he was dead. . . . [He was] granted immunity from prosecution on 66 terrorist counts, including murder.

'As John Graham, Bennett took to Derby's underworld like a fish to water. Three years later he was arrested for armed robbery and found himself again being looked after by the authorities. This time he stood in the defendant's box and was jailed for ten years.

'Joe Bennett was very resourceful. He got a new life and a new girlfriend without anyone realising his past. She told journalists after his trial: "It was a tremendous shock when I heard about his past. I knew he had a cheque every month, but I just thought it was from the authorities".'

Source: A. Bellos, 'Nowhere Men', *Guardian*, 17 Aug. 1996.

HOW do we know whether the quiet, respectable man that we met at a party—the one who told us that he was a chartered accountant—is really a terrorist supergrass living under a false identity? Even Joe Bennett's girlfriend did not know his real name, his past life, or where his money came from. How do we know that our neighbour is not a serial killer? Might the apparent conformist really be a deviant?

In fact, the whole question of identity is far more complex than these questions imply. It is a very unusual person today who has only one identity: we live in a society of multiple identities, both conformist and deviant. Someone may be a woman and black, married, working as a doctor, involved in extramarital affairs with other women, aged 50, born in Glasgow, and an occasional user of cannabis. What is her identity? Is she a woman, black, a doctor, a wife, a lesbian, middle-aged, Scottish, or a drug user? She is, of course, *all* of these, since each grasps a particular aspect of her life; but she is also *none* of them, as they isolate one aspect of her life from all others. People will see her at different times as one or the other of these identities, and she will also see herself in varying ways.

People in modern societies, then, have numerous identities, and the way that they identify themselves to others will depend upon the particular situations in which they find themselves and the expectations that others have about their likely behaviour. Nevertheless, the reactions of others are sometimes so powerful and compelling—because they think that they know who you really are—that you may yourself accept their point of view and see that identity as somehow fundamental to your whole personality. This is particularly the case with the views of experts and officials, because they are given a considerable authority in our society. Their views count for far more than ordinary lay opinions. In this chapter, we try to uncover the ways in which certain deviant identities may come to be seen in exactly this way.

UNDERSTANDING DEVIANCE AND CONTROL

Deviance is non-conformity to social norms or expectations. For many people, the word deviance is used only in relation to moral, religious, or political norms. The 'deviant' is seen as someone whose behaviour departs from normal moral standards (for example, those concerned with sexual behaviour), or who deviates from a political or religious orthodoxy. The sociological concept of deviance, however, takes a broader point of view and recognizes that there can be deviation from social norms of all kinds.

Along with sexual deviants, political deviants, and religious deviants must be counted those whose behaviour runs counter to legal or customary norms more generally—criminals, the mentally ill, alcoholics, and many others. What makes these people deviant is the fact that their behaviour seems to run counter to the norms of a social group. It is this that the homosexual, the prostitute, the child molester, the schizophrenic, the suicide, the radical, the heretic, the Ecstasy user, and the burglar all have in common. All of them seem to engage in behaviour that is not normal in their society.

No form of behaviour is deviant in and of itself. To judge behaviour as deviant is to judge it from the standpoint of the norms of a particular social group. Even where there is a consensus over standards of behaviour within a society, these standards may change over time. What was formerly considered as normal, conformist behaviour may come to be seen as deviant. High levels of consensus are uncommon, and it is more typical for there to be rival definitions of normality and deviance within a society. In these circumstances, conformity to the expectations of one group may mean deviating from the expectations of another. Revolutionary terrorists, for example, may be regarded as deviants from the standpoint of established social groups, but they are seen very differently by members of their own political movement.

In all such contested situations, it is the views of the powerful that prevail, as they have the ability to make their views count. This insight is particularly associated with a so-called **labelling theory** of deviance that is closely linked to symbolic interactionism. According to this point of view, it is the fact of being labelled as a deviant by the members of a powerful or dominant social group that makes an action deviant. This is why ethnic minorities are in many societies treated as deviant groups if they are seen as violating the normal customs and practices of the majority ethnic group. Similarly, those women who depart from what is seen as normal female behaviour by, say, entering what are regarded as male occupations, might be regarded as deviant by many men and by some other women. Whether the behaviour of a person is deviant depends upon whose values are taken as being the basis for determining what is normal or conformist behaviour.

In this section we will look at a number of forms of deviance. We will look at the formation of deviant

Deviance

The defining statement for the sociological study of deviance is Becker's justly famous claim that

'**Social groups create deviance by making the rules whose infraction constitutes deviance, and by applying these rules to particular people and labelling them as outsiders. From this point of view, deviance is *not* a quality of the act the person commits, but rather a consequence of the application by others of rules and sanctions to an "offender". The deviant is one to whom that label has successfully been applied; deviant behaviour is behaviour that people so label.'** (Becker 1953: 9).

identities through interaction between deviants and the agents of social control. We will show that what is deviant in one context may be conformist in another, and that the critical element is the social reaction that labels behaviour one way or another. Having discussed some of the features that are common to all forms of deviance, we will look in more detail at criminality, drug use and abuse, and sexual difference.

BIOLOGY AND DEVIANCE

In the past, and also in some more recent discussions, the social dimension of deviance has often been ignored. Deviant behaviour has been seen in purely individual terms and as something to be explained by biology. From this point of view, all 'normal' individuals conform to social expectations, and so those who differ must have something wrong with them. A deviant body is seen as explaining a deviant mind and deviant behaviour. Such a claim ignores the fact that no behaviour—except, perhaps, purely automatic reflexes such as blinking in bright sunlight—can be seen independently of the meanings that it carries and the social contexts in which it occurs.

Evolution, race, and deviance

For many writers on difference and deviance in the nineteenth century, and still for many today, biology provides the key to explaining human behaviour. Nineteenth-century evolutionary theory led to the widespread acceptance of the idea that there was a 'great chain of being', an evolutionary hierarchy of species that connected humans to apes and to the lower animals. The supposed racial divisions of the human species that we discuss in Chapter 4, pp. 143–4, were all accorded their place in this evolutionary hierarchy.

It was widely believed that individuals 'recapitulate' the evolution of their species in their own biological development. They go through various animal-like stages in their foetal development and during their later development outside the womb. Particular races, it was held, had developed only to the particular level that was allowed by their biology: the white races had developed the furthest, while the black races showed an inferior development. White children, for example, were seen as having reached the same stage of evolution as black adults, who had not developed beyond these more 'child-like' characteristics and forms of behaviour.

These assumptions underpinned contemporary views of deviance. Down, for example, classified various forms of mental disability in terms of the 'lower' races to which their characteristics corresponded. He argued that some 'idiots' were of the 'Ethiopian' variety, some of the 'Malay' or 'American' type, and others of the 'Mongolian' type. His special study of the genetics of the latter group meant that those with Down's syndrome were, for many years, known as 'Mongols'—a derogatory label that continued to be very widely used until the 1970s. Each society tends to see its own members as being the highest, most-evolved exemplar of the human species. The Japanese, for example, saw themselves as being at the pinnacle of evolution and civilization, and their term for Down's syndrome was 'Englishism'.

Cesare Lombroso

Cesare Lombroso (1836–1909) was born in Verona, Italy. He worked as an army surgeon and later became a Professor of Forensic Medicine and Psychiatry at Turin. He carried out extensive investigations into the appearance and biological characteristics of convicted criminals, publishing his results in his book *L'uomo delinquente* in 1875. This book was never translated into English, but had a great influence through the presentation of its ideas in a summary form in 1911 and in the work of his disciples Ferri and Garafalo. Lombroso's ideas lived on among many psychiatrists interested in criminal behaviour.

The most notorious of these evolutionary approaches to deviant behaviour was the theory of crime set out by Cesare Lombroso, who held that many criminals had been born with 'atavistic' features. Criminals had definite biological failings that prevented them from developing to a fully human level. They showed, perhaps, certain ape-like characteristics, or sometimes merely 'savage' features that gave them the distinct anatomical characteristics from which they could easily be identified: large jaws, long arms, thick skulls, and so on. These atavistic features, Lombroso argued, also led them to prefer forms of behaviour that are normal among apes and savages, but are criminal in human societies. These criminal tendencies were apparent, Lombroso claimed, in their other 'degenerate' personal characteristics: the criminal, he believed, is idle, has a love of tattooing, and is a frequent participant in orgies. Lombroso claimed that about 40 per cent of all criminals were 'born criminals' of this kind. They were driven into criminality by their biology. Other law-breakers were simply occasional, circumstantial offenders and did not have the 'atavistic' characteristics of the born criminal.

The excesses of Lombroso's theory and the racial assumptions that underpinned it have long been discarded. However, many people still see criminality as resulting from innate characteristics. Violence and aggression, for example, are often seen not only as specifically male characteristics, but in their extreme forms as being due to genetic peculiarities. It has been proposed, for example, that many violent criminals have an extra Y chromosome in their cells. The link between biology and social behaviour is not this straightforward. While there may, indeed, be a biological basis to violent behaviour—and the matter is still

hotly debated—the ways in which this is expressed and the consequences that flow from it depend upon the meanings that are attached to it and the particular social situations in which it occurs.

The behaviour of a soldier in time of war involves violence that is channelled into disciplined action against a national enemy. This violence is condoned and encouraged, and it may even be rewarded as heroism or bravery. The behaviour of someone at a football match who attacks a member of the opposing team's supporters involves far less violence, but it is likely to be condemned and denounced as hooliganism that must be stamped out. No biological explanation of violence can explain why one act is that of a hero and the other is that of a villain. Of course, this is not to make the absurd claim that it is only the social reaction

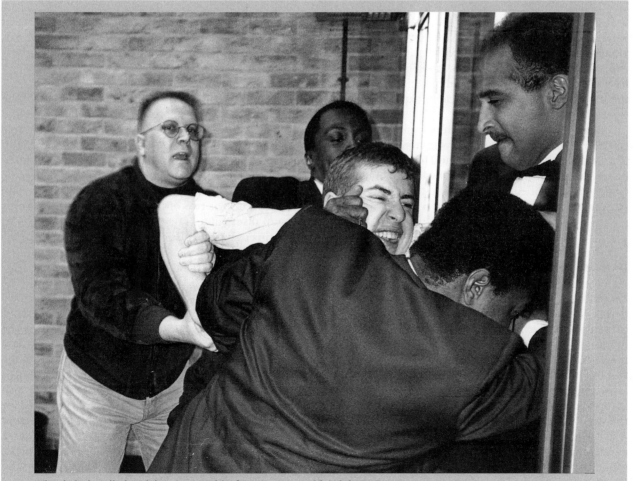

What is it that distinguishes 'acceptable' from 'unacceptable' violence?

Genes and violence

'Pimping and petty theft appear to be genetically conditioned but a person's genes have little influence on their propensity for committing crimes of violence. . . . Two American studies comparing identical twins, who share the same genes, with non-identical twins, have supported the contentious suggestion that some criminals may be born, not made.' (*Independent*, 15 Feb. 1994)

'A series of psychological studies of Danish men, schoolboys in York and murderers on California's Death Row all point strongly to biology—and specifically mild brain dysfunction in early life—playing a crucial role in determining whether a young boy turns into a violent man. The upshot is that better health care for pregnant women in inner cities to avoid birth complications could help to reduce violent crime by more than 20 per cent in the next generation.'   (*Independent*, 8 Mar. 1994)

▶ **How well justified are these claims?**
What further evidence would you want in order to assess them?

that differs between the two cases. The point is that, while some people may have a disposition towards violent behaviour, a biological explanation can, at best, explain the disposition. It cannot explain when and how that disposition is expressed in social action, or is inhibited from expression. Nor can it explain the reactions of others to violence.

An explanation of deviance must refer to the processes of socialization through which people *learn* to give meaning to their behaviour and to the processes of discipline and regulation through which some people come to be identified as deviants and to be processed in particular ways by a system of social control.

SOCIAL REACTION AND DEVIANCE

There are three levels of explanation in the study of deviant behaviour. A first level of explanation is concerned with the existence of the many different forms of human behaviour that occur in any society. Biology may contribute towards an explanation of this diversity, but it can never provide the whole explanation. It is always necessary to take account of processes of socialization. A second level of explanation is concerned with the variation in norms between social groups, as manifested particularly in cultural and subcultural differences. Socialization takes place within particular social groups, and it is the norms of these groups that provide the standards for the identification of particular kinds

of behaviour as deviant. The third, and final, level of explanation is concerned with the ways in which particular individuals are identified as deviants by others and so come to develop a deviant identity. This is a matter of social reaction and control.

In the rest of this section we will outline some of the general processes that are involved in deviance and control and the processes that are common to a range of deviant and conformist identities. You may like to read this through fairly quickly, not worrying about all the details, and then go on to the discussion of specific forms of deviance in the following sections. When you have read one or two of these sections, return to this general discussion of deviance and control and try to work through its details.

Primary and secondary deviation

Two key concepts in the study of deviance are primary deviation and secondary deviation, which were first systematized by Lemert (1967). **Primary deviation** is the object of the first two levels of explanation that we identified above. It is behaviour that runs counter to the normative expectations of a group, and is recognized as deviant behaviour by its members, but which is 'normalized' by them. That is to say, it is tolerated or indulged as an allowable or permissible departure from what is normally expected. It is ignored or treated in a low-key way that defines it as an exceptional, atypical, or insignificant aberration on the part of an otherwise normal person.

The **normalization** of the deviant behaviour defines it as something that is marginal to the identity of the deviator. Many justifications for the normalization of deviant behaviour are employed: a man is seen as aggressive because he is 'under stress' at work, a woman behaves oddly because it is 'that time of the month', a child is being naughty because he or she is 'overtired', an elderly woman steals from a supermarket because she is 'confused', a middle-aged man exposes himself in public because he has a 'blackout' and 'did not know what came over him', and so on.

What Lemert calls **secondary deviation**, or deviance proper, is the object of our third level of explanation. It arises when the perceived deviation is no longer normalized and is, instead, stigmatized or punished in some way. The social reaction and its consequences become central elements in the deviator's day-to-day experiences and it shapes their future actions. When public opinion, law-enforcement agencies (police, courts, and tribunals), or administrative controls exercised by the welfare and other official agencies react in an overt and punitive way, their reaction labels the person as a deviant of some kind (a thief, a welfare fraudster, a junkie, and so on). This labelling stigmatizes the behaviour and the person, who must now try to cope with the consequences of the stigma.

Stigmatization

Stigmatization is a social reaction that picks out a particular characteristic and uses this to devalue a person's whole social identity. The term was introduced by Goffman (1963b) to describe the reaction of many people to those with physical disabilities. Such reactions define people as 'disabled' and others respond to them in terms of that label. The term 'stigma' has been applied more widely to any characteristic that is regarded as abnormal or unusual and that is seen as a reason for denigration or exclusion.

Stigmatization may involve the rejection, degradation, exclusion, incarceration, or coercion of the deviant, who becomes the object of treatment, punishment, or conversion (Schur 1971). Those who are stigmatized find that their lives and identities come to be organized around their deviance. They may even come to see themselves *as* a deviant—as a 'thief', as 'mentally ill', and so on—taking on many of the stigmatizing attributes of the popular and official images. Even if the deviator rejects this identity, the fact that he or she is identified in this way by others becomes an important factor in determining future behaviour.

The development of secondary deviation may, initially, involve an acceptance of the negative, stigmatizing stereotypes that others hold of the deviant. Deviants may often, however, be able to construct a more positive image of their deviance and build an identity around a rejection of the stigma. They accept the label, but, instead of merely reflecting back the public stereotype, they construct an alternative view that reflects their own experiences and those of people like them. They construct accounts—narratives—of their coming to be the kind of people that they are, and these narratives become central features of the construction and reconstruction of their identity (Plummer 1995: ch. 2). In much the same way that the Black Power movement constructed more positive images of black identity, so such movements as Gay Pride have led to the construction of positive images of homosexuality.

Not all deviance results from the conversion of primary deviation into secondary deviation through an external social reaction. Deviators may, for example, escape the attention of those who would label them, remaining 'secret deviants'. Such people may, nevertheless, move into secondary deviation precisely because of their attempts to keep their deviant behaviour secret. By *anticipating* the reactions of others, they begin to act towards themselves in terms of the stigmatized deviant identity, even if they do not embrace this identity themselves. The man who engages in homosexual acts in private, for example, may become even more drawn into association with other gay people because the risks of his inadvertent exposure as gay in other social situations are too great.

There is also the possibility of false accusation. Someone who has not violated expectations may, nevertheless, be labelled as a deviant and processed accordingly. Such people will experience many of the same consequences as those who have been correctly labelled. Although they may feel a sense of injustice about their wrongful accusation, they may—as a result of their experience of stigmatization—come to act in ways that are quite indistinguishable from other deviants. Such highly publicized cases of wrongful imprisonment for terrorist bombings as those of the Birmingham Six and the Guildford Four highlight the more general situation of false accusation that is apparent in, for example, the child who is wrongly punished by a teacher for cheating or the political dissidents in the Soviet Union who were officially designated as mentally ill.

Primary deviation that is not normalized does not always result in secondary deviation or commitment to a deviant identity. Many people *drift* in and out of deviant behaviour without being committed to it at all (Matza 1964). Because they are not committed to their deviant acts—they do not see them as a fundamental expression of their identity—they are able to abandon them whenever they choose, or when the circumstances are not right. Conversely, of course, they may feel able—though not required—to deviate whenever the opportunity and the inclination are present. Drift, then, is an important aspect of the structuring of deviant behaviour. Matza suggests, for example, that juvenile delinquency rarely becomes a matter of secondary deviation, precisely because juveniles drift back and forth between deviant and conformist behaviour without ever becoming committed to delinquency as a way of life.

Many of those who become involved in crime do not embrace a deviant identity—they do not see themselves as criminals, burglars, or housebreakers. Rather, they see their involvement in criminal activities as an aspect of the larger social situation in which they find themselves. They may, for example, be long-term unemployed, in serious financial hardship, and faced with the opportunity of illegal gain. Such people drift into crime for situational reasons, and may become secondary deviants merely because of the constraints that they face. Certain opportunities will be denied to them, while other courses of action will be made easier. The whole structure of interests within which they act—the advantages and disadvantages, rewards and punishments—will tend to force them into continued deviance. Those who have been imprisoned for theft or burglary, for example, may experience restricted employment and promotion opportunities in the outside world that make it difficult for them to abandon their criminal life and to enter or re-enter conventional occupations.

Where people do take on a deviant identity, however, their behaviour will be shaped by commitment as well as constraint. Those who have become committed to a deviant identity will be committed to a whole range of behaviours that are associated with that identity. These ways of behaving will seem more 'natural' to them than any others, and they will identify with the behaviours as much as with the label itself. Commitment and constraint generally operate together: a firmly committed deviant is more likely to face disadvantaged opportunities, and a tightly constrained deviant is more likely to feel a sense of difference from others. If their circumstances change, and these constraints alter, they may find it possible to drift out of crime once more.

Deviant roles and careers

Where deviance has become a central feature of a person's identity and way of life, it can take the form of **role deviance**. In this situation, their lives become organized into a distinct and recognizable social role to which particular normative expectations are attached. The deviant is expected to act in deviant ways: conformity to these particular role expectations confirms the person's deviant identity! Male homosexuals, for example, are widely expected to exhibit their deviance by behaving in 'effeminate' ways, and a homosexual man who conforms to these expectations has adopted the public, stereotyped homosexual role.

Deviant roles, like conformist roles, often have a career structure. This is particularly likely where the role is defined within a group of deviants, rather than by public stereotypes alone. Where the deviant role involves a particular sequence of events and experiences that are common for all its occupants, role deviance becomes what has been called **career deviance**. This may be highly formalized, paralleling the kinds of career structures that are found in conventional occupations. Full-time thieves, for example, may be members of teams who make their living from their deviance and that have their own internal structures of leadership, reward, and 'promotion' (Sutherland 1937).

When organized as career deviance, the deviant role is likely also to involve what Goffman (1961b) has called a **moral career**. This term describes the internal or personal aspects of a career, the specific sequence of learning experiences and changes in conceptions of self and identity that occur as people follow their deviant career. It is a process through which people come to terms with their stigma and their commitment to a deviant identity. With each phase of the public career associated with the role, its occupants must reconsider their past in an attempt to make sense of their new experiences. They single out and elaborate, with the benefit of hindsight, those experiences that they believe can account for and legitimate their present situation. This is a continuous process in which their personal biography—their life story—is constantly constructed and reconstructed in the light of their changing circumstances.

Deviant groups and communities

Career deviants are especially likely to become involved with groups that support and sustain their identities and that help them to come to terms with the constrained opportunities that they face. Gangs and cliques are formed, clubs and pubs are colonized as meeting places, and organizations and agencies are set up to promote shared interests or political goals. With advances in technology, new forms of support and communication become possible. The spread of the telephone allowed people to maintain distant communication far more effectively than was possible through writing letters, and computer technology now allows global communication through the Internet and e-mail. Those who are involved in two or more of these groups will tie them into larger social networks that bond the groups into cohesive and solidaristic communities with a shared sense of identity.

Criminal gangs, for example, may be involved in localized networks of recruitment and mutual support, to which individual criminals and juvenile gangs may also be attached. These networks form those subcultures of crime that comprise an underworld. The subcultures are means through which skills and techniques can be learned and in which criminals can obtain a degree of acceptance and recognition that is denied to them by conventional groups.

Goffman (1963b) has argued that the groups of 'sympathetic others' that form the supportive subcultures of deviance comprise two distinct types of people: the own and the wise. The **own** are those who share the deviant identity. They have a common understanding of stigmatization from their personal experiences, and they may be able to help in acquiring the tricks of the trade that allow a deviant to operate more effectively, as well as by providing emotional support and company in which a deviant can feel at home. The own help people to organize a life around their deviance and to cope with many of the disadvantages that they experience.

The **wise**, on the other hand, are 'normals' who have a particular reason for being in the know about the secret life of the deviants and for being sympathetic towards it. They are accepted by the deviants and are allowed a kind of associate membership in their activities. They are those for whom the deviants do not feel the need to put on a show of normality or deviance disavowal: they can safely engage in back-region activities with them. The wise can include family members and friends, employees, and even some control agents (such as nurses or police) who have day-to-day contact with them. The own and the wise together form a network of contacts and connections that support deviants in the construction of their narratives of identity.

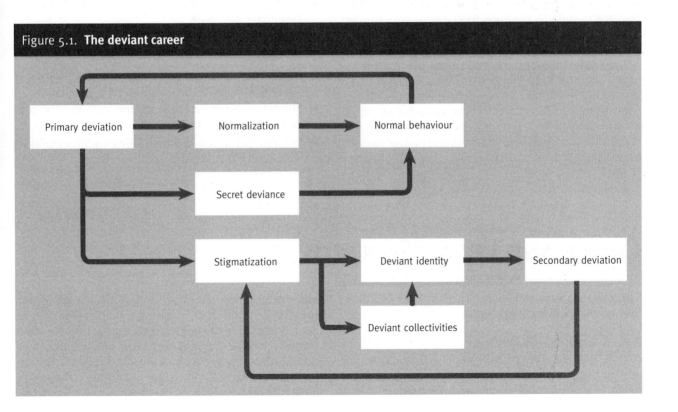

Figure 5.1. **The deviant career**

Look back at our discussion of Goffman's work on self-presentation in 'Social-Construction Theory', Chapter 4, pp. 131–4. You might check, in particular, the argument about front regions and back regions.

Some of the wise may actively support deviants in sustaining their deviance, though there are limits on the willingness of people to become too closely involved in activities where the stigma of deviance is likely to 'rub off' onto them. Active support, then, is most likely to come from the own, and this is particularly true where there is a need for representatives to speak or act for their interests and concerns in public. Such representatives may sometimes become very active and make a living—and a new identity—out of their role as spokespersons for particular deviant groups. They make a 'profession' of their deviance in quite a novel way, perhaps appearing in the press and on radio and television whenever issues of concern are discussed. There are, of course, limits to this. Only certain forms of deviance are allowed to have the legitimacy of their stigmatization debated in public. Gays and the mentally ill, for example, have active and important organizations that can lobby for their interests, while thieves and burglars do not. Pressure groups on behalf of those involved in serious crime are, for the most part, limited to campaigns for prison reform and are led by the wise and by reformed offenders.

The general account of deviance and control that we have presented (summarized in Figure 5.1) must be treated with caution, as all of its elements will not apply equally to every case of deviance and stigmatized identity. It is a general framework that provides the concepts that can sensitize researchers to the specific issues that occur in particular cases. We will illustrate

this by considering a number of forms of criminal behaviour, drug abuse, and sexual deviance. In the following chapter we will show that certain aspects of illness can also be understood as forms of deviance.

SUMMARY POINTS

In this section we have looked at the relationship between biological and social factors in the explanation of deviance and the formation of deviant identities. In reviewing our discussion of biology and deviance, you may like to look back to our discussion of the biology of race in Chapter 4, pp. 143–5. The main points we made in this section were:

▶ Early approaches to deviance drew on now-discredited evolutionary ideas. Lombroso, for example, saw 'born criminals' as 'atavistic' evolutionary forms.

▶ Deviance is never a purely biological fact. It depends on an act of social definition, of labelling.

In considering the nature of the social reaction to deviance and its consequences, we showed that:

▶ It is important to distinguish between primary and secondary deviation.

▶ Many people drift in and out of deviance without becoming committed to it.

▶ Much deviation is normalized, but some is stigmatized.

▶ Stigmatized secondary deviation may involve role deviance and a deviant career.

▶ Deviant groups and communities are important in supporting and sustaining role deviance.

CRIME AND LEGAL CONTROL

Crime is that form of deviance that involves an infraction of the criminal law. Not all laws are 'criminal'. Lawyers recognize civil law, constitutional law, and various other categories of legal norm.

Civil law, for example, concerns relations among private individuals, such as the contractual relations that are involved in such areas as employment relations

and consumer purchasing. A person who breaks a contract by, say, unfairly dismissing someone from her or his job or failing to supply goods that are 'fit for their purpose' has infringed the civil law, and action can be taken only by the particular individual affected (the dismissed person or the unhappy consumer). The police have no right to become involved, and a completely separate system of courts is involved in hearing any civil case. The outcome of a successful civil case is some kind of 'restitution', such as financial compensation or 'damages'.

The criminal law, by contrast, consists of those legal norms that have been established by the state as a *public* responsibility and which the police and the criminal courts have been designated to enforce. Someone who infringes the criminal law can be arrested, charged, and tried at public expense and, if found guilty, will be subject to repressive or punitive penalties such as a fine or imprisonment.

The criminal law of a society can cover a wide range of actions. In Britain, for example, it includes such things as driving above the legal speed limit, stealing a car, breaking into a house, possessing certain drugs, forging a signature on a cheque, murdering someone, and arson. Penalties attached to these offences range from small fines for speeding to life imprisonment for murder, and execution for treason. The crimes that are most visible or that are perceived to be the most threatening are not necessarily those that have the greatest impact in real terms. In practice, many minor crimes are normalized: few people report cases of speeding or dropping litter, and the police may often choose to disregard such offences. Figure 5.2 shows the main types of serious offence (officially termed 'notifiable offences')

recorded in the criminal statistics for England and Wales.

Public concern over crime relates mainly to such crimes as theft and violence, which are regarded as being serious enough to warrant sustained attention from the police. This concern, reflected in periodic moral panics, tends to ensure that many of those who are involved in theft and criminal violence do so as a form of secondary deviation. As a result, many of them develop a criminal identity. In this section we will look at forms of professional and career crime and at those normalized forms of crime commonly called white-collar crime. We will also look at the gendered nature of criminal activity, in relation both to the undertaking of criminal acts and to becoming the victim of crime.

PROFESSIONAL AND CAREER CRIME

Theft—stealing property belonging to another person—is one of the few forms of crime to have a highly organized character and to offer the chance of a career or profession to those engaged in it. Theft includes burglary (theft from houses), robbery (theft with violence), forgery, confidence tricks, pickpocketing, and numerous other fraudulent activities. Not all of these are organized as career crime, of course, and not all of those who drift into theft even make the transition from primary deviation to secondary deviation. Schoolchildren who steal from shops, for example, rarely continue into a career of thieving. Nevertheless, theft is, indeed, one of the most organized forms of crime.

Career crime is nothing new. Mary McIntosh (1975) traces it back to the actions of pirates, bandits, brigands, and moral outlaws who often combined criminal with political aims. If the Robin Hood image of the rural outlaw is a rather idealized fiction, it nevertheless grasps an important element in pre-modern theft (Hobsbawm 1969). With the growth of towns in the early modern period, opportunities for street and house crime became much greater, and there was a growth in the amount of what McIntosh calls **craft crime**. This is the small-scale, skilled theft of the pickpockets, cutpurses, and confidence tricksters. These forms of career crime proliferated through the eighteenth and nineteenth centuries and remain an important part of everyday crime. McIntosh traces the origins of what she calls **project crime** to a later period. This is large-scale robbery and fraud and became fully

Offence	1981	1995
	(thousands)	
Theft and handling stolen goods	1,603	2,452
Burglary	718	1,239
Criminal damage	387	914
Violence against the person	100	213
Fraud and forgery	107	133
Robbery	20	68
Sexual offences	19	30
Drug trafficking	—	21
Other notifiable offences	9	29
TOTAL	2,964	5,100

Figure 5.2. Notifiable offences recorded by the police, England and Wales, 1981 and 1995

Note: notifiable offences are those that are regarded as most serious by the legal system.

Source: *Social Trends* (1997: 155, fig. 9.4).

Serious crime

'Organised rustling of sheep from remote moorland grazing areas is costing Britain's farmers millions of pounds a year. . . . The problem has been particularly serious for farmers on Dartmoor and in other parts of south-west England, where an estimated 10,000 sheep valued at £1 million were stolen last year. . . . Livestock rustling costs the industry more than £7 million a year . . . and the overall level of farm crime soared to more than £85 million last year—up from £78.7 million in 1995. Around three-quarters of the loss comes from the increased theft of farm machinery, tools and equipment.'

Source: Guardian, 26 June 1997.

established only in the early years of the twentieth century. It has become the predominant form of theft only since the 1950s.

Crime and the underworld

Where rural bandits and outlaws were enmeshed in the surrounding social life of the rural communities from which they were drawn, urban craft crime tended to be based in a distinct criminal **underworld**. The growth of such criminal areas was first reported in the sixteenth century, but it was in the eighteenth and nineteenth centuries that they achieved their fullest development. The criminal underworld of a city such as London comprised various 'rookeries' that formed the dwelling places and meeting places of craft criminals of all kinds. Segregated from the rest of society, the underworlds provided for the security, safety, shared interests, and concerns of the craft thieves. The underworlds were rooted in the surrounding slum districts of the poor working class. Poverty, unemployment, overcrowding in poor physical conditions, and a lack of leisure opportunities other than the pub, were the conditions under which many people drifted into crime and some became confirmed in a criminal career (T. Morris 1957; John Mack 1964; see also M. Kerr 1958).

An urban underworld formed an occupational community with a subculture that established norms of criminal behaviour, a slang and argot, and an *esprit de corps* that sustained the shared identity of the thieves. Central to the underworld code was the injunction not to 'squeal', 'squawk', 'grass', or inform on others. Association with other thieves, and a lack of association with the targets of their theft, inhibited any concern for

the feelings of the victims of crime. It also meant that thieves could learn from other thieves the techniques and skills that would help them in their own crimes. In addition, their leisure-time associates formed a pool of partners in crime. They were able to find markets for their stolen goods, and they could attain a degree of protection and insulation from detection and law enforcement (Chesney 1968; McIntosh 1975: 24).

The underworld, however, has been fundamentally altered by the urban redevelopment of the inner-city areas and the dispersal of population to the suburbs. One of the principal roots of the London underworld was to be found in the Spitalfields and Cable Street districts of the East End, where there has been much redevelopment. While certain central pubs and clubs remain important venues for career criminals, much activity is now more dispersed through the city, and the underworld forms an extended social network rather than a particular physical locale. Even in the 1960s, however, Spitalfields retained a surviving tradition of craft crime, while the surrounding district had high levels of crime: there were especially high levels of burglary, violence against the person, gambling, and prostitution. Much crime, however, was 'petty, unsophisticated, unorganized and largely unprofitable—if often squalid and brutal' (Downes 1966: 150).

A subculture of crime continues to sustain career crime, which has, however, changed its character. Alongside the older craft crime, project crime has become more significant, and this has also helped to transform the structure of the underworld. Where craft theft involved the stealing of small amounts of money from large numbers of people, project crime involves a much smaller number of large thefts. Growing affluence and, in particular, the increasing scale of business activity have meant that the potential targets of theft have become much bigger. As a result, criminals have had to organize themselves more effectively and on a larger scale if they are to be successful against these targets. Improved safes, alarm systems, and security vans can be handled only by organized teams of specialists: safe-breakers, drivers, gunmen, and so on. Such crimes, organized as one-off projects, require advanced planning and a much higher level of cooperation than was typical for craft crime.

Teams for particular projects are recruited from the cliques and connections that comprise the underworld, and these may sometimes be organized on a semi-permanent basis. The criminal underworld that existed in the East End of London from the Second World War until the 1960s, for example, contained numerous competing gangs that were held together largely by the violent hegemony of the Kray twins and their associates. The east London gangs engaged in violent feuds with their counterparts (the Richardsons) from the south London underworld, and the leading members of the East End and south London gangs occasionally met on the neutral ground of the West End (Hobbs 1994).

The subculture of crime is the basis of socialization into a criminal identity, whether that of a craft thief or a project thief. The professional thief, like the professional doctor, lawyer, or bricklayer, must develop many technical abilities and skills. He (the thief is generally male) must know how to plan and execute crimes, how to dispose of stolen goods, how to 'fix' the police and the courts, and so on. These skills must be acquired through long education and training, and it is through his involvement in the underworld that the thief can acquire them most effectively.

Based on his detailed study of a professional thief, Sutherland (1937) has shown how the person who successfully learns and applies these techniques earns high status within the underworld. The beginning thief, if successful, is gradually admitted into closer and closer contact with other thieves. It is they who can offer him 'better' work and from whom he can learn more advanced skills. Once successful, the thief dresses and behaves in distinct ways and proudly adopts the label 'thief' in order to distinguish himself from mere 'amateur', small-time criminals. As well as gaining respect within the underworld, he may also gain a degree of recognition and respect from police, lawyers, and newspaper crime writers. These people are aware of his activities and have often evolved forms of accommodation towards professional crime: apart from the corruption that sometimes occurs, there are also shared interests in not reacting immediately and punitively towards all crime.

Burglary as a way of life

One of the few contemporary investigations of career theft in Britain is an investigation of domestic burglaries carried out by Maguire and Bennett (1982). Burglary is illegal entry into a building with the intent to steal. Domestic burglary was, for a long time, subject to the death penalty, and from 1861 to 1968 it carried a maximum sentence of life imprisonment. Following the Theft Act of 1968, the maximum penalty has been fourteen years' imprisonment. In practice, only just under a half of convicted burglars have been given custodial sentences.

Recognizing the problems involved in assessing rates of crime, Maguire and Bennett have concluded that about 60 per cent of all burglaries were committed by a relatively small number of persistent, career criminals. The remaining 40 per cent were committed by juveniles

The professional thief

In 1930 Edwin Sutherland, a sociologist at the University of Chicago, carried out lengthy research with Chic Conwell, a man involved full-time in theft between 1905 and 1925. Using the life-history method pioneered at the university, Sutherland obtained a biographical account of Conwell's life, which he used as the basis for his interpretation of thieving (Sutherland 1937).

Conwell was born in the 1880s and, after a short period of theatre work, got involved in the use of drugs and became a pimp. Through his pimping, he acquired a knowledge of other forms of crime and he worked in Chicago as a pickpocket, a shoplifter, and a confidence trickster. He spent a number of periods on prison, though only one of his sentences was for theft. He gave up both thieving and drug use after release from prison in 1925 and worked regularly until his death in 1933.

Sutherland specialized in the study of crime. He developed a view that stressed differential association: people learn criminal behaviour by coming into contact with others who define criminality in positive ways. In addition to his study of professional theft he pioneered the study of white-collar crime (Sutherland 1949).

Sutherland's position on the professional thief was that

'a person can be a professional thief only if he is recognized and received as such by other professional thieves. Professional theft is a group-way of life. One can get into the group and remain in it only by the consent of those previously in the group. Recognition as a professional thief by other professional thieves is the absolutely necessary, universal, and definitive characteristic of the professional thief. . . . A professional thief is a person who has the status of a professional thief in the differential association of professional thieves.' (Sutherland 1937: 211)

who had drifted into delinquency and would, for the most part, drift out of it again.

 Criminal statistics are notoriously unreliable, mainly because of the non-reporting of crimes. You will find a fuller discussion of this in 'Using Official Statistics', Chapter 3, pp. 107–9.

Maguire and Bennett interviewed a number of persistent burglars, most of whom were committed to their criminal careers. They had, typically, carried out between 100 and 500 break-ins during their careers. They combined this with involvement in car theft, burglary from commercial premises, and cheque forgery. They were mainly young, single, and with no dependants. The men described themselves as 'thieves', or simply as 'villains', and they described their crimes as 'work' from which they could earn a living and from which they would eventually retire. Maguire and Bennett are, however, more critical of this self-image than Sutherland had been. In particular, they highlight a number of ways in which the thieves sought to neutralize the moral implications of their actions through self-serving rationalizations.

Thieves claimed, for example, that any distress suffered by the victims was no concern of theirs. They were simply doing a job, carrying on their trade, and this distress was an unavoidable consequence of their routine, professional activities. This claim was further bolstered by the claim that, in any case, they stole only from the well-to-do, who could easily afford it and who were well insured (Maguire and Bennett 1982: 61). In fact, many of their victims were relatively poor council house residents who could ill afford to be burgled.

Similarly, the thieves sought to boost their own status by disparaging the amateurism of the majority of 'losers', 'wankers', 'idiots', and 'cowboys' who carried out unsuccessful thefts. It is more accurate, Maguire and Bennett argue, to see the persistent career thieves as divided into low-level, middle-level, and high-level categories on the basis of the scale of their crimes. Thieves move up and down this hierarchy a great deal over the course of their careers.

High-level burglaries are undertaken by the thieves who are members of small networks of committed criminals who keep themselves separate from other, small-time criminals. Sometimes they work alone, and sometimes in pairs, but always they keep their principal criminal contacts within their network. Middle-level burglaries are carried out by those who are involved in larger and less exclusive networks of thieves with varying abilities and degrees of commitment. There is less consistent adherence to the code of mutual support, and less effective contacts with receivers of stolen goods and with other specialist criminals. Finally, low-level burglaries are undertaken by individual thieves with only loose connections to one another and who are indiscriminate in both their criminal connections and their choice of crimes.

It is at the lower level that people first enter burglary, as the loose social networks are closely embedded in the surrounding structure of the local community. In most cases, this is a process of drift by some of those who have previously been involved in juvenile delinquencies. The thieves themselves, however, minimized the element of drift and presented a self-image of people who had chosen to enter careers of crime. Those who drift into lower-level burglary and become at all successful may graduate, in due course, to middle-level or high-level burglary by virtue of the contacts and connections that they make.

Those in the networks carrying out the high-level burglaries were, in a sense, at the pinnacle of the career hierarchy, though Maguire and Bennett show that they are unlikely to be at all involved in large-scale project crimes undertaken by the London gangs. Their activities are confined to housebreaking, shop-breaking, car theft, shoplifting, and cheque forgery. They had little or no involvement in such specialist crimes as hijacking lorries, bank raids, or embezzlement.

Very few burglars—even those at the high level—made a major financial success of their chosen careers, and most spent at least one period in prison. Imprisonment is not, however, a purely negative experience, as it gives the burglar an opportunity to 'widen his circle of criminal acquaintances, learn new techniques and be encouraged to try his hand at more lucrative offences' (Maguire and Bennett 1982: 67). Nevertheless, few burglars continued with burglary beyond their thirties or forties. Most drifted into what they hoped would be safer forms of work. Entry into legal employment is difficult for someone with a criminal record, and few make the transition successfully. Walsh (1986: 58–9) has shown that some burglars are able to combine career crime with a continuing involvement in legitimate employment—typically short-term jobs in the building and construction industry or in other casual work such as catering and cleaning. It seems likely that some who retire from burglary may be able to continue or to re-enter such casual and temporary work.

Career crime has probably never been a completely self-contained, full-time activity. Even in the heyday of the Victorian underworld of the East End, criminal activities were combined with casual labour and street

Figure 5.3. **Unemployment and crime**

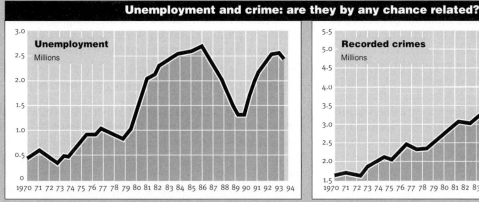

Unemployment and crime: are they by any chance related?

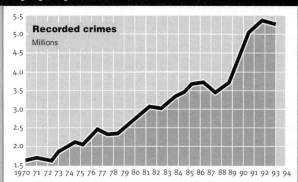

Source: *Independent on Sunday*, 4 June 1995.

▶ **What conclusions would you draw about crime from the two graphs above? Take a few minutes to think about this. Look at our discussion of unemployment measures and the crime statistics in Chapter 3, pp. 107–11, and see if you would want to change any of your conclusions.**

trading, one type of work supplementing the earnings from the other (Mayhew 1861*b*). Hobbs (1988) has shown how the East End has long been organized around an entrepreneurial culture of wheeling and dealing, trading and fixing, that makes little sharp distinction between legal and illegal activities.

Theft may, indeed, be career crime, a way of life, but it does not take up all of a thief's time and cannot usually provide him with a regular or substantial income. Those involved in thieving, then, must combine it with other ways of gaining an income. Casual labour is combined with their own thieving and the performance of the occasional criminal task for other, more successful thieves. Those who are themselves more successful may be involved as much in trading and dealing as in thieving, and their entrepreneurial activities are likely to range from the legitimate, through various 'shady' deals, to the criminal. The full-time criminal is not a full-time thief, even if he stresses this aspect of his life in constructing his own identity. Much thieving is undertaken by those who are in low-paid or semi-legitimate work or who are unemployed (see Figure 5.3).

There is considerable evidence that the growth of the drugs market in the 1980s has sharpened a distinc-

tion between the full-time criminal and the mass of ordinary thieves. The establishment of a large and extensive market in drugs has connected together the criminal networks of London, Manchester, Birmingham, Glasgow, and other large cities. This has allowed a greater degree of organization to be achieved in the project crimes that sustain drug-trafficking. Those who are involved in this organized crime, however, have highly specialized skills—for example, in relation to VAT fraud—and are very different from those who steal hi-fis and videos from domestic premises. The significance of the drug market for ordinary thieves, as we show later in this chapter is that it offers possibilities for casual and occasional trading in small quantities of drugs that supplement their more established sources of income (Hobbs 1994: 449, 453–4).

GENDER, ETHNICITY, CLASS, AND CRIME

The public perception of crime concentrates on robbery, burglary, theft, mugging, rape, and other crimes of theft and violence. The popular view sees this crime as male, working-class activity. Professional crime is seen as the work of certain adult males and as expressing conventional notions of masculinity.

This point of view does get some support from the criminal statistics, which seem to show the very small number of women who are convicted of criminal offences (see Figure 5.4). While 44 per cent of all men in England and Wales have been convicted of a criminal offence at some time in their lives, this is the case for only 15 per cent of women. It also appears that the kinds of crimes committed by women are less 'serious' than those committed by men. Figures for all parts of Britain show that women have very little involvement as offenders in domestic or commercial theft, vehicle theft, or street violence, though they are often, of course, involved in these as victims. They are, however, more heavily involved in shoplifting than are men, prostitution is an almost exclusively female crime, and only women can be convicted of infanticide. There is some evidence, however, that the number and type of crimes committed by women may have altered since the 1960s (Heidensohn 1985).

Figure 5.4. Indictable offences by gender, England and Wales, 1995 (000s)

Offence	Males	Females
Theft and handling stolen goods	160.9	60.1
Drug offences	71.9	7.9
Burglary	43.9	1.9
Violence against the person	41.8	7.7
Criminal damage	12.2	1.2
Sexual offences	6.8	0.1
Robbery	5.3	0.5
Other indictable offences	52.4	5.0
TOTAL	395.2	84.4

Source: Social Trends (1997: 159, fig. 9.12).

In a similar way to the crimes of women, many middle-class crimes are not generally regarded as 'real' crimes. While there is a great public fear of street violence and domestic burglary, there is relatively little concern about fraudulent business practices, violations of safety legislation, or tax evasion. While such offences, arguably, have much greater impact on people's lives than does the relatively small risk of theft or violence, they are either invisible to public opinion or are not seen as 'crimes'.

In this section we will assess the adequacy of these views of crime, exploring aspects of the crimes of women, ethnic minorities, and the affluent.

Distribution by gender, ethnicity, and class

The kinds of crimes that are committed by women, like those committed by men, reflect the gender-defined social roles that are available to them. Both men and women are involved in shoplifting, for example, but women are more likely to steal clothes, food, or low-value items. Men are more likely to steal books, electrical goods, or high-value items. This reflects the conventional domestic expectations that tie women to shopping for basic household goods in supermarkets, while men are able to shop for luxuries and extras. Put simply, both men and women tend to steal the same kinds of items that they buy (Smart 1977: 9–10). Similarly, men (especially young men) are heavily involved in vehicle crimes, including car theft, while women are heavily involved in prostitution. This involvement in prostitution can be seen as an extension of a normal feminine role that allows implicit or explicit bargaining over sex.

This connection between crime and conventional sex–gender roles is particularly clear in the patterns of involvement that women have in offences related to children. Those who are most responsible for childcare are, other things being equal, more likely to be involved in cruelty to children, abandoning children, kidnapping, procuring illegal abortions, and social-security frauds. Theft by women generally involves theft from an employer by those involved in domestic work or shop work. Even when involved in large-scale theft, women are likely to be acting in association with male family members and to be involved as receivers of stolen goods rather than as thieves.

There are, of course, problems in estimating the actual number of offences from the official statistics (as we show in Chapter 3, pp. 108–9), but the overall pattern is clear. Because women are less likely to be arrested and convicted for certain offences—something that we look at below—the difference between male and female involvement in crime is exaggerated by the official figures. The differing patterns of offence do, however, exist. Only in the case of sexual offences is the pattern for male and female involvement more equal, the apparent predominance of women resulting from the fact that their sexual behaviour is more likely to be treated in ways that result in conviction. The sexual double standard means that the authorities normalize much male sexual delinquency, but express moral outrage at female sexual delinquency.

Crimes of women

'None of these types of offences requires particularly "masculine" attributes. Strength and force are unnecessary and there is only a low level of skill or expertise required. The women involved have not required training in violence, weapons or tools, or in specialised tasks like safe breaking. On the contrary the skills required can be learnt in everyday experience, and socialization into a delinquent subculture or a sophisticated criminal organisation is entirely unnecessary.'

Source: Smart (1977: 15–16).

There is growing evidence that members of ethnic minorities in Britain have become more heavily involved with the legal system since the 1960s. They are now especially likely to appear as offenders and, more particularly, as victims of crime and as police suspects. Housebreakings and other household offences show little variation among the various ethnic groups, around one-third of all households being victims of such crime.

African-Caribbeans, however, are almost twice as likely as whites to be the victims of personal attacks. This is, in part, a consequence of the fact that African-Caribbeans live, disproportionately, in inner-city areas where such crimes are particularly likely to take place. However, they also have a racially motivated character. The growing victimization of black and Asian people reflects a real growth in racial violence and racist attacks by members of the white population. While criminal acts carried out during the urban riots of the 1980s (see Chapter 11, pp. 435–7) often had a racial aspect to them, blacks and Asians are far more likely to be the targets of racial crimes than they are to commit them. There has, nevertheless, been a growing involvement of young African-Caribbeans in many kinds of street crime.

The police hold to a widely shared prejudice that African-Caribbeans, in particular, are heavily involved in crime and that special efforts need to be taken to control them. Many studies have shown the racism inherent in police actions that stop black people in the street and subject them to closer scrutiny than other members of the population (Hall *et al.* 1978; Gelsthorpe 1993). African-Caribbeans are more likely than whites, and members of other ethnic minorities, to be approached by the police on suspicion, to be prosecuted, and to be sentenced. This is reflected in a growing hostility of ethnic minorities towards the police, who are seen as racists rather than as neutral defenders of law and order.

Offences carried out by men (and women) from the middle classes are generally described as **white-collar crime** (Sutherland 1949; Croal 1992). This term originally referred to crimes and civil-law infractions committed by those in non-manual employment as part of their work. It is now used a little more broadly to refer to three categories of offence:

▶ *Occupational crimes* of the affluent: offences committed by the relatively affluent and prosperous in the course of their legitimate business or profession. Examples are theft from an employer, financial frauds, and insider dealing in investment companies.

▶ *Organizational crimes*: offences committed by organizations and businesses themselves—that is, by employees acting in their official capacities on behalf of the organization. Examples are non-payment or under-payment of VAT or Corporation Tax, and infringements of health and safety legislation leading to accidents or pollution.

▶ Any other crimes committed by the relatively affluent that tend to be treated differently from those of the less affluent. An example is tax evasion, which is treated differently from social-security fraud (Nelken 1994: 362–3).

The concept of white-collar crime, then, is far from clear-cut. It does, however, help to highlight the class basis of much crime. The numbers of people involved in white-collar crimes is barely apparent from the official statistics, as many go unrecorded. Its status as hidden crime, however, is paradoxical in view of its financial significance. It has been estimated that the total cost of reported fraud alone in 1985 was £2,113 million, twice the amount accounted for by reported theft, burglary, and robbery (Levi 1987; see also M. Clarke 1990).

The relatively low representation of women in recorded crime is the main reason why female criminality has been so little researched. Lombroso and Ferrero (1895) set out a deterministic theory, based on the claimed peculiarities of female biology, which still has some influence in the late 1990s. They held that women were less highly evolved than men and so were relatively 'primitive' in character. They were less involved in crime, however, because their biology predisposed them to a passive and more conservative way of life. They were, however, weak willed, and Lombroso and Ferrero saw the involvement of many women in crime as resulting from their having been led on by others. The female drift into crime was a consequence of their weak and fickle character.

The extreme position set out by Lombroso and Ferrero has long been abandoned, but many criminologists do still resort to biological assumptions when trying to explain female criminality. Pollak (1950), for example, held that women are naturally manipulative and deceitful, instigating crimes that men undertake. What such theories fail to consider is that, if women do indeed have lower rates of criminality, this may more usefully and accurately be explained in terms of the cultural influences that shape sex–gender roles and the differing opportunities available to men and to women.

Like the crimes of women, the crimes of the affluent have been little researched. Early discussions of white-collar crime were intended as criticisms of the orthodox assumption that criminality was caused by poverty or deprivation. Those who carried out thefts as part of a successful business career, Sutherland (1949) argued, could not be seen as acting out of economic necessity. Sutherland's own account stressed that white-collar crime was *learned* behaviour and that, in this respect, it was no different from other forms of criminality. All crime, he held, resulted from the effects of 'differential association' on learning: those who interacted more frequently with others whose attitudes were favourable to criminal actions were themselves more likely to engage in criminal acts.

This implies that patterns of conformity among the affluent and the deprived, among men and among women, are to be understood in the context of their wider role commitments and the interactions in which they are involved with their role partners. Those who are predisposed to see criminal actions as appropriate will, if the structure of opportunities allows it, drift into crime. There is no need to assume that women are fundamentally different from men, or that the working classes are fundamentally different from the middle classes.

Women and crime

It appears, then, that women, like men, drift into criminal actions whenever the structure of opportunities is such that it seems a reasonable response to their situation. The particular situations in which they find them-

selves are determined by the ways in which sex–gender identities are institutionalized in their society, and so their patterns of criminality are gendered. Cultural stereotypes about men and women, as we will show, are also a major influence on the nature of the social reaction to female criminality. The absence of strong punitive responses to most forms of female crime means that the progression from primary to secondary deviation is less likely to occur. Women may drift into crime, but they only rarely pursue criminal careers.

A form of female crime that seems to be the principal exception to this rule is prostitution. In law, a prostitute is someone who sells sex, and this is almost invariably seen as a female offence. Men involved in prostitution, other than as clients, tend to be seen as engaged in acts of 'indecency' rather than of 'soliciting' for prostitution. Under the British law, a woman who has been arrested and convicted for soliciting is officially termed a 'common prostitute' and is liable to rearrest simply for loitering in a public place. As most prostitution is arranged in public, on the streets, it is difficult for women so labelled to avoid the occasional spell in custody. They may also find it difficult to live a normal life off the streets: 'It is virtually impossible for them to live with a man or even another woman as it is immediately assumed that such people are living off immoral earnings, thereby making themselves vulnerable to a criminal charge. Also, the legal definition of a brothel, as a dwelling containing two or more prostitutes, makes it difficult for two women to live together even where only one is a prostitute' (Smart 1977: 114).

 You might like to consider street prostitution in relation to our discussion of the gendering of space in Chapter 11, pp. 416–18. A good discussion can be found in McKeganey and Barnard (1996). While you are looking at the gendering of space in the city, you might also think about the way in which urban space is used by various ethnic groups (see pp. 430–2 in the same chapter).

The reaction of the police is critical in determining whether a woman who breaks the law is defined as a criminal. Police work is structured around the cop culture (Reiner 1992), a culture that strongly emphasizes masculinity and that underpins the harassment and abuse of female police officers and the derogation of many female offenders.

Prostitutes, for example, are seen as flouting the domesticity of the conventional female role and have been subject to harassment and entrapment. Nevertheless, prostitutes are often able to establish a mutual accommodation with the police, an arrangement in which each can get on with their job with the minimum of interference from the other. When there is pressure on the police to take action, however, such arrangements break down. In these circumstances, prostitutes are highly vulnerable and can be quite susceptible to police persuasion and suggestion. On the other hand, women who conform to conventional role expectations are seen as in need of protection, and cautioning is more widely used for female offenders than it is for males (S. Edwards 1984: 16–19).

There is some evidence that this differential treatment of male and female offenders also occurs in the courts. Sexist assumptions in court practices have led some to suggest that women experience greater leniency than men (Mannheim 1940: 343). Others, however, have suggested that greater harshness is more likely (A. Campbell 1981). Heidensohn (1985) correctly points out that this may simply reflect the well-known lack of consistency in sentencing, though she reports evidence that supports the view that women are treated more harshly (Farrington and Morris 1983).

Indeed, Edwards (1984) has suggested that women are subjected to much closer scrutiny in courts precisely because the female offender is seen as unusual or unnatural. Women are on trial not only for their offence but for their deviation from conventional femininity. Their punishment or treatment is intended to ensure that they adjust themselves back to what is seen as a natural feminine role.

Very few convicted women are given custodial sentences. Men are two or three times more likely to be imprisoned for an offence than are women, and their sentences tend to be longer. The women who are imprisoned are mainly those who have been convicted of such things as theft, fraud, forgery, or violence. Prisons do make some attempt to recognize that women's domestic commitments are different from those of men, and a number of mother-and-baby units have been set up. Some well-publicized cases have been reported, however, of pregnant prison inmates who have been forced to give birth while manacled to a prison officer. Studies of female prisons in the United States have shown how these prisons are important sources of emotional and practical support for their inmates (Giallombardo 1966), often involving the establishment of lesbian family relationships. This appears to be less marked in Britain.

Crimes of the affluent

The crimes of the affluent, the prosperous, and the powerful can be explained in terms of the same motives as any other criminal act. They differ from 'ordinary' theft and burglary only in terms of their social organization and the social reaction to them. The character and motivation of those involved are no more, and no less, pathological than those of any others who drift into crime. White-collar crimes, however, are much less likely to result in full-time criminal careers. The nature of the social reaction makes the development into secondary deviation much less likely.

Much corporate and occupational crime takes place in the financial services industry, where changing patterns of regulation have created greater opportunities for illicit activities. The British financial system was, for much of the nineteenth and twentieth centuries, regulated in a highly informal way. Recruitment to banks, insurance companies, and other financial enterprises took place through an old-boy network centred on the public schools and the Oxford and Cambridge colleges. The Stock Exchange, as the central institution in the financial system, was at the heart of this system of informal regulation. The system rested on trust and loyalty: those who had been to school together and shared a similar social background felt that they could trust one another in their business dealings. The motto of the Stock Exchange was 'My word is my bond', and many deals were sealed on the shake of hands rather than with a written contract (Lisle-Williams 1984; M. Clarke 1986).

Recruitment to the boards of the financial enterprises that make up the City of London financial system is one aspect of the recruitment to elites and top positions in British society. You might like to look at our discussion of elites and the ruling class in Chapter 17, pp. 701–4, where we look in more detail at the part played by schooling and informal social networks.

During the 1970s the government introduced a number of changes to this system of regulation in response to the growing internationalization of the money markets. This culminated in the so-called Big Bang of October 1986, when the Stock Exchange was finally opened up to foreign competition. New codes of practice were introduced to reflect the more diverse social base of recruitment of those involved in the buying and selling of currency, shares, and

Banking crimes

The most notorious case of white-collar crime in the 1990s is, perhaps, that of Nick Leeson, who worked for the Singapore branch of the London firm of Barings. Leeson's job was to buy and sell financial assets on behalf of his bank, but he established a series of secret accounts and built up a massive hidden fortune until a trading mistake transformed this into a loss of £830 million and the bankruptcy of Barings. Leeson was tried in Singapore and, after plea bargaining, was given a sentence of six and a half years in Changi jail. Leeson's offences, though punished, may not result in secondary deviation. While in prison, he has negotiated an advance of £450,000 for writing a book about his crimes, and he has agreed a £3 million contract for the film rights.

Nick Leeson is brought back from Malaysia by police officers.

commodities. The old system of trust could no longer be relied on, and more formal mechanisms were required. The Bank of England was given greater powers of control and supervision, and in 1997 the Labour government created a new Securities and Investment Board to regulate the whole system.

The offences with which the new system of regulation has had to deal are those that have been made possible by the changing structure of the financial system. The investment management firm of Barlow Clowes, for example, set up new offshore investment funds to provide high returns to its wealthy clients who wanted to minimize their tax bills. The head of the company was found to have financed an extravagant lifestyle at the expense of the investors in the funds (M. Clarke 1990: 167–70). The growth of domestic takeover business made possible massive fraud by some directors and managers associated with Guinness and its financial advisers in 1986. These directors and managers manipulated share dealings to keep up the price of Guinness shares on the stock market and to help its takeover of another company. Their actions were the subject of an official inquiry and, later, a criminal trial that resulted in some of them being imprisoned.

Much white-collar crime is low in visibility. It tends to occur in the context of normal business routines, and it is less likely to be noticed, even by its victims. Fiddling business expenses, for example, is almost undetectable, and many employers treat it as a source of tax-free perks for their employees (Mars 1982). Large-scale fraud, when discovered, is more likely to result in an official reaction, though it will often be hushed up if it might suggest a failure of supervision or control by senior managers.

Crimes of the affluent are far more likely to be regulated by specialized enforcement agencies than by the police, and this has important consequences for the nature of the social reaction. These agencies—the Health and Safety Executive, the Factory Inspectorate, the Inland Revenue, and so on—generally have a remit to maintain and promote high standards of business and trading, and the enforcement of the criminal law is only one part of this remit (Croal 1992: ch. 5). Their officials, therefore, develop 'compliance strategies' that stress persuasion and administrative sanctions aimed at crime prevention, rather than the detection and punishment of offences. The level of prosecutions is, therefore, very low. Few cases go to court, and very few result in imprisonment. In these ways, the transition to secondary deviation is avoided.

SUMMARY POINTS

In this section we have looked at professional and career crimes and at the relationships between gender, class, and crime. We started out by showing that not all deviation from legal norms is criminal activity. Criminal actions involve deviation from the criminal law. In considering theft and career crime, we showed that:

▶ Theft has undergone a series of transformations as the wider society has changed.

▶ Much theft has been organized in relation to an extensive underworld, a subculture of crime that supports and sustains criminal activities.

▶ Career thieves adopt an identity as professional thieves, though their involvement in theft is quite variable.

▶ Much burglary is combined with low-paid, semi-legal, and casual work, or is carried out by those who are unemployed.

We explored the popular viewpoint that crime is a male, working-class phenomenon. Looking at gender, ethnicity, class, and crime, we showed that:

▶ Patterns of male and female crime differ, and they reflect differences in conventional sex–gender roles.

▶ Female criminality is often explained in terms of female biology, ignoring cultural conceptions of femininity and the structure of opportunities open to women.

▶ There are significant variations in the attitudes of police and the courts to men and to women.

▶ African-Caribbeans are twice as likely as whites to experience personal attacks. Many of these crimes are racially motivated.

▶ Members of ethnic minorities are more likely than whites to be stopped by the police and prosecuted in court.

▶ White-collar crime includes a diverse range of crimes of the affluent. Its economic impact is far more extensive than is often assumed.

▶ Crimes of the affluent are more likely to be normalized or to be regulated by bodies other than the police and the criminal courts.

▶ Trends in white-collar crime are related to changes in the structure of the financial system and the wider economy.

DRUGS AND DRUG ABUSE

The use of drugs is now one of the most widely discussed forms of deviance. In its most general meaning, a drug is any chemical that can have an effect on the human body and, perhaps, a physical effect on the mind. Some drugs occur quite naturally in many widely used drinks and foods. Caffeine, for example, is found in both coffee and tea, alcohol is the basis of beer, wine, and spirits, and vitamins are found in fresh fruit and vegetables. Many drugs are used as medicines, usually under the control of doctors. Morphine, penicillin, and steroids, for example, are used very widely and under a variety of commercial trade names in hospitals, clinics, and surgeries. Many other medical drugs are freely available for purchase without prescription: aspirin, codeine, ibuprofen, and numerous other analgesic (pain-killing) drugs can be bought in any high-street pharmacy and in many supermarkets.

This broad, dictionary definition of 'drugs', however, is not what newspaper columnists, politicians, and social commentators mean when they use the word. These people generally use the word in a much narrower sense to refer to the non-medical use of drugs. This is the deliberate use of chemical substances to achieve particular physiological changes, simply for the pleasure or the other non-medical effects that they produce. It is in this sense, for example, that many parents and teachers rail against the use of drugs by children and young people. The non-medical use of drugs in the twentieth century has, indeed, been largely an activity of the young. Drug use, then, is seen as a deviant activity, as non-medical drug *abuse*. It becomes, therefore, a matter for social control. For this reason, the non-medical use or possession of many drugs has been made illegal.

There is a great deal of ambiguity over how widely this meaning of the word drug is to be taken, and whether all non-medical drug use is to be regarded as a deviant activity. Many freely available products have the same characteristics as illicit drugs. Tobacco, for example, can be freely bought in shops and it is a major source of tax revenue for the government. At the same time, however, it contains nicotine, an addictive stimulant to the nervous system that is a major health hazard both to those who smoke and to those around them. Similarly, alcoholic drinks, which can have serious physiological and psychological effects if taken in large quantities, are an accepted and even encouraged part of a normal social life for most people. Like tobacco, alcohol is available in shops and supermarkets, it is a multi-million pound industry, in which many people find legitimate employment, and—unlike cigarettes—it can be advertised freely on television.

Some chemicals with domestic or industrial uses, but which can also be used to produce 'high' feelings, can be purchased quite legitimately and with even fewer restrictions. Glues and solvents, which are used as stimulants and hallucinogenics (mood-changers) by many young people, can be purchased in hardware and do-it-yourself shops. The use of heroin, cocaine, or Ecstasy (MDMA), on the other hand, is widely disapproved of and their use is surrounded by numerous legal restrictions over their acquisition and sale. Many such drugs are the objects of advertising campaigns that are aimed at discouraging their use by encouraging people to 'say no' if offered them. They can usually be obtained only from illegal sources.

LEARNING DRUG USE

The idea of **addiction** to drugs is central to discussions of their non-medical uses. Addiction is seen as occurring where people have become physiologically dependent on the use of a particular drug and suffer serious and persistent withdrawal symptoms when its use is

---

Feeling the rush

'Marijuana could be a "gateway" drug that primes the brain for dependence on harder drugs, scientists say. . . . The active ingredient in hemp cannabis does its work in the same region of the brain and uses the same triggers as heroin. . . . This region, known as the limbic system, is where the addictive drugs nicotine, cocaine and the amphetamines are most active. . . . Neuroscientists in California have further discovered that people who get a "rush" from chocolate do so because something in the bar mimics the action of cannabinoids, which do the work in marijuana.'

Source: Guardian, 27 June 1997.

▶ **Why do you think there are such wide variations in the social reaction to the use of cannabis, nicotine, and chocolate?**

---

stopped. However, dependence is as much a psychological as a physiological fact and, as such, it is shaped by social factors. People must learn how to use particular drugs, and they become committed to their use only through complex social processes from which physiological dependence cannot be isolated. 'Addiction' is a medically constructed label and a social role that combines elements of the sick role and, in some cases, the criminal role.

 We look at the idea of the sick role in Chapter 6, pp. 210–11. You may want to read our discussion now.

Drugs do, of course, have specific physiological effects: alcohol and barbiturates depress mental activity, cocaine and caffeine stimulate it, and LSD distorts experiences and perception. Their full effects, however, depend upon the social context in which they are used. Individuals who use drugs learn from one another not only the techniques that are necessary for their use, but also how to shape and to experience the kinds of effects that they produce. The non-medical use of drugs, then, is a deviant activity that, like all forms of deviance, is surrounded by normative frameworks that structure the lives of users and lead them to experience particular deviant careers and associated moral careers. 'Drug addiction' is a deviant identity that reflects a specific deviant career.

Becoming a cannabis user

In an influential study of deviant activity, Becker (1953) documented the career stages that are involved in becoming a marihuana (cannabis) user. He showed that people drift into cannabis use for a variety of reasons. Once they begin its use, however, they will—if they persist—follow a particular sequence of stages. Becker called these stages the 'beginner', the 'occasional user', and the 'regular user'. As users follow this career sequence, cannabis-smoking becomes an ever more important part of their identity. Becker shows, however, that cannabis use rarely involves full-blown secondary deviation, despite the fact that its use is illegal. Cannabis use is a low-visibility activity that rarely comes to the attention of those who might publicly stigmatize users, and so these users are less likely to progress to secondary deviation.

Becker's research was undertaken in the early 1950s, and public attitudes have altered somewhat since then. There was an increase in cannabis use in both the United States and in Britain during the 1960s. It has, since then, become accepted or tolerated in many situations. In California in 1996, for example, legal restrictions were relaxed in order to allow for its medical use in the treatment of certain cancer patients. Indeed, it has been suggested that cannabis use has become normalized for many people. Research suggests that almost a half of 15 and 16 year olds in Britain have tried cannabis and that they regard it in the same way that most adults regard alcohol and tobacco.

When Becker undertook his research, cannabis use was both illegal and surrounded by social meanings that associated it with irresponsibility, immorality, and addiction. Becker showed that, while the drug is not physically addictive, its image and its illegality led to specific patterns in its use. Unlike cigarettes, cannabis could not be bought at the local newsagent or the supermarket—though it can be obtained in this way in the Netherlands. Most people, therefore, had neither the opportunity nor the inclination to smoke it. Those who were most likely to begin to use the drug, Becker argued, were those who were involved in social groups where there was already a degree of cannabis use. It was here that there were likely to be opportunities for new users.

Becker saw the typical locales for exploratory drug use as organized around values and activities that oppose or run counter to the mainstream values of the larger society. When he undertook his research, these had their focus in social groups around jazz and popular music, students, and 'bohemians'. These groups tended to have a more critical and oppositional stance towards conventional social standards. Participants were likely to see many other people using the drug, and their own first use was likely to become a real possibility if an opportunity presented itself. Someone enters the *beginner* stage in the use of cannabis when he or she is offered the opportunity to smoke it in a social situation where others are smoking, where there is a degree of social pressure to conform to group norms, and where the group itself provides a relatively safe and secluded locale away from the immediate possibility of public censure.

Howard Becker

Howard Becker was born in 1928 and was trained at the University of Chicago. His work draws heavily on symbolic interactionism, but he places this in the larger context of the power struggles among social groups. His early work on drug use was followed by work on student doctors (Becker *et al.* 1961), education (Becker *et al.* 1968), and artistic production (Becker 1982). He has also published a number of important methodological essays (Becker 1970). His work on drug use was republished in the early 1960s (Becker 1963), when it made a major contribution to the labelling theory of deviance.

Becker shows that people who move from the stage of the beginner to that of the *occasional user* must learn a number of skills and abilities associated with the use of the drug. Someone willing to use the drug may know that it causes a 'high' feeling, but they are unlikely to know exactly how to produce this. The principal skill that must be learned, then, is the actual technique for smoking cannabis. This is different from that used in tobacco smoking. Only if the smoke is inhaled in the correct way, with an appropriate amount of air, can cannabis have any significant effect on a person's body and mind. Group membership is essential for the easy learning of this skill, as the new user is surrounded by those who can demonstrate it in their own smoking. Those who fail to learn the proper technique will never experience the physical effects of cannabis and so are unlikely to persist in using the drug.

A user must also acquire the ability to perceive the effects of the drug and, therefore, must learn what it is to be high or stoned. This is not as strange as it may seem. Users may have experiences that they fail to recognize as effects of the drug, but that others recognize as central features of their high state. Through interaction with others, new users begin to learn what signs and symptoms to look out for and what, therefore, can be taken as indicating that they have successfully learned the smoking technique. Last, but not least, they must learn to enjoy the effects of cannabis. They must learn to treat dizziness, tingling, and distortions of time and space as pleasurable experiences, rather than as unpleasant and undesirable disturbances to their normal physical and mental state. Only those who successfully acquire these skills and abilities—the smoking technique, the ability to perceive the effects, and enjoyment of the effects—will persist as cannabis users.

As occasional users, cannabis smokers acquire further justifications and rationalizations for its use, and these reinforce their continued use of the drug. The subculture of the group provides ready-made answers to many of the conventional objections to cannabis use that may be raised in their minds. Users may claim, for example, that cannabis is less dangerous than the alcohol that is tolerated and encouraged by conventional opinion. They are also likely to hold that cannabis smokers are in complete control of when and where they choose to use the drug; that the drug is not in control of them.

The regular user of cannabis seeks ways to neutralize the conventional image of the 'dope fiend' or 'dope head', which they fear might be applied to them by non-users. People do not become regular users if they continue to hold on to the stereotype of addiction or to the idea that they are likely to escalate towards the use of hard drugs. If ideas of addiction, escalation, and mental weakness cannot be neutralized, smokers may revert to occasional use, rather than becoming committed, regular users. Becker showed, for example, that regular users tested their dependence on the drug by stopping its use for a while, so that they could prove to themselves that they could live without it. Similarly, they would claim that they were aware of their psychological need to smoke and, because of this awareness, they really remained in control of it.

To protect themselves from stigmatization, regular users try to learn how to control the effects of the drug, inhibiting its effects at will, so that they are able to pass as normal in front of non-users. They must, nevertheless, run certain risks of detection, as regular use requires access to illegal dealers whose criminal activities may bring the user to the attention of the police. In order to minimize their chances of discovery as users, they are likely to spend more and more of their time in the company of their own, the other regular users who can provide a supportive and relatively safe environment in which to smoke.

PATTERNS OF DRUG USE

People learn how to use drugs in particular social contexts. Becker's work explored cannabis use in the specific context of post-war America, though his conclusions have a much wider application. In this section we will look at the changing context of drug use in Britain. We look first at an account of deviant drug use in the 1970s, and then we turn to the contemporary, normalized use of drugs by young people.

Deviant drug use

Although it was developed in the 1950s, Becker's argument retains much of its relevance for contemporary patterns of cannabis use, and it has much to say about the use of other drugs. This was first confirmed in a study undertaken by Jock Young (1971) in London. Young's primary concern, however, is the origins of the negative social reaction to cannabis use. Why is it, he asks, that there is no similar social reaction to the use of tobacco? He holds that the reason is to be found not in the drug, but in the motivation that people are seen as having for using it. Drugs that are seen as being used to aid productivity are likely to be tolerated, while those that have a purely hedonistic (pleasure-seeking) purpose are seen as 'drug abuse'.

European and North American societies tolerate or even encourage the drinking of coffee and tea, and the smoking of tobacco when working under pressure or as a 'release' from the pressure of a heavy work schedule. The worker 'earns' the right to 'relax with a smoke and a drink' after work, and people may be allowed to smoke at work if it 'helps them to concentrate'. Alcohol is widely used, and it is tolerated as a way in which people may, periodically, ease the transition from work to leisure. It is culturally normalized. It is only when alcohol is used to excess and interferes with normal, everyday activities that its use is defined as deviant. No such tolerance is allowed for the user of cannabis, which is not seen as linked in any way to work productivity. Young also points out that there can be cultural variations in response to the same drug. Andean peasants use cocaine (in the form of coca leaves) as an aid to work, and it is a normalized feature of their society. In Britain and the United States, however, cocaine is regarded very differently.

Young has shown that these variations in response to drugs can be explained in terms of the relationship between a dominant set of social values and a secondary *subterranean* set of values (Matza 1964). The dominant values of contemporary societies stress work and everyday routines, but they coexist with other values that stress the need for excitement, leisure, and pleasure. These hedonistic, or pleasure-oriented, values are subterranean because they concern experiences that can be pursued only when the demands of employment and family life have been met. It is through their work—paid employment and unpaid work in the household—that people acquire the 'right' to freely enjoy their leisure activities and to pursue the subterranean values. Young sees this as involving a socialized conflict between the desire for pleasure and the repression of this desire as people engage in their everyday activities (Marcuse 1956). Through their socialization, he argues, adults acquire a feeling of guilt about any expression of these hedonistic values that has not been earned through hard work. Subterranean values can be exercised only with restraint and only so long as they do not undermine the normal everyday realities of work and family life.

The drugs that have come to be seen as problematic in contemporary societies are those that are used to induce an escape from everyday realities into an alternative world where hedonistic values alone prevail. They are seen to be associated with subcultures that disdain the work ethic and enjoy pleasures that have not been earned through work: 'It is drug use of this kind that is most actively repressed by the forces of social order. For it is not drugtaking *per se* but the culture of drugtakers which is reacted against: not the notion of changing consciousness but the type of consciousness that is socially generated' (J. Young 1971: 137). In contemporary societies, Young argues, this kind of drug use is to be found in the inner-city subcultures and certain of the youth subcultures.

Young found an overwhelming emphasis on drug use in the 'Bohemian youth culture' of the hippies of the 1960s. The use of mind-altering drugs was raised to a paramount position as one of the fundamental organizing principles for the identities of its members. This subculture—primarily a subculture of middle-class, student youth—was organized around spontaneity and expressivity and a rejection of work. It was in hippie culture that the main structural supports for cannabis use were found, and in the late 1960s Young documented its increasing emphasis also on the strong hallucinogenic drug LSD. What he called the delinquent youth culture, on the other hand, was more characteristic of some working-class areas. Young saw this as generating an ambivalent attitude towards drug use. While the delinquent subculture was organized around its strong emphasis on subterranean values, drug use was merely tolerated or allowed—it was not required.

Normalized drug use

Young's work was undertaken in a period of full employment and relative affluence. The period since he wrote has seen the emergence of mass unemployment and economic insecurity, exacerbated by a global recession. His conclusions must now be somewhat qualified. Illegal drug use today is not so focused on hippie youth who reject the work ethic. It is now more strongly emphasized by the inner-city unemployed who have no experience and no prospect of regular paid employment. Some glimpses of this were apparent in Young's references to the subculture of inner-city black Americans, as it has developed from the 1920s. He saw this as strongly supportive of cannabis use and as a principal source of heroin use. Their poverty and inferior status forced them into a rejection of conventional values and an embrace of subterranean values (Finestone 1964). Indeed, this was one of the principal contexts of drug use studied by Becker. This group has recently been identified as the core of a so-called underclass—an idea that we examine in Chapters 14 and 15.

In the 1970s, 'conformist youth culture' could still be seen as fully embracing conventional culture and its conditional commitment to hedonistic values. Its members were committed to work and to family, and their leisure-time activities posed no challenge to the dominance of the conventional values. Young saw this culture as having little significance for deviant drug-taking, holding that conformist youth simply made illicit use of alcohol (which they were not supposed to buy until aged 18) for the same purposes as their parents. It seems clear, however, that cannabis use has become common within this culture since the 1980s and that there was a growth in the use of Ecstasy in the 1990s. Declining employment opportunities in a period of recession broke the link between conventional work values and hedonistic values for many young people. Where there was little or no employment, the question of 'earning' pleasure simply did not arise.

Drug use has increased among all sections of youth. Almost a half (47 per cent) of 16 year olds in Manchester in 1992 were reported to have used an illegal drug, generally cannabis, and just under three-quarters (71 per cent) had been in situations where drugs were available and on offer. In a national survey of 15–16 year olds in 1996, 42 per cent had used an illegal drug (Parker and Measham 1994). Class and gender show little association with drug availability and take-up, but ethnicity does. Black youths are rather more likely to come into contact with drugs than are white youths, as suggested in an earlier study by Pryce (1986), and Asians are far less

The availability of drugs is now a normalized feature of youth culture.

likely to do so: only 32 per cent of young Asians in Manchester in 1992 reported having been offered drugs.

The ease of access to drugs such as cannabis—44 per cent of boys and 38 per cent of girls in 1996 had used it—shows that Becker's view of the importance of subcultures to occasional users must now be qualified. Changes in the urban and class conditions that sustained 'delinquent' subcultures in the past, combined with a more commercialized structure of illegal drug-trading, have resulted in a wider availability of drugs.

Drug use is now an integral, normalized part of a generalized 'conformist' youth culture, and not of specific class-based or deviant subcultures. Even the police are tolerant towards its use and will merely caution those cannabis users who come their way. Along with music, clothes, magazines, and a love of fast cars, drugs and alcohol are a part of the everyday, pleasure-seeking experience of virtually all young people. The countercultural Bohemian and hippie orientations that Young identified in the 1960s are no longer an important part of this youth subculture, which is now a consumerist and leisure-oriented subculture organized around the pursuit of pleasure that is disconnected from the requirement to 'earn' it through productive work.

Despite its high profile in the news media, Ecstasy (MDMA) is far less widely used than cannabis. In a national survey in 1996 9 per cent of boys and 7 per cent of girls reported having taken Ecstasy. Amphetamines (such as 'speed' and 'whizz'), LSD ('acid'), and solvents are all more widely used than Ecstasy: 20 per cent of boys and 21 per cent of girls had used solvents. Ecstasy, amphetamines, and LSD were all associated with regular involvement in dance clubs and raves; but in these venues, cannabis remains the most widely used illegal drug. Indeed, alcohol—consumed under age—was even more widespread: 94 per cent of 15–16 year olds in a national survey reported that they had consumed alcohol, generally on a regular basis. Over one-third were tobacco smokers, the rate of use and the rate of growth in use being higher among girls than among boys (Ettorre 1992, Oakley *et al.* 1992). These findings support the claim that there is now a 'poly-drug' culture in which users are not confined to the use of any one drug. Cannabis remains the drug of preference, but it is taken alongside other drugs (see Figure 5.5).

Not all drugs used by young people are normalized features of the conformist youth culture. Heroin use, for example, is found among less than 2 per cent of young people, and these generally have little involvement in consumerism and conventional family life. Indeed, 'conformist' drug users tend to regard heroin as a drug that would undermine their lifestyle. It is something to be avoided in favour of the more 'pleasure-oriented' drugs (M. Collison 1994). Auld *et al.* (1986) show that there is a characteristic *episodic user* of heroin: neither the occasional nor the regular user, but someone who has periods of sustained heroin use, followed by periods 'coming off' (see also Dorn and South 1987).

Retreatism and withdrawal from what is perceived as a hostile world are principal motives for those who have experienced a lifetime of emotional and physical abuse in broken families and poor districts (Ruggiero and South 1995: 116 ff). Such users find it difficult to band together for mutual support in the deprived city areas where the homeless congregate, and their lifestyle forces them into close association with a vast criminal underworld of dealers and organized crime (Dorn *et al.* 1992). In these circumstances, heroin users are very likely to make the transition from primary to secondary deviation.

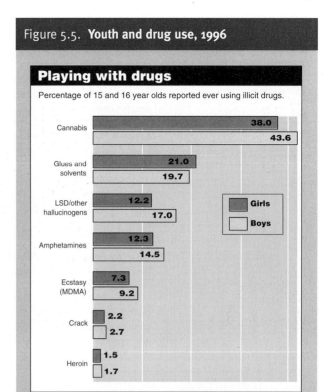

Figure 5.5. Youth and drug use, 1996

Playing with drugs

Percentage of 15 and 16 year olds reported ever using illicit drugs.

Drug	Girls	Boys
Cannabis	38.0	43.6
Glues and solvents	21.0	19.7
LSD/other hallucinogens	12.2	17.0
Amphetamines	12.3	14.5
Ecstasy (MDMA)	7.3	9.2
Crack	2.2	2.7
Heroin	1.5	1.7

Source: *Guardian*, 16 August 1996, drawing on a report in the *British Medical Journal*.

The feature film *Trainspotting* highlighted the relationship between drugs and crime.

Large-scale and small-scale dealing

'The largest drugs investigation ever run by Customs and Excise . . . code-named Operation Stealer, spanned three continents and led to the seizure of £65 million worth of cocaine and cannabis and 44 arrests. . . . Many of those convicted enjoyed expensive holidays in the Far East, the West Indies and the United States and some owned what the court was told were 'very expensive toys' including a £240,000 yacht, a £47,000 Mercedes convertible and a Harley Davidson motorbike.

'The operation targeted men who were believed to be deeply involved in the drugs trade between South America and Europe. It involved co-operation with law enforcement agencies in France, Switzerland, Spain, Italy, Brazil, Belgium, Colombia, Venezuela and the United States.' (*Guardian*, 1 July 1997)

'The world's drug trade has grown dramatically over the last decade and is now bigger that international trade in iron and steel and motor vehicles, according to a United Nations Report.' (*Guardian*, 26 June, 1997)

Professional traders are part of the same networks as small-time dealers:

'A sniffer dog found a teddy bear stuffed full of heroin when police raided a Colchester House. Nineteen packets of the drug were found in Lorraine Kelly's house . . . Cannabis was also found inside her bra.

'The judge told Kelly: 'You were storing heroin prepared for resale in individual smaller quantities for the supplier. You were part of a team who were dealing in heroin. Your role was to store the drugs. . . . He jailed her for a total of three years.'   (*Essex County Standard*, 18 July, 1997)

In the inner-city areas, the growth of an informal economy has been associated with the expansion of an extensive fringe of irregular activities—street-level thieving, dealing and exchange of stolen and illicit goods of all kinds (Auld *et al.* 1986). The unemployed residents of these areas seek to make more than the bare public assistance level of income through involvement in these activities. Cannabis has, since the 1960s, become more closely tied to professional drug-dealing and, along with hard drugs such as heroin and cocaine, is traded on the streets. It has been estimated that, by 1997, the number of drug deals in London alone had reached an annual total of 30 million, with a total value of £600 million. Only around 1 in 4,000 street deals results in an arrest.

Through their involvement in this irregular economy, the unemployed can easily become involved in drug-dealing, and the opportunities for use are great. Small-scale users and others become drawn into large networks of organized drug crime. There is a hierarchical division of labour in the supply of drugs, and the largest rewards tend to go to those who are furthest removed from street-level dealing.

SUMMARY POINTS

In this section we have looked at how people learn to obtain and to use drugs for pleasure, and we traced the growing normalization of certain types of drug use.

▶ It is not easy to define the meaning of the word 'drug' or to distinguish the medical and non-medical uses of drugs.

▶ People drift into drug use for a whole variety of reasons, and not all enter a career of persistent drug use.

▶ Persistent drug users pass through a series of stages in which their experiences and identities alter.

▶ The use of drugs is closely involved with ideas of work, leisure, and pleasure.

▶ Use of certain drugs has been normalized in youth culture. Rates of use are now very high.

▶ The use of drugs and trading in them on the streets and in clubs is closely tied into large international networks of drug-trafficking and organized crime.

SEX AND SEXUALITY

In Chapter 4 we looked at sex differences in relation to the concept of sex–gender differences in social life. We define these in relation to the biological categories of male and female. The word 'sex' is also used in another, related sense to describe physical, erotic behaviour between men and women. Use of the word in this latter sense originated in nineteenth-century biology, which saw sexual behaviour as the mechanism of reproduction in all animal species. Through some kind of sexual relations, male and female animals produce offspring that grow into the parents of the next generation. Erotic behaviour between men and women—sexual intercourse—was, then, seen as the natural form of human reproduction. Sex, it was held, is a natural, instinctive drive that impels people to engage in the very behaviour that ensures the reproduction and survival of the human species.

This biological view of sexual behaviour might appear quite straightforward, but matters are not that simple. We have already seen how sexual differences are socially constructed into sex–gender differences. It should come as no surprise to find that sexual behaviour is also a socially constructed reality. The view of sexual behaviour as a natural drive, oriented towards reproduction, is inextricably linked with conventional ideas about sex–gender differences. Sexuality cannot be considered apart from the social meanings that are given to it. What counts as normal sexual behaviour in a society depends upon how sex–gender differences are defined in that society.

SEX AND SEXUAL DIFFERENCE

Through their socialization, people come to learn both the public norms concerning sex and the more implicit rules and meanings that structure sexual activity and establish a conception of normal sex. These social meanings confront people as social facts, objective realities that are deeply embedded in their everyday life. In contemporary societies, this idea of normal sex is linked firmly to gender identities, romantic love, and family relationships. Normal sex takes place between a man and a woman who are involved in a long-term marital relationship; it is a private activity that takes place only at certain times and in certain places; and it is an activity that involves only certain kinds of physical act.

Sex can be a pleasurable activity. Whatever reproductive purposes it may have in family relationships, it is also engaged in for its own sake. The erotic and sensual aspects of sex underpin and make possible its reproductive uses. Much sexual behaviour has pleasure—not procreation—as its purpose. This autonomy of erotic sex from sexual reproduction is clear from such practices as the widespread use of contraception—to *prevent* reproduction—and the continuation of sexual activity by women who are past the age at which conception is possible.

The autonomy of the erotic from the function of reproduction highlights the great diversity that can exist in sexual behaviour between men and women. It also shows the wide range of objects and situations that can acquire a sexual or erotic meaning: people can be 'turned on' by shoes, photographs, rubber clothes, and their own thoughts, as well as by the actual presence of a sexual partner. This also makes it very clear that such erotic concerns have no necessary connection to male–female (heterosexual) interactions. Homosexual and 'autoerotic' activities are widespread and, in terms of their pleasurable, erotic dimensions, cannot be distinguished from heterosexual activities. The stereotype of normal sex misunderstands the socially constructed nature of sexual behaviour, and misrepresents the type and range of sexual activity that does, in fact, occur.

Normal sex

Contemporary views on normal sex draw on a view of the past. The situation today is often related to a supposed 'decline' in standards today. What accurate information we have about sexual behaviour in the past suggests that this view contains a rather idealized version of the past. Indeed, it seems that each generation criticizes young people in terms of standards that they, mistakenly, believe their own parents to have observed. For example, 44 per cent of those interviewed in a large national survey in 1949 thought that sexual standards were declining (J. Harrison 1949).

Premarital sex seems to have increased throughout the twentieth century. Nineteen per cent of married women born before 1904 reported that they had sex before their marriage. The proportion rose to 36 per cent among those born between 1904 and 1914, and by

The national sex survey

Planning for the *National Survey of Sexual Attitudes and Lifestyles* began in 1986. With the support of the Department of Health, the Health Education Authority, and various scientific bodies, a proposal for funding was put forward. A pilot study was undertaken and the proposal was sent for ministerial approval. Instead of receiving approval, fieldwork plans were halted while the project was passed to a senior Cabinet committee for consideration. The press soon leaked the fact that the then Prime Minister, Margaret Thatcher, had directly intervened to block the survey, arguing that an investigation into sexual behaviour was an inappropriate way to spend public money. Faced with this decision, the researchers sought private funding from medical charities, and the main survey was eventually able to go ahead.

The survey collected data through face-to-face interviews, each lasting just under one hour, and self-completion questionnaires. It used a sample of adults at addresses drawn from the Post Office register (the Postcode Address File). Just under 30,000 addresses containing adults aged 16–59 were drawn at random, of which 63.3 per cent (18,876 people) agreed to be interviewed. The interview schedule contained sixty-four lengthy questions, and the self-completion questionnaire a further twenty-one. Fieldwork was carried out by 488 interviewers in 1991. Full details can be found in Wellings *et al.* (1994).

1934 it had reached 43 per cent. There is some evidence that these rates varied by class. Virginity at marriage seems to have been most likely in poorer families and least likely among wealthier families. This must, in part, reflect the relative lack of opportunities for premarital sex for those who lived in small, cramped houses. A study of sexual behaviour in the working-class districts of Bolton in 1939 reported that for most young, unmarried couples the streets, parks, and back alleys were all that were available for their 'courting'. For this reason, large numbers of those interviewed in a survey in 1946 said that they would have had sex before marriage if they had the opportunity to do so (Burke 1994).

The first half of the twentieth century was, however, a period of considerable sexual ignorance for most people. They knew little about human anatomy and even less about the causes of pregnancy. Knowledge about contraception was very limited. This ignorance meant that rates of illegitimacy, abortion, and sexual disease were high. Nevertheless, rates of illegitimacy fell from the 1870s until the 1940s. This suggests that, when premarital sex resulted in pregnancy, a marriage rapidly followed. Sexual ignorance continued after marriage. For many couples—and particularly for women—the sex that occurred, on average, about twice per week was hardly a source of pleasure (Hall 1991; see also T. Harrison 1949).

The most comprehensive investigation into sexual behaviour in Britain was that undertaken in a large survey carried out in 1991 (Wellings *et al.* 1994), from which a number of important conclusions can be drawn.

The national survey of 1991 showed that heterosexual experiences began quite early in life—at age 13 or 14 for the youngest people in the sample—and that first sexual intercourse occurred around three or four years later. These average figures, of course, hide a number of age, gender, and ethnic differences. More detailed figures show a decline in the age of first sexual intercourse over the century. Women born in the early 1930s first had sex at about 21, for those born in the late 1940s the age had fallen to 19, and for those born since the middle of the 1960s it was 17. Among men, the corresponding ages were 20, 18, and 17.

A quarter of young men and almost one in five young women had sex before they were 16 years old. This was especially marked among those in manual work and those who left school at the minimum leaving age. Those who identified themselves as Indian, Pakistani, or Bangladeshi showed a much higher than average age for first sex, while those who saw themselves as black began sexual activity much earlier than the national average. Religion had much less effect, though Roman Catholics were more likely to begin sexual activity at an earlier age than were non-Christians or those who described themselves as Church of England.

For most people, sex took place in established and stable relationships, though the meaning of the relationship differed somewhat between men and women. Among men, first sex was seen, most commonly, as resulting from curiosity about 'what it would be like'. Women, on the other hand, said that their first sex occurred because they were 'in love'. Once involved in a partnership, whether married or cohabiting, most people remained monogamous. Nevertheless, about 3 per cent of married people and 11 per cent of cohabitees reported having had two or more sexual partners during the year before the interview. This was especially marked among men.

Married and cohabiting partners typically had sex once or twice per week, with the frequency of sex declining somewhat with age and with the length of the relationship. Their sexual activities were not, however, confined to the conventional image of normal penetrative intercourse. While this was, indeed, the most common form of sex, 80 per cent of men and 75 per cent of women had engaged in mutual masturbation, and 75 per cent of men and 70 per cent of women had engaged in oral sex. These rates showed little association with age, rates of oral sex among people aged over 45 being 62 per cent for men and 50 per cent for women. Sixty-four per cent of all married men and 58 per cent of all married women had oral sex in the year before the interviews.

Most people in the survey reported exclusively heterosexual relationships, but homosexual experiences were far from uncommon. Six per cent of men and 3 per cent of women reported having had some homosexual experiences. These involved genital contact in about half of all cases. Rates for homosexual activity were higher among non-manual than among manual workers, and they were higher in London than in any other part of the country. Exclusively homosexual relationships were reported for just 0.3 per cent of men and 0.1 per cent of women, rates of bisexual experience being much higher at 3.4 per cent and 1.7 per cent. The validity of the results of the survey on these highly sensitive matters, however, has been questioned, and levels of homosexual experience are believed to be very much higher than recorded in the survey (Stanley 1995).

The national survey found that people's attitudes were often, though not always, different from their behaviour. While three-quarters of people did not consider premarital sex to be wrong, nearly 80 per cent thought that adultery (extramarital sex) was wrong. About one-third of men and two-thirds of women thought casual 'one-night stands' were wrong. Attitudes towards homosexuality were far harsher. More than two-thirds of men and over a half of women said that sex between men was always or mostly wrong, though they were marginally more tolerant towards sex between women. These levels of intolerance towards homosexuality are similar to those found in the United States.

Deviant forms of sexual behaviour are labelled as such against the backdrop of what is taken for normal in a particular society. Sexual behaviour is no mere natural, biologically rooted drive. It is a meaningful social activity that is defined and produced in socially variable ways. As Weeks has argued in his admirable summary of this whole question: 'The physiology and morphology of the body provides for human sexuality. Biology conditions and limits what is possible. But it does not cause the patterns of sexual life' (Weeks 1986: 25).

Becoming homosexual

The fact that sex is not a purely biological matter means that, while biological factors clearly play a part in sexual activity, those forms of sexual activity that come to be defined as 'deviant' cannot simply be assumed to be biologically different from normal ones. There has, for example, been much media comment about a possible genetic influence on homosexuality, leading some to speculate on the existence of a 'gay gene'. Even if there does turn out to be a genetic basis to sexual preference, the meanings that are attributed to this biological predisposition and the ways in which it might be expressed in behaviour are highly variable and are not themselves matters of biology.

Activities that are conventionally labelled as homosexual today, and therefore as deviant, have been seen as perfectly normal activities in many societies, including ancient Greece and traditional Japan. It is only recently that homosexuality has been seen as an identity-defining characteristic. No historically *specific* identity or role can properly be explained in terms of *universal* genetic characteristics alone. A

Genetic controls

'James Watson, the Nobel prize winner who discovered DNA, the human genetic code, has provoked outrage by claiming that women should be allowed an abortion if their unborn babies are found to be carrying a gene for homosexuality: "Some day a child is going to sue its parents for being born. They will say: my life is so awful with these terrible genetic defects and you just callously didn't find out. Or, you knew and you didn't do anything about it."'

Source: Sunday Telegraph, 16 February 1997.

▶ **What sociological response might there be to such claims?**

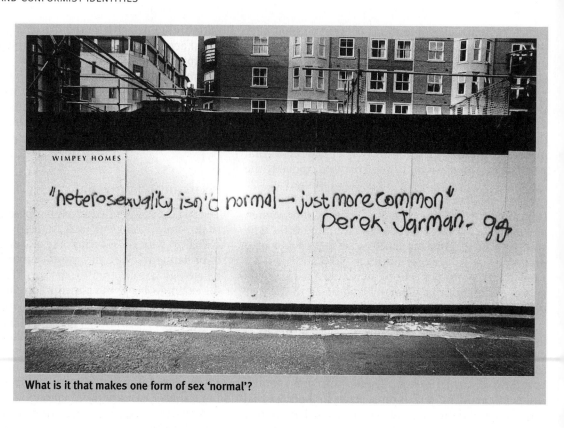

What is it that makes one form of sex 'normal'?

sociological perspective on sexual deviance shows that, whatever natural differences there may be among individuals, these are always subject to social definition.

Contemporary Western ideas of normal sex developed within a framework of Christian thought. This emphasized marriage and reproduction, and it established a view of non-marital sex as sinful. The secular medical and psychiatric discourses of the eighteenth and nineteenth centuries transformed this view of sexual deviance from one of 'sin' to one of 'perversion' or 'abnormality' (Foucault 1976). There were concerns about the morality of non-reproductive sex and the need to protect the domestic ideal of womanhood and the family. These were apparent in

☞ **You will find a discussion of medical and psychiatric discourse in Chapter 6, p. 193. There is no need to read that now, but you may like to return briefly to our discussion of normal sex when you have worked through 'Sex, Bodies, and Populations' in that chapter, pp. 191–4.**

the treatment of prostitution as a major social danger and in the hostility that there was towards the use of contraceptive measures. The medical and psychiatric viewpoint also defined a whole range of sexual 'perversions'.

The principal 'perversion' that came to be identified in nineteenth-century scientific discourse was male homosexuality. Along with the homosexual, a number of other sexual types were recognized, each with its own specific nature. The transvestite, the sado-masochist, and the paedophile all joined the homosexual as popular folk devils. The homosexual was seen as having specific psychological characteristics that reflected his inescapable nature. Homosexuality was seen as a personality disorder that resulted from biological pathology. In a related vein, psychoanalytic theory saw homosexuality as resulting from failures of socialization that occurred among boys with domineering mothers and weak fathers. Such boys, Freud argued, remained 'fixated' at an immature stage of sexual development. Homosexuality, then, came to be seen as a psychiatric disorder, as a form of mental illness. It was officially defined in this way by the American Psychiatric Association until the 1970s.

The work of Ken Plummer (1975) has shown very

clearly that sexual deviance—specifically, male homo-sexuality—can best be understood if it is seen as a process of social learning. Plummer argues that sexual socialization involves learning to define oneself as sexual and then continuing to manage that definition and its consequences for other aspects of one's life. People gradually become committed to a particular sexual identity and to the actual or anticipated sexual practices that are associated with it. Core sexual ideas are built up at the same time that gender identities are initially established, during primary socialization, but the period of adolescence is critical for adult sexual identity. At a time when the biological changes of puberty are occurring, sexual identity is crystallized around the already established gender identity. It is in the peer group, rather than the family, that this adoles-cent sexual socialization takes place.

Plummer's study shows that this is a time when boys tend to enter into casual and irregular exploratory sexual encounters with other boys. Mutual masturba-tion, for example, has been especially common at single-sex boys' schools. In most cases, these are tran-sient encounters, and the behaviour is normalized by all concerned. It takes place in private or semi-private places, it is not usually visible to non-participants, and many non-participants, in any case, are tolerant or 'turn a blind eye'.

In some circumstances, however, boys may come to identify these activities and their own involvement in them as signs or indications of homosexual inclina-tions. This is likely if they have other reasons for feeling different from other boys. These feelings may involve an over-concern about what are believed to be 'proper' male activities. A boy may, for example, be more inter-ested in art, literature, or hairstyles than in football or aggressive sports, and he may, as a result, be seen as 'sissy'. Such boys are particularly likely to feel that their apparent cultural difference from other boys is a sign of their sexual difference. This self-identification is most likely if parents, teachers, or other boys pass remarks about their 'effeminacy'—they are 'a bit of a girl'—or stigmatize a homosexual encounter by describing them as 'queer'.

Most boys are able to deny these thoughts of sexual difference. They see their sexual experiences as merely passing phases and as having no lasting significance. Some who are isolated are more likely to persist in their self-identification. They have no attachments to social groups that can support their denial and a homosexual identity may become crystallized. In these circum-stances, feelings of guilt or shame are aroused by the negative image that homosexuality has in the wider culture. As a result, the boy's feelings about his identity

are kept secret and he may become more and more soli-tary. This solitude reinforces his sexual identity because it cuts him off from the possibility of hetero-sexual experiences.

Some people may persist in this way for the whole of their lives, passing as normal. Others, however, com-plete the transition to secondary deviation by 'coming out' as homosexuals. Coming out is an open avowal of homosexuality. It allows someone greater, and more open, contact with others who are perceived to be similar to them. Meeting their own people, those who share their identity and with whom they can feel at ease, brings them into contact with alternative, more positive views of homosexuality, and they are able to reconstruct their sense of self in more positive terms. They fully enter the homosexual role (McIntosh 1968) and become committed to a 'gay' identity. Through contacts with other homosexuals in clubs, pubs, and elsewhere, they are drawn into a subculture of homo-sexuality that sustains possibilities for meeting sexual partners and provides meanings that legitimate their new sexual identity.

Participation in a subculture of homosexuality allows men to reject the conventional stereotype of the effeminate homosexual, if they so wish, and allows them a greater choice of identity. This choice, of course, reflects the range of meanings available in the subcul-ture of homosexuality. During the 1970s, for example, 'camp' forms of behaviour that parodied conventional ideas of masculinity and femininity gave way to more 'macho' styles and identities. For many, however, the subculture of homosexuality simply gives them the confidence and possibility to 'be themselves', pursuing the very activities and interests that once defined them as different. The subculture of homosexuality also pro-vides opportunities for political involvement in move-ments of social change aimed at altering the status and life chances of gay and lesbian people. Indeed, the very word gay came to be adopted during the 1950s and 1960s as a deliberate strategy for politicizing homosex-uality and constructing a more positive self-image.

Telling sexual stories

We now live in a world in which 'it's good to talk' and there is great encouragement to verbalize one's feel-ings. Plummer (1995) has explored the ways in which sexual identities of all kinds are explored and recon-structed through the production of narrative accounts of personal biography. These personal sexual narratives arise out of the various social worlds in which a person is involved, including the subculture of homosexuality and other sexual subcultures. They may, however, contribute to the reproduction or transformation of the very cultural imagery on which they draw. Plummer saw the collection of sexual narratives as an important way of understanding the changing meanings of sexuality. Some sexual narratives are published in books, magazines, or broadcasts, but Plummer also wanted to collect the private narratives that are recounted only among small circles of friends or, perhaps, only to oneself. Although using the word story to describe these accounts, Plummer is not implying that they are fictional accounts. A **sexual story** is a reconstruction of a person's sexual biography from the standpoint of his or her current situation. It is a genuine attempt to make sense of his or her experiences and moral career.

 In addition to published sources, Plummer used a wide range of personal contacts to encourage people to write down their sexual stories or to provide them in interviews. Look at our discussion of documentary research in Chapter 3, pp. 91–4, and see what problems you can identify in this research design. You might like to look at Plummer's own methodological discoussion in his book *Documents of Life* (Plummer 1983).

Plummer shows that the sexual narratives of those who came out as gay during the 1960s and 1970s, when it first became possible for such stories to be made public on any scale, show a particular pattern. They present biographical accounts that follow a linear, deterministic structure that 'explains' a 'truth' about the person's life. They tend to revolve around a common pattern in which sexual suffering is survived and then surpassed or overcome:

'Stories of suffering, surviving and surpassing are personal experience stories which speak initially of a deep pain, a frustration, an anguish sensed as being linked to the sexual. They speak of a silence and a secrecy which may need to be broken. They are stories which tell of a need for action—something must be done, a pain must be transcended. There is a move from suffering, secrecy, and an often felt sense of victimisation towards a major change: therapy, survival, recovery or politics. Often harboured within is an epiphany, a crucial turning point marked by a radical consciousness raising. The narrative plot is driven by an acute suffering, the need to break a silence, a 'coming out' and a 'coming to terms'. These are always stories of significant transformations.'   (Plummer 1995: 50)

The most significant act in the development of homosexuality is coming out and announcing one's gayness to others. Those who have come out recount their stories to friends, colleagues, and others. The telling of sexual stories in a gay club, for example, helps to reinforce the identities of the storytellers through their shared experiences and creates a sense of solidarity that can sustain them in the future.

Gay and lesbian accounts of coming out, Plummer argues, tend to follow a common storyline. This begins with a frustrated or stigmatized erotic desire for someone of one's own sex, and moves on to explorations into one's childhood and youth in an attempt to uncover 'motives' and 'memories', feelings of unhappiness and 'difference', that would 'explain' this desire. The accounts then proceed to a crisis or turning point—perhaps a 'discovery'—that leads to a complete reconsideration of one's past and the building of a new identity, often with the help of others who are in the same situation. A sense of identity and community is established. Subcultures of homosexuality—gay social worlds—are crucial conditions for the production of these accounts.

Plummer suggests that a similar pattern is found in other sexual stories—stories of sexual abuse, of 'sex addiction', of pornography, of fetishism, and of rape experiences. In the case of rape, for example, he suggests that from the 1960s and 1970s there was a recasting of women's narratives of rape in the same 'suffering, surviving, and surpassing' structure that has just been described. These accounts were sustained by the women's movement and contributed to its focal concerns. Rape stories generally begin with the denial or non-recognition of an act of sexual violence that leads to a felt need to remain silent and in a state of constant fear. The turning point comes when it is discovered that other women have suffered in the same way. The women come to see their private troubles as being a public issue. Rape is seen as part of a wider continuum of sexual violence—domestic violence, sexual harassment, and so on—and women see a need to support one another in countering this male violence. Through this recognition, women are helped to 'fight back' and to become 'survivors' rather than 'victims'.

These sexual stories, as they become public, enter into a new politics of what Plummer calls 'intimate citizenship'. They contribute to a broadening of cultural self-understanding. The dominance of the expert or the authority figure—the doctor, the psychologist, and even the sociologist—is finally broken, and participants are able to make their own views known and to begin to shape a more autonomous cultural and political agenda. The formulation and publication of sexual stories are part of an emancipatory politics that has been sustained by the gay movement and the women's movement (see also Giddens 1992). As this emancipation proceeds, Plummer argues, so it is possible for new kinds of sexual stories to emerge, stories that depart from the linear, deterministic structure inherited from the past and that begin to explore diversity, difference, and multiplicity in personal and sexual identities.

SUMMARY POINTS

In this section we have looked at sexual behaviour and the ways in which some forms of this behaviour come to be defined as deviant.

▶ Ideas of normal sex are quite variable over time and from one society to another. People come to learn what is 'normal' through their socialization.

▶ Evidence on sexual behaviour shows great diversity in practices and shows that people engage in a far wider range of activities than they would admit in public. This was as true in the past as it is today.

▶ Homosexuality is a social role that is learned and is reinforced by social experiences. Many boys engage in homosexual behaviour, but this is rarely a significant aspect of their social identity.

▶ The crucial factor in shaping homosexuality is public labelling and stigmatization.

▶ Those who come out as gay are likely to find support and encouragement in a subculture of homosexuality.

▶ People explore their identity by telling sexual stories that account for it to themselves and to others.

REVISION AND EXERCISES

Review the various Summary points in this chapter. You may find it useful to consider these in relation to our discussion of socialization and identity in Chapter 4. The topics that we considered can usefully be revised in three groups: the most general issues raised about deviance, issues related to crime and criminality, and issues related to conformity and deviance in the pursuit of pleasure.

DEVIANCE, REACTION, AND IDENTITY

In 'Understanding Deviance and Control' we set out a number of general ideas that were applied to deviance in later parts of the chapter:

▶ **How would you distinguish between 'difference' and 'deviance'?**

▶ **What were the three levels of explanation that we identified in the study of deviance?**

▶ **Make sure that you understand the meaning of the following terms: labelling, primary deviation, secondary deviation, stigmatization; secret deviant, drift, role deviance, career deviance; differential association; the own, the wise.**

▶ **Familiarize yourself with the key ideas on deviance that are associated with: Becker, Lemert, Goffman, Lombroso.**

Many writers and commentators on deviance still look to biology for the causes of crime. Look back at our discussion of biological and cultural determinism in Chapter 4, pp. 121–4, and then consider the following questions:

▶ Lombroso and other biological theorists used terms such as 'atavism', 'degenerate', 'lower races', and 'born criminal'. Can these be considered to have any scientific meaning, or are they mere value judgements?

▶ How much attention should sociologists give to recent developments in genetics that have claimed to identify the genes responsible for particular kinds of behaviour?

CRIME AND CRIMINAL CAREERS

We began our discussion of crime with an account of the distinctive features of the criminal law, distinguishing it from civil law, constitutional law, and other specialist forms of law. We then looked at criminal behaviour as a specific form of deviance. A number of the issues that we looked at concern the formal and informal social organization of crime:

▶ What do you understand by the following terms: craft crime, project crime, underworld, white-collar crime?

▶ How plausible is it to describe career crime as a job? Why are women less likely than men to engage in a career of theft?

▶ What problems are involved in calculating the economic significance of corporate crime?

One of the central issues in the study of crime is to assess its extent and distribution and then to look at how these are related to social conditions:

▶ Compare the data in Figures 5.2 and 5.4. Why are the numbers in each category of offence so different in the two tables? Which type of crime reported to the police is most likely to result in a conviction or caution? And which is the least likely?

▶ How are small-scale theft and drug-dealing related to contemporary economic conditions?

Finally, you will need to review the ideas of the main theorists of crime that we have discussed:

▶ Make sure that you are familiar with the key ideas of McIntosh and Sutherland.

SEX, DRUGS, AND PLEASURE

Our sections on drugs and sexuality looked at diverse ways in which people pursue pleasure, and we paid particular attention to the ways that their actions come to be seen as conformist or deviant:

▶ Why is there such great diversity in the social reaction to different drugs and other mood-changing substances?

▶ How useful is it to relate prostitution to sex–gender roles and normal patterns of sex?

▶ How would you define the following terms: occasional user, regular user, addiction, hedonism, retreatism, normal sex, sexual narrative, intimate citizenship.

▶ Make sure that you understand the main ideas of Becker, Young, Plummer.

You should give some attention to the particular methodological problems involved in trying to find accurate information about these matters. You will find some useful background in Chapter 3:

▶ Using the data in Figure 5.5, draw pie charts of drug use for both girls and boys. Are the data in the figure likely to be reliable? Why is this?

▶ What are the main problems involved in obtaining accurate information about sexual behaviour?

FURTHER READING

Good overviews of the subjects in this chapter are:

Becker, H. S. (1963), *Outsiders: Studies in the Sociology of Deviance* (New York: Free Press). This is a landmark study that still repays a close reading.

Heidensohn, F. (1985), *Women and Crime* (London: Macmillan). A very useful and comprehensive overview of the gendering of criminal activity.

Croal, H. (1992), *White Collar Crime* (Buckingham: Open University Press). An up-to-date account of the nature and significance of white-collar crime.

Weeks, J. (1986), *Sexuality* (London: Tavistock). A thorough, lively, and readable introduction to the sociology of sex.

Plummer, K. (1975), *Sexual Stigma: An Interactionist Account* (London: Routledge). A classic study of homosexuality that makes powerful use of symbolic interactionist theory.

Further and more detailed information can be found in:

Matza, D. (1964), *Delinquency and Drift* (New York: John Wiley & Sons). An important work that emphasizes the fact that much criminal behaviour results from 'drift' and circumstances, rather than from commitment to a criminal career.

Goffman, E. (1963), *Stigma* (Englewood Cliffs, NJ: Prentice-Hall). Like all of Goffman's work, this is very readable and has been massively influential. He sets out a general model of the stigmatization of deviance and difference.

Wellings, K., Field, J., Johnson, A., and Wadsworth, J. (1994), *Sexual Behaviour in Britain: The National Survey of Sexual Attitudes and Lifestyles* (Harmondsworth: Penguin). An encyclopædic, though flawed, survey of contemporary sexual lifestyles. Worth looking at for a consideration of research methods.

Dorn, N., Murji, K., and South, N. (1992), *Traffickers* (London: Routledge). An important book by some of the leading figures in the study of the organized criminal drug trade.

Young, J. (1971), *The Drugtakers* (London: McGibbon & Kee). Young's emphasis on the hippies now seems a little outdated, but the book has much to say about the relationship between work, pleasure, and social control.

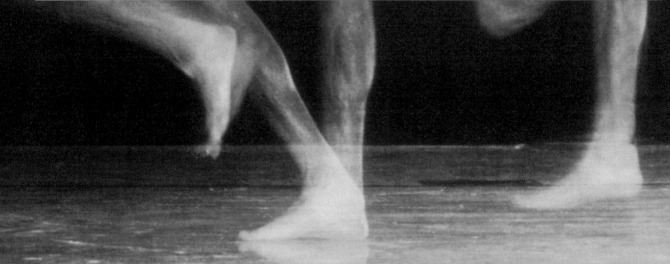

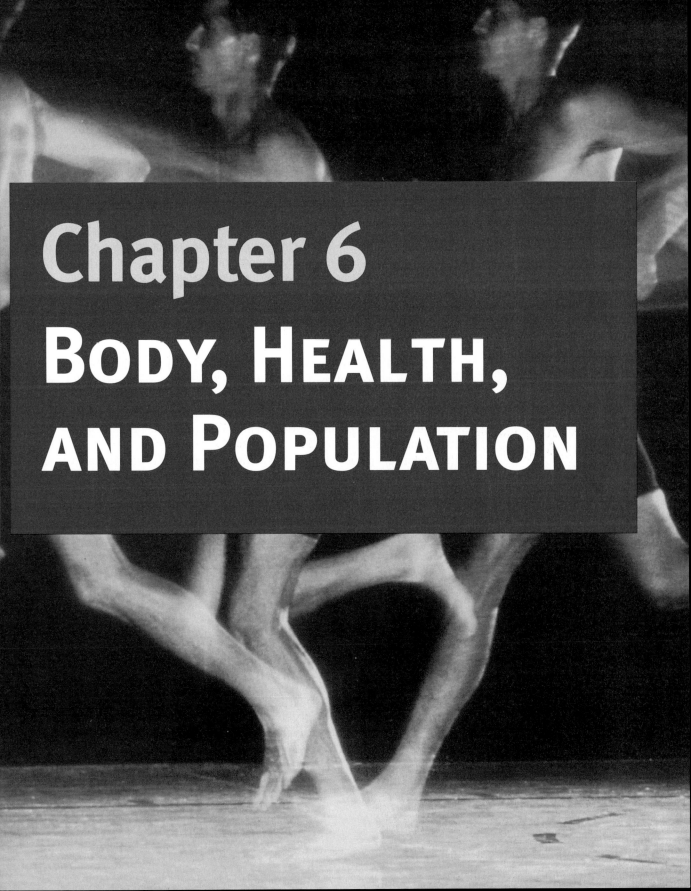

Chapter 6
BODY, HEALTH, AND POPULATION

A psychiatric career

'My psychiatric "career" began in 1991, when I felt everything was closing in and I couldn't cope. So I took an overdose. . . . I started to overdose because I felt so desperate and depressed.

'Eventually I was put on a compulsory section under the Mental Health Act because I said I was a risk to myself, and I remained in hospital for about eight months because of my "difficult" behaviour. . . . This was due to depression and was my way of coping with feelings by attempting to annihilate myself and everything.

'On discharge, I stayed out of hospital for six months, but found it difficult coping with my job living once again in the community. I found colleagues tended to treat me as one might an individual with a disability. . . . After about six months the depression was more severe and I was taking more overdoses. . . . I was taken back to the psychiatric hospital.

'When I left hospital I had to fight to see a community psychiatric nurse. . . . I was not told what benefits I was entitled to and had to find out for myself when I felt able. This led to me losing benefits I was entitled to. . . . Before leaving hospital, I had lived a lie and kept saying I felt well as I desperately wanted to leave hospital and make a go of things and try to survive. But I could not cope on leaving hospital.'

Source: Deborah Tallis, *Guardian*, 5 Feb. 1997.

DEBORAH Tallis is one of a growing number of women whose depression leads to long periods of medical treatment. She has moved continually from the community to hospital and back again over a period of more than six years. When she is in hospital, she wants only to be outside again. When she is released, her difficulties in coping and getting welfare benefits make her long for the relative security of hospital.

What is depression, and why is it so difficult to treat? If it is an illness, why does it seem less responsive to treatment than other diseases? In this chapter we will look at the ways in which both psychiatric and physical illnesses are subject to a process of social construction. They are the products of a long-term transformation in medical understanding that began in the eighteenth century, and they have become the objects of the political and economic activities of the state. Control over the minds and bodies of its population have become a major feature of state policy, and the nature of contemporary medicine cannot be understood in isolation from this. Deborah Tallis would be the first to recognize that her personal troubles are inextricably linked to the public issues of financing medical and welfare provision.

In the section on 'Understanding Bodies' we look at the ways in which individual bodies and populations have been controlled, examining the arguments of Foucault. Aspects of individual health and population demography are considered in 'Population, Health, and Modernity', where we present an account of the consequences of the development of industrial societies. In the final section on 'Medicine, Minds, and Bodies' we look at the medical control and regulation of bodies, in life and in death, and at the shaping of mental problems by medical interventions. We also consider how these interventions are related to cultural conceptions of femininity and beauty.

UNDERSTANDING BODIES

The role of the state in controlling the bodies of its members has been described in some detail by Michel Foucault. His work provides an essential context for understanding the development of the medical profession and of modern forms of medical practice. He relates these to the transformation of states and their capacities to exercise powers of surveillance over their populations.

SEX, BODIES, AND POPULATIONS

Foucault sees the late eighteenth century as the crucial point in the rise of what he calls a **disciplinary society**. This was a form of society in which there was a growing concern to secure the human base of national wealth by introducing new forms of social power over human biology. These forms of power were the demographic control (or *regulation*) of whole populations, and the anatomical control (or *discipline*) of individual human bodies.

Regulating populations

The idea of a national 'population' came into use as an economic and political category as the leading nation states strived to expand their national wealth and productive powers at the end of the eighteenth century. A population was seen not as an aggregate of individuals but as an entity in its own right, having specific properties of its own. These properties were what Durkheim (1895) was to call 'social facts'. They concerned characteristics of the nation as a whole: its level of productivity, rate of employment, rate of growth, level of national wealth, and so on. Nation states recognized that these variables depended, to a crucial degree, on the size and well-being of their population and the productive powers of its members. These, in turn, depended on the sexual behaviour of its members. As Foucault (1976: 25–6) put it: 'At the heart of this economic and political problem of population was sex: it was necessary to analyse the birth rate, the age of marriage, the legitimate and illegitimate births, the precocity and frequency of sexual relations, the ways of making them fertile or sterile, the effects of unmarried life or of the prohibitions, the impact of contraceptive practices.'

Thus, a whole new range of social facts were identified for study: rates of birth and death, trends in life expectancy, rates of suicide, levels of health and disease, patterns of diet, and so on. At a national level, there was a growing concern to suppress all forms of sexuality that were not directly linked to procreation and, therefore, to the reproduction of the population. The sexual conduct of the population became the object of analysis and a target for intervention by nation states.

The fertility, health, and welfare of a population, the crucial conditions for its reproduction, are all linked to sexual activity. Sex became a public issue to be

---

Michel Foucault   Michel Foucault (1926–84) was born in Poitiers, France. He was the son of a doctor and studied philosophy at the École Normale Supérieure in Paris. While there he joined the Communists, though he left the party in the early 1950s. Disillusioned by the failure of philosophy to provide him with answers to the great questions of human existence, he turned to the study of psychology and psychopathology. He spent the period from 1952 to 1955 carrying out research into psychiatric practices in mental hospitals, and he wrote a short book on mental illness.

During academic visits to Sweden and Poland he switched his attention to the history of philosophy and science, and particularly to the history of medical science. He soon completed his first major book in this area, *Madness and Civilization* (1961), and this was soon followed by *The Birth of the Clinic* (1963).

More general works in history and theory and a diverse array of specialized investigations led to his masterly *Discipline and Punish* (1975). By this time he had already begun the research for what he intended to be a six-volume history of sexuality, though only parts of this (1976, 1984a, 1984b) were to appear before his death.

regulated through techniques of surveillance and intervention. Observation of birth, death, and marriage rates in censuses and surveys, the compilation of official statistics by government agencies, the undertaking of public health and housing schemes, and control over migration were all developed as ways of regulating the 'social body'.

Foucault saw the introduction of these demographic controls as the establishment of a **biopolitics** of the population. This involved new forms of discourse that shaped and gave direction to the demographic controls. Statistics and later demography, for example, defined ways of mapping a population in numerical terms and measuring its key characteristics. These new forms of knowledge became central to state policy. Indeed, the word 'statistics' has its origins in the idea of collecting facts relevant to the state. In a related way, political economy provided ways of mapping the resources that were available to a population and the division of labour through which these resources were used. The emergence and growth of sociology itself, with its concept of 'society', involved a recognition that human populations had come to be defined by nation-state boundaries and could not be seen as mere aggregates of individuals.

Medical experts played a key part in this reorientation of social thought. According to the medical point of view, populations were complex organic wholes—social bodies—that could exhibit 'pathological' social problems that required effective treatment. This treatment could be achieved through an informed social policy that was aimed at restoring normal 'health'. The health of the social body was seen as dependent, in large part, on the health of the individual bodies from which it was composed. Public-health measures, such as sanitation and housing improvements, were seen as means to improve the general health of the population. Fear of the effects of such diseases as cholera and typhus were eventually met by the introduction of sewerage and freshwater schemes, urban paving and rebuilding, by regulations over the burial of dead bodies, and through the expansion of hospital medicine. These public health measures were linked to other techniques of regulation that were massively expanded during the nineteenth century. The police and the prisons, the workhouses and poor-law welfare administration all contributed to the regulation and control of human populations.

Disciplining the body

The second form of power, anatomical control, involved new disciplines of the body. Foucault describes these as comprising the **anatomo-politics** of the body. This form of power rested on a view of the body as a mechanism with capabilities and skills that had to be optimized in order to increase its usefulness and to integrate it into efficient economic systems.

Until the eighteenth century, physical controls over the body had as their main aim the reaffirmation of the power of the state and the deterrence of others. In many cases this took the form of public spectacles of torture and execution, such as hanging, burning, disfigurement, or dismemberment. Foucault summarized the public execution that was set out for anyone who attempted to murder the French king:

'The flesh will be torn from his breasts, arms, thighs and calves with red-hot pincers, his right hand, holding the knife with which he committed the said parricide, burnt with sulphur, and, on those places where the flesh will be torn away, poured molten lead, boiling oil, burning resin, wax and sulphur melted together and then his body drawn and quartered by four horses and his limbs and body consumed by fire.'   (Foucault 1975: 3)

Anatomical controls were not, however, purely physical in nature, and Foucault traces a shift in social control from attempts to shape the *flesh* of the body to attempts to shape its *mind*. New techniques of social control sought to operate on the body only as a means of influencing the mind. From the late eighteenth century, new techniques of social control were developed that affected the body only as a way of influencing the mind. Surveillance and the shaping of motives, operating through consciousness and language, were seen as more effective methods of control than force and coercion. This kind of control involved harnessing and intensifying the energies of the human body through treatment and training.

Disciplines of training into new habits of behaviour were the tasks of the new prisons, clinics, schools, workshops, and barracks that brought people together for various purposes. These kinds of organizations began to be established from the sixteenth century, but they were massively expanded with the consolidation of the capitalist market in the nineteenth century. The emergence of scientific medicine was central to the establishment of new disciplines of the body in these organizations. Medicine and reform—the clinic and the prison—were particularly closely associated, as many forms of criminal behaviour were seen as the results of medical conditions that could be treated. The growth of psychiatric medicine, in particular, involved a close association between the criminalization and the medicalization of behaviour (Scull 1979).

Criminals were controlled through private and enclosed disciplines aimed at their reform. Prison discipline has only incidentally been concerned with physical intervention on the body. Methods of punishment were principally concerned with altering the mind in order to shape a person's motivations and desires. Inmates of the prisons were trained in new ways of behaviour so as to produce conforming, obedient individuals who could, in due course, be returned to a 'normal' and productive life. Moral training and industrial training in work habits were at the heart of this new discipline of the body.

☞ In Chapter 16, pp. 647–50, we discuss more fully the nature of the 'carceral' organizations in which this discipline takes place. You will find this a useful background for the present discussion and our discussion of Goffman's work on the hospital treatment of mental patients later in this chapter.

Conceptions of health and illness in traditional societies had made little distinction between disorders of the body and disorders of the mind. They saw illness in religious terms and linked 'sickness' with 'sin'. Physicians and surgeons did not exist in most societies, and there was little or no medical treatment. Where it did occur, it was barbaric and used unfounded techniques. Even this kind of intervention was largely confined to the aristocratic and professional strata. The illnesses and emotional problems of labourers and peasants were of little concern to anyone else. For the most part, those in the rural villages remained dependent on herbal and folk remedies that were passed down by word of mouth from one generation to the next and were sometimes meted out by the local wise man ('wizard') or wise woman.

The expansion of scientific medicine in the eighteenth and nineteenth centuries changed all this and introduced characteristically modern ways of handling physical and psychological disorders. A new bio-medical model of illness was established, and doctors—as the possessors of this knowledge—established themselves as the 'experts' in the treatment of bodily ills. Centralized hospital medicine allowed doctors to use their control over knowledge to build a power base for themselves. The shift from aristocratic **client control** over medicine to autonomous **professional control** by doctors themselves meant that doctors were able to define the nature of health and to determine forms of treatment (Jewson 1976; see also T. Johnson 1972; I. Waddington 1973). Initially in the private clinics and the workhouses, and later in large public hospitals, forms of hospital medicine and general practice were slowly established through an increasingly complex division of labour that involved doctors, nurses, and other professionals, along with administrators and ancillary workers.

Central to the rise of scientific medicine was a new orientation towards the sick. The **medical gaze** was a specific way of seeing, a style of perception that entailed specific forms of investigation, teaching, and clinical intervention. The medical gaze built an image of the 'sick body' as something that could be technically manipulated. The sick were no longer seen as persons, but simply as 'pathological' or dysfunctional bodies. They were systems of organs, cells, and tissues that required treatment whenever they were subject to 'disease'. This new viewpoint culminated in the germ theory of disease that was systematized during the 1870s and 1880s. As scientific technicians, doctors could adopt a detached, neutral, and disinterested orientation towards a particular 'case' and its 'symptoms'. Each case could, furthermore, be given a clinical description that could be bureaucratically organized and filed as a 'case record'.

In all countries, medical experts have become the core members of an administrative apparatus that comprises the various levels of staff that run the wards, consulting rooms, and dispensaries. Bureaucratically organized staff have expanded continuously since the nineteenth century, and include many different categories of 'specialist' doctor (physician, surgeon, psychiatrist, dentist, geriatrician, gynaecologist, paediatrician, etc.), nurses (midwives, psychiatric nurses, district nurses, health visitors), technicians (radiographers, audiologists, haematologists), social workers, and managers. Medicine has expanded into specialized organizations (asylums, sanatoriums, isolation hospitals) and into associated and subsidiary positions and organizations: Medical Officers of Health, general-practice surgeries, health centres, pharmacies, school and occupational nursing, family-planning clinics, old people's homes. Administrative apparatuses vary considerably in their levels of organization into health regimes. Even where state centralization has resulted in the establishment of such organizations as the National Health Service, the degree of coordination has generally been quite loose (Freidson 1970).

This looseness and lack of coherence in health regimes led Foucault to reject the concept of a health 'system'. The 'disciplinary society' is one in which organizations and agencies are interconnected in complex and extensive networks of power. However, they are rarely formed into tight and centralized systems. Foucault describes such a network as an 'archipelago'—

literally, a group of islands—so as to emphasize that there is only a loose interconnection among the constituent organizations.

Controlling sexuality

Central to the new techniques of anatomical control, according to Foucault, was the attempt to discipline sexuality, which came to be seen as a central and potentially dangerous force that had to be channelled in appropriate and productive directions. In all areas of social life there was an attempt to define and to consolidate images of normality: the good worker, the well-educated child, the law-observing citizen, and so on. The 'pathologies' of the feckless, unemployed poor, the ill-educated truants, and criminals had to be controlled so that they did not 'infect' the 'healthy' members of society. The norm of sexuality was defined in relation to an image of the heterosexual couple. This was the 'Malthusian couple', whose sexual activity was limited to the procreation of children and, thereby, to increasing the size of the population. On this basis, norms of sexual development were defined that described the behaviours that were felt to be appropriate.

Public attention was directed towards the maintenance and protection of the marital, heterosexual sexuality of the normal family. There was a corresponding 'medicalization of the sexually peculiar' and a 'psychiatrization of perverse pleasure' (Foucault 1976: 44). 'Unusual' and 'unnatural' forms of sexuality were identified as 'lesions', 'dysfunctions', or 'symptoms' that reflected deep organic disturbances of the body. Those who were sexually different were fixed in the medical gaze and isolated as objects of investigation and treatment. They were seen as suffering from 'nervous disorders' and sexual 'perversions'. Medical power drew out, isolated, and solidified these sexual disorders and made them objects of public concern, transforming many types of sexual conduct into behaviours that could be criminalized.

Childhood masturbation, for example, became a major target of medical attention. Described as 'onanism' and as a wasteful and dangerous activity, it was seen as something for which parents, teachers, and others needed to be constantly observant. Similarly, the male medical establishment saw female sexuality as dangerous and in need of control. Many female disorders were seen as sexual in origin. 'Idle' or 'nervous' women, for example, were seen as suffering from 'hysteria'—literally, a disorder of the uterus. Such women were in need of medical treatment that could restore them to a healthy state and, therefore, to their domestic, childbearing, and family roles.

A whole range of sexual practices came to be identified as distinct *types* of 'perversion'. Psychiatric opinion recognized not only the 'homosexual', but also the 'zoophile' and the 'zooerast', the 'auto-monosexualist', the 'mixoscopophile', the 'gyneco-mast', the 'presbyophile', and so on (Foucault 1976: 43). Many of these categories had only a short medical life, before being superseded by newer ones. Today, for example, the 'homosexual', the 'sado-masochist', and various types of 'fetishist' form the core elements in the sexual mosaic of contemporary society.

Several perversions were also seen as carrying the threat of other forms of illness. Diseases linked to sex, such as the venereal diseases of syphilis and gonorrhoea, were seen as ever-present consequences of unnatural sexual pleasures, much as AIDS is now seen. Concern about the spread of these diseases in the nineteenth century led to great public concern over prostitution, which itself reflected male attitudes towards female sexuality.

Foucault has provided a very powerful account of the disciplines of the body and the regulation of populations in modern societies. His argument, however, tends to present a highly flexible picture of the body that recognizes few significant physical limits to how the human body can be shaped by social forces. The body is known only in and through discourse and, as a result, Foucault tends to play down the importance of the physical, material aspects of bodies that exist independently of medical and other forms of discourse. Later in this chapter we will look at some of these material features of populations and bodies before going on to consider the social construction of health and illness through medical discourse. First, however, we must give some further consideration to the idea of surveillance.

SURVEILLANCE OF POPULATIONS

Regulation and discipline depend on practices of **surveillance**. Those who are to be controlled through the new techniques of bio-politics and anatamo-politics must be observed and monitored by the various agencies whose job it is to supervise and superintend their behaviour. The power of surveillance has been central to the growth of nation states, which have developed complex apparatuses for collecting and processing information on those who live within their boundaries. In this section we will look at the establishment of censuses and surveys along with mechanisms for the analysis and reporting of official statistics.

The birth of the census

Central to systems of surveillance were new mechanisms for counting the population and keeping track of its growth. In Britain and in many other countries, the churches had been responsible for the regulation of births, marriages, and burials, together with occasional local censuses, since the sixteenth century. The new systems of the eighteenth and nineteenth centuries, however, established national systems backed by the full force of the law. In 1800 an Act of Parliament established a regular census, a full count of the whole English population. The first national census took place the following year and, with the sole exception of 1941, a census has been taken every ten years since then. In 1837 a national system of 'civil registration' was set up for England. Under this system, all births, marriages, and deaths were registered at a local office that returned these to a national office. A few years later, similar systems were set up for Scotland and Ireland (Scott 1990: ch. 4, see also Nissel 1987).

Similar moves occurred in other countries. By the middle of the nineteenth century, registration and statistical services had been established in virtually all of the major European countries, in the United States, in Australia and New Zealand, and in Japan. Alongside the collection of data on their populations, states also began to compile statistics on crime, health, and a whole array of economic matters. Publication of statistics on court trials, for example, began in Britain in 1805, and this was followed by prison statistics in 1836 and police statistics in 1857. By the time that Durkheim carried out his investigations into suicide (Durkheim 1897), official statistics on this subject were available for a large number of countries.

The censuses in Britain are carried out by local enumerators, who issue standard forms to each household in their area. These forms require information on the names, ages, sexes, places of birth, and occupations of all members of the household, together with an indication of their marital status and their relationship to each other. To this core of information is added a varying set of questions concerning travel to work, education, housing conditions, car ownership, and ethnicity. The household forms, when completed, are used for the compilation of registers and, in recent years, computer records, and they are stored by the Office of Population, Censuses and Surveys (OPCS).

Civil registration records are also stored by OPCS, and it is from these registers that birth, marriage, and death certificates are produced. The birth registers record the name, sex, place of birth, and date of birth of each child, together with the names of its parents, the occupation of its father, and the name and address of the person (usually a parent) registering the birth. A marriage register records the date of the marriage, the names, ages, and occupations of both partners, the names and occupations of their fathers (but not of their mothers), and whether the partners were bachelor, spinster, or widowed at the time of the marriage. The death registers are much shorter, giving simply the name age, sex, and occupations of the deceased, the cause and place of death, and the name and address of the informant.

The original records and registers from the census and civil registration are stored under conditions of official secrecy, though the census records are opened for public examination after 100 years. Staff in OPCS, however, have full access to all the original records and they use them to produce periodic statistical reports. Civil registration data are summarized quarterly in a publication now called *Population Trends*, while census data are summarized in national and country reports and in the so-called small area statistics. Taken together, the census and civil registration data provide regular benchmark counts of the whole population and a record of trends between these benchmark years. In addition to aggregate totals, the statistical summaries give breakdowns and comparisons by age, sex, class (as computed from occupational data), and a whole variety of other factors.

The OPCS came into being in 1970 as a result of the merger of the old General Register Office with the Government Social Survey (GSS). The GSS had begun in 1939 as a part of the Ministry of Information. It had the task of monitoring public morale during the war. Drawing on the successes achieved by many private and academic surveys, the GSS used sampling methods to obtain national data that would complement the more comprehensive data that came from the census and civil registration. The GSS produced detailed information on a whole range of topics much more cheaply than could a complete census. Some of the early wartime surveys looked at the availability of steel for corset production and shortages in domestic brushes and brooms, though more long-lasting results came from surveys on food consumption and attitudes towards sexual disease.

In the post-war period, a number of regular national surveys were established, including the Family Expenditure Survey, the General Household Survey, and the Labour Force Survey. Reports are produced from each of these annual surveys, and their statistical results are combined with census and civil registration data in such compilations as *Social Trends* (from 1970). Together with health service and other data, they have been used for periodic reports on drinking, smoking, dental

Government social surveys

In addition to occasional surveys and alongside the census and civil registration, OPCS is responsible for three major social surveys that provide essential information for planners and academics.

The **Family Expenditure Survey** began in 1957 and carries out interviews with people in 11,000 households. These people keep detailed records of their expenditure over a period, and they provide details on their incomes. In addition to providing information on tax changes and on income distribution, typical patterns of expenditure can be identified. These data are used in the preparation of the Retail Price Index.

The **General Household Survey** began in 1970. It undertakes annual interviews with those aged over 16 in 12,500 households. Topics covered include household composition, housing, employment, education, health, and income. Additional topics are added from year to year. It was reduced in scope in the 1980 cost-cutting review, and in 1997 it was announced that it was being suspended for a year in order to save money.

The **Labour Force Survey** began in 1973. It was carried out every two years until 1983, annually from 1984 to 1991, and is now a quarterly survey. It draws its information from a regular 'panel' of individuals in 60,000 households. Questions covered in the interviews cover employment, hours worked, vocational training, education, job-search methods, nationality, and ethnicity.

---

health, disease and illness, employment, and numerous other issues.

The Office of National Statistics oversees the statistical publications of OPCS and coordinates them with those from other government departments. Criminal statistics are collected in the Home Office, which publishes *Criminal Statistics* and various reports from the regular *British Crime Survey*; health statistics are collected by the Department of Health; employment and unemployment statistics as well as educational statistics are collected by the Department for Education and Employment, which publishes the *Employment Gazette*; and financial and trade statistics are collected in the Treasury. A cost-cutting review in 1980 made substantial cutbacks in the statistical service in order to reduce its public-service role and limit its work on social statistics, but there is still a massive output of statistical data.

SUMMARY POINTS

In this section we have examined the growth of regulation and discipline in the control of populations and human bodies. We used the ideas of Foucault to bring together a number of concerns.

▶ The development of nation states and the idea of a national population was an important feature of the growth of surveillance and control. Medicine and statistics were central to this.

▶ Medicine introduced new techniques of social control aimed at the shaping of the body and the influencing of the mind. The medical gaze introduced conceptions of the sick body and of professional expertise.

▶ Control over sexuality became central to control over populations. You may like to consider this point in relation to our discussion of normal sex in Chapter 5, pp. 179–80.

We also looked at the ways in which new techniques of measurement through censuses, surveys, and registration became central to social surveillance. This resulted in the collection and compilation of official statistics.

▶ Nation states have established regular population censuses and a number of regular surveys aimed at collecting data about their people.

▶ Criminal statistics, unemployment statistics, demographic statistics, and a variety of other statistics are shaped by the bureaucratic procedures through which they are produced. They reflect administrative concerns rather than sociological concepts.

POPULATION, HEALTH, AND MODERNITY

Foucault's work highlighted the importance of examining the ways in which populations are regulated and individual bodies are disciplined. In this section we will look at the material aspects of each of these. We will look at the material structure of populations—what Durkheim called 'social morphology'—and at the material health, disease, and diet of individual bodies. We will show that both social morphology and individual health have undergone a distinctive pattern of change since 1800.

FERTILITY, MORTALITY, AND MIGRATION

Total world population seems to have fluctuated at a level of around half a billion until the modern period, when it began to climb steadily. By 1950 it had risen to 2.5 billion, and in 1995 it stood at 5.7 billion. The United Kingdom, with a population of just over 58 million, is the seventeenth largest country in the world. It has 0.1 per cent of total world population. Within the European Union, it has about the same size of population as France and Italy, but it is significantly smaller than Germany. In geographical extent, however, it is quite small, which means that it has a very high population density of 241 people per square kilometre. The European average is 153 people per square kilometre. (More detailed demographic figures, from which our account draws heavily, can be found in Coleman and Salt 1992 and *Social Trends* 1996.)

Europe's total population (see Figure 6.1) is about half as big again as the total population of the United States (263 million people). This, in turn, is half as big again as the population of Japan. Europe, the Americas, and Africa are roughly equivalent to each other in terms of population size, but by far the most populous area of the world is Asia. Almost two-thirds of the world's population lives in Asia, and almost a quarter of the world's population lives in China. The significance of this is clear when population is compared with economic development, an issue that we discuss more fully in Chapter 12. Just 20 per cent of the world's population lives in the most developed areas (North America, Europe, Australia, New Zealand, and Japan). The remaining 80 per cent of people live in the world's poorest countries, where population growth is also most rapid. The population of India, for example, increased by 30 per cent between 1971 and 1981.

The British population figure of 58 million is a substantial increase over the figure of 38 million that was recorded in 1901. The population is estimated to rise to 62 million by the year 2031. Despite this substantial increase, the *rate* of growth in the twentieth century has been much lower than it was in the nineteenth century. The first census, in 1801, recorded a population of just over 10 million, a figure which had doubled by 1851 and had almost doubled again by 1901. By contrast, the estimated population size for 2031 is less than double the 1901 figure. The fastest period of population growth this century was during its first decade, and the growth rate has declined since then. Despite a small boom in the 1960s, this decline in the rate of growth has been especially rapid in the last thirty years of the twentieth century and it is expected to continue. These trends are summarized in Figure 6.2.

Figure 6.1. **World population, 1995**

Region	Population (m.)	%
Europe		
European Union	371.3	
Other north and south Europe	45.6	
Eastern Europe	308.7	
Total	727.0	12.7
Americas		
North America	292.8	
Latin America, Caribbean	482.0	
Total	774.8	13.5
Asia	3,458.0	60.5
Africa	728.1	12.7
Oceania	28.5	0.5
Total	5,716.4	

Note: figures do not total exactly because of rounding in the original source.
Source: Social Trends (1996: table 1.20).

Figure 6.2. **UK population, 1851–2031** (000s)

Year	England	Wales	Scotland	Northern Ireland	United Kingdom
1851	16,764	1,163	2,889	1,443	22,259
1901	30,515	2,013	4,472	1,237	38,237
1931	37,359	2,593	4,843	1,243	46,038
1961	43,561	2,635	5,184	1,427	52,807
1971	46,412	2,740	5,236	1,540	55,928
1981	46,821	2,813	5,180	1,538	56,352
1991	48,208	2,899	5,107	1,601	57,807
1994	48,707	2,913	5,132	1,642	58,395
2031 (projected)	52,435	2,977	4,998	1,831	62,241

Sources: Coleman and Salt (1992: table 3.1); Central Office of Information (1995: table 1); *Social Trends* (1996: table 1.3).

The British population is very unevenly distributed. Most of this population lives in England, and population densities are much sparser elsewhere. Wales and Northern Ireland have much lower population densities than does England, while Scotland is extremely sparsely populated. About one-third of the British population lives in the south-east of England, with almost seven million people living in Greater London itself. The second largest city is Birmingham (just over one million people), followed by Leeds, Glasgow, and Sheffield. The least densely populated areas, as might be expected, are rural areas such as East Anglia and the Highlands of Scotland. Over the second half of the century there has been a geographical redistribution of population as people have moved from the north to the south. Areas such as Merseyside, Tyneside, and Strathclyde have lost population, and the fastest growing areas in the country are Cambridgeshire and Buckinghamshire.

Marriage and fertility

The size of a population and its rate of growth or decline are largely determined by the balance between fertility (births) and mortality (deaths). Whenever the birth rate is higher than the death rate, there is an increase in the so-called natural growth rate of the population. This terminology is a little unhelpful, as it implies that changes in population that are due to other factors are somehow 'unnatural'. Nevertheless, it remains the case that the balance between births and deaths is fundamental to the development of any particular population.

The basic measure of the **fertility** of the population is the so-called crude birth rate. This is the annual number of live births per 1,000 population. This widely used figure gives a result that is very similar in form to a percentage figure, but it is calculated on a base of 1,000 rather than 100. The crude birth rate in Britain stood at 35.2 per 1,000 between 1860 and 1870. It declined very rapidly from the 1870s to the 1920s, reaching 27.2 in the period 1901–10. The drop in the rate was particularly sharp while men were away at the front during the First World War. The rate increased in the years immediately after the war, but the decline set in again fairly rapidly and continued through the 1930s.

Despite the onset of the Second World War in 1939, the birth rate increased through most of the wartime years, and there was a substantial baby boom in the years 1945–8. From a low point in the middle of the 1950s, the birth rate increased through the 1960s. This was a period of relative prosperity and affluence, and there was a second baby boom between 1957 and 1966. Following this boom, the rate declined once more, and it has continued to decline. The decline since the 1960s has been especially rapid. The crude birth rate fell from a level of 18.8 in 1964 to one of 13.1 in 1993.

As its name implies, this 'crude rate' is a very rough-and-ready figure, which does not directly reflect changes in the age and sex composition of the population. What is called the 'general fertility rate' does a rather more precise job of measurement. This is the number of births per 1,000 women in the usual child-bearing age range of 15 to 44. Figures show that this rate fell from 94 to 62 between 1964 and 1993. The general fertility rate, however, is also a little misleading, as it obscures the variations that exist from one age group to another. Age-specific fertility rates show, for example, that there were 117 births per 1,000 women aged 25–29 in 1992, compared with 87 births per 1,000 women aged 30–34.

Changes in the age-specific rates—and, therefore, in the overall birth rate—are consequences of changes in the age of marriage and the age at which childbearing begins. If people marry late, then there will be fewer years of marriage in which they can have children. Similarly, if married women delay having their first child, they will also reduce the total number of years that are available for childbearing. The age at marriage for women was between 25 and 26 throughout the period from 1990 to 1940. The age at marriage for men in the same period was between 27 and 28 After 1940, people began to marry much earlier, and the average marriage age had fallen to 22 for women and 24 for men by 1970. During the 1980s and 1990s, however, age at marriage began to increase once more. At the turn of the century it stands at about 24 for women and 26 for men.

Late marriage is especially marked among professional and managerial workers. Late marriage, however, does not necessarily mean that people begin their families later. As we show in Chapter 10, the rate of marriage itself has fallen as more and more people choose to cohabit. Many 'late' marriages take place between people who have already been cohabiting for some time. Nevertheless, the so-called age of maternity—the age at which a woman has her first child—has increased. In 1951 the average age at maternity was 28.4 years. This fell to 27.3 in 1964, and 26.5 in 1977. During the 1980s and 1990s the age of maternity increased, and by 1993 it had risen to 28.1.

Mortality

The basic measure of **mortality** is the crude death rate, the annual number of deaths per 1,000 population. Death rates were very high in the eighteenth century, but began to fall during the nineteenth century. By 1870 the rate stood at 23.0 per 1,000, and this had dropped to 13.5 by 1910. Death rates have altered very little during the rest of the century, though high rates were recorded—for obvious reasons—in the wartime years. The death rate is currently between 10 and 11 persons per 1,000.

The aggregate figures, of course, mask significant differences among the age groups. There are fewer than one per 1,000 deaths among those aged between 1 and 15 years, while there are 44.7 per 1,000 among those aged 65–79 and 141.4 per 1,000 among those aged 80 or

more. If crude death rates are compared across the country, the highest death rates—for obvious reasons—appear in those areas where there are relatively large numbers of retired persons. Many of these deaths are among people who have retired to the seaside. About a third of the population in East Sussex and the south of the Isle of White are over pension age, and these areas have the highest death rates in the country.

A more useful comparison of death rates involves the use of the so-called standardized mortality rate, which takes account of the age structure of the population. A figure of 100 indicates that an area or group has exactly the death rate that would be expected among people of its age composition; a figure above 100 indicates higher-than-average death rates, and a figure below 100 indicates lower-than-average death rates. Using age-specific measures for Great Britain as a whole, death rates are lowest in East Anglia and the south-west, and they are highest in Scotland and the north of England.

Mortality rates reflect the increase in life expectancy that has taken place over the century. People are now living longer than ever before, and women live longer than men. Life expectancy for a male born in 1996 was about 74 years, compared with almost 80 for a female. The corresponding life expectancies for 1901 were 49 for men and 52 for women, an increase in average life span of 50 per cent. A hundred years earlier, in 1801, life expectancy was around 37 years (Coleman and Salt 1992: 38).

This does not mean, however, that large numbers of people died at age 37 in 1801 and at around 50 in 1901. Life expectancy at birth is very low when rates of infant mortality are high, but those who survive their childhood can expect to live rather longer than these minimal figures suggest. Although life expectancy at birth in 1901 was around 50, those who actually managed to survive until age 45 could certainly have expected about another twenty-five years of life. Changes in life expectancy, then, reflect two quite separate changes: the rate of infant mortality and the rate of post-infant mortality.

One of the major changes in mortality during the twentieth century has been the reduction in levels of infant mortality. This is officially measured by the number of deaths of infants aged under 1 year old per 1,000 live births. At the end of the nineteenth century, infant mortality accounted for one in five of all deaths. Most of these were due to diarrhoea, dysentery, and other forms of gastric infection. These were diseases of poverty, poor sanitation, and bad hygiene (Coleman and Salt 1992: 54). The rate of infant mortality has fallen constantly over the course of the century. It fell from 147 in 1901 to 70 in 1931, 32 in 1951, 23 in 1961, 10 in

1981, and 6.9 in 1994. The greatest improvements in infant health have been those that have increased survival chances during the critical first four weeks of life. These so-called neonatal mortality rates fell from 15.8 per 1,000 in 1961 to 4.2 per 1,000 in 1993.

Infant mortality is not constant across the country, but varies quite considerably from one region to another. Rural areas of Oxfordshire, Cambridgeshire, and Warwickshire, like the affluent districts of London, Surrey, and Hampshire, have infant mortality rates of between 5 and 6 per 1,000. The poorer urban areas of Birmingham, Wolverhampton, and Bradford have rates that are more than double these levels. Rates of infant mortality also vary by ethnicity: rates for infants born to mothers from the Caribbean and Africa are one and a half times those for mothers born in Britain. Rates for mothers born in Pakistan were double the British-born rate.

Migration and demographic divisions

We showed earlier that the so-called natural growth of a population depends upon the balance between its birth rate and its death rate. A further variable that has an effect on population—and which should by no means be regarded as 'unnatural'—is migration. **Immigration** (the movement of people into a country) tends to increase the population, while **emigration** (the movement of people out of a country) tends to reduce it. The net effect of migration on a population is the balance between its levels of immigration and emigration from year to year.

Migration has generally had only a relatively small effect on overall population trends in Britain, as the numbers involved have been so small in relation to the numbers of births and deaths. For the first thirty years of the twentieth century, Britain experienced a net loss of population through migration (emigration was greater than immigration). The reason for this was that large numbers of Britons migrated to Canada, Australia, South Africa, and other parts of the Empire. Rates of immigration increased from the late 1940s, and from the middle of the 1950s into the early 1960s there was a net gain through migration (immigration was greater than emigration). This occurred as large numbers of people from the Commonwealth (as the 'Empire' had become) were recruited into the expanding industries and public services, generally into low-paid work. The number of Asian and Caribbean immigrants declined after that, partly because of legal

Migrants from the West Indies arrived in Britain in large numbers from the 1940s to the 1960s. What can you learn about identities by comparing the photograph with that on p. 139?

restrictions on immigration, and the immigrants that have arrived since then have mainly been the dependants of those who had already settled here.

During the 1960s there were about a quarter of a million immigrants to Britain each year, but in every year until the middle of the 1980s they were more than balanced by an even larger number of emigrants. Almost a half of all immigrants in this period came from Australia, New Zealand, and Canada (the 'Old Commonwealth' in the official terminology), the United States, or the European Community. These numbers were counterbalanced by the return of short-term migrants to the same areas and by the emigration of Britons to join relatives in the 'Old Commonwealth' or to work in other parts of Europe. Immigrants to Britain from India, Pakistan, and the Caribbean were generally long-term or permanent migrants, but they were very few in number: in the middle of the 1980s there were 21,000 migrants from the Indian subcontinent, 11,000 from African Commonwealth countries, and 3,000 from the Caribbean. Only since the middle of the 1980s has there again been a net balance of immigrants over emigrants.

Although migration into Britain has a long history, it is the successive waves of migration since the early nineteenth century that have had the most impact on the ethnic composition of the population. As a result of migration from Ireland, the Irish accounted for 2.9 per cent of the population of England and Wales by 1851. Their descendants, together with more recent Irish migrants, are estimated to account for up to 10 per cent of the mainland British population today. Jewish migrants from Germany and Eastern Europe in the late nineteenth century and the early part of the twentieth century settled in large numbers in the East End of London and in other major urban centres. Since the 1940s people from the Caribbean, India, and Pakistan have further increased the ethnic diversity of the British population.

While it is notoriously difficult to formulate survey questions that will accurately uncover people's felt sense of ethnic identity, some indications of this ethnic diversity can be found in the 1991 Census. This was the first census to ask people about their ethnic identity. People were asked an open question about how they would define their own ethnicity, with the results shown in Figure 6.3.

More than three million people in England and Wales (5.5 per cent of the population) identified themselves as members of a non-white ethnic group. Almost a half of these people claimed a broadly Asian identity, identifying themselves as Indian, Pakistani, or Bangladeshi, and around a third defined themselves as

black. It has been estimated that around 40 per cent of the British ethnic minority population were born in the United Kingdom, showing the inadequacy of the common popular designation of them as 'immigrants'. Almost a half of the total ethnic minority population lives in Greater London, the second biggest concentration being in Birmingham. Other concentrations of the non-white population can be found in West Yorkshire (Bradford and Leeds), Greater Manchester, and Leicester.

Figure 6.3. **Ethnic composition of the population, England and Wales, 1991**

Ethnic identity	%
White	94.5
Black-Caribbean	0.9
Black-African	0.4
Black other	0.3
Indian	1.5
Pakistani	0.9
Bangladeshi	0.3
Chinese	0.3
Other	0.9

Source: Mason (1995: table 4.1), summarizing census data. For earlier estimates based on the Labour Force Survey, see Joshi (1989: 183) and Skellington (1992).

The population is also, of course, diverse in terms of its gender and age structure. Very slightly more than a half of all births are male, and males outnumber females in the population throughout childhood and the early years of adulthood. Death rates for males, however, are higher than they are for females at all ages, and women tend to live longer than men. As a result, women outnumber men from about the age of 50. Amongst those who are 80 years old or more, there are twice as many women as men.

The age composition of the population can vary quite considerably from one period to another. From the middle of the nineteenth century until the 1920s, there were relatively large numbers of infants and young children. About one-third of the population was aged 15 or less in 1901. At the same time, there were very small numbers of people aged over 70. As a result, the British population was, overall, quite young. A decline in the birth rate, however, has meant that the total number of children in the population has declined from its earlier level. About one-fifth of the population is now aged under 16, while one-sixth of the population is aged 65 or more. Baby booms in the 1940s and the 1960s (peaking in 1964) have produced bulges in the age distribution of the population in successive years as the members of these cohorts have aged. At the same time, there has been a growth in the number of elderly people. In 1993, 18.3 per cent of the population were of retirement age or above (60 for women, 65 for men), the corresponding figure having been 6.2 per cent in 1901 (see Pilcher 1995: figure 1.2).

It is estimated that 23 per cent of the population will be aged 65 or over in 2031, and about a third of these people will be aged 80 or more. Those over 80 will be the survivors of the post-war baby boom, while those in their sixties will be the survivors of the 1960s baby boom. Looking at these trends in the numbers of the young and the old from a different angle, those of working age (16 to 65), whether actually working or not, had fallen to 63 per cent of the population in 1994 and they will have fallen to 58 per cent by 2031 (see Figure 6.4).

Britain is not unusual among advanced industrial societies in this respect, although its population is now somewhat older than the European average. There are major differences, of course, from the non-industrial societies, which tend to have much younger populations. About one-third of the Chinese population is under 15 years old, and only 6 per cent are aged 65 or more. Where Britain is unusual among industrial societies is in the ethnic composition of its ageing population. Members of ethnic minorities (predominantly black and Asian) are significantly younger than the rest of the population. In 1995 almost one-third was under 16 and only 6 per cent were aged over 60. In 2031, if present trends continue, the population of working age will be disproportionately black and Asian, while the retired population will be disproportionately white.

Figure 6.4. **Age and gender, United Kingdom, 1961–2031**

Year	% of population				
	under 16	16–39	40–64	65–79	80 or over
1961	25	31	32	10	2
1971	25	31	30	11	2
1981	22	35	28	12	3
1991	20	35	29	12	4
1994					
male	22	36	29	11	2
female	20	33	29	13	5
all	21	35	29	12	4
2031 (projected)	18	28	30	16	7

Source: *Social Trends* (1996: table 1.5). See also Pilcher (1995) and Vincent (1995).

An ageing population

The increase in the overall age of the population has been seen as posing major problems for social policy. The pensions and health care of a large retired population, for example, must be met from the work of a much smaller working population.

▶ **What other problems of policy and welfare do you think will result from an ageing population?**

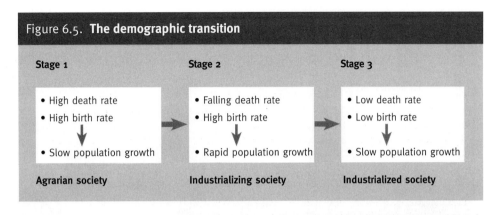

Figure 6.5. **The demographic transition**

Stage 1	Stage 2	Stage 3
• High death rate • High birth rate ↓ • Slow population growth	• Falling death rate • High birth rate ↓ • Rapid population growth	• Low death rate • Low birth rate ↓ • Slow population growth
Agrarian society	**Industrializing society**	**Industrialized society**

Malthus on population

Writing at the end of the nineteenth century, during Stage 2 of the demographic transition, Thomas Malthus (1798) tried to anticipate future population trends. He saw that the population of Britain was growing rapidly and he expected this to continue into the future. He calculated that population would increase at an 'exponential' rate, doubling every generation. The supply of food, on the other hand, could not expand so rapidly, as there were limits to the productivity of agriculture. As a result, population would outstrip food supply; Britain was heading for a famine that would reduce its population.

The only way to prevent this catastrophe, Malthus held, was for people to exercise 'moral restraint' by postponing marriage, remaining chaste before marriage, and having sex less often during marriage. This restraint would lower the birth rate. Malthus rejected the use of contraception on religious grounds, as being counter to God's law. While attitudes towards contraception have changed since Malthus's time, the Roman Catholic Church is still opposed to it.

The demographic transition

Population trends in industrialized societies have been described as showing a particular pattern called the **demographic transition** (W. S. Thompson 1929; Kingsley Davis 1945). According to this point of view, population change shows a succession of three stages (see Figure 6.5). Stage 1, which in Britain preceded the Industrial Revolution of the eighteenth century, is a period of high death rates combined with high birth rates. As a result, population growth is fairly slow. Industrialization initiates the transition to Stage 2, where death rates begin to fall as the improved food supply increases longevity and reduces infant mortality. Birth rates, however, remain high, and so population begins to increase rapidly. This period of rapid population growth ended in Britain at the close of the nineteenth century, when birth rates began to fall. Stage 3, then, is a period of low death rates combined with low birth rates, resulting in only slow population growth.

The late and more rapid industrialization of other European countries meant that they underwent the demographic transition somewhat later than Britain. It is now the common experience of all the industrialized societies. It has been suggested that the non-industrialized countries of the world today will eventually undergo a similar transition as they industralize. Many think that this will resolve the problem of overpopulation that the poorer countries currently face. However, these countries have been able to learn from the European experience. They have been able to adopt many measures to improve individual and public health, so lowering death rates, before improved industrial productivity can have any effect on their birth rates. As a result, Stage 2 of the demographic transition has shown a much more dramatic increase in population than occurred in Britain. This makes it much less likely that Stage 3 will be entered. Large families remain the norm, and there are often religious proscriptions against birth control. Some governments, such as the Communist regime in China, have tried to

Family size has declined since Victorian times. What have been the main factors responsible for this?

encourage family limitation, but with only limited success. While the death rate in China has fallen to 8 per 1,000, the birth rate stands at 27 per 1,000. In India, death rates of 12 per 1,000 are countered by birth rates of 33 per 1,000. The demographic transition *may* describe the future of the newly industrializing countries, but it is by no means an inevitable transition for them. This become clear if the reasons for changes in birth and death rates in Britain are examined.

Birth rates in Britain have been shaped by both economic and cultural factors. The costs involved in having and bringing up children are considerable, and they include the costs of housing, education, and food. They also include the lost earnings of a parent who takes responsibility for child care, or the costs of paying for a professional nanny or child care. These costs lead people to have fewer children when times are bad and there is much unemployment or less full-time work. They also have fewer children if they seek to improve

the standard of living of their existing family. In the former case, parents may simply *defer* births. In the latter case, however, they are more likely to *reduce* family size. The effects of these economic influences depends upon cultural factors. These include changing ideas about the appropriate or ideal number of children in a family, expectations concerning the age of marriage, attitudes towards contraception, and the normative expectations that are attached to female identity. If, for example, there is a weakening of the traditional ideal of female domesticity and an increase in opportunities for women to take on paid employment, there is likely to be a reduction in the number of children born.

In general, the long-term population trend in Britain has resulted from a desire for improved standards of living and an increase in the number of women who enter or remain in paid work. Both of these factors imply that women and men have made conscious and deliberate decisions to reduce the number of children that they wish to have (Banks 1954). A crucial condition for this decision, however, has been the availability of effective forms of contraception. Methods of 'family planning' have become both more easily available and more acceptable over the course of the century, making it possible for people to translate their decisions about family size into practice. This was not possible, for most people, before the end of the nineteenth century. The desire to reduce family size was not, in any case, so strong until then. For much of the nineteenth century, children were seen as a source of income for a family—and this was true for even quite young children. Restrictions on child labour and the introduction of compulsory education in 1870 turned young children into more of a financial burden, altering the calculations that parents made about family size. The average number of children per family was seven in the 1860s, but this had fallen to four by 1900.

Although contraceptives were more easily available from the 1920s, they were not used by the mass of the population until the 1950s. It was in this period that family size reached its famous and much-parodied level of 2.4 children. The introduction of the contraceptive pill in the 1960s allowed far more effective planning of births and allowed the increasing numbers of women who took on paid employment to defer or end their childbearing period.

Death rates since the middle of the nineteenth century have been influenced mainly by changes in medical treatment and public-health provision. In the nineteenth century and the first part of the twentieth century, public health was of the greatest significance in this respect. Improved sanitation, better living and working conditions, changes in diet and nutrition, and many effects of increasing disposable income all helped to reduce the *incidence* of disease by making

people less susceptible. Medical treatment, on the other hand, has mainly had an effect since the early years of the twentieth century, when techniques of vaccination and immunization improved the survival chances of infants. We look further into this in the following section.

HEALTH, DISEASE, AND DIET

One of the concerns of writers like Malthus was the fear that population growth would outstrip food production and that this would result in famine, disease, and death on a large scale. The most pessimistic expectations have not materialized, but patterns of death and disease have changed quite markedly since the end of the nineteenth century.

The health transition

In parallel with the demographic transition that we have described, there has been a change in patterns of disease. This can be described as a **health transition**. This transition, shown in Figure 6.6, involves a change in the nature and scale of the principal diseases that have been responsible for ill health and death as societies have industrialized.

Stage 1 of the health transition is that of pre-modern, agrarian societies. The principal causes of illness and death are acute infectious diseases. These are spread from one person to another through direct contact, through polluted water, or through parasitic carriers such as fleas and mosquitoes. Diseases such as tuberculosis, malaria, and plague are endemic in these societies, along with cholera, typhus, leprosy, and sleeping sickness. Young children are particularly susceptible to

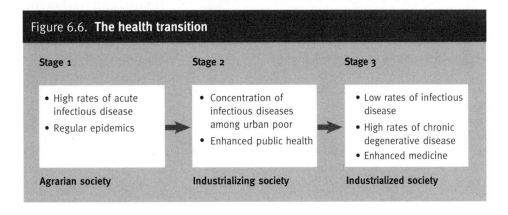

Figure 6.6. **The health transition**

measles, smallpox, and diphtheria. Whole populations are at risk from these diseases, and only the very wealthy have a degree of immunity. The incidence of these diseases is greatly affected by poor harvests and by warfare, which reduce or disrupt food supply and result in deteriorating living and working conditions. In these circumstances, epidemics are regular occurrences.

Stage 2 of the health transition, corresponding to the period of industralization, involves some improvement in the standard of living for many people, though the problem of urban poverty increases. Acute infectious diseases (particularly tuberculosis, cholera, and typhus) remain at a high level. They are, however, particularly concentrated among the new urban poor, whose living conditions make them the most vulnerable. Tuberculosis accounted for 13.2 per cent of all deaths in Britain in 1880, typhus, dysentery, and cholera accounted for 7.3 per cent, measles, scarlet fever, and whooping cough each accounted for just less than 1 per cent. Alongside these infectious diseases, respiratory diseases such as pneumonia accounted for 17.6 per cent of all deaths. Improved public health through sanitation, housing, and nutrition had some effect on the diseases of the poor, but it served mainly to confine the diseases to the poor districts and to insulate the majority of the population from their worst effects.

In Stage 3 of the health transition there is an enhanced control over infectious diseases, which fall to low levels. It is not always realized how little direct effect medical treatment had until comparatively recently. The decline in tuberculosis, for example, began in about 1850, but the tubercle bacillus was not discovered until 1882, and drug treatment was not available until 1947. Nevertheless, vaccination and the use of antibiotics from the 1930s and 1940s did have a significant effect on health, particularly on that of children. This was possible once the underlying improvements in living conditions had been made. There has been a rapid growth in medical and surgical techniques since the 1940s (McKeown 1979). As a result of these medical advances, there have been the significant falls in infant mortality and the general increase in life expectancy that we have already discussed.

In Stage 3, rates of the degenerative diseases, such as cancer, heart disease, and strokes, are high. They become the principal causes of chronic illness and death. These diseases result largely from bodily deterioration with age, or from environmental conditions (such as dietary changes and the use of alcohol and tobacco) that have their greatest effects as bodies age. People now live long enough to suffer from different kinds of disease. Respiratory diseases continue to account for around one in ten of all deaths in Britain, but tuberculosis now accounts for only a fraction of 1 per cent. Circulatory diseases (those of the heart and blood vessels) now account for 46 per cent of all deaths, compared with just 7 per cent in 1880. Another major cause of death is cancer, which now accounts for 25 per cent of deaths (2.5 per cent in 1880). The incidence of lung cancer among men has declined since 1951, but among women both lung cancer and breast cancer have increased sharply since the 1960s.

Britain is now above the European Union average for both circulatory disease and cancer. The highest rates of death from cancer among European women are found in Denmark, Ireland, and Britain; the lowest rates are in Greece, Spain, and France. Among men, the highest rates of death from circulatory disease are found in Austria and Germany, and the lowest rates are those of France and Spain.

Changes in patterns of death in the twentieth century reflect, in part, a real increase in the level of such diseases as cancer as a result of changes in living conditions. An increase in smoking in the first half of the century, for example, was responsible for the increase in the prevalence of both lung cancer and heart disease. However, these trends also reflect increased life expectancy. Putting matters crudely, a greater control over infectious diseases means that people are now living long enough to face the circulatory and cancer problems of old age that their parents and grandparents avoided because they died much younger. These diseases are, therefore, commonest among the oldest age groups. By contrast, over a half of deaths among men aged 15 to 39 result from injury or poison (associated with drugs or alcohol), and not from disease at all. Many of these injuries result from road-traffic accidents, which account for nearly 40 per cent of all accidental deaths.

Health and well-being

Of course, not all people suffer from serious illnesses. A national survey in 1993 found that over three-quarters of adults rated their own health as 'good' or 'very good'. Nevertheless, around 40 per cent reported that they had a long-standing illness or disability.

On average, people see their doctor about four times each year, and it is he or she who provides most of the medical treatment that people receive. More serious illnesses are often referred on for more specialist treatment at hospitals, though this may involve a long wait until a clinic appointment or hospital bed is available.

In 1997 almost one and a quarter million people in England were on waiting lists for in-patient treatment, and 57,000 had been waiting for more than a year. The British health care system is not typical. In the United States, for example, the bulk of the health system operates on a private basis rather than as a public service, and it is normal for paying patients to make direct approaches to specialist practitioners.

For all age groups—and among both men and women—problems of the musculo-skeletal system (arthritis and rheumatism) were among the most common long-standing disorders. Among those aged 45 to 64, 22 per cent reported these kinds of problems in 1993. For those aged 65 or over, the proportion increased to 26 per cent for men and 39 per cent for women. Among older men, however, heart and circulatory problems outweighed arthritis and rheumatism. The most common heart and circulation problems faced by older people were high blood pressure and angina, though large numbers of people experienced diabetes or abnormal heart rhythms. Most older people, of course, experienced both musculo-skeletal problems and circulatory difficulties, along with other long-term disorders.

Among the medical conditions that affect large numbers of people and that are chronic rather than physically dangerous are fatigue and sleep problems, irritability and worry, anxiety, depression, and 'stress'. People aged 35 to 54 are particularly likely to report that they have experienced stress or pressure in their life; men and those in non-manual jobs are more likely to report this than women and those in manual jobs. A growing amount of evidence, however, shows that medically diagnosed stress is more common among manual workers than non-manual workers. On the other hand, rates of depression are much higher among women than among men, and they are especially great among women in manual-working households.

Asthma has shown an increased incidence during the 1980s. This is an illness that is particularly likely to affect children and that has been linked to growing levels of air pollution. Many other childhood diseases, however, have shown a long-term decline. Measles and whooping cough, despite occasional epidemics, are at a lower level than they were earlier in the century, and diseases such as diphtheria (which killed around 10,000 children each year in the second half of the nineteenth century) and polio are kept under control through immunization programmes.

A major health issue of the 1980s was AIDS (acquired immune deficiency syndrome). This is sexually transmitted, but can also be contracted through infected blood. It can often prove fatal. The number of new cases reported in the United Kingdom increased from 298 in 1986 to 1,785 in 1994, and the total number of known cases in 1995 was 11,051. Of these known cases, about 6 per cent resulted from infection as a result of the injection of drugs. About the same number were contracted through infected blood (generally from a transfusion), and 73 per cent were as a result of unprotected homosexual intercourse. To put these numbers in context, the incidence of many less serious sexually contracted diseases is much higher, and also increasing. The number of cases of gonorrhoea and syphilis has decreased substantially, but just under 100,000 people in 1994 were treated for genital warts, 71,000 were treated for thrush, and figures for other sexually transmitted diseases were almost as high.

Diet and fitness

The health and fitness of a population reflect a whole complex of environmental factors. Among the most critical have been patterns of eating and exercise. Under-nourishment was chronic throughout the eighteenth and nineteenth centuries, when large numbers of people died in the Irish famines. A lack of food left many people unhealthy and prone to infectious diseases. At the time of the Boer War (1899–1902), 38 per cent of potential army recruits were rejected as being undersized or unfit for military service.

During the twentieth century, the quality of the national diet has generally improved. Levels of poverty have declined, though lack of food remains a problem for many people. Many of the poor are forced into eating cheap but unhealthy diets. Although the quantity of food eaten by the majority of the population has increased over the century, its nutritional quality has not always increased at the same pace. Compared with the typical nineteenth-century diet, there has been a reduction in fibre intake and an increase in fat, sugar, and salt intake, as well as a greater consumption of alcohol and tobacco.

There have been major changes in diet since the 1960s. Most significant has been a shift from red meats (beef and lamb) and dairy products to poultry and vegetables. The increased consumption of vegetables reflects a growing level of vegetarianism and concern for healthy eating, especially among the young (P. Atkinson 1983; Twigg 1983). There has also, however, been a decline in the consumption of fresh vegetables and an increase in the consumption of processed vegetables. This is associated with a growth in the consumption of 'convenience foods' of all kinds, including sweets and snacks. A national survey for 1993 found that young people in the 16–24 age group were especially likely to eat confectionery and to do so on five or six days of each week. These trends are, perhaps, reinforced by the decline in the idea of the 'family meal' as the focus of family life. Households of all kinds rely more and more on convenience foods, rather than the traditional 'hot meal' with a 'pudding', and household members eat at different times of the day (Blaxter and Paterson 1982; Murcott 1982; Charles and Kerr 1988).

Smoking has declined considerably since the early 1970s. In 1972, 52 per cent of men and 41 per cent of women were smokers. By 1994 these figures had fallen to 28 per cent and 26 per cent respectively. The fall levelled off, however, and there appears to be a growth in smoking among those in the 20–24 age group. Similarly, the incidence of excessive drinking—consumption of alcohol above medically approved limits—is highest among both men and women in the 18–24 age group.

These changing diets and eating habits are connected with weight problems. As a result of both poor diets and overeating among the relatively affluent, many British people are medically overweight. Few people engage in any strenuous activity during an ordinary day. They drive to work, are mainly involved in sedentary, non-manual work, and take little or no exercise. Less than half of the population is at a weight that is medically recognized as appropriate for their height and body shape. In 1980, 39 per cent of men and 32 per cent of women were medically overweight, and by 1993 these figures had risen to 57 per cent of men and 48 per cent of women. Thirteen per cent of men were classified as 'obese' or dangerously overweight. This increase in the problem of overweight was also apparent in the United States, though levels were somewhat lower there. In 1994, 33 per cent of American men and 36 per cent of women were overweight (see Figure 6.7). The incidence of these conditions was lowest among young people and increased with age. It has been linked with the incidence of heart disease and other serious medical disorders.

There is also a serious problem of an 'underweight' population. This problem affected between 5 and 7 per cent of those surveyed in 1993. This is predominantly a problem of youth, and is caused principally by a deliberate restriction of food intake (for example, as part of a slimming diet). In the 16–24 age group, 14 per cent of males and 18 per cent of females were underweight. Lack of body weight is linked to menstrual and fertility problems in women, as well as to such conditions as osteoporosis (brittle bones).

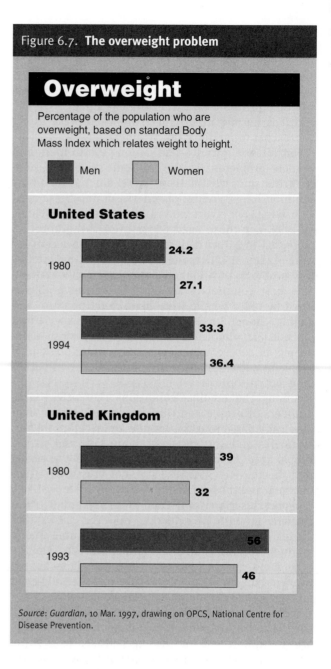

Figure 6.7. **The overweight problem**

Source: *Guardian*, 10 Mar. 1997, drawing on OPCS, National Centre for Disease Prevention.

SUMMARY POINTS

This section has presented a large number of statistics about population and health, and these cannot be summarized here. You will find it useful to glance back over the various tables and diagrams that we have given.

▶ Population change is the result of the balance between fertility, mortality, and migration.

▶ In modern societies, changes in population can be described in terms of a demographic transition.

▶ Causes of illness and death have altered considerably with the development of industrial societies.

▶ The demographic transition is associated with a parallel health transition.

MEDICINE, MINDS, AND BODIES

Illness is now generally seen as having an objective, physical reality. It is a result of the influence of germs, viruses, and other specific biological agents. Our discussion in 'Population, Health, and Modernity' may have seemed to accept, rather uncritically, the idea that there can be an objective and straightforward definition of health. It should be clear from our discussion of Foucault, however, that this is not the case. It is now necessary to return to this theme and look more critically at the ideas of health and illness.

The conditions that are recognized as illnesses vary quite considerably from one society to another, as do the particular ways in which they are defined and treated. For the sociologist, health comprises whatever is regarded as the normal biological condition of an individual in a society that emphasizes a medical conception of reality. Illness is any perceived departure from this condition that is subject to medical treatment (Freidson 1970).

People in different societies may be affected by a similar viral infection, but their conditions may be socially defined quite differently. In contemporary societies, such a person is likely to be seen as 'ill'. In many pre-modern societies, which lack a concept of 'virus' and have no institutionalized medicine, they may be seen as suffering from the effects of witchcraft or evil spirits. In the same way, it is only recently—and still only in part—that those who suffer from persistent fatigue and depression have been defined as suffering from chronic fatigue syndrome (sometimes called ME or myalgic encephalomyelitis) rather than being seen as malingerers. The social construction of health and illness makes it impossible to set out any kind of general and absolute idea of what it is to be healthy. Conceptions of health are inextricably linked to ideas of personal identity and social acceptability.

Consider the case of dental health. It might be thought that this could be defined in terms of the presence or absence of tooth decay. Much dental treatment, however, is preventive and opens up many ambiguous areas of treatment. The removal of crowded teeth, the straightening of crooked teeth, and the whitening of yellowed teeth are treatments that owe as much to cosmetic considerations as they do to preventive dentistry. It is impossible to decide with any certainty which particular dental interventions are necessary for good health.

In the same way, it might be thought that those who are overweight are unhealthy. However, it is impossible to define what is meant by being overweight independently of social considerations. Conceptions of what it is to be overweight, as we show below, are impossible to disentangle from ideas of what it is to be slim and attractive. This kind of ambiguity has drawn doctors into medical treatments aimed at slimming and into various types of cosmetic surgery.

Sociologists do not, of course, deny that there is a biological basis to illness, nor do they fail to recognize physical suffering. This would be obviously absurd. Two fundamental points are being made in theories of the social construction of illness:

▶ Even biological concepts of health are imprecise. The World Health Organization defines health in relation to 'well-being', for example, but the Royal College of General Practitioners sees it as 'adjustment' to circumstances. Medical definitions leave many areas of uncertainty that can shift as medical knowledge changes. This medical knowledge is itself the product of a complex social process of clinical and scientific investigation.

▶ Social contexts shape both the meanings that are given to biological conditions and people's reactions to them. While doctors need to employ biological conceptions of illness in order to diagnose and treat particular disorders, the sociologist is more interested in the social behaviour of those who are labelled as 'sick' and those who do this labelling. Medicine and sociology have complementary concerns. An understanding of health and illness requires both a biological knowledge of the causes of illness and a sociological understanding of how sick people behave and how others react to their sickness.

MEDICAL CONTROL AND THE BODY

Foucault (1976) showed the way in which the medical gaze transformed the prevailing view of the human body and introduced new disciplines of anatomical control. Organized medicine has been expanding its power by extending its claims to competence to more and more areas of social life. Matters that used to be the responsibilities of priests, social workers, teachers, and others are now seen as 'medical' matters. Illich (1977) sees this **medicalization** as undermining the power of ordinary people to make their own decisions. The right to make decisions is handed over to the technical 'expert' (see also Zola 1975).

In this section we will look at the idea of the sick role, which has been widely used as a way of understanding how these disciplines of the body have been organized in contemporary societies. We will also look at some of the reproductive technologies through which the fertility and sexuality of women have been disciplined. Finally, we look at the discipline of the body in death.

The sick role

In his discussion of health and illness, Talcott Parsons (1951) described the emergence of what he called the **sick role**. This role is defined by normative expectations that people who are ill should behave in ways that minimize the disruptive effects that their illness can have on ordinary social life. Those who are ill may not be able to continue with their usual activities, or they may behave in unacceptable ways. In either case, there may be much disruption of normal, everyday life. Minor forms of illness and disability are often disregarded, but those disorders that are long-lasting or debilitating are likely to cause particularly pressing problems for others as well as for the sufferer. The deviance that might result from such illnesses can be minimized and normalized if the ill person conforms to the expectations of the sick role. Through their knowledge of the sick role—a knowledge that is acquired during their socialization—people learn how to be ill in socially acceptable ways.

There are three principal elements in the normative expectations that define the sick role:

▶ a sick person is exempted from any personal responsibility for her or his illness;

▶ a sick person has permission to withdraw from many normal family and work commitments;

▶ a sick person is obliged to seek medical help and to become a 'patient'.

In our society, illness is not seen as something that sufferers bring upon themselves. It is something that is beyond their control. The physical or organic character of an illness is seen as having no direct connection with the previous behaviour of the sick person. This general principle is not, of course, completely clear-cut, and there are many areas of ambiguity. The health risks that result from heavy smoking are now well known, and there has recently been some discussion about whether heavy smokers should be entitled to medical treatment for lung cancer. Even more controversially, public opinion on AIDS has sometimes tended to see it as a 'self-inflicted' illness. It is seen as a consequence of deviant sexual behaviour and, therefore, as less deserving of treatment than are other illnesses. These are, however, highly problematic and contentious areas. In most cases, exemption from responsibility is given to the sick person, who is then permitted to act in ways that would not normally be tolerated.

The recognition of 'sickness', then, is one way of normalizing deviant behaviour. When people are recognized as suffering from a sickness for which they have no responsibility, they are seen as having a legitimate right to abandon many of their normal day-to-day responsibilities. They may be entitled to take time off work without loss of pay, they can take to their bed and leave domestic chores to other household members, and they may even be able to disregard some of the normal niceties of polite behaviour. None of these dispensations would usually be allowed to people experiencing problems that were seen as their responsibility. The person who becomes incapable of work because of

---

Self-inflicted illness?

'In 1993, Harry Elphick, 47, was refused treatment for a heart condition because he was a heavy smoker. Consultants at Wythenshawe Hospital in Manchester told him that tests to show if a by-pass was needed were not carried out on smokers. Mr Elphick quit his 25-a-day habit, but died a week before he was due to see the doctors again.'

Source: Independent, 28 Jan. 1997.

a drinking spree, for example, is not normally seen as having a legitimate right to take a day off. Those who find themselves in such a situation may often invent a 'bug' or a bout of 'flu' to legitimate their time off work. In doing so, they trade on the social acceptability of the sick role.

This permission to withdraw from normal commitments is not absolute, but is conditional on the person seeking medical help. The sick role is a temporary role, and the sick person must see her or his state of sickness as undesirable, as something to be escaped from as soon as possible. Those who 'wallow' in their illness and who show no sign of trying to recover will rapidly find that the permission to withdraw from normal interaction and the exemption from responsibility are taken away from them. They will be seen as 'malingerers'. The normal assumption is that real sufferers will visit a doctor's surgery or arrange a visit from a doctor to her or his home. It is normally doctors who confirm that a person is ill and so legitimate occupancy of the sick role. The sick person is permitted to continue in this role by those family members, friends, and work colleagues who accept the medical definition of the illness. Doctors authorize the sick person's withdrawal from normal life and make available their medical expertise to treat her or him as a patient.

Central to an understanding of the sick role, then, is the doctor–patient relationship. The relationship between the role of the doctor and the role of the patient is one of authority. There is a fundamental difference in power between the two, rooted in the claim that the doctor makes to scientific expertise (T. Johnson 1972). The patient must submit to the doctor's power, because continued occupancy of the sick role rests upon an acceptance of medical authority. People who deny the authority of a doctor, must give up any claim to have a legitimate sickness. They may, indeed, be ill, but they cannot expect any allowance to be made for this by others because they have rejected the institutionalized requirement to seek and to accept medical help.

This difference in power between doctor and patient is brought out in the use of the very word 'patient', a word that originally described someone who exercises 'patience' and is, therefore, 'passive'. This power difference is magnified when there are also differences of class, gender, or ethnicity between doctors and their patients.

Reproductive bodies

The difference in power between doctors and their patients is especially marked in the medical care of pregnancy and childbirth. In these medical encounters, the doctors are overwhelmingly male and the patients are exclusively female. Their power relations are shaped by the wider context of gender differences and gender inequalities. Medical intervention in childbearing is, in fact, an intervention in the central defining characteristic of sex–gender roles in contemporary societies.

There has been a major shift in the way in which childbearing has been controlled over the last century and a half. Until well into the nineteenth century, childbirth was an event that took place within the private sphere of the home, perhaps with the help and support of female relatives and neighbours. The rise of modern medicine that we have traced brought childbirth and the whole surrounding area of sexuality, pregnancy, and child health into the medical arena, under the control of doctors. Obstetricians, gynaecologists, and paediatricians, supported by midwives and other nurses, achieved a high level of control over these aspects of women's lives (Oakley 1984). By 1927, 15 per cent of all births took place in hospital; by 1980 this figure had reached 98 per cent.

Pregnancy and childbirth are not, of course, illnesses. Their incorporation under the medical gaze, however, has eliminated or reduced many of the dangers to health that women and their babies previously faced. Death during childbirth, for example, was once far more common than it is today, and we have also shown how much neonatal and infant mortality have been reduced. A consequence of this involvement of medical experts has been that pregnant and would-be pregnant women have been required to adopt a variant of the sick role that legitimates the further medicalization of their lives. As a patient, they must accept the authority of the doctor (H. Roberts 1985). They must subordinate their own knowledge of their body and their control over it to the expertise of the doctor. The obstetrician, for example, expects to have the same degree of control over a woman's reproduction as a neurosurgeon has over patients during brain surgery.

The medicalization of reproduction has involved the expansion of a whole complex of reproductive technologies, under the control of doctors. Many of these technologies have, of course, made childbirth safer, but they have also introduced new risks to health. Indeed, the expansion of medical technology has resulted in a significant increase in the health risks that women face when undergoing treatment.

There are four principal technologies of reproduction:

▶ contraception technologies;

▶ childbirth technologies;

▶ foetal technologies;

▶ conception technologies (Stanworth 1987: 10–11).

Contraception technologies are among the oldest available and include a whole array of techniques for preventing and terminating pregnancies. The legalization of abortion in Britain in 1968 reduced the very large number of deaths and injuries that resulted from illegal 'back-street' and self-induced abortions. The technology of termination, however, means that abortion of a foetus is now possible at a much later age. There have been renewed debates about the ethics of abortion and who has the right to decide whether an abortion should take place. Condoms and barrier methods of contraception have been used for a very long time, but one of the greatest revolutions in contraceptive technology has been the introduction of the contraceptive pill (see Figure 6.8). As a technology, working through the regulation of hormones in the woman's body, it is highly effective. It has, however, been linked with thrombosis and some forms of cancer.

Childbirth technologies include such procedures as the long-established caesarean section and the somewhat newer induction of deliveries. Drug technologies for inducing births have allowed hospitals to schedule childbirth to correspond with staff shifts and rotas, reducing the number of overnight births, but induction is not without its dangers to women and their babies. Particularly important forms of childbirth technology have been those concerned with monitoring and treating the pain and distress of the mother and baby. Painkilling injections and foetal-monitoring equipment, for example, were introduced as ways of making childbirth more comfortable and of increasing the chances of the baby being born healthy.

Foetal technologies have been introduced and extended in order to monitor foetal development and eliminate birth defects. These technologies include the use of ultrasound and X-ray to examine the foetus, amniocentesis to identify genetic problems, and, most controversially, the expanding area of genetic engineering. The results of monitoring programmes have been used to identify potential 'problems'—such as a foetus that is likely to develop into a baby with Down's syndrome—and to recommend terminations. The aspiration of many medical scientists involved in the area, however, is that it may be possible, instead, to intervene directly and alter the genetic material of the foetus.

Finally, *conception technologies* ae concerned with the promotion of pregnancy and the treating of infertility. Informal arrangements for the 'donation' of ova and sperms and for 'surrogate motherhood' have long existed, but the medical profession has increasingly become involved in formalizing and medicalizing these arrangements. The development of drug treatments for infertility and the use of *in vitro* fertilization (so-called test-tube reproduction) have expanded the power that the medical profession has to decide who may have children and when they may have them.

The development and expansion of new reproductive technologies must be seen in the context of the occupational strategies of medical experts. While they may, indeed, remove some dangers, they create new risks, and their introduction and use have not been led by their health effects alone. Doctors involved in such high-profile work at the leading edge of research are able to enhance the status of their professional specialism and strengthen their arguments for higher levels of funding. The expansion of reproductive technologies is also driven by the interests of the big drug and medical supply companies, for whom reproduction has become big business.

In this context, women can become quite powerless. For this reason, feminists have seen it as critical to the whole debate over women's health and the control over their own bodies (Dworkin 1983). Reproductive technologies allow the medical profession to weaken—and perhaps to break—the link between sex and mother-

Figure 6.8. **Methods of contraception**

Contraception

Contraception methods, women aged 16–49

Sterilization: **24%**   Pill: **25%**   IUD: **4%**

Safe period: **1%**
Withdrawal: **3%**
Condom: **18%**
Cap: **1%**

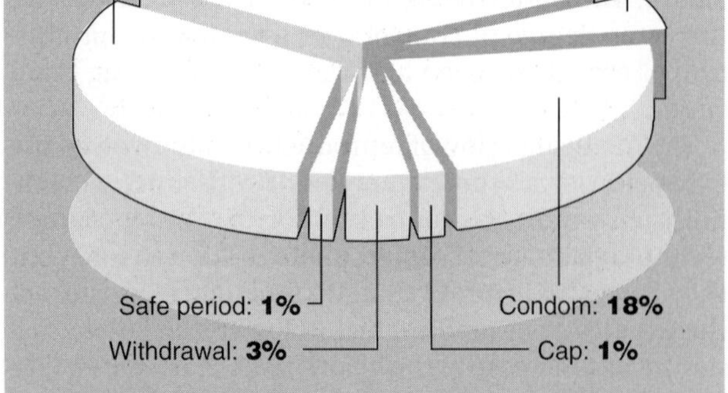

Source: Guardian, 18 Mar. 1997, drawing on General Household Survey, 1995.

hood. A predominantly male medical profession usurps activities that were formerly a primary concern of women, making women's bodies into objects of the new technologies. Reproductive technologies are integral parts of the socially structured medical practices that centralize control over the regulation of populations and human reproduction.

Learning to die

It may be accepted that physical illness is socially constructed in various ways, but surely death is an undeniable biological fact? In one sense, of course, this is true, though there are numerous differences of medical opinion as to exactly when someone can be regarded as 'dead'. There are very real medical difficulties involved in determining the moment of death and in deciding whether those in a persistent vegetative state on a life-support machine are, in fact, 'dead'. This has generated much debate over the rights of relatives to switch off the life-support systems of patients who are in long-term comas. In a wider sense, however, death must also be seen as a socially constructed event around which there are all sorts of values and norms. While people do, of course, die—an undeniable physical event, however difficult it might be to identify in some cases—there are numerous and very different subjective meanings that can be given to this event. For some, death is the end of their existence, for others it is merely a point of transition to some higher, 'spiritual' life, and for yet others it may mark the point at which the 'soul' is released for rebirth in another body. Physical death is the end stage of a social process of 'dying', and this can be understood in the same way as other forms of social behaviour.

Dying, then, must be understood as a social process. This view was one of the central insights of Durkheim's (1897) great study of suicide. Durkheim showed that suicide could be understood only if it was recognized that rates of suicide varied quite considerably from one social group to another. Douglas (1967) extended this argument, showing the varying social meanings that are given to unexpected deaths by the perpetrator (for example, in a suicide note), by friends and relatives, doctors, the police, coroners, and others.

In their powerful study of death, Glaser and Strauss (1965) have shown that, except in cases of sudden accidents that result in instantaneous death, a person's death is a process that takes time. Sometimes this is days, sometimes weeks, sometimes years. In many cases, dying is the final phase of a long occupancy of the sick role, and it involves the continued 'management' of the patient, which today generally takes place in a hospital. Relatives and medical staff will have certain expectations about when and how a patient will die, and they construct a **death trajectory** that they expect the patient to follow. The trajectory becomes, in effect, a role that is expected of the dying person.

It is difficult for these role expectations to be imposed on a dying patient if the patient is unaware that he or she is dying, and Glaser and Strauss have shown the considerable variations in role behaviour that occur with varying degrees of awareness. Doctors and nurses make medical assessments of a patient's condition, which they record in case notes and that influence their behaviour towards the patient. The medical professionals must decide how much of this information is to be passed on to the patient and to his or her relatives. In some cases, patients and relatives may be made fully aware of the situation, while in others they may be kept in the dark.

The various participants in a death, therefore, act on the basis of varying states of awareness. Where all the participants share a common state of awareness, there may be a high degree of consensus over the death trajectory that will be followed. When awareness varies, however, there will be much scope for conflict and misunderstanding and for deviance on the part of the dying patient. The person may, for example, be perceived as dying in unexpected or 'inappropriate' ways. Glaser and Strauss identify four different **awareness contexts** that surround dying in hospitals. These are:

▶ *closed awareness*: the patient is kept in ignorance of the condition and does not know that he or she is dying;

▶ *suspected awareness*: the patient suspects that he or she is dying;

▶ *mutual-pretence awareness*: both staff and patient know, but maintain the fiction that the patient does not know;

▶ *open awareness*: patient and staff are all fully aware.

In a closed-awareness context, the patient does not know his or her true condition, and the medical staff will strive to ensure that this remains the case. To this end, they employ various tactics to prevent the patient from even suspecting the truth. Doctors will not tell patients that they are dying, unless asked a direct question, and all staff may talk 'around the houses' in order to avoid making any direct statements that would give the game away. There is a structure of collusion and secrecy among the staff and the relatives, all of whom try to construct plausible accounts of events and experiences that might otherwise lead the patient to question his or her chances of recovery. In these circumstances, it is difficult to make patients conform to expectations about how to die properly, as they do not know that they are dying.

Because of the collusion and the potential for misunderstanding, closed awareness is difficult to sustain, and it often slips into a situation of suspected awareness or open awareness. Where a patient discovers the truth, he or she may, nevertheless, pretend not to have done so, and the staff—if they are aware of this pretence—are also likely to try to maintain the fiction. This context of mutual pretence is also particularly difficult to sustain.

An open-awareness context is far easier for staff to manage. In this situation, expectations of proper behaviour can be explicitly imposed on patients. Their awareness means that they can be seen to have responsibility for their own actions as dying persons: not for the fact that they *are* dying, but for *how* they die. When people know that they are dying, they are expected to present a *dying self* to the world, and this self-presentation is expected to conform to particular standards that define a 'proper' death:

> 'The patient should maintain relative composure and cheerfulness. At the very least, he [*sic*] should face death with dignity. He should not cut himself off from the world, turning his back upon the living; instead he should continue to be a good family member, and be 'nice' to other patients. If he can, he should participate in the ward social life. He should co-operate with the staff members who care for him, and if possible he should avoid distressing or embarrassing them. A patient who does most of these things will be respected. He evinces what we shall term "an acceptable style of dying".'   (Glaser and Strauss 1965: 86; see also Glaser and Strauss 1968)

Patients who do not die 'properly' are sanctioned in attempts to make them conform to the role expectations. They will be reprimanded, scolded, and ordered; they will be coaxed and coached in how to behave; and they may even be offered rewards for cooperation. Staff may be more likely to be friendly and helpful if the patient cooperates with ward routines, and the relatives of the patient are drawn into this process of social control.

MEDICALIZATION AND THE MIND

We have looked at the sick role in relation to physical illnesses, but there exists a whole array of other illnesses that are seen as having mental rather than physical effects. Schizophrenia, depression, and other mental illnesses are often seen as having an organic basis and as being treatable through drug therapies. They are,

however, generally seen as a different type of illness from the purely physical.

Mental disorders are seen in a rather more ambiguous light than are physical and physiological disorders. There is a lack of public understanding about the nature of mental disorders, and there is often an unwillingness on the part of sufferers to recognize their own symptoms. There is, in a very real sense, public disagreement over whether mental illness is really an illness at all. Many people feel that those who are depressed should 'pull themselves together', that psychological states are less 'real' than physical states, and that, in many respects, people are responsible for their own mental states.

If people are seen as having at least a degree of responsibility for their own illness, then the sick role cannot be played in the usual way. From this point of view, mental illness—unlike physical illness—comes to be seen as a type of deviant behaviour itself. Mentally ill people not only deviate from expectations about normal, everyday behaviour, they also deviate from the expectations surrounding the sick role. Many of the ambiguities and contradictions that are inherent in the treatment of the mentally ill and in the low prestige of psychiatric doctors can be explained by this ambivalence over the character of mental *illness* itself.

Becoming schizophrenic

Scheff (1966) has set out a model of those forms of mental illness that are diagnosed by psychiatrists as forms of 'schizophrenia' or 'psychosis' (see also Coulter 1973). These diagnoses are usually employed where people experience serious delusions or hallucinations and are seen as a threat to themselves and to others. Scheff aims to show that these forms of mental illness, which often involve long periods of hospitalization, can be understood as forms of deviant behaviour.

Schizophrenia is rooted in what Scheff calls **residual rule breaking**. 'Residual rules' relate not to specific kinds of interaction and relationship, but to the very nature of social interaction itself. These rules involve deeply embedded assumptions about the nature of ordinary, day-to-day encounters. They specify such things as the expectation that people who are engaged in a conversation should face one another, maintain a certain distance, take proper turns in the conversation, remain attentive to what is going on, and so on. Those who violate these expectations on a regular basis or in especially visible ways tend to be seen as particularly strange, bizarre, or frightening. They violate the very expectations without which 'normal' interaction is impossible. Their behaviour is seen as unreasonable (Busfield 1996).

Behaviour that may be seen as violating residual rules includes withdrawal, hallucination, muttering, unusual gesturing or posturing, and distraction. Many of these behaviours are acceptable in some contexts, but objectionable in others. Kneeling down, muttering, and hallucinating, for example, are regarded as perfectly acceptable behaviour in a Christian Church—they define a devout act of prayer—but they are not regarded as appropriate in a job interview. It is when such types of behaviour occur in inappropriate situations and in ways that threaten normal interaction that they are likely to be seen as deviant behaviour.

Nevertheless, residual rule breaking is quite frequent in everyday encounters. We all, quite regularly, encounter those who seem to be distracted while we talk to them, or who continually interrupt and refuse to allow others to speak. In most cases, this behaviour goes unnoticed, is ignored, or is explained away—it is normalized in one way or another. People are seen as 'tired', 'busy', 'under the weather', or as in some other way experiencing difficulties that account for their behaviour in terms of 'normal' motivations. When residual rule-breaking is normalized, it has little continuing significance for any of those concerned.

In some cases, however, the behaviour goes beyond the bounds of what is regarded as normal, exceeding the normal tolerance levels of friends, family, or work colleagues. It may, for example, be particularly visible, extreme, or long-lasting. In these circumstances, the behaviour is seen as being unreasonable, abnormal, and incomprehensible. It is seen, therefore, as needing to be acted upon. In contemporary societies, such behaviour is likely to be labelled as a symptom of 'mental disorder'. In other societies, argues Scheff, the same behaviour might be seen as symptomatic of 'spirit possession' or of 'witchcraft' (see Szasz 1970). The term 'mental disorder' is likely to be used today because our culture has become permeated by medical and psychiatric concepts—often only partially understood—that make the imagery of mental 'abnormality', 'madness', and 'insanity' central aspects of our culture.

Stereotyped images of mental disorder are learned from early childhood, and they are reinforced in the mass media. These images are conjured up through the use of such terms as 'crazy', 'loony', 'mad', 'insane', or 'deranged'. In appropriate circumstances, these labels may be applied to others or even to ourselves. People grow up with a particular image of mental disorder and, therefore, of the ways in which they expect those who suffer from it to act. As a result, there is a specific version of the sick role, the **insanity role**.

Many forms of depression and anxiety may be normalized by families, or treated within the conventional framework of the sick role; those who seem to experience seriously disruptive mental problems are more likely to be treated in terms of the insanity role. As with the sick role proper, the medical profession is called in to accredit the insanity. The person's friends and family may, for example, call in the general practitioner, who may refer the case to a psychiatric specialist. In these ways, residual rule-breaking is medicalized, and the medical professionals initiate a process of treatment.

When people act in terms of the insanity role, incorporating it into their sense of identity, residual rule-breaking is transformed into the form of secondary deviation that is called 'mental illness':

'When the deviance of an individual becomes a public issue, the traditional stereotype of insanity becomes the guiding imagery for action, both for those reacting to the deviant and, at times, for the deviant himself. When societal agents and persons around the deviant react to him [sic] uniformly in terms of the traditional stereotypes of insanity, his amorphous and unstructured rule-breaking tends to crystallise in conformity to these expectations, thus becoming similar to the behaviour of other deviants classified as mentally ill, and stable over time. The process . . . is completed when the traditional imagery becomes a part of the deviant's orientation for guiding his own behaviour.'   (Scheff 1966: 64)

But why should anyone conform to such a role? Scheff argues that this occurs because residual rule-breakers are encouraged by others to accept the image of insanity as an 'explanation' for the problems that they have been experiencing. At the same time, they are refused the opportunity to act in more conventional ways: if mentally ill people deny their illness and do not accept the treatment, then this simply shows how ill they really are. They may, for example, find it difficult to enter or to retain employment or to continue with normal domestic responsibilities. The people labelled are, furthermore, likely to be highly suggestible to the opinions of others. The hostility that they may feel and the strength of the opinions held by professionals all leave them feeling highly vulnerable.

To see schizophrenia as a form of deviance is not to deny that many people do face serious mental problems and that they may need help in dealing with them. Nor is it to deny that there may be a biological basis to some forms of residual rule-breaking. The point that Scheff is making is that mental illness is always to be seen as a social fact as well as a physical fact. Psychiatric diagnoses—such as 'schizophrenia', 'phobia', and 'neurosis'—are made in social contexts and are applied to people who have already been labelled as a problem by others. It is only those who have come to be seen as problematic by non-psychiatrists—by friends, relatives, or colleagues—who come to the attention of psychiatrists. For this reason, psychiatrists have most of their professional contact with those who have entered the stage of secondary deviation and are already playing the insanity role. In this context, psychiatric diagnoses cannot be seen as neutral acts that are independent of processes of social control.

The moral career of the mental patient

Goffman (1961*b*) has also explored the life of seriously ill schizophrenics and psychotics, paying particular attention to their 'moral career'. This term refers to the changing sense of self that develops as they experience the particular contingencies and constraints that occur with their hospitalization.

Goffman sees the transition from primary deviation to secondary deviation for the mentally ill as involving a movement from the status of a *civil person* to that of a *patient*. Whereas the civil person is an individual with full civil rights as a member of society, the patient loses certain rights and powers. Hospitalized mental patients in Britain, for example, cannot vote in general elections, and hospital staff have the power to act on their behalf in many areas of life. As we show in Chapter 16, the admissions procedures adopted by mental hospitals emphasize the new status that the person has acquired. With the status of patient, the person fully enters the insanity role, and a career of mental illness becomes possible.

The patient stage of the insanity role is seen by Goffman as involving three phases. First, there is the *home-patient phase* (Goffman calls this the pre-patient phase). This is when the person remains at home, but is under the supervision of a general practitioner. Second is the crucial *in-patient phase*, when the person has been hospitalized, voluntarily or forcibly, and begins a period under the close control of hospital staff. Third is the *ex-patient phase* that follows the patient's release. Ex-patients experience a continuing public reaction, and may face many constraints on their opportunities. They are seen in terms of their status as a former mental patient and this may, for example, make it difficult for them to get a job. Many ex-patients relapse into illness, re-entering the hospital for further in-patient treatment. Goffman's argument is summarized in Figure 6.9.

Goffman's own work was concerned mainly with the in-patient phase. He saw the mental hospital as an arena in which staff and patients struggle with each other to define the reality of the patient experience. Patients will initially respond to hospitalization by denying that they are sick. They selectively draw on pre-hospital experiences that allow the presentation of a convincing and self-respecting account of the reasons for their new status: 'It's all a mistake', 'I was under a lot of pressure', 'I'm not like all the other patients', and so on. These kinds of accounts are difficult to sustain in the long term, as they are incompatible with the medical definition of the situation that staff are constructing.

This medical definition is embodied in the case notes and underpins the treatment that is carried out. It is structured into the very power relations of the hospital. The staff construct the image of the patient as a sick person. He or she is seen as someone who has suffered some kind of collapse or breakdown on the outside and is currently unable to act in his or her own best interests. As the patient attempts to put a positive interpretation on his or her situation, so staff will make comments or highlight evidence that contradicts this. when patients attempt to show staff how 'normal' they are, this is simply taken as a sign of how ill they are: they are so ill that they cannot even recognize their own illness.

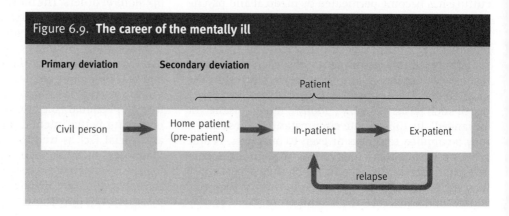

Figure 6.9. **The career of the mentally ill**

Striking evidence in support of Goffman's argument comes from a remarkable study carried out by Rosenham (1973). In this study, Rosenham and seven colleagues feigned psychiatric symptoms—they claimed that they heard voices—and they got themselves admitted to psychiatric hospitals in various parts of the United States. Following admission, they gave up the pretence of hearing voices and began to act in 'normal' ways once more. In all cases, it was some considerable time before staff accepted that they were 'well enough' to be discharged. One of the researchers remained in hospital for a month and a half before being released. On their release, being ex-patients, none of the researchers was defined as having been 'cured' or as having returned to mental health. All were diagnosed as being 'in remission', a diagnosis that meant that the doctors felt that their 'illness' could recur at any time.

Goffman's study focused on the activities that were undertaken by staff to manage the lives of their patients. The staff included not only the doctors and the nurses, but also cleaners, porters, administrators, athletics instructors, therapists, and many others. When in hospital, Goffman argued, patients must conform not only to the medical definition of their 'case', but also to the demands of the organizational routines on which staff work activities depend. Patients must, for example, fit into ward routines and staff shift patterns, they must receive their meals and post at times convenient for the catering, delivery, and cleaning staff, they must have their visits properly regulated, and so on. The hospital—like any organization—is a *negotiated order*, a stable system of recurrent relationships and interactions that results from conflict, bargaining, and compromise among the various participants. Each participant has different kinds and amounts of power resources that they can bring to the situation (Strauss *et al.* 1963). The patient, of course, is the least powerful participant. He or she is enticed into accepting the staff definition of the situation by the rewards that can be offered for conformity.

A key to this system of rewards in the hospitals that were studied by Goffman was the ward system. The various wards were arranged in an informal hierarchy of conditions, facilities, and privileges, and patients could be moved from one ward to another in accordance with their perceived 'progress'. This progress, of course, was measured by the extent to which the patient had come to accept the staff definition of their situation as that of a person in need of treatment. Protestations of sanity and rejection of the hospital routines were regarded as signs of illness or of a lack of insight. Patients with such signs could be punished

through being 'demoted' from a privileged ward to a less privileged one. A patient who accepted the medical staff's definition of the situation and cooperated with attendants and orderlies was seen as developing an insight into his or her illness. Such patients could be rewarded through 'promotion' up the ward system.

Deprived of the social supports that sustained their self-image in the outside world, patients are particularly vulnerable to these processes of control. They are, therefore, likely to show a gradual submission to staff views. In order to achieve a speedy release from hospital, 'The patient must "insightfully" come to take, or affect to take, the hospital's view of himself' (Goffman 1961*b*: 143). By accepting the staff definition of the situation, patients reconstruct their biographies as those of people who are 'ill', but are 'getting better'.

'Community' care

Both Scheff and Goffman looked mainly at the situation of schizophrenics and psychotics, and especially at those who receive hospital treatment. With the expansion of psychiatry, however, there has been a shift away from the nineteenth-century model of the asylum as the principal focus of psychiatric treatment. Figure 6.10 shows that the total number of patients in mental hospitals in England and Wales increased continually until its peak year of 1954. After this year, however, the number declined constantly, despite an increase in the total population over the same period. Thus, the rate per 10,000 people declined to a level in 1980 that was

Figure 6.10. Mental hospital patients, England and Wales, 1850–1980

Year	Number	No. per 10,000 popn.
1850	7,140	4.03
1880	40,088	15.73
1900	74,004	23.05
1930	119,659	30.14
1954	148,100	33.45
1960	136,200	29.48
1970	103,300	21.02
1980	75,200	15.15

Source: adapted from Scull (1984: tables 4.1 and 4.3). Rates for 1960–80 calculated by the authors using census data for 1961, 1971, and 1981.

close to its level of 100 years before. Data for the United States show a similar pattern, the peak year for hospitalization being 1955.

What was happening over this period is that more and more patients were being treated 'in the community', rather than as hospital in-patients. This is the process of decarceration that we discuss in Chapter 16, pp. 674–80. This change in treatment was associated with a shift in the psychiatric gaze. The expansion of psychiatry led its practitioners to give relatively less attention to the severe psychotics and schizophrenics and relatively more attention to the less severe 'depressive' disorders. Depressive states had long been recognized as illnesses by the psychiatric profession, but it was only during the twentieth century that more precise diagnostic criteria were established. At first, such patients were treated in hospital, but they rapidly became candidates for out-patient treatment.

> ☞ Read our discussion of Goffman's concept of the total institution in Chapter 16, pp. 649–50, and consider how useful you think it is in understanding mental hospitals. Look also, in the same chapter, at our discussion of decarceration on pp. 674–6.

It has been suggested that new drug therapies using tranquillizers such as Largactil (chlorpromazine) were responsible for this change in treatment, but this has been overstated. These drugs undoubtedly had some effect in controlling symptoms and so allowing patients to be treated at home, but the shift away from treatment in a mental hospital began before tranquillizer treatment was at all widely available. Scull has convincingly argued that decarceration became a possibility only because of changes in the system of welfare provision. With the establishment of improved welfare systems from the 1930s, and especially since the Second World War, the cost of hospital treatment has been far greater than the cost of out-patient treatment for a person receiving welfare benefits. Given the choice, then, medical authorities have preferred to treat patients in the community rather than in the asylum.

By the 1960s a formal policy of 'community care' had been adopted. Long-term patients thought not in need of active medical treatment were processed through hostels, 'halfway houses', and training centres, while others remained at home. Instead of becoming or remaining in-patients, they have the status of home patient and the task of care is placed upon their families and their neighbours. Many mental problems are

Community care.

now treated by general practitioners and a growing number of counsellors. This process was especially rapid in the 1980s, as Thatcherism promoted the commercialization of care by encouraging private hostels and residential care homes. It has been estimated that the total cost of community care for elderly people suffering from dementia, depression, or anxiety was £2 billion in 1997. These costs include not only medical treatment but also the cost of such things as home helps and meals on wheels. The Labour Government has announced its intention to reverse this policy.

The lack of proper funding for community-care programmes has meant that many schizophrenics and psychotics who are released from the mental hospitals have had to live in rundown hostels or have become homeless. These are the very conditions that perpetuate their difficulties and that may allow them to drift into other forms of primary deviation.

There have been a number of well-publicized cases of schizophrenics in community care who have become

Schizophrenia and community care

There have been a number of notorious cases of schizophrenic patients released into the community and subsequently carrying out violent acts. Christopher Clunis, for example, stabbed a perfect stranger in the street, killing him. Clunis's career as a mental patient had included treatment at ten different hospitals before the events of 1992. He had also stayed in a probation hostel, two prisons, a sheltered housing scheme, and five bed-and-breakfast hotels. He had been seen by five different Social Services departments. The family of the victim, Jonathan Zito, pressed for an official inquiry, which found that Clunis's records had not been properly kept, that there had been no proper plan for his care after his last release into the community, and that no one had overall responsibility for supervising his case.

When you have read our discussion of the meaning of community in Chapter 11, you might like to return to this case and think about the implications for the idea of care in the community.

involved in dangerous actions or crimes of violence that would not have been possible if they had been hospitalized.

Depression, stress, and gender

The largest number of people suffering mental disorders and being treated 'in the community' are those suffering from depression. Like many psychiatric diagnoses, 'depression' is only loosely defined. It is seen as involving feelings of general helplessness, and is closely associated with 'anxiety' and 'stress', as well as with extreme lethargy, loss of appetite, and with both suicide and attempted suicide. The disorder is highly gendered, and women form the core of those receiving treatment for depression.

Studies of depression (Busfield 1996: ch. 10) have come to focus on various distressing experiences that put people under 'stress' and so predispose them to feelings of depression and anxiety. Events associated with stress have been said to include job change, moving home, divorce, bereavement, loss of work, being the victim of crime, illness, heavy demands at work, and so on. Stress levels have been found to vary with subordination and oppression, as people in these situations are more likely to experience unemployment, ill health, family breakdown, violence, poor housing, and crime. Women and the poor, for example, have higher rates of diagnosed and self-reported depression than have men and the more affluent. It has been estimated that between 12 per cent and 17 per cent of women have suffered from clinical depression at some stage in their life, compared with only 6 per cent of men. Women are also far more likely to be taking or to have taken tranquillizers: 23 per cent of the population in 1984 had

been prescribed tranquillizers at some stage in their life, and women were twice as likely as men to have used them (Blackburn 1991: 103).

In practice, the idea of 'stress' is difficult to define with any precision. The question of what is and what is not stressful is very much a subjective matter, and it may be as much a *consequence* of depression and anxiety as it is a *cause*. The fact that women are far more likely to experience depression than men, for example, has been related to the way in which emotions are structured into gender identities. Conventional gender identities involve an expectation that women will express their emotions and take on the 'emotional work' of dealing with others, and this has become a central part of their responsibilities within families (Duncombe and Marsden 1993; see also Hochschild 1983). Men, on the other hand, are expected to 'hold things in'. When men do express their emotions, this is more likely to be outwardly, in the form of violence or in the use of alcohol. The inward direction of emotions by women has been seen as responsible for the self-blame and lower self-esteem that predisposes them to depressive responses to stress. It has been suggested, for example, that because women tend to have more emotionally charged relationships with others to whom they are close, they are, themselves, more likely to be emotionally affected by the problems faced by others in their family and the circle of close friends.

These issues were explored by Brown and Harris (1978) in their investigation into the links between potentially stressful life events and depression in a large sample of women in south London. They show that women who become depressed are far more likely to have experienced serious and severe stressful events (life-threatening illness in the family, loss of job, and so on) over a long period than were those who did not become depressed. They argue, however, that the susceptibility of women to stressful events depends upon what they call 'vulnerability'. By this they mean the social supports that are available through social ties and social networks and that help, or hinder, people's ability to cope with stress. They identify four particular 'vulnerability factors' that predispose certain women to depression:

▶ the absence of an intimate relationship;

▶ employment outside the home;

▶ having three or more children under 14 at home;

▶ loss of their own mother before the age of 11.

Those women who have these experiences—especially the first one—are far more likely to experience depression if they are faced with stressful events. Women with an intimate partner, with few or no small children, without paid employment, and who have not lost their mothers appeared to find it easier to cope with stressful events and were less likely to fall into depression. The important point made by Brown and Harris is that these factors do not, in themselves, induce depression: they make people more or less vulnerable to the stressful events which actually trigger depression (see Figure 6.11). Further stress after the onset of depression reinitiates the process and deepens depression.

The vulnerability factors are clearly linked to conventional gender roles and to ideas about the domesticity of women. Having small children at home and being responsible for them is a central feature of the *captive*

wife described by Gavron (1968). It is the combination of this with involvement in paid work that has placed conflicting pressures on many employed women in contemporary Britain. Their two principal roles—employee and mother—involve contradictory expectations and may make it more difficult to cope with stress. Those factors that help women to combine the two roles may, thereby, reduce the impact of stressful events on them. The availability of effective childcare facilities, for example, helps those who have many small children.

FEMININITY, MEDICINE, AND BEAUTY

As the boundaries of medicalization have expanded, there has also been a counter-movement in which patients are, at least in formal terms, seen by governments as 'consumers' of health with the right to choose in medical matters in the same way that they choose the education of their children, the type of car that they drive, and the kind of food that they eat. The power of patients to choose is limited in a whole variety of ways, just as their powers to choose in other areas of life are limited. However, the growing popularity of alternative medicines is a sign, perhaps, of the weakened authority of doctors. Indeed, patients are able to exercise a degree of consumer power in areas such as 'beauty', where medicine has stretched beyond the more clear-cut boundaries defined by notions of 'disease' and 'illness'.

In this section, we will look at two very different ways in which people 'choose' their own state of health. We

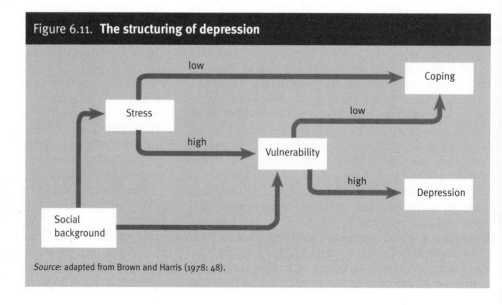

Figure 6.11. **The structuring of depression**

Source: adapted from Brown and Harris (1978: 48).

will look at cosmetic surgery and eating disorders as responses to contemporary images of femininity.

Images of femininity

There is, in contemporary Western culture, a strong positive value attached to the idea of the slim, attractive woman, who is seen as both independent and self-assured. This cultural ideal contrasts sharply with the traditional image of female domesticity. The conventional image was vociferously challenged by the women's movement of the 1960s and 1970s in the wake of Friedan's (1962) critique of the 'feminine mystique'. This critique encouraged the view that caring for a family is a mundane and undemanding task and that women needed to develop their potentialities outside the home.

The new image of feminity closely combines conceptions of 'beauty' and 'attractiveness' with conceptions of 'health' and 'fitness' (Wolf 1991; Kathleen Davis 1995). A whole complex of industries and processes surround this image. The cosmetics industry, the fashion industry, pharmaceuticals companies, and other organizations concerned with dieting and 'healthy eating', as well as the medical profession itself, are all involved in perpetuating the new cultural ideal. These are, in turn, reinforced by advertising images of all kinds, and not only by advertising for 'beauty' products themselves. Consumer pressure groups and television programmes that publicize the health implications of food also tend to reinforce the image of the healthy and fit women.

Cultural ideals can change rapidly, and the ideal body of the 1960s has become the 'full figure' of the 1980s and 1990s. It has been shown that, over the period from 1959 to 1979, the average size of women depicted in fashion and other magazines decreased substantially. At the same time, changes in diet have meant that average weight in the population as a whole has increased. Pressures to be slim have grown and the size of the ideal body image has diminished (Mennell *et al.* 1992).

 You might find it useful to turn to Chapter 8 and look at our discussion of images of women in the media in 'Representation', pp. 294–5.

Through their socialization, women have come to internalize this conception of feminity and to accept it as an ideal. The strength of the image is such that the great majority of women learn to scrutinize and monitor their size, shape, and food intake. They compare themselves with the cultural ideal, and feel themselves to have some kind of spoiled identity (Goffman 1963*b*). They may feel that they are overweight or fat, or they may feel that they have some particular blemish that marks them out as different from other women: their nose is the wrong shape, their breasts are too small or too big, or they have too many wrinkles.

The tyranny of the cultural ideal means that it is almost impossible not to develop a negative self-image. In pursuit of the cultural ideal, women seek to control and to shape their bodies in the desired direction. Dieting—restricting the amount of food that is eaten—becomes, for many, a normal part of their life. Large numbers of women are drawn not only into diet, exercise, and jogging, but also into body-building, the use of slimming pills, and increasingly into cosmetic surgery. Young girls are also exposed to these pressures and grow up feeling that it is unusual not to diet for weight loss. Their attitudes are affected by the views about health and fitness held by their own families and friends and by the classes on 'healthy eating' that now figure in the school curriculum.

We will look at two different responses to this situation, both of which are attempts at empowerment and control. In the case of those women who choose to undergo cosmetic surgery, we will show that control is sought through a faith in medical experts and the quick surgical fix. In the case of those women who experience eating disorders, we will show that control is sought through the adoption of a strict and disciplined way of life.

The surgical fix

Various forms of plastic surgery have been performed for many centuries in the past, but it was not until the Crimean War that these techniques became at all reliable. These surgical techniques were driven by the need to repair the war-ravaged bodies of male soliders, and great advances were made in the two world wars. Only in the second half of the twentieth century has plastic surgery for the aesthetic improvement of healthy bodies become a major area of medical specialization.

Indeed, plastic surgery is now the fastest growing medical specialism. Cosmetic surgery now accounts for about 40 per cent of all plastic surgery. About two million Americans received cosmetic surgery in 1988. Ninety per cent of them were women who were given face lifts, breast augmentations, liposuction (fat removal), and so on. This is, perhaps, the clearest expression of a consumerist 'choice' orientation in contemporary medicine. Having a new nose or new breasts is almost seen in the same way as having a new hair style: it is something chosen by a woman in order to achieve a particular, desirable presentation of self.

Kathleen Davis (1995) has shown that cosmetic surgery is seen as an option by those women who, comparing themselves with others, develop a fear and loathing of a particular feature of their own body. This feature comes to be seen as a blemish that in some way discredits them as women. Their nose, their breasts, or their buttocks, for example, do not fit with the image of what they feel they 'really' look like. It does not match the rest of their body.

Having a face lift

'I saw a face lift performed—the surgeon's hand inside the woman's face, punching and tearing, her separated skin only anchored at the nose and mouth. . . . The laser has added a further dimension to face lifting. The woman's face is now cut, separated, trimmed and reattached, the skin then burnt with a laser to get rid of the fine lines around the mouth.

Source: *Guardian*, 18 Feb. 1997.

Davis argues, then, that these women are not in search of absolute perfection or an exceptional beauty. They are, rather, responding to a perceived stigma. She notes, however, that the perceived stigma is rarely disfiguring, or even apparent, in any objective sense. The cultural pressures on women, however, have led many to be hypersensitive towards their appearance. They are constantly concerned about anything that is 'not quite right'. They hope to rectify a specific blemish that, they feel, prevents them from appearing 'ordinary' and is responsible for their (actual or imagined) exclusion and derogation by others. They feel different and they feel that they are constantly noticed by others because of their assumed peculiarity. These women use the word 'ordinary' when they mean having an appearance that is within the normal aesthetic range for contemporary women. An ordinary women is not noticed in her everyday encounters. Their perception of normality, however, is heavily influenced by the cultural ideal of femininity.

The first step towards cosmetic surgery, then, is a feeling of being blemished. The second step, however, is coming to a decision that cosmetic surgery is an appropriate solution to this. In a society where more and more areas of life have become medicalized, the surgi-

cal fix becomes a more realistic possibility for ever-increasing numbers of people.

Those that take this decision, Davis argues, are involved in a renegotiation of their identity and sense of self. It is seen as a last-ditch attempt to rectify a situation that is perceived to be unbearable: 'Cosmetic surgery is not about beauty, but about identity. For a woman who feels trapped in a body which does not fit her sense of who she is, cosmetic surgery is about exercising power under conditions which are not of one's own making. In a context of limited possibilities for action, cosmetic surgery can be a way for an individual woman to give shape to her life by reshaping her body' (Kathleen Davis 1995: 163).

Women come to believe that by controlling their bodies they are controlling their lives. Cosmetic surgery comes to be seen as a way of enhancing their power. Their identity is renegotiated, however, in relation to a prevailing image of femininity and a medicalized definition of reality. Their freely chosen option of the surgical fix is as much a sign of subordination as it is of empowerment. The dilemma of cosmetic surgery is that the desire for power and control is pursued by subordination not merely to a cultural ideal of feminity but also to the power of the medical profession.

Femininity, weight, and eating

There has been growing public concern in recent years over anorexia nervosa. Indeed, there has been something of a moral panic. Anorexia comprises a number of physical symptoms that revolve around an abnormally low body weight for the age, height, and sex of the sufferer. This is brought about by a sustained and deliberate restriction of food intake. Although the condition first appeared as a medical diagnosis in the middle of the nineteenth century, it is only since the 1970s that it has become of epidemic proportions. The condition is found mainly, but not exclusively, among young, white, and relatively affluent women, and it is the causes and consequences of anorexia in this group that have been so keenly discussed. Its incidence is difficult to gauge, but it is thought to be a serious problem for one in every 200 or 250 women between the ages of 13 and 22. The number of deaths is small, but they may amount to around 10 per cent of those who receive long-term medical treatment as hospital in-patients.

The loss of body weight in anorexia may vary from a condition of being mildly underweight to a state of extreme emaciation. Medical discussions have tended to suggest a physiological model in which the former leads inexorably to the latter. The medical view does, however, correctly identify a number of physiological changes that result from extreme weight loss and that characterize established sufferers. These physical effects include secondary amenorrhoea (cessation of menstruation as a result of hormonal changes), feelings of extreme coldness as a result of a lowered rate of metabolism and blood circulation, disturbed sleep, the growth of fine body hair, and a thickening of head hair. There are also likely to be stomach and intestinal upsets, such as constipation and abdominal pain. These are, however, much worse in the related problem of bulimia, where 'binge' eating is followed by induced vomiting or diarrhoea. Abstinence from food over a long period of time reduces body weight below the level at which normal physiological mechanisms can operate to regulate the state of the body, and total physical breakdown is, indeed, inevitable unless treatment is accepted (Palmer 1980).

In relatively affluent and comfortable families, there is often great pressure on children to succeed in their lives. In the case of young women, this is likely to involve an encouragement—experienced as pressure—to take up opportunities that were not available to earlier generations of women. This encouragement involves a rejection of, or at least an ambivalence towards, the traditional feminine role and an implicit endorsement of the new cultural ideal. This new ideal of independent and assertive femininity, however, is something that many young women find difficult to accept. They are anxious about their ability to meet these expectations, concerned about how they could ever compare with the ideal.

It is these anxious individuals, it seems, who are especially likely to be drawn into anorexic behaviour (Bruch 1973, 1979; Chernin 1985). Their anxiety leads them to be uncertain about their own goals, unable to decide what to do. They become confused about who they are and what they might be in the future. This uncertainty over their identity, and the associated feeling that they have no control over their own lives, leads them to focus their attention on more immediate goals that are set by parents and teachers. Educational success, for example, becomes an end in itself, and, striving to please, they tend to adopt a perfectionist attitude towards their school work. In doing so, they set unrealistic goals and so are constantly unable to meet their own rigorous standards. If they do meet these standards, they feel that they must, after all, have been too low. This is the classic example of the inferiority complex described by Adler (1928).

In their search for a solution to their problems of identity, these young women have not completely abandoned the cultural ideal of femininity. It is something that is still important to them, but about which they feel ambivalent and inadequate. Like others of their age, and like many of their mothers' generation, they are drawn to the ideal and to the practices of bodily control that are associated with it. Slimming and fitness training, for example, may be adopted as exploratory experiments in their ability to meet this ideal. Such experiments often begin around the time of puberty and are associated with the natural weight gain and changes in body shape that occur at this time. For those who misinterpret the nature of these changes, they can be seen as signs that they are getting 'fat'. It is in these circumstances that the drift into anorexia becomes a possibility.

Many young women begin to diet, perhaps by avoiding what they see as unhealthy or fatty foods. Many—perhaps most—are unsuccessful in losing weight and may drift in and out of dieting for the rest of their lives. Some of those who are successful, especially the anxious perfectionists, are likely to feel a degree of pleasure in having achieved their goal. They enjoy the feeling of accomplishment and control that it gives them. Achieving a weight loss provides a sense of purpose that seems to resolve some of the confusions that they feel about the direction that their lives should take. Dieting becomes one area of life where it seems possible to exercise total control (Bordo 1993: 148–50).

The anorexic solution

The person who drifts from experimental dieting into incipient anorexia is one who gets great satisfaction from finding, at last, something that she has chosen and that she is good at. Dieting seems to resolve her sense of identity even more than immersion in school work. It becomes something that is very difficult to give up. If it is the one area where she feels that she can 'succeed', then what does she have left if she gives it up? She becomes committed to the activity into which she has drifted, gaining satisfaction and even enjoyment from it. Continued weight loss, rather than a fixed target weight, becomes her goal. The original aspiration to achieve attractiveness and independence is partially displaced into a mastery of the body for its own sake. She begins to enter what we describe in Chapter 5, as secondary deviation. She begins a *career* of anorexia, which becomes a way of life that, paradoxically, becomes increasingly detached from the cultural ideal of femininity.

The anorexic way of life revolves around a commitment to *ascetic* practices and values that are deeply rooted in our culture and were first explored by Max Weber (1904–5; see also B. Turner 1996). The asceticism of the early puritans, he argued, was the basis of their business success. In the favourable circumstances of seventeenth- and eighteenth-century England, it helped the expansion of the capitalist system. These values subsequently became much weakened, but they became the basis of a so-called work ethic that limited consumption and leisure by subordinating them to the expansion of production. As we suggest in the discussion of drug use in Chapter 5, the work ethic involves the idea that consumption and leisure can be enjoyed only *after* work commitments have been met in full. The right to enjoy one's leisure must be earned through hard work (J. Young 1971).

> 👉 Asceticism is the pursuit of a disciplined life of self-denial and abstention from material comforts and pleasures. We discuss Weber's argument in Chapter 9, pp. 323–4, and you might find it useful to review what we say there. You might also find it useful to look at our discussion of hedonism and the work ethic in Chapter 5, pp. 174–5. These issues are well covered in Lupton (1996).

The work ethic is linked to a specific structuring of sex–gender roles. Participation in the 'public' world of paid work and politics has been mainly an activity of men. Women have largely been confined to the 'private' domestic world of unpaid work. In the conventional family household, women have been responsible for intimate and emotional matters and the man has been the 'breadwinner'. It is precisely this feminine role that many young women today reject, reflecting a fundamental cultural shift that has involved a weakening of the work ethic and a possibility for the more open pursuit of pleasure.

For those who are ambivalent towards the contemporary images of femininity and who drift into anorexic practices, the adoption of a purer form of asceticism, closer to the Puritan original, is highly conducive. In this sense, the anorexic way of life is an ascetic way of life. Asceticism for the anorexic is a response to anxiety and inner loneliness, as much as it was for the Calvinist. In her case, however, the anxiety does not concern religious salvation but personal autonomy and independence.

Bordo (1993) sees these women as in a state of implicit 'protest' against the culturally institutionalized images of feminity that, in crucial respects, they fear and seek to avoid. This is not, however, an absolute rejection, and their feelings are highly ambivalent. As young girls, they are socialized into an acceptance of these images, which become deeply embedded parts of their sense of self. Nevertheless, they find it impossible

The fashion industry is often seen as reinforcing — and exaggerating — cultural images of slimness and beauty.

to embrace them wholeheartedly as examples to follow in their own lives. The anorexic, then, is in protest against these prevailing images of women—attracted by both, but fearing and rejecting aspects of them as well. This protest, however, is not a conscious and planned political protest, but a *bodily* protest. The anorexic engages in what Orbach (1986) calls a 'hunger strike' against contemporary femininities.

In the stage of secondary deviation that is marked by the adoption of an ascetic way of life, the central element in the young woman's identity is no longer an aspiration to a cultural ideal of femininity. Instead, it is the maintenance of an image of a person who is in control of her own life through her control over her own body. The anorexic way of life establishes a regime in which size must be constantly reduced. The search for a slender, controlled body involves a constant watch for any increase in weight and for any unwanted bumps that must be eliminated. With continued weight loss to well below 'normal' levels, the sufferer becomes committed to being thin rather than to meeting the cultural ideal of femininity itself. Being thin—and so being 'straight' rather than 'curvy'—is *safe*, as it allows her to withdraw from the competitive pressure to be an attractive and independent woman. A return to normal weight is feared for the problems of identity that would return with it.

As the goal becomes that of attaining ever greater slenderness, any soft flesh comes to be seen as unsightly, as fat. Sensations of emptiness become a sign of health and achievement, while eating above the very restricted level that has been adopted leads to feelings of being 'bloated' and, therefore, 'fat'. Paradoxically, the slimmer a woman gets, the more obtrusive becomes any normal roundness in body shape, and the greater becomes the internal pressure towards continued size reduction. As the sufferer gets drawn further into these patterns of behaviour, so the inevitable physical hunger pains and other physical symptoms of starvation also come to be seen as things that must be suppressed or ignored and, therefore, controlled. This victory over pain may even be secretly enjoyed as yet another sign of control.

It has been suggested that a sufferer from anorexia experiences perceptual distortions as a direct result of her physical condition—she misdescribes her own body as fat rather than thin. This view, however, has been contested. It may simply be that there is a verbal obscuring of her new, secret identity as someone who has escaped from contemporary femininity through the hunger strike. By describing herself as fat, the anorexic legitimates the continuation of the ascetic practices that she believes have helped her to escape from the tyranny of the cultural ideal.

As her physical condition worsens, however, a sufferer may begin to feel that there is something wrong with her. This is tempered by a continuing commitment to her lifestyle and new identity as someone who is in control. Wearing many layers of clothing will keep her warm, partly offsetting the physical coldness that she feels; but it may also help to hide the extent of her weight loss from friends and family. She continues to tell herself that she fears putting on weight because she would no longer be attractive or healthy, and she may put these arguments to others if challenged about her appearance or behaviour. These explanations, however, become less convincing.

From reading magazines, watching television, and talking to others, the anorexic adopts the idea of an 'eating disorder' to account for her behaviour. As she struggles to understand her own feelings, she may come to accept, in private, the idea that she is suffering from anorexia. Because anorexia has been socially defined as abnormal or unacceptable—by family, by friends, and in the media—this self-definition is likely to remain a private matter. Outwardly, the anorexic wishes to appear as normal, but privately she feels that only she may know the practices and routines through which this appearance is produced. The idea of anorexia is incorporated into her identity and given a positive interpretation, but it must remain secret, something that can be admitted only in private. By maintaining an outward front-region appearance of normality and conformity, she can feel that she is able to remain in control.

In the back region—in the privacy of her bedroom—the sufferer voraciously consumes books about anorexia and eating disorders, and she comes to redefine and to reconstruct her biography in the same terms that they use. There is, however, a curious ambivalence about the medical diagnosis. This is likely to be rejected at the same time as many of its features are accepted. There can be no easy acceptance of the idea of being ill when the sufferer feels that she is in control.

Successful reversal of the anorexic condition has been shown to depend upon a self-recognition of it and an acceptance of the need to struggle against the illness. Such a decision is by no means easy, as a positive view of anorexia has become a central feature of the sufferer's identity. Any departure from the ascetic regime that she has been following for so long is likely to result in feelings of guilt, and guilt is likely to lead to readoption of the regime in an even more rigorous form. The ascetic shaping of the body and its physical consequences reinforce one another. Eventually the deteriorating physical condition of the sufferer may destroy the possibility of any proper control and autonomy. Lack of energy, depression, and sheer starvation make almost all physical and mental activity impossible. The search for control *over* the body can all too easily end in the control of the searcher *by* her own body.

SUMMARY POINTS

In this section we have looked at the medicalization of ever more areas of life. We looked not only at physical health and mental health, but also at the medicalization of reproduction and beauty.

▶ There is no necessary conflict between medical and sociological views of health and illness. Both are important, but they have differing purposes and concerns.

▶ Illness in contemporary society is organized in terms of a sick role that establishes norms of behaviour for the sufferer and for others. Death is also disciplined through definite role expectations.

▶ Schizophrenia has its origins in the social reaction to residual rule-breaking. Hospital treatment involves a definite moral career for patients.

▶ Depression has its origins in particular life conditions that are experienced most particularly by women.

We argued that the medicalization of life raises important questions about the meaning of 'health'.

▶ Reproductive behaviour has increasingly come to be defined in medical terms. Sex and motherhood have both come under the medical gaze.

▶ Contemporary concerns about feminine beauty have had a major impact on women's lifestyles. They have been a major causal factor in the growth of cosmetic surgery and eating disorders.

REVISION AND EXERCISES

Review the various Summary Points in this chapter. You may find it useful to consider these in relation to our discussion of socialization, identity, and deviance in Chapters 4 and 5. We considered a number of substantive areas, as well as the methodological problems of using official statistics.

MEDICINE, HEALTH, AND ILLNESS

In our discussion of medicine, we looked at both physical illness and mental illness. We showed that each must be seen as socially constructed:

▶ **Make sure that you understand the following terms: medical gaze, medicalization; client control, professional control; sick role, insanity role, death trajectory, awareness context; residual rules, moral career; community care; reproductive technologies.**

▶ **What kinds of medical intervention are covered by each of the following terms: contraception technologies, childbirth technologies, foetal technologies, conception technologies?**

▶ **Try to grasp the key ideas associated with: Foucault, Parsons, Glaser and Strauss, Scheff, Goffman, and Brown and Harris.**

POPULATION AND THE SOCIAL BODY

Foucault figures again in our review of population. You should spend a little time thinking about the links between his views on medicine and his arguments about population:

▶ **How does Foucault distinguish between regulation and discipline?**

▶ **How would you define the following: anatamo-politics, bio-politics, surveillance; demographic transition, health transition?**

Understanding population requires a little bit of statistical knowledge, and you should try to practise some of your skills and consolidate your knowledge of the statistical concepts used to study populations:

▶ **What do you understand by the following demographic measures: crude birth rate, crude death rate, age-specific fertility, standardized mortality rate, life expectancy, neonatal mor-**

tality, ageing population? Do not worry about giving precise definitions, but just ensure that you understand the general idea.

▶ Using the figures in Figure 6.1, draw a pie chart to show the distribution of world popuplation across the various regions.

▶ Using the data in Figure 6.2, calculate the periods in which UK population increase has been most rapid. You may find it useful to draw a line graph.

▶ How would you word a question on ethnic identity for use in a government social survey? How would you expect the results in Figure 6.3 to be affected by a change in question wording?

FOOD, BEAUTY, AND LIFESTYLE

Issues of beauty and eating have increasingly come to be seen in medical terms, and we discussed a number of matters that have arisen. Issues of health and lifestyle are now closely associated with each other:

▶ What is the significance of the idea of the family meal? What factors have contributed to its decline?

▶ Why do you think there has been a growth in smoking among young people?

▶ Why do you think that the cultural ideal of femininity is so important to most women?

▶ What do you understand by the following terms: cosmetic surgery, asceticism, hunger strike

FURTHER READING

Good general discussions of the issues covered in this chapter can be found in:

Foucault, M. (1963), *The Birth of the Clinic* (New York: Vintage Books, 1975). Hard going, but it repays the effort.

Coleman, D., and Salt, J. (1992), *The British Population: Patterns, Trends and Processes* (Oxford: Oxford University Press). A large and comprehensive summary of population trends since the nineteenth century.

Pilcher, J. L. (1995), *Age and Generation in Modern Britain* (Oxford: Oxford University Press). A very useful and well-written overview of population issues related to age and ageing.

Freidson, E. (1970), *The Profession of Medicine* (New York: Dodd Mead). An important study of the medical profession and its power.

Goffman, E. (1961), *Asylums: Essays on the Social Situation of Mental Patients and Other Inmates* (New York: Doubleday). Once again, we recommend a book by Goffman. This one was said to have inspired the feature film *One Flew Over the Cuckoo's Nest*.

The issues are explored in greater depth in:

Douglas, J. (1967), *The Social Meanings of Suicide* (Princeton: Princeton University Press). A classic critique of Durkheim's work on suicide, written from a phenomenological point of view.

Lupton, D. (1996), *Food, the Body and the Self* (London: Sage). A useful overview of the sociology of food that considers many of the issues discussed in this chapter.

Busfield, N. J. (1996), *Men, Women and Madness: Understanding Gender and Mental Disorder* (London: Macmillan). A good, recent account of the gendered character of mental illness.

Stanworth, M. (1987) (ed.). *Gender, Motherhood and Medicine* (Cambridge: Polity Press). Important for Stanworth's Introduction and for other contributions on the new reproductive technologies.

Bordo, S. (1993), *Unbearable Weight: Feminism, Western Culture, and the Body* (Berkeley and Los Angeles: University of California Press). A collection of Bordo's papers that examine anorexia from a feminist standpoint.

Wolf, N. (1991), *The Beauty Myth: How Images of Beauty are Used against Women* (New York: Wm. Morrow). A good critique of the cultural ideal of beauty and how it constrains and coerces women.

Chapter 7
EDUCATION AND TRAINING

More choice or less?

'Imagine a town where parents have a wide choice of school. There are two grammar schools, single-sex schools, schools which have opted out of local authority control and even one which has not, for those on the Left who object to the rest. It looks like a place which fulfils every Conservative's parental choice dream. In fact, it is a parental nightmare.

'The town is the London borough of Bromley, where Harriet Harman's son, Jo, is in his second term at St Olave's grammar school, and its story is a cautionary tale about the perils of competition in education.

'The trouble began when one grant-maintained school, Hayes, applied to the Secretary of State for Education for permission to select 25 per cent of its pupils. Last July, the 13 heads of the other schools got together and agreed that they would all select 15 per cent of their pupils to stop Hayes siphoning off the cleverest children. They are not allowed to select more without permission from the Secretary of State.

'Selection inevitably reduces choice for those who are not selected. But, to make matters worse, all except one of the schools picking 15 per cent set their entrance exams on the same day. So parents were forced to choose just one of them. . . .'

Source: Judith Judd, 'The Great School Lottery', *Independent*, 5 Feb. 1997.

SCHOOL life is one of the few things that we have all experienced. It is hard to imagine growing up without spending many years in school. It is only in the last century or so, however, that children in Britain have had to go to school and schools have been provided for all. Britain was an industrial society long before it was an educated one.

Although education for all was slow to develop in Britain, everyone now has access to free education up to the age of 16, and up to 18, if they do well enough in their exams. The free provision of education suggests that it is the one thing that is equally available to everyone. It has, indeed, been argued that it is education that provides equality of opportunity. Educational success leads to occupational success and everyone has an equal chance to succeed in education. But do they? Does everyone start equal or do some have advantages because of their class background, their gender, or their ethnicity? This has been one of the central concerns of the Sociology of Education and is one of the main issues that we discuss in this chapter.

By the 1970s the structure of British education seemed well established but it was about to enter a new period of transformation in the 1980s and the 1990s. The provision of greater choice for parents was one of the main changes, though, as our opening extract shows, choice was sometimes made very difficult. Other aspects of this transformation were a new pressure on educational institutions to compete and a centralization of control over the curriculum and standards of education that was quite new in Britain. We examine these changes in the last part of the chapter.

UNDERSTANDING EDUCATION

The central issues of the Sociology of Education focus on the relationship between education and society. In this first section of the chapter we take up three key issues of this kind. The first of these is the significance of education in the socialization process, the way in which educational institutions provide a bridge between the family and society. The second is the issue of inequality, for education has been central to the discussion of both equality of opportunity and the transmission of inequality. The third is the relationship between education and capitalism, for education is crucial to the supply of labour to the economy, while the recent transformation of education in Britain resulted largely from the economic crisis of the 1970s.

EDUCATION AND SOCIALIZATION

Education plays a crucial part in the process of socialization. As we show in Chapter 4, pp. 124–8, *primary* socialization is carried out within the family, but this takes the process only so far. Both Durkheim (1925) and Parsons (1959) have argued in their different ways that education plays a key role in *secondary* socialization by performing functions that the family cannot perform.

One way in which education has done this is by providing the skills needed to perform the specialized occupations characteristic of industrial societies. As the division of labour became more specialized, it was no longer possible for skills to be handed down within the family. Children could acquire these skills only through formal education. How well schools perform this function has, however, become a matter of growing concern in Britain, as the development of technology has changed the skills required.

Education also turns children into members of society by socializing them into the common values of that society. Through education children learn the religious and moral beliefs of the society they live in. They also develop a sense of national identity through education. Indeed, this has been one reason for the emphasis placed on education by governments seeking to weld the members of diverse ethnic groups into a single nation. Education has been an important part of the project of nation-building, for it is through education that children learn national languages, the symbols of nationality, and the history of the nation.

Durkheim was particularly concerned with the moral aspects of making children members of their society. It was through school discipline that children learned to behave in a moral way. Punishment and the authority of the teacher played an important part in this. He emphasized, however, that it was not just a matter of forcing children to obey but also of getting them to appreciate the moral basis of society. They needed to understand the reasons for moral behaviour, so that they behaved morally not because they were forced to do so but because they wanted to. Social rules had to become internalized as part of the individual's personality, so that discipline became self-discipline.

Durkheim emphasized the moral aspect of education because he was concerned with the increasing individualism of nineteenth-century French society. For Durkheim the key function of education was that it subordinated the individual to society and made people aware of their responsibilites to each other and to the wider collectivity. This view of education has more recently been expressed by Hargreaves (1982), who drew extensively on the work of Durkheim. He argued that British schools and teachers had become dominated by a culture of individualism. They were far too concerned with meeting the needs of the individual child and too little concerned with the school's functions for society. He called for schools to promote social solidarity by generating a sense of community among their pupils and linking this to the wider community and society as a whole.

Parsons too recognized the moral significance of education, but in the rather different social context of mid-twentieth-century America he placed more emphasis on the value of individual achievement. According to Parsons, it was through education that children learned to achieve and came to accept the value of achievement. This value was central to the functioning of an industrial society but families could not instil it in children, for families treated children in a *particular* way according to who they were. In school, however, success depended upon achievement and this was measured by the universal standards of examinations, which took no account of who you were and simply measured how well you performed.

Although they differed in their emphasis, both Durkheim and Parsons saw education in terms of the functions it performed for society. Education does do the kinds of things that Durkheim and Parsons saw it as

The Islamic Education Trust in Leicester.

Muslim schools receive state funding

State funding was granted in January 1998 to two Muslim (and two Jewish) primary schools. Muslims had complained for years that the state funding of Anglican and Roman Catholic schools meant that white, middle-class parents could obtain free education in religious schools for their children, while Muslim, often working-class, parents had to pay for their children to go to religious schools. The Secretary of State for Education emphasized that the schools concerned were required to teach the national curriculum and to treat boys and girls equally, like all state-funded schools. According to Department of Education officials, previous applications for the state funding of Muslim schools had been turned down because the buildings or curriculum had been unsuitable or there were already too many school places in the area.

Source: Independent, 1 Jan. 1998.

▶ **What did Durkheim consider to be the key functions of education? Do religious schools perform these functions?**

doing but, as we show in Chapter 2, pp. 30–2, there are certain problems with the functionalist approach and these have led to criticism of their views.

First, functionalists argue in terms of the needs of society as a whole. Does education perform functions for society or does it rather serve the interests of those who rule the society and control education? Does edu-

cation impose the views of the majority on minorities? This leads to a second problem.

Functionalists tend to assume that the members of a society share common values. A diversity of cultures exists within most societies, however, and there are many conflicts, often grounded in religious differences, over moral and cultural issues. Conflicts of this sort occur also in relation to nationality, which in many countries is a disputed issue. The particular values and beliefs transmitted by schools are open to challenge by those who do not hold them and they may well set up alternative educational institutions. Education may perpetuate particular and disputed cultures as well as create a sense of membership of a common society.

EDUCATION AND INEQUALITY

The relationship between education and inequality has been one of the central issues of the Sociology of Education. It has also been a central concern of educational policy in Britain, which has gone through two major processes of reform aimed at producing greater equality. The 1944 Education Act and the later movement to introduce comprehensive schools both claimed to provide equality of opportunity.

Here we shall consider some of the main theories of the relationship between education and inequality. We start with the theory that education provides equality of opportunity and then move on to the arguments of those who believe that it cannot do this.

Equality of opportunity?

As we have seen, Parsons argued that education instilled the value of achievement. This was closely linked to another shared value, a belief in equality of opportunity, which was also central to the functioning of industrial societies. It was crucial to the allocation of human resources, since it enabled people with ability to find their way into the jobs that required those abilities. In industrial societies status was not determined by birth but by achievement, and, according to Parsons, equality of opportunity enabled those with ability to achieve success.

It also performed another crucial function in getting those who did not succeed to accept their failure. Industrial societies motivated people to achieve by providing them with superior rewards. This inevitably resulted in inequality, but those who did not succeed accepted this because they believed that everyone had had an equal opportunity to succeed. Thus, the belief that equality of opportunity existed legitimated the stratification of society.

Parsons saw education as the main mechanism of equality of opportunity. In schools there was competition on equal terms, for examinations applied universal standards and performance in examinations determined educational success. Those who succeeded educationally did so on the basis of superior performance. Furthermore, it was clear to all that success was the reward for achievement. The key values of achievement and equality of opportunity were transmitted through education.

> **We discuss equality of opportunity and the related concept of meritocracy in Chapter 14, p. 555.**

The problem with this approach is that it assumes that there is competition on equal terms in schools. Others have argued that this is not the case and we now need to consider their views.

Class, culture, and language

There is first the argument that class background shapes educational success through material advantages and disadvantages. The better off can buy educational success, either through buying entry to better schools or by buying assistance with education, such as private coaching or extra books. It is not just money that counts, however, for it has been shown that such factors as health and quality of housing, which are related to class background, influence educational success (see Lee 1989).

Others have argued that it is not so much a matter of *material* as *cultural* advantages and disadvantages. One approach of this kind has been labelled **cultural-deprivation theory**. It argued that working-class children have been disadvantaged in the educational system by working-class values and beliefs. These placed a low value on education and focused on the immediate rewards of earning money rather than *deferring gratification* until educational qualifications had been obtained. This could, for example, result in a lack of parental interest in education, which Douglas (1964) found to be the single most important factor in explaining children's educational attainments. It could result in children leaving school early in order to earn money. Similar arguments have been put forward to explain some ethnic minorities' lack of achievement in education.

Such approaches have been criticized for the negative views they present of particular class or ethnic-minority cultures. These views often seem to reflect prejudices rather than real knowledge of the culture concerned. It is also difficult to separate out cultural from situational factors. Leaving school early, for example, may not mean that education is undervalued but rather that a family desperately needs money. A lack of interest in education may reflect *material* rather than *cultural* deprivation.

These criticisms indicate that one must be careful in relating educational achievement to culture, but they should not lead us to rule out cultural explanations, for people's values and beliefs do shape their behaviour. Culture must, however, be placed in its social context, for culture and social situation are closely interrelated. This can be seen in Bernstein's theory of the relationship between speech patterns and educational success.

Bernstein developed an approach to class differences centred on differences in the use of language. In his early work (1961), he distinguished between two speech patterns:

▶ *Restricted codes.* This refers to speech patterns where meanings are implicit. They are typical of situations where people have so much in common that they do not have to spell out what they mean. Few words are needed. Sentences tend to be short and have a simple grammatical structure. Much may be communicated by gesture or tone of voice rather than the words themselves. While this form of language works well in situations where people know each other, its capacity to communicate is limited because it is *context bound* to a particular situation.

▶ *Elaborated codes.* This refers to speech patterns where meanings are made explicit. People spell out fully what they mean in longer and more complex sentences. While restricted codes are *particularistic*, elaborated codes are *universalistic*. They are *context independent* and enable people who do not share a particular social situation, or who do not know each other, to communicate.

Educational success requires an ability to use elaborated codes. These are the language of instruction. Restricted codes are no use for essay-writing! Children need, therefore, to be able to communicate in elaborated codes if they are to be successful in education. Bernstein argued that, while middle-class children can typically communicate in both restricted and elaborated codes, working-class children are generally accustomed to restricted codes only and are therefore likely to be less successful in education. He did, however, recognize that schools can teach elaborated codes to those who have not acquired them beforehand.

These cultural differences were linked by Bernstein to differences in class situation. Middle-class people speak in elaborated codes because their non-manual occupations require more complex verbal skills. There are also differences in family structure. Working-class families tend to be *positional* in character—that is, their members treat each other according to their position in the family. Relationships are unambiguous and can be expressed through restricted codes. Middle-class families tend to be *person centred*. They are more individualized and relationships are worked out through discussion which involves the use of elaborated codes (Bernstein 1977).

This is an influential theory which links educational success to class culture and class situation through language rather than values and beliefs. It has been criticized for the rather crude distinctions that it makes between the middle and working classes, and for

Language and class	Language and context	Restricted code	Elaborated code
	Speech forms	Small vocabulary and short, simple sentences	Large vocabulary and longer, more complex sentences
	Meaning	Implicit	Explicit
	Communication	Particularistic and context bound	Universalistic and context independent
	Family structure	Positional	Person centred
	Class	Working	Middle

▶ **Imagine that a parent is telling a child to switch off the television and go to bed. How would this be expressed in speech using restricted and elaborated codes?**

Pierre Bourdieu

Pierre Bourdieu (1930–) was born in south-eastern France. He trained initially as a philosopher in Paris in the early 1950s. His two years as a conscript in the French army in Algeria had a major impact upon him. He was shocked by the gap between the views of Parisian intellectuals and his experiences from the Algerian war. At this time he began to move towards sociology via anthropology. In the 1960s he established himself as a leading sociologist in Paris, where he became a Professor of Sociology at the College of France in 1981. His best-known work on education is *Reproduction in Education, Society, and Culture* published in 1977. Other influential works are *Distinction* (1984) and *Homo Academicus* (1988). Richard Jenkins (1992) provides a helpful account and discussion of his life and work.

having insufficient evidence to back up its statements (Rosen 1974). Bernstein (1997) has rejected criticisms of this sort, however, and claims that the theory is supported by a large body of research carried out under his leadership.

Cultural capital

The French sociologist Bourdieu argued that success depends not just on having appropriate language abilities, as Bernstein's work suggests, but on having a broader **cultural capital**. Cultural capital consists of various cultural advantages that can be turned into economic gains. Bourdieu (1997) identifies three forms that it can take:

▶ *The embodied state.* This consists of what Bourdieu calls 'long-lasting dispositions of the mind and body'. Put crudely, this is the culture that we carry around with us 'in our head'.

▶ *The objectified state.* This is the culture that is found in 'things'. It is the culture that exists in possessions, such as books or paintings or clothing.

▶ *The institutionalized state.* This is typically culture as represented in qualifications.

Thus, certain ways of thinking and speaking, a stock of cultural possessions, or examination certificates can all provide people with cultural advantages.

The term 'cultural capital' may seem a strange one, but it has become a widely used concept in the Sociology of Education. It reflects the importance of culture in occupational success, for this does not just depend on material resources. Money alone cannot enable a person to become, say, a successful and high-earning architect or barrister (though it may well help the process along). Examinations have to be passed and professional qualifications acquired.

Bourdieu argued that success in examinations depended on possessing the right culture. Educational standards appeared to be objectively established and unrelated to the class structure but in reality they reflected this structure. It was the dominant culture of those who ruled the society that established standards of excellence in schools. The dice were therefore loaded against the lower classes from the start. Those whose family backgrounds enabled them to acquire the dominant culture before they come to school had a hidden advantage. They already possessed a cultural capital that enabled them to do well in examinations. In this way education simply maintained the existing class structure by assisting those from the top and excluding those from the bottom. To put it another way, education led to the **reproduction of class**.

Education also maintained the class structure in another way. It legitimated inequality by making the success of upper-class children and the failure of lower-class children appear to be the result of objective procedures. Those who succeeded did so because examination procedures were stacked in their favour but it appeared as though they had superior ability. Similarly, those of lower-class origin who failed had stood little chance of succeeding, but failure appeared to be the result of their own inadequacies. Furthermore, some did succeed and this made the system appear fair and reinforced the idea that those who fail do so because of their own failings. Bourdieu here made a very similar point to that made by Parsons, who argued that competition on equal terms at school made inequality acceptable to the unsuccessful, though Bourdieu would not, of course, consider the terms equal.

Acquiring cultural capital was not just a matter of passing exams and gaining qualifications. Bourdieu argued that correct manners, the right 'taste' in, say, dress, and an appreciation of 'high culture' were all part of cultural capital. They could be crucial in determining whether someone got a high-status job or gained admission to elite circles. Having the right accent has often, for example, been considered necessary for occupational succcess in Britain.

A number of criticisms have been made of Bourdieu's analysis of education (Jenkins 1992: 15–19). It has been criticized for overemphasizing the way in which education reinforces inequality and allowing insufficiently for the opportunities it provides for those of lower-class origin. It assumes that it is the legitimation of inequality by education that maintains the social order. This may not actually be the case at all and workers may accept inequality not because they see it as justified but because there is little that they can do about it. Bourdieu also presents a rather circular picture of class structures endlessly reproducing themselves through static cultural mechanisms. This makes social and cultural change appear almost impossible but both do happen.

While these criticisms are well founded, Bourdieu has provided important insights into the interrelationships between class, culture, and education. His concept of cultural capital has been widely used. There has been wide acceptance of the idea that apparently objective exam procedures actually embody the values of a dominant culture and load the dice in favour of the bearers of that culture. A similar point has been made by those who argue that apparently objective tests for grammar-school entry in Britain actually favour children from superior class backgrounds.

The influence of the school

According to these approaches, education cannot provide equality of opportunity because success in education is determined by social and cultural background. They also imply that the kind of school that a person goes to or what happens in the school make no difference to people's life chances. This was quite openly argued by Jencks *et al.* (1972), who concluded from US data on educational achievement that the quality of schools made no difference. These approaches suggested that attempts to create equality of opportunity by tinkering with institutions were pointless. In this vein, Bernstein (1970) wrote a well-known article entitled 'Education Cannot Compensate for Society'.

Others are, however, less pessimistic and argue that schools do have an impact on educational success. Various aspects of the school and what goes on within it have been related to educational achievement. Studies have shown that the composition of a school's intake affects performance. It has been argued that the organization of a school, whether it streams its pupils or

Subcultural capital

Thornton has taken up the concept of cultural capital and applied it to social success in the world of clubbing.

'Subcultural capital confers status on its owner in the eyes of the relevant beholder. It affects the standing of the young in many ways like its adult equivalent. Subcultural capital can be *objectified* or *embodied*. Just as books and paintings display cultural capital in the family home, so subcultural capital is objectified in the form of fashionable haircuts and carefully assembled record collections (full of well-chosen, limited edition 'white label' twelve-inches and the like). Just as cultural capital is personified in 'good manners' and urbane conversation, so subcultural capital is embodied in the form of being 'in the know', using (but not over-using) current slang and looking as if you were born to perform the latest dance styles. Both cultural and subcultural capital put a premium on the 'second nature' of their knowledges. Nothing depletes capital more than the sight of someone trying too hard. For example, fledgling clubbers of 15 and 16 years old wishing to get into what they perceive as a sophisticated dance club will often reveal their inexperience by over-dressing or confusing 'coolness' with an exaggerated cold blank stare.'   *Source*: Thornton (1997: 202–3).

▶ **How do you think that subcultural capital is acquired?**

▶ **What kind of advantages do you think that subcultural capital confers on those who have it?**

▶ **Can it be converted into economic capital?**

not, affects their performance. The expectations of teachers can affect the performance of children, and, although these expectations may stem from attitudes current in the wider society, they are also linked to the culture of a particular school and can be modified through training. Other studies have shown that the character of a school makes a considerable difference to rates of success in obtaining qualifications.

We will take up these issues again in 'Inequality in British Education', pp. 246–56.

EDUCATION AND CAPITALISM

As we showed on pp. 231–3, the functionalist approach to education assumed that education met the needs of society. Marxist writers on education have argued that we should not refer to society as a whole, for there is a fundamental conflict of interest between capital and labour. According to this approach, education does not meet the needs of society but serves the interests of the owners of capital.

The supply of labour

Bowles and Gintis (1976) carried out the classic study of the relationship between capitalism and education through an examination of the development of education in the United States.

To Bowles and Gintis, education was the main means by which capital subordinated labour. Capitalism required obedient and disciplined workers prepared to

carry out boringly repetitive work in a highly unequal society. Labour could not be subordinated by the use of force alone, either within the factory or in the society at large, because force on its own was self-defeating and generated resistance. Effective subordination depended on getting workers to accept the capitalist system and it was education that produced this acceptance. Thus, education not only led to the reproduction of class, it was also crucial to the **reproduction of labour**.

In explaining how education does this, Bowles and Gintis referred not to the *content* of education but to the *structure of social relationships* in education. Their key concept is the 'correspondence principle' (Bowles and Gintis 1976: 131). The structure of social relationships at school corresponded to the structure of relationships at work. Thus, relationships of authority at school corresponded with those at work. Competition between students in school corresponded to the competition between workers which employers seek to encourage. Students were *externally* motivated by the award of grades not the satisfactions of learning, just as workers were motivated by pay not the satisfactions of work. Children were prepared for work because schools taught them how to behave like workers.

In focusing on these aspects of education, Bowles and Gintis drew attention to what Illich (1973) called the hidden curriculum. While students may have thought that the purpose of education was to provide them with skills, knowledge, and qualifications, the hidden curriculum taught them how to work and obey.

The correspondence principle also operated in another way by relating levels in education to occupa-

Illich and the 'hidden curriculum'

Ivan Illich (1926–) was born in Vienna, studied theology and philosophy in Rome, obtained a Ph.D. in history at the University of Salzburg, and became for a time a Catholic priest. His career led him to Latin America, where he became a severe critic of economic development. He saw it as destroying the skills, knowledge, and self-sufficiency of pre-industrial societies and forcing people into a passive dependence on experts and organizations.

One of his most well-known books is *Deschooling Society* (1973), where he called for the abolition of schools. He argued that education has been confused with schooling and that most learning occurred outside schools, which do nothing for the poor and turn people into passive consumers.

Illich originated the widely used concept of the **hidden curriculum**. This strikingly expressed the idea that schools do not just teach the subjects of the formal curriculum. They also teach values, attitudes, and patterns of behaviour through the organization and social relationships of the school. It is argued that this hidden curriculum maintains the existing social order and has a far greater influence on social life than the formal curriculum of subjects taught. While this is an important insight, the concept has been used in a widely varying way to refer to almost any aspect of education outside the formal curriculum. It is in some ways a misleading term, because it does not refer to an identifiable curriculum but to the whole context of education in the school.

tional levels. The lower levels of education emphasized obedience to rules, as required in low level occupations. Intermediate levels in education required students to work independently without continuous supervision, as did middle-ranking positions in organizations. In higher education students were expected to internalize the institution's norms, so that they were self-motivated and self-disciplined, just as those in senior posts in organizations were expected to be. If students were unable to make it to the next stage of education, they moved into the occupational level corresponding to the stage they had reached. Thus, while reproducing labour, education also reproduced the occupational divisions of the class structure.

While this approach started from a different theoretical perspective, it did, however, overlap in many ways with the functionalist approach. The points made by Bowles and Gintis about the importance of school discipline and competitiveness to life in the wider society were quite similar to those made by Durkheim and Parsons. Although Bowles and Gintis saw education as serving the interests of capital rather than the needs of society, they too were examining the importance of education to the socialization process and the maintenance of social order.

By assuming that education actually performed these functions, they also laid themselves open to one of the main criticisms made of the functionalist approach. Does education actually produce subservient students or workers who accept authority? Does it actually provide employers with the workers they need? We now take up these issues.

The workers the employer needs?

A general problem with the Bowles and Gintis approach is that it treated the working class as culturally passive, absorbing and accepting the values of the school and the employer. In doing this, they argued in a similar way to those who have claimed that there is a *dominant culture* imposed by the ruling class on the rest of the population. Another stream of research has, however, examined the way that resistant *subcultures* grow out of the experience of the working class.

We discuss the concepts of dominant culture and subculture in Chapter 8, pp. 280–1, and you may find it helpful to refer to this discussion.

In *Learning to Labour* Willis (1977) carried out a well-known study of the emergence of an oppositional subculture in a secondary-modern school. He argued that this subculture was hostile to authority, rejected the value of mental work, and celebrated physicality and violence. The authority of teachers was constantly challenged but in subtle ways that undermined it while stopping short of open confrontation. Willis argued that this oppositional culture was generated by the school itself, though its content was provided by the wider culture of the working class.

His study was based mainly on the observation of twelve working-class 'lads', who were selected because they were members of a minority opposition group. They cannot therefore be considered representative of the boys in the school or of working-class boys in general. Brown has indeed argued that most children adopt a strategy of limited compliance. They recognize the importance of qualifications for jobs and go along sufficiently with the school to 'achieve modest levels of attainment' that will improve their job prospects. Brown (1989: 242) points out that this too is a typical working-class response to school. Thus, while Willis certainly showed that schools did not automatically produce obedient workers for employers and could have a quite opposite effect, the extent of an oppositional culture should not be exaggerated.

Willis too demonstrated a correspondence between school and work. The oppositional culture in many ways prepared pupils for the realities of work. It corresponded closely to the oppositional culture of the workplace, while its celebration of physical work prepared boys for the boring and repetitive tasks they would have to carry out at work. Most of them stood no chance of the kind of occupational success promoted by the academic culture of the school and the oppositional culture was therefore much more realistic.

If education does not always produce subservient workers, perhaps in other respects it does not always produce the labour that the capitalist economy needs. It has been argued that one of the reasons for Britain's poor economic performance during the twentieth century was that the educational institutions set up in the nineteenth did not produce the skills required by modern industry. This was to become a key issue in the 1970s. The declining competitiveness of the British economy and rising levels of unemployment led to much discussion of the reasons for British economic decline. A movement pressing for the reform of education to make it more relevant to economic needs emerged amongst politicians, employers, and trade unionists.

This was not just a matter of old institutions. The changing requirements of the economy were central to the growing dissatisfaction with education. The decline of traditional industries and occupational changes meant that there was less need for unskilled manual labour. Furthermore, as we show in Chapter 13, p. 529, the changes associated with post-Fordism led to employers seeking adaptable, committed, and cooperative workers rather than simply obedient ones. They wanted workers who could cope with the demands of technical change, turn their hands to whatever job needed doing, and produce the high-quality goods and services demanded by customers.

The kinds of workers that Bowles and Gintis saw the education system producing no longer corresponded to the needs of the employer. Similarly, the oppositional culture's celebration of manual labour no longer corresponded to the realities of work. Opposition itself was no longer acceptable to employers seeking a high level of commitment from their workers. This was not just a problem for the capitalist employer, however. It was also a problem for those boys who identified with a working-class culture that fitted them for a kind of work that was in decline.

The approach taken by Bowles and Gintis draws our attention to the importance of the relationship between education and the capitalist economy. As we show in 'Education, Training, and National Revival', pp. 257–69, an understanding of this relationship is certainly crucial to an understanding of recent changes in British education policy. It is also clear that there is nothing automatic about the relationship. Education did not correspond to work and it was this lack of fit between the two that led in the 1980s to the 'new vocationalism', the expansion of post-16 education, and the attempt to raise educational standards, which were central aspects of the transformation of education in the 1980s. This transformation required, however, the extensive intervention of the state.

SUMMARY POINTS

In this section we have examined different approaches to the relationship between education and society. We first considered the part played by education in the process of socialization:

▶ According to Durkheim, education provided a sense of common membership in society and taught moral behaviour and self-discipline.

▶ According to Parsons, education transmitted values of achievement and taught children to achieve.

The relationship between education and inequality has been one of the central issues in the Sociology of Education.

▶ According to Parsons, education provided equality of opportunity and also legitimated inequality.

▶ Bernstein showed that differences in speech patterns related to class situation shaped educational success and failure.

▶ Bourdieu argued that examinations were biased in favour of those with cultural capital.

▶ One problem with approaches that locate the sources of inequality in the wider society is that they do not take sufficient account of the influence of the school.

While functionalists saw education as meeting the needs of society, Marxist writers argued that it served the interests of the owners of capital.

▶ Bowles and Gintis claimed that education provided obedient and appropriately trained workers for the capitalist employer.

▶ Willis showed, however, that education could generate an oppositional culture as well.

▶ Dissatisfaction with the contribution of education to the economy led to extensive changes in British education during the 1980s and 1990s.

THE DEVELOPMENT OF EDUCATION IN BRITAIN

As we showed in 'Understanding Education', the Sociology of Education has centred on the discussion of the relationship between education and society. In Britain the key issues have been whether educational institutions have provided equality of opportunity and met the needs of the economy. Before examining these questions further, we need to set these issues in context by outlining the development of educational institutions in Britain.

In this section we examine the development of British education up to the 1970s. We deal separately with the major changes of the 1980s in 'Education, Training, and National Revival', pp. 257–69.

THE NINETEENTH-CENTURY GROWTH OF EDUCATION

At the beginning of the nineteenth century there was nothing approaching a national system of education. Elementary education for the poor was provided by charity and church schools, and various local private schools which charged parents for widely varying standards of usually very basic education. Secondary education was not widely available and was provided mainly by the so-called public schools, which catered not for the public but mainly for fee-paying pupils, and a scattering of grammar schools in the towns. The only universities in England were Cambridge and Oxford, which were very exclusive institutions admitting only about 300 fee-paying students a year in the mid-eighteenth century (Royle 1987: 368). They were primarily concerned with educating the sons of the upper class to become Anglican clergy.

In Scotland education was rather more developed at both ends of the spectrum. There was a system of publicly funded local schools, and the local schoolmaster was expected to be a graduate able to teach up to university-entrance level. Five universities existed and university education was far more accesssible than it was in England and Wales. About a quarter of the students at Glasgow university at the end of the eighteenth century were of working-class origin (Royle 1987: 373).

Education of all kinds expanded in the nineteenth century. Elementary schooling for the poor grew initially through church education, but after the 1870 Education Act through state education. The public schools also expanded, with the founding between 1837 and 1869 of thirty-one new boarding schools providing a classical education (Royle 1987: 360). The founding of the University of London in 1828 was the key step in the growth of higher education, and towards the end of the century colleges were set up in the provinces and the industrial cities, many of them becoming universities around 1900.

It has often been argued that education is linked to economic development. Britain was industrializing at the time and it would be easy to conclude that the expansion of education was driven by an industrial society's need for a more educated labour force. This was not really the case, however. At this stage of economic development, practical workshop skills rather than technical knowledge or even literacy were required. Indeed, employers opposed the expansion of elementary education because they did not want to lose children as a cheap labour force. As we showed above, education was more developed in Scotland, although Scotland was less developed economically than England.

The expansion of elementary education had more to do with religious, moral, and political than economic concerns. Religious organizations competed to set up schools in the cities. Schools for the poor were seen as a means of establishing order in the new industrial cities through school discipline. They could also counteract the dangerous influence of radicals by teaching respect for the existing social and political order. But there was also a popular demand for education, and radicals called for it to be taken out of religious hands and made available to all on a free and equal basis. Education became a battleground between conservatives and radicals, though both agreed that more education was needed.

The expansion of 'public-school' education for the middle and upper classes was linked to state and empire rather than commerce and industry. The bureaucratization of the nineteenth-century state (see Chapter 16, pp. 650–1) meant that there was a growing emphasis on qualifications. The route to office in the growing apparatus of the imperial state was through success in school, university, and civil-service examinations. As Royle (1987: 390) has put it: 'Ambitious middle-class parents knew they would have to make the

Control through education

'The great object to be kept in view in regulating any school for the instruction of the children of the labouring class, is the rearing of hardy and intelligent men, whose character and habits shall afford the largest amount of security to the property and order of the commmunity.'

Source: Sir James Kay Shuttleworth, 1838, quoted by Digby and Searby (1981: 118).

much education was seen as threatening the social order. The public schools provided education for the upper class and those members of the middle class who could afford them. Grammar schools too provided education for the middle class. Some of these schools did actually become increasingly exclusive, as the children of the local poor were kept out because fee-paying parents did not want their children rubbing shoulders with those from a lower class (Royle 1987: 360).

necessary sacrifices to buy a public-school education for their sons if they were to make their marks in the world. Purchase of office had been the eighteenth century method; purchase of education replaced it in the nineteenth.' The public schools, together with Cambridge and Oxford universities, produced a cohesive ruling class with bureaucratic skills, the shared culture of a classical education, and a gentlemanly set of norms and values centred on public service and sportsmanship.

Nineteenth-century education clearly reproduced the class stucture. Elementary education was considered the most that the working-class required and too

STATE SCHOOLS FOR ALL

The state did gradually become more involved in schooling. From 1833 it provided increasing funds for schools through religious societies. In 1856 the Education Department was created and it promptly set up a Royal Commission to investigate the state of elementary education. Concern with rising levels of state spending on education led to the introduction of 'payment by results' in 1862. Under this system, schools would in future be funded only if they had a certificated teacher, secured regular attendance, and their pupils passed examinations set by Her Majesty's Inspectors. Standards at six levels were laid down (Griggs 1989*a*).

On the playing fields of Harrow: boys at a public school in the 1940s.

Development of a national school system in England

Elementary education

1833 The state began to provide some funding for religious schools.

1844 Factory Act required children in employment aged 8–13 to spend half the week in school.

1870 Education Act to provide cheap, publicly funded local schools.

1880 Attendance made compulsory up to the age of 10.

1891 Right to free elementary education established.

1893 School leaving age raised to 11.

1899 Leaving age raised to 12.

Secondary education

1902 Education Act to create national secondary education: state grants for grammar schools in exchange for some 'free places' for children from elementary schools; new state-funded secondary schools created on grammar-school model.

1918 School leaving age raised to 14.

1944 Education Act introduced tripartite system of grammar, technical, and secondary-modern schools. Free secondary education for all.

1947 School leaving age raised to 15 (1972 to 16).

Concerns with teacher quality, attendance, grading, and inspection have a long history!

A national system of schooling was slowly constructed in England between 1870 and 1944. The 1870 Education Act established the principle of state elementary education, though initially state education was seen as filling the gaps left by existing provision. A system of free and compulsory elementary education was then gradually built up during the twenty years or so afterwards. The 1902 Education Act began to create a national system of secondary education, though it was not until the 1944 Act that free secondary education was made available to all.

The 1944 Act has been seen as a major social advance which transformed education. It completed the construction of a national system by providing free secondary education for all, but in other ways the structure it produced was not national at all. It was argued in the early 1940s that there would only be a truly national educational system if the 'public schools' were included in it. They were, however, left out of the reorganization of secondary education by the 1944 Act.

The Act also created not one state secondary school for all but a *tripartite* structure, consisting of three different types of school for children of different abilities. There were grammar schools for the academic, technical schools for those with technical abilities, and secondary-modern schools for the rest. This was a selective system that distributed children into type of school

on the basis of their performance in examinations at age 11. It was described as meritocratic (see Chapter 14, p. 555), because it supposedly allocated children to schools entirely on the basis of their ability or merit. It certainly exemplified the *correspondence principle* of Bowles and Gintis, for types of school corresponded to occupational levels.

If private education is included, there were not three but five distinct levels in secondary education:

▶ public schools;

▶ direct-grant grammar schools (charging fees);

▶ grammar schools;

▶ technical, central, and trade schools;

▶ secondary-modern schools.

This structure maintained a hierarchical educational system. The top two categories provided superior education for those who could afford it. The grammar schools were kept as the elite institutions of the state sector. The fourth category was never widely available and the 1944 system has been labelled by some as *bipartite* rather than *tripartite*, since for most of the population state education meant either a grammar school or a secondary modern (Chitty 1993). Secondary moderns were essentially a continuation of elementary education for the working class. As Simon (1991: 74) has put it: 'after all the discussion and legislation, the country emerged with an hierarchical educational structure almost precisely as planned and developed in the mid-late nineteenth century . . .'.

Although grammar and secondary-modern schools were supposed to be different but equal, grammar schools were inevitably seen as superior. The tripartite system was soon rejected by the Labour Party. Most working-class children ended up in secondary moderns and the *Early Leaving Report* of 1954 showed that over half those who did get into grammar schools dropped out or failed to get three GCE passes (GCE was the examination that preceded GCSE). There was also some middle-class dissatisfaction, for those middle-class children who failed the 11+ examination also ended up in secondary moderns. From a national point of view, an elitist system wasted talent and created social divisions. Comparisons were made with other economically more successful countries, like the United States, that did not have selective state education.

Comprehensive schools were put forward as an answer to these problems. The principle of comprehensive education was that all the children within a particular area would go to the same secondary school, which would cater for children of all abilities. Education was gradually reorganized along comprehensive lines through local-authority action and the 1964 Labour government's education policy. The process was eventually halted in the 1980s and selection returned to favour, a reversal of policy which we will examine in 'Diversity and Selection', p. 262, but comprehensive schools by then predominated.

The fact that selective schools (and private education) still existed and 'creamed off' many of the more able students meant, however, that a genuinely national *system* had still not been established. Further-more, the selective principle still operated *within* most comprehensive schools through the streaming of children into different ability groups.

HIGHER EDUCATION FOR SOME

The founding of the University of London in 1828 broke the Oxbridge monopoly of education in England and established a major new institution that soon became by far the biggest in the country. It was also a centre for the spread of higher education, for the colleges emerging in the industrial cities taught external London degrees until they had acquired the expertise and status to award their own.

The founding of 'red-brick' universities around the turn of the century extended university education to the provinces and the industrial cities. By the 1930s there were twenty-one universities in Britain but higher education was still relatively undeveloped, especially in England, as comparison with comparable industrial countries shows (see Fig. 7.1 on p. 244).

It has, indeed, been argued, notably by Wiener (1980), that the character of British education largely accounts for Britain's failure to keep pace with other industrial countries and eventual economic decline in the 1960s and 1970s. Wiener argued that an anti-industrial culture developed in elite educational institutions during the nineteenth century. This left Britain ill-equipped to meet the intensification of international competition as other countries industrialized.

British industrialists concerned with increasing international competition had played an important

Open wide but not wide open: the Oxford student body.

Figure 7.1. **Higher education in industrial countries, 1934**

Country	Number of inhabitants per university student
Great Britain	885
England	1,013
Scotland	473
Wales	741
Italy	808
Germany	604
Holland	579
Sweden	543
France	480
Switzerland	387
United States	125

Source: Simon (1991: 30).

part in establishing the new colleges in industrial cities during the 1870s and 1880s. Civic leaders insisted, however, that these colleges taught the liberal arts as well as applied studies, and they eventually became universities teaching a broad range of subjects. Any educational institution with aspirations tended to model itself on the public schools or on Cambridge and Oxford universities, where the arts were dominant. Where science was taught, it was pure rather than applied science. Comparisons with Germany show that technology was much more highly valued there and that there was a much greater provision of education in technology and applied science.

In the 1950s and 1960s attempts were made to develop education in technology with the creation of Colleges of Advanced Technology and Polytechnics. These too, however, acquired arts departments and gradually lost much of their technological distinctiveness as they modelled themselves on the universities. According to Royle, the attempt to expand technological education in the 1960s failed because 'students could not be found in the same numbers and of the same quality as humanities students to fill the places provided for them' (1987: 396). This suggests that the problem lay not only in educational institutions but also in wider attitudes towards technology.

Mass higher education began with the expansion of higher education between the 1950s and the 1970s. The Robbins Report of 1963 established the principle that all those who could benefit from higher education should have access to it and planned almost to triple student numbers by the mid-1980s. Expansion was actually driven, however, by the demand for higher education. During the five years between 1957/8 and 1962/3, before the Robbins Report had been published, student numbers had already doubled in a quite unplanned way. Growing demand was linked to rising numbers of 18 year olds and the growing proportion of 18 year olds obtaining the A-level qualifications needed for university entry.

During the years 1957–72 the number of full-time students in higher and further education rose from 148,000 to 470,000 (Simon 1991: 597). Slowness in expanding higher education had meant that further education too grew rapidly to meet the rising demand. In the 1970s the expansion of higher education slowed down and barely kept pace with the growing number of 18 year olds until there was a new burst of expansion in the late 1980s.

The 1960s expansion of higher education took a binary form. Robbins had proposed a unitary system of higher education based on universities. The 1964 Labour government decided, however, to halt the creation of new universities and build up a distinct public sector from existing colleges and new polytechnics. The rationale for this *binary system*, as it was called, was that a separate public sector would boost the development of new, vocationally relevant institutions of higher education that would not be dominated by the elite universities. It inevitably created, however, a two-class system of higher education with the polytechnics being seen by many as second class rather than different institutions. The polytechnics themselves tried to become more like universities by awarding degrees and developing university-type courses. They were eventually allowed to take the title of university with the abolition of the binary system in 1991.

BRITISH EDUCATION IN COMPARATIVE PERSPECTIVE

We have been examining the development of British education up to the 1970s. We will now briefly consider the distinctiveness of the British system by placing it in comparative perspective.

The 1944 Education Act had established a national system of education which was less centralized than the French system but rather more centralized than the

American. There was no centrally controlled national curriculum as in France. There was, none the less, more of a national system in Britain than in the United States, where funding was much more decentralized and local communities had more control. In Britain state education was centrally funded and school organization was at least shaped by national education policies. But the British system was an untidy one that allowed the competing principles of the 'tripartite' structure and comprehensive schooling to coexist according to local decisions. In most European countries there was a uniform national structure.

Selection and specialization took place early in British education, whether this involved selection for schools or for streams within schools. In Sweden, by contrast, there was not only a fully comprehensive system of education up to the age of 16 but also mixed-ability teaching within schools. Mixed-ability teaching had been introduced in British comprehensives but on a local not a national basis. As in Britain, there was a major specialization at age 16 but less selection, for in Sweden far more pupils stayed on in schools, some 90 per cent staying on after 16 (A. Gould 1993: 205).

We showed above that the expansion of higher education was slow in Britain. In spite of the expansion of the 1960s, a far lower proportion of 18 year olds entered higher education than in comparable countries (Halsey 1997: 642). On the other hand, those who did had their fees paid by the state and, at that time, a generous system of maintenance grants rather than the loans found in, say, Sweden. British higher education was also elitist in another way, for the more vocational polytechnics were widely considered to be lower in status than universities. Although the polytechnic institutions of France, Germany, and Sweden were not strictly comparable, they were high-status institutions, indeed often having higher status than universities.

It is difficult to compare educational systems, though Hopper (1968) produced a typology that tried to provide a framework for doing so. This is partly because there is so much variation within systems. For example, private schooling is highly developed in Britain but higher education is overwhelmingly funded by the state. It is also because educational systems change and many aspects of British education were transformed in the 1980s. It is, furthermore, difficult to penetrate beyond institutional differences to differences in the way that education is actually experienced. The above comparisons do, however, show that the system of education that developed in Britain was quite distinctive and had been shaped by a very particular history.

SUMMARY POINTS

In this section we have outlined the development of educational institutions in Britain:

▶ The expansion of elementary education in the nineteenth century was driven by religious, moral, and political concerns rather than economic needs.

▶ The first step in the construction of a national system of education was the establishment of the principle of state elementary education in 1870.

▶ Free state secondary education for all was not provided until the Education Act of 1944, which created a tripartite structure of state education with selection at age 11.

▶ Concerns with the unreliability, unfairness, and waste that resulted from selection at age 11 led to a movement to introduce comprehensive schools.

▶ Higher education was slow to develop and Britain's economic problems have been blamed on an anti-industrial culture in elite educational institutions.

▶ Mass higher education began with the expansion of universities in the 1960s and the Robbins Report's principle that all those who could benefit from higher education should have access to it.

▶ British education was internally divided, selective, and elitist in comparison with other industrial societies.

INEQUALITY IN BRITISH EDUCATION

As we showed earlier (see pp. 233–6), education has been considered the main source of equality of opportunity, though others have seen it as transmitting inequality from one generation to the next. We showed in 'The Development of Education in Britain' that there has been much concern with this issue in Britain and major attempts were made to reform education in order to increase equality of opportunity. Whether these reforms did so or not has been the subject of considerable research in sociology. In this section we draw on this research to examine the impact of these changes on patterns of inequality. We start by considering class inequalities and then move on to those of gender and ethnicity.

CLASS

Nineteenth-century education reproduced the class structure. First the 1944 Education Act and then the reorganization of schools along comprehensive lines were intended to provide equality of opportunity, irrespective of class background.

The tripartite system

The 1944 Act made free secondary education available to all, with access to grammar schools determined by performance at the 11+ examination alone. Did this create equality of opportunity?

In a classic study, Halsey, Heath, and Ridge examined the impact of organizational changes in education on patterns of class inequality. They studied the educational careers of 8,529 men by examining the careers of four age 'cohorts' (an age cohort consists of all those born between two dates). Two of their cohorts were educated before the 1944 Education Act came into operation and two afterwards. This enabled them to examine the effects of the 1944 Education Act.

Under the tripartite system, entry to selective schools was crucial in determining educational success. Only those going into these schools could obtain academic qualifications and have a chance of going on to university. They found that class continued to determine boys' chances of getting into these schools. That education in grammar schools was now free and children were selected for them on the basis of success in the 11+

examination made no appreciable difference to class differentials. Around a fifth of the working-class children in their earliest (1913–22) cohort and their last (1943–52) cohort entered selective schools (Halsey *et al.* 1980: 63).

Performance at the 11+ examination was clearly crucial in determining future educational career. The 11+ examination was basically an intelligence test, which assumed that there was some general, underlying ability called intelligence, which could be measured objectively. Any such ability was not, however, independent of class (or ethnicity). Tests of this sort have been shown to embody cultural and linguistic assumptions that are themselves linked to class and ethnic background (see Chapter 14, pp. 563–5). Performance at intelligence tests can, anyway, be improved through training and families with superior resources can buy in assistance that will improve their child's chances. As we showed above, Bourdieu argued that examinations are not objective because they are framed by the dominant culture. The greater success of those from higher classes in intelligence tests and examinations reflected both their material and cultural advantages.

Class differences then carried through to university entrance. The increasing availability of university places meant that the proportion of working-class children getting into university certainly increased but so did the proportion of those from higher classes. Indeed, while the proportion of working-class children tripled, the proportion of service and intermediate class children went up by nearly four times (see Figure 7.2). Furthermore, if one looks at *absolute* increases, the service class clearly benefited far more than the other classes. Their attendance increased by 19 per cent as compared with an increase of 6 per cent for the intermediate classes and a mere 2 per cent for those at the bottom.

Comprehensive schools

Did the reorganization of education on comprehensive lines make any difference? It is difficult to explore this question because a fully comprehensive system was not created. Since selective schools could 'cream off' the more academically successful children, comparisons between the tripartite system and comprehensive schools could not easily be made.

Heath (1989) has argued that comprehensive reor-

Figure 7.2. Attendance at university by birth cohort, 1913–1952 (%)

Father's social class	Birth cohort	
	1913–32	1943–52
I and II (service)	7.2	26.4
III, IV, and V (intermediate)	1.9	8.0
VI, VII, and VIII (working class)	0.9	3.1

Note: This study used the Goldthorpe class categories (see Chapter 3, p. 99).
Source: adapted from Halsey et al. (1980: 188).

ganization made no real difference, but his conclusion has been challenged by McPherson and Willms (1989). They examined later data from Scotland, where comprehensive reorganization had been more extensive. Their evidence showed that, since comprehensive reorganization, the gap between the examination performance of working-class and middle-class children had narrowed slightly, as working-class children started to catch up. Differences remained great, however, and it is clear that the performance of children in comprehensive schools was still substantially related to their class background.

Ball's (1981) case study of 'Beachside' comprehensive school showed some of the reasons why. Like many comprehensives, Beachside was internally streamed into three ability bands. He found that banding reproduced the traditional academic/non-academic split in British education. Band one, the academic band, consisted mainly of middle-class children, bands two and three of working-class children. On entry children were allocated to bands on the basis of primary-school reports. There was a sorting-out process in the first term which involved some movement between bands but little movement after this point, certainly little movement into band one. Band differences in curriculum, syllabus, teaching methods, and relationships with teachers created two different kinds of education within the school.

The significance of primary-school reports for banding showed that selection originated largely at the previous stage of education. Success in primary education was, therefore, critical to future success in education. In this connection, Douglas et al. (1968)

demonstrated that the social-class composition of the primary school had a persistent influence on secondary-school performance. Children from predominantly working-class primary schools did less well in whichever type of school they went on to at age 11.

Beachside comprehensive did make a limited shift to mixed-ability classes, against some resistance from the staff. This shift occurred largely it seems because of persisting discipline problems in band-two classes, where an oppositional culture had established itself. The mixing of children with different abilities was, however, limited. 'Sets' for children of different abilities emerged in some subjects, notably Maths and Languages, while mixed-ability classes came to an end after the third year.

Ball argued that mixed-ability classes did not, anyway, change teacher attitudes. Teachers still classified children in terms of their ability and treated them accordingly. He made the important point that the classroom mixing of children of different abilities did not mean that there was mixed-ability *teaching*, if children were still taught differently. His research did show that the shift to mixed-ability classes brought about some changes. It enabled the more effective socialization of children into the school and better control of their behaviour. The social divisions found within banding were, none the less, broadly reproduced in mixed-ability classes.

Class differences certainly persisted in entry to higher education, as the data assembled by the Dearing Report (1997) showed (see Figure 7.3 on p. 248). The expansion of entry to higher education meant that the participation of each socio-economic group increased during the 1990s. Indeed, the proportion entering from the lowest group actually doubled. There was no perceptible lessening of class differentials, however, and the absolute increase in the proportion from the highest group was clearly by far and away the greatest. The participation gap between the professional group and all other groups widened considerably.

Class background or type of school?

It would be easy to conclude from all this that class background is decisive in shaping educational success and that schools do not matter. As we showed in the opening section of this chapter, it has been argued that the material, cultural, and linguistic advantages of children from higher social classes mean that they will inevitably be more successful in education. Was Bernstein (1970) right in declaring that 'education cannot compensate for society'?

Halsey et al. (1980) certainly believed that the school

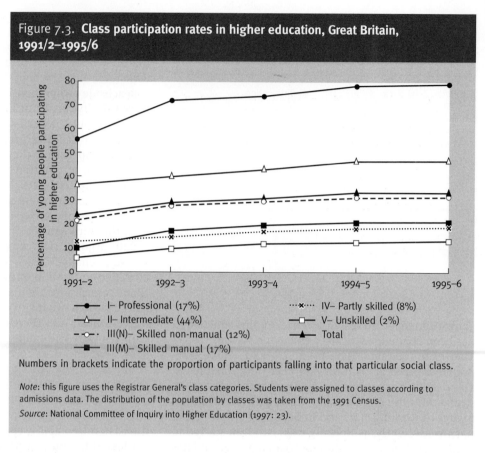

Figure 7.3. **Class participation rates in higher education, Great Britain, 1991/2–1995/6**

I– Professional (17%)
II– Intermediate (44%)
III(N)– Skilled non-manual (12%)
III(M)– Skilled manual (17%)
IV– Partly skilled (8%)
V– Unskilled (2%)
Total

Numbers in brackets indicate the proportion of participants falling into that particular social class.

Note: this figure uses the Registrar General's class categories. Students were assigned to classes according to admissions data. The distribution of the population by classes was taken from the 1991 Census.

Source: National Committee of Inquiry into Higher Education (1997: 23).

mattered. They did conclude that whether children went to public schools or grammar schools made little difference to their examination performance. It was, however, critical whether they went to selective schools (public and grammar) or secondary moderns. Boys with similar social backgrounds and similar abilities fared very differently according to this decision. Class had a major influence on the kind of school a boy ended up in, but its influence then diminished as the school took over. It has, indeed, been argued that grammar schools, with their strong academic culture, provided a better route upwards for those working-class children who managed to get into them than comprehensive schools could do.

Rutter *et al.* (1979) carried out a rather different study that enabled them to identify differences within one type of school. They studied twelve non-selective secondary schools in the London area. They found that, although the composition of a school's intake influenced academic success and delinquency rates, neither was wholly explained by this. Differences in the schools as 'social institutions' were systematically related to their results. They list such factors as teaching practices, school values, and the amount of respon-

sibility given to children. These all to some degree depended on a school's staff and training and were not determined by its social environment. Furthermore, they not only operated independently; they interacted to give a school an overall character, which itself influenced results.

Mortimore has recently reviewed the literature on school differences and concludes that they do account for about 10 per cent of variations in examination performance (1997: 479). This may seem a very low proportion. It does, after all, mean that performance is mainly determined by factors over which the school has no control. Mortimore points out, however, that this 10 per cent variation can have a crucial effect on the qualifications achieved and future educational and occupational career. A 10 per cent difference in performance at GCSE could amount to the difference between obtaining seven C and seven E grades.

This shows that we should be wary of overdeterministic explanations of educational success that relate it solely to class background and do not take account of the character of the school. Parental interest in school choice indicates that parents are in little doubt about the significance of the school.

Phillip Brown (1995) argues that middle-class interest in school choice has increased as middle-class jobs have become more insecure. Organizational changes, intensifying international competition, and declining security of employment mean that the middle class can no longer rely on an easy passage for its children into stable bureaucratic and professional careers. On the other hand, mass higher education has produced larger numbers of graduates seeking entry to such careers. Middle-class parents have responded by seeking to use their material and cultural capital to maximize their children's educational advantages.

This has been translated into a pressure for greater choice in education. The more choice there is, the greater the opportunity for middle-class parents to use their advantages to get their children into higher-quality, higher-status institutions. We will return to this issue on pp. 260–3, where we examine the provision of greater choice in education during the 1980s.

GENDER

The literature on education and class has been mainly concerned with the persistence of inequalities in educational achievement. In examining gender inequalities we find not so much persistence as transformation. Historically girls were excluded and sidelined but in recent years they have overtaken boys in educational achievement.

The separation of girls

According to the nineteenth century domestic division of labour, women were destined for housework and child-rearing, and therefore had little need for formal education beyond elementary level.

 Since the education of women reflected nineteenth-century ideas of their place in the world, you may find it helpful to refer to our discussion of this in Chapter 10, pp. 366–7.

By 1880 elementary education was compulsory for all children up to the age of 10. The limited skills taught were differentiated by gender, girls learning domestic skills and boys basic craft skills and elementary arithmetic. Education was considered less necessary for girls and their truancy was treated more permissively than that of boys, because it was considered reasonable for girls to stay at home helping their mothers and acquiring domestic skills (Abbott and Wallace 1990).

Secondary schools for upper- and middle-class girls were gradually established during the second half of the century. One model for their education was provided by Cheltenham Ladies College, founded in 1854, which saw its function as providing an improved training for women's traditional roles. North London Collegiate, which opened as a day school for girls in 1850, had the very different mission of providing an academic education for girls. Its founder believed that middle-class girls should be educated for employment, for, if they remained single, they would have to earn their living, usually as governesses. It provided a model for the Girls' Public Day School Company which was funding thirty-eight schools by 1901 (Royle 1987: 363). Secondary schools for girls were well established by the beginning of the twentieth century but far less numerous than those for boys.

Women were excluded from universities for most of the nineteenth century but feminists increasingly pressed for entry to be opened to them. Their breakthrough was made at the University of London, where they were for the first time allowed to take degrees in 1878. Cambridge and Oxford were particularly slow to open their doors to women. Separate colleges for girls were established around 1880, but the struggle to achieve full recognition was a long one. Women were not allowed to receive full degrees until 1920 in Oxford and 1948 in Cambridge. The numbers of women in higher education remained low for a long time. In 1961 only 13 per cent of students at Cambridge and Oxford were women (Royle 1987: 381).

Integration and discrimination

The 1944 Education Act made free secondary education available to all and established a school leaving age of 15. State secondary education for girls did not, however, mean that they pursued the same curriculum. In secondary-modern schools especially, the idea persisted that girls should take different subjects in order to prepare them for a domestic and reproductive role. It was not just a matter of the formal curriculum, however, for, even when girls and boys were integrated in the same classes in co-educational comprehensive schools, a *hidden curriculum* differentiated between them.

The role expectations of both staff and students steered girls and boys towards specialization in different subjects as they moved higher up the school and into higher education. Even when all subjects were available to both boys and girls, girls moved towards subjects that were extensions of the domestic role and boys towards technical and scientific ones. This was clearly not just a function of the school, for it involved gender-role expectations in the wider society and different patterns of employment. These expectations were often built into the language and content of teaching materials. The introduction of a national curriculum in the 1980s counteracted this to some extent by establishing the same curriculum for boys and girls, though this applied only up to age 16, when choices of subject had increasingly to be made.

Requiring girls and boys to take the same subjects did not, anyway, remove gender issues from the curriculum, as the debate over the gendering of science shows (Heaton and Lawson 1996). Feminists argued that science was taught in a 'masculine' way. Three responses to this problem emerged:

▶ *girl-friendly science*: Making science more attractive to girls by introducing topics that interest them;

▶ *feminine science*: replacing competitive masculine behaviour in the laboratory with a more cooperative feminine approach;

▶ *feminist science*: challenging masculine ways of thinking by arguing that scientific method should give more weight to feminine intuition.

This debate exemplifies the conflict between the liberal and radical tendencies in feminism (see Chapter 16, pp. 663–5, for a similar debate about organizations). Liberal feminism seeks equal opportunities for women within the existing system, but radical feminism argues that this requires women to think and act like men. Masculine ways of behaving and thinking should be challenged and replaced by feminine ones. This, however, can lead to the response that scientific method, as it stands, is essential to science and if it is masculine this means that girls cannot be as good at science as boys.

Research by Spender (1982) and Stanworth (1983) showed the importance of different gender-role expectations in the classroom. This applied not only to subject choice but also to other aspects of student–teacher interaction. Boys got more attention and interest than girls. Boys tended to receive higher marks than girls for comparable work and were expected to perform better in examinations. This was not just due to teacher expectations but to the expectations of the children and the way that boys and girls behaved. Boys, for example, demanded more attention. This has led some to conclude that girls would be better off in girls' schools or girls' classes in mixed schools.

Is science masculine?

Single-sex classes

'One of the top five education authorities in England has decided to pilot single-sex teaching in its secondary schools with a view to separating boys and girls for lessons across the board. The decision by Barnet in north-west London follows the success of single-sex teaching at one school where the number of pupils gaining five or more good GCSE passes has risen from 40 per cent to 69 per cent in the three years since it was introduced.

'Boys at the school admit that they work better without feeling pressure to "play-up" to girls or risk being regarded as "swots". Girls say they make more progress when science subjects are presented as "people-oriented" and the boys are not hogging the teachers' attention. . . .

'Anne Jarvis, the education committee chairman, said parents often sought places in girls' schools because they saw boys as pushy and demanding in class. Research showed that girls did better in single-sex classes, she said.

'Most schools are co-educational but a handful have moved back to teaching the sexes separately, largely prompted by individual head teachers attempting to remedy the under-achievement of boys. Barnet is the first to consider an authority-wide policy.'

Source: Liz Lightfoot, 'Authority to Pilot Single-Sex Classes in GCSE Schools', *Daily Telegraph*, 8 Nov. 1997.

▶ **Is a change of this sort likely to benefit boys or girls most?**

The educational superiority of girls

In spite of their well-documented disadvantages, girls have increasingly performed better than boys in public examinations (see Figure 7.4). In 1996, in England and Wales, girls performed better than boys in all of the fifteen most popular GCSE subjects and in thirteen of the fifteen most popular A levels (see Figure 7.5 on p. 252).

The growing educational success of girls in schools has been reflected in their access to further and higher education. If those on part-time courses are included, the number of women in further education overtook the number of men during the early 1980s, and by the middle 1990s there were substantially more women than men entering undergraduate courses in higher education. Women have not yet caught up with men on postgraduate courses, but they have been steadily closing the gap (see Figure 7.6 on p. 252).

How is girls' greater success at examinations to be explained?

There is, first, the argument that attempts to counteract discrimination against girls have worked. These include such initiatives as GIST (Girls into Science and

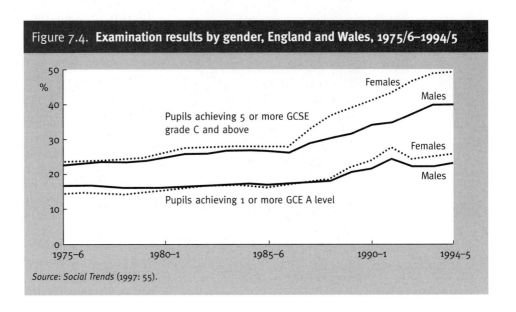

Figure 7.4. **Examination results by gender, England and Wales, 1975/6–1994/5**

Source: Social Trends (1997: 55).

Figure 7.5. Examination results in selected subjects, United Kingdom, 1996 (%)

Percentage of entrants from state schools awarded grades A–C

GCSE			A level		
Subject	Boys	Girls	Subject	Boys	Girls
English Literature	49.2	65.5	English Literature	54.6	56.5
English Language	41.4	60.5	English Language	48.9	51.6
Maths	40.4	40.8	Maths	56.2	61.2
Double Science	45.1	45.6	Physics	51.8	56.0
Technology	45.6	53.9	Chemistry	51.9	56.3
Art and Design	42.4	62.9	Art and Design	54.6	63.8
Geography	44.2	51.2	Sociology	44.0	51.5

Source: Denscombe (1997: 21).

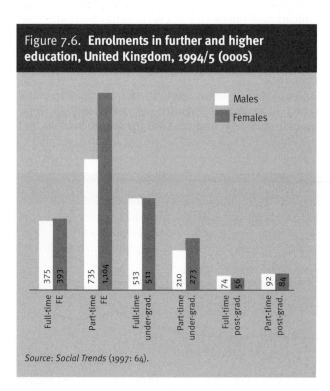

Figure 7.6. Enrolments in further and higher education, United Kingdom, 1994/5 (000s)

Males
Females

	Males	Females
Full-time FE	375	393
Part-time FE	735	1,104
Full-time under-grad.	513	511
Part-time under-grad.	210	273
Full-time post-grad.	74	56
Part-time post-grad.	92	84

Source: Social Trends (1997: 64).

Technology) and the introduction of single-sex classes. More generally, there has been a greater awareness of and sensitivity to gender issues in schools. There are indeed now calls for boys-only classes to assist boys to catch up. It is clearly possible that single-sex classes can benefit both boys and girls. It is difficult, however, to argue that single-sex classes can both lead to girls improving their performance relative to boys and enable boys to catch up with girls.

There is, secondly, the argument that it is changes in the relationship between education and work that account for the superior performance of girls. Reference is made here to the growing employment of women and the declining employment of men (see Chapter 13, p. 539). It is argued that the growing employment of women has raised girls' expectations and confidence. The decline of traditional male jobs involving physical labour has led to the disillusionment and disaffection of many boys, who no longer bother with education and take refuge in an oppositional culture, of the kind decribed by Willis (see p. 238). Weiner *et al.* (1997) suggest that the impact of organizational downsizing and a growing insecurity of employment in middle-class male careers may have had similar effects on middle-class boys. These theories are linked to wider notions of a male identity crisis, which we discuss in Chapter 10, pp. 390–2.

Although plausible, these explanations tend to make

general statements about boys and girls that take insufficient account of class location or of different responses to change. Thus, the greater employment of women in paid work does not just mean that educationally qualified girls are moving into professional or managerial careers. As Mac an Ghaill (1996) points out, many girls are moving into low-paid, part-time, and insecure jobs, which they have to combine with traditional domestic duties. He also emphasizes that a range of male peer groups and masculinities, not just oppositional cultures of the kind described by Willis, can be found in schools. For some working-class boys new vocational routes are opening up into areas such as business studies, technology, and computing.

The educational success of girls should also not be taken to mean that older patterns of male domination have disappeared. Thus, gender still plays a part in subject choice, which steers men and women towards different careers. The introduction of a national curriculum has reduced gender differences in subject choice before age 16, but by A level traditional gender differences have re-emerged and these continue in higher education. Males tend to opt for the natural sciences and females for arts and social-science subjects.

Male domination of education has also persisted in other ways. This can be seen in higher education and managerial positions in education. Early 1990s studies showed that women comprised only some 20 per cent of full-time university staff, and a much smaller proportion of senior staff. In the 'old' universities, only 6 per cent of senior lecturers were women and only 3 per cent of professors (Bagilhole 1994: 15). This meant that not only were teaching and research dominated by men but also university procedures and decision-making. Senior positions in schools, governing bodies, Local Education Authorities (LEAs), and the Department of Education and Employment have also been male dominated (Weiner *et al.* 1997).

ETHNICITY

We now turn to consider the relationship between ethnicity and education. Variations in educational achievement have also been linked to ethnicity, though, as we shall see, the relationship between ethnicity and achievement is complex.

Ethnicity and achievement

A growing concern with ethnic variations in educational achievement led to the Rampton Report of 1981

The head teacher of an East London primary school with a group of pupils.

and the Swann Report of 1985, which showed that there were ethnic differences in attainment.

A considerable literature developed to explain the relationship between ethnicity and educational achievement. Some explanations related to *out-of-school* factors. Herrnstein and Murray (1994) have argued that ethnic differences in educational achievement can be explained by inherited differences in intelligence. According to cultural explanations, African-Caribbean culture places a low value on education, while some Asian cultures highly value it. Alternatively, it has been suggested that growing up in a white-dominated society with few positive 'black' role models leads to low self-esteem, low aspirations, and low educational achievements.

> We examine biological explanations of ethnic differences in Chapter 4, pp. 143–4, and biological explanations of differences in intelligence in Chapter 14, pp. 563–5.

Another set of explanations referred to *in-school* factors. It has been argued that, as with gender, teacher and child expectations interact to influence subject choice, career guidance, performance, and assessment. A study by the Commission for Racial Equality (CRE 1992) showed that Asians tended to be placed in lower sets than their ability warranted, while expectations also influenced the handling of discipline problems. The content of the curriculum also matters, for it tends to reflect the majority culture. Some history and geography textbooks have embodied racist views of non-white peoples, in, for example, accounts of imperial history. This could alienate ethnic-minority children from education.

This literature has been reviewed by Rattansi (1988), Troyna and Carrington (1990), and Mason (1995), who have pointed out many problems with it.

There is, first, the problem of *ethnic categories*. The collective term 'ethnic minorities' conceals great differences in culture and achievement between them (see Figure 7.7). Some ethnic minorities are performing at higher levels than the white majority, some at substantially lower ones. The category Asian is equally problematic, given the differences between, say, those of Pakistan/Bangladeshi and those of Indian origin (the 'other Asian' category includes those of Chinese culture). There are also many other minorities, such as Cypriots or Jews or Irish, who rarely figure in these comparisons or are lumped together in spite of their differences. Generalizations about the 'ethnic minorities' are therefore meaningless.

There is, secondly, the difficulty of distinguishing between *ethnicity* and *class*. Particular ethnic groups, such as African-Caribbeans or Bangladeshis, that apparently perform badly may do so because of their class rather than their ethnic composition. A larger proportion of these groups than of whites or Asians in general is working class.

There is, thirdly, the existence of *gender variations* within ethnic groups. Figures on the performance of ethnic groups may conceal considerable gender variations. Studies have shown that African-Caribbean girls obtain considerably higher educational qualifications than boys (Mirza 1992). This may well be linked to a distinctive African-Caribbean family structure, which we discuss in Chapter 10, pp. 384–5.

It is, fourthly, important to take account of *change*. The notion of deep-rooted ethnic differences is undermined by the evidence of improving educational performance. Rattansi (1988: 254) notes that, when the LEAs studied by the Rampton Report were restudied for the Swann Report, African-Caribbean children were found to be doing around twice as well at age 16 and 18. Mason (1995: 66) concludes that there is a 'narrowing qualifications gap' between the ethnic majority and the ethnic minorities in post-16 education.

In an important study of nineteen 'multi-racial' comprehensives in the early 1980s, Smith and Tomlinson (1989) explored the significance of ethnicity for educational achievement. They found ethnic differences at age 16 in GCE/CSE grades (the examinations that preceded GCSE), but class was far more strongly related to attainment than ethnicity. It is also quite possible that the ethnic differences that they found reflected class differences. Thus, the relatively low score achieved by those from families of West Indian and South Asian origin could well have resulted from their mainly working-class backgrounds.

Smith and Tomlinson concluded that the performance of children depended, above all, on the school they attended. As we showed earlier (see p. 248), Rutter *et al.* (1979) demonstrated that school character made a difference. Smith and Tomlinson went further than this. They argued that school character far outweighed ethnic background in determining educational success. What really mattered was the quality of the school attended. This led them to the policy conclusion that 'the measures that will most help the racial minorities are the same as those that will raise the standards of secondary education generally' (1989: 307).

Rattansi (1988), Troyna and Carrington (1990), and Mason (1995) have all been very sceptical of the notion that ethnic minorities in Britain 'underachieve'. Some ethnic minorities clearly do suffer from disadvantages that make it more difficult for them to achieve educational success, but these disadvantages do not necessarily stop them achieving it. It is also not clear that these disadvantages have much to do with their ethnicity as such.

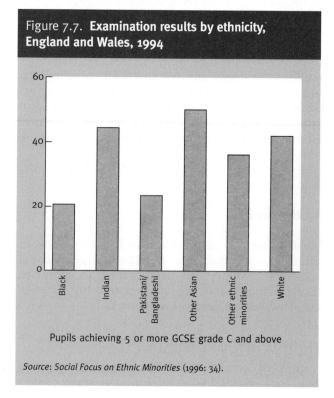

Figure 7.7. **Examination results by ethnicity, England and Wales, 1994**

Pupils achieving 5 or more GCSE grade C and above

Source: Social Focus on Ethnic Minorities (1996: 34).

Racism in schools?

While notions of the underachievement of ethnic minorities have been criticized, there is no doubt that ethnic minorities have met discriminatory attitudes and practices in education.

Ethnographic studies, such as that by Cecile Wright (1988), have documented this. These studies have used observational and interview techniques to investigate the interaction between different ethnic groups and teachers in schools. They have shown teachers interpreting the behaviour of African-Caribbean children as disruptive and reacting in a punitive way that was inappropriate to the situation. This is consistent with the much higher rate of exclusion of black children from school because of 'bad' behaviour. According to research carried out by the Commission for Racial Equality, black boys are six times as likely as white boys to be excluded from school (CRE 1996).

Rattansi refers to the *institutional racism* embedded in taken-for-granted features of school organization and curriculum (see Chapter 14, p. 557, for a discussion of this term). By this he means the way that such matters as dress requirements or school meals arrangements or aspects of the curriculum fail to take account of non-white cultures.

Mason recognizes the existence of these practices but is concerned that the term racist has become overused (1995: 9). He argues that practices of this sort should be viewed as *ethnocentric* rather than *racist*. They show an ignorance and disregard of other cultures that is typical of a widely found ethnocentrism. These practices are in principle no different from practices that discriminate against the customs and cultures of, say, people from Ireland or Poland who live in Britain. Mason prefers to keep the term racism for beliefs that involve the idea that there are biologically distinct races.

He argues that racism defined in this more limited way is found in schools. There are many examples of racially motivated attacks on members of ethnic minorities, both in schools and on the way to and from the school. Racism of this sort can clearly have a very serious, sometimes life-threatening, impact on ethnic minorities and their educational success. The advantage of this approach is that it enables us to make a clear distinction between racism and an unthinking ethnocentrism, which both pose problems to the members of ethnic minorities but rather different ones.

As we showed in the case of class, disadvantage and discrimination do not themselves lead to failure to achieve. Much depends on the response to this situation. Brah and Minhas (1988) describe the emergence of an oppositional response by Asian schoolgirls. These girls were well aware of the existence of ethnocentric stereotypes in their schools. They responded to the notion that Asians had language difficulties by pretending not to understand their teachers' instructions and by speaking Urdu in class. Their resistance to the ethnocentric culture of the school took a collective form as they created mutual support groups.

On the other hand, it has been argued that some African-Caribbean girls responded to low teacher expectations by combining defiance with educational success (Fuller 1983). They were well aware of the importance of educational qualifications and demonstrated that they could achieve results as good as anyone else's. This can be linked to the significant gender differences in African-Caribbean educational achievement.

It is not just the response by the children that matters, for there have also been policy responses to ethnocentrism and racism in schools.

The first of these was *multicultural* education, which recognized cultural diversity and tried to treat cultures as different but equal. It involved changes to the curriculum that would better reflect cultural diversity by, for example, bringing black writers into the study of literature and recognizing religious diversity, but it has come under much criticism. It provoked a hostile reaction from those who believed that it threatened British national identity. It was also criticized by black activists for colluding with *cultural racism* and trying to assimilate minorities into a racist society which it did not openly challenge.

> ☞ We discuss these complex identity issues, the problems with a multicultural approach, cultural racism, and black responses to it in Chapter 12, pp. 486–7. You might find it helpful to refer to that discussion.

The second more radical response was *anti-racist* education. This more directly challenged racism by insisting that it must be recognized and confronted. It sought to raise awareness of all aspects of racism and train teachers in anti-racist policies. It involved a broad definition of racism that treated all forms of disadvantage or discrimination affecting ethnic minorities as racist in character. It labelled as racist practices which Mason would consider ethnocentric rather than racist in character. It certainly brought racism out into the open but has been criticized for intensifying and racializing conflict between ethnic groups.

CLASS, GENDER, AND ETHNICITY

Class, gender, and ethnicity have all been sources of inequality of opportunity in education. Similar mechanisms are involved in each case. There are patterns of class, gender, and ethnic disadvantage. The expectations of parents, children, and teachers may be shaped by stereotypes of class, gender, or ethnicity. These are sometimes expressed in open hostility or discrimination but are often hidden in ways of thinking and behaving that are taken for granted. They may be buried in a *hidden curriculum* or embedded in organizational structures.

Factors both outside and inside educational institutions produce patterns of disadvantage. Employment, occupation, housing, health, and wealth affect educational success from outside education. Stereotyped expectations originate and operate outside education but can be reinforced within it. Selective processes within schools through streaming, option choice, and career guidance can reproduce external structures of disadvantage.

It is important to stress, however, that educational institutions can also counteract these structures. Studies of the 'school effect' show that school character can be more influential than social background in determining outcomes. This makes all the more important the selective processes that lead to children going to one school rather than another. Patterns of discrimination may also be openly countered through equal opportunities policies and programmes to make teachers sensitive to the effects of disadvantages and expectations.

Inequalities both persist and change. Class inequalities seem very persistent. Changes in the organization of education appear to have had only marginal effects upon them. Gender inequalities in educational achievement do, however, seem to have diminished, indeed to have been reversed, though, as we have seen, this does not mean that gender-based role expectations or structures of male domination have disappeared. There is some evidence too that ethnic differences have declined. Where inequalities are linked primarily to beliefs and expectations, social movements and policy changes can have an impact. Where they are linked to the more material factors associated with class position—employment, occupation, income, and housing—or to the possession of cultural capital, they seem to persist more strongly.

While we have considered class, gender, and ethnicity separately, they intersect in complex ways. As we have seen, ethnic differences are difficult to separate from class differences and it may well be that much of the difference in educational achievement between ethnic groups is explained by differences in their class composition. On the other hand, average figures for classes or ethnic groups may mean little if there are major internal gender differences. This means that we should not deal with class, gender, or ethnicity in isolation from each other and should always take account of location along all three dimensions. It also means that we should not see class, gender, and ethnicity as cumulative sources of inequality.

SUMMARY POINTS

In this section on inequalities in education we first considered the impact of educational reforms on class inequality:

▶ It has been demonstrated that selection at age 11 on the basis of ability had no significant effect on class differences in boys' entry to selective schools.

▶ Although there is evidence that comprehensive schools have marginally reduced class differences in educational achievement, internal streaming has reproduced them.

▶ There is also evidence that the character of a school has some impact on educational achievement.

We then considered the significance of gender:

▶ During the nineteenth century girls were educated separately and largely excluded from higher education.

▶ Although the schooling of boys and girls became increasingly integrated, gender differences persisted through both the formal and the hidden curriculum.

▶ Recently girls have generally overtaken boys in educational performance, though gender differences persist in subject choice.

Variations in educational achievement have also been linked to ethnicity:

▶ It has been shown that ethnic groups vary in their educational achievement, though their success rates also change.

▶ It has been argued that much of this variation may be explained by class differences and there are also important gender differences within ethnic groups.

▶ Discriminatory attitudes and practices disadvantage ethnic minorities, but their impact on achievement depends also on responses to them.

EDUCATION, TRAINING, AND NATIONAL REVIVAL

In the 1980s and 1990s British education went through a series of fundamental changes. There was a new emphasis on gearing education to the needs of the economy and developing its training function. Parental choice and competition between schools and colleges exposed education to market forces. Local Education Authorities (LEAs) lost much of their control over education, but central state regulation increased with the introduction of a national curriculum, national tests, and new inspection procedures. The proportion of students staying on in education after the age of 16 rose sharply and higher education entered a new phase of rapid expansion.

In this section we will first examine the relationship between education, training, and the economy before moving on to the education market place and state regulation. Although similar changes affected schools and higher education, we will deal with higher education separately because of its institutional differences. Finally we will consider the general role of the state, which was largely responsible for the 1980s transformation in education and training.

EDUCATION, TRAINING, AND ECONOMY

The background to the growing concern with education's contribution to the economy lay partly in Britain's economic decline and growing unemployment in the 1970s. As we showed on p. 243, education was held responsible by some for Britain's declining international competitiveness. There has also been an increasing international awareness of the links between education and economic success.

Education and economic success

At the heart of this awareness was the issue raised by Bowles and Gintis (see p. 237)—the supply of labour by education to the capitalist economy. *Manual* work, particularly unskilled manual work, was in decline and *non-manual* work was growing in importance. The production of goods was increasingly carried out in a highly automated fashion requiring much less manual labour. The spread of information technology into all areas of life meant that new skills in processing and communicating information were needed. Knowledge and the capacity to use and communicate it were vital to economic success. Education became crucial to economic competitiveness.

It has also been argued that changes in the relationship between the economy and the state lay behind government concerns with education. Increasing global integration had made it more difficult for governments to manage national economies. It became, for example, much harder for them to protect industries against foreign competition. One of the few things that governments could do was to try to ensure that education contributed to national economic competitiveness. Education policy had become one of the few ways in which governments could influence the success of national economies (P. Brown *et al.* 1997: 8).

It is now widely agreed that education is important to economic success, but which aspects of education matter most to the economy? Four different answers to this question can be identified:

▶ *Technical skills.* Education needs to train workers in the particular skills required by industry. Industry needs, for example, workers trained in information technology.

▶ *Transferable and interpersonal skills.* In a more competitive, more uncertain, and rapidly changing environment, employers are looking less for training in specific skills, which may soon go out of date, and more for adaptable and flexible workers with transferable skills. Employers need workers with skills of communication and teamwork, who can work well with others.

▶ *Level of education.* Economies require workers educated and trained to higher levels. Competitive economies need well-developed systems of post-16 and higher education.

▶ *Standards.* It is not so much the content or the level of education that are problematic but the standards reached. Standards of literacy and numeracy especially need to be improved.

While it is clearly possible for governments to try to improve all these aspects of education, given limited resources they imply conflicting priorities. Thus, the improvement of general numeracy requires higher investment in schools, while the raising of the overall

Training the workers of the future.

level of education suggests that more money should be put into further and higher education.

The need to improve the contribution of education to the economy might seem self-evident, but Levin and Kelley (1997) view the claims made for the relationship between education and productivity with some scepticism. They point out that Japanese companies setting up car factories in the United States have been able to increase productivity with the existing labour force. They also emphasize that education alone cannot generate high labour productivity. Too much emphasis on education could distract attention from the organizational and managerial aspects of improving productivity.

This does suggest that some of the attention recently paid by governments to education policy reflects not so much the labour needs of the economy but, as argued above, the diminishing scope for other kinds of intervention in economic matters. Governments show that they are doing something by intervening in education.

The new vocationalism in Britain

The concern to improve education's supply of labour to employers led to the emergence of what Whiteside has called a 'loose alliance' of politicians, civil servants, industrialists, and trade unionists (Whiteside

et al. 1992: 3). This alliance advocated the 'new vocationalism'.

Vocational education is education for work. The 'new vocationalism' of the 1980s sought to transform education so that it could more effectively meet the economy's requirements for labour. It challenged the

Does education make any difference to productivity?

General Motors (GM) and Toyota set up a joint venture in California which began producing cars in 1985. Toyota designed the factory and took responsibility for production, leaving the marketing to GM. Eighty per cent of the workers were recruited from a factory closed down by GM because of its poor-productivity, high absenteeism, poor-quality production, and industrial conflict. Toyota were able to achieve a 50 per cent increase in productivity with virtually the same labour force. Absenteeism declined. Productivity and quality were comparable to their Japanese plants. These improvements were due to changes in organization, personnel policy, and company training. They were not due to changes in the education of American workers.

Source: Levin and Kelley (1997: 244).

established liberal and academic traditions of British education. The liberal approach to education aimed to develop an individual's full potential in all aspects of life and did not particularly concern itself with education for work. The academic tradition valued knowledge for its own sake and was not concerned with how it was used.

At the heart of the new vocationalism was the belief that education needed to develop the transferable skills relevant to a rapidly changing economy. Knowledge was considered less important than the capacity to learn, communicate, and work cooperatively with others.

The alliance argued for a more vocational, more motivating, more student-involving education that would raise the numbers of 16–19 year olds staying on in education. There were calls for the following kinds of changes:

▶ *Course construction.* Modularizing courses into shorter, more flexible units. Specification of objectives, so that students are clear about what they are expected to achieve.

▶ *Skills.* A shift of focus from knowledge to skills. The acquisition of 'core' skills in communication, problem-solving, and personal management by all students. Where appropriate to the subject, the development of skills in numeracy, information technology, and modern-language competence.

▶ *Learning.* More emphasis on student-centred learning through project work rather than teaching factual information. Group cooperation rather than individualist competition.

▶ *Assessment.* Profiles and records of achievement to recognize what has been achieved and replace traditional grading, which is demotivating because it values only high grades. Certification that a defined level of competence had been reached. More assessment through coursework rather than examination.

It was no good, however, developing work-relevant skills if they were not valued by the educational system or employers or indeed the students themselves. This was a deep-rooted problem in Britain, where academic qualifications had always been more highly valued than vocational ones. The response to this problem was to build a new system of National Vocational Qualifications (NVQs), which tested not just knowledge but competence in specific work situations. General NVQs (GNVQs) were developed to meet the requirements of groups of related occupations, such as health care, and provide a vocational route into further and higher education. Advanced GNVQs or 'vocational A

Academic education versus the new vocationalism

Academic education	New vocationalism
▶ Teaching	▶ Learning
▶ Knowledge	▶ Competence
▶ Subject specific skills	▶ Transferable skills
▶ Individual achievement	▶ Team work

levels', as they were called by some, were created to give equality of status with A level and provide a route into higher education through vocational qualifications. Smithers (1994) has described this creation of new qualifications as 'a quiet educational revolution'.

The new vocationalism may have brought about a quiet revolution but it upset some on both the Right and the Left of politics. It was resisted by Conservative supporters of the academic tradition. They saw the traditional knowledge and subject-based A level as a 'gold standard' that should be defended at all costs. Proposals to change A level to provide a less specialized and broader-based education of the kind favoured by industry and found in other countries were defeated in the 1980s. Critics on the Left argued that it subordinated education to the requirements of work in a capitalist economy. It seemed to vindicate the Bowles and Gintis analysis of the relationship between education and the capitalist economy. Was education only for work?

▶ Think about the course that you are taking.

▶ Does it reflect the changes that we have listed?

▶ If it does not, why do you think that this is?

From school to work

Attempts were made to bridge the gap between education and work in other ways by introducing work experience into schools and by expanding post-16 education and training.

Work experience was introduced into the school curriculum by schemes such as the Technical and Vocational Education Initiative (TVEI). Its aim was to prepare students for employment and it typically involved from one to three weeks' paid work for a local employer. Shilling (1989) found that, although it could be a positive experience for many of the students

The equivalence of academic and vocational qualifications

NVQs		GNVQs	Academic
5. Professional and managerial		—	Higher education
4. Higher technician and junior management		—	—
3. Technician and supervisor		Advanced	2 A levels
2. Craft		—	5 GCSEs at grades A–C
1. Foundation		Foundation	GCSEs at lower grades

Source: Smithers (1994).

involved, it could also be disappointing and alienating when they were left on their own to carry out boring tasks for very little pay. This may not have been the kind of preparation intended, but it certainly confronted them with the realities of low-paid work in a capitalist society.

A series of training schemes linking school and work have followed one upon another. The Youth Training Scheme (YTS) was developed in the 1980s but widely criticized for providing low-level, low-quality training by poorly qualified trainers. It appeared to be not so much a training for work as a way of reducing unemployment. Employer actions seemed to confirm this. When the demand for labour increased in the later 1980s, many employers pulled out of YTS and recruited school-leavers directly. It became Youth Training in 1991, a more flexible scheme that could lead to NVQs (Malcolm Maguire 1992).

In 1989 youth training was handed over to local bodies controlled by employers, the Training and Enterprise Councils (TECs), a move described as 'the most significant government policy innovation' in vocational education during the previous two decades (Malcolm Maguire 1992: 95). Its basic idea was that local, employer-led bodies were best placed to know what training needs were. Maguire questions whether this is the case, for British employers are not noted for their commitment to training or the development of long-term policies to improve skills. Local provision might be appropriate for jobs requiring low-level skills but not to provide the intermediate and higher-level skills, which Britain is often said to lack.

The training initiatives of the 1980s have also been criticized from the Left. Finn (1984) and Clarke and Willis (1984) argued that YTS was a source of cheap labour. Employers could substitute YTS trainees for regular workers. It was also a low-cost way for the government to disguise the true level of unemployment by reducing the unemployment figures.

Numbers staying on in education and training after the age of 16 increased rapidly. The proportion of 16–18-year-old boys in England in full-time education or training rose from 52 per cent in 1985 to 75 per cent in 1995, the proportion of girls from 54 per cent in 1985 to 76 per cent in 1995 (Social Trends 1997: 63).

Expansion was driven by the government, which linked funding to student numbers and encouraged institutions to compete for students. Demand for places in further and higher education increased as improved examination performance at age 16 produced more students qualified to continue their education. Higher levels of unemployment and the withdrawal of income support from 16–17 year olds meant that many had little alternative to continued education. On the other hand, as more students continued on to acquire higher qualifications, competition for jobs forced others to seek higher qualifications as well.

A REGULATED MARKET PLACE

The government was not just concerned with the supply of labour; it also sought to change education in other ways. These involved the introduction of market principles, the provision of greater diversity and choice, and the establishment of national standards. All of these changes were driven by the belief that the contribution of education to the economy could be improved. Similar processes of change went on in all sectors of education but we will consider changes in schools and colleges in this section and higher education on pp. 264–7.

Market forces

The introduction of market principles reflected the government's general belief that the British economy could be revitalized by allowing market forces to operate more freely. This involved two key interacting processes, greater competition between institutions and greater parental choice.

Before the 1980s reforms, entry to state schools was based on catchment areas. Children were allocated to schools by the LEA according to the area they lived in. If parents did not like the local school, they either had to educate their children privately or move house into the catchment area of a 'good' school. Schools did not have to compete for children and parents had very little choice within the state system, unless they were prepared to move house.

The 1980 and 1988 Education Acts gave parents the right to choose which school their children attended. Catchment areas still existed, but parents had the right to go outside them. The removal of restrictions on entry meant that in theory popular schools could expand, while unpopular schools might be forced eventually to close. Schools now had to compete for pupils. Each school had to persuade parents that they should send their children to it and glossy brochures multiplied.

Competition was also encouraged by reducing LEA control over schools. The delegation of management and budget control to schools gave them greater freedom to compete, for they could themselves decide how to use their resources most effectively. As LEAs lost control of day-to-day management, governing bodies acquired greater powers and parents were given more influence on them (Deem 1997). Schools could indeed 'opt out' of local-authority control, if a majority of parents agreed, and funding would then be provided by a central state agency. Schools could increase their resources by attracting more pupils, but in this new competitive climate they also began to raise more money from parents, sponsors, and commercial operations.

Similar changes occurred in further education.

Schools sell

'Pupils as young as 11 could be targeted with advertising for products such as fast food and sportswear on their school walls. Three hundred secondary schools have signed deals which offer £5,000 a year in return for providing 10 poster sites within their buildings. The poster boards will be placed wherever pupils congregate or pass by regularly, including corridors, libraries, gyms, and dinner halls. Only classrooms will be out of bounds. The company which promoted the scheme has drawn up a rough list of products it would favour, but heads and governing bodies will have the final veto on the content of posters . . .

'[The] list of preferred advertisers includes the Central Office of Information, which might provide anti-drugs or smoking health warnings; universities promoting courses; employers advertising evening or weekend jobs; and banks and building societies offering junior savings accounts. Driving schools, bus companies, rail firms and toiletry manufacturers would also find favour.

'A second list, described as "harmless but maybe a little more contentious", includes music retailers, food manufacturers, cinemas and "places to go", such as theme parks.

'A so-called "banned list" would cover sugary drinks, confectionery and sportswear. However, if schools wished, they could accept advertisements for sports goods or fast-food chains.'

Source: Lucy Ward, 'School Ads may Sell Burgers and Trainers', *Independent on Sunday*, 10 Aug. 1997.

▶ **Is there any reason why advertising should not be allowed in schools?**

▶ **Why do you think that distinctions have been made between the different groups of products?**

▶ **Who should decide what products should be allowed? Is there a role for the state here?**

Schools enter the market place

Before 1980	After 1980s reforms
▶ Catchment areas	▶ Open entry
▶ LEA allocation of places	▶ Parents' right to choose
▶ LEA coordination of provision	▶ Competition between schools
▶ LEA control	▶ Governor authority, delegation of management, opting out
▶ LEA services	▶ Private services

Further Education Colleges were removed from local-authority control and their funding was transferred to a national funding council appointed by the government. They were now controlled by new governing bodies on which local industry was heavily represented. Funding linked to student numbers forced the colleges into competition with each other and also with schools providing post-16 education.

Competition has also been introduced in another way. Educational services had previously been provided by the LEAs, which had built up a large staff to provide services as various as in-service training or grounds maintenance. Schools could now choose whether to buy LEA services or go to private suppliers. The LEAs now had to compete on the same basis as private companies to win contracts from schools. Education services, just like many other local-authority services, had been privatized.

Diversity and selection

In principle, more choice could also be provided through greater diversity in schools. It was argued that children's needs differ and one type of school could not meet the needs of all children. A range of different types of school would enable parents to match the needs of their particular child with what a school had to offer. There were three main ways in which the Conservatives tried to increase school diversity.

First, there was specialization. The development of colleges specializing in technology and languages increased diversity and also met other objectives by making education more relevant to economic needs. New City Technology Colleges (CTCs), partly funded by industry, were established. These were colleges for 11–19 year olds that gave special emphasis to maths, science, and technology. They were to be partly funded by industry. Other existing schools were encouraged to become colleges specializing in technology or modern languages. By 1996 the government had created 15 CTCs, 30 language colleges, and 151 technology colleges (Chitty 1997).

Secondly, there was the encouragement of selective education in the belief that this alone could enable children of high academic ability to maximize their potential. Right-wing circles in the Conservative Party had long been opposed to the standard, all-embracing, comprehensive school and sought to protect and revive grammar schools, some 163 of which still existed in Britain in the 1990s. Attempts to create new ones largely failed, however, because of local opposition. Middle-class parents, who might be expected to support grammar schools, did not relish the prospect of their children finishing up in inferior schools if they failed the entry examinations (Chitty 1997).

Selective education was therefore developed in other ways. Existing schools were allowed to become more selective. This applied particularly to grant-maintained schools, which had opted out of what was left of local-authority control, and the specialized colleges. Before the 1997 general election, the government put forward far-reaching proposals to give schools more power to select but its defeat stopped them going any further.

Thirdly, there was the Assisted Places scheme, which provided a number of state-funded places in private schools for 'bright children from less affluent homes'. This too was highly selective. Furthermore, it supported private education with public funds. Private education expanded under Conservative rule, with the percentage of the school population in private schools rising from 5.8 per cent in 1979 to 7 per cent in 1994.

Diversity is, however, a rather misleading term. It implies that a range of equal but different schools is available to all. As we have seen, greater diversity in practice meant increasing selection. A growing emphasis on selection inevitably strengthened the hierarchical tendencies in British education. The existing top layers of the private schools and the grammar schools flourished, while new layers of selective education were constructed underneath them.

Choice and inequality

The operation of choice too produces hierarchy. As money follows pupils, resources flow to popular schools. If there is a high demand for places, popular schools can be more selective in deciding whom to accept. At the other extreme, 'sink' schools emerge which face a downward spiral of pupils, resources, and results. Inequalities between schools increase.

How to get children into the school of your choice

'Faced with the reality that one in five children is now denied their first choice of school (rising to one in two in London), parents desperate to squeeze their children into flourishing schools with high league table placings will resort to desperate measures. Their tactics include claiming they are on the verge of moving into an area, using a relative's address, or even temporarily splitting up, renting a flat for one partner close to the preferred school and registering it as the child's address, and then "reconciling" once an offer of a place has been made. Others are prepared to pay as much as £2,500 a month in rent for property within a catchment area. To secure places in church schools, which generally score high in league tables, parents will begin to attend church with pious regularity, and may rush to have their children confirmed.'

Source: Lucy Ward, 'The Parents who Cheat for their Children', *Independent*, 17 Apr. 1997.

The opportunity to choose schools has, however, turned out to be illusory for many people. Recent studies suggest that somewhere between a quarter and a half of parents do not get their children into their school of choice (Judd 1997). There are two quite simple reason for this. First, although money follows pupils, popular schools simply cannot expand sufficiently to accommodate the demand for places in them. Secondly, as we have just seen, schools have been encouraged to become more selective. When it is in their interests, schools can also sabotage choice by parents, as the extract at the beginning of this chapter shows. Those parents who cannot get their children into their school of choice have to settle for schools lower down the hierarchy. Alternatively they can move or pretend to move into the chosen school's catchment area.

The capacity to exercise choice effectively is related to social class. There are straightforward material factors, such as the availability of transport and the pressures of work which limit working-class choice. Income clearly has a bearing on the use of the expedients described by Lucy Ward (see box). There are differences of a more cultural kind, which relate to career expectations and aspirations. Cultural capital, to use Bourdieu's term, also plays an important part, since knowledge of education and how schools work helps parents to get their children into better schools. This is particularly the case when schools are selective and entry is competitive.

In a study of school choice in Greater London during 1991–2, Ball *et al.* (1995) found two patterns of choice that corresponded to social class:

▶ *Working-class locals.* Their choice was governed by practical considerations and immediate concerns, such as transport arrangements.

▶ *Middle-class cosmopolitans.* They gave higher priority to school reputation and longer-term career concerns.

As we showed on p. 249, Phillip Brown (1995) argues that a growing competition for jobs and the inflation of qualifications by mass higher education led middle-class parents to use their full weight in the education market in order to give their children a competitive edge. To do this, they needed greater choice. Thus, the Conservatives' belief in the virtues of choice coincided with the economic interests of the middle class. Brown claims that there has been a shift in the ideology of the middle class from *meritocracy* to *parentocracy*. He contrasts these two ideologies through two equations:

▶ *meritocracy*: ability + effort = merit;

▶ *parentocracy*: resources + preference = choice.

Greater choice inevitably increases inequality. It increases inequality between schools. It creates a new line of division between those who get the school of their choice and those who do not. It reinforces existing inequalities, since those with superior material and cultural resources are better placed to pursue their preferences and obtain the education they want for their children.

State regulation

The government did not, however, simply leave education to the operation of market forces and the exercise of parental choice.

The 1988 Education Act introduced a national curriculum of three core and seven foundation subjects for pupils aged 5 to 16. This was a fundamental change in British education, which had never experienced before such a regulation and standardization of its content. The actual content of the curriculum was not particularly innovatory, however, for it consisted largely of traditional subjects. Technology was introduced, but subjects such as economics, politics, psychology, and sociology were all left out. After industrial action by teachers forced the government to review this system, the compulsory content for 14–16 year olds was, however, reduced to 40 per cent of school time.

With the national curriculum went national testing. GCSE already provided a national test at age 16 but new tests were introduced at the ages of 14, 11, 7 (and later 5). The requirements of the national curriculum and the testing of all subjects overloaded teachers and led to heavy protests from the teaching unions and teacher boycotts of testing. This resulted in a slimming-down of the curriculum and the restriction of testing to the three core subjects in 1994. The principle of a national curriculum and national tests had, however, been established.

National testing enabled the construction of league tables that allowed the comparison of schools' performances. A major problem with these tables was, however, that performance was largely determined by a school's intake. This created a powerful incentive for schools to be more selective in their intake and exclude children likely to perform badly. Education professionals argue that what really matters is the *value added* by the school. The quality of a school should be judged not by its results but by the amount of improvement it has brought about.

An alternative league table produced on this basis showed that some inner-city schools which did badly in the official table had actually brought about great improvements in performance. Schools in Liverpool, Tower Hamlets, and Lambeth which ranked 98, 105, and 100 respectively in the official league table rose to positions 7, 8, and 9 in the value-added table (*Observer*, 20 Mar. 1994).

It was not only pupils that were tested, for a new system of school inspection run by the Office for Standards in Education (OFSTED) was introduced. This involved not only the inspection of the workings of the school but also meetings with parents at which teachers were not present. OFSTED reports were then made available to parents. This fitted well with the government's belief in parent power, which it had increased by giving parents more influence on governing bodies.

In their day-to-day running schools had been given greater freedom from local-authority control. They now, however, had to face not only the disciplines of the market but also heavier demands from parents and tighter control by the central state. Schools were caught in a vice of increasing parental and state control.

HIGHER EDUCATION

The changes in schools were in many ways paralleled by those taking place in higher education but we are dealing with it separately because of its organizational differences.

Renewed expansion and financial squeeze

After its rapid expansion in the 1960s and early 1970s, higher education (HE) grew more slowly until the end of the 1980s, just about keeping up with the growing number of 18 year olds. The proportion of 18 year olds in higher education reached 14 per cent in 1973 and did not reach 15 per cent until 1988. It then doubled to reach 30 per cent by 1994 (see Figure 7.8).

Expansion resulted partly from the growing demand for places. The number of 18 year olds rose during the 1980s and they became better qualified, as their GCSE and A-level results improved. New routes opened up for older students through Access courses. Demand became to some extent self-generating, as rising numbers of jobseekers with degrees forced others to obtain degrees as well, if they were to compete. A high level of unemployment anyway encouraged students to stay on in education.

The great increase in the proportion of 18 year olds going into higher education was, however, largely driven by the government. HE institutions were pressed to expand by changes in funding, which in the late 1980s became more closely linked to student numbers. Higher education began to grow more rapidly than the government had intended, and in 1992, alarmed by rising costs, the government put the brakes on.

Education as a whole has been financially squeezed but higher education has suffered particularly. Funding per student was in decline during the 1980s but dropped particularly sharply during the 1990s (see Figure 7.9 on p. 266). Universities have responded by allowing the number of students per lecturer to rise. In the 'old' universities student–staff ratios rose from 10.3 to 1 in 1986 to 14 to 1 in 1994. In the 'new' universities (the ex-polytechnics) they rose even more sharply from 12 to 1 in 1988 to 18.7 to 1 in 1993. Staffing levels in key university services also failed to keep up with increasing student numbers.

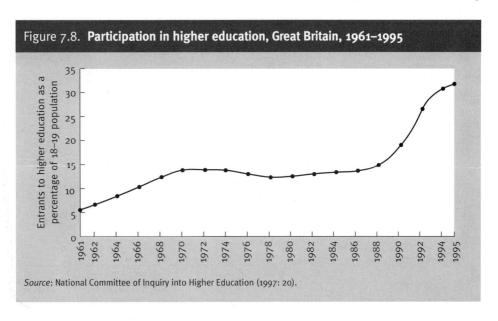

Figure 7.8. **Participation in higher education, Great Britain, 1961–1995**

Source: National Committee of Inquiry into Higher Education (1997: 20).

Universities have tried to find new sources of income and save on costs. The government halted the expansion of home undergraduate numbers, so universities have recruited more overseas students (who pay much higher fees), expanded postgraduate courses, and developed distance-learning programmes. They tried to raise more money from renting out their accommodation, from commercial sponsorship, and appeals to their alumni. They saved on costs by reducing staff and allowing buildings to deteriorate.

Pressures on students increased in various ways. The most obvious was the freezing of the student grant,

which forced students to rely increasingly on loans (see Figure 7.10 on p. 266). They have also increasingly earned their way through university by taking paid work in term-time as well as vacations. Students have also come under other forms of pressure through library, equipment, and accommodation shortages, larger classes, and cramped conditions in university buildings. One likely result of all this is higher drop-out rates.

Research funding has been squeezed as well. University researchers have been forced to seek funds increasingly from private industry or government departments. This means that research is increasingly directed by outside organizations seeking the information that they need, which they may not want disclosed to competitors or to the public. Competition for research money from the Higher Education Funding Council has become more intense since the polytechnics became universities and began to seek a share of the limited funds available.

Competition, flexibility, and control

Under these pressures, universities, like other organizations, have had to become more competitive and more flexible in their internal workings.

More flexible course structures have been created through modularization and the standardizing of credits. The modularization of many courses has created smaller course units, which can be more flexibly combined into varying degree packages. Standardized credits make transfers easier between courses and also enable the gradual accumulation of credits

Applicants visiting a Midlands university.

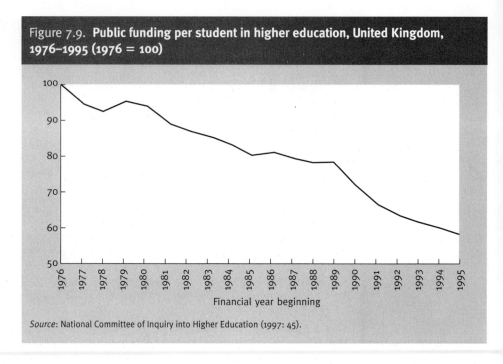

Figure 7.9. **Public funding per student in higher education, United Kingdom, 1976–1995 (1976 = 100)**

Financial year beginning

Source: National Committee of Inquiry into Higher Education (1997: 45).

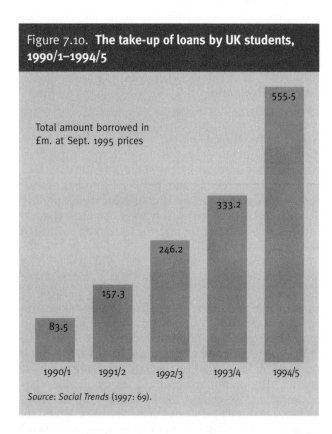

Figure 7.10. **The take-up of loans by UK students, 1990/1–1994/5**

Total amount borrowed in £m. at Sept. 1995 prices

Source: *Social Trends* (1997: 69).

over longer periods of study, possibly interspersed with periods of paid work.

Universities have, like schools and many other employers, moved towards greater flexibility of employment (see Chapter 13, pp. 530–2). They have a *core* of full-time, permanent staff members and a *periphery* of part-timers and staff on short-term contracts. This provides them with what is called 'numerical flexibility', so that they can more easily respond to financial crises by reducing their staff costs.

Greater organizational flexibility has been created by decentralizing management and the control of budgets to departments. As with schools, this kind of decentralization has, in principle, allowed greater freedom to operate in a more competitive environment. Resources have, however, been tightly controlled by university administrations trying to cope with the consequences of the financial squeeze.

Universities, like schools, have also come under closer state scrutiny, as their teaching and research have been inspected and graded by the Higher Education Funding Council. Each subject in turn undergoes an inspection of teaching, called Teaching Quality Assessment (TQA), on an eight-year cycle (six yearly in Scotland). TQA reports are public documents and TQA scores enable the construction of national league tables for each subject. Research too is evaluated through four- (in some cases six-) yearly assessments of its quality. Again results are published and league tables are constructed. Research performance is linked to funding but teaching performance has not yet been.

Thus, although greater flexibility has been introduced into the organization of higher education, there has also been tighter bureaucratic control by the state. Both teaching and research have come under closer surveillance. Student numbers have in recent years been closely controlled. The institutions of higher education have lost much of their earlier autonomy and now have to operate within a framework imposed by the state.

This was an inevitable consequence of the funding of almost all higher education by the state. Higher education in Britain is here quite different from that of some other countries, such as Japan and the United States, where a large proportion of HE institutions are private.

EDUCATION AND THE STATE

Education had been more thoroughly transformed by government during the 1980s and the 1990s than ever before. In this section we will review the state's role in Britain and consider what difference a Labour government is likely to make to education policy.

The Conservative education revolution

The Conservatives' concern to increase Britain's international competitiveness by improving education's contribution to the economy was not distinctive to the Conservative Party. As we showed in 'The New Vocationalism in Britain', p. 258, a broad alliance had formed on this issue across the political spectrum.

What was distinctive about the Conservative approach was its belief in the market principle. The *neo-liberal* ideology of the New Right was here central to its transformation of education. The neo-liberals believed that British education could most effectively be reformed by introducing market principles. This led to the policies that increased competition between schools, reduced local-authority control over them, and provided more choice for parents. The rise of neo-liberalism must itself be placed in the context of the growing economic crisis of the 1970s, for neo-liberal policies were a response to that crisis.

The state regulation of the curriculum and the introduction of national testing might, at first sight, seem to contradict the Conservatives' belief in market forces. They were less contradictory than they appeared to be, for they took the control of education out of the hands of LEAs. The Conservatives believed that education

needed to be rescued from what they saw as the distorting influence of 'progressive' teachers and left-wing ideologists in local authorities. The national curriculum and national testing also provided a framework within which competition and choice could operate. National testing enabled the construction of league tables, which encouraged competition and provided parents with the information they needed in order to make informed choices.

This linked to another strand in Conservative policy, a truly conservative appeal to the beliefs and values of ordinary people, which has been labelled *authoritarian populism* (Dale 1989). Populism rejected the views of experts and called for a return to the common sense and 'natural instincts' of the people. It was associated with 'parent power' and parental choice; calls for a return to Christian education; stricter school discipline; the teaching of patriotic versions of British history. It was also concerned to maintain traditional subjects, 'chalk-and-board' teaching methods, traditional examination methods, and A levels. This strand of Conservatism came into conflict with many of the reforms sought by the new vocationalists and the alliance for change.

 We discuss Conservative ideology and the Conservatives' transformation of the state in Chapter 18, pp. 748–9. *Neo-liberalism* and *authoritarian populism* were two different strands of Conservative thinking, which were to some extent in conflict but also complemented each other.

While politicians generally agreed on the importance of education, they were also under pressure to control state expenditure. There was a tension in education policy between the need to reform education and put more resources into it and the need to keep public spending under control. Schools were squeezed financially through the government's control of local-authority spending. There were frequent calls on higher education to make 'efficiency gains' as the government reduced the value of the student fee paid to the universities. The Conservatives also gradually shifted the funding of students' maintenance from a grant to a loan basis.

The proportion of national income spent on education did actually decline, particularly in the 1980s. As a proportion of UK Gross Domestic Product, state spending on education dropped from 5.5 per cent in 1980/1 to

Aspects of the Conservative transformation of education

Aspects of Conservative government	Policy in education
▶ Neo-liberalism	▶ Competition and market forces. Increased choice.
▶ Authoritarian populism	▶ Parent power. Discipline. Traditional values and methods.
▶ Improvement of economic performance	▶ New vocationalism. Expansion of post-16 education. Raising standards.
▶ Increased state regulation	▶ National curriculum and national tests. Inspection. Assessment of HE teaching and research.
▶ Control of expenditure	▶ Financial squeeze on schools, colleges, and HE. Declining value of grant.

4.8 per cent in 1990/1 and was at 5.2 per cent in 1994/5 (*Social Trends* 1997: 69). The proportion of young people in higher education had more than doubled over this period but the state was spending a lower proportion of the national income on education at the end of it than it was at its beginning.

Labour government and education

Many of the changes introduced by the Conservatives were opposed by the Labour Party. In 1997 the Labour victory in the general election led to the formation of a Labour government. Will the Labour government reverse the Conservative revolution in education?

Selection has been a key issue in the politics of education and historically the two main parties have taken very different attitudes towards it. The Labour governments of the 1960s and 1970s promoted comprehensive schools, while the Conservatives have supported diversity and selection. The Labour Party remains in principle opposed to selection at age 11, but the 'New Labour' government of 1997 has not signalled any intention to return to old Labour policies aimed at ending selective

education. Indeed, so far as selection within schools is concerned, the government has stated that it will end mixed-ability teaching and require 'setting' by ability, unless a school can demonstrate the effectiveness of an alternative approach.

Policy statements suggest that the existing diversity and hierarchy of state schools will be largely left alone. Grammar schools will continue to exist. Grant Maintained Schools will lose their financial advantages and return to LEA funding but will be allowed to retain their distinctiveness as 'foundation schools'. Schools will be allowed to continue to specialize and select children on the basis of their ability in the area of specialization.

There has, however, been a shift away from a reliance on market forces to raise standards towards more emphasis on direct state intervention. The national curriculum and national testing will remain in place, though league tables will provide more 'value-added' information. There will be a tighter central control over quality matters. The government has declared that improvement targets will be set at every level, with 'zero tolerance of failure'. Penalties for failure will include the faster dismissal of bad teachers, the closure of failing schools, and the suspension of the powers of failing LEAs.

The government has also declared its commitment to parent power and an intention to involve parents further, but also to place more responsibility on parents. There will be no return of control over the management of schools to LEAs. There are proposals to increase parent representation on school governing bodies and give parent governors representation on each LEA committee. These proposals would also give parents greater responsibility for their children's education through 'home–school' contracts, covering such matters as attendance, homework, and discipline. Parents would be liable to fines of up to £1,000 if their children persistently truant.

So far as higher education is concerned, the main things that emerged during the government's first months were the requirement for students and their families to make a contribution to fees, unless family income is less than £23,000 per year, and the abolition of maintenance grants. Both clearly continued in the direction set by the Conservatives. The expansion of higher education, the financial crisis of the universities, and constraints on public spending made it more or less inevitable that students would be required to contribute to the costs of higher education. The abolition of maintenance grants simply continued the process of shifting student funding from grants to loans.

There are differences of emphasis and detail between Conservative and Labour education policy, but there

Fees, loans, and equality?

Will the government's abolition of maintenance grants and introduction of a student's contribution to higher-education fees result in a more or less equal society? In considering this question, you should take account of the following points:

▶ Only students from families with an annual income higher than £35,000 have to make the full contribution of £1,000 per year. Those from families earning less than £23,000 do not have to make any contribution.

▶ It is estimated that maintenance and fee payments will cost at least £10,000 per student for a three-year course.

▶ The Dearing Report estimated that higher education increases a person's earning capacity by an average of 11–14 per cent.

▶ Student loans will become repayable only when earnings reach a certain level.

▶ The middle class has benefited far more from state expenditure on education than the working class (see our discussion of this in Chapter 18, p. 742).

▶ Some elite universities have been threatening to 'go it alone' by introducing 'top-up' fees.

seems to be more continuity than change. The Labour government of 1997 has the same concerns as the previous Conservative government with controlling state expenditure, maintaining economic competitiveness, raising standards, and keeping middle-class political support. It appears unlikely that it will make major changes to the system it has inherited from the Conservatives.

SUMMARY POINTS

In this section we have examined the transformation of education in the 1980s and 1990s. The background to this transformation was the economic crisis in 1970s Britain:

▶ Changes in occupational structure and in the relationship between the economy and the state led governments to place greater emphasis on the economic role of education.

▶ This led in Britain to a new emphasis on training and vocational education.

▶ Attempts were made to bridge the gap between school and work through work experience schemes and the expansion of post-16 education and training.

Schools were also subjected to market forces and greater state regulation:

▶ The introduction of market principles involved less LEA control, greater competition, and increased parental choice.

▶ Greater diversity and increased selection strengthened the hierarchical tendencies in British education.

▶ Selection and choice led to greater inequality.

▶ There was increased state regulation through the national curriculum, national testing, and intensified inspection.

Similar processes occurred in higher education:

▶ Higher education began to expand rapidly in the late 1980s.

▶ Under the pressures of higher numbers and a financial squeeze, universities became more commercial, more competitive, and developed greater organizational flexibility.

▶ Standards of both teaching and research came under closer surveillance.

The transformation of education was driven by government policy:

▶ Conservative policies were driven by the imperatives of international competition, neo-liberal beliefs, authoritarian populism, and the control of state expenditure.

▶ The 1997 Labour government seems unlikely to reverse the main features of the Conservative education revolution.

REVISION AND EXERCISES

EDUCATION AND INEQUALITY

In 'Understanding Education' we examined different theories of the relationship between education and inequality. In 'The Development of Education in Britain' we outlined the tripartite system and the introduction of comprehensive schools:

▶ Make sure that you are familiar with the main ideas of Parsons, Bernstein, and Bourdieu.

▶ What do you understand by the following terms: material and cultural deprivation, restricted and elaborated speech codes; cultural capital, subcultural capital; hidden curriculum; tripartite system, comprehensive education?

In 'Inequality in British Education' we examined patterns of class, gender, and ethnic inequality:

▶ What is the evidence for the persistence of class inequalities after the 1944 Act? Why do you think that comprehensive education has had little impact on class differences in educational achievement?

▶ What possible explanations are there of girls' superior exam results? Do they signal the end of the male domination of education?

▶ Do ethnic differences in educational achievement show that ethnicity is related to educational success? In what sense can racism be found in schools?

The issue of inequality also came up in our discussion of the 1980s policy of introducing greater parent choice, in 'A Regulated Market Place':

▶ Why has there been so much concern with choice?

▶ What were the consequences of greater parental choice for patterns of inequality?

▶ What do you think is the most important thing that parents can do to ensure the educational success of their children?

EDUCATION AND LABOUR

We considered theories of the relationship between education and labour in 'Understanding Education':

▶ Make sure that you are familiar with the main ideas of Durkheim, Parsons, Bowles and Gintis, and Willis.

▶ What do you understand by the following terms: primary and secondary socialization; correspondence principle, hidden curriculum, oppositional subculture?

When we outlined the 'Development of Education in Britain', we referred to the idea that Britain's lack of economic competitiveness was a result of the character of British education. We took this issue up again in 'Education, Training, and National Revival':

▶ What reasons are there for supposing that British education has failed to provide the kind of labour force required by the economy?

▶ Make a list of the main changes made to education and training during the 1980s and 1990s. In what way could each change be seen as improving the economic performance of education?

▶ Did greater state regulation contradict the Conservative government's belief in market forces?

▶ In what ways do the 1980s and 1990s changes in education provide evidence for the approach taken by Bowles and Gintis? Do they suggest any weaknesses in their argument?

▶ **What changes have been made to education policy by the 1997 Labour government? Has it merely continued Conservative policies?**

FURTHER READING

The following cover most of the issues dealt with in this chapter:

Heaton, T., and Lawson, T. (1996), *Education and Training* (London: Macmillan). A clearly written and up-to-date text which deals not only with the traditional inequality issues but also recent changes in educational policy.

Cosin, B., Flude, M., and Hales, M. (1989), *School, Work, and Equality* (London: Hodder & Stoughton). A generally useful reader which covers organizational aspects of the school, inequality issues, and the transition from school to work.

Halsey, A., Lauder, H., Brown, P., and Stuart Wells, A. (1997) (eds.), *Education: Culture, Economy, and Society* (Oxford: Oxford University Press). A very comprehensive and quite advanced reader, which deals with all the latest debates and issues, and will be a standard work for some time to come.

Particular topics can be followed up through:

Ball, S. (1981), *Beachside Comprehensive: A Case-Study of Secondary Schooling* (Cambridge: Cambridge University Press). A participant observation study of a comprehensive school, covering the introduction of mixed-ability teaching.

Gillborn, D. (1992), *'Race', Ethnicity, and Education* (London: Unwin Hyman). Reviews the literature and debates on this issue.

Stanworth, M. (1983), *Gender and Schooling: A Study of Sexual Divisions in the Classroom* (London: Hutchinson). A classic study of the gendered aspects of classroom interaction between teachers and students.

Ashton, D. N., and Lowe, G. (1991), *Making their Way: Education, Training and the Labour Market in Canada and Britain* (Milton Keynes: Open University Press). A collection of readings on the transition from education to work.

Illich, I. (1973), *Deschooling Society* (Harmondsworth: Penguin). A classic critique of schooling which argues that education should not be confused with what goes on in schools.

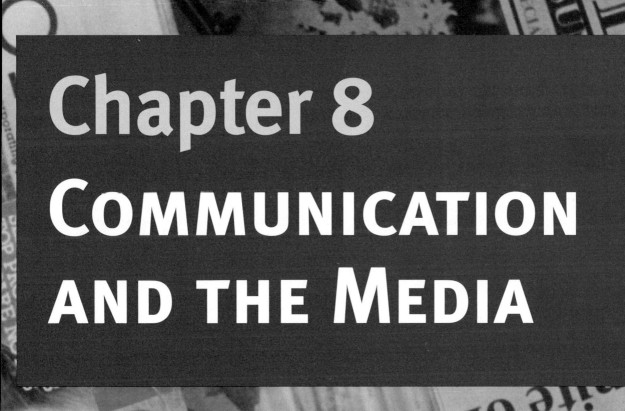

Chapter 8
COMMUNICATION AND THE MEDIA

Why *EastEnders* is Scarier than Tarantino

'The television violence debate reignited yesterday with the revelation that children and teenagers are more disturbed by violence in soap operas such as *EastEnders* than in Hollywood action movies. The difference was that violence in soaps occurred in a real-life setting, they told researchers for a Broadcasting Standards Council report into the attitudes of 10–16-year-olds, *Young People and the Media*.

'"When Bruce Willis blows away a load of villains it's a laugh. You know it's not real. I think violence in *EastEnders* is more shocking because it's real life," one 16 year old said.

'The BSC researcher agreed. . . . "We had some 12 to 13 year old girls who saw a TV programme called Backup in which a man was thrown off a block of flats. You saw blood oozing slowly from his body. But instead of being disturbed by the scene, some complained that the blood wasn't the right colour. Most 15 year olds would laugh at you if you said *Pulp Fiction* was disturbing."'

Source: Marianne MacDonald, 'Why "EastEnders" is Scarier than Tarantino', *Independent*, 13 Dec. 1996.

WE live in a media-saturated world. On average people in Great Britain spend between three and four hours a day watching television and over two hours a day listening to the radio. Well over half the adult population reads a national daily newspaper and over two-thirds read a Sunday paper (*Social Trends* 1997: 218).

The media consume a lot of our time but what influence do they have on the way we feel, think, and act? Do newspapers influence the way that we vote? Does the enjoyment of a Hollywood film mean that we absorb American values? Does screen violence make us behave more violently? As the opening extract suggests, violence is very much a matter of context and perception. A lot of research has gone into trying to answer these questions and we shall examine in this chapter the issues that they raise.

Another set of questions is raised about the content of the media. Who determines what we read in the newspapers? Is it the journalists, the editors, or the owners of the papers? Or are they all simply trying to give us what we want in order to maximize sales? Does it matter that Rupert Murdoch's companies own a large part of the British press and control satellite television? We shall examine patterns of ownership and their significance for media content.

The media in general, and television in particular, have been transformed by technical change. There is suddenly a bewildering amount of choice, as terrestrial, satellite, and cable delivery systems provide us with hundreds of channels. But is this sense of choice illusory? Will it actually diminish as growing competition forces the media to chase larger audiences? Can the BBC's tradition of public-service broadcasting survive? Does state censorship and political manipulation distort the increasing amount of information that flows at us through the media? We shall also examine recent changes in broadcasting and the pressures generated by commercialization and state intervention.

UNDERSTANDING THE MEDIA

COMMUNICATION AND LANGUAGE

Animals communicate but only humans communicate through language. The distinctive feature of language is that words carry meanings, which we learn initially through socialization and education. Communication through language depends upon these meanings being shared.

We also communicate in many non-verbal ways, through gestures or posture (commonly called body language), but the same processes of attaching and learning meaning apply. Thus, we learn that the 'thumb's up' sign means that 'things are OK'. We communicate through images too. A holiday snap can communicate our well-being on holiday and inform people that we have visited a fashionable resort. The term 'image' has, indeed, been extended to mean not just a representation of something but also the impression of ourselves that we communicate to other people. We create an image through the style we adopt, and the clothes that we wear communicate a great deal about us. These non-verbal ways of communication carry learned and shared meanings and may also be considered languages of a kind.

Languages are much more than a means of communication, for they also express and shape the way that we see the world and the way that we see ourselves. If you say that you are British, this does not just state which country you live in. It presupposes a way of seeing the world that divides it up between nation states. It indicates that you see yourself as British, rather than, say, English or Scottish, and carries with it ideas of national character. The importance of language is not only that it allows us to communicate, but also that it gives us an identity. Without it we would not know who we are.

Communication occurs not only through face-to-face interaction but also through various forms of recorded and transmitted images and sounds. These means of communication are generally termed **media** (the plural of medium), because they mediate between those who give information and those who receive it. We usually use the term 'the media' to refer to television, newspapers, and radio, sometimes films, and this chapter will be mainly concerned with these media, but we should bear in mind that there are many others, such as paintings, books, tapes, and grafitti, which all enable communication over distance and/or time. The time dimension should not be forgotten, for the media not only spread information; they also store it for future use.

THE MEDIA AND SOCIETY

The media are central to the way our society functions. Television, newspapers, and radio are the principal means through which people obtain information. Indeed, if the media do not cover an event or an issue, it is unlikely that anyone other than those immediately involved will know anything about it. The media not only inform us selectively about events; they actually shape them. Politicians or public relations agencies or advertisers construct events in ways that will maximize their coverage by the media and create an image of a particular kind. The term 'media event' has entered the language.

The media play an important role in cultural, economic, and political activities. They largely create popular culture. They are crucial to the functioning of the economy because of their role in the marketing of goods and services. Politicians use them to manipulate voters and elections may well be won or lost through them. Indeed, one of the first things that the leaders of any revolution or military *coup* will try to do is seize control of the radio and television studios.

The relationship between the media and society has

What do our clothes say about who we are?

theory, industrialization and urbanization had *atomized* society, which had become a mass of isolated individuals after traditional community and family structures disintegrated. Social isolation meant that people were particularly open to influence by the media.

> ☞ Louis Wirth's notion of an 'urban way of life', which we discuss in 'Urban Society', Chapter 11, pp. 403–4, embodied ideas very similar to those of mass-society theory. He too argued that the decline of community led to social disintegration and instability in the city.

Mass-society theorists, such as Kornhauser (1960), were much concerned with the dangers of both political and commercial manipulation. The fascist leaders of the 1930s, such as Hitler and Mussolini, had been very skilful at using the media to mobilize and control people. As Strinati (1995: 5) has put it, mass-society theorists believed that 'mass media equalled mass propaganda equalled mass repression'. These theorists also believed that the rise of a 'culture industry' would result in the creation of a highly standardized and highly commercialized mass culture, which we discuss further in 'The Media and Culture', pp. 279–81.

The **dominant-ideology** approach too saw the media as highly influential, though it held a very different

been discussed from a number of perspectives and in this section we will examine the main approaches that have emerged.

Manipulation and domination

The development of the media opened up new opportunities for the manipulation and domination of people by both governments and business. Technological innovation enabled the media to reach ever larger numbers of people, particularly with the invention of radio and television which could *broadcast* messages to huge audiences simultaneously. The media became **mass media** in the sense that they could reach masses of people.

The manipulative possibilities offered by the mass media have been explored by **mass-society** theory. This theory was based not only on the capacity of the media to reach large numbers of people but also on their new vulnerability to manipulation. According to this

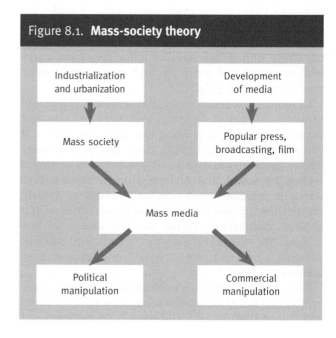

Figure 8.1. **Mass-society theory**

view of the nature of society (see also our discussion of this in Chapter 17, p. 690). It rejected the idea that industrialization and urbanization produced a mass of isolated and disorganized individuals and drew from Marxist theory the concept of a society divided into classes. It argued that *subordinate* classes are dominated by the ideas and beliefs of a *ruling* class. In Marx's famous words: 'The ideas of the ruling class are, in every age, the ruling ideas: i.e. the class, which is the dominant *material* force in society, is at the same time its dominant *intellectual* force' (Marx 1845–6: 93).

This approach to the media has been much influenced by the ideas of Gramsci, who was critical of the economic determinism of some later Marxists and argued that they failed to recognize the importance of ideas in class domination and class conflict. According to Gramsci, the ruling class maintained its authority not just by coercion but by establishing hegemony. By **hegemony** he meant the ideological domination of society by the ruling class, which persuaded other classes to accept its values and beliefs so that a general consensus emerged around them. According to Gramsci, the reason why socialist and communist movements had failed was that the ruling class had won the battle of ideas. A revolutionary movement could not succeed unless it first challenged the hegemony of the ruling class and wrested the control of ideas from it.

Miliband (1969) argued that the ruling class's control of the mass media was one of the main means through which it influenced people's ideas. The media were largely in private ownership, which was concentrated in a few hands. The owners of the media were not only major capitalists in their own right but also closely connected with ruling circles. They used their control of the media to support right-wing parties by presenting ruling-class interpretations of events and preventing the discussion of alternative interpretations. More generally, it has been argued that the media play a key role in getting people to accept inequality, for they gain most of their knowledge of the world from the media, which treats inequality as a normal, natural, and inevitable fact of life. The media also divert people's attention from the exploitation and inequality characteristic of capitalist society by glorifying and encouraging consumption (Murdock and Golding 1977).

But how dominant is the dominant ideology? There is a tension in this approach between the notion of a dominant ideology and the idea that subordinate classes have their own beliefs based on their class situation (J. Clarke *et al.* 1976). These beliefs can provide the basis for challenges to the dominant ideology. Furthermore, such challenges can be assisted by analyses of the media which reveal the ways in which people are manipulated.

The significance of ideology has also been queried. Abercrombie *et al.* (1979) recognized that a dominant ideology exists but argued that its importance in maintaining capitalism had been exaggerated. They held the view that capitalism is maintained primarily by what Marx called the 'dull compulsion of economic relations'. Workers accept capitalism because they have no real choice. They have to work in order to live and it is the capitalist economy that provides them with employment. Their beliefs have little to do with it.

Consumption and production

Both mass-society and Marxist theory assume that the content of the media is shaped by those who own and control them. An alternative approach is to argue that the content of the media is determined by market forces. Thus the content of, say, newspapers is determined not by their owners but by the readers who buy them. Newspapers and broadcasters are ultimately concerned with circulation and audience figures. The market rules and the media will serve up whatever the consumer wants.

The problem faced by this approach is that it cannot explain why the readers hold the views they do. It takes these views as given. It also treats those who own and control the media as passive, when there is plenty of evidence that many of them hold strong opinions and see the media as vehicles for their political beliefs. It is none the less true that most media operations have to

Antonio Gramsci

Antonio Gramsci (1891–1937) was born in Sardinia. He studied at the University of Turin but left to become a socialist journalist. He was closely associated with the factory-councils movement of the Turin workers, which sought to establish a system of direct industrial democracy. He was one of the founders of the Italian Communist Party in 1924 and was arrested because of his political activities in 1926. He died in prison in 1937. It was during his years in prison that he wrote his major work *Prison Notebooks*. Unlike most Marxist theorists, he developed his ideas not in a university context but out of his practical experience of political work. His most well-known contribution to Marxist theory is the concept of hegemony. An introduction to his work can be found in Ransome (1992).

make profits and cannot afford to alienate readers or audiences. This applies to the British Broadcasting Corporation (BBC) too, for it can only justify the licence fee if its audience consists of a substantial part of the population.

Yet another approach argues that it is the producers who determine the content of the media. Journalists and programme producers have an important degree of autonomy. They are professionals with their own values and their own occupational associations. There is certainly some truth in this view, for the media do depend on creative people with specialized occupational skills. An understanding of media content does require the study of those who produce it, as in Tunstall's (1971) classic study of journalists at work.

Tunstall certainly recognized, however, that the professionals work under constraints of various kinds. They have to operate within the organizations that employ them. They are controlled by editors, who are ultimately controlled by owners. Their careers depend on the approval of others and they are in competition with colleagues. They are also dependent on those who provide them with information (Tunstall 1995). At most, they have a very limited autonomy.

We will take up this issue again in 'Constructing the News', pp. 291–3.

A public sphere?

The autonomy not only of media professionals but also of a public sphere has been an important issue in the study of the media. The concept of a public sphere is of an area where people can freely discuss matters of general importance to them as citizens. The eighteenth-century idea of human rights, especially the right to vote, and the rights to free speech and free assembly, was crucial in establishing this notion.

Habermas developed an influential theory of the development and decline of the public sphere. He saw this as first emerging in eighteenth-century coffee houses, where people of any kind could meet and freely discuss any matter in a non-commercial atmosphere uncontrolled by Church or State. He considered that the rise of the mass media led to the decline of the public sphere and regarded them as commercialized and manipulative. The picture he drew of the coffee houses has, however, been considered rather idealistic, since they were hardly accessible to all. His view of the media has also been criticized, for they do in various ways allow for the discussion of matters of public interest. In Britain the BBC was established within a public-service framework and public-service ideals remain influential in British broadcasting. His ideas have, none the less, struck a chord amongst those concerned with the decline of the public functions of the media (Boyd-Barrett 1995).

The relationship between the state and the public sphere has been a complex one. The public sphere needs protection from both commercial and political pressures if it is to flourish. Protection from commercial pressures requires state regulation, and this has performed an important role in limiting the effects of commercialization on the content of British television. The state is in other ways, however, an enemy of the public sphere, for governments seek to control or manipulate the political content of the media and turn them into an instrument of government. The BBC has had an uneasy relationship with governments and, as we shall show later, its ideal of public service has at times appeared to mean service to the state. In ' Decline of the Public Sphere', pp. 309–13, we shall examine the

---

The principles of public service broadcasting in the 1990s

▶ Broadcasts should be available to the whole population.
▶ Programmes should cover a broad range of tastes.
▶ At least one broadcaster should be funded by licence fee or tax.
▶ Broadcasters should be institutionally protected from commercial/political interests.
▶ Political, state, and sporting events of national interest must be covered.
▶ Emphasis on national concerns must not be at the expense of ethnic, cultural, or demographic minorities.
▶ Broadcasting should be organized to promote quality rather than pursuit of audiences.
▶ Public guidelines should free rather than restrict programme-makers.

These principles are based on a survey of influential broadcasters and politicians by the Broadcasting Research Unit.

Source: Franklin (1994: 57).

increasing pressures on it from both governments and commercial interests.

The idea of a public sphere also implies some distinction between public and private matters. Media space and time have become increasingly taken up with material from private life, which tends to push out the discussion of public matters. While commercial pressures have largely driven this, as the media have sought audiences and readers by revealing details of people's private lives, politicians and other public figures have played their part by using the media to project their personalities and families. Media revelations can, however, do public figures considerable damage, and this has led to calls for privacy legislation to regulate *unwelcome* media intrusions into private life. Significantly, the concern is with the protection of privacy rather than the maintenance of a public sphere where matters of general interest to citizens are discussed.

THE MEDIA AND CULTURE

Culture has been central to the issues that we have been discussing. If the media shape the way that people think and live, then it is largely through popular culture that they must do this. There has been a growing interest in the Sociology of Popular Culture and in this section we will examine what we mean by this term and the main approaches to it. We first need to set popular culture in the context of the development of types of culture.

> **We discuss the general meaning of the term 'culture' in Chapter 1, pp. 14–15, and you might find it helpful to refer to this discussion.**

Folk, high, and popular culture

The distinction between **folk culture** and **high culture** has been applied to pre-industrial societies in Europe, where there was a *high* culture of the aristocratic elite that was separate from the *folk* or *low* culture of the ordinary people. Folk culture consisted of local customs and beliefs that were handed down by word of mouth from one generation to the next. While high culture was associated with the arts, folk culture was associated with the crafts.

With industrialization and urbanization a new, increasingly commercialized culture emerged amongst the people. It was a mixture of elements of the old folk culture and the new way of life in the industrial cities. On the one hand, it influenced the content of the media, as they sought larger circulations and audiences, but, on the other hand, it was in turn shaped by media influences. This new form of culture came to be called popular culture.

While the term 'popular culture' is widely used, it is not easy to specify what it means. Three different meanings are commonly found:

▶ *That which is not high culture.* This elitist way of defining popular culture assumes that we know what high culture is and implies that popular culture is inferior. Even within its own terms it is difficult to apply, for the boundaries between the two are hard to establish and particular items of culture move across them. Thus, Shakespeare and Dickens originated as means of popular entertainment but are now treated by many as high culture.

▶ *What most people like and do.* This raises the issue of how popular a cultural trait has to be in order to be classified as popular. Pop songs are commonly regarded as part of popular culture but the latest fashion in pop may not actually be at all popular in

Pavarotti in the park

'Even the most rigorous defenders of high culture would not want to exclude Pavarotti or Puccini from its select enclave. But in 1990 Pavarotti managed to take 'Nessun Dorma' (None Shall Sleep) to number one in the British charts. . . . On 30 July 1991, Pavarotti gave a free concert in London's Hyde Park. 250,000 people were expected, but due to heavy rain, the number who actually attended was around 100,000. Two things about the event are of interest to the student of popular culture. The first is the enormous popularity of the event. . . . Second, the extent of his popularity would appear to threaten the class exclusivity of a high culture/popular culture divide. It is therefore interesting to note the way in which the event was reported in the media. All the British tabloids carried news of the event on their front pages. The *Daily Mirror*, for instance, had five pages devoted to the concert. . . . When the event was reported on television programmes the following lunchtime, the tabloid coverage was included as part of the general meaning of the event. Both the BBC's 'One O'Clock News' and ITV's '12.30 News' referred to the way in which the tabloids had covered the concert, and, moreover, the extent to which they had covered the concert. The old certainties of the cultural landscape suddenly seemed in doubt.'

Source: Storey (1993: 8–9).

this sense. The notion of a culture of the majority does not, anyway, fit easily with the diversity of culture, which varies, for example, by class and ethnicity.

▶ *Culture created by the people.* This gets round the problem of how popular something needs to be in order to be part of popular culture. Folk music, pigeon-fancying, train-spotting, and rugby league—the list is endless—can all be regarded as popular in this sense, even if they are all minority interests. But does pop music originate from the people or from recording studios funded by transnational corporations? The notion of 'the people' is, anyway, more than a little vague. Does it include the middle class?

We may find it difficult to sort out precisely what popular culture means but it is, none the less, an area of study that is thriving. It is anyway characteristic of an expanding field that its boundaries are not clear and people are not too worried about where they lie. It has certainly focused attention on previously neglected aspects of our culture that are central to the lives of most people.

Mass culture, dominant culture, and subcultures

According to mass-society theory, which we examined above, popular culture was **mass culture**. The 'genuine' folk culture of the people was destroyed by a highly commercialized and standardized mass culture, which also undermined the standards of high culture.

Adorno and Horkheimer, prominent members of the Frankfurt school, used the term 'culture industry' to describe this transformation of culture. Culture had become something that was made and sold, just like any other industrial product, in order to make a profit. It was, according to this view, imposed on the masses by the culture industry and turned people into passive consumers of material that did not meet their 'real needs'. Mass culture was also crucial to the maintenance of a capitalist society. Workers were willing to accept boredom and exploitation at work because they could escape during their leisure hours into the pleasures of popular culture, by watching films or listening to popular music.

A debate between **elitist** and **populist** interpretations of popular culture has run through the literature on it. The elitist view valued the high culture of the arts and treated popular culture as commercial and trivial. Populist views, on the other hand, recognized the vitality and creativity of popular culture and argued that it expressed the experience of ordinary people. They saw popular culture as rooted in *subcultures* related to ethnicity or class. We shall return later to the conflict between these interpretations in the section on 'Culture', pp. 297–8.

Subcultures are the cultures of particular groups within society. The term is generally used to refer to youth cultures or the cultures of subordinate classes. The concept of subculture, which essentially means an 'under-culture', implies the existence of a dominant culture, a notion similar to that of dominant ideology, which we discussed above.

Some Marxist writers have seen subcultures based in subordinate classes as resisting the **dominant culture** and, potentially at least, challenging the social order. Thus, the subcultures that emerged amongst the young in the working class and middle class in the 1960s were described as 'counter-cultures' (Clarke *et al.* 1976). The 1960s styles of the 'mods', 'teds', and 'skinheads' were interpreted as challenges to the dominant culture (Hebdige 1979). As we noted in our discussion of the dominant-ideology approach, there is a tension in this literature between the idea of the imposition of a dominant culture by the ruling class and the possibility of subcultural resistance to this culture.

This discussion situates the analysis of culture within the framework of class relationships in a capitalist society and enables us to make important links between the structure of a society and its culture. It helps us not only to understand the content of culture

The Frankfurt school

The Frankfurt school is the name given to a group of left-wing thinkers associated with the Frankfurt Institute of Social Research. Founded in 1922, the institute moved to New York during the Nazi period, returned to Frankfurt in 1949, and was disbanded in 1969. Theodor Adorno (1903–69), Erich Fromm (1900–80), Max Horkheimer (1895–1973), and Herbert Marcuse (1898–1979) were prominent members of the school. Jurgen Habermas (1929–) has continued to develop their ideas.

The Frankfurt school found much of its inspiration in the work of the young Karl Marx on alienation (see Chapter 13, p. 504, for a discussion of this concept). It emphasized the way that the culture industry integrated workers into a capitalist society. The growth of mass consumption gave capitalist societies more stability, though there were still crisis tendencies in capitalism. Habermas (1973) has produced an influential theory of a sequence of crises that spread from the economic through the political to the cultural sphere.

but also how the existing structure of a society can both be maintained and periodically challenged through culture. One problem with this literature is, however, that it tends to neglect those aspects of culture linked to gender, ethnicity, and nationality, and the conflicts taking place between dominant and subordinate groups along these other dimensions of inequality.

MEDIA INFLUENCE AND THE AUDIENCE

The mass-society and dominant-ideology approaches both assume that the media do actually have some influence on what people think and do. Whether they have such an influence has been extensively debated and researched. In this section we will first examine the main positions that have emerged in the literature on the influence of the media. We then go on to consider the main methods that have emerged in the study of the media and their impact on the audience (for short-hand purposes readers and viewers, as well as listeners, are treated as audiences).

Models of media influence

Three main models of media influence can be found in the literature:

▶ the media-effects model;
▶ the active-audience model;
▶ the media-themes model.

Also known as the 'hypodermic model', the *media-effects* model assumes that audiences are passive and simply absorb injections of material from the media. It is characteristic of mass-society theory, some Marxist theories, and those who blame the media for the ills of society. Its passive view of the audience has been challenged by the second model.

According to the *active-audience* model, audiences do not simply receive messages from the media. American research in the 1950s demonstrated that local 'opinion leaders' influenced the way that people responded to the content of the media. There was then a growing emphasis on the way that members of an audience selected what *they* wanted from the media and interpreted media messages according to their existing ideas and beliefs. To put it in a nutshell, 'they heard what they wanted to hear'. Indeed, it was argued that this process meant that the media tended to reinforce rather than change people's views.

While this emphasis on selection and interpretation provided a healthy correction to the previous notion of influential and all-powerful media, it went in some ways to the opposite extreme. As Eldridge *et al.* (1997) point out, it exaggerated the freedom and choice of the audience. The *media-themes* model pursues more of a middle path. It is advocated by the Glasgow University Media Group (GUMG) and is based on their studies of television news. It recognizes that audiences are active but argues that the media none the less influence them. In many ways it combines the insights of the other two approaches.

The GUMG found that the themes of media reporting corresponded closely with the ideas of audience groups. This was a matter not just of the central arguments expressed in a programme but also of subtler themes in the language used and the images created. Indeed, members of the audience might reject opinions that did not fit their pre-existing beliefs but still pick up ideas and images that affected their view of the topic. Media influence was reinforced by social interaction. Thus, particularly striking events or stories acquired 'social currency' and were passed around in conversation, which reinforced them in people's minds. The GUMG studies have shown how perceptions of key social issues, such as those surrounding AIDS, child abuse, food panics, mental illness, sexual violence, strikes, and the conflict in Northern Ireland, were affected in this way by media coverage (Eldridge 1993*a*).

The GUMG has brought the idea of media influence back in, but its model of it is much more complex than the media-effects one. It recognizes that audiences are selective and interpretive and argues that audience activity actually increases media influence by involving the audience's interest and emotions. If an audience member is passive, the message may, so to speak, 'go in one ear and out of the other'. An active response is far more likely to result in something being carried away from a programme, discussed with others, and incorporated into ways of thinking and acting.

Methods of media research

Methods issues have been quite central to the debate over media influence, for different approaches have tended to use different methods. Here we will examine the advantages and disadvantages of the three main methods used:

▶ content analysis;
▶ textual analysis;
▶ audience research.

Audience understandings of AIDS

The GUMG study of media influence on the knowledge and understanding of AIDS showed the importance of both the words and the pictures used by the media, and the associations created by media coverage.

Words. Content analysis showed that the media made frequent reference to 'mixing bodily fluids' and the 'exchange of bodily fluids'. Audience research found that these words had stuck in people's minds and led them to fear that kissing could cause AIDS through contact with saliva, even though scientists had rejected this idea.

Pictures. Media coverage often showed AIDS sufferers looking thin, haggard, and depressed. This image too stuck in some people's minds and led them to think that this appearance would enable them to recognize people with the AIDS virus. This undermined the health-education message that people with this virus can look quite normal for many years before they develop AIDS symptoms.

Associations. Much of the early media coverage associated AIDS with homosexuality. There was little reference to lesbians but this association led people to think wrongly that lesbians were a high-risk group.

Source: adapted from Kitzinger (1997: 6–11).

Early approaches focused on **content analysis**. Typically this involved quantitative studies of how often a particular item was covered by the media. These could establish the amount of coverage of a topic and certain basic aspects of the way that it was covered, whether, for example, in news reports, editorials, or commentaries. It could provide useful information on such matters as, say, how often strikes were reported in newspapers or on television.

There are two main problems with this approach. There is, first, the problem of meaning, for researchers are interested not just in how a topic is covered but in the significance of the coverage. It is not just a matter of how often a newspaper covers strikes but also of how it reports and interprets them. Does it adopt a managerial or a union perspective? A purely quantitative analysis of content cannot tell us this. There is, secondly, the problem of effect. Content analysis cannot tell us anything about how a given article or programme affects the audience.

The problem of meaning was addressed by the more qualitative techniques of **textual analysis**. As this name suggests, this approach drew on the techniques developed to analyse the meaning of literature. It was also influenced by the study of the meaning of words and images by semiotics, the study of the meaning of signs, and is sometimes called the semiotic approach. It sought to penetrate behind the actual words or images used to uncover their meaning. The words or pictures used in reporting a strike could, for example, present a managerial account of it by emphasizing the stoppage of work and the loss of production. Alternatively, they could present a union perspective by focusing on the grievances of the workers. Through careful analysis of the text of the programme, its meaning could be revealed and its bias identified.

This approach also faced problems, however. There was the problem of its lack of objectivity. The researcher had to make assumptions about the meaning of the text and other researchers might interpret the same text quite differently. Would ordinary readers or viewers interpret it in the same way? There was also yet again the problem of effect. This approach too could not, on its own, tell us anything about the impact of the text on the audience.

To overcome these problems it was necessary to carry out **audience research**. A commonly used method for doing this was to show a programme to an audience and assess its effect by making before and after comparisons. While this approach did address the problem of the effect of a programme, it ran into other problems of its own. There was, first, the problem of the research situation. This involved putting an audience into a contrived situation where people's attention was drawn to a particular programme and they concentrated on it. Would they react to the programme in the same way outside this laboratory situation? There was, secondly, the problem of long-term effects. Studies of this kind could not get at the long-term and cumulative effects of exposure to the media. Do people gradually build up a way of looking at things through repeated exposure to a particular perspective? There was, thirdly, the social context of influence. Assessing the impact of a programme on members of an audience could show how they were affected as individuals. It could not deal with the way they thought about it later, after discussion with others.

All research methods have advantages and disadvantages. Thus, while content analysis can only take one so far, it is an important starting point, which can identify issues for audience research by establishing a map of the way that the media deal with a given topic. It can also deal with some important questions, such as whether the media report on events in a balanced way, giving equal time, for example, to the views of different political parties. Audience research, whatever its problems, is, however, the only way of addressing the question of media effects. It has also become more

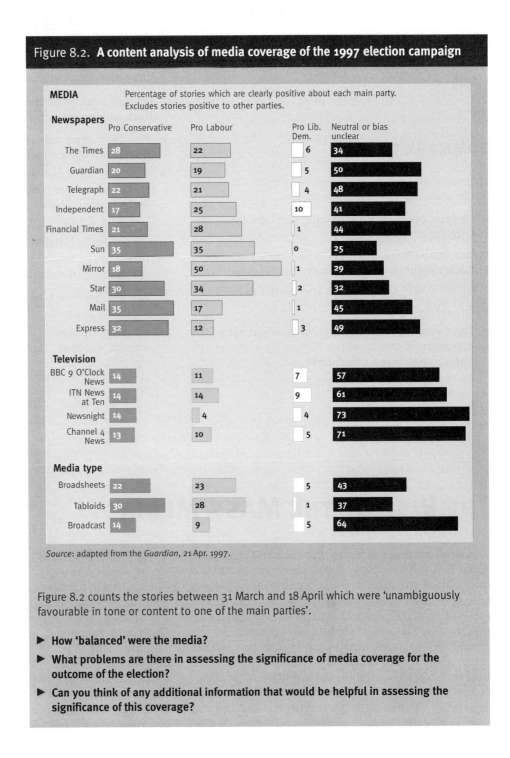

Figure 8.2. A content analysis of media coverage of the 1997 election campaign

MEDIA — Percentage of stories which are clearly positive about each main party. Excludes stories positive to other parties.

Newspapers

	Pro Conservative	Pro Labour	Pro Lib. Dem.	Neutral or bias unclear
The Times	28	22	6	34
Guardian	20	19	5	50
Telegraph	22	21	4	48
Independent	17	25	10	41
Financial Times	21	28	1	44
Sun	35	35	0	25
Mirror	18	50	1	29
Star	30	34	2	32
Mail	35	17	1	45
Express	32	12	3	49

Television

BBC 9 O'Clock News	14	11	7	57
ITN News at Ten	14	14	9	61
Newsnight	14	4	4	73
Channel 4 News	13	10	5	71

Media type

Broadsheets	22	23	5	43
Tabloids	30	28	1	37
Broadcast	14	9	5	64

Source: adapted from the *Guardian*, 21 Apr. 1997.

Figure 8.2 counts the stories between 31 March and 18 April which were 'unambiguously favourable in tone or content to one of the main parties'.

▶ How 'balanced' were the media?

▶ What problems are there in assessing the significance of media coverage for the outcome of the election?

▶ Can you think of any additional information that would be helpful in assessing the significance of this coverage?

sophisticated in order to deal with the problems raised above. The GUMG, for example, has developed discussion-group techniques and script-writing exercises in order to probe into longer-term effects and examine the social context of media influence (Kitzinger 1997).

Particular pieces of research should not be rejected because of these problems but rather interpreted in the light of them. It is certainly important to bear them in mind when considering any research on the media.

SUMMARY POINTS

We began this section by considering the nature of communication and the role of the media:

▶ Human beings communicate through languages with shared meanings.

▶ The media are central not only to communication but to cultural, economic, and political activity.

We then outlined the main approaches to the study of the relationship between the media and society:

▶ The concept of the mass media emerged out of the mass-society theory of the atomizing of society by industrialization and urbanization.

▶ Dominant-ideology theory emphasized the part played by the media and their owners in maintaining ruling-class hegemony.

▶ Other approaches have suggested that consumers and producers as well as owners and controllers shape the content of the media.

▶ The media can perform important functions for the public sphere, but these are threatened by commercialization, political pressures, and a weakening of the distinction between the public and the private.

We went on to consider different conceptions of culture and the meanings of popular culture:

▶ Popular culture emerged out of a folk culture distinct from high culture.

▶ Elitist and populist views provide competing interpretations of the relationship between the media and popular culture.

We concluded the section by examining the various models of media influence that have emerged in the literature and the advantages and disadvantages of different methods of research:

▶ We distinguished between media-effects, active-audience, and media-themes models.

▶ Research into media influence used methods of content analysis, textual analysis, and audience research.

THE RISE OF THE MASS MEDIA

Industrial societies not only produce and distribute goods and services; they also produce and distribute information and entertainment. Industrialization not only generated mass production, it also created the mass media of the popular press, film, radio, and television. In this part of the chapter we will examine the growth of the mass media and situate this within the development of a capitalist industrial society. We start with a brief account of the invention of printing, before going on to the growth of newspapers, the emergence of a film industry, and the rise of radio and television.

THE PRINT REVOLUTION

The key step in the development of printing technology was the invention in Germany around the year 1450 of a printing press using movable metal type. Johannes Gutenberg is generally credited with this invention, but, like many inventions, his printing press was actually but the last step in a gradual process of technical development. Presses already existed and Gutenberg's key contribution was the creation of movable type. Printing was not in fact a European invention and had long existed in the Far East. The earliest known book was printed in China in the year 868 and metal type was in use in Korea at the beginning of the fifteenth century.

The print revolution took place in Europe, however. This shows the crucial importance of European capitalism, for it was this that transformed printing from an invention into an industry. Right from the start, book printing and publishing were organized on capitalist lines. The biggest sixteenth-century printer, Plantin of Antwerp, had twenty-four printing presses and employed more than 100 workers (Febvre and Martin 1976: 126). Only a small minority of the population was literate, but the production of books none the less grew at an extraordinary speed. By 1500 some 20 million volumes had already been printed (Febvre and Martin: 1976: 248).

The immediate effect of printing was to increase the circulation of works that were already popular in a handwritten form, while less popular works went out of circulation. Publishers were interested only in books that would sell fairly quickly in sufficient numbers to cover the costs of production and make a profit. Thus, while printing enormously increased access to books by making cheap, high-volume production possible, it also reduced choice. It was the first step on the road to the mass production of the written word.

The great cultural impact of printing was that it facilitated the emergence of national languages. Most early books were printed in Latin, for this was the language of educated people. The market for Latin books was, however, limited, and in its pursuit of larger markets the book trade soon started producing translations into the national languages that were emerging at this time. Printing indeed played a key role in standardizing and stabilizing these languages by fixing them in print, and producing dictionaries and grammar books. Latin then became obsolete, as national literatures were established in the sixteenth century.

NEWSPAPERS

Newspapers first established themselves in Britain in the eighteenth century. They were initially concerned mainly with providing the middle class with information relevant to its business activities, but a radical press grew up at the end of the eighteenth century and played a key role in the growth of nineteenth-century radicalism (E. P. Thompson 1968). The popular press first emerged in the 1820s, in the form of Sunday papers containing stories of murders and executions, and it was these papers that led the expansion of newspaper

reading. Then in the second half of the nineteenth century the *Daily Telegraph* pioneered the growth of a cheaper, more popular middle-class press. In the 1890s the *Daily Mail,* followed by the *Daily Express* and the *Daily Mirror*, created a mass market for daily newspapers.

A key step in the growth of newspaper readership was the 'freeing of the press' during the 1850s. This refers to the abolition of restrictive taxes, which created the conditions for a larger readership by making newspapers much cheaper (Curran and Seaton 1991). A decisive and far-reaching change had taken place in the relationship between the press and the state. The government had previously tried to suppress the radical press through repressive laws and taxation but without much success. Commercial interests eager to develop press advertising now wanted to get rid of restrictions. This was the era of liberal capitalism, and state regulation was increasingly opposed by those who believed in market forces and the freedom of the individual. Leading figures in the campaign for a free press argued that a cheap commercial press, staffed by 'responsible' members of the middle class, would drive the radical press out of business. It did.

> ☞ **We discuss the stage of liberal capitalism and the changing relationship between the state and the economy in Chapter 18, pp. 735–6.**

Expanding demand stimulated the introduction of new technologies during the second half of the nineteenth century. The spread of the railways enabled the national distribution of dailies. High-volume production made newspapers cheaper and led to further increases in demand. Newspaper publication had become a mass production industry by the end of the century.

The financial basis of newspapers changed as advertising became a greater source of newspaper earnings. Papers could become cheaper than ever, because they were increasingly funded by advertising, but a large circulation was also now more important than ever. Founded in 1896, the Daily Mail spearheaded the growth of a new kind of mass circulation daily newspaper. Raymond Williams (1961) interestingly linked this change in the press to wider changes in the economy. He argued that there was a growth of display advertising in the 1890s because of a change in marketing strategies linked to changes in economic organization. The growing size of industrial corporations made them dependent on large and stable markets. They tried to create these not by competing on price but

The commercializing of the Daily Mirror

The front pages of the *Daily Mirror*, 2 Nov. 1903 and 11 March 1932

▶ **How many differences between these two front pages can you find?**

by organizing and controlling the market place through advertising. Mass-circulation newspapers were part of an increasingly organized capitalism.

As the popular press became a mass medium seeking to maximize readership, newspapers changed in character. Headlines became bigger and there was more illustration. Coverage of political and economic matters declined, while sport, crime, sex, and human-interest stories increased. Between 1927 and 1937 the *Daily Mirror* halved the proportion of its news covering political, social, economic, and industrial issues (Curran and Seaton 1991: 67).

We discussed earlier the idea of a public sphere. It could be argued that the rise of mass-circulation newspapers extended this sphere by making news and views available to larger numbers of people. The radical press, which in the early nineteenth century generated political debate by challenging the dominant ideology, had, however, been driven out of business by the growth of a more commercial and more popular press. Furthermore, the decline of serious content in the mass-circulation newspapers, as the popular press became more concerned with entertainment than information, hardly promoted public discussion.

The transformation of the press into a mass-production, mass-circulation industry led to the concentration of ownership. Production had become capital intensive and large amounts of money were needed to set up a newspaper, while costs were reduced if the machinery was used to produce more than one. Small-circulation papers could not compete with the new mass dailies and were driven out of business.

Newspapers owned by the Harmsworth brothers in 1921

Lord Northcliffe (Alfred Harmsworth)
The Times, Daily Mail, Weekly Dispatch, London Evening News

Lord Rothermere (Vere Harmsworth)
Daily Mirror, Sunday Pictorial, Daily Record, Glasgow Evening News, Sunday Mail

Sir Lester Harmsworth
A chain of local papers in the south-west of England

Source: Curran and Seaton (1991: 50).

Already in 1910, 67 per cent of national daily circulation was in the hands of three owners and 69 per cent of national Sunday circulation in the hands of another three. By 1921 the Harmsworth brothers owned papers with a circulation of over 6 million (Curran and Seaton 1991: 51–2).

The era of the press barons, most famously Lord Northcliffe and Lord Beaverbrook, raised acutely the question of the influence of the press and the power of those who owned it. The barons made no secret of their intentions to use their papers for political purposes. They certainly exercised a detailed control over editorial content. But did their views influence those of their readers? Examples can be found of them apparently influencing election outcomes, but they also often failed in their political campaigns. Curran and Seaton argue that it was not so much their direct as their indirect influence that mattered: 'Their main significance lay in the way in which their papers provided cumulative support for conservative values and reinforced opposition, particularly among the middle class, to progressive change' (1991: 61).

The political influence of the barons was not, anyway, simply a matter of their influence on readers, for they used the large circulations of their papers to influence politicians. They claimed to represent their readers and argued that politicians should listen to them because their papers had large circulations. Politicians certainly became keenly aware of the power of those who owned the press. The barons are said to have forced a change of prime minister in 1916, though they failed in their attempt to unseat the leader of the Conservative Party in 1930 (Boyce 1987).

The era of the press barons has gone but ownership has remained concentrated and the issues it raises have not gone away. We will return to these questions in the very different context of the period after the Second World War in 'Ownership and Control', pp. 306–9.

FILM

The history of the press is long and readership built up steadily over a long period, but 'movies' burst upon the world at the end of the nineteenth century. Raymond Williams (1983) cautions us, however, against the idea that films were simply something new. He points out that film continued the tendency established by the popular press of moving the media away from political content towards the telling of entertaining stories. It also further developed tendencies in nineteenth-century popular theatre towards melodrama, elaborate costumes and scenery, and special effects to represent such events as fires, volcanic eruptions, railway crashes, and naval battles.

Movies arrived in England in 1896 and by 1914 there were already 500 cinemas in London. As Corrigan (1983: 27) puts it, 'by 1914 going to the picture palace had become a normal activity'. The reproducibility of film meant that multiple copies could be made and films could be shown simultaneously to audiences across the world.

Going to the cinema could become a mass activity, however, only if ordinary people had the time and money for it. The reduction of working hours provided more leisure time, and in the 1920s and 1930s cinemas benefited from the enforced leisure resulting from higher levels of unemployment. The introduction of unemployment benefit meant that the unemployed could afford cheap seats. Films appealed particularly, however, to the young and to women. Eldridge *et al.* (1997) suggest that film-going was for women the first permissible leisure activity outside the home.

Films are often seen as an art form, with inspirational directors drawing on the creative talents of writers, actors, and camera crew to craft unique products. Such films were made, but most were produced on an industrial basis. Picture houses in Britain were eventually showing two new programmes each week, each typically containing two feature films. To meet this demand, studios had to churn films out on a routine basis and to a tight schedule. Like any other form of mass production, they were large-scale operations with a high division of labour and a bureaucratic structure.

Production and distribution were integrated and concentrated in the hands of Hollywood companies,

Mass entertainment in the 1930s.

the 'Big Five'—and the 'Little Three', which, unlike the Big Five, did not own cinemas. Control of distribution was crucial, for this guaranteed outlets for production and shut out the competition. Distribution networks

The Hollywood star system

'Far more than the type of movie, stars were the commodities that most consistently drew audiences to the movies. A "star vehicle", a movie constructed around the appeal of one or more particular stars and sold on that basis, was bound to have a set of conventional ingredients. . . . An Elvis Presley movie, for instance, offered its star several opportunities to sing, a number of girls for him to choose his romantic partner from, and a plot in which he would be misunderstood by older characters. The repetition of these standard ingredients created an audience expectation of these elements. . . . The studio system was committed to the deliberate manufacture of stars as a mechanism for selling movie tickets, and as a result generated publicity around the stars' off-screen lives designed to complement and play upon their screen images.'

Source: Maltby and Craven (1995: 89).

were able to dominate the market, because film copies were cheap to produce and could be rented to a large number of cinemas at the same time. The distributors kept their grip on the cinemas by establishing a system of block booking, which required them to take a block of up to fifty movies, good, bad, or indifferent. They also built up chains of cinemas which gave them direct control of outlets. They kept their grip on audiences through the star system, for stars were the best guarantee of a large audience for a film.

By 1914 Hollywood already had 60 per cent of the British market. In the 1920s it became completely dominant, producing 95 per cent of the films shown in Britain in 1925 (Corrigan 1983: 26). In the 1930s and 1940s Hollywood accounted for 60 per cent of world film production (Maltby and Craven 1995: 66).

Why was Hollywood so dominant? The huge English-language market provided both British and American capital with a great opportunity, but a slow British response gave American companies a head start. The First World War then halted the growth of European film production at a critical time in the industry's development. Once Hollywood domination had been established it was hard for any other industry to contest it. The United States also provided the largest market and films that had paid for their costs in America could be distributed cheaply abroad and undercut the competition.

As with the popular press, there has been a concentration of ownership and control in a small number of large corporations. With films, however, there is the additional twist that ownership and control have been internationally concentrated in the hands of American corporations. This raises the issue of the Americanization of popular culture, which we discuss on p. 298.

RADIO AND TELEVISION

Radio and television are broadcasting media, which are quite different in character from film. This can be shown by contrasting television with film. Although television shares with film the combination of image and sound, and has, indeed, become a major medium for the showing of films, it is fundamentally different for the following reasons:

▶ *Domesticity*. Television is a domestic medium that penetrates into the ordinary life of family and household.

▶ *Continuity*. It provides continuity through an endless daily programme rather than a one-off entertainment.

▶ *Immediacy*. It has the capacity to go 'live' and communicate events to an unlimited audience as they happen.

▶ *Variable usage*. When people go to the cinema they do little else but watch the screen for a fixed period of time, while television watching can be combined with many other activities.

Television shares all these features with radio, and in Britain its early organization was, in fact, modelled on radio. In the 1920s radio had come under the control of a publicly owned monopoly, the British Broadcasting Corporation (BBC), while television, as another broadcast medium, developed under the BBC's control during the 1930s. Broadcasting took this form in Britain less because of the particular characteristics of radio than a general tendency towards the public ownership of important services and resources at this time. Water supply and forestry, for example, had come under the control of public corporations.

BBC radio was established as a public service by Reith, the first Director-General of the BBC, on two basic principles. The first of these was universality. BBC radio had to provide a national service, though with some

---

The BBC and the General Strike

The General Strike of 1926 lasted eight days. It was called by the TUC in support of the coal-miners, who were in conflict with the mine-owners and the government over wage cuts.

The BBC suddenly became immensely important, because the newspapers were shut down, apart from the government-controlled *British Gazette*, and radio was the only source of news. Some government ministers wanted to take control of the BBC and use it for propaganda purposes. Reith certainly believed that the BBC should act in the national interest, which in this situation meant siding with the government, but he successfuly resisted direct state control. He argued that the BBC could best help to end the strike by gaining the trust of the strikers as an 'impartial' source of news.

BBC coverage was in reality not at all impartial, for it paid no attention to the causes of the strike and no union representative was allowed 'on the air'. As Curran and Seaton (1991: 143) have put it: 'Called by some workers the "British Falsehood Corporation", the BBC learnt how to censor itself during the strike in order to forestall government intervention. Nevertheless the General Strike marks the end of the propaganda based on lies and the start of a more subtle tradition of selection and presentation.'

Source: Curran and Seaton (1991).

---

regional programmes. As Scannell and Cardiff (1991: 14) have put it, 'broadcasting equalized public life through the principle of common access to all'. Secondly, programming should be mixed. Listeners should have a wide and varied range of programmes, providing education, information, and entertainment, and catering for different tastes and interests.

As we argued above, the changing character of the press was at this time making it less appropriate as a vehicle of the 'public sphere'. The control of British broadcasting by an independent public corporation meant that first radio and then television were able to take over this function to some degree, though the BBC had a somewhat uneasy relationship with the state. Reith wanted to develop the political functions of broadcasting, in particular to deal with matters of political controversy and to broadcast parliamentary debates. A properly informed public needed to be well informed about politics. In this he was, however, thwarted by the government, which expected the BBC to be a cooperative instrument of the state. It refused to allow the BBC to cover matters of political controversy or to make parliamentary broadcasts. Indeed, during the General Strike of 1926 the BBC found itself assisting the government to bring the strike to an end.

British broadcasting was transformed in the 1950s by the breakthrough of television and the ending of the BBC's monopoly. Although television had existed in the 1930s, it had faced many technical problems, and its growth was slow. Radio continued to dominate broadcasting during the Second World War and it was only during the 1950s that television began to reach a mass audience. The number of TV licence-holders rose from 344,000 in 1949/50 to 1,165,000 in 1959/60 (Curran and Seaton 1991: 196). In 1954 a law was passed to introduce commercial television or 'Independent Television' (ITV), as it was misleadingly but cleverly called. Pressure from the advertising and entertainment industries had combined with the Conservative Party's belief in market forces to end the BBC's monopoly.

The ending of the BBC's monopoly did not, however, destroy the public-service tradition. Indeed, it led in some ways to television becoming a more effective medium for the public sphere. The prohibition on dealing with matters of political controversy gradually disappeared during the 1950s, as the arrival of commercial television loosened up the relationship between politics and television, while politicians themselves became increasingly interested in using television for their own purposes (Wagg 1994). Both radio and television were able to develop their political function of informing the public about political debates and presenting opposition as well as government views. As their exclusion from politics was lifted, the key issue became one of 'balance', of fairly covering the range of political views.

There was some danger that commercialization and the competition for audiences would undermine public-service principles, but their effects were limited by state regulation. The new companies had to operate within a system of regulation by the Independent Broadcasting Authority (IBA). This restricted the amount of advertising, required that non-fiction programmes occupy one-third of airtime, and limited repeats and imports. There was also a concern to protect minority interests. The creation of a second BBC channel (BBC2) and a commercial channel for minority interests (Channel 4) showed that considerations of public interest still mattered. The public-service tradition survived, as a 1990s survey of broadcasters showed (see Box, p. 278).

The effects of competition were also limited by monopolistic tendencies within the industry. There was little competition between ITV companies once

The concentration of media ownership

Concentration of ownership became a feature of all areas of the media, with a higher level of concentration in these industries than in industry generally. In Britain:

▶ two companies dominated the production of gramophone records by the 1930s;

▶ two companies dominated cinema by the 1940s;

▶ five companies accounted for about 70 per cent of newspaper circulation in the 1950s;

▶ commercial television in the 1960s was dominated by five network companies with monopoly positions in particular regions.

Source: J. Scott (1990: 142).

they had won their franchises, for they operated as a national network with regional monopolies. Competition was also limited by programming conventions. Thus, the BBC and ITV learned to schedule unpopular programmes at the same time. This maximized the audiences for, say, documentaries in the interests of both organizations. After an initial period of frantic rivalry, BBC and ITV settled down to live quite comfortably with each other during the 1960s and the 1970s. A period of more drastic change did, however, await them in the 1980s, as we shall show later in the section on 'The Limits of Choice'.

SUMMARY POINTS

The growth of the mass media reflected the general features of the development of capitalist industrialism:

▶ Large, capital-intensive enterprises mass produced newspapers and films for mass consumption.

▶ They gained control of markets by integrating production and distribution, and by driving out competitors.

▶ Ownership became highly concentrated and competition declined.

In 'Understanding the Media', we discussed the idea of a public sphere that enabled a free exchange of information and views on matters of public concern:

▶ After the 1850s newspaper readership grew but commercial pressures diminished 'serious' content.

▶ The BBC was set up on public-service principles but the government initially refused to allow the BBC to cover matters of political controversy.

▶ The BBC was also forced at times to act as the servant of the state.

▶ Commercial television was introduced in the 1950s, though continued public-service regulation and limited competition restricted the effects of commercialization.

Now that we have examined the growth of the mass media, it is time to move on to consider their influence upon society.

THE INFLUENCE OF THE MASS MEDIA

The development of the mass media had created organizations with an enormous potential for influencing populations. Industrial techniques gave newspapers and films a huge production capacity, while their distribution networks enabled them to reach large numbers of people at more or less the same time. The broadcast media could reach people simultaneously and give them the illusion of being present as events happened. The concentration of ownership gave great power to the small number of organizations that controlled each of the media industries, in some cases putting this power in the hands of individual owners prepared to use it to further their political ends.

But how much influence could those who control the media actually have on their audiences? This has been the central issue in the study of the media. As we showed in the first part of the chapter, there is no consensus on this point and different models of media influence have led people to very different conclusions. In this section we will examine the research and debate on media influence in a number of key areas—the media production of information, their representation of people, and their impact on culture and on morality. In reading this part of the chapter, you should bear in mind the different models of media influence that we discussed in 'Media Influence and the Audience', pp. 281–4, and the issues of method that we raised there.

INFORMATION

The mass media are the most important sources of information in our society. We rely on 'the news' to tell us of important events and report them in a truthful and accurate way. Journalists and editors assure us that their professional values require them to provide accurate and objective information, and a balanced and representative range of opinions. But do they provide this? Is it even possible for them to do so?

Constructing the news

The starting point of the sociological study of the news is its social construction. The facts never speak for themselves. Space and time are limited and editorial *gatekeepers* select what goes into newspapers and news programmes. The news also has to be trimmed and packaged to fit newspaper layout or the structure of a broadcast news programme. Furthermore, news does not just arrive on the editor's desk. Information is gathered by journalists, who do not collect it randomly.

Journalists are organized into a reporting network by their newspaper or broadcaster, which directs and distributes them, steering them towards information of one kind rather than another. International reporting shows this particularly well. It is inevitably patchy and decisions to send journalists to one country rather than another can have an enormous bearing on international coverage. A searchlight can be trained on a country with a particular problem, say the destruction of rainforest in Brazil, by sending a camera team to cover it for television. Problems that are not highlighted in this way hardly exist on the world stage.

The journalists themselves are guided by 'news values', which shape what they find newsworthy. They often claim that these are objective and self-evident, and Galtung and Ruge (1965) did find some evidence for this. Certain underlying principles seemed to govern the selection of events as worth reporting. The more recent, the closer, and the bigger an event, the more likely it was to be covered. Other aspects of news-gathering are, however, not objective at all and are shaped by the requirements of a particular organization. As Tunstall (1996) puts it, each newspaper looks for the 'good story for us', the story that fits the style of a paper and its political slant.

Journalists are well aware of the need to find stories of this kind and present them in the way required by their organization. They have occupational values of objectivity and impartiality that may well lead them to seek out information that is unpalatable to their employer but they are also socialized into the values of the particular organization they work for. When *occupational* and *organizational* values come into conflict, journalists can be forced to conform to editorial policies and the views of owners, if they want to keep their jobs. Editors can bring strong pressures to bear on them and owners ultimately control editors.

This was shown well by what happened to the *Sunday Times* after it was bought in 1981 by Rupert Murdoch, who shifted its political stance to the right. A new editor was appointed and journalists were pressed to conform through the editorial hierarchy. Their articles were amended through editing. If they resisted, they could find that their pieces appeared less often, facing them with 'professional death'. It was also easier to conform than struggle every day to maintain their views. Isobel Hilton has suggested that many ended up internalizing these controls and becoming their own censors. In the end, the choice was to give in or resign. Curran and

A journalist under pressure

Isobel Hilton, the Latin American correspondent of the *Sunday Times* in the early 1980s, describes the pressures she experienced after its takeover by Murdoch:

'What would happen is that you would write a story and it would disappear. The copy would vanish around the building and people would write little things into it and take out other things. It would eventually appear in a very truncated form with the emphases changed. It had all been done at stages along the way. To try and make a fuss about this on a Saturday when everything was very busy was very difficult. . . . The sense of intimidation was so strong that people actually started censoring themselves because it is very unpleasant to get into this kind of argument all the time. It is not just a collection of incidents, it's a collection of incidents *and* the atmosphere, which is in the end so depressing. You stop functioning as a journalist. There are things that you just don't bother to pursue because you know you just won't get them into the paper.'   Quoted by Curran and Seaton (1991: 104)

Reporting a bombing

'If the PLO bomb a bus load of kids in Tel Aviv, VISNEWS would not describe that as an atrocity; we would not describe the PLO as terrorists, nor would we describe them as freedom fighters; nor would we ourselves refer to that specific event as a tragedy. We might well quote somebody else as saying it was a tragedy. The reason is quite simple. To many of our subscribers the PLO blowing up a bus load of children anywhere might be a victory for the oppressed people of Palestine. There are no militarists in VISNEWS; there are no freedom fighters. We have to choose this very precise middle path.'

Source: A former VISNEWS executive quoted in Gurevitch (1996: 210).

▶ **The PLO is the Palestine Liberation Organization. Is it possible to refer to this organization in a neutral way?**

Seaton (1991: 104) report that at least 100 journalists left the *Sunday Times* between 1981 and 1986.

Much of the news is not, anyway, gathered by journalists so much as made available to them. News agencies are an important source of material, particularly from other countries. International news agencies do try hard for purely commercial reasons to present information in a neutral way, for they have to sell it into countries with widely varying cultures and political regimes. Gurevitch (1996) points out that this does, however, make it easier for national editors to manipulate the material for their own purposes. Furthermore, sources are not generally given for agency material, which frequently originates from state news agencies. An apparently neutral agency commentary does not make the news objective.

It is considerably easier for journalists to write stories on the basis of information they have been given. It is this that keeps the public-relations industry in business providing material that presents its clients in a favourable light, and the capacity to employ public-relations companies clearly depends on resources, which are unequally distributed. In practice, this means that business corporations and the political parties they support are able to dominate the flow of information to the media.

The construction of the news provides many opportunities for governments to influence it. According to the account given by Bob Franklin (1994), some of the main ways in which British governments can influence the media are as follows:

► *Censorship.* The media are not allowed by the Official Secrets Act to publish information on 'sensitive' military or security matters or obtained in confidence from foreign governments or international organizations. The broad wording of these restrictions leads editors to play safe, which considerably widens the effect of censorship.

► *Control of the BBC.* The BBC depends on the government for increases in the licence fee to cover rising costs. Governments have at times threatened to withhold increases. The government also appoints the BBC's Board of Governors.

► *Provision of information.* Briefings by the Prime Minister's Press Secretary through the lobby system are an important source of information for journalists. This system feeds government information from unattributed sources into the media. State agencies generally are a key source of information, which can be released to suit their purposes, or suppressed altogether.

► *Pressure on investigative journalists.* There are well-known examples of governmental attacks on specific programmes, such as the 1988 Thames television documentary *Death on the Rock*, which investigated the shooting of three unarmed members of the IRA in Gibraltar. Thames Television's failure to obtain renewal of its franchise in 1991 has been attributed to its conflict with the government over this programme.

► *Relationships with newspaper owners.* The newspapers take up political positions and those favourable to the government can become a mouthpiece for its views.

While all governments seek to use every means in their power to influence the media, it is important to take account of differences between societies in the relationship between the state and the media. Thus, in the United States the law on Freedom of Information makes material available to the media which the British Offical Secrets Act keeps from them. On the other hand, in societies like China the media are an arm of the state, under direct state control.

Balance and contest

It is not just a matter of how information is obtained but also of how events are explained. The GUMG has demonstrated how the news favours explanations that reflect the views of dominant groups in British society. Their content analysis of strike coverage makes this point particularly well, for it is characteristic of strikes that management and union provide contrasting explanations of them. The television reporting of strikes did recognize that there were two views but generally privileged the managerial account. Managerial explanations came up more often, were highlighted in headlines and summaries, and were adopted by the journalists themselves. An illusion of balance was

Live television news coverage

Television coverage might seem to avoid the problem of government control of information. During the Gulf War of 1991 satellite television coverage relayed pictures of events as they happened. Robert Fisk, who reported the war for the *Independent*, found that his reporting role was being superseded by live television coverage. This was, however, subject to far greater state control. Governments could control cameras and television crews much more easily than they could newspaper reporters.

'The import of satellite dishes, the operation of camera crews, the travel of television reporters, is invariably restricted, especially in times of crisis. The need for pictures means that television will always submit to the demands of government. . . . With the shining exception of some Independent Television News teams and a few French crews, almost all the free and uncensored reporting of the Gulf War was undertaken by print journalists.'

Furthermore, editorial control led to the editing out of the worst scenes of the war from television reports.

'In the hours after the ceasefire north of the Iraqi border, it was almost impossible to drive on the highway without running over parts of human bodies. I watched wild dogs feasting on Iraqi flesh and camera crews filmed all this. But scarcely a frame reached television viewers. Faced with the reality they supposedly craved, nearly all television editors decided that 'good taste' would restrict their reports now that government officials were no longer there to censor them.'

Fisk concluded that satellite television has not supplanted newspaper journalism but has rather made it more important 'to the functioning of democracy' than it has ever been before.

Source: Robert Fisk, 'Challenging the Might of the Sound-Bite', *Independent*, 8 Jan. 1992.

created because both views were represented, but there was no real balance because they were weighted differently (Philo 1990: 169–70).

It may be said that two views were at least given, while in other societies, where television is more closely controlled by the state, that would not be the case. On the other hand, the creation of an illusion of balance is more manipulative. It can lead people to think that they are receiving a fair account, and therefore make them more likely to accept it as objective.

The study of the process of news construction and the analysis of news content have demonstrated that the news is neither objective nor impartial. Broadly speaking, those with power and wealth are able to dominate the flow of information and interpretation through the media. But it is important to recognize that this domination is not always effective. Investigative reporting exists. Governments and business corporations are at times seriously embarrassed by the activities of journalists.

As Eldridge (1993a: 20) has put it, 'the media occupy space which is constantly being contested'. Subordinate groups organize and challenge the dominant ideology. Conflicts within the elite itself often provide journalists with leverage through the leak of information that governments would like to keep quiet. This is where the journalists' occupational values of independence, objectivity, impartiality, and balance are very important. Even if these values do not and cannot produce objective news, they can enable the voice of dissent to be heard.

REPRESENTATION

The media can influence their audience not only through the information they provide but also through the way they represent people. They do this through language but also through images, which can have a subtle and powerful effect on an audience. In this section we will consider the representation of class, gender, and ethnicity.

Class

Dodd and Dodd (1992) argue that in the late nineteenth century middle-class commentators created an image of the British working class which shaped later representations of it. The working class was invariably situated in industrial communities of the north. It was contrasted with the middle class by making a set of oppositions which represented workers as physical and practical in character rather than intellectual; decent and simple rather than sophisticated; local rather than national figures.

This image of the working class persisted through the twentieth century and can be found in the writings of Orwell, Hoggart, and Sillitoe, and in 1960s films like *Saturday Night and Sunday Morning* or the much later *Letter to Brezhnev* of the 1980s. It can also be found in soap operas, as in *Coronation Street's* close-knit community located in a northern city. The Dodds note, however, that with *Coronation Street* there was a shift away from the domination of the community by men, probably because 'the street' was aimed at a female audience. According to the Dodds (1992: 126), 'it appears that strong, sexualized middle-aged working-class women characters are one of the major reasons for its abiding popularity'.

Continuities can be found with the 1980s soaps, *Eastenders* and *Brookside*, but these also broke new ground. Although they too focused on local communities, they were concerned 'not so much with what holds a community together but with what threatens to splinter or disrupt it' (Geraghty 1992: 137). These soaps were aimed at a wider audience that included male and young viewers and tried therefore to break away from the *Coronation Street* model. There was more emphasis on social diversity, conflict, deviance, and crime. *Eastenders*, for example, recognized the multi-ethnic character of the British working class and included black, Asian, and Turkish-Cypriot families. As the Dodds point out, the values of community were still there, however, for the community is defended against the criminal and racist forces threatening it from the outside.

Although the image of the working class was created by the middle class, it was adopted by intellectuals of working-class as well as middle-class origin. It was then adapted to the audience needs of television and became part of popular culture through the soap opera. The extent to which it has shaped conceptions of the working class is an open question, but the soap operas have certainly reached a mass audience. At a time when class communities were in decline, as we show in Chapter 11, pp. 429–30, the only working-class community in the lives of most people was the community in the soap opera.

Gender

Feminists have criticized the media for the way that they reinforce traditional gender stereotypes. Tuchman reviewed evidence on the representation of women by the American media during the period from the 1950s to the 1970s. She claimed that women were portrayed mainly in terms of their sexual attractiveness and their performance of domestic roles. When they were shown in occupational roles, the occupations were extensions of the domestic role. Women appeared as nurses rather than doctors, as secretaries rather than lawyers. The exclusion, marginalization, and trivialization of women's activities resulted in what Tuchman (1981: 183) called the 'symbolic annihilation of women'.

This reinforcement of stereotypes has been particularly evident in advertising. Cumbernatch carried out a study of television advertising in Britain in 1990 and analysed the content of 500 prime-time television adverts. He found that there were twice as many men as women in the adverts, while 89 per cent of them used a male voice-over. The women portrayed were on average younger and there was more emphasis on their attractiveness. Men were twice as likely as women to be shown in paid employment. When housework was shown, men were more likely to be shown doing it, which might appear to go against gender stereotypes. Women rather than men were, however, shown doing the routine tasks of washing and cleaning. While men were more likely to be shown cooking, this was not everyday cooking for the family but was rather for a special occasion or involved particular skills (Strinati 1995).

These studies of the representation of gender by the media make a clear point, but, as we pointed out in our discussion of methods of media research, content analysis of this kind can go only so far. It can count the number of times that a particular way of representing

women appears, but it has to make assumptions about the meaning and significance of these representations. It cannot address the issue of their impact on the audience.

McRobbie's well-known study of the teenage magazine *Jackie* addressed these issues of meaning and importance (McRobbie and McCabe 1981). This study tried to penetrate behind the content of the magazine to identify the ideology of femininity which it communicated. The importance of *Jackie* was that, as a magazine for teenage girls, it influenced them at a formative stage in their lives, preparing them for the adult roles that they were soon to take on. Thus, its treatment of these issues can be considered more important than their treatment in women's magazines, which would reinforce rather than shape gender roles.

McRobbie argued that the stories, images, problem pages, and articles on fashion, beauty, and pop music combined to focus girls on personal and emotional matters, as though these were the only things that they should be concerned with. Relationships between boys and girls were treated solely in 'romantic' terms. As McRobbie put it, 'the girl is encouraged to load all her eggs in the basket of romance and hope it pays off' (McRobbie and McCabe 1981: 118). Furthermore, *Jackie's* light and entertaining style made it enjoyable to read, and this enabled it to get its hidden messages through to its readers.

This approach went well beyond content analysis by using techniques of textual analysis to discover hidden meanings. However, in order to do so, it had to make assumptions about the meaning of the text. Martin Barker (1989) examined McRobbie's analysis and came up with a different reading of the texts that she analysed. He argued that they at times undermined rather than reinforced the romantic love model. McRobbie's approach also treated the reader as a passive receiver of messages. Frazer (1987) studied reader responses to *Jackie* through discussions amongst seven groups of girls. She found that they distanced themselves from the fictional characters, criticized the magazine, and were well aware of the process through which it had been produced.

It is also important to take account of the way that representations change. This did, indeed, come out in Barker's examination of *Jackie*. He showed that after 1975 there was 'a real decline of confidence in romance's possibilities' (M. Barker 1989: 178). Others have pointed out changes in the representation of women in police series (A. Clarke 1992) and soap operas (Dodd and Dodd: 1992). Stereotypes have a certain inertia, but the media do also have to take account of social change if they are to keep their audiences.

What features of gender stereotyping does this OXO advert display?

Ethnicity

The media have reinforced racial as well as class and gender stereotypes. Solomos and Back argue that media racism has two core features. The culture of black people is presented as alien to the British way of life and their presence is seen as a threat to British culture (Solomos and Back 1996: 184).

 It is important to bear in mind the cultural form taken by racism in Britain. As we show in Chapter 12, pp. 485–7, the discrediting of an openly biological racism led to its replacement by a 'new racism' emphasizing national cultural differences.

The press in particular has presented a negative image of black people, though the content of this image has shifted over time. Solomos and Back suggest that in the 1960s the image was of the 'welfare scrounger', in the 1970s the 'mugger', in the 1980s the 'rioter' (1996: 183). The emphasis was on the problems presented by black people rather than their contribution to British society, or the problems that British society created for them. Thus, welfare scrounging was emphasized rather than the contribution of black immigrants to the staffing of the National Health Service. The black mugger was highlighted rather than rising numbers of racist attacks on blacks by whites. Headlines such as

Does this Benetton advert promote ethnic integration or ethnic division: can this question be answered by analysing the content of the advert?

'Black War on the Police' presented the disorders in 1980s British cities as 'race riots', in which blacks attacked the police, rather than as the outcome of urban deprivation, exclusion, or changes in methods of policing (we discuss these disorders in Chapter 11, pp. 435–7).

It is not only a matter of how blacks are presented; it is also a matter of their absence. While soap operas have recognized the existence of blacks in British society, there has been little recognition of them in advertising. The ordinary family in the television advert has generally been a white family. Tuchman's term 'symbolic annihilation' would seem appropriate here too.

Multi-ethnic adverts did become fashionable in the late 1980s (Solomos and Back 1996). These presented people from different ethnic backgrounds and emphasized their harmony and unity. Thus, a 1995 British Airways campaign featured a Danish woman next to an Indian woman, with the caption 'there are more things that bring us together than keep us apart'. The rationale for adverts of this kind is easy to see. They fit nicely into the marketing strategy and image of transnational corporations selling products across the globe.

Solomos and Back point out, however, that these apparent celebrations of ethnic difference could reinforce racist stereotypes. They might seem to be anti-racist in their positive representation of ethnic diversity and their emphasis on harmony between different peoples. They could also reinforce racial stereotypes by emphasizing the physical characteristics that

Racial representations of science-fiction aliens

Jones and Jones (1996) have argued that racist colonial imagery is reproduced in science-fiction programmes that revolve around stories of the colonization of other planets. Asian or black ethnic-minority characters are often used to portray aliens. The aliens are often represented as 'primitive savages' inferior in intelligence to the colonizing whites, though often superior in physical strength and closer to nature. As the authors emphasize, there is no intention to be racist, but racist images and stereotypes from the imperial past are none the less reproduced and communicated by the 'white eye of television'. They note that these programmes are often targeted at a younger audience and wonder how such images are received by young, black viewers.

Source: Jones and Jones (1996).

these are based on. Thus, for example, in one Benetton advert a blue-eyed blonde white child is flanked by a 'negroid' black child and an 'oriental' Asian child.

As with much of the discussion of representations, what we do not know, however, is the impact they make on the audience. The analysis of content is an important starting point, as we emphasized in our earlier discussion of methods, but it does leave open the whole issue of the *effect* of representations. How important, for example, are negative images of blacks in shaping their sense of identity? As we shall show in the discussion of culture, audiences identify with media representations in complex ways.

CULTURE

Now we turn to examine the broader impact of the mass media on the development of culture. We argued on p. 280 that two broad views of popular culture have emerged. The *elitist* view regards popular culture as commercial, standardized, and manipulative. The *populist* view argues that, on the contrary, it is creative, diverse, and rooted in experience. Here we will discuss these views in relation to audience involvement and Americanization.

Audiences: Passive or active?

The media are successful commercial enterprises because people enjoy their products but those who hold a manipulative view of the media regard audience pleasure as dangerous. When people enjoy a magazine story, a film, or a television programme their guard is down and they are most likely to absorb media ideologies. Thus, feminists have argued that women who enjoy romantic films or stories receive a powerful reinforcement of traditional conceptions of womanhood by identifying with the heroine. The implication is that people should boycott material that misrepresents women, blacks, workers, etc. Alternative films and stories with more appropriate messages should be produced.

Apart from the practical difficulties of producing an alternative and persuading audiences to buy it, the problem with this approach is that it disparages the daily pleasures of millions of people. One researcher into the content of women's magazines has expressed this nicely: 'I felt that to simply dismiss women's magazines was also to dismiss the lives of millions of women who read and enjoyed them each week. More than that *I* still enjoyed them, found them useful, and escaped

with them. And I knew I couldn't be the only feminist who was a closet reader' (Winship 1987: p. xiii). As we showed in our discussion of the representation of women in teenage magazines, readers are anyway not passive and can retain their critical faculties while they enjoy reading.

Identifying with a vampire

'I knew I was supposed to feel relieved when the vampire got staked. I didn't. . . . I knew I was supposed to find vampires frightening, and my home, family, and their expectations of me comforting, safe. I didn't. I identified with the vampires. *They* were the rebels I wanted to be. They didn't have elders bugging them. I dreamed of independence and revelled in the vampires' anarchic force: they spurned families, marriage and other social conventions. . . . Although loners themselves, they found others like them and were united by a shared difference against the mass of humanity.'

Source: quoted in Eldridge *et al.* (1997: 153).

Research on audience response has shown that people do not simply absorb representations. They frequently identify with film and television characters in unexpected ways. Eldridge *et al.* (1997) list many examples of this. A study of responses to Westerns showed that some Native Americans rejected them and were critical of the way that 'Indians' were portrayed but others actually identified with the Indian-hating John Wayne because they appreciated the freedom of the cowboy way of life. Audience members can also identify with minor or deviant characters, even with vampires (see box above). The term identification is itself misleading, for it suggests that people simply accept the character presented. In reality they select aspects of a given character, say beauty or cleverness or strength, to identify with. They can interpret and reconstruct characters to suit their particular needs and fantasies.

Television is usually treated as the medium which induces most passivity. Viewers are often regarded as 'couch potatoes' who soak up whatever 'the box' throws at them. This is, however, a quite misleading notion of what viewers actually do. Researchers have mounted video cameras inside television sets and watched the watchers. They have found that viewers engage in all sorts of other activities while watching and frequently do not watch at all, and, when they do watch, do so with widely varying degrees of (in)attention (Abercrombie 1996).

This may seem an obvious finding but it has considerable implications for assessments of the impact of television. Viewing figures based on reports of hours spent watching or programmes watched are likely greatly to exaggerate actual watching time. The term 'watching' is itself misleading, since it implies that people are either watching or non-watching, when in reality they may well be 'half-watching'. While television is in some ways the most powerful of the media, since it penetrates into the private life of a household, this very feature also lessens its impact. It is part of everyday life, which goes on around it, and watching is combined with a great deal of non-watching, which dilutes its impact.

The notion of an active audience corrects the misleadingly passive view of audiences embodied in many theories of the impact of the mass media on popular culture. As Eldrige *et al.* (1997) point out, it does, however, carry with it the danger of uncritically celebrating the way that people enjoy and use the media. It can all too easily suggest that content no longer matters, that there are no representation issues, that it does not really matter who owns and controls the media. The fact that people select and interpret does not mean they are uninfluenced, as the GUMG's research has shown (see p. 281).

Americanization

The conflict between *elitism* and *populism* has taken another form in the debate over the Americanization of popular culture, which has been analysed by Strinati (1992*b*). It was the domination of film production by Hollywood which raised this issue, but almost any item of popular culture may be American in origin, whether we are aware of it or not. If we eat a 'big Mac' or wear jeans, we are consuming items of American culture.

American culture was certainly exported on a massive scale. As we showed on p. 288, Hollywood dominated world film production in the 1920s and 1930s. American interests continued to control film production and distribution into the television age. It is claimed that in the early 1970s American films still occupied more than half of 'world screen time' (Hebdige 1988: 73). Given this dominant position even films produced, financed, and distributed by non-American interests were likely to be influenced to some degree by the Hollywood model.

Those holding *elitist* views of culture have been hostile to Americanization. They have viewed it as popular, commercial, and generally responsible for the mass culture which threatened to swamp British cultural traditions. This view of Americanization treated audiences as passive recipients of American influence.

Americanization has been interpreted very differently from a *populist* perspective, which saw audiences as active rather than passive. This view argued that America was popular not because American dominance of the media shaped what people liked but because American culture gave them what they actually wanted. America was a source of democratic and popular forms of culture that had been suppressed in a class-dominated Britain. Young members of the working class could draw on American culture to create their own subcultures that enabled them to resist and challenge the dominance of middle-class culture. According to this view, America was a diversifying rather than a standardizing influence on British culture. The elitist reaction to Americanization itself reflected elite fears of democratization.

The populist view may seem a healthy corrective to the rather patronizing treatment of American culture by elitists, but the import of American culture does present problems, such as the preservation of other national cultures and the maintenance of production and employment in other countries. We will return to these issues again when we consider whether globalization has led to Americanization (see p. 304).

MORALITY

In this section we focus more specifically on the way that the media handle behaviour judged to be criminal or immoral. On the one hand, they have been held responsible for criminal or immoral behaviour. On the other hand, they have been accused of generating moral panics through the exaggerated and distorted reporting of events.

Sex and violence

Almost as soon as films were introduced into Britain, concerns were raised about the way that they would undermine morality (Eldridge *et al.* 1997). They were seen as generating crime, promiscuous sex, and violence. There was particular concern because of the large numbers of women and children who went to the cinema. Some claimed that children learned how to commit crime by seeing crimes on the screen. Others worried that screen stories of romantic love affairs would undermine marriage and threaten the family. The film industry decided to stave off state regulation by setting up its own British Board of Film Censors in 1912.

This issue did not go away and periodically resurfaces. A recent example of this was the James Bulger case in 1993, when the murder of a 2-year-old child by two 11-year-old chidren was blamed on horror videos. One particular video, *Child's Play 3*, was generally associated with this murder, though there was no evidence that either of the children had seen it (Newburn and Hagell 1995). Violent films and videos particularly attract moral condemnation, though, as the opening extract to the chapter suggests, they may well have a less disturbing impact than apparently less violent events in a more ordinary and familiar setting.

The question of whether the media cause violence has attracted a lot of attention and has been much researched. It is, however, an exceptionally difficult issue to research, because of the problem of defining violence. It is hard to define it objectively, because what some would consider a violent act, others would not. Is smacking a child a violent act? Furthermore, forms of violence considered acceptable by some people are not accepted by others. Boxing, for example, is considered by some but not others to be a legitimate form of violence, as is military violence. It is similarly difficult to assess the amount of violence involved in different kinds of violent act. This applies to both attempts to measure violent behaviour and attempts to assess the amount of violence in the media.

Defining violence

► a cruise missile attack
► a fatal shooting
► a brutal but non-fatal 'beating up'
► a boxing match
► verbal abuse
► corporal punishment

► **Which of these would you consider 'violent'?**

► **Can you rank them in terms of degree of violence?**

► **What do you think makes one act more violent than another?**

It is then difficult to isolate the effect of media violence from the wide range of other factors which may be said to cause violent behaviour. Experiments can be designed to do this by exposing groups in laboratory situations to different amounts of violence and then measuring their aggressiveness. Such experiments have demonstrated a relationship between exposure and aggressive attitudes. These studies are, however, open to the criticism that the experimental situation is quite artifical and bears no relation to the social situations in which people actually watch the screen. Non-experimental survey studies, on the other hand, find it very difficult to isolate the effect of the media.

A recent review by Newburn and Hagell (1995) concludes that, although well over 1,000 studies have been made, the case for a link between media violence and violent behaviour is 'not proven'. Their own research examined the assumption that young offenders prefer and watch more violent television programmes than non-offenders do. They found no evidence from their study that this was the case. The viewing preferences and viewing habits of both offenders and non-offenders were very similar.

Although many studies may be flawed and the case may not be proven, this clearly does not mean that there is no relationship between media violence and violent behaviour. Crude notions that one causes the other do not stand up to examination, but the research by the GUMG (see p. 281) has shown that on a number of issues the media do influence the audience in a subtle and long-term way. The discussion of moral panics shows how complex this influence may be.

Moral panics

The literature on 'moral panics' provides another approach to these questions. The argument here is not that the media cause people to behave badly but rather that the media report bad behaviour in an exaggerated and distorted way. This results in a societal reaction out of all proportion to the initial problem and this reaction can itself generate deviance.

The concept of the **moral panic** was first developed in Stanley Cohen's (1972) study of the 'mods and rockers' of the 1960s. These were rival youth groups which engaged in some minor violence in Clacton during the Easter weekend of 1964. The newspapers reported widespread violence and large numbers of arrests with such headlines as 'Day of Terror by Scooter Groups' (*Daily Telegraph*) and 'Youngsters Beat Up Town—97 Leather Jacket Arrests' (*Daily Express*). These exaggerated reports generated public fear and a hostile reaction to the youth groups, which were seen as a major threat to public order. Mod and rocker subcultures received publicity, which led more teenagers to adopt these styles, further increasing public fear. Mods and rockers became what Cohen called the *folk devils* of their time.

Cohen's analysis of this moral panic made an important contribution to the theory of deviance, which we outline in Chapter 5, pp. 156–61. Its two key notions were:

▶ *The labelling of behaviour.* What were little more than subcultural styles, the riding of scooters and the wearing of leather jackets, became defined as deviant behaviour.

▶ *Deviance amplification.* The social reaction to *primary* deviance, the minor violence in Clacton, generated *secondary* deviance, the spread of deviant subcultures. This developed the distinction between *primary* and *secondary* deviation made by Becker and Lemert, though Cohen used the term deviance rather than deviation.

Moral panics

▶ **Can you think of a recent moral panic?**

▶ **What form did the primary deviance take?**

▶ **What role did the media and the politicians play in its amplification?**

▶ **Were any folk devils created?**

▶ **Can you identify any secondary deviance that resulted from this process?**

▶ **Why do you think this moral panic occurred?**

You may find it helpful here to return to the discussion of deviance in Chapter 5, pp. 156–60.

Cohen's model of the moral panic was taken up and developed at the Birmingham Centre for Contemporary Cultural Studies, where it was applied in particular to the issue of mugging. The Birmingham researchers focused on the functions of the moral panic for the maintenance of social order. They argued that it enabled the courts to take a tougher line when punishing offenders. The creation of a moral panic over mugging was, they suggested, a means of legitimating state repression at a time of social crisis in the 1970s. They linked this to the *populist authoritarian* strand of Thatcherism, which generated much of its political support (see Chapter 18, p. 748). Their analysis has been criticized as too conspiratorial in approach and lacking evidence for some of its arguments (Eldridge *et al.* 1997).

It does, none the less, usefully raise the issue of the relationship between the state and the press. Governments do run law-and-order campaigns in which folk devils, such as strikers, drug pushers, football hooligans, or paedophiles, undoubtedly figure. Politicians can certainly play a role in the creation of a moral panic. On the other hand, moral panics generated by the media can also conflict with government policy. Thus, Eldridge *et al.* (1997) point out that the *Sun*'s representation of AIDS as a disease largely of homosexuals and junkies conflicted with government efforts to target both heterosexuals and homosexuals in its campaign for safe sex.

The concept of a moral panic was a useful addition to the vocabulary of sociology. It identified important mechanisms in the media representation of deviance and showed how the media could amplify it. The main problem that it faces is the extent to which a moral panic actually affects people's attitudes and behaviour. A readership accustomed to exaggerated media stories may well view them with some scepticism. Newspapers may also pander to *existing* popular taste in constructing folk devils. The effects of media labelling and amplification may therefore be limited.

SUMMARY POINTS

In this section we have been examining the various ways in which the mass media have been said to influence the way that people think and act. We first examined the media presentation of information:

▶ The social construction of the news shapes the way that information is presented by the media.

▶ The superior resources of those with wealth and power enable them to influence but not wholly determine the content of the news.

We moved on to consider the way in which the media represent class, gender, and ethnicity:

▶ The media reproduce stereotypes, though representations do change.

▶ While media research demonstrates the existence of stereotypes, it tends to assume rather than demonstrate their influence on audiences.

We then explored the influence of the media on culture:

▶ Elitist views of the influence of the media on culture treat audiences as passive, while populist views treat them as active.

▶ Elitists are critical of the Americanization of culture, while populists view it as liberating and diversifying.

Lastly we considered the debate on the moral influence of the media:

▶ Research has been unable to demonstrate convincingly that media violence causes violent behaviour, though this does not mean that there is no relationship between the two.

▶ According to the concept of the moral panic, the media can create deviance by labelling behaviour as deviant and amplifying it.

THE LIMITS OF CHOICE

We have examined the growth of the mass media and their influence on culture and society. In recent years the media have lost some of their previous mass character. In British television, for example, there has been a movement from the BBC1 or ITV model, where a channel provides a broad range of programmes aimed at the whole audience, to specialized provision on the Sky Sports model. As channels have multiplied, they have become more specialized and their programmes are increasingly targeted at particular rather than mass audiences. Broad-spectrum mass products clearly still exist, but, as the media become more specialized, the term 'mass media' becomes less appropriate as a collective term for the media in general.

Greater media diversity has apparently increased consumer choice. Until the 1980s there were three television channels in Britain—BBC1, BBC2, and ITV. A large number of channels now compete for audiences. Choice has also been enhanced by the globalization of the media, which has made programmes internationally available. Similar changes have happened in other media, as cinemas have gone multiplex and a huge range of special-interest magazines has appeared on newspaper stalls.

We also have to be aware, however, of the limits to choice. It depends upon access to the alternatives. It may be illusory if product variety declines under the pressures of greater competition. It may be diminished in other ways by the concentration of ownership, for, if ownership becomes more concentrated, the range of political views expressed by the media may decline, even if there are more channels. Choice may be diminished if commercialization and government intervention weaken the free exchange of views in the public sphere. As for globalization, it has arguably led not to international diversity but to a growing global domination of the media by American corporations marketing American culture.

These are the issues that we shall take up in this section. We begin by examining the diversification of the media, its implications for greater choice, and the issue of access to this diversity.

DIVERSITY AND CHOICE

Greater choice has come about through a combination of technical, economic, political, and cultural changes. Technical advances have attracted most attention but technical change does not happen of its own accord and must be placed in the context of broader social changes.

> In this section we situate changes in the media within the context of broader changes in the economy, in politics, and culture. It will help you to understand these changes if you follow up the cross-references in the text to other chapters that deal with these changes in more detail.

Technology or politics?

Technological change has opened up new ways of delivering information to the household. The introduction of the new delivery systems of satellite and cable, together with digital transmission, has made it possible to have hundreds of channels. Satellites have also made programmes available across national boundaries. The Internet is an alternative delivery system that can provide almost limitless digital material down telephone lines.

Choice has also been enhanced by the use of the video cassette recorder (VCR) and videotapes, because it is no longer restricted by what is immediately available either on TV or at the local cinema. Indeed, as with books, audiotapes, and CDs, a personal store of video material can be accumulated and accessed at will, which has resulted in some shift of control from the distributor or programme scheduler to consumers. The development of telephone delivery technology may take this process further by making programmes available on the 'magazine model'. This would allow them to be bought at any time in the same way as magazines on particular topics. Pay-TV is already moving in this direction.

Politics, however, provided much of the driving force behind change. The post-1979 Conservative government held a neo-liberal ideology that advocated deregulation and competition (see the discussion of Thatcherism in Chapter 18, pp. 748–9). It was argued that greater competition would result in more choice for the consumer, though this was not the only motivation for it. Greater competition would also cut costs by forcing programme producers to be more efficient and could be used to break the power of the unions, which were seen as having a stranglehold over BBC and ITV production.

Competition has indeed increased as cable and satellite delivery systems have been allowed to develop and also as the regulation of ITV has changed. The ITV companies were forced into greater competition by the 1990 Broadcasting Act, which put ITV franchises out to competitive tendering. The highest bid would get the franchise, though certain quality requirements still had to be met. The IBA, which regulated commercial television, was replaced by a 'lighter-touch' Independent Television Commission that allowed the commercial companies to operate more freely. All this led to a major shake-up in ITV, as a number of established companies lost their franchises and others were taken over by rivals.

While greater competition can increase choice by enabling new companies to enter the market and sell their products, it is important to recognize that it can also diminish diversity. The growing competition for audiences has, for example, led to more frequent episodes of popular soap operas, driving other programmes from peak viewing times. The multiplication of commercial channels is also spreading advertising funds more thinly and driving down the rates that the companies can charge advertisers. This was indeed one of the main reasons why advertisers were enthusiastic

supporters of the introduction of Channel 5. Expensive minority programmes that could be afforded when ITV held a monopoly of popular commercial television and could charge advertisers monopolistic rates may disappear from the schedules as funds start to dry up.

Thus, competition may apparently increase choice by providing more channels to choose from, but the commercial pressures generated by greater competition may then diminish the diversity of programmes.

Post-Fordism and post-modernism

Product diversity has also been increased by the broader changes in production and consumption that have been labelled 'post-Fordism' (see Chapter 13, pp. 528–30). The saturation of markets with mass-produced goods led to the production of a more diverse range of products aimed at niche markets rather than *mass* markets. Advertising has similarly become more sophisticated and increasingly seeks to target particular niche markets. Market researchers can now provide advertising agencies with detailed information on the segmentation of markets by age, class, and gender, so that they can more effectively aim their campaigns at the particular groups most likely to buy their products.

These changes have been reflected in the media too. The creation of Channel 4 in 1982 has been seen in terms of a public-service concern to provide programmes for minorities. It also made commercial sense, because these minorities provided niche markets for advertisers. Entirely specialized television channels or radio stations have taken this process one stage further. Classic FM provides a case in point. There is also the proliferation of special-interest magazine titles. If you are selling pesticides to gardeners, the best way to reach them is to put adverts in a gardening magazine or attach them to a gardening programme on commercial radio or television.

Another important post-Fordist change has been the emergence of more flexible forms of organization that contract out functions to a network of smaller specialist firms (we discuss network organizations in Chapter 16, pp. 661–2). This has occurred in television with the introduction of the *publisher* model to replace the *producer* model.

Both the BBC and the ITV companies were traditionally *producer-broadcasters*—that is, they largely made the programmes that they transmitted. Channel 4 was set up as a *publisher-broadcaster* to commission programmes made by others. The 1990 Broadcasting Act forced both BBC and ITV companies towards the publisher model by requiring them to take at least 25 per cent of their

The sources of diversity

Technology	New delivery and storage systems
Politics	Deregulation and competition
Consumption	Niche marketing
Production	Post-Fordist product diversification
Organization	Publisher broadcasting
Culture	Pluralism and pick and mix

output from independent producers. Small and often short-lived independents providing programmes for the networks have multiplied. This has diversified production and enlarged the range of products available. It has also greatly reduced security of employment and weakened the union organization of workers in the television industry.

The cultural changes associated with post-modernism (see Chapter 2, p. 66) have contributed to diversity in other ways by creating a non-hierarchical plurality of cultures. The distinction between *high* and *popular* culture has become ever more blurred, as the domination of an elite *high* culture has been increasingly challenged by *popular* forms of culture disseminated by the media. Culture has also became less hierarchical as diverse class, ethnic, and national subcultures have become increasingly valued in their own right.

It is, however, not only the coexistence of a plurality of cultures that is characteristic of post-modernism. It is also the way that they are mixed and combined. People move more freely across cultural boundaries, as they consume culture just like any other product. They adopt styles and follow fashions in dress or food, picking and mixing from the various cultural resources available to them. Styles from different places and times are artistically combined, whether in architecture or popular music. This can be done for effect, to surprise and attract attention by deliberately breaking cultural rules. As Strinati (1992*a*) points out, there is often a subversive jokiness in the combination of apparently incompatible styles.

Access

Diversity may make choice possible, but, as always, the exercise of choice depends on income, knowledge, time, and control.

Almost everyone in Britain has access to a television, but access to satellite, cable, digital transmissions, and video recording requires extra expenditure. It is not simply a matter of equipment, as subscription channels and Pay-TV become steadily more common and displace 'free' television funded by licence fee and advertising. The exercise of choice will more and more depend on income, and those living in poverty will become increasingly excluded from media participation. Thus, a section of the population will be deprived of what is increasingly regarded as a normal part of social life (see 'Poverty and Deprivation', Chapter 14, pp. 583–90).

Knowledge, time, and control are closely related to the division of labour and distribution of power in the household. Gray (1992) studied household use of VCRs. She found that men had more knowledge of the technology and exercised more control over the choice of programmes. Housework, anyway, reduced the time, especially uninterrupted time, available to women for television-watching. Indeed, some of the women she interviewed saw television and VCR as a last-resort leisure activity. Household obligations meant that many felt that at home it was difficult to escape work and preferred to go out. Arguably, as greater choice has made television and VCR use more attractive to children and men, women's opportunities to enjoy outside leisure activities have diminished. Thus, Gray found that women benefited less than men from the opportunities for increased choice and some found that their choice of leisure activities had actually shrunk.

It should not then be assumed that the availability of a more diverse range of media products creates greater choice for all. Issues of choice and access are also raised by globalization, which we turn to next.

Choice?

► Look at one of the weekly magazines listing television programmes.

► How many channels are listed?

► How many do you have access to?

► Try making a list of the factors that you think limit your choice of viewing.

GLOBALIZATION

Global communication has made television a 'window on the world'. It has brought world events, from the Olympics to the Gulf War, into the household as they happen. It has also brought in programmes from other countries, for satellites do not respect frontiers. *Potentially*, this has made available a wide diversity of experiences and cultures.

Another aspect of globalization is, however, the growth of global corporations, which largely control what is actually available (see Chapter 12, pp. 478–9, for a discussion of this). Many of the biggest corporations are American owned and globalization may therefore in practice mean Americanization. We have already discussed the American domination of the film industry and the issues that this raised. In this section we consider the American dominance of world media corporations and its consequences for local cultures. There are two main approaches to this question, one emphasizing Americanization and the other the growth of cultural pluralism. The following discussion draws on Sreberny-Mohammadi's (1996) analysis of this issue.

American global domination

The Americanization approach argues that the world's media are dominated by American corporations, which diffuse American culture and American views of the world. A UNESCO study based on data from the later 1980s showed that seven of the world's top ten media corporations and ten of the top fifteen, as defined by the size of their sales, were at that time American. America's Cable News Network (CNN) has established itself as the chief global provider of news. Recent mergers have created even greater concentrations of media ownership in American hands. In 1995 Time-Warner merged with Turner-Broadcasting (the owners of CNN) to create the world's largest media grouping.

On the other hand, it must immediately be said that American corporations do not monopolize the corporate media world. Australian, European, and Japanese corporations also appear in the top ten of the later 1980s. As Sreberny-Mohammadi notes, it is the absence of certain countries that is perhaps the most striking feature of the UNESCO table, for the seventy-eight companies listed did not include a single one from a Third World country. The United States may be regarded as the dominant member of a small group of countries that dominate the corporate media world. This gives some support to the notion of **media imperialism**—the idea that the countries that once dominated the world through their empires continue to do so through the media.

But does American domination of global sales figures mean American dominance of world markets? The American penetration of particular television markets varies greatly. Some Asian markets have been little penetrated by media imports, and a 1994 study reports that in India and Korea 92 per cent of television programming is of domestic origin. This is much higher than in Europe, though there are considerable variations between European countries, with Sweden producing 81 per cent, but Italy producing only 58 per cent of its output. The figures for Australia were lower still at 46 per cent (Sreberny-Mohammadi 1996: 188).

Access to television is also a crucial issue, for American control of the media can influence local cultures only if people are exposed to media influence. Although many viewers may watch one set, the ownership of television sets gives some indication of access to programmes. As Figure 8.3 shows, access to television varies enormously between different areas of the world.

Cultural pluralism

The Americanization approach is opposed by those who argue that the emergence of local production has led to a growing cultural pluralism. Sreberny-Mohammadi lists a number of ways in which national cultures can resist media imperialism:

▶ *The domestication of output.* Home-produced programmes can oust imports because they are more attractive for linguistic and cultural reasons.

▶ *Reverse flows.* Ex-colonial countries can start to export their own programmes to the old imperial societies. Increasing international migration has paved the way for this.

▶ *Going global.* Local producers can themselves create transnational corporations. For example, ZEE TV, a Hindi-language Indian commercial station, took over TV Asia in Britain.

▶ *Controls on distribution.* Television imports to Britain have been limited to a quota of some 14 per cent of programmes. It is more difficult to control satellite television, but some countries, such as Singapore, Malaysia, Saudi Arabia, and Iran, have banned the sale of satellite dishes.

Notions of Americanization or cultural imperialism anyway tend to follow the *media-effects* model that we

Figure 8.3. **The ownership of television sets in different areas of the world, 1970 and 1992**

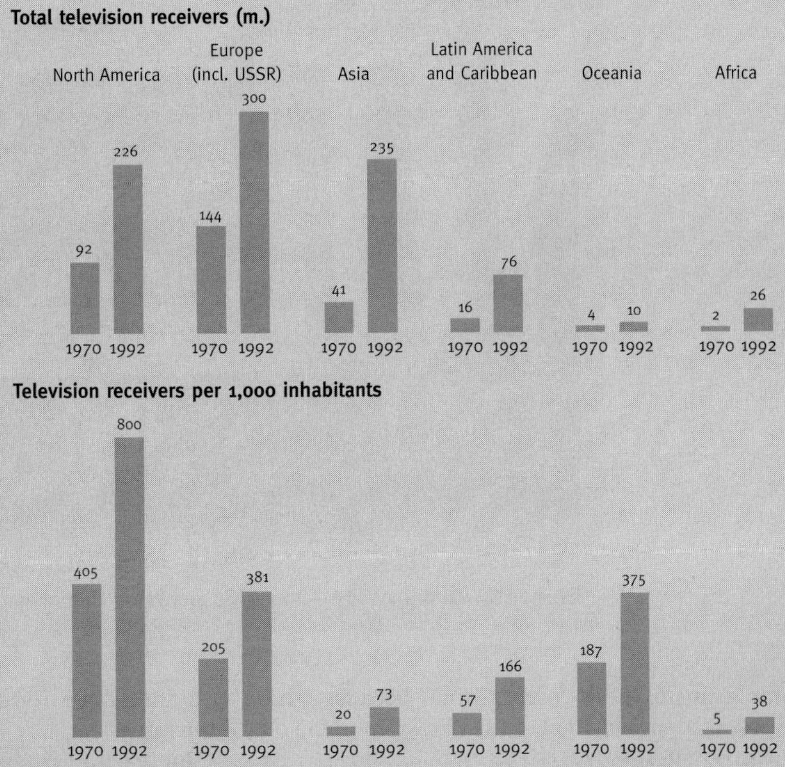

Total television receivers (m.)

	North America	Europe (incl. USSR)	Asia	Latin America and Caribbean	Oceania	Africa
1970	92	144	41	16	4	2
1992	226	300	235	76	10	26

Television receivers per 1,000 inhabitants

1970	405	205	20	57	187	5
1992	800	381	73	166	375	38

Source: Sreberny-Mohammadi (1996: 182)

▶ **Think about the relationship between American influence and television ownership.**

▶ **Which area of the world has provided the largest and which the smallest market for television programmes?**

▶ **Which area of the world has had most access to television and which the least?**

▶ **Can figures on the ownership of television be used as an indicator of exposure to American influence?**

discussed on p. 281, and assume that foreign programmes inject American values. Studies of the impact of the American *Dallas* series, which was exported to more than ninety countries, have demonstrated that it is not as simple as that. *Dallas* apparently celebrated the values of American capitalism, but Ang (1985) has shown that Dutch viewers were perfectly capable of enjoying the story and its emotions while disapproving of its values and rejecting them. As we showed earlier, audience identification with film characters is a complex process. The audience may simply reverse the apparent values of a Hollywood film by siding with the 'bad guys' rather than the 'good guys'. People respond to cultural imports within the context of their own situation and values.

Global corporations anyway recognize that they can market their products more effectively by adapting them to local needs. Indeed, the term 'glocalization' was invented to describe the Japanese marketing strategy of adapting global products to meet local requirements (Robertson 1992: 173). In the case of the media, this may often, however, mean adapting to the requirements of the national state. An example of this was Murdoch's decision to drop the BBC World programme

Reverse flows: Bollywood—Bombay's answer to Hollywood—takes over a Leicester cinema.

from Star transmissions over China because the Chinese government objected to the BBC's reporting of human-rights issues.

There are, then, dangers in uncritically celebrating the local. As Sreberny-Mohammadi points out, so-called local producers will generally be national producers under the control of the national state, which may well be trying to stamp out local resistance to its authority. Similarly, the banning of satellite dishes may be little to do with preserving local culture and a lot to do with maintaining the existing social order. In patriarchal societies, male domination may be threatened by the import of programmes embodying a more liberated conception of the role of women. Thus, the debate over the control of media imports must be placed in the context of conflicts of interest and authority relationships *within* society as well as the context of conflicts *between* cultures and international relationships.

OWNERSHIP AND CONTROL

We showed in our discussion of diversity and choice that government policy in the 1980s sought to reinvigorate market forces and generate more competition. It was believed that greater competition would increase product diversity and provide more choice for the consumer.

Increasing competition suggests that ownership is becoming more widely spread, but the reality is that the concentration of ownership has if anything increased. This raises the question of the importance of ownership. Does it really matter? Koss (1984) argues that the current owners of the media are interested in profits alone and do not influence media content or interfere in politics as the press barons of old did. We must first consider the pattern of ownership.

Ownership

As we showed on pp. 286–7, ownership became more concentrated as the media developed. This process has continued in a number of important ways:

▶ concentration within media;
▶ cross-media ownership;
▶ ownership across delivery systems;
▶ transnational ownership.

Ownership has become concentrated *within* particular media. The ownership of British newspapers has become highly concentrated. In 1988 the largest three newspaper groups accounted for 81 per cent of national

Sunday circulation and 73 per cent of national daily circulation (Curran and Seaton 1991: 91). Murdoch's News International papers accounted for one-third of the weekly sales of national papers in 1993 (B. Franklin 1994: 34). The ownership of ITV companies became more concentrated after the easing of ownership restrictions by the 1990 Broadcasting Act. As in any other area of the economy, concentration is a way of increasing profits by eliminating competitors and creating economies of scale.

Even more striking has been the growth of *cross-media* empires. Conglomerates have emerged with wide-ranging interests spanning newspapers, book and magazine publishing, television companies, film studios, and radio stations. Rupert Murdoch's News International provides a good example of this (see box on p. 308). Ownership across the media facilitates the promotion of related products, and the pooling of communications expertise. Books, for example, are published to coincide with related television series.

The conglomerates also cut across the competing *delivery systems* in complex ways. Thus the ITV companies Carlton and Granada have interests in the satellite company BSkyB. This joined with Carlton, Granada, and the BBC to create British Digital Broadcasting, in order to bid for digital terrestrial channels. Ownership across delivery systems enables companies to hedge their bets at a time when competition is intensifying, technical change is rapid, and it is uncertain how successful each system will be.

The major media conglomerates are *transnational* corporations with a global reach. Murdoch's News International, for example, has major interests in Australia, Britain, Hong Kong, and the United States and minor interests in many other countries.

Newspaper politics

But does ownership matter? In this section we focus on the consequences of the concentration of newspaper ownership for the political process.

There is little doubt that newspapers were moving to the political right during the period from the 1960s to the 1980s. The *Daily Mirror* continued to support the Labour Party but became much less radical and much less political in its content (Pilger 1997). The *Sun* moved from supporting Labour to supporting the Conservatives in 1979. *The Times* and the *Sunday Times* too moved to the right. There is no doubt that the Labour Party faced a largely hostile press in the 1980s. By 1987 papers supporting the Conservative Party accounted for 72 per cent of national daily circulation (Curran and Seaton 1991: 124). The press as a whole was hostile to the

unions, attacked the Labour left, and supported the central values of Thatcherism.

Their shift to the right can be explained in two different ways. There is firstly the argument that it resulted from the interests of capital. The owners of newspapers are major owners of capital and have a general interest in maintaining capitalism, which was in crisis in the later 1970s and early 1980s (see Chapter 18, pp. 747–8.). More specifically, their profits are heavily influenced by their labour costs, and they therefore have a direct interest in 'bashing the unions'. Tunstall (1996) suggests that their support for Thatcherism was linked to its attack on union power. The anti-union legislation passed by the Thatcher government certainly helped Rupert Murdoch to take on and defeat the print unions in the crucial battle over the movement of newspaper production to Wapping in 1986. This defeat destroyed their previously considerable control of newspaper production.

The alternative explanation is in terms of market pressures. In the end profits depend on selling newspapers and no owner can run a paper at a loss for long. People are unlikely to buy papers on a regular basis if they express unpopular views. The electorate undoubtedly shifted to the right in the later 1970s and it can be argued that the newspapers simply followed it in order to maintain their sales.

The rightward shift of the press in the 1970s probably involved both these processes. Ownership undoubtedly mattered, for the impact of changes of ownership on the press can be clearly traced and the shift of the press to the right followed changes in ownership. But owners had to operate within the constraints of the capitalist system and the market for newspapers.

The significance of this shift to the right is more difficult to assess. The *Sun*'s support for the Conservatives has been considered a major factor in their election victories, but, as our previous discussion of these issues has shown, it is very difficult to demonstrate media effects on behaviour. It is claimed, however, that a study of the 1987 election showed that the *Sun* and the *Star* markedly influenced politically uncommitted readers towards voting Conservative (B. Franklin 1994). We may conclude that, in its support for Thatcherism, the press probably played some role in the transformation of British politics in the 1980s, but it is difficult to assess how important this was. The labour movement was weak during the 1980s for many other reasons and its weakness cannot be attributed to a hostile press alone.

This was not, however, the end of the story, for in March 1997 the *Sun* changed sides (as did some other right-wing newspapers). It announced that it was going

Rupert Murdoch's News International in 1993

News International is 37 per cent owned by the Murdoch family

Area	Newspapers	Book and magazine publishing	Television, radio and film
Global	—	Harper Collins UK, US, and Australia Inc. (Operations in 30 countries)	20th Century Fox Film Corporation
Asia	*Hong Kong Sunday Morning Post Wha Khi Yai Po*	—	Star TV (satellite covering China and India)
Australia	*The Australian* 108 regional papers	12 magazine titles	Seven Network
United Kingdom	*The Times Sunday Times News of the World Sun Today*	*Shoppers' Friend The Times* supplements *TV Hits Inside Soap*	BSKYB (satellite) (50%) SKY Radio
United States	*Boston Herald New York Times*	*Mirabella TV Guide*	Fox Broadcasting Company 8 Fox Television Stations
Other	Interests also in Fiji and Papua New Guinea		Latin America El Canal Fox

Source: G. Williams (1994: 36).

▶ Note that this list is far from complete.
Can you add any recent acquisitions or other changes to it?

to support the Labour Party. Contacts between Rupert Murdoch and the Labour leadership had been developing since 1994. Tony Blair's new Press Secretary was seeking to prevent tabloid attacks on the Labour Party of the kind that had occurred during the 1992 election, while Murdoch was interested in meeting 'rising political stars'. In 1995 Blair flew to Australia to address a conference of Murdoch's top executives and further meetings in London followed. In March 1997 Murdoch's main concerns were reported to be that there should be no new legislation that would restrict his expansion into digital television and no privacy laws to interfere with the operations of his tabloid papers. As it happens, Blair did announce in March 1997 that there would be no new laws of this kind but rather 'a request for sensible behaviour'. It is reported that Blair and Murdoch 'have never directly discussed cross-media ownership' (*Independent on Sunday*, 23 Mar. 1997).

The Sun's change of sides

▶ Why do you think that the *Sun* changed sides? In thinking about this question, consider the political situation before the 1997 election and the development of the Labour Party's policy during the 1990s (we discuss this in Chapter 18, pp. 756–8).

▶ What are the implications of the *Sun*'s change for our discussion of the relationship between media ownership and the political process?

Newspapers may try to influence the outcome of elections, but they also need to make sure that they end up on the winning side.

DECLINE OF THE PUBLIC SPHERE

We showed on p. 290 that, although commercialization reduced the serious content of the British press, broadcasting was set up within a public-service framework, which survived the introduction of commercial television in the 1950s. In the 1980s the public sphere came under new pressures from commerce and government, and we examine these pressures in this section.

The commercialization of the media

Here we consider first the continued commercialization of the press and then the commercialization of broadcasting.

The popular press came under growing commercial pressures because of rising costs, falling circulations, and the shift of advertising to commercial television. Its serious content declined sharply between the 1940s and the 1970s. Curran and Seaton have shown that the space devoted to 'public affairs' dropped by at least half between 1946 and 1976. By public affairs they mean political, social, economic, industrial, scientific, and medical news and features. More space was given to human-interest stories, entertainment features, sports pages, and women's articles. This process was accelerated by the arrival of the *Sun*, which established a new, highly commercial form of popular journalism. Competition for readers then forced the rest of the popular press to follow its lead. If the *Sun* is compared with the *Daily Herald*, which it replaced, the proportion of the paper devoted to public affairs dropped from 45 to 14 per cent between 1946 and 1976 (Curran and Seaton 1991: 113–16).

A widening gap emerged between the popular and the so-called quality press, where coverage of public affairs was maintained, and in some cases increased. Curran and Seaton argue that this gap was maintained by advertising pressures. Advertisers targeting a middle-class readership wanted the quality press to remain exclusive. They were not interested in paying higher rates for advertisements because circulation amongst other groups had increased. When *The Times* tried in the 1960s to adopt a more popular style and increase its circulation, it lost advertising and had to revert to being a 'middle-class paper'.

Curran and Seaton argue that this gap in the press had important political consequences, for it meant that working-class readers were denied serious coverage of public affairs. They reject the idea that this happened because there was no popular demand for this material. Market research showed that 'substantial minorities within the mass market' wanted it. The problem was that lack of purchasing power in these groups meant that advertisers were not interested in supporting newspapers that might meet this demand. They conclude that: 'An elite press thus came to dominate by default the field of serious journalism, thereby reinforcing elite domination of political life' (Curran and Seaton 1991: 118).

The introduction of commercial television in 1950s did not end public-service broadcasting. The BBC

The quality of digital television

'The quality of television will fall when digital services start broadcasting, Virginia Bottomley, the Heritage Secretary, admitted yesterday. She said the Independent Television Commission (ITC) would have to allow standards to drop "so that the aeroplane can get off the ground". She told members of the National Heritage Select Committee: "We should not expect the same quality from the multiplicity of channels if we want to be sure that digital television will fly. We have to let it be successful first. Then let the government and the ITC change the standards if they want."'

Source: Alison Boshoff, 'Quality Will Fall on Digital Television', *Daily Telegraph*, 12 Feb. 1997.

▶ **What do you think is meant by the 'quality' of television? Refer back to our discussion of 'the media and culture'.**

▶ **Is there any objective basis to judgments of 'quality' or is it simply a matter of personal preference?**

continued to keep commerce at arm's length, while commercial television was supervised by the IBA, which tried to keep advertising completely separate from programming. Both the BBC and the ITV network have, however, come under heavier commercial pressures. The BBC's licence fee was not increased sufficiently during the 1980s to cover its rising costs and it needed to find alternative sources of money, by, for example, obtaining commercial sponsors for programmes. ITV companies came under greater commercial pressure as franchises became more expensive, while the arrival of Channel 5 intensified the competition for audiences and advertisers.

One of the effects of commercialization has been the steady breakdown of the barrier between programme content and advertising. Advertising agencies seek to break through this barrier because advertising that is *integrated* with content is more effective than advertising *segregated* in slots. Integrated advertising enables advertisers to use what Vance Packard (1963) famously called 'hidden persuaders'. It also reaches a larger audience through repeats and international sales, and cannot be bypassed through use of the 'zapper', in the way that separate advertising slots can.

Murdock (1992) has traced this process. In the early 1980s both BBC and IBA came to accept programme sponsorship. The televising of sport was a key battleground, for advertisers wanted to associate their products with healthy activities and reach large, often international, sport audiences. The BBC gave way and by 1986 it was showing in one year some 350 hours of sport sponsored by tobacco companies, which were not allowed for health reasons to advertise their products in ITV slots. ITV sponsorship rules were then relaxed by the 1990 Broadcasting Act, which allowed sponsorship of an increasing range of programmes, including weather forecasts but excluding news programmes.

Sponsorship is now an accepted part of television. Does it really matter if programmes are funded by sponsors? The current regulatory body, the Independent Television Commission, bans the influence of programme content by sponsors, but there is clearly a risk that those who fund programmes will find ways of doing this. It has certainly happened in other countries, particularly through 'product placement', which inserts branded products into programmes. Although this is banned in British television, Murdock notes that advertisers try to 'beat the system' and that since the 1980s it has occurred increasingly in films.

He points out that sponsorship anyway affects programme-making, by giving commercial interests the power to determine which programmes are made, and warns that sponsorship threatens broadcasting as a public sphere: 'The result is a programme system in which commercial speech is increasingly privileged over other voices by virtue of its financial leverage and where corporate interests regulate which other voices may be heard' (Murdock 1992: 229).

Commercialization operates in other ways, by, for example, mixing information with entertainment to produce 'infotainment'. Hallin (1996) has examined

Product placement

'The present intensification of placement activity dates from 1982, when the alien in *ET* was enticed from his hiding place by a trail of Reese's Pieces sweets, producing a 300 per cent increase in the brand's sales. Since then, placement has become an integral part of Hollywood film-making, with Associated Film Promotions and similar agencies continually scanning new scripts for placement opportunities for their clients. Sums for onset promotions regularly range from the $100,000 Kimberly-Clark paid to have Huggies nappies used in *Baby Boom* and to use its infant star in publicity, to Philip Morris's $350,000 outlay on *Licence to Kill* to have James Bond use their Lark cigarette brand.'

Source: Murdock (1992: 227).

this process in American television. In the 1960s professional journalism became well established in the networks' news divisions, which were insulated from commercial pressures. Increasing competition led, however, to the spread of what was called 'reality-based programming' in the 1980s. This mixed news and entertainment in magazine-style programmes which became the main output of the news divisions. One consequence of this was a greater interest in the private lives of public figures and presidential elections in the United States came to revolve largely around personalities rather than policies. Politicians were, of course, happy to manipulate this interest in their private lives, especially when it focused on the less savoury aspects of the private lives of their rivals, but commercial pressures lay behind this shift of news content.

Hallin does see some virtues in a more popular and less elitist presentation of news, but he is concerned about the consequences of commercialization for the political process: 'The nation's political agenda, its stock of social knowledge, its style of political discussion, all are shaped by the news media, and there is no reason to suppose that they will be "optimized" by profit-seeking programmers and advertisers' (Hallin 1996: 259).

The state and the public sphere

The public sphere needs protection from political as well as commercial pressures. In the 1980s the availability of information grew and this in many ways benefited the public sphere, but more information also meant more attempts to control and direct its flow.

The flow of information to the media about politics and policies increased enormously. Television gained access to parliament, with the admission of cameras to the House of Lords in 1985 and the House of Commons in 1990. Information on hospital waiting lists, school tests, and examination results, and the quality of university teaching and research, has become available from state agencies.

The other side of this process was increasing manipulation. What Bob Franklin (1994) calls the 'packaging' of politicians and policies for the media rapidly developed. The political parties increasingly employed media consultants, public-relations experts, and advertising agencies to promote their policies and personalities.

While all political parties did this, the governing party had control of the apparatus and resources of the state. The government increasingly used the media for promotional purposes. The Prime Minister's Press Secretary more actively managed and coordinated the flow

of information to journalists. There was also a massive increase in expenditure on the promotion of government policy. By 1989 the government had become Britain's biggest advertiser. Huge amounts of money were spent on campaigns to promote both privatization and the highly unpopular and eventually abandoned Poll Tax.

 You might find it helpful here to refer back to 'Constructing the News', pp. 291–3.

There were also growing government attempts to restrict media activities and censor information. The government attacked media coverage of the Falklands War and the conflict in Northern Ireland. New bodies were established to regulate broadcasting, the Broadcasting Complaints Commission of 1981 and the Broadcasting Standards Council of 1988. The 1990 Broadcasting Act required the practice of 'due impartiality' in matters of 'political or industrial controversy or relating to current public policy'. This apparently reasonable requirement was motivated by a concern that television news coverage was becoming more left-wing, and Franklin notes that, although this part of the Act has not yet been invoked, it has the potential to become a means of censorship.

The state's relationship to the public sphere is ambiguous. There have been calls for greater state regulation of the press through privacy laws to prevent journalists intruding into people's private lives. As we showed in the previous section, the control of the commercialization of television also depends on state regulation. The state is both the main protector of the public sphere and the greatest potential threat to it, for the state is also an instrument of governments seeking to manipulate and restrict the information available to the public.

The revival of the public sphere by the Internet?

Arguably, as the state weakens the media's contribution to the public sphere, the Internet can take over this function. The Internet can link any computer with access to a telephone line to any other computer in the world with such access. The World Wide Web is the main means of exchanging information, which is stored on web pages at web sites. Pages can contain text, graphics, photographs, sound, and video material. They also contain links to other pages at other sites. Any

The state and the public sphere

The state's positive contribution

▶ Public service framework of TV
▶ Regulation of commercial interests
▶ Provision of information
▶ Privacy laws? (Could be negative by hindering investigative journalism)

The state's negative contribution

▶ Censorship
▶ Pressure on the media
▶ Promotion of government policy
▶ Selection and presentation of information
▶ Manipulation

organization or any individual can establish a web site and provide freely or sell information through the Web. The big problem with such a network is to know what information is available on which pages at which sites and how to locate it. Web browser software provides the means of doing this.

From a public-sphere perspective the key thing about the Internet is its freedom from commercial and political pressures. Information can be exchanged at low cost without as yet much possibility of interference from the state. It is not, however, clear how long the uncontrolled anarchy of the Internet can last. Access to web sites is provided through web servers run by commercial organizations, which currently provide this service very cheaply but may not continue doing so. The free exchange of information is not liked by governments, who are seeking ways of policing use of the Internet. While it is extremely difficult to prevent the production of information, which can originate from any computer anywhere, it is possible to identify its source and trace users of it. People accessing pornographic material have, for example, been prosecuted and web servers have closed access to sites producing such material. There would seem to be no reason why other kinds of material, such as that produced by political or religious organizations, could not be traced or suppressed in the same way.

The ingenuity of Internet users has so far run well ahead of attempts to police the Net, but there are other reasons for doubting whether it can replace the media as the main vehicle of the public sphere. The first of these is access, which requires technical skills as well as equipment. Although it is often suggested that this is no real barrier, for computers are becoming ever more available and knowledge of how to use them is spreading fast, the Internet is still a long way from becoming as accessible as radio, television, or newspapers. There is, secondly, the problem of the interface between information exchange and politics. There is much exchange of information and opinion on the Net, but currently no real connection between its world and mainstream political discussion and communication. Internet hype notwithstanding, the media are still the main vehicle of political communication and appear likely to continue to be.

SUMMARY POINTS

In this section we have examined the movement from a small number of mass media towards a world of more specialized multiple media. Greater media diversity has in principle provided more choice, but in practice this has been limited by other processes of change:

▶ Technical change, neo-liberal politics, post-Fordist organization, and post-modern culture have broadly resulted in greater media diversity.

▶ The exercise of choice depends, however, on access, which requires resources, knowledge, time, and control.

Globalization has potentially provided access to a far greater range of cultures and experiences but may, however, result in a loss of cultural diversity through Americanization:

▶ American corporations dominate world media sales but the import penetration of national markets varies greatly.

▶ Other societies can develop local production and resist American influence in various ways.

Increasing competition may suggest that ownership has become more widely spread, but in reality the concentration of ownership has increased not only within particular media but also across the media and across delivery systems:

▶ Newspaper owners shifted the press towards the political right between the 1960s and the 1980s, and arguably played a significant part in the Thatcherite transformation of British politics.

▶ Newspaper owners as owners of capital had an interest in the success of Thatcherite policies, but the political views expressed in newspapers are also constrained by market considerations.

A flourishing public sphere enabling the free exchange of information and opinion requires protection from commercial and political pressures:

▶ Commercial pressures resulted in the declining coverage of public affairs in the popular press and a widening gap between the popular and the 'quality' press.

▶ Commercial pressures have broken down the barriers between television programming and advertising.

▶ The flow of information about politics and policies has increased but so have the political manipulation of the press and attempts at censorship.

▶ The Internet may provide an alternative to the media as a means of information exchange and discussion.

REVISION AND EXERCISES

MASS MEDIA

One of the main approaches to the study of the media treats them as 'mass media'. We examined this approach in 'Understanding the Media':

▶ **Make sure that you are familiar with the ideas of the mass-society theorists, Gramsci, Miliband, and the Frankfurt school.**

▶ **What do you understand by the following terms; the media; mass society, mass media, dominant ideology, dominant culture, subculture.**

▶ **Why did mass-society theorists think that people could be manipulated by the mass media?**

We also identified three models of media influence:

▶ **Which model was adopted by the mass-society approach and what problems does it face?**

We moved on to outline the rise of the mass media. We argued that this was linked to mass production and mass consumption.

▶ **What does the development of the cinema tell us about these relationships?**

We also examined the influence of the mass media on information, representation, culture, and morality:

▶ **Assess the influence of the mass media on each of these areas.**

In 'The Limits of Choice' we considered recent changes in the media:

▶ **What grounds are there for thinking that the media are no longer 'mass media'?**

▶ **Make a list of your five favourite television programmes. What audiences do you think that they are aimed at? Do you think that television is still a 'mass medium'?**

CULTURE

One of the central issues of the debate on the influence of the media is their effect on culture:

▶ **What do you understand by the terms: high and folk culture; popular culture, mass culture; elitist and populist interpretations; dominant culture, subculture.**

▶ **What is the relationship between popular culture and high and folk cultures?**

▶ **Compare and contrast the mass society and Marxist theories of popular culture.**

▶ **How do elitist and populist views of the audience differ?**

▶ **Compare their views with the models we identified of media influence.**

The elitist and populist approaches have provided different interpretations of Americanization. We showed that Hollywood came to dominate world film production in the section on 'Film' and discussed the issues raised by Americanization in the sections on 'Americanization' and 'American Global Domination':

▶ **How would you account for Hollywood domination?**

▶ **Contrast the elitist and populist interpretations of American influence.**

▶ **Do you think that globalization has resulted in the American global domination of culture?**

What were the last three television programmes that you watched?

▶ **Where was each of these programmes produced?**

▶ **Did any of them show signs of American influence? Consider the type of programme, its format, and its style when answering this question.**

▶ **Did these programmes reflect British culture in any way?**

A PUBLIC SPHERE

There has been considerable debate over the contribution of the media to a 'public sphere':

▶ **Make sure that you are familiar with the main ideas of Habermas and the main criticisms that have been made of his discussion of the public sphere.**

▶ **What do you think are the key features of the public sphere?**

▶ **How does such a sphere relate to the economy, politics, and private life?**

We outlined the development of newspapers and broadcasting, and discussed their significance for the public sphere:

▶ **How has the development of the press affected its capacity to act as part of the public sphere?**

▶ **The BBC was established on public-service principles. What problems did it face in providing a service to the public?**

In 'Decline of the Public Sphere' we examined recent pressures on the public sphere:

▶ **What pressures have come from commercialization?**

▶ **What pressures have come from politicians?**

▶ **Do you think that the state has protected or threatened the public sphere?**

▶ **Do you think that the Internet provides a new arena for the public sphere?**

There has been much recent discussion of the need for privacy to be protected by the law:

▶ **Why do you think that the protection of privacy has become a matter of increasing concern?**

▶ **What do you think that the consequences of such a law would be for the public sphere?**

We listed some principles of public-service broadcasting on p. 278:

▶ **Do you think that these principles operate?**

▶ **Do you think that the state should intervene to maintain them?**

▶ **Should the content of the media be left to market forces and consumer choice?**

FURTHER READING

The following cover most of the issues dealt with in this chapter:

Eldridge, J., Kitzinger, J., and Williams, K. (1997), *The Mass Media and Power in Modern Britain* (Oxford: Oxford University Press). A wide-ranging and up-to-date discussion of the power of the media, dealing with all the media, examining their history, and reviewing different approaches to media influence.

Curran J., and Gurevitch, M. (1996) (eds.), *Mass Media and Society* (2nd ed., London: Arnold). A wide-ranging and up-to-date reader covering all the main issues of the Sociology of the Media.

Particular topics can be followed up through:

Abercrombie, N. (1996), *Television and Society* (Cambridge: Polity). A very clear and full analysis of all aspects of the Sociology of the Media, with reference to television.

Curran, J. and Seaton, J. (1991), *Power without Responsibility: The Press and Broadcasting in Britain* (4th edn., London: Routledge). A theoretically informed account of the development of the press and broadcasting from the nineteenth century onwards.

Negrine, R (1994), *Politics and Mass Media in Britain* (2nd edn., London: Routledge). A comprehensive introduction to the relationship between politics and the media in contemporary Britain.

Strinati, D. (1995), *An Introduction to Theories of Popular Culture* (London: Routledge). A clear and comprehensive account of theories of the media, focusing on popular culture but generally useful as a guide to the various theoretical positions.

—— and Wagg, S. (1992) (eds.), *Come on Down: Popular Media Culture* (London: Routledge). A diverse selection of readings on popular culture.

Tunstall, J. (1996), *Newspaper Power: The New National Press in Britain* (Oxford: Clarendon Press). A lively and very detailed account of the recent development of the press, based on a study of journalists, editors, and executives.

Chapter 9
RELIGION, BELIEF, AND MEANING

Talking to God

'It is midnight in Leicester Square. About 100 people stand in a circle with their eyes shut, arms raised high above their heads. They sway in time to the sound of guitars, a banjo and cymbals. "It's your blood that puts my faith in redeeming sacrifice," they say, to a catchy soul tune, "washes me whiter than the snow."

'The singers laugh and hug each other. Their talk of love and peaceful revolution has a whiff of the 1960s but it is not drug-induced. The love of which they talk is not human, but spiritual. They are members of a Baptist sect, the Jesus Army, and they have devoted their love to God.

'Today, the Jesus Army expects 2,000 people to attend its Celebrate Jesus meeting at Liverpool Philharmonic Hall, which will include singing, healing, and exorcism.

'As the singing and dancing in Leicester Square reaches fever pitch a man collapses on the ground as if in a coma. Another man is held by two Jesus Army recruits who are trying to convert him: "Feel the Holy Spirit moving inside of you," they whisper. "Moving up and down you. Ask the Spirit to come into you. Confess it with your lips." One of the recruits rolls back his eyes and utters an unintelligible phrase which roughly transcribes as "hasialalabaruslamarula."

'The recruit . . . later explains he was speaking in tongues. He believes this is a gift from God which allows him to communicate directly with the Creator.'

Source: Guardian, 10 Oct. 1992.

F OR every person in Britain today who has such emotionally charged religious views, there are many more whose religious beliefs are more low key and taken for granted. For these people, religion is something for Sundays and holy days. It does not lead them to give up their routine, everyday concerns and take on a life of talking in tongues, faith healing, the exorcism of evil, or evangelistic conversion. In many societies in the past, levels of religious activity were much greater than they are for most people in Britain. Even today, many societies have high levels of religious activity. In fact, the strength of religious commitment is quite variable from one type of society to another. What, then, is religion, and what part does it play in social life?

In this chapter we will look at religions of all kinds and, in particular, at the historical trend of religion and belief in modern societies. In the section on 'Understanding Religion' we consider the nature of religion and the major sociological theories of religion. The second section on 'Religion in Modern Society' examines the idea that modern societies have undergone a process of secularization in which religious beliefs and practices have declined. The final section on 'The Rise of New Religions' looks at the significance of the many new religions that are today experiencing a growth in membership.

UNDERSTANDING RELIGION

A religion is a system of beliefs through which people organize and order their lives. This is often thought to involve a belief in a god or gods, but this is not the case for all religious beliefs. The central meaning of the word religion is, in fact, simply the way in which shared beliefs establish regulations, rules, or bonds of obligation among the members of a community. In its broadest sense, then, religion can be seen as involving devotion or attachment to a system of beliefs that defines the moral obligations and responsibilities that people have towards one another. These beliefs define a code of behaviour that regulates personal and social life. It is notoriously difficult to produce any generally acceptable definition of religion. Wallis and Bruce, however, have come up with a useful, if rather complex, definition. According to these writers, a religion comprises the 'actions, beliefs and institutions predicated upon the assumption of the existence of either supernatural entities with powers of agency, or impersonal powers or processes possessed of moral purpose, which have the capacity to set the conditions of, or to intervene in, human affairs' (Wallis and Bruce 1992: 10–11).

While this definition contains a number of quite complex ideas, it is a good starting point for our discussion, and you will find it useful to return to it from time to time.

THE SACRED AND THE SECULAR

Religious beliefs and rites have generally been organized around objects and activities that are held to be sacred because they are seen as having superior power or dignity to the objects and activities of everyday life. Sacred things have 'a quality of mysterious and awesome power' (Berger 1969: 34; see also Durkheim 1912; Pickering 1984). They have a spiritual quality that leads them to be venerated as holy and to be set apart from everyday things. By contrast with natural objects, they are *supernatural*. These sacred objects are the basis of the moral standards by which the non-sacred, or *secular* world is judged. Religious activity involves special forms of communication and action—such as prayer and ritual—through which those in the secular world can come into contact with the sacred world.

Religion forms what Berger (1969) calls a *sacred canopy*. By this he means an overarching framework of meanings that gives a larger, cosmological significance to the ordinary world of practical action. Everyday matters can be seen as significant if they have a place in a wider context of meanings. When covered by a sacred canopy, routine, day-to-day social reality comes to acquire a significance that goes beyond the immediate, practical interests and concerns of everyday life. Instead of appearing as arbitrary and precarious, it appears as part of some larger purpose. People conform to the expectations defined by this social reality because they feel a sense of duty or obligation to something beyond themselves.

Religions differ from one another in terms of those particular things that they regard as sacred or holy. Typically, the ultimate sacred object is some kind of higher power, such as a god, though this may often be seen in highly abstract terms. What are called theistic religions are those that involve devotion to a superhuman or controlling power that is seen as being the source of all moral values and that requires an attitude of reverence or awe. Such a sacred power becomes the object of worship. The major monotheistic religions—Judaism, Christianity, and Islam—have all accorded this kind of devotion to a single, personified God. In Christian theology, for example, representations of God are at the heart of the spiritual significance given to sacred texts (especially the Bible), to sacred buildings (churches and chapels), and to sacred music and works of art.

Polytheistic religions, on the other hand, are organized around a large number of separate gods. The religions of ancient Greece and Rome, for example, were polytheistic. In fact, they invoked a similar set of gods. For the Greeks, Zeus ruled the spiritual world from Mount Olympus, along with such other gods as Athena, Poseidon, Hermes, and Artemis. For the Romans, the counterpart gods were the spiritual ruler Jupiter, together with Minerva, Neptune, Mercury, and Diana. In both religions, the events of the natural and social worlds reflected the relations of cooperation and competition that existed among the various gods.

In practice, however, the distinction between monotheistic and polytheistic religions is difficult to draw with any precision. Early and medieval Christianity, for example, saw God—personified always in male terms—as standing at the head of a celestial hierarchy of other spiritual beings: seraphim, cherubim, thrones, dominations, virtues, powers, principalities, archangels, and angels. The various prophets and saints inspired by God also became objects of religious devotion, as did—above all—Mary, the mother of God. In this system of religious belief, then, monotheism was combined with the recognition of a vast number of lesser spiritual beings.

Not all religions are theistic. Buddhism, for example, has no conception of a personal god, although it does require that people regulate their lives by specific values and standards. It sees people as going through a series of reincarnations until they achieve an enlightened, sacred state that releases them from their earthly existence. They achieve 'nirvana'. The moral standards that Buddhists must follow, therefore, have an ultimate, supernatural significance, but they are not derived from the demands of any supernatural being. Though recognizing no personified gods, Buddhists do revere those people who have achieved perfect enlightenment. They are termed Buddhas and Bodhisattvas

and are held up as exemplars for others to follow. The founder of the religion—often referred to simply as Buddha—was Sidartha Guatama, the most important of the Buddhist saints. Buddhism merges easily with other religions, and many of the gods of the traditional Brahman religion of India, from which Buddhism originated, were simply transformed into Buddhas. The number of holy entities recognized in some forms of Buddhism can, in fact, be very high.

Buddhism is a religion in which the ultimate state of existence (nirvana) is *transcendent*. That is to say, it goes beyond the everyday world and exists only on a purely spiritual plane. Similarly, the Christian heaven is an ultimate state that transcends the everyday world. In some non-theistic religions, however, the ultimate state of existence is *immanent* rather than transcendent. This means that it is rooted in the natural, practical world itself and is seen as an actual state of affairs that can or will result from practical actions. The secular world—as it is or as it might become—is itself given a sacred status.

Buddhism is a contemplative religion that places great emphasis on withdrawal from everyday activities.

Soviet Communism, for example, justified commitment to the existing political order in relation to the ideal Communist society that was being built. The state's role in building this ideal legitimated conformity to its demands. Despite the absence of gods and transcendent states of existence, Soviet Communism was a religion as we have defined it. Marxist-Leninist ideas were drawn upon to construct images of such sacred entities as the proletariat and the party, and these became the objects of reverential attachment. Exemplary thinkers and practitioners of Marxism were accorded a holy status, and some became the objects of cult attachments. Marx, Engels, Lenin, and Stalin were all treated in this way. Lenin's body, for example, was preserved in a special mausoleum in Moscow and was the focus of many ceremonies of state. Party Congresses and other party meetings provided the ritualized contexts in which these ideas and values could be reaffirmed. Even after the collapse of the Communist regime, cult attachments persisted, and the new authorities did not rush to remove Lenin's body from public display.

THEORIES OF RELIGION

The pioneer sociologists of the nineteenth century recognized the central part that religion has played in human history. They were particularly concerned, however, with the implications that modern science had for traditional forms of religion. Both Comte and Marx saw the specifically supernatural aspects of religious belief as being incompatible with an acceptance of modern scientific knowledge. Both of them held that traditional forms of religion would disappear as modern societies matured. Their claim concerned the secularization of modern society, or the declining significance of religion in the day-to-day lives of people in the modern social world.

The founders of classical sociology—most particularly Durkheim and Weber—drew on these ideas and developed them into more sophisticated understandings of the social significance of religion and scientific knowledge. Durkheim, like Comte, saw modern society as evolving new forms of religion that were more compatible with scientific knowledge and with the structures of complex, advanced societies. Weber was more pessimistic. He anticipated the complete disappearance of all religion and held that individuals would, therefore, be unable to make any sense of their lives. Weber undertook a range of comparative and historical studies of religion, looking particularly at the link

between religion and the rise of capitalism. A useful overview of theories of religion can be found in Beckford (1989).

Comte and Marx: Religion and science

Comte saw traditional religions as having either a theistic or a metaphysical character. They constructed sacred canopies around ideas of supernatural beings or of abstract forces and powers. The Catholic Church in medieval Europe was typical of such a traditional religion. These kinds of religious ideas, Comte held, have been undermined by the growth of modern science. In the modern world, he argued, no theistic or metaphysical religion can stand up to the advance of scientific knowledge. He held, however, that modern societies did still require a system of beliefs that would function as religion had in the past to regulate social activities and produce social order. This new form of religion he found in science itself.

Positive, scientific thought, Comte held, would become the basis of a new kind of religion that could provide the cohesion and consensus that is necessary for social integration. It could do this without resorting to theistic or metaphysical ideas. Only a scientifically based religion could provide sacred ideas and a moral code that were compatible with the modern scientific outlook. Central to all religious beliefs are ideas about the nature of social life itself, and Comte therefore held

Catholicism

Christians believe that Jesus was the Son of God, the Messiah prophesied in the Jewish religious texts. Christianity was adopted as the official religion of the Roman Empire in the fourth century AD. The Roman Church termed itself Catholic because it claimed to be a universally valid religion for all who lived within the Empire. The Roman Catholic Church always had a centralized structure and is headed by the Pope, who has ultimate, infallible authority over its members. The authority of the Church is exercised through a hierarchy of cardinals, archbishops, bishops, and priests.

With the fall of the Roman Empire, the Roman Catholic Church was separated from the Eastern Orthodox Church, a federation of independent churches that rejected the authority of the Pope but retained the core beliefs and rituals of the Roman Church. The Orthodox Church remains strong in Greece, the Balkans, and Russia, while the Roman Catholic Church is strongest in Italy, Spain, and Latin America.

that the science of society—sociology—would be at the heart of this new religion. Comte set out to help build a positivist religion of humanity that could provide the necessary cement to hold modern societies together (B. Turner 1991: ch. 2).

 You might like to look back at our review of the development of sociological theory in Chapter 2. There you will find accounts of Comte and the various other theorists that we look at in this section. Comte's religion of humanity followed from his law of the three stages, which we discuss on p. 28.

A more radical view of religion was taken by Marx, though he too recognized the role that it played in furthering social cohesion. Like Comte, Marx believed that theistic forms of religion would disappear as modern societies matured. He believed, however, that this would occur only when the capitalist features of these societies had been abolished and they had become socialist societies.

Marx saw the theistic and metaphysical religions as expressions of the deepening alienation that people experienced in a modern capitalist society. Traditional religious thought was simply a distorted reflection of the real class relations that connected and divided people from one another. In a capitalist society, Marx held, class divisions took a particularly sharp form, but were obscured by religious ideas of unity and common brotherhood. The cohesion and integration that this produced simply served the interests of the dominant class and not the whole of society.

According to Marx, then, traditional religion had an *ideological* function and could not be understood apart from the underlying social divisions and conflicts of a society. Although it appeared to provide a sense of meaning for those who were subject to economic exploitation, this was an illusion. It merely obscured their subordination and oppression and made it less likely that they would challenge the existing social order. Religion deflected social conflict by encouraging people to accept their social position. It was, in Marx's words, both 'the sigh of the oppressed' and 'the opium of the people'. By providing illusions to live by, it effectively drugged people into the acceptance of social relations that exploited and alienated them. Religion would be swept completely away when capitalism was overthrown and when, in consequence, alienation and class divisions finally disappeared from human history.

Durkheim: Religion and individualism

Durkheim followed Comte in recognizing the part that was played by religious belief and ritual in social cohesion and social integration (Beckford 1989: 25–31). He also agreed with Comte that the theistic aspects of religion would disappear in modern society. Though he rejected Comte's religion of humanity, he did say that modern societies would come to be organized around a 'cult of man' or cult of individualism.

Durkheim approached religion from an analysis of its most primitive or elementary forms. These he found in the **totemism** of tribal societies. All forms of religion, he argued, had their origins in totemistic beliefs, though he believed that these survived only among native Australians and some North American tribes. These tribes, he argued, were divided into clans, which were the real bases of social solidarity. People felt strong sentiments of attachment to their clan, because it defined their relations to all other members of their tribe. Each clan identified itself with a particular animal or plant. This was its emblem or totem, and it symbolized the clan. Members of a clan might say, for example, that they were the fox clan, and that they were quite distinct from the beaver clan. These totems were, then, marks of social identity.

Because clan membership was fundamental to the whole way in which people lived their lives, the totem had a sacred quality. It was in this imputation of sacredness to particular objects that Durkheim found the basis of all religion. In more advanced forms of totemism, sacredness was not so likely to be seen in natural objects such as animals, plants, winds, stars, rocks, rivers, and so on. Instead, social identity became focused around spiritual entities such as souls, demons, spirits, saints, or gods. A people might, for example, regard themselves as the 'chosen people' of a particular god. The further development of religion, as societies advanced beyond the tribal stage, led to the complete disappearance of its totemistic elements. The sacred objects of a society became even more abstract.

Durkheim had only a rather limited knowledge of the Australian tribes, and his views on totemism have been seriously questioned by later writers (Lévi-Strauss 1962). What has not been challenged, however, is his general view of the relationship between the sacred sphere and the religious attitude, on the one hand, and the structure of society, on the other.

Durkheim, like Marx, saw religion as having a social basis. The origin of the idea of the sacred was to be found in society itself. Religious forces and entities are, he held, mere representations of the moral forces and constraints that people experience in their social relations. In their social interaction, people build what Durkheim called **collective representations**. These include shared images and ideas about the moral obligations that they feel to bind them together as members of their society. These representations are so fundamental to their social relations that they come to have a sacred character. They are, under some circumstances, personified as gods or other spiritual beings. The idea of god is an expression of society itself.

Ideas of divinity, then, are reflections of the ways in which people attempt to understand their social relations with one another. Religion is also central to the production of a sense of moral community. It is through religion that the symbols and ideas that sustain social life and that underpin the social order are sustained. Durkheim called these symbols and ideas, in French, the *conscience collective*. This is a difficult term to translate, and so is generally left in the French. It refers to both the consciousness that is shared among the members of a society and the moral ideas that form their consciences. Because the *conscience collective* is so central to social life, Durkheim held, the disappearance of religion would mean the disappearance of social order itself. For this reason, he concluded that any society that is to persist must have some form of religion. This is why Durkheim is often said to have focused his attention on the functions of religion in creating social solidarity.

Although traditional forms of supernatural religion disappear as societies become more modern, other forms of religion will take their place. This new form of religion, Durkheim argued, centres around the idea of the individual. Individualism is the system of ideas most compatible with the social division of labour and the market relations that are central to modern society. This is manifested in moral systems that emphasize human rights, freedom, and equality, and in the encouragement of individual autonomy and choice in all things. Moral individualism, centring around a cult of the individual, is, according to Durkheim, the normal form taken by religion in modern society.

 Read our discussion of Durkheim's wider theoretical ideas in Chapter 2, pp. 35–40. We show there how he saw anomie and egoism as pathological expressions of the normal condition of moral individualism in modern societies. Can you see why religion was so important in Durkheim's theory of suicide?

Weber: Religion and capitalism

Weber's particular concern in his sociology of religion was to look at the relationship between religious values and economic action. He carried out comparative studies of the religions of China, India, and ancient Israel, but his most important study was set out in a book on *The Protestant Ethic and the Spirit of Capitalism* (Max Weber 1904–5). The problem that he set himself to examine was why modern capitalism developed first in Western Europe, and he found the answer in its particular religious pattern.

Weber saw the central characteristic of modern capitalism as its spirit, its particular cultural attitude towards commercial activity. The **spirit of capitalism** is a system of beliefs that encourage the accumulation of income and assets through productive activity. This spirit encourages people to see excessive consumption as wasteful and, therefore, as something to be avoided. The profits of business have to be reinvested rather than consumed in luxurious and extravagant expenditure. This spirit emerged first among those who became active capitalist entrepreneurs in the seventeenth and eighteenth centuries, and Weber wanted to uncover its origins. He concluded that these origins were to be found in certain characteristics of the Protestant religion.

Weber looked, in particular, at the Calvinist forms of Protestantism that developed from the ideas of John Calvin. Calvinists believed that only a small minority—the elect—were destined by God for salvation and would join Him in heaven. The remainder were destined for eternal damnation. Nothing that people did during their lives could make any difference to their destiny, which reflected God's choice, and there was no way in which any individual believer could know whether he or she was destined for salvation or damnation. As a

Religion and society

'Religious force is only the sentiment inspired by the group in its members, but projected outside of the consciousnesses that experience them, and objectified. To be objectified, they are fixed upon some object which thus becomes sacred' (Durkheim 1912: 229).

Durkheim's statement is quite complex, and you will not fully understand it the first time that you read it. Read it through once or twice, picking out the key words and try to get the gist of what he is saying. The key words are 'sentiment', 'projected', and 'objectified'. Can you see how he applied these ideas to totemism?

result, Calvinists experienced what Weber called 'inner loneliness'. They were completely on their own, as to whom they could turn for authoritative guidance on their eternal destiny.

Protestantism

This is a Christian religion that originated in Martin Luther's 'protestation' against the authority of the Roman Catholic Church in the sixteenth century. Luther emphasized the authority of the Bible, as the direct word of God. He rejected the Catholic view that priests were able to interpret God's wishes. Luther held that each individual must open his or her mind to God and must rely on conscience as the sole guide to conduct.

This extreme anxiety about their fate caused great uncertainty about how they should behave. Protestant ministers and teachers responded to this by stressing those other aspects of Calvinism that might help to resolve the anxieties of their parishioners. Calvin had said that success in a person's calling might be seen as a sign that he or she was destined for salvation. A calling or vocation was the particular way of life to which one had been called by God. Calvin's followers concluded that God would hardly allow worldly success to those whom he had damned. The Puritan sects of the seventeenth century—especially the Quakers and the Baptists—developed an ethic that saw success in an occupation, business, or profession as giving people some indication of whether they were saved or damned. They began to encourage their members to be diligent and hard-working in their work and disciplined in all aspects of their lives. Those who worked hard found that they were, indeed, likely to be successful, and this helped to lessen their sense of anxiety about their destiny (G. Marshall 1982).

Weber described this lifestyle as one of *asceticism*. The ascetic lifestyle involved hard work, discipline, the avoidance of waste, and the rigorous and systematic use of time. This rational and calculative attitude was applied in all aspects of life. In the Puritan world-view, eating and sexuality were seen as stimulating the bodily appetites and, therefore, as things to be controlled. Fasting, the avoidance of non-reproductive sex, and, outside marriage, a life of chastity and celibacy were all seen as means of self-control through which a mastery of the body could be attained (B. Turner 1996).

The pursuit of these values by seventeenth-century merchants in the Puritan sects led them to greater business success than their counterparts in other religions. Their ascetic way of life stressed the avoidance of excessive income and wasteful or luxurious consumption, and this led them to plough back their profits into their businesses and so to expand their scale of operations. Asceticism gave a new meaning to practical economic life. A distinctively modern view of commercial activity and an ethic of hard work were encouraged, and it was this new outlook and orientation that allowed capitalist business enterprises to expand on an unprecedented scale in the eighteenth and nineteenth centuries. The Protestant ethic, Weber argued, had given birth to the spirit of modern capitalism.

In the favourable conditions provided by the nation states of Western Europe in the seventeenth and eighteenth centuries, this spirit helped to produce the modern capitalist system of production. This system rapidly spread across Europe and into the wider world. In the longer term, however, the success of the capitalist system undermined sacred, religious meanings. In expanding capitalist societies, Weber argued, individuals are driven to work through economic necessity, and not by any spiritual commitment to it as a calling. For most people there is simply no alternative to capitalist economic activity: if employers do not make a profit, then the pressures of competition will force them out of business; and if employees do not work hard, they will be sacked and replaced by those who will. The spirit of modern capitalism disappears, and modern life becomes increasingly empty and meaningless.

SUMMARY POINTS

In this section we have looked at the nature of religion and the principal sociological theories about the development of religion in modern societies.

▶ A religion is an overarching system of beliefs and practices that helps the members of a society or community to organize and order their lives.

▶ Central to religious thought is a distinction between the sacred and the secular.

We sketched the views of the main sociological theorists of religion. Their ideas are relevant to the many issues that we discuss in the rest of this chapter.

▶ Comte saw a conflict between religion and science, though he held that science could itself become the basis of a new religion and a new form of social cohesion.

► Marx related religion to class divisions and alienation. It is an important factor in the legitimation of social divisions.

► Durkheim saw modern societies as organized around a religion of moral individualism that corresponded to its social differentiation and division of labour.

► Weber gave an account of the rise of modern capitalism that saw the social ethic of the Protestant churches as a crucial factor in generating the attitudes and outlook of the capitalist entrepreneur.

RELIGION IN MODERN SOCIETY

It is often claimed that belief in God is less common in Europe and America today than was the case in the past. Those who hold to this see this loss of traditional religious belief as showing that modern societies must be seen as increasingly secular societies. This was one element in Comte's argument that positive, rational knowledge would free people from traditional forms of religious belief. Atheists have seen secularization in a favourable light, seeing it as an opportunity to liberate people from superstitious and irrational beliefs. Those who remain committed to traditional forms of religious faith, on the other hand, have seen secularization in more negative terms. For them, it undermines morality and destroys the possibility of a disciplined communal life. Most sociologists prefer not to take sides on these theological issues, seeing religious faith as a purely personal matter. They concern themselves only with the actual question of whether modern societies have, in fact, undergone a process of secularization.

SECULARIZATION AND MODERNITY

The sociological concept of **secularization** involves two closely related ideas. First, it implies that there has been a *disengagement* of religion from public institutions. This means that religious beliefs and practices are detached from major social institutions and become purely private matters of individual belief and choice. Indeed, the word secularization was originally used to denote the removal of a territory from the legal control of a church. It was generalized from this to mean the declining public significance of religion. The idea of secularization also implies that there has been a *disenchantment* of social life. A society is disenchanted when sacred ideas are no longer of any relevance to people

and practical matters are, in consequence, emptied of any ultimate spiritual significance. Disengagement involves a *privatization* of religious belief; disenchantment involves a *loss* of spiritual concerns.

The disengagement of religion

Disengagement is 'the process by which sectors of society and culture are removed from the domination of religious institutions and symbols' (Berger 1969: 113). This is apparent in the separation of church and state, the removal of education and welfare from control by religious bodies, and the withdrawal of churches from their attempts to regulate economic behaviour and control matters of morality. In Europe, this disengagement was apparent in the transformation and weakening of the Roman Catholic Church.

Medieval Europe was built around the cultural dominance of the Catholic Church, which was allied with all its major states and was the main focus of unity across the continent. The Catholic Church established a virtually compulsory framework for religious observance. People were born into membership of the Church, just as they were born into membership of a particular state. There was no choice about either. Place of birth fixed a person's subjection to church and state. The Church hierarchy was closely allied with the political hierarchies of the states of the Christian world, and the Pope was at least the equal of the European kings and princes.

Sociologists introduced the term **ecclesia** to describe the specific form taken by religion in this period. This type of religious organization is sometimes referred to simply as a church, but this word is now used so widely and in such a general sense that it has lost its original and more specific meaning. A church, in its broadest sense, is any form of association that is organized

Secularization

Secularization involves the two interrelated processes of disengagement and disenchantment. The *disengagement* of religion from public life involves the separation of economic and political institutions from religion and the privatization of religious belief. The *disenchantment* of the world is the process through which the ultimate spiritual meaning of practical life recedes as individuals lose their traditional religious beliefs.

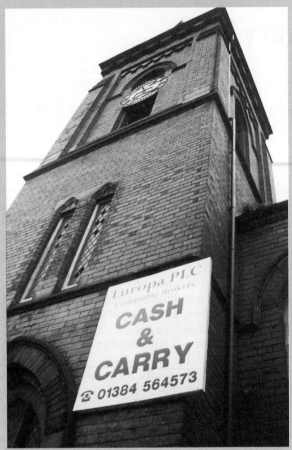

Secularization means that there is need for fewer church buildings, which have to find alternative uses.

around the relations of its members to a sacred sphere of meaning and action. The word church is even used to refer to the buildings in which religious activities take place.

An ecclesia is a specific kind of church, most clearly illustrated by medieval Roman Catholicism. It is a uni-versal and inclusive religious organization that claims total spiritual authority over all of those who live within a particular territory. It generally claims a degree of political authority too. The medieval Catholic Church claimed spiritual authority over virtually the whole of Europe. An ecclesia is organized around an orthodox doctrine. This is a systematically codified body of beliefs that is protected as the one true faith and is given authoritative interpretation by the church's leaders. People are born into membership of an ecclesia and they are socialized into its beliefs and practices. An orthodox doctrine may be the basis of a rigid social conformity: heretics (deviants from the reli-gious orthodoxy) are not tolerated and may be relent-lessly persecuted.

The ecclesia can be distinguished from the **denomi-nation**. A denomination is a church that is organized around *voluntary* rather than compulsory membership. It occurs where there is a separation between church and state. A denomination is a church that is disen-gaged from the many political and public functions undertaken by an ecclesia. A denomination claims no monopoly of religious truth and it accommodates itself to the legitimacy of secular states and to the beliefs of other denominations. This contrast between ecclesia and denomination is important when comparing dif-ferent forms of religion (Martin 1962; see also Niebuhr 1929).

By the nineteenth century, neither Roman Catholicism nor Anglicanism could be regarded as ecclesia. They had come closer to being mere denomi-nations. Anglicanism had, and still has, certain privi-leges and powers in relation to the State. It forms the established 'Church of England'. However, it is far weaker than it was in the past (B. R. Wilson 1966: 252). In virtually all the societies of Europe, religion became denominational, and states have gradually come to tol-erate the existence of numerous separate denomina-tions. At the same time, the various denominations tend to be more tolerant of one another than any ecclesia would be towards unorthodox beliefs and prac-tices. In Britain, for example, such churches as the Methodists and the Baptists emphasize voluntary com-mitment to the church and accommodation to other religions.

Denominations often have a social base in a particu-lar social class or ethnic group, and religious struggles in a denominational society can often be closely associ-ated with the social struggles of these groups for power. For example, nonconformist (i.e. non-Anglican) Protes-tantism was strongest in nineteenth-century England in the working-class communities of the industrial north. Methodist, Baptist, and Congregationalist

Ecclesia and denomination

The contrast between the ecclesia and the denomination—often discussed as a contrast between 'church' and denomination—is of great importance. According to Weber, an ecclesia is a form of administration that organizes religion into a structure of what he called 'hierocratic coercion'. It is characterized by:

▶ a claim to universal authority: control that is not restricted by kinship, ethnicity, or other particularistic claims;

▶ a systematic dogma and set of rites, generally recorded in texts that are objects of disciplined training;

▶ a professional priesthood, having specific duties and being controlled through salaries and promotions;

▶ compulsory membership for all who live within the territory over which it claims authority.

A denomination, on the other hand, exercises fewer and more restricted controls over its members. Although it may have a professional priesthood, these do not have the powers held by priests in an ecclesia. Specifically, the denomination is characterized by

▶ a tolerance towards other religions, which are recognized—in principle—as having an equally legitimate right to attract members and spread their views;

▶ a voluntary membership based on an act of choice made by a believer.

Examples of ecclesia are medieval Catholicism and Islam. Examples of denominations are the Methodist and Baptist churches in nineteenth- and twentieth-century Britain, and the many branches of Buddhism in Japan. Anglicanism is intermediate between the ecclesia and the denomination.

---

chapels provided a focus for communal cohesion and bases for opposition to the Established Church. The conflict between 'chapel' and 'church' became an important thread in British politics, persisting well into the twentieth century. In big cities, where there were substantial numbers of Irish migrants, Catholicism played a similar part in building the solidarity of the Irish working-class communities.

The disenchantment of the world

The second aspect of secularization is what Max Weber called the *disenchantment* or 'desacralization' of the world. By this he meant that modern societies experience a loss of the spiritual meaning that had been provided by traditional religious belief. While it is important not to overstate the depth and the consistency of religious belief in the past, Weber correctly identified a major difference between the medieval and the modern world-view.

Most ordinary people in the medieval world did hold to a broadly Christian world-view. The details of Christian theology and its specific doctrines were often unfamiliar or poorly understood, but Christianity provided a taken-for-granted sacred canopy that helped them to organize their everyday lives. The spiritual content of this religion was reinforced by equally strong beliefs in a whole array of supernatural and magical powers. For most people, witches, spirits, and fairies were every bit as real as the angels and saints of orthodox Christianity. These heretical views were tolerated by the Catholic Church, so long as its own position was not threatened. More systematic and intellectually consistent Christian beliefs were held by the literate, though even here there was a willingness to believe in magical forces (K. Thomas 1971). Medieval people, then, lived in an enchanted world, a world in which the secular activities of everyday life were permeated by supernatural forces.

The Reformation of sixteenth-century Europe challenged the Catholic orthodoxy and popular beliefs. The new Protestant beliefs recognized far fewer spiritual beings and emphasized a much greater degree of doctrinal purity. In a wider context, this helped to produce the fundamental shift in intellectual outlook that has been described as the Enlightenment. In one sphere of intellectual enquiry after another, knowledge was freed from religious constraints and opened up to rational criticism (Merton 1938a). As Comte had recognized, an increasingly scientific world-view gave greater priority to rational considerations over matters of faith. Protestantism and Enlightenment thought together destroyed the medieval world-view, encouraging a separation of religious from practical matters. Protestantism eliminated much of the spiritual content from religion, and scientific knowledge soon began to challenge any kind of theistic religion. Traditional religious beliefs could no longer be taken for granted, and they became progressively more difficult to sustain.

Many people, then, experienced a loss of faith in traditional religious ideas. Miracles, mysticism, saints, and sacraments all played a much smaller part in everyday life when religion took a specifically rational form and placed less emphasis on the supernatural. As Berger (1969: 117) has written, 'The Protestant believer no longer lives in a world on-goingly penetrated by sacred beings and forces.' In the modern world, it is science and technology that are looked to for solutions to practical problems. While most people do not have the knowledge that would allow them to assess scientific ideas critically, their faith is now placed in the powers of the scientific expert rather than the world of the spirits.

With the growing rationalization of modern culture, the sense of spiritual meaning that had formerly been provided by religion was lost. Weber took a particularly pessimistic view of this. He saw people living in a cold, soulless, and calculating world. They no longer had any sense of mystery about supernatural forces that could be understood only through magic or religion. They had lost sight of any values or goals except those that were tied to their immediate economic and political concerns. Modern society was becoming a vast and relentless machine, and individuals became mere 'cogs' in this machine. They played their parts out of necessity and not for any ultimate spiritual purpose.

In these circumstances, Weber held, it becomes more and more difficult to justify a commitment to any values and ideals (B. R. Wilson 1976; Wallis 1984). Individuals no longer feel that they have any basis for choosing the values by which to live their life. They must make arbitrary choices among the competing values that face them, and they cannot rely on the guidance formerly provided by traditional religions. Such arbitrary choices provide them with no foundation for moral commitment to the rational and impersonal world in which they live. Practical matters lack any moral legitimacy.

Durkheim was less pessimistic than Weber. Like Comte, he accepted that there had been a decline in

Anomie

Anomie is a term that was introduced by Durkheim to describe a failure of moral regulation. The word literally means 'without norms', and Durkheim used it to mean the absence of a normative framework or sacred canopy. Individual desires and interests for wealth and power are left uncontrolled.

Anomie is seen as a pathological condition that exists when the moral basis of modern society (moral individualism) has not properly developed. The full development of moral individualism produces the organic solidarity that Durkheim saw as the key to social cohesion in modern societies.

In Chapter 2, p. 40 and pp. 49–50, we look at how Durkheim and Merton defined anomie. We will use Merton's ideas later in this chapter.

people's willingness to believe in spiritual beings and forces. He recognized, however, that a new form of religion—moral individualism—was developing and that this could give a moral significance to social life. Moral individualism, as it developed, would help to offset the calculative and soulless aspects of modernity that Weber had identified. Only where moral individualism had not fully developed did modern life break down into anomie. For Durkheim, then, disenchantment could be seen as involving a decline in traditional religious beliefs, but not a decline in religion as such. Religion had been transformed, but not displaced. Religion in the modern world may be less spiritual and less theistic, but it could still sustain a sacred canopy.

Differentiation and religious pluralism

In medieval society, the Catholic Church was able to claim a monopoly of moral authority. In a secular society, there are numerous denominations and they must compete for believers. In this situation, religion becomes much more a matter of individual choice and preference (Berger 1961a, b). The roots of this religious pluralism and the need for choice can be traced to certain central features of Protestant Christianity itself.

The Protestantism of Luther and Calvin, as we have shown, rejected the authority of priests and of the church hierarchy. It emphasized, instead, the need for each individual to read the Bible and to listen directly to the voice of God. Individuals had to use their powers of reason to arrive at their own decisions about what is right and what is wrong. The Protestant obligation to consider all matters rationally and critically encouraged, albeit unintentionally, the very existence of God to be questioned. By the nineteenth century, all the major elements of traditional Christian belief—the Trinity, miracles, and the Virgin birth—were legitimate subjects for rational debate. They were no longer simply matters of faith (B. R. Wilson 1966). In this cultural context, religious denominations felt an increasing need to ensure that their doctrines and teachings would appear plausible to rational believers. They could not rely on an uncritical acceptance of traditional authority.

These features of Protestantism have meant that none of its denominations has found it easy to maintain a plausible claim to a monopoly of truth. It has been said that 'Protestantism is essentially fissile': it tends always to split into competing schools of thought (Bruce 1985, 1986). Unlike Roman Catholicism, there is no unified and coherent system of Protestant doctrine and practice. Existing interpretations of the word of God are always open to challenge in the light of rational argument or personal inspiration, and so there is a strong tendency to schism and sectarianism. Protestant churches must compete to maintain the loyalty of those who have the obligation to make their own religious choices.

When religion is a matter of personal choice and private belief, societies face a problem of moral legitimacy. Traditional religion can no longer provide an authoritative guide for moral decision-making. There can be no intellectually convincing statement of what is right and what is wrong. Modern societies must live with the possibility of moral relativism. The moral individualism of modern society provides only a very weak basis for a shared commitment to any other ideals.

Contemporary societies are not, however, in a chronic state of anomie. In addition to the bonds of moral individualism, there do remain certain areas of *shared* belief. It is those who are most concerned with intellectual matters who are the most likely to pursue the rational criticism of accepted values. Most people, for most of the time, do not question the values into which they have been socialized. While these values are, in principle, subject to rational criticism, they are generally taken for granted in everyday situations. People are born into specific cultural and religious traditions, and these shape the way that they approach religious and moral questions. Religious commitment becomes weaker, but religious and moral beliefs tend to be relatively standardized throughout a society. As a result, competition between religions tends to be limited in scope. They can compete through the marginal differentiation of their ideas within a broadly shared religious framework.

Individual attachment to this framework is, however, weak and precarious. It is constantly subject to intellectual criticism, and there is always the danger that individual adherents will take these intellectual problems seriously. The inherited religious framework is in constant danger of erosion in the face of the secularizing tendencies built into modern society. Religious attachment must also compete with other calls upon people's time. When religion becomes a matter of individual preference, people see it as a leisure-time activity to be engaged in on a purely voluntary basis. It must, therefore, compete with the many other leisure-time activities that have become such important aspects of modern life. As B. R. Wilson has argued, choice in religion becomes equivalent to the consumer choice between 'pushpin, poetry, or popcorn' (1976: 96).

RELIGION IN BRITAIN

One of the most characteristic features of Protestantism is that its churches have tended to be organized as sects. A **sect** is a schismatic group, a body of people whose views diverge from those of others within the *same* religion. Following the Reformation, the number of sects multiplied as they diverged from one another within the broadly Protestant framework. The sociological concept of the sect was used by Troeltsch (1912) in his study of how the early Baptists, Quakers, and Methodists split from the Anglican and other Protestant faiths in the seventeenth and eighteenth centuries.

Like the ecclesia, the sect claims to possess a monopoly of religious truth, but it is organized on a voluntary basis rather than through compulsory membership. Members are recruited through the conversion of non-members or through their personal decisions to join. People are born into an ecclesia, but they *choose* to join a sect. Sects establish sharp boundaries between members and non-members, and they expect a high level of involvement and commitment from their members. They stress the earnestness of individual faith and there is a heightened sense of commitment and morality. They tend, therefore, to be highly emotional in character and to adopt an evangelistic stance towards non-members. Where a denomination is tolerant towards other religions, a sect stresses its sole and exclusive claim to religious truth.

Sects also place a great emphasis on individual decision and choice. This has meant that they tend to show greater lay involvement in religion. There is far less differentiation between lay people and clergy than there is in either the ecclesia or the denomination, and so they have more fluid and democratic structures of leadership. Niebuhr (1929) showed that sects tended to evolve into denominations as they grew and matured. The early Protestant sects in Britain, for example, had gradually been transformed into denominations by the nineteenth century. The Protestant sects had rejected Episcopalianism—rule by bishops—and relied, instead, on quite informal and democratic structures of leadership. In their denominational forms, church government was formalized into congregational or presbyterian structures.

It was this transition from sect to denomination that allowed the secularizing potential of Protestantism to make itself felt in Britain. The emerging denominations relaxed their earlier claims to possess a monopoly of religious truth, and they accommodated to one another and to Anglicanism. This pattern of denominational pluralism—the competition of rival but mutually tolerant denominations—became the characteristic religious pattern in Britain and the United States. Sects such as the Jehovah's Witnesses and the Seventh Day Adventists have survived only through very active proselytization and conversion.

Church and nation

The high point of religious participation, for all denominations, was the second half of the nineteenth century, after which it declined quite considerably. Rates of church attendance and of membership fell rapidly, and only a quarter of adults in England were even nominal members of a religious group by the 1950s (B. R. Wilson 1966; Martin 1967). Between 10 per cent and 15 per cent of the population were regular Sunday churchgoers, compared with around 40 per cent a century earlier. This decline in membership and attendance was especially marked during the last decades of the nineteenth century. Decline began first among Anglicans, and it then set in among the nonconformist denominations.

The decline in membership was greater in towns and cities than in rural districts, though the extent of the decline varied quite considerably from district to district within the major cities. Inner-city and working-class housing estates, for example, had very low rates of churchgoing, while middle-class suburbs showed significantly higher rates. The Catholic Church in Britain was more successful in retaining relatively high levels of church attendance, partly because of the large numbers of those who migrated to England from Ireland. For this reason, Catholics came to form a large proportion of the total churchgoing population.

While Protestantism in Britain took this highly pluralistic form, the Church of England remained the religion of the majority until well into the twentieth century (B. R. Wilson 1966: 119). The Church is the Established Church, having a constitutionally defined role in relation to the monarchy and the political system. The monarch is both Head of State and Head of the Church, appointing all bishops and archbishops and acting as 'Defender of the Faith'. The Church retained a strong association with the major social institutions of British society. As the Established Church, it was very much the church of the aristocracy, the old professions, and the middle classes.

Despite its official status, however, the Church of England is a denomination, not an ecclesia. It is a state church whose religious monopoly is limited by the existence of a substantial bloc of dissenting religion (Davie 1994). It has consistently sought to accommodate its practices to those of the leading Protestant denominations that have split from it over the years. Methodism, for example, has been particularly successful in attracting large numbers of working-class adherents, but the two churches have cooperated in a number of religious and secular activities

A majority of people in England in mid-century (just under two-thirds) continued to describe themselves as 'Church of England' when asked. A nominal affiliation to the Church was seen as a part of what it was to be 'English'. It was an expression of English national identity and allegiance to English social institutions (B. R. Wilson 1966: 24). Other religions in Britain had much

Surviving sects

Jehovah's Witnesses believe in the literal truth of the Bible. They hold that the world was actually created in seven days and that there will soon be an apocalyptic battle between God and Satan. The sect actively recruits new members through a door-to-door ministry.

Seventh Day Adventists believe that Jesus Christ will soon return to earth and will rule for 1,000 years. Founded in the 1840s when William Miller prophesied the end of the world, the sect is active in missionary work and has Saturday as its holy day.

smaller numbers of adherents. About one in ten people were Catholics, and there were similar numbers in the Church of Scotland. There were as many Jews as there were Catholics, and one in ten of the population were members of smaller nonconformist denominations. In 1966 these smaller denominations included about 700,000 Methodists, 280,000 Baptists, 200,000 Congregationalists, and about 250,000 people in total spread among the Unitarians, Presbyterians, Quakers, and the Salvation Army. Between 1 and 2 per cent of the population were affiliated to small sects, such as the Christian Scientists and the Jehovah's Witnesses. Religious pluralism was especially high in Wales, where there were many dissenting sects and denominations. As in England, however, religion was linked with national identity. The chapels were the carriers of a distinctively Welsh identity, nurturing generations of Liberal and Labour supporters and politicians.

Only a very few people were willing to describe themselves—at least in public—as non-religious. An opinion poll in the middle of the 1960s found just 6 per cent of the English population stating 'none' as their religion. Only 9 per cent claimed that they had no belief in a 'spirit, god or life-force'. Almost a half of the people (43 per cent) claimed that they said regular prayers, and the majority wished to retain religious instruction in schools (Forster 1972).

Britain was a nominally Christian nation, and for the majority it was an Anglican nation. Although the level of emotional commitment to religion was low, involvement in the major rituals of the Christian calendar persisted. Church services were important markers of various critical stages in the life course. Two-thirds of all children were baptized into the Church of England between 1885 and 1950, and a quarter of the population in the early 1960s had been confirmed into the Church. One fifth of children attended Sunday school over the period from 1895 to 1940. In this period the marriage

rate was high and marriage in church was very common. The proportion of church marriages declined from the high level of 70–80 per cent that it achieved between 1850 and 1880. Nevertheless, over a half of all marriages were still being solemnized in the Church of England until after the Second World War.

RELIGION IN THE UNITED STATES

While England had a national church, and there were similar institutions in Scotland and Wales, this was not the case in the United States. While the US Constitution guaranteed religious freedom for all its citizens, it gave no privileged position to any denomination. Political differences in the United States did not, therefore, take a religious form—there were no nonconformist or dissenting churches that could link religious opposition to an established religion with political opposition to an established state (Tocqueville 1835–40). The numerous religions that migrant settlers brought from their home countries to the United States all found their place within a strong pluralistic structure. Some of the older Protestant sects did retain a sectarian form, though they have often found it difficult to survive. The Shakers, for example, have died out, while the Amish have been much reduced in numbers.

Despite their different histories, Britain and the United States have moved towards similar forms of denominational pluralism (B. R. Wilson 1966: ch. 6). Levels of church membership in the United States have been higher than in Britain, however, and church involvement has substantially increased since the turn of the century. Twenty per cent of the US population were church members in 1880, and by 1962 the figure had increased to 63 per cent. Membership of Protestant denominations, for example, increased from 27 per

Declining sects

Shakers originated in the United States in the eighteenth century. They were celibate communities that lived apart from the rest of society and followed a simple life. They originally practised religious activities that involved shaking, trembling, or convulsions. There are no longer any Shaker communities, and they are now famous for their highly valued antique furniture, produced in their communities to simple, clean designs.

Amish originated in a Swiss sect of Anabaptists in the seventeenth century. They now live in isolated communities in Pennsylvania and the mid-West. They maintain a strict Puritan lifestyle, living apart from the world in isolated communities. Contemporary 'Old Order' Amish still dress in the same way as their founders and they make no use of modern technology such as cars and televisions (Sim 1994).

cent of the population in 1926 to 35 per cent in 1950. The number of Catholics increased from 16 per cent to 23 per cent over the same period. Until well into the post-war period, almost a half of all Americans attended church every week.

The religious melting pot

These high levels of church attendance and membership do not mean, however, that the United States is not a secular society. An important study by Herberg (1955) showed that mainstream religions in the United States were losing their specifically theological character and were coming to be more closely identified with a sense of national identity. Herberg traces this to the particular experience of migration in the United States.

The United States is a nation of migrants. Successive waves of migrants arrived with their specific ethnic identity and religious affiliation. There was never a single, dominant denomination, and nor was there a single, dominant ethnic group. While the great bulk of all nineteenth- and twentieth-century migrants were white, they were ethnically diverse: there were Germans, Poles, Irish, Dutch, Norwegians, Russians, and many others. This produced what has been called an ethnic 'melting pot' (Glaser and Moynihan 1963). While first-generation migrants retained strong emotional ties to their home countries, second- and third-generation migrants tried to forge stronger identities for themselves as Americans and identified themselves closely with the social institutions of American public life.

Central to the American way of life—or so it seemed to the newcomers—was regular churchgoing, and members of the ethnic minorities sought acceptance by mainstream American society through their own churchgoing. At church, they met those who had already successfully completed the process of migration and settlement, and they could get much needed practical help, including help with the language. Most importantly, they could acquire a sense of belonging in their new society. In their dealings with others, religious differences were minimized, as they built a shared sense of being religious and, therefore, of being 'American'.

Commitment to a church was a matter of practical commitment to the American way of life and American national identity. It was not a sign of high levels of religious faith or devotion. High levels of church membership and attendance, then, went hand in hand with secularization. Religions in the United States were disengaged and American society was disenchanted. It was the particular situation of the United States as a nation

of migrants that led to such high levels of church involvement in a secular society. Churchgoing was an expression of one's citizenship, of being a 'good American'. To be a good American did not, however, require adherence to any particular religion. Someone could be a good American by being a good Protestant, a good Catholic, or a good Jew.

The various denominations identified themselves with the American state and society and the American way of life. As a result, the moral teachings of the principal religions became more and more similar, and their theologies became looser and more liberal in character. Once religiosity is identified with national identity in this way, a withdrawal from or denial of religion comes to be seen as a withdrawal from or denial of the American way of life. People are locked in to high levels of church attendance and to the public espousal of religious values. To do anything else would be 'un-American'. Churchgoing strengthens a sense of national community. It reinforces the symbolically bounded imagined community that unites all together in a common activity and with a common identity.

CIVIL RELIGION

In both Britain and the United States there has been a close association between religion and national identity. In Britain, this took the form of the nominal affiliation of a majority of the population to the Church of England. In the United States, it took the form of high levels of church attendance. This identification of religion and national community has led many sociologists to suggest that secular societies can be seen as organized around a characteristic pattern of **civil religion**.

In a civil religion, the secular world itself has a sacred character (Bellah 1967, 1970; Bocock 1974; see also Warner 1953). Secularized religions of this kind are a result of the partial, but not complete disenchantment of the modern world. Despite growing disenchantment, modern societies have been able to rely on a residue of traditional attachment to established social institutions. The traditional symbolism of national identity provides a common cultural framework for all members of society, cutting across differences between particular denominations. The nation itself can become an object of religious veneration, and distinctive civic rituals are focused on it. Presidential Inaugurations, Thanksgiving, Independence Day, Veteran's Day, and other public occasions in the United States, for example, provide opportunities for the expression and reaffirmation of a sense of shared national identity and commitment.

Bellah, like Herberg, sees the United States as having been united by a religious belief in the sacred character of Americanism and a consequent loyalty to the American nation. God is almost seen as being American. Where children's prayers end with 'God bless Mummy and Daddy', political speeches end with 'God bless America'. Saintly figures from American history have been central to the maintenance of American values. The story of Abraham Lincoln's rise 'from the log cabin to the White House', for example, is central to the mythology of America as an open, classless society and to the maintenance of the 'American Dream'.

Involvement in civic rituals is a way in which existing religious organizations can maintain a role for themselves in a secular society. In Britain, for example, the Church of England remains the nationally Established Church. It is closely involved in major parliamentary occasions and in the celebration and commemoration of national values and events. The Royal Family has for long been associated with the civic rituals of the major national occasions. Many specific rituals surround the Royal Family itself: the Coronation, the Queen's Birthday, the Christmas speech, the Trooping of the Colours, the State Opening of Parliament, Remembrance Day, and so on. The link between the nation, the monarch, and the Church has been central to the legitimation of the state.

This view of religion and ritual in British society was first explored in an influential article on the Coronation of Queen Elizabeth II in 1953 (Shils and Young 1953). The Coronation was seen as one of a number of occasions—others might be royal weddings—in which a sense of national community could be affirmed and the basic moral values of the society reinforced. The Coronation of 1953 was the first major televised spectacular in which a large mass audience could simultaneously participate in the same civic ritual. Twenty million viewers watched seven hours of live coverage of the Coronation. Even in 1981, 39 million people watched the televised wedding of the Prince of Wales, and there was a doubling in sales of video recorders.

The idea of civil religion offers, perhaps, the best framework for understanding the religious character of Soviet Communism that we mentioned earlier. The Marxist-Leninist creed identified the revolutionary role of the proletariat with the Soviet state and its leaders, and many public ceremonials and rituals reinforced its moral values and legitimated its power (C. Lane 1981). Public occasions were marked by the parading of portraits of Communist leaders as national symbols from

> ☞ **You will find it useful to look at what we say about national identity in Chapter 12, pp. 451–3. Pay particular attention to the idea of nationalism as allegiance to an imagined community.**
>
>   **The situation that we are describing is that which existed in its strongest form until the 1960s. How far do you think it still applies to Britain? How have the personal problems of the Royal Family affected the Church of England and its role in civil religion? What does public reaction to the death and funeral of Diana, Princess of Wales, tell us about religious beliefs and attitudes towards the monarchy.**

Public reaction to the death of Diana, Princess of Wales: an aspect of civil religion?

the Communist past. On the anniversary of the Communist Revolution, the major national event of the year, lengthy military and industrial parades marched past the political leaders in their enclosure above Lenin's mausoleum. The Red Flag, the Red Army, and Red Square were the symbols of Soviet identity.

It is important not to overemphasize the consensual character of civil religions (K. Thompson 1992). For many people, involvement in public ceremonies and rituals reflects a pragmatic acceptance of them rather than any kind of normative commitment. In a disenchanted society, people may not be individually and genuinely committed, in terms of their personal and private beliefs, to the moral authority of political leaders and national symbols. They may, nevertheless, conform to the rituals and observances as public acts, and as part of the routine of their daily lives. This conformity may reflect the power of taken-for-granted attitudes, or the wish not to deviate from what is taken to be public opinion. It may result from calculations of personal advantage, or it may be enforced by coercive political authorities (Abercrobie *et al.* 1979).

 We look at the political structure of the Soviet Union in greater detail in 'Totalitarianism and Command Societies', in Chapter 17, pp. 703–8. You may like to return to our discussion of civil religion when you read that chapter. What evidence is there from television and newspapers of a civil religion in the new post-Communist Russia?

SUMMARY POINTS

In this section of the chapter we have looked at patterns of secularization in modern society. We began by looking at the concept of secularization itself.

▶ Secularization can be seen in terms of the two processes of disengagement and disenchantment.

▶ In Europe, secularization involved a transition from the Catholic ecclesia to a situation of denominational pluralism. Many denominations evolved from earlier sects.

▶ In modern societies, religious belief has become more of a private matter and, therefore, a matter of choice. Religious activities have to compete with the other activities among which individuals must choose to allocate their time.

We then turned to reviewing religious practices and beliefs in Britain and the United States from the middle of the nineteenth century to the 1960s.

▶ There was a decline in religious participation in Britain, but a majority of the population continued to see themselves as nominal members of the Church of England.

▶ There was an increase in religious participation in the United States, where a nation of migrants saw church membership as a symbol of American national identity.

▶ Religious patterns in both Britain and the United States can be seen in terms of the idea of civil religion, a secularized form of religion that identifies religion with national identity.

THE RISE OF NEW RELIGIONS

In the previous section we traced patterns of religious belief and practice up to the 1960s. As in so many other areas, the 1960s were a turning point for religion. Since then old and established forms of religion have declined, and those that have prospered have done so by adapting their beliefs and practices to the new times. Moreover, civil religion has weakened, and now exists in only a very feeble form. The residue of traditional social attachment on which it could trade in the past has continued to decline in the face of growing disenchantment. Traditional authority in the state and other social institutions is increasingly difficult to sustain, and, with the decay of tradition, so civil religion is weakened. At the same time, however, new religious sects and cults have multiplied. While the scale of religious involvement remains quite low, new forms of religion have become an important element in the lives of many people.

BELONGING AND BELIEVING

The post-war period in Britain has seen a continued decline in church membership and attendance. Although church involvement in the United States remains higher than in Britain, membership is no longer growing and attendance seems to be falling. There has been a considerable weakening of religious belonging. People are now less likely to belong to organized religions or to be actively involved in their rituals and practices. There has not, however, been a comparable decline in religious belief. The majority of people continue to subscribe to broadly religious beliefs, though their adherence is very loose. Their beliefs are not tied to particular doctrines or practices and they are a matter of only very low-key adherence.

For many people, then, religious belief is a real, but rather unimportant part of their lives that has no particular significance for their moral or political attitudes. For a minority, however, the common religion does not suffice. These are the people who are attracted into active and reinvigorated Protestant sects or into new, non-Christian forms of cult religion. In this section we will look at trends in religious behaviour and the nature of the common religion, and we will then turn to a discussion of the variety of new religions.

From civil religion to common religion

The proportion of the British population who actually belong to a Christian church fell from 19 per cent in 1970 to 12 per cent in 1990. This was less than a half the level that it had been at the turn of the century. About two-thirds of church members were Protestants and one-third were Catholics. Just under 4 per cent of the adult population were active members of the Church of England in 1990 (Bruce 1995: 37). Only one-fifth of the population now attend church at least once each month. Some estimates have put this figure even lower, though a survey in 1978 found just over a third of English Catholics to be regular church attenders.

Church membership and attendance are highest among older women and among non-manual workers than they are, in general, among men and manual workers. Among those who see themselves as 'frequent' or 'regular' church attenders, two-thirds are women. Among Protestants, members of the Anglican denominations (the Church of England, the Church in Wales, the Episcopal Church in Scotland, and the Church of Ireland) were in a minority. The great majority of active Protestants are members of Presbyterian, Methodist, or Baptist denominations (Davie 1990). Church membership remains particularly high in Northern Ireland,

among both Catholics and Protestants. About a quarter of Catholics in England are first-generation migrants from Northern Ireland or the Republic.

Britain has one of the lowest levels of church membership in Europe. Although comparative figures are notoriously difficult to compile, it seems that around 15 per cent of the adult British population are members of one church or another, compared with just over 20 per cent in France and Denmark, and around 30 per cent in Finland and Norway. Overt religious activity is still very high in the United States. Over two-thirds of the population of the United States claim to be church members, and just over a half of the population still attends a church at least once each month.

Figures 9.1 and 9.2 show some recent trends in church membership and church allegiance in Britain. A comparison of the two tables brings out clearly the discrepancy between the numbers claiming a nominal

Figure 9.1. Active membership in Christian Churches, United Kingdom, 1975–1992

Church	1975	1985	1992
Anglican	2,297,571	2,016,593	1,808,174
Roman Catholic	2,518,955	2,204,165	2,044,911
Presbyterian	1,641,520	1,384,997	1,242,406
Other Protestants	1,345,273	1,318,644	1,346,951
Orthodox	196,850	223,686	275,805
Total	8,000,169	7,148,085	6,718,247

Source: Davie (1994: 46, table 4.1).

Figure 9.2. Expressed Church allegiance, United Kingdom, 1975–1995

Church	Allegiance (millions)		
	1975	1985	1995 (est.)
Anglican	27.2	27.0	26.7
Roman Catholic	5.5	5.6	5.6
Presbyterian	1.9	1.7	1.5
Other Protestants	3.2	3.1	3.3
Orthodox	0.4	0.4	0.5
Total	38.2	37.8	37.6
Scientology	0.1	0.3	0.4
Hindus	0.3	0.4	0.4
Jews	0.4	0.3	0.3
Muslims	0.4	0.9	1.1
Sikhs	0.2	0.3	0.6
Others	0.6	0.8	0.9
Total	2.0	3.0	3.7
Totals	40.2	3.0	3.7

Source: Davie (1994: 48, table 4.2).

▶ How do you think a question on religious allegiance might have been worded for this survey?
▶ Is it useful to study religious beliefs using survey methods?

adherence to a religion and the numbers who are actively involved as members of one or another church. About 40 million people in 1995 claimed to have some kind of religious allegiance, over a half of them claiming to be Anglican. Very few of these nominal Anglicans were active members or attended church regularly. It would seem that only about one in twenty of those who claim to be Anglicans are actually members of the Church. This discrepancy was less marked for other denominations. In most cases, about a half or more of their adherents were active members.

The Anglican and Catholic churches both lost large numbers of members between 1975 and 1992. The Protestant sects and denominations have held up slightly better than the Anglicans. Nevertheless, the Baptists lost 20 per cent of their members between 1970 and 1990, and the Methodists and the Presbyterians have each lost 25 per cent. Among Christian churches, only the Orthodox Church has shown an increase in numbers, largely as a result of migration over the period.

The proportion of children who were baptized into the Church of England had fallen to a half by 1960. This figure had stood at two-thirds between 1885 and 1950. By 1993 the figure had dropped to only just over a quarter. Less than one in ten children were then attending Sunday school, compared with one in five during the period from 1895 to 1940. There was also a decline in church marriages, as couples became more willing to have a civil ceremony. One-third of English marriages were civil marriages in the period from 1952 to 1962, compared with one quarter in 1929 and just one in eight in 1879 (Wilson 1966: ch. 1). By 1990, however, almost a half of all marriages took place in a register office rather than a church, and marriage itself had become less popular (see Chapter 10, pp. 374–8).

These falls in membership and attendance have been associated with organizational changes for the churches. The number of Church of England vicars declined from over 20,000 in 1900 to less than 10,000 in 1990, and the number of Methodist ministers declined from 3,800 to 2,500 over the same period. The number of Catholic priests in England and Wales, by contrast, increased for a while as the number of migrants from Eire and Northern Ireland also increased. It has now fallen back in line with declining membership. In Scotland, the number of ministers in Presbyterian denominations has fallen from 3,600 to less than 1,500 (Bruce 1995: 32–3).

These trends show, then, a decline in religious *belonging*, as measured by conventional churchgoing and church involvement. They do not, however, give any direct evidence of a decline in religious *believing* (Davie 1994). In fact, religious belief appears to remain quite strong. A survey carried out in the 1980s found that 76 per cent of people in Great Britain believed in God, 50 per cent engaged in regular prayer, and only 4 per cent described themselves as atheists. In 1990, 71 per cent claimed to believe in God, 53 per cent prayed or meditated, and 44 per cent said that they drew personal strength from their religious beliefs. Fifty-three per cent of people believed in 'Heaven', and 25 per cent believed in 'the Devil' and in 'Hell' (Davie 1994: 79, see also Jowell *et al.* 1991). In a survey in 1995, only 11 per cent said that they definitely did not believe in God, while 21 per cent had no doubts at all about the existence of God (see Figure 9.3). During 1996, the then leaders of all three major political parties claimed that they prayed regularly to God.

In the United States, religious belief seems to be somewhat higher. A massive 95 per cent of the population claim to believe in God. In many cases, Americans subscribe to creationist ideas that run counter to the conclusions of contemporary science. In the early 1980s, a survey reported that 44 per cent of Americans believed that God had created human beings within the last 10,000 years.

Though most people in Britain and the United States describe their religious beliefs as 'Christian', they are not those of conventional Christianity. For many people, Christian and non-Christian ideas have been fused into loose and amorphous systems of personal belief. They claim no specific biblical or priestly authority for these beliefs, regarding them as things that they simply accept or have worked out for themselves. Forty two per cent of those who believed in God saw this god

---

Figure 9.3. Belief in God, Great Britain, 1995

	(%)
Do not believe in God	11
Do not know if God exists and cannot find evidence for God's existence	15
Believe in a higher power of some kind	12
Believe sometimes	12
Doubt, but believe	23
God exists, with no doubts	21
Can't choose/not answered	7
	100

Source: *Social Trends* (1997: table 13.23).

as 'some sort of spiritual or vital force' rather than as the personal God of traditional Christianity (Bruce 1995: 50).

Beliefs in a god are directly and closely linked with 'superstitious' beliefs and practices and with beliefs in astrology, psychic phenomena, ghosts, and paranormal experiences. Just under a quarter of the British population in 1991 believed that good-luck charms were effective, just over a quarter believed in the accuracy of horoscopes, and 40 per cent believed in the powers of fortune tellers (Jowell *et al.* 1991). For many people, these beliefs were held alongside beliefs in alternative medicine, the power of crystals, and reflexology.

This was true also of those who identified themselves as Catholics, a significant number of whom held unorthodox beliefs or rejected certain aspects of traditional Catholicism. These 'heterodox Catholics' formed a majority among Catholic non-attenders at Church. They were younger than the average English Catholic—two-thirds of them were under 35—and they were more likely to be second or later generation than recent migrants. A survey of their attitudes concluded that they might never have been anything more than nominal Catholics (Hornsby-Smith *et al.* 1982; see also Hornsby-Smith 1987, 1991).

Organized religion, both conventional denominational religion and state-orientated civil religion, is no longer a major factor in the lives of most people. Those religious beliefs that they do retain are loose and free-floating and are not organized into any formal participation in churches or rituals. Mainstream religious belief in Britain is no longer tied to conventional Christianity or to regular church attendance. What Davie (1994) has termed the common religion is a non-sectarian and eclectic form of religious belief. People 'continue to believe in God, but . . . are reluctant to express this belief in either churchgoing or church membership' (Davie 1990). Their conception of God, furthermore, bears little relationship to the scriptural God of the Christian tradition. The common religion is a private system of belief that draws on a pool of shared ideas that derive from both Christian and non-Christian sources.

What is striking, however, is that the common religion has no significant moral implications for how people should live in society. There is some sign of a growing sense of the environmental implications of these religious beliefs—of the need to protect the earth and its natural resources—but there is no equivalent sense of any need to build or to defend particular kinds of social order. The common religion does not provide the moral bonds and regulations that were central to traditional religion. In a secular society, the uncommitted mainstream religion of the vast majority of the population is a sprawling and amorphous array of beliefs that form a framework of taken-for-granted ideas that, for most people, are an integral, if rather marginal, aspect of their day-to-day lives. This raises the question of whether such collective beliefs can still be said to constitute 'religious' beliefs in the fullest sense of the term.

What is religion?

The idea of the common religion raises questions about the definition of religion. What do you think about this? Look back at the definition given on p. 319 at the beginning of the chapter. You might like to talk to friends and family about their beliefs to see if they are similar to those described here.

Varieties of new religion

The common religion is a widely shared framework of ideas, but for many people it is not enough. Nor does the more general framework of moral individualism meet their need for truly spiritual values. Some of these seekers after the sacred have turned to more fundamental forms of traditional Christianity, but others have found a greater appeal in new religions. The number of these new religions, both Christian and non-Christian, has increased since the Second World War, in both Britain and the United States. This growth has been especially rapid since the 1960s. These new religions are often described as cults, though this term has been given a wide variety of meanings.

In the original definition given by Troeltsch (1912), the **cult** was contrasted with the sect. Troeltsch defined the cult as a loosely organized grouping without sharp boundaries and with no exclusive system of beliefs. Cult beliefs are not rigid and exclusive; they are open and flexible. They comprise a set of common themes and ideas, and individual members are able to contribute their personal views to the pool of ideas. A cult is very open to new recruits, it is tolerant towards other beliefs, and it makes no demand that its members should completely abandon their other beliefs. Many people today, for example, adhere to cult beliefs in UFOs and alien abductions. These beliefs are remarkably diverse, and those who adhere to such beliefs are united by little more than their common concern and interest. There is no central organization or rigidly codified and enforced set of beliefs.

Cults are often short-lived. They depend upon the personal leadership of a founder or key member, and they dissolve when this leader dies. An example of a long-lasting cult is spiritualism, which has drawn its adherents from the membership of many churches, as well as from those who are members of none (Nelson 1969). Troeltsch argued that, if a cult can establish a more secure base of recruitment, it can establish a more permanent organization. Such a cult may even develop into an ecclesia, as happened when early cult Christianity was taken up by the Roman emperor and became the Roman Catholic Church. On the other hand, however, cults may remain apart from political and economic power and evolve into sects.

The word 'cult' has also been used in popular discussions, but here it tends to be a derogatory term. For many people, then, a cult is a contemporary religious organization, often a tight and exclusive sect, whose aims and methods they reject. Cults are accused of brainwashing or kidnapping those who join them, and they are often accused of financial, sexual, or political deviance. Because the original sociological meaning of cult has been obscured by its contemporary popular use as a label for religious deviance, many sociologists now prefer to use the more neutral term 'new religious movement'. This term, too, can be a little misleading, as all religions were, at some stage, new, and many of the growing religions of the 1960s have long-established roots.

The established Christian and non-Christian denominations and sects—Methodists, Baptists, the Reformed Church (Presbyterian and Congregationalist), Anglicans, Catholics, Jews, Spiritualists, Mormons, Jehovah's Witnesses, and the Salvation Army—have, in general, continued to decline in numbers or have, at best, maintained their membership through active proselytizing. The big growth in numbers of members and believers has largely occurred among those sects that have returned to or have emphasized the fundamental beliefs of their faith and those religions that have based themselves on radically new sets of ideas that are often non-theistic in character.

In the rest of this chapter, we will look at the four main forms of religion in which there has been a growth of activity. They are:

▶ inspirational Protestantism;

▶ world-rejecting religions;

▶ world-affirming religions;

▶ religions of ethnic protest.

Inspirational Protestantism comprises a number of fundamentalist, reformed, and evangelical sects and denominations that have split from the established denominations or that have been set up in direct opposition to them. Examples are the Pentecostalist churches and the Southern Baptist Convention. World-rejecting religions are a variety of generally non-Christian sects and cults that reject established religion and many aspects of modern society. They adopt a 'utopian' or millennial point of view. Examples are the Unification Church and Krishna Consciousness. World-affirming religions, on the other hand, include a variety of sects and cults that embrace the values of modern society. They aim to provide their members with better means to achieve them. Examples are Scientology and Transcendental Meditation. Finally, religions of ethnic protest are religions of migrants and

Sect and cult

We have identified four concepts that form a typology of religious organizations. These are ecclesia, denomination, sect, and cult. Review the definitions of ecclesia and denomination on p. 327.

A sect is characterized by:

▶ a claim to a monopoly of religious truth;

▶ voluntary, not compulsory membership;

▶ a high level of emotional commitment;

▶ non-hierarchical forms of leadership.

In so far as the concept of a cult can still be used in its original sociological sense, it refers to religious groups that are characterized by:

▶ great openness to all who wish to join;

▶ loosely defined beliefs and concerns;

▶ non-institutionalized forms of leadership.

ethnic minorities who have been excluded from full participation in the mainstream of modern society. The religion becomes a means of protest and opposition to their exclusion and oppression. Examples are Rastafarianism and some contemporary forms of Islam.

INSPIRATIONAL PROTESTANTISM

Those who are attracted to inspirational Protestantism do so in reaction to the increasingly liberal religious attitudes of the mainstream Protestant denominations. As we have shown, Protestant beliefs have encouraged and reinforced the tendency to secularization, and this has meant that the beliefs of the Protestant denominations themselves have been marked by a disenchantment. To those who look for traditional religious beliefs, the Protestant denominations have little to offer. In moving in an increasingly liberal direction, the Protestant denominations have estranged many of their own adherents.

These people decry the loss of any distinctively religious content in the teachings of the churches. They resent the abandonment of what they still regard as religious certainties, especially when it is bishops and other senior leaders of the churches who seem to be denying the central tenets of their belief. When, in the early 1990s, the Bishop of Durham gave a rational, liberal interpretation of the Virgin birth, many of the most active members of the Church felt that he was no longer speaking as a truly Christian clergyman.

Those who retain traditional Christian beliefs lose confidence in a church that they see as moving rapidly away from them in an increasingly secular direction. They reject attempts to be relevant to contemporary concerns and to update the liturgy and rituals. They disapprove of the translation of the Bible into contemporary English. The involvement of the churches in social work and political controversies is seen as a departure from their primary purpose of preaching the gospels. The Protestant denominations have lost members, at least in part, because their liberal beliefs are out of line with the more conservative religious beliefs and attitudes of many of their members. These disaffected Protestants are attracted to the more fundamentalist Protestant sects that have managed to increase their memberships in recent years. These sects have prospered by retaining traditional beliefs in an increasingly secular age. As Bruce (1983: 466) has argued, 'The group of Protestants who do most to preserve their faith from the ravages of the secular world have survived the last

quarter century in better shape than have those who argued for compromise with the modern world.'

Most of the Presbyterian denominations in both Scotland and Northern Ireland, for example, have experienced declining membership over the course of the century. The more conservative Free Presbyterian Churches, however, have experienced huge increases in membership since the middle of the 1950s. Ian Paisley's Free Presbyterians have built up a massive 10,000 membership in Northern Ireland since its formation in 1951, its role as the defender of the 'loyalist' ethnicity of Ulster Protestants having helped to strengthen its appeal (Bruce 1983).

The Protestant sects that have attracted this growth in membership have been the inspirational sects and we now need to look a little closer at the nature of inspirational Protestantism and those who support it.

Fundamentalism and Pentecostalism

Two principal forms of inspirational Protestantism can be identified in Britain and the United States. These are fundamentalism and Pentecostalism. Fundamentalists adopt a particularly conservative attitude towards their religion. They subscribe to the Protestant reliance on the Bible as the direct word of God and, therefore, as the fundamental source of all knowledge, and they hold that its meaning is self-evident to all who read it. The Bible requires no interpretation by priests or others: it is not allegorical or mythical, it is literally true. God's will and the truth of human creation are claimed to be discoverable by a simple and direct reading of the Bible.

Things are not, of course, this simple, as no text can be understood in a strictly literal sense, without interpretation. The meaning of the Bible, or, indeed, of any other text, is far from straightforward. This is clear from the fact that there are divergent forms of biblical fundamentalism. There are, for example, differences between reformed and evangelical Protestantism. Calvinist or Reformed Protestants believe in a doctrine of predestination according to which only a small group of the elect are destined for salvation. Evangelical forms of fundamentalism, on the other hand, encourage people to choose God and, through being 'born again', to *achieve* salvation.

In reality, then, fundamentalism must rely on the authoritative interpretations given to the Bible by the preachers and teachers who have played a leading role in the social organization and development of the particular sects. Fundamentalists are inspired by the direct word of God, as recorded in the Bible, but they must rely on charismatic, inspiring preachers to guide their reading. Fundamentalist readings of the Bible are attractive to those who, by prior belief or social background, are predisposed towards conservative responses to its message.

Pentecostal Christians also subscribe to the literal truth of the Bible, but they combine this with an over-riding emphasis on personal religious experiences, such as spiritual possession, speaking with tongues, healing, and the working of miracles (Bruce 1985). In this kind of religion, the word of God in the Bible is supplemented by the direct voice of God. Pentecostalists believe that they can learn God's wishes for them through opening their hearts and minds to His spirit. They believe that they can learn from direct spiritual inspiration and from observing the religious experiences and inspiration of others in their church.

Large numbers of Pentecostalists in Britain are African-Caribbean. First-generation migrants arrived in Britain in the 1950s with more conservative religious attitudes than most of the white population. They were particularly attracted by Pentecostalism. It has been estimated that 17 per cent of African-Caribbeans attend church regularly, about four-fifths of them attending Pentecostal churches. Pryce (1986) has shown the high level of support for Pentecostalism in the area of Bristol that he studied. African-Caribbeans in Bristol reported that they were oppressed as both black and working class. Their religion helped them to minimize the significance of this oppression while they awaited sal-

vation in the next world. Black Pentecostalism, then, is a form of *cultural defence* (Bruce 1995: 78) for African-Caribbean ethnicity.

The new Christian right

The social and political influence of fundamentalism grew particularly rapidly in the United States during the 1960s and 1970s. Underlying this growth was a feeling that a weakening of the civil religion and an associated spiritual decline in American society into permissiveness and moral relativism was something that needed to be reversed through a reassertion of traditional Christian values. Moral individualism, also, was felt to be unsatisfying in itself because it lacked the enchantment and spirituality of traditional religion. Specific targets were the liberal intellectuals who were seen as responsible for this spiritual decline.

This demand for moral revival emerged in what Bruce has called conservative social milieux or subcultures. These are loose networks of individuals and organizations that are united by shared beliefs and values but are not formed into any single organization or political movement (Bruce 1984: chs. 3 and 7). These milieux are particularly strong in the Southern states, but they extend nation-wide. Those who live in the conservative milieux build supporting institutions that strengthen it and allow it to extend its influence. Separate and distinct schools and colleges, for example, have allowed conservative Protestants to socialize their children away from the permissiveness and liberalism that they saw in the mainstream schools. Similarly, the publication of fundamentalist books, films, and music helps to enlarge the subculture of fundamentalism. Most recently, these cultural efforts have been solidified through radio and television evangelism. There are now a number of satellite and cable television channels dedicated to evangelistic Protestantism and its charismatic leaders.

Evangelical crusades have been of major significance in attracting new recruits to particular churches, and in preventing the sons and daughters of subcultural adherents from falling away from their faith. Conservative Protestant movements have, however, recruited mainly from those who were already predisposed towards traditional, conservative forms of religion. The principal recruits have been the children of people who were already associated with one or another of the conservative Protestant churches. The crusades have been occasions for reviving and revivifying the religious beliefs of those who are already predisposed towards conversion.

When existing religious world-views lose their plau-

Pentecostalism

According to the Bible, the Holy Spirit descended on the disciples on the fiftieth day (Greek *pente koste*) after the Passover festival. The Holy Spirit gave the disciples gifts of prophecy, healing, and speaking in foreign tongues. In the contemporary Christian calendar, this is celebrated at Whitsun.

Pentecostal churches believe that these gifts are still available to true believers, and their services are designed to create the conditions for this. Services involve loud and joyful singing and prayer, and members of the congregation may exhibit signs of the Spirit's 'gifts'. The Pentecostal movement began in the United States around 1900 and soon spread to Britain. The principal Pentecostal church in the United States is the Assemblies of God. In Britain, most Pentecostalists are members of the Elim Pentecostal Church or the Apostolic Church. There are also many independent black Pentecostalist churches.

Religious crusades

'The people who go forward are almost all the sons and daughters of believers. What they signify with such a move is not that they have found a new and previously alien belief-system convincing but rather that they have come to make a positive commitment to a set of beliefs with which they are already familiar.'

Source: Bruce (1984: 102).

sibility, many young people in the conservative milieux find the message of the fundamentalist churches attractive. This cultural affinity builds on the close personal links that they and their families have to the churches and other institutions of the subculture of fundamentalism. Personal social relations are also able to reinforce their commitment once their religious choice has been made. More than a half of all converts to the conservative Protestant churches are recruited between the ages of 12 and 20, and they have generally been introduced to the church through a parental Christian influence (Bruce 1984: 56–7). For these reasons, fundamentalist churches have made few converts from outside the milieux, and the evangelical crusades have not resulted in the mass conversion of the uncommitted.

It was from these conservative cultural milieux that the so-called new right emerged in the 1970s. Media evangelists were key figures in mobilizing cultural support for the Moral Majority, which was formed in 1979 as an organizational focus for the new Christian right. Conservative Protestants formed the leading members of the new right in the political sphere, though it also built its support through alliances with right-wing thinkers in the Catholic, Jewish, Mormon, and other churches. This movement built a large bloc of support that helped to secure the election of Ronald Reagan in his first term as President.

☞ **If you want to know more about the growth and influence of the new right in the United States and Britain, turn to Chapter 18, pp. 748–9.**

The processes that helped the formation of the new Christian right in the United States were much weaker in Britain. The conservative Protestant churches have, however, been the least likely to embrace the move to toleration and secularism in politics. Bruce has shown

that smaller religious organizations in Scotland and Northern Ireland, especially those with a predominantly working-class membership and a strong regional identity, have maintained a sectarian stance towards other churches and have opposed moves that would undermine their own particular identity (Bruce 1986). In Northern Ireland, conservative Protestantism has developed into a strong social force with an anti-Catholic character, and these fundamentalist churches have been particularly important social bases of support for the Orange Order, a Masonic body that pursues charitable and, above all, political goals. Orangeism in Northern Ireland, drawing widely in its recruitment from among the Protestant population, has been especially strongly shaped by the views of those associated with the conservative Protestant sects.

WORLD-REJECTING AND WORLD-AFFIRMING RELIGIONS

The religious needs of many people can no longer be met through any of the conventional forms of Christianity. They seek forms of religion that seem to be more in accord with contemporary life. To understand this, we can draw on the work of Merton, whose ideas on anomie we looked at in Chapter 2, pp. 49–50. Merton looked at the strains and tensions that can occur in cultural systems and at the varying responses that individuals may make to these. The growth of affluence and consumerism in the 1950s and 1960s generated two characteristic responses to the mainstream religious culture on the part of those who felt unable to achieve their goals through the conventional means available to them:

▶ *Retreatism*: this involves a rejection of the goals and means of the conventional society and a withdrawal from it;

▶ *Innovation*: this involves seeking out alternative ways of achieving the conventional goals.

Wallis (1984: 4–6, 9ff.) argued that each of these responses was associated with the growth of a particular kind of religion. Corresponding to the retreatist response are the **world-rejecting** religions that denigrate the central values and assumptions of the modern world. Examples of such religions are The International Society for Krishna Consciousness (ISKCON) and the Unification Church. ISKCON—popularly known as Hare Krishna—is based around a form of Hinduism that requires a particular ascetic and communal way of life from its followers. Corresponding to the innovative response are the **world-affirming** religions such as Transcendental Meditation (TM) and Scientology. These religions embrace many of the central cultural goals and values but claim to offer new means to achieve them. TM, founded by the Maharishi Mahesh Yogi, stresses the personal and practical benefits of regular meditation, while Scientology uses methods closer to psychotherapy.

Many of these religions take a cult form. They engage in worldly activities and allow people to drift in and out of participation as they sample the beliefs on offer. TM, for example, is associated with a political party (the Natural Law Party) that fights general elections on policies that advocate the benefits of TM and 'yogic flying' for solutions to individual and social problems. Even such groups as the Unification Church and Scientology, which are relatively closed to outsiders, do not typically hold onto their members for long periods.

Utopian religion and world rejection

World-rejecting, utopian religions grew rapidly in the 1960s, when many young people were attracted by retreatist responses. In the early 1960s this had been expressed in the hippie, drug-user subculture of American and European youth, which, as Jock Young (1971) showed, rejected the work ethic and the impersonality and bureaucracy of modern society. In place of these values, hippies emphasized spontaneity and hedonism. The subculture proved especially attractive to white, middle-class, college drop-outs. It was the perceived failure of hippie utopianism to achieve its aims that produced many recruits for new religions that offered more radical solutions. Those who identified with the values of the hippie culture, even if they had not directly experienced it, sought new ways of meeting its values of community and fellowship.

☞ **You might like to read the discussion of Jock Young's work in Chapter 5, pp. 174–5. This will give you an overview of the hippie subculture.**

These religions see present-day problems as symptoms of a departure from an authentic and more natural way of life, and their appeal derives not so much from the specific content of their beliefs as from the communal lifestyles with which the groups have been identified. Familiarity with the beliefs generally came *after* young people had joined the groups. Potential members have been attracted by the communal

Moonies

A characteristic world-rejecting religion is the Unification Church, popularly known as the 'Moonies' after its founder the Reverend Moon. Drawing on both Christian and Buddhist sources, the religion rejects the materialism of the contemporary world and advocates a disciplined, ascetic lifestyle. It requires that its members should give their income and assets over to the use of the church. Moonies see their task as bringing about a physical kingdom of God on earth that actualizes the spiritual kingdom that had been established by Jesus. The Reverend Moon is believed to be the new Messiah who leads adherents towards this goal. A good study is E. Barker (1984).

group solidarity that the religions espouse, and it is this—rather than brainwashing—that has tied people to them. These religious communities appeared to offer an escape from the impersonality of modern society and a solution to the perceived loss of community in the wider society.

These religions tend to have a clear and specific conception of a god or gods, regarded as the source of moral norms and obligations. They have a sense of their religious mission that is sometimes allied with a search for political influence and social change. Some, however, are millenarian. That is to say, they anticipate the destruction or collapse of the world, followed by their own salvation. The Children of God, for example, await the return of Jesus to save the world. Yet other groups anticipate the arrival of extra-terrestrial life forms (Festinger *et al.* 1956). What such groups tend to hold in common is a view that

'the prevailing social order . . . [has] departed substantially from God's prescriptions and plan. Mankind has lost touch with God and spiritual things and, in the pursuit of purely material interests, has succeeded in creating a polluted environment; a vice-ridden society in which individuals treat each other purely as means rather than ends; a world filled with conflict, greed, insincerity and despair. The world-rejecting movement condemns urban industrial society and its values, particularly that of individual success as measured by wealth or consumption patterns. It rejects the materialism of the advanced industrial world, calling for a return to a more rural way of life, and a reorientation of secular life.'   (Wallis 1984: 10)

The religions tend to organize themselves as total institutions, and there is a great emphasis on their separate, enclosed, and disciplined communal life. This often involves engaging in economic and fund-raising activities that help to provide for the group's own subsistence. Those religions that have been particularly successful in this and have become very wealthy have often attracted external criticism, especially when their wealth seems to provide extravagant lifestyles for the leadership.

Social control within the group operates mainly through a *persuasion* that draws on people's commitment to the group and their love for its leaders, its ideals, and their fellow members. In these circumstances, individual identity is subordinated to collective identity. Although the exercise of coercion over members is not usual, it does occur, and a degree of coercive control may be accepted by members as necessary to maintain the group in a hostile environment. In some extreme cases, suicide may be accepted as a necessary way to affirm the group's identity and beliefs when they are under threat from the outside. This is known to have been the case with the mass suicides of members of the Heaven's Gate group in San Diego in 1997, and it is thought to have played a major part in the destruction of the Branch Davidian group in Waco, Texas, in 1993. Durkheim (1897) called this fatalistic suicide.

The end of the long period of sustained affluence in the mid-1970s was marked by static or declining membership for the world-rejecting religions. In response, some of them became more world-accommodating in character and have since recruited older people. The term **world-accommodating** describes those religions that adopt an attitude of mild disapproval or of acceptance of the world as it is, rather than an attitude of complete rejection. In such groups, religious beliefs often come to be seen as separate from the principal activities of everyday life (Wallis 1984). As religions become world-accommodating, they tend to attack established religious organizations rather more than they do the secular world, and they recruit those who are searching for a more direct experience of the sacred than established religions can provide. The religions provide a feeling of certainty in a relativistic culture, and Wallis suggested that world-accommodation is the end-stage for all world-rejecting sects and cults.

Therapeutic religions and world affirmation

The second response that we identified to the mainstream religious culture is the innovative response of the world-affirming religions. These religions have a worldly character. That is to say, they embrace the goals and values of modern society. They combine their religious orientation with an acceptance of magical and manipulative techniques that allow their members to achieve conventional goals through unconventional means.

Many of these religions adopt a psychotherapeutic stance towards the solution of their members' problems, and they 'straddle a vague boundary between religion and psychology' (Wallis 1984: 35). They generally lack any developed theology or ritual, and their conception of God, if any, is that of a diffuse, universal force that manifests itself in individuals. They are oriented towards the perfectibility of the individual through specific therapeutic practices, and they work towards promoting individual achievement within the existing society. They might claim, for example, that they can unlock a person's potential by providing him or her with the appropriate discipline or training. These advantages are held to be open to anybody who joins the group and learns its techniques.

These religions have deeper roots and a more long-lasting base of recruitment than do the world-rejecting religions. They expanded considerably during the 1950s and 1960s, and they recruited from among relatively affluent people in their twenties and thirties who were seeking ways of helping themselves towards greater individual achievement, happiness, and success in a consumer society (B. R. Wilson 1966: 216).

While Scientology has tended to adopt a sectarian form of organization, the so-called New Age movement is a much looser world-affirming cult. It combines elements of Eastern religions with mythology and Jung's psychoanalysis to form a complex and diverse system of beliefs that embraces crystal healing, the use of essential oils, astrology, acupuncture, herbalism, dowsing, UFOs, Paganism, certain aspects of witchcraft, and various other strands. New Age ideas became especially popular in the 1980s, and they have had an impact on mainstream culture beyond its own adherents. Those who see themselves as part of the New Age movement promote their preferred therapies and ideas through advertising, setting up shops, and publishing books. These promotional activities bring non-believers into contact with the movement, and they have been behind the massive popularity of such techniques as aromatherapy. This technique, which involves the use of essential oils, appeals to those, for example, who are also attracted to the forms of alternative medicine and personal strategies of well-being that challenge the authority of medical experts.

Despite the growth in their numbers, the world-rejecting and world-accepting religions together comprise only a very small proportion of the population. The membership of any one group is tiny. There have, for example, never been more than 1,000 'Moonies' in

World-rejecting and world-affirming religions

	World-rejecting	World-affirming
Conception of god	Personal entity distinct from humanity	Element of every human life
Present world	Debased; its values all contrary to the ideal; in need of total transformation	Much to offer if one has the means to secure the good things available
Commitment required	Complete, including separation from family and career. Movement is a 'total institution'	Partial, a largely leisure-time pursuit while one continues one's activity in the world
Economic base	Wealth and labour of converts, supplemented by street solicitation of donations	Fees for goods and services marketed by the movement
Sexual morality	Ascetic (i.e. tightly regulating sexual activity) or antinomian (permitting promiscuous sexual relationships)	Largely indifferent to regulating general sexual conduct
Conversion	Rapid, abrupt after contact, attitude of 'surrender' required from outset	Typically a sequence of stages of progressive personal transformation
Leader	God's emissary or representative	Technical innovator
Social organization	Communal	Corporate
Examples	Unification Church ISKCON Children of God People's Temple Manson's Family	Transcendental Meditation Human Potential Movement Est (Erhard Seminars Training) Silva Mind Control Scientology

Source: Wallis (1984).

Britain. There are less than 500 members of ISKCON, and only a few hundred members of TM (E. Barker 1989).

RELIGIONS OF ETHNIC PROTEST

Religious beliefs have long played a central part in defining and developing ethnic identities. In many religions, a particular ethnic community is seen as being in some way special to the gods. Jewish holy texts, for example, define the Jews as the chosen people of God, and the indigenous religious beliefs of Japan trace the origins of the Japanese to *Ama-terasu*, the sun goddess. As A. Smith (1991: 7) has shown, for most of human history, religion and ethnic identity have been very closely entwined, each people having its own gods and sacred texts, and its distinctive religious practices, priests and places.

Migration into Britain and the births of second- and later-generation members of migrant families have altered the religious mix. Migrants from the Caribbean, as we have shown, brought conservative Protestant religions with them, but migrants from elsewhere have brought about an expansion of non-Christian religions. Those from India, Pakistan, Bangladesh, and East Africa

Scientology

A characteristic world-affirming religion is Scientology. Founded by the science fiction writer L. Ron Hubbard, Scientology draws on psychotherapy to provide practices and techniques that alter the consciousness of its members and enable them to act in more positive and effective ways to achieve their worldly goals: a better job, a higher income, or greater happiness in what they are doing. It claims to give its members spiritual powers, such as the ability to see, hear, and manipulate people and objects at great distances, purely by mental forces. The religion works through training and therapy sessions in closed communities, but it has many similarities to a conventional business operation: recruits pay fees for their training and counselling, and many full-time workers are employed to manage the church. An enquiry in the 1990s alleged widespread financial fraud on the part of the church. A good description is in Wallis (1976).

Scientology recruits new members through high street operations such as this one in London.

have swelled the numbers of Hindus, Muslims, Sikhs, Jews, and others. This religious diversity is increased by the divisions that exist within each religion. About one in ten British Muslims are Shi'as, while most of the rest are Sunnis. The Sunnis, however, are divided into Barelwi, Deoband, and Tablghi Jamaat branches. Similarly, Hindus are divided into loose traditions, as well as being divided by caste (Bruce 1995: 79 ff.).

There are now more than one million Muslims in Britain, there are just under a half a million Hindus, and there are the same number of Sikhs. Membership of these religions has tripled since 1970. The state has long financed denominational schools—through the system of voluntary aid—for Anglicans, Catholics, Methodists, and Jews, and there is a growing demand for similar support for Muslims.

Growth in the numbers of those affiliated to ethnic minority religions is not, however, what is meant by the term religions of ethnic protest. A multi-ethnic, multi-religion society is an essential condition for the emergence of religions of ethnic protests, but it is not the same thing. Religions of ethnic protest are those that have grown within particular ethnic-minority communities and are used by their members to voice their protest at their exclusion, on the grounds of their ethnicity, from full participation in their society.

 You will probably find it useful to remind yourself about what we say on ethnicity and ethnic identity in Chapter 4, pp. 143–5. You will also find useful our discussion of ethnicity and national identity in Chapter 12, pp. 452–3. Finally, you might want to read 'Migration and Demographic Divisions', Chapter 6, pp. 200–2.

Islam

Islam is a monotheistic religion that shares much of the old testament tradition with Jews and Christians. Its main beliefs, however, are contained in the Qu'ran, which contains the teachings of the sixth- to seventh-century prophet Muhammad. The Qu'ran is seen as the revealed will of God (Allah). It has no priestly hierarchy or authoritative interpretation of its orthodoxy, and no distinction is made between the spheres of religion and politics. Sunni Muslims are the more orthodox, while Shi'ahs have added to the original teachings of Muhammad. About one-fifth of the world's population is nominally Muslim. The largest areas of settlement are in the Middle East, the Indian subcontinent, South East Asia, Turkey, and West Africa. The largest single community is found in Indonesia. In Western Europe, the largest numbers of Muslims are in France, mainly migrants from north and west Africa, with smaller groups in Britain and Germany.

Reciting the Qu'ran is an important part of Muslim religious practices.

Rastafarianism and the Nation of Islam

The two most characteristic religions of ethnic protest in contemporary Britain are Rastafarianism and the Nation of Islam.

The deeply felt experience of deprivation and exclusion that is found in the poor, inner-city districts of Britain where many African-Caribbean people are forced to live contrasts sharply with the optimistic expectations of the migrants who arrived in Britain during the 1950s and 1960s. Many of the first generation, as we have shown, have given voice to their situation through inspirational Protestantism. Those of the second and third generations—like their young white counterparts—have sought answers in newer and more

radical forms of religion. Among these people, Rastafarianism has had a particularly strong appeal, as its social ethic seems to talk directly to their experiences.

Membership grew particularly during the 1970s with the success of the singer Bob Marley and the popularization of reggae. Its musical style, along with its style of dress and the use of cannabis (ganja), have sprung from and contributed to the wider growth of a consciousness of black identity (Alexander 1996). Its lifestyle and ethic of social nonconformity were attractive to many inner-city African-Caribbeans. Many of these adherents were attracted by its musical and fashion styles, and they did not necessarily make any serious commitment to its religious beliefs and practices. The committed Rastafarian refuses to become involved in crime and deviance for its own sake, stressing the need to build a sense of black dignity (Pryce 1986).

Drawing on a shared memory of the African diaspora, this black consciousness forms part of what Gilroy (1993) has called the 'Black Atlantic', a cultural framework that links Africa, Britain, the Caribbean, and the Americas. This consciousness, however, is not without its divisions. In 1996, Rastafarians attended a service for the dead Crown Prince of Ethiopia at an Ethiopian Orthodox church in London. The Rastafarians saw the Prince as the son of a God (Haile Selassie), a direct descendent of King Solomon and the Queen of Sheba. He was also heir to the throne of their spiritual homeland. The Ethiopian Orthodox Church, part of the Eastern Orthodox Church, refused to be publicly linked with these claims, and many Ethiopians resented the presence of the Rastafarians in their church.

The Nation of Islam (NOI) was central to the civil-rights movement in the United States. One of its principal aims is the promotion of black consciousness, and it was a major force behind campaigns stressing 'Black Power' and 'Black is Beautiful'. Those who were excluded from the ethnic melting pot also felt excluded from any sense of American identity and participation in the civil religion. Total membership in the United States is estimated at about 100,000. Membership in Britain, where they began recruiting in 1986, is relatively small, and is thought to be about 2,500. In the United States, it takes a high-profile stance in

Rastafarianism

Rastafarianism originated in Jamaica. Marcus Garvey had claimed that Africans were the 'lost tribe' of biblical Israel, and that this tribe had been further dispersed across the world by the enslavement of Africans and their transportation to the West Indies and the Americas. Africans, African-Americans, and African-Caribbeans were, therefore, seen as a chosen people of God. Their oppression and exploitation could be ended only by a return to Africa and the establishment there of societies free of colonial and post-colonial domination. Seeing the former Emperor of Ethiopia Haile Selassie (otherwise known as Ras Tafari) as a Messiah, Garvey advocated and encouraged such a return. There are estimated to be about 70,000 believers worldwide, but the religion is not united under a single leadership.

A Rastafarian takes communion at a service in the Eastern Orthodox Church.

Nation of Islam

The Nation of Islam, also known as the Black Muslims, was founded in the United States by Fard Mohammad and his deputy Elijah Muhammad in the 1930s. They promoted the adoption of Islam by African–Americans as a return to the pre-slavery religion of their ancestors. Those who join the NOI adopt new Muslim names, and many of the men wear smart suits and a bow tie as a mark of their membership. For many years the chief spokesman for the group was Malcolm X, but he was expelled in the 1960s. The beliefs of the group are far from pure Islam, and there is much reliance on the Christian New Testament. Some activists hold that the founders of the NOI are orbiting the earth in a spaceship.

African-American politics. Its leader, Louis Farrakhan, has been at the centre of attempts to build cross-faith solidarity amongst African-Americans (Lincoln 1973).

The British Nation of Islam, which is more closed and secretive in its organization than the American, is in some rivalry with the Rastafarians for recruits. It has been suggested that those African–Caribbeans who identify with Africa are attracted to the Rastafarians, while those who identify with black Americans are attracted to the Nation of Islam. In many respects, the Nation adopts conservative attitudes, stressing traditional morality and the value of the family. To this moral conservatism, however, it adds a radical political programme of black consciousness-raising and black segregation.

Islam in a global context

The globalization of economic, political, and cultural relations has posed a threat to many local, indigenous communities that had not previously been drawn directly into the modern world. As we show in Chapter 12, pp. 469–73, these communities have not been isolated from the expanding world-system—far from it— but they have not until now been so directly penetrated by forces that come from outside their own immediate world. In many parts of Africa, the Middle East and the Far East, for example, strongly anti-modern and, therefore, anti-Western sentiments have been aroused. Similarly, migrants from these areas to Western and Central Europe have generally experienced an exclusion from mainstream society that reinforces their sense of difference from white Westerners. The post-colonial experience—in the metropolitan centres and in the local communities—provides fertile ground for an emphasis on 'traditionalism' and traditional religion.

Fundamentalism occurs in areas that have been relatively secure from outside influence and have suddenly experienced major disruptions to their way of life. In those parts of the world that have a Christian tradition, as we have shown, Christian fundamentalism has attracted large numbers of adherents, while Muslim areas—which make up a significant proportion of all areas that are greatly affected by the forces of globalization—have shown a growth in Islamic fundamentalism.

This fundamentalism stresses that traditional religious truths, far from being undermined by modern society, have an ever-greater relevance to its problems. Essential religious truths are reaffirmed in a context where the globalizing forces of modernity have disrupted highly valued traditional ways of life. The fundamentalist reassertion of traditional ideas and values, however, is not a simple restatement of an unchanging tradition. It is, rather, a creative reinterpretation of that tradition through a selective drawing on inherited social meanings in the light of their present circumstances. Islamic fundamentalism is a reworking of the shared values and beliefs of a Muslim community aimed at uncovering their 'fundamental' basis in the face of modernizing forces seen as imposing a 'western' or even 'American' way of life. This need to rework and re-create tradition is made all the more necessary by the fact that migration and the globalization of cultures make each local group more aware of the diversity that exists within Islam. No set of beliefs can any more be simply taken for granted. They have to be taken back to their fundamental principles.

A key characteristic in Islamic fundamentalism, then, has been its development in reaction to a specifically *Western* form of modernization. This form of fundamentalism achieved its earliest success in Iran in 1979, where it produced a revolutionary overthrow of the pro-Western regime of the Shah and established a Shi'ite Islamic Republic. Powerful and important Islamic fundamentalist movements played a major role in the Lebanon, in Egypt, in Syria, and in Afghanistan, and fundamentalist regimes have been established in Algeria and Sudan. Moderate—generally Sunni—forms of Islam are the official creeds of many Arab states. The growth of fundamentalist regimes has been greatest wherever globalization results in the oppression or exclusion of those from a particular ethnic group—in many cases, therefore, fundamentalism strengthens a sense of national identity.

The image of fundamentalist Islam in the West focuses on its links with the political violence, kidnapping, and hijacks undertaken by groups such as

Hezbollah, though these are minority activities. More typically, fundamentalists argue their position in peaceful, though forcible, discussion. Nevertheless, political regimes based on fundamentalist principles have tended to take a very restricted view of personal and political rights, such as those of women.

There is some evidence of a growth of fundamentalist views among some young second-generation Muslim migrants in Britain. While many have abandoned their religion altogether, the experience of unemployment, poor housing, and racial discrimination leads others to be receptive to radical solutions. Just as disadvantaged African-Caribbean youths have embraced Rastafarianism rather than the Pentecostalism of their parents, so many young Muslims find fundamentalist ideas appealing.

SUMMARY POINTS

In this section we have looked at the emergence of a number of new forms of religious belief and practice and at how there has also been a growth of traditional beliefs.

▶ There has been a continuing decline in both church attendance and church membership.

▶ The civil religion has weakened, in both Britain and the United States.

▶ There is strong evidence for the existence of a loose and unorthodox common religion that has little similarity with traditional Christianity.

We looked at how the growth of liberal Protestantism has encouraged many believers to seek out more inspirational forms of Christianity.

▶ Conservative Protestantism takes two main forms: fundamentalism and Pentecostalism.

▶ These forms of conservative Protestantism have been closely associated with the new right and the moral majority.

The new religions that have grown in numbers have tended to be non-Christian sects and cults.

▶ World-rejecting religions are utopian or millennial and reject many aspects of contemporary social life.

▶ World-affirming religions are therapeutic and tend to embrace the values of modern society.

We finally looked at the relationship between religion and ethnicity. We showed how Britain had become a multi-ethnic, multi-religious society, and we examined global changes in religion.

▶ There has been growing support for religions of ethnic protest.

▶ Islamic fundamentalism is one of the fastest-growing religions in the world.

REVISION AND EXERCISES

In addition to looking at the main overarching theories of religion, this chapter has looked at the long-term trend of secularization and its implications for mainstream religions. It has also looked at a number of new and expanding religions.

THEORIES OF RELIGION

▶ Make sure that you are familiar with the main ideas of the following theorists: Comte, Marx, Durkheim, Weber.

▶ What do you understand by the following terms: sacred canopy, totemism, conscience collective, anomie, moral individualism, spirit of capitalism, asceticism.

SECULARIZATION AND MAINSTREAM RELIGION

The idea of secularization has dominated discussions of religion in the modern world. We drew on the work of Weber to explore some of its implications. We started off by seeing secularization as involving the two processes of disengagement and disenchantment:

▶ How would you define (*a*) disengagement and (*b*) disenchantment?

▶ What do you understand by the following terms: ecclesia, denomination, sect, cult; ethnic melting pot, civil religion, common religion.

▶ What examples of denominations can you give? Is the Church of England an ecclesia or a denomination?

▶ We have presented some evidence to show that women are more likely to be active church-goers than are men. In view of this, why do you think that there was such opposition to the ordination of women in the Church of England.

▶ What does Bruce mean when he says that 'Protestantism is essentially fissile'?

▶ Figures 9.1 and 9.2 give some evidence on church membership and church attendance in Britain. How do you think that these data might have been collected? What other kinds of data would be useful to assess the extent of secularization?

NEW RELIGIONS AND GROWING RELIGIONS

We examined a number of new and growing forms of religion, some of which are renewed and more strident expressions of traditional religious beliefs:

▶ What do you understand by the following terms: world-rejecting religion, world-affirming religion, world-accommodating religion; inspirational Protestantism, religion of ethnic protest?

▶ Look again at the definitions of ecclesia, denomination, sect, and cult. Which description is most appropriate for each of the following contemporary religions: Krishna Consciousness, Jehovah's Witnesses, Children of God, Pagans, Hinduism, Shinto, Unification Church, Scientology, Rastafarianism, Nation of Islam. If you are not familiar with the beliefs and organizations of these religions, use your library resources to find out more about them.

▶ How would you go about collecting evidence on the extent and significance of New Age beliefs in Britain today?

▶ How useful is it to see the spread of Islam as a response to globalization?

The study of religious belief raises some of the most fundamental questions about the nature of knowledge and the role of science. You might like to consider some of these issues. (We do not expect you to come up with the answers!):

▶ What is religion? Do you think that the definition given by Bruce and Wallis (p. 319) is useful?

▶ Are the claims of religion and science compatible with one another? Is it possible to be both a rational scientist (for example, a sociologist) and a religious believer?

FURTHER READING

Extremely good general accounts of religion can be found in:

Turner, B. (1991), *Religion and Social Theory* (2nd edn., London: Routledge). A useful overview of theories that discusses many of the key issues.

Bruce, S. (1995), *Religion in Modern Britain* (Oxford: Oxford University Press). A brief and very readable account of contemporary trends in British religion.

Wilson, B. R. (1976), *Contemporary Transformations of Religion* (Oxford: Oxford University Press). One of the key sources by the principal writer on contemporary forms of secularization.

Wallis, R. (1976), *The Road to Total Freedom* (London: Heinemann). A study of Scientology.

——(1984), *Elementary Forms of the New Religious Life* (London: Routledge & Kegan Paul). A classic account of the variety of new religions. You should follow this with a reading of Wallis (1976) and Barker (1984).

Barker, E. (1984), *The Making of a Moonie* (Oxford: Basil Blackwell). A study of the Unification Church.

More detail can be found in the following. You should *try* reading the books by Durkheim and Weber, but be warned that they are rather difficult.

Festinger, L., Riecken, H. W., and Schachter, S. (1956), *When Prophecy Fails* (New York: Harper & Row). A wonderful case study of a millenarian, flying-saucer cult. The methodological appendix is particularly good for highlighting the practical and ethical problems of participant observation. The research was fictionalized in Alison Lurie's novel *Imaginary Friends*.

Herberg, W. (1955), *Protestant, Catholic, Jew* (New York: Doubleday). A classic study of mainstream American religions in relation to ethnicity.

Lane, C. (1981), *The Rites of Rulers: Ritual in Industrial Society—the Soviet Case* (Cambridge: Cambridge University Press). A useful investigation of ritual in Soviet society, which brings out the religious aspects of Communist systems.

Durkheim, E. (1912), *The Elementary Forms of the Religious Life* (London: George Allen & Unwin, 1915). Sets out Durkheim's argument about totemism and the origins of religion.

Weber, Max (1904–5). *The Protestant Ethic and the Spirit of Capitalism* (London: George Allen & Unwin, 1930). Sets out Weber's account of the part played by religion in the rise of modern capitalism.

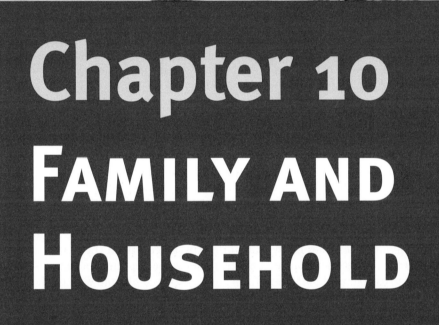

Chapter 10
FAMILY AND HOUSEHOLD

The rise of the Sinmoos

'After the Dinkies, meet the Sinmoos. If "Dual Income No Kids" households were the phenomenon of the 1880s, then the 1990s have been marked by the rise of the "Single Income Never Married Owner Occupier". . . .

In 1977, there were 370,000 single never married owner occupiers; today, there are three times as many and they make up nearly one in 12 of all households. The number of under-45 Sinmoos has risen sixfold in 20 years, from 100,000 to 660,000 . . . .

The growth of one-person households is one of the principal reasons why an extra 4.4 million homes need to be built between now and 2020. Of these new households, almost 80 per cent—3.5 million—are expected to come from one-person households. . . .

Between 1991 and 2016, the number of one-person households formed by unmarried men and women aged between 30 and 64 is projected to more than double.'

Source: Philip Johnston, 'Rise of the Home-Alone Generation', *Daily Telegraph*, 9 May 1997.

MOST of us have experienced family life in some form and many of us will then have gone on to build our own families. Family relationships have probably been the most important relationships in our lives. This intimate knowledge of family life can easily lead us to think that we know from experience all there is to know about it.

Our experience is, however, of particular families in particular societies at a particular time. It is also the experience of one member of the family, who is emotionally involved in it and not able to make objective statements about it. The sociological study of the family enables us to locate our experience within the whole range of forms that the family has taken and understand how specific our experience is. It also enables us to gain some detachment from our own experience and view the family as a social institution in a non-emotional way.

In this chapter we begin by considering what we mean by 'the family' and different approaches to it. We then go on to discuss the historical emergence of the modern family, before examining a range of contemporary issues to do with family life.

We consider the impact of the 1960s sexual revolution on marriage, the rising divorce rate, and their consequences for households, which, as our opening extract shows, are changing significantly in size and character. We also discuss their consequences for parenting and children. Changes in family life are set in the context of growing ethnic diversity. The issue is raised of the impact of the growing employment of women on the domestic division of labour and male identity. We also consider whether family violence and sexual abuse within the family have increased or simply become more visible.

UNDERSTANDING FAMILIES AND HOUSEHOLDS

WHAT IS THE FAMILY?

This might seem a question that does not have to be asked. Surely we all know what a family is. When we refer to 'our family' or indeed someone else's family there is usually little doubt about what we mean.

A little reflection shows, however, that it is far from clear what we mean by 'our family'. We may be referring to the immediate family with which we share a household. We may mean a wider group which includes parents and children, whether or not they live with us. Divorce(s) and remarriage(s) may make this an extensive and complex group with uncertain boundaries. We may mean a much wider group of relatives who have occasional contact by phone or at family meetings and parties. We may mean a group of blood relatives, extending perhaps to cousins, grandparents, uncles, and aunts, which includes people with whom we have no contact at all.

Defining what is meant by the family is not as straightforward as it appears to be, and there has, indeed, been much discussion in sociology of how the family should be defined. We now move on to examine the issues raised by this discussion.

FAMILIES, HOUSEHOLDS, AND KINSHIP

The definition of the family needs to be discussed with the related concepts of household and kinship. We start here by discussing how the family should be defined and then go on to the other two concepts.

A major problem with the definition of the family has been the political debate over the form that the family *should* take. The New Right, which took over the Conservative Party in the 1970s, tried to revive traditional notions of the family centred on marriage and a domestic division of labour between a breadwinning husband and a housewife responsible for childcare. A definition of the family in these terms excludes single-parent families, and unmarried couples, heterosexual or homosexual, even though they may consider themselves to be families and act together in family ways. This definition also builds the domestic division of labour into the family, instead of treating it as just one way in which families can organize their work lives.

To avoid this problem, Gittins (1993) argued that instead of referring to 'the family' we should refer to 'families'. By doing this we could recognize the various forms taken by the family and avoid privileging any one form. This practice has now been widely adopted in sociology. It does not really solve the definitional problem, however, for families must have something in common that leads them to be called families. Some distinction must also be made between families and other social groups, such as, for example, communities. There is still the problem of what we mean by the term 'family'.

Families may be said to have two things in common:

▶ *The closeness of family relationships.* There is a sense that relationships are closer within a family than with people outside it. There is a boundary around a family, a sense of family identity, that separates it off from other people.

▶ *A sense of obligation and responsibility.* Members of a family give higher priority to each other's needs than those of other people. Family responsibilities are not fixed and are continually negotiated by family members, but there is, none the less, something distinctive about them which makes family commitments different from, say, those to friends.

The **family** may then be defined as a small group of closely related people who share a distinct sense of identity and a responsibility for each other that outweighs their commitments to others. This group is commonly, but not necessarily, based on marriage, biological descent, or adoption.

Sociologists distinguish between families and households. A **household** consists of a person or group of people living in a particular residential unit. The Labour Force Survey defines a household as 'a single person, or a group of people who have the same address as their only or main residence and who either share one meal a day or share the living accommodation'. This is a very precise definition for survey purposes which is a little too narrow for general use in sociology. In some nomadic societies a household may not have an address. This definition does indicate, however, that the members of a household must in some meaningful way share its facilities. It must, in other words, be *more than* a group of people who have the same address.

One definition of the family

'The family is a social group characterized by common residence, economic co-operation and reproduction. It includes adults of both sexes, at least two of whom maintain a socially approved sexual relationship, and one or more children, own or adopted, of the sexually cohabiting adults.'

Source: Murdock (1949: 1).

▶ **This is a well-known and much-quoted definition of the family. What problems do you think that it faces in the light of the discussion in the text?**

▶ **Have a look at other definitions in dictionaries and sociological works (use indexes to locate definitions). How well do they cope with these problems?**

▶ **Do you think that the definition that we offer is a satisfactory one?**

The members of a family may well live in different households. When children leave home and set up their own households, this does not mean that they leave their family. On the other hand, while the members of a household *may* consist of members of one family, they may well not be bound together by family ties. Indeed, some groups opposed to the idea that people should live in families have created communal households based on community rather than family (see 'Alternatives', p. 361).

Sociologists also distinguish between family and kinship. **Kinship** refers to a network of relatives (kin) who are connected by common descent or by marriage. Common descent means that all can trace their ancestry back to the same person, though this does not necessarily mean that they are biologically descended from this person, for kinship structures can sometimes be based on a myth of descent from a particular individual. Kinship extends well beyond the smallish group that we usually take the term 'family' to mean, though there is also an intermediate term, the 'extended family', which we shall discuss shortly.

Kinship structures have been central features of small-scale societies, such as hunting and gathering bands or tribes, and social anthropologists have discovered many different principles of kinship in these societies. They have, for example, distinguished between *matrilineal* structures that trace descent from a female ancestor, and *patrilineal* structures that trace descent from a male. These differences have been very important in stateless societies, because they were largely organized around kinship. While contemporary societies are not primarily structured in this way, kinship networks are certainly found within them and perform important functions for their members.

Nuclear and extended families

The most common forms of the family distinguished in the literature are nuclear and extended families. The **nuclear family** is usually defined as a two generation unit consisting of parents and unmarried children. A distinction is generally made here between the **family of origin** and the **family of destination**. People who have children will have been members of at least two nuclear families, the family of *origin* into which they were born and the family of *destination*, which they created themselves. Divorce and remarriage may, indeed, mean that they have been members of a series of such families.

The **extended family** includes other family members. It extends *vertically* to include at least three generations—that is, at least grandparents and grandchildren. It extends *horizontally* to include 'in-laws', cousins, aunts, and uncles, though how far it extends will vary and depends upon perceptions of the extent of the family. It is important to recognize that terms such as aunt are not universal. The language of kinship and the kinds of relationships that exist between family members vary greatly between societies. In some societies, for example, aunts on the mother's side are distinguished from aunts on the father's side and there is no common word for aunt.

There has been much debate over the relationship between these two forms of the family. Talcott Parsons argued that industrialization resulted in a shift from the extended family characteristic of traditional societies to the nuclear family typical of industrial societies. Against this view, the historian Peter Laslett claimed that in Britain the nuclear family has always been the dominant form. On the other hand, in their famous study of Bethnal Green, Michael Young and Peter Willmott found that the extended family was alive and well in the 1950s.

One problem with this literature is that there has been some confusion of the household with the family. Laslett showed that households in Britain have generally consisted of nuclear rather than extended families. From the sixteenth century through to the nineteenth the average household contained less than five people (Laslett and Wall 1972). This did not, however, mean that extended family networks did not exist or were unimportant.

O'Day (1994) argues that there is plenty of evidence that in pre-industrial Britain wider family connections were very important to people and were carefully maintained. They provided the support that enabled families to continue to function when key members died, which happened often at a time when death rates were much higher. The extended family existed as a structure of collective responsibility for its members even if they did not all live together in the same household.

Nuclear family households are perfectly compatible with the existence of extended family networks. When we speak of the development of the nuclear family, we do not mean that the extended family ceased to exist. It is rather that the nuclear family became a more distinct and independent unit.

Michael Young

Michael Young (1915–) was born in Manchester and educated at Dartington Hall and the London School of Economics. He was an influential thinker in the Labour Party and became Secretary of its Research Department In 1945. His work on education, inequality, the family, and the community has been influential in sociology and the development of social policy. His book *The Rise of the Meritocracy* (1958) had a considerable influence on the rise of the comprehensive movement in education. His interest in communities led to the classic study of Bethnal Green, *Family and Kinship in East London* (1957), which he wrote with Peter Willmott. This was followed by another well-known study, also written with Willmott, *The Symmetrical Family* (1973). In 1978 he was given the title Lord Young of Dartington. In 1982 he was one of the founders of the University of the Third Age.

The nuclear family is usually defined in residential terms, as parents and children living together on their own, but in many ways its key feature is less a matter of who lives with who than of the family's relationship to other people. The nuclear family is a relatively isolated and inward-looking unit that is centred on domestic life and held together by close emotional relationships. It is this rather than whether or not a grandparent lives in the household that really marks out the nuclear family. Shorter has expressed this view of the nuclear family in a typically striking passage.

'The nuclear family is a state of mind rather than a particular kind of structure or set of household arrangements. It has little to do with whether the generations live together or whether Aunt Mary stays in the spare bedroom. Nor can it be understood with kinship diagrams and figures on family size. What really distinguishes the nuclear family—mother, father, and children—from other patterns of family life in Western society is a special sense of solidarity that separates the domestic unit from the surrounding community. Its members feel that they have much more in common with one another than they do with anyone else on the outside— that they enjoy a privileged emotional climate they must protect from outside intrusion, through privacy and isolation.' (Shorter 1976: 205)

The nuclear family has often been linked to a division of labour between the breadwinning male and the housewife. Talcott Parsons saw a domestic division of labour of this kind as a central feature of the nuclear family. While historically the emergence of such a division of labour was associated with the rise of the nuclear family in societies like Britain, it is not essential to it. Nuclear families certainly exist where both parents go out to work and share housework and child-rearing or where there is a female breadwinner and a house-husband.

THEORIES OF THE DEVELOPMENT OF THE FAMILY

Here we examine more closely three theories of the development of the modern family, which respectively explain its emergence by reference to industrialism, capitalism, and patriarchy.

Industrialization and the family

Parsons (Parsons and Bales 1956) took a functionalist approach to the development of the family. This approach starts from the assumption that social institutions develop to meet the basic needs of society.

Parsons argued that there were two such needs that the family met and that only the family could meet. These were the needs for primary socialization and personality stabilization. Primary socialization is the process through which children acquire the basic values of society during their early years. Family life also stabilizes the adult personality by providing emotional support through marriage and enabling adults to satisfy childish impulses which cannot be indulged in public, by, for example, playing games with their children.

Parsons's theory of the development of the family is set in a more general theory of social change. He argued that the pre-industrial extended family was a multifunctional unit that met most of people's needs. Modernization involved institutional differentiation, as specialized institutions emerged to meet particular needs. The family lost many of its functions to these other institutions. Production moved from the household to the workplace. Education and health care were provided by specialist occupations and organizations. The family itself became more specialized around its core functions of socialization and personality stabilization.

> 👉 We deal with primary and secondary socialization in Chapter 4, pp. 124–8, and you will find it helpful to refer to this chapter for a more detailed discussion. We discuss the functionalist approach in Chapter 2, pp. 50–2, and Parsons's theory of social change, also in Chapter 2, pp. 52–3.

Parsons argued that the nuclear form of the family was particularly well suited to an industrial economy. Within this unit roles were specialized, with one adult earning money through paid work and the other bringing up the children. There was a high rate of change in an industrial society, which required a mobile workforce prepared to move to where there was work. The small nuclear family without obligations to an extended family and with only one 'breadwinner' could be geographically mobile. This close fit between the nuclear family and the requirements of the economy integrated the institutions of industrial society.

The nuclear family also fitted an industrial society in another way. An industrial society was based on values of *achievement* and *universalism*. People were rewarded according to their achievements and were judged according to universal standards of qualification and competence. The family operated on the basis of the opposite values of *ascription* and *particularism*. In the family, status was ascribed—that is, it depended on *who* one was—husband, wife, child, or grandparent, etc. The particular relationships of the family governed family behaviour—parents did their best to advance their children, whatever their children's abilities might be. If family units and work units overlapped, as they did in earlier times, there would be endless tension and conflict between the incompatible value systems of work and family relationships. With the nuclear family the two worlds were kept separate and linked only by the male breadwinner.

Parsons's approach has been much criticized. It appeared to justify the patriarchal family with a gendered division of labour by arguing that it alone met the requirements of an industrial economy. It emphasized the fit between the nuclear family and industrial society and did not take account of the tensions

between the two. It said nothing about observable variations in the structure and composition of families in industrial societies. It also treated the family as a harmonious institution and did not deal with its internal conflicts and their consequences. Nor did it consider alternative ways in which the functions of socialization and personality management could be met, through different forms of the family or through non-family community organizations. These issues will become clearer as we examine other approaches shortly.

Capitalism and the family

An alternative theory of the development of the family was put forward by a 1970s group of Marxist writers (see Walby 1986 for a critical review of their work). They explained the development of the family in terms of the needs of a capitalist economy.

Their central argument was that the capitalist system exploits the free domestic labour of the housewife. Housework and child-rearing are not family activities *outside* the operation of the capitalist economy but rather an *essential* part of it. There is a **domestic division of labour** between the worker and the housewife. The male breadwinner can work long hours for the employer only because the domestic work of looking after the household and bringing up children is done by the housewife. The family also begins the process of producing submissive workers, which is then continued by education (see Chapter 7, pp. 237–8). Crucially, although domestic labour is essential to the capitalist economy, employers pay only for the work of the male breadwinner. If the housewife was paid for her labour, the wage costs of the capitalist employer would increase sharply.

It has also been argued that the family provides an outlet for the tensions and frustrations generated by the alienating work of a capitalist economy. Workers are under constant pressure from the employer to work harder and faster, often carrying out boring and repetitive work in very poor conditions, over which they have little control. Family life provides a temporary escape and a means of relieving the tensions generated by work, which may well be at the expense of wife and children, particularly if it takes a violent form. Thus, the bullied worker may restore his self-esteem by bullying his family. The build-up of an explosive discontent at work is avoided through the safety valve provided by the family and the emotional labour of the wife.

Many housewives do, however, work in paid employment and have always done so. Since the main role of the woman in the nuclear family was to be a housewife and the male breadwinner earned a 'family wage' to support the whole household, employers could pay women low wages. They could also treat women as a 'reserve army' that could be drawn into work when there was a labour shortage and returned to the home when demand was slack. Thus, the nuclear family also provided employers with a useful additional supply of cheap labour.

This analysis shares with the functionalist approach the assumption that a particular form of the family fits the requirements of the economy. It treats the nuclear family with a gendered division of labour as the standard form of the family, much as Parsons did, and similarly says little about variations in the structure and character of the family. It was an approach that was taken up by some Marxist feminists, such as Beechey (1987), who see the dynamics of capitalism as central to the subordination of women.

> We discuss alienation and the relationship between work and leisure in Chapter 13, pp. 507–8. We discuss the employment of women in paid work, and the concept of a 'reserve army', also in Chapter 13, p. 522.

Patriarchy and the family

An alternative feminist approach focused in a similar way on the domestic division of labour but rejected the idea that it can be explained by capitalism. This approach argued that the domestic division of labour preceded the rise of capitalism and resulted from an age-old domination of women by men. This was the kind of approach taken by another group of feminist writers, called radical feminists (see Chapter 4, p. 141, for a discussion of radical feminism). To this group of feminists it was not capitalism that was the problem but patriarchy.

While the term **patriarchy** has been commonly used simply as a shorthand term for male domination, radical feminists saw patriarchy as the source of this domination. By patriarchy they meant a universal structure of male authority that is found in all societies but expressed in many different institutional ways. It is the power that men have over women, not the dynamics of capitalism, that explains the inequalities between men and women.

Delphy (1977) saw this exploitation as rooted in 'the domestic mode of production' not the capitalist mode of production. She used this term to emphasize that productive work went on in the household, as well as in

the factory, for housework was, in her view, as productive as any other kind of work. Within the domestic mode of production men held a superior position and controlled the distribution of money and goods within the family to their advantage, exploiting through marriage the labour of women. The family was, therefore, an institution for the exploitation of women by men. Delphy rejected the idea that women held the same class position as their husbands. Since they were economically exploited by their husbands, they should be treated as a separate class. Similarly, she argued that middle-class educational advantages were gender specific, since they were passed on to sons rather than daughters. These ideas were further developed by Delphy and Leonard (1992).

Walby (1986) too rejected the idea that capitalism accounts for male domination but emphasized that there are other patriarchal structures besides the family. It was not so much that men kept women subordinated in the home as that men excluded them from the paid employment that would enable them to be independent. The capitalist employer wanted to employ women as a cheaper source of labour. It was the state and the trade unions that excluded women from work. Thus, Walby argued that women's domestic labour was a *result* of the exclusion of women from paid work rather than a *cause* of it. Patriarchy operated through the unions and the state as well as the family.

Explanations that rely on the concept of patriarchy have, however, been strongly criticized (see Acker 1989; Bradley 1989; Pollert 1996). While patriarchy may be a useful term for male domination, an *explanation* of male domination in terms of the universal existence of patriarchy appears more than a little circular. The only way out of the circle would seem to be a biological determinism, for, if patriarchy is universal, it must be biological in origin, as indeed some have argued (see Chapter 4, pp. 141–2). Biological determinism has been rejected by Walby and many other feminists, but without it patriarchy appears to hang in the air without any explanation of why it should exist. Furthermore, if patriarchy is a universal feature of human society, it cannot help us in understanding differences and changes in gender relationships.

The concept of patriarchy has played an important role in drawing attention to patterns of male domination and conflicts of interest between men and women. Its explanatory power is, however, doubtful. We use it in this book to mean male domination, without implying that this is some universal or permanent feature of society. Gender relationships may become more or less patriarchal depending on social changes at work or in the family or in other institutional areas.

IS THE FAMILY IN DECLINE?

Since the 1960s there has been much concern with the decline of the family. Here we first outline the beliefs of those who think the family is in decline and then consider critics of the family. We go on to consider briefly the development of alternative non-family ways in which people live with each other.

Family values

Those who claim that the family is in decline commonly refer to what they call 'family values'. This is the kind of position taken up in Britain by right-wing political and religious circles. According to Jewson (1994), the notion of family values makes four main assumptions:

▶ It assumes that there is a normal form taken by the family. This is essentially a married couple with children. Other forms, such as one-parent families, are abnormal.

▶ It assumes a gendered division of labour and the authority of the male breadwinner.

▶ It considers that responsibility for welfare is a matter for the family rather than the state.

▶ It involves a belief that sex should take place only within marriage. This is generally associated with a hostility to homosexuality, sex education, and abortion.

Marriage is central to this view of the family. A rising divorce rate is, therefore, symptomatic of the decline of the family and there are calls for divorce to be made more difficult. Those holding this view do not consider that cohabitation is an acceptable alternative to marriage and commonly believe that mothers should look after their children rather than take paid work.

Single-parent families headed by lone mothers have particularly come under attack. It is argued that the absence of a father weakens family control of children and deprives boys of a male role model. Fatherless families are blamed for rising crime, educational failure, disinterest in work, and dependence on state welfare. Indeed, the American social scientist Charles Murray blames fatherless families for the emergence of an underclass. British sociologists too, such as Dennis and Halsey, have argued that there is evidence to support these views. We will return to this issue in our discussion of 'parenting and parenthood'.

Those opposed to this interpretation argue that it is not the single-parent family that is responsible for

In what ways does this picture of a family represent family values?

these problems but the poverty of such families and the low level of state support for them. More generally, it can be argued that the focus on the decline of the family as the source of social problems diverts attention from their broader economic and political sources.

The critique of the family

Barrett and McIntosh (1991) present a quite opposite view of the family in their book *The Anti-Social Family*. They do not consider that it is in decline but, on the contrary, emphasize how strong it is. They stress the negative rather than the positive consequences of this strength. To them, it is not the decline of the family that is the problem but rather the strength of family values.

They argue that the family is the central mechanism through which inequality is passed on from one generation to the next through the inheritance of wealth. They also emphasize what is often called the 'dark side' of family life. The family is not so much a refuge from the pressures of the world as a form of imprisonment, which isolates women, leaves them vulnerable to domestic violence, and generates mental illness. Marriage subordinates women financially and sexually to men. The family is one of the main sources of the oppression of women through marriage and the domestic division of labour.

The problem with the family is not only what it does to people but also that it is a 'privileged institution' which devalues life outside it. As Barrett and McIntosh (1991: 77) put it, 'the family ideal makes everything else seem pale and unsatisfactory'. Non-familial institutions, such as old people's homes, nurseries, or children's homes, may well provide better care or a more stimulating environment than the family, but they are always viewed in negative terms because of the dominance of the family ideal. Furthermore, people become so wrapped up in family life that they do not have time and energy for other relationships and institutions.

The family is presented here as an exclusive and suffocating institution. In another striking phrase, Barrett and McIntosh (1991: 78) assert that 'the family sucks the juice out of everything around it, leaving other institutions stunted and distorted'.

These consequences of family life are certainly recognizable, and, as we shall see in 'Domestic Violence and Abuse', pp. 392–5, there is plentiful evidence for the 'dark side' of family life. This critique of the family also played an important role in balancing the idealizing of family life by those who believed in family values. It does, however, attribute too much to the family itself. As we showed in our discussion of patriarchy, the family is not the only patriarchal structure in society and cannot, for example, be held solely responsible for inequalities between men and women.

Alternatives

In the 1960s there was much interest in communes as an alternative way of life. Communal living was particularly associated with the hippie movement (see Chapter 5, p. 175). Many different kinds of commune came into existence, but the one thing that they had in common was a rejection of the family. As an alternative way of life, they faced two main problems (Weeks 1991).

First, they did not generally provide a way of living *within* society. The commune movement tended to reject the wider society, seeking to establish separate communities that were egalitarian or lived in harmony with the environment. This limited the appeal of a commune to those who held certain beliefs and meant that they were not an alternative for those seeking to lead ordinary lives within the existing social order. It also meant that communes easily became isolated.

The last children's house

'Since 1949 the children of the *kibbutz* at Baram in northern Galilee have been reared together in special children's houses and not by their parents. Tsvi Benayoun, the *kibbutz's* economic manager says:

"Children lived together and performed all activities together from the age of eight months until they entered the army. It was a long, sustained—and by no means unsuccessful—attempt to bypass the nuclear family as the centre of a child's life. Instead, children were expected to give their first loyalty not to their parents, brothers and sisters but to each other and to the members of the *kibbutz* as a group."

After prolonged and angry debate, Baram, a prosperous community of 566 adults and children just south of the border with Lebanon, last month became the last *kibbutz* out of some 250 in Israel—many of which once brought up their children together—to abandon the system. For the first time this month the children sleep at home and the neat four-bed rooms in the children's houses are empty at night.

Mr. Benayoun said the main reason for returning children to their parents was "pressure from the mothers. The children themselves said they wanted to be in the children's house".'

Source: Patrick Cockburn, 'End of the Kibbutz Dream', *Independent*, 26 July 1997.

▶ **Perhaps the most striking thing about this story is that the experiment had lasted so long. Can you think of any reasons for this?**

▶ **Can you think of any institutions in British society which are similar to the 'children's house'? In what ways are they different from it?**

Secondly, family values tended to reassert themselves. This has happened in the Israeli kibbutz. The kibbutz was a relatively successful form of the commune, which, unlike most other forms, was certainly plugged into society and made a productive economic contribution to it, for the kibbutzim were highly successful agricultural enterprises. They were based on the principle of separating children from their families, so that they would grow up together and develop a wider collective solidarity, but the family has re-emerged within them. This is shown most dramatically by the closing of the last 'children's house' (see box on p. 361).

The commune movement has waned, and, instead of rejecting family life, critics of the family tend now to argue that we should recognize that there are many alternative ways in which people can live together *as families*. This involves accepting the claims of homosexual couples that they are families and recognizing the different forms of the family associated with ethnic diversity. It also avoids stigmatizing one-parent families as in some way irresponsible or deficient and comes to terms with the complex structures of families reconstituted through divorce and remarriage. The concept of the family is widened to include many different groups and ways of living.

SUMMARY POINTS

We began this part of the chapter by considering the definitional issues raised by the study of the family:

▶ We emphasized that a sociological definition of the family must be distinguished from political views of the form that families should take.

▶ We distinguished between the family, the residential unit of the household, and the wider kinship network.

▶ We also distinguished between the nuclear and extended forms of the family, though we emphasized that the nuclear family was compatible with the continued existence of an extended family network.

We went on to discuss different theories of the development of the family.

▶ Parsons argued that the nuclear form of the family became dominant because it was particularly suited to the requirements of a capitalist economy.

▶ Marxist writers argued that the domestic division of labour characteristic of the nuclear family resulted from the needs of a capitalist economy.

▶ An alternative approach taken by radical feminists claimed that the domestic division of labour preceded the development of capitalism and resulted from the patriarchal domination of women by men.

Lastly we considered the issue of the decline of the family.

▶ Those who believe in family values have argued that the decline of the family has caused many of the problems of contemporary society.

▶ Others have criticized the family and argued that the problem is not its decline but its continued strength.

▶ Those critical of the family have either proposed non-familial alternatives such as the commune or called for an acceptance of greater diversity in family forms.

THE DEVELOPMENT OF THE FAMILY

Many aspects of family life get taken for granted. It is taken for granted that the family is a domestic unit, that there are strong emotional bonds between its members, and that there is a division of labour in most families between what men do and what women do. It is commonly assumed that people naturally pass from childhood to adulthood as they grow up, that they become middle-aged and at some point old. As we shall show in this chapter, these various aspects of family life are not, however, natural to it and have developed and changed throughout its history.

We begin this section by considering the important changes that took place in the pre-industrial family. We then go on to the impact of industrialization and the development of the family in industrial society. Lastly, we consider changes in the stages of life and their implications for the family.

THE PRE-INDUSTRIAL FAMILY

The classic studies of the development of the family were carried out during the 1970s by Aries (1972), Shorter (1976), and Stone (1977). They have been labelled the 'sentiments approach' by Michael Anderson (1980*a*), because of their focus on the emotional aspects of the development of the family. We shall make frequent references to these studies, but it is important to bear in mind that their work, and later work too, has faced two big problems of method.

▶ They were reliant on documentary sources and it is inevitably very difficult to draw conclusions about the emotional quality of relationships or the way that people actually behave from sources of this sort.

▶ Documentary sources become scarcer as one moves down the social order. The discussion of changes in the family tends to be dominated by evidence from upper- or middle-class families.

The emergence of the nuclear family

As we argued earlier, the nuclear family is usually defined as a residential unit consisting of parents and unmarried children, but in many ways what really matters is not so much its precise composition as its relationship to the society. The nuclear family is a relatively isolated and inward-looking unit that is centred on domestic life.

According to the classic model of the development of the family, the extended family unit of pre-industrial society gave way to the nuclear family of industrial societies. In pre-industrial societies production largely depended on the amount of family labour available to work the land, and the extended family was the most appropriate unit. In industrial societies, the household became increasingly separated from production and the nuclear family became the dominant form. This was the view presented by Parsons. It needs considerable qualification, however, in the light of later historical research.

The nuclear family was emerging long before industrialization. According to Stone, in the upper and middle classes the isolation of the nuclear family from the extended family began as early as the sixteenth century. Before this time there was no boundary between the extended and the nuclear family. Relationships between husbands and wives, parents and children, were no closer than relationships with other relatives or neighbours. From this time on, the family became increasingly focused on the upbringing of children and the emotional needs of their parents. By the eighteenth century the nuclear family had become 'walled off' from the community and the wider network of relatives.

In line with this view, Davidoff (1990) has argued that the family life of at least a section of the upper class became more private and more domestic during the eighteenth century. There was less involvement in public life and a greater interest in the pleasures of home and family. In the country house, the life of the household became less centred on the semi-public great hall and more on the small private rooms of the family. One important architectural change was the building of corridors, which allowed people to go from one room to another without disturbing each other's privacy. Servants were increasingly segregated in their own quarters away from the family proper.

Hall has shown how a similar domesticity was also emerging in the middle class. During the eighteenth century the better-off shopkeepers became no longer content with living over the shop and wanted their homes to be separate from their workplace. Their wives 'were furnishing their living apartments elegantly, putting their servants into livery, and refusing to be seen in the shop themselves, as it was not considered to be ladylike' (C. Hall 1982*a*: 4).

In the family lives of the lower classes, the great change in the eighteenth century was the break-up of the household as a unit of production. This prepared the way for the emergence of the nuclear family as a domestic unit centred on the home.

During the stage of household production all members of the family were expected to engage in productive activities—working on the land, keeping animals, producing craft goods, collecting wood or foraging for food. Young people often became servants or apprentices in the larger households, where they were closely controlled by the head of the household, and treated as members of the family. Indeed, the family at this time meant all members of the household. According to Davidoff (1990), apprentices and servants had the same status and were treated in much the same way as members of the biological family.

The pre-industrial development of wage labour broke up the household as a unit of production. With the growth of capitalism in eighteenth-century Britain, production was carried out not by members of the family but by workers paid a wage for their labour. The family began to become a unit of *consumption* rather than *production*, as its members no longer worked together but rather used the wages they had earned to buy goods which they consumed as a family unit.

The family also became a unit based on kinship. Its members were linked now only by marriage and birth (or possibly adoption). Apprentices and servants were no longer members of the family, though both apprenticeship and service continued in a different form. Apprentices learned their trade in the workplace, while servants increasingly themselves became wage workers. The family had become both biologically and emotionally a tighter unit, focused on the home.

This resulted in a sharper break when children left the family home. On the one hand, they remained longer within the family home. Instead of being apprenticed to a household and living in that household, they went out to work from home on a daily basis and their wage made them valuable contributors to the family's economy (Gillis 1974). On the other hand, young people could become more independent of both family and community. They could now move directly on to the labour market, travelling about to find work, and taking lodgings near their work. They could marry and establish their own household earlier than they could before. This also freed them from the traditional community controls which had kept a grip on family life in rural villages (Davidoff 1990).

Husbands and wives

According to the sentiments group of historians, family members have not always been bound together by strong emotional relationships. They argue that there was no affection in the relationships of the early family. It was only with the emergence of the nuclear family that family life developed an emotional quality.

Stone called this process the 'growth of affective individualism' (affective simply means emotional). People began to treat each other as unique individuals with personal and emotional needs. Family relationships took on a new quality as its members became concerned with their own feelings and their feelings for each other. The main function of the nuclear family increasingly became the satisfaction of emotional needs.

He argued that these changes could be seen in marriage. In the sixteenth century, marriage in the upper ranks of society was a means of joining together two kinship groups, for economic or political purposes. Mate selection was controlled by parents and the wider

family. By the end of the eighteenth century love had become much more important to marriage. Economic considerations and parental influence still mattered, especially when large fortunes or landed estates were at stake, but love and companionship were also seen as essential. Rejection of a chosen partner on the grounds of incompatibility was allowed and choice based on mutual attraction was becoming more common. It was also recognized that loveless marriages would lead to extramarital affairs.

One sign of these changes was the growth of matchmaking institutions for upper-class families. Balls, card parties, and events in the assembly rooms that were being built in eighteenth-century towns enabled young members of the elite to meet potential marriage partners. A national marriage market, centred in London and Bath, became established.

Lower down the social order, in the lower middle class and amongst skilled workers, economic considerations were still central to mate selection, because capital was scarce and crucial to economic success. Amongst the propertyless poor there was less at stake and premarital sex was common. Partners were freely chosen, and discarded, or abandoned. Desertion and bigamy were, according to Stone, common, while 'wife sales' by 'mutual consent' provided an unofficial means of divorce.

As marriage became more emotional, it also became less stable. The nuclear family was held together less by

Eighteenth-century wife sales

'As described in 1727, the husband "puts a halter about her neck and thereby leads her to the next market-place, and there puts her up to auction to be sold to the best bidder, as if she were a brood mare or a milch-cow. A purchaser is generally provided beforehand on these occasions". This procedure was based closely on that of the sale of cattle. It took place frequently in a cattle market like Smithfield and was accompanied by the use of a symbolic halter, by which the wife was led to market by the seller, and led away again by the buyer. . . . In the popular mind, this elaborate ritual freed the husband of all future responsibility for his wife, and allowed both parties to marry again. Very often, perhaps normally, the bargain was pre-arranged with the full consent of the wife, both purchaser and price being agreed upon beforehand.'

Source: Stone (1977: 40).

▶ **What does the symbolism of this ritual tell us about the relationship between husband and wife?**

wider kin relationships and depended more on internal bonds. Women found themselves torn between the demands of their children and their partners as family relationships became emotionally more intense. The eighteenth-century changes in marriage resulted in 'very severe stresses' for the institution (Stone 1977: 404).

Shorter argued that similar changes took place in France as love and affection became a central part of marriage in the later eighteenth century. He linked the new importance of romance in marriage to a revolution in attitudes to sexual behaviour at this time. His evidence for these changes was the great increase in children born outside marriage during the century from 1750 to 1850. He argued that rising illegitimacy showed that there was much more sexual activity before marriage. Courtship was transformed as affection and personal compatibility became much more important in the selection of partners.

He explained this change in terms of the spread of capitalism, which broke down community control and generated a selfish individualism. He saw this as occurring primarily amongst workers and particularly linked it to the growing employment of women in paid work, which enabled them to be independent. According to Shorter (1976: 259), 'the sexual and emotional wish to be free came from the capitalist market-place'.

Stone agreed that there was a loosening of moral control and a transformation of sexual behaviour in the later eighteenth century, but his account was in important respects different. Rising illegitimacy was nothing to do with freedom and resulted from the economic deprivation and sexual exploitation of women in both domestic service and the early factory. He also argued that this transformation was in the nineteenth century largely, if temporarily, reversed by a revival of religion and Victorian morality. This applied particularly to the middle class, for growing poverty and greater geographical mobility continued to weaken parental and communal control over the poor.

While their interpretations of these changes were significantly different, both Shorter and Stone emphasized the decline of moral, communal, and parental control over sexual behaviour and marriage as it became increasingly centred on an emotional relationship.

Parents and children

Shorter and Stone argued that, just as the relationships between husband and wife became more emotional, so did the relationship between parents and children. It was, however, the pioneering work of Aries on the history of childhood which started the discussion of this aspect of the family.

According to Aries, childhood did not exist in medieval times. Once children no longer required constant care, they were treated like adults. This was shown by the way that they were dressed. Until the seventeenth century there were no special clothes for children, who were dressed as though they were adults. Children did not lead separate lives and generally mixed with adults. They were expected to earn their keep, and to fight in war, as soon as they were physically able to do so.

The sentiments historians argued that relationships between parents and children were at this stage unemotional. Adults took no pleasure in their relationships with children and were indifferent to their emotional needs. They left children alone for long periods, put them out to wet-nurses, and showed little concern when they died, which they often did, for infant mortality was very high. Indeed, this meant that it was best not to invest too much emotion in them. The lack of parental feeling for children was shown by the harsh punishments that were used to discipline them.

It was in the seventeenth century that attitudes began to change in the aristocracy and amongst educated people. Parents began to take pleasure from watching and playing with children, and began to treat them as different from adults. Clothes, games, toys, and stories specifically created for children made their first appearance. Also, a sense of special parental responsibility for the welfare and success of children began to emerge. Child-rearing now became a central function of the family in a way that it had not been before.

The idea that parents had previously lacked emotional feelings for their children has, however, been challenged by Pollock (1983). She used diary and autobiographical material to show that sixteenth-century parents grieved for their children when they died and did not treat them as harshly as the sentiments historians had suggested. Cunningham (1995) has reviewed the literature on this issue and concludes that there were, none the less, significant changes in attitudes towards children, particularly in the eighteenth century. A greater concern for the welfare of children and a greater sense of parental responsibility emerged in the middle class and spread downwards to the working class after industrialization.

Patriarchy and the domestic division of labour

The development of the family involved not only changes in the emotional quality of relationships but also changes in power relationships. The discussion of power has focused on the issue of patriarchy or male domination, which we discussed on p. 359.

The discussion of patriarchy in industrial societies has linked it closely to the domestic division of labour. Men went out to work and controlled the family income, while women were confined within the home doing the housework and bringing up children. According to Marxist writers, it was industrial capitalism that brought about this domestic division of labour. There is, however, plentiful evidence of the existence of a pre-industrial division of labour between men and women.

Bradley (1989) has reviewed the literature on this question. Women were certainly engaged in a wide range of productive tasks in pre-industrial Europe but tended to carry out those that were of lower status and linked to the home. Segalen's (1983) study of French peasant households showed that women worked in the house, the barn, the farmyard, and the garden more often than in the fields. Middleton (1979) argued that women in medieval Britain did carry out many different agricultural tasks, but it was the men who did the high-status work of ploughing. In towns women were engaged in a variety of occupations but the main crafts were male dominated and women took part in craft-work in a less specialized and more intermittent way, generally through family connections.

This general picture of male domination needs to be qualified. There was considerable local variation in the division of labour between men and women, and this resulted in differences in the status of women. In some places they were very active in trade and in shopkeeping, which could give them independence and lead to their playing important public roles. Widows and unmarried women could indeed be heads of households in the same way as men. Bradley stresses that the gendering of the pre-industrial division of labour was quite flexible. She suggests that the greater uncertainties of life in pre-industrial societies made it necessary for the members of the household to cooperate in a flexible way.

It is then clear that patriarchy and the domestic division of labour did not originate with industrialization. Both were well established in pre-industrial society but with a lot of local variation and flexibility according to circumstances. It was this variability and flexibility that were largely to disappear with industrialization.

THE FAMILY IN INDUSTRIAL SOCIETY

Here we consider the impact of industrialization and urbanization on the family and its development within an industrial society. We begin by considering the separation of male and female spheres and then go on to examine the changing relationship between the nuclear and extended family.

 We refer here to many important processes of change which impacted on the family and which we discuss in more detail in other chapters. The separation of production from the household and its consequences are discussed in Chapter 13, pp. 518–26; urbanization and suburbanization in Chapter 11, pp. 416–17; changes in community in Chapter 11, p. 429; the privatizing of leisure and consumption in Chapter 13, p. 544.

The separation of male and female spheres

As we showed earlier, family life had become increasingly focused on the home during the eighteenth century. This process continued during the nineteenth century as Britain became an industrial and predominantly urban society.

In the middle class, home life became sharply separated from work life. This can be seen in the building of distinctively middle-class areas in nineteenth-century cities. Middle-class residential areas, such as Edgbaston in Birmingham, or Bloomsbury and Islington in London, were built well away from the business and industrial parts of these cities. In these areas interest grew in the furnishing of houses and the stocking of gardens. The invention of plate glass made large windows possible, so that the garden became an extension of the house. Davidoff (1990) points out that the setting of the house in a garden was one way of insulating domestic life from the outside world. This separation of home life from work life was taken further by the spread of residential suburbs at an ever greater distance from work.

The separation of home from work led to a sharper separation of male and female spheres. The world of business outside the home became a male sphere and the world of home and children a female one. Catherine Hall (1982b) notes that informal business partnerships between husbands and wives gave way to formal business partnerships between men. The woman's business was now to look after home and children, with the assistance of servants. Domesticity not only cut off women from the business world; it also excluded them from public activities in general, which became increasingly a male preserve.

Davidoff (1990) has related this separation of spheres to the construction of contrasting gender identities. In the nineteenth-century middle-class family, women were expected to be dependent, child-like, and home-centred, while men were required to be strong, protective, and active in the public world. These conceptions of masculine and feminine character strengthened patriarchal ideology and practice by making it appear as though the different roles of men and women were due to differences in their nature.

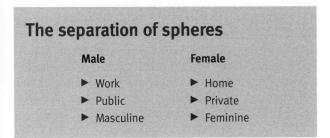

The separation of spheres

Male	Female
▶ Work	▶ Home
▶ Public	▶ Private
▶ Masculine	▶ Feminine

The situation for workers was initially somewhat different. The rise of capitalist production had certainly begun the process of separating the home from production. The creation of the industrial factory then massively extended this separation, so that it became a normal feature of most workers' lives. The separation of home from production did not, however, automatically result in the domestic division of labour characteristic of the modern nuclear family. It was not only men that were increasingly employed in wage labour but women and children too.

The employment of women generated a male reaction. It was seen as threatening the authority of the male head of the household and it also conflicted with the strengthening of patriarchy in the middle-class family. Furthermore, it weakened the bargaining position of male workers, for women and children were paid lower wages.

This reaction led to attempts to exclude women from work. The Factory Acts (see Chapter 18, p. 737), restricted the employment of women (and children). The trade unions of craftworkers excluded women from employment in the more skilled and better-paid trades. This was part of a union strategy to keep wages as high as possible by controlling the supply of labour (see Chapter 13, p. 509). Later, during the twentieth century, when the demand for labour was such that women could no longer be wholly excluded, they were restricted by the unions to lower-paid and lower-status occupations.

The idea of the 'family wage' became established.

This embodied the belief that the male breadwinner should provide for his family. It did not mean that wives stopped working for money but it did establish the principle of a domestic division of labour between male breadwinner and housewife in the nuclear household. Women's wages were treated as a supplementary source of income and women's paid work could not be allowed to interfere with their unpaid domestic work. Furthermore, employers could pay women less, since the family's standard of living depended on the man's wage. Thus, women still worked but they were paid less than men, excluded from many occupations, and left financially dependent on their husbands.

The domestic division of labour and patriarchy were not the result of capitalist industrialization. It is quite clear that both existed in pre-industrial societies, but, as Bradley argued, in pre-industrial societies there was far more local variation and the division of labour was quite flexible. Capitalist production, industrialization, and the emergence of distinct residential areas in cities more uniformly separated the home from work and this separation resulted in a more systematic division of labour between breadwinner and housewife.

The persistence of the extended family

Domesticity did not, however, mean that the nuclear family cut itself off from contact with relatives. According to Davidoff (1990), the nineteenth-century middle-class family was typically large, with families interlinked by marriage into a network that blurred the boundaries between them. People kept in touch with their relatives through letter-writing, visiting, and the exchange of gifts. The domestic focus of the middle-class household clearly did not prevent important relationships with a wide circle of relatives. Technological change later made it easier to maintain such relationships, with the telephone providing a new means of keeping in contact and eventually car ownership making visits much easier.

In the working class, the modern pattern of the nuclear family focused on home life and separated from work had become generally established in the nineteenth-century industrial city, but this did not mean that the working-class family was isolated from a wider network of relatives or from the community.

First, the extended family still performed important functions in people's lives. Michael Anderson (1971) examined the impact of industrialization and urbanization on the family in nineteenth-century Lancashire. He found that industrial employment did enable children to become independent of their parents at an early age in a way that was impossible in rural areas. But this did not mean that the wider family lost its significance, for 'critical life situations' led to a continued dependence on the family. These situations occurred through illness, death, unemployment, difficulties in finding work or accommodation, and the problems of old age. In such circumstances it was only the family that people could fall back on. The extended family remained a crucial means of support.

Secondly, the tendency towards the isolation of the nuclear family was partially reversed by the growth of stable working-class communities. After the population movements of the period of rapid urbanization had slowed down, working-class communities established themselves in the industrial city. Working-class family households were typically less isolated from the surrounding society than those of the middle class.

In their well-known study of Bethnal Green, Young and Willmott (1957) found that the extended family was still alive and well in a stable working-class community in the 1950s. They particularly emphasized the importance of the mother–daughter relationship. Even when daughters had married and set up their own households, mothers and daughters relied upon each other for help and advice, and had frequent contact. In their sample, a fifth of those married couples who had parents that were still alive had them living in the same street. This was not just a feature of family life in Bethnal Green, for similar family relationships were found in other places, such as Liverpool, Wolverhampton, and Swansea (Willmott 1988).

Communities of this sort did then change as the extensive rehousing of inner-city communities dispersed their members to other locations during the 1960s. Willmott and Young (1960) showed that the rehousing of Bethnal Green families to a housing estate in Greenleigh broke up extended family relationships and led people to lead a more isolated life focused on the nuclear family household. Women now depended much less on their mothers and more on their husbands. It was not only a matter of community upheavals, for changing leisure patterns, the rise of home ownership, and increasing domestic consumption led to a growing focus on the private life of the family.

Some recent local studies have shown that contacts with the extended family still survive, to a perhaps surprising degree. In a study of part of North London, Willmott (1986) found that two-thirds of couples with young married children saw relatives at least weekly. Working-class couples saw their relatives more often than middle-class couples did, though the differences were not great. O'Brien and Jones (1996) found similarly that 72 per cent of households in an area of East London had been visited by a relative during the previous week. Indeed, they concluded that contact with relatives had not changed significantly since a study of the area carried out by Wilmott in the 1950s.

There are grounds for thinking that in both the middle and working classes the extended family has actually been becoming more important in people's lives again. As life expectancy has increased, the number of old people has risen and they have required more care, but state care for the old has declined with the closing of local-authority homes and geriatric wards. Similarly, with the closure of mental hospitals, care of the mentally ill has been shifted back into the community via community care, but inadequate resources mean that in practice a growing burden has fallen onto families (see Chapter 6, pp. 217–19 for a discussion of community care). Increasing numbers of working women, especially the working mothers of small children, have probably made extended family assistance with childcare, particularly through grandparents, more important.

As Finch (1989) has emphasized, the amount of support provided by relatives is a matter not just of family structure but also of people's *need* for support and the *capacity* of relatives to provide it. Demographic

Main stages in the development of the nuclear family

1. Pre-industrial emergence of domesticity;
2. pre-industrial break-up of the household as a unit of production;
3. increasing focus of the family on emotional life;
4. separation of home from work by capitalist production and industrialization;
5. separation of male from female sphere and standardizing of a domestic division of labour;
6. further isolation of the nuclear family through the break-up of communities and the privatizing of leisure and consumption.

changes, the economic context, and changes in social policy all change both needs and capacity.

There is then plentiful evidence that the extended family has remained important to people in industrial societies. Extended kin are still a source of help and support, and this function may well have revived. This does not contradict the idea that the nuclear family has become increasingly isolated. The separation of production from the household, the rise of domesticity, the spread of home ownership, the decline of community, and a growing focus on private life have all gradually isolated the nuclear family. It does, however, show that the notion of a transition brought about by industrialization from the extended to the nuclear family is oversimple.

LIFE STAGES AND GENERATIONS

We have so far been examining the changing relationships between family members. We have, for example, explored the changing relationships between children and adults. However, children not only have relationships with adults; they also *become* adults as they move through life. Here we examine the stages of life through which a person passes and the way these stages have changed as the family has developed, drawing on Pilcher's (1995) analysis of these changes. We also consider how these changes in life stages have led to changes in the relationships between generations, and their impact on family structures.

The term 'life cycle' has often been used to describe this process but **life course** is preferable. The term life cycle carries with it from biology the idea of a fixed sequence of stages through which the body passes as it ages. The stages of life are, in fact, socially constructed. Conceptions of these stages vary between societies and have changed as the family has developed. Life course is a more flexible term that allows for this variability. As Pilcher has pointed out, it also carries with it a sense of the cumulative character of a person's movement through life. Thus, the way that a person starts the course and moves through it will shape the way that they finish it.

Childhood and youth

The idea that the stages of life are socially constructed, not biologically fixed, comes out most strikingly when we consider childhood. Indeed, Aries, whose work we discussed on p. 365, claimed that childhood did not exist in medieval times.

As we showed earlier, attitudes towards children were changing, in the upper levels of society at least, by the seventeenth century, but childhood, as people think of it today, did not become clearly established for the mass of the population until the nineteenth century. Two key changes during this century were the restriction of child labour by the Factory Acts and the development of compulsory education, which was gradually lengthened until the school-leaving age reached 16 in 1972. These changes created a space for childhood between infancy and adulthood and kept children in the parental home for a longer period.

Recent changes have to some extent undermined the distinctiveness of childhood. Television's penetration into the household has given children a virtually unrestricted access to the adult world. They early become fully fledged consumers of adult products, or smaller-size versions of them, rather than special products designed for children. Children have also become increasingly treated as individuals in their own right. Thus, the Children's Act of 1989 made changes in their legal status, treating them less as minors without rights and more as individuals, with the right to have their wishes and feelings taken into account by, for example, the courts or those running children's homes (Lavalette 1996; Winter and Connolly 1996).

On the other hand, there has been a reaction against these changes that has sought to emphasize the distinctive status of children. There has been a growing concern with the protection of children from drugs, violence, sexual abuse, exploitative child labour, and 'adult' television. There has also been much political concern with a need to reassert parental authority over children and establish parental responsibility for their behaviour. The status of children in the contemporary family has become a source of tension in the family and a major political issue.

Between childhood and adulthood comes youth, though it is a less clearly defined stage in the life course. Pilcher suggests that it is best treated as a stage of transition between the two, which involves two particular transitions:

▶ from compulsory, full-time education to employment;

▶ from family of *origin* to family of *destination*.

Modern conceptions of youth as a distinct stage date in Britain from early in the twentieth century, when special prisons, courts, employment, and welfare agencies for young people were established. Special organizations and institutions were required to deal with teenagers who were no longer really children but not yet recognized as adults.

The life course

It was not until the 1950s and 1960s, however, that distinctive youth cultures emerged. During these years of growing affluence teenagers found jobs quickly and could earn large amounts. Pilcher (1995: 67) cites a 1950s study that showed real earnings of young people increasing by over 50 per cent between 1938 and 1958, growing at twice the rate of adult earnings. Their spending power and minimal financial obligations to the household made them important consumers and industry responded by creating products that marked youth out as having a distinctive style of clothing and leisure. Their earnings, their greater independence, and their lifestyle brought them into conflicts with 'the older generation' that sharpened awareness of age differences.

The affluence of the young was not to last, however, and with the changes of the 1980s the *celebration* of youth arguably gave way to its *marginalization* (Coffield 1987). The spending power of youth declined because of unemployment, insecure employment, and the lengthening of education. A much higher proportion of young people now stay in some form of education or training to the age of 21. The ending of maintenance grants and the introduction of student contributions to higher education fees will lead to more dependence on the family during higher education.

The transition to economic independence has become longer and more difficult, and this is reflected in the delayed transition from family of *origin* to family of *destination*. Young people are marrying later and in the UK the average age of mothers at the birth of their first child rose from 24 in 1974 to 28 in 1994 (*Social Trends* 1996: 60).

Adulthood, middle age, and old age

Adulthood became a more distinct stage as its boundaries with childhood and old age grew sharper. We have just considered childhood. Old age became more distinct with the notion of retirement from work and the creation of the old-age pension in 1908. Adulthood became seen as the time between education and old age during which people made a productive contribution to society.

A 'new middle age' covering the later years of this period and extending into what used to be considered 'old age' has, however, emerged. There has been a reconstruction of this period as an active phase of life with its own distinctive features. This is most apparent in the idea of a *third age*.

Since the 1970s, changes in employment and welfare have created the potential for a period of active non-work. Earlier retirement released people from the

> ## The four ages of life
>
> ▶ The *first age* is the period of childhood, characterized by socialization and dependent status.
> ▶ The *second age* is the period of full-time employment, family-building, and adult responsibility.
> ▶ The *third age* covers the years 50–74 and is the age of active independent life, post-work and post-parenting.
> ▶ The *fourth age* is old age proper, characterized by increasing dependence on others.
>
> *Source*: Pilcher (1995: 89).

constraints of paid work, while state-subsidized occupational pension schemes provided them with the means to maintain a reasonable standard of living. The growing purchasing power of the over 50s led to the creation of special products for them, such as magazines, holidays, insurance schemes, and retirement homes. The University of the Third Age was set up to provide an educational forum for the exchange of accumulated occupational expertise.

Pilcher emphasizes, however, that the capacity to enjoy a leisurely and affluent *third age* is not equally available to all. Lower-paid jobs and intermittent work histories, because of child-rearing, mean that women may have to resume or continue paid work into the *third age*, while there is no retirement from housework. Redundancy may bring employment to an end before sufficient pension contributions have been accumulated to provide for a comfortable retirement. Those in lower-paid work without occupational pensions have to rely on state pensions, whose value relative to earnings has been declining since 1982, when they were linked to changes in prices rather than earnings. Some ethnic minorities are disproportionately represented in this group. The *third age* may largely be inhabited by white, middle-class, males.

In contrast with the active, up-beat presentation of the *third age*, images of the *fourth age* tend to be negative, treating old age as a period of dependence, disability, and decline. It is important to understand that these images are not simply descriptions of the characteristics of old people. Like the other stages of life, old age is socially constructed not biologically fixed.

There are two main ways in which people become classified as old. The first is their chronological age. Old age is often taken to mean the age at which people become entitled to the state pension, which in the past meant that men became old at 65 and women at 60, though in future both will become old at 65. The second is the way that they look. Grey hair and wrinkles are, for example, commonly taken to indicate that people are old.

Once people are classified as old, they tend to be treated as dependent and as physically and mentally incapacitated, irrespective of their characteristics as individuals. This stereotyping of old age has led to those who would conventionally be considered old rejecting the term as inappropriate for them. People who *look* old frequently state that they do not *feel* old. There is, as Pilcher points out, a tension between interpretations of external appearance and sense of identity.

The stereotyping of old age has been associated with patterns of prejudice and discrimination labelled **ageism**, in the same way as patterns of racial and sexual prejudice and discrimination are called racism and sexism. In the case of older women, ageism tends to be combined with sexism, for women are judged more in terms of personal appearance than men are. Old women have also been particularly caricatured in folk tales and children's stories.

The stages of life are, therefore, anything but fixed. The boundaries between one stage and another have often shifted. New stages have been created as views of the life course have altered. Changes in the life course also mean that the relationships between generations have been in constant change and this has impacted in important ways on the structure of the family and relationships within it, as we shall show next.

Generations and families

Here we examine changes in the relationships between generations and their implications for families. We first need to be clear about the meaning of the term **genera-tion**. This is commonly used in two senses:

▶ *Those born during a particular period.* Examples of this usage are the 'Sixties generation' or the 'pre-war generation' or 'my generation'.

▶ *Kinship groups defined by parent–child relationships.* Children and their cousins; their parents, aunts, and uncles; their grandparents, great-aunts, and great-uncles; (and so on) each constitute a generation within a family.

Pilcher argues that this double usage of the term creates confusion. It is best to use the term **cohort** for all those born in a particular year or group of years and reserve generation for kinship groups. The term 'inter-generational relationships' then refers, for example, to relationships between parents and children or grandparents and grandchildren within a family.

An inter-generational relationship.

Changes in the life course changed families by altering the relationships between family generations. The nineteenth-century changes in the life course profoundly altered the relationships between children, adults, and old people. As children and old people were excluded from the labour market, they became increasingly dependent on the adults of the family. The creation of the old-age pension increased the independence of the old, though, as we argued above, changes in social policy have since led to a return to greater dependence on the family.

Another important change has been the growing numbers of multi-generation families that include grandparents and great-grandparents. Two long-term demographic changes operating since the nineteenth century were the main causes of this:

▶ Greater longevity meant that the older generations lived longer.

▶ The earlier age of childbearing reduced the age gap between generations. If a couple aged 30 have a child, who also has a child at age 30, there is a sixty-year gap between grandparents and grandchildren. But if a couple aged 20 have a child, who also has a child at age 20, this gap drops to forty years.

As people live longer, four- and five-generation families are becoming more common. Thus, around a half of all people over the age of 65 are now great-grandparents.

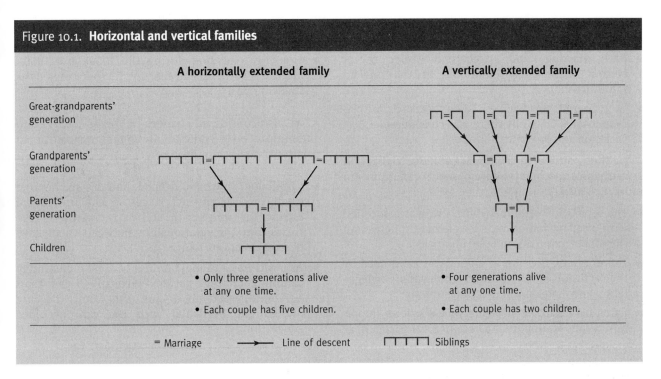

Figure 10.1. Horizontal and vertical families

A horizontally extended family

A vertically extended family

Great-grandparents' generation

Grandparents' generation

Parents' generation

Children

- Only three generations alive at any one time.
- Each couple has five children.

- Four generations alive at any one time.
- Each couple has two children.

= Marriage   ⟶ Line of descent   Siblings

Increasing longevity has combined with a lower birth rate to restructure the family. On the one hand, the family has become multi-generational. On the other hand, a lower birth rate means that people have fewer siblings. This has led to the structuring of family networks by relationships *between* generations rather than relationships *within* them. Families have been extended *vertically* rather than *horizontally* (see Figure. 10.1).

Increasing longevity, in combination with 1980s changes in social policy, means that the care of the old has become more of a burden on the young. It has been estimated that during the twentieth century the number of people in England and Wales aged 65 or over will have increased more than six times faster than the population as a whole (Allan 1985: 126). Social policy changes have, as we argued above, in practice shifted more of the care of the old onto the family. Finch (1989) emphasized that the burden has increased as the capacity of the young to look after the old has diminished. Smaller families mean that there are fewer children to share the responsibility for care of the old. Care of the old tends to fall on daughters rather than sons and the increasing employment of women means that daughters have less time available.

There is some danger, as we noted above, of treating the old as merely a burden. They can clearly make a very positive contribution to family life. Grandparents can, in particular, assist with childcare as mothers increasingly go out to work. On the other hand, the old do require more care as they get older and more of this care seems to be descending on the family at a time when it is less able to provide it. There is the potential here for a growing conflict between generations. In this context, the problem of 'elder abuse', which was 'discovered' in the United States during the 1980s (Gelles and Cornell 1987), may become a more serious issue in the future.

Thus, changes in the life course have had important consequences for family structure, family relationships, and family life. As we have shown, the family gradually became more focused on the nuclear, domestic unit, but extended family relationships remained important. These extended family relationships have, however, themselves changed as families have become vertically rather than horizontally extended. Changes in social policy have then led to these vertical relationships placing a greater burden of care on the nuclear family at a time when it is strained by other processes of social change.

SUMMARY POINTS

In this part of the chapter we have examined the development of the nuclear family as a distinct domestic unit. We began by considering the development of the family during pre-industrial times:

▶ The nuclear family emerged before industrialization and urbanization.

▶ Both marriage and parent–child relationships became increasingly emotional as the nuclear family developed.

▶ A gendered division of labour existed in pre-industrial society but there was considerable local variation and flexibility.

We then considered the impact of industrialization and urbanization, and the development of the family in industrial society:

▶ The separation of home from work was associated with a separation of male and female spheres and the construction of gendered identities.

▶ The domestic division of labour was reinforced by the exclusion of women from employment by legislation and male-dominated trade unions.

▶ Extended family relationships were still an important means of support and became stronger again as stable working-class communities established themselves.

▶ Housing relocation during the 1950s and 1960s, along with other social changes, further isolated the nuclear family.

We also considered changes in the life course and their impact on the stages of life and inter-generational relationships within the family:

▶ Childhood, youth, adulthood, and old age became established as distinct stages in the life course during the nineteenth and early twentieth centuries, but the relationships between them have been in constant change.

▶ As multi-generational families became increasingly common, families became vertically rather than horizontally extended, and the family became increasingly burdened with the care of older generations.

AWAY FROM THE NUCLEAR FAMILY

By the middle of the twentieth century the nuclear family had become established as the main form of the family in Western industrial societies. This did not mean, as we have shown, that extended family relationships ceased to be important. The nuclear family was, none the less, a distinct unit centred on marriage and children, focused on domestic life, and based on a gendered division of labour. This form of the nuclear family had also become ideologically dominant. It was enthroned as 'the family', a standard model of the family against which other forms of the family were measured and judged.

Since the 1960s, however, the dominance of this form of the family has been undermined in various ways:

▶ The institution of marriage was challenged by the sexual permissiveness of the 1960s and rising divorce rates.

▶ Separation, divorce, and remarriage resulted in one-parent families and more complex reconstituted family structures.

▶ The domestic division of labour was challenged by feminists and by the growing employment of women in paid work.

▶ A growing awareness of the 'dark side' of the family, of the violence and abuse that took place within it, revealed the negative aspects of the private and emotional nuclear family.

▶ The greater ethnic diversity generated by international migration led to more diverse family structures.

This has led to the debate over the decline of the family (see pp. 360–1). On the one hand, those who believe in family values have defended what they see as the model family against the changes that are undermining it. On the other hand, those critical of this model have argued that change has not been happening fast enough and have called for a greater acceptance of the new forms of the family that have been emerging.

In this part of the chapter, we shall work through these changes in family relationships and attitudes towards the family, and discuss the issues that they raise.

SEX, MARRIAGE, AND DIVORCE

We start by considering the so-called sexual revolution of the 1960s and its consequences. Marriage was a cornerstone of the established form of the family. Has the sexual revolution changed this? Rates of marriage have certainly declined and the divorce rate has increased. Does this mean that marriage is in decline?

A sexual revolution?

While Shorter considered that there had been an earlier sexual revolution in the eighteenth century (see p. 365), his evidence for this was at best indirect. It is, however, generally agreed that such a revolution did take place in the 1960s.

Weeks (1991) has set this sexual revolution in the context of post-war changes in capitalism and their impact on the working class in particular. Drawing on the ideas of the Frankfurt school, which we examine in Chapter 8, p. 280, he argued that economic growth after the Second World War was based on a mass consumption that commercialized all aspects of life and ended the social isolation of the working class. Social barriers were broken down and attitudes towards sexual behaviour changed. There was a shift from the traditional bourgeois virtues of self-denial and careful saving to compulsive spending. He speculated that this was associated with a new pleasure-seeking attitude towards life, which spilled over into sexual behaviour and was manipulated through the more explicit use of sexual images in advertising.

Weeks considered that it was women who 'experienced the most obvious sexualization' (1991: 256). A redefinition of female sexuality took place as sex became a source of pleasure rather than a means of producing children. The commercial manipulation of sexual images played some part in this, but new birth-control techniques, especially the contraceptive pill, were crucial, while some religious and political leaders helped the process along by taking a more permissive stance on their use. According to Weeks (1991: 258), the result was that 'women were asserting their own perceived sexual needs, though largely within a heterosexual framework and in the terms allowed by commercialism'.

Whether these were really their own needs has been a matter of debate. Weeks's insertion of the word 'perceived' is here crucial. To some feminists this has not been a liberation of women at all, for an essentially male sexual culture was imposed upon them. According to this view, the sexual revolution involved the sexual exploitation of women and led to their adoption of casual and indiscriminate male behaviour patterns.

The sexual revolution changed attitudes towards unmarried sex but not to extramarital sex. F. R. Elliot has reviewed the literature and concludes that 'sexual intercourse seems to have become an integral part of

unmarried heterosexual relationships' (1996: 13). Surveys have shown that, while premarital sex has become generally accepted, this is not the case with extramarital sex, which still meets with general disapproval. This does not, of course, mean that extramarital sex is uncommon. Annette Lawson's review of British and US research suggested that in Britain a quarter to a half of married women and at least a half of married men had at least one extramarital affair after marriage (1988: 75).

The sexual revolution changed not only attitudes to unmarried sex but also attitudes to sex in marriage. A growing importance was attached to the sexual side of the marital relationship and a satisfying sex life became one of the expectations of marriage (Richards and Elliott 1991). Thus, marriage itself had changed as a result of the sexual revolution. This can be seen as continuing the process of changing marriage from a primarily economic to a primarily emotional relationship, which, as we showed earlier, started long ago.

> ☞ You may find it helpful to place this account of changes in the relationship betwen sex and marriage in the context of our discussion of patterns of sexual behaviour and the social construction of sexuality in Chapter 5, pp. 179–81.

While heterosexual relationships between unmarried people had become accepted as normal, the same cannot be said of homosexual relationships. There were, none the less, some important changes in attitudes towards homosexuality. Homosexual behaviour was substantially, if far from completely, decriminalized in the United Kingdom by the 1967 Sexual Offences Act. The toleration of the emergence of gay villages in some cities indicates a limited acceptance of gay lifestyles. Significantly, gay couples have increasingly laid claim to the same legal status as married couples and have called for the right to marry, which indeed shows the continued normative significance of the institution of marriage.

Weeks emphasized that the new permissiveness also provoked a 'new moralism'. The rise of the New Right in the 1970s, in combination with the spread of AIDS, which the New Right saw as clear proof of the dangers of sexual liberation, led to a growing conflict between liberationists and moralists. By the 1980s the moralists of the New Right were making the running and seeking to introduce laws that would roll back permissiveness.

376 FAMILY AND HOUSEHOLD

A gay marriage

'A gay male couple, both of whom are disabled, declared their determination to have a child of their own yesterday, despite opposition from doctors, social workers and health managers. Russell Conlon, 39, and his partner Stephen, 32, are seeking a lesbian couple prepared to enter a surrogate arrangement to provide them with a baby, after being turned down as foster carers by their local social services department. In return they say they would provide the sperm for the lesbian couple to have a baby of their own.

'Mr Conlon, who "married" his gay partner last year in a ceremony blessed by a priest after an on/off relationship lasting ten years, told the *Independent* yesterday of his lifelong desire for a child. "It would be worth more to me than winning £10 m on the lottery. We can give a child as much love, care, understanding, and discipline as any heterosexual couple can," he said. "We are married in the eyes of God, we have a marriage certificate, we wear rings, and our marriage was blessed by the Church. Whether you are single, married, disabled, straight or gay you still have the right to try for a child".

'The couple, from north Manchester, applied to the Manchester social services department to adopt or foster a child, but were turned down on the grounds of their disability.'

Source: Jeremy Laurance, 'Stephen and Russell are Gay, Disabled and Want a Baby . . .', *Independent*, 28 May 1997.

▶ **Do you think that either their disability or their homosexuality are grounds for rejecting them as foster parents?**

▶ **Is there any difference, apart from their sex, between a homosexual and a heterosexual couple?**

Marriage and cohabitation

The permissiveness of the 1960s was seen as a threat to the institution of marriage. The number of marriages per year has certainly gone down. Whether this indicates that marriage itself is in decline is a more complex matter, which we will discuss below.

Statistically marriage is certainly in decline. The number of first-time marriages taking place each year has been going down since the late 1960s (see Figure 10.3 on p. 379). Another way of measuring the extent of marriage is to consider the proportion of households that contain a married couple. In Great Britain this has fallen from 74 per cent in 1961 to 58 per cent in 1995/6 and is projected to fall to 42 per cent in 2016, if current trends continue (*Social Trends* 1997: 40). More people have been staying single or cohabiting.

The proportion of single-person households in England and Wales has doubled since the 1960s, rising from 14 per cent in 1961 to 28 per cent in 1995/6. It is projected to rise to 33 per cent in 2006 (see Figure 10.2).

Cohabitation—that is, unmarried couples living together—has increased rapidly. In 1979 11 per cent of single women in Great Britain aged 18–49 were in cohabiting relationships, but by 1995 this figure had risen to 25 per cent (*Living in Britain* 1996: 23). Cohabita-

tion relationships need to be differentiated, however, and fall into three different categories:

▶ long-term relationships similar to marriage, which are often called consensual unions;

▶ short-term relationships with little commitment;

▶ pre-marriage relationships, a group that to some degree overlaps with the other two, for relationships can clearly change.

Cohabitation as an alternative to marriage has become particularly established in Scandinavia, especially in Sweden. It is much more common there than in other European countries and has become institutionalized as a stable relationship very similar to marriage. The proportion of Swedish women who marry is consequently much lower than in other countries. In 1988 the proportion of women married by the age of 50 was only 55 per cent, as compared with 78 per cent in England and Wales (F. R. Elliot 1996: 15).

Although cohabitation as an alternative to marriage has been increasing in Britain too, it commonly takes the form of a pre-marriage relationship. The proportion of women cohabiting before marriage has increased greatly. Only 19 per cent of women in Great Britain aged 18–49 who got married for the first time in the years 1975–9 cohabited before their marriage, while 51 per

Figure 10.2. **One-person households, England and Wales, 1971–2016**

Gender and age	One person households as a percentage of all households					
	1971	1981	1991	1996	2006	2016
Males						
Under 65	3	5	7	9	12	13
65 and over	2	3	3	3	4	4
Females						
Under 60	3	3	4	5	6	6
60 and over	10	12	12	11	11	12
All one-person households	18	23	27	29	33	36

Note: figures for 1996–2016 are 1992-based predictions.

Source: *Social Trends* (1997: 41).

▶ **What are the main changes that have taken place in the composition of single-person households since 1971?**

cent of those who got married during the years 1985–9 did so (F. R. Elliot 1996: 16). The rising rate of cohabitation clearly does not then mean that marriage is correspondingly in decline, for cohabitation often leads to marriage.

It is very important when considering the statistical decline of marriage to set marriage within the life course of the individual. The declining proportion of the population in marriages has been taken to mean that people increasingly prefer to live on their own or cohabit rather than marry. This is no doubt the case to *some* extent, but the decline in part reflects the smaller part of their lives that people spend in marriage. Thus, the later age of first marriages, which has been increasing since around 1970, inevitably reduces the proportion of the population who are married at any one time. Marriage may be delayed for various reasons, such as the lengthening of education, but this does not mean that any one person is less likely to become married.

Sexual behaviour has no doubt changed since the sexual revolution, but marriage clearly remains an important institution in people's lives. They may delay marriage and cohabit for a time, but the continued disapproval of extramarital sex suggests that attitudes towards marriage have not changed that much. Indeed, surveys show that well after the sexual revolution most young people in Britain still wanted to marry, wanted their marriages to be lifelong, and expected sexual fidelity (F. R. Elliot 1996: 17). Changes in marriage practices should not be confused with the decline of marriage as an institution.

Divorce and remarriage

While people are still keen to get married, the divorce rate has risen. Does a rising divorce rate indicate that marriage is in decline?

The number of divorces in the UK has risen steadily since the 1960s. It was during the years 1960–80 that divorces rose most sharply, but they continued rising until 1994, when there was a small drop (see Figure. 10.3 on p. 379). The divorce rate per thousand married people in England and Wales rose from 2.1 in 1961 to 11.9 in 1981, a sixfold increase, and by 1995 had risen to 13.1 (*Social Trends* 1997: 48).

This might suggest that marriage as an institution has declined, that it has become less stable and more likely to break down. There are, however, two reasons for qualifying such a conclusion. First, the divorce rate reflects not only the state of marital relationships but also the ease of separation. Secondly, there is also the high rate of remarriage.

Let us first consider ease of separation. An unhappy marriage leads to divorce only if the couple are able to end the marriage. Permissive changes in the law have here been crucial and invariably followed by a rise in the divorce rate. The 1969 Divorce Reform Act made divorce far easier and was followed by the big rise in divorce (see Figure 10.3). The 1984 Act allowed divorce after one rather than three years of marriage and the number of divorces after less than two years of marriage then rose (see Figure 10.4).

Crossing a threshold.

Ease of separation depends not only on the law but also on the practicalities of life after divorce. The growing employment of women in paid work and the availability of state benefits have made it easier for wives in particular to live apart from husbands.

By the 1990s a countertendency had, however, emerged. The earlier legislation had made divorce easier, but, although the 1996 Act in some ways continued this process, in other ways it made divorce more difficult. This Act removed the need for evidence of breakdown, and by introducing 'no-fault' divorce tried to take some of the conflict out of it. This was because one of the most damaging aspects of divorce for children was considered to be the conflict generated by the divorce process. On the other hand, the 1996 Act also slowed down the process by forcing people to wait and undergo a process of conciliation. This change was motivated by a belief that divorce had become too easy and people resorted to it too quickly when problems arose within relationships.

As the divorce rate went up at the end of the 1960s, so did the number of remarriages (see Figure 10.3). Two-thirds of women who get divorced in Great Britain under the age of 35 have remarried within ten years (*Social Trends* 1997: 48). People have, therefore, become more likely to pass through more than one marriage. The term *serial monogamy*—that is, a sequence of marriages—is used to describe this process. The rate of remarriage seems to have been dropping slightly during the 1990s, but it is important to bear in mind that a declining *rate* of remarrriage may simply mean that people are cohabiting longer before remarrying.

In assessing whether marriage has declined, much depends on the view taken of it. If marriage is taken to mean a lifelong relationship, which provides the only permissible framework for a sexual relationship, sexual permissiveness, increasing cohabitation, and a rising divorce rate undoubtedly mean that it has declined. This is the view of marriage put forward by those who believe in family values. If the essence of marriage is taken to be a mutually satisfying relationship, it has arguably been strengthened rather than weakened by cohabitation and divorce. Neither has stopped people marrying, while both can be seen as improving the quality of marital relationships. Cohabitation enables a more informed selection of partners and a preparation for marriage, while the greater ease of divorce makes 'empty-shell' marriages less likely.

PARENTING AND PARENTHOOD

We now move on from the marital relationship to consider parenting. The model of family relationships enshrined in family values sees marriage as essential to parenting. According to this view, the only right way to bring up children is within the marriage that has produced them.

Marriage has, however, become increasingly dissociated from parenthood. This has occurred in three main ways:

Figure 10.3. **Marriages and divorces, United Kingdom, 1961–1994**

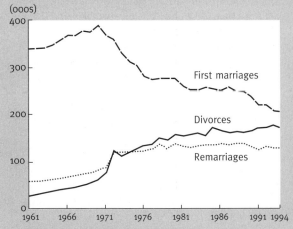

Source: Social Trends (1997: 46).

Figure 10.4. **Duration of marriage at divorce, United Kingdom, 1961–1993 (%)**

Duration (years)	1961	1981	1993
0–2	1	2	8
3–4	10	19	14
5–9	31	29	28
10–14	23	20	18
15–24	14	22	22
Over 25	21	10	9

Source: Social Trends (1996: 59).

▶ Note that the duration categories in Figure 10.4 are of different lengths.

Divorce and the law

Main laws	Main provisions
1857 Divorce Act	Made divorce available through the courts rather than special Act of Parliament. Husbands could divorce wives on the basis of adultery but wives had to prove other offences, such as cruelty and desertion as well. The expense of the procedure made it unavailable to the mass of the population.
1923 Divorce Reform Act	Wives now allowed to divorce husbands on adultery grounds alone.
1937 Divorce Reform Act	Allowed divorce on the basis of desertion, cruelty, and insanity as well as adultery.
1949 Legal Aid and Advice Act	Legal aid for divorce procedings made divorce available to the poor.
1969 Divorce Reform Act	Irretrievable breakdown made the only basis of divorce. Evidence of breakdown is adultery, unreasonable behaviour, desertion, or separation (two years with consent or five years without).
1984 Matrimonial and Family Proceedings Act	Divorce now allowed after one rather than three years of marriage.
1996 Family Law Act	A wait of nine months (fifteen if there are children) required after a statement of marital breakdown and conciliation meetings. No evidence of breakdown required.

▶ What have been the main changes in patterns of divorce since 1961?
▶ What effect do you think that legislation has had on divorce?
▶ Why do you think that the divorce rate has increased?

Sharon's marital career

Age

17   Sharon begins her sexual career. Before she is 19 she has a series of sexual partnerships with varying degrees of commitment. During this time she is living at home with her parents.

19   Sharon briefly shares a flat with female friends and then moves into rented accommodation with her boyfriend, Simon.

20   Sharon has a son and she gives up full-time employment but works in the evenings, filling shelves in a supermarket.

21   Sharon's relationship with her boyfriend breaks up and with her child she temporarily moves back to live with her parents. She finds this situation unsatisfactory, but efforts to secure alternative accommodation prove difficult. After an argument she leaves home, is judged homeless by the local housing department, and given bed and breakfast accommodation. At this time Sharon's only source of income is income support.

23   Sharon begins another relationship with William. He has been divorced for two years and has two children by his first marriage who live with his ex-wife. Sharon and William decide to live together. Sharon's mother has now retired and agrees to look after Sharon's son.

Sharon returns to working part-time as a secretary in an insurance office. Sharon and William take out a mortgage on a house.

25   Sharon and William get married.

29   Sharon has had two more children and temporarily decides to give up employment.

31   Sharon and William separate.

32   After a brief and unsuccessful attempt at reconciliation, Sharon and William divorce. Their house is sold and Sharon and her three children are rehoused in local-authority rented accommodation.

34   Sharon meets Mark, who eventually moves into Sharon's house.

40   Sharon and Mark get married.

62   Mark dies and Sharon becomes a widow.

Source: adapted from Chandler (1993: 5).

▶ **Which aspects of contemporary marriage does this (fictional) biography illustrate?**

▶ **Does the biography of Sharon suggest that marriage is in decline?**

▶ **Biography is one method used in sociology. What are the advantages of using a method of this sort in studying family life?**

▶ The number of childless couples has been rising.

▶ Children are increasingly born outside marriage.

▶ The rising rate of separation/divorce splits up children's parents.

We will not concern ourselves here with childless couples but concentrate on the consequences of this dissociation for the parenting aspects of family life. One result is increasing numbers of single-parent families. Another is more complex stepfamilies when parents remarry after divorce.

Single-parent families

The proportion of families with dependent children headed by single parents has tripled since the beginning of the 1970s (see Figure 10.5). There are two main routes to single-parenthood—the birth of children outside marriage and divorce.

The proportion of children born outside marriage has risen sharply in the United Kingdom, from 5 per cent in 1961 to 33 per cent in 1995 (see Figure 10.6). This is an internationally high figure, though France and the United States have comparable rates, and Scandinavian countries with institutionalized cohabitation substantially higher ones.

Many of these children are, however, born into a household with two parents. Cohabitation relationships may, as we showed above, be less stable than marriages, but they do mean that two parents are present and they may well lead to marriage. There is evidence that a much higher proportion of children born outside marriage are now born to mothers in a stable relationship of this sort. The joint, as opposed to sole, registration of births is taken as an indicator of a stable relationship. In England and Wales in 1971 less than half the children born out of marriage were joint registered but by 1995 well over three times as many were joint rather than sole registered (*Social Trends* 1997: 50). There is also evidence that well over a half of the mothers of children born outside marriage marry later (A. Brown 1986).

Divorce and separation also lead to single-parent families and are responsible for nearly twice as many as

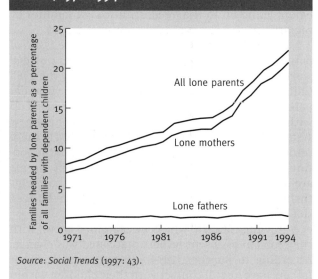

Figure 10.5. **Families headed by lone parents, Great Britain, 1971–1994**

Source: *Social Trends* (1997: 43).

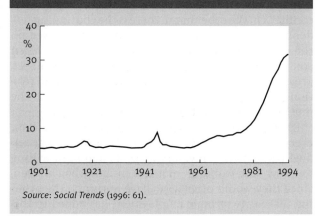

Figure 10.6. **Live births outside marriage as a percentage of all births, United Kingdom, 1901–1994**

Source: *Social Trends* (1996: 61).

unmarried mothers. Single-parent families are overwhelmingly headed by women (see Figure 10.5).

Single-parent families have become the focus of much debate. To right-wing commentators they are a defective form of the family that cannot function properly. This approach tends to treat them as the result of a lack of moral responsibility that is often blamed on the permissiveness of the 1960s. Those on the political left

attribute their problems to poverty and see them as needing support rather than criticism.

This debate has particularly centred on whether single-parent families are a source of social problems. It has been argued that the absence of a father results in inadequate socialization, particularly for boys without an appropriate male role model, who fail to learn correct patterns of male behaviour. Dennis has distinguished between families with publicly *committed* and *uncommitted* fathers and pointed to evidence that the children of the latter suffer more deprivation and show more behaviour problems (Dennis and Erdos 1992; Dennis 1993).

 Charles Murray has argued that single-parent families are largely responsible for the creation of an underclass. We discuss his theory of the underclass in Chapter 14, pp. 562–3. You may also find it interesting to compare this theory of paternal deprivation with the theory of maternal deprivation discussed in Chapter 4, pp. 137–8.

But is it the absence of a father that leads to problem behaviour? Rodger (1996) reviews many alternative explanations. The key factor may be not whether fathers are *present* but whether they are actively *involved* in upbringing, and this applies to two-parent families as well. Children in single-parent families may be disturbed not because of the absence of a father but because of the conflict and disruption caused by separation and divorce. Single-parent families experience greater deprivation than two-parent families and it may be the poverty of the household rather than the absence of a male role model that is crucial. Rodger reports that research on delinquency in children has, anyway, related it not to 'broken' but to 'bad' homes, to the way children are treated, supervised, and disciplined rather than the composition of the household.

Another key policy issue has been the rising cost to the state of supporting one-parent families. This led to the Conservative government's establishment of the Child Support Agency (CSA) in 1993 to make absent parents support their children financially. This did not, however, lead to any greater support for children, for state benefits were reduced in line with maintenance payments from the father. Women not on benefit who tried to secure the assistance of the CSA in obtaining financial support from absent fathers found that they were placed at the end of the queue. The result was not only a male backlash but also a loss of support amongst

Not only a male backlash: a demonstration against the CSA.

tinue working out their relationship as parents. Remarriage may then lead to complex parenting relationships. Here, we first consider parenting after divorce, before going on to the 'reconstitution' of families by remarriage.

Neale and Smart (1997) have explored the issue of parenting after divorce and the change from *custodial parenthood* to *joint parenting* brought about by the 1989 Children's Act. Under the earlier system of custodial parenthood, one parent, usually the mother, ended up with responsibility for care of the child. Under the new system of joint parenting, parents are required to share responsibility and are expected to cooperate in the continued care of their children. Disputes between parents are to be settled by a process of mediation that helps them work out their relationship rather than by decisions in the courts.

A growing concern, which we examined above, with the problem of absent fathers motivated this change. According to Burghes (1994), 40 per cent of absent fathers have lost all contact with their children within two years. This is a problem not only for the children but also for the father and there has been a reassertion of fathers' rights after divorce.

This issue has been linked to broader changes in family relationships by Beck and Beck-Gernsheim (1995). On the one hand, the combination of a growth in the employment of women with their continued responsibility for childcare has led to growing marital conflict. On the other hand, there is the continuing tendency for families to become increasingly focused on the emotional relationships of their members. When conflict between husband and wife increases, both seek greater emotional satisfaction in the parent–child relationship. If divorce leads to children staying with the mother, fathers feel emotionally deprived.

Furthermore, the notion that their wives now 'have everything', both a career and the children, has generated resentment. Previously, fathers had been willing to allow 'non-working' mothers to have the children, since they would otherwise 'have nothing'. The growing insecurity of male employment has added to this sense of injustice. Men have found themselves liable to end up with neither jobs nor children. They have therefore claimed that 'true equality' means that, just as women are entitled to a career, men are entitled to the emotional satisfactions of parenthood. An assertion of fathers' rights has combined with a social-policy concern with absent fathers to promote a model of joint parenting after divorce.

Neale and Smart carried out a study of post-divorce parenting. They found that the problem with the co-parenting model (they preferred this term to joint

women, who found that they benefited little from it, and risked losing whatever their (ex-)husbands were paying if they tried to obtain more through the CSA (Toynbee 1997). The CSA ran into other problems because of clashes with the courts, inadequate staffing, and difficulties in enforcing its decisions. The 1997 Labour government has, none the less, committed itself to reforming the CSA in order to make it work.

The 1997 Labour government has also set out to tackle the problem in another way, by getting single parents back to work through its Welfare to Work programme. This involves providing more state-funded childcare and putting pressure on the mothers of school-age children to seek work.

Parenting after divorce and remarriage

Divorce is generally seen as ending a marriage but it does not end a couple's relationship, at least where children are involved, for the divorced partners have to con-

parenting) and the 'true-equality' argument was that both presupposed an equality that did not actually exist. In many cases men were using the equality argument but their (ex-)wives did not have full-time employment. Furthermore, the man may not have contributed much to childcare before the divorce.

Neale and Smart argue that the demand for co-parenting may actually be generating more problems than it solves, by creating greater conflict between parents over their children. They also suggest that the old model of custodial parenting had certain advantages, since it allocated responsibility clearly and therefore enabled both parties to have greater control over their lives. Their sample was not a representative one but they did find that the custodial model remained both common and popular. They point out that there is a danger that changes in social policy will impose one model on a diversity of situations, which call for varying solutions.

Post-divorce parenting has been made more complex by the reconstitution of families after remarriage. These new families have been variously called stepfamilies, reconstituted families, and hybrid families. This kind of family is not, however, new, for the death of one parent led frequently to the reconstitution of families in earlier centuries. The commonness of a divorce background gives the contemporary reconstituted family a special character, however, and special problems. In 1995 8 per cent of families in Great Britain with dependent children contained one or more stepchildren, most of whom were from the woman's previous marriage, as Figure 10.7 shows.

Reconstituted families are generally regarded as experiencing additional tensions and problems. The marital relationship itself is likely to be less stable, since the divorce rate for second marriages is higher than that for first marriages. Children have to establish new relationships with step-parents and possibly step-siblings. They experience conflicts of loyalty between their parents and between parents and step-parents. Parents may well have to juggle feelings and responsibilities between biological children and stepchildren. Ex-partners generally have access rights and the conflicts of the previous marriage and family may well re-emerge and cast a shadow over the new one. Joint parenting arrangements may well increase these conflicts. The process of working out all these relationships is a long and complex one (Robinson and Smith 1993).

This somewhat gloomy view of the reconstituted family has been challenged. It has been argued that it compares stepfamilies with an idealized and unrealistic image of the nuclear family. This does not, for

Figure 10.7. Stepfamilies by family type, Great Britain, 1995

Family type	%
Couple with child(ren) from the woman's previous marriage	86
Couple with child(ren) from the man's previous marriage	10
Couple with child(ren) from both partners' previous marriages	4
Total	100

Note: statistics for families where family head is aged 16–59; includes children from previous cohabitations.
Source: Living in Britain (1996: 4).

example, take account of the negative aspects of this kind of family, which we discussed on pp. 360–1. It also neglects the advantages of the new form of extended family created through remarriage (see box on p. 384). A more complex but more extensive family network is created. In such a family a child can draw on the support and resources of a far greater array of relatives. Family life can be flexible and adaptable, with no fixed boundaries and an opportunity for considerable choice of relationships within the family network.

One policy response to these changes in parenting has been to defend and try to revive the traditional family, on the basis that this is the only context in which proper parenting can take place. The alternative response is to accept the growing diversity of family life, recognize that there are positive aspects to other forms of the family, and provide appropriate support for the new kinds of family that are emerging.

ETHNICITY AND FAMILY DIVERSITY

Ethnic diversity due to increasing international migration is another source of family diversity. It is, however, important to bear in mind the diversity *within* as well as *between* ethnic groups, as Westwood and Bhachu (1988a) have argued. Family forms are also changing all the time. Static stereotypes that exaggerate the differences between groups and ignore the diversity and change within them must be avoided.

It is particularly important to avoid contrasting ethnic-minority households with a mythical British

A new form of extended family

Figure 10.8. Jennie's extended family

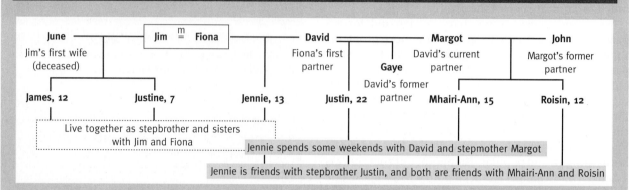

'Alongside the nuclear family of parents and their children, a new social organism is developing: the extended network of stepparents, stepchildren, cousins, aunts, uncles and grandparents. It is a grouping that is simply reflecting demographics, expanding and adapting to increased rates of divorce and remarriage. . . .

'Take Jennie, 13, whose mother Fiona, 38 . . . separated from her partner David six years ago to marry Jim, 45. She now enjoys strong relationships with both sets of parents and their respective partners as well as various step- and half-relations across the country. For Jennie there have been many positive aspects to this complex merger of relatives and strangers.

'"I like having this sort of family," says Jennie. "My mum seems much happier and so does my dad. I also feel I've got more people to support and care for me—I've always got lots of different relatives to visit and things to do."'

Source: Emma Cook, 'The Nuclear Family is Dead: Long Live the Extended Family' *Independent on Sunday*, 11 Nov. 1996.

---

nuclear household. Most British households do not consist of husband, wife, and children. In 1996 in Britain as a whole only 23 per cent of households consisted of a married couple with dependent children (*Social Trends* 1997: 40). Differences between ethnic minorities may also be greater than differences between a minority and the majority (see Figure 10.9).

We consider here both African-Caribbean and Asian family structures. In each case, we begin by outlining family structures in the area of origin and then consider how these have changed in the context of British society. We draw considerably here on F. R. Elliot's (1996) discussion of these issues.

African-Caribbean families

The literature on family patterns in the Caribbean suggests that the lower-class Caribbean family is particularly centred on the role of the woman. Marriage is weakly institutionalized, men 'wander', and it is common for women to head households. Relationships between mothers and children are much stronger than those between fathers and children. The family is held together by a network of women. Children are cared for through this network and women other than the biological mother often take on a mothering role.

According to Foner (1986), the Caribbean pattern of the household headed by the woman persists amongst migrants to Britain and their descendants, though men have been more involved in family life than in the Caribbean. Evidence from the 1980s shows that families headed by lone mothers were much more common amongst African-Caribbean than other ethnic groups. According to Haskey (1991), 44 per cent of African-Caribbean households took this form, as compared with 13 per cent of white households.

It seems that this woman-centred pattern re-established itself amongst later generations after first-generation migrants moved away from it. This should not, however, be seen simply as the re-emergence of a cultural tradition, for it has also been explained in terms of increased black male unemployment or the assertion of black cultural identity in response to patterns of racist exclusion (see Chapter 12, p. 486, for a discussion of the politics of identity).

Figure 10.9. **Ethnicity and household composition, Great Britain, 1991** (%)

Household composition	Black	Indian	Pakistani/ Bangladeshi	Other ethnic minorities	White
One person	27	10	7	22	27
Two or more unrelated adults	6	3	3	7	3
One family					
Couple					
No children	13	14	7	16	28
Dependent children	20	50	60	37	24
Non-dependent children only	6	8	4	5	9
Lone parent					
Dependent children	21	4	7	8	5
Non-dependent children only	6	3	2	3	4
Two or more families	1	9	9	2	1
All households (=100%) (000s)	328	226	132	185	21,027

Source: Social Focus on Ethnic Minorities (1996: 20).

▶ **What are the main differences between ethnic groups in the size of households and their composition?**

▶ **What evidence can you find in this table to support the points made in the text about ethnic differences in family life?**

F. R. Elliot (1996) argues that this African-Caribbean family pattern is associated with a high involvement of women in economic activity and distinctive attitudes to work. African-Caribbean women have been more economically active than women from any other ethnic group. They see paid work as a basis for financial independence and are more likely to control the use of their earnings than Asian or white women. This high involvement in economic activity is made possible by the sharing of the mothering role with other women.

Asian families

Although there are considerable cultural differences between the various South Asian nationalities that have come to Britain, there are certain underlying similarities. Families from rural areas in South Asia typically take a more extended form. They include three generations in the household, and are organized through a network of males. They are also strongly bound together by ideas of brotherhood and family loyalty. Marriages are arranged and seen as a contract between two families. This type of family structure contrasts strongly with both the contemporary nuclear family in Britain and the mother-centred African-Caribbean family.

Migration to Britain severely disrupted extended families of this kind and many women especially found themselves socially isolated at home and unsupported by kin. A period of dislocation was followed by the rebuilding of extended family structures. The family network was an important resource for the individual, as well as a source of identity, a means of maintaining cultural distinctiveness, and a defence against local hostility.

F. R. Elliot argues that South Asian communities have adapted to the British environment but according to 'their own cultural logic' (1996: 52). Sikh households have become more focused on couples and women have renegotiated traditional authority patterns through the greater independence paid work has given them. They were able to do this because Sikh religious traditions emphasized equality and allowed Sikh women a degree of independence (Bhachu 1988). In contrast, women from Pakistani and Bangladeshi cultures have been limited to homework or work in family businesses by the Islamic prohibition of contact with unrelated men. This can lead to the exploitation of women as cheap labour and their confinement within the home. They have, none the less, become more assertive and influential within the family, and have also developed some independence through their own neighbourhood networks (Werbner 1988).

Divorce rates are very low within the minorities of Asian origin. Divorce is permitted under certain circumstances but strongly discouraged. This lower rate of divorce can be linked to the greater strength of communal and kinship bonds, to the patriarchal control of women by men, and the lower involvement of women in paid employment outside the family. There is evidence that the family life of young Asian couples has become more focused on the marital relationship and less involved with wider kin networks but that they have, none the less, a strong sense of obligation to the extended family.

Elliot goes on to relationships between parents and children. Some commentators have pictured young Asians as caught between cultures and in conflict with their parents, particularly over arranged marriages. Ethnographic studies have suggested that they have been able to make compromises between cultures or find ways of combining them. Thus, they have accepted the institution of the arranged marriage but have become more involved in the arrangement process and have been allowed to defer the marriage until they have completed higher education. Conflict does clearly occur, however, and some young Asians have rejected their parents' plans, chosen their own partners, or engaged in secret relationships.

Both the African-Caribbean and the various Asian patterns of family life originated in agrarian societies but have persisted in a modified form within British industrial society. Since both are quite different from the standard nuclear family, their adaptation to life in an industrial society leads one to question Parsons's notion that the nuclear family is the form appropriate to an industrial society. They similarly show that family forms are culturally diverse and that the standard nuclear family is not really standard at all but just one cultural form that the family has taken.

WORK, MONEY, AND IDENTITY

The standard nuclear family has also been challenged by changes in employment patterns and we now move on to consider the impact of these changes on gender roles within the family. As we showed on pp. 366–7, the form of the nuclear family that developed in Britain was characterized by the separation of male and female spheres, a domestic division of labour between the male breadwinner and the housewife, and the patriarchal authority of the husband/father.

We begin by discussing whether the growing employment of women has led to changes in the domestic division of labour. We then move on to consider whether it has affected the management of money in the household. Lastly, we discuss whether it has led to the emergence of the 'new man'.

 The discussion of the domestic division of labour should be placed in the context of changing employment patterns, which we examine in Chapter 13, pp. 536–41.

A changing domestic division of labour?

Changes in employment have challenged the rationale for the domestic division of labour. It is not only that there has been a growing employment of women in paid work. It is also that the employment of men has declined. Does this mean that the domestic division of labour is coming to an end?

The domestic division of labour established in nineteenth-century Britain was gendered. It was a division of labour between the male *breadwinner* and the *housewife*. This was not, however, an absolute division of labour. First, men did some household tasks. These two were gendered, for some tasks, such as gardening and house repairs, were defined as men's work, while others, such as routine cleaning and childcare, were defined as women's work. Secondly, as we showed on p. 367, women too did paid work, but this was regarded as secondary to their domestic work. It has often been said that women in this situation had to carry a *double burden* or work a *double shift*, because they were still expected to carry out their domestic work.

A 1990 study by Warde and Hetherington (1993) of households in the Manchester area showed that the domestic division of labour still operated. Housework was overwhelmingly done by women rather than men. There was also a clear division of household tasks between men and women. Women did the more routine cleaning, cooking, and childcare tasks. Men mainly did jobs such as home repairs, home improvement, car maintenance, and also various intermittent tasks such as brewing alcohol, cooking barbecues, and

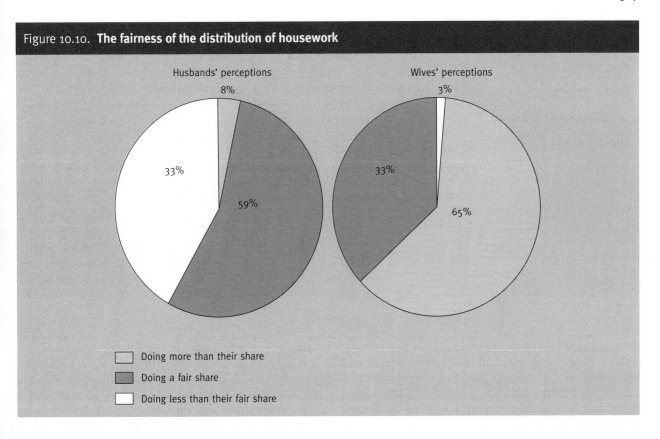

Figure 10.10. **The fairness of the distribution of housework**

Husbands' perceptions

8%

33%

59%

Wives' perceptions

3%

33%

65%

Doing more than their share

Doing a fair share

Doing less than their fair share

collecting takeaways. Weeding the garden appeared to be the only ungendered task.

The Warde and Hetherington study also addressed the issue of whether this division of labour was perceived as fair. As Figure 10.10 shows, they found unsurprisingly that most men thought that they did their share of household tasks, though most women disagreed and considered that women did more than their fair share.

Does this mean that the growing employment of women has made no difference? Do they still carry a double burden?

Gershuny (1992) challenged the notion of a continuing double burden on the basis of time-budget studies. These used detailed diaries to measure the time spent by men and women on their various daily activities. Gershuny argued that, even if the distribution of housework was still far from equal, the proportion of housework done by men had been increasing and the total work done by men and women had become almost equal. This was not just a matter of changing shares, for Gershuny claimed also to have shown that since the 1960s the time spent by women on housework has

declined because of the introduction of more machinery into the household (Gershuny 1988: 587–8).

Gershuny argued that a process of *lagged adaptation* was taking place. His data showed that a gap still existed between the total amount of work done by men and women, but he held that there was inevitably a lag between women taking on paid work and households adapting to change. There was evidence to show that they did adapt, for the longer that a woman had been in paid employment, the more equal had become the sharing of the total household workload. Gershuny argued that there was also a generational dimension to change, for children socialized in a changing household may be expected to acquire different conceptions of gender roles.

While the Warde and Hetherington study showed that in many ways there was an unchanging domestic division of labour, some of its findings were consistent with change. When women were in full-time employment, there was a more equal distribution of household tasks. It is also significant that a substantial proportion of men thought that they were doing less than their fair share. This suggests that, even

Household responses to high male unemployment, north-east Britain, 1980s	Type of household	Wife's hours of work per week	Husband's domestic tasks	Gender segregation ideas
	Traditional	Around 12 hours	A few minor tasks only	Traditional
	Traditional flexible	A wide range of hours[a]	A few major and some minor tasks	Some belief in sharing
	Sharing	Around 20 hours	Some major and a range of minor tasks	Strong belief in sharing
	Exchange of roles	30 hours or more	A range of major tasks	A few residual traditional beliefs

[a] No relationship was found between this type and the number of hours worked by the wife.

Source: adapted from Wheelock (1990: 111, 114, tables 4.2, 4.3).

though there was little sign of behavioural change, some attitudinal change had taken place. Warde and Hetherington also found that the household tasks carried out by sons and daughters were less gendered than those done by their parents, which fits Gershuny's adaptation model.

In her study of an area of high male unemployment in north-east Britain during the 1980s, Wheelock (1990) found that the families that she studied were adapting to change. They were evenly distributed between four types of household organization, which showed, broadly speaking, a relationship between the number of hours worked by the woman and the amount of sharing of household tasks, though there was also clearly some lagging-behind of traditional practices and beliefs.

The domestic division of labour has then persisted, in spite of the growing employment of women, but there is certainly evidence of change. The growing employment of women has had some effect on the domestic division of labour.

This discussion has been concerned primarily with housework in Britain, but, as is often the case in sociology, international comparisons can be highly instructive. Figure 10.11 presents data on the distribution of certain housework tasks in Britain, China, and Japan.

The contrast between China and Japan is particularly striking, with Britain lying in a middle position between them. Interestingly, China, the economically least developed country, had gone furthest towards an equal distribution of tasks. Also, China and Japan originally shared a culture that sharply separated the tasks of men and women but then diverged. China has passed through a communist revolution involving a thoroughgoing programme of cultural change which proclaimed that 'women hold up half the sky' and emphasized equality between men and women. This comparison suggests that rapid change in gender roles is possible and brings out the significance of politics and ideology for the distribution of housework.

There are a number of hidden issues in this discussion that need to be brought out. There is first the problem of the definition of housework. Does this, for example, include gardening or car maintenance? Different conclusions will be reached according to the range of tasks included in a study. Time budget studies may well reach different conclusions from other studies because of their all-inclusive nature.

Secondly, a focus on the amount of work done does not take account of its meaning. When men carry out an increasing share of housework, do they take on the boring routine jobs that are particularly soul-destroying? Or do they focus on intrinsically more interesting activities, such as gardening, which could reasonably be considered leisure rather than work (see our discussion of these issues in Chapter 13, pp. 504–8)? There is also evidence that women are more likely to do multiple tasks simultaneously, to combine work and leisure activities, and to experience interruptions that fragment their activities (O. Sullivan 1997).

Thirdly, the listing of tasks takes no account of the hidden 'emotion work' that women do. Duncombe and Marsden (1995) carried out a study of forty couples who

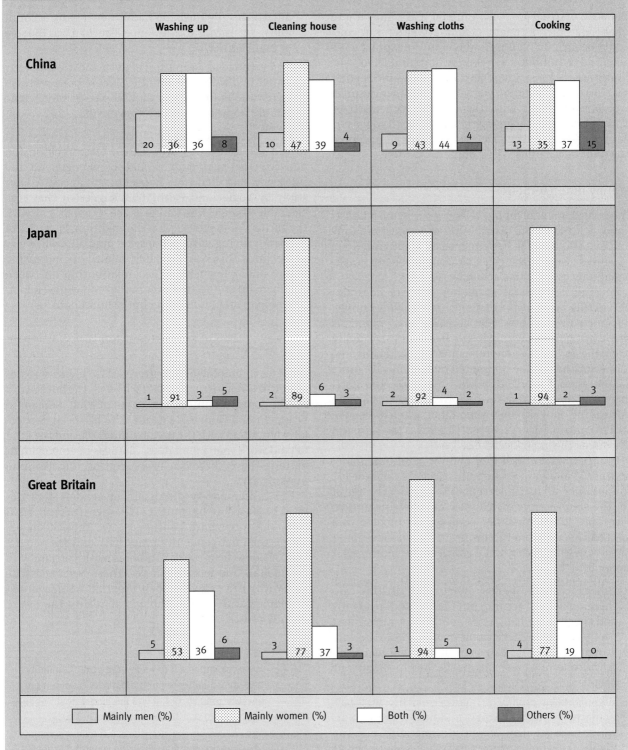

Figure 10.11. **Who does the housework in China, Japan, and Great Britain?**

	Washing up	Cleaning house	Washing cloths	Cooking
China	20 36 36 8	10 47 39 4	9 43 44 4	13 35 37 15
Japan	1 91 3 5	2 89 6 3	2 92 4 2	1 94 2 3
Great Britain	5 53 36 6	3 77 37 3	1 94 5 0	4 77 19 0

Mainly men (%)   Mainly women (%)   Both (%)   Others (%)

Source: Stockman *et al.* (1992: 4).

▶ What are the main differences in the domestic division of labour between the three countries?

▶ Can you identify any patterns that the three countries have in common?

▶ What are the implications of these data for the achievement of equality between men and women?

had been married for at least fifteen years. They found what they called a general gender asymmetry in emotional behaviour. Men were reluctant to express emotions and the emotion work of the household had to be done by the women. It has been argued (see p. 558) that it is through the emotion work of the wife that the male breadwinner copes with the tensions generated by work in a capitalist economy. It has also been suggested that this additional emotion work means that women carry not a *double* but a *triple* burden.

Money management

The management of money is a key issue in most households. Studies of the distribution of tasks commonly find that this is one that is either shared or mainly done by women. Does this mean that women control household finances and that patriarchy is a myth?

Routine *management* of money matters does not neccesarily mean *control* of money. It may, for example, mean sorting out how the 'housekeeping' money is spent, but not deciding how much is to be allocated to it. Furthermore, as Crompton points out, when income is low, sorting out the household budget may be 'more a chore than a source of power' (1997: 92). The statement that both partners are involved may also be quite misleading, for Pahl (1989) found that, when both were said to control finances, in practice it was the husband who made the major decisions.

Pahl (1993) identified four main ways of organizing household money in a randomly selected sample of 102 couples, who all had at least one child under the age of 16. The couples were sorted into the following groups according to whether they pooled their income in a joint bank account and according to the wife's response to the question 'Who really controls the money that comes into the house?'

▶ *Husband-controlled pooling* (39 couples). In this case there was a joint account but the husband paid bills and checked the bank statement. This arrangement was typical of higher income groups where the wife was not in paid employment. If the wife had a job it was one of lower status than her husband's or part-time.

▶ *Wife-controlled pooling* (27 couples). This was particularly common amongst middle-income groups, where both partners were in full-time paid work. The higher the wife's earnings and educational level, as compared with the husband's, the greater the wife's financial control.

▶ *Husband control* (22 couples). This occurred typically on the traditional model of a housekeeping allowance. The husband had his own bank account and gave his wife an allowance. The man was the sole or main earner.

▶ *Wife control* (14 couples). This was most commonly found in low-income families, where both partners were unemployed and household income came mainly from social-security payments.

Thus, women had most control when there was least to control. There was otherwise a clear relationship between the paid employment of women and the influence they had over household finances. A later study by Vogler and Pahl (1993) suggested that considerable change was taking place. Comparison with the earlier study showed that the traditional practice of husbands giving wives a housekeeping allowance was in decline. This was probably related to increasing male unemployment. The relationship between employment and control over money shows how important employment is to power in the household.

The 'new man'?

Changes in employment patterns raise identity issues as well. It is not just a matter of who does the housework or who controls family finances but of what it means to be a man or a woman. Male identity has been particularly bound up with the breadwinner role and the kind of paid work that a man does. Changes in employment patterns have therefore been seen as undermining masculinity.

The contemporary discussion of gender identities must be placed in the context of the identities inherited from the nineteenth century. As we showed on pp. 366–7, the emergence of domesticity and the separation of home from work combined with patriarchy to create male and female spheres. These became associated with distinct gender identities that were regarded as biological in origin, though in reality they were socially constructed.

 It is very important to understand that femininity and masculinity are not biologically fixed but are socially constructed. If you are in any doubt about this, refer to our discussion in Chapter 4, pp. 139–42, where we also discuss the development of feminism. You may also find it helpful to refer to Chapter 13, pp. 539–41, where we discuss changing patterns of male and female employment.

These identities came into question because of changes in employment patterns and the feminist challenge to traditional gender roles. The identities attached to the gendered division of labour have been undermined by the growing employment of women in paid work. Furthermore, the growth of women's employment has been not only in traditional women's jobs in, for example, caring occupations. Women have also broken into high-status professional and managerial occupations that were previously considered a male preserve. Girls have also been overtaking boys in education (see Chapter 7, p. 252).

Moreover, male unemployment rose sharply in the 1980s as employment in traditional industries collapsed. Men found it more difficult to sustain the male breadwinner role and came under pressure to do more domestic work, while their wives went out to earn money. Nor was it only unemployment that was the problem, for job expectations had changed as well and men found themselves called upon to be more flexible, to behave as members of a team, and to be more responsive to clients and customers (see Chapter 13, p. 529). Men were, in other words, expected to show both inside the home and at work the caring and cooperative qualities traditionally associated with women.

One response to these changes has been the notion of the 'new man', who shares housework and childcare with his partner. Young and Willmott (1973) argued that changes in employment patterns would lead by the end of the twentieth century to the emergence of a 'symmetrical family' in which men and women would be equal. They would both have demanding jobs outside and inside the household. The notion of the 'new man' went beyond this, however, to claim that differences in gender identity would disappear. The 'new man' would be caring and cooperative, abandoning masculine aggressiveness and competitiveness.

As we showed above, a gendered division of labour within the household has, none the less, persisted. There is little evidence that many 'new men' have appeared on the scene. Indeed, there has arguably been a reassertion of masculinity.

Connell (1995) has shown this reassertion occurring within, what he calls, masculinity therapy. This grew up in the 1960s in response to the feminist challenge to traditional gender roles and was initially concerned with the development of the 'new man'. Men were to be cured of masculinity through therapy. In the 1980s, however, masculinity therapy completely changed in character and now meant the restoration of a traditional masculinity. Men went off to 'bush camps' where they engaged in drumming, hunting, and warrior activities in search of the 'deep masculine' within them.

Masculinity was asserted in other ways, such as the emergence, particularly in the United States, of movements celebrating the gun and defending the right to carry it. Another was 'gay-bashing', for the coming-out of gays threatened the heterosexual component of traditional masculine identity. Yet another was the reassertion of patriarchal authority by religious movements.

Connell also argues that the questioning of male identity should not lead us to suppose that men are losing their grip. He emphasizes their continued power in industry, politics, and the media. He suggests that globalization has in fact led to the extension of Western patriarchy throughout the world. As he puts it, the 'active defence' of 'hegemonic masculinity' has 'formidable resources' and has been 'impressively successful' (1995: 216).

Tim Edwards (1997) has examined changes in masculinity from a refreshingly different perspective. He focuses on the rise of male fashion, particularly through the boom in men's fashion magazines, and the part it has played in shaping conceptions of masculinity. His starting point is not a male identity crisis caused by changing employment patterns and feminism but rather the expanding market for male fashion. This was generated by the individualist consumerism of the 1980s and the high purchasing power of young men in

The Promise Keepers

A men-only Christian movement with this name has emerged in the United States, and has organized large gatherings and marches. It is based on the idea that men should commit themselves to follow seven moral and religious promises. Men are urged to form close relationships with other men in order to help them keep these promises. Its beliefs emphasize the importance of family values, male authority in the family, and responsible male behaviour. In its stress on male authority and leadership it is clearly a reassertion of patriarchy. Its concept of masculinity emphasizes male responsibility, however, and it recognizes that many American social problems are the result of men's sexual behaviour, violence, and neglect of their family responsibilities. While its patriarchal tendencies have been attacked by feminists, some women have supported it because of its promotion of responsible male behaviour.

growing occupations, such as financial services, advertising, and marketing. Demographic changes meant that there were more single men and childless couples, with money to spend on fashion products.

Edwards too detects the continuation of traditional conceptions of masculinity. He recognizes that some change has occurred. Male fashion and the manipulation of male sexuality in advertising broke with the traditional focus of male identity on work and production. The rise of an openly expressed and consumption-oriented gay culture also played some part in the growth of male fashion. However, even while seeking to attract gay consumers, the men's magazines retained a dominantly heterosexual orientation and traditional images of masculinity:

'Images of masculinity are pumped through the media, witnessed on trains, splashed upon posters and endlessly paraded in mail-order and high-street shopping. Yet despite this apparent plethora, the content of these representations remains quite extraordinarily fixed. The men concerned are always young, usually white, particularly muscular, critically strong-jawed, clean shaven (often all over), healthy, sporty, successful, virile, and ultimately sexy.' (T. Edwards 1997: 41)

Changes in employment patterns and gender relationships have not destroyed masculinity. Instead of the emergence of a 'new man' indistinguishable from woman, there has been a reassertion and commercial exploitation of masculinity that involve much of its traditional content. This does not, however, mean that the 'old man' has simply persisted. Traditional conceptions of masculinity have been reconstructed and refashioned into something new that is more appropriate to the times. Distinct gender identities still exist, but, in a world of constant change, they too are changing.

DOMESTIC VIOLENCE AND ABUSE

The established form of the nuclear family has come into question not only because the domestic division of labour and established gender roles have been challenged but also because of an increasing awareness of what is often called the 'dark side' of the family. The family home is not only a place of comfort and affection but also a place where violence and sexual abuse occur.

Both family violence and sexual abuse have become major issues. There are three possible explanations of this:

▶ *Changes in behaviour.* The behaviour concerned has been increasing. This is the explanation that first springs to mind. While it may certainly be part of the

explanation, two other possible explanations must also be considered.

▶ *The redefinition of behaviour.* Behaviour once considered acceptable or only a minor form of deviance has been redefined as unacceptable or serious. The beating of children or 'date rape' are examples of this.

▶ *Increasing awareness.* Unacceptable behaviour that was previously concealed has come to light. Much of what goes on in families is hidden from view. There has been a process of rediscovering and investigating the 'dark side' of the family since the 1960s.

Child abuse and child protection

The problems of separating out changes in behaviour from changes in attitudes and reporting apply to both violence towards children and the sexual abuse of children.

Violence against children is nothing new, but it is only since the 1960s that it has been described as physical abuse. Corporal punishment and firm discipline within the family had long been considered essential to the maintenance of social order. In the 1960s, however, the 'battered-baby syndrome' was discovered, and in 1973 the death of Maria Colwell at the hands of her stepfather led to a Public Inquiry that established child abuse as a problem. The work of professionals in medicine and childcare was clearly important in bringing child abuse to light, but Hendrick (1994) argues that it became a major issue because the post-war political consensus had collapsed and ideological conflict was increasing at that time. The Colwell case was used by the New Right to highlight the dangers of permissiveness and moral decline.

The reported physical abuse of children has certainly increased rapidly in Britain. The number of child-injury cases registered with the National Society for the Protection of Children doubled between 1976 and 1986 (Creighton 1992: 64). We are, however, dealing here with rates of around one case per thousand children and changes in reporting can easily have a big effect. The media gave considerable publicity not only to the Maria Colwell case but to a number of other tragic cases at this time.

There is actually some evidence from the United States of decreasing violence. Straus and Gelles replicated a 1975 national survey in 1985 and found that, although the overall level of violence towards children had changed little, both severe and very severe violence had considerably declined. The proportion of children experiencing severe violence had declined from 14 to 10.7 per cent, and the proportion experiencing very severe violence from 3.6 to 1.9 per cent. Straus and Gelles argue that a decline of violence is consistent with a number of changes during these years: increased birth control leading to fewer unwanted children; improved economic conditions, and therefore less financial stress on families; improved child-protection services; and greater publicity given to the child-abuse issue. This study relied, however, on interviews with parents, and the authors recognize that growing publicity may have led to a greater reluctance to report violence.

The discovery of the physical abuse of children was followed shortly by the discovery of sexual abuse. This happened in the United States in the 1970s and in Britain in the 1980s.

There is some American evidence of a long-term increase in the sexual abuse of children (see box below). In the United States there was also a large increase of 71 per cent in reported cases during the three years 1976–9 (Russell 1986: 75). An increase of this scale over such a short period can only be due, however, to changes in reporting or definition. Varying definitions of sexual abuse certainly have an enormous affect on reported rates. Faith Robertson Elliot (1996: 156) points out that different definitions have resulted in estimates of its prevalence in Britain ranging from 3 to 46 per cent of children. A key issue here is whether non-contact offences, such as exposure or obscene telephone calls, are included.

In Britain there was an upsurge of concern with the sexual abuse of children in the family during the 1980s. High publicity was given to certain cases. In 1987 545 complaints of child sexual abuse were referred to Cleveland Council and action was taken in 265 cases to protect the children involved. Social workers advised by doctors using new techniques of diagnosis removed a large number of children from families suspected of child abuse. According to Rodger (1996), the main reason why these cases (and the subsequent Orkney cases in 1981) caused so much shock was that they involved apparently normal middle-class families. According to recent studies, child sexual abuse is equally likely to be found in all social classes (F. R. Elliot 1996: 160).

Intense publicity was also generated by the very public conflict in Cleveland between the police, on the one hand, and social workers and doctors, on the other. The police rejected the medical evidence of sexual abuse and refused to act on it. Gittins (1993) interprets this as a conflict between a patriarchal police force denying the existence of child sexual abuse, which is mainly carried out by men, and social services seeking to protect children. Media coverage largely took the side of the police, and social workers found themselves under attack from the media and from politicians. They were, in fact, under a double attack for both failing to protect children and overzealously removing them from their families.

There has subsequently been a shift towards a more legalistic and formal system of child protection. Social work has become more bureaucratic, defensively concerning itself with rules and procedures in order to avoid criticism. It has also focused increasingly on the investigation and surveillance of families rather than family support. Rodger argues that a concept of the 'dangerous' family has replaced notions of the

The increasing sexual abuse of children in the United States

Russell (1986) carried out a study of sexual assaults through a survey of 930 women in San Francisco in 1978. Women of all ages (aged 18 or above) were interviewed and rates of abuse could therefore be established for women born from the early years of the century up to the early 1960s. Russell concluded that rates of both incestuous and non-familial child sexual abuse had increased fourfold between 1909 and 1973. Instances of incestous abuse amounted to 16 per cent of the total reported child abuse. There were, however, problems with the representativeness of these findings, since 36 per cent of those approached refused to participate.

Why had child sexual abuse increased in this way? The main explanations suggested by Russell related to changes in sexual behaviour and gender relationships. She pointed to the increasing availability of child pornography and the permissiveness generated by the sexual revolution of the 1960s. She also suggested that a reaction against women's demands for sexual equality might be involved. Women's challenge to male power deflected men towards children as sexual objects, for children were dependent on adults and less able to resist their demands. This is consistent with the generally accepted explanation of child sexual abuse as due to the availability and vulnerability of children rather than their sexual attractiveness.

'vulnerable' or 'troubled' family (1996: 188). While the Cleveland and Orkney cases, the publicity surrounding them, and the public inquiries that followed them clearly had a considerable impact, longer-term changes were also at work.

Parton (1996) links changes in child protection to the changing relationship between the state and the individual since the 1970s. During the 1970s people became increasingly sceptical of the idea that state intervention was 'for the good of the people' and more concerned with protecting the individual against the state. During the 1980s social policy in general became much more individualist (see Chapter 18, pp. 750–3). This was reflected in attitudes towards the handling of child-abuse cases, where interventions by social workers were widely condemned. There was a growing emphasis on the rights of the individual and it was in this context that an increasingly legalistic approach was taken towards child protection.

There is no way of knowing whether child abuse has increased or whether there is simply greater awareness of it. It is clear from all this that the publicity given to child abuse and policy towards it have little to do with child abuse itself and much to do with changes in professional interest, ideology, and politics.

Marital violence and coercion

Attitudes towards violence between husband and wife have also changed markedly since the 1960s. Feminism has here played a crucial role in exposing the hidden violence within marriage and challenging the idea that it is simply part of normal married life. The idea that marital violence is solely the violence of husbands against wives has, however, been challenged by research in America, which claims that husband-battering is as much a problem as wife-battering.

Dobash and Dobash have shown that a large part of criminal violence occurs within the home and that this is overwhelmingly the violence of men against women. Their analysis of domestic violence in Glasgow and Edinburgh demonstrated that over a third of criminal violence offences actually occurred within the family. Some 26 per cent of violence offences were assaults on wives, as compared with under 1 per cent that were assaults on husbands or cases of mutual assault (Dobash and Dobash 1980: 247). According to these authors, violence was a means through which men sought to control women. Violence against women was typical of a patriarchal society.

Changes were made in British law during the later 1970s to provide greater protection for women. Housing rules were changed so that women leaving home because of male violence were no longer regarded as making themselves homeless and therefore losing the right to council housing. New laws gave women greater legal protection against violent husbands through injunctions that could be issued quickly by magistrates and followed by imprisonment if breached. Abbott and Wallace (1990) conclude, however, that lack of implementation means that these Acts have not in practice done much to give greater protection to wives, let alone those in cohabiting relationships.

Marital rape is a key issue in the study of changing attitudes to domestic violence. This is because marital rape was until recently not treated in most countries as a crime. Indeed, it was regarded as a legal impossibility. The law assumed that men were entitled to sexual intercourse whenever they wished it, while married women were required by their marriage vows to obey men. In the United States the law on this point was changed in most states by 1990 (Russell 1990). In Britain, it was not until 1991 that a House of Lords ruling established that rape could occur within marriage.

Russell carried out a pioneering study of marital rape, using material from the same 1978 survey that she used for her study of child sexual abuse (see box on p. 393). Definitions of rape vary from the narrow legal definition of forced intercourse to the much broader notion of forced sexual activity of any kind. Russell adopted an intermediate definition that included forced oral and anal sex and forced digital penetration as well as intercourse. She found that 14 per cent of the married women in her sample reported that they had experienced rape or attempted rape by a husband or ex-husband. Marital rape was a common form of rape, and 38 per cent of the rape *incidents* reported were carried out by husbands or ex-husbands (Russell 1990: 57, 67).

Marital rape as defined in this way has been regarded as but an extreme form of sexual coercion. Indeed, it has been argued by some feminists that there is a continuum from entirely mutual sexual acts to rape, which then becomes a somewhat arbitrary line drawn across the continuum at a certain point. Russell argues that 'much conventional sexual behaviour is close to rape' (1990: 74). Twenty-six per cent of Russell's sample reported some kind of 'unwanted sexual experience' with their husbands, and interviewers then had to probe further to establish whether this experience fell into the study's definition of rape.

This emphasis on husbands' violence against wives has been challenged by other research in the United States. Thus, the 1985 national survey carried out by Straus and Gelles (1986) showed that women were, in the domestic situation, at least as violent as men. The most common situation involved violence by both parties. After this, violence by women against men was more common than violence by men against women. Even in the severe-violence category, wives were violent more often than husbands (see Figure 10.12). Straus and Gelles argued that these findings were supported by a number of other studies. They recognized, however, that wife-to-husband violence could be very different from husband-to-wife violence in its meaning and consequences. The greater strength and weight of men meant that their violence was likely to be more damaging. More fundamentally, much of the violence of women was a response to male violence or was violence in self-defence.

This approach has been heavily criticized on a number of grounds. Dobash and Dobash (1992) argue that the sheer weight of evidence from many different sources shows that most marital violence is directed against women. They claim that the survey methods and measurement tools used by Straus and his colleagues were not appropriate to the study of marital violence, because of the complexity of the issues it raises and the difficulty of defining violence. F. R. Elliot recognizes the force of these arguments but still concludes that the American surveys have shown that 'in a significant minority of relationships only the woman is violent' (1996: 164).

Although the problems of carrying out research in this area and the sensitivity of the issues that it raises make it difficult to arrive at clear conclusions, there is no doubt that it has revealed a 'dark side' of family life. The inward focus of the nuclear family and its charac-teristic isolation of family life from wider kin and community networks have hidden violence and abuse from public view. Furthermore, the growing emotionality of family relationships as the nuclear family developed may well have created an emotional intensity that finds expression in greater violence and abuse. Those who believe in family values face the problem that the very form of the family which they defend may also be the form that is most likely to generate behaviour which violates other widely held norms and values.

SUMMARY POINTS

This part of the chapter has been concerned with recent challenges to the standard nuclear family. We began by considering the sexual revolution and changes in marriage:

▶ The sexual revolution of the 1960s changed attitudes to both unmarried sex and sex in marriage.

▶ The rate of marriage has declined and cohabitation has increased, but cohabitation often leads to marriage and attitudes towards marriage seem largely unchanged.

▶ Divorce rates have risen but so has the rate of remarriage.

We then moved on to consider changes in parenting:

▶ Parenting has become increasingly separated from marriage.

▶ This has led to rising numbers of single-parent families, post-divorce conflicts over children, and the reconstitution of families after remarriage.

▶ One response to parenting problems has been an attempt to revive the traditional family, but others have argued for an acceptance of diversity, a recognition of its positive aspects, and the provision of greater support.

A growing ethnic diversity has been another source of family diversity:

▶ African-Caribbean backgrounds are associated with households headed by women supported by a network of other women and with women's high involvement in economic activity.

▶ Asian backgrounds are associated with strong extended family networks, though differences of religion have affected the way that the Asian family has adapted to British society.

We then moved on to consider the effect of the growing employment of women in paid work on the

	Husband and wife	Wife-to-husband	Husband-to-wife
Overall violence	158	121	113
Severe violence	58	44	30

Figure 10.12. **Marital violence in the United States, 1985** (per 1,000 couples)

Notes: acts of severe violence were: kicked, bit, hit with fist; hit, tried to hit with something; beat up; threatened with gun or knife; used gun or knife. Overall violence included minor acts as well: threw something; pushed/grabbed/shoved; slapped or spanked.

Source: Straus and Gelles (1986: 470).

domestic division of labour, the management of money, and gender identities:

▶ The domestic division of labour and the double burden have persisted, though there is evidence of changes in attitude and some adaptation of households to the employment of women.

▶ Men more commonly control household finances than women, but control of money is related to employment and employed wives have more financial control.

▶ Changes in gender relationships and employment patterns have challenged traditional masculinity, but this has re-emerged in a new form.

The standard nuclear family has also been challenged by a growing awareness of the 'dark side' of family life:

▶ There has been a growing concern with child abuse and the legal protection of children.

▶ There has also been a growing awareness of domestic violence by men against women, though there is also evidence of violence initiated by women.

REVISION AND EXERCISES

INDUSTRIAL CAPITALISM AND THE FAMILY

In 'Understanding Families and Households' we outlined different approaches to the development of the family:

▶ **Make sure that you are familiar with the main ideas of Parsons, and Marxist and feminist writers, on the relationship between industrial capitalism and the family.**

▶ **What do you understand by the following terms: family and household; extended and nuclear families; patriarchy; the domestic division of labour; the family wage?**

In 'The Development of the Family' we examined various aspects of the development of the nuclear family:

▶ **What are the main features of the nuclear family?**

▶ **Did industrialization result in a transition from the extended to the nuclear family?**

▶ **What consequences did urbanization have for the family?**

▶ **In what ways did family relationships change as the nuclear family developed?**

▶ **Was a gendered division of labour the result of industrialization?**

▶ **What was the significance of the family wage for gender roles in the household?**

▶ **How have the relationships between generations changed as the family has developed?**

FAMILY DECLINE OR FAMILY DIVERSITY?

In 'Understanding Families and Households' we discussed the definition of the family and compared different approaches to recent changes in it:

▶ **What problems are there in defining the family?**

▶ **How should the family be defined?**

▶ **Make sure that you are familiar with the ideas of those who believe that the family is in decline and those who are critical of the family.**

In 'Away from the Nuclear Family' we examined recent changes in the family, its growing diversity, and challenges to the standard nuclear family:

▶ **How did the sexual revolution change the relationship between sex and marriage?**

▶ **Do you think that marriage is in decline?**

▶ **In what ways has parenthood become separated from marriage? What have been the consequences of this separation?**

▶ **How are the African-Caribbean and the Asian family different from the standard nuclear family? What are the implications of ethnic diversity in family forms for theories of the relationship between industrial capitalism and the family?**

▶ **Has the growing employment of women resulted in the decline of the domestic division of labour?**

▶ **Do you think that distinct gender-roles will disappear?**

▶ **Why has there been a growing concern with violence and abuse in the family?**

FURTHER READING

The following cover a wide range of issues in the sociology of families and households:

Allan, G. (1985), *Family Life: Domestic Roles and Social Organization* (Oxford: Basil Blackwell). A clear introductory text on the study of the family.

Elliot, F. R. (1996), *Gender, Family, and Society* (Basingstoke: Macmillan). A detailed and comprehensive review of the literature on recent changes in the family, focusing on ethnic differences, unemployment, ageing, violence and sexual abuse, and AIDS.

Gittins, D. (1993), *The Family in Question: Changing Households and Familiar Ideologies* (2nd edn., London: Macmillan). A critical examination of the gulf between the ideology of family values and the realities of family life, which challenges the whole idea of 'the family' and argues that only 'families' exist.

Morgan, D. H. J. (1996), *Family Connections: An Introduction to Family Studies* (Cambridge: Polity). Not so much an introduction as a thoughtful discussion of current issues in the Sociology of the Family, arguing that it should be studied through the notion of 'family practices'.

For further reading on specific topics, see the following:

Anderson, M. (1980), *Approaches to the History of the Western Family* (London: Macmillan). A concise and critical review of the classic studies of the history of the family.

Barrett, M., and McIntosh, M. (1991), *The Anti-Social Family* (2nd edn., London: Verso). A classic critique of the family.

Pilcher, J. L. (1995), *Age and Generation in Modern Britain* (Oxford: Oxford University Press). A clear and thorough account of changes in the life course, which examines each of its stages from childhood to old age and discusses the changing relationships between generations.

——and Wagg, S. (1996) (eds.), *Thatcher's Children: Politics, Childhood, and Society in the 1980s and the 1990s* (London: Falmer). A reader that covers a wide range of contemporary political and social issues relating to children.

Rodger, J. J. (1996), *Family Life and Social Control* (Houndmills: Macmillan). Examines the literature on a range of contemporary issues concerning the family from the perspective of social policy and social control.

Walby, S. (1986), *Patriarchy at Work* (Cambridge: Polity Press). A review of theories of the relationship between patriarchy and capitalism, and a historical study of the way that it has changed.

Chapter 11
CITY AND COMMUNITY

The privatizing of Coventry

'Coventry is being privatised. The West Midlands city destroyed by the Luftwaffe then rebuilt as the capital of the car industry is being recreated again, this time as a US-style privately-run district. A limited company will take over the running of the city centre in June. Instead of the local council, the company will be responsible for keeping the streets clean, safe, and secure; car parking, litter bins, shopping streets, pavements, toilets, street lights, cycle paths, Christmas decorations and closed-circuit security cameras will all be its responsibility. A team of 75 "ambassadors" will be recruited to work in the city centre, welcoming shoppers and visitors, and urging them "to have a nice day". . . .

'The change is the brain-child of Labour-controlled Coventry council. Running the city centre, which was largely rebuilt in the Fifties and Sixties, costs £1.6 million a year, and the council cannot afford to spend any more. Councillors believe Coventry, which has suffered as nearby out-of-town shopping and its arch-rival, Birmingham, have boomed, will only thrive again if business is involved in running the city. The carrot, they say, is giving business more power and more say. So business, along with community representatives, will be given seats on the company board, and encouraged to invest. . . .'

Source: Catherine Pepinster, 'Coventry Ltd Means Business', *Independent on Sunday*, 5 May 1996.

IN two centuries we have moved from a mainly rural to a mainly urban world. Britain was the first country to become urban and by 1851 half its population lived in cities. The United Nations predicts that by the year 2005 over half the world's population will do so. In Britain the growth of cities has, however, halted and they have begun to lose population to their surrounding areas. In this chapter we will examine both the growth of cities and the question of whether they are now in decline.

But what is it that makes living in cities different from living in the countryside? There has been much debate about this. Some have argued that there are strong communities in rural areas which integrate people and give them a sense of identity, while in cities there are only isolated individuals with little sense of belonging together. Others claim that strong communities *can* form in the city. As for the rural community, some suggest that this is a myth. We examine this debate in the first part of the chapter and later explore the impact of change on communities in both urban and rural areas.

Cities are dynamic places in a state of constant change. In this chapter we consider both the centralization of the city and its recent decentralization. We examine the growth of the local state as cities began to provide public services for their inhabitants and the recent privatizing of the city, as exemplified by our opening extract. We examine the decline of the inner city and recent attempts to regenerate it. We also discuss the rise of a new type of 'global city', which directs and controls processes of growing world economic integration.

Changes in the city are most obvious in its buildings, in the derelict factories of its inner areas, or the new retail and leisure complexes along the motorways that ring it.

The changes in buildings are, however, closely linked to changing social relationships. We examine changes in the relationships between classes, between men and women, and between ethnic groups. We discuss increasing inequality and rising violence. In the changes of the city we see in concentrated form the changes that have been taking place in society as a whole.

UNDERSTANDING CITIES AND COMMUNITIES

The development of an urban society where most people lived and worked in cities was closely linked to the growth of industrial capitalism. In this section we first examine the connections between the development of the city, the rise of capitalism, and industrialization. We then go on to consider the question of the differences between urban and rural life.

This leads us to a second set of issues concerning community. We consider different approaches to its study and the debate on whether communities can exist in cities. Lastly, we consider the usefulness of the concept of locality, which has been developed as an alternative way of approaching the study of local society.

CAPITALISM AND THE CITY

Our cities are in constant change as the dynamic forces of capitalism transform them, but cities have also played an important part in the development of capitalism itself. In studying the city it is important to be aware of its role as a source of social change.

In his work on the city, Max Weber was primarily interested in the part played by the *medieval city* in the rise of modern capitalism in Europe. To Weber the medieval city was 'a fusion of fortress and market'. It was there that the markets central to the rise of capitalist economies were first established. It was also in the city that legal and political institutions emerged to protect property, establish the rights of citizens, and enable cities to govern themselves. These institutions enabled the growth of market economies based on trade, for they gave city merchants and craftsmen the stability and security they needed to engage in their economic activities. The independence of the city was crucial too, for this allowed capitalism and citizenship to emerge within a feudal society hostile to both, which

is where the fortress came in, for political independence depended on military security.

A network of independent cities provided a framework for the early development of international capitalist trading in Europe. These early cities did not, however, maintain their leading economic and political role. Although the medieval European city created the economic and political conditions that enabled the early growth of capitalist *trading*, they later inhibited the capitalist transformation of *production*. Capitalist production developed outside the city, for detailed guild regulations in the cities protected traditional crafts and new forms of production could be more easily established elsewhere. Cities also lost their independence with the development of the political and administrative structures of the nation state.

These changes were symbolized by the dismantling of medieval city walls, which not only marked the city's subordination to the modern state but also its incorporation within a national economy. City walls obstructed the free movement of goods, while land-use was increasingly determined by the requirements of a capitalist economy.

 You may find it helpful here to refer to Chapter 12, pp. 459–61, where we examine the rise of the nation state, and Chapter 13, pp. 501–2, where we discuss capitalism and industrialism.

Capitalist production led to industrialization and the emergence of a new kind of city, the *industrial city*, in the nineteenth century. It was largely the growth of the industrial city that resulted in the urbanization of society. Industries employed large numbers of people and became the centres of new concentrations of population that were far greater in size than the older cities dating from medieval times.

The industrial city was quite different in character from the medieval city. This can be seen in the city's physical structure. The medieval city was shaped by the contours of the land, for its streets and walls followed the land's shape. In a capitalist society urban land was not just ground that was suitable to be built on but had a market value. It was bought and sold. As Mumford (1961) emphasized, the spatial patterns of the capitalist city were not *dictated* by the shape of the land but were *created* by a market in land. And re-created, for cities have been involved in a constant process of restructuring as developments in production, communication, and consumption have changed property values and altered land use.

Industrial capitalism shaped the city not only through these economic transformations of its physical structure but also through the changing relationship between capital and labour. This aspect of the city was explored by Castells, a French Marxist, whose work greatly influenced the development of urban sociology in the 1970s.

Castells (1977) argued that capitalism could function only if the employer was provided with an educated, healthy, and housed labour force that was able to work. Employers, if they were to make profits, could not bear the costs of providing schools, hospitals, and housing themselves. Such costs were, therefore, increasingly borne by the state through what Castells called **collective consumption**. By this he meant that the education, health, and housing consumed by labour were not obtained from the market on an individual basis but collectively provided by the state, largely though local authorities in cities. Labour movements played an important role in forcing the state to provide these services.

As services were expensive to provide, collective consumption eventually led to crisis and conflict. Thus, in the 1970s the state cut back on services and came into conflict with urban political movements struggling to maintain them. Because Castells believed that collective consumption was essential to the maintenance of capitalism, he saw no way out of this crisis. In the 1980s, however, public services were privatized and consumption became increasingly individualized, a process that we examine on pp. 432–4.

With Castells the study of the city had become an aspect of the study of capitalism. What happened in

Capitalism and the city	Type of city	Relationship between capitalism and the city

	The medieval city	▶ Cities as early centres of capitalist trading
		  • Markets
		  • Citizenship and self-government
		  • Military and political independence
		▶ A network of trading cities controls the European economy

	The industrial city	▶ New centres of industrial production emerge outside the medieval city ▶ Industrial cities shaped by capitalism ▶ Nation state incorporates the city ▶ Development of collective consumption shaped by the needs of capital and by class conflict
	The global city	▶ Cities become control centres of emerging global economy ▶ Imperial cities control empires ▶ Post-imperial global cities are headquarters of TNCs and manage the global flow of money ▶ New network of cities outside national control

cities was to do with the needs of capital, the class conflict that capitalism generated, and the state's response to the demands of capital and labour. His focus was, however, on consumption and the conflicts that emerged around consumption issues, and he has been criticized for paying insufficient attention to the city's role in the production of goods and services.

Certain cities have indeed come to play an increasingly important role in directing the development of the world economy. What have been called *global or world* cities emerged as centres of a growing worldwide economy, which we discuss in Chapter 12. Global cities, such as London, New York, and Tokyo, have become the headquarters of transnational corporations and are the financial centres that manage the flow of money and investment around the world. They form a new network which directs economic forces that have an enormous impact on national economies but are largely outside the control of the nation state. We examine the growth of global cities on pp. 440–2.

The independence of the medieval city enabled the emergence of an early form of capitalism within it. Cities lost their independence, however, with the rise of the nation state, while capitalist production developed outside them. New industrial cities grew up that were shaped by industrial capitalism, class conflict, and state intervention. With the growing importance of a network of global cities, the city has, however, regained some of the autonomy that it had in earlier times.

URBAN SOCIETY

The new industrial cities presented a sharp contrast to the predominantly rural societies in which they emerged. This raised the question of whether the social life of the city was different from life in rural areas.

The urban way of life

Louis Wirth (1938) has made the most well-known attempt to identify the differences between urban and rural life. He saw the defining characteristics of the **city** as:

▶ the large size of its population;
▶ its high population density;
▶ its social diversity.

These features of the city resulted in a quite distinctive **urban way of life**, though he was careful to emphasize that the city's influence on surrounding areas meant

that this way of life was found to some degree outside the city. The large and dense population of cities resulted in a high division of labour. People performed specialized roles and this meant that social relationships were segmental and secondary.

Louis Wirth

Louis Wirth (1897–1952) was born in Germany but pursued his career in the United States. He received his doctorate at the University of Chicago and spent almost the whole of his career there. He was a member of the Chicago School of Sociology, which established Urban Sociology as a specialized field in its own right. He believed that the urbanization of society had done more to shape its character than either industrialization or capitalism. His short 1938 essay on *Urbanism as a Way of Life* is generally considered to be the most influential piece in urban sociology. He was not only an academic, for he also acted as a consultant to numerous housing, anti-poverty, and planning agencies.

Relationships were **segmental** because people did not know each other as rounded individuals and saw only the segment or section of personality related to a person's role as, say, shop assistant, employer, or union organizer. This contrasted with rural society, where people knew about many different aspects of each others' lives and had all-round relationships that were not limited to particular roles.

The term secondary referred to a distinction made by Cooley (1909), another member of the Chicago School of Sociology, between *primary* and *secondary* groups. **Primary groups** involved face-to-face interaction, of the kind found in the family or amongst friends. **Secondary groups** were much larger associations in which relationships were distant and impersonal, as in organizations, such as factories, unions, or political parties, where the members of the organization did not all know each other as individuals.

According to Wirth, urban society was weakly integrated. City-dwellers had frequent but brief and superficial encounters with a wide variety of people rather than enduring relationships. Their involvement in the organizations that dominated city life was limited to the task or activity concerned. Although population density was very high, people felt isolated and 'on their own'. This weak integration meant that city life was unstable and social order was liable to break down. People living in cities were more likely than those living in rural areas to suffer mental break-downs, commit suicide, or become victims of crime. Weak integration and instability also meant that city-dwellers were easily manipulated by politicians and the media.

Wirth's notion of a distinctive urban way of life was criticized by Gans (1968). He argued that Wirth focused too much on the inner city and ignored the majority of the urban population who lived in quite stable communities which protected them from the worst consequences of urban living. He also argued that in the inner city itself there was not just one way of life. Five different ones could be distinguished.

▶ *Cosmopolites.* These were students, artists, writers, musicians, entertainers, and other intellectuals and professionals, who chose to live in the city for cultural and educational reasons. Insulated from city life by their subcultures, they had no wish to be integrated and were detached from the neighbourhood they lived in.

▶ *The unmarried and childless.* These tended to be geographically mobile and lived in areas of high population turnover. They were not interested in local services because of their stage in life. They too had little interest in the neighbourhood in which they lived, did not seek local ties, and did not suffer from social isolation.

▶ *Ethnic villagers.* These were groups with a common ethnic background. Heavily reliant on kinship and the primary group, they were little involved with secondary associations and lived outside the formal controls of society in highly integrated communities that identified strongly with their neighbourhood.

▶ *The deprived.* These were the poor, the emotionally disturbed and handicapped, single-parent families, and people who experienced racial discrimination. Forced to live in deprived areas with the cheapest housing, they did suffer from social isolation.

▶ *The trapped.* These were old people on small pensions, or the downwardly mobile, who had been left behind when others moved out to the suburbs and had to continue to live in an area after its character had changed. They had lost their social ties and they too suffered from social isolation.

Of these five ways of life, only two, the *deprived* and the *trapped*, experienced the social isolation that Wirth saw as typical of urban life. Gans argued that ways of life depended not so much on people's urban or rural location as on their class situation and stage in life. He con-cluded that there was no such thing as 'an urban way of life'.

In a similar vein, he has also argued that there was nothing distinctive about suburban life either (Gans 1995). There is a popular notion that life in the suburb is somehow different in quality and character from life in the city, but Gans considered this to be a myth and argued that American suburbs were not significantly different from the other residential areas of cities. Suburbs varied just as other residential areas did, and these variations were greater than those between the suburbs and other residential areas. Gans argued that the age of an area and the cost of its housing had a greater bearing on the characteristics of the people who lived in it than its location.

Giddens (1981) too has rejected Wirth's idea that there is a distinctive urban way of life. He argued that there were sharp differences between urban and rural society at the time of the pre-capitalist city. Modern capitalism has, however, eliminated these differences. Whether people live in the city or the countryside makes little difference, for capitalism has transformed both urban and rural life. What really matters is that they sell their labour to an employer in return for a wage. They then buy similar goods with these wages and live a similar lifestyle. It is wage labour, not where people live, that shapes their lives.

In a short essay Wirth had provided a coherent, wide-ranging, and forceful analysis of urban life that has been highly influential but also much criticized. Although he mentioned some of the positive sides of city life, notably the greater choice, freedom, and toler-ance it provides, the image he presented of it was, on the whole, negative and emphasized its loneliness, insecurity, and superficiality. There was an anti-city bias in Wirth's approach which reflected a widely found nostalgia in industrial societies for the life of the rural village.

Urbanism and community

Wirth believed that city life was incompatible with community. A contrast has commonly been drawn between the integrated communities of rural society and the isolation of the individual in the city. It has also been argued, however, that this contrast is misleading, that city life is perfectly compatible with community, while plenty of conflict can be found in supposedly integrated rural communities. In this section we will examine the debate on community and the issues that it raises.

Wirth followed in the steps of the nineteenth-century theorists who contrasted traditional commu-

Rural integration and urban isolation

		Rural integration	Urban isolation
	Ferdinand Tonnies	**Community**	**Association**
		▶ Emotion	▶ Reason
		▶ Unity	▶ Individuality
		▶ Custom	▶ Contract and law
		▶ Loyalty to place	▶ Non-attachment to place
	Louis Wirth	**Ruralism**	**Urbanism**
		▶ Primary group	▶ Secondary association
		▶ 'All-round' personality	▶ Segmental roles
		▶ Personal relationships	▶ Impersonal relationships
		▶ Integration	▶ Isolation and disorder

nities with the urban industrial society they saw emerging around them. The best-known exponent of this view is Ferdinand Tonnies, who distinguished between community (*gemeinschaft*) and association (*gesellschaft*).

According to Tonnies (1887), in *communities* there were strong and emotional bonds of unity based on kinship and sustained by close, personal relationships within a small population. In contrast, *associations* were characterized by rational and impersonal relationships between isolated individuals. These relationships were typical of business enterprises and large populations, such as those of the industrial city or the nation state. While custom ruled in communities, relationships were regulated by contract and law in these larger groups and organizations. In communities there was a strong emotional attachment to the place where people lived but this was absent in the city. Tonnies's distinction between community and association corresponded closely to Wirth's distinction between primary groups and secondary associations.

But is urban society so hostile to community life? Gans demonstrated that communities of what he called 'ethnic villagers' could be found in American cities. Young and Willmott (1957) showed that a strong working-class community still existed in Bethnal Green in 1950s London (we discuss the working-class community on pp. 414–16.

Indeed, it can be argued that urban life actually enables the formation of communities through a process of community gravitation. Fischer has argued that cities allow thinly spread minorities, such as artists or students, to gravitate together to produce a 'critical mass' that enables them to establish 'thriving social worlds' (1975: 1326). This kind of argument can also be applied to ethnic or religious minorities, who in cities can form communities that would be impossible in rural areas or small towns, where they would be isolated and excluded.

Savage and Warde have, however, come to Wirth's defence and argue that his critics have overstated their case. They suggest that those studying communities have found evidence of social integration partly because they were looking for it. They have tended to neglect isolated people, who are inevitably less visible and more difficult to contact. Furthermore, people move through many different situations in their daily lives and can sometimes behave as members of a community but at other times experience social isolation.

Changing views of the relationship between cities and communities

Communities and cities incompatible	**Wirth, Tonnies**
Communities do exist in cities	**Gans, Young, and Willmott**
Cities facilitate formation of communities	**Fischer**
Social isolation is nonetheless a feature of city life	**Savage and Warde**

In other words, membership of a city community does not mean that people live their whole lives within it. Savage and Warde conclude that Wirth's essay does contain 'important insights into the nature of life in modern cities' (1993: 109).

COMMUNITY

The debate over the impact of the city on community raises the issue of what we mean by community. This term has been given many different meanings and used in countless different ways. It is often used loosely to refer to any group that is assumed to share a common way of life, as in references to the diplomatic community or the black community, or simply to those who live in the same place, the local community. Community care is another such usage that assumes that those living in an area are members of a community.

These everyday usages should be distinguished from the use of the term in sociology, where it indicates that a group has certain sociological characteristics. Thus, if those living in a particular place do not manifest these characteristics, they are not a community.

What is community?

While sociological definitions themselves vary in their emphasis, they do share certain common features. A **community** may be said to have the following characteristics:

▶ *Common situation.* Those living in a community will share some common feature which binds them together. This may be their place of residence, but may also be their class, their ethnicity, their religion, or some other feature. A distinction is commonly made between *residential* and *non-residential* communities.

▶ *Common activities.* Communities involve all-round relationships between people. They are all-round in the sense that they are not limited to work or politics or sport or any other single activity but extend into most areas of life.

▶ *Collective action.* People have some sense of a common interest, and may well organize collective action in pursuit of this common interest. Thus those living in a particular place may organize action to prevent a road being built through it or to raise money for a community centre.

▶ *Shared identity.* There is a sense of belonging to a distinct group that has an identity. With this identity goes a certain emotional charge, a feeling of belonging to a larger unit and a certain loyalty to it.

In studying communities it is not simply a matter of whether a community exists or not, for many social groups may be in an intermediate position, showing some of the features of community but not in a strongly developed form. It makes sense to refer to *degree* of community as a dimension of social groups. This was the approach taken by Frankenberg (1966), who arranged communities along a *rural–urban continuum* stretching from the 'truly rural' situation of scattered populations in the countryside at one extreme, through villages and towns, to the urban housing estate at the other.

Definitions are important not only for what they contain but also for what they leave out. In the above definition we deliberately make no reference to integration or place, which are commonly seen as characteristics of community. This is because there has been much argument over their links with community and we will now examine the issues they raise.

The classic discussions of community assumed that communities were unified or integrated. This was particularly considered to be the case with rural communities. Those who have studied rural society have often found high levels of conflict, however.

Thus, Frankenberg found plenty of conflict in the Welsh village that he studied in the 1950s. One example of this was the conflict within the village football committee over whether outside players, who would increase the team's strength but diminish its local character, should be selected. The conflict in the committee was apparently settled by resignations but then spread into the wider community, as those who had left sabotaged the committee's actions. Eventually the conflict became so intense and so widespread that village football collapsed and village interest switched to other activities. These went through the same cycle of intensifying conflict followed by collapse. There was no apparent end to these sequences, though some of the people involved were driven out of the village or left.

Features of the community that are commonly thought to produce integration actually generated a conflict that weakened it. Thus, the emotionality of community life, its frequent face-to-face contacts, and the multiple connections between those involved made conflict more intense and harder to resolve through avoidance or compromise. In the end village unity could only be maintained by 'adopting an enemy, real or imagined, outside' (Frankenberg 1966: 273).

Which aspects of community does this scene show?

It is also commonly assumed that communities are identified with places. Community studies have certainly demonstrated the importance to many communities of a sense of place. This is a feature of most residential communities, but there are also non-residential communities whose members do not live in the same place.

The significance of spatial location has been particularly questioned by those who have studied social networks. One of the features of the city is that ease of travel enables the creation of *network communities* spanning large areas. Communities can be created that are not tied to a particular locality. In the city, community relationships can indeed be liberated from the constraints of place. They do not even require face-to-face contact. The invention of the telephone enabled the creation of voice-to-voice networks well beyond the confines of the city. Arguably, the ultimate liberated community is provided by the spatially unlimited global villages of the Internet.

Flanagan (1993) has emphasized that it is important to understand that people who live in an area where there is a residential community may not be a part of that community. Their particular social network may connect them more strongly with people in other parts of the city or nation or world. The cosmopolites identified by Gans provide a good example of this, for local people may well be strangers to the cosmopolite. This is probably more than ever true, for global communications and extensive international migration mean that local people may hardly figure in some social networks.

Flanagan also makes the point that 'each of us lives in our own city'. Each person has a personal map of the city, where the areas that they know and use are highlighted. Two people who say that they live in the same city may have very different personal maps and therefore, in Flanagan's terms, actually live in two quite different cities. As Flanagan also points out, the fact that we each have a personal map also means that much of the physical city will be unknown to us and a 'world of strangers' (1993: 39–40).

For and against community

Why, you might ask, has there been so much concern with community? Built into much of the literature is the idea that communities meet deep human needs for

Personal maps

▶ Photocopy a local map and distribute it to several different people. Ask them to mark with a highlighter pen the places they have visited during the past week and the routes they have taken.

▶ Compare the maps. From what you know of the people concerned, how would you explain the differences between their personal maps?

(You could develop this into a small project by administering a short questionnaire to find out their occupational status, family situation, leisure patterns, etc.)

integration, identity, and mutual support. Tonnies and Wirth, for example, clearly believed that community life was desirable and held negative views of the city because they thought that city life was incompatible with it.

Tonnies and Wirth were reacting against the growth of large cities, but a belief in the virtues of community is still very much alive today. It is found, for example, amongst architects and planners who want to reconstruct our cities in order to revive community. The ideal of the community has also recently experienced a political revival in the *communitarian* movement associated with the American sociologist Amitai Etzioni.

Communitarians advocate the strengthening of community structures—the family, the local school, the neighbourhood—so that people will take a shared local responsibility for what happens to them (Etzioni 1995). They are opposed to the neo-liberal belief in the need to revive individual freedom and responsibility. They are equally opposed to the left-wing idea that the state should bear responsibility for people's welfare. They argue that people should take a collective, mutually supportive responsibility for each other's well-being through the institutions of the local community. It is these institutions that should mediate between the individual and the wider society.

☞ Communitarianism needs to be placed in the context of neo-liberalism and different approaches to social policy, which we discuss in Chapter 18, pp. 731–4. There are many similarities between this movement and the pluralist approach to politics, which we examine in Chapter 17, pp. 709–10.

It might seem that, like apple pie and motherhood, no one could be against community, but Richard Sennett has written a powerful critique of the community ideal. He argued that communities are based on a belief in sameness, that 'people feel they belong to each other, and share together, because they are *the same*' (Sennett 1973: 40). This belief led to conformism, an intolerance of difference and deviance, and the risk of violent confrontations with other communities. It resulted in the dangerous myth of the 'purified community'. These dangers were particularly great where a community defined itself in terms of a shared religion or shared racial characteristics.

Your community?

▶ Can you identify any communities in the area where you live? What makes you think that they are communities? Do they meet the criteria that we listed in our definition?

▶ Do you think that people should be encouraged to form communities? Does it matter what kind of community they form?

To Sennett, communities were an immature adolescent response to the uncertainties and insecurities of life. He believed that people had to come to terms with their differences and conflicts, and learn to deal with each other in an adult way. This could occur only if they had frequent contact with many different kinds of people. He condemned any attempt by planners either to construct communities or zone activities in ways that would reduce these contacts. To him, the great thing about cities was that they made such contacts possible through their high population density and their diversity. Sennett celebrated exactly those aspects of city life which Wirth criticized.

In some people's minds the word 'community' may conjure up images of harmonious village life, but in other people's minds it may be associated with racism and 'ethnic cleansing'.

LOCALITY

The problems posed by the term community have led some sociologists to develop alternative terms. Stacey rejected the concept of community and proposed 'local social system' instead (1969: 139). More recently, others have argued that the concept of **locality** is preferable.

Cooke (1989) argued that locality was a more neutral term that allowed a greater recognition of local diversity and local initiative. Those who studied communities were preoccupied in an inward-looking way with the integration and identity of those who lived in a particular place rather than with their activity in the world. The very word 'community' focused attention on stability and continuity rather than innovation and change. Instead of referring to local societies as communities, we should refer to them as localities.

He also criticized Marxist writers, such as Castells and Harvey, for treating local society as though it was wholly subject to external economic forces. They saw local changes too much as the result of broader changes in the capitalist system, such as the movement of capital or the growth of transnational corporations, and took insufficient account of local initiative and the local generation of economic activity.

Cooke argued that there are plentiful examples of a local cultural or economic dynamism that cannot be comprehended by either of these approaches. He pointed to the success of cities that had developed as cultural centres, giving the examples of opera at Salzburg, the Cannes film festival, and country and western music at Nashville. As we shall show later in the chapter, some cities have responded to the decline of traditional industries by engaging in a *cultural restructuring* that has provided the basis for local economic revival by making them attractive to both tourists and investors. He also drew attention to the emergence of centres of advanced technology in cities such as Boston in America or Cambridge in Britain.

Should we then refer simply to localities rather than cities or communities? The term 'locality' is certainly less loaded with the concerns of the past than the terms 'city' or 'community'. It avoids the issue of whether a place is urban or rural, or somewhere in-between. It does not carry with it the emotional baggage of community. It has enabled researchers to escape old controversies which they found burdensome and helped them to take a fresh look at what is happening in particular places.

Day and Murdoch argue, however, that 'although badly wounded, "community" is a concept that will not lie down'. In a study of social life in Welsh villages they found that 'the notion of "community" plays a central part' (1993: 85, 108). The old issues raised by the discussion of city and community continue to generate debate. Planners and architects still discuss how 'urban villages' can be created in cities, while, as we saw above, the communitarian movement is seeking to revitalize local communities.

Cooke is also right to point out that those who examine the local from the perspective of the dynamics of capitalism tend to see the local as determined by the global and pay insufficient attention to differences in local response. The local does, however, have to be put in its global context. The inner areas of many old industrial cities in Britain and other industrial societies were devastated during the 1980s by the rise of more competitive industries in the Far East and the movement of capital to areas where costs were lower. There was initially very little that local responses could do about this.

Locality is a useful addition to the vocabulary of sociology, for it does provide a relatively neutral way of referring to local society that avoids the problems associated with the terms community and city. The term 'community', in particular, has, as we argued earlier, been extensively misused. The locality approach does not, however, replace these earlier approaches and the concepts associated with them, for the issues with which they were concerned have not disappeared and remain important.

SUMMARY POINTS

We began this section by considering the relationship between the development of the city, capitalism, and industrialism:

▶ A network of medieval cities was at the heart of the development of capitalism until they lost their leading economic and political role.

▶ The character of industrial cities was shaped by the requirements of industrial capitalism and the rise of collective consumption.

▶ With the growth of a capitalist world economy, global cities emerged as centres of a new network directing economic development.

We went on to consider the issue of the distinctiveness of urban society:

▶ Wirth defined cities in terms of their size, population density, and diversity, which he saw as producing a distinctive urban way of life.

▶ Gans and Giddens argued that way of life is shaped by class, life cycle, and capitalism rather than location.

▶ Wirth and Tonnies saw the city as incompatible with community but others have argued that communities can thrive in cities.

We then discussed the issues raised by community:

▶ Communities are not necessarily associated with integration or location.

▶ Sennett has drawn attention to the negative side of community life.

Some have argued that the problems posed by the concept of community are such that it should be replaced by locality:

▶ Locality does provide a more neutral way of referring to local society and avoiding the implications of the terms community or city.

▶ The issues raised by community and the impact of global changes in capitalism remain, however, central to the study of cities.

URBANIZATION AND CENTRALIZATION

In this section we outline the process of urbanization in Britain and the growth of large, centralized cities. We discuss the ecological approach to the analysis of these cities and examine the impact of urbanization on class, ethnicity, and gender. We also consider the creation of local state structures centred on the city.

URBANIZATION

Urbanization, in the broad sense of the growth of cities, began with the earliest known civilizations. It was not until the eighteenth and nineteenth centuries, however, that urbanization, in the sense of a shift of population from rural to urban areas, really got under way. It is with urbanization in this second sense that we are concerned here.

Industrialization and urbanization

Industrial capitalism turned Britain into a predominantly urban society by the second half of the nineteenth century. Only a third of the population lived in towns or cities in 1801, but by 1851 half the population was living in urban centres and by 1901 80 per cent. Rapidly growing industrial cities, such as Birmingham, Leeds, Liverpool, Manchester, and Sheffield, were largely responsible for this shift to urban living.

It was not only that Britain had become a predominantly urban society, it was also that the size of these new industrial cities was of a quite different order from those that had preceded them. Leaving aside London, which we discuss below, the five largest cities in early eighteenth-century Britain—Bristol, Exeter, Newcastle, Norwich, and York—had populations of under 20,000. By 1851 Liverpool had 376,000 inhabitants, Manchester 303,000, and Birmingham 233,000. There had been an urban as much as an industrial revolution in Britain.

Urbanization was linked also to changes in travel and leisure. In the second half of the nineteenth century the spread of the railways led to the growth of Swindon, Crewe, York, and Derby as railway centres. There was also another kind of urban growth associated with the railways—the rise of the seaside holiday resort. Blackpool and Bournemouth grew enormously in the later years of the nineteenth century (Lawless and Brown 1986: 12–15). Industrialization led to urbanization not only because of the building of factories. It also resulted in new patterns of travel and leisure (which we examine in Chapter 13, pp. 523–6) and these too contributed to urbanization.

Urbanization was not just, however, the result of industrialization and its consequences. Any account of the urban transformation of Britain must deal also with the growth of London.

Imperialism and urbanization

In 1500 London already had a population of some 60,000 and by the mid-eighteenth century this had risen to 700,000—a considerable process of urbanization by any standards and occurring well before industrialization had made much progress. Trade was at the heart of

The Urbanization of Britain

Figure 11.1. The urbanization of British society 1801–1901

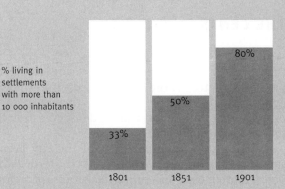

% living in settlements with more than 10 000 inhabitants

- 1801: 33%
- 1851: 50%
- 1901: 80%

Source: Lawless and Brown (1986: 18).

Figure 11.2. The growth of the British industrial city, 1801–1851

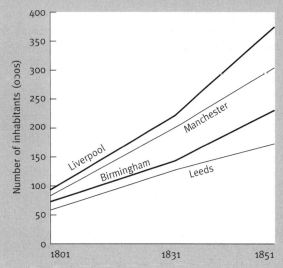

Number of inhabitants (000s)

Liverpool, Manchester, Birmingham, Leeds

Source: Lawless and Brown (1986: 14).

Figure 11.3. The rise of the seaside resort, 1851–1911

Resort	1851	1911
Bournemouth	700	78,000
Blackpool	4,000	60,000

Source: Lawless and Brown (1986: 14).

Figure 11.4. The growth of London, 1500–1935

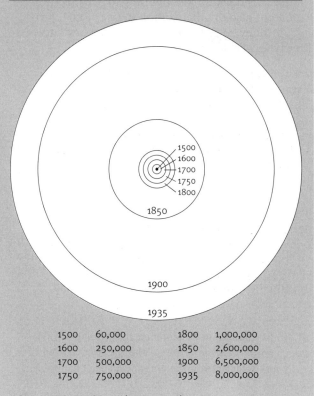

1500	60,000	1800	1,000,000
1600	250,000	1850	2,600,000
1700	500,000	1900	6,500,000
1750	750,000	1935	8,000,000

Source: Lawless and Brown (1986: 6, 14, 18).

London's growth, and something like a quarter of London's population depended on port employment in the eighteenth century. During the nineteenth century employment in financial and administrative, as well as trading, activities grew rapidly. By the mid-1930s London and its suburbs contained eight million people, around a fifth of the British population. While London had by then become a major industrial city, its growth had been driven mainly by its role as a global centre of trade and finance.

London's global role was closely linked to its position at the heart of the world's largest overseas empire, and this was reflected in its buildings. During the early twentieth century the area around Trafalgar Square and the Strand was rebuilt to accommodate the administration of the Empire with the opening of Australia House (1914), India House (1924), Canada House (1925), Africa House (1928), and South Africa House (1933). In the inter-war period companies based on imperial trade, such as ICI, Shell, and Unilever, built impressive corporate headquarters, which employed large numbers of clerical workers on sites along the Thames. The growth of other British cities too, such as Bristol and Liverpool, Glasgow and Dundee, was based on the import and processing of raw materials from the Empire.

Imperialism was linked not only to urbanization in Britain but also to urbanization in its colonial territories. Anthony King (1990: 33) distinguishes between three types of colonial city:

▶ the *metropolitan capital*, such as London or Paris;

▶ the *colonial capital*, such as Delhi or Canberra;

▶ the *colonial port or regional capital*, such as Calcutta or Hong Kong.

This hierarchy of cities provided a network of control for the overseas empires that divided up the world during the nineteenth century. It also established the framework within which a global process of urbanization took place during the nineteenth and twentieth centuries. The colonial cities became the 'mega-cities' of the ex-colonial states during the later twentieth century. Third World urbanization is often treated as a separate field of study, but the growth of London and the growth of, say, Calcutta were linked together.

☞ The process of globalization, the dividing-up of the world between empires, and the urbanization of ex-colonial territories are examined in Chapter 12.

Thus, while industrialization certainly resulted in urbanization, it is important to see this as a global process that was generated by the broader growth of a world economy.

THE CENTRALIZED CITY

We now turn to examine the structure of the large cities that urbanization produced. After considering the physical structure of the city, we discuss the ecological approach to the study of the city, and then examine the processes of ethnic, class, and gender segregation that took place within it.

As cities grew, different parts of the city became specialized in different activities, and the term *differentiation* is often used to describe this process of area specialization. Thus, particular areas became devoted to factories, shopping, leisure, finance, and housing. Commercial and industrial activities were concentrated in the centre and residential areas spread outwards to the edge of the city and beyond. Residential areas themselves became differentiated by their class or ethnic composition.

One form taken by area specialization was the growth of the residential suburb. Suburbs began to appear around the edges of British cities towards the end of the nineteenth century and then grew steadily, achieving their greatest growth after the Second World War. It was indeed the suburb that made possible the growth of large cities by providing new residential areas.

The city had a recognized centre and most people living in the city would travel into the centre for work, shopping, and entertainment. It also became centralized in other ways, as centrally organized services and local government developed with important planning and regulatory functions (an aspect of the city that we take up in 'Managed Cities', pp. 418–22).

Although suburbanization involved some decentralization of population from overcrowded central areas, and eventually led to some decentralization of employment and services, suburbs were very much part of a centralized structure. They were tied to the city centre, for this was where employment, services, leisure facilities, and shops were concentrated. The development of urban transport systems, based first on railways and trams and later on the car and the bus, linked the suburb to the centre and made suburbanization possible.

The ecological approach

The field of urban sociology first developed through the study of processes of differentiation by sociologists working in Chicago during the period from the 1910s to the 1930s. They mapped out the way that the various areas of a city became specialized around particular activities and occupied by different groups (see Figure 11.5). Prominent members of this group were Burgess, Park, and Wirth.

Their approach is commonly described as **urban ecology**, because of the use by Park and Burgess in particular of an ecological model of the city derived from biology. They argued that, just as specialized plant forms occupied particular habitats in the natural environment, different social groups colonized areas of the urban environment. Like plants, these groups then competed for dominance and areas periodically changed hands. It is important to stress that this approach is labelled ecological not because of any concern that its members had with preserving the natural environment but because they treated the city

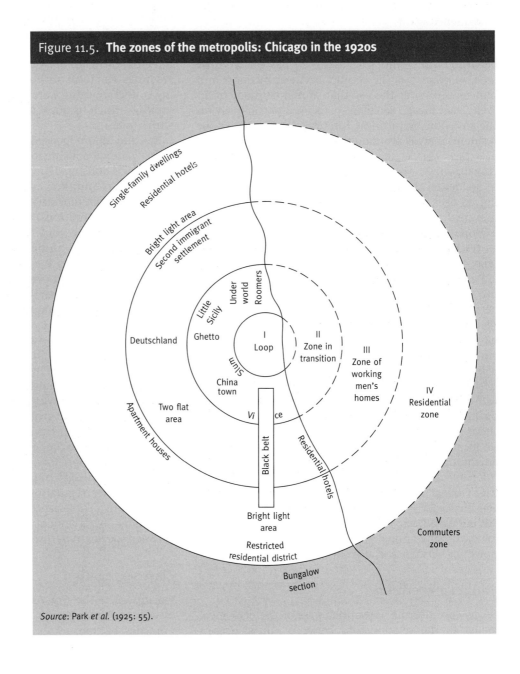

Figure 11.5. **The zones of the metropolis: Chicago in the 1920s**

Source: Park *et al.* (1925: 55).

as though it was such an environment. They particularly emphasized that groups competed for dominance in the city in the same way that species competed for habitats in nature.

Park saw this process as going through a series of stages:

▶ competition between groups within an area;

▶ establishment of dominance by one group;

▶ succession as dominant group takes over area from the defeated group;

▶ invasion of a new area by this group, starting the sequence again.

One example of this process was the competition between ethnic groups or classes for possession of an area. Another was the conflict between business and homeowners over the use that should be made of an area. The Chicago sociologists focused particularly on the invasion by business interests of the innermost residential areas around the central business districts of cities. This created what they called a **zone of transition**. As the inner city became less attractive to residents, those who could move out did so, leaving an area of decline occupied by the poor, and by marginal and deviant groups. This area was seen as exemplifying the disintegrated character of urban life, as described by Louis Wirth, whose ideas we discussed on p. 403.

Processes of area specialization, and changes in the use and social composition of areas, have undoubtedly been important aspects of the development of urban society. The biological assumptions of urban ecology have, however, been strongly criticized as inappropriate to the analysis of social behaviour.

In nature, if one species is better adapted to a particular environment, it will force out other, less-well-adapted, species, as grey squirrels have gradually pushed out red ones in most of Britain. But in a city there may be successful local resistance to invasion, for local people can organize to keep out the invaders. Furthermore, local politicians and planners may well intervene and control changes in the occupation and use of areas. Thus, the zoning of areas for different uses was characteristic of British town planning after the Second World War. The ecological model does not allow for the organizational and political aspects of the relationships between social groups.

Ethnic competition

Let us consider the appropriateness of the ecological model to the relationships between ethnic groups in cities. Rex and Moore (1967), in their well-known study of race relations in Birmingham, found the ideas of the Chicago school useful, especially the notion of competition for areas and the concept of a zone of transition. Their analysis also demonstrated, however, the importance of external intervention, for the control of areas was not simply a matter of competition between groups and depended on the allocation of housing.

They examined the role of urban **gatekeepers**, such as landlords, building-society managers, and Housing Department officials, in the distribution of accommodation. These were quite literally gatekeepers, since they controlled access to housing, though the term has also been used in a more general way in sociology to refer to those who control access to or availability of any resource. The local authority's procedures for allocating council housing were particularly critical in determining which groups occupied which housing in which areas.

Rex and Moore focused particularly on the distribution of council housing to ethnic minorities. Eligibility for council housing depended first on being a resident for five years and then on the number of points accumulated, which took account of such matters as existing housing conditions, health, war service, etc. Rex and Moore pointed out that these criteria inevitably disadvantaged the ethnic minorities, who were forced into lodging houses by the residence rule. Furthermore, when they had met this requirement and accumulated enough points, they generally found that they were allocated poor-quality housing in slum areas. The kind of council housing offered depended on a visit to the applicant by a Housing Visitor, who could offer a newly built house or a dilapidated one awaiting demolition. The criteria used by the Housing Visitor were not made public, and, although it could not be proved that this occurred, there was plenty of scope here for discrimination on racial grounds.

This study demonstrates well the limitations of an ecological model of the Chicago kind in understanding ethnic competition for areas. Such competition has certainly occurred but within a framework of local-authority regulation and a structure of ethnic relationships. These aspects of city life cannot be comprehended by a model based on the competition between species in nature.

Class segregation

The growth of the city led to the segregation of classes as well as ethnic groups. Distinct working-class communities became established in the inner areas of

Local support.

cities, while suburbanization created separate middle-class areas.

As we showed in our earlier discussion of community, nineteenth-century theorists and their twentieth-century followers thought that urbanization led to the decline of community because city life was incompatible with it. This was far from the case. When the turbulence of industrialization and the population movements of nineteenth-century urbanization had settled down, relatively stable communities could emerge, these were later dispersed through the slum clearance and relocation policies implemented by the local state (see pp. 429–30).

There were many features of working-class life which encouraged the growth of strong communities. The workers in one area would often be largely employed in one particular trade, such as mining or dock-work, and sometimes largely by a single local employer. Conflict with this employer and the growth of trade unions generated local solidarity. The deprivations and insecurities of life in industrial cities before the rise of the welfare state made people reliant on local structures of support. Opportunities for social or geographical mobility were limited and most people lived most of their lives within a restricted area. Common situation, collective organization, mutual dependence, and

social segregation produced the kind of conditions in which strong communities could become established.

Once such communities were established, the strength of their networks, organizations, and identities enabled them to perpetuate themselves and resist external changes. In the most famous study of a working-class community in Britain, that of Bethnal Green in 1950s London by Young and Willmott (1957), the authors expected to find that post-war social changes were leading to the breakdown of community but instead discovered that it was alive and well.

The middle-class became concentrated in the suburbs. The rise of the suburb was closely related to the growth of the middle class. The building of suburbs was financed by the sale of houses to owner-occupiers, and middle-class people were more able to afford home-ownership, and more able to pay the costs of travelling in and out. Suburban living also enabled the middle class to separate itself off socially by spatially distancing itself from the working class. Thus, the growth of white-collar occupations generated a demand for new housing away from the working-class areas of the inner city.

As Savage and Warde (1993) have argued, suburbanization reinforced social inequality, for, by excluding those with lower incomes from new residential areas, it consolidated a distinctive middle-class culture and strengthened middle-class solidarity. Suburbanization itself contributed to class formation.

Working-class suburbs too were created. In Britain, slum clearance led to the building of some council estates in suburban locations. In other societies, such as Australia and the United States, working-class owner-occupier suburbs have been more common, though, as Savage and Warde point out, they have typically been built at a greater distance from city centres and with fewer amenities than middle-class suburbs. Middle-class and working-class suburbs have generally been spatially separated.

Where mixed-class suburbs have existed, other ways have been found to maintain class segregation. Willmott and Young (1960) studied a mixed suburb, Woodford, in 1950s Britain. They found that there were considerable and increasing similarities of housing and way of life but there were still 'two Woodfords'. The middle and working classes were spatially separated within Woodford into distinct areas, while social inter-action was kept to a minimum by different patterns of friendship. In one famous case, walls were built in the 1930s to separate working- and middle-class areas of suburban Oxford (see box below).

Gendered urban space

The growth of the city was also associated with gender segregation, which was linked to the separation of home life from work life in the nineteenth-century city (see Chapter 10, pp. 366–7).

The public life of the city became dominated by men, who could travel freely through it, and there has been much discussion in the feminist literature of the 'male gaze' of the wandering man or *flâneur* (the French term generally used), which expressed male domination and treated women as sexual objects. The presence of women in public places was associated with prostitu-tion, as in the term 'street-walker'. The male domina-tion of public space was particularly apparent in the predominantly male character of sporting events and sports places. As Doreen Massey observes, this started early in life (see box on p. 417).

Elizabeth Wilson cautions us, however, against taking this view of the male domination of the city too far, for the city was also a place of opportunity for women (1995: 69). Employment in the city gave women a possible escape from unpaid labour in the household, while shopping became a legitimate public activity for women. The growth of female white-collar work in the city and the rise of the department store led to the spread in late-nineteenth-century cities of a range of eating places, specifically designed for women.

So, women too could wander in the city, albeit within certain limits. Men could not keep women out of public life and Wilson suggests that their attempts to do so reflected not so much male domination as the threat to males posed by women in public places and the greater independence of women in cities. Wilson is critical of

The Cutteslowe walls

'I went to see the walls and they certainly provided a striking sight. Approaching from the side of the private estate one passed along a very ordinary road much like thousands of others to be found in the suburbs of British cities. The houses were semi-detached and of the type one imagines to be favoured by school teachers, bank clerks, business executives, and other minor professionals and white-collar workers. . . . The road, however, did not continue as most roads do, nor did it make a junction with another road. Instead it was brought to an abrupt end by one of the walls. The wall itself was a substantial structure. Some seven feet tall it was supported at intervals by buttresses, and it was topped by a set of formidable revolving iron spikes which ran its entire length. The wall extended right across the road, across the footpaths at each side of the road and into the front gardens of the adjacent houses where it was linked to the garden fences by a tangle of barbed wire. It provided a completely impassable barrier . . . One had to leave the private estate altogether and make a long detour in order to get into the neighbouring council estate.'

Source: P. Collison (1963: 13).

The male domination of space

'I can remember very clearly a sight which often used to strike me when I was nine or ten years old. I lived then on the outskirts of Manchester, and "Going into Town" was a relatively big occasion; it took over half an hour and we went on the top deck of a bus. On the way into town we would cross the wide shallow valley of the River Mersey, and my memory is of dank, muddy fields spreading away into a cold, misty distance. And all of it—all of these acres of Manchester—was divided up into football pitches and rugby pitches. And on Saturdays, which was when we went into Town, the whole vast area would be covered with hundreds of little people, all running around after balls, as far as the eye could see. . . . I remember all this very sharply. And I remember, too, it striking me very clearly—even then as a puzzled, slightly thoughtful little girl—that all this huge stretch of the Mersey flood plain had been entirely given over to boys.'

Source: Massey (1994: 185).

▶ **Is this male domination of open space still the case?**
Observe your local park at the weekend and see who makes most use of its space and sporting facilities.

feminist accounts of women in the city that treat women as passive victims.

Suburbanization hardened the separation of gender roles in the household. The male breadwinner commuted into the city, while the housewife remained at home with little else to do but engage in housework and child-rearing. As compared with the inner city, there was unlikely to be much local employment for women. Furthermore, transport was designed to meet the needs of the male commuter, and the poor provision of local public transport within the suburb confined the housewife even more to the home. Distance from other members of the family intensified the housewife's social isolation and substituted telephone for face-to-face contact.

Thus, suburbanization not only segregated classes, it also segregated men and women, reinforcing gender as well as class inequality.

MANAGED CITIES

As we argued on pp. 401–3, the development of the city must be set in the context of the development of capitalism, class relationships, and state intervention, which led to the emergence of the managed city and collective consumption.

In Britain the local state was constructed by the national state in the nineteenth century. Parliament passed laws that enabled the development of local democratic institutions and empowered local government to develop a wide range of authorities and services. In the 1830s elected local councils and new town corporations were created. These initially focused their attentions on the problem of social order before moving on to tackle health, education, and housing. It was at the local level that the labour movement first established its political presence through representation on local councils and local school boards. What has been called *municipal socialism* resulted in councils taking water and gas supply into public ownership, and developing modern transport systems, first through the tram and later the bus. The management of the city later extended to the planning of the use of land.

We examine elsewhere the issues of order (Chapter 16, pp. 650–4), health (Chapter 6, p. 206), and education (Chapter 7, pp. 240–2). We concentrate here on the public provision of housing and the development of planning.

Housing classes

Perhaps the best example of collective consumption in the city is the public provision of housing. In this section we outline the growth of public housing through the building of council houses before examining the concept of *housing classes*.

The nineteenth-century construction of the local state

Laws	Key provisions
1834 Poor Law Amendment Act	Established the work house to provide indoor relief for the poor.
1835 Municipal Corporations Act	Created town corporations and required towns to appoint constables.
1846 The Liverpool Sanitary Act	Gave the council of 'the unhealthiest town in England' responsibility for drainage, sewerage, and street-paving.
1848 Public Health Act	Extended these powers to all towns.
1851 Common Lodging Houses Act	Required registration of lodging houses and gave the police the power to inspect.
1868 Artisans and Labourers Dwelling Act	Gave councils the power to demolish slums.
1870 Forster's Education Act	Created locally elected school boards for England and Wales.
1875 Public Health Act	Layed down building regulations.
1888 Local Government Act	Established modern framework of local government.
1890 Housing of the Working Classes Act	Gave councils the power to build houses.

Source: Lawless and Brown (1986).

The rapid growth of the industrial city in the nineteenth century soon produced severe problems of overcrowding in poor-quality housing and calls for slum clearance and house-building programmes. The 1890 Housing Act enabled both processes to start, but it was not until the years after the First World War that large-scale clearance and building got under way. The state's responsibility to provide housing to meet local needs was established by the 1919 Housing and Town Planning Act. Economic crisis and Conservative political dominance then led to a switch of priority to subsidies for private house-building. During the inter-war period some 4 million houses were built, of which 1.1 million were council houses.

After the Second World War slum clearance and council house-building accelerated. The Labour Party inclined more to public housing than the Conservative Party, but both tried to win votes through ambitious building programmes that combined public and private provision. The process of clearing old houses and building new ones became particularly rapid in the 1960s. In London, for example, one in ten houses was demolished between 1967 and 1971. At its high point in 1979 the public sector amounted to a third of British households.

The social significance of the ownership and control

How does this illustrate collective consumption?

of housing had been rather neglected in sociology, but Rex and Moore tried to remedy this through their concept of **housing classes**. This started a debate over whether housing situation should be treated as a separate dimension of stratification.

The housing classes of Rex and Moore

1. Owner-occupiers
2. Council-house tenants
3. Tenants of whole private houses
4. Owners of lodging houses
5. Tenants of rooms in lodging houses

In their study of race relations in Birmingham (see p. 414), Rex and Moore argued that lack of housing was a more serious problem in people's lives than lack of employment. They claimed that ownership of domestic property was as important in determining class situation as the ownership of industrial property. They concluded that 'there is a class struggle over houses and this class struggle is the central process of the city as a social unit' (Rex and Moore 1967: 273).

Housing class was not, however, a matter of ownership alone, for there were important differences within the categories of owners and non-owners. There were, for example, differences between council-house tenants and those renting rooms from private landlords. As we showed on p. 414, they also argued that 'urban gatekeepers' played a key role in determining the distribution of housing.

This analysis has been criticized on a number of grounds. The class categories are open to question because of important variations within them. In defence of Rex and Moore, they did in fact distinguish between, for example, council tenants in houses with a long life and those in houses awaiting demolition. People's views on the desirability of different kinds of housing also varied, making it difficult to establish an objective ranking of housing situations. It has also been argued that the focus on urban gatekeepers attached too much importance to relatively minor officials with little discretion, as opposed to those who shaped the policies and structures within which they operated.

More fundamentally, the whole idea of separate housing classes has been found wanting, since position on the housing market is so closely related to other aspects of stratification. If housing situation is largely determined by income, there is nothing to be gained by creating a separate housing dimension of stratification. While these criticisms of the concept of housing classses are sound, Jewson (1989) points out that Rex and Moore did demonstrate that access to housing was not *only* a matter of income. They also showed how the local state played an important role in distributing 'life chances' and reinforcing patterns of inequality.

 The ideas of Rex and Moore can be linked to the debate between Marxists and Weberians on stratification. Rex and Moore followed the Weberian tradition in arguing (1) that stratification is multi-dimensional and (2) that class situation is not simply a matter of ownership or non-ownership, for there are important variations within these categories. These issues are discussed in 'Class and Status', Chapter 15, pp. 604–10.

Planning

Nineteenth-century British cities grew but twentieth-century cities were increasingly planned, and the planning process has shaped the environment in which we now live.

Planning was strongly influenced by conceptions of the ideal city. Two influential conceptions were Howard's *garden city* (Figure 11.6) and Le Corbusier's *radiant city* (Figure 11.7). Howard's garden city sought to combine the advantages of urban and rural life. Le Corbusier presented the radiant city as a 'vertical garden city' that would preserve open space for grass and trees and prevent urban sprawl but in a more realistic way compatible with large concentrations of population. The radiant city was, none the less, radically different from the garden city in its size, architecture, and transport arrangements.

Jane Jacobs has argued that, in spite of their differences, both these conceptions were fundamentally anti-urban in spirit, since they devalued street life, imposed conformity, forced activities into zones, and left no space for the spontaneity, diversity, innovation, and dynamism which she saw as the essence of urban life (1961: 16–23). Their elitist blueprints catered for the interests of planners, architects, and engineers but did not allow for popular involvement, for people to have any say in the construction of the environment in which they would have to live, travel, and work.

Garden and radiant cities

Figure 11.6. Ebenezer Howard's garden city

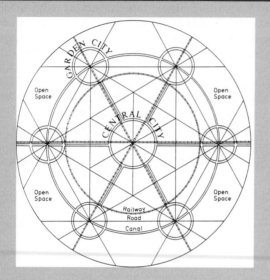

Source: Howard (1898).

Figure 11.7. Le Corbusier's radiant city

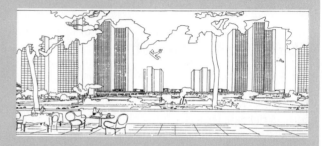

Note: The centre of the city seen from one of the terraced cafés surrounding the Great Central Station square. The station can be seen between the two sky-scrapers on the left, only slightly raised above ground level. Leaving the station the 'speedway' is seen continuing to the right in the direction of the Park. We are in the very centre of the city, the point of greatest density of population and traffic; there is any amount of room for both. The terraces containing the cafés are much frequented and serve as boulevards. Theatres, public halls, etc., are scattered in the open spaces between the sky-scrapers and are surrounded by trees.

Source: Le Corbusier (1947: 258–9).

Published at the end of the nineteenth century, this vision of the city envisaged a group of six garden cities, each the size of a small town, surrounded by green belts, and linked to a somewhat larger central city, the whole complex comprising a 'Social City'. Each garden city would be self-sufficient, with its own industries, residential areas, and central cultural, recreational, and service facilities. The residential areas would be divided into neighbourhoods in order to facilitate the growth of communities. There would be an emphasis on public transport, and cycling would be encouraged. Housing would be small scale and traditional. Howard believed in the collective ownership of land and the development of public welfare services at local level.

This 1920s vision of the city saw it as 'towers in a park'. Population density would be far higher than in the garden city or, indeed, than existing cities, but the construction of tower blocks sixty storeys high would leave most of the land free of building and given over to green spaces for sport and leisure. There would be a great central open space for restaurants, cafés, and various public buildings. The techniques of mass production would be used to standardize building and cut its costs. The city would be designed for the car, with arterial roads, one-way systems, and underground routes for heavy vehicles and deliveries. Although Le Corbusier too believed in the public ownership of land, there was less concern for community in his vision of the city, which sought to maximize the freedom of the individual by, for example, facilitating travel by car.

More down-to-earth concerns with the growing size of cities, overcrowded housing, and uncontrolled building motivated politicians. Legislation, especially the 1947 Town and Country Planning Act, established a framework for planning, and local government applied it. Implementation involved the locally elected bodies of councils and their planning committees and officials, the planners who influenced and implemented local planning decisions.

The operations of a wide range of economic interests are affected by decisions about land use and building design. Developers, builders, architects, industrialists, and transport firms, to name only the most obvious examples, have shown a keen interest in these decisions and sought to influence the planning process at all levels—as have local inhabitants and national pressure groups, such as those concerned to protect historic buildings or conserve the natural environment.

What has been the impact of planning on the development of towns and cities? The construction of self-sufficient 'new towns' and the preservation of green belts around cities showed the influence of Howard's ideas. These fitted well with the anti-urban sentiments of the British elite, which has always valued country life rather than city life. The protection of the countryside and agricultural land was one of the main themes of British planning. In spite of these views, population growth after the Second World War and a rising demand for homes in suburban and rural areas created pressures that could not be resisted and led to selective development in rural areas. Some villages were earmarked for development, some for preservation (Murdoch and Marsden: 1994).

sented as consistent with the character of an area. In general, employment, transport, and housing were higher priorities and the reshaping of the urban environment continued apace.

Planning is a bureaucratic process carried out by experts, but group interests are heavily involved and exert heavy pressures on the bureaucrats. Thus, incoming middle-class residents seek to conserve rural areas, while farmers often want to sell their land to developers, and local workers are primarily interested in new economic activities that will provide employment. Conservation Areas in cities have been used

Garden city versus radiant city

Garden city	Radiant city
▶ Small population	▶ High population density
▶ Decentralized	▶ Centralized
▶ Green belts	▶ Green spaces
▶ Neighbourhood housing	▶ Tower blocks
▶ Public transport and cycling	▶ Cars and trucks
▶ Collectivist	▶ Individualist

The situation in cities was different, for here the emphasis was on planned transformation rather than preservation. Le Corbusier's conception of the city has been highly influential. The high density and industrial building techniques that he advocated enabled cheap solutions to the problem of overcrowded cities and badly built slums. His ideas were seized upon by city councils, architects, engineers, and builders, and his influence is highly visible in the tower blocks, system building, and urban motorways of British cities.

In the 1960s there was some shift of emphasis from transformation to conservation. The 1967 Civic Amenities Act gave local authorities greater power to protect listed buildings and trees. Particular areas of historic or architectural interest could be designated Conservation Areas. Development in Conservation Areas was, however, allowed, so long as it could be pre-

Figure 11.8. **New towns, Great Britain**

Source: Lawless and Brown (1986: 134).

by the urban middle class to protect the quality of its environment and increase the value of its property. So-called slums in working-class areas were cleared without much concern for conservation and little reference to the people whose homes were demolished.

Those who are most organized and have most resources are most able to represent themselves effectively, pay for professional assistance, and influence planning procedures. This not only means that the middle class is likely to be more effective than the working class in protecting its interests; it also means that the interests of capital tend to prevail over those of conservation groups seeking to halt development. Planning is not a neutral bureaucratic process, for decisions are shaped by class interests and class power.

SUMMARY POINTS

In this section we have outlined the process of urbanization:

▶ Industrialization led to the urbanization of British society, not only through changes in production but also through other changes in travel and leisure patterns linked to industrialization.

▶ Urbanization also resulted from the growth of global trading and financial activities and the creation of overseas empires.

We went on to examine the structure of the centralized city and the relationships that emerged within it:

▶ The Chicago School of Sociology analysed it from an ecological perspective that treated the city as though it were a natural environment.

▶ City space was segregated by ethnicity, class, and gender.

▶ Although urbanization disrupted communities, they re-established themselves in working-class areas of the city.

One important feature of the development of the centralized city was the growth of the local state and collective consumption:

▶ Public-sector housing was provided through council-house building, particularly during the period from the end of the Second World War to the 1970s.

▶ Land use in the managed city was increasingly planned by public officials, though organized interest groups had a considerable influence on the planning process.

DEURBANIZATION AND DECENTRALIZATION

Since the 1970s there has been a general transformation of the city which has reversed many of the tendencies that we have examined in 'Urbanization and Centralization'. Deurbanization and decentralization have spread the city out and blurred its boundaries with rural areas. Depopulation and industrial decline have turned the inner city into a problem area, though some parts of it have been recolonized through a process of gentrification. Long-established communities have been broken up, though some new ones have also emerged. The local state lost power and resources, while social order was threatened by a return of the urban riot. In this part of the chapter we turn our attention to these changes and their consequences for life in the city.

Cities have not just experienced decline, however.

They have responded with regeneration programmes and developed new kinds of economic activity. While global economic changes inflicted considerable damage on industrial cities, some of the so-called global cities have benefited greatly from these changes. In the later sections of the chapter we consider these dynamic and expansive aspects of the contemporary city.

DEURBANIZATION OR DERURALIZATION?

The halting of city growth and the decline of city populations in countries such as Britain and the United

Figure 11.9. **Decades of deurbanization**

Size of settlement	Percentage population change	
	1961–71	1971–81
Greater London	−6.8	−10.1
All conurbations	−4.3	−8.1
Cities over 100,000	+2.6	−1.6
Cities 50–100,000	+9.4	+2.2
Towns under 50,000	+13.0	+5.5
Rural areas	+17.0	+9.7
(Pop. of England and Wales)	(+5.7)	(+0.5)

Source: Wallman (1993: 63).

States suggest that some degree of deurbanization has been taking place in the old industrial societies. On the other hand, it can also be argued that the influence of the city has extended further into rural areas. Has deurbanization or deruralization been taking place?

Urbanization had been going on for such a long time that it seemed an unstoppable process, but in the 1950s it began to slow down and eventually reverse in both Britain and the Unites States. Large cities lost population to towns and rural areas—a process called **deurbanization** (sometimes counter-urbanization). One interesting aspect of this process was that, the greater the size of an urban concentration, the faster its population decline, while the more rural the area, the faster its growth (see Figure 11.9).

As we showed in our earlier discussion of planning, the belief that cities were becoming too large led to attempts to halt their growth by constructing green belts and building new towns. This containment set limits to the size of cities but cannot explain deurbanization, which relates to more fundamental changes.

First, urban employment has declined. Between 1951 and 1981 some two million manufacturing jobs were lost in the larger cities. Between 1961 and 1978 Greater London itself lost 47 per cent of its manufacturing jobs, though increasing service employment partially compensated and the decline in total employment was only 17 per cent. The decline of urban employment was due in part to a general collapse of manufacturing but also to a shift of employment towards the outskirts of cities,

the smaller towns, and rural areas (Lawless and Brown 1986: 188–92; D. King 1987: 226–30).

This loss of employment was linked to increasing international competition and the global integration of national economies. The manufacturing industries of the old industrial societies found it increasingly difficult to compete with the newly industrializing countries of the Far East. The problem for the cities was partly that so much of the manufacturing of the old industrial societies was concentrated in them, partly that the location of many factories in the inner city made them uncompetitive. Some simply closed, while others moved to the edge of the city or outside it. Land and labour were cheaper there and companies could escape the old buildings, small plots, and poor access of the inner city.

Secondly, those who worked in cities increasingly lived outside them. Road- and house-building, together with the spread of car and homeownership, made it easier for people to live in preferred or cheaper rural or semi-rural locations and commute. Motorways and rail electrification brought a huge area of the country, including the Midlands, East Anglia, and even parts of Wales and Yorkshire, into commuting range of London. Information technology enabled some to telework and made it possible for them to pursue city careers a long way from cities.

There is more recent evidence, however, that suggests some movement of population back into inner-city areas. Thus, inner areas of London such as Southwark, Tower Hamlets, Islington, Camden, and Hackney gained population during the 1980s, though not sufficiently to make up for previous losses. These gains were associated with processes of gentrification and urban regeneration (see pp. 426–8 and 438–40).

It is also important to emphasize that the decline of city populations has occurred only in a limited number of rich countries. In most countries of the world urbanization has continued. The world as a whole is becoming more urban. We discuss the continued urbanization of poor countries in Chapter 12, pp. 475–7.

Are we, anyway, really talking about deurbanization or **deruralization**? Large cities may lose population, but if people with an urban culture and urban living patterns are dispersed into rural areas, which are closely linked by commuting and shopping patterns to the cities, do not these areas become urbanized? Furthermore, declining employment in an ever more capital intensive agriculture has led village people to seek urban employment. The new stores and services around the edge of cities are accessible from rural as well as urban areas. There are also proposals to build a new wave of new towns to accommodate rising numbers of households, and this suggests further urbanization of the countryside.

Rural areas have also become increasingly given over to the provision of leisure pursuits for city-dwellers. Are the golf courses, theme parks, and garden centres that take up increasing areas of the countryside in any sense rural?

The term 'deurbanization' certainly draws our attention to important changes in the distribution and location of population and employment, but it must be placed in the context of a broader urbanization of rural areas that makes it ever more difficult to argue that social life in rural areas is distinctive. As we saw in 'Urban Society', pp. 403–6, some sociologists have been sceptical of the notion that urban and rural societies were different from each other. There was certainly a case for arguing that they were different during the period of city growth, when cities were becoming centralized and city populations looked inwards to the city centre. The processes we have just been examining suggest, however, that there is no longer much difference between urban and rural society.

THE DECENTRALIZED CITY

We now turn to examine the emergence of a new type of city, the decentralized city, with multiple centres and activities dispersed to the city's periphery. Cities have spread out and incorporated outlying towns and villages into an urban network. Urban development is focused on the periphery of the city as new stores, warehouses, leisure facilities, hotels, schools, and hospitals are built around the edge of the city. People increasingly travel out of the city for shopping or leisure, and many now work on the city's edge. Indeed, the term 'edge city' has come into use as another name for this new kind of city.

Decentralization is associated with a process of dedifferentiation that has reversed the process of differentiation that we discussed earlier (see p. 412). The various parts of a city have become less specialized in their activities and land use. Retail stores are spread through the city and no longer concentrated in a shopping district. While at one time there were distinct industrial areas, numerous small industrial estates are dotted through and around the city.

These changes are linked to changes in communications. The centralized city typically had radiating railway lines, which brought people in and out of the centre and connected one city with another. The decentralized city has a network of motorways that link its multiple centres and give access to the periphery. The prime location for many commercial organizations is now the motorway junction.

The best and probably only example of a totally decentralized city is Los Angeles, which has no discernible centre. Cities generally retain some centralized structures, but the above tendencies are superimposing a decentralized pattern of economic

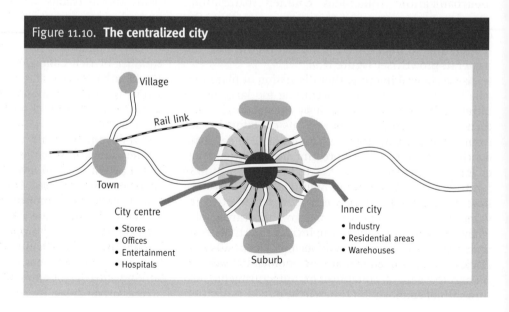

Figure 11.10. **The centralized city**

Village

Rail link

Town

City centre
• Stores
• Offices
• Entertainment
• Hospitals

Suburb

Inner city
• Industry
• Residential areas
• Warehouses

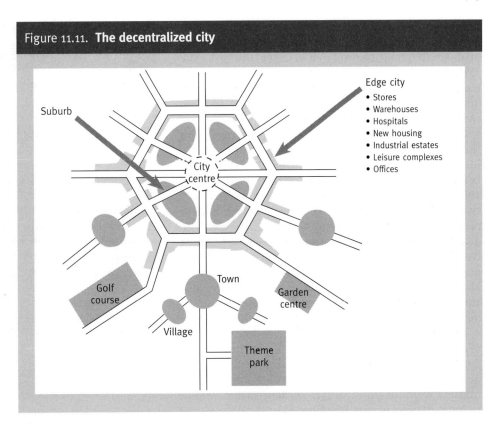

Figure 11.11. **The decentralized city**

activity on them. The great problem of the contemporary city is how to reconcile the centralized structures inherited from the past with the decentralizing tendencies of the present and produce a working city out of them. The diagrams in Figures 11.10 and 11.11 contrast the two structures.

Inner-city deprivation

Decentralization has 'hollowed out' the city, as the loss of economic activity, employment, and population from inner areas has drained resources from them and concentrated deprivation in them. Also, changes in the character of the local state, such as privatization and a tighter control of local funds, which we examine later, have in many ways made the problems of the inner city worse.

The growing problems of the inner city in the 1970s and 1980s have been described in Harrison's study of Hackney, one of London's inner-city boroughs. Jobs in manufacturing, the main source of employment for those who lived there, declined from 45,500 in 1973 to 27,400 in 1981, a drop of 40 per cent. The decentralizing processes examined above and Britain's growing problems of industrial competitiveness were mainly responsible for destroying local jobs. Furthermore, the industries that were left—for example, in clothing and footwear—were labour intensive and highly vulnerable to competition from poor countries with cheaper labour. Then, in the early 1980s, employment by Hackney Council, the largest employer in the borough, was hit by various government policies aimed at reducing local-authority expenditure. By 1982 the unemployment rate was 22 per cent and it continued to rise until 1986 (P. Harrison 1985: 49–51).

Rising unemployment was accompanied by growing homelessness in the 1980s. The number of people in England recognized as homeless by local authorities more than doubled between 1979 and 1988, rising from 57,000 to 118,000. Homelessness was worst in the big cities, especially in Manchester and inner London. During the 1980s housing provision for the poorest declined as council houses were sold, council-house building plummeted, and private renting continued a long decline. The figures for those in local-authority temporary accommodation, such as hostels and bed-and-breakfast hotels, indicate the size of the housing problem that had accumulated in inner London by the early 1990s (see Figure 11.12). The appearance in 1980s London of a 'cardboard city' of people living in boxes and others 'sleeping rough' in streets and shop doorways also bore witness to the scale of the problem.

Poverty and ill health are linked and concentrated in the inner-city. The concentration of deprivation in the inner city was demonstrated by the 1985–6 study of London by Townsend and his colleagues (Townsend 1991). Of the ten most deprived wards they studied, only two were in outer London. They also showed a clear relationship between deprivation and death rates. The death rate for those under the age of 65 was almost twice as high in the most deprived areas as in the least deprived. Townsend reports that other studies of Manchester, Birmingham, and Liverpool have also shown a clear link between inner-city deprivation, ill heath, and premature death.

The London study also investigated people's feelings of deprivation by asking respondents whether a list of deprivations had been experienced as major problems during the past year. Concerns about a whole range of matters were linked to degree of deprivation with a remarkable consistency (see Figure 11.13).

Figure 11.13. The experience of deprivation, London, 1985–6 (%)

Form of deprivation	Percentage experiencing deprivation as a major problem in	
	Most deprived areas	Least deprived areas
Health of someone in the family	33.8	29.1
Vandalism and theft	30.3	14.5
Poor public transport	20.4	11.2
Unemployment	20.1	6.7
Street/estate violence	17.7	4.6
Poor housing	16.4	1.3
Being alone and isolated	12.1	6.9
Poor local schools	8.2	3.0
Conflict at home	7.1	4.5
Racial harassment	7.0	1.4

Source: adapted from Townsend (1991: table 5.6).

Figure 11.12. The accumulating housing shortage, inner London, 1980–1991

Inner London borough	Households in temporary accommodation per 1,000 households	
	1980	1991
Hackney	3.8	55.4
Haringey	0.7	42.5
Hammersmith and Fulham	2.1	28.7
Tower Hamlets	0.8	24.6
Brent	2.7	23.8
Newham	0.2	21.5
(Greater London)	1.0	10.3
(Rest of south-east)	0.2	2.1

Source: Willmott and Hutchison (1992: 60).

The evidence of inner-city deprivation is overwhelming, but we must be careful about the conclusions that we draw from this. We must not assume that it is only in the inner city that such deprivation is found. Meegan (1989) has described the intense deprivation experienced by those living on estates in Kirby and Speke on the edge of Liverpool. The fortunes of this area changed drastically in the 1970s and 1980s, when the transnational corporations that had invested there during the 1950s and 1960s either closed their plants or sharply reduced their labour forces. All studies of these problems also emphasize that some inner-city areas are not deprived and that in the least deprived areas some people experience great deprivation.

Gentrification

Inner-city decline has resulted in deprivation for some but opened up opportunities for others. In some parts of inner cities property developers and middle-class owner-occupiers have moved in to 'upgrade' areas, a process known as gentrification. Changes in class composition have led to the appearance of boutiques, galleries, delicatessens, restaurants, and similar enterprises that have also helped to revitalize inner-city areas.

Gentrification can be said to have partially reversed the process of suburbanization. Instead of moving out to the suburb, some middle-class people have moved into central areas of the city. Tim Butler (1996) points out, however, that gentrification involves not so much the return of those who had left as decisions by young people, typically singles and childless couples, to settle in the inner city rather than the suburbs.

Following Warde (1991) **gentrification** can be defined as involving four processes:

▶ the displacement of one group of residents by another of higher social status;

▶ the transformation of the built environment as housing is renovated and new shops and services arrive;

▶ the emergence of a new urban lifestyle with a distinctive pattern of consumption;

▶ rising property values.

Why does gentrification occur? The decline of the inner city itself provides an opportunity, for lower property prices in the inner city attract both developers and owner-occupiers. Property developers have typically organized gentrification in the United States. Middle-class owner-occupiers have led the way in a rather more piecemeal fashion in Britain.

Savage and Warde (1993) link gentrification to changes in household formation, composition, and employment. Rising population after the post-war baby boom led in the 1960s to a greater demand for housing, which could not be satisfied by suburban house-building. Gentrified areas provided housing particularly suitable for the smaller households that have become steadily more common. The growing employment of women in salaried occupations was also a factor, for living in the city suited dual-career couples by giving easier access to work and paid domestic labour.

What may loosely be called cultural reasons for preferring to live in the inner city have played a significant part in the process. These may involve access to the cultural facilities of big cities or a rejection of suburban values and lifestyles. Some people are attracted into the city by the opportunity to pursue deviant lifestyles in a more anonymous, more tolerant urban society.

Suburbanization, as we showed earlier, segregated

The advantages of living in central London

'Cany Ash and Robert Sakul are both architects in their thirties. They set up home together in Bloomsbury in central London in 1984, moving from Wapping and Islington respectively, and now have three children under nine. Home is an open-plan, converted, light industrial mews building on two floors, with three bedrooms and a roof garden.

'"The centre's a brilliant place to live, because we're exactly half-way between the West End and the City," says Robert. "We work around the corner. So we don't commute, and things like rail and tube strikes just wash over us. London is a wonderful city, but the worst thing about it is travelling in it; if you don't have to travel in it, however, it's ideal."

'"I suppose if we sold this house we could probably buy a much bigger house in the suburbs, so in that sense, living in the centre is more expensive than living out. But on the other hand, we save on fares because we cycle everywhere. We do have a car but it only gets used at weekends. But our moving here wasn't really a financial issue for us, because we bought this place for £30,000 and did it up. We also rent car parking spaces on our property to some lawyers who work nearby, so that also helps."

'"What we love about living in this particular part of London is that you can still hear the wind, and the birds singing—it's very, very peaceful."'

Source: Scott Hughes, 'The Centre is a Brilliant Place . . . the Suburbs Feel like a Ghetto in Comparison', *Independent*, 20 Aug. 1996.

▶ **How many aspects of gentrification can you identify in this piece?**

classes residentially, while gentrification is a movement of middle-class groups back into predominantly working-class areas. Has it reversed class segregation? Tim Butler (1996: 104) points out that in gentrified areas of Hackney 'there is little evidence that spatial togetherness leads to any lessening of social distance'. Furthermore, while gentrification upgrades areas, it pushes house prices out of working-class reach, reduces the rented accommodation available to those who cannot afford to buy houses, and generally displaces the lower paid. There is little to suggest that gentrification has diminished class differences or class segregation.

The degendering of urban space?

We argued earlier that the spatial differentiation of the metropolis, especially the growth of the suburb, contributed to the separation of the spheres of home and work and intensified the segregation of gender roles. Suburban life distanced housewives from the public life of the city centre and left women isolated in the home, often without transport. Have recent decentralizing and dedifferentiating tendencies reversed this process?

Decentralization means that the local availability of services has increased in most suburban areas, as have employment opportunities, and suburban isolation has therefore diminished. The new superstores and leisure services on the edge of cities offer part-time work consistent with the domestic role. Public transport to the city edge may be poor, however, so access to many of these decentralized activities may still be dependent on car ownership and car availability, which is itself gendered, since men tend to control car use.

Gentrification too has arguably contributed to the degendering of the domestic division of labour (we discuss this in Chapter 10, pp. 386–8). One of the attractions of inner-city living is that it provides easier movement between workplace and home for dual-career households trying to juggle with the competing demands of work and family.

The situation in declining areas of the inner city is quite different. Single-parent families with small children and, after the collapse of many city communities, without extended kinship networks to support them are confined to the home by the demands of childcare. Their incomes are not high enough to buy it and state nursery provision in Britain has been minimal, though this situation may be changing under the 1997 Labour government. The decline of employment with the collapse of inner-city manufacturing has forced many women to take up low-paid homework and work for very long hours within the home.

New housing estates with leisure facilities often limited to male-dominated clubs and pubs may leave women with little alternative, apart from bingo, to private leisure in front of the TV. Bingo is a predominantly female activity, which, according to Dixey (1988: 126), 'plays a vital role in providing a semi-public space which is local and handy, and, as an extension of the community, brings feelings of rootedness and "at-homeness"'.

Taylor, Evans, and Fraser (1996) certainly found that the male domination of urban space persisted in Manchester and Sheffield. Their street survey found that, in public spaces, men consistently outnumbered women at all times of day and night. Male dominance was particularly marked at night, and, according to K. Evans (1997), in the streets during the early evening hours the researchers came across only thirty-one women for every 100 men. Women's use of the city was shaped by safety concerns and a 'landscape of fear', which identified areas to be avoided. These varied according to the time of day, and shopping areas that attracted women in daytime became a 'dead space' that was avoided or passed through hastily at night.

A landscape of fear?

► Have you ever felt frightened in a public place? If so, when did this last happen? At what time of day did it happen? Where did it happen?

► What frightened you about the situation that you were in? Is there any part of the city you live in (or a city that you visit) which you would avoid visiting? During the daytime? At night?

► In what ways do you think that the city could be made safer?

► Try comparing male and female responses to these questions.

As Valentine (1992) points out, a vicious circle comes into operation. The male dominance of public space in cities leads to women avoiding some areas by day and all areas by night, which increases male dominance, which intensifies women's fears. The response of both the police and the media to incidents of violence against women reinforce the landscape of fear by suggesting that women are partially to blame for violence against them, through putting themselves at risk by being on their own in dangerous places. Increased surveillance, design changes of subways and car parks, and safer transport could reverse this process by restoring women's confidence, but local-authority initiatives of this kind have generally fallen foul of public expenditure cuts.

There is in the end little to suggest that recent changes in the city have done much to degender urban space.

CHANGING COMMUNITIES

The changes in the city that we have been examining have had various consequences for the decline and the formation of communities in both urban and rural areas. In this section we will examine their impact on different kinds of community.

Declining working-class communities

Although, as we discussed on p. 415, working-class communities were still flourishing in the 1950s, this situation was about to change. Slum clearance and relocation shattered the residential base of many such communities in British cities during the 1950s and 1960s. Willmott and Young followed what happened to forty-seven young married couples who moved from Bethnal Green to Greenleigh, a council housing estate twenty miles away.

The move to Greenleigh immediately broke up the extended kinship network that was a prominent feature of Bethnal Green, while fewer public meeting places meant less opportunity for social interaction. In Bethnal Green there had been one pub for every 400 people and one shop for every fourteen households, but in Greenleigh there was one pub for every 5,000 people and one shop for every 300 (Willmott and Young 1960: 142). Greenleigh also brought together people from many different places who lacked common backgrounds and were strangers to each other. People lived a much more private existence focused on the household and the nuclear family.

Some of these features of Greenleigh may have been temporary and transitional, as Willmott and Young themselves suggested. Given time people are more likely to develop relationships, improve local facilities, and establish local identities. But time alone cannot turn a housing estate into a community in the absence of the conditions that enable residential communities to form.

The changes that we have examined in the inner city weakened the working-class communities that were left. The decline of manufacturing destroyed their economic base. This was a matter not only of loss of employment but also of the loss of local-authority funds as the local tax base declined, at the very time that rising unemployment and growing deprivation meant that these funds were more needed than ever before. Those left in inner-city areas were disproportionately the old, the unemployed, one-parent families, the homeless, and those suffering from long-term illnesses. Socially isolated, they looked to support from the welfare state rather than from relatives or community.

Where communities survived these changes, they were weakened by the more general privatizing tendencies that we examine in Chapter 15, p. 632. These focused people's energies increasingly on home and household. When Holme restudied Bethnal Green thirty years after Young and Willmott, she found that it had become much more home-centred (see box on p. 430). It was more like the suburb of Woodford, which Willmott and Young had studied in the 1950s and found to be markedly more focused on the home than Bethnal Green (Willmott and Young 1960: 15–27).

Conflict in the rural community

Decentralization and deurbanization also had an impact on rural communities. The spread of urban commuters into rural areas meant that the dividing line between the urban and the rural came to run *through* villages rather than *between* the village and the city. As commuters leading essentially urban lives became an increasing proportion of village inhabitants, the village community could be weakened and divided. Pahl commented on this as long ago as the 1960s: 'The middle-class people come into rural areas in search of a meaningful community and by their presence help to destroy whatever community was there' (1965: 18).

In his study of class relations in East Anglia, Newby (1977) interpreted this kind of situation rather differently. He argued that a common opposition to newcomers had strengthened the sense of community between agricultural workers and farmers. In the nineteenth century the landowners had tried to create a spirit of community between themselves and labourers but with little success. The class structure and the conflicting interests of landowners and labourers generated an oppositional culture amongst the latter. This culture had, however, been weakened by the decline in the number of agricultural workers. The invasion of outsiders from the city then strengthened the bonds

Bethnal Green revisited

'One striking difference was how home-centred most Bethnal Green families had now become. In the 1950s, this had been a feature of the Woodford families. Mothers with a three month old child are, of course, likely to spend more time in the home than outside it. But it was noticeable how many husbands in Bethnal Green today were almost as much around, when they could be, as Woodford husbands. DIY, even in rented property, and television—not to mention the baby—were clearly strong competitors of the pub and the football ground. . . .

'But whatever the draw towards the home, or occupation within it, the corollary in Bethnal Green to this new home-centredness was the emptiness of the streets and corridors and staircases in the housing estates. Markets still flourished. Children sometimes played outside. Small groups of adults occasionally congregated. But no longer could it be said that people in Bethnal Green were (in Young and Willmott's words) "vigorously at home in the streets" . . .'

Source: Holme (1985: 45).

between farmers and their workers, because of their shared hostility to the newcomers.

Thus, according to Pahl, the incomers destroyed the existing community, while, according to Newby, they stimulated the emergence of a community that had not previously existed. In spite of their rather different conclusions, these apparently conflicting interpretations are, none the less, perfectly compatible with each other, for Pahl and Newby were referring to different kinds of community. Pahl was concerned with the decline of the residential community as village unity and identity became weaker, while Newby drew attention to a closing of the ranks of farmers and workers in the face of an invasion from the outside.

As we showed in our earlier discussion of community, one of the problems in using the term is the different meanings that it has been given. In evaluating any study of a community, you must first determine the way in which the term has been used.

Ethnicity and community

Ethnicity as well as class has provided a basis for city communities. As we showed in the first part of the chapter, Gans argued that *ethnic villages* had a distinctive way of life based on strongly integrated communities. Immigrant communities are by no means new, and have always been found in large cities, particularly in the United States, but increased immigration in the 1950s and 1960s built up ethnic minorities in British cities.

 It is important to be clear about the meaning of *ethnicity* and its relationship to *race*, which we discuss in Chapter 4, pp. 143–5. In Chapter 12, pp. 483–7, we examine international migration and growing ethnic diversity.

Various aspects of the situation of ethnic minorities facilitate community formation. They tend to be spatially concentrated, while ethnicity itself provides a strong basis for community because of the distinctive linguistic, cultural, and religious traditions that can bind members of an ethnic minority together. This is reinforced by the ethnic conflicts and racism that commonly accompany ethnic diversity. Racism is, as Jewson (1990: 171) has put it, 'a particularly intrusive, explicit, involuntary, and powerful determinant of collective identity'. Ethnic communities are not just the product of shared customs and beliefs. They are also the result of common experiences of exclusion and discrimination, and the creation of organizations for mutual support and protection.

While attention has been focused on the ethnic communities of black and Asian minorities, whites too have an ethnic identity and ethnicity has provided a basis for white communities as well. Jeffers, Hoggett, and Harrison (1996) have examined the emergence of what they call 'defended communities' amongst whites in the East End of London and on the Beaumont Leys estate in Leicester. These communities saw themselves as threatened by blacks and Asians, though, as Jeffers *et al.* point out, this did not mean that any actual threat existed. The scarcity of housing and jobs in these areas easily generated fears and conflicts. As we discussed on p. 414, ethnic competition for housing has been a long-standing feature of city life.

Ethnicity as a basis for community comes into conflict with attempts to develop multi-ethnic residential communities out of those living in a particular area. Community Relations Councils and Community Associations provide examples of efforts to 'improve race relations' by creating local organizations that would bring different ethnic groups together.

Jeffers *et al.* have examined the interrelationships between these conflicting principles of community. They studied the success of seven community initiatives in overcoming ethnic and racial divisions in Bristol, Leicester, and Tower Hamlets in London. They concluded that one important factor in the success of such initiatives was whether the various ethnic groups were interdependent. When they were interdependent because they shared a common interest, which might be in a sporting activity or in improving a housing estate, an appropriately organized initiative could reduce ethnic and racial conflict.

They argued that the form taken by state initiatives could have a considerable bearing on these relationships. Government funding strategies that encouraged competition for public resources often generated ethnic conflict in British cities during the 1980s. Ethnically based groups competed for funds and claimed that they had 'special needs'. This competition led them to emphasize ethnic distinctiveness, and ethnic identities were reinforced.

On the Bancroft estate in Tower Hamlets, both blacks and whites were, however, dependent on a multi-ethnic Tenant Management Committee for access to the funds needed to modernize the estate. Racial conflicts on the estate declined. Blacks and whites at least came to 'cohabit the same space in a friendly and peaceful fashion'. Jeffers *et al.* suggest that this example shows that interdependence can be promoted if government interventions are designed appropriately.

They point out that much also depended on how such initiatives were conducted. They needed to strike a difficult balance between working against racism in public and allowing people to maintain their private attitudes and feelings, even if these were racist in character. It was important that cultural differences were not ignored or suppressed but instead recognized and accommodated. The Easton Community Association in Bristol was successful because it was able to deal with conflicts in this way.

Ethnicity has then provided a basis for community in the ethnically diverse city of contemporary Britain, but ethnic communities were not only generated by the distinctive customs and cultures of groups. They also arose because of patterns of exclusion, racial discrimination, and the competition of groups for resources. Attempts have been made to reduce ethnic conflicts by constructing multi-ethnic organizations, which have tried to establish communities on a residential rather than an ethnic basis.

Initiatives of this sort show again the deficiencies of the ecological approach to the study of relationships in cities, for this approach cannot easily comprehend interventions of this sort.

Gay villages

The hollowing-out of the city has provided the space for another kind of community to emerge, one based on sexual orientation. Taylor, Evans, and Fraser (1996) have examined the growth of a gay village in the centre of Manchester.

They advance an argument similar to Fischer's 'gravitation' theory in suggesting that the sheer size of the city's population meant that it contained a sufficient number of gay people to sustain an openly identifiable gay area (Taylor *et al.* 1996: 182). The existence of various ethnic communities in Manchester, including a Chinatown and distinct Indian and Jewish areas, facilitated tolerance of a gay village as just one more minority culture. As Zukin (1995) points out, even though it is not based on ethnicity, a gay community can be presented as an ethnic minority (see box on p. 432).

The emergence of gay communities must be set in the context of changing attitudes towards sexual orientation. The partial decriminalizing of gay sexuality by the Sexual Offences Act of 1967, the rapid spread of openly gay pubs and clubs in the 1970s, and the emergence of a distinctive gay lifestyle prepared the way for the establishment of gay villages. But these were not simply the result of a growing tolerance that enabled gays to associate openly in public.

Indeed, Taylor and his colleagues suggest that the 1980s resurgence of political and media hostility to gays, partly occasioned by the association of AIDS with gay sexual activity, precipitated a withdrawal of gays into their own space. Gay communities are the result of 'gay-bashing' as well as gay association. Indeed, while gay villages clearly require a degree of tolerance, they also stem from a more general intolerance. It is this that leads gays to travel considerable distances to find an area where they can be open, relaxed, and at home.

Gay communities and city interests: the 1994 Gay Games in New York

'The games are more than an athletic competition for a special group. They are supposed to exemplify the solidarity and pride of homosexuals, burnished by political organizations and ravaged by AIDS. In the publicity surrounding the games, as well as in the athletic and cultural program, homosexuality is represented as if it were an ethnicity with its own traditions and roots. It is also represented as a lifestyle, with its own entertainment forms and consumption choices. Lifestyle is inescapably linked to marketing, as it is often pointed out that most individual homosexuals in the United States have higher incomes than most households. Thus the Gay Games have drawn the support of large corporate sponsors (manufacturers of consumer goods), feature T-shirts and other commercial memorabilia, and are praised for bringing tourist dollars to the city.'

Source: Zukin (1995: 264).

The creation of a gay village was also a form of gentrification, since it upgraded a derelict area of inner-city warehouses. Commercial interests and local-authority regeneration strategies became involved. The Manchester gay village required investment in shops and places of entertainment, and the renovation of buildings and streets. The so-called pink pound, the exceptional spending power of gay consumers, with their lower family and household commitments, attracted the interest of entrepreneurs, both gay and straight. To a local authority, a gay village could be a means of reviving a flagging local economy, revitalizing a derelict area of the city, and attracting tourists. Zukin's description of the Gay Games in New York shows the same forces at work there.

Community diversity

This section has shown that the relationship between the city and the community is a complex one. This is partly because there are many different kinds of community. Changes that weaken one kind of community may enable another kind of community to establish itself. Thus the decline of the inner city weakened traditional working-class communities but then provided the opportunity for gentrifying processes to establish new ones. We have examined the interesting case of the emergence of gay communities, but, arguably, gentrification has also enabled new middle-class communities to form within previously working-class areas. As we have also shown, ethnicity has become a more prominent basis for community but is in conflict with attempts to create multi-ethnic residential communities.

Generalizations are often made about the decline of the community in the city. It is clear, however, that, while some communities decline, others establish themselves. No general statements can really be made about the community in the city, for there are many different kinds of community that respond differently to the processes of urban change.

THE DECLINE OF CITY MANAGEMENT

While urbanization had led to the growth of a local state to manage the city and provide collective consumption, this process was reversed in the 1980s. As decentralization transformed the structure of the city and cities faced mounting problems, local authorities found that their capacity to manage a growing urban crisis was weakened. This was partly because the economic decline of the inner city reduced the resources available to them, but it was also due to political changes. In this section we examine the decline of collective consumption with the privatization of the local state, and the increase in urban disorder.

Privatization

In Britain the local state came under attack from a Conservative government seeking to reduce local-government powers and spending after the election of 1979. This government also initiated an extensive programme of privatization that had a major impact on local services.

The privatizing of Coventry

► The extract at the beginning of the chapter described the plan to privatize Coventry's city centre.

► Have any similar changes taken place in any city that you know?

As we showed earlier (pp. 402–3), Castells believed that collective consumption was necessary to the maintenance of capitalism, for it provided the capitalist employer with a supply of healthy, educated, and housed workers. In the 1980s, however, **privatization** resulted in a shift from collective to individual consumption. According to Castells, this was but a temporary reversal of the growth of collective consumption at a time of crisis.

Saunders has taken a very different view of privatization. According to Saunders (1986: 316), collective consumption was not a requirement of capitalism but rather a 'holding operation' that covered people's basic consumption needs until they were able to take responsibility for meeting these needs themselves. Privatization enabled them to do this. In future most people would satisfy their consumption requirements through private purchases, leaving a minority that was unable to do so dependent on what was left of the welfare state. This was, furthermore, not something that was forced on people by the government, for it met their real needs for greater control over their lives. Privatization was not, therefore, something that Saunders expected some future Labour government to reverse.

As part of its general programme to 'roll back the state', the 1980s Conservative government set out to privatize local-authority services and property. It is important to bear in mind that city life was also greatly affected by national privatizations. Thus, privatizing changes in the National Health Service impacted on local hospitals, local doctors, and, of course, their patients.

 These changes in the local state need to be placed in the context of changes in the state as a whole and the general crisis of capitalism in the 1970s and 1980s that lay behind these changes in the state. We discuss all this in Chapter 18, pp. 745–58, and also consider there the 1997 Labour government's attitude to privatization.

Some of the main forms taken by privatization in the city were:

► compulsory competitive tendering;
► delegation of education budgets;
► deregulation of bus services;
► sale of council houses;
► privatizing of public space.

Compulsory competitive tendering required local authorities to allow private companies to compete for contracts to provide local services. Contracts had to go to the cheapest provider. This meant that local-authority organizations were, in effect, privatized, since they had to behave like private companies in order to compete with them. Services such as refuse collection, road maintenance, street cleaning, and school-meals provision were privatized in this way. This was linked to the *delegation of education budgets* to schools. The funds for local education authority services were largely transferred to schools, which could then buy in the services they chose to have from a provider of choice.

The *deregulation of bus services* meant that municipal bus companies lost their monopoly of local routes, which were now open to a virtually unregulated competition. Municipal companies had to behave like private companies or go out of business. Deregulation did indeed enable large national companies to force out of business many local ones, whether publicly or privately owned. These companies were also able to buy into rail transport when the railways were privatized.

The *sale of council houses* too was driven by government policy, which forced local authorities to allow their tenants to buy their houses. Between 1981 and 1989 1.5 million council houses were sold. Public-sector housing provision also declined because new council-house building dropped and rent subsidies to council-house tenants were reduced.

While the sharp decline of council housing in the 1980s was clearly the result of government policy, it should be placed in the context of a steady increase in owner-occupation during the twentieth century (see Figure 11.14) and a cultural preference for home-

Figure 11.14. Housing tenure changes, Great Britain, 1914–1991

	%		
Year	Types of tenure		
	Owner-occupiers	Council tenants	Other rented
1914	10	0	90
1945	26	12	62
1961	43	27	31
1971	53	31	16
1981	54	34	12
1991	67	24	10

Sources: Jewson (1989: 130); *Living in Britain* (1996: 229).

ownership. Saunders (1990) points out that house ownership is particularly high in Britain and societies originally settled by the British—Australia, Canada, New Zealand, and the United States—as contrasted with continental Europe, and argues that it is related to a strong culture of individualism going back to medieval British society.

Saunders saw private ownership as meeting people's real needs. Homeownership gave people greater control over their lives. It also gave them a sense of security and identity. Home was a place under their own control where people could take refuge and a place where they could truly be themselves. Homeownership did have its disadvantages too. For some people, it turned into a personal disaster, when they lost their jobs, found themselves unable to pay the interest on their loans, and lost their homes. Others found that what they thought to be a safe investment was anything but sound when the bottom dropped out of the housing market at the end of the 1980s. In enabling greater homeownership the Conservative government in the 1980s did, however, generate considerable popular support, particularly in the working class, which helped it to stay in government for such a long period.

Another less obvious form taken by privatization was the *privatizing of public space*, which had been one of the central features of urban life. This process has gone further in the United States but it is certainly present in Britain (Bianchini and Schwengel 1991). Examples of it are:

▶ *Shopping malls.* The essentially public shopping street has been replaced by privately owned or pri-

vately managed shopping malls. Access to these is controlled by private security companies, who can exclude activities such as busking and expel 'undesirables'.

▶ *Privately controlled streets.* Homeowners' Associations in the United States have formed Common Interest Developments with authority to carry out surveillance and control the streets. Similarly Business Improvement Districts allow business and property owners to take responsibility for the upkeep and control of streets in business areas (see the chapter's opening piece).

▶ *Fortified estates.* Walled estates with controlled entry, surveillance by camera, and patrol by private security companies have been built, particularly in American cities. Private security companies have also offered their services in suburban areas of Britain (M. Davis 1990).

▶ *Privately managed parks.* The transfer of park management to private companies is commonly found in American cities. Zukin describes the privatizing of Bryant Park in New York. She notes that it was relandscaped to increase surveillance by removing hidden areas. Private security firms were brought in to patrol the park (Zukin 1995).

The privatizing of public space reflects not only the spread of private ownership but also a growing concern with public order and a more general decline of public welfare provision. The exclusion of 'undesirables' is in part a response to rising crime, the growth of begging and busking, squatting in shop doorways, and 'sleeping rough' in the parks. This has all resulted from unemployment, homelessness, declining public welfare provision, and the closing of mental hospitals (on this see Chapter 16, pp. 674–6).

This process is also linked to the privatizing of law enforcement. The financial crises of the state, local and central, have led to the transfer of security and policing to the private sector, because it pays lower wages and provides a cheaper service. According to Zukin (1995: 40), in California there are 3.9 private security employees for every public security employee. This process has gone further in the United States, but there is plenty of evidence that it is taking place in Britain too (see Chapter 18, p. 756).

Privatization is often seen in terms of the sale of public companies to the private sector. It is, however, a much broader process that involves the decline of collective consumption at local level, the extensive sale of public housing, the privatizing of public space, and the related privatizing of law enforcement.

Urban disorder

Riots were a common feature of the pre-industrial and early industrial city, but during the nineteenth century conflict became increasingly organized, managed, and contained. The main form it took was class conflict and this was organized in the industrial sphere by unions or in the political sphere by parties. Open conflict still occurred, most obviously in the form of strikes and demonstrations, but these too were highly organized by unions and political organizations. They were generally non-violent, followed a well-established pattern, and were tolerated as legitimate means for the expression of discontent. Violent riots did occur from time to time but these were considered exceptional events.

In the 1980s, however, open conflict became more common, with more violent strikes, such as the miners' strike of 1984–5, and more frequent riots. There were waves of rioting in particular years and a higher background level of minor rioting in between. Beatrix Campbell (1993: p. xi) goes so far as to claim that 'riot became routine' in the 1980s and 1990s.

The one thing that most riots have had in common is their occurrence in working-class areas with high levels of unemployment and deprivation, whether of the *inner city*, such as Brixton, or the *outer estate*, such as Meadowell. While this suggests that the higher unemployment of the 1980s and 1990s was one of the important conditions that led to rioting, it cannot provide a complete explanation of the riots. They have not occurred in all areas of high unemployment and were not a feature of the 1930s, when unemployment and deprivation were much higher.

Jewson (1990) has suggested that another common feature of the 1980s riots was the involvement of ethnic minorities experiencing racial discrimination and exclusion from full participation in British society. He argues that in Britain political organization has been on class lines and there is no tradition of organized ethnic politics. Ethnic minorities have not, therefore, been politically incorporated in the way that they have in the United States, where there is a much greater representation of ethnic minorities in city government. Jewson points out that, since the rioting of the 1960s, American cities have been relatively quiet.

The ethnicity dimension is linked to another feature of the riots in British cities—conflict with the police. Discrimination and exclusion generated a counter-culture associated with drug-dealing and petty crime, which brought people into conflict with the police. Relations between the police and ethnic minorities deteriorated because of new police stop-and search tactics that seemed to discriminate against blacks. There were suspicions of racist attitudes in the police force, and there was anger at the apparent failure of the police to deal with racist attacks on members of the minorities.

Incidents involving the police have certainly often triggered off riots. This applies to the United States as well, and the Los Angeles riot of 1992, which set off disturbances across the United States, was triggered by the

Major riots of the 1980s and 1990s

1980s			1990s		
1980	Apr.	Bristol (St Paul's)	1991	Aug.	Cardiff (Ely)
				Sept.	Oxford (Blackbird Leys)
1981	Apr.	London (Brixton)		Sept.	Tyneside (Meadowell)
	July	London (Brixton)			
	July	London (Southall)	1992	May	Coventry (Wood End)
	July	Liverpool (Toxteth)		July	Bristol (Hartcliffe)
	July	London (Brixton)			
			1995	June	Bradford (Manningham)
1985	Sept.	Birmingham (Handsworth)		July	Leeds (Hyde Park)
	Sept.	London (Brixton)		July	Luton (Marsh Farm)
	Oct.	London (Broadwater Farm)		Dec.	London (Brixton)

Brixton in July 1981.

acquittal of four white police officers who had been videotaped beating a young black man.

Racism was not a major factor in generating the *outer estate* riots of the early 1990s, but other forms of exclusion were involved. According to Beatrix Campbell (1993: 303), 'these estates had been living with permanent high unemployment and decline, while they were encircled by evidence of prosperity and renewal'. Campbell gives as an extreme example of this the proximity of the Scotswood Estate to the Gateshead Metro centre (see box on p. 442). Conflicts with the police were also a feature, for the estates had become centres of burglary, car theft, ram-raiding, and joy-riding.

Campbell argues that crime was not, however, simply a response to deprivation and exclusion. Criminal activity resulted also from a 'gender struggle over space'. The traditional gendered division of labour had broken down. Unemployment meant that males had lost their power and status, while women were no longer confined within the home and became the organizers of community self-help and mutual support. According to Campbell, this threatened male control of public life, and young men reasserted themselves by creating criminal fraternities and engaging in public violence.

In understanding and explaining riots it is important to separate out:

▶ the underlying social conditions;

▶ the dynamics of conflict generation;

▶ the triggering incident;

▶ later responses to the situation;

▶ the explanations of those involved.

The *underlying social conditions* can be linked to the changes in the city that we have examined earlier in this chapter. The decline of the inner city, the dispersal of population to isolated peripheral housing estates, rising unemployment, concentrated deprivation and increasing inequality, and a growing ethnic diversity created the social conditions in which riots could occur.

The *dynamics of conflict generation* involved the vicious circles that easily developed around issues of race relations, policing, and criminality, which intensified discontent and created a combustible situation. Some

Anatomy of two riots	Elements of a riot	Brixton, April 1981	Meadowell, Sept. 1991
	Location	Inner city area of London	Outer estate on Tyneside
	Social context	Strong African-Caribbean minority	White working class
	Unemployment	25% of black workers unemployed	25% of young males under 24 unemployed
	Conflict with police	Over 'stop and search' policy	Police decide to tackle estate crime
	Precipitating incident	'Operation Swamp' street search	Death of two young men after police car chase
	The events	Battles between police and young men using bricks, bottles, and petrol bombs over two days. Large number of injuries, looting, and damage to buildings	Petrol bombing of shops, starting with those owned by Asians, followed by general looting. Police surround and occupy estate

Source: Campbell (1993).

incident, very often of a quite minor kind, then ignited the riot, but the way the riot unfolded depended on *responses* to the situation and it might take on a quite new character in its later stages.

After the riot those involved provided their own *explanations*, which derived from their own particular experiences, their beliefs about social conditions in their society, and their concern to justify their actions. Rioters focused attention on the injustice or unfairness of the incident that precipitated the riot and accused the police of worsening the situation by overreacting to legitimate protests. The 'authorities' denied that legitimate grievances played any part in generating a riot and accused extremists or looters of engineering it for their own purposes. Alternatively, the media were blamed for publicizing previous riots and triggering off 'copycat' incidents. It is important to emphasize that there is no single or simple reason why such a complex event as a riot occurs. It passes through many stages in its development and at each one new factors can influence its course. It involves complex interactions between many different groups of people with differing perceptions of what is going on. The explanation of a riot must take account of the whole process and not fasten on one particular stage of it or one particular group's view of it.

URBAN REGENERATION AND GROWTH

We have given much attention to changes that are symptoms of urban decline—deurbanization, the flight of commercial activity to the periphery, the problems of the inner city, the decline of the local state, and the return of the riot. Although cities have experienced growing problems during the last thirty years of the twentieth century, they have also been centres of regeneration and growth. We now examine the part played by culture, sport, and the state in urban regeneration. We also discuss the rise of a network of global cities with thriving economies.

Cultural restructuring

Culture has become an increasingly important part of the city economy. Zukin argues that what she calls 'cultural consumption' has become a central activity of the contemporary city.

With the disappearance of local manufacturing industries and periodic crises in government and finance, culture is more and more the business of cities—the basis of their tourist attractions and their unique competitive edge. The growth of cultural consumption (of art, food, fashion, music, tourism) and the industries that cater to it fuels the city's symbolic economy.   (Zukin 1995: 2)

By the 'symbolic economy' Zukin means the production and distribution of images rather than goods. Tourism, for example, sells sights, captured as images by the camera, rather than objects. Employment has steadily increased in a range of occupations concerned with the symbolic economy. Advertising, public relations, the media, designers, and software companies in various ways all make and sell images. Goods are, of course, still produced, but their design has become an ever larger component of their value. How it looks and what it signifies become a more important aspect of the product than what it does and how it works. It is not the cloth of the T-shirt that matters but the symbol on it and what that tells you about the wearer.

The image of the city itself has become an important means by which cities compete to attract investment. Culture, tourism, and investment are closely tied together. Cultural attractions enable image-makers to sell cities to tourists, who bring money into the city, make it more widely known, and attract corporate investment. The growth of global tourism (see Chapter 12, pp. 482–3) is yet another aspect of the increasing integration of cities in the global economy.

Education too is tied into this complex, for universities are major employers and an important source of consumer demand. Sheffield, for example, has been one of Britain's major industrial cities, but Sheffield University has become the city's third largest employer (Taylor *et al.* 1996). The image of the city is important in attracting students as well as tourists.

The growing economic importance of culture, tourism, and education have made *cultural restructuring* one of the chief ways of regenerating cities in economic decline. The revival of Glasgow provides perhaps the best-known case of this in Britain, but the process is going on in towns and cities up and down the country.

Lancaster provides another example that at least started with the advantages of a castle, a museum, and lots of listed buildings. The same can hardly be said for Wigan, another Lancashire town, which has had to make the most of its non-seaside pier. An undistinguished canal pier, its sole claim to fame is that it appears in the title of George Orwell's well-known account of working-class life, *The Road to Wigan Pier*, but it is now the focus of the Wigan Pier Heritage Centre, with 'a colourful market and elegant shops, excellent sports facilities, attractive pubs and restaurants, and

---

Cultural restructuring

'As industry has departed from the city centre Lancaster has been reconstructed as a modern consumption centre preserving the shells of past rounds of economic growth to house new functions—the old customs house as a maritime museum, the warehouses of the riverfront as gentrified homes, canal-side mill buildings as new pubs. One of the main thrusts of all of this is to construct 'Lancaster' as an object of the tourist gaze. It has many of the ingredients of a modern tourist mecca: a castle (which in 1991 will become entirely usable for tourist purposes); a river and a gentrified river front; the folly on the hill (Ashton Memorial) just restored at a cost of some £1.5 million; four museums, three of which have been recently completed; well-conserved old, interesting streets with 270 listed buildings; cultural events including the Lancaster Literature festival, and so on.'

Source: Bagguley *et al.* (1990: 161).

▶ **Can you think of any examples of cultural restructuring in the area where you live?**

delightful canal-side walk-ways' (Lash and Urry 1994: 214–15).

As employment in manufacturing has collapsed, the heritage industry has turned industrial landscapes into tourist attractions. This not only provides local employment and brings in tourists but also makes places better to live and work in, and therefore attracts other unrelated businesses.

Sport cities

The attraction of major sporting events can perform a similar function to cultural activity in promoting an image, attracting tourists and investment, and improving city facilities. Taylor, Evans, and Fraser (1996) have discussed the part played by sport in the regeneration of Manchester and Sheffield.

Manchester's bids for the Olympic Games were an important part of that city's regeneration strategy, and the (so far unsuccessful) bidding process alone has attracted funds and improved facilities. Taylor, Evans, and Fraser note, however, that Sheffield's success in attracting the World Student Games in 1992 was a mixed blessing, for, although it generated jobs and sports facilites, it also imposed a financial burden on the city which led to cuts in local-authority services and jobs. None the less, the intense competition to host major sporting events certainly bears witness to the importance that cities attach to them.

Cultural restructuring and the attraction of major sporting events both depend on a positive local response to change. They require investment by local entrepreneurs and the active involvement of local authorities in promotion, coordination, restoration of the urban landscape, and the provision of facilities. On p. 409 we showed that one of the problems with some accounts of the effect on the city of global changes in capitalism is that they present cities as victims of changes outside their control. In studying the city we must take account not only of the impact upon it of movements of capital but also the local response, for this response can have a major influence on where the capital flows.

Government schemes

Having contributed more than a little to the creation of an urban crisis through its cuts in local-authority spending, central government eventually became involved in urban regeneration.

The Conservative government's first initiative in the 1980s was the creation of Enterprise Zones. These were

Canary Wharf: urban regeneration or degeneration?

typical of its general approach to policy, since they assumed that economic recovery would come from freeing business from state interference. Planning regulations would be relaxed in these zones and companies would be exempt from certain taxes. As with the Free Trade Zones established in such countries as Mexico (see Chapter 12, pp. 480–1), capital would be attracted by creating a favourable environment for it. Lawless and Brown (1986: 228–9) note, however, that the more successful of the zones were precisely those where public agencies were actively involved in developing them.

A more interventionist approach followed with the creation of twelve Urban Development Corporations, the most well known of which is the London Docklands Development Corporation (LDDC). These were administered by local business people and bypassed local authorities. They could compulsorily purchase large areas, invest in infrastructure, and ignore normal planning restrictions. As the LDDC has shown, they could have a big impact on the environment, but whether this benefited the people who lived there was another matter. The LDDC certainly attracted international capital to build the office blocks, most famously at Canary Wharf, that now dominate the east London skyline, but they did not provide much employment for local people accustomed to dock-work and other kinds of manual labour. Similarly, there was a huge expansion of private housing in the area but the prices were out of the reach of most locals, while funding cuts halted council-house building (Coupland 1992).

The City Challenge programme of 1993 differed importantly from its predecessors. It was targeted at small areas, and included within its remit the tackling of housing, education, and crime problems, because these diminished an area's attractiveness to investors. It also involved local authorities as major partners, though they had to compete for funding, were required to form partnerships with other bodies, and had to deliver specified results within a fixed period. City Challenge took more account of local needs and local people, though it was still firmly controlled by central government. This meant that there was plenty of scope for conflict between a programme driven by central government and the priorities and procedures of local authorities (Pratt and Fearnley 1996).

The involvement of the Conservative government in urban regeneration was typical of its general policy towards local government. It kept close control of funding, forced projects to compete for limited funds, and involved the private sector as much as possible.

Global cities

The picture of urban decline that we presented earlier must be qualified not only by the evidence of urban regeneration and local initiative but also by the emergence of a distinct group of global cities which benefited from the processes that were generating problems in other cities.

Globalization led to the emergence of a new kind of **global** or **world city** which was centrally involved in the growing economic integration of the world. The rise of the global city and the shifting of capital out of the old industrial cities were part of the same process. In her study of *The Global City* Sassen (1991) argued that the *dispersal* of production from the old industrial societies to other parts of the world made greater coordination necessary and therefore led to the *concentration* of control in a small number of global cities. These are the 'command' cities, where transnational corporations and financial institutions have located their headquarters (Sassen 1991: 5).

 Globalization and growing global economic integration are discussed in Chapter 12, pp. 477–83.

Definitions of the global city vary and different lists are accordingly produced. Knox has produced a list of twenty-nine (see Figure 11.15), from which five—Brussels, London, New York, Paris, and Tokyo—stand out because so many international organizations and transnational organizations (TNCs) have located their headquarters in them. Sassen concentrated her attention on London, New York, and Tokyo and argued that these three cities have become increasingly alike because of their similar global functions, although they have very different histories, cultures, and national traditions.

According to Sassen, these three cities are linked together in a global financial network that has produced 'one transterritorial marketplace' (1991: 327). Their geographical positioning means that, as one closes down at the end of the day, the next one to the West is just opening for trading. Sassen also argues that the global role of these cities has partially unhooked them from the societies in which they are located. She points out that they follow patterns of economic growth different from those of the national economy. At a time in the 1980s when industrial cities in Britain, America, and Japan were in decline, the global cities themselves were booming.

Figure 11.15. **Global cities**

Source: Knox (1995:9).

Note: This map shows cities that have at least one major TNC headquarters *and* at least one headquarters of an international non-governmental or inter-governmental agency.

These cities produce the services and financial innovations required by TNCs and the international financial industry. They are therefore centres of managerial, legal, insurance, marketing, communications, public relations, design, and accountancy occupations. They are also centres of innovation where the latest technologies are applied to the development of these services. Sassen actually rejects the distinction between goods and services and emphasizes that 'the "things" a global city makes are services and financial goods' (1991: 5).

While these global functions have revived the fortunes of the cities concerned and provided them with new sources of employment, it is important to bear in mind that not all of those who live in them have benefited. As we showed on p. 425 when we considered the state of the inner city, a global city like London contains areas that have experienced severe deprivation as growing global economic integration has led to the decline of their traditional industries.

Also, a growing inequality has resulted from the occupational changes generated by London's global financial functions. While higher-paid managerial and professional occupations have expanded, so have various low-paid occupations, such as those of the clerical workers, cleaners and security staff employed in the office blocks. Other low-paid occupations, such as those of restaurant workers, bar staff, and shop-assistants, have expanded to meet the consumption needs of the higher-paid professionals. Low-paid home-work too has increased, partly to produce fashion prod-ucts for the higher paid. Sassen suggests that this gap between the higher and lower paid has been widened by the global city's orientation to world markets and diminished sensitivity to local poverty, local problems, and local politics.

The notion of the newness of global cities is in some ways misleading. As we showed earlier (pp. 410–12), London and other comparable cities have long per-formed global functions. They did so, however, largely within the framework of the imperial state, and there is certainly something new in the emergence of a network of global cities with distinctive occupational structures that are partially unhooked from national economies. As we argued on p. 403, this network has opened a new chapter in the evolving relationship between capitalism and the city.

THE POST-MODERN CITY

The idea that cities have recently entered a new stage in their development has led to the notion of the **post-modern city**, which is similar to the concepts of post-Fordism and post-modern organization and related to the changes that they describe. In this section, we use the concept of the post-modern city to draw together the various changes that we have examined in this part of the chapter and link them to changes in city culture and city life. We contrast the post-modern city with the modern city of the 1960s and 1970s, which had developed out of earlier processes of change.

Like the post-modern organization (see Chapter 16, pp. 665–6), the post-modern city is decentralized and dedifferentiated. The shifting of production and ser-vices to the periphery has hollowed out the city and decentralized its activities. The specialized zoning characteristic of the modern city has also declined, as activities that used to be differentiated by their concen-tration in particular parts of the city have been dis-persed through it.

The economy of the post-modern city is based less on the production and consumption of goods and focused more on the production and consumption of culture. The significance of culture is linked to the rise of tourism and the growth of a *symbolic economy* concerned

with making and distributing images. City politicians have recognized these changes and tried to revive their economies through cultural restructuring and the improvement of the city's image to draw in tourists, investors, and consumers in general.

The manufacturing of goods still, of course, goes on, but style and image have become a more important aspect of the product. This is linked to the post-Fordist changes in production that we discuss in Chapter 13, pp. 528–30. Product diversity has become increasingly important and variations in style are one means of cre-ating this. Furthermore, a style can extend across a range of products, so that furnishing, clothing, and per-sonal appearance can be combined to create a certain image. The projection of an image lies at the heart of the attractiveness of a style.

In modern cities function shaped appearance, and products and buildings were mass-produced in stan-dard forms, but in the post-modern city style and appearance rule. Modernism produced efficiently func-tioning structures that were universally applicable and virtually indistinguishable. One tower block looked like another. Post-modern architecture has reacted by playfully creating façades that have nothing to do with the function of the building, often borrowing and com-bining styles from the past.

This emphasis on style and surface appearance took on an all-embracing form through theming. This can

A themed shopping centre

'Looking across the river from Scotswood, the residents see another miracle of the Enterprise Zone, the £200 million Gateshead Metro Centre, Europe's biggest retail park, which was built on 115 acres of derelict land, and was fuelled by tax allowances and an exemption from rates until 1991. It provided a creche for customers, but not for its projected four thousand workers. Looking like an eyeless fortress, topped with stiff plastic flags around its periphery, the Metro Centre is a cornucopia of pastiche—customers walk around two million square feet of retail space down colour-coded routes, along 42nd Avenue, or around the Grecian Terrace, or through the Victorian Arcade lit darkly with a night sky all day long. People go for the day to the Metro Centre; they have been seen with flasks and sandwiches as if they were on holiday. The Metro Centre is a shopping resort.'

Source: B. Campbell (1993: 305).

The city centre fights back: an inner city retail park in Leicester.

be seen in themed hotels, themed shopping centres, and theme parks, which seek to construct a complete world into which people can escape. In the modern city people went to the cinema to transport themselves into another world, for this was the only way that most people could 'escape reality'. The film industry has, however, created in the various versions of Disneyland complete cities, which we can visit and where we can for a time stay in another world and accompany its characters. The emphasis on style, image, and appearance is associated with the simulation of experience in a safe and sanitized environment.

The post-modern city is also a more private place. This is partly because of broader processes of change that have led people to focus more on their private lives. It is also the result of the privatizing changes that we

Modern and post-modern cities

The modern city

▶ Specialized or differentiated zones
▶ Centralized
▶ Manufacturing
▶ Function
▶ Faceless architecture
▶ Sameness
▶ Reality
▶ Collective consumption
▶ Public life
▶ Integration

The post-modern city

▶ Dedifferentiation
▶ Decentralized
▶ Symbolic economy
▶ Style
▶ Facades
▶ Diversity
▶ Simulation
▶ Private consumption
▶ Private life
▶ Fragmentation

have examined in this chapter, the privatizing of consumption, homeownership, and space.

All these various changes have resulted in urban society becoming more fragmented in the post-modern city. It has been fragmented by decentralization and the dispersal of population. The public life and public space that once brought people at least superficially together have declined and are increasingly seen as dangerous and best avoided. Cities have become more divided by inequality and ethnic diversity. The well-off have withdrawn behind their walls, and the poor have been isolated in inner-city areas of deprivation and outer-city estates without employment. Ethnic fragmentation has produced some strong communities but also juxtaposed cultures that do not communicate much with each other.

It would be misleading to suggest that the city has wholly changed. Decentralization does not mean that city centres no longer exist, and central shopping areas have fought back against the peripheral stores, often by creating a kind of inner periphery of their own shopping malls or retail parks. There are still rush hours, as those living in suburbs travel into work in the centre, while city centre discos and clubs still pull in people from suburban areas at night.

The post-modern city is superimposed on the modern city, which still surrounds us and still structures our lives. While being aware of continuities, we do, however, need to find ways of grasping change, and the notion of the post-modern city helps us to do this. It enables us to highlight the reversal of many previous tendencies and connect together into a coherent pattern many of the features of the contemporary city.

SUMMARY POINTS

We began this section by considering whether the decentralization of the city had led to deurbanization or deruralization:

▶ Both population and employment had shifted from the larger cities to smaller towns and rural areas.

▶ Rural areas had, however, become increasingly urbanized.

Decentralization led to the dispersal of activities from the centre and the development of the periphery:

▶ The hollowing-out of the city resulted in severe inner-city deprivation.

▶ There was a reverse movement of population back into inner-city areas through gentrification, though there is little evidence of any reversal of the class segregation brought about by suburbanization.

▶ There was some reversal of the intensified gender-role segregation brought about by suburbanization, but city space has remained highly gendered.

We went on to consider the effects of urban change on communities:

▶ Some existing urban and rural communities were weakened but other communities formed.

▶ Ethnic communities established themselves, but attempts were also made to construct multi-ethnic communities.

The local state was weakened by central government actions and collective consumption declined:

▶ Services, housing, and space were privatized.

▶ Urban rioting became a regular feature of city life in the 1980s and early 1990s.

▶ Riots were associated with patterns of social exclusion and changes in policing.

Although cities showed many symptoms of decline, there were also processes of regeneration:

▶ Regeneration was associated with cultural restructuring, the competition to host major sporting events, and various state initiatives.

▶ Global cities benefited from the processes hollowing out the industrial city and created a global network that was partially unhooked from national economies.

REVISION AND EXERCISES

CAPITALISM AND THE CITY

In 'Understanding Cites and Communities' we discussed different approaches to the relationship between capitalism and the city:

▶ **What do you understand by the following terms: capitalism (see Chapter 13, p. 501); medieval city, industrial city, and global city; collective consumption; locality?**

▶ **Make sure that you are familiar with the main ideas of Weber, Giddens, Castells, and Saunders (see p. 433) on this issue.**

In 'Urbanization and Centralization' we examined the impact of the development of industrial capitalism on the city:

▶ **What were the main ways in which industrial capitalism shaped the development of the city?**

▶ **Was urbanization the result of industrialization?**

▶ **How did 'managed cities' develop?**

▶ **How useful is the concept of housing classes?**

In 'Deurbanization and Decentralization' we discussed the relationship between recent changes in capitalism and changes in the city:

▶ **Why did the inner city decline?**

▶ **In what ways has collective consumption declined?**

▶ **How would you explain the regeneration of the city?**

▶ **What is it that makes the global city distinctive and how has its global function affected urban society?**

URBANISM

In 'Urban Society' we discussed whether there is a distinctive urban way of life:

▶ **What do you understand by the following terms: urban way of life; segmental relationships, primary groups, and secondary groups; cosmopolites and ethnic villagers.**

▶ **Make sure that you are familiar with the main arguments on this issue of Wirth, Gans, and Giddens.**

▶ **What are the distinctive features of the city and urban society?**

▶ **What are the main arguments against the notion that there is a distinctive urban way of life?**

In 'The Centralized City' we discussed the approach taken by the Chicago School of Sociology to the study of the city:

▶ **What do you understand by the following terms: differentiation; the ecological approach; succession and the zone of transition; gatekeeper.**

▶ **How useful is the ecological approach to the study of cities?**

In 'Decentralization and Deurbanization' we examined later changes in the city and their impact on the relationship between urban and rural areas:

▶ **What impact have deurbanization and decentralization had on the differences between urban and rural areas?**

▶ **Why do some people prefer to live in suburbs and others in gentrified areas of the inner city?**

▶ What do you think are the differences between living in the city and living in rural areas? Make a list of the differences and a list of the similarities. Do you think that the differences justify maintaining a distinction between urban and rural ways of life?

COMMUNITY

We discussed various issues related to community in 'Urban Society' 'Community', and 'Class Segregation':

▶ What do you understand by the following terms: community and association; community gravitation; network community and residential community; locality.

▶ Make sure that you are familiar with the main ideas on this issue of Wirth, Tonnies, Etzioni, and Sennett.

▶ What are the key features of a community? Is high integration one of its defining features? How important is identification with a place?

▶ Is city life compatible with community life?

▶ Should the term community be replaced by locality?

In 'Changing Communities' we examined the effects of various social changes on a range of communities:

▶ What impact have changes in the city since the 1950s had on the community? Consider here the significance of decentralization for both urban and rural communities.

▶ How would you explain the emergence of gay villages?

▶ Under what conditions can multi-ethnic communities form?

▶ Do you consider that communities are a desirable feature of urban life?

FURTHER READING

Clear and comprehensive coverage of the main issues and the literature can be found in the following texts:

Flanagan, W. (1993), *Contemporary Urban Sociology* (Cambridge: Cambridge University Press).
Savage, M., and Warde, A. (1993), *Urban Sociology, Capitalism and Modernity* (London: Macmillan).

Wide-ranging collections of articles and extracts can be found in these readers:

Jewson, N., and MacGregor, S. (1997) (eds.), *Transforming Cities: Contested Governance and New Spatial Divisions* (London: Routledge).
Kasinitz, P. (1995) (ed.), *Metropolis: Centre and Symbol of our Times* (London: Macmillan).
Legates, R. T., and Stout, F. (1996) (ed.), *The City Reader* (London: Routledge).
Westwood, S., and Williams, J. (1997) (eds.), *Imagining Cities: Scripts, Signs, and Meanings* (London: Routledge).

For further reading on particular topics:

Butler, T., and Rustin, M. (1996) (eds.), *Rising in the East: The Regeneration of East London* (London: Lawrence & Wishart). A collection of pieces on the economic, political, religious, ethnic, and cultural aspects of regeneration.
Campbell, B. (1993), *Goliath: Britain's Dangerous Places* (London: Methuen). A lively and perceptive account of the return of the urban riot that places it in the context of changes in gender relationships.

Knox, P. L., and Taylor, P. J. (1995) (ed.), *World Cities in a World-System* (Cambridge: Cambridge University Press). Contains an up-to-date discussion of global or world cities and summaries of the current state of research on them.

Lawless, P., and Brown, F. (1986), *Urban Growth and Change in Britain: An Introduction* (London: Harper & Row). A full and clear account of the process of urbanization in Britain from the eighteenth century onwards.

Taylor, I., Evans, K., and Fraser, P. (1996), *A Tale of Two Cities: Global Change, Local Feeling, and Everyday Life in the North of England. A Study in Manchester and Sheffield* (London: Routledge). A plentiful and fascinating source of material on recent changes in these two cities and how they have affected many different aspects of the lives of those who live in them.

Zukin, S. (1995), *The Culture of Cities* (Oxford. Blackwell). Highly readable analysis of cities as centres of cultural consumption and production, which examines, amongst other things, the Disneyfication of the city.

Chapter 12
NATION AND WORLD

A global oil spill

'Built in Spain; owned by a Norwegian; registered in Cyprus; managed from Glasgow; chartered by the French; crewed by Russians; flying a Liberian flag; carrying an American cargo; and pouring oil on to the Welsh coast. But who takes the blame?

'As salvage teams last night succeeded in refloating the stricken *Sea Empress* tanker there was growing confusion over where the responsibility for the disaster lay. . . .

'Britain's Marine Accident Investigation Branch will have to examine shipping records from Cyprus, Norway, France, and Scotland just to establish who owns and manages the Sea Empress. The Spanish-built tanker was carrying crude oil from the North Sea for the American multi-national Texaco. It was chartered from a French company and was sailing under a Liberian flag of convenience.'

Source: James Cusick, Peter Victor, and Rebecca Fowler, 'But Who Takes the Blame?', *Independent*, 22 Feb. 1996.

A S our opening extract shows, we live in a world that is ever more integrated economically but still divided between nation states. This chapter examines the rise of the nation state, the growth of global integration, and the relationship between the national and global levels of social organization.

We examine the problems created by the tension between nations and nation states, and the impact of global changes on national identity. Does living in a nation state make one a member of that nation? The British nation state has been challenged by those who feel that they belong to the Scottish, Welsh, or Irish nations rather than a British one. Increasing international migration has created an ethnic diversity within Britain which raises the question of what it means to be British. From another direction, British national identity is also threatened by growing European integration.

Does living in a nation state mean that one lives in a national society? If in some unimaginable way Britain was cut off from the rest of the world, ordinary life would collapse. Factories and offices would close, supermarket shelves would empty, garages would run out of petrol, the satellite dish would no longer provide televised sport, and sooner or later there would be no new episodes of *Neighbours*. While nation states claim to be independent, they have become more and more dependent on each other. This interdependence between countries suggests that we live in a global as much as a national society.

Although nation states have become increasingly dependent on each other, that does not mean that they have become more equal. Great differences in wealth and power exist between them and we shall examine the origins and persistence of the international inequalities between rich countries and poor ones. We shall also consider the efforts made by poor countries to develop, the significance of economic aid, the strategies that they have adopted, and the problems they have faced.

It is often said that the world is in crisis, that 'planet earth' is threatened by exploding populations, sprawling cities, ever-increasing pollution, and diminishing resources. We consider the conflicts that arise from these problems and the growth of new global movements that seek to address them. We also discuss the United Nations' attempts to coordinate policies to protect the environment through 'earth summits' and international treaties.

This leads us on to discuss the UN's role as a 'world government' and the rise of other supra-national bodies like the European Union. Is the age of the nation state now coming to an end?

UNDERSTANDING NATIONS AND WORLDS

Nation states are the world's basic political units and in this part of the chapter we begin by examining nation states and their relationship to nations. Most of the world's nation states were created after the collapse of the European empires and we move on to consider the issues raised by the development of these states and theories of the relationship between developed and developing societies. We also discuss whether the developing societies should still be labelled a Third World. Does it make sense to speak of different worlds when the world as a whole is becoming increasingly integrated? This leads us to the issue of globalization and what this term means. We consider different approaches to globalization and the debate around the consequences of globalization for the nation state.

NATION STATES, NATIONS, AND NATIONALISM

We first consider the relationships between nations, nation states, and nationalism. Although these relationships might seem self-evident, there are many issues here that need careful exploration.

Nation states and nations

The contemporary world is divided up into nation states and we begin by considering what is meant by the nation state. A **nation state** can be defined as a political unit with national citizens, a national territory, and a national administration.

Nation states are based on the idea that their citizens are members of a nation. The nation is considered to be those living within a territory with defined borders. This territory comes under a unified administration, which, formally speaking, treats all citizens in the same way. They are all subject to its laws, all entitled to its protection, and all have the same rights and responsibilities. This national character of the state, the claim that it is the political embodiment of a nation, is an essential element in its legitimacy. Thus, government actions towards both its citizens and other governments are often justified by the claim that the government represents the nation.

It is important to bear in mind, however, that not all those who live within the territory are treated as full citizens. Until they reach a certain age, children are not considered citizens. In many nation states women were for a long time not considered to be full citizens. Migratory workers from other countries are often not considered citizens, though their position varies greatly from one country to another.

The distinctiveness of the nation state becomes clearer when we compare it with the **dynastic states** that preceded it in Europe. These states were the family possessions of their ruling dynasties. Their territories would change as a result of marriage, which could instantly more than double the size of a state. There was no sense that all those who lived within the state were members of the same nation. There was no unified administration. Each territory would largely run its own affairs, with its own institutions of government and its own laws. The state's inhabitants were the ruler's *subjects*, not *citizens* with certain rights, and the ruler's actions required no justification, for monarchs ruled by 'divine right'.

Nation states are based on the idea that political units correspond to nations. But what is a nation? A **nation** may be defined as a people with a sense of

Dynastic states and nation states	Aspects of the state	Dynastic state	Nation state
	Territory	Possessions of ruling family	Land occupied by nation
	Administration	Local institutions	Unified structure
	Inhabitants	Subjects of ruler	National citizens and dependents
	Legitimation	Ruler's divine right	Embodiment of nation

identity. While a nation state is defined objectively by its territorial and administrative structure, a nation is defined by the feeling that its members have something in common that distinguishes them from others. Max Weber expressed this idea by defining a nation as a 'community of sentiment' and referred to 'a specific sentiment of solidarity in the face of other groups' (1920: 922).

Anderson has developed this approach in an influential definition of nations as 'imagined communities'. They have the force of a community because they possess a strong sense of fraternity or comradeship, powerful enough to motivate people to die for their country. They are imagined because 'the members of even the smallest nation will never know most of their fellow-members, meet them, or even hear of them, yet in the minds of each lives the image of their communion' (B. Anderson 1991: 6).

What then is the relationship between the nation and the nation state? Here we need to distinguish between the emergence of a sense of national distinctiveness and the construction of nations by the state, two sources of nationality that often come into conflict with each other.

Anthony Smith (1994) emphasizes that the 'ethnic elements' of nationality existed long before the nation state. He argues that those who have concerned themselves mainly with the construction of the modern nation state have tended to neglect the ethnic origins of the nation in the emergence of distinct peoples with their own languages and cultures. This distinctiveness is expressed in myths of their historic origin, which commonly refer to an ancestor or a deity, from which the nation is said to be descended.

These ethnic elements provided what one might call the raw material of nationality, but it was the state that forged the modern nation out of this material. Giddens (1985) argued that a nation does not exist until the state has developed a national administrative structure that stretches over its territory. In other words, it is the state that unifies its citizens into a nation. Indeed, when nation states were later created from the colonies of the European empires there was often no previous sense of national identity. One of their governments' first tasks was to 'build a nation'. The term *nation-building* expresses well this approach to the nation, for it is essentially something that is constructed.

The ethnic elements of nationality and its construction by the state may well, however, be in conflict. Nationalities created by the state may be strongly resisted by peoples within its territory that either already have a sense of national identity or stretch across state boundaries. Such peoples may feel strongly

A Kurdish nation?

'The Kurds trace their history, with some irony, to the defeat of the Assyrians by the Medes at Nineveh, north of Mosul, in the first millennium BC. The Assyrians, a highly disciplined and warlike people, lived in what is now Iraq. But from then on, the Kurds consistently appear as a separate people committed to national self-determination, despite the continuous efforts of the states which still control Kurdistan to deny them their own identity.

'The Kurds are scattered across the territory of what is now Syria, Turkey, Iraq, Iran, Armenia and Azerbaijan. It is difficult to estimate how many people would form a Kurdish state, or what its borders would look like. The Minority Rights Group says there were about 9.6 million Kurds in Turkey in 1987, 5 million in Iran, 4 million in Iraq, 900,000 in Syria and maybe 300,000 in the former Soviet Union.'

Source: Christopher Bellamy, 'Fighters Find a Bitter Irony in History', *Independent*, 7 Sept. 1996.

that they should have the right to form their own nation states. Thus the British state has been opposed by those who identify with the Irish, Scottish, and Welsh nations. The Kurds form sizeable minorities in a number of states and are in almost constant revolt against them as they seek to build their own state. Nation states and nations often do not coincide and this has been a most potent source of conflict in our world.

Nationalism

We must now consider what is meant by **nationalism**. Nationalist movements typically seek to create states on the basis of a particular nation. Thus, Scottish nationalists seek to build a nation state that will correspond to the Scottish nation. Nationalists claim that a people has the right to its own nation state, to independence or 'self-determination'. This has made nationalism a powerful force in the break-up of empires, and this applies to the nineteenth-century Austrian empire in Europe, to the colonial empires of European states, and, indeed, to Soviet Russia, which was an empire of sorts.

Nationalism is more than this, however, for it asserts that national unity and national identity should take priority over membership of any other group. It claims that one is first and foremost a member of a nation rather than a member of a family or a class or a religion. One's obligations as a member of a nation must take priority over any other duties or responsibilities. Thus, nationalism does not come to an end once an appropriate nation state has been constructed. Nationalism is, indeed, generated by conflicts between nation states.

It is important to understand that nationalism is not just some natural outgrowth of feeling from the nation. It is an ideology that can be used by many different groups in pursuit of their own purposes and interests. Politicians excluded from government may launch a nationalist movement to set up a breakaway state as a vehicle for their ambitions. Governments seeking to mobilize a population for war will use the rhetoric of nationalism to justify it and motivate people to fight for their country. Employers faced with troublesome unions may accuse them of dividing the nation. Racists may seek to justify their actions by wrapping themselves in the national flag and claiming that they are defending national identity.

An awareness that nationalism is an ideology has led to some denying that nations have any real existence. This has been particularly the case with those writing in the Marxist tradition, who tend to treat nationalism as a class ideology, a means by which the owners of capital control labour. While many different uses may be made of nationalism, this does not, however, mean that the nation is just an invention of those seeking to manipulate people. Nationalism does strike a popular

Nation-states and national identities do not always correspond.

Your nation?

▶ **What nation state are you a citizen of?**

▶ **Make a list of the main rights and obligations that citizenship of your nation state involves.**

▶ **What do you consider your nation to be?**

▶ **What do you think are the distinguishing features of your nation?**

▶ **Does your nation correspond with your nation state?**

chord. If there was not something in the idea that nations exist, nationalism would not be the powerful force in the world that it is.

DEVELOPMENT, MODERNIZATION, AND UNDERDEVELOPMENT

The post-colonial emergence of a large number of new nation states raised the issue of their future development. The field of the Sociology of Development grew up around the study of the post-colonial nation states of Africa, Asia, and Latin America. Many different meanings have, however, been given to the term development. We discuss these briefly in this section, before moving on to different theories of development, and the concept of a Third World.

Development

When sociologists refer to the **development** of the industrial societies, they usually mean by this the broad historical process through which these societies acquired their modern occupations, organizations, and institutions (see Chapter 2, pp. 25–30). When this term is applied to the ex-colonial societies of Africa, Asia, and Latin America, it generally has the much narrower meaning of economic growth.

During the 1950s and 1960s it was thought that growth could be quite easily achieved and would enable the new nation states to make up for lost time and acquire the living standards enjoyed by those living in the developed societies. This optimism resulted in the use of the term 'developing nations' for the ex-colonial countries. Later on the terms 'more developed countries' (MDCs) and 'less developed countries' (LDCs) came into fashion. These drew less sharp a contrast and more realistically did not imply that much development was taking place.

The meaning given to the term 'development' itself changed, as rates of growth turned out to be much slower than expected and the problems of population growth, disease, and unemployment much worse. There was less emphasis in the 1970s and 1980s on economic growth as such and development was taken to mean meeting people's basic needs for food and water, shelter, and clothing, for education and health. This was later extended to include broader needs, such as employment, personal security, and civil rights (Hulme and Turner 1990: 5).

A growing concern with the environmental consequences of development has led more recently to the concept of **sustainable development**. This is development which does not damage the environment in ways that will reduce the prospects for development in the future. We will discuss this notion further in 'One Earth?', pp. 490–2.

These approaches to development have always defined it in terms of the aspirations of policy-makers, which reflect both beliefs about what a 'good society' should be like and more practical concerns with what seems to be achievable. The term development does not have a fixed or agreed meaning. As policy objectives have changed, so has the meaning of development.

Modernization or underdevelopment?

There have been two main approaches to the study of development. The first of these is generally called 'modernization theory'. It was an approach widely adopted in the 1950s and 1960s by both academics and policy-makers.

Modernization theory started from a distinction between traditional and modern societies. Traditional societies were typically pre-industrial and modern societies industrial. Modernization theorists emphasized the differences in values and attitudes between traditional and modern societies, arguing, like Parsons, that modern societies held values of achievement and universalism that were not found in traditional societies (see Chapter 7, p. 231). Development was then treated as a process of **modernization**, which involved traditional societies becoming modern through industrialization and changes in values and attitudes.

A key feature of this approach was that it saw this process as the same for all societies. It was the process that the developed industrial societies had gone through and it was the process that the modernizing countries of Africa, Asia, and Latin America would go through. Becoming modern therefore meant becoming like the already developed countries of the West.

The modernization approach put forward a diffusion model of economic growth. By **diffusion** is meant the spread of modernity from the developed to the developing world. Development would typically occur through the adoption of modern technology, modern production methods and organization, and modern ideas and attitudes. The main obstacles to development were traditional institutions and traditional attitudes. Once these were overcome, development would occur.

The economic growth that modernization theorists expected to flow from diffusion was, however, much slower than expected. In the later 1960s they turned to examine what had gone wrong. Failure was blamed on the selfishness or incompetence of the governments and elites of the (non)developing countries.

Another approach began to question the whole basis of modernization theory. This approach originated from the *dependency theory* which emerged amongst radical Latin American economists during the 1930s. Dependency theory argued that, although Latin American countries were *politically independent*, they were still *economically dependent* on the industrial societies. This relationship of dependence kept Latin American societies undeveloped. Far from the developed countires diffusing modernity to undeveloped ones, they actually prevented them developing.

The most well-known exponent of this view was Andre Gunder Frank (1967). He rejected the idea that countries were undeveloped because they were traditional societies that had not yet been incorporated in the modern world. The real situation was the exact opposite of this. Their lack of development was due to their involvement in the international capitalist economy and their exploitation by the developed societies.

In using the phrase 'the development of underdevelopment' he went further than the dependency theorists. He argued that it was not only a matter of the developed societies holding back the undeveloped ones. The developed societies had actually reduced the level of development in the rest of the world. The so-called undeveloped societies had been more developed earlier and had experienced a process of **underdevelopment**. Thus, one of the consequences of industrialization in Europe and the United States was that cheap industrial goods drove manufacturing crafts in other parts of the world out of business. As the industrial societies became more developed, the rest of the world became less developed.

This was not simply a matter of the developed countries exploiting the undeveloped ones, for the ruling classes of underdeveloped countries were also involved in this exploitation. It was, for example, not only the coffee importers in London who exploited coffee producers in Brazil. It was also the merchants exporting coffee from Brazil and the landowners, who enjoyed a good lifestyle at the expense of the landless agricultural workers who actually produced the coffee. Furthermore, the merchants and landowners were quite content for Brazil to remain a dependent coffee producer, even if this condemned the society as a whole to remain undeveloped and at the mercy of international coffee prices.

A chain of exploitation relationships ran between what Frank called *metropoles* and *satellites*. Each metropolis exploited its satellites, each satellite then acting as a metropolis for its own satellites, and so on down to the peasantry at the bottom. Underdeveloped societies would develop only if these links were broken by a socialist revolution.

Frank's metropolis–satellite relationships: the example of Chile

Metropolis	New York	Capital of Chile	Provincial cities	Estates
Satellite		Capital of Chile	Provincial cities	Landed estates	Peasantry

The conflict between these two approaches dominated the Sociology of Development for many years. Each of them drew attention to an important aspect of the relationship between the developed and undeveloped societies, but each was at the same time one-sided. While the modernization approach could not really explain the failure of many poor countries to develop, the underdevelopment approach could not account for the success of countries like Singapore. As Foster-Carter (1991) points out, neither of them left much scope for local variations and initiatives.

As we show in Chapter 11, p. 408, those studying urban and rural areas in Britain have developed the concept of locality to enable them to break free from old debates, take account of varying local responses, and allow for local initiatives. Foster-Carter suggests that a similar approach is needed in the study of developing countries. David Booth (1993) has drawn attention to an alternative action approach that emphasizes people's capacity to act rather than seeing their behaviour as determined by the constraints of wider structures.

Booth also points out, however, that there is the danger that an action approach may open a gap between the study of local situations and wider structures. Apparently flourishing local initiatives can, for example, be suddenly destroyed by economic changes or wars originating at national or international level. Furthermore, globalization, as we shall show shortly, means that different areas of the world have become ever more closely connected with each other, which means that distant changes may have a much greater local impact.

While the Sociology of Development must take account of local initiative and local diversity, it must always set the local within the context of national and international relationships. The value of the modernization and underdevelopment approaches is that they draw attention to important aspects of these relationships and therefore provide a useful starting point.

An obituary for the Third World

'The Third World is disappearing. Not the countries themselves, nor the inhabitants, much less the poor who so powerfully coloured the original definition of the concept, but the argument. Third Worldism began as a critique of an unequal world, a programme for economic development and justice, a type of national reformism dedicated to the creation of new societies and a new world. It ends with its leading protagonists either dead, defeated or satisfied to settle simply for national power rather than international equality; the rhetoric remains, now toothless, the decoration for squabbles over the pricing of commodities or flows of capital.'

Source: Harris (1986: 200).

The Third World

The ex-colonial societies have been commonly regarded as a **Third World**. This term came into use in the very different economic and political context of the 1950s and 1960s, but it is still widely used today as a short-hand label. It does, after all, avoid the vexed question of whether these countries should be called undeveloped, developing, less developed, or underdeveloped!

Why were these countries called the Third World? This term distinguished them from the First World of the industrial-revolution countries and the Second World of the Soviet bloc, which had pursued a socialist rather than a capitalist route to modernity. There was also the belief that the ex-colonial societies could somehow develop together in their own way and avoid the evils of both capitalism and socialism. Thus, the Third World also referred to countries taking a third route to modernity.

These distinctions now appear more than a little dated. Any idea of the ex-colonial countries pursuing a common path disappeared quickly, as the cold war between the United States and the Soviet Union forced them to align themselves politically with one or the other. The Second World then collapsed with the break-up of the Soviet bloc and the general abandonment of the socialist route. It is, anyway, difficult to see the countries of the Third World as any longer sharing common features. While the economies of Malaysia, Singapore, South Korea, Taiwan, and, of course, Japan—the so-called Asian Tigers—rival the old industrial societies, some African countries seem stuck in an almost permanent condition of deprivation and poverty. Writers such as Harris have, therefore, suggested that it is time to abandon the notion of a Third World (see box above).

Increasing global integration now makes the notion of distinct worlds quite out of date, though this was always somewhat misleading. There have always been close relationships between the so-called First, Second, and Third World countries. As we shall show on pp. 461–2, a single capitalist world economy has long existed and it has never made much sense to distinguish three different worlds within it.

Rich countries and poor countries do, of course, still exist. The relationships of influence and exploitation between those that are rich and powerful and those that are poor and weak are as important as ever. The 1980 Brandt Commission distinguished between the rich 'North' and the poor 'South', and these labels have also been widely used. But, although most rich countries are in the northern hemisphere and most poor countries in the southern, rich countries like Australia and poor countries like North Korea simply do not fit these categories. The simplest solution is to refer to rich countries and poor countries, and that is what we will do in this chapter.

GLOBALIZATION

The central concept of a sociology of one world is globalization. In this section we will first discuss the meaning of this term and then go on to consider its impact on the nation state.

What is globalization?

The term **globalization** refers to the growing integration of societies across the world. Since this has taken a number of different forms, it is difficult to discuss in a general way. Indeed, most uses of the term attach it to one of the particular forms it has taken. Thus, some use the term to refer to the economic integration of the world but others use it to refer to people's growing awareness that they are members of a single species inhabiting one world. These are, of course, not unconnected and it is important to bear in mind the inter-relationships between the various processes of globalization. The main forms taken by globalization are:

▶ global organization;

▶ global interdependence;

▶ global communication;

▶ global awareness.

Three main types of *global organization* can be distinguished. The key aspect of each type is the relationship between the organization and the nation state.

1. **Empires**. Overseas empires became global organizations that integrated many different parts of the world within administrative and economic structures. They were, however, essentially extensions of the nation state.

2. **Transnational organizations**. These are organizations that operate across national boundaries. Transnational corporations (TNCs) produce their goods and services in more than one country. Although TNCs are generally seen as the prime example of transnational organizations, there are many other kinds, such as transnational religious organizations and transnational social movements.

3. **International organizations**. Organizations like the United Nations bring nation states together and have a certain **supra-national** character. This means that they involve some transfer of authority from the nation state to a higher body. They operate, however, through the nation states that make them up.

Globalization also involves a growing *interdependence* between different parts of the world. This is particularly evident in economic matters, and the growth of a world economy is indeed one of the main aspects of the globalization process. Thus, vegetables from Kenya or wine from New Zealand or video recorders from Japan or software programmes from California are produced for a global market. On the other hand, the local superstore is dependent on producers around the world to supply it with goods. As the piece on 'Vegetables from Zimbabwe' shows, this interdependence can result in such close relationships that producers in one country and distributors in another become part of the same organization.

The development of *global communication* has made it possible for different parts of the world to become more closely connected with each other. It is often said that the world has become a smaller place through the 'compression' or 'shrinking' of the globe. By this it is meant simply that faster communications have made places seem closer together. Indeed, telecommunications and information technology can be said to have destroyed distance by making possible the almost instant

Vegetables from Zimbabwe

When you next buy vegetables from Asda or Marks and Spencer, they may well have come from Zimbabwe. It is cheaper to fly them 5,000 miles than bring them in from a market garden down the road. Zimbabwe has certain climatic advantages—it can grow crops around the year and therefore provide a regular supply to the superstores—but it is the lower cost of labour in Zimbabwe that makes the operation economic. Cheap air transport is also crucial, but what is not so obvious is the key role of information technology and organization. The planting of the vegetable seeds is dictated by a British-based marketing company, which analyses the pattern of past superstore sales to predict future demand. The picking and packing of the vegetables is similarly controlled by information about the previous day's sales. The Zimbabwe producers are not simply exploiting cost advantages to out-compete local producers. They are part of an internationally integrated production and marketing organization.

Source: Michael Prest and David Bowen, 'Vegetable Magic'; *Independent on Sunday*, 7 July 1996.

▶ What do you think would happen if the workers in Zimbabwe asked for higher wages?

▶ What would happen if the airline increased its charges?

▶ What would happen to the superstore if the supply links broke down?

▶ Who controls the 'organization'?

transmission of information to any point on the world's surface that can receive it. People, money, and information can now move very rapidly around the world, which raises the important question of whether states can any longer control their borders.

Yet another aspect of globalization is *global awareness* and this is particularly emphasized by Robertson (1992). Advances in the technology of communication and travel have made people much more aware of other parts of the world. Environmental concerns have intensified this awareness of the world as a whole, as Waters nicely and somewhat breathlessly demonstrates with reference to Tasmania. According to Robertson, people now see themselves less as members of this community or that country and more as members of humanity, of a single threatened species. His approach makes culture and identity central to the process of globalization, for what has changed above all is the way that people see themselves and their relationships with each other.

Tasmania too is part of one world

'Tasmanians know that they live on one planet because other people's aerosol sprays have caused a carcinogenic hole in the ozone layer over their heads, because their relatively high rate of unemployment is due to a slump in the international commodities markets, because their children are exposed to such edifying role models as Robocop and The Simpsons, because their university is infested by the managerialist cultures of strategic planning, staff appraisal and quality control, just like everyone else's, because British TV-star scientists may drop in for a week to save their environment for them, and because their Gay community may at long last be able to experience freedom of sexual expression because it has appealed to the human rights conventions of the United Nations.'

Source: Waters (1995: p. xi).

It is important to be aware of the long-term character of globalizing processes. People tend to be conscious of the way that the world has 'shrunk' since the 1960s, with the introduction of wide-bodied passenger jets and geostationary satellites. TNCs grew rapidly during this period and capital began to move around the world much more freely. Globalization might appear to be a rather recent phenomenon. Robertson (1992) considers that, on the contrary, it began in the fifteenth century with the European voyages of discovery and the beginnings of the European colonization of the world. Simi-

larly, Wallerstein, whose ideas we will examine below in 'a global economy', argues that a capitalist world economy was already in existence at this time.

Hirst and Thompson have advanced a rather different argument that challenges what one might call the 'onwards and upwards' notion of globalization as a continuous and ever-increasing process. They claim that the world economy was more integrated by trade and finance during the period before the First World War than it is today, though they do recognize that some globalizing processes, such as the growth of TNCs, have recently accelerated. They also reject the idea that a new global economy exists that is somehow above and beyond national control, a point that we will take up below. They declare that 'globalization, as conceived by the more extreme globalizers, is largely a myth' (Hirst and Thompson 1996: 2).

Globalization and the nation state

The relationship between globalization and the nation state is at the heart of the current debate on globalization and is the central theme of this chapter.

Globalization initially took place within the framework of the nation state. Overseas empires were extensions of the nation state and it was the growth of these empires which first created economic, political, and administrative structures that integrated distant parts of the globe. These empires also, however, divided the world up between them and this led to the global conflicts of the world wars and the cold war.

The collapse of the overseas empires resulted in the multiplication of nation states but also in the emergence of global challenges to the nation state. The development of global communications has led to the greater movement of money, information, goods, and people across national borders and threatened the nation state's control of its territory. The growth of transnational corporations has challenged the nation state's control of national economies. International migration and the growing ethnic diversity of societies have threatened national identities. New supranational political organizations have challenged the sovereignty of the nation state.

Does this mean that the nation state is becoming a structure of the past? There are certainly some who think so. Thus, Stuart Hall (1991*b*) believes that the nation state is in decline, though reacting to decline by asserting national identity in a dangerous and racist way. In *The Borderless World* Ohmae (1990) argues that the global flow of information is 'eating away' the boundaries between states. Waters (1995) claims that the globalizing of culture means that people are less willing to accept the authority of the nation state and increasingly appeal to international organizations on the basis of their human rights.

Against views of this sort, Hirst and Thompson reject the idea that the nation state is in decline. They argue that TNCs have national headquarters, national cultures, and depend on the nation state's institutions and support for their activities. They also argue that international political bodies have not taken authority away from the nation state. Nation states are represented in such bodies and participate in their decision-making, while these bodies depend on nation states to implement their policies. Hirst and Thompson conclude that government has become a multi-layered matter, but the nation state is still central to it and will remain so (1996: 184–7, 190).

The impact of globalization on the nation state raises a range of important questions, which are in many ways the most pressing issues of the world today. We will come across them at many points in this chapter and we conclude it with a discussion of the relationship between globalization and the nation state.

SUMMARY POINTS

We began this chapter by considering the nation state, and its relationship to the nation and to nationalism:

▶ Nation states are based on the principle that those who live within a territory with defined borders are national citizens.

▶ A nation is a people with a distinct and common sense of identity.

▶ Nations and nation states often do not overlap and this is a major source of conflict.

▶ Nationalism is based on the belief that nation states should correspond to nations and that nationality should take priority over all other affiliations.

We then considered the issues raised by the development of the post-colonial nation states:

▶ We noted the different meanings that have been given to the term 'development'.

▶ We compared the contrasting approaches to development provided by modernization and under development theory and the problem they both faced of accommodating local diversity and local initiative.

▶ We argued that the Third World was no longer an appropriate term for the ex-colonial countries, if indeed it ever had been.

Finally we examined the process of globalization. We argued that globalization involved a number of interrelated processes:

▶ the rise of global organizations.

▶ the increasing interdependence of different parts of the world.

▶ the growth of global communication.

▶ a developing awareness of the world as a single place.

We concluded this section by considering the issues raised by the impact of globalization on the nation state:

▶ Some argue that globalization is making the nation state obsolete.

▶ Others argue that global organizations are dependent on nation states.

NATIONAL EMPIRES IN A GLOBAL ECONOMY

In this part of the chapter we deal with the rise of nation states and the imperial stage of globalization. We outline the growth of a world economy and its integration by industrialization. We go on to consider the huge movements of population that resulted from empire-building and global economic integration, and their consequences for ethnic diversity and racial divisions. Lastly, we consider the role of empires in dividing the world and globalizing warfare. The combined effects of these processes transformed the lives of those who lived in every corner of the world.

FROM NATION STATE TO EMPIRE

The origins of the European nation states can be traced far back in history. Anthony Smith (1994) argues that the ethnic elements of nationality already existed in medieval times. The various peoples of Europe had a sense of their distinctiveness because of differences of language and culture, and historical myths that traced their origins back to distant ancestors.

Linguistic diversity had always existed in Europe but distinct national languages had to be created. We must remember that in medieval Europe educated people communicated with each other through the international language of Latin. On the other hand, the spoken languages of ordinary people were no more than local dialects. The creation of national languages involved the displacement of Latin, the consolidation of dialects into a standard and stable language, and the elimination of rival languages within a country. The fifteenth-century invention of the printing press and the growth of the print trade played a crucial role in this process (see Chapter 8, pp. 284–5).

At this time Europe was divided up between dynastic states, of the kind that we described on p. 451. The centralizing monarchs of the sixteenth and seventeenth centuries began, however, to build new administrative structures that gave them more control over their populations and resources. Royal administrations to collect taxes and maintain order began to emerge within distinct territories with defined borders. The nation state as such had not yet come into existence, but national territories and administrative structures were starting to appear. As part of the process of unifying their territories, rulers encouraged the growth of national languages within their territories.

 Other closely related aspects of the development of states are discussed elsewhere. The bureaucratization of the state is discussed in Chapter 16, pp. 650–1, and the development of the ruler's authority in Chapter 18, pp. 728–9.

Interstate conflict played an important part in the process by driving rulers to find new ways of raising armies and financing wars. As Giddens (1985) emphasized, the growth of nation states can be understood only if they are seen as parts of a system of nation states. The nation state and international relations emerged together. The importance of relationships between nations in the growth of the nation state can be seen clearly in the British case.

The key steps in the creation of a British nation state were taken in the eighteenth century. According to Colley (1992), it was the long eighteenth-century conflict between Britain and France, lasting until the defeat of Napoleon in 1815, which forged the British nation. It made three crucial contributions to the formation of the British state:

▶ *national administration.* The conflict led to the founding of the Bank of England, the creation of an effective system of national taxation, and the building of what Colley calls a 'massive military machine'.

▶ *British identity.* The periodic wars with France created a British identity. Colley notes that religion played an important part in this, for war with Catholic France unified the Protestant nations of Great Britain and Northern Ireland.

▶ *Empire.* It was in the eighteenth century that Britain first carved out an overseas empire through its conflicts with France in the Americas and India. The combined involvement of the various British nationalities in creating, administering, and exploiting the Empire helped to unify them into a British nation.

The building of the modern nation state was then completed in the nineteenth century. Unified national administrations were constructed through an administrative revolution, which we examine in Chapter 16, pp. 650–1. The railways, improved postal services, and the telegraph created national communication systems.

Within this framework other changes integrated and strengthened the nation. The French Revolution of 1789, the European revolutions of 1848, and the nineteenth-century democratization of government brought peoples into politics. State education, state employment, and national military service generated loyalty to the state. Governments standardized national languages, built national monuments, revived ancient myths of national origin, and generally glorified the nation (Hobsbawm 1977: ch. 5). Industrialization and urbanization broke people's local ties and brought them together in larger groupings where they could acquire a greater sense of what Benedict Anderson (1991) called the 'imagined community' of the nation.

The rise of the nation state and the construction of overseas empires were closely connected with each other. Conflicts over territory in Europe extended to conflicts over territory elsewhere in the world. The first overseas empires were those of Spain and Portugal, which in 1494 ambitiously signed a treaty dividing up the world between them. Other European countries gradually got into the act and in the seventeenth century the British, French, and Dutch were busily establishing their own empires. On the other hand, overseas rivalries contributed to nation-building in Europe, as Colley showed in the British case.

The construction of empires must be set in the context of economic as well as political change and we now go on to consider the emergence of a global economy.

A GLOBAL ECONOMY

The beginnings of a global economy can be found in the late-fifteenth-century expansion of Europe through the voyages of exploration that led to trading relationships with other continents. But it was nineteenth-century industrialization which integrated this world economy. In this section, we first discuss Wallerstein's notion of a 'capitalist world economy' and then go on to examine industrialization and the establishment of an international division of labour.

The capitalist world economy

The idea of a **capitalist world economy** comes from the work of Immanuel Wallerstein. It is very important to bear in mind that in using the term 'world', he was referring not to the world as a whole but to what he called a 'world system'. In his terms this is a unit within which there is a division of labour that extends across various ethnic and cultural groups. It is a world in the sense that a complete range of specialized activities takes place within it. According to Wallerstein (1974), world systems took the form of either a *world empire* or a *world economy*.

World empires had a single political centre and were held together by a bureaucratic administration. Examples of such empires were those of Rome and China. They extended across huge territories and included a wide diversity of peoples. They appeared to be complete worlds to those that ruled them and those that lived in them.

World economies had multiple political centres and were integrated economically rather than politically. Wallerstein's example here was the capitalist world economy that established itself in Europe during medieval times and then gradually extended to include the whole world. Wallerstein argued that no world empire was able to establish itself in Europe after the collapse of the Roman Empire. Europe's political fragmentation eventually resulted in the growth of various nation states that were linked together by a world economy. The capitalist merchants in the trading cities of north-west Europe created the network of economic relationships that held this world economy together. It was, therefore, a *capitalist* world economy.

The central feature of this world economy was the relationship between a *core* and a *periphery*. The world economy was initially dominated by a group of *core* countries in north-west Europe—Britain, France, and the Netherlands—but later included Germany and the United States as well. These were the economically most advanced areas, where the manufacturing of goods was already well established and which were later to be at the centre of the Industrial Revolution. Other countries, such as Spain and Portugal, which he called the *semi-periphery*, were not part of the core but assisted its exploitation of the periphery.

The *periphery* supplied raw materials to the core and imported manufactured goods from it. The periphery initially consisted of Eastern European countries, but in the late fifteenth century it began to expand to include Africa, Asia, and Latin America. Military domination by the strong states of the core countries kept state structures weak in the periphery. The construction of overseas empires played an important part in this, though the core also dominated the periphery by financial means.

The importance of Wallerstein's approach is, first, that he established the principle that we should not examine national economies in isolation but always consider their place in the whole system of economic relationships. Secondly, he showed how from its very beginnings the development of capitalism lay behind a growing economic integration of the world. Thirdly, he argued that the end of empire did not end the core's domination of the periphery. Thus, when Latin American countries became independent from Spain and Portugal, their domination by core countries continued, for Britain and the United States still controlled their economies.

Industrialization and the international division of labour

While a world economy was *created* in the sixteenth century, it was industrialization that really *integrated* it. Industrialization generated a much greater interdependence between the core countries and the periphery.

This interdependence resulted from the establishment of an **international division of labour** in the nineteenth century. The industrial societies specialized in the production of manufactured goods and the rest of the world in the production of raw materials and food (usually called primary products, to contrast them with the secondary, processed goods made in the industrial countries). This global division of labour was said to be to the advantage of all, since each country could concentrate on producing what it was best at. Each group of countries became dependent on the supply of products from the other, while each was also dependent on the markets provided by the other.

But, as always happens with a division of labour, interdependence meant that some were more dependent than others and the result was international inequality. The primary producers found that most of the benefits of the international division of labour seemed to go to the industrial countries. It was the growing awareness of this that led to the rise of the *dependency* theory of the relationship between the industrial and primary producer countries that we discussed earlier.

There were a number of reasons for a growing international inequality between the industrial societies and the primary producers:

▶ *Profit on capital.* The industrial countries were the source of the capital that financed the construction of tea estates in India or rubber plantations in Malaya, and the profits from primary production largely ended up in the industrial countries.

▶ *Control of prices.* These were controlled by trading corporations and markets located in the industrial countries. The prices of industrial goods were kept high, while raw material prices tended to fall.

▶ *Product dependence.* The economies of the industrial countries were highly diversified, but the economies of the primary producers were often dependent on one product, such as coffee in Brazil or bananas in the Caribbean. A fall in the price of these products had a catastrophic effect on these countries.

▶ *Imperialism.* Through their empires the industrial countries were in political, administrative, and military control of many of the primary producers, and could make sure that colonial economies were subordinated to imperial interests.

Nineteenth-century empire-building was indeed in part a consequence of industrialization. The spread of industrial methods of production from Britain through Europe to the United States led to an increasing international competition for markets and raw materials. The best way to protect markets and raw-material supplies was to construct an imperial fence around them.

Although industrialization and imperialism were linked in this way, some important qualifications must be made. First, while a *belief* in economic benefits

might motivate colonization, the imperial power might not actually benefit much from a particular colony. As Hobsbawm (1987) has pointed out, Britain obtained greater benefits from areas, such as Latin America, that were politically independent than from most of its colonial territories. Secondly, economic concerns were not the only motivation behind imperial expansion. Having an empire was regarded as one of the defining characteristics of a 'great power' and latecomers to the competition, such as Germany and Italy, scrambled for areas of little obvious economic value.

A WORLD DIVIDED BY RACES

The creation of a world capitalist economy generated a series of migrations which created ethnically diverse societies. At a time when people were learning to identify themselves as nations, they also began to think of themselves as belonging to distinct races. While the world was becoming economically more integrated, it was also becoming racially divided.

Movements of people

It is estimated that between 1500 and 1800 some six million Africans were transported by the slave trade from Africa to the colonies of America and the Caribbean (Emmer 1993: 67). This was not, it should be emphasized, the only slave trade, for there was also an extensive trading of slaves from parts of Africa to the Islamic states of North Africa and the Middle East.

The defining characteristic of slavery is that it treats people as property. Slaves are the possessions of slave-owners, who can buy and sell them at will. The infamous story of the slave-ship *Zong* demonstrates this all too well.

The labour provided by slaves was central to the emerging capitalist world economy. They were used to work the gold and silver mines of South America, to produce sugar in Brazil and the Caribbean, to grow tobacco and cotton in North America. Native populations had often been exterminated by a combination of colonial conquest and the diseases that invariably followed the colonists, or else they were hard to subdue into a reliable labour force. Slaves transplanted from their societies of origin and forced into submission were a cheap and controllable source of labour, though this did not mean that there was no resistance. There were some slave revolts, but the slave-owners usually crushed them with little difficulty.

The slave-ship Zong jettisons its cargo

The *Zong* was a Liverpool slave-ship that sailed in 1781 from West Africa to Jamaica with a cargo of slaves. On the initiative of its captain, and with the compliance of the crew, 131 sick slaves were thrown overboard as it approached its destination, in order to save drinking water and make a claim on the ship's insurers. When this became known, Granville Sharp, a leading campaigner against the slave trade, tried to bring a prosecution against the crew for murder.

Two cases came to court in 1783, though these were concerned not with the murder of the slaves but with the shipowner's insurance claim, which was contested by the underwriters. The Solicitor-General represented the slave-owners and declared in court that a prosecution for murder 'would be madness: the blacks were property'. The judge agreed and stated that 'the case of the slaves was the same as if horses had been thrown overboard'.

The only response of the British state to this and similar cases seems to have been the Act of 1790 which ruled out insurance claims 'on the account of the mortality of slaves by natural death or ill treatment, or against loss by throwing overboard of slaves on any account whatsoever'.

Source: Walvin (1993: 18–21).

This trade in people was also central to the capitalist world economy in another way, for it formed one side of the Atlantic trade triangle of the eighteenth century. Goods shipped from Britain and France were used to buy slaves on the West African coast. These were transported across the Atlantic and sold to plantation-owners. The ships could then return to Europe with a cargo of colonial products, typically sugar or tobacco or cotton. Slaves were not just labour. They were also a valuable commodity that could be bought and sold at a profit like any other. The growing wealth of cities such as Bristol and Liverpool depended largely on this triangular trade (see Figure 12.1 on p. 464).

While most people have at least heard of the slave trade, the far greater transportation of the indentured labour that succeeded it during the nineteenth century, after the abolition of slavery, is often forgotten. Some thirty million indentured workers were transported from India to other British colonies, to work, for example, on sugar plantations in the Caribbean or to build railways in East Africa. China was another source of indentured labour for the European empires but also for America both North and South (Massey and Jess 1995: 12).

Unlike slavery, indentured labour involved the payment of wages, but in other respects it was little different. People were forced to sign contracts that bound them to work for a particular employer for a number of years. Their wages and work conditions were generally very poor. Their contracts gave them no protection and required them to submit to the demands and obey the orders of their employer. Like African slaves they were removed from their society of origin and transported to distant and alien lands.

There was also an extensive migration of settlers from Europe to the 'new world', particularly during the nineteenth century (see Figure 12.2 on p. 465). An estimated sixty million people left Europe for America, Africa, and Australasia combined between 1815 and 1914 (Hirst and Thompson 1996: 23). Between 1860 and 1920 an estimated thirty million emigrated to the United States alone (Castles and Miller 1993: 51).

This migration is often described as voluntary, to distinguish it from the forced migrations of African slaves and the coercive recruitment of indentured labour. There clearly was a difference, but the term voluntary is more than a little misleading. How voluntary was the migration of nearly two million Irish people to the United States during the potato famine in the 1840s? How voluntary was the migration of the Jews who were persecuted in Eastern Europe? Some migrants were motivated by dreams of making their fortunes in the colonies or on the American frontier, but for many emigration was the only means of escaping from hunger, poverty, and death.

Ethnic diversity and racialization

International migrations created ethnically diverse colonial societies with ethnic groups occupying different positions. Thus, a hierarchy of ethnic groups emerged in the United States, with white Anglo-Saxon Protestants (WASPS) in a dominant position, other groups of European origin, such as Italians, Irish, and Poles, below them, and the black descendants of African slaves at the bottom. In many British colonial territories Asians occupied an intermediate position between the British settlers and native populations.

These hierarchies resulted from differences in power and wealth, but notions of superiority and inferiority were quickly attached to ethnicity. Stereotyping resulted in crude characterizations of different peoples, which were then used to justify inequality. The ethnic stratification of these colonial societies was seen

Figure 12.1. The transatlantic slave-trade triangle

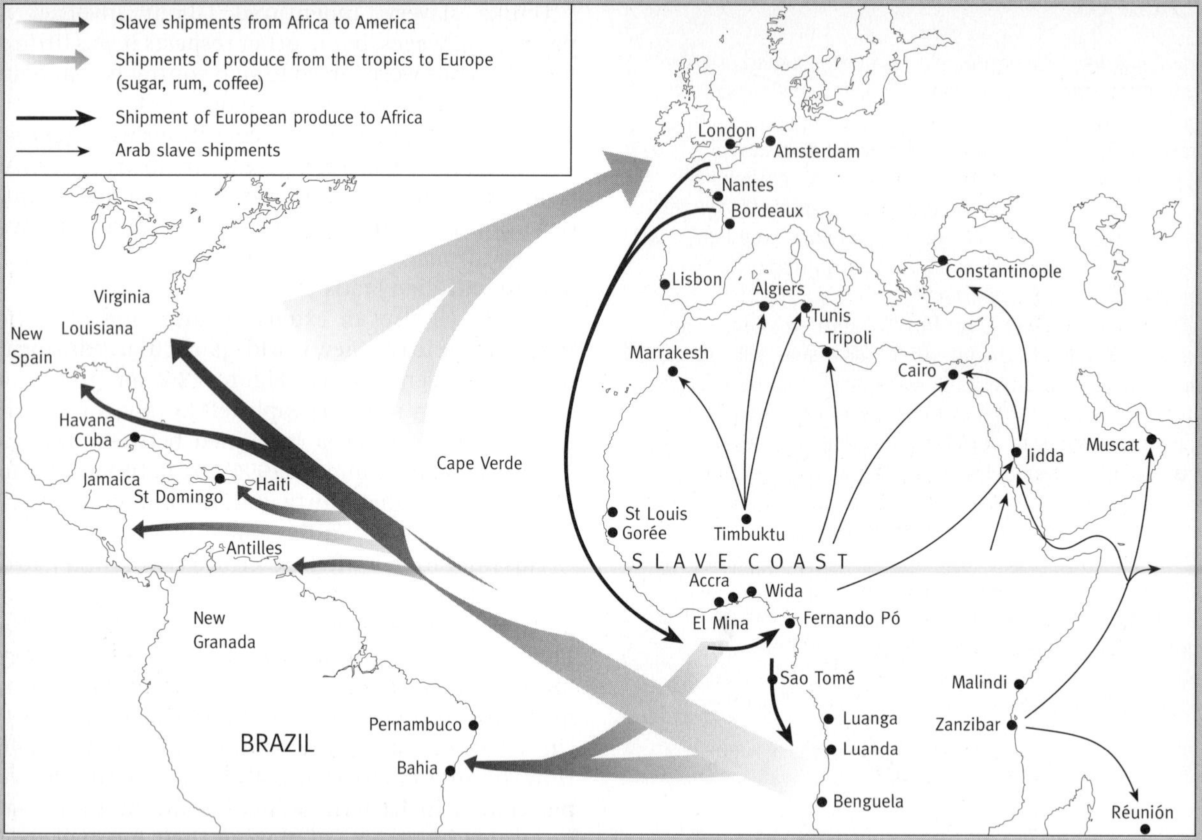

Slave shipments from Africa to America

Shipments of produce from the tropics to Europe
(sugar, rum, coffee)

Shipment of European produce to Africa

Arab slave shipments

Source: Potts (1990, 42).

as reflecting in-born characteristics rather than resulting from power and wealth.

> ☞ We discuss race and ethnicity in Chapter 4, pp. 143–5, and stratification in Chapter 15, pp. 602–4. You may find it helpful to refer to these discussions while reading this section.

Ideas of the inferiority and superiority of different peoples eventually took the form of racism. This is often associated in people's minds with slavery but, although slave-traders and plantation-owners treated slaves in inhuman ways, they did not think of them as a distinct race but, as we showed above, as property. Malik (1996) points out that, when the movement to abolish slavery got under way in the later eighteenth century, its defenders did not argue that slaves were an inferior race. They put forward economic arguments, such as the claim that slave labour was necessary for production in tropical areas.

At the end of the eighteenth century the term 'race' began to come into use but in a different context. Initially it had nothing to do with skin colour. Malik (1996) emphasizes that the idea of separate races first became established in nineteenth-century Britain as an explanation of the persistence of inequality *within* British society. The social inferiority of workers was seen by the elite of British society as resulting from their racial characteristics. Race was, therefore, defined in terms of social status and, according to Lorimer (1978), black people were not regarded as a separate social group in Britain until mid-century.

The notion of race was then given an increasingly biological character. The rise of science had led to the

Figure 12.2. **International migrations, 1820–1910**

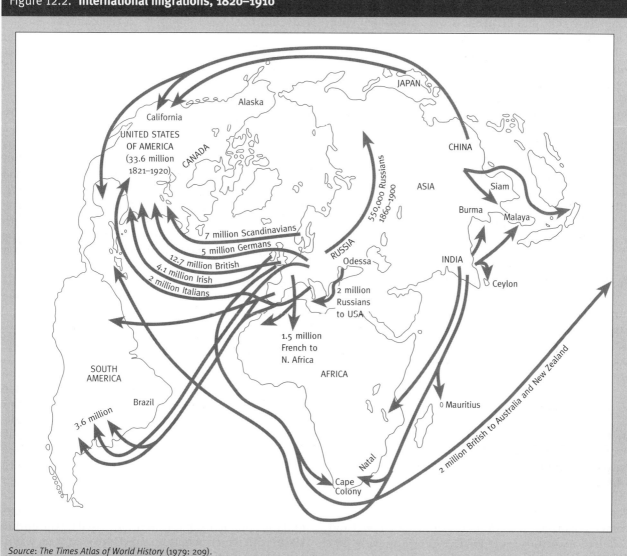

Source: *The Times Atlas of World History* (1979: 209).

belief that human as well as natural behaviour was governed by natural laws. Human differences had therefore to be explained by natural differences. It was believed that ethnic differences must in some way be biologically explained and social superiority must mean biological superiority. Just as there was a hierarchy of species in the natural world, there was a hierarchy of races in the human world. Racist thinking acquired a pseudo-scientific character, though, as we argue in Chapter 4, pp. 143–4, there is no scientific basis for the concept of race.

It was imperialism that led to the identification of race with skin colour. Europeans justified their rule over Africa and Asia by claiming the superiority of the white race over the black, brown, and yellow peoples of the world. As Malik (1996: 118) has put it, '"the colour line" now became the chief way of understanding and dividing the world'. This was not just a matter of racial thinking, for the creation of 'colour bars' excluded non-whites from particular areas or jobs.

With imperialism race also became a matter of popular belief that helped to unify the class-divided societies of Europe. The British workers who had been treated by the upper class as an inferior race could now see themselves as members of a superior white race that ruled the world. Race and nationality became linked together at this time. The possession of an empire had become an important aspect of being British. Imperialism, white rule, and Britishness were associated with each other.

It is important to emphasize that international migration, ethnic diversity, patterns of ethnic inequality, and ethnic stereotyping were not new. The history of Europe was a history of migratory peoples and European societies were littered with ethnic stereotypes. Anti-Semitism, for example, was widespread in medieval Europe. What was new, however, was the stereotyping of people according to skin colour and the categorizing of people into races on this basis. Thus, the idea that the peoples of the world could be divided into a hierarchy of races defined by skin colour emerged in the context of late-nineteenth-century imperialism.

A WORLD DIVIDED BY EMPIRES

Imperialism also divided the world in another way. Empires not only integrated distant parts of the world economically and administratively; they also divided it between rival empires. Globalization not only led to world trade; it also led to world wars.

Dividing up the world

By the nineteenth century, Britain, France, Holland, Spain, and Portugal had constructed overseas empires. Belgium, Germany, Italy, and Russia then joined in, while the United States carved out its own sphere of influence in the Caribbean, Latin America, and the Pacific. Towards the end of the century, another newcomer, Japan, began to follow the European model and acquired its first overseas territories by annexing first Taiwan and later Korea.

Virtually the whole of the world was divided up by these rival empires. Where they did not formally incorporate territories, they established competing zones of influence, as in China. Most of Latin America had become politically independent during the early nineteenth century, but the United States considered that it properly belonged within its sphere of influence and through the Monroe doctrine warned other countries to keep out.

Expansion overseas not only gave these countries new territory; it also consolidated them as nation states at a time when their labour movements were growing and they were increasingly threatened by class conflict. Imperial expansion provided various ways of containing and managing internal discontent. The economic

benefits of imperialism produced employment and higher wages, while those who were discontented or adventurous could emigrate to the colonies. Empire also provided a sense of national superiority that strengthened popular identification with the nation. Hobsbawm (1987: 69) has noted that the politicians of the time were well aware of what they saw as the social benefits of imperialism.

Unlike Wallerstein's world empires, which we discussed above, these overseas empires were part of a system of nation states. The empires of Rome and China were for a time at least contemporary civilizations, but they were isolated from each other and each had established a 'world of its own'. Although the overseas empires of the nineteenth century called themselves empires and often associated themselves with the empires of the past, they were not empires in the same sense. They were extensions of nation states that were in constant competition with each other. It was, indeed, this rivalry which largely drove forward the process of imperial expansion. It also drove them into war with each other.

World wars

Industrial production, national railway systems, and bureaucratic administrative structures provided nation states with a new capacity for war. It was now possible to organize and mobilize the whole population and the whole economy for 'total war'. They had also generated a popular nationalism which motivated and legitimated mobilization for war, and did so with an effectiveness that exceeded the expectations of their governments. Hobsbawm (1987: 325) notes how at the beginning of the First World War both governments and the opponents of war were surprised by the enthusiasm with which people plunged into a war that was to kill at least twenty million of them.

Imperialism made war a global affair. Periodic warfare between rival overseas empires had begun as soon as they acquired colonies, but the nineteenth-century division of the world brought about a more intense economic, political, and military competition between them. It also led to the construction of complex alliances sretching across the world. Britain's 1902–21 alliance with Japan to contain the expansion of Russia provides a striking example of this. What Hobsbawm (1987: 315) has called a 'globalization of the international power-game' had taken place.

Given the nation state's mobilization capacity and the system of alliances, a small incident could escalate into a big war. This is essentially what happened in 1914, when an incident in Bosnia, the assassination of

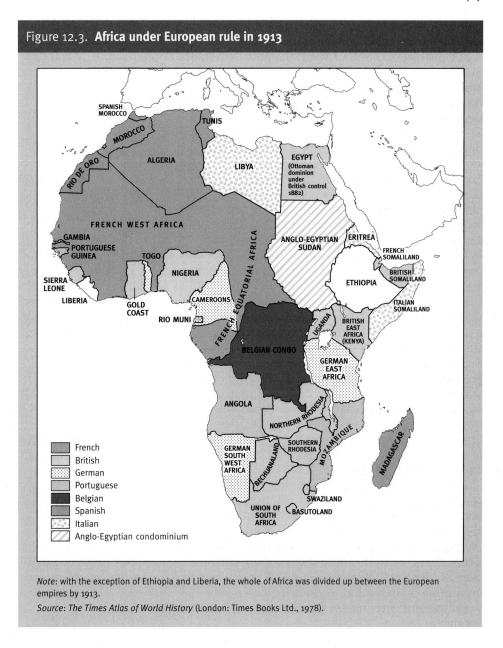

Figure 12.3. **Africa under European rule in 1913**

French
British
German
Portuguese
Belgian
Spanish
Italian
Anglo-Egyptian condominium

Note: with the exception of Ethiopia and Liberia, the whole of Africa was divided up between the European empires by 1913.

Source: *The Times Atlas of World History* (London: Times Books Ltd., 1978).

an Austrian archduke in Sarajevo, triggered off the First World War. Once the European states had gone to war, their imperial territories were drawn in and eventually the United States as well.

The First World War was still essentially a European war with a global dimension, but the Second World War was truly global in scope. Conflicts in Europe and the Far East were linked together. In Europe German expansion resulted in something of a rerun of the First World War. In Asia the expansion of the Japanese Empire collided with the imperial interests of Britain,

France, the Netherlands, and the United States. The European and Pacific 'theatres' of war, as they were called, were linked by global alliances, which joined the United States to the Soviet Union, Britain, and France and joined Japan to Germany and Italy.

The cold war was a world war of a different kind. It was a war between alliances led by the Soviet Union and the United States. It started as the Second World War ended and lasted some forty years until the Soviet Union began to collapse at the end of the 1980s.

The world was more divided into two blocs than ever

before and Third World countries that tried to maintain neutrality found themselves under heavy pressure to join one side or the other. While the globally destructive power of nuclear weapons made 'hot war' too dangerous, war was carried on by other means. Many countries were split by civil wars or political struggles between forces sponsored by one side or the other.

The cold war in some ways marked the end of the imperial stage of globalization. The European colonial empires collapsed as the cold war developed, partly because the United States and the Soviet Union supported independence movements. There was also an ideological dimension to the cold war conflict between 'capitalism' and 'socialism' that was absent from the earlier conflicts between the colonial empires.

There were, none the less, continuities with the imperial past, for the United States and the Soviet Union can be considered the last two empires. The United States continued to regard Latin America, the Caribbean, and the Pacific as its sphere of influence and took military action against Soviet attempts to penetrate them. Much of the Soviet Union was not ethnically Russian and consisted of countries conquered by the pre-revolutionary Russian Empire, while its 'allies' were controlled by military occupation. These continuities suggest that the cold war can be considered the last phase of imperialism. The collapse of the Soviet Empire during the years around 1990 and the building of a new wave of nation states give some support to this view.

The conflicts between nation states had led to the construction of empires that both integrated and divided the world. They integrated the world by bringing almost all peoples into a small number of political, and military structures that stretched across the continents. They divided the world because these structures were in economic, political, and military conflict with each other. Empires and world wars meant that the world was both more integrated and more divided than ever before.

SUMMARY POINTS

We began this section by outlining the development of nation states, which became the centres of overseas empires:

▶ The ethnic elements of nationality already existed in medieval times.

▶ National administrations emerged as rulers sought greater control over their territories in the context of increasing interstate conflict.

▶ The modern nation state was constructed in the nineteenth century through the administrative revolution, democratization, and various nation-building processes.

We then considered the growth of a world economy.

▶ A capitalist world economy emerged in a politically divided Europe and then expanded to include the world as a whole.

▶ Nineteenth-century industrialization brought about an international division of labour that created a global interdependence between countries.

▶ This led to a growing international inequality between the industrial societies and the primary producers.

While globalization integrated the world, it also divided it by creating racial divisions:

▶ Globalization led to the international movement of peoples through the slave trade, indentured labour, and migration.

▶ Increasing ethnic diversity within societies resulted in ethnic patterns of stratification and ethnic stereotyping.

▶ The concept of biologically defined races emerged as a means of explaining inequality in the nineteenth century and imperialism led to the association of races with peoples of different skin colour.

Lastly, we examined the way that empires had divided up the world and generated world wars.

▶ By the late nineteenth century most of the world had been divided up between a small number of empires.

▶ The modern nation state's capacity to organize and mobilize populations and resources for war, in combination with imperial rivalries and global alliances, led to world wars.

▶ The cold war between the American and Soviet empires brought the imperial stage of globalization to an end.

DEVELOPMENT AND GLOBALIZATION IN POST-COLONIAL TIMES

The European overseas empires collapsed after the Second World War and the Soviet Empire some forty years later. In this section we examine first the problems of development faced by the post-colonial nation states, going on to discuss the issues raised by population growth and urbanization. We then consider globalization in the post-colonial era and discuss global economic integration and the emergence of a new international division of labour. We also examine increasing international migration, the response of the state to it, and its implications for national identities. This leads us into a discussion of the impact of globalization on the nation state.

THE DEVELOPMENT OF NEW NATION STATES

We begin by outlining the foundation of most of the world's nation states during the post-colonial era. We then examine the role of economic aid in their development and their development strategies. We also consider whether patterns of international inequality have changed.

From empires to state nations

Western imperial domination, which had appeared so inevitable and so permanent at the end of the nineteenth century, was self-destructive. The European states could not administer their huge colonial territories without involving and educating local people to do most of the work for them. Education brought local people into contact with the political movements and democratic institutions of the home countries. Nationalist movements calling for the same institutions to be established in the colonial territories inevitably emerged. The conflicts between the empires anyway weakened their control over their colonial territories. The Second World War had particularly destructive consequences for the European empires in Asia. The Western empires were initially defeated by Japan, which also encouraged nationalist movements for its own purposes.

The post-war political climate was not favourable to the colonial empires. World politics were dominated by the United States and the Soviet Union. The United States was opposed to colonialism and wanted the European empires opened up to its exports. The Soviet Union supported independence movements in the hope of establishing politically favourable regimes in the ex-colonial countries, and this led the United States to sponsor rival ones. The cold war between the two superpowers meant that nationalist leaders could find powerful backers to support them. As for the Soviet Union, in the end its economy was unable to sustain the military expenditure required by the cold war and its collapse brought the last of the European empires to an end.

Between its foundation in 1945 and the 1990s the membership of the United Nations tripled from around 50 to over 150. This was mainly because of the collapse of the European empires and the creation of new nation states from their territories. Another wave of states joined with the collapse of the Soviet Union in the 1990s.

The ex-colonial nation states faced difficult political problems. They rarely corresponded to a people with a sense of national identity. Their boundaries were determined by the way the empires had divided up territory between them, sometimes by simply drawing straight lines on a map across 'unknown' territories. They often included ethnically diverse peoples, with different languages and different cultures. They had, therefore, to construct new nations within their state boundaries and for this reason have been called *state nations* rather than *nation states*.

The new state apparatus would often be dominated by one ethnic group at the expense of others, and subordinate ethnicities frequently found this situation intolerable. Military *coups* and civil wars became a common feature of the newly independent states.

Economic aid

The new states faced the question of how they could catch up with the developed industrial societies. Would the rich countries of the West, which had exploited them for so long, assist them to do so? According to modernization theory, which we examined earlier (see p. 454), economic growth would spread from the rich to the poor countries. Economic aid could help this process along.

More economic aid has often been seen as the solution to the continuing problems faced by the new states. The United Nations has called on rich countries to give 0.7 per cent of their gross national product annually as aid. Few have given as much as this and there are often calls for the rich countries to be less selfish and give more. Arguably, the problem with economic aid is, however, not so much whether there is enough of it as whether aid can actually do much to help poor countries.

The economic significance of aid is problematic. This is partly because other aspects of the economic relationship between the rich and poor countries outweigh the impact of economic aid. Many poor countries are heavily dependent on the export of one product. The price of, say, bananas or tea is far more important to them than the amount of aid they receive. It is also because when aid takes the form of a loan, debt repayments become a major burden, particularly when interest rates rise. Poor countries have in fact been regularly paying out more annually in interest payments than they have received in aid. Economic aid has anyway often been misdirected into large and highly visible projects, typically dams, that turn out to be of little

Aid or narco-dollars?

It is reported that drug barons have been offering to lend billions of 'narco-dollars' to poor countries. The drug barons have been finding it increasingly difficult to launder their profits, as governments have increased their surveillance of financial transactions and forced banks to check the sources of funds. It is estimated that some $85–100 billion a year is laundered annually into the global financial system and this compares with total global aid to poor countries of around $60 billion a year. Narco-dollars may provide countries that have difficulty meeting the requirements laid down by the World Bank and the International Monetary Fund or simply do not wish to abide by their conditions with an alternative, though rather risky, source of funds.

Source: *Independent*, 6 Feb. 1996.

benefit to the poor and may well cause serious damage to the environment.

Aid-giving countries also generally attach 'strings' to aid. It may be given on condition that it is spent on projects that benefit exporting companies in the donor country or linked to weapons contracts. Aid has often been steered politically to countries adopting the 'right' political and ideological stance. Loans have been made conditional on governments pursuing 'correct' economic policies. Thus, in the 1980s the World Bank and the International Monetary Fund made loans conditional on structural adjustment programmes that required governments to cut state expenditure and privatize state enterprises. Conditions of this kind could lead some countries to explore alternative sources of money.

It is then more than a little doubtful whether the aid-receiving countries have benefited much from economic aid. In many ways it seems to be of greater benefit to those who give it.

States and strategies

If development was to occur, it depended largely on the efforts of the poor countries themselves. What strategy should they pursue? Industrialization initially seemed to be the best way to achieve economic growth. As we showed earlier, the international division of labour was not to the benefit of all, which suggested that the new states needed to industrialize if they were to achieve economic independence and have the standards of

Britain helps Malaysia to build a dam

In 1990 the British government agreed to contribute £234 million towards the building of the Pergau dam in Malaysia, although this project was widely criticized as economically unnecessary and highly damaging to the environment. The project and its funding were reported to be highly beneficial to members of the Malaysian elite involved in the development and privatization of the Malaysian electricity supply industry.

In 1990 the Malaysian government decided to buy arms worth £1.3 billion from British companies. Was this a coincidence? The British government denied that there was any link between the dam and the arms contract. In 1988 the British Defence Secretary had signed with the Malaysian government an outline agreement (later withdrawn) that proposed a formula linking aid to arms deals.

Source: *Sunday Times*, 27 Feb., 27 and 13 Mar. 1994.

living enjoyed by those who lived in the industrial societies.

How was industrialization to be achieved? The strategy advocated in the 1950s and 1960s was *import substitution*. This generally involved the state setting up industries and protecting them against cheap imports from the industrial countries by erecting tariff barriers. While this policy could rapidly establish new industries, these could then devour state resources and become out of date and inefficient in the absence of competition.

The emphasis shifted in the 1970s to *export-oriented* industry. Japan had taken this approach and very successfully penetrated the markets of the West. A group of other countries, notably South Korea, Taiwan, Singapore, Brazil, and to some extent Mexico, which were labelled the newly industrializing countries (NICs), have also followed this path. The problem was that their very success made it difficult for others to follow, since the NICs dominated world markets. Their success seems anyway to have resulted from specific features of their situations, histories, and cultures, such as the Confucianist values of the East Asian success stories, that were not present elsewhere.

A problem with the emphasis on industrialization was that a focus on the production of manufactured goods could lead to the neglect of agriculture. The economies of most of the new states were mainly agricultural and it made little sense to ignore agricultural development.

Some countries tried to increase agricultural production within small-scale traditional units, sometimes combining this with land reform to break up large estates and return the land to those who worked it. Taiwan is commonly cited as an example of the success of this strategy. Cooperatives and community development projects were set up in many countries to help traditional farmers to raise production by pooling their resources, acquiring modern technology, and improving organization. Results were, however, generally disappointing, largely it seems because inappropriate structures imposed by unresponsive state bureaucracies alienated local people. This led to a call for a more flexible 'learning process approach' that gave locals more involvement and more choice (Hulme and Turner 1990).

The opposite strategy was to invest capital in large, modern units with economies of scale and the latest technology, which could produce for export markets. The technological advances of the 'green revolution', which produced new, more productive crop varieties, required this kind of unit. Countries such as Colombia,

Far from the green revolution: traditional agriculture in Zimbabwe.

Mexico, and the Philippines went down this route. It could work well but only within fertile areas, leaving most of rural society with its productive potential untapped. Success, anyway, tended to be short term, for these crops needed an ever greater use of expensive and environmentally damaging fertilizers and pesticides.

There are a number of problems with the whole notion of a *development strategy*. First, this can lead to the adoption of the latest fashion, whether or not it is appropriate to the country concerned. This is not to say that strategies do not ever work. It is rather that there is no universally appropriate one. What works in Korea will probably not work in Somalia.

Secondly, strategic thinking also tends to be top down. There is a general danger that plans are imposed from above without recognizing local diversity, involving local people, or drawing on local initiative. Indeed, the latest thinking on development emphasizes the local role and argues that the most that the state can do is to provide the conditions within which local initiatives can flourish.

Thirdly, there is the problem of the political and ideological aspects of policy. Discussion of development strategies tends to proceed as though policies can operate in isolation from the concerns and interests of the groups that control the state. All strategies will have distributive consequences, benefiting workers at the expense of peasants, or city-dwellers more than villagers, or one ethnic group at the cost of another. Choice of strategy will therefore depend on the outcome of political conflicts between interest groups. It will also depend on the kind of society that a given political leadership seeks to achieve. The value placed on increased production, for example, has to be set against the value placed on religious customs, which may well be undermined by economic and social change.

Lastly, it is somewhat naïve to believe that economic policy is ever governed simply by development considerations, since it is often a means of lining the pockets of rulers and their families. This is particularly the case where military takeovers have resulted in regimes that are not answerable to parliamentary bodies or political parties. Leaders such as Marcos of the Philippines, Mobutu of Zaire, and Suharto of Indonesia accumulated enormous wealth, much of it safely stashed away outside their countries, at the expense of their peoples.

While much of the discussion of development strategy has revolved around ways of increasing industrial or agricultural production, globalization has produced new opportunities of a rather different kind. One of these is global tourism (see pp. 482–3). Another is the utilization of global communication links to process

Forced labour in Burma

'Starved of international funding since the economic embargo by the World Bank and others, in response to the 1988 military takeover . . . the government seeks to lure foreign currency spenders, in the form of tourists. But the infrastructure is run-down; the roads unsuitable for tourist coaches, the railways slow and unreliable— you can wait at Rangoon for two days before the train leaves for Mandalay—and the archaeological sites and beauty spots are not up to accommodating mass tourism. So the generals have turned the country into one huge slave-labour camp. The rich can buy their way out or pay for someone else to do the work. For the rest there is no escape. One of the largest projects is the fort at Mandalay—the fabled City of Kings. . . . Today, the fort and moat swarm with hundreds of prisoners and villagers, repairing walls and dredging mud. They are watched by armed soldiers, unpaid and fed only by a midday meal of rice.'

Source: Vivien Morgan, 'In Bondage on the Road to Mandalay', *Independent*, 19 Jan. 1996.

▶ **What does this account suggest about the role of aid, development strategies, and the state in generating economic growth?**

data or develop software for customers in the rich countries. The growth of transnational corporations has led many countries to seek to attract investment by creating Export Processing Zones, where foreign companies can operate with a minimum of regulation and taxation. We discuss these below in the section on 'global economic integration'.

How successful have the new states been in developing their economies? Since the 1960s the output of manufactured goods has grown slightly faster in the developing countries than in the industrial countries (Hulme and Turner 1990: 102–3). International inequality remains extreme, however, and actually increased between 1960 and 1989 (see Figure 12.4). While the NICs have done well, other countries, such as Zaire and Somalia, have gone backwards. A telling indicator of international divergence is that, while fifty-four of the world's countries increased their gross domestic product (GDP) during the 1980s, in forty-nine countries GDP actually fell (*New Internationalist* 1990: 17). This diversity reinforces the arguments, which we discussed earlier (see p. 456), for abandoning any notion of a Third World.

Figure 12.4. **International inequality, 1960–1989**

Country groupings	Percentage share of global GNP	
	1960	1989
Richest countries	70.2	82.7
Poorest countries	2.3	1.4
Other countries	27.5	15.9
Total	100	100

Note: richest = those with the richest 20% of world population; poorest = those with the poorest 20% of world population.
Source: United Nations Development Programme (1992: 36).

POPULATION GROWTH AND URBANIZATION

As they struggled to develop, poor countries found themselves faced with a rapid growth of population. It was argued that a 'population explosion' and a resulting 'over-urbanization' threatened their growth prospects and endangered the environment. In this section we examine these arguments and their implications.

Overpopulation?

After the Second World War the population of poor countries began to rise rapidly. Population increase is basically a matter of there being more births than deaths, though migration may have some impact on population size when the population is small. The post-war population increase in poor countries was quite simply the result of rapidly falling death rates as the technology of disease control spread from the industrial countries.

Death-rates had, of course, fallen in the industrial countries too but this had happened gradually over the previous century and the effect of falling death rates was more or less cancelled out by falling birth rates. Industrial countries had passed through what is called the demographic transition (see Chapter 6, pp. 203–5). This means that they moved from one relatively stable state to another as they shifted from high birth and death rates to low birth and death rates (see Figure 12.5

on p. 474). In the poor countries death rates fell very rapidly but birth rates remained very high. Thus in the mid-1950s birth rates in the industrial societies ranged between 15 and 25 births per 1,000 people per year but in most poor countries they were between 40 and 50 births per 1,000 (Hurd 1973: 70).

It is easy to see why death rates declined so rapidly in poor countries, but why have birth rates stayed so high? Before answering this question, we need to consider why birth rates declined in the industrial societies. This was basically because people needed large families less and wanted smaller ones, as children became less a source of additional income and more a cost, with education becoming a longer and more compulsory process. Family income would be maximized by women going out to work rather than having children. Also, pensions, state health care, and old people's homes meant that there was less need for children as an insurance policy to provide support in old age.

In poor countries most of this did not apply. Much of the population was still engaged in agriculture and more children meant more farmhands. Child labour was and still is common not only in agriculture but also in workshops and factories, in some countries in mining. In the cities children make good beggars, thieves, and scavengers. Thus, a larger family meant a larger income and more support in illness or old age.

By the 1960s there was a growing concern with what was seen as a *population explosion*. Although having more children might be a rational strategy for the individual household, an increasing population had serious consequences for countries trying to develop. It led to higher unemployment and increased welfare expenditure, pressure on the land and over-urbanization. It resulted in growing poverty, which might lead to a disorder which threatened the regime in power. There was also much concern with the impact of a rising world population on the environment.

The conquest of Malaria in Sri Lanka

The death rate in Sri Lanka fell gradually from 27 deaths per 1,000 people in the 1920s to 20 per 1,000 in 1946. Malaria spread by mosquitoes had long been the major cause of death and in 1946 a campaign began to spray DDT on the places where mosquitoes lived. In one year the death rate fell from 20 to 14 deaths per 1,000 people. In Britain a similar fall had taken around thirty years, from 1880 to 1910.

Source: Hurd (1973: 62).

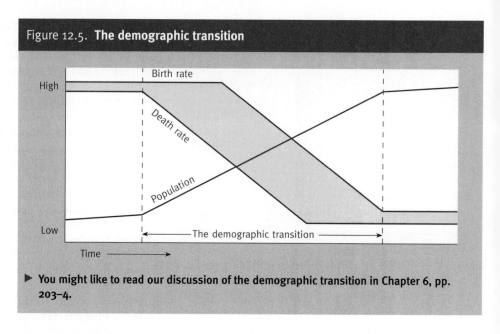

Figure 12.5. **The demographic transition**

▶ **You might like to read our discussion of the demographic transition in Chapter 6, pp. 203–4.**

If population increase was a serious problem, what was to be done about it? The first approach was to try to spread birth-control techniques by establishing networks of family-planning clinics and providing free contraception. Contraceptive technology had advanced rapidly in the industrial societies and seemed to provide the solution. High birth rates were blamed on ignorance, which could be overcome through instruction in modern techniques. The problem with this approach was that, as argued above, many people in poor countries had good reasons for producing large families and this, rather than ignorance, was the main reason why birth rates have stayed so high.

One response has been to bribe or coerce people to limit their families. A coercive policy was followed in China, where a one-child-per-family policy was adopted. In terms of results, this policy was highly successful and a birth rate of 37 births per 1,000 people in 1952 was reduced to 17.9 per 1,000 by 1979 (Hulme and Turner 1990: 125). Policies of this kind were only possible, however, in an authoritarian society.

A growing understanding of the reasons for high birth rates led international agencies to change their approach in the 1980s. High birth rates were now seen as a consequence as well as a cause of poverty. More emphasis was placed on programmes to alleviate poverty and improve general education, especially the education of women.

Some doubts about the seriousness of the population explosion have been expressed. It has been argued that much of Africa, Asia, and Latin America is now moving through its own demographic transition to greater population stability. Indeed, it is claimed that develop-

ing countries are moving through it faster than the developed countries did (Holdgate 1996: 11).

One recent analysis suggests that some of the more extreme projections of world population increase are unlikely to be correct. It predicts that the rate of

Empowering women to control population increase

'The population explosion in the developing world is best controlled by education, giving young women an alternative to perpetual motherhood, the head of the United Nations Population Fund said yesterday. . . . "If we had paid more attention to empowering women thirty years ago and had listened to their needs, we might well have been ahead of the game as far as population numbers are concerned," Dr Sadiq said. "The fact is that women have been, and still are, disregarded and undervalued for everything they do apart from having children, preferably boys. Despite the advances of the past two generations, there is still a wide gender gap in both education and health care in most developing countries" . . . .'

Source: Steve Connor, 'Women Hold Key to Population Curb', *Independent*, 18 Aug. 1994.

▶ **Why might more education for women lead to lower rates of population increase?**

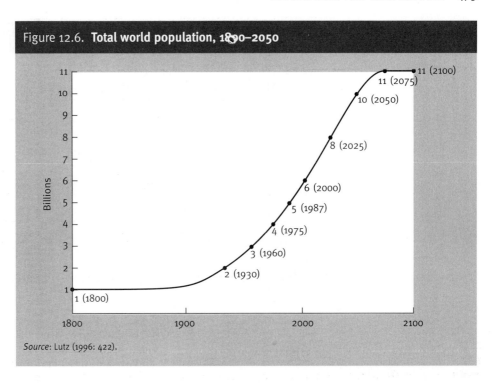

Figure 12.6. Total world population, 1800–2050

Source: Lutz (1996: 422).

increase will slow down and the world's population will probably peak at around 11 billion during the second half of the twenty-first century (see Figure 12.6). The declining Chinese birth rate plays an important part in this, for nearly one-quarter of the world's population lives in China and the current birth rate there is lower than that needed to replace those dying. Birth rates are also at last falling in sub-Saharan Africa, mainly it is suggested because of the increased education of women. On the other hand, AIDS and apparently conquered but now resurgent diseases such as cholera, malaria, and tuberculosis are causing death rates to rise.

There are, of course, many variables operating here and this study identifies other less probable outcomes, ranging from a world population of 17 billion to one of 6 billion in the year 2100. Even if the likeliest peak of 11 billion is correct, it is, anyway, almost double the world's population of 5.8 billion in 1995 (Lutz 1996: 422).

Over-urbanization?

Like population growth, urbanization in poor countries is often treated as though it is out of control. League tables are produced that show the cities of Asia, Africa, and Latin America overtaking in size those of Europe and North America (see Figure 12.7 on p. 476).

Terms such as 'mushrooming cities' or 'the urban explosion' are used. It is often argued that 'over-urbanization' is taking place.

The notion of **over-urbanization** is based partly on the idea that urbanization in the poor countries of Africa, Asia, and Latin America has been much faster than it was in the developed countries at a comparable stage in their development. The rate of urbanization in nineteenth-century Britain did not get much above 1 per cent a year, while annual rates in poor countries during the period 1950–90 were commonly between 3 and 6 per cent.

It is argued that cities in poor countries are *parasitic* rather than *generative*. They are said to drain resources from rural areas and contribute nothing to them, instead of creating economic growth as cities are supposed to do. Urban elites have been criticized for leading unproductive lives, focused on the consumption of imported goods, and assisting foreign capital in the exploitation of their societies.

It is also argued that cities have become too big to cope with their increasing populations. Employment opportunities have not kept pace with the growing urban population and large numbers of people have been forced into the informal economy, which shades into activities such as begging, scavenging, and prostitution, in order to survive. Many of them have to live in shanty towns without decent housing or sanitation.

Figure 12.7. The world's largest five cities, 1950–2015

1950		1990		2015 (projected)	
City	Population (m.)	City	Population (m.)	City	Population (m.)
1. New York	12.3	1. Tokyo	25	1. Tokyo	28.7
2. London	8.7	2. New York	16.1	2. Bombay	27.4
3. Tokyo	6.9	3. Mexico City	15.1	3. Lagos	24.4
4. Paris	5.4	4. Sao Paulo	14.8	4. Shanghai	23.4
5. Moscow	5.4	5. Shanghai	13.5	5. Jakarta	21.2

Source: United Nations Population Fund (1996: 32–3).

Rio de Janeiro: city and shanty town.

Unmanageable concentrations of population have built up that cannot be provided with proper services and are a source of crime and disorder.

There are, however, a number of criticisms that can be made of the over-urbanization thesis. There are two main kinds of criticism. One argues that this thesis exaggerates the differences between urbanization in rich and poor countries. The other argues that the over-urbanization approach paints too negative a picture of conditions in the cities.

A recent UN report claims that urbanization rates in the old industrial societies have often been as high as those in developing countries or, indeed, higher. In the United States between 1820 and 1870 the annual increase in urban population was 5.5 per cent, a rate of increase similar to contemporary rates in poor countries (UN Centre for Human Settlements 1996: 25).

This report also points out that comparisons of city populations in rich and poor countries fail to take account of boundary changes. Many cities in poor countries have grown larger by extending their boundaries, while some cities in the old industrial countries have failed to extend theirs to take account of growth. Thus, London has retained administrative boundaries that give no real idea of its spread. Greater London in 1991 had a population of 6.4 million, which made it the twenty-third largest city in the world, but a definition in terms of its metropolitan region would have given it a population of 12.5 million, which would have made it the world's sixth largest city (UN Centre for Human Settlements 1996: 17).

The concept of 'over-urbanization' also presents too negative an image of city life in poor countries. The UN report argues that the generative role of cities in the economy has too often been overlooked. Another point is that, although there may be insufficient employment in the formal economy to absorb the population, migrants are drawn to cities because they none the less offer better prospects than the areas the migrants come from. Conditions may be bad in the cities but they are worse elsewhere. This negative view also neglects the success of community-based self-help initiatives in improving the urban environment in many cities.

Flanagan suggests that, if high levels of unemployment and a growing informal economy indicate over-urbanization, this is due to 'the dynamics of the international economy', which affect all cities. On this basis, Britain too is over-urbanized. He concludes that the study of the Third World City has been a separate field for too long and now needs to be integrated with the study of the cities of the developed world (Flanagan 1993: 127–9).

Have poor countries become over-urbanized?

Aspects of urbanization	Yes	No
Rate of urbanization	Higher than in rich countries	Comparable rates at a similar stage
Size of cities	Larger than in rich countries	Differences in boundary definitions
Contribution to economy	Parasitic	Generative
Living conditions	Cities unable to provide decent living conditions	Living conditions better than in rural areas

The 'street-finders' and 'collectors' of nineteenth-century London

'These men, for by far the great majority are men, may be divided, according to the nature of their occupations, into three classes:

1. The bone-grubbers and rag-gatherers . . . the pure-finders, and the cigar-end and old wood collectors.
2. The dredgermen, the mud-larks, and the sewer-hunters.
3. The dustmen and nightmen, the sweeps and the scavengers.

The first class go abroad daily to *find* in the streets, and carry away with them such things as bones, rags, 'pure' (or dogs' dung), which no one appropriates. These they sell, and on that sale support a wretched life. The second class of people are also as strictly *finders*; but their industry, or rather their labour, is confined to the river, or to that subterranean city of sewerage unto which the Thames supplies the great outlets. . . . The third class is distinct from either of these, as the labourers comprised in it are not finders, but *collectors* or *removers* of the dirt and filth of our streets and houses, and of the soot of our chimneys.'

Source: Mayhew (1861a: ii. 136).

▶ **Were conditions in nineteenth-century British cities much different from those in poor countries today?**

GLOBAL ECONOMIC INTEGRATION

As Flanagan suggests, it no longer makes much sense to treat the Third World as a separate area of study. Globalizing processes are producing a more integrated and definitely single world. In this section we will first outline changes in communications, before considering the growth of transnational corporations, the emergence of a new international division of labour, and the spread of global tourism.

A shrinking world

In the nineteenth century, a revolution in communications 'shrank' the world. Steam power transformed travel with railways and steamships. It was not only that steam travel was so much faster, but also that it was regular, reliable, and less dependent on the weather. It also enabled the movement of larger quantities of goods and greater numbers of people.

Air travel has now made it possible to reach most of the world within a day or so. Speed is certainly important, and the growing speed of travel is shown in Figure 12.8 on p. 478, but too much emphasis can be placed on this alone. The regularity and cheapness of transport are fundamental to global integration. The wide-bodied passenger jets introduced in the 1960s made cheap mass travel possible. The container revolution enormously cheapened the transport of goods by sea during the 1970s and enabled a huge growth in the volume of trade.

It is not only travel that matters but also the communication of information. The invention of the telegraph in 1837 and the telephone in 1876 'destroyed distance' by separating communication from travel. With the telegraph it was possible to send messages across the globe without sending someone with them. After the laying of submarine cables, London could communicate with Australia and New Zealand in four days rather than the seventy taken by surface mail (Leyshon 1995: 26). Global communication became instant with international phone calls. As Giddens (1990: 141) points out, the telephone made it possible to be in more intimate and private contact with someone on the other side of the globe than someone on the other side of the room.

It was, however, the launching of geostationary satellites in the 1960s and 1970s that transformed communication. These made global communication cheap and enabled the transmission of large amounts of information. Digital transmission has subsequently increased greatly, through compression, the amount of information that can be sent.

Transnational corporations

Faster communication facilitated transnational economic organization through the **transnational corporation** (TNC). The key feature of the TNC is that it does not just *trade* across borders. International trading is as old as national borders. TNCs *produce* goods and services in more than one country. They first emerged in the nineteenth century, but it was the new economic conditions stemming from the collapse of empire and increasing international competition in the 1960s and 1970s that made them a dominant force in the world economy.

Increasing international competition and declining profits drove companies in the old industrial countries to set up production in countries where labour costs were lower. Another strategy for dealing with international competition was to buy up or merge with the opposition in other countries and become a TNC by this means. On the other hand, the multiplication of states and increasing international competition generated threats of tariff barriers to protect domestic producers. One way of forestalling this was to produce goods and

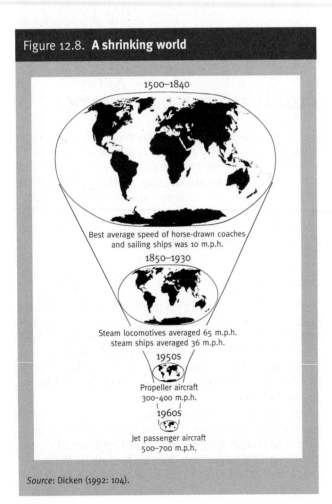

Figure 12.8. **A shrinking world**

1500–1840

Best average speed of horse-drawn coaches and sailing ships was 10 m.p.h.

1850–1930

Steam locomotives averaged 65 m.p.h. steam ships averaged 36 m.p.h.

1950s
Propeller aircraft
300–400 m.p.h.

1960s
Jet passenger aircraft
500–700 m.p.h.

Source: Dicken (1992: 104).

Plastic bags from China

When you next put your supermarket purchases in a plastic bag, the chances are that it is a bag made in China. In 1995 British Polythene Industries closed its Shropshire factory, with the loss of 150 jobs, and moved production of supermarket plastic bags to China. Wages in China were one-tenth those in Britain and a bag made in China was about 20 per cent cheaper. The cost savings on an individual plastic bag were, however, minute, since one bag cost only around 1p to make. Why then was it worth shifting production to China? The factory made 21 million bags per week and to the superstore chains which gave out large numbers of them a 20 per cent saving was worth making. The company did not move production to make higher profits but because this was the only way that it could stay competitive as world plastic bag prices were driven down by Asian production.

Source: Simon Hoggart, *The Hollow State*, BBC2, 28 Sept. 1996.

Figure 12.9. **The destruction of distance**

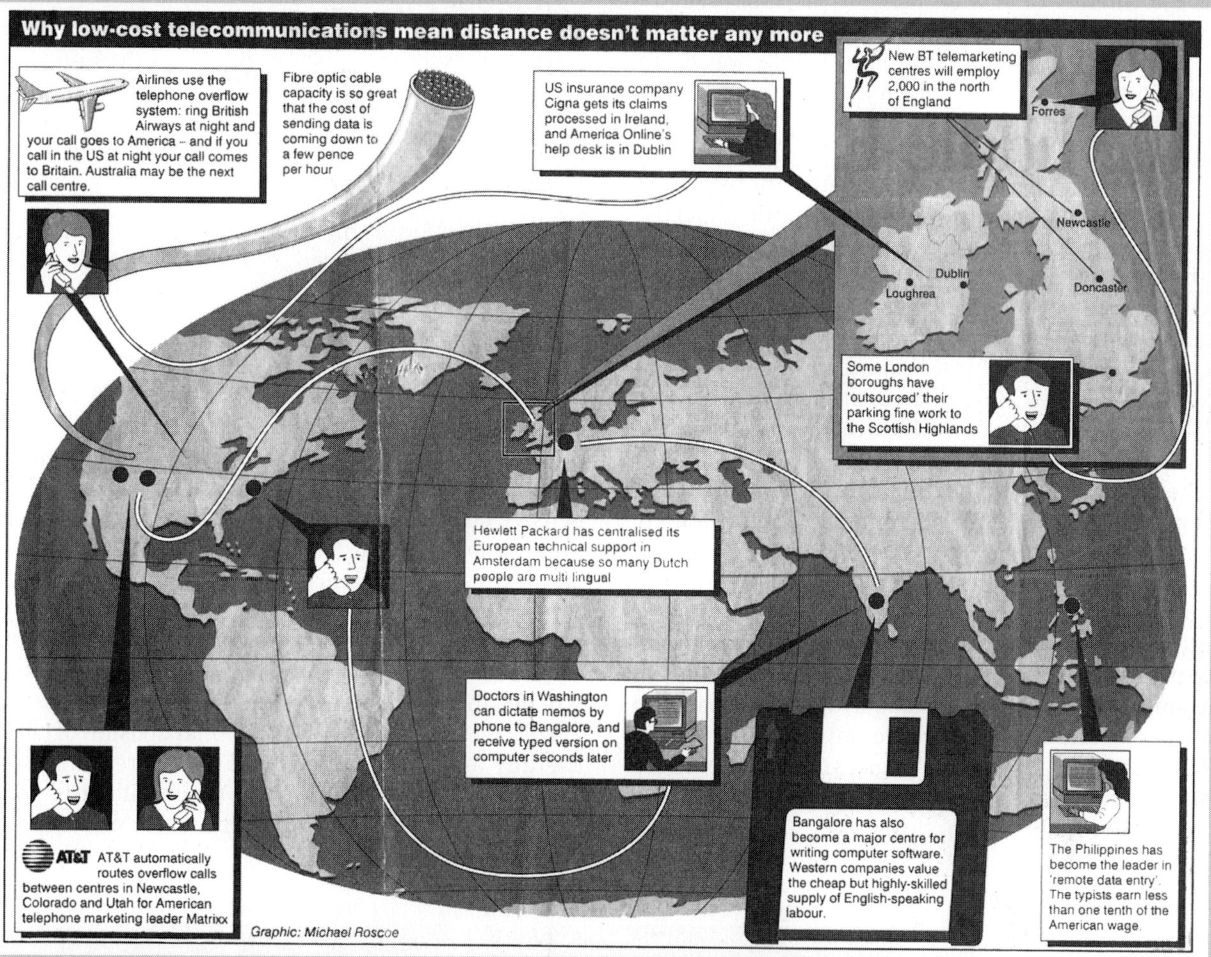

Why low-cost telecommunications mean distance doesn't matter any more

Airlines use the telephone overflow system: ring British Airways at night and your call goes to America – and if you call in the US at night your call comes to Britain. Australia may be the next call centre.

Fibre optic cable capacity is so great that the cost of sending data is coming down to a few pence per hour

US insurance company Cigna gets its claims processed in Ireland, and America Online's help desk is in Dublin

New BT telemarketing centres will employ 2,000 in the north of England

Some London boroughs have 'outsourced' their parking fine work to the Scottish Highlands

Hewlett Packard has centralised its European technical support in Amsterdam because so many Dutch people are multi lingual

Doctors in Washington can dictate memos by phone to Bangalore, and receive typed version on computer seconds later

Bangalore has also become a major centre for writing computer software. Western companies value the cheap but highly-skilled supply of English-speaking labour.

The Philippines has become the leader in 'remote data entry'. The typists earn less than one tenth of the American wage.

 AT&T AT&T automatically routes overflow calls between centres in Newcastle, Colorado and Utah for American telephone marketing leader Matrixx

Forres, Newcastle, Dublin, Loughrea, Doncaster

Graphic: Michael Roscoe

Source: Independent, 12 Jan. 1998.

---

services inside other countries' frontiers. That is one of the main reasons why Japanese companies built factories in Europe.

TNCs provide services as well as goods, and there are, for example, global hotel chains, global advertising agencies, and global car-rental companies. These global service corporations are sometimes seen as the camp followers of global manufacturers. Up to a point they are, but this is not the whole story. Hilton hotels do not just provide standard rooms for travelling American business executives. They also provide standard rooms for tourists (see 'Global Tourism', pp. 482–3).

Changes in culture and way of life are also very important. The global expansion of McDonald's was not just to provide burgers for American travellers, whether business executives or tourists. It more importantly provided a standard and fashionable fast food for local people. The popularity of McDonalds was largely a result of the globalization of the media, which has spread American culture and the consumption of American products world wide. The growth of TNCs is linked to global changes in culture and living patterns as well as the economic advantages of production in other countries.

> ☞ The globalization of the media is an important aspect of globalization. We discuss this, and the issue of Americanization, in Chapter 8, pp. 304–6.

A new international division of labour

One of the main consequences of the growth of TNCs was the emergence of what Frobel *et al.* (1980) called a **new international division of labour**. As we showed earlier, an international division of labour was established in the nineteenth century. The industrial societies specialized in exporting manufactured goods, while Africa, Asia, and Latin America provided primary products. With the spread of TNCs the industrial societies increasingly exported capital and expertise instead, while poor countries provided cheap labour for manufacturing.

One feature of this new international division of labour was the creation of Export Processing Zones or Free Trade Zones. To attract capital, governments cut taxes and allowed unregulated production in these zones, as the example of the Mexican *maquiladoras*, the local name for these zones shows.

The exploitation of cheap labour in poor countries has resulted in the increasing employment of women. According to Mitter (1986: 41), 80 per cent of the workers in Free Trade Zones are women. TNCs prefer to employ young women workers, for they can be paid less and are seen as easier to control than male workers, and easier to dispose of by returning to the household if the employer needs to shed labour. Western images of the docility and dexterity of oriental women attracted TNCs to the Far East, and Mitter gives examples of Asian countries reinforcing this stereotype in their efforts to draw in foreign capital.

Changes in the international division of labour (IDOL)

Groups of societies	Old IDOL	New IDOL
Industrial societies	Manufactured goods	Capital and expertise
Rest of the world	Primary products	Cheap labour

Child labour has similar advantages and is widely exploited in many poor countries. The Director-General of the Pakistan Workers' Education Programme is quoted as saying that: 'There's little doubt that inexpensive child labour has fuelled Pakistan's economic growth. Entire industries have relocated to Pakistan because of the abundance of cheap child labour and our lax labour laws' (*Independent on Sunday*, 26 Apr. 1996). It has been reported that the footballs used in the World Cup, the Premier League, and the Cup Final were stitched together by children in Pakistan.

The concept of a new international division of labour usefully draws our attention to the increasing use of cheap labour in poor countries to manufacture goods for rich countries, but it is in some ways misleading.

Young women in a Sri Lankan free trade zone making clothes for British stores.

Export Processing zones in Mexico

'The companies, whose plants are known as *maquiladoras*, or simply *maquilas*, were enticed by a Mexican programme that allowed foreign firms to import parts and raw materials duty-free, provided the finished product was exported. Since the programme was introduced in 1965, more than 2,000 manufacturing and assembly plants have been built along a 12 mile band on the Mexican side of the border, thriving on tariff exemptions and wage rates lower than in Taiwan and Korea. The programme has pumped millions of dollars into the Mexican economy. But years of unchecked industrial growth have transformed the entire border region into an environmental nightmare, where companies operate outside the constraints of the US Environmental Protection Agency and the Occupational Safety and Health Administration. . . .'

Source: Jeff Silverstein, 'Tax Breaks Poison the Atmosphere for Mexico's Workers's, *Independent*, 10 Apr. 1992.

Pakistan children hand-stitch footballs

'The children, often engaged in a modern form of slave labour, spend long hours in workshops around Sialkot, a Punjabi town near the border with India. . . . Sialkot is the source of most of the world's hand-stitched footballs, its produce snapped up by household names such as Adidas, Reebok, and Mitre. Many of the children are unable to attend school because their families need the 10p an hour they earn. . . . Many of the children in the Sialkot football workshops are bonded labourers, working to pay off loans taken out by their parents. . . . Mudassar, 11, has worked for two years making footballs alongside three of his brothers. "I wanted to go to school but I have to work so I will probably never go," he said. Two-thirds of the 1,500 children in his village make footballs . . .'.

Source: Caroline Lees and Simon Hinde, 'Scandal of Football's Child Slavery', *Sunday Times*, 14 May 1996.

First, this new division of labour has not replaced the old one. Although the old industrial societies lost some manufacturing to the NICs, they still have important exporting industries. Furthermore, poor countries are still heavily involved in producing food and raw materials for the rich countries (see Figure 12.9 on p. 479). The old international division of labour lives on.

Secondly, much of the cheap labour carried out in poor countries involves little investment, if it is done in small workshops or at home. This applies particularly to international telework, which is spreading as companies based in rich countries seek to have their software written or their data processed by cheap labour in poor countries. Since this work can be carried out in small offices or at home, it requires little investment. There may, in other words, be very little transfer of capital to the poor country where the goods or services are produced.

Thirdly, most transnational investment is between rich countries. Europe, Japan, and the United States, the main sources of international capital, have been directing most of their investment not to Africa, Latin America, or the poor countries of Asia, but to each other. The share of global investment going to Africa and Latin America has actually fallen steadily since the 1960s. Asia is different, because of investment in the 'tiger' or 'would be tiger' economies of Singapore, Hong Kong, Malaysia, South Korea, Thailand, and Taiwan,

but, as Allen (1995) points out, this is a very select group of Asian countries.

Fourthly, rich countries too attract capital by providing cheap labour. Thus, in the mid-1990s Korean capital was drawn into Britain, particularly to Wales, where the closure of steelworks and coal mines had depressed wage levels. The tables had been truly turned with Third World countries investing in First World ones,

Dresses for the Middle East from London via Cyprus

'In 1983 the Observer newspaper reported that a British company, Wearwell, based in London's East End and headed by Turkish-Cypriot millionaire Asil Nadir, was shipping out 15,000 ready-cut women's and girls' dresses per week to Cyprus for assembly by 500 to 1,000 homeworkers. The dresses were sent back to London for finishing and then exported mainly to Arab countries. The company, whose profits in 1982 were £4,200,000 and which had twice received the Queen's Award for Exports, was paying the homeworkers 22p per dress.'

Source: Phizacklea (1990: 41).

and First World countries courting this investment with grants and incentives.

The concept of a new international division of labour does, therefore, give an oversimple picture of the complex international relationships between capital and labour. It is, however, quite correct in drawing attention to the way in which cheap labour in poor countries has been drawn increasingly into the production of manufactured goods and services for rich countries.

Global tourism

The discussion of global economic integration usually concerns itself with the trading and production of goods and services but makes no mention of tourism. Yet, according to Cater (1995: 184), tourism has become the most important activity in world trade.

International tourism has grown at a remarkable speed (see Figure 12.10). Global tourism is clearly a consequence of faster and cheaper international travel but has also generated this itself, by increasing the demand for travel and opening up routes to new destinations, which have often acquired airports in order to receive tourists. Similarly, greater global awareness through global media coverage has stimulated tourist interest in new holiday destinations, but tourist travel has also generated a demand for travel programmes on television, travel books, and information about far-off places. Global tourism results from globalization but also promotes it.

As with the circulation of money, the circulation of tourists is mainly between the rich countries of the world, between the United States, Europe, and Japan. Tourism has, none the less, become very important to the economies of many poor countries. In 1984 it was already the main source of foreign earnings in Barbados, Haiti, Bermuda, Panama, the Philippines, Thailand, and India. Given the rapid growth of international tourism since then, it is now no doubt the main 'export' of many other poor countries (D. Harrison 1994: 236–7).

Tourism has become in many ways the spearhead of global capitalism. It can penetrate rapidly into areas of the world that have little capacity to produce goods or other services for the world market. Indeed, the most traditional societies attract tourists because of their traditionality. Their religious festivals, cultural objects, and way of life suddenly acquire a monetary value. Tourism creates employment in paid labour in bar and hotel work, and prostitution. It generates a greater demand for food production and transport, and may well provide the basis for the local manufacturing of souvenirs and faking of relics. The earnings from tourism will increase the circulation of money, lead to the import of manufactured goods, and establish new consumption patterns.

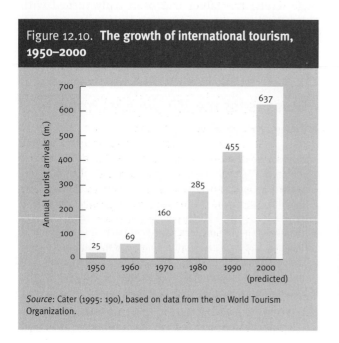

Figure 12.10. **The growth of international tourism, 1950–2000**

Source: Cater (1995: 190), based on data from the on World Tourism Organization.

Sex tourism

Sex tourism is one form of global tourism that has grown rapidly. It is another example of the exploitation of the cheap, unregulated labour available in poor countries by people from rich countries. Tourists can engage in immoral or illegal activities, such as sex with children, more cheaply, more easily, and more safely, than they can in their own countries. In 1995 Christian Aid suggested that there were over 200,000 child prostitutes in India, some 200,000 in Thailand, 60,000 in the Philippines, 15,000 in Sri Lanka, and an unknown number in many other countries of South-East Asia, Africa, and Latin America. Prostitution in sex tourist destinations is largely organized by local entrepreneurs, though expatriates from the countries that supply the tourists have also become involved. O'Connell Davidson (1998) argues, however, that 'the airlines which transport prostitute users half way around the globe and the hotels (many of which are owned by international conglomerates) in which they stay, as well as the travel agents which arrange their flights and accommodation, are probably the prime beneficiaries of sex tourism'.

The question of who gains from tourism has been much discussed. Poor societies apparently gain a new economic activity that generates employment, encourages local businesses, and earns foreign currency. But how much of the benefit stays in the country concerned? Global tourism is organized by TNCs, which return most of the profits on tourism to the rich countries. Agriculture may well suffer from ecological damage or a shortage of labour as people take up new jobs, while tourism may be seasonal and not support people through the year. Land and property prices may be pushed out of the reach of local people.

This leads to the wider issues of the cultural, social, and environmental impact of tourism. Customs may lose their authenticity when commercialized, though, on the other hand, commercialization may at least keep them alive in some form. Traditional patterns of authority will probably be undermined, which may be destabilizing, from one perspective, but liberating, from another. Hotel-building and the sheer weight of tourist numbers may damage the natural environment, but tourists may also provide an incentive to preserve vanishing species and maintain natural environments. Much depends on the kind of tourism involved. The rise of 'alternative tourism' and 'eco-tourism' may mean that a tourism more compatible with preservation has become commercially viable.

Whether tourism benefits poor countries is a complex matter, which ultimately depends on value judgements, on the relative value attached to employment, the environment, culture, and so on. What can be said is that surveys indicate that ordinary people in poor societies take a positive view of tourism and say they want more of it (D. Harrison 1994: 251).

MIGRATION, DIVERSITY, AND IDENTITY

Globalization brought not only an international flow of tourists but also increasing numbers of people seeking to work or settle in other countries. Immigration became a major issue in many societies and has been increasingly controlled and regulated by the state. The ethnic composition of societies has changed, challenging existing ideas of nationality, and raising problems of identity. The literature on globalization has given a lot of attention to global movements of capital and has neglected the global movement of people and its social consequences.

International migration after 1945

As we showed earlier, there was an extensive international migration during the nineteenth century but this died down after 1914. A new wave of international migration developed after 1945 and it is estimated that by 1990 there were some 80 million migrants world wide (Castles and Miller 1993: 4).

During the 1950s and 1960s the booming economies of North America, north-west Europe, and Australia sucked in labour from both the peripheral countries of Europe and the colonial and ex-colonial territories of Africa and Asia. Some countries, such as Germany and Switzerland, drew in 'guestworkers' on a temporary basis and gave them no rights of residence. At the other extreme, countries such as Australia and the United States, with a recent history of population through migration, allowed migrants to settle, though they restricted the numbers they allowed in. In between, there were ex-colonial countries such as Britain and France, which initially allowed in migrants from their colonies and ex-colonies but then increasingly restricted entry and settlement.

Worsening conditions in many poor countries increasingly drove people to seek entry to rich ones. Population pressure, the failure of economic growth, famine, and war all generated emigration. The governments of some poor countries have promoted migrant labour because of the foreign earnings that it brings.

Eco-tourism

The Belize government decided to develop an environmen-tally sensitive eco-tourism that would benefit local people. Around one-third of the country's land area has been designated as nature reserves and the small-scale development of tourist facilities has been encouraged. There are examples of tourist enterprises based on cooperatives of local people. The need to attract foreign investment and achieve a sustainable tourist industry has led, however, to the involvement of foreign-owned TNCs, the foreign ownership of coastal land, the building of large hotels, the clearing of mangrove swamps, and rapidly increasing numbers of tourists. There is already evidence of damage to coral reefs and overfishing to satisfy tourist demands. Eco-tourism cannot avoid all the problems generated by conventional tourism but Cater concludes that it is 'a lesser evil than uncontrolled mass tourism'.

Source: Cater (1995: 227–31).

Migrant labour from the Philippines

The Philippines have been one of the main sources of migrant labour with some 600,000 workers leaving annually in the early 1990s. Migrant filipinos have been widely employed as seamen, nurses, and domestic workers. The state was heavily involved in the migratory process. The Overseas Employment Administration made labour-supply agreements with many countries. Under the Marcos regime those working abroad were required to send 30 per cent of their earnings (70 per cent if they were seamen) back to bank accounts monitored by the state. Failure to do so would lead to the withdrawal of passports. In practice, these rules could not be enforced, illegal recruitment agencies emerged, and travel documents were forged.

Source: N. Harris (1995: 66).

The perils of international migration

'More than 100 would-be refugees from the Middle East and Asia have been granted asylum in Sweden and neighbouring Nordic states after a nightmare journey to the West. The refugees, most of whom are Iraqui Kurds claiming political persecution, set out almost two years ago, travelling to the Baltics via Moscow, having paid thousands of US dollars to smuggling gangs. They were captured in Latvia last year and spent more than two weeks being shunted back and forth by train to Russia and Lithuania. None of the three countries wanted to accept them. After protests from the UN High Commissioner for Refugees they were moved to a Latvian prison. Sweden has agreed to take 52 of the 108 refugees, with Denmark, Finland and Norway accepting 25, 20 and 11 apiece.'

Source: Adrian Bridge, 'Sweden Ends Refugees' Nightmare', *Independent*, 6 Dec. 1996.

The number of refugees also rose and by the early 1990s there were an estimated 20 million worldwide (Castles and Miller 1993: 84).

Since the mid-1970s the pattern of international migration has changed. European countries restricted entry, while the rapidly growing economies of the Asian NICs and the oil-rich countries of Arabia drew in migrants. International migration was less dominated by colonial relationships and became increasingly global in character, as more countries became both suppliers and receivers. Also, growing transnational economic activity led to the international circulation of businessmen, managers, and professionals.

Another change has been the increasing migration of women (Phizacklea 1995). In rich countries the demand for female labour has been rising. Service occupations that typically employ women have expanded, as has paid domestic work. In the Gulf States the growing employment of women in professional and managerial occupations led to the recruitment of Asian maids to do the housework, and this has happened in Hong Kong and London too. Female migrants have been drawn into prostitution and sex tourism, while there has also been a growing trade in 'mail-order' brides. Asia was their main source initially but more recently they have come from Eastern Europe, after the collapse of the state socialist economies led to increased unemployment there. Female migrants have also continued to provide cheap labour in manufacturing industries, often through homework, which we discuss in Chapter 13, pp. 541–2.

After entry barriers rose in the 1970s illegal immigration grew. Worsening conditions in many poor countries increased the pressure to migrate, at the very time that Western European countries were trying to close their doors. The result was more illegal immigration, which has led to a further tightening of controls. In Britain airlines are penalized if they bring in people without valid travel documents. Employers have been made responsible for ensuring that they do not employ illegal migrants. There have also been proposals to use public employees, such as health administrators and college admission tutors, to track down illegal entrants.

Some employers actively seek to bring in and employ illegal entrants. Indeed, economies can become dependent on them. In the United States, the 1986 Immigration Act introduced fines and imprisonment for employers hiring illegal migrants, but huge protests from agricultural and industrial interests followed, particularly in California and New Mexico, where there was also a widespread employment of illegal migrants in housework and gardening. Concessions were made and enforcement was ineffective. It was its very illegality that made Mexican and Central American labour so cheap, for illegals were extremely vulnerable and willing to work for very low wages, while their employers avoided having to make social-security payments (N. Harris 1995).

While it is mainly the poor who want to migrate, in the hope of a better life elsewhere, it is easy to buy your way into countries if you have wealth. Thus, the United States Immigration Act of 1991 allowed the entry of up to 10,000 migrants willing to invest one million dollars and create ten jobs within six months. Australia and Canada operate similar schemes with lower requirements. Harris argues that there is an international competition to attract wealthy immigrants, with one country trying to outbid another.

Racist immigration laws?

It was part of the ideology of the British Empire that all those who lived within its territories had the right to enter Britain and rights to citizenship, but these were steadily withdrawn from the 1960s.

There has been some debate over the reasons for immigration control. A slowing-down of economic growth meant less need for labour and more concern with unemployment, but the 1962 Act in Britain occurred well before this slowing-down. There can be little doubt that it was a political response to a growing white backlash. Whites had, for example, attacked blacks in the highly publicized 'race riots' in Notting-

ham and London in 1958. Immigration legislation was not, on the other hand, just a response to a popular racism. Solomos (1993) points out that British politicians had been discussing entry controls since the 1940s. There was little difference between the main political parties on this issue, for the Labour Party opposed the 1962 Act but a Labour government passed the 1968 Act.

Were these laws racist? It was claimed that immigration legislation was not racist, for it was concerned with protecting the British way of life and integrating existing ethnic minorities. Frequent reference was made to the danger that immigration would 'swamp' British culture and generate a violent response, as in the famous television interview given by Margaret Thatcher in 1978, shortly before she became prime minister (see box on p. 486).

The problem with this argument was that immigration laws had created entry categories that allowed in most white but kept out most black and Asian migrants. Martin Barker (1981) claimed that these

The main British immigration laws

Main laws	Main provisions	Main laws	Main provisions
1962 Commonwealth Immigrants Act	Distinguished between British passport holders and those holding the passports of independent Commonwealth countries. Restricted the entry of Commonwealth citizens to those with employment vouchers, which were issued in limited numbers.	1971 Immigration Act	Distinguished between *patrials* (see above) holding British and Commonwealth passports and *non-patrials*. Commonwealth citizens who were non-patrials were now treated as no different from any other foreigner. Non-patrials entering with employment vouchers were given work permits and had no right to settle.
1968 Commonwealth Immigrants Act	Restricted entry of British passport-holders resident outside Britain (British passports had been given to a number of Asians living in East Africa). British passport holders could enter only if they (1) had passports issued in Britain or had a parent or grandparent born in Britain (patrials), or (2) came from a Commonwealth country that had become independent by 1948.	1981 British Nationality Act	Not an immigration law as such but a law defining British nationality. The previous category of Citizen of the United Kingdom and Commonwealth was now divided into three categories. The new category of 'British citizen' applied to patrials (see above) only. They alone were given 'full right of abode' in Britain.

▶ Examine each of these laws. Does each law have equal consequences for blacks and whites? Are those excluded mainly black or 'white'?

▶ This is only the briefest summary of each law. If you can, look up a more detailed account in, for example, Solomos (1993) or Mason (1995)

Protecting British culture

'If we went on as we are, then by the end of the century there would be four million people of the New Commonwealth or Pakistan here. Now that is an awful lot and I think it means that people are really rather afraid that this country might be swamped by people with a different culture. And, you know, the British character has done so much for democracy, for law, and done so much throughout the world, that if there is a fear that it might be swamped, people are going to react and be rather hostile to those coming in. . . . We are a British nation with British characteristics. Every nation can take some minorities, and in many ways they add to the richness and variety of this country. But the moment a minority threatens to become a big one, people get frightened'.

Source: Margaret Thatcher, quoted in the *Guardian*, 31 Jan. 1978.

Defending national identity: a Conservative Party rally at the Royal Albert Hall.

cultural arguments were manifestations of a 'new racism'. Its key feature was the use of the language of cultural difference rather than the language of biological inferiority, which had become discredited by Nazism.

Cultural justifications for immigration control do not stand up to examination. British culture is treated as though it is an agreed and clearly defined thing, but it is actually far from clear what it is. It is rather easier to establish what being English, Welsh, or Scottish means. Migrants from Caribbean islands are arguably closer than the Scots to the English character, since they do after all play cricket, and closer than the Welsh-speaking Welsh, since their 'mother tongue' is English. If the Scots and the Welsh are British, why were people from Jamaica treated as non-British? The real answer sems to be that it was because they were black. The cultural-differences argument turns out to be racist, for the only cultural differences that it considers significant are those that follow the lines of skin colour.

Ethnicity, race, and national identity

Exclusion not only took the form of restrictions on black and Asian immigration. Black and Asian people living in Britain were also excluded by cultural racism from the British nation. They might have British passports and full rights of citizenship but this did not make them truly British. As Margaret Thatcher's interview showed, they were regarded as culturally distinct ethnic minorities, which could be tolerated, so long as they did not grow too large.

Stuart Hall (1991) has argued that globalization has intensified racism. Global economic integration and the rise of supra-national political structures threaten the nation state, which has responded with a 'defensive exclusivism'. As Hall (1991a: 26) puts it, with Thatcherism in mind, 'one can see a regression to a very defensive and highly dangerous form of national identity which is driven by a very aggressive from of racism'.

One response to exclusion by whites was the assertion of a counter-ideology of blackness. This originated in 1960s America with the notion of 'black power' and the slogan 'black is beautiful'. As Hall explains from his own experience, 'black' became a political category. In the 1970s this led the black political movement to reject the language of ethnicity and multiculturalism. It appeared to be progressive, for it recognized the value of different cultures and treated people as different rather than superior or inferior. It was also divisive, however, since it emphasized the differences between, for example, Asians and African-Caribbeans, though they experienced the same racism. It concealed the realities of discrimination and colluded with the new cultural racism that we examined above. To Hall, ethnicity and multiculturalism were 'the enemy'.

While the black identity movement and black nationalism enabled blacks to fight back, there has been a growing concern with the negative side of black identity politics. Asians felt that their distinctive cultures were being submerged. Furthermore, not all of those who saw themselves as black accepted the kind of black identity presented. Masculinist versions of black identity were unacceptable to gay blacks and black women. In response to these arguments, Stuart Hall has called for a 'plural blackness' that accommodates internal differences, but he insists that so long as racism exists there will be a need for a black struggle against it (1991b: 56).

Gilroy has argued that an exclusive black nationalism is as bad as an exclusive white one. He rejects the idea that cultures are pure and mutually exclusive. Elements from different cultures can be combined with each other. People can construct their identities from many sources. Thus, blacks in Britain draw elements of their culture from other black communities across the Atlantic but also from British culture (Gilroy 1993: 15). Solomos (1993: 220) has claimed that 'we are witnessing the emergence and flowering of "new ethnicities" which challenge the boundaries of national identity by asserting the possibility of being both black and English'.

This raises the whole issue of the implications of ethnic diversity for national identities. When national identities have a strong ethnic component, a growing ethnic diversity challenges them. The immediate response may be exclusion, and, as we have seen, this was very much what happened in Britain. The argument that immigration was a threat to British culture raised, however, the question of what Britishness actually meant. As Solomos (1993: 220) has put it:

'There is no longer, if there ever was, any certainty about the meaning of 'Englishness' and 'Britishness' in the current political environment. Such uncertainty is certainly not new in the context of British history . . . but what we are seeing at the present time is a profound debate about the definition of the 'nation' and its boundaries in the context of internal social change and external patterns of political transformation.'

Increasing international migration and ethnic diversity generated an exclusive response in Britain, which tried to preserve the racial basis of its existing national identity by restricting immigration and sealing off black and Asian migrants as non-British ethnic minorities. This brought British identity itself into question, however, at the same time as nationalist movements within Britain and European integration were challenging the British nation state.

GLOBALIZATION AND THE NATION STATE

Hall saw globalization as threatening the very existence of the nation state. As we showed in 'Understanding Nations and Worlds' there are a number of arguments of this sort. It is claimed that:

▶ nation states can no longer control their borders;

▶ power has shifted to transnational corporations;

▶ global social movements are challenging governments;

▶ the nation state has lost authority to higher political bodies.

On the other hand, the number of nation states has been multiplying and there is no sign that nationalism has become a less potent force in the world. In this final section of this chapter we examine the relationship between globalization and the nation state.

Uncontrolled communication?

As we showed earlier on pp. 477–8, information can more easily cross national borders than ever before. States have found it increasingly difficult to control the international flow of information and money, which in its electronic form is essentially digital information.

The volume of money circulating electronically between the world's financial centres has now become

---

How blacks became Black

'I was brought up in a lower class family in Jamaica. I left there in the early fifties to go and study in England. Until I left, though I suppose 98 per cent of the Jamaican population is either Black of colored in one way or another, I had never ever heard anybody either call themselves or refer to anybody else as "Black". Never. I heard a thousand other words. My grandmother could differentiate about fifteen different shades between light brown and dark brown. When I left Jamaica, there was a beauty contest in which the different shades of women were graded according to different trees, so there was Miss Mahogany, Miss Walnut etc. . . . But the word "Black" was never uttered. Why? No black people around? Lots of them, thousands and thousands of them. Black is not a question of pigmentation. The Black I'm talking about is a historical category, a political category, a cultural category. . . . I heard Black for the first time in the wake of the Civil Rights movement, in the wake of the de-colonization and nationalistic struggles. Black was created as a political category in a certain historical moment.'

Source: S. Hall (1991b: 53–4).

staggeringly large. In the 1990s global trading in currencies was running at a rate of more than one trillion (a million million) US dollars a day. The movement of money in and out of a country's currency alters its exchange rate, which in turn affects many important aspects of its economy, such as the competitiveness of its exports and the cost of imports. International currency dealing has long existed, but the huge sums of money now moving around the globe mean that exchange rates can change rapidly without governments being able to do much about it. Furthermore, government policies themselves can easily trigger off these movements. Governments seeking to maintain a particular rate have to pursue policies that are considered non-inflationary, for money will otherwise move elsewhere and this will push the exchange rate down.

Governments have also found it increasingly difficult to control the flow of information. Any person with access to a phone line can use a fax or modem to communicate large amounts of information to any other person with receiving equipment anywhere in the world. Similarly, anyone with appropriate equipment can access and download via the Internet large amounts of information from other countries. Dissidents, for example, can transmit anti-government material across frontiers.

Lash and Urry (1994: 6) suggest that to comprehend these changes we need a 'sociology of flows' rather than national structures. Information does not, however, simply flow around the world in an uncontrolled way. It has to originate somewhere, and has to be transmitted and received. States can intervene at all these points. They can also restrict the availability of the technology needed and access to it.

Furthermore, while the amount of information, goods, and people moving around the world has increased, so has the state's surveillance technology. Indeed, in their attempts to control terrorism and drug-trafficking, states rely now not on random searches at borders but on intelligence-gathering operations.

Communications technology is, therefore, at the service of a state as well as those who wish to undermine it. This is not just a matter of surveillance but also one of manipulation. A modem in every house could, in principle, give people uncontrolled access to uncensored information on the Internet, but a television in every house can enable a government to flood the nation with its own account of events by manipulating the news. The idea put about by Internet enthusiasts that technology has taken the world into a new age of individual freedom should be treated with some caution.

Thus, while being aware of the growing problems faced by states in controlling the movement of information and money across their borders, we must also take account of the state's increased capacity to control and manipulate.

TNCs and the state

TNCs pose a particular threat to the authority of the nation state, for they threaten its control over the economy. By shifting investment from one country to another they can move capital and employment between countries. They can also move profits to countries where taxes are low, through internal transfers between their operations. All this makes it hard for the state to control them or organized labour to oppose them. If they do not like a government or a labour movement, they can move their operations elsewhere or, at least, threaten to do so. They can put pressure on states to act in ways that will maximize their profits and on unions to toe the management line. Arguably, we now live in a world where governments and unions have to dance to the tune of the TNC and power has shifted from the nation state to the transnational corporation.

But are TNCs really so powerful and so independent? Hirst and Thompson (1996) argue that very few TNCs are really transnational. Overseas operations will often be concerned primarily with assembling and marketing components produced in the TNC's country of origin. TNCs almost always have a clear national base where their headquarters, research and development division, and main production facilities are located. They benefit from national educational and financial institutions, and from supportive relationships with central and local government. The TNC's management style and corporate culture may also be distinctively national (see Chapter 16, pp. 672–4).

This usefully corrects the idea that TNCs are somehow free floating and detached from nation states. They can, none the less, still move production, employment, and profits across borders. They may depend on their nation state of origin, but they are much less dependent on the other states in which they operate. Governments certainly compete to attract investment by offering TNCs grants and subsidies. While TNCs are rooted in particular countries, their transnational organization does give them some autonomy and considerable leverage on national governments.

Global social movements

The transformation of communications has been linked to new globally organized social movements, which mobilize people across frontiers and bring pressure to bear on both governments and TNCs.

Until the 1980s labour movements were the most powerful social movements. They were focused on the nation state and tried to gain control of the national state apparatus, which they could use to advance the interests of labour. They went into decline in the 1980s, partly because of the increasingly international organization of capital, which they could not match. Although they had international ambitions and connections and often allied themselves with labour movements in other countries, they were not very successful in building international organizations.

☞ **We discuss social movements in a number of other chapters. Our main discussion of them is in Chapter 17, pp. 718–21, and you may find it helpful to look this up as you read this section. You may also find it interesting to link our discussion of environmental issues here with the notion of 'positive welfare', which we discuss in Chapter 18, pp. 761–3.**

New social movements that were more international in character emerged in the 1960s, notably the feminist, peace, and environmental movements. Believing that the world as a whole was at risk from nuclear or environmental disasters, the peace and environmental movements showed a high level of global awareness. The feminist movement became concerned with the growing world wide exploitation of women's labour. There was also a sense that the world's problems were largely due to the activities of TNCs, which could be opposed effectively only through the global organization of political movements.

These movements both reflect and create a new awareness of our individual responsibility for the fate of the world. Beck (1992) and Giddens (1991) have explored these changes in the way that people see themselves and their actions.

There is, first, a growing *sense of insecurity and risk*. People are increasingly aware of the dangers of the world they live in. They are less concerned with the old issues to do with the distribution of wealth and income, and more concerned with the avoidance of risks, such as nuclear war or pollution, that affect the whole world and everyone in it.

There is, secondly, a growing *distrust of experts*. According to Giddens, trust in experts was one of the main features of modern life. In traditional societies people had relied on the personal knowledge and experience of those around them. Industrialization, urbanization, and the growth of nation states led them to depend increasingly on the impersonal knowledge of the expert. They are now, however, more aware of the deficiencies of science and the failure of technology to solve the problems of the world. Scientists and engineers are indeed often held responsible for the world's problems, through, for example, their development of nuclear technology and polluting industrial processes.

Thirdly, there is increasing **reflexivity**. This is the process whereby people observe what happens to them and others, reflect upon life, and decide on courses of action. With the growing distrust of expertise and institutions, individuals increasingly try to puzzle their own way out of the uncertainties and risks surrounding them. Instead of leaving things to the experts, they take personal responsibility for the state of both society and nature.

Political action has begun to take new forms, such as:

▶ direct action against destruction of the environment or harm to animals;
▶ consumer boycotts of environmentally harmful products or goods manufactured by child labour or exported by politically unacceptable regimes;
▶ personal conservation activities such as recycling;
▶ the purchase of rainforest to prevent its destruction.

These movements can successfully bring pressures to bear on nation states and TNCs, which find themselves faced by global organizations that are well able to manipulate the media. Thus, in 1995 the Greenpeace orchestrated threat of an international boycott of Shell products forced the company to reverse its decision to dump a derelict oil rig in the North Sea. Although the

---

Transnational Greenpeace

'It can hardly be denied that, in order to pursue its environmental concerns around the world, Greenpeace has developed into a form of transnational organization comparable in principle and in the global extent of its activities to some of the companies which it opposes. It draws expertise from different nation-states and deploys technology according to its strategic plans. It has learned to lobby governments and to mobilize public support, taking advantage of the global media and the raised consciousness of a global movement.'

Source: Spybey (1996: 146).

Greenpeace vessel *The Rainbow Warrior* could not stop the French nuclear tests in the Pacific in 1995, the publicity it generated led the French Prime Minister to call off all future tests.

'Green consumerism' has also stimulated some stores to switch to 'green products', which they claim are environmentally friendly. This has been viewed with some scepticism, for it can just mean relabelling existing products in order to cash in on the 'green market'. Yearley points out that companies make such changes to their products, where they can do this easily and cheaply, to create a 'green' image and distract attention from other practices. On the other hand, campaigners can then draw attention to those practices that do not fit the image and press a company to justify itself. He concludes that 'on balance, green consumerism is likely to benefit the environment' (Yearley 1991: 100).

Global social movements have certainly won some victories in particular cases. It is more difficult to do anything about the accumulating effects on the environment of steadily rising population, production, and consumption. It is also more difficult to change widespread economic practices, such as child labour, or to change the character of political regimes that systematically violate human rights. When the goals of global social movements collide with the central economic and political interests of nation states, the movements find that they have little real muscle.

The part played by these movements in the UN organized 'earth summit' at Rio in 1992 perhaps sums up their influence. They attracted a lot of publicity, and strongly influenced the debate. They were, however, active mainly at the 'talking shops' of the Global Forum and the Earth Parliament. Although they had some influence on the national delegations, they were largely excluded from the formal sessions. The international agreements that emerged from them were negotiated by the representatives of nation states (Adams 1995).

This raises the issue of what international organizations can achieve in controlling the policies of nation states in environmental matters.

One earth?

Environmental issues are generally considered a key area for global political organization. The radiation from nuclear disasters, such as Chernobyl, or nuclear weapons-testing, circled the globe. Pollution does not recognize national boundaries. Deforestation in one country affects the climate of another. The consequences of climate change due to global warming impact on all countries. It has been suggested that dis-

Can social movements stop the destruction of the rain-forest?

putes over environmental issues, such as water supplies and pollution, are increasingly a cause of international conflict and civil war.

But has global political organization developed far enough to regulate the environmental relationships between nation states? We will examine this question by considering the role of the United Nations (UN), which has taken on the function of coordinating national responses to ecological issues. Its Conference on the Human Environment at Stockholm in 1972 was followed by the founding of its Environment Programme and in 1992 a further conference, generally known as the 'Earth Summit', at Rio de Janeiro.

These world conferences have demonstrated not so much a common interest in 'saving the earth', as a conflict of interest between rich and poor countries. At the Stockholm conference, the rich countries' concerns with resource conservation and pollution control clashed with the poor countries' development goals. The poor accused the rich, who were undoubtedly the world's main polluters and consumers of raw materials, of trying to solve the problems that they had created by restricting the growth of other countries (see Figure 12.11). The poor countries referred pointedly to what they called the 'pollution of poverty'. This conflict led to the compromise notion of *sustainable development* which came into widespread use as a way of trying to reconcile environmental and developmental concerns.

At the Rio conference greater prominence was given to development issues but the same conflict re-emerged between development and conservation. The twenty-seven principles of the Rio Declaration included the sovereign right of countries to develop, which the US

Figure 12.11. Carbon emissions from fossil fuel burning, top ten emitters, 1994

Country	Total emissions (m. tons)	Emissions per person (tons)	Emissions growth 1990–4 (%)
United States	1,371	5.26	4.4
China	835	0.71	13.0
Russia	455	3.08	−24.1
Japan	299	2.39	0.1
Germany	234	2.89	−9.9
India	222	0.24	23.5
United Kingdom	153	2.62	−0.3
Ukraine	125	2.43	−43.5
Canada	116	3.97	5.3
Italy	104	1.81	0.8

Source: Brown *et al.* (1996: 30).

▶ **What is the significance of carbon emissions for the world?**

▶ **Do you think that China and India really belong in this list of the 'top ten' emitters?**

▶ **Which countries pose the most serious threat in the future?**

▶ **What is the significance of this table for international action to protect the environment?**

Pollution and civil war

'Bougainvillea is probably the clearest example of an environmentally induced conflict, in which some 1,000 people have died in the past seven years. Fighting erupted when rebels demanded independence from Papua, New Guinea, after a dispute caused by massive pollution from a copper mine at Panguna. Water was polluted, waterways clogged and fish died as a result of debris from the mine, which polluted one fifth of the island. In 1988 local people demanded changes and compensation. By the end of the year the mine was attacked by saboteurs, and in May 1989 it was closed. The conflict continues, however.'

Source: Christopher Bellamy, 'How Nature is Inflaming the Wars of the World', *Independent*, 29 Oct. 1996.

Sustainable development

The most common and influential definition of sustainable development is 'development which meets the needs of the present without compromising the ability of future generations to meet their own needs' (Brundtland Commission quoted by Adams). More specifically, sustainable development recognizes the need for economic growth but this must be growth that conserves natural resources, maintains the productivity of the land, and protects genetic diversity.

Source: Adams (1995: 355).

▶ **Compare this concept of development with the other definitions discussed in the section on 'development'.**

▶ **Is development generated by global tourism compatible with this definition?**

▶ **Do you know of any examples of sustainable development taking place in your country?**

delegation dissociated itself from. Some $125 billion dollars was required by the United Nations to implement the programme agreed at Rio, but only $2.5 billion was actually pledged, let alone delivered (Adams 1995: 367).

International agreements have emerged from the UN's efforts, but they tend to be vague, since governments will not agree to anything that significantly restricts their freedom of action. International cooperation has had some successes—for example, in reducing the production of chemicals that destroy the ozone layer—but in this case alternative chemicals were available. There is little sign of effective action on the more intractable problem of global warming. Attention is turning from *prevention* to *adaptation*, though those countries that will be totally submerged by rising sea levels may find this difficult.

World government?

Has the United Nations been any more successful in other areas of activity?

It was founded in 1945 at the end of the Second World War as a forum for the discussion of international issues and the settlement of disputes, but it has steadily acquired new functions. International bodies were needed to manage and regulate the increasing movement of people, goods, money, and information between countries. Awareness grew of the global scope of problems such as poverty, disease, and pollution and international organizations were created to coordinate attempts to deal with them. A cluster of such organizations has developed around the United Nations, which by 1996 employed almost 60,000 people.

The United Nations and its organizations have, however, been *international* in character rather than *transnational*. International organizations are importantly different in character from transnational ones. While transnational organizations cut across nation states and threaten their authority, international ones are constituted by nation states, which control them, and also have to act through nation states.

Thus, the United Nations' actions are constrained by the principle of national sovereignty. It can intervene forcibly and effectively if one state attacks another, as the Gulf War showed, but rarely intervenes in the internal affairs of nation states. The UN has no military force of its own. When it sends a military force into a country, this force is composed of units from national armies, which remain largely under the control of their respective nation states. The United Nations is entirely dependent for its resources on contributions from nation states, which are often slow to provide them and may withhold them.

The creation of the United Nations did not change the fact that world politics were dominated by the most powerful nation states. Indeed, the Security Council, the key UN body in peacekeeping matters, is itself dominated by a select and unrepresentative group of nation states, the Second World War victor states—Britain, China, France, Russia, and the United States. For some forty years after its creation, the rivalry between the United States and the Soviet Union anyway shaped world politics. These superpowers settled international issues between them, making little reference to the UN.

The collapse of the Soviet Union fundamentally changed the situation and a 'New World Order' has been proclaimed. It was said that the UN could now assume a more important role in the world and its successful response to Iraq's invasion of Kuwait in 1991 showed that it was able to do this. In practice this new order actually meant American domination. The Gulf War was dominated by American policy and military power and UN interventions are generally dependent on the agreement and resources of the United States.

It may, anyway, be more accurate to refer to a 'New World Disorder'. Although the collapse of the Soviet Union apparently confirmed American political dominance, it also loosened America's grip on its allies, which are no longer forced to take sides by the cold war. Furthermore, it created many new and independent-minded nation states out of the territory of the Soviet Union. The result may be a new disorder, as nation states new and old act more independently, with neither the UN nor the USA having much control over them.

Thus, the nation state does not seem to have lost much of its authority or sovereignty to global political organization. The essentially international rather than transnational character of political organization at the global level leaves the nation state intact. If anything, the UN strengthens rather than undermines national sovereignty. New nation states seek membership because acceptance into this body strengthens them, by giving them recognition, legitimacy, a voice in international affairs, and some protection against attack by other states.

The European Union

Political integration has gone much further at the level of the regional bloc of countries, as in the case of the European Union. It is also at this level that the defenders of the sovereignty of the nation state have shown most concern, at least in Britain.

States have lost some of their law-making and judicial powers to European bodies. Thus, in some matters people can appeal to European law and European courts, which take precedence over national law and national courts. Closer economic union through a single currency will, if it occurs, constrain the economic policies of national governments. Some of their policies, as in the area of agriculture and fishing, are already largely determined within European institutions.

European unification has also diminished national control of frontiers. Control over borders has always been a key issue in nation states, for their territorial integrity and the implementation of national policies depends on the existence of frontiers. One of the features of European integration has been the virtual disappearance of border controls within the EU. The weakening of border controls has made it more difficult for some national policies to be maintained. Thus, the UK government is under pressure to bring its taxation of alcohol and tobacco products into line with other countries, because the massive inflow of these products from countries with lower taxes is threatening the markets of British producers.

European integration has threatened the integrity of nation states in another way. Subnationalisms have been boosted by the links that regions within nation states have made with Brussels, thereby bypassing national capitals. The thirty-two regions of the Atlantic seaboard have formed an organization called the Atlantic Arc. They have a sense of common interest, to some extent a common Celtic culture, and seek financial aid directly from European institutions.

Nation states are, however, involved in the making of European law. They do so by making the treaties, such as the Maastricht Treaty, which provide the framework of the Union. They also negotiate and decide policy through the Council of Ministers. The Presidency and other positions in the European Commission rotate between countries. This means that, although each state has lost some autonomy, it has also gained some influence, which it did not previously have, over other countries.

Nation states also implement European laws and policies. While the European Commission supervises and monitors the application of European laws and treaties, they are implemented by national administrations. There is no European police force or European army. Thus the European Union can only act through the apparatuses of the nation states that make it up.

 This section raises a number of issues related to the definition and development of the state, which we discuss in Chapter 18, pp. 727–9.

Interpretations of the impact of the European Union on the nation states that make it up vary widely. It can be seen as a threat to the nation state or as a structure

Is the nation state in decline?	Areas of change	Arguments for decline	Arguments against
	Advances in communications	Loss of control over borders	Increased surveillance and manipulation of populations
	Transnational organization	Rise of the TNC	TNC dependence on the state
	Global social movements	State policies challenged	Movements ignored and resisted by state
	International government	Authority lost to international bodies	State participation in international regulation
	National identity	Revival of sub-nationalisms and ethnic diversity	New nation states

based on nation states. Hirst and Thompson (1996: 190) conclude that government in Europe has become a more complex and multi-layered process, but the nation state remains at the heart of it.

This issue has become a particularly sensitive one in Britain, perhaps because of the fragility of British national identity. Subnationalisms were strongly established in Britain and British identity was forged through war and empire (see p. 460). With European wars a thing of the past and the Empire gone, there is less holding the British nation together. To use Colley's (1992) terms, the British can no longer bounce their identity off the historic 'non-British others'. The defenders of British identity have tried to maintain it by defining it against the 'others' of ethnic minorities and a Franco-German dominated European Union.

SUMMARY POINTS

Globalization was well advanced by the end of the nineteenth century but it had taken place largely through the structures provided by overseas empires. We began this part of the chapter by examining their collapse and the creation of most of the world's current nation states. We then considered the problems of development faced by these states and the strategies they adopted:

▶ Aid from developed countries has been a mixed blessing that has contributed little to development.

▶ The new nation states adopted varying strategies of industrial and agricultural development, though there are many difficulties with the notion that development can be directed by strategies.

▶ The gap between rich and poor countries has continued to increase.

Poor countries have been seen as facing problems of overpopulation and over-urbanization:

▶ Declining death rates but a continued high birth rate led to rising populations, but some of the more extreme predictions of world population increase may be too high.

▶ One consequence of rising population has been the rapid growth of cities in poor countries and there

has been considerable debate over whether this has led to over-urbanization.

In the wake of the collapse of empire, new forms of global economic integration emerged:

▶ The development of communications technology increased not only the speed of communication but also its cheapness and capacity.

▶ Increasing international competition stimulated the growth of TNCs.

▶ A new international division of labour emerged, though some important qualifications have to be made to this concept.

▶ Global tourism grew rapidly and integrated new areas into the capitalist world economy.

Another important aspect of globalization was the increase in international migration after 1945:

▶ Migration increasingly involved women, refugees, and professional and business people.

▶ A growing ethnic diversity challenged established national identities.

▶ Patterns of ethnic exclusion in Britain were justified by a new racism based on cultural differences, which raised the issue of what it meant to be British.

Globalization challenged the authority and integrity of the nation state:

▶ Global communication made control of borders harder, and TNCs were able to shift capital and jobs between countries.

▶ Globally organized social movements challenged the authority of the state.

▶ Nation states faced cross-border environmental problems but UN attempts to coordinate policies to protect the environment generated conflicts between rich and poor countries.

▶ The United Nations' international rather than transnational character meant that it did not threaten the authority of the nation state.

▶ The growth of the European Union has weakened the nation state's authority in some ways, though it is still nation states that take policy decisions and implement EU policies.

REVISION AND EXERCISES

THE DEVELOPMENT OF NATION STATES

In 'Understanding Nations and Worlds' we examined the relationship between the nation and the nation state, and different approaches to the development of post-colonial nation states:

▶ **Make sure that you are familiar with the main ideas on these issues of Weber, Anderson, Smith, Giddens, and Frank.**

▶ **What do you understand by the following terms: dynastic states, nation states, state nations, and nationalism; development, sustainable development, modernization and underdevelopment; the Third World.**

In 'From Nation State to Empire' we examined the rise of nation states in Europe:

▶ **What were the main processes involved in the development of the modern nation state?**

▶ **What was the relationship between nation states and overseas empires?**

We then considered the new nation states and the problems of development that they faced:

▶ **Do you think that more eonomic aid from rich countries will help poor countries catch up?**

▶ **Is development a matter of adopting the right strategy?**

▶ **Have the problems of overpopulation and over-urbanization been exaggerated?**

▶ **What do you think is the main problem faced by poor countries in achieving improved standards of living?**

▶ **Do you think that the term 'Third World' is still of any use?**

In 'One Earth' we discussed 'sustainable development':

▶ **Do you think that this is a viable option for poor countries?**

GLOBALIZATION

In 'Understanding Nations and Worlds' we discussed the meaning of globalization and later we outlined the ideas of Wallerstein on the growth of 'a world economy':

▶ **What do you understand by the following terms: globalization; international organization and transnational organization; world empires, world economies, and the capitalist world economy; the international division of labour and the new international division of labour?**

In 'National Empires in a World Economy' we examined the first stage of globalization:

▶ **What part did industrialization play in the growth of a world economy?**

▶ **Did the construction of empires unify or divide the world?**

We then examined globalization in post-colonial times:

▶ **What are transnational corporations and how would you explain their rise?**

▶ **How useful is the concept of a 'new international division of labour' in describing the changing relationship between rich and poor countries?**

▶ **What is the significance of global tourism for the process of globalization?**

▶ **Have either global social movements or transnational corporations challenged the nation state?**

► Has the nation state lost its authority to supra-national organizations?

► Do you think that it is correct to say that nowadays people live on 'one earth'?

MIGRATION, RACISM, AND IDENTITY

Globalization involves not only the movement of money and information around the world but also the movement of people:

► **What do you understand by the terms slavery and indentured labour; ethnicity, race, and racialization? (See Chapter 4, pp. 143–5, for a discussion of the last three terms.)**

In 'A World Divided by Races' we examined movements of people and their consequences for the relationships between ethnic groups:

► **What were the main forms taken by the international movement of people?**

► **How did the term 'race' arise?**

► **Why did races become associated with differences of skin colour?**

In 'Migration, Diversity, and Identity' we discussed the new wave of international migration that developed after 1945:

► **Why did international migration increase again and what have been the main changes in patterns of migration?**

► **Why has illegal migration increased?**

► **What reasons are there for considering British immigration legislation to be racist?**

► **Why did the black political movement reject the multicultural approach to ethnic differences and what problems were generated by its emphasis on black identity?**

► **What do you think is meant by Britishness and why is British national identity under challenge?**

FURTHER READING

This chapter covers a wide range of topics and the further reading is therefore divided by topic.

The nation state

Anderson, B. (1991), *Imagined Communities: Reflections on the Origin and Spread of Nationalism* (2nd edn., London: Verso). An unusual and influential collection of essays on the history of the nation.

Hutchinson, J., and Smith, A. D. (1994), *Nationalism* (Oxford: Oxford University Press). A comprehensive reader which contains extracts from the writings of a wide range of authors.

Development

Hulme, D., and Turner, M. M. (1990), *Sociology and Development: Theories, Policies, and Practices* (New York: Harvester Wheatsheaf). Comprehensively covers all aspects of the Sociology of Development.

Spybey, T. (1992), *Social Change, Development and Dependency: Modernity, Colonialism, and the Development of the West* (Cambridge: Polity). Wide-ranging examination of theories of development, relating them to the rise of the West, the nation state, imperialism, the 'Third World', the NICs, and the resurgence of Islam.

Globalization

Allen, J., and Hamnett, C. (1995), *A Shrinking World?: Global Unevenness and Inequality* (Oxford: Oxford University Press). An interesting and varied collection of chapters on communications, transnational corporations, cities, pollution, and global tourism.

Dicken, P. (1992), *Global Shift: The Internationalization of Economic Activity* (2nd edn., London: Paul Chapman Publishing). A mine of information on the economic aspects of globalization.

Waters, M. (1995), *Globalization* (London: Routledge). Provides useful summaries of the various theories of globalization and reviews its economic, political, and cultural aspects.

International migration, ethnicity, and racism

Castles, S., and Miller, M. J. (1993), *The Age of Migration: International Population Movements in the Modern World* (London: Macmillan). Covers all aspects of international migration, and examines different national responses to it.

Mason, D. (1995), *Race and Ethnicity in Modern Britain* (Oxford: Oxford University Press). Provides a very clear and up-to-date examination of the complex issues surrounding migration, ethnic diversity, immigration legislation, and its implications for citizenship.

Solomos, J. (1993), *Race and Racism in Britain* (London: Macmillan). Thoroughly examines the theories and the history of racism, immigration policies, and nationalism.

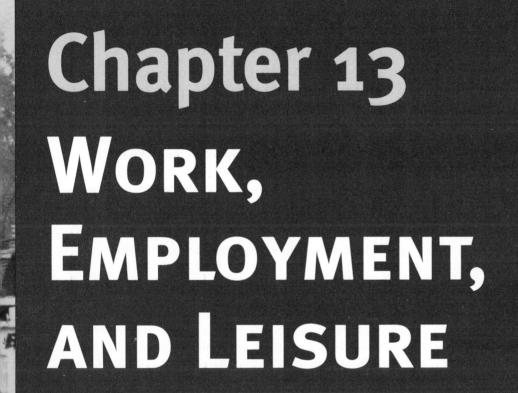

Chapter 13

WORK, EMPLOYMENT, AND LEISURE

The industrialization of catering

'Much of catering is still run along traditional lines; but rationalizing trends are evident everywhere. Sophisticated technology, standardized products, fragmented and routinized production, careful planning are dramatically changing the appearance of eating and drinking places. Frozen food processed in food factories, which at times resemble assembly lines and at times petro-chemical refineries, finds its way not only on fast-food trays, but also in school dining-rooms and hospital wards as well as in *haute-cuisine* restaurants. Even the jargon begins to sound like that of industrial production—cooks reclassified as material handlers, waiters as interface workers, others as crew-members or thawers-outers.'

Source: Gabriel (1988: 8).

W HEN we speak of 'going to work', we have in mind leaving home and travelling to a workplace. We take this for granted, but it was not a regular feature of daily life before industrialization. It was this that created a world of work with its own distinctive relationships and conflicts, organizations, and experiences. It also created employment and unemployment, for work now generally meant work for an employer and the loss of a job resulted in unemployment. And it created leisure, as a distinct part of life, for daily life became divided into work and leisure periods. New industries then emerged to provide products and services for leisure time. In this chapter we examine the impact of industrialization on both work and non-work.

In exploring the world of work, we consider not only the factory and the office but also the home, for the home too is a workplace. Thus, we examine the relationship between paid work in employment and unpaid domestic labour. We discuss the work of servants, the mechanization of housework, and the rise of do-it-yourself. We also take account of homework, which in this context means paid work in the home for an outside employer. This has remained an important source of employment for many people and has indeed recently been growing.

There have been major recent changes in the organization of production, industrial relations, and patterns of employment. We consider the shift of employment into services, which have themselves become industrialized, as our opening piece suggests. We examine the introduction of more flexible forms of production and employment. We also discuss the so-called new industrial relations in Britain and the decline of trade unions. We explore the reasons for the rise of unemployment to a much higher level, the growth of part-time work, and the increasing employment of women in paid work. Lastly we consider the implications of these changes for work at home, the informal economy, and the relationship between work and leisure.

UNDERSTANDING WORK, EMPLOYMENT, AND LEISURE

Our experience of work, employment, and leisure has been shaped by two powerful forces that have transformed the world—capitalism and industrialism. We begin by discussing the meaning of these terms and the relationship between them. We then move on to consider the emergence of a distinct world of work and the relationship between home and workplace, work and non-work.

INDUSTRIAL CAPITALISM

Capitalism and industrialism have been closely linked, for it was their combination in the form of industrial capitalism that led to the transformation of the world. They must, however, be carefully distinguished, for they refer to quite distinct aspects of economic organization.

Capitalism

The basic feature of **capitalism** is the financing of economic activity by the investment of capital in the expectation of making a profit. Capital simply means accumulated money that is available for investment. Money can be invested in this way in any economic activity, in trade, in production or in services, or in agriculture. Capitalism did indeed first develop in trading activities during medieval times and it was not until much later that capitalist production became established. It was, however, capitalist production that transformed society and it is on capitalist production that we shall focus.

Karl Marx (1848) first systematically analysed the nature of capitalist production. He argued that its central feature was the private ownership of the means of production. The **means of production** were the workplace, the tools, and raw materials which made the production of goods possible. It was the capitalist who provided the money to set up a workplace, equip it with machinery, and buy the necessary raw materials. These means of production were therefore the private property of the capitalist and were not owned by the producers, the workers who actually made the goods.

Capitalist production was carried out by **wage labour**. Capitalists employed workers to produce goods in exchange for a wage. Instead of being able to consume or sell what they had made, workers received a wage in return for their labour. The producers had therefore lost control of the product of their labour, which was owned by the employer. They worked not in order to produce something that they could use or sell but in order to earn wages. They had become, as Marx put it, 'wage slaves'.

Market relationships came to dominate capitalist societies. In order to make a profit, the capitalist had to sell products in the market. Equally, producers could not consume what they had produced or produce what they needed to consume. Instead, they had to use their wages to buy in the market everything that they needed or wanted. The link between production and consumption had been broken and was now mediated by market relationships.

Marx emphasized that under capitalism those who produced lost control not only of the *product* of their labour but also the *process* of production. The capitalist employer determined what machinery should be used, how the work should be divided between employees, the hours of work, and the speed of work. This loss of control over the product of work and the process of work resulted in the *alienation* of the worker, a concept which we discuss in 'The Meaning of Work', p. 504.

The interests of the owners of capital and labour were, according to Marx, in conflict. The employer's concern to maximize profits by squeezing as much work as possible out of labour, while keeping wages and salaries as low as possible, meant that the interests of the owners of capital and their employees were inevitably opposed. Marx argued that this conflict of interest would lead to the division of society into two classes, the capitalist bourgeoisie and the working class (see Chapter 15, pp. 613–16 for a discussion of Marx's theory of class conflict). Increasing conflict between these two classes would lead eventually to a revolutionary transformation of society that would bring capitalism to an end.

Industrialism

Capitalist production existed before the Industrial Revolution. In sixteenth- and seventeenth-century Europe

Marx and Engels on capitalism

Although Marx's name is associated with attempts to overthrow capitalism and replace it with communism, he was greatly impressed by the enormous productive potential of capitalism. In the *Communist Manifesto* of 1848, Marx and Engels wrote that

'the bourgeoisie, during its rule of scarce one hundred years, has created more massive and more colossal productive forces than have all preceding generations together. Subjection of nature's forces to man, machinery, application of chemistry to industry and agriculture, steam-navigation, railways, electric telegraphs, clearing of whole continents for cultivation, canalization of rivers, whole populations conjured out of the ground—what earlier century had even a presentiment that such productive forces slumbered in the lap of social labour.' (Marx and Engels 1848: 85)

production in households and workshops was increasingly financed and controlled by the owners of capital. These then began to bring their workers together in larger units called factories and in the eighteenth century developed the techniques of industrial production in order to make higher profits on their capital.

Industrialism refers to the new method of organizing production that became fully established in the nineteenth century. While the development of *power-driven machinery* was central to industrialization, the defining feature of industrialism was the way that production was organized. It was *concentrated* in factories, where work was *divided into specialized tasks* and *coordinated by managers*.

Production was transformed through the introduction of *power-driven machinery*, initially driven by water but then by the steam engine. It was the nineteenth century introduction of steam power that led to the rapid spread of industrialism, for steam engines could be set up anywhere, while travel was transformed by the steam-driven locomotive and the steamship. Hand tools had been controlled by the worker, but in a real sense the worker was now controlled by the power-driven machine, for this determined the speed of work and shaped the work environment.

Industrialization involved the *concentration* of production in large workplaces. Workers could be controlled more easily and more closely if they were brought together under one roof, while the harnessing of water and steam power made it necessary to concentrate production in factories with power-driven machinery. The factory changed the social character of work, bringing large numbers of workers together and enabling them to organize themselves in unions.

The development of technology and the concentration of production led to the *division of labour* into specialized tasks. The division of labour did not begin with industrialization, but factory production resulted in a much more systematic division of work into specialized tasks than had existed before. This made workers highly dependent on each other, for the work of each depended on the work of others.

A whole new range of functions and occupations emerged to enable the *management and control* of the workplace. The concentration of labour, the introduction of new technology, and the specialization of tasks in the industrial factory generated new problems of coordination, expertise, and control. Employers could neither ignore these problems nor handle them on their own and began to employ professional and increasingly specialized managers.

Capitalism and industrialism have been closely related because it was the capitalist's pursuit of more profitable ways of organizing production that drove industrialization forwards. We do, therefore, frequently refer to *industrial capitalism*, but it is important to distinguish between capitalism and industrialism. As we have shown, capitalist production existed before production was organized on industrial lines. Furthermore, capitalist industrialism has not been the only form of industrialism.

The main alternative form of industrialism was developed in state socialist countries. Nineteenth-century socialists considered that the exploitation, inequality, and meaningless work which they saw as typical features of the new industrial society were the result of capitalism, not industrialism. If the *private* ownership of the means of production could be replaced by *common* ownership, a new society could be created where production would be in the interests of all. Attempts were made to create a non-capitalist form of industrial production in some state socialist countries, notably in the Soviet Union, its satellite countries in Eastern Europe, in China and Cuba. State socialism was, however, in the end unable to establish itself as a viable alternative and it collapsed at the end of the 1980s (see Chapter 17, pp. 705–7).

THE WORLD OF WORK

The development of capitalist production and industrialization separated production from the household.

Capitalism and industrialism

Capitalism	Industrialism
▶ Profit drives economic activity	▶ Power-driven machinery
▶ Private ownership of means of production	▶ Concentration of production
▶ Employment of wage labour	▶ Systematic division of labour
▶ Control of process of production by employer	▶ Coordination of production by specialized management
▶ Conflict of interest between capital and labour	▶ Organization of workers in unions

Previously, most production had been carried out in the household, or a workshop attached to it, or on a family farm. Under industrial capitalism the workplace became a world of its own, the world of the factory, the office, the laboratory, the superstore, the factory farm. Indeed, people now spoke of the world of work as though it was quite separate from the rest of life.

Industrial relations

A distinct set of social relationships emerged between employers and workers. These involved, on the one hand, the organization and management of work and, on the other hand, industrial relations. We examine organization and management in Chapter 16, pp. 653–6. In this chapter we consider the development of industrial relations.

The term *industrial relations* refers to the bargaining relationships that developed between employers and workers, not only in factories but also in offices and all other kinds of workplace, in stores or schools or hospitals or restaurants. These relationships became a distinct area of organizational and institutional development.

The process of organization was initiated when workers began to form unions because they were individually weak in the face of the employer. They were dependent on employment for the wages that provided them with a living, but the employer could easily dismiss them and replace them with other workers from the labour market. In exceptional circumstances, such as an employer's need for particular skills in short

supply or an acute general labour shortage, individual workers could have some power over the employer. Generally speaking, however, they have been in a weak position as individuals and have acquired strength only through collective organization. Worker organization then stimulated counter-organization by employers, who created employers' associations.

Organization led to the gradual **institutionalization of industrial conflict**. This refers to the process by which conflict became increasingly organized and regulated by institutional arrangements. Unions and employers entered into collective agreements which regulated the relationship between them. These agreements specified matters such as wage rates and conditions of employment but also laid down procedures for dealing with disputes and for negotiating agreements.

It was the unions that initially pushed for collective agreements, for these reflected the collective strength of workers and protected the individual worker. Employers often fought against collective agreements to start with but then generally came to recognize that they were in their interests too, for they regulated worker behaviour, reduced disruption, and generally made industrial relations more stable and more peaceful. The first collective agreements operated within particular factories or companies, but the growing organization of both sides of industry led to the negotiation of industry-wide agreements. In Sweden, where both workers and employers became more organized than in any other country, the practice of negotiating central agreements covering all workers and all employers became established in the 1930s (Fulcher 1991a).

Institutionalization has often resulted in the development of procedures of *mediation* and *arbitration*. Mediation occurs when an outsider is brought in to help the two sides reach agreement. Arbitration goes further by giving the outsider the power to decide a settlement. Governments have frequently become involved in the process of institutionalization by creating institutions of mediation or arbitration in order to avoid as much as possible the disruption and disorder resulting from open conflict.

It is important to emphasize that the institutionalization of conflict did not mean that it came to an end. Conflict took place within the framework of the negotiation procedures set up to regulate it. Open conflict anyway still occurred when negotiations broke down. Institutionalization also itself generated conflict, for it led to conflicts between the leaders of organizations and their members. One consequence of institutionalization was the rise of unofficial strikes, when workers took action locally in defiance of the agreements reached by their leaders.

We examine the relationship between institutionalized and open conflict in 'Industrial Conflict', pp. 508–12.

The meaning of work

The creation of separate workplaces also meant that the experience of work now became a distinct part of life. Those in paid work were spending a considerable proportion of their daily lives in the workplace. Furthermore, this experience was shaped by aspects of the work situation that were largely outside their control. The technology, the pace of work, and the work environment were controlled by the worker's employer.

According to Marx (1844), work had been a creative means of self-expression, but the development of capitalism turned it into a non-creative activity. Traditional craftsmen had worked at their own pace in their own way in their own workshops with their own tools, creating whole and unique products, which belonged to them. The pace of factory work was set by a machine in an environment controlled by the employer. Work was fragmented by the division of labour and workers had no sense of making a complete object. They produced standard and characterless goods owned by the employer. Instead of work being a means of self-expression, it was merely a means of earning a living.

This loss of the creative aspects of work was characterized by Marx as a process of **alienation**. There are four main aspects of this idea:

▶ Since the worker had lost control of the product, it had become an alien object. The worker had no feelings for it, no attachment to it, or pride in it.

▶ With loss of control over the product went loss of control over the process of production which dominated the worker as an alien and oppressive force.

▶ Workers also became alienated from each other. Competition for employment in a labour market made it difficult for them to cooperate with each other.

▶ To Marx creativity through work was central to human nature. The loss of creativity meant that humanity had become *alienated from its true self*. Work under capitalism was therefore dehumanizing.

Durkheim (1893) challenged this view and argued that the growing division of labour would not have such degrading consequences, because it created a new interdependence between workers. This interdependence would give a sense of participation in a common enterprise that would make work more rather than less meaningful. Instead of producing alienation and conflict, the division of labour would lead to cooperation and harmony. Durkheim used the analogy of the human body, where organs were specialized but worked together in a harmonious fashion to produce what he called an organic solidarity.

Durkheim's views were not as far apart from those of Marx as they appear to be, for Durkheim did recognize that the division of labour would have these integrative consequences *only if* people were able to carry out freely chosen tasks appropriate to their abilities. The difference between them was that Marx believed that this was quite impossible in a capitalist society, while Durkheim thought that it would normally be the case. When it was not, perhaps because social change had been too rapid, society was, according to Durkheim, in an abnormal state of anomie (see Chapter, 2, p. 40).

Marx and Durkheim were concerned with the impact of industrial capitalism on work, but many different kinds of work situation have emerged within industrial societies, and we examine these on pp. 512–18.

OUTSIDE THE WORLD OF WORK

Industrialization not only created a new world of work, it also changed people's ways of thinking about their work and non-work activities.

Work at home

We discussed the experience of work as though work always means paid work outside the home. Commonly used phrases such as 'going to work' or 'hours of work' define work in this way, as does the term workplace. Where, however, does this definition of work leave housework or homework?

One of the problems in this area is that the definitions of the various kinds of work that go on in the household are far from clear. It is important first of all to distinguish two key terms:

▶ **Domestic labour.** This refers to all work concerned with maintaining the household. It includes both housework and domestic production, as well as other tasks that we discuss below.

▶ **Homework.** This is not writing essays at home but paid work carried out at home for an outside employer.

Domestic labour in the household takes up a large part of people's daily lives. Although it has not tradi-

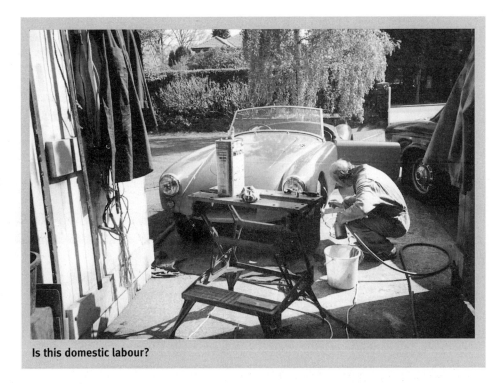

Is this domestic labour?

tionally been counted as economic activity, it undoubtedly makes an enormous contribution to the economy. People can only carry out paid work if they are fed, clothed, housed, and kept both mentally and physically well, but most of the work that goes into maintaining them in this state is provided by unpaid domestic labour. Its importance has recently been recognized in official attempts to measure its contribution (see p. 506).

Domestic labour consists of a wide range of different kinds of work. The routine cleaning and maintenance tasks of *housework* are different from *domestic production*, such as baking cakes, making clothes, or growing vegetables. Other tasks, such as roof repair or decoration, are concerned with *domestic capital*, for they maintain or increase the value of property. There are also *management* tasks which deal with family finances, the distribution of domestic labour between its members, and the supervision of their work. *Emotional labour* is yet another kind of task, which is not concerned with the physical maintenance of the household but with its members' emotional needs (see Chapter 10, p. 388).

Domestic labour can also be carried out in various ways. There is, first, the *unpaid labour* of the household members. There is, secondly, *waged domestic labour*, when, for example, maids, gardeners, or au pairs are paid to carry it out. There is, thirdly, an important and often omitted source of labour, *informal cooperation*. This can range from reciprocal baby-sitting arrangements to local systems for exchanging tokens that represent amounts of labour.

This focus on domestic labour should not lead you to think that this is the only kind of work carried out at home. There is also homework. Since industrialization, most people have earned their living in a separate workplace but some have continued to carry out paid work for an employer at home. Much of the finishing-off work in the textiles industry has been done by homeworkers. The development of communications and information technology has given homework in the form of telework a new lease of life in recent times. Most of this book has been written and edited at home!

The home is then a workplace, within which many different kinds of work go on. The Sociology of Work should concern itself not just with paid work outside the home but with all work going on in the society. Glucksmann has developed the concept of the *total social organization of labour* (TSOL) in order to express this idea. The TSOL refers to 'the manner by which all the labour in a society is divided up between and allocated to different structures, institutions, and activities' (Glucksmann 1995: 67). This concept makes central to the study of work the relationships between the different forms that it takes. It enables Glucksmann to

The value of unpaid labour

Government statisticians have used data on how people spend their time to calculate the value of unpaid labour. They estimate that unpaid labour is worth somewhere between £341 billion and £739 billion pounds a year to the economy of Great Britain. The lower figure makes it worth 56 per cent of the gross national product (GNP), while the higher figure makes it worth 122 per cent of GNP—i.e. making a significantly greater contribution than the whole of the formal economy. The big difference between these figures reflects differences in the valuation of work. If it is valued at a wage rate that is average for the economy as a whole, the result is the higher of the two figures. If it is valued at the much lower wage rates typical of paid work in catering and childcare, the lower figure is arrived at.

Unpaid labour consisted of travel to work (labour services), routine housework activities such as food preparation (domestic current), and unpaid work for others (voluntary work).

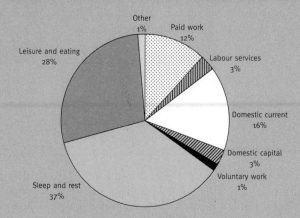

Figure 13.1. **Time use by adults, Great Britain, 1995**

Source: Murgatroyd and Neuberger (1997: 67).

▶ **The valuation of unpaid labour presents one major problem in arriving at these estimates. What other problems can you think of? How, for example, would you classify shopping or gardening in the time use categories?**

examine, for example, the relationship between mass production and changes in domestic labour, an issue that we will take up later in 'Home as a Workplace', pp. 518–20.

Employment and unemployment

With industrialization, work became identified with employment. Those who made their living by providing goods and services without working for an employer were now the exception rather than the rule. This was shown by the way they became described as *self-employed*. If people lost their jobs or were unable to find paid work, they now fell into the new category of those who were *unemployed*. If they were unemployed, they were considered 'out of work', however hard they might be working, say, to forage for fuel or grow their own food or make their own clothes.

The definition of unemployment presents many problems. The employed are not simply all those who are not in paid work, for those who are ill, retired, or in full-time education are not considered unemployed. To be unemployed people must at least be *available* for paid work and availability is not so easy to determine. Some people may be available for work but not actually seeking it, because, for example, they have developed an alternative lifestyle. Should they be considered unemployed?

The official definition of unemployment determines the size of the figure for the unemployed. This is a polit-

> ▶ **Which of the following would you consider to be unemployed?**
> - All those not in employment?
> - People who are 'out of work' and available for it?
> - Those who are out of work who are seeking it?
> - Part-time workers unable to find full-time work?
> - Retired people who still want to work?
> - Students unable to find vacation work?
> - People who are between jobs?
> - Those receiving unemployment benefit?
> - House-husbands and housewives?

ical matter, for the number of unemployed is a politically sensitive issue. As we show in Chapter 3, pp. 109–11, there have been many changes in the official definition of unemployment, which have mostly had the effect of reducing it.

Unemployment is sometimes described as enforced leisure. This presents, however, a quite misleading image of it. The search for work is hardly a leisure activity. The experience of unemployment, as we show on pp. 520–3, has seriously damaging consequences for those involved. It may lead people to engage in new forms of unpaid work, as they seek to provide goods and services for themselves in a non-market way. The drop in income suffered by the unemployed makes it much more difficult for them to participate in many normal leisure activities, such as taking holidays.

Work and leisure

In daily life we commonly distinguish between work and **leisure**. This distinction makes a sharp division between work and non-work activities and commonly treats them as opposite in character. Work is seen as alienating, while leisure is a time of freedom, individual choice, self-expression, and creativity.

Should, however, such a sharp distinction be made? Stanley Parker (1976) showed how in some situations work is not sharply distinguished from leisure. He identified three different work-leisure patterns and linked them to differences between occupations:

▶ *The segmentalist pattern.* This broadly matched the conventional work–leisure distinction. It was found amongst routine clerical or unskilled manual workers, particularly those, such as fishermen or miners, working in harsh or dangerous conditions. These workers saw work as a means to earn a living, found that it provided few opportunities for work satisfaction, and had little control over their work. Leisure was an escape from alienating work. (See 'The Working-Class World', Chapter 15, pp. 617–19.)

▶ *The extension pattern.* This did not fit the conventional distinction. In this case work interests spilled over into non-work time. It was characteristic of business people, professionals, and skilled workers, whose work was involving and satisfying. Those who worked in these occupations did not treat work as a negative experience and leisure as an escape from it.

▶ *The neutrality pattern.* This was an intermediate pattern, where there was no sharp opposition between work and leisure but also no extension of work into leisure time. It was typical of semi-skilled manual and clerical workers.

The extension pattern shows that a contrast should not be drawn between work as a negative experience and leisure as a positive one. While work can be a positive experience, leisure may not always be as positive as the work–leisure distinction suggests. The emergence of leisure industries, and the manipulation of the consumer by the mass media and advertising, suggest that leisure may not simply be a time of choice, freedom, and creativity. There are pressures to consume as well as pressures to work. Furthermore, the pressure to consume may lead to passive forms of leisure, such as television-watching. Indeed, some work activities may well be more creative and self-expressive than many leisure activities.

It has also been argued that the work–leisure distinction reflects a particularly male way of looking at the world. It does not take account of the housework that has been the main daily activity of many women, for housework is neither paid work nor leisure. Furthermore, when women are employed in paid work, they generally have to carry out housework at other times. Thus, non-work time can only become leisure if the housework is done by someone else. It could be done by the wage labour of maids and cooks, etc., but in twentieth-century Britain it has most commonly been done by housewives. The work–leisure distinction has applied, therefore, most clearly to the lives of married men in full-time employment with full-time housewives.

There are then many problems with the distinction between work and leisure. As we shall show in 'The Development of Leisure', pp. 523–6, industrial capitalism did, however, lead to a separation of work and leisure activities in workers' lives. While we must be aware of the problems it poses, we must also consider that it did become a meaningful distinction. Whether it is still meaningful is another matter, which we discuss in 'A Leisure Society?', pp. 543–5.

SUMMARY POINTS

We began by discussing the meaning of capitalism and industrialism, and the relationship between them:

▶ Capitalism refers to the investment of capital in any economic activity in the expectation of making a profit, and is characterized by the private ownership of the means of production and wage labour.

▶ Industrialism refers to the mechanized production of goods or services organized on the principles of concentration, the systematic division of labour, and specialized management.

We went on to discuss the emergence of a separate world of work:

▶ A distinct set of organizations and institutions emerged to regulate conflict at work.

▶ Marx and Durkheim provided conflicting interpretations of the impact of industrial capitalism on the experience of work.

We then examined the relationship between workplace and home, and work and non-work:

▶ The home too should be considered a workplace, where various forms of domestic labour are carried out, partly on the basis of waged labour, and paid work is sometimes carried out for outside employers.

▶ There are many problems with the work–leisure distinction, but industrial capitalism did lead to a separation between work and leisure activities in workers' lives.

THE IMPACT OF INDUSTRIAL CAPITALISM

In this section we examine the main features of the new world of work created by industrial capitalism. This concentrated labour in the workplace and generated industrial conflict. It made the experience of work a distinct and central feature of people's lives, and it separated work from non-work—the workplace from the home, the employed from the unemployed, and work from leisure.

INDUSTRIAL CONFLICT

Industrial capitalism generated industrial conflict. Capitalist production brought about a conflict of interest between the owners of capital and wage labour. This was quite simply because profits depended on keeping labour costs to a minimum by paying workers as little as possible for as much work as possible. Industrialization then concentrated workers together in large units and made it easier for them to organize themselves in unions and stand up to the capitalist employer.

Workers organized themselves in different ways, however, and pursued different strategies, while employers too became organized and developed counter-strategies. Before considering industrial conflict, we need first to consider the process of organization on both sides of industry.

Organization and strategy

Historically the first organizational form was the *craft union*. The first strong unions in Britain were the craft unions that established themselves during the second half of the nineteenth century. They were based on the principle of organizing workers within a particular craft or occupation, such as printing. Indeed, the term **trade union** originally meant an organization that brought all members of a trade or craft together, though it was later generalized to refer to any collective organization of workers.

The main strategy pursued by craft unions was to control entry to an occupation. They kept wages high by keeping the supply of labour under their control, which they were able to do because their members were skilled workers, who had acquired their skills through training controlled by the craft. They used their control of labour to get employers to accept the principle of the *closed shop*—that is, that only those who were members of the union could be employed in a particular workshop. Employers countered this strategy by seeking to employ less skilled labour, a process known as *deskilling*. This could be done by breaking work down into simpler tasks or by introducing machinery that could be operated by workers with less skill (we discuss deskilling on p. 514).

This form of worker organization tended to be exclusive and divisive, for its main objective was to create and maintain a monopoly of jobs for its members. The British craft unions often opposed the organization of unskilled workers, which they saw as a threat to their control of employment and their superior wages. They were also highly patriarchal and excluded women from membership. It was not until 1943, when the demand for labour generated by the Second World War had led to the widespread employment of women in factories, that the main British engineering union allowed them to become members (Walby 1986: 196).

 The nineteenth-century exclusion of women from employment is discussed in Chapter 10, p. 367.

A similarly exclusive strategy has been operated by professions, whose associations have operated rather like craft unions. They too have established their bargaining power by restricting entry and controlling the training and certification of members. Thus, during the nineteenth century the British medical profession established control of entry through the registration of medical practitioners and the control of medical education. As with the craft unions, this involved the exclusion of women from membership (Witz 1992).

The second form of organization was the *industrial* or *general* union, which was created by less skilled workers unable to control entry to particular occupations. Examples of industrial unions are unions of textile workers or steelworkers. General unions organized unskilled workers across industrial boundaries and typically emerged where strong craft unions blocked the development of industrial unionism, as in much of British industry.

Industrial and general unions relied on collective bargaining and use of the strike weapon. They were inclusive in character, seeking to organize as many workers as possible, regardless of their skill. Because of their open and inclusive character they have tended to adopt socialist ideologies based on the principle of class organization and class action. They have also been associated with centralizing tendencies to develop national union federations that could mobilize the strength of the working class as a whole.

Employers responded to the development of this kind of unionism by developing counter-organizations.

Faced by unions that stretched across a whole industry, they organized themselves into matching employers' associations. National union federations were countered by national employer confederations. Employers' associations developed the weapon of the lockout. If faced with strikes within an industry, they would often respond by locking out all union members, seeking to exhaust the unions' funds by forcing them to support large numbers of out-of-work members.

The third main form of organization was the *labour* or *social democratic* party. Labour parties have provided an alternative means of advancing the collective interests of labour through political rather than industrial action. In a democratic political system they could bring to bear the numerical advantages of the working class, for workers' votes far outweighed those of the employers. In this situation, the employers' strategy was to themselves support and fund political parties and use their influence over the state to counter the actions of a labour government.

 We discuss labour movements and the development of the British Labour Party in Chapter 17, pp. 694–6. In Chapter 18, 730–1, we discuss the relationship between labour movements and the state.

Strikes

The term industrial conflict is often taken to mean strike action, but this is quite wrong. When considering industrial conflict it is important to make a number of basic distinctions:

▶ between *institutionalized* and *open* conflict;

▶ between *different forms* of open conflict;

▶ between *collective* and *individual* expressions of conflict.

We discussed the *institutionalization* of industrial conflict in 'Industrial Relations', pp. 503–4. As we argued there, institutionalization did not mean that conflict ceased, even if there was no open conflict taking place.

Open conflict commonly takes the form of strike action, but in some situations it may be more effective to use other weapons. Workers can bring considerable pressure to bear on employers by refusing to work overtime or going slow. One form of going slow is the work-to-rule, which involves working to the letter of workplace rules. Workers can carry out 'non-strike

Labour organization, strategy, and response

Labour organization	Membership	Strategy	Employer response
Craft union	Skilled workers	Control of entry	Deskilling
Industrial union	All workers in an industry	Collective bargaining	Employer associations
Labour party	All workers	Use of political power	Influence on parties and state

actions' of this sort without breaking agreements or contracts and can continue to draw their pay. Open conflict may also be initiated by employers declaring lockouts.

In situations where workers are unorganized or unable to act collectively, discontent may take the form of *individual* action, such as going sick or simply staying away from work. The term absenteeism is used for this kind of individual refusal to work. The line between individual and collective action may, however, become blurred, for unions may advise their members to go sick or may coordinate absenteeism.

While industrial conflict must not be confused with strikes, they have been the most disruptive weapon used by workers and have been extensively studied. The most common method used in studying them has been to analyse trends and variations in the amount of strike action, though there have also been some important case studies of particular strikes (Gouldner 1965; Lane and Roberts 1971; Friedman and Meredeen 1980). In Britain the main source of information on strikes has been the Department of Employment (this information is now collected by the Office of National Statistics). Since 1980 the periodic Workplace Industrial Relations Surveys have collected important data on both strikes and non-strike action (Millward and Stevens 1986; Millward *et al.* 1992).

As we show in Chapter 3, pp. 107–8, there are many problems with official statistics. The official statistics on British industrial disputes present three main difficulties:

▶ reporting;
▶ definition;
▶ measurement.

Reporting. The initial source of information for those collecting the statistics is either press reports or reports by employers. For a strike to be reported by an employer, a work stoppage must first be defined as a strike. Batstone *et al.* (1978) have shown that the decision to treat a work stoppage as a strike is itself a social process. Depending on their situation, managers may take a tough line with workers and define a stoppage as a strike or prefer not to do so because they do not wish it to be known that they have a 'strike problem'.

Definition. If a strike is reported, there is a further definitional problem because the official statistics exclude very small disputes that involve fewer than ten workers or last less than one day, unless they result in the loss of more than 100 worker days. The official definition also excludes political strikes. The official definition does not, however, distinguish between strikes and lockouts.

Measurement. There are two main ways of measuring the amount of strike activity. The first is *annual worker days lost* per thousand employees. This figure reflects both the size of strikes and their length. The second is *strike frequency* per thousand employees. Strike frequency data are important as an indicator of the readiness of workers to take strike action, but they are less reliable. Most strikes are short, and, the shorter the strike, the less likely it is to be reported or included by the official definition. The figure of worker days lost, on the other hand, is mainly determined by large or long strikes that are certain to find their way into the statistics. The problems with frequency data particularly affect international comparisons, for reporting and definitional practices vary considerably between countries.

Let us first consider the trend of strikes. In a well-known study, Ross and Hartman (1960) argued that there had been a general decline of the strike in all the main industrial societies as industrial conflict became institutionalized. They rather rashly characterized this as 'the withering away of the strike'. In Britain there

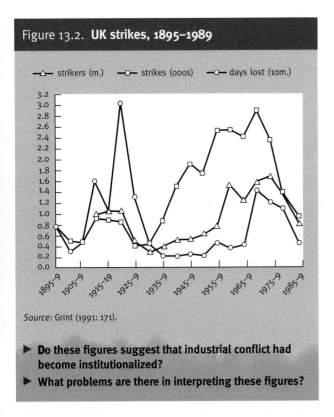

Figure 13.2. **UK strikes, 1895–1989**

—△— strikers (m.)   —□— strikes (000s)   —○— days lost (10m.)

Source: Grint (1991: 171).

▶ **Do these figures suggest that industrial conflict had become institutionalized?**

▶ **What problems are there in interpreting these figures?**

had certainly been a considerable decline in the worker days lost through strike action after the 1920s. Strike frequency, however, was considerably higher in the 1950s and 1960s than it had been earlier in the century. Furthermore, the figure for worker days lost rose again in the 1970s (see Figure 13.2).

Why did industrial conflict increase during these years? Strikes in the 1950s and 1960s were mainly unofficial, which means that they were initiated by workers or local leaders without the approval of the central leadership. Two main explanations have been provided for the rise of the unofficial strike:

▶ the bureaucratization of unions;

▶ the inadequacy of institutions.

The gap opened up by bureaucratization between the leaders and members of unions is one explanation of unofficial strikes. Unions became increasingly bureaucratic as they grew in size and appointed officials to manage their internal affairs and represent their members. According to Roberto Michels's famous 'iron law of oligarchy' (oligarchy means rule by a few), these officials became a self-perpetuating group that cooperated with employers and no longer represented the interests of their members. Unions became undemo-cratic organizations in which decisions were taken by the leaders without reference to the membership (Michels 1912). Research has shown that, although there are plentiful examples of unions that have developed in this way, their internal relationships have varied considerably (Hemingway 1978).

It was also argued that British institutions had become inadequate and unable to channel and regulate industrial conflict effectively (H. A. Clegg 1976). Archaic organizational and institutional structures had been inherited from the nineteenth century. Complex patterns of trade unionism meant that in many workplaces there were competing unions representing different groups of workers. Union leaders were frequently in conflict with shop stewards, local union officials who were widely blamed for unofficial strikes. Employer organization too came under heavy criticism, for it had not kept pace with changes in industrial structure and industrial relations. British industrial relations were in a disorderly state.

Large strikes then reappeared in the 1970s with the return of the official strike. This marked a broad shift by the union leadership from cooperation with the government to conflict. Union leaders became increasingly concerned at the growth of membership discontent over their cooperation with government incomes policies. There were also a number of major conflicts as the unions defied government industrial relations reforms and incomes policies.

Major attempts were made in the 1960s and early 1970s to reform British industrial relations, but these failed and merely brought governments into disastrous conflicts with the unions. The conflicts had very important consequences, however, since they prepared the way for the legislative onslaught on union power in the 1980s, which we examine in 'Industrial Conflict and the State', pp. 533–4.

 It is important to put this industrial-relations disorder and the attempts to reform industrial relations in the context of a wider economic and industrial crisis. We discuss this in Chapter 18, pp. 745–8.

The strike rate has varied considerably across industry and this has led to theories of the strike-proneness of industries. Kerr and Siegel (1954) showed that what they called the 'isolated mass' industries were particularly strike-prone. Miners, lumberworkers, dockers, and seamen lived in isolated, single-occupation communities where worker solidarity was very high and there were frequent, large, and long conflicts with

Figure 13.3. **Changes in strike rates in selected industries, United Kingdom, 1980–1996**
Working days lost per 1,000 employees

Year	Mining, energy, and water	Manufacturing	Services	All industries and services
1980	259	1,961	42	520
1985	7,518	183	86	299
1990	245	228	44	83
1996	9	24	71	59

Source: Sweeney (1997: 222).

▶ **Which area of the economy had the highest strike rate in each of these years?**

▶ **Do these figures suggest that some industries are more strike-prone than others?**

employers. There is certainly evidence to support this theory but it does not provide a complete explanation of strike patterns. Car-industry workers, for example, have not lived in isolated communities of this sort, but the car industry has been highly strike-prone in Britain (H. A. Turner *et al.* 1967).

The whole notion of the strike-proneness of particular industries is in fact hard to sustain. There are, first, international variations in strike rates. As Hyman (1972) has pointed out, the steel industry has been highly strike-prone in some countries but not in others. There are, secondly, considerable variations between companies or workplaces in particular industries, as Herbert Turner *et al.* (1967) showed in their study of the British car industry. There are, thirdly, changes in the relative strike rates of different industries (see Figure. 13.3).

It is difficult to arrive at any general explanation of strike rates. The reason for this is that strikes occur only after a complex sequence of events in which many factors are involved. Let us consider the steps that must be gone through before a strike occurs.

For a strike to occur, workers must be sufficiently discontented to be willing to take action and lose pay. Discontent is not enough, however, for strikes require solidarity and organization. Divisions within a workforce may weaken solidarity. The leaders of the union may discourage strike action because they have just

negotiated an agreement with the employer or because the union has insufficient funds to support a strike. A strike may not, anyway, be the most appropriate form of action and other tactics, such as a work-to-rule, may be more effective. Action of any kind may not be necessary if the employer decides to make concessions and avoid the disruption that a strike would cause. A settlement may be negotiated and the threat of strike action may be enough to force concessions from the employer.

There are patterns in strikes, but they are complex patterns that do not lend themselves easily to simple explanations. For a strike to occur a whole set of conditions must be met and at any point a change in one of these conditions can lead to the strike being called off. What mainly matters, of course, to those involved is not whether a strike occurs but whether their demands are met or whether an acceptable compromise can be reached.

THE EXPERIENCE OF WORK

We now turn to consider the impact of industrial capitalism on the experience of work. We discuss, first, the effects of different technologies and then examine the way in which the experience of work has been shaped by factors outside the work situation. In considering these issues, we examine both manual and clerical work.

Technology and the meaning of work

Writing in the nineteenth century, both Marx and Durkheim were concerned with the impact on work of the new system of industrial capitalism that was establishing itself at that time. Industry has changed greatly since, and many different work situations have been created. From the much later standpoint of the mid-twentieth century, Blauner (1964) explored the issue of variations in alienation. The interest of his study lies not only in its subject matter but also in the way that he developed and applied the concepts of Marx and Durkheim, which we discussed earlier on p. 504.

Blauner considered that technology was central to the way that work was organized and experienced. He saw technology as developing through four stages:

▶ craft production;
▶ machine-based factory production;
▶ assembly plants;
▶ automation.

Although these were historical stages in the development of technology, each of them still existed. He took printing as his example for craft production, textiles for the machine-based factory, the car industry for the assembly plant, chemicals for automation.

These examples were appropriate at the time of his study in the 1950s, but it is important to bear in mind the changes in technology that have happened since. Printing, for example, has been transformed by the development of information technology and can no longer be considered an example of craft production. The car industry still operates on assembly-line principles but many operations have been automated and are carried out by computer-controlled machinery. All the technologies examined by Blauner do, none the less, still exist. Craftwork, for example, has not disappeared and the demand for craft products has if anything increased in recent years.

In order to study the effect of different technologies on the experience of work, Blauner had to operationalize the concepts developed by Marx and Durkheim so that he could measure the degree of alienation experienced by workers. His first step was to sort out the different ways in which the work situation could affect the worker. From the writings of Marx and Durkheim he extracted four dimensions of alienation:

▶ powerlessness;
▶ meaninglessness;
▶ isolation;
▶ self-estrangement.

Self-estrangement largely resulted from the effects of the other three dimensions on the experience of work. It referred to workers' inability to express themselves through their work or involve themselves in it. It is very similar to Marx's idea that workers are alienated from their true selves. As Blauner (1964: 26) put it: 'When work encourages self-estrangement, it does not express the unique abilities, potentialities, or personality of the worker'.

Each of these dimensions then had to be broken down into aspects of the work situation that could be measured. Indicators had to be found for each of his dimensions. Blauner established the following indicators for the powerlessness dimension:

▶ non-ownership of the means of production and the product of labour;
▶ inability to influence general managerial policies;
▶ lack of control over the conditions of employment;
▶ lack of control over the immediate work process.

Scope for making work more meaningful?

So far as non-ownership was concerned, he agreed with Marx that this characterized all workers under capitalism. All therefore experienced some degree of alienation. His other indicators of powerlessness varied, however, from industry to industry, producing different degrees of alienation.

Blauner then applied all four of his dimensions to each of his four industries, using data from a survey of attitudes to work in the United States and case-study material (see Figure 13.4 on p. 514).

He found that printing retained much of the character of a pre-industrial craft and showed low levels of alienation. Workers had high security of employment and considerable control over the work process. They experienced their work as meaningful and were well integrated into an occupational community. They were consequently involved in their work and expressed themselves through it. They were not self-estranged.

Textiles workers, who exemplified machine-minding technologies, had little economic security and little control over their work, which they found repetitive and unfulfilling, but they too were strongly integrated into their local small-town communities. The bonds of family, religion, and neighbourhood counteracted to some degree an alienating work situation and made work a meaningful activity.

Car workers on assembly lines also had little control over work or employment and their highly subdivided

Figure 13.4. **Operationalizing the concept of alienation**

MARX **Alienation**	DURKHEIM **Anomie**

BLAUNER   **Dimensions of alienation**
1. Powerlessness
2. Meaninglessness
3. Isolation
4. Self-estrangement

Indicators of powerlessness	Printing	Textiles	Cars	Chemicals
1. Separation from ownership	✓	✓	✓	✓
2. Inability to influence management	✗	✓	✓	✗
3. Lack of control over conditions of employment	✗	✓	✓	✗
4. Lack of control over work process	✗	✓	✓	✗

▶ Try applying Blauner's dimensions to any work situation that you have experienced.

▶ In Chapter 3, pp. 95–6, we discuss whether Blauner accurately operationalizes Marx's ideas. Look at what we say there and see what you think.

work was even less satisfying than that of textiles workers. Furthermore, social integration did not compensate for alienating work conditions, for they worked in large, anonymous plants, had few social contacts at work, and lived in large cities. They were the least involved in their work and the most alienated.

Chemical workers, who operated highly automated processes, had greater security of employment and more control over their work. Their responsibility for large-scale operations gave them a sense of involvement in their work, though they could experience periods of boredom when everything was running smoothly. They were well integrated into work teams in a relatively small labour force. Like the printers, they showed low levels of alienation.

This led Blauner to conclude that alienation increased with industrialization, until it reached its maximum with the assembly plants of the car industry, but with automation it returned to a level characteristic of pre-industrial work. Much of the alienation generated by industrial capitalism could be removed by the development of more advanced technologies that made work satisfying and meaningful again. Although Blauner had accepted that under capitalism workers inevitably experienced some degree of alienation, his study presented industrial work in a much more positive light than Marx had done.

The idea that automation has reversed the tendency towards increasing alienation has, however, been challenged by later work. Braverman has been particularly important in the discussion of the consequences of automation. His starting point was that automated work was said to require higher levels of education, intelligence, and mental effort, but there was growing evidence that it produced unsatisfying and meaningless work (Braverman 1974: 3). How were these contradictory perspectives on automation to be reconciled?

Braverman argued that the labour process under capitalism is characterized by **deskilling**, which is essentially the separation of mental work from manual work. Mechanization enabled management to turn work into a series of simple, repetitive tasks that required little training and little mental effort. Mental work was concentrated in management, in the occupations that planned, organized, and controlled the work process. The advantages of deskilling to the employer were that it made labour cheaper and increased employer control of the work process. According to Braverman, automation was but the latest stage in this process.

Is the worker in control?

He was very sceptical of Blauner's argument that workers in the chemical industry had meaningful work. The monitoring of chemical processes was a routine matter that required little skill. The only knowledge it needed was the capacity to read a dial. A case study by Nichols and Beynon (1977) supported this view of work in the chemical industry and argued that control work could be lonely and meaningless. However automated an industry was, it did anyway still employ many workers carrying out traditional kinds of manual work.

So why did people think that automation led to more skilled and meaningful work? Braverman argued that it could result in a limited and temporary increase in such work. In its early stages it created a small number of highly skilled jobs concerned with installing and programming the machinery, planning the work process, and sorting out teething troubles. Once auto-

mated production had been established, operations became routine and tasks were deskilled.

Critics of Braverman argued that he did not take account of workers' capacity to resist deskilling or of the generation of new skills. Paul Thompson (1983) reviewed the literature and concluded that, although technological change may at times generate new skills or workers may for a while resist attempts to deskill their jobs, deskilling remained the central tendency of the capitalist labour process. There is, however, as we shall show later, some evidence of rising skill levels in the 1980s.

A more general issue is, however, raised by the work of both Blauner and Braverman. What is the significance of technology for the meaning of work? Is this determined by technology in the way that both in their different ways suggest?

The significance of technology?

While Blauner considered that it was technology that had the main influence on the degree of alienation experienced by workers, his own study showed that this was not the only factor. The social isolation of machine-work in the textiles industry was, for example, reduced by integration in the community. Similarly, the degree of powerlessness must be related to the strength of trade-union organization, which cannot be explained by technology alone.

Work tasks are determined not by technology but by the social organization of work. Braverman focused his analysis on the *scientific management* approach, which dominated management thinking in the United States, and emphasized the division of labour and the detailed managerial control of the work process (see Chapter 16, pp. 655–6). The later *human-relations* school of management thinking sought to raise productivity by integrating workers and providing more satisfying work. Boredom could be relieved by moving workers between tasks (job rotation), expanding a worker's range of tasks (job enlargement), or giving workers more responsibility for the organization of their work (job enrichment). Nor was this solely a matter of management initiative, for workers themselves have some scope for varying their work and making it more meaningful (see photo on p. 513).

 We discuss the development of managerial thinking on the organization of work in Chapter 16, pp. 666–8. The *Affluent Worker* study is discussed in Chapter 15, pp. 631–2.

Catering work

Gabriel has examined the experience of work in catering. One of the workplaces that he studied was the catering department of a community centre in a northern British city. He found that it demonstrated well Braverman's analysis of scientific management (sometimes called Taylorism after Frederick Taylor, its most prominent exponent):

'The cook-freeze kitchen was a faithful adoption of Taylorist principles in mass catering, splitting up cooking from planning, breaking up work-tasks into simple and tightly controlled routines, and reducing the skill, initiative and thinking required of the cooks to a virtual minimum. . . . All freedom and creativity, the hallmarks of craft cooking, are eliminated through rules aimed at preventing the cooks

from 'messing about with the recipes'. Monotony and lack of variety prevailed, each day being the same as the next.' (Gabriel 1988: 87–8)

He also found, however, that the women who worked in this kitchen made their work more meaningful by taking responsibility for meeting production targets, and controlling the pace and distribution of work. Their shared interests and common home backgrounds also made work bearable by generating a feeling of togetherness that 'provided consolation for jobs devoid of interest'. They, none the less, felt trapped in their jobs and unable to seek more interesting work, because the department's work hours and holiday periods were compatible with their domestic and childcare obligations.

But was the meaning of work simply a matter of what went on in the work situation? The *Affluent Worker* study by Goldthorpe, Lockwood, Bechhofer, and Platt (1968a) of workers in Luton during the 1960s argued that the attitudes that people *bring to* work shape their experience of it. This was a study of workers in three companies in Luton during the 1960s. It covered three of the technologies examined by Blauner, the Vauxhall car assembly plant, machine-based work at the Skefko ball-bearing factory, and automated production at Laporte Chemicals.

This study found that technology was related to the amount of *work satisfaction* experienced by these workers, but also that there was remarkably little variation in their *attitudes* to their work. These were instrumental, for they saw work as a means to earn the money they needed, rather than a means of self-expression. Their work was not in fact a *central life interest*. What mattered in their lives was not their work experience or relationships but their private life at home, their possessions, and their families. Since their work situations were so different, these attitudes could not come from an alienating work experience and must have been brought into the workplace.

The *Affluent Worker* study introduced the important concept of **orientation to work** to describe the attitudes that workers brought with them to work. Orientations were shaped by prior socialization, social background, earlier experiences of life, and the influence of the media. Orientation to work then mediated between the characteristics of the workplace, such as its size and technology, and workers' experience of it. The Luton workers typically held an *instrumental* orien-

tation to work, but Goldthorpe, Lockwood, *et al.* also identified *bureaucratic* and *solidaristic* orientations to produce a typology of orientations. The solidaristic one was typical of the more traditional worker community, the bureaucratic one of white-collar workers.

The Luton workers were not typical of workers in general. The high wages of this area had attracted mobile workers from all over the country. Highly instrumental workers had been selected out. The authors of the study were well aware of the distinctive character of the Luton labour force and, indeed, studied it for this very reason.

The importance of this study is that it challenged the assumption that attitudes to work were simply a response to the work situation. It would be wrong, however, to go to the other extreme and conclude that the work situation is of no significance. Other studies of more stable and less extreme workforces have shown that variations in technology do affect attitudes to work (Beynon and Blackburn 1972; Wedderburn and Crompton 1972). Orientations to work should not, anyway, be seen as wholly external to the workplace, for they will be shaped in part by a worker's previous work experiences or, indeed, those of other people.

So far we have considered studies of British and American workers, operating within a basically Anglo-Saxon culture. Gallie's (1978) study of oil refineries in Britain and France examined international differences in orientations to work. His choice of highly automated plants also meant that he could test Blauner's theory that automation would lead to declining alienation.

Gallie concluded that Blauner's theory was cultur-

Orientations to work

Orientation	Meaning of work	Involvement in organization	Involvement in work	Relationship between work and non-work life
Instrumental	Work as source of income	Calculative only	Work not a central life interest.	Sharp separation
Bureaucratic	Service to organization in exchange for career	Moral obligation to organization	Career a central life interest	Social aspirations and status related to career
Solidaristic	Work as a group activity	Identification with enterprise or work group	Work a central life interest	Strong occupational community

Source: adapted from Goldthorpe and Lockwood *et al.* (1968a: 38–41).

ally specific. The British refineries did broadly fit his model, for the workers were integrated and had few grievances. In France, however, they were in a continual state of conflict with an arrogant and exploitative management, whose authority they did not accept. The French workers believed there should be a general extension of worker control over all areas of management. The British workers certainly criticized management but their criticisms were mainly of managerial inefficiency. This highlighted the differences between the British and French plants, for criticisms of this kind implied an acceptance of managerial goals and did not challenge the legitimacy of management. Although the British and French refineries operated the same technology, worker attitudes were very different.

In accounting for these differences, Gallie first referred to differences of management. In Britain, management was willing to negotiate with the unions and conceded some control over work organization to union representatives, but in France the unions were excluded and managers were uncompromising. While this stance generated conflict with labour, it was also a response to the French labour movement, which was more radical, more politicized, and more threatening to management. Gallie could not explore the origins of these differences, given the limits of his study, but he had demonstrated that attitudes to work which appeared to be the result of technology were in fact culturally specific.

White-collar work

White-collar work has often been treated as quite different from manual work. In the classic British study of white-collar workers Lockwood (1958) argued that in the 1950s their work, market, and status situations differed from those of manual workers. They had a more personal relationship with their superiors, while 'much clerical work is specific, non-repetitive, requiring a modicum of skill and responsibility and individual judgement' (Lockwood 1958: 42–3). As we showed above, Goldthorpe, Lockwood, *et al.* considered that a distinct bureaucratic orientation to work was associated with white-collar work. According to Braverman, however, the same deskilling processes have operated in white-collar as in manual work and its distinctiveness has entirely disappeared.

☞ **Braverman and other Marxist writers have argued that a process of proletarianization turned white-collar workers into members of the working class. We discuss changes in the class situation of white-collar workers in Chapter 15, pp. 621–3.**

The clerk's situation was changed by bureaucratization and mechanization. Bureaucratization led to the creation of large offices with standard procedures that took much of the discretion and personal contact out of clerical work. The career opportunities for the white-collar worker declined as the number of routine jobs grew. Braverman argued that the mechanization of clerical work and the application of the principles of scientific management led to the subdivision of tasks and deskilling, just as it had done with manual work.

In a study of white-collar workers carried out between 1979 and 1981, Crompton and Jones (1984) examined the effects of automation on a largely female workforce of clerks in three types of workplace—local-authority departments, an insurance company, and a bank. The result was a greater fragmentation of work into specialized, low-skill, routine tasks. Instead of giving the clerks more control over their work, automation actually shifted control into the hands of senior administrators. Automation had increased alienation. Crompton and Jones did, however, find that their greater contact with the public did make work more satisfying and more meaningful for the bank clerks.

Crompton and Jones also examined the significance of the career, which was central to the notion of a bureaucratic orientation to work. Here they made two main points. First, white-collar occupations have become increasingly stratified by a promotion barrier. There were a relatively small number of positions involving skill and responsibility which had good promotion prospects and were filled by entrants with high educational qualifications. The broad mass of routine clerical jobs involved little skill and little likelihood of significant promotion. Secondly, it was mainly the men who got promoted. The lower grades were largely filled by women, whose promotion prospects suffered because of lower educational qualifications and career breaks to have children.

Crompton and Jones considered whether women had a different orientation to work. They expected to find that women's socialization into domestic roles would lead to less interest in work but they found that women's attitudes to work were very similar to those of men. There was no evidence that women were less involved in their work.

Women were less *career* oriented than men, though this difference required careful interpretation. Young women with qualifications seemed as eager for promotion as young men. Interest in promotion fell off rapidly with age, marriage, and children, suggesting that career interests were abandoned as women took on traditional family roles. Leaving work to rear a family had more effect than anything else on attitudes towards promotion. Thus, 79 per cent of young, unmarried women showed an interest in promotion as opposed to 29 per cent of those who returned to work after bringing up children (Crompton and Jones 1984: 156).

Crompton and Jones pointed out, however, that one should not assume that the younger women in their sample would follow down this track, for their generation had grown up in a different world where equal opportunities had become a more important issue. They also had more qualifications than the older women. Career attitudes resulted, therefore, from a complex interaction between socialization, education, work situation, stage in the life courne, and generation.

WORK AND NON-WORK

In pre-industrial society, people worked, enjoyed themselves, and looked after their homes but they did not use the concepts of employment, leisure, and housework to describe these activities. It was the shift of production from the household by industrialization that created these ways of categorizing the activities of daily life. We now move on from industrial work itself to consider the impact of the development of industrial capitalism on work and non-work outside the factory.

Home as a workplace

Industrial capitalism separated the production of goods and services from the household. As we argued earlier, the home remained a workplace, however, in which many different kinds of work took place.

Paid work depended on the unpaid work of women in the home to reproduce labour. Women did become employed in industrial work, particularly in the textiles industry, but they were excluded from most other industrial occupations. Paid work was anyway treated as secondary to their main role as housewives and they were expected to do the housework as well.

Routine housework was not the only unpaid labour that was carried out by women in the home. They continued to carry out important productive tasks. Thus, the household's clothing was not just provided through the purchase of factory made-clothes. Some clothing was still made at home. Indeed, production at home was facilitated by one of the new industrial products, the sewing machine.

Paid work was not carried out only in the workplace. Employers could economize on workplace costs and pay very low wages by giving work that did not require factory machinery to women at home. They were in a weak bargaining position because of their isolation

Women were not only housewives: an early twentieth century dress-making factory.

and their domestic responsibilities. A lot of this kind of work was carried out in the textiles industry, where spinning, weaving, and dyeing were carried out in factories but the 'finishing-off' of clothes was done by homeworkers. Although industrialization had shifted the bulk of production out of the household, it had also resulted in the emergence of a new form of homework.

☞ We discuss the reproduction of labour in Chapter 10, p. 358, and the domestic division of labour and its relationship with industrialization in Chapter 10, pp. 366–7.

Most women who took paid work were not in fact employed in the textiles industry but in waged domes-

tic labour in middle-class households. Women's employment in domestic service was not new, but the character of this employment had changed. They had previously been treated as members of the family but they were now increasingly seen as wage labour. Thus, the development of industrial capitalism led not only to wage labour in factories but also wage labour in the home.

Domestic labour changed in character during the twentieth century with the growth of clerical work and mass production. The cost of labour rose as the demand for women's labour in offices and factories grew. As the employment of domestic servants dwindled, the gap they left was filled in three different ways. First, mass-produced labour-saving machinery reduced the time taken to do some household tasks. Secondly, domestic production declined and finished products, particularly food products such as bread, were increasingly

Figure 13.5. Distribution of the labour force by sex and occupation, Great Britain, 1841 (%)

Occupation	Women	Men	Total
Domestic service	14.3	3.7	18
Textile etc.	8.1	12.8	20.9
Agriculture and fishing	1.2	21.1	22.3
Professional	0.7	1.6	2.3
Food and drink	0.6	3.9	4.5
Manufacturing	0.6	9.6	10.2
Transport etc.	0.1	2.8	2.9
Mining	0.1	3.2	3.3
Armed forces	0.0	0.7	0.7
Commercial	0.0	1.4	1.4
Building	0.0	5.4	5.4
Public administration	0.0	0.6	0.6
All others	0.6	6.9	7.5
Total occupied	26.3	73.7	100

Source: Grint (1991: 66).

▶ **What does this table tell us about the work done by women in the nineteenth century?**

Figure 13.6. Housework and industrial work

Workers	Percentage experiencing		
	Monotony	Fragmentation	Speed
Housewives	75	90	50
Factory workers	41	70	31
Assembly-line workers	67	86	36

Source: Oakley (1974: 87).

bought. Lastly, middle-class wives found themselves having to do more housework. Indeed, the time spent by working-class and middle-class housewives on routine domestic tasks had become virtually the same by the 1960s (Gershuny 1988).

In the 1970s, Oakley carried out a path-breaking study of housework as work. She examined the experience of housework in the same way that industrial sociologists like Blauner had studied industrial work and found that housework was characterized by monotony, the fragmentation of tasks, time pressure, and social isolation. When she compared her findings with data on work satisfaction from the *Affluent Worker* study, she found that housework was not only more alienating than industrial work in general; it was apparently more alienating than assembly-line work, the most alienating form of industrial work.

Oakley found no relationship in housework between technology and work satisfaction, but, as she pointed out, the relationship between machine and worker is different in housework. In industrial work the pace of the machine controls the speed of work, but the house-

wife controls the pace and rhythm of housework. The alienation of housework is not, therefore, related as closely to technology as it is in industrial work. The pressures of housework were different, for they came from the standards and routines that governed its performance. Dusting could, for example, be done several times a day, once a week, or considerably less often. While mechanization could in principle save time, it also led to the more frequent repetition of tasks.

Oakley argued that in the absence of a wage the housewife had to find other rewards of a psychological kind, and it was in the meeting of standards that housewives obtained what satisfaction they could from housework. These standards varied considerably and were defined by the housewife but became powerful constraints that seemed to her to be external forces. Standards originated largely from the socialization process which transmitted norms of housework from one generation to the next, though there were other influences, such as the media.

Oakley demonstrated that housework, like industrial work, could be analysed in terms of the satisfaction or dissatisfaction that it gave, but also that it was different in character. The routines of housework were not imposed in the same way. But because they were psychological, the pressures generated by standards were greater than the external pressures of paid work. Paid workers could also leave the workplace and, at least temporarily, escape from its pressures. The housewife could not do this so easily.

Unemployment

The distinction between employment and unemployment goes back to the emergence of industrial capitalism. Work came to mean work for an employer. If their

Work in pre-industrial times

'A labouring family around 1700 normally got its support, not from just one or two sources, but from a variety of activities. . . . Even in places where few commons existed, many people had small cottage gardens where they could grow potatoes, cabbages, peas and beans; cottagers very commonly kept a pig or two, which could be fattened on almost anything; some had chickens or geese, a few kept bees . . . Some of this produce they sold in the market, much of it they consumed directly. For most of them farm labour was an important source of income; and increasingly country people were taking up ancillary employments—spinning, weaving, knitting, glove-making, metalworking, and the like—to supplement the livelihood they gained from agricultural wages, a smallholding, or common rights.'

Source: Malcolmson (1988: 58).

paid work ceased, workers became unemployed. A new category of people, the unemployed, had come into existence.

People were often out of work in pre-industrial societies, but their pattern of work was so irregular and included so many different economic activities that a clear distinction between the employed and the unemployed could not be made. Thus, a household could combine farming activities with craftwork, collecting the products of the countryside, and paid work when it was available.

Industrialization changed all this. Industrialists required their employees to work continuously for long hours so that expensive machinery did not stand idle and the profits on the capital invested in production were maximized. No longer could work in manufacturing be combined with other kinds of work. When, however, production became unprofitable, there was no basis for continued employment and factories closed. Unemployment then had a devastating effect on workers and their families, for they had become entirely dependent on paid work for their livelihood. Furthermore, the concentration of particular industries in cities or regions meant that, when an industry went into recession, the possibility of finding alternative work was minimal.

Industrial capitalism by its very nature has provided insecure employment. The economic cycle has generated periods of intense work as the economy booms, followed by slumps when demand collapses, production

ceases, and people are thrown out of work. Intense competition can also lead to the sudden closure of companies driven out of business. The high rate of technical change can result in the replacement of workers by machines and whole occupations can become obsolete. As industry spread, international competition increased and new industries elsewhere could take away markets.

Unemployment has had serious consequences for the individual and the society. For most of the population of working age, employment in paid work is the main source of income, but the impact of unemployment on the individual is not just financial. Warr (1983) has listed six benefits of employment that are lost when unemployment occurs:

▶ *Money.* Employment is the main source of income.
▶ *Activity.* It enables the development of skills and competences.
▶ *Variety.* The experience of work gives greater variety to life and by providing income makes possible activities and experiences, for example through holidays, not otherwise available.
▶ *Temporal structure.* Work hours and work routines give a structure to daily life.
▶ *Social contacts.* Employment provides the main means through which people make social contacts outside the family.
▶ *Personal identity.* For many people their work is central to their identity and the means by which they make a contribution to society.

The experience of unemployment has also been seen as going through a number of stages. Four have been commonly identified:

▶ *shock*: the initial shock on learning the news;
▶ *optimism*: an initially optimistic search for work;
▶ *distress and pessimism*: a growing concern about the future and a lowering of expectations when the search fails;
▶ *resignation and adjustment*: acceptance of the situation.

While there is evidence to support these analyses of the effects and experience of unemployment, they present universal models that do not take account of varying social situations. Ashton (1986) has argued that the meaning of unemployment varies. Those in middle-class occupations are more likely to be financially cushioned through savings but may suffer a serious psychological loss, because their work allows self-expression and is important to their identity. Skilled workers may well experience unemployment in a similar way and have some cushioning through redundancy payments. Unskilled or semi-skilled workers are in a different situation. They are less likely to receive redundancy payments and are more affected by loss of income but suffer less from a loss of identity, for they express themselves less through their work and take an instrumental attitude towards it.

 You might like to compare our discussion of the impact of unemployment with our earlier discussion of the meaning of work and orientations to it on pp. 512–16.

The effects of unemployment also depend upon its duration. The longer people have been unemployed, the more difficult it becomes to re-enter employment, partly because motivation diminishes, partly because technologies and occupations change, so that previous experience becomes out of date. Long-term unemployment leads to poverty and dependence on the state. A vicious circle can develop that makes unemployment self-perpetuating.

Unemployment has wider consequences for society as a whole. There is plentiful evidence that it leads to higher levels of physical and mental illness, divorce, crime, and violence (Ashton 1986; Gallie and Marsh 1994). Unemployment and other social-security benefits paid to the unemployed may seem inadequate to those receiving them but they are a major item of state expenditure, while unemployment also reduces the state's tax revenue and, therefore, its capacity to pay out benefit. So far as the economy is concerned, unemployment reduces spending power and therefore the demand for goods and services, thereby throwing other people out of work and threatening to cause a cumulative decline of economic activity.

The problem posed by unemployment eventually generated political, ideological, and welfare issues that became central to the politics of industrial societies. The first government response to unemployment was to help people cope with it on an individual basis by providing labour exchanges and national insurance. Unemployment benefit was introduced by the National Insurance Act of 1911. The experience of mass unemployment in the 1920s and 1930s led to the 1940s acceptance of Keynesian economic policies (developed by the economist John Maynard Keynes) designed to prevent unemployment by managing the economic cycle. Welfare provision and economic management had become functions of the state.

It must also be recognized that unemployment has some positive consequences for employers and for the state. It provides a *reserve army* of people available for work, which helps to keep down wage levels, undermine collective bargaining, and reduce union membership and militancy. It has been argued that a certain level of unemployment is beneficial, because it damps

The reserve army of labour

The concept of the **reserve army of labour** played an important part in Marx's theory of capitalism. He argued that, as capitalism developed, labour was increasingly replaced by machinery. This created a reserve army of the unemployed, which made workers available for the further expansion of production. The reserve army also kept wage-levels down and forced workers to submit to a more intense exploitation of their labour, by increasing the competition between workers for jobs. Indeed, Marx believed that wage levels were wholly determined by the size of the reserve army. While it is generally accepted that the amount of unemployment has a considerable effect on wages, this argument took no account of the role of trade unions in pushing up wages through collective bargaining or the part that the state can play in fixing wage rates.

The notion of a reserve army has been taken up by feminist writers, such as Beechey (1987), who argues that married women in particular are part of the reserve army. They can be drawn into production when there is a shortage of labour and returned to the household to resume their primary role as housewife when no longer required. This happened in Britain during the First and Second World Wars but also in the 1960s, when a labour shortage developed in British industry. The growth of part-time work enabled women to continue performing their domestic role. Women's wage rates are lower than those of men, because their domestic role is their primary role, so the availability of female labour depresses wage levels. Beechey emphasizes that it is the 'sexual division of labour' and traditional assumptions about the role of women that make them part of the reserve army.

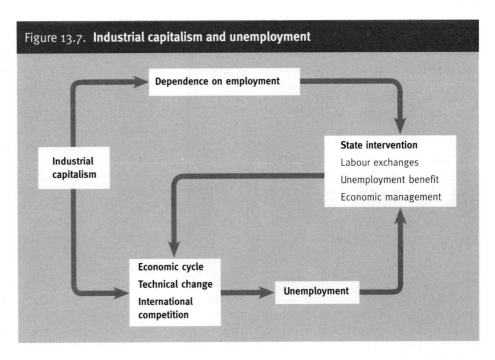

Figure 13.7. **Industrial capitalism and unemployment**

down inflation, forces people to work harder in order to keep their jobs, and increases international competitiveness. Governments that give a higher priority to these matters may decide, as in the early 1980s, to allow the level of unemployment to rise.

The development of leisure

Recreational and creative activities, such as sport or play or painting or conversation, that are commonly regarded nowadays as leisure pursuits have existed since the earliest known human societies. The idea of leisure as something distinct and separate from work was, however, another result of the impact of industrial capitalism on daily life. It is important to understand that 'leisure' is not simply a descriptive term for these activities but a way of thinking about them.

In pre-industrial times, the days of the landed gentry were largely occupied with activities such as field sports, gambling, social occasions, reading, eating, and drinking. These were seen not as recreational activities for non-work hours but as normal pastimes. Work activities were considered inappropriate to their class and socially demeaning. Their wealth enabled them to employ others to carry out both the management of their estates and the running of their households. Their lifestyle demonstrated their wealth and signified their high social status to others.

The poor necessarily spent most of their time in productive activities as they tried to provide themselves with a living, though there were some clear non-work times in their lives. There were seasonal festivals, such as Christmas and Easter, and saints' days, when there were fairs and sporting events. But there was no clear distinction between work and leisure time in daily life, for work hours were generally irregular and often seasonal. At harvest-time, for example, work would be day-long, while at slack periods of the year there might be no work available. Work and leisure activities were not sharply separated. Thus, the pre-industrial craftsman determined his own pace of work and could combine it with other activities. Craftwork, anyway, had a creative quality and work was not a meaningless activity that had to be balanced by recreation outside work hours.

Industrialization was associated with a very different attitude towards work. Capitalist entrepreneurs put their time and energy into *generating* rather than *spending* wealth, while their employees were required to work regularly and continuously in a disciplined manner.

This focus on work might seem opposed to the whole notion of leisure but it had the effect of creating leisure as a distinct part of people's lives. Since the regulated, supervised and continuous work typical of the factory did not permit the mixing of work with non-work

Clocking on.

and children. Sunday Observance Laws were enforced and extended to prohibit most commercial activity on Sundays. In 1871 four bank holidays were created. Later, in 1938, the Holidays with Pay Act was passed and paid holidays gradually became a normal feature of work-life.

The creation of 'free' leisure time for workers did not mean that they could simply be left to enjoy their leisure as they pleased. As early nineteenth-century factory-owners sought ways of controlling the work behaviour of their employees, a campaign began to regulate and 'improve' their non-work lives as well. This was not just due to the employer's need for disciplined labour, important though this was, for there was also the problem of maintaining order in the cities. The urban poor, who worked and lived in appalling conditions, engaged in disorderly, sometimes violent, political and recreational activities.

Leisure activities became increasingly regulated and organized. Traditional popular pastimes, such as drinking, bull-baiting, cock-fighting, and dog-fighting, could be tolerated and contained within the established and relatively stable framework of rural communities but endangered social order in the cities. By 1835 a law had been passed to prohibit sports involving cruelty to animals. From 1830 to 1914 a series of laws increasingly restricted the opening hours of public houses. Disorderly pre-industrial sports were brought within a framework of increasingly detailed rules of behaviour. Local sporting activities were organized within the framework of the club, with its members, officials, rules, and committees. Sports eventually came under the control of bodies, such as the 1863 founded Football Association, which regulated competition nationally.

activities, work and leisure became separated and leisure time had to be created for such activities. Employers themselves concluded that it was better to channel leisure into clearly organized holiday periods when their factories shut down than have production interrupted and disorganized by workers taking time off during traditional holiday periods. Then, as workers became organized, their unions pressed for shorter working days and a fixed number of working hours per week.

The state too played an important part in the development of leisure by creating a legal framework for it. Health and welfare concerns, the pressure from religious movements to protect Sundays, and demands from the labour movement for shorter hours and restrictions on the work of women and children, all put pressure on governments to pass laws that extended and protected leisure time. The Factory Acts of the 1840s and 1850s restricted the hours of work of women

Why did seaside resorts grow in the nineteenth century?

New leisure activities were developed, particularly by the growing middle class and the 'respectable' skilled section of the working class. They established their social status though leisure activities that were different from both the traditional pastimes of the landed gentry and the popular entertainments of the poor. They sought 'improving' recreations compatible with their religious values, and the growth of a civic, municipal culture in the new cities led to the emergence of publicly funded colleges, libraries, museums, and art galleries to improve the mind. Local clubs for sports such as cricket, bowling, cycling, and swimming improved the body. Tennis, golf, and croquet became popular and socially exclusive sports for the middle class.

In a capitalist society the growth of leisure also gave new opportunities for profit-making and led to the rise of leisure industries. The emergence of the weekend stimulated the commercialization of sport, particularly through the Saturday afternoon football match. Football itself became a capitalist enterprise towards the end of the nineteenth century, and the popularity of football and horse-racing provided the basis for the development of a gambling industry. By the 1930s sixteen times as many people gambled through the

football pools on the results of matches as actually went to watch them (Royle 1987: 269).

The spread of the railways enabled cheap and fast travel to sporting fixtures and seaside resorts. Organized tourism dates from 1841, when Thomas Cook of Leicester arranged a railway trip to a temperance meeting at the neighbouring town of Loughborough

Key steps in the nineteenth-century commercialization of football

▶ Charging for entry to matches
▶ Wages for players
▶ Transfer fees
▶ Investment of capital by local businessmen
▶ Formation of a union by players
▶ Emergence of professional management
▶ Clubs becoming limited companies
▶ Formation of Football League (1888)

▶ **Can you think of any further examples of commercialization that have happened since?**

for some 400 people. Cook went on to organize international holidays, pioneer the conducted tours and the guidebook, arrange travel and hotel bookings, and ultimately create the package holiday. As Lash and Urry (1994: 262) have put it: 'Cook's was responsible for a number of innovations which transformed travel from something that was individually arranged and full of risks and uncertainty into one of the most organized and rationalized of human activities based on considerable professional expertise'.

During the twentieth century new manufacturing industries emerged to provide the *mass-consumer* products, such as cars, televisions, and washing machines, that became used during non-work time by most people. *Mass production* depended on a steady demand for products and this provided an opportunity for the rise of yet another industry, advertising. Leisure time, leisure activities, and the marketing needs of both consumer goods and leisure industries in turn provided the conditions in which the modern *mass media* could emerge (see Chapter 8, pp. 284–90).

The significance of leisure had changed since the early years of industry. The first industrialists tried to make their employees work long hours, for this enabled them to keep their costs low and maximize their profits. But by the twentieth century the economy increasingly revolved around the consumption of goods and services during leisure time. One person's leisure provided another person's employment. Production had now become dependent in a quite new way on the earnings, non-work activities, and spending patterns of the population as a whole. Mass consumption also made it possible for governments to manage the economy in Keynesian fashion by controlling purchasing power through taxation or control of credit. Consumption, production, and state economic management had become interdependent by the 1950s.

SUMMARY POINTS

In this section we first examined the generation of conflict in the workplace:

▶ Workers became collectively organized but labour strategies varied between the control of entry, collective bargaining, and political organization.

▶ The institutionalization of conflict eventually led to a decline in the worker days lost through strike action but strike frequency later increased and large conflicts returned in the 1970s.

We went on to consider the experience of work and the ways in which it has varied:

▶ Blauner demonstrated that the degree of alienation varied within industry and related this variation mainly to differences in technology.

▶ The experience of work does not depend solely on technology, however, because the social organization of work also varies, while workers' attitudes to their work reflect their orientation to it and differences in culture.

We then examined the changing relationship between work and non-work:

▶ Although industrial capitalism separated production from the household, this remained a workplace, where housework, domestic production, and homework all took place.

▶ It resulted in workers becoming dependent on employment and frequently experiencing unemployment because of the instability and change characteristic of capitalist economies.

▶ It also led to the creation of leisure, which became organized and increasingly commercialized, as leisure industries grew and mass production generated mass consumption.

THE TRANSFORMATION OF WORK, EMPLOYMENT, AND LEISURE

During the period of economic expansion from the end of the Second World War to the early 1970s industrial capitalism continued to develop along the lines established before the war. Mass production and mass consumption flourished, while the high demand for labour resulted in full employment. In Britain the labour movement continued to grow and Labour governments alternated with Conservative ones. The unions saw off various attempts to reform them.

All this changed in 1970s and 1980s Britain. Established industries went into decline. Unemployment rose sharply and new forms of insecure, part-time, and temporary employment emerged. Men lost jobs, while women became increasingly employed in paid work.

The labour movement declined, while the Conservatives entered an eighteen-year period of government and passed a series of laws to control union behaviour. The development of communications and information technology transformed both work and leisure. In this section we examine the main changes in work, industrial relations, employment, and leisure since the 1970s.

THE CHANGING CONTEXT OF WORK

International competition began to increase in the later 1960s and the profitability of industry began to fall, particularly in the old industrial societies. The rise of new industrial societies, especially in the Far East, created powerful competitors. This increasing competition was also linked to global economic integration. Rapidly improving international communications and advances in information technology made it possible to shift people, goods, and money rapidly around the world.

> 👉 We refer here to important processes of change that are discussed in more detail elsewhere. We discuss 'The crisis of the 1970s' in Chapter 18, pp. 745–8. We examine 'Global Economic Integration' in Chapter 12, pp. 477–83.

One response to the falling profitability of industry was the rise of the New Right, which became politically dominant in the 1980s and sought to revive the ailing economies of the old industrial societies by making them profitable again. Its strategy for doing this was to stimulate market forces, remove obstacles to their operation, and restore the freedom of the individual. While this led to policies of deregulation and privatization, it also resulted in a thoroughgoing attack on union power, for unions were seen as a major obstacle to the operation of market forces.

As the traditional industries declined, there was a major shift of employment from manufacturing into services. In the United Kingdom employment in manufacturing dropped by 51 per cent during the years 1971 to 1995 and employment in services rose by 42 per cent (*Labour Market Trends*, Jan. 1996). Employment grew in: financial services; distribution; travel and tourism; communications and the media; leisure activities; personal services such as hairdressing, catering, and cleaning; education and health; care and welfare. This led

some to argue that society had become post-industrial in character.

A post-industrial society?

The concept of **post-industrial society** is primarily associated with Daniel Bell's work (1973). His starting point was the well-known shift of economic activity from the production of *goods* to the provision of *services*. Manual work was in decline and machine operators were being replaced by robots, while non-manual service occupations were expanding. These service occupations were engaged in the processing of knowledge and information. For example, financial occupations, teachers, advertisers, market researchers, scientists, and social workers all worked with different kinds of information. According to Bell, economies were now driven not by the search for more efficient ways of producing goods but by the generation of knowledge and the processing of information. Indeed, he used the term **information society** to describe a world in which knowledge was the prime resource.

The specific changes described by Bell were, and indeed still are, happening, but should they be described as post-industrial? The generation and communication of knowledge have always been central to production. Industrial production has been based on the systematic development and application of knowledge to create more productive machines and operate them more efficiently. Technological change has certainly reduced the need for manual labour but this too is nothing new. The steady shift of work and employment from production to services has been a characteristic feature of industrial societies ever since the Industrial Revolution. People have certainly become increasingly employed in service occupations that process information, but this does not make society post-industrial.

Services have themselves become increasingly organized along industrial lines. Industry should not be confused with factories. As we argued in the section on 'Industrialism', pp. 501–2, industry refers to the way in which production is organized and the same principles of organization have been applied outside the production of goods to the way that services are produced. The characteristic features of industrialism listed earlier are found, and found increasingly, in service organizations as well. Catering, for example, is considered a service, but Gabriel, who carried out research on it in the 1980s, was in no doubt that it was becoming industrialized (see box on p. 500).

There are similar problems with the term **deindustrialization**. Traditional industries have declined and the particular communities that lost shipyards or coal

The industrialization of health care?

▶ **Mechanization:** the use of ever more sophisticated machinery to investigate and treat illness and injury.

▶ **Concentration:** the emergence of large regional hospitals and the closure of small local ones; the concentration of particular health-care functions, such as accident and emergency work or childbirth, in the hospital.

▶ **Specialization:** the specialization of hospitals, as particular ones become transplant centres or centres for the treatment of particular conditions, such as spinal injury; the specialization of medical, surgical, and nursing occupations, with, for example, physicians, surgeons, and nurses specializing in cancer care.

▶ **Management:** the creation of a distinct stratum of professional managers who distribute resources and develop policy.

▶ **Do you think that health care is an industry?**

▶ **Can you identify similar changes taking place in your school, college, or university?**

▶ **Do you think that education has been industrialized?**

mines or steel mills no doubt had a strong sense that a process of deindustrialization was taking place. There has, however, been no deindustrialization of society as a whole. Coal, ships, and steel are still being produced on an industrial basis but increasingly outside the old industrial societes. New industries, such as those concerned with the production of electronics or biotechnology or software, have grown up in the old industrial societies. As we have just argued, services are still undergoing a process of industrialization. The term deindustrialization confuses the decline of particular industries in particular places with a reversal of the process of industrialization.

Post-Fordism

Post-Fordism is a similar but more specific term that has come into use to describe changes in production but, before discussing it, we need to consider briefly what Fordism means.

Fordism refers to the system of mass production created by Henry Ford in the car factories he set up in the United States during the years 1908–14. This became the model for the low-cost production of standardized goods for a mass market. Fordism exemplified the deskilling of work that Braverman considered characteristic of capitalist production. In Blauner's terms, its assembly-line technology maximized alienation.

Work was fragmented into small tasks which could be carried out repeatedly by low-skilled labour with very little training. There was a clear division between a mass of semi-skilled workers and a small number of skilled workers carrying out key tasks. Production was controlled by a centralized management, which was sharply separated from labour. A divided labour force was in Britain represented by many different unions and there was a high level of open conflict.

The very success of Fordism meant, however, that markets became saturated. Once a household had a vacuum cleaner, it did not need to buy another one for a while. As competition increased, quality, product

Fordism and post-Fordism

Aspects of production	Fordism	Post-Fordism
▶ Product	▶ Standard	▶ Diverse
▶ Priority	▶ Cheapness and quantity	▶ Quality
▶ Work-tasks	▶ Fragmented and repetitive	▶ Multiple and varied
▶ Skills	▶ Mainly semi-skilled work	▶ Multi-skilled worker
▶ Labour force	▶ Occupationally divided	▶ Integrated and flexible
▶ Management	▶ Centralized	▶ Decentralized
▶ Industrial relations	▶ Conflictual	▶ Co-operative
▶ Trade unionism	▶ Multiple	▶ One union per plant

Figure 13.8. From Fordism to post-Fordism at Ford's Dagenham plant

DAGENHAM 1975

DAGENHAM 1995

Clock—nearly 5 and time to knock off

Clock—the time is irrelevant

PRODUCTIVITY TARGETS: APRIL

Team effort boosts morale and output

Union card—the workers united will never be defeated

Multi-tasking—the last of today's jobs completed ahead of schedule—as usual

STRIKE FOR 10% NOW!

Wonkey bumper—'not perfect but it'll pass - and it's not my job anyway'

Quality's the name of the game— no detail is too small to check

Work area so clean you could eat your lunch off it

Source: *Independent*, 20 Apr. 1995.

diversity, and innovation became crucial in the market place. Long production runs were replaced by frequent changes of product and small batch production, to meet particular market opportunities and respond to changes of style. The Ford company had been famous for the production of the standard model T Ford, which could be obtained in any colour, 'so long as it was black'! Car factories now provide a wide range of models, each with many variations in style and engine power, and many optional extras.

The concept of **post-Fordism** was introduced to describe the way in which production was reorganized to meet the requirements of quality, diversity, and innovation. This involved interrelated changes in the organization of work, personnel policies, and industrial relations. Greater skill, flexibility, and commitment were required from labour. Workers were expected to be adaptable and multi-skilled, which made trade unions organized on craft lines less appropriate. Flexible production and quality products implied a highly motivated and highly trained labour force, a more decentralized management, and a more cooperative, less conflictual style of industrial relations.

The concept of post-Fordism has generated considerable debate. It challenged the notion that capitalism continually deskilled and degraded labour and claimed that work would become multi-skilled and more varied. Paul Thompson (1993) has been sceptical of this view and argues that requiring workers to do a wider range of tasks does not upgrade their work or increase its skill content. He suggests that it would be more accurate to describe this as multi-tasking than multi-skilling. Wood (1989) has similarly argued that many of the post-Fordist changes in work organization and management are merely minor modifications to basically Fordist methods. He preferred the term neo-Fordism—that is, a new form of Fordism—to post-Fordism.

According to Gallie (1996), national surveys have shown that skill levels in Britain did rise during the 1980s and early 1990s. There were observable tendencies to give workers more responsibility and work had become more varied. The experience of work had been enriched rather than degraded, though Gallie notes that there was also a negative aspect to these changes, for work pressures had intensified and people felt under greater stress. The surveys also showed, however, that it was only skilled workers, technicians, supervisors, lower professionals, and managers that had experienced this upgrading of work. Semi-skilled and unskilled workers had not experienced changes of this sort. These findings are therefore not wholly inconsistent with the scepticism of Thompson and Wood.

It must also be said that in some industries Fordism is on the increase. Gabriel (1988) has described the changes taking place in catering as it has become industrialized. The mass production, fragmentation of work, deskilling, centralized control, and authoritarian management typical of Fordist production were spreading in catering.

It is also important to emphasize that post-Fordist production remains capitalist production. Employers still seek to maximize their profits and minimize their labour costs. Managers still control the production process. If anything, more is demanded from labour than before, for workers are required to produce higher quality work, to work at a greater range of tasks, and work as long as it takes to complete the job. The weakening of labour movements was probably a condition of these changes, for it enabled management to take greater control of the workplace.

The flexible firm

The flexible use of labour was central to the post-Fordist organization of production. John Atkinson (1984) has contructed an influential and widely discussed model of the flexible firm which particularly focuses on this issue.

> ☞ The flexible use of labour is closely linked to new organizational forms, which we discuss in Chapter 16, pp. 660–2.

Atkinson identified three different kinds of flexibility—functional, numerical, and financial:

▶ *Functional* flexibility. This required workers to carry out any task assigned by management.

▶ *Numerical* flexibility. This enabled management to vary the size of the labour force according to the demand for labour.

▶ *Financial* flexibility. This referred to financial changes, such as performance-related pay, that enabled companies to increase their functional and numerical flexibility.

This model particularly drew attention to the importance of numerical flexibility. The uncertainties generated by greater competition and faster change, together with the need to minimize costs, led employers to seek ways of adjusting the size of the labour force to their actual need for labour. One way of doing this is to employ more workers on a part-time basis, as when stores employ extra staff at checkouts during peak shopping times. Another way is to offer short-term contracts, perhaps for a particular production run or, in education, the duration of a course. An extreme example is the zero-hours contract, which requires

The advantages of employing temporary workers

One of the key reasons given for the return of the Raleigh bicycle factory in Nottingham to profitability after heavy losses in the 1980s was the greater use of temporary workers. Between 250 and 350 employees were hired on a temporary basis to supplement a core workforce of 1,000 workers when demand for cycles was high, as in the pre-Christmas period. This enabled the company to meet surges in demand quickly, halve the time it took to respond to orders, and carry lower stocks.

Source: Financial Times, 1 Feb. 1996.

employees to be available for work but does not specify their hours of employment and only pays them when the employer calls them in.

The flexible firm created a new division within labour, between *core* and *periphery* (see Figure 13.9). The *core* consisted of permanent, full-time employees with security of employment, promotion prospects, and company benefits of various kinds. In exchange for these privileges, they were expected to be loyal and flexible employees. The *periphery* was composed of those with a looser and less secure relationship to the organization. Atkinson divides it into two groups. The first consists of full-time workers with less security and fewer career prospects than the core groups. These workers have jobs rather than careers and can be returned to the labour market if there is no work for them. The second group consists of various kinds of temporary or part-time workers. Further flexibility is provided by an outer ring of workers brought in under contract but not employed by the organization.

This division between core and periphery had important consequences for the organization of labour, for it weakened the collective solidarity of workers. Coates (1989) has argued that the working class as a whole has been split by this new line of division.

Like post-Fordism, the model of the flexible firm has been much criticized (see Pollert 1991). It has been argued that the features of work organization and employment that it identifies are nothing really new. Capitalist employers have, for example, always tried to cut their employment costs at the expense of the security of labour and are simply finding new, or rediscovering old, ways of doing this. Thus, the practice of contracting out work rather than directly employing workers is long established.

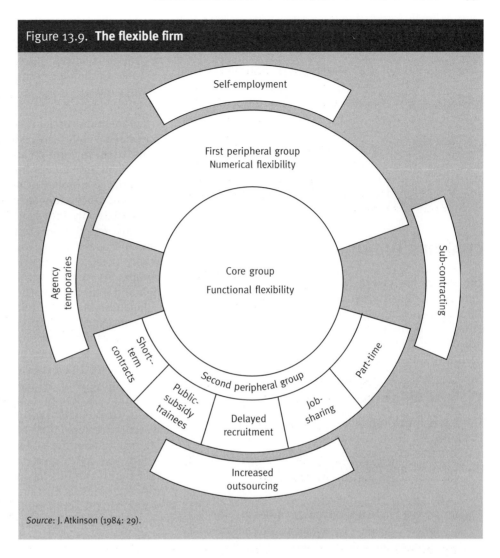

Figure 13.9. **The flexible firm**

Self-employment

First peripheral group
Numerical flexibility

Core group
Functional flexibility

Agency temporaries

Sub-contracting

Short-term contracts

Public-subsidy trainees

Second peripheral group

Part-time

Job-sharing

Delayed recruitment

Increased outsourcing

Source: J. Atkinson (1984: 29).

It has also been argued that the term 'flexibility' gives too positive an image of change. Greater numerical flexibility can also be described as the *casualization* of labour. The labour movement has long struggled to improve the security of employment by getting rid of casual work, only to find it re-emerging under the banner of flexibility. Pollert (1988) has, indeed, argued that the flexible firm is an essentially political notion that is part of a government and employer campaign to spread and justify changes in employment relationships that result in greater insecurity for workers.

One argument against the flexible firm is that greater flexibility can have negative as well as positive consequences from an employer's point of view. In-secure employees are likely to be poorly motivated and unreliable. It has been reported that some companies have indeed gone back to employing labour on a more secure and stable basis in order to improve product quality and reliability.

Like post-Fordism, the concept of the flexible firm usefully highlights changes in employer practices. It is important to see both concepts not as descriptions of work organization or employment relations but as simplified models of reality that help us to grasp processes of change by drawing contrasts and suggesting the interrelationships between them. The critics of these concepts do, however, rightly point out the dangers of exaggerating change and emphasizing its positive rather than its negative consequences.

CHANGES IN INDUSTRIAL RELATIONS

The changes we have just outlined were linked to major changes in industrial relations, industrial conflict, and labour organization. In this section we examine the so-called new industrial relations of the 1980s, the regulation of industrial conflict by the state, and the dramatic decline in union membership since 1979.

The 'new' industrial relations

There was much talk of a new industrial relations in 1980s Britain. Here we examine two aspects of this, the introduction of a new Japanese-style pattern of industrial relations and the decline of collective bargaining.

 Japanese industrial-relations practices are closely linked to Japanese organizational structures and management, which we discuss in Chapter 16, pp. 662–3 and pp. 669–70.

Before considering Japanese-style industrial relations, it is worth considering briefly the character of Japanese industrial relations proper (Dore 1973). In Japan workers are expected to be flexible, committed, and loyal members of the company, willing to subordinate themselves totally to the company's requirements. Worker integration and identification with the company are fostered in the following main ways:

▶ *Life-time employment*. Workers normally stay with one company throughout their working lives.

▶ *Company welfare*. The company provides welfare for employees, through, for example, company housing.

▶ *Management–worker integration*. Workers are integrated through, for example, the adoption of a common uniform, and social mixing during work-breaks and company-organized leisure activities.

▶ *Enterprise unions*. Unions are organized on company lines, so that, for example, there is a Nissan union, a Sony union, etc.

Japanese industrial relations and personnel policies have been widely taken as a model, but it is important to place them in context. Japanese industry developed a dual structure consisting of some very large units and a large number of very small ones. The pattern described above has been characteristic of the large companies only. Indeed, the large companies can offer lifetime employment only because fluctuations in demand are absorbed by the small company sector, where there is no security of employment. The large companies contract work out to the small ones when demand is high and withdraw it when demand falls.

Japanese industrial relations must also be placed in the context of greater employer domination and the particular form taken by the Japanese state. Enterprise unionism was imposed on workers by their employers and reflects the historic weakness of the Japanese labour movement, which was periodically crushed by the state. Although company welfare schemes are often attributed to traditions of employer paternalism, workers are dependent on their employers for welfare because state welfare is less developed in Japan.

Japanese-style industrial relations should not be confused with the full Japanese model. Japanese companies operating in Britain have certainly tried to bind workers to the company and have used the same kind of integrative techniques that they employ in Japan. They have not, however, been able to make workers dependent on the company through lifetime employment and company welfare, which are not compatible with British institutions. Britain's tradition of independent trade unionism ruled out enterprise unions, though Japanese employers have moved some way towards company unionism through single-union deals. This practice has resulted in unions competing to make themselves attractive to the employer and win 'beauty contests' to select which union should represent the workers.

Japanese-style industrial relations in Britain have had the following main features (Bassett 1987):

▶ *A single union agreement*. Only one union is allowed to represent workers.

▶ *Binding arbitration agreements*. In conflict situations arbitrators select the position taken by one side or the other. This is often called pendulum arbitration, because it forces both sides towards a middle position likely to be adopted by the arbitrator.

▶ *Consultation and participation.* Committees are established where workers' representatives can meet with management, bypassing the union and integrating workers into the company.

▶ *Single status.* Manual and non-manual workers have the same conditions of employment.

This prescription fitted well with the post-Fordist emphasis on flexibility and integration, but the Japanese model has had little impact outside a small number of well-known, highly publicized, and mainly Japanese-owned companies (Bassett 1987; Wickens 1987). The Workplace Industrial Relations Survey (WIRS) found little evidence of its adoption in British industry as a whole. The 1990 survey showed, for example, that only 1 per cent of the workplaces surveyed had pendulum arbitration (Millward 1994: 123).

The main change identified by the WIRS was the decline of union recognition and collective bargaining. The proportion of workplaces recognizing unions fell from 64 per cent in 1980 to 53 per cent in 1990. The proportion recognizing manual workers' unions in the private manufacturing sector fell particularly sharply, from 65 per cent to 44 per cent. The proportion of employees covered by collective bargaining fell from 71 per cent in 1984 to 54 per cent in 1990. This fall occurred across the economy, in both the private and public sectors, in manufacturing and services (Millward *et al.* 1992: 70, 94).

Why did this decline occur? Had employers become hostile to unions or had they lost worker support? There were cases when employers derecognized unions, but there is no real evidence of employers becoming anti-union during the 1980s. The local surveys conducted by the Social Change and Economic Life Initiative during the later 1980s showed that employers still found unions useful or considered that the costs of getting rid of them outweighed any possible benefits (Gallie *et al.* 1996). Nor did these surveys find any evidence of a declining worker commitment to unions. According to Millward (1994), the likeliest explanation is that this was a period of major structural change, when many highly unionized workplaces closed and new ones opened where unions were not recognized.

Millward considers that government hostility to the unions played an important role in this. In 1980 the Conservatives repealed the 1976 law that assisted unions to gain recognition from unwilling employers. When new workplaces opened, unions were therefore in a weaker position to obtain recognition. There was also a lot of anti-union legislation, which we shall

examine shortly. Although there was little sign of attitudes changing locally, there had been important changes at national level which made the local organization of unions more difficult.

There had certainly been major changes in British industrial relations during the 1980s, but it was not a Japanese-style transformation so much as a decline of collective institutions. The previous century had seen the growth of collective bargaining but this tendency was apparently reversed during the 1980s.

Industrial conflict and the state

The Conservative government elected in 1979 broke sharply with the previous relationship between the state and the unions. During the 1960s and the 1970s governments had tried to find a way of bringing the unions into the state management of the economy (see Chapter 18, p. 740). In the 1980s the Conservatives reversed this approach and tried to regenerate the economy by reviving market forces and, as they saw it, restoring the freedom of the individual. This brought them into conflict with the basic principle of trade unionism, the subordination of individual to collective interests in order to protect the individual from the market. The unions promptly found that their representatives were removed from a wide range of state organizations and committees.

They also found themselves subject to greater state regulation. Laws passed at roughly two-yearly intervals through the 1980s and into the 1990s placed the unions in a legal framework that regulated their organization and behaviour. We cannot examine these laws in detail, but it is important to understand the main changes that they made in the unions' capacity to use their industrial power.

▶ *Secondary action made illegal.* Industrial action in support of workers employed elsewhere was made illegal. This attacked one of the key principles of labour movements, that workers in conflict with an employer can obtain support from other workers.

▶ *Restrictions on picketing.* Picketing refers to the practice of placing strikers at the entrance to a workplace to discourage or prevent workers from entering. It is crucial to effective strike action and had been used to great effect in the miners' strikes of the 1970s, when 'flying pickets' of miners shut down power stations and prevented the distribution of coal. The 1980s laws restricted picketing to a worker's own place of work and the number of pickets to six. Unions were no longer allowed to discipline members who crossed picket lines.

▶ *Balloting.* Industrial action became subject to membership ballots, which meant that the unions had to follow complex and detailed procedures. If a union failed to ballot its members correctly, a strike became illegal. The election of union officials and union financial support of political parties, in practice the Labour Party, were also made subject to membership ballots.

▶ *Banning of political strikes.* Strikes for political purposes or against legislation or privatization were made illegal. To be legal, industrial action had to be concerned with a worker's own conditions of work.

These may seem reasonable restrictions on union behaviour. They can be justified on the grounds that they protect the individual, prevent unions abusing their power, and require unions to act democratically. They must also be placed in the context of class conflict, for they weakened the collective power of workers and strengthened the power of the employer. They fundamentally changed the relationship between unions and employers, reversing the 1906 Trade Disputes Act, which had given unions immunity from the law in order to prevent employers using the courts against them.

Passing laws was one thing, enforcing them another. In 1971 a Conservative government had passed a massive law to reform industrial relations but had been quite unable to enforce it in the face of union opposition. In the 1980s the Conservatives acted more carefully and more effectively. They passed a series of laws that gradually built up restrictions and made it possible to learn from experience. They avoided the imprisonment of union members who disobeyed the law, for this had strengthened the opposition in the 1970s, and instead introduced financial penalties. If a union broke the law, it was fined. If it refused to pay the fine, it had its assets, which included its funds and offices, seized by the courts. Some unions did travel down this path and soon found themselves unable to function and forced to submit.

Enforcement also depended on the use of old laws and police action. The government's struggle with the unions came to a climax in the 1984–5 miners' strike. During this strike the government used the criminal law against the strikers. Close to 10,000 arrests were made and over 4,000 prosecutions were brought, largely on the basis of public-order offences. There were battles between the police and the miners at the mines and power stations, and the police set up roadblocks to intercept and turn back miners moving across the country on picket duty (Pery-Smith and Hillyard 1985).

Government policy to some extent increased open conflict, but its long-term effect was to diminish it. Initially it led to major confrontations with the unions, not only with the miners but also with printers, seamen, and dockers. During the 1980s and the 1990s, however, the long-term tendency has been clearly downward (see Figure 13.2 on p. 511). The legislative reforms have made it more difficult for the unions to strike, but other changes have also been involved. As we showed above, collective bargaining has declined and, as we shall show shortly, union membership has gone down steadily. The decline in the strike rate reflects the general tendency for collective organization and collective action to decline.

It should not be thought that the strike is dead. In 1996 there were 244 strikes in the United Kingdom, involving 364,000 workers, and resulting in the loss of 1.3 million working days (Sweeney 1997: 220).

The decline of trade unions

The fall of union membership has been quite dramatic. The number of union members in Great Britain fell from 13 million in 1979 to 7 million in 1996. This reversed a long period of union growth and has taken union membership back to the level it was at in the late 1930s.

The absolute number of union members is not, however, the best measure of the extent of union mem-

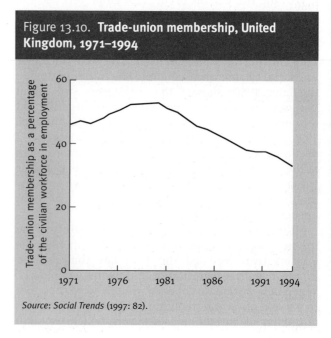

Figure 13.10. **Trade-union membership, United Kingdom, 1971–1994**

Source: Social Trends (1997: 82).

bership because it does not take account of the size of the labour force—that is, the number of potential members. The extent of membership is best measured by *union density*, which is the proportion of employees who are members of unions. This measure is also useful for comparing the rates of different groups of workers. Union density in 1979 was 55 per cent and by 1996 it had fallen to 31 per cent.

How is this dramatic fall to be explained? Many of the changes that have taken place in Britain since the 1970s have weakened trade unionism and it is difficult to separate out their effects.

One possible explanation is the higher level of unemployment after 1979. Unemployed workers tend to leave unions. Unemployment also weakens their bargaining power and enables anti-union employers to recruit non-union workers or refuse recognition. It is, however, clear that the level of unemployment cannot provide the main explanation of falling union membership. When unemployment dropped in the later 1980s, union membership continued to fall. One of the striking features of the decline in union membership is that it has fallen each year since 1979, right through the economic cycle.

Another possible explanation is the changing occupational and industrial structure of the British economy. Union density varies greatly between occupations and industries, and employment has shifted from highly to weakly unionized ones. Many highly unionized workplaces in heavy industry and manufacturing were closed down during the recession of the early 1980s. Some services that have grown in employment have very low union densities. Hotels and restaurants have a union density of only 7 per cent, wholesale and retail distributors a density of 11 per cent (Cully and Woodland 1997: 237). Other such changes were towards part-time work and employment in smaller workplaces, both of which are associated with lower union densities.

The decline of union density has been too widespread, however, to be explained solely by changes of this kind. Indeed, it is groups of workers with the highest rates of union membership that show the greatest decline (see Figure 13.11). This has resulted in the union density of many groups converging towards a lowish rate just above 30 per cent.

How is this general, decline in union density explained? As we showed in 'The "new" industrial relations', pp. 532–3, there is no evidence that employers have become more hostile to unions. As we have also shown, the Conservative governments of 1979–97 were, however, hostile. Since there has been a general decline in union density and an anti-union government was in

Figure 13.11. **Changes in union density, 1989–1996** (%)

Variations in density	1989	1996	1989–96
Men	44	33	−11
Women	33	29	−4
Full-time work	44	35	−9
Part-time work	22	20	−2
Manual work	44	32	−12
Non-manual work	35	32	−3
Production	45	32	−13
Services	37	32	−3
Workplaces with 25+ workers	49	39	−10
Workplaces with less than 25	20	16	−4

Source: Cully and Woodland (1997: 233).

▶ **Why do you think that small workplaces and part-time workers have lower union densities?**

▶ **Why do you think that women have had a lower union density than men? Can the growing employment of women explain declining union membership?**

power for eighteen years, it is plausible to argue that this made some contribution to membership decline, but there is no easy way of assessing how important this was.

One particular way in which government policy may have contributed to the decline of union membership is through privatization. The aspect of work which is most related to union density is whether employment is in the private or the public sector. In Great Britain in 1996 the union density of the public sector was 61 per cent, as compared with 21 per cent in the private sector. Privatization might, therefore, be expected to lead to falling union membership, though it has not yet had this effect in the privatized utilities, for, in gas, electricity, and water supply, union density was still at a level of 61 per cent in 1996 (Cully and Woodland 1997: 237).

Is the 1997 election of a Labour government likely to reverse the unions' membership decline? The Labour Party has promised the unions that it will introduce legislation to enable them to obtain recognition if there is majority support in a workplace for the union. This would, however, increase union membership only in workplaces where the employer has refused to recognize the union and the union has majority support.

There may not be many situations of this kind. It seems unlikely that the 1997 Labour government will do much to strengthen the unions' overall position. It has indicated that it will not take away the restrictions on strike action. The Labour Party has been distancing itself from the unions and seeking more support from employers.

Whether union membership continues to decline also depends on the unions' response to it. As Gallie *et al.* (1996) have emphasized, we should not see union membership as wholly determined by the environment within which unions operate. It depends greatly on their actions too. One response has been to merge, but, although this has maintained the strength of individual unions, it has done nothing for the size of the movement. Another response has been to target recruitment on groups with a lower than average rate of membership, such as women and young workers. To be attractive to these groups unions have had to change their image and their character.

They have indeed been doing this. Having once been highly patriarchal organizations, they have gone through a process of feminization, though the feminizing of the leadership has lagged behind the feminizing of the membership (Rees 1992). They have also been developing financial and legal services for their members. Collective bargaining remains a key function, but they have adapted to increasing individualism by placing less emphasis on collective action and more on services to the individual. These changes may lead to more successful recruitment in the future.

While the decline of union membership is clear, unions remain major organizations. After many years of decline, the unions in Great Britain still had some seven million members in 1996.

CHANGES IN EMPLOYMENT PATTERNS

The 1980s not only saw changes in industrial relations; there were also major changes in employment patterns. Unemployment rose to a much higher level and employment became more flexible with the spread of part-time work, which was linked to the growing employment of women.

Higher unemployment and its causes

In the 1980s there was a huge rise in British unemployment, and, although there have been large fluctuations

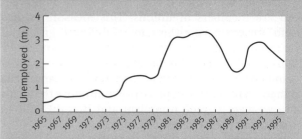

Figure 13.12. **Unemployment in the United Kingdom, 1965–1996**

Note: this graph is based on administrative unemployment rates and there have been many changes in the official definition of unemployment (see Chapter 3, p. 110).

Sources: Denman and McDonald (1996: 7); *Labour Market Trends*, Nov. 1997: S24.

since, it has not yet dropped back to the level of the 1960s and 1970s (see Figure 13.12). The scale of the increase is not in doubt, though the way that unemployment is measured has changed and different ways of measuring it have a considerable impact on the figure (see Chapter 3, pp. 109–11).

When considering unemployment, it is important to look not only at national rates but also at the distribution of unemployment, for it is not evenly spread through the labour force. Some of the main differences in rates of unemployment are shown in Figure 13.13.

Length of unemployment too varies considerably

Figure 13.13. **High and low rates of unemployment, United Kingdom, 1996** (%)

Variations in unemployment	High		Low	
Age (men)	16–19	21	45–54	6
Area	Merseyside	16	Oxfordshire	4
Educational qualification	No qual.	14	Above A-level	4
Ethnicity[a]	Black	21	White	9
Gender	Men	10	Women	6

[a] Ethnicity figures are for 1995.

Note: ILO definition of unemployment is used.

Source: *Social Trends* (1996: 83; 1997: 84–6).

between social groups. In the United Kingdom in the spring of 1996 46 per cent of unemployed men but only 28 per cent of unemployed women had been unemployed for more than a year. One in two unemployed blacks and Pakistani/Bangladeshis had been out of work for more than a year as compared with only one in twenty unemployed whites. Length of unemployment is also related to age. Thus, 32 per cent of unemployed men aged 50–64 had been unemployed for more than three years as compared with 16 per cent of those aged 20–29 (*Social Trends* 1997: 85).

How is the big rise in unemployment in the 1980s to be explained? It is first necessary to distinguish between the economic cycle and longer-term changes. Unemployment rises and falls with the cycle of economic activity. You can see an example of such a cycle taking place during the 1980s in Figure 13.12. While the economic cycle partly explains the high rate of unemployment in the mid-1980s, it cannot explain the higher level since the later 1970s, which has persisted through the cycle.

One popular explanation is the impact of technological change on employment, as machines replace workers. Automation has steadily reduced the need for manual labour in manufacturing, most dramatically through the introduction of computer-controlled robots. Advances in information technology have led to heavy and continuing job losses in areas such as banking.

This process of substituting machinery for labour has, however, been going on since the Industrial Revolution. Redundancies and closures hit the headlines, but technical change also generates employment. The introduction of computer technology has made many clerical and manual workers redundant, but it has also led to the growth of computer hardware and software industries. It has created new occupations, such as

Figure 13.14. **Unemployment rates, selected countries, 1976–1993**					
Country	1976	1981	1986	1991	1993
United Kingdom	5.6	9.8	11.2	8.8	10.3
Sweden	1.6	2.5	2.7	2.7	8.2
United States	7.6	7.5	6.9	6.6	6.7
Germany	3.7	4.4	6.4	4.2	5.8
Japan	2.0	2.2	2.8	2.1	2.5

Note: ILO definition of unemployment is used.
Source: *Social Trends* (1995: 76).

computer programming, and new consumer products, such as video games. Technological change does certainly result in particular individuals becoming unemployed, but it is less easy to argue that it explains the *level* of unemployment in a society.

Increasing international competition provides an alternative explanation. This has led to the collapse of some old industries, such as shipbuilding, and a general pressure to reduce costs by employing less labour. While this seems quite a powerful explanation, rates of unemployment in industrial societies have varied greatly, which raises the issue of different responses to increasing competition (see Figure 13.14).

 We discuss in Chapter 18, pp. 746–7, the idea that the crisis was particularly severe in Britain because of certain legacies from the nineteenth century. You might find it helpful to link the discussion of different national responses to Esping-Andersen's typology of state welfare (see Chapter 18, pp. 742–4 and 760–1).

The loss of jobs in banking

'Another 75,000 jobs will be cut from Britain's banking industry, according to the chief executive of one of the big four banks. Sir Brian Pitman, chief executive of Lloyds Bank, said last week that about one-fifth of the existing industry workforce would go, on top of the 90,000 jobs that have been lost in the past six years, as the banks drive to increase their efficiency and combat intensifying competition.'

Source: *Sunday Times*, 2 Apr. 1995.

There are two main approaches to the explanation of varying levels of unemployment, which we can call the *labour-movement* theory and the *flexibility* theory.

Therborn (1986) has advanced the labour-movement theory. He divided countries into high and low unemployment categories according to their rates of unemployment during the years 1974–84. He argued that the main difference between them lay in their economic policies. His high-unemployment countries—Belgium, the Netherlands, and the United Kingdom—had pursued deflationary policies. They had weak labour movements, which allowed right-wing governments to take power. His low-unemployment countries—Austria, Japan, Norway, Sweden, and Switzerland—were more of a mixed bag, but they all pursued full employment policies. Three of them—Norway, Sweden, and Austria—had strong labour movements, but in Japan and Switzerland full employment policies resulted more from a government concern to maintain social stability.

The flexibility theory, which informed Conservative policy in Britain, advances a quite different explanation of international differences. According to this approach, it is countries with flexible labour markets that have low rates of unemployment, for flexibility allows wage rates to adjust to market conditions. If wages become low enough, employers will take on workers. If wages are kept high by strong labour movements, there will be higher unemployment. Similarly, flexible low-cost labour will attract foreign investment, which creates jobs. Those who support this theory argue that the 1997 Labour government's proposed minimum-wage legislation will increase unemployment if it sets the minimum wage at too high a level.

The explanation of international variations is complex because there are many differences between countries and it is hard to isolate one source of variation from another. Evidence can be found to support both theories. The flexibility theory is supported by falling unemployment in 1990s Britain and its continued high level in the more regulated labour markets of France and Germany. Extensive Japanese investment in Britain arguably shows that the flexibility strategy works. America's flexible labour market and lower rate of unemployment are also often said to prove this theory. The theory cannot explain, however, a long history of low unemployment in countries with strong labour movements and highly regulated labour markets, such as Sweden. On the other hand, while Sweden fitted Therborn's argument at the time that he was writing, unemployment there has risen sharply during the 1990s.

The growth of part-time employment

While there is no denying the importance of unemployment, too sharp a contrast should not be made between employment and unemployment. In between these two states are a number of steadily growing intermediate forms of limited or temporary work.

Perhaps the most striking feature of the changing pattern of employment in the United Kingdom is the growth of part-time work. In 1951 only 4 per cent of workers were employed part-time but by 1993 25 per cent were. Most of these jobs, 85 per cent of them in 1996, are done by women, though the number of men in part-time work has also been rising. Significantly, the reasons given by men and women for taking part-time work are very different. Most women do not want full-time work, while most men do. Gender differences in the attitude to part-time work are particularly marked amongst those in the 25–49 age group, where most men (nearly 60 per cent) say that they take part-time work because full-time work is not available, while the vast majority of women (nearly 90 per cent) say that they prefer it (Naylor 1994: 480).

The explanation of women's preference for part-time work has been the subject of an important recent debate (J. Elliot 1997). Explanations of women's involvement in part-time work have generally argued that women have had to take it because of their domestic responsibilities. Against this view, Hakim (1995, 1996) has put forward a *rational choice* explanation. She argues that part-time work is not forced on women but freely chosen. According to Hakim, there are two kinds of women, *career centred* and *home centred*. Home-centred women work part-time because they prefer to do so. Hakim believes that this preference should be considered a quite rational decision by women, who are perfectly able to make up their own minds about what they want to do and are not forced into part-time work against their will.

Her argument has, however, been strongly criticized by Ginn *et al.* (1996) and Crompton and Harris (1997). They argue that Hakim fails to explain why some women are home centred and others not. She takes insufficient account of the childcare difficulties faced by women seeking to combine their work and domestic roles. She also ignores the socializing processes that shape women's roles and expectations. This is not to say that women have no choice but rather that their choices are constrained by the structures within which they live. The critics reject Hakim's rational-choice model as sociologically inadequate.

Part-time work is clearly linked to childcare responsibilities. The amount of part-time work taken by women is related to the age of the dependent child, while those without dependent children are more likely to work full-time (see Figure 13.15). An important factor here is the historically low level of care provided by the state for pre-school children in Britain, which has been the lowest in Europe (Phillips and Moss 1988).

Another issue is whether part-time work has devel-

Figure 13.15. **Economic activity status of women, United Kingdom, 1996**				
	%			
Activity Status	Age of youngest dependent child			No dependent children	All women aged 16–59
	0–4	5–10	11–15		
Working full time	17	22	34	47	37
Working part time	31	43	41	24	29
Unemployed	5	5	4	4	5
Inactive	46	30	21	25	29
All women (= 100%) (m.)	3.1	2.2	1.5	10.2	17.0

Notes: data for women aged 16–59. ILO definition of unemployment is used.

Source: *Social Trends* (1997: 75).

oped because of women's preference for it or employers' need for it. According to Crompton (1997), when demand for labour was high during the years after the Second World War, the only way that employers could get women to work for them was to make available part-time work that could be fitted in with their domestic responsibilities. Part-time work became a means by which employers could tap into the reserve army of women's labour (see p. 522). The situation changed in the 1970s, when the demand for labour dropped and unemployment rose. Employers now, however, began to want more part-time workers for other reasons.

This was partly because of the shift of employment from manufacturing to services, where the demand for labour fluctuates, with, for example, periods of peak demand in stores or restaurants. It was partly because part-time workers have been *replacing* full-time workers. Thus, the proportion of part-time workers *within* most branches of the British economy increased between 1984 and 1994 (Naylor 1994). The replacement of full-time by part-time jobs increased labour flexibility and cut costs. Part-time workers were anyway cheaper to employ because their weekly wages could be kept below the point at which employers had to pay national-insurance contributions for them. Employers could also avoid many of the obligations

and costs laid on them by employment legislation by employing workers for less than sixteen hours a week.

The growing employment of women

In discussing part-time work we have already been dealing with one of the main ways in which women's employment has increased. In this section we explore more generally the reasons for the growing employment of women.

The involvement of women in paid work has risen steadily in the second half of the twentieth century in Great Britain. In 1951 43 per cent of women aged 15–59 were economically active, a term that includes both the employed and the unemployed, but by 1996 this figure had risen to 71 per cent. During the same period the proportion of men aged 15–64 who were economically active declined from 96 per cent to 85 per cent (Hakim 1993: 99; *Social Trends* 1997: 21). The gap between men and women has been steadily closing, though one must bear in mind the much higher proportion of women employed in part-time work.

Women's availability for paid work has increased in various ways. A declining birth rate has reduced the time required for childcare. The mechanization of housework has reduced the time needed to carry it out. There is also some evidence that men are taking an

Women have often been employed in jobs that are an extension of their domestic role.

increasing share of housework, though this is still mainly done by women.

 The employment of women in paid work and the domestic division of labour raise closely linked issues. We discuss the domestic division of labour and its relationship to changes in the family in Chapter 10, pp. 386–90.

Greater availability for paid work does not itself explain the growing employment of women, however. Men may do more housework *because* women are going out to paid work. The birth rate may have gone down *because* women are giving a higher priority to paid work. It may be the higher household incomes due to the money earned by women that make possible the purchase of domestic machinery. It is far from clear what is cause and what is consequence and it appears likely that there is a complex process of interaction at work here.

One reason for women taking paid work is the growing financial pressure on households. The costs of increasing homeownership, the media pressure to acquire consumer goods, and rising levels of debt in a society where credit has become much more freely available have led to increasing financial demands on households. Furthermore, male unemployment has been rising and state benefits have been cut. On the other hand, higher divorce rates have forced more women onto the labour market in order to support themselves, while the number of lone-parent families headed by women has increased. Financial pressures have been particularly acute for ethnic minorities, and, according to Phizacklea and Wolkowitz, this may well have led to a higher rate of full-time employment amongst women in these groups.

'In Britain today many more ethnic minority women work full-time than white women (70 per cent as against 50 per cent). The vast majority of these ethnic minority women have not 'chosen' to pursue a career over the homemaker role; they work full-time through financial necessity, a necessity which is linked to higher rates of black male unemployment, larger family size, lower household incomes and the necessity of working longer hours to bring home something approximating a living wage.' (Phizacklea and Wolkowitz 1995: 13)

These financial pressures probably account for a considerable rise in the number of working mothers. The change has been particularly marked for women with children under the age of 5. In the United Kingdom

their participation in the labour market has gone up from 37 per cent in 1984 to 54 per cent in 1996. The 1997 Labour government's 'welfare-into-work' programme has put more pressure on lone mothers to find employment.

Financial pressures are not the whole story, however, since many women want to do paid work anyway. As we showed on p. 521, employment performs many functions for people. For many women it is a means of establishing independence and escaping confinement in the home. According to a 1992 national survey, 67 per cent of women in paid work said that they would continue to work in the absence of financial need (Hakim 1996: 104).

The growing employment of women must also be placed in the context of changes in the demand for labour. Occupational recruitment patterns are gendered, and the occupations that tend to employ women, such as those involving clerical and secretarial work, sales, and personal services, have been expanding, while predominantly male jobs, such as those in manufacturing, mining, and construction, are in decline. As we showed on pp. 538–9, the part-time work that disproportionately employs women has been growing at the expense of full-time work.

The traditional gendering of occupations has, however, been challenged, and this too partly explains the growing employment of women. There has been a dramatic increase in the entry of women to managerial and professional careers. The proportion of solicitors who were women rose from less than 1 per cent in 1946 to 31 per cent in 1994 (J. Elliot 1997: 12). The proportion of women who were administrative and executive local-government officers rose from 20 per cent in 1971 to 51 per cent in 1990. Women entering medical school now slightly outnumber men (Crompton 1997: 46). Women in these occupations still face the problem of getting through the 'glass ceiling' into the senior and better-paid posts, but there has clearly been an opening-up of these occupations that has greatly increased opportunities for women.

Equal-opportunities legislation and the pressure exerted by the feminist movement have contributed to the opening-up process, but the increasing education of women has here been crucial (see Chapter 7, pp. 249–53). Women's growing educational success has generated higher occupational aspirations and enabled women to compete with men and challenge the male domination of graduate and professional jobs.

The explanation of the growing employment of women in paid work is not a simple matter. Mothers forced to take poorly paid work in factories and super-

Possible explanations of the growing employment of women in paid work	The demand for women's labour	Availability for employment	Financial pressures	Challenges to patriarchy
	▶ Occupational change ▶ Growth of part-time work ▶ Economic pressures to employ cheap labour	▶ Mechanization of housework ▶ Lower birth rate ▶ Changing domestic division of labour	▶ Rising male unemployment ▶ Divorce and rise of single-parent households ▶ Home ownership, growing debt, benefit cuts	▶ Education of women ▶ Feminist movement ▶ Equal opportunities legislation

markets are in a very different situation from highly educated single women pushing their way into male-dominated professions. Changes in the household and the economy interact in complex ways. Account must also be taken of changes in education and the challenging of patriarchy through the organization and political action of women.

HOUSEHOLD AND ECONOMY

The changes in patterns of employment that we have been examining have been associated with many changes in the home as a workplace. We discuss their consequences for the domestic division of labour in Chapter 10, pp. 386–90. Here we examine changes in the relationship between the household and the economy. Homework, waged domestic labour, and informal economic activity were thought to be relics of the past but have all increased in recent years. We also consider changes in the relationship between work and leisure.

Homeworking and teleworking

The growing employment of women in paid work meant that more women were going out to work. More women were also staying in to work—as homeworkers—though it is difficult to establish quite how much homework is going on. It is not a particularly visible activity and homeworkers are often anxious to keep their work secret from officialdom, in the form of tax inspectors or health-and-safety officials.

It is also hard to define who should be considered a homeworker. The Census defines homeworkers as all those who 'work mainly at home or who live at their workplace'. On this basis, the 1991 Census showed that there were 1.2 million homeworkers in Great Britain, some 5 per cent of the working population (Felstead and Jewson 1995). This definition included not only the manual and clerical workers that people usually have in mind when they refer to homeworkers, but also others such as farmers, who in a sense work at home, shopkeepers who live on the premises, and resident hotel owners. Using a much narrower definition that includes only those employed at home in manufacturing and lower-level service jobs, Felstead (1996: 230) arrives at a figure of 300,000 homeworkers in Great Britain in 1994, as compared with 100,000 in 1981.

Employers' increasing use of homeworkers can be seen as another example of the tendency towards greater flexibility of employment, since homeworkers are often paid not by the hour but by the number of garments they sew or the number of phone calls they answer. Homeworkers are, anyway, cheap to employ, partly because employers can avoid overheads but also because homeworkers will work for very low wages. They have always been vulnerable to exploitation because they are isolated, unorganized, and often unable to compete for jobs on the open labour market, because, for example, of childcare responsibilities.

Homeworking is sometimes presented as a choice made by those who prefer to work at home. This may be the case for some, but Phizacklea argues that many who work at home have no real choice, because of both internal and external constraints. By internal constraints she means the socialized expectation that any paid work done by women should take account of the demands of childcare and housework. External constraints include high local unemployment, and the operation of the state benefit system and immigration law, which push both wives of unemployed men drawing benefit and illegal immigrants out of regular employment. They also include a lack of transport, qualifications, or affordable childcare. Phizacklea

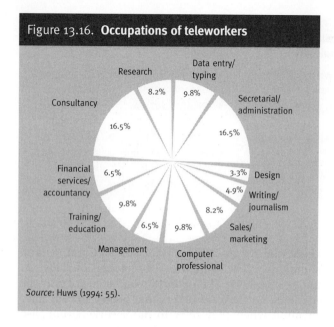

Figure 13.16. **Occupations of teleworkers**

Source: Huws (1994: 55).

(1995: 68) concludes that 'the social inequalities which arise from class, "race" and gender relations are simply replicated and reproduced in the homeworking labour force, structuring women's access to different types of work and pay and conditions'.

Teleworking has a quite different image from the 'sweated labour' traditionally associated with homework, though whether this image is justified is another matter. A teleworker is basically a homeworker who uses information technology. Telework is often taken to refer to consultants, designers, and writers working creatively in rural settings far removed from the city office but also includes those carrying out routine secretarial, clerical, or sales work from ordinary homes in the suburbs. Figure 13.16 shows that the two largest occupational groups engaged in telework are consultants *and* secretarial/administrative workers (Huws 1994: 55).

Teleworking has much the same advantages and disadvantages as any other kind of homework. If it allows some the freedom to work when they choose where they choose, it also isolates them and may lead to frequent domestic interruptions to work. It can also mean for others that home provides no escape from work, that the employer or customer can always reach them, interrupt their activities, and demand attention. It is both the most flexible and the most intrusive form of homework.

Teleworking has, however, brought about one major change in homework, which historically was locally based, with networks of homeworkers linked to nearby factories. Information technology has given homework a global reach, for satellite links can be used to employ teleworkers in cheap labour countries to carry out telephone-answering, data-processing, or software production (see Chapter 12, p. 479).

Waged domestic labour

As we showed on p. 520, waged domestic labour was the main source of paid work for women in the nineteenth century. As labour costs increased, it declined, but during the 1980s it expanded again, along with small businesses organizing and providing it.

The re-emergence of waged domestic labour is related to the employment of women in two different ways. It is, first, one response to the growing employment of middle-class women, though Gregson and Lowe (1994) emphasize that it is found in only a minority, possibly a third, of dual-career households. It is, secondly, a source of expanding employment for working-class women at a time when other working-class occupations have been shrinking.

The revival of waged domestic labour has complex implications for social inequalities. To the extent that it facilitates women's careers and reduces women's unpaid housework, it promotes equality between men and women. It does so, however, at the expense of greater *class* inequality.

The return of waged domestic labour

'Running parallel with the explosion in the small ads have been increasing levels of demand reported by employment agencies specializing in the recruitment and/or supply of domestic staff, and an expansion in the number of firms specializing exclusively in home-cleaning services . . . Moreover, in the late 1980s brightly coloured vans (with appropriate "mop and bucket" or "Victorian maid" logos, advertising services such as "The Maids", "Upstairs Downstairs", "Poppies" and "Dial a Char") were to be seen everywhere, particularly in the "affluent south". Such vans ferried teams of cleaners, many of them uniformed, to their client middle-class households, there to perform the regular weekly service, spring cleaning or, indeed, pet care, gardening, ironing or even granny minding.'

Source: Gregson and Lowe (1994: 4).

There has been a reconstruction of what Gregson and Lowe call (1994: 234) 'a class-mediated hierarchy of domestic tasks'. The more pleasurable housework and child-rearing activities are carried out on a shared basis by the middle-class couple, while the routine cleaning tasks are left to waged working-class labour. Waged domestic labour results in the growing employment of women in lower-paid, unorganized, and unregulated work. It often provides work for migrant labour but at the cost of exploitative conditions of employment. These conditions are often made worse by the illegal status of migrants, as with Mexican migrants to California (see Chapter 12, pp. 483–5).

The informal economy

With the development of industrial capitalism, both goods and services were increasingly obtained from the market. The formal economy of transactions involving money became dominant and, as we argued earlier, the formal economy was increasingly treated as though it was the only economy. In recent years there has, however, been a growing interest in the informal economy of the non-market provision of goods and services.

The **informal economy** consists not only of unpaid labour within the household but also non-market exchanges within local networks and the acquisition of goods through 'foraging'. An example of non-market exchanges would be mutual baby/pet/granny-sitting arrangements within a group of households or barter exchanges 'in kind' of, say, garden produce. Such activities have sometimes been partially formalized through local systems for the exchange of tokens that represent amounts of labour. Foraging activities range from traditional hunting and gathering activities, such as fishing, through refuse gleaning to shoplifting and other forms of pilfering and theft (Mars 1982). Somewhere between the formal and informal economies lies a grey area of transactions that involve cash but are untaxed, often illegal, and certainly outside the laws that regulate formal economic activity. This would include non-taxed household repairs by craftsmen, car-boot sales, prostitution, and the sale of illegal drugs.

Attention has been drawn to the informal economy not only because it refers to important work activities that are generally excluded from the study of work but also because of its growing significance. Many activities that were previously part of the formal economy have shifted into the informal economy through the growth of *self-provisioning*. Instead of paying workers to repair houses, shop assistants to serve us, or agricultural workers to harvest crops we increasingly use DIY,

self-service, and 'pick your own'. Increased self-provisioning can be linked to declining hours of paid work, rising unemployment, the development of domestic machinery, and the growth of a DIY industry.

Pahl referred to a 'shift out of employment into work', which he linked to the decline of employment in the formal economy and the growth of 'patterns of getting by' that combined whatever paid work a household could get with greater activity in the informal economy (R. Pahl 1984: 179, 190). The increased taxation and regulation brought about by state-managed capitalism have also played their part by driving activities out of the formal into the informal economy.

This rise of the informal economy reversed the previous tendency to commercialize all goods and services and revived the pre-industrial pattern of combining household production with foraging and paid work (see p. 521). As we showed above, there are also opposite tendencies, such as the recent growth of waged domestic labour. In a society where inequality is increasing, a widening gap has emerged between two-career households at the top, which can afford to buy time by paying for services, and unemployed ones at the bottom, which can afford plenty of time but little else.

While the informal economy is an alternative source of goods and services, it is important to realize that it is also dependent on the formal economy. Thus, self-provisioning depends on central features of the formal economy, such as the mass production, marketing, and distribution of a whole new range of do-it-yourself products for home, car, and garden. Furthermore, while households with low incomes may turn towards self-provisioning in order to acquire the goods and services they want, they need sufficient income to buy the means of self-provisioning. Raymond Pahl (1984) found that employment was, for this reason, crucial to self-provisioning. The modern informal economy is dependent on and generated by the formal economy.

A leisure society?

As industrial societies developed, increasing productivity and growing automation promised a world where machines rather than people would do most of the work. The daily hours of paid work declined and 'work-free' weekends and holidays became established, as we showed on p. 524. Working lives also became compressed between a lengthening education at one end and earlier retirement at the other.

With mass production and mass consumption, leisure activities became a more important part of people's lives. The deskilled and meaningless work characteristic of mass production was associated with

Figure 13.17. **The privatizing of leisure**

Participation in home-based leisure activities, Great Britain, 1977–1993/4 (%)

Activity	1977		1993/4	
	Males	Females	Males	Females
Watching TV	97	97	99	99
Visiting/entertaining friends or relations	89	93	95	96
Listening to radio	87	87	91	88
Listening to records/tapes	64	60	79	75
Reading books	52	57	59	71
DIY	51	22	57	30
Gardening	49	35	51	45
Dressmaking, needlework, knitting	2	51	3	38

Note: figures are percentage of those aged 16 and over participating in each activity in the four weeks before interview.

Source: *Social Trends* (1997: 215).

▶ **In which home-based activity has participation diminished? How would you account for this?**

▶ **Does the growing participation in home-based activities mean that 'leisure' has increased?**

an instrumental orientation to work that treated work merely as a means to leisure (see p. 516). The commercialization of leisure, the growth of leisure industries, and the marketing of their products through the mass media made leisure pursuits the main focus of life. Patterns of consumption rather than work occupation became the main source of identity for most people. According to Dumazedier (1967), changes of this sort were leading towards a leisure society.

Leisure became privatized as leisure activities *at home* became increasingly important in people's lives. The Affluent Worker study argued that the mobile and well-paid workers it studied in Luton during the 1960s had developed a privatized style of life (Goldthorpe, Lockwood, *et al.* 1969). The spread of home and car ownership, and the ever greater development of the domestic machinery of leisure, have continued this process.

There have recently been some counter-tendencies, such as, for example, a sustained rise in visits to the cinema, but the time spent on these activities is dwarfed by the time spent watching television. This is *the* dominant leisure activity, with adults in the United Kingdom watching on average over twenty-five hours of television per week in 1995 (*Social Trends* 1997: 216).

The privatizing of leisure has been reinforced by the globalization of culture (see Chapter 8, pp. 304–6). Satellite communications have connected homes to a global entertainment and information network. Global media corporations produce global products, whether sports events, soap operas, nature and arts programmes, or news coverage, for domestic consumption. This connection of the global to the domestic bypasses local activities and increases the privatizing of leisure.

While mass consumption established new leisure habits, the post-Fordist shift to greater diversity has enabled individuals to tailor leisure activities to their own requirements. The multiplication and diversification of television channels, radio stations, and weekly magazines aimed at specific market niches rather than mass markets provide examples of this (see Chapter 8, pp. 301–3).

Lash and Urry (1994) argue that the decline of the package holiday is another example, for the package holiday exemplified Fordist patterns of consumption. It involved:

▶ a complete package that combined holiday destination, travel, accommodation, catering, and entertainment;

▶ a standard product, with limited variation in accommodation or resort;

▶ advertising through the mass media and sale through travel agent chains;

▶ high volume to keep prices low.

Although cheap air travel boosted the package holiday in the 1950s, it has recently shown signs of decline, with a drop in the number of such holidays from a peak of 11 million in the 1980s to 9 million by the end of the decade. Package holidays themselves have also changed in character to provide more choice. Holiday destinations have spread globally, while packages have become more varied, and a range of new holiday and travel experiences, often tailored to minority interests, have emerged. Lash and Urry draw attention to the rise of a more diverse 'green' tourism sensitive to particular local environments (see Chapter 12, pp. 482–3). They point out that the Thomas Cook company, whose founder created the package holiday,

The creator of the package holiday: Thomas Cook outside Leicester railway station.

for the household. The same amount of housework still has to be done during 'non-work' hours, unless waged domestic labour is employed to do it, and it appears that only a minority of even middle-class households employ this. So, leisure time is squeezed.

Leisure time has also diminished as unpaid domestic labour has increased in other ways. Self-provisioning has invaded leisure time. Furthermore, rising longevity, and the decline of public-sector care and state benefits, mean that many households have to spend more time looking after the old, the ill, and the disabled.

The separation of work and leisure into distinct time compartments has become less sharp. There are now few blocks of time when most people are at leisure. This is partly because employment in leisure services has increased, so more people have to work during leisure periods. It is also because of the lifting of restrictions on trading and opening hours. Twenty-four-hour, Sunday, and bank-holiday shopping mean that many have to do their paid work during leisure time.

Industrialization separated work and leisure activities in the lives of industrial workers. It also led to the creation of distinct periods of time when most people were not engaged in paid work. This stimulated the growth of leisure industries and leisure activities became a more important part in people's lives. In recent years leisure time has for many people diminished, however, while work and leisure time have increasingly overlapped. The division of daily life into periods of work and leisure now seems specific to a particular historical period that has passed.

has reorganized itself into a global operation that specializes in providing holiday *information*, so that customers can construct their own packages instead of buying one out of the brochure. They also suggest that travel could be replaced by what they call the 'post-tourist' experience of other places through 'travel by television' (see box opposite).

As leisure possibilities have increased, the time available to enjoy them has, however, diminished. The historic decline in the hours of work does not mean that leisure time has increased. There has been increasing pressure on people to work until tasks are completed instead of working specified hours. It is also important here to consider household units rather than individuals, for the growing employment of women, children, and students means that there are increasing numbers of multiple-earner households. If the time spent by households in paid work rises, there is less leisure time

Post-Tourism

'The post-tourist does not need to leave his or her house in order to see many of the typical objects of the tourist gaze. With TV and VCR most such objects can be gazed upon, compared, contextualized, and gazed upon again. The typical tourist experience is anyway to see *named* scenes through a *frame*, but this can now be experienced in one's living room at the flick of a switch, and it can be repeated again and again. It can be suggested that there is little difference between seeing a particular view through the viewfinder of one's camera and through the television set. The latter of course causes far less environmental damage. Tourism through virtual reality may be the twenty-first century solution.'

Source: Lash and Urry (1994: 275).

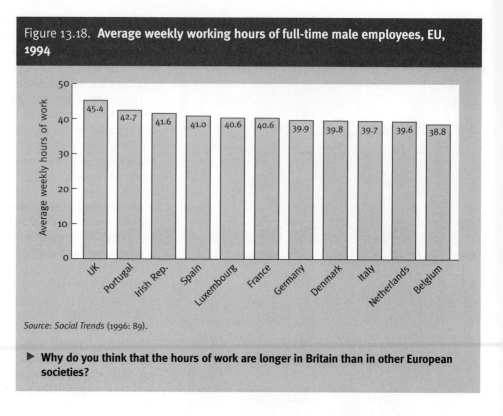

Figure 13.18. **Average weekly working hours of full-time male employees, EU, 1994**

Source: Social Trends (1996: 89).

▶ **Why do you think that the hours of work are longer in Britain than in other European societies?**

SUMMARY POINTS

We began this section by discussing changes since the later 1960s in the social and economic context of work and in the organization of production:

▶ As international competition increased, old industries declined, employment shifted into services, and the New Right became politically dominant.

▶ A post-Fordist reorganization of production was associated with changes in the organization of work, personnel policy, and industrial relations.

▶ Companies adapted to increasing competition and greater uncertainty by developing greater functional and numerical flexibility.

Changes occurred in industrial relations, in the regulation of industrial conflict, and in union organization.

▶ Although Japanese-style industrial relations became fashionable in Britain, they were not widely adopted and the main change was a decline in union recognition and collective bargaining.

▶ Industrial conflict became highly regulated by the state and the strike rate declined.

▶ Union membership declined steadily after 1979 and unions responded by merging and changing in character.

We moved on to consider changes in employment relations:

▶ Unemployment rose to a much higher level in Britain in the 1980s.

▶ Part-time work has been increasing steadily and is associated with the growing employment of women in paid work, the shift of employment from manufacturing to services, and the general pressure on employers to reduce labour costs.

▶ The growing employment of women can be explained in terms of the expansion of occupations that mainly employ women, their greater availability for employment, financial pressures on households, the greater education of women, and the challenging of patriarchy.

Lastly we considered the impact of these various changes on the relationships between home and work, and work and leisure:

▶ There is evidence that homework has been growing, in part through the growth of telework.

▶ Waged domestic labour in middle-class households has also increased and is associated with international labour migration.

▶ Informal economic activity has grown as an alternative source of goods and services, though it is dependent in various ways on the formal economy.

▶ Leisure activities have become more important in people's lives but leisure time has for many people diminished, while the distinction between work hours and leisure time has largely disappeared.

REVISION AND EXERCISES

INDUSTRIAL CONFLICT

In 'Industrial Capitalism' we outlined the concepts of industrialism and capitalism, and the relationship between them:

▶ **What do you understand by the following terms: capitalism, capital, private ownership of the means of production, wage labour, market relationships; industrialism, the concentration of labour, the division of labour, and management?**

▶ **Why is there a conflict of interest between capital and labour?**

In 'Industrial Conflict' we examined the organization of workers and employers, and the development of industrial conflict:

▶ **Why did workers become collectively organized?**

▶ **What have been the main forms of worker organization and how have employers responded to them?**

▶ **What is meant by the institutionalization of industrial conflict and what effect did it have on strikes?**

▶ **How useful is the notion of the strike proneness of industries?**

In 'The Changing Context of Work' and 'Changes in Industrial Relations' we considered recent changes in patterns of industrial conflict:

▶ **What do you understand by the term post-Fordism and what are its implications for industrial conflict?**

▶ **Were industrial relations Japanized in 1980s Britain?**

▶ **In what ways did the state regulate industrial conflict in the 1980s?**

▶ **How would you account for declining union membership in Britain and do you think that it is irreversible?**

THE EXPERIENCE OF WORK AND NON-WORK

In 'The World of Work' and 'The Experience of Work' we discussed various approaches to the experience of work:

▶ **Make sure that you are familiar with the main ideas of Marx and Durkheim, Blauner and Braverman.**

▶ What do you understand by the following terms: alienation, self-estrangement, deskilling; orientation to work; instrumental, bureaucratic, and solidaristic orientations.

▶ How did Blauner *operationalize* the concepts of Marx and Durkheim? (If you are unsure about the meaning of this term, see our discussion of it in Chapter 3, pp. 95–6.)

▶ Does technology shape the way that work is experienced?

In 'Employment and Unemployment' and 'Unemployment' we considered the meaning and experience of unemployment:

▶ What do you understand by the following terms: employment and unemployment, the functions of employment, the stages of unemployment, Keynesian policy?

▶ Why is unemployment a characteristic of industrial capitalism?

▶ Does unemployment affect everyone in the same way?

In 'Work and Leisure' we discussed the work–leisure distinction and the issues that it raises:

▶ What do you understand by the following terms: segmentalist pattern, extension pattern, neutrality pattern?

▶ What problems are raised by the work–leisure distinction?

In 'The Development of Leisure' and 'A Leisure Society?' we examined the development of leisure and recent changes in its relationship with work:

▶ Why did industrial capitalism lead to the growth of leisure?

▶ Why have leisure activities become more important in people's lives?

▶ Do you think that we now live in a leisure society?

WORK AT HOME

In 'Work at Home' we discussed the different kinds of work that go on in the home:

▶ What do you understand by the following terms: domestic labour and homework, waged domestic labour, the total social organization of labour?

In 'Home as a Workplace', we examined the relationship between work at home and industrial production:

▶ What were the consequences of the separation of production from the household?

▶ What effect did the growth of mass production have on domestic labour?

▶ How does the experience of housework compare with the experience of factory work?

In 'Household and Economy' we examined the changing relationship between the home and the wider economy:

▶ Is telework a distinctive form of homework?

▶ Why has waged domestic labour increased and what effect does it have on social inequality?

▶ What do you understand by the terms informal economy and self-provisioning?

▶ Why do you think that the informal economy has grown?

▶ Is the informal economy an alternative to the formal economy as a means of providing goods and services?

FURTHER READING

Books do not generally range across the topics covered in this chapter, which each have their own literatures. The following items do, however, cover a range of topics:

Grint, K. (1991), *The Sociology of Work: An Introduction* (Cambridge: Polity). This covers the standard topics of the Sociology of Work in an interesting way and links them well to the main theoretical traditions of sociology but also deals with housework, gender, and ethnicity.

Noon, M., and Blyton, P. (1997), *The Realities of Work* (London: Macmillan Business). A refreshing look at work, focusing on issues such as the significance of time for the experience of work, emotional labour, survival strategies in the workplace, and informal work.

For reading on specific topics, see the following:

Batstone, E., Boraston, I., and Frenkel, S. (1978), *The Social Organization of Strikes* (Oxford: Basil Blackwell). A detailed analysis of the process by which strikes are organized in the workplace and a case study of a near strike in the car industry.

Critcher, C., Bramham, P., and Tomlinson, A. (1995), *The Sociology of Leisure* (London: Chapman & Hau). A wide-ranging collection of pieces on leisure and its relationship to work.

Crompton, R. (1997), *Women and Work in Modern Britain* (Oxford: Oxford University Press). A clearly and strongly argued analysis of women's work that examines the growing employment of women, setting this in the context of change in both the family and the economy, and examining international differences.

Gabriel, Y. (1988), *Working Lives in Catering* (London: Routledge Kegan Paul). A lively exploration and discussion of many of the traditional issues of the Sociology of Work in an understudied and generally ignored area in which large numbers of people are employed.

Gallie, D., Marsh, C., and Vogler, C. (1994), *Social Change and the Experience of Unemployment* (Oxford: Oxford University Press). This contains a wealth of material on the experience of unemployment from the local studies carried out under the Social and Economic Life Initiative.

Garrahan, P., and Stewart, P. (1992), *The Nissan Enigma: Flexibility at Work in a Local Economy* (London: Mansell). A revealing study of the realities of Japanese-style industrial relations and flexible work.

Pahl, R. (1984), *Divisions of Labour* (Oxford: Basil Blackwell). Based on research on the Isle of Sheppey, this is a classic study of the informal economy, self-provisioning, and the domestic division of labour.

Phizacklea, A., and Wolkowitz, C. (1995), *Homeworking Women: Gender, Racism and Class at Work* (London: Sage). An informative and highly readable account of a generally overlooked area of work, dealing with teleworking as a form of homeworking.

Chapter 14

INEQUALITY, POVERTY, AND WEALTH

Family poverty

'Annie Oliver is 27 and has a five year old son called Alex. She has been living on benefits for six years. She receives a total of £80.10 a week for herself and Alex, made up of £47.90 income support, £16.45 child benefit, £10.55 family premium and £5.20 lone parent benefit.

'In a good week, when there are no bills, Annie can spend up to £30 a week on food. In a bad week she may have as little as £8. Then she will survive on toast to feed Alex, with basics like soap powder forgone for food. . . . Poor parents have very few choices when it comes to feeding their children, and being unable to afford healthy food makes parents feel very guilty. In her local shop, six Wagon Wheels cost less than three pre-packaged apples, and she is constantly forced to buy cheap food that's full of fats, sugars and E-numbers.

'For a woman of her age, Annie doesn't have much of a social life, being unable to afford new clothes or even invite a friend over for a cup of tea, much less dinner. . . . She was excluded from everyday activities that most of us take for granted.'

Source: The Great, the Good and the Dispossessed, Channel Four Television (1996).

HOW many Annie Olivers are there in Britain today? How much poverty is there? These are remarkably difficult questions to answer, as it is extremely difficult to measure poverty. Even the continued use of the word 'poverty' has been questioned by some, who hold that standards of living are far higher today than they were in the past. A Secretary of State for Social Security, responsible for welfare provision, said in 1989 that 'Not only are those on lower incomes not getting poorer, they are substantially better off than they have ever been before'. Is this an accurate judgement on the lone parent with a weekly income of £80.10?

The question of poverty cannot be considered separately from the question of inequality. It is structures of social inequality that generate both poverty and wealth. One of Annie Oliver's fellow citizens, Paul Raymond, is estimated to have assets that generate an income in excess of £1 million a week, and Sir Paul McCartney is reported to earn £3,750 an hour from his composer royalties alone.

In this chapter we will look at the evidence on the distribution of income and assets and on the patterns of deprivation and privilege that result from this. We will try to answer the big question with which we began: how extensive is poverty today? Wherever possible, we will look at societies other than Britain so as to put the British pattern into an international context. These are highly contested political issues, and we will look at the various explanations and justifications that have been given for the existence of social inequality. We begin with an evaluation of the view that social inequality is inevitable—and therefore acceptable—because it is a simple consequence of natural human differences.

UNDERSTANDING SOCIAL INEQUALITY

Social inequalities comprise patterns of advantaged and disadvantaged **life chances**. A person's life chances are the opportunities that they have to acquire income, education, housing, health, and other valued resources. Many discussions of social inequality have attempted to clarify which, if any, of these inequalities can be seen as natural and, therefore, as necessary and inevitable features of any human society. Natural inequalities are those social inequalities that result, ultimately, from innate or genetic differences among people. All other inequalities are purely conventional in character and so are possible objects of social reform and social change.

There are, of course, many biological differences in human populations. These range from such minor details as hair and skin colour, through differences of height, weight, and physique, to differences of sex and, more contentiously, of innate intelligence. In Chapter 4, we look at the difficulty of defining these differences with any precision, especially those that are involved in the construction of gender and ethnic identities. Some biological differences are, of course, determinants of human abilities: the ability to run fast, for example, is determined by physique, and the ability to undertake mathematical tasks may reflect innate intelligence. These abilities may, in turn, determine success or failure in achieving those kinds of resources that produce social inequalities: being able to run fast may allow someone to achieve success in competitive sports, while being able to do maths may allow him or her to achieve success in the competition for highly paid jobs.

But this does not mean that there is a simple translation of natural differences into social inequalities. Social factors shape natural differences in all sorts of ways. A person's physique and running skills, for example, can be transformed through regimes of training, while mathematical skills develop only if intellectual capacities are cultivated through appropriate socialization and education. There are also other determinants of success and failure. Success in competitive sports, for example, depends upon whether a person is selected for a particular team and whether the team's organizers are able to resource and plan its activities. Similarly, success in the competition for jobs reflects such factors as the connections and contacts that a person is able to mobilize, the existence of prejudice, discrimination, or other sorts of bias in recruitment,

and so on. The successful conversion of any 'natural' ability into a social advantage depends upon socially structured opportunities and circumstances.

For these reasons, it is difficult—if not impossible—to separate out 'natural' from 'artificial' aspects of social inequalities. Indeed, in the debates over intelligence that we will examine later in this chapter, there has been much discussion over whether it is at all possible to distinguish the genetic from the environmental aspects of measured intelligence. In the section on 'Equality and Inequality' we will look at how these issues have been debated in discussions of the relationship between intelligence, inequality, and social justice.

EQUALITY AND INEQUALITY

Debates about equality and inequality bring together sociological and moral ideas that are sometimes difficult to separate. Although sociological arguments should never be pre-empted by value judgements and political opinions, it is important to be aware of the ethical and political implications of sociological ideas and research.

Citizenship and equality

Equality is an ideal that has attracted many political philosophers and political activists, though they have differed considerably in what they take the term to mean. Critics of equality—most notably those associated with the New Right—have argued that inequality is inevitable and morally acceptable. However, these critics have often gone on to say that inequality is acceptable only if the structure of inequality is 'open'. As we will show, this idea of openness itself depends on a particular view of equality: equality of opportunity. The meaning of equality, then, is highly contested, and a sociologist who attempts to contribute to this debate must be clear about which of the many possible ideas of equality is under consideration.

A useful starting point for clarifying these issues is the work of T. H. Marshall (1949). His particular concern was to show how the development of welfare policies has been shaped by specific ideas about the rights and obligations of **citizenship**. A citizen is a full member of his or her society. It is the rights and obligations that are institutionalized in state policies and in the practices of state agencies that define what it means to be a full member of a society. Full members have rights and obligations that are denied to others who live in the same society. For example, adults in contemporary Britain have a whole set of rights and obligations that are not allowed to children, and these rights and obligations are only gradually extended to people as they age. No one age is critical in acquiring citizenship rights in Britain today, though most major rights are acquired by the age of 21.

Until quite recently, citizenship rights were restricted to certain sections of the population. For example, those who held no substantial property—the great majority of the population—were denied voting rights in elections until well into the nineteenth century. Marshall shows that state policy in Britain since the eighteenth century has gradually extended citizenship rights to all adults.

Initially, civil and political rights were slowly extended from mainly male property-owners to both men and women, regardless of property. It was not until 1928, however, that all women received full voting rights in elections. Social rights to full participation in the cultural and communal life of a society were established towards the end of the nineteenth century. These social rights covered such matters as education, health, and welfare. Marshall saw these social rights as having been fully established in the major policy reforms of the 1940s.

The extension of citizenship rights reflects changing views about the respects in which the members of a society should be treated as equal to one another. The central theme in many discussions of equality is that all citizens should enjoy broadly similar life chances (B. Turner 1986). There are, of course, many different views as to *how similar* and in *what respects* life chances should be equalized. It is possible to recognize three different conceptions of equality:

A selection of age-related citizenship rights, England and Wales	Age and citizenship	Rights
	0	Have a bank account, borrow money, be named on parent's passport
	5	Start full-time education, drink alcohol in private, see U or PG film unaccompanied
	7	Open a National Savings account
	10	Be convicted of a criminal offence, be fingerprinted, photographed, and searched in custody
	12	Buy a pet animal
	13	Be employed part-time, with restrictions
	14	Enter a pub, own a rifle, shotgun, or airgun
	15	See a 15 certificate film
	16	Get married with consent, drive a moped, consent to sex (females), get a passport with parental consent, drink alcohol with a restaurant meal, leave school, get a National Insurance number, join a trade union, buy cigarettes, buy fireworks, work full-time, join armed forces (males), change name by deed poll, pay NHS charges (if not in education), consent to medical treatment
	17	Drive a motor vehicle, emigrate, join armed forces (females), no longer subject to care order
	18	Vote in elections, get a passport, sue or be sued, serve on a jury, qualify for basic rate income support, marry, make a will, consent to homosexual act (males)
	21	Stand for election, hold a licence to sell alcohol
	25	Qualify for higher-rate income support
	65	Qualify for state pension

Note: Some rights and obligations, and the ages at which they apply, differ in Scotland and Northern Ireland.

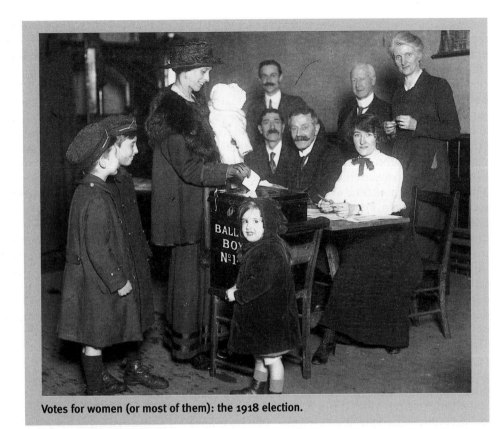

Votes for women (or most of them): the 1918 election.

▶ equality of opportunity;

▶ equality of outset;

▶ equality of outcome.

Those who promote **equality of opportunity** hold that access to all social positions should be governed by universalistic criteria. That is, they should be open to all, on the basis of merit and not through birth or social background. Advocates of this view stress a need to move from *ascription* to *achievement* in recruitment to social positions. They have stressed that education should be the central mechanism of occupational recruitment and mobility, as this allows occupational achievement to reflect innate and cultivated talents (intelligence and skills). This close association between individual merit and social achievement has been called **meritocracy**.

Proponents of **equality of outset** hold that equality of opportunity makes sense only if people start out from similar positions. Using the model of a competitive race for social advantage, advocates of equality of outset hold that a fair and equal competition requires that all participants begin from the same starting line. If some enjoy advantages at the start, then the outcome of the race will not result merely from differences in merit. Thus, equality of outset has often been seen as a necessary condition for equality of opportunity. Advocates hold that social reform must create the conditions that allow equality of opportunity to be truly effective.

Advocacy of **equality of outcome** is the most radical position, as it holds that all should enjoy the same standard of living and life chances. For some, complete equality of outcome is an absolute goal in its own right, while others hold that equality of outset can never occur without equality of outcome: winners of one race will have advantages at the start of the next. Supporters of this kind of equality, then, hold that the rewards that are received by the successful should be no greater than those that go to the runners-up and the losers. Views differ on whether this equality should be absolute and complete, or whether a limited degree of inequality can be allowed in order to motivate people to try to win.

Structured inequality

These views of equality, for all their differences, agree in seeing it as involving universalistic standards in the judgement of behaviour. **Universalism** involves treating all people in the same way, without any consideration of their particular or unique characteristics. Universalistic standards reject any arbitrary limitations on people's opportunities to participate fully in public life. Universalism is often contrasted with particularism. In a universalistic system, all are free to achieve social goals through their own individual efforts. A **particularistic** system, on the other hand, restricts opportunities to particular social groups and categories. This contrast is sometimes presented as one between achievement and ascription. In contemporary societies, the extension of citizenship rights has been based on the idea that economic resources should be distributed on a purely universalistic basis.

Universalism has generally been seen as operating most effectively through either a market mechanism or a bureaucratic mechanism. In a market system, individuals are rewarded according to the supply and demand for their skills or abilities. No account is taken of their particular circumstances or characteristics. The wages paid to engineers, for example, would depend on their technical knowledge and not on their gender or ethnicity. In a bureaucratic system, on the other hand, payments to individuals are based on political considerations that, again, should not vary with an individual's background. Someone who receives a welfare benefit would receive it because he or she has a specific need: the Jobseeker's Allowance, for example, is paid to all those who are unemployed, not to those from particular ethnic groups.

> ☞ The distinction between market and bureaucratic systems for the provision of welfare is sometimes described as one between commodified and juridified provision. These terms are defined and applied in Chapter 17, p. 719, and Chapter 18, pp. 732–3.
>
> At this point, you might want to look again at our discussion of sex–gender and of ethnicity in Chapter 4, pp. 139–45.

Actual markets and bureaucracies do not, of course, work in quite this way. Even where universalistic standards are formally acknowledged, for example, women and members of ethnic minorities have often been excluded or disadvantaged on grounds that have nothing to do with their abilities or needs. Purely universalistic principles can be undermined by the informal and unofficial use of particularistic principles. Employers may, for example, discriminate against women, even when they are fully qualified for a job.

Social inequalities, then, are structured by a combination of formal and informal processes. The formal mechanisms of the job market and the welfare bureaucracy have been expected to operate according to universalistic standards, but this has been offset by unofficial forms of bias and discrimination. Indeed, official policies themselves have sometimes been built around particularism and discrimination. The most important way in which universalistic principles have been undermined is through ethnicity and gender.

Ethnic differences have most often been translated into social inequalities through their racialization. That is to say, skin colour and other visible markers of ethnic difference are seen as creating racial characteristics that are used to justify the exclusion of some people from the rights and advantages that are enjoyed by others. Terms such as black and white, for example, are widely used in Britain, the United States, and elsewhere as signs of racial difference. Although the

Discourse

In its most general sense, the word **discourse** refers to a more or less systematic argument, whether spoken or written. It has come to be used in literature and social science to refer to any system of statements, arguments, and theories that is organized around particular underlying themes, concepts, and assumptions. So, a racist discourse consists of a whole set of shared ideas about 'race' and racial difference. Foucault has emphasized that any discourse embodies and reinforces the power relations among the groups to which it refers. A racist discourse advantages some ethnic groups and disadvantages others. It is in this sense that Foucault has said that 'knowledge' always implies 'power'.

Discourse analysis is particularly associated with the method of deconstruction that is associated with the so-called post-structuralist writers. They argue that discourses tend to be confusing and lacking in coherence, reflecting any inconsistencies and contradictions that exist in the underlying concepts. The deconstruction of a discourse involves digging down below its surface content to these underlying inconsistencies and contradictions. You do not need to worry too much about the details of this position, but you might like to look at our discussion of Foucault in Chapter 6, pp. 191–4, and Chapter 16, pp. 648–9.

concept of race has no biological foundation, it is used by many who seek to disparage or to disadvantage members of other ethnic groups. Through prejudiced attitudes and stereotyped identities, one ethnic group asserts its superiority over another.

The idea of race, then, becomes the basis of **racist** discourse. A racist discourse is a set of ideas that serves to advantage some 'races' and to disadvantage others. A racist discourse has its greatest social impact when it is translated into actions and becomes embodied in social institutions that discriminate against certain ethnic groups. The term **racism** has been used to describe the structures and processes of disadvantage and inequality that are built around a racist discourse.

Some writers have used the term 'institutional racism' to describe those situations where an ethnic group is systematically disadvantaged by the ways in which social institutions that are not built around explicit racist ideas nevertheless operate. People may not employ racist ideas and they may disavow them, but they are, nevertheless, involved in structures that systematically disadvantage certain ethnic groups. This is a racism that is inscribed within social institutions and their effects and not only, if at all, in the attitudes and beliefs of those who participate in them. It seems less confusing, however, to describe such a situation as one of institutionalized ethnic disadvantage, reserving the term racism for those systems of institutionalized ethnic disadvantage that do involve explicitly racist ideas.

Some similar distinctions can be made in relation to sex–gender differences. A **sexist** discourse is a system of ideas in which sex–gender categories play a central part and that has the effect of disadvantaging women in relation to men. There may also, but far less often, be a sexist disadvantaging of men in relation to women. As with a racist discourse, it is the use of particular language or categories, rather than the intentions of people, that is so important in producing discrimination and disadvantage. To object to racist and sexist language is not to be 'politically correct', it is to recognize the impact that language can have on people's life chances.

Sexism is a complex of structures and processes of discrimination and inequality that are built around a sexist discourse. Sexism can be distinguished from the broader idea of institutionalized gender disadvantage. Institutionalized gender disadvantage occurs when, for example, women with young children are unable to take certain jobs because of a lack of childcare facilities. They would experience sexism if they were denied job opportunities simply because they were women.

A number of Acts have been passed in the attempt

Sexism in employment

'The employment of married women in schools and in certain other capacities was discussed by the London County Council yesterday. The matter arose upon a joint report of the General Purposes Committee making recommendations that, with certain exceptions, married women should not be employed in the schools.

'Sir John Gilbert said that . . . the Council had a more than sufficient supply of well-qualified women and there was no evidence that the work of the Council had suffered through the non-employment of married women.'

Source: Manchester Guardian, 17 Feb. 1926.

to limit racism and sexism. These Acts have often been introduced only after long political struggles on the part of the excluded groups. Some legislation, however, restricts citizenship rights and may itself be an expression of racist or sexist ideas. Immigration into Britain, for example, has been regulated through a series of Acts that have defined nationality in restrictive ways in order to limit the numbers of immigrants from particular countries (Layton-Henry 1984). This kind of legislation may conflict with other Acts that aim to regulate discrimination.

POVERTY, INEQUALITY, AND CITIZENSHIP

The distribution of economic resources creates a structure of social inequality in which there will usually be extremes of poverty and wealth. Attempts have been made to draw a poverty line—and more recently a wealth line—to highlight the points at which these extreme conditions occur. Poverty has often been seen in terms of basic subsistence requirements: the poor are seen as those who are unable to meet the basic human needs for food and housing. These attempts have not, however, been successful. It has been realized that poverty and wealth can be understood only if they are seen in relation to whatever is the normal standard of living in a particular society. In this section we will look at how useful definitions of poverty and wealth have emerged from research on social inequality and debates over the establishment of citizenship rights.

<table>
<tr><td>

Acts of discrimination

</td><td colspan="2">

The main acts that have regulated nationality and discrimination on the grounds of gender and ethnicity are listed below, though sections in many other Acts are also relevant.

</td></tr>
<tr><td></td><td>British Nationality Act 1948</td><td>Distinguished 'UK and Colonies' citizens from 'Commonwealth' citizens</td></tr>
<tr><td></td><td>Commonwealth Immigrants Act 1962</td><td>Limited rights of immigration for Commonwealth citizens</td></tr>
<tr><td></td><td>Commonwealth Immigrants Act 1968</td><td>Limited rights of immigration for UK and Colonies citizens</td></tr>
<tr><td></td><td>Immigration Act 1971</td><td>Introduced restrictions on Commonwealth citizens who did not have a British parent or grandparent</td></tr>
<tr><td></td><td>British Nationality Act 1981</td><td>Distinguished British citizens from two categories of overseas and dependent territories citizens</td></tr>
<tr><td></td><td>Race Relations Act 1965</td><td>Made illegal discrimination on the basis of 'race, colour, or ethnic or national origin' in public places</td></tr>
<tr><td></td><td>Race Relations Act 1968</td><td>Made racial discrimination illegal in employment, housing, and other areas</td></tr>
<tr><td></td><td>Race Relations Act 1976</td><td>Set up Community Relations Commission and allowed cases to be taken to industrial tribunals</td></tr>
<tr><td></td><td>Representation of the People Act 1928</td><td>Gave full voting rights to all women over 21</td></tr>
<tr><td></td><td>Equal Pay Act 1970</td><td>Required equal pay for men and women doing work that was the same or similar</td></tr>
<tr><td></td><td>Sex Discrimination Act 1975</td><td>Made illegal sexual discrimination in employment, education, and other areas</td></tr>
<tr><td></td><td colspan="2">for more information on laws concerning immigration see Chapter 12, pp. 485–6.</td></tr>
</table>

Drawing a poverty line

From the very earliest days of the Poor Law, poverty was seen as a matter of subsistence. Human beings were seen as having certain physiological requirements for food, clothing, and shelter that can be established with scientific certainty and that can be used to draw a sharp poverty line that distinguishes the poor from the rest of society. People were said to live in poverty if their income was too low for them to be able to afford all of the things that they required for their subsistence.

Rowntree (1901), for example, used medical studies of nutrition to identify the calorie intakes that are required for individuals of different ages and sexes. The cheapest and most basic foods that would supply these needs made up what he called the standard diet. He then estimated the cost of this food and added an estimate of the amount that he thought was needed for basic clothing, fuel, and housing. Rowntree's standard diet was based closely on the diet of the inmates of the York workhouse. It was, therefore, tied closely to official estimates of the minimum standard of living that was thought appropriate for people at the time.

No single monetary value could be assigned to the poverty line, as Rowntree recognized that the amount of food and the type of housing that people need depend upon the size and composition of their household. A couple needed more money than a single person, and those with children needed more than the childless. He calculated, for example, that a family with two adults and three children needed, in 1899, a weekly income of 21s. 8d. (about £1.08 in decimal currency). In order to be able to draw a single poverty line in the distribution of resources, Rowntree used this household as an example, assigning households to positions above or below the line according to whether their actual income was equivalent to that which was needed by the example household.

This method might seem to provide an obvious and plausible approach to the definition of poverty. Its particular attraction to policy-makers is that it seems to offer the possibility of a clear and attainable poverty policy. The aim of a poverty programme can be to ensure that the whole of the population has sufficient income to meet all its physiological subsistence needs, and governments and others can monitor progress

The standard diet

Rowntree (1901: 99–102) gives long and complex day-to-day tabulations of the food needed for men, women, and children. To illustrate his method, the list below shows the diet that he specified for one particular day (Monday) for a man, a woman, and a child aged 3 to 8.

	Breakfast	Dinner	Supper	cals.
Man	bread 8 oz margarine $^1/_2$ oz tea 1 pt	boiled bacon 3 oz pease pudding 12 oz	bread 8 oz margarine $^1/_2$ oz cocoa 1 pt	3,560
Woman	bread 4 oz porridge 1 pt	potatoes with milk 20 oz bread 2 oz cheese 1$^1/_2$ oz	bread 6 oz vegetable broth 1 pt cheese 2 oz	2,987
Child	bread 2 oz new milk $^1/_2$ pt porridge $^1/_2$ pt sugar $^1/_2$ oz	potatoes with milk 12 oz bread 2 oz cheese $^1/_2$ oz	bread 5 oz new milk $^1/_2$ pt	1,824

Note: 1 oz = 28.3 g.

towards this goal. Rowntree was, in fact, very influential among those who were responsible for official policy on poverty.

Some commentators have gone even further than Rowntree and have said that people can be said to be living in poverty only if they are so lacking in resources that they are close to starvation. This leads them to claim that the absence of starvation conditions in contemporary Britain shows that the struggle against poverty has been won. It is, of course, very important to distinguish between starvation and other kinds of human hardship. It is also true that the incidence of starvation is much lower in Britain today than it was in the nineteenth century. Similarly, it is very much lower than it is in many Third World countries today. However, poverty is still real, even when it does not lead to starvation or near-starvation.

Harsh as it was, Rowntree's subsistence standard was not a starvation standard. To his basic physiological subsistence measure, he added estimates for the kind of housing and clothing that he and others of his time felt it was appropriate for people to have. There was, then, a cultural element in his definition of poverty. Even the standard diet itself was based on customary ideas about appropriate kinds of food: it is, after all, possible to meet a particular calorie intake with caviar and smoked salmon as well as with bread and potatoes. Rowntree's conclusions about what could be allowed

in the basic budget of a household reflected his culture-bound judgements and not simply the requirements of nutrition.

Recognizing this point, Townsend (1974) argued that poverty can be defined only in relative terms and never in absolute terms. A subsistence standard might appear to be absolute and physiologically determined, but this is not the case. It always involves standards that are historically and culturally relative. Researchers and policy-makers, therefore, must use a concept of **relative poverty**. People can be said to be living in poverty if their way of life is deprived relative to the standard of living that is customary in their society. Customary standards change over time, and so the poverty line also alters. What might have been a minimum acceptable diet in Victorian Britain is not acceptable to people today. Townsend concluded that poverty must always be measured in relation to whatever standards of acceptability and unacceptability actually prevail in a society. To be deprived in a particular society—to live in poverty—is to be excluded from the kind and level of living that is regarded by people themselves as normal for members of that society.

This view of poverty rests on a particular understanding of citizenship. To be a citizen, a full member of a society, is to be able to meet the expectations that are attached to parenthood, work, politics, neighbourliness, and friendship. Central to citizenship in modern societies are its social rights: rights to health, education, and welfare, and to the basic income that allows people to meet the normal obligations and standard of living expected of them. Customary expectations of what is to count as a normal or acceptable way of life are institutionalized and become the basis for people's perceptions of deprivation.

With the establishment of an idea of citizenship, demands for improved welfare facilities and for redistributive taxes can be made on the grounds that the existing distribution of resources does not allow everybody to participate fully as citizens of their society. Those who lack the necessary resources are denied the opportunity to exercise their citizenship rights in full. People live in poverty, then, if their lack of material resources deprives them of the opportunities that are normally open to citizens. They can neither meet their obligations, nor exercise their rights as citizens. The

Relative and absolute poverty

An absolute view of poverty tries to measure it in terms of a fixed and unchanging baseline. Poverty is seen as defined by physiological subsistence or fixed human needs. A relative view of poverty measures it in terms of changing social standards of need. Poverty is defined relative to the level of comfort that is enjoyed by the majority of people in a society and is socially recognized as normal or desirable for all.

poverty line is a line in the distribution of resources that divides the deprived from the rest of the population.

Wealth and the wealthy

Wealth can also be defined most usefully in relative terms. Where the poor are excluded from full public participation, the wealthy have resources that allow them to enjoy benefits and advantages that are not available to others in their society. The poor are deprived or excluded from public life; the wealthy, or the rich, are privileged because they can deny their special advantages to the general public (J. Scott 1994).

The standpoint from which both poverty and wealth are judged is the accepted view of what is normal for citizens in a particular society. The wealthy are able to enjoy life chances and life styles that are superior to those that are recognized as normal. They are able to enjoy things that are culturally regarded as privileges, luxuries, or advantages. Poverty and wealth, then, are conditions that differ, in opposite directions, from the normal lifestyle of the citizen.

The poverty line is the point towards the bottom of the distribution of resources at which deprivation begins. The wealth line, on the other hand, is the point towards the top of the distribution at which privilege begins. The wealth line divides the rich from everybody else. This line is more difficult to draw, and it has been far less well researched than the poverty line. It is, nevertheless, just as real. The poverty line and the wealth line are important lines of social division, and they may often become significant lines of social fracture. Poverty and wealth are polar positions in the distribution of resources, and one cannot be understood without the other. The causes of poverty cannot be separated from the causes of wealth, and policies aimed at reducing poverty will have repercussions for the existence of wealth.

The changing value of money

It is very difficult to compare incomes over time, because of the changing value of money. As prices rise, a given *money wage* loses its purchasing power. As a very rough guide, £1 in the 1890s bought about fifty times as much as £1 in the 1990s. To overcome this problem, money wages are often converted to *real wages* that reflect their purchasing power. Wages for 1899 and 1998, for example, can be compared 'at 1998 prices'.

In many studies, however, only money wages are given, so here are some comparisons that may help you. In 1899, unskilled manual workers were paid an average of £1.05 per week, while skilled manual workers received £2 per week. In 1995 (the latest year for which comparisons are available), average weekly earnings were £369 for a man and £268 for a woman. The table below sets out some official comparisons of prices for various years.

Food	Price in pence		
	1914	1947	1995
500 g beef	5	7	236
250 g cheese	2	2	115
1 kg potatoes	1	1	77
large loaf	1	2	74
1 kg sugar	2	3	72
1/2 dozen eggs	3	4	59
1 pt milk	1	2	36

The changing face of housing for the workers. Nineteenth-century working-class housing in Islington, now prosperous middle-class housing; twentieth-century working-class housing in Manchester.

Poverty and wealth, understood as economic conditions that are *relative* to social standards of citizenship, are very likely to be integral features of any system of inequality. They could disappear only if there was a very flat and egalitarian distribution of resources, or if there was no consensus over minimum or maximum citizen entitlements. A society that accepted the legitimacy of whatever inequalities were generated by the free and unfettered operation of the market mechanism would have its extremes of income and assets, but it would have no poverty or wealth. This is why Conservative governments of the 1980s and 1990s began to deny that there was any poverty in Britain and abandoned the collection and publication of official statistics on poverty. However, this view was not widely shared, and the claim was contested. In the wider society, there was still a recognition that there ought to be both a floor and a ceiling to the distribution of resources and life chances.

A task for sociology is to chart the extent of inequality that exists in a particular society and to try to identify the levels at which deprivation and privilege begin. The numbers in poverty and wealth can then be counted and their lifestyles uncovered.

POVERTY, INTELLIGENCE, AND HEREDITY

One of the most contentious issues in recent discussions of social policy has been the idea of the so-called underclass. Politicians on the New Right, and some on the left, have used the term underclass as a way of denying that these people suffer from racism, sexism, or other forms of institutionalized disadvantage. Many of those who live in long-term poverty are members of ethnic minorities or are living in lone-parent, female-headed households. The argument of the New Right is that the poor are poor because of natural, innate inequalities that divide people. The poor have certain innate biological characteristics that predispose them towards poverty.

The undeserving poor and the underclass

These ideas have a long history. In the eighteenth century, Malthus (whose views we look at in Chapter 6, p. 203) saw poverty as related to population growth.

Malthus argued that a restriction in the levels of welfare—then already very low—would give people an incentive to work and to limit their families to a size that they could support from their own wages. Where this so-called moral restraint was absent, Malthus held, poverty would increase and there would be a 'redundant population' of vicious, indolent, ignorant, and dependent individuals, who deserved nothing better than to perish in the struggle for subsistence.

These people were called the undeserving poor, and they were believed to refuse work, even when it was available. Commentators and social investigators made some attempts to distinguish the undeserving poor from others who happened to live in poverty. In a remarkable account of life in the slum districts of London between the 1840s and the 1860s, Henry Mayhew showed that employment opportunities were not equally distributed. Many people could obtain only irregular or casual work that did not pay them enough to escape a life of poverty. These people were *forced* into degrading conditions by their circumstances. Nevertheless, there were others who *chose* a life of degradation by avoiding any form of steady work and who maintained themselves through street trading, begging, and criminal activities. Mayhew's work saw the distinction between the deserving and the undeserving poor as one between 'those who cannot work' and 'those who will not work'. He saw this moral distinction as having a biological basis. The undeserving poor were, almost literally, a 'race' apart, a group whose biological traits predisposed them towards a culture of poverty that encouraged habits of vice, ignorance, and barbarism.

This outlook dominated Victorian thought. The poor were seen as deserving public or charitable support only if they were willing to embrace the norms and values of respectable society and help themselves to escape from their poverty. These 'respectable poor' were deserving of help because their poverty was a temporary condition that could and should be alleviated. On the other hand, those who rejected respectability and pursued a life of degradation and crime were seen as 'undeserving'. They were described as the 'dangerous classes' because of the threat that they were thought to pose to social order. (For a general review of this idea, see Stedman Jones 1971 and L. Morris 1994: ch. 1.)

Marx took a much more critical view of Victorian capitalism, which he saw as generating ever greater levels of poverty for all the working class. Movement in and out of poverty depended, among other things, on the incidence of unemployment. Those who were put out of work in times of economic stagnation, he argued, became a reserve army of labour that could be called back into work when the economy was growing again. Marx saw a segment of the long-term unemployed as a 'stagnant' group that could hope only for casual, irregular, and low-paid work. Their circumstances brought them closer and closer to the vagrants and criminals that Marx called the lumpenproletariat. Marx's contrast between this stagnant proletariat—who were forced into pauperism—and the 'depraved' lumpenproletariat—who chose it—repeated the conventional distinction between the deserving and the undeserving poor.

The growth of poverty in recent years has led to the revival of the notion of the undeserving poor in the form of the **underclass**. While this term has been used in a tentative and careful way in social research, many political commentators associated with the New Right have given it a moral dimension. In their hands, it has become a pejorative label that blames the victims of poverty for their own deprivation. They argue that there is a genetically inferior underclass of welfare recipients whose poverty is a consequence of their lack of intelligence and their cultural outlook rather than of any structurally determined differences in opportunity and advantage.

While some sociologists have shared these views, many have not. However, those who have tried to use the word in a neutral, analytical sense have often found that their research has been distorted by political commentators. This is, of course, the fate of much sociological research, but it has been a particular problem in poverty research. In this and in the following chapter we will set out some criticisms of the idea of an underclass. We will show that, even when it is stripped of its moral dimension and used as a purely analytical concept, it misrepresents the realities of contemporary economic divisions.

The immediate source for much recent discussion of the underclass is work undertaken in the United States. Charles Murray's *Losing Ground* (Murray 1984), attempts to identify those of the poor who deserved support through the public welfare system and those who did not. Drawing on sociological research by Frazier (1932) and Moynihan (1965) on life in African–American districts, Murray documents the poverty and 'social pathology' of the inner-city ghettos. The residents of these areas, he says, live in a culture of poverty (see Lewis 1961, 1966) that encourages fatalism and an acceptance of their situation as in the nature of things. Their concern is for the present and for immediate gratification. There is no interest in planning for the future. The inhabitants of these areas, Murray argues, show high levels of indolence, illegitimacy, drunkenness, and criminality. He places particular emphasis on the effects of being brought up in lone-parent, female-headed households. In these households, he claims, discipline is poor and boys have no appropriate male role models to show them the virtues of the work ethic and the morality of responsible parenthood.

The existence of large numbers of lone-parent households, Murray argues, is a result of the high level of welfare benefits. Dependence on these benefits, he argues, prevents people from taking responsibility for their own lives. When welfare levels are high, unmarried women are encouraged to have children that they could not otherwise support. Murray advocates a reduction in benefits, believing that this would encourage more self-reliance. Faced with reduced benefits, many more young women would remain childless and would go out to work, or they would marry a man who would support their children.

Murray and a number of others have tried to link the intelligence of those in the underclass with 'race' (Jensen 1969, Herrnstein and Murray 1994; for critical commentaries, see Flynn 1980 and S. Fraser 1995). They have claimed that the disadvantaged position of African-Americans can be explained by their lower intelligence than white Americans. Hernstein and Murray, for example, have estimated that the median intelligence of black Americans is much lower than that of white Americans. This is a highly contentious claim, and all its various elements have been questioned.

Averages

There are a number of ways of measuring the 'average' figure in a distribution. The most common is what is technically called the *mean*. This comes the closest to what is meant by the word average in everyday life—for example, in the points average of a football team. The mean for a set of figures is calculated by adding them all up and then dividing by the total number of cases. So, the mean income for a group of people is the total of all their incomes, divided by the number of people.

Other measures of average are the median and the mode. The *median* is the middle value in a distribution, the point at which it divides evenly in half. There are as many people above the median as there are below it. When a distribution, such as that of income, is skewed towards the top, the mean income will be higher than the median income. The *mode* is less widely used, but is the most frequently occurring value in a distribution. The mode is the 'typical' or most 'popular' value.

Intelligence: heredity *versus* environment

Many aspects of Murray's argument have their roots in nineteenth-century discussions that gave rise to the idea of 'eugenics'. The growing acceptance of Darwin's ideas on 'natural selection' after the 1860s led many to argue that there should be a scientific selection of those with the most desirable physical and moral qualities. Eugenecists believed that human populations could be bred for appropriate characteristics, much as horses, domestic animals, and farm animals are bred for their speed, strength, or food value. They suggested that social arrangements should discourage the undeserving, unintelligent poor from breeding, while still encouraging the middle classes and other respectable members of society to increase their numbers. Poverty could be eliminated by selective breeding.

Some eugenecists combined an emphasis on biological factors with a belief in the reality of race differences. Many of the poor were Irish or Jewish migrants, and eugenecists blamed their poverty on their assumed racial characteristics. A policy of eugenics can lead, all too easily, to a policy for the elimination of particular racial groups aimed at improving the genetic stock of the population.

A looser form of eugenics lay behind the development of attempts to measure intelligence and to associate it with social inequalities (Galton 1869). According to this point of view, the role of environmental factors had to be recognized alongside the part played by 'heredity'. This work led to the construction of IQ (intelligence quotient) tests to measure intelligence. The measurement of IQ originated in the work of the statistician Spearman (1904), who introduced the concept of 'g' (general intelligence) to describe the general cognitive ability that he thought lay behind specific abilities and forms of intelligence (linguistic, mathematical, spatial, musical, etc.). The development of these tests seemed to promise the possibility that the relationship between material inequalities and social inequalities could be studied with mathematical precision.

Arguments that link inherited intelligence to social disadvantage rest on four assumptions:

▶ General intelligence (g) is a cognitive ability that underlies all other specific forms of intelligence and can be accurately measured by IQ tests.

▶ Measures of social advantage and disadvantage correlate highly with measures of general intelligence. Because the distribution of advantages and disadvantages reflects the distribution of intelligence, it can be seen as determined by differences in general intelligence.

IQ

IQ is measured through tests of logic and mathematics. Tests are devised so that the mean score will be 100. Particular scores are represented as ratios of this average: an IQ of 110 is 10 per cent above average, while an IQ of 85 is 15 per cent below average. The tests are also derived so as to produce a 'normal distribution' of results. This is a statistical distribution of the frequency of scores that, when drawn as a graph, is described as a 'bell curve'. In the normal distribution, most people cluster around the mean and relatively few have very high or very low scores. The normal distribution has particular mathematical properties that make it useful for statistical purposes.

Figure 14.1. A bell curve

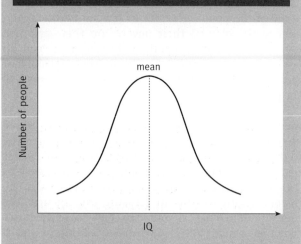

Attempts by Burt (1946) to use the idea of IQ in educational research have been seriously questioned after it was found that he had fraudulently manipulated some of his results (see Hearnshaw 1979; but see also Joynson 1989, Fletcher 1991, and Mackintosh 1995). A useful overview is in Gould (1981).

▶ Intelligence is genetically determined. It is, therefore, fixed from birth: education and other environmental factors have little or no effect on the level of intelligence.

▶ The genes that determine racial differences also determine intelligence.

Each of these assumptions can be questioned. The concept of general intelligence has been heavily criticized, and there is no agreement that there is any such common factor behind particular abilities. Mathematical and verbal intelligence, for example, are not perfectly associated with one another. It may be more useful to regard intelligence as a set of intellectual capacities rather than a single one. Even if it is allowed that general intelligence exists, however, there is the problem of how it is to be measured.

Many have questioned the value of the IQ score as a measure of intelligence. Tests have been shown to be culturally biased towards Western (American and European) culture and, within this, towards white, middle-class men. The cultural differences that shape the ability to perform in the tests do not necessarily reflect any differences in intelligence. More fundamentally, perhaps, there are doubts about whether performance in pencil-and-paper tests can be a proper measure of a person's ability to perform in 'real' situations. Indeed, there are wider doubts about whether performance in A level, degree, or other examinations is an adequate measure of a person's understanding of a subject or ability to apply it in real-life situations.

Intelligence is a complex process that brings together numerous aspects of brain function, and doubts have been raised about its genetic basis. It is inherited not as a fixed quantity but as a capacity to learn the kinds of skills and understandings that make up a particular ability. The realization of this capacity depends on the stimulation that is received in the first few years of life and, to a much lesser extent, in later life. It has been found that pre-school, primary socialization is critical in raising or lowering measured intelligence. Formal education can have a continuing, if smaller, effect, and educational action programmes can significantly raise the IQ of children who enter them with relatively low IQ. Cross-cultural studies have shown that the relatively high IQ of East Asians, as compared with North Americans, is due to the length and type of schooling, the extent of parental support, and the cultural support for disciplined work.

 Look back at our discussion of educational achievement in Chapter 7, pp. 253–5, for more information on the effects of schooling on different ethnic groups.

As we show in Chapter 4, most reputable scientists long ago rejected the concept of race. It is hardly surprising, then, to find that differences in intelligence do not directly reflect genetic differences. All the attributes that have been treated as racial characteristics show much greater variation *within* categories than they do *between* them. While the measured IQs of blacks and whites do show a difference in median scores, many blacks have higher IQs than the average white, and many whites have a lower IQ than the average black. This is one reason why the evidence garnered by Hernstein and Murray shows such a low level of association between IQ and social disadvantage. If intelligence is not genetically determined, but is partly influenced by environmental factors, then the impact of purely *inherited* intelligence on social disadvantage must be very slight.

The ability to perform well or badly in a test of IQ is, to a very great extent, a consequence of the whole way of life of a group. It reflects education and social class, as well as ethnicity. The fact that those labelled black may score lower in intelligence tests has nothing to do with their skin colour.

OPENNESS AND MERITOCRACY

The eugenic theories that we looked at in the last few pages have tried to relate social inequalities directly to natural inequalities. Genetic differences among individuals are seen as determining their intelligence and talents, and these, in turn, are seen as the basis of social inequalities. Those who are successful and those who fail have the positions that they deserve on the basis of their naturally given abilities. Even if the genetic basis of this argument is rejected, however, there still remains the question of the relationship between social inequalities and the actual distribution of abilities. These abilities may be the product of environmental factors, rather than hereditary factors, but is it the case that structures of social inequality directly reflect their distribution? If they do, then the structure of inequality can be seen as a meritocracy. These issues have been examined in the debate around the so-called functionalist theory of inequality.

The functionalist theory of inequality

The functionalist theory of inequality (Davis and Moore 1945) is a much misunderstood theory, not least because of some of the rather simplistic statements made by its own supporters. Nevertheless, it does offer a useful, if partial approach to openness and inequality.

The theory assumes that the various social positions in a society require different skills and abilities for their performance. It is important that people with skills (or with the ability to acquire them) are encouraged, trained, and recruited to the appropriate social

positions. This is especially important for those social positions that are critical for the survival of the society or for the maintenance of its essential characteristics. The theory concludes that societies will tend to develop a system of values that recognize the differing **functional importance** of social positions Attaching high rewards to important positions makes it possible to ensure that people with the required skills and abilities will, in fact, be motivated to take them on and to perform them effectively. The theory suggests, for example, that an industrial capitalist society that fails to recognize the functional importance of engineers and entrepreneurs for the continued production of goods that can be sold at a profit is likely to decline relative to its competitors, even if this decline takes some time (M. J. Weiner 1981; but see Rubinstein 1993).

 This theory of inequality adopts the general functionalist approach that we discuss in Chapter 2, pp. 47–53. If you are uncertain about this theory, you might like to look at that discussion now.

The theory rests upon a model of supply and demand. It holds that, if the skills and abilities that are required for a social position are not especially unusual, and so are in easy and plentiful supply, there is no need for any great reward to be attached to them. This is the case no matter how important a position may be: an important job that is easy to do is likely to recruit sufficient people so long as its wages are not too low in relation to alternative and similar occupations. If, on the other hand, the requisite skills and abilities are difficult to acquire, or are possessed by only a few people, they are likely to be in short supply. In these circumstances, high rewards will have to be attached to the position or not enough people will be recruited. This model is set out in the diagram shown in Figure 14.2.

There are many problems with the functionalist theory of inequality. It tends to assume a high level of consensus in societies, and it assumes that people are motivated purely by rational economic considerations. Most significantly, it is not at all clear that it is possible to distinguish important from unimportant occupations in any clear-cut way.

The theory's main limitation is that it applies in whole only to those societies where social mobility is easy and typical among its various social positions. The theory has no place for ascriptive social factors and material inequalities (of outset or of outcome) that

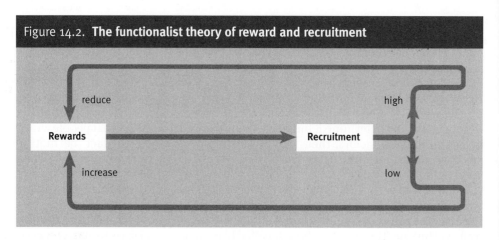

Figure 14.2. **The functionalist theory of reward and recruitment**

might prevent social mobility. There may be a considerable waste of talent whenever these occur on any scale, as talented individuals are prevented from rising into the positions where they could best exercise their talents. There may also be a dangerous incapacity at the top, as incompetents would face no pressure towards downward mobility.

In spite of this limitation, the functionalist theory of inequality does provide a useful, if partial explanation of the mechanisms that are responsible for social inequality in actual societies and of some of the ways in which particular structures of inequality may change over time.

A parable of functional importance

The rulers of the planet of Golgafrincham decided to rid themselves of those in useless occupations: personnel officers, public-relations executives, hairdressers, and telephone sanitizers. These people—all rather dim— were told that the planet was doomed and that it was to be evacuated for another, safer planet. The telephone sanitizers and others were to be sent off into outer space as an advance party. One of them said:

'the idea was that into the first ship, the "A" ship, would go all the brilliant leaders, the scientists, the great artists, you know, all the achievers; and then into the third, or "C" ship, would go all the people who did the actual work, who made things and did things; and then into the "B" ship—that's us—would go everyone else . . . And we were sent off first.'

A chronicler continues the story:

'It was . . . an eccentric poet who invented the spurious tales of impending doom which enabled the people of Golgafrincham to rid themselves of an entire useless third of their population. The other two-thirds stayed firmly at home and lived full, rich and happy lives until they were all suddenly wiped out by a virulent disease contracted from a dirty telephone.'

Source: adapted from Douglas Adams, *The Restaurant at the End of the Universe* (London: Pan Books, 1980).

SUMMARY POINTS

In this section we have looked at the relationship between equality, natural differences, and the openness of social structures.

▶ Social inequalities cannot be reduced to natural, biological differences. They are the outcome of complex social processes.

▶ Ideas of the underclass and the undeserving poor tend to confuse moral judgements with factual judgements.

We also looked at how ideas of equality and inequality must be seen in relation to the idea of citizenship, and we looked at some of the ways in which sexism and racism affect social inequality.

▶ Conceptions of citizenship rights and obligations set the basis for understanding poverty, wealth, and equality. Poverty must be distinguished from starvation and must be seen as a socially relative condition.

▶ Racism and sexism are major causes of systematic social disadvantage. For this reason, the association between intelligence and social inequality is far more complex than is often assumed.

Inequalities in modern societies are organized around property and occupations. We looked at a set of issues related to the merit, skills, and functional importance of occupations.

▶ The functionalist theory of inequality offers a useful, but partial explanation of social inequal-

ity in terms of supply, demand, and cultural values.

▶ The functional importance of an occupation is difficult to measure. Judgements of functional importance can often involve value judgements.

TOWARDS WELFARE AND EQUALITY

An open society can be an unequal society, and an unequal society may still have extremes of poverty and wealth. Sociological research must explore the extent of inequality, both of outset and of outcome, as well as its openness. This involves an assessment of the level of poverty and wealth and of changes in this level over time. In this section we will look at how these matters have been handled and at the conclusions that have been drawn from empirical research.

GREATER EQUALITY

Central to the structure of inequality in modern societies is the distribution of economic resources to individuals and households. The economic resources of a household determine its opportunities to purchase consumer goods, to obtain housing and to use transport facilities, to provide for the future welfare of its members (for example, through saving for a pension or taking out an insurance policy), and to purchase such things as private health treatment and private schooling. The distribution of economic resources, then, underlies the whole range of household life chances.

Income and assets

Economic resources are important to people as income and as assets. **Income** is the flow of resources that a person or household receives in a particular period. It is the number of pounds, dollars, or marks that they receive each week, month, or year. Income may take the form of wages or salaries from employment, interest on savings and other personal investments, and profits from business or trading. It may also include income in kind, such as the provision of a company car, cheap housing, and so on. Incomes of all types are usually

subject to taxation. This can be direct taxation such as income tax, or indirect taxation such as council tax and VAT. The rate of tax can vary with the type of income and the personal circumstances of the recipient. It is usual to distinguish between measures of income distribution before tax and after tax in order to recognize the redistributive effects of the tax system.

Assets, on the other hand, comprise the total stock of economic resources that a person or household has been able to accumulate. These may be physical assets such as land or houses, or financial assets such as bank deposits, shares, or unit trusts. Assets often generate an income. A bank deposit, for example, earns interest. Similarly, an income may help someone to accumulate assets, as when part of an income is invested rather than spent. Assets are often referred to as 'wealth' by economists, but our earlier definition of wealth and the wealthy uses the word in a sense that is closer to its everyday meaning. To avoid any confusion, then, we will use only the word assets to refer to a person's stock of economic resources.

Much information on the distribution of economic resources comes from official statistics, and we show in Chapter 3, pp. 107–11, how difficult it is to rely on these for precise information. Nevertheless, there are comprehensive and long-standing series of statistics on these matters, and many statisticians and economists have gone to great lengths to clarify them and to make them more useful for social researchers (see especially A. B. Atkinson 1983). As a result, it is possible to arrive at a clear picture of overall trends in the distribution of economic resources.

The pattern of distribution

In terms of both income and assets, Britain was a highly unequal society over the whole of the first half of the twentieth century. This is clear from a whole series of

Slicing the distribution

In a study of the distribution of economic resources, individuals and households are arranged in a hierarchy according to the size of their income or the value of their assets. This hierarchy can, then, be sliced in various ways to identify the top 1 per cent, top 5 per cent, bottom 10 per cent, and so on. It is then possible to report the percentage of total income or assets that is held by those in each of these slices.

In an egalitarian society, any 1 per cent of the population would hold close to 1 per cent of assets, and any 10 per cent of the population would receive around 10 per cent of all income. Reporting the income and assets of various slices, then, is a way of showing how much a particular society departs from this egalitarian situation.

Each 1 per cent slice of the hierarchy is technically termed a percentile, each 10 per cent slice is a decile, and each 20 per cent slice is a quintile. Thus, there are 100 percentiles, ten deciles, or five quintiles in any distribution. The median value is that which corresponds to the fiftieth percentile, or third quintile.

studies in which the distribution of total income or assets is divided up according to the percentage that is held by particular 'slices' or statistical categories in the population. This makes it possible to look at the percentage of income or assets held by, say, the top 10 per cent of the population over a long period of time.

The particular slices identified in distributions of income and assets—the top 1 per cent, top 5 per cent, and so on—are not, of course, real social groups. They are simply categories identified for statistical purposes. For this reason, it must not be assumed that, say, the top 1 per cent of income recipients are precisely the same people as the top 1 per cent of asset holders. The statistical evidence does, nevertheless, allow us to draw some conclusions about the overall shape and extent of social inequality.

The top 1 per cent of the population—a useful approximation to the wealthy in British society—held 69 per cent of all personal assets in 1911. Their share declined to just over a half in 1938, and during the 1940s and 1950s it slipped below this level to stand at 44 per cent in 1956 (see Figure 14.3). The relative share of the richest section of the population, then, fell over this period of half a century by almost one-third. The share of the top

Figure 14.3. Distribution of personal assets, Britain, (1911–1971)

Percentage share of assets

	England and Wales				Great Britain				
	1911	1923	1930	1938	1950	1955	1961	1966	1971
top 1%	69	61	58	55	47	44	37	31	29
top 5%	87	82	79	77	74	71	61	56	53
top 10%	92	89	87	85	—	—	72	70	68

Sources: Revell (1965); Hills (1995: table 14).

You will be looking at a number of similar tables later in this chapter, so make sure that you understand this one now. Plot the data onto a graph that shows trends over time. You should show the dates along the horizontal (bottom) axis and percentage of assets held along the vertical (side) axis. Draw a separate line on the graph for each of the three categories listed.

What other kinds of graph or chart might be used to illustrate these figures?

5 per cent declined from over 80 per cent to 71 per cent over the same period, a much more limited rate of decline (A. B. Atkinson 1983: 168; Rubinstein 1986: 95). Looking at these figures from a different angle, it can be seen that, in 1956, 95 per cent of the population held only just over a quarter of all personal assets.

Income has always been more equally distributed than assets. Nevertheless, the earliest systematic study of income distribution showed that the top 3 per cent of the population received just over a third of all income in 1903 (Chiozza-Money 1905: 28, 42). If income had been equally distributed, each person would have received about £40 a year. In fact, those in the top 3 per cent slice of the population had incomes that were above £700 a year, while the very richest manufacturers and owners of large businesses each received more than £2,000 a year. At this time, average workers' wages were between £1 and £2 per week. Just a few years later, in 1910, it was found that 327 people received incomes over £45,000 a year—more than 800 times the wage of an unskilled labourer.

There seems to have been some slight redistribution of income away from those at the very top during the 1920s, and by 1938 the top 1 per cent of the population was receiving 16.6 per cent of before-tax income. Its share continued to decline until well into the post-war period, falling to 11.2 per cent in 1949, 8.2 per cent in 1964, and 6.2 per cent in 1974 (Rubinstein 1986: 80).

Both income and assets moved towards greater equality over the first sixty or so years of the century, although assets were more unequally distributed than income. A combination of economic change and social policy reduced the great inequalities that had been generated in the Victorian period, and those at the top saw a continuous, if limited erosion of their relative position. Much of this redistribution at the top, however, consisted of a redistribution of assets within large extended families. The massive fortunes that had been made from land, finance, and manufacturing in the nineteenth century were entering their third or fourth generation by the middle of the twentieth century, and the assets were being spread among ever larger numbers of heirs. At the same time, many wealthy families sought to avoid estate duty (inheritance tax) by transferring assets to children before the death of the head of the family. Nevertheless, the continuity of great wealth is striking. Over the nineteenth century and into the first half of the twentieth century, sixty-seven families each had three or more of their members leaving at least £0.5 million on their deaths (Rubinstein 1981).

Economic inequalities shape the other advantages and disadvantages that people experience. In Chapter

Figure 14.4. **Inequalities of death (males), Great Britain, 1910–1953**			
Occupational group	1910–12	1930–2	1949–53
Professional and managerial	88	90	86
Technical	94	94	92
Skilled manual and non-manual	96	97	101
Partly skilled	93	102	104
Unskilled	142	111	118

Note: 100 indicates average mortality rate for population as a whole.
Sources: Stacey (1987: table 8); Black *et al.* (1980: table 7).

6, pp. 199–200 and 205–7, we show the ways in which a number of measures of health and mortality have varied over time and from one group to another. The evidence that we present in that chapter shows how health and mortality are related to gender and ethnic differences. Figure 14.4 shows how mortality rates vary from one occupational group to another. In this table, numbers above 100 indicate that a group has an above-average rate of mortality, while numbers below 100 represent below-average mortality. The highest-paid occupations, the professional and managerial ones, have mobility rates that have been below average for the whole of the first half of the twentieth century. Mortality rates for unskilled workers—the lowest-paid group in the population—improved substantially between 1910 and 1953, but they were still significantly above average. In each year, there is a very clear gradient in mortality rates from the highest paid to the lowest paid.

 If you are unclear about the meaning of the standardized mortality rate, read our discussion of this in Chapter 6, p. 199. You will need to understand this if you are to make the best use of the evidence presented in this chapter.

MAPPING POVERTY

The Victorian upper and middle classes had been haunted by the prospect of a growth in urban poverty, especially that in London's East End. Journalists, novelists, reformers, and the early social researchers were explorers of poverty in what came to be called 'Darkest England'. Best-known among these writings are the novels of Charles Dickens, but systematic social investigations were also undertaken. In the 1840s, Friedrich Engels, Marx's collaborator, produced a report on the condition of the poor in Salford and Manchester, and in the 1860s, Mayhew (1861a) and Hollingshead (1861) produced sensational reports on conditions in London. Mayhew's surveys contain lively and vivid descriptions of the lives of the poor, and they remain among the major social documents of the nineteenth century. It was in the later work of Charles Booth and Seebohm Rowntree, however, that the parameters of poverty were to be uncovered with statistical precision.

Deprivation in deepest England

Booth began his work in 1886 with a study of social conditions in East London and some related analyses of Central London and Battersea. From this base, he broadened his enquiries into a comprehensive survey of the whole of London. His first priority was to devise a set of categories into which he could organize his materials. He defined eight categories of people according to the

level and type of earnings that were available to their members (see Figure 14.5). These categories were seen as social classes, a claim that we look at in Chapter 15. Booth's main purpose was to use his categories to show the distribution of the population according to their various levels of living.

Booth saw poverty in relative terms. It was, he said, an inability to maintain 'the usual standard of life in this country' (Booth 1901–2: i. 33). He calculated that a family of five would require at least 21s. per week in order to achieve this standard of living (see also Pember-Reeves 1913). Those living in the 'ordinary poverty' of categories C and D, with incomes between 18s. and 21s. (90p to £1.05p) had insufficient means and could barely scrape by. Those who depended upon intermittent, irregular earnings lived a particularly precarious existence, as they faced the ever-present possibility of falling into deeper poverty. 'Chronic want', the lot of the very poor in categories A and B, occurred whenever income fell below 18s. The very poor relied, at best, on casual earnings from temporary and seasonal work or from small-time street trading. The 'loafers' of category A, forming what many now describe as an underclass, were the poorest of all. They had little in the way of

ASYLUM FOR THE HOUSELESS POOR, CRIPPLEGATE.

For many people in the past, some partial relief from poverty was possible only in the workhouse or in a hostel. How does the position of the homeless differ today?

Charles Booth

Charles Booth (1840–1916) was a wealthy Liverpool shipowner and merchant. He felt a responsibility to improve the conditions in which ordinary people lived, but was convinced that radical claims about the extent of poverty in London were overstated. He decided to undertake an investigation that would produce accurate figures on its true extent. Booth was surprised to discover that there were even more people living in poverty than the radicals had claimed. His work helped to shape the introduction of old-age pensions in 1908.

The work that Booth carried out was pioneering empirical sociology, although he was untrained in sociological theory or research methods. He originally intended to compile a full census of all residents of the East End, but he soon realized that this was an impossible task to undertake through house-to-house methods. Alternative methods were required. Booth gathered his information indirectly from School Board visitors and others who had a detailed knowledge of local residents. In this way, he was eventually able to extend his research to the whole of London, producing detailed street-by-street accounts of poverty in a massive work of seventeen volumes (Booth 1901–2). He compiled his results into a large-scale map of London, colouring each street: black or blue for poverty, red for comfort, and yellow for wealth.

Figure 14.5. The Booth class scheme

Category	Percentage in London (1889)	
H Upper middle class (and above)	5.9	
G Lower middle class	11.9	
F Higher class labour **E** Regular standard earnings	51.5	} Working class
		— 21*s*. line
D Small irregular earnings **C** Intermittent earnings	22.3	Poor
		— 18*s*. line
B Casual earnings	7.5	} Very poor
A Lowest class of occasional and semi-criminals	0.9	

Source: J. Scott (1994: table 2.1).

Figure 14.6. Distribution of poverty in London, 1886–1889

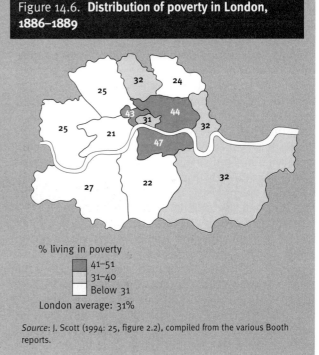

% living in poverty

- 41–51
- 31–40
- Below 31

London average: 31%

Source: J. Scott (1994: 25, figure 2.2), compiled from the various Booth reports.

legitimate income from employment, they drifted in and out of crime, and they were beset by vices of all kinds.

Booth's researches showed that 30.7 per cent of the whole population of London were living in poverty as he defined it. The bulk of these people were the ordinary poor who were dependent on low or intermittent pay, but a hard core of 8.4 per cent lived in chronic want. Poverty was heavily concentrated in the East End and a vast swathe of south London, where approaching 50 per cent lived in poverty. However, even the western boroughs had substantial amounts. Kensington and Chelsea, for example, had 21 per cent of their residents living below the poverty line. The localities with the highest levels of poverty were Southwark, Greenwich, and Clerkenwell, all of which had over 60 per cent living in poverty, while the wealthiest areas were Dulwich (1.3 per cent poverty), Mayfair (2.7 per cent), and Belgravia (5.0 per cent). This distribution is shown in Figure 14.6.

Booth saw the level and regularity of earnings as

being at the heart of the problem of poverty. Among the ordinary poor (categories C and D), 43 per cent had only casual or irregular pay and a further 25 per cent were on regular but low pay. Most of the very poor (categories A and B) suffered from similar problems, but Booth saw those he termed the 'loafers' as *choosing* to avoid employment. They were, he held, responsible in part for the depths of their own poverty. Even among the ordinary poor, Booth identified 13 per cent whose suffering he thought was made worse by their wasteful spending of money on alcohol that should have been spent on food. Others on similar incomes managed just about to scrape along because of the thrifty housekeeping of a 'good wife' (Booth 1901–2: i. 50). A substantial number of those living in ordinary poverty were in such dire straits because of the size of their families. Their incomes were insufficient to support the large numbers of children that they had. In other cases, he claimed, poverty was due to serious illnesses that prevented people from working.

Booth wanted to find out more about the employment conditions that were responsible for low pay and irregular earnings, so he carried out an investigation into the London labour market. Of particular interest are his studies of those trades that employed women in large numbers. There were, for example, nearly 400,000 domestic servants in London, and 85 per cent of them were women. Many female servants were recruited as young girls directly from the workhouses, where they had been given a basic domestic training. At 13 years old, their pay averaged £5.30 a year, rising to £17.70 a year for those over 30. Many women had casual or irregular employment as homeworkers, employed to finish textile goods or assemble matchboxes. Such 'sweated' conditions, Booth held, were typical of all the East End trades. Both men and women had to work long hours in unsanitary conditions for low and irregular pay. In the docks, for example, casual labourers received between 60p and 75p per week, and they often had to go for weeks without any work at all.

 You will find a discussion of contemporary forms of homeworking in Chapter 13, pp. 541–2.

Poverty and the welfare state

Shortly after Booth's research, Rowntree began an investigation of poverty in his home city of York. Rowntree wanted to see whether the amount of poverty found in London was typical of the rest of the country. His major survey was carried out in 1899, but he

Seebohm Rowntree

Benjamin Seebohm Rowntree (1871–1954) was the son of Joseph Rowntree, the founder of the large cocoa and chocolate business. The family were prominent Quakers and philanthropists. Seebohm worked in the family firm as labour director. He introduced a pension scheme, a works council, and arrangements for profit-sharing. He was Chairman of the company from 1925 to 1941. Rowntree was given responsibility for the welfare policy of munitions workers during the First World War and was centrally involved in the planning of post-war housing policy. Rowntree's researches (1901, 1941; Rowntree and Lavers 1951) provide a long-term overview that stresses, in particular, the impact of age and the life cycle on poverty.

updated this in 1936 and 1950. He used similar research methods to Booth, but he also carried out a house-to-house survey.

We have already looked at the rather restrictive, absolute view of poverty that Rowntree adopted. Nevertheless, his poverty line, set at £1.08 per week, was actually a little higher than that drawn by Booth. Using this poverty line, Rowntree concluded that 9.91 per cent of the population of York was living in what he called primary poverty. They simply had insufficient income for their own survival. A further 17.89 per cent had incomes that were above the poverty line, but were unable to budget properly and so experienced the 'obvious want and squalor' of what he called secondary poverty (Rowntree 1901: 115). Those in secondary poverty, he held, could escape this through better budgeting. In all, 27.8 per cent of York's population were living below the subsistence standard, a figure that was not much less than that found by Booth in London.

Rowntree saw the immediate cause of primary poverty, in more than a half of all cases, as low pay. He concluded that the wages that were then paid to unskilled labourers were insufficient to maintain a normal family. He held, however, that the life cycle also had a major impact on poverty. The same family could pass from poverty to a degree of comfort as its members moved from child-rearing to maturity, but the husband and wife might move back into poverty in their old age (see Figure 14.7).

Studies by later researchers suggested that the level of poverty fell during the first three decades of the twentieth century. Rowntree decided to test this claim in a new study for 1936. He updated his primary poverty line to £1.53 per week for a family of five, and he found that

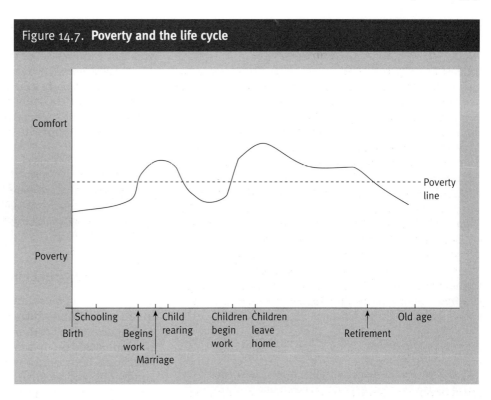

Figure 14.7. **Poverty and the life cycle**

just 3.9 per cent of the York population were then living in poverty. The amount of primary poverty, then, had fallen by two-thirds, and this finding was in line with the claim that income had become more equally distributed in the first part of the century.

This new study, however, also used a relative concept of poverty. This measure recognized that an absolute measure of subsistence income had to be combined with an allowance for insurance, newspapers, holidays, and various other things that could be regarded as necessities for most people. This new relative poverty line was set at £2.18 per week in 1936, and on this basis Rowntree found that 17.7 per cent of the York population were living in poverty (see Figure 14.8).

Rowntree recognized, however, that he had still produced only a minimum estimate of the number of people who might actually experience poverty at some stage in their life. Some of those who had been poor in the past might be living in relative comfort at the time of his survey, because of the particular stage in their family life cycle. Similarly, many of those who were comfortable at the time of the survey might be expected to fall into poverty at some time in the future. Rowntree concluded that the numbers of these people needed to be estimated. He suggested that over a half of all manual workers would experience poverty at

some stage in their life, even though a much smaller number would actually be living in poverty at any one time.

The principal causes of poverty, Rowntree argued, were old age (responsible for 14.6 per cent of all poverty), unemployment (28.6 per cent), and low pay (32.8 per cent). He therefore concluded that improvements in pension provision, an increase in the level of employment, and an increase in average pay would eventually lead to the disappearance of poverty.

Rowntree, in common with many of his contemporaries, thought that by 1950 these very changes had come about. Unemployment was much lower than it had been in the 1930s and the country was coming out of a period of post-war austerity and entering a new era of affluence. Most importantly, the Beveridge proposals for establishing a welfare state had been implemented. Rowntree's own work from the 1930s had been taken up by William Beveridge (later Lord Beveridge) as the basis of his proposals on the level of welfare benefits. The key change, Rowntree felt, was improved old-age pensions. Rowntree set out to examine the consequences of these changes in a third, and final, survey of York (Rowntree and Lavers 1951). Setting his relative poverty line at £5.00 per week, he found that just 1.66 per cent of the population were poor, far fewer than there had been in

Figure 14.8. Poverty in York, 1936 and 1950

1936		1950	
Class or weekly pay (£)	% of population	Class or weekly pay (£)	% of population
Middle class (and above)	35.0	Middle class (and above)	not recorded
3.18 or more	20.5	7.30 or more	34.98
2.68–3.17	8.0	6.15–7.29	11.90
2.18–2.67	10.8	5.00–6.14	11.48
1.68–2.67	9.6	3.85–4.99	1.43
Less than 1.68	8.1	Less than 3.85	0.23

Relative poverty line

Note: pay levels identified by Rowntree have been converted to decimal currency.

Source: J. Scott (1995: table 2.16).

▶ The percentage figures do not add up to 100 per cent because Rowntree excluded servants and those living in public institutions, such as workhouses and hospitals. Do you think that the amount of measured poverty would increase or decrease if they had been included? What further evidence would you need to answer this question?

the 1930s. The welfare state had, it seemed, confirmed a move towards equality.

OPENNESS AND CLOSURE

The distribution of income and assets—and, therefore, the levels of poverty and wealth—are largely determined by the ownership of property and earnings from employment. For all but the very rich, in fact, it is their occupational earnings that determine their life chances. It is for this reason that an investigation into the occupational structure can tell us so much about a society. The openness of a structure of social inequality can be measured by the amount of **occupational mobility**, the amount of movement from one occupation to another.

An **open** structure of inequality is one in which people have the opportunity to rise from lowly paid occupations to those that give them superior income,

assets, and prestige. Conversely, a **closed** structure is one in which people's chances in life are fixed at birth and they cannot rise, or fall, through their own efforts or achievements. An open structure, according to the functionalist theory of inequality, is one in which the ambitious and the talented are able to rise, and in which those without merit will fall. Britain may be an unequal society, but is it, nevertheless, a meritocracy?

 We look in more detail at occupational mobility in Chapter 15, where we consider the question of when social *inequalities* are formed into patterns of social *stratification*.

Social mobility in Britain

The earliest and most important study of this question in Britain was undertaken by David Glass and a team of colleagues at the London School of Economics in 1949. Glass allocated occupations to seven categories, each of which was homogeneous in terms of income, working conditions, and prestige. He was then able to compare the occupations of parents and children and to look at the occupational mobility of people over their working life. The research showed that positions in life were not completely fixed at birth. There was a degree of fluidity or movement from one type of occupation to another.

Glass found that there was rather more upward than downward mobility, but even this was very limited in scope. Most occupational mobility was short range: it was movement within a particular occupational category or between categories that were close to one another in the occupational structure. People were unlikely to move into occupations that were very different from those of their parents or from those in which they had started their own working lives.

Glass concluded that the existence of only a limited amount of occupational mobility showed that Britain was far from being a truly open society. Openness was assessed against the yardstick of **perfect mobility**. This is the amount of mobility that we would expect to find if ability was randomly distributed and there were no barriers to the mobility of the able. In fact, there was nothing like perfect mobility in Britain. There was a kind of inertia that produced a pattern of *occupational closure*: people were more likely to remain where they were born than they were to rise or to fall.

This occupational closure was especially marked at the top and at the bottom of the occupational structure. The top category in Glass's schema contained the professional, administrative, and managerial occupa-

Glass and social mobility

David Glass's 1954 study of mobility in England, Wales, and Scotland used a sample of 10,000 adult men and women who were aged over 14 in 1949. His interviewers collected biographical details on each individual, especially on their education, qualifications, and work history. They also collected information on fathers' (but not mothers') occupations.

The occupational categories that were used in the Glass study are those of the Hall–Jones Classification. These are often seen as social-class categories, and we discuss these more fully in Chapter 3, p. 98. You may like to keep that discussion in mind.

The two central concepts used in mobility studies are *inter-generational* mobility and *intra-generational* mobility. Intergenerational mobility is movement between generations and is measured by comparing a person's occupational level with that of his or her parents. In practice, most mobility studies have looked only at the father's occupation, a highly contentious approach. Intra-generational mobility is movement within a single generation and is measured by comparing a person's current occupational level with that of his or her own first job.

tions that enjoyed superior life chances to all other occupations. If there was perfect mobility and openness, then everyone would have an equal chance of attaining one of these jobs. On this basis, only 3 per cent of the children of people already in these occupations would be expected to enter the same kind of jobs. In fact, 40 per cent of them followed in their fathers' footsteps. Those who went into lower-level occupations than their fathers only rarely had to enter manual work. Their chances of remaining in some kind of relatively privileged non-manual work were very high.

Occupational achievement

The argument that modern societies are characteristically open societies with no sharp boundaries between one level of living and another has been extensively explored in American sociology. It is useful to look at those studies for what they tell us about the United States and because the methods used have been taken up by British sociologists. The most important study in this area is that of Blau and Duncan (1967).

The amount of occupational mobility was measured in the same way as it had been by Glass. They used an

index of association that compared the actual mobility rates between two categories with those that would be expected solely on the basis of chance. In a completely open society—one with perfect mobility—this index would be 1.0. In fact, Blau and Duncan found that there was a high degree of self-recruitment, or closure, in the United States. The index of association was as high as 11.7 in the case of self-employed professionals. Despite the existence of a high level of self-recruitment throughout the occupational structure, there was also a great deal of upward mobility. There was a small amount of downward mobility, but only rarely did this involve mobility between non-manual and manual jobs or between manufacturing and agricultural work.

Blau and Duncan

Peter Blau and Otis Dudley Duncan studied occupational achievement using a sample of more than 20,000 men aged between 20 and 64 (Blau and Duncan 1967). Data were collected in 1962, using interviews and questionnaires. The fieldwork was undertaken in association with the US Bureau of Census.

The occupations of their respondents were initially allocated to seventeen occupational categories (salaried professionals, managers, clerical, manufacturing, labourers, etc.) that were similar in terms of their life chances and social experiences. These seventeen categories were ranked according to the income and education of their incumbents. By comparing respondents' occupations with those of their fathers, Blau and Duncan were able to study inter-generational mobility.

The high level of upward mobility was seen as being a consequence of a massive growth in the numbers of non-manual and service-sector jobs, together with a corresponding decline in the number of manual and agricultural jobs. There was a surplus of non-manual jobs and a surplus of manual workers' children ready to fill them. Most of this movement was short-range mobility. There was little of the kind of long-range mobility that would indicate a truly open structure of inequality.

This was confirmed in some comparative work by Lipset and Bendix (1959), who undertook a secondary analysis of research into occupational mobility. Using a rather crude distinction between manual and non-manual occupations, they found similarities in all advanced industrial societies. Adding together the total amount of upward and downward mobility, they found the highest levels of overall vertical movement in Germany (31 per cent) and the United States (30 per cent). Levels in Britain and Sweden stood at 29 per cent, while France and Japan had levels of 27 per cent.

These similarities in levels of mobility were seen by Lipset and Bendix as reflecting certain common patterns in the development of industrial societies. It was only the less-advanced societies of Italy and Finland that had lower rates of mobility. The expansion of non-manual occupations as industry advanced, they argued, meant a growing demand for highly qualified workers. The children of those who were already in such jobs were too few to fill all the vacancies, even if none of them were downwardly mobile. As a result, opportunities for upward mobility were created simply because of the changing occupational division of labour. In these circumstances, education became especially important for occupational recruitment, and it is those who acquired educational credentials through school, college, and university who were able to move into managerial, technical, and professional occupations in large numbers.

Blau and Duncan looked at how occupational achievement, the occupational level to which people can rise or fall, was related to social origins. They asked how people's social background shaped their occupational destinations and, in particular, what part was played by education in linking origins and destinations. To explore these issues, they abandoned their initial seventeen occupational categories and used a quantitative measure of occupational prestige to place the occupations in a hierarchy. They held that the prestige of an occupation was closely associated with its income. They went on to construct causal path diagrams of the factors involved.

Figure 14.9 shows the causal model produced by Blau and Duncan to describe occupational achievement in the United States. The higher path coefficients are treated as the more important causal links. Assessing causation is not straightforward, as correlation is not the same thing as causation. Correlation means only that there is a mathematical association between two measures. This can be used as evidence for a causal relationship only if we have good reason to think that all the important variables have been included in the model. Blau and Duncan believed that they had measured everything that was important, and they draw conclusions about their relative importance.

It can be seen from Figure 14.9 that the greatest influence on both initial and current occupation was a man's level of education, which was itself influenced by his father's education and occupation. The direct effect of father's occupation, independently of educational factors, was very small. People's social origins determine their occupational achievements largely through the influence that they exert on their education.

Path diagrams

The first steps in constructing a causal model are to guess at the most likely causal relations and to draw a flow chart of these influences. The next step is to calculate the actual strength of the various relations. Correlations among the variables are calculated and regression coefficients are used as *path coefficients* to indicate the strength of a particular causal influence. You do not need to understand the mathematics of this, so long as the general principles are clear.

Correlation is a measure of how closely associated two variables are. If one changes in line with another, they are said to be correlated. The measure of how closely associated they are is called the correlation coefficient, but you do not need to know how to calculate this. Perfect correlation (one variable changing in direct proportion to another) has a coefficient of 1, while complete randomness has a coefficient of 0. The closer the value is to 1, the greater is the association between the two variables. If two factors vary in opposite directions (one going up while the other goes down), the coefficient has a negative value.

☞ You might like to review our discussion of educational selection in Chapter 7, pp. 233–7, and see what further light it throws on these claims.

The biggest causal influences in the diagram, however, are the so-called *residuals*, the unknown or unmeasured factors that are left over when all the known factors are measured. While the path linking education and occupation had a coefficient of 0.394, the unknown influences on occupation had a combined effect of 0.753. Blau and Duncan argued that this did not undermine their model, as they claimed to have uncovered the single most important set of factors determining occupational achievement. Jencks (1972), however, has suggested that the massive size of the residuals indicates that factors such as 'luck' (for example, being in the right place at the right time to get a job) are far more important than any of the structural factors measured by Blau and Duncan.

Blau and Duncan gave particular attention to the

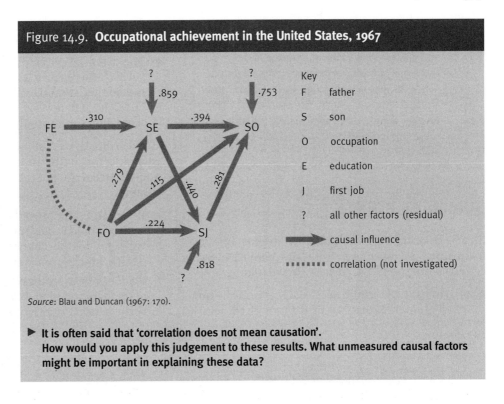

Figure 14.9. **Occupational achievement in the United States, 1967**

Key
F   father
S   son
O   occupation
E   education
J   first job
?   all other factors (residual)
→   causal influence
▪▪▪▪▪▪▪   correlation (not investigated)

Source: Blau and Duncan (1967: 170).

▶ **It is often said that 'correlation does not mean causation'.**
How would you apply this judgement to these results. What unmeasured causal factors
might be important in explaining these data?

effects of ethnicity on occupational achievement. The economic disadvantages that were experienced by African-Americans, they argued, were due to their educational disadvantages. Because they had less chance of an education at high school, college, or university, African-Americans were disadvantaged in the competition for jobs. These disadvantages reflected the existence of prejudice and racism. Even well-educated African-Americans faced worse opportunities than did whites with a similar level of education. Because of the poorer educational facilities and economic opportunities that existed in the southern states, those living there were especially disadvantaged by comparison with those living in the north. Blau and Duncan (1967: 238) argue that 'It is the cumulative effect of the handicaps Negroes encounter at every stage in their lives that produces the serious inequalities of opportunities which they suffer.'

Occupational achievement in the United States, they conclude, was largely regulated by the universalistic values that are displacing more particularistic standards and ascribed characteristics. The effects of universalism, however, are partially counteracted by the persistence of racism and of disadvantages linked to ethnicity.

By contrast, the descendants of recent white migrants to the United States (Germans, Italians, Poles, and others) had patterns of occupational achievement that were similar to those of the long-established white migrants. It took two or more generations for these patterns to appear, because of the strong influence that was exerted by parental background, but Blau and Duncan present much evidence to support the idea that, so far as white ethnic minorities are concerned, there was an ethnic melting pot that unified the life chances of indigenous and migrant groups.

Blau and Duncan saw the drive to universalism as persisting. Education has become ever more central to occupational achievement, they argued, because it measures ability and accredits academic success in the abilities that are required by the industrial system. This growing universalism is also apparent in the materialistic character of people's orientations. Material success, in the form of the pursuit of income and consumer goods, becomes the yardstick of occupational success. People are motivated by the material rewards that are attached to occupations. Like many observers, however, Blau and Duncan were pessimistic about the long-term impact of universalism on the ethnic disadvantages of African-Americans.

Blau and Duncan's emphasis on universalism and materialism shows their acceptance of the functionalist theory of inequality. You might also notice the way in which their view connects with Merton's theory of anomie (discussed in Chapter 2, pp. 49–50) and Parsons's theory of stratification (discussed in Chapter 15, pp. 606–7).

SUMMARY POINTS

In this section we have examined trends in social inequality and openness from the late nineteenth century until the 1950s. We have shown that

▶ Britain has had a a high degree of economic inequality over the whole of this century, though the level of concentration in both income and assets declined over the period considered.

▶ The extent of poverty in London and in York at the turn of the century was extremely high. Booth estimated that around one in three of the London population lived in poverty. Rowntree suggested that this had fallen substantially by the 1950s.

We went on to show the connections between economic inequality and other aspects of life chances, and we tried to put our figures in a comparative context.

▶ Inequalities in income and assets are associated with a whole range of other advantages and disadvantages in life chances. These include those of health, housing, and mortality.

▶ Evidence from studies of occupational mobility suggests that rates of mobility in Britain were similar to those in other industrial societies.

TOWARDS NEW INEQUALITIES

The view that poverty had been eliminated persisted for some time into the post-war period. Gradually, however, academic commentators came to realize that the hopes that lay behind the establishment of the welfare state had proved over-optimistic. Poverty was rediscovered, and greater attention was given to charting the overall extent of economic inequality. While a trend towards the equalization of incomes could be observed, poverty persisted. Social policy through the 1960s and 1970s continued to be concerned with alleviating poverty, eliminating the conditions that produce it, and promoting greater equality. From the late 1970s, however, government policy became more concerned with reducing the level of spending on welfare provision and promoting greater enterprise, effort, and inequality. By the 1980s, many politicians were denying that there was, any longer, any poverty. If the welfare state had failed to eliminate poverty, it appeared to many that the 'enterprise economy' had done so.

Those who held that poverty no longer existed tended to use an absolute concept of poverty. They argued that living standards were far higher than they had been during the early years of the century. Those who have not only food and shoes, but also cars, televisions, and washing machines, they held, cannot be regarded as poor in any meaningful sense.

Much of the discussion over the existence or non-existence of poverty and inequality has revolved around official figures derived from the public-assistance programmes of the welfare state. Although there has never been a truly official poverty line in Britain, the basic social-assistance level has been widely used for this purpose. Social assistance—variously called National Assistance, Supplementary Benefit, and Income Support—defines minimum incomes for households of different sizes, and welfare benefits are available, under certain conditions, to those whose incomes fall below these levels.

The social-assistance level is the official view of what ought to be the minimum standard of living for a full member, a citizen, of British society. This level of living has been institutionalized through Acts of Parliament and administrative regulations. The level at which it is set varies with the financial constraints that a government currently faces, and it is also shaped by prevailing political prejudices and ideologies. Nevertheless, it does provide a benchmark level for estimating the officially recognized level at which poverty or deprivation occurs. Direct research on public perceptions of poverty have produced figures that are broadly comparable with those that have been arrived at by using the social-assistance level (Mack and Lansley 1985). The social-assistance level, then, is the closest thing that there is to an official poverty line. Conservative ministers of the 1980s and 1990s were the first politicians to seriously challenge this view. Their rejection of the concept of poverty was linked to an attempt to cut back the level of welfare benefits.

The drive towards greater European integration during the 1970s and 1980s, however, has led to moves in the opposite direction. There have been a series of Community-wide and Union-wide poverty and aid programmes, and in these an alternative poverty line has been employed. The European poverty programme measures the percentage of individuals and families whose *disposable income*—the amount that they actually have to spend after direct taxes—is 50 per cent or less of the national average income. This definition has become the effective official poverty line for the European Union. It has been seen as the level at which people's resources 'exclude them from a minimum acceptable way of life in the Member State in which they live' (Article 1.2, 85/8/EEC).

This is, it must be noted, a relative definition of poverty. The line is drawn at a level of income that is felt to prevent people from participating fully in the society of which they are citizens. It defines the acceptable social minimum in precise statistical terms. It is a matter not of particular administrative criteria (as with the social-assistance level) but of the way in which a social consensus is actually institutionalized in the structure of income distribution. Poverty is defined relative to the particular pattern of income distribution that is maintained by custom, by official policies, and by the economic processes of a society.

There are, then, two official poverty lines. The social-assistance line, which came increasingly under attack by Conservative critics in the 1980s and 1990s, and the European Union poverty line. Academic research on poverty has employed both of these poverty lines, recognizing that neither of them can give a perfect measure of the extent of relative poverty. This research into poverty has been allied with a considerable amount of research into the structure of the income and asset distributions within which poverty and wealth are generated.

GREATER INEQUALITY

Both of the official definitions of poverty see it in relative terms. Poverty is not a matter of absolute physiological subsistence, but of a standard of living that is deprived relative to the range of acceptable standards of living in a society. It is only possible to assess poverty

in the context of a wider understanding of the extent of economic inequality and the differences in life chances with which these are associated.

Income and earnings

Income distribution changed only slightly between the Second World War and the middle of the 1960s. Between 1963 and 1977, however, there was a move towards much greater equality. This equalization was a result of government policy that could build upon a period of affluence and economic growth. From 1978 to the end of the 1980s, however, policy and economic conditions were reversed. Unemployment increased as recessions became more persistent, and there was a rapid increase in the level of inequality. This growth in inequality levelled off during the 1990s, by which time most of the post-war equalization had been reversed.

The top 20 per cent of the population's share of income before tax rose from 44 per cent in 1972 to 50 per cent in 1988 (Social Trends 1992). The share of the top 10 per cent increased from 21 per cent to 24 per cent over the same period, and the share of the top 1 per cent also increased. At the other end of the scale, the bottom 10 per cent received 4 per cent of all income in 1979, and their share had fallen to 2 per cent by 1991. Figure 14.10 shows the increase in income inequality since the late 1970s.

A major reason for this growth in income inequality during the 1980s, as we have suggested, was a growth in unemployment, which brought more and more people into dependence on low welfare benefits. The number of households in which neither partner was in employment grew particularly rapidly. At the same time, benefit levels were being reduced as the government

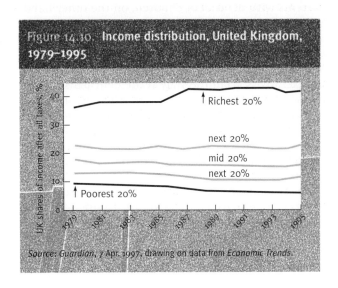

Figure 14.10. Income distribution, United Kingdom, 1979–1995

Source: Guardian, 7 Apr. 1997, drawing on data from Economic Trends.

tried to reduce the level of state expenditure. Relative to average earnings, the state retirement pension and unemployment benefit have both fallen. In 1970 Unemployment Benefit (now termed the Jobseeker's Allowance) was just over 40 per cent of average income, but in 1992 it was less than 30 per cent of average income.

There has also been an increase in the inequality of incomes attached to particular jobs. The distribution of income among manual workers, for example, remained virtually unchanged over the almost 100 years from 1886 to 1976. During this period, incomes of all manual workers tended to rise together by very much the same amount. From the late 1970s, however, this was no longer the case. Long-established relativities were destroyed by an increasing demand for qualified and experienced workers, and by a decline in unionization and other mechanisms of wage regulation (see Chapter 13, pp. 534–6). Competitive, deregulated labour markets increased differentials among workers, and in very much the direction predicted by the functionalist theory of inequality.

Another factor responsible for the increase in inequality during the 1980s was the huge growth in investment incomes and other high incomes as a result of the deregulation of the financial markets and the creation of a tax climate that encouraged a so-called enterprise culture. A quarter of all Chairmen and Chief Executives of large companies in 1986 had received salary rises of 23 per cent, and one in ten of them had been given a rise of 42 per cent in the year.

By 1995 average gross weekly earnings (before tax) stood at £369 for a man and £268 for a woman. The typical family of two parents and their dependent children received gross earnings of £537 per week, 88 per cent of this being received as salaries or wages. Lone parents with dependent children, on the other hand, averaged an income of just £203 per week, with welfare benefits accounting for 49 per cent of their income. Among retired households, there was a growing division between those who derived their incomes mainly or exclusively from the state retirement pension and those who were in private pensions schemes. In 1979 44 per cent of pensioners had occupational pensions, and the number had risen to 55 per cent by 1989. The average income of these private pensioners was far higher than the average income of those who depended on the state pension alone.

These inequalities become clearer if they are seen in relation to particular occupations. Figure 14.11 presents some pay comparisons. The pay of a cleaner, a typical low-paid job, is used as the baseline for comparing the earnings of other workers. Gross earnings of

Figure 14.11. Weekly earnings of selected occupations, Great Britain, 1981–1995

Occupation	£ per week in		
	1981	1991	1995
Doctor	569	691	764
Solicitor	379	610	585
Secondary teacher	324	403	435
Social worker	254	313	340
Nurse	194	308	329
Carpenter	230	269	274
Receptionist	139	179	188
Cleaner	175	186	181
Waiter	143	166	161

Note: figures are real wages, based on 1995 prices.

Source: Social Tends (1996: table 5.7); see also Social Trends (1997: chart 5.7).

▶ You might like to calculate the mean income in 1995 for the occupations listed in this table.

▶ How does your result compare with figures for average earnings that we have given in the text?

▶ Why do you think that it is different?

cleaners have been fairly static in real terms at around £180 per week throughout the 1980s and 1990s. In 1981, nurses and assembly-line workers (not shown in the table) earned only a few pounds more than a cleaner, but they were earning much more by the end of the 1980s. By 1995, an assembly-line worker was earning just under £300 per week, and a nurse was earning almost twice as much as a cleaner. Solicitors earned more than twice as much as cleaners in 1981; ten years later a typical solicitor was earning over three times a cleaner's wage. Doctors were already receiving more than three times a cleaner's wage in 1981, and by 1995 a doctor was earning four times as much as a cleaner.

These comparisons, of course, give only an estimate of the differences. The actual differences are often much greater. A cleaner's wage shows little variation with age and experience, but solicitors and doctors are generally on progressive salary scales that allow many of them to earn far more than the incomes shown here. This is particularly true of many management careers. Pay for graduate entrants to a managerial career is broadly similar to that of a nurse who is well established in a career, but the pay of top directors and executives goes well beyond the conventional scales. The highest paid directors in large British companies receive, on average, at least ten times as much in income as a typical doctor, or forty times the income of a cleaner. The highest-paid director in 1990 received almost 150 times as much as the person who cleaned his office.

At the end of the 1990s, nearly one in twelve workers earns less than £3 an hour. This gives a maximum of £112.50 for a typical working week, though many low-paid workers are in part-time jobs that give them total incomes of only £40 to £50 per week. Most part-time workers are women, which goes much of the way towards explaining the lower earnings of women as compared with men. However, women in full-time work earn less than men in full-time work. Over a half of all women employed full-time in 1996 earned less than £250 per week, compared with only a third of men. These differences are reflected in the households of married or cohabiting partners: in more than a half of couples, the man earns at least £100 per week more than his female partner.

Incomes show great variation by industry and region. Earnings are highest in banking, finance, and insurance, and in the privatized energy and water industries. They are lowest in agriculture and fishing, in retail and wholesale distribution, and in hotels and restaurants. Wages and salaries are highest in London, Surrey, and Berkshire, and only slightly lower in the adjoining counties of West Sussex, Wiltshire, Hertfordshire, Buckinghamshire, Oxford, and Bedfordshire. In the north of England, only Cheshire, Redcar, and Cleveland are high-income areas, while Aberdeen is the only Scottish city in this category. The lowest incomes are found in parts of Wales, the Scottish border counties, and the Highlands (*Social Trends* 1997: chart 5.6 and table 5.8).

Gross earnings tell only a part of the story, as taxation has a considerable effect on the final income that is available to people. Because of the system of allowances and varying tax rates, the proportion of a person's income that is paid in tax varies with the level of her or his income. Those earning less than £100 a week in 1996 paid little or no income tax, while those on £200 a week paid around 9 per cent of this in tax. Those earning between £400 and £500 a week paid about a quarter of their income in tax, while those earning nearly £2,000 a week (£100,000 a year) paid over one-third of this in income tax (*Social Trends* 1997: table 5.12). National Insurance contributions make a further reduction to most incomes, but these are not so progressive in their effects as income tax.

Disposable income has actually increased overall in real terms since 1971. This increase, however, has been greater for higher earners than for lower earners, leading to an increase in the gap between top and bottom. A couple with two children fall into the bottom 20 per cent of family households if they have an income below £181 per week. The disposable income of those at the bottom of the distribution was only slightly higher in 1994 than it had been in 1971. Disposable income for those in the top 10 per cent, however, increased from about £280 per week in 1971 to £470 per week in 1994.

About one-fifth of disposable income, on average, goes towards such indirect taxes as VAT and Customs Duty. Direct taxation is *progressive* in its effect—the tax rate rising with income—but these indirect taxes are *regressive*. That is to say, the proportion of income paid in indirect taxes is greater in low-income households than it is in high-income households. For this reason, a shift from, say, income tax to a tax on food or fuel has a redistributive effect in favour of highly paid households.

It is extremely difficult to compare statistics for one country with those for another, but it is important to try to put the British figures in context. The share of total income going to the top 1 per cent of the population in 1970 seems to have been lower in Britain than it was in any other European country. In Belgium, Germany, and France, almost one-third of total income went to the top 10 per cent, while in Britain the figure was a quarter. On the other hand, the share of the bottom 20 per cent (just over 6 per cent) was broadly similar in Britain, Belgium, and Germany. Only France and Italy had a greater imbalance, probably reflecting the large agricultural population in these two countries.

Sir Paul McCartney: reputed to earn over £3,750 per hour from his composer royalties.

Outside Europe, Britain and Australia were comparable in terms of economic inequality, but Japan and the United States were both considerably more unequal during the 1970s. By the middle of the 1980s, the growth of inequality in Britain had been more rapid and more marked than in any other country except New Zealand. Income in Britain was more unequally distributed than it was in Germany, the Netherlands, Sweden, and Canada, but it was less unequal than it was France, Italy, New Zealand, and the United States (Hills 1995: 64; see also J. Scott 1994: ch. 5). Income distribution in Britain and the United States, however, is very similar. In 1992 the top 20 per cent of the population in the United States received 47 per cent of all income, while the bottom 20 per cent received just 4 per cent.

Britain's tax rates are currently low by international standards. While an average of 16.3 per cent of income in Britain in 1994 was taken in direct taxes and National Insurance contributions, the tax burden in Germany was much higher at 21.4 per cent. Canada, France, Italy, and the United States all had higher levels of taxation than Britain, and only Japan had a lower rate (13 per cent).

Assets and expenditure

We have been looking, so far, only at income distribution. The distribution of personal assets must also be examined. Assets, it will be recalled, are the total stock of economic resources that a person or household has been able to accumulate. Inequality in the distribution of personal assets narrowed continually from the 1920s to the 1970s, but it has not changed very much since then. Assets are, however, more concentrated than income. The share of the top 1 per cent of the population declined from 47 per cent in 1950 to 17 per cent in 1993, most of this decline occurring during the 1950s and 1960s (see Figures 14.3 and 14.12). Figure 14.12 shows that the share of the bottom 50 per cent of the population in total personal assets has barely altered since 1976. In fact, the principal change in the distribution has been a slight shift from the top 10 per cent to the next 40 per cent, reflecting the impact of the growth in home ownership over this period.

The top 1 per cent of asset holders in the United States had 20.7 per cent of all assets in 1972, compared with the figure of 29 per cent found for Britain (Rubinstein 1986: 147). In 1986, 160 American families had assets in excess of $200 million. These included such families as the Du Ponts, Fords, Gettys, and Rockefellers. The bases of these huge fortunes were financial, industrial, and commercial businesses, which have remained

Figure 14.12. Distribution of personal assets, United Kingdom, 1976–1993

	Percentage share of assets				
	1976	1981	1986	1991	1993
Top 1%	21	18	18	17	17
Top 5%	38	36	36	35	36
Top 10%	50	50	50	47	48
Top 25%	71	73	73	71	72
Top 50%	92	92	90	92	93
Bottom 50%	8	8	10	8	7

Source: Social Trends (1997: table 5.25).

➤ Extend the graph that you drew for Figure 14.3 and add the data in this table. Add lines for the extra slices shown. Do these extra data throw any new light on the trends that you have observed?

➤ Why not try drawing some pie charts for these data? Figure 14.13 shows a pie chart of the 1993 data.

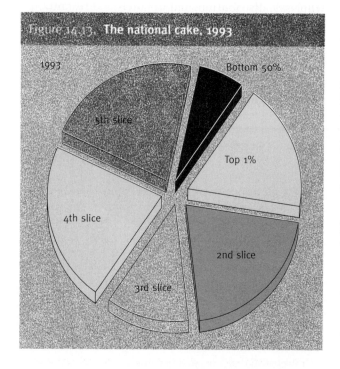

Figure 14.13. The national cake, 1993

important sources of wealth throughout the century. In France, the top 5 per cent of households in 1992 held 40 per cent of all personal assets, while the bottom 25 per cent had just 1 per cent. The assets of a person in the top 10 per cent were five times the average for the French population as a whole, and almost 800 times the average for those in the poorest 10 per cent. In 1997 the richest person in the world was the Sultan of Brunei, with total personal assets of $38 billion. Second to him, with $36.4 billion, was Bill Gates, the founder and head of Microsoft.

Personal assets include houses, cars, and household goods, but the bulk of personal assets are held in monetary form. These include bank or building society current accounts, unit trusts, Independent Savings Accounts (ISAs), Personal Equity Plans (PEPs), and company shares. Just under a half of all adults have a building society savings account, but very few people hold any other kind of financial asset. For many people, however, their bank account is simply a temporary store for their income before the bulk of it is paid out again on household running costs. Indeed, in some cases, monetary assets are negative, as goods bought on credit or mortgage represent debts rather than assets.

The great bulk of financial assets are held by a small number of the very wealthiest households. The top 5 per cent of asset-holders in 1961 held 96 per cent of all personally owned company shares. The number of shareholders has increased since then, and in 1995 around 17 per cent of the population were shareholders. About three-quarters of these shareholders owned shares in fewer than four companies. These were generally enterprises that had recently been privatized or converted from building societies. For comparison, around 19 per cent of families in the United States own shares, with the top 1 per cent holding a half of all privately owned shares. These same wealthy families also held almost one-seventh of all cash and bank deposits and one-seventh of all land and housing.

Just over a quarter of all household expenditure in Britain goes on food and housing costs, with a further 18 per cent going on the costs of car ownership and public transport. While the costs of food and housing have declined since 1971, the proportion of income that is spent on transport has increased, and the total spent on these basic costs has remained at just under a half of all household expenditure. Spending on alcohol, tobacco, and fuel costs has reduced, and there has been a corresponding increase in the proportion of income spent on entertainment, sport, and electrical goods.

Spending on alcohol and tobacco is higher in Britain than in all other European Union countries except Ireland. In 1994, the average British household's weekly spending included £12.45 a person on alcohol and tobacco, £8.30 on clothing and footwear, and £13.84 on recreation, entertainment, and education (*Social Trends* 1997: table 6.4). Over 90 per cent of households now have colour televisions, telephones, and washing machines, 79 per cent have video recorders, 70 per cent have microwave ovens, and over a half have CD players and tumble driers. Around a quarter of households have personal computers, and one-fifth have dishwashers.

However, patterns of expenditure are not uniform across different income groups. Food accounts for a quarter of expenditure in the bottom 20 per cent of income recipients, but only 14 per cent among top income recipients. Fuel accounts for 8 per cent of spending by poorer households and 3 per cent by richer households. Leisure takes just 12 per cent of the spending of poorer households, compared with 19 per cent of spending by richer households. Pensioners who are mainly dependent on the state pension spend 26 per cent of their income on food and 10 per cent on fuel (*Social Trends* 1997: tables 6.7 and 6.8).

POVERTY AND DEPRIVATION

Recognition of the fact that poverty had not declined so much as Rowntree had expected, despite the introduction of the welfare state, was largely due to the work of Peter Townsend. A number of early papers and a major study of the poverty and circumstances of the elderly (Townsend 1963) were followed by a large national survey that set the scene for all later debates. Townsend's survey documented the scale of poverty in the 1960s, and he followed this with a survey of London that showed how the poor had fared during the 1970s and 1980s.

Poverty in the United Kingdom

Townsend undertook a full-scale national investigation of the extent and distribution of poverty in the 1960s, following in the tradition of Booth and Rowntree. His study of poverty in London in the 1980s was designed to allow direct comparisons to be made with Booth's work of 100 years before.

Using the official poverty standard, based on social-assistance levels, Townsend showed that 7.3 per cent of households in Britain were living below the poverty line in 1968. A further 23.3 per cent were living on the

Poverty in the United Kingdom

Townsend's national survey (1979) involved interviews in 2,052 households drawn from a sample of 2,495, a completion rate of 82 per cent. These households contained 6,098 individuals, and the aim was to interview 'the housewife and all wage-earners' in each household. The interview schedule contained 175 questions on such topics as housing and living conditions, employment, income and savings, health, and disability. The main survey was carried out in 1968–9.

A number of related investigations were undertaken in various localities, but the main follow-up study was a survey of London carried out in 1985–6. A sample of 2,700 adults was used, and more detailed investigations were made in Hackney and Bromley (Townsend *et al.* 1987).

The official poverty line for a couple with two young children in 1968 was about £10.40 a week, excluding housing costs. In 1986 it was £70.15, and in 1996 it was £119. A survey for 1996 found that a majority of people in a national sample thought that a weekly income of £276, after tax, was necessary for such a family to avoid poverty.

Figure 14.14. Poverty in the United Kingdom and London, 1968–1989

| | Percentage of households | | | |
	UK 1968	UK 1979	UK 1989	London 1986
In poverty	7.3	12.0	20.0	13.3
On the margins	23.3	10.0	9.0	13.3
TOTAL	30.6	22.0	29.0	26.6

Sources: Townsend (1979: table 7.2), Townsend *et al.* (1987: table 5.2), Oppenheim (1993: fig. 1).

margins of poverty: they had incomes that were only just above the income-support level and were in danger of falling below it. The corresponding figures for London in 1986 were 13.3 per cent living in poverty and a further 13.3 per cent living on the margins (see Figure 14.14). The top 1 per cent of households in Townsend's survey, corresponding closely with those who can be regarded as the wealthy, had incomes 1,000 or more times larger than those living in poverty. If those below the poverty line and those on the margins are added together, these findings of 30.6 per cent of households nationally and 26.6 per cent of households in London compare strikingly with Booth's discovery of 30.7 per cent of London households living in poverty (see Figure 14.5).

Townsend showed that poverty was a condition of relative deprivation. He measured deprivation using twelve indicators: going without a week's holiday in the previous year, going without a cooked meal in the last fortnight, not having exclusive use of a toilet, sink, bath, or cooker, and so on. Most households experienced one or two of these deprivations, but 28 per cent of men and 30 per cent of women experienced true *mul-*

tiple deprivation (see also Coates and Silburn 1970). A family of four with an annual income of £2,500 or more in 1976 might experience two types of deprivation, but a similar family with an annual income of £600 was likely to suffer from five or more types.

One of the most important aspects of multiple deprivation was the condition of a person's housing. Of those actually living in poverty, 86 per cent experienced one or more serious housing problems from a list of major structural defects such as damp, leaking roof, etc. Twenty-six per cent had three or more defects (Townsend 1979: table 13.11). Almost three-quarters of those on the margins of poverty had homes with one or more structural defects.

However, the poor were not, by any means, sharply divided from the larger category of manual workers. Townsend showed, for example, that among semi-skilled and unskilled manual worker families

▶ 23 per cent lacked exclusive use of an indoor toilet, and 22 per cent did not have exclusive use of a bath or shower;

▶ 31 per cent lived in houses with serious structural defects;

▶ 54 per cent had only one room heated in winter;

▶ 91 per cent were without a telephone, and 35 per cent were without a vacuum cleaner.

These people, he argued, were living a precarious existence, and it needed only a relatively small change in their circumstances to tip them into the multiple deprivation of true poverty. Low pay or loss of earnings through unemployment could trigger the slide into

Child poverty is a great problem for families at the bottom of the income distribution.

poverty. Unemployment was, perhaps, the most significant factor. Two-fifths of unskilled and a quarter of semi-skilled males had had ten or more weeks of unemployment in the year of Townsend's survey, and a further 17 per cent had had at least one week of unemployment (Townsend 1979: table 17.4). Unskilled and semi-skilled workers who moved in and out of employment, who took on low-paid, seasonal, or casual work, or who, in general, had a precarious and marginal position in the labour market, faced the greatest risk of poverty. Forced into a dependence on welfare benefits, they often found it impossible to get by, especially when they had large families. They moved in and out of the margins of poverty, and periodically they fell into actual poverty.

The highest levels of poverty found by Townsend, both nationally and in London, were among single-person households (predominantly the elderly) and households where there were large numbers of children. Women are more often found in poverty than are men. This *feminization of poverty* is a result of the concentration of women in low-paid jobs and their disproportionate dependence on welfare benefits. Poverty was especially marked among men and women aged over 65. Over a half of all people of pensionable age were living in poverty or on the margins of poverty. The life-cycle effect on poverty that Rowntree had highlighted in his research was confirmed by Townsend, and this

goes some way to explaining why there was a considerable turnover among those living in poverty.

The London survey found that the labour market operated in such a way as to concentrate poverty in certain areas. While the overall London unemployment rate in 1986 was 11.9 per cent, it was more than twice this level in Hackney and Tower Hamlets. Townsend noted an increasing polarization between 'poor' boroughs such as Hackney, Tower Hamlets, Islington, Lambeth, and Newham, and affluent boroughs such as Harrow, Sutton, Bexley, Bromley, and Havering (see Figure 14.15). He also found there to be a *racialization of poverty*, as members of ethnic minorities became concentrated in the occupations and boroughs that were especially likely to experience high levels of poverty. Young African-Caribbean and Asian men, for example, had rates of unemployment that were almost three times the London average. Later research has shown that unemployment among young Asians in parts of Bradford in 1996 stood at 45 per cent, three times the national average level.

Growing poverty

Townsend's research showed the persistence of poverty into the post-war period. Although it did seem to decline somewhat during the 1960s and 1970s, it increased again during the 1980s (see Figure 14.14).

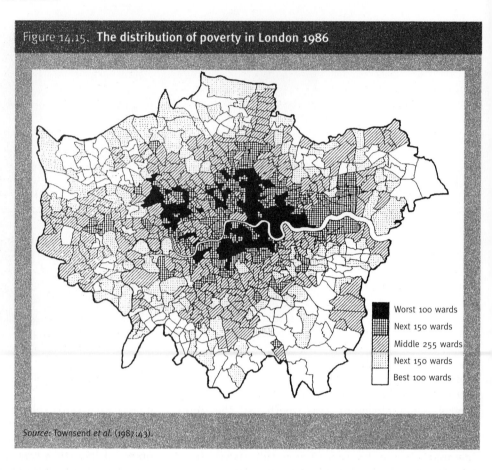

Figure 14.15. The distribution of poverty in London 1986

Worst 100 wards
Next 150 wards
Middle 255 wards
Next 150 wards
Best 100 wards

Source: Townsend *et al.* (1987:43).

This was a period of rapidly growing inequality, and poverty also deepened. The incidence of poverty was especially great among women and members of ethnic minorities.

The number of people in Britain whose final income after tax was less than a half of average income—the official European Union poverty level—amounted to around 10 per cent of the population through the 1960s. The proportion fell below this level in the mid-1970s, but since 1978 it has increased. Although it fell back slightly after 1992, it rose to just under 20 per cent (Barclay 1995: 17).

Those in the bottom 20 per cent of the income distribution include single people earning up to £77 a week and family households earning up to £181 a week. This bottom quintile of the income distribution includes large numbers of pensioner households and lone parents with dependent children. The most recent figures available, for 1993, show that one-third of the poor are in low-paid employment, a quarter are unemployed, and a quarter are retired. In a growing number of two-adult and family households, neither partner is able to find regular employment and the whole house-

hold is plunged into poverty. This has created particular problems of child poverty. Thirty two per cent of children lived in poverty, the highest rate of any country in the EU.

Black and Asian households are also over-represented among the poor. Around two-thirds of Pakistani and Bangladeshi families are in the bottom one-fifth of the income distribution. Black and Asian households suffer from extremely high levels of unemployment, and Asian women in particular are disproportionately involved in low-paid home-working. Differences in unemployment worsened during the 1980s, with ethnic minorities being desperately hit by job losses. African-Caribbean, Pakistani, and Bangladeshi males are more than twice as likely to be unemployed than are white males, and Bangladeshi females have an unemployment rate that is four or five times the rate for white females. Nearly a half of all young blacks and Asians were unemployed in 1982.

Those in employment experience a racialized employment structure. Just under 19 per cent of white males in 1982 were employed in professional and managerial work, but this was the case for only 5 per cent of

African-Caribbeans and 13 per cent of Asians. Conversely, while 16 per cent of white males were employed in semi-skilled and unskilled manual work, this was the case for more than a third of African-Caribbean and Asian men. As one of the most important studies in this area found, male ethnic-minority workers earn between 10 per cent and 15 per cent less than white male workers (C. Brown 1984).

☞ **You might like to look at Chapter 13, pp. 536–41, for some data on trends in work and unemployment.**

Black women are doubly disadvantaged in the labour market. As black people and as women, they experience both racism and sexism. The employment rate for white women in 1995 was 68 per cent, but rates for Asian women ranged from 13 per cent for Bangladeshis to 17 per cent for Pakistanis. 'Sweated' textile trades of the kind studied by Booth are now important sources of low-paid work for many Asian and black women who work from home or in small workshops. It has been estimated that in the 1980s the pay of such women averaged 90p an hour, though some were earning as little as 10p an hour (Mitter 1986).

Using the official European poverty line, comparative research has shown that the countries with the lowest levels of poverty in Europe in 1985 were Belgium, the Netherlands, and Germany, each with around 7.8 per cent of their households living in poverty. The European average was 13.9 per cent of households, and the level in Britain was just below this. France, with 17.5 per cent of households in poverty, was just above the European average. The highest concentrations of poverty were found in Portugal, Greece, Ireland, and Spain, which all had massive problems of rural poverty. Research in Europe has highlighted the growth of poverty among ethnic minorities, women, and young people across the whole Union. Migrant workers from Turkey and North Africa, for example, have been especially heavily hit by unemployment and recession in France, Germany, and the Netherlands (Room 1990).

Poverty in the United States, as measured by an official subsistence measure, remained between 12 per cent and 14 per cent throughout the 1970s and 1980s. On the basis of the official European poverty measure, however, the level of poverty in the United States would be 17 per cent, about the same as in France. About a third of those in poverty were rural or urban African-Americans. 2.4 million people were living in the inner-city ghettos of Chicago, New York, and other big cities, where poverty rates exceeded 40 per cent. Two-thirds of these ghetto residents were African-Americans, and a quarter are Mexicans or Puerto Ricans (W. J. Wilson 1987). Levels of unemployment among African-Americans were more than twice those of whites during the 1980s, and wages for those in employment were about three-quarters of white male wages.

It was findings such as these on the United States that led to the debate over the so-called underclass of urban poor. We have already discussed some aspects of this idea and the attempts to castigate them as the undeserving poor. Central to this debate has been the idea of a culture of poverty and an associated *cycle of deprivation*. According to this view, poor children are born into a culture that socializes them into inappropriate work habits and prevents them from overcoming their poverty. As they grow up in poverty, their own children are born in poverty, and so the cycle continues.

☞ **You should already be thinking about our earlier remarks on the underclass. If you were not, you should quickly review what we said in 'The Undeserving Poor and the Underclass', pp. 561–3.**

The evidence that we have reviewed most certainly supports the idea that extremes of poverty still persist and that this poverty is particularly concentrated in those areas where large numbers of ethnic minority and lone-parent households are to be found. On the other hand, it provides little support for the idea that people are trapped in an underclass by a cycle of deprivation. Those living in poverty are not sharply divided from other manual workers, and households continually fall in and out of poverty.

Work undertaken by the British Household Panel Study showed that over a half of those with incomes less than half the average in 1991 were no longer living in poverty by 1994. This was mainly due to those who had been unemployed finding employment, though a person's position was also improved whenever other members of the same household (for example, a husband or wife) increased their earnings. Most of those who had moved out of poverty had moved into its margins, and not all would eventually escape the risk of falling back into poverty in the future. This is confirmed by the fact that others had fallen from the margins into true poverty. Families falling into poverty were the victims of redundancy, divorce, or the death of a partner, all of which seriously reduced family incomes. Almost a third of the whole population had some experience of poverty in the four-year period of the study. Those who were most trapped in long-term poverty, lasting four years or more, were pensioners and lone parents (S. Jenkins 1996).

Poverty is not the condition of a distinct underclass, it is endemic to the lives of unskilled manual workers and their families, and it is an ever-present possibility for many other manual workers. A full exploration of this issue, however, depends upon a proper understanding of what it is to be a class, and we will return to the question of the underclass once more in the following chapter.

Disadvantaged life chances

Inequalities in economic resources are significant because of the differences in life chances that they produce. In this section we will explore the deprivations that correlate with economic inequalities, and we will show how they are structured by gender and by ethnicity. We will concentrate on deprivation in health and housing.

> ☞ We look at overall trends in health, fertility, and mortality in Chapter 6, pp. 197–200 and 206–7. You might want to look at this as background for our discussion of inequalities in this section.

The normal length of a healthy pregnancy is somewhere between 38 and 41 weeks, but the actual length of pregnancy has been found to vary with the occupational position of the mother. Pregnancies run to normal term in about 80 per cent of women from professional backgrounds, but this is the case for only 70 per cent of women from a manual-worker background. Children born into manual-worker families are far more likely than those born into professional families to have been over-term or premature. These inequalities continue after birth, as the length of pregnancy, along with the mother's own health, affect the birthweight and the child's later health. Birthweight is, in fact, significantly lower in manual-worker families than among the professions (I. Reid 1977: Tables 4.1 and 4.2). Figure 14.16 shows that rates of infant mortality are also higher among those born into manual-working households. Rates of infant mortality have declined for all occupational categories over the course of the century, but they are still almost twice as high among unskilled manual households than they are among professional and managerial families. Among those children who survive the first year of life, health chances in later life also vary by occupational background. Figure 14.16 shows that rates of immunization for major childhood diseases are much lower in unskilled manual households.

These and other health inequalities persist in later life. Rates of death, general health problems, and specific problems such as total tooth loss are lower among professional and managerial workers than they are among manual workers (I. Reid 1977: Tables 4.11 and 4.13). In this and a number of other similar health

Occupations and social class

Many discussions of inequality use occupational categories that are treated as social classes. This raises many important questions that we pursue in Chapter 15. For the present discussion we treat these purely as convenient occupational categories.

The classification used in Figure 14.16 is the Registrar General's Classification, which has the following categories:

| | professional and managerial occupations
II | technically qualified occupations
III (N) | routine non-manual occupations
III (M) | skilled manual occupations
IV | partly skilled manual occupations
V | unskilled occupations

High income & prestige

Low income & prestige

The Registrar General's Classification is discussed more fully in Chapter 3, pp. 97–8. After reading Chapter 15, you may wish to return to this section to see what the use of the concept of social class adds to the conclusions that we draw.

Figure 14.16. Infant mortality and immunization, United Kingdom, 1921–1989

Occupational category	Deaths under 1 year per 1,000 live births				Percentage of children not immunized for diseases (1965)		
	1921	1950	1970	1989	smallpox	polio	diphtheria
I	38	17	12	6.0	6	1	1
II	55	22	14	6.1	14	3	3
III (N)	76	28	16	7.0	16	3	3
III (M)				7.5	25	4	6
IV	89	33	20	10.4	29	6	8
V	97	40	31	11.0	33	10	11

Sources: Black *et al.* (1980: table 17), and *OPCS Monitor* (1992).

chances, there is an occupational gradient that shows an association between health and economic resources.

Unskilled workers are two and a half times more likely to report the quality of their own health as merely fair or poor than are professional and managerial workers. Research into the causes of death has found that rates of tuberculosis and bronchitis show the same occupational gradient, and it is only slightly less marked for heart disease. Many of these inequalities are associated with differences in smoking behaviour, which, for both men and women, follow the same occupational gradient (Black *et al.* 1980: table 34). Crude death rates, for both men and women, follow the same pattern. These occupational differences intersect with gender differences: standardized male mortality rates are twice the female rates in every occupational category.

Health inequalities also reflect ethnic differences. Figures 14.17 and 14.18 show rates of child mortality and adult causes of death according to place of birth. Still births in the United Kingdom are lowest for British-born mothers and highest for mothers who were born in Pakistan or in Bangladesh. British-born mothers show the same relatively low risk of having children that die in their first year of life, while Pakistan-born and Caribbean-born women have much higher rates. A contrast between mothers born in Britain and those born in the Caribbean or the Indian subcontinent is also found in statistics on low birth weight and in such childhood diseases as rickets (deficiency of vitamin D). Among adults aged 20 or more, those born outside the

Figure 14.17. Infant mortality and ethnicity, United Kingdom, 1990

Mother's place of birth	Rate per 1,000 live births	
	Still births	Neonatal deaths
UK	4.4	4.3
Bangladesh	8.6	3.9
India	5.3	5.1
Pakistan	9.1	7.8
East Africa	6.9	5.6
Caribbean	5.7	8.4

Source: Hunt (1995: table 1).

▶ **In this table, place of birth is used as an indicator of ethnic identity.**
What problems are there with this approach?
Look at our discussion of ethnic identity in Chapter 4, pp. 143–5, for some clues.

United Kingdom showed higher than average rates for a number of death-inducing illnesses and accidents. Only in the case of bronchitis were rates consistently lower for the non-UK-born.

Some of these differences can be explained by differences in lifestyle (for example, differences in diet and in

Figure 14.18. Causes of death, United Kingdom, 1970–1978

Place of birth	Higher rates	Lower rates
Africa	Strokes, high blood pressure, violence and accidents, maternal deaths, tuberculosis	Bronchitis
India/Pakistan	Heart disease, diabetes, violence and accidents, tuberculosis	Bronchitis, some cancers
Caribbean	Strokes, high blood pressure, violence and accidents, diabetes, maternal deaths	Bronchitis

Source: Culley and Dyson (1993: fig. 2).

Figure 14.19. Housing and ethnicity, United Kingdom, 1991

Ethnic category	Percentage of households		
	Overcrowded	Self-contained	Without exclusive use of bath or toilet
White	1.8	0.9	1.2
Black-Caribbean	4.7	2.0	1.4
Black-African	15.1	6.5	5.1
Other black	5.6	3.2	2.4
Indian	12.8	1.0	1.1
Pakistani	29.7	1.2	1.7
Bangladeshi	47.1	1.3	2.0
Whole population	2.2	1.0	1.3

Source: Mason (1995: table 7.4).

the use of cooking fats), but far more significant is the over-concentration among ethnic minorities of those social conditions of low pay, unemployment, and poor housing that are known to increase the chances of these health problems among all groups. People are made ill not by their ethnicity but by their poverty.

Housing conditions are, we have shown, central to multiple deprivation. Those who are poor are more likely to live in poor-quality housing, and poor housing is a major cause of health problems. Very few of those in professional and managerial occupations live in homes that are overcrowded (the official criterion is more than 1.5 people to each room), but this is not unusual for unskilled workers. Townsend's research showed how this overcrowded housing is often in a poor state of repair. Problems of cold and damp housing are especially significant for childhood and adult health.

Inequalities in housing were a massive problem for first-generation overseas migrants to Britain in the 1950s and 1960s. New migrants did not qualify for public housing and frequently lived in shared and poor-quality accommodation: in 1961 about a half of African-Caribbean households were overcrowded, and even in 1974 almost two-fifths of ethnic-minority households lacked sole use of a bath, hot water, and indoor toilet. Migrants and their families were largely confined to run-down inner-city housing. By the 1980s, rates of over-crowding were far lower, although Figure 14.19 shows that major inequalities persisted.

According to the 1991 Census, an average of just 2.2 per cent of the whole population was living in over-crowded conditions, but the rate was 47.1 per cent among those identifying themselves as Bangladeshi, and 29.7 per cent among Pakistanis. Rates among black Britons were lower, though there were sharp differences between Caribbean and African identifiers. Those identifying themselves as Black African had 15.1 per cent overcrowding, and they were less likely than the average household to live in self-contained accommodation. They also showed higher rates for the lack of basic bath and toilet facilities. (See also Ratcliffe 1981; Karn *et al.* 1985.)

CONTINUING CLOSURE

The Glass study of occupational mobility showed that Britain was far from being an open society in the first half of the twentieth century. The situation seems to have changed little in the second half of the century. A series of projects directed by John Goldthorpe have demonstrated this well and have put the British situation in its international context.

Occupational mobility and stability

Goldthorpe's Oxford Mobility Study threw considerable doubt on the idea that Britain can be characterized

The Oxford Mobility Study

The study was carried out by John H. Goldthorpe and others, at Nuffield College, Oxford, in 1972. They used a sample of 10,000 adult males (aged 20–64) in England and Wales. A follow-up study in 1974 collected data on attitudes. The original intention was to compare the 1972 results with those from the Glass study, but detailed comparisons proved impossible as the original Glass data no longer existed. Goldthorpe analysed the 1972 data in terms of seven occupational categories (see pp. 99–100), which differ from those used by Glass. Like the Glass categories, however, these were intended to form a social-class

classification, and we discuss this aspect of the work in Chapter 15, pp. 607–9. For some purposes, Goldthorpe followed Blau and Duncan, and assigned occupations to individual scores on a 124 point-scale that reflects their income and prestige.

The main publications are *Social Mobility and Class Structure* (Goldthorpe 1980) and *Origins and Destinations* (Halsey *et al.* 1980), both of which are summarized in Heath (1981). A companion study for Scotland was undertaken by Payne (1987a), though this followed a different theoretical line.

by openness, meritocracy, and equality of opportunity. The study showed that there were still sharp barriers to social mobility in England and Wales. Openness had barely altered since the 1940s.

Figure 14.20 shows Goldthorpe's findings on **outflow mobility**. Outflow mobility measures the proportion of individuals who have moved out of the category in which they began their lives. The Oxford study found that the highest levels of self-recruitment are among the higher professionals and the less-skilled workers. Clerical and supervisory workers show much lower levels of self-recruitment. Of the mobility that does occur, much is simply short-range movement into neighbouring categories. There are particularly high rates of mobility between the two professional and administrative categories and between the routine occupations and the professional and administrative ones. Between a half and two-thirds of professionals and administrators were in the same kind of occupations as their fathers, and almost the same proportion of sons of less-skilled workers were found in manual work.

There was very little long-range mobility, which Goldthorpe defined as movement from less-skilled manual jobs to professional or administrative ones. Eight per cent of sons of men in category II were downwardly mobile to unskilled work, and just under 8 per cent were upwardly mobile between the same two categories. Nevertheless, large numbers of manual workers did move up the occupational hierarchy: 18.4 per cent of the sons of skilled manual workers entered the higher professions, as did 15.4 per cent of the sons of supervisors. This reflects the opening-up of opportuni-

ties that occurred with the expansion of professional and administrative work in the post-war period, and the contraction of manual work over the course of the whole century. It was found, for example, that upward mobility had increased for people born after 1928. These were people who entered their working careers in the 1950s and 1960s. Those born since the 1930s were the first to go through the secondary schools that were reformed in the 1940s, their improved educational prospects coinciding with an expansion of occupational opportunities.

Manual occupations are far more homogeneous in terms of social background than are non-manual occupations. This is particularly clear from data on **inflow mobility**. This measures the proportion of individuals within a particular category who have come from specific other categories. An analysis of inflows shows that nearly three-quarters of manual workers are second-generation manual workers, and many of these are third or later generation. On the other hand, only just over a third of professional and administrative workers are the sons of men in the same kind of work. As Blau and Duncan (1967) discovered for the United States, the professional and administrative categories had expanded so rapidly that they had to recruit from outside their own boundaries and so they are today very diverse in their background. The contraction of manual work, on the other hand, means that it has been unnecessary to recruit large numbers from outside.

Figure 14.21 presents the Oxford results in the same form as Blau and Duncan's data for the United States (see Figure 14.9). This shows that virtually all the relationships were weaker than they are in the

Figure 14.20. Outflow mobility, England and Wales, 1972

Fathers' social class

Sons' social class

	I	II	III	IV	V	VI	VII		Total
I Higher professional and administrative	48.4	18.9	9.3	8.2	4.5	4.5	6.2		100
II Lower professional and administrative	31.9	22.6	10.7	8.0	9.2	9.6	8.0		100
III Routine non-manual	19.2	15.7	10.8	8.6	13.0	15.0	17.8		100
IV Small employers, proprietors, and self-employed	12.8	11.1	7.8	24.9	8.7	14.7	19.9		100
V Lower technical and manual supervisory workers	15.4	13.2	9.4	8.0	16.6	20.1	17.2		100
VI Skilled manual workers	18.4	8.9	8.4	7.1	12.2	29.6	25.4		100
VII Semi-skilled and unskilled manual workers	6.9	7.8	7.9	6.8	12.5	23.5	34.8		100

LONG RANGE (above VII I/II cells)

LONG RANGE (vertical, by VII column)

Downward mobility

Upward mobility

Source: Heath: (1981: table 2.1).

Figure 14.21. Occupational attainment, England and Wales, 1972

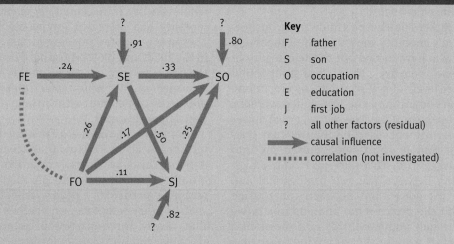

Key

F   father
S   son
O   occupation
E   education
J   first job
?   all other factors (residual)
→   causal influence
▪▪▪▪▪▪▪▪   correlation (not investigated)

Source: adapted from Heath (1981: diagram 5.2).

You can find a full list of the Goldthorpe categories in Figure 3.7.

▶ In a table showing outflow mobility, as above, the percentages are calculated across the rows. A table of inflow mobility looks very similar, but the percentages are calculated down the columns. Why is this? Would it make any sense to add up totals for the columns above?

▶ Whenever you look at a table, make sure that you read the percentages in the correct direction.

United States, though the general model is confirmed. The residuals are, once more, very high. As has been indicated before, however, low residuals would suggest a society in which there was no freedom of action and everything was preordained by the facts of birth.

Although the Oxford study collected information only on men, Heath's (1981) summary used data from the General Household Survey to try to rectify this problem. Comparing women's occupations in 1975 with that of their fathers (still not their mothers), Heath found that the concentration of women's employment in routine white-collar work and in semi- and unskilled work means that there are very high levels of downward mobility for those born into pro- fessional or administrative families. As we show in Chapter 3, pp. 100–2, however, there is much evidence to suggest that women's occupations are badly handled in these occupational classifications. Nevertheless, the rates of downward mobility for women do seem to be significantly higher than those for men. An assessment of these gender inequalities, however, depends upon an understanding of patterns of marriage and household formation and the structuring of gender roles within families.

The conclusions so far come from an analysis of the **absolute mobility** that results from changes in the occupational structure. Goldthorpe, however, attaches particular significance to the measurement of relative mobility. Absolute mobility is a measure of the propor- tion of individuals in a particular category who have been socially mobile, whether upwards or downwards. **Relative mobility** refers to the chances of one group compared with another. The expansion of professional and administrative occupations may have increased the opportunities for all to rise up the occupational structure, but there can be continuing differences in the chances of those from one category relative to another.

Calculations of relative mobility are very complex, and they need not detain us here. Goldthorpe shows, however, that the chances of the son of a manual worker rising into a professional or administrative occupation are a half of the chances of the son of a non- manual worker rising to a similar level, and a quarter of the chances of the son of a professional or administra- tive worker following directly in his father's footsteps. Looking at trends over time, Goldthorpe concluded that absolute rates had changed because of occupa- tional change, while relative mobility rates were largely unaltered. The apparent openness of British society is an illusion that results from a focus on absolute mobility.

A comparative view

Goldthorpe and his co-workers have recently extended their work to the international level and have produced an important comparative study of social mobility (Erikson and Goldthorpe 1993). The research has com- pared the British situation with that found in various European and non-European countries. This investiga- tion involved the use of data from twelve national studies that had been undertaken between 1970 and 1978, and the original England and Wales data from the Oxford Mobility Study formed a part of it. As with the original Oxford study, a major limitation of the research is that it concerns only men aged 30 or over. Women and their experiences of social mobility are not considered.

The international study did not simply reanalyse existing data from the various countries. This would have meant replacing a variety of schemes with a crude division between manual and non-manual workers, as Lipset and Bendix had done. Instead, Erikson and Goldthorpe undertook a systematic recoding and re- examination of the original data from the projects, using a new set of occupational categories. The original categories used in the Oxford study were modified to take account of the different occupational structures in the various countries. Separate categories for farmers and for agricultural workers were added, small employ- ers were separated from routine non-manual workers, and various other changes were made.

Erikson and Goldthorpe had hoped to uncover pat- terns of international variation in occupational mo- bility, but they found little evidence of significant variations. There is, in fact, what they call a standard pattern of mobility. Rates of mobility are slightly below the norm in Ireland and in Poland, and they are above it in Hungary, but these three countries seemed to be beginning to converge towards the standard pattern. It might be expected, however, that the final collapse of Communism in Eastern Europe will further alter pat- terns in Hungary and Poland.

Typically in the advanced societies, about one-third of sons enter the same kind of occupations as their fathers. Between a half and three-quarters have experi- enced some degree of social mobility, and there has been little change in this over time. For those men born in the 1930s and the 1940s, then, there is much greater cross-national similarity in their occupational mobility experiences than there had been for those born a gen- eration earlier. There is a tendency for mobility to increase at an early stage of industrialization, but thereafter there is no particular trend of increase or decrease in mobility. Overall, Erikson and Goldthorpe summarize the cross-national pattern of mobility as one of 'trendless fluctuation': mobility rates go up and down, almost at random, with no structural variations between societies over time.

This is rather a surprising conclusion. It might have been expected, for example, that there would be significant and systematic differences between Western and Eastern Europe, between areas with different national cultures, and between economies with different industrial structures. All of these expectations were disproved, so far as absolute mobility patterns were concerned. All the major countries were remarkably similar, and there were no particular trends over time. The results of the research lead Goldthorpe and his colleagues to support the hypothesis first set out by Featherman, Jones, and Hauser (1975) that there is a broad *similarity* in mobility patterns in industrial societies: the similarities in mobility patterns outweigh any minor national differences (see also Lipset and Bendix 1959 for the earlier period).

To explore this idea further, they construct what they call a *core model*, to which the patterns of social mobility in England and France corresponded most closely. In this core model, the salaried managers and professionals are at the top of the hierarchy of occupational desirability and advantage. They have the greatest resources and the greatest barriers to entry from outside. Non-skilled jobs are at the opposite pole of the hierarchy and are the easiest to enter for those who are unable to maintain or to improve their social position. There is, for all occupational categories, a strong tendency towards the inheritance of occupational position.

The sectoral division between agriculture, on the one hand, and industry and services, on the other, forms a major barrier to mobility, as this economic boundary also tends to coincide with cultural and geographical differences. Mobility is fairly high between small business and the professional and administrative category, and between skilled and non-skilled manual work. Variations from this core model were relatively minor and were due largely to particular historical circumstances and political policies. The broad picture, however, was

one of similarity. Inheritance of occupational position was strongest in Ireland and weakest in Sweden, and Sweden appeared, overall, as the most open society. This was not simply a European pattern. Evidence from the United States, Australia, and Japan showed no great departure from the core model.

SUMMARY POINTS

In this section we have looked at the rediscovery of poverty in the 1960s and the growing social divisions that have emerged during the 1970s and 1980s.

▶ Inequality of assets has stabilized and inequality of income has increased since the 1970s. This reflects changing economic conditions and shifts in government policy.

▶ From an international point of view, Britain today is a more unequal society than Germany and Sweden, but less unequal than France and the United States.

▶ Investigations into poverty show that, depending on how it is measured, the amount of poverty in Britain remains very great. On the official European poverty standard, just under 20 per cent of the British population are living in poverty.

▶ Disadvantaged life chances are a feature of poverty. These have increasingly been feminized and racialized.

To develop your understanding of the impact of racism and sexism on social inequality, you may find it useful to look back at our discussions of sex–gender and ethnicity in Chapter 4. The final point that we made in this section concerned trends in openness over time.

▶ Openness has barely altered since the 1940s, despite the apparent increase in social mobility. Patterns of mobility are broadly similar in all the advanced societies.

REVISION AND EXERCISES

Look back over the Summary Points in this chapter. You will find it useful to revise our arguments in relation to the conceptual issues involved in studying inequality, the problem of measuring poverty, and the question of occupational mobility and openness.

EQUALITY, INEQUALITY, AND CITIZENSHIP

▶ What are the three conceptions of equality that were identified? How would advocates of each view regard (*a*) sexism and (*b*) racism?

▶ What do you understand by the following terms: eugenics, undeserving poor, heredity, functional importance; absolute poverty, relative poverty, poverty line?

We considered a number of theoretical issues in the study of inequality, and you should ensure that you are familiar with the key ideas that we mentioned:

▶ Make sure that you are familiar with the arguments of the following: Marshall, Murray, Malthus, Mayhew, Marx.

▶ What are the major criticisms that you would make of the functionalist theory of inequality? Why is it called a 'functionalist' theory?

Finally, we looked at a number of problems in using biological factors to explain social inequalities. You might like to compare what we say here with the discussion of biological explanations of deviance in Chapter 5, pp. 154–6:

▶ What is meant by the underclass? Is it a useful sociological concept? How does it relate to the idea of a culture of poverty?

▶ What is IQ? To what extent can sociologists use evidence on IQ differences in their theories of social inequality?

MEASURING POVERTY AND INEQUALITY

It is not easy to measure poverty, and definitions are often contested by politicians who wish to minimize the amount of poverty. We have, however, introduced a number of ideas that will help you to understand poverty and wealth:

▶ What do you understand by the following terms: standard diet, real wages, wealth line, income, assets; life chances, occupational mobility, primary poverty, secondary poverty, before-tax income, after-tax income, direct taxes, disposable income,

▶ Make sure that you are familiar with the arguments of the following: Booth, Rowntree, Townsend.

▶ Booth's language for describing the categories of the population carry obvious moral judgements. Does the use of such words as 'loafers' and 'vicious' undermine his factual conclusions?

You will need to have some grasp of basic statistical ideas if you are to get the most out of published studies on poverty and inequality:

▶ Make sure that you understand the general ideas behind the following statistical terms: percentile, mean, median.

▶ If you are still not happy with tables and graphs, try the exercises suggested under Figures 14.3, 14.11, and 14.12.

OPENNESS AND MOBILITY

You will find that a good grasp of occupational mobility helps you to approach questions of inequality and opportunity. We look at some other aspects of occupational mobility in Chapter 15:

▶ **How would you distinguish between inter-generational mobility and intra-generational mobility?**

▶ **What do you understand by the following terms: non-manual work; prestige; core model, absolute mobility, relative mobility, inflow mobility, outflow mobility.**

▶ **Make sure that you are familiar with the arguments of the following: Glass, Goldthorpe, Blau and Duncan.**

The study of occupational mobility has become a very complex area in sociology, and we have only touched upon some of the many issues here. You need to know only some very basic ideas:

▶ **Make sure that you understand the general ideas behind the ideas of correlation and the path diagram. Do not worry if you do not understand this in detail. Try to concentrate on grasping the general principles. If you ever need to calculate correlations, you can always get someone else to do the maths for you!**

FURTHER READING

Good general coverage of the topics in this chapter can be found in:

Fraser, S. (1995) (ed.), *The Bell Curve Wars* (New York: Basic Books). This collection of papers gives a good critical review of the arguments of Herrnstein and Murray.

Hills, J. (1995), *Joseph Rowntree Inquiry into Income and Wealth*, ii (York: Joseph Rowntree Foundation). One of the most up-to-date and thorough investigations into inequality and deprivation. Very useful tables and charts.

Mack, Joanna, and Lansley, S. (1985), *Poor Britain* (London: George Allen & Unwin). A report on a survey into poverty undertaken for a television series on 'Breadline Britain'. Now a little old, but raises a lot of important issues.

Scott, J. P. (1994), *Poverty and Wealth: Citizenship, Deprivation and Privilege* (Harlow: Longman). A comprehensive overview of the distribution of poverty and wealth. Concentrates on Britain, but puts this in an international context. Covers many of the issues raised in this chapter.

Heath, A. (1981), *Social Mobility* (Glasgow: Fontana). A useful compendium of the results of various studies of occupational mobility, presented in a digestible form. Should soon appear in a new, updated edition.

For more detailed considerations of specific issues, you might like to look at:

Black, D., *et al.* (1980), 'The Black Report', in P. Townsend and N. Davidson (eds.), *Inequalities in Health* (Harmondsworth: Penguin, 1992). A landmark study that the Conservative government tried to suppress. One of the first things that the 1997 Labour government did was to ask Sir Douglas Black to produce a new review of evidence on health inequalities.

Goldthorpe, J. H. (1980), *Social Mobility and Class Structure* (Oxford: Clarendon Press). The basic report of the Oxford Mobility Study. Complex in places, but essential reading.

Erikson, R., and Goldthorpe, J. (1993), *The Constant Flux* (Oxford: Clarendon Press). Puts the British results of Goldthorpe (1980) in an international context.

Townsend, P. (1979), *Poverty in the United Kingdom* (Harmondsworth: Penguin). Townsend's *magnum opus*. A massive report of more than 1,000 pages. A landmark study.

Wilson, W. J. (1987), *The Truly Disadvantaged* (Chicago: University of Chicago Press). Influential and contentious. Wilson's radical view of the underclass was soon overtaken by Murray's conservative view. Worth reading for the data and ideas about the ghetto poor, but be wary about taking on the terminology of 'underclass'.

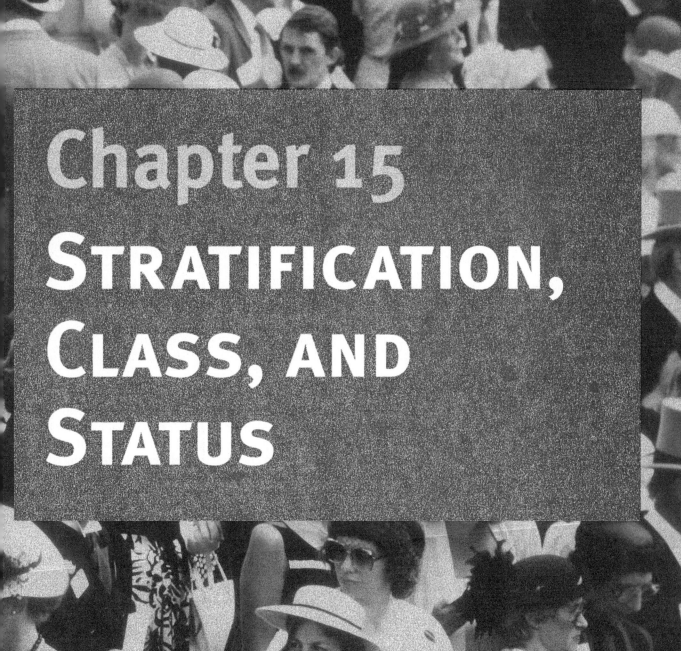

Chapter 15
STRATIFICATION, CLASS, AND STATUS

Knowing your place

The rich man in his castle.
The poor man at his gate.
God made them high and lowly
And ordered their estate.

('All Things Bright and Beautiful',
Mrs C. F. Alexander, 1848.)

In the summer of 1997 a mass rally for the countryside arrived in Westminster to lobby Parliament against the proposed abolition of hunting and other field sports:

'They rolled up for the dawn special in their Range Rovers, Mercedes, and mud-spattered off-roaders—the rich men from the castle, the poorer folks at the gate. . . . In the sunrise . . . the high and the lowly merged into one, green-jacketed mass.

'Hunting is more than killing. "Its a good way of linking social classes," explained the Duke of Roxburgh (Guy to his friends), occupying a first class compartment with the young Duchess (Virginia), and daughter Lady Rosie Innis-Kerr. . . . "But this is also about what goes with the hunt. In a big way we're bringing the countryside together with lots of related social activities—cricket, tennis, and things for the children like pony clubs".'

Source: Guardian, 11 July 1997.

Members of seven hunts demonstrate against the Anti-Hunting Bill

T HE idea of 'class' inherited from the past is summed up, for many people, in the image of English society presented in Mrs Alexander's popular hymn and in the picture of the countryside described by the Duke and Duchess of Roxburgh. Class is a matter of social hierarchy and knowing your place; it is something that ties people together into a cohesive rural world. According to this view, a person's class is all a matter of breeding, of social background, and is reflected in social attitudes and lifestyle, in accent, and in style of dress. These social differences have been seen as the source of snobbery and prejudice, leading many to conclude that Britain is a peculiarly class-ridden society.

Other aspects of a modern, urban, and industrial society point in a different direction. While trains and planes still divide passengers into first and second class, this is now done on the basis of their ability to pay. More significantly, class has, for a long time, been seen by many people as a matter of economic division and power. This is aptly summarized in one woman's comments on the contrasting fates of herself and her schoolmate William Hague. Why, Jo Pearson asked, had he become leader of the Conservative Party with his own office at the House of Commons, while she was still living in a council flat? Her answer was that their common schooling had, in fact, been divided by class differences: 'William absorbed the values and aspirations of his property and business-owning parents and the confidence of their economically-stable background. . . . I absorbed the values and feelings of *my* parents and the community around *me*: insecure and frustrated men' (*Guardian*, 7 July 1997). Class differences in attitude, for Jo Pearson, were rooted in the ownership and non-ownership of property, and these economic and social differences were perpetuated and multiplied over the generations.

How, then, are we to see class? Is it a matter of hierarchy, cohesion, and deference? Or is it, rather, a matter of ownership, division, and disadvantage? Is Britain actually any more bound by class than other societies? And have there been any significant changes in class relations in recent years? We will consider these issues by looking at the idea of social stratification and its relationship to social inequality. We will distinguish between class and status, and we will show how the arguments of Marx and Parsons can be used to study these varying patterns of social stratification. In the section on 'The Making of a Class Society' we will look at the development of the upper class, the middle class, and the working class in Britain and the establishment of a class society. In the section on 'A Fragmentary Class Society' we will look at the contemporary disruption of class relations that has led some people to suggest that Britain—and other advanced societies—are no longer class societies.

UNDERSTANDING STRATIFICATION

Social stratification is not the same thing as social inequality. The inequalities that we describe in Chapter 14 are central to any understanding of social stratification, but social stratification itself is something more than simply differences in life chances. **Social stratification** exists only when social inequalities are associated with the arrangement of individuals into *strata* or classes that lie one above another in a hierarchy of advantaged and disadvantaged life chances. When this happens, a society is said to be stratified.

The idea of stratification comes from geology, the science that studies the ways in which rocks of various kinds are formed into the levels or strata that make up the earth's crust and its surface layers of deposits. The concept of *social* stratification borrows these ideas to describe the formation of individuals into the levels or layers of a social hierarchy of advantages and disadvantages. What is borrowed from geology, of course, is simply the general metaphor and image of stratification. Social strata are not lifeless objects, like rocks, but are actual social groups that are conscious of themselves and can act together. An upper class, for example, lies on top of a middle class that, in turn, lies on top of a lower class. Like rock strata, however, social strata will usually have a history of division and fragmentation. They are also likely to have experienced structural changes, and they may come into contact with newer strata that have risen from below to higher positions.

Some of these ideas are illustrated in Figure 15.1.

The first diagram shows the simplest image of social stratification: three social strata are arranged in a simple hierarchy of relative advantage and disadvantage in their life chances. As we show in Chapter 3, pp. 96–102, many official and academic models of social stratification in contemporary society have taken just this form. In these classifications, however, it has been usual to recognize five, six, or seven social strata, not just three. However many strata are recognized, the simple image of stratification remains the same.

The second diagram in Figure 15.1 suggests how the idea of stratification can be extended to describe more complex structures with cross-cutting social divisions. Some commentators have described ethnically divided societies in these terms. They see two ethnic groups, a majority and a minority, divided from one another by a difference in colour or some other ethnic difference. Each ethnic group is internally stratified. Relations between whites and African–Americans in the United States, for example, have been seen in this way (Warner 1936; Myrdal 1944).

A **social stratum**, then, is a group of individuals with similarly advantaged or disadvantaged life chances. It is not a mere collection of individuals defined in statistical terms. The members of a stratum are tied together through social relations and interactions that forge them into a real and cohesive social group. These social ties are those of occupational mobility, marriage, kinship, and informal association that close off one

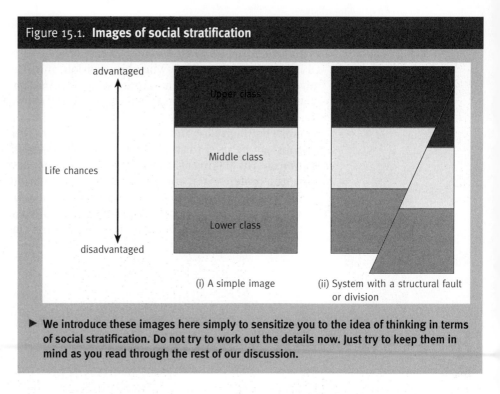

Figure 15.1. Images of social stratification

advantaged

Life chances

disadvantaged

Upper class

Middle class

Lower class

(i) A simple image

(ii) System with a structural fault or division

▶ We introduce these images here simply to sensitize you to the idea of thinking in terms of social stratification. Do not try to work out the details now. Just try to keep them in mind as you read through the rest of our discussion.

stratum and divide it from another. People who are unequal are in different strata if there are social boundaries across which they rarely move: if, for example, they do not usually marry or interact with each other. Social strata are bounded social groups that are reproduced over time and across the generations. Social strata may, therefore, develop their own distinctive attitudes and values and may come into conflict with one another. A system of social stratification must be seen as a dynamic system that is shaped by shifting relations of antagonism or cooperation among the social strata.

STRATIFICATION AND POWER

The advantages and disadvantages that people possess as members of social strata are aspects of their **power**. This power comes from the various resources that they have. To have the kind of property that generates a substantial investment income and which can, in turn, be used to buy education, housing, or health care is to have power. It is for this reason that Max Weber claimed that social stratification was to be seen as a principal aspect of the distribution of power in society.

Much ink has been spilled in attempts to discover a fundamental basis for social power and to build this

into a universal theory applicable to all systems of social stratification. For Marxists, as we show later in this chapter, property and other economic resources are seen as the bases of social power. This argument has much to commend it, but we will show that it tells only a part of the story. Dissatisfaction with the Marxist position has led to the production of other all-inclusive theories. The two most important of these have focused, respectively, on sex and race. Each of these has a part to play in a comprehensive account of stratification, but neither can be taken as providing a complete theory of stratification. Indeed, it is doubtful if any such universal, single-factor theory could ever be workable.

Sex, race, and stratification

For many feminist writers, social strata have been seen as rooted in relations of sexual power that are built around biological differences of sex. According to Shulamith Firestone (1971), all societies are divided into opposed 'sex classes' that are the basis of gender inequalities. She holds that 'all men' oppress 'all women', and that the struggle between men and women is the driving force in human history. Arguments such as this were central to the women's liberation movement as it developed in America and Europe from the 1960s. They helped to open up the whole ques-

Stratification and unequality are both gendered and racialized.

tion of sex–gender systems. Through their impact on discussions of inequality and difference, they have transformed the whole intellectual context in which these social issues are discussed.

Theories of sexual stratification have been allied with political strategies of liberation and emancipation, but this is not the case with most theories of racial stratification. These have often been associated with more repressive political positions. The argument that social strata are rooted in racial differences that are built around inherited differences in human biology was particularly influential in the nineteenth century. Writers such as Ludwig Gumplowicz (1885) saw ethnic and racial conflict as the fundamental mechanism of social development. Social stratification was a result of the conquest and domination of one ethnic group by another, which is an inescapable fact of human history. For Gumplowicz, this was a positive thing, as he believed that the conflict of races would lead to the survival of the fittest.

This racial interpretation of social stratification was taken up by more extremist political writers, and it was often allied with the eugenic arguments that we discuss in Chapter 4, pp. 143–4, and Chapter 14, pp. 563–5. The most extreme formulations have been those of Gobineau (1853–5) and Chamberlain (1899), who popularized the idea of racial stratification and justified the repression of 'inferior' races. Their ideas underpinned the later racialist program of Adolf Hitler (1925), who advocated the dominance of the 'Aryan' or 'Nordic' master race and whose policies before and during the Second World War involved the extermination of those seen as inferior races.

Theories of sexual and racial stratification have undoubtedly recognized some of the key elements needed in any account of social stratification. Ethnic and gender divisions are, in different ways, central aspects of social inequality, and they play an important part in many systems of social stratification. They are not, however, forms of stratification themselves.

You might find it useful to review what we say in 'Gender and Ethnic Identities', Chapter 4, pp. 139–45. We show how these are involved in patterns of social inequality in Chapter 14.

While ethnic divisions are fundamental in many systems of social stratification, this is not the case for *all* systems of stratification. Ethnic identities are cultural expressions of a sense of difference that is rooted in history, origins, language, religion, or some other ascribed group characteristics. These identities are relevant to social stratification when they rest on assumptions about the superiority or inferiority of particular ethnic groups. These assumptions of ethnic superiority, however, can play a part only if combined with economic or political resources that are not themselves simply a result of ethnic differences. A theory of social stratification must look at all of these factors together, and not just at ethnicity alone. An emphasis on ethnic stratification becomes especially misleading, of course, if ethnic differences are assumed to involve real biological differences of race. As we show in Chapter 4, pp. 143–4, there is no scientifically justifiable concept of biological race. For this reason, there can be no valid theory of racial stratification.

Theories of sexual stratification must also be rejected if they attempt to reduce all social divisions and struggles to biological differences of sex. The fundamental problem with these theories is that, while they have recognized a significant aspect of *social inequalities*, they have not—and cannot—account for the long-term *stratification* of a society. Social strata reproduce themselves over time, ultimately through the sexual reproduction of their members. Separate social groupings of men and women cannot do this.

Sex and ethnicity affect relations of stratification in many very important ways—as we will show—and they have, of course, a major significance in areas of social life other than social stratification. Social inequalities are, indeed, both gendered and racialized, and no theory of stratification can afford to ignore this. A more comprehensive understanding of social stratification, however, requires a different starting point. This has been provided for us by Max Weber.

CLASS AND STATUS

Weber saw social stratification as a central feature of social life, and it figured in all his sociological studies.

Yet his theoretical discussions of it were very brief. These discussions have, however, been enormously influential. The distinctions that he made between class, status, and party have become commonplace in sociology, as has his related definition of authority. Here we will review Weber's key ideas, building on them where necessary, in order to provide a comprehensive framework for understanding social stratification. (See J. Scott 1996 for a fuller discussion.)

Weber identified three distinct aspects or dimensions of the distribution of power within societies. These can be called the economic, the communal, and the authoritarian. Each of these aspects of power has a separate effect on the production of advantaged and disadvantaged life chances. In summary, he holds that

▶ *economic* power is the basis of class relations;

▶ *communal* power is the basis of status relations;

▶ *authoritarian* power is the basis of authority relations.

We will look at each of these, concentrating on class and status, and we will show how other writers have helped to develop ideas about these issues.

Class and economic power

Class relations and class divisions have an economic basis because they result from the distribution of property and other resources in the capital, product, and labour markets. It is possession and non-possession of economic resources that give people their power to acquire income and assets from their involvement in market relations. What Weber called **class situation** is a person's position in the capital, product, and labour markets as determined by the kinds of resources that they have available to them. People occupy a similar class situation whenever they have similar abilities to secure advantages and disadvantages for themselves through the use of their marketable resources.

Someone who owns company shares, for example, will earn an investment income on them and may be able to sell them for a profit on the stock market. Similarly, someone with educational credentials and a particular technical expertise may be able to demand a higher income in the labour market than someone without this skill. A carpenter and an electrician both have skills that allow them to earn higher wages in the labour market than an unskilled labourer.

A person's economic power is, Weber said, a **causal component** in the determination of their life chances. What he means by this is that the inequalities in life chances that we examine in Chapter 14 are determined, to a greater or lesser extent, by differences in property and market position. A person's class situation not only determines their life chances; it also determines the interests that they have in protecting and enhancing these life chances. This is very important, as Weber held that people are often likely to act, individually or collectively, in pursuit of their class interests. Weber accepted many of the views that Marx set out in his analysis of class relations, and it is possible to use some of Marx's ideas to broaden out the understanding of class divisions that Weber has given us.

Central to Marx's theory was the claim that all societies, except for the most primitive tribal ones, were, in fact, class societies. This view was summarized in a famous statement that 'The history of all hitherto existing society is the history of class struggles' (Marx and Engels 1848: 79). For all the apparent differences that there are between feudal Europe, traditional China, ancient Egypt, and contemporary capitalism, these societies were all seen by Marx as being stratified by class. He did not, of course, ignore the many things that distinguished them from one another, but he did regard them as being of secondary importance.

Marx saw property ownership as the key factor in all social divisions. Above all, it is property in the means of production—the ownership and non-ownership of factories, machines, land, and other economic resources—that gives rise to class relations. In some societies, these class relations may be masked or obscured by religious, ethnic, or other cultural differences, but they are always there as the fundamental determinants of people's actions.

The class that owns the means of production in a society, Marx argued, has the greatest amount of power and is able to oppress and to exploit the class of non-owners. In a capitalist society this creates a fundamental opposition between a 'bourgeoisie' or **capitalist class** and a 'proletariat' or **working class**. Capitalist property-owners have their historical origins in the merchant burghers of the medieval towns, but they include a whole range of property-owners who are directly concerned with the acquisition and use of capital in commerce, finance, and manufacturing. Proletarians, on the other hand, are those who have no capital and so must rely on the sale of their own labour power for a wage. Only by securing employment from a capitalist can a proletarian obtain the money that is required to meet his or her needs.

Capital

Marx used the word 'capital' to refer to any physical or financial asset that is used in the economic sphere and so is a source of value. The personal assets of an individual or family, then, are not 'capital', in the strict sense, if they are simply consumed or enjoyed. A house, for example, becomes a form of capital only if its owners let it out for rent, rather than living in it themselves. The most important forms of capital are those assets that are used in production and finance. Capitalists are people who derive all or most of their income from their capital and who are involved in controlling the use of this capital.

Marx on class

Although the idea of class was central to virtually everything that he wrote, Marx never set out a systematic statement of his views. Those who have followed him have had to reconstruct a theory of class from his many writings, leaving much scope for rival views of 'what Marx really meant'. Nevertheless, his core ideas are clear enough. The main sources from which his views on class can be derived are the *Communist Manifesto* (Marx and Engels 1848) and the various volumes of *Capital* (see especially Marx 1864–5). Much of his work, including the *Communist Manifesto*, was written jointly with his collaborator, Friedrich Engels, but it is usual to refer to the principal ideas as being those of Marx alone. Marx's arguments were developed by many later Marxist writers. Of particular importance in relation to the study of class in British society are Miliband (1969) and Westergaard and Resler (1975).

Marx used the term 'exploitation' to describe the class relation that exists between capitalists and their employees. The workers' wages are only a small part of the total value of the commodities that they produce during the working week, and by controlling this extra value—Marx called it the surplus value—the capitalist benefits at the expense of the worker. Surplus value is the source of the profit that funds investment in machinery and allows a business enterprise to grow, and it is also the source of the personal income of the capitalist. The exploitation of labour, then, is the basis for both the accumulation of capital and the accumulation of wealth.

The class situations of capitalists and proletarians, therefore, are quite distinct. One is based on the ownership and control of capital, and the other is based on the exercise of labour power as an employee. Capitalist class situations include those of industrial entrepreneurs, bankers, and landowners, as well as those who simply live on income from company shares. Proletarian class situations include those of people involved in skilled work, manual labour, office work, and so on.

Marx's account of class cannot be accepted as it stands. Class relations are more complex than Marx's two-class model implies. Nevertheless, it is an extremely useful starting point. Weber's main objection to Marx's account was that it involved an economic determinism. It tried to explain everything in terms of economic factors. Weber wanted to recognize the importance of non-economic factors in social stratification. Class situation is a causal component in life chances, but it is only *one* causal component. The other causal components are to be found in the non-economic factors of status and authority relations.

Status and communal power

Status relations and status divisions have a communal basis because they emerge from the distribution of prestige or social honour within a community. In its most general sense, a person's status is his or her standing or reputation in the eyes of others. People appraise each other as superior or inferior in relation to the values that they hold in common with the other members of their society or with some group within it. Those whose actions conform to these values receive wide approval and a great deal of prestige. They have a high status in their community. Those who deviate from these values or who conform to less-central values are given a lower status and may be rejected as outsiders.

> ☞ You might recognize some similarities with our discussion of deviance in Chapter 5. Try thinking about the idea of deviance as a social status.
> You might also like to look at the way in which community is defined in Chapter 11, pp. 406–8.

In small-scale societies, and in many face-to-face situations, status differences are based on the detailed personal knowledge that people have about each other. They know one another as individuals through frequent interaction in many different situations, and they can easily arrive at an overall judgement of reputation or social standing. Weber was more concerned with status in complex societies, where this kind of detailed knowledge is not usually available. In these

societies, a person's status does not depend on all of the many ways in which their actions can be evaluated. It is the appraisal of their **style of life** that is crucial.

What Weber meant by this is the way in which people carry out the tasks associated with their most important social positions and the customs and practices that they follow as members of particular social groups. Occupations, gender roles, and ethnic group membership are all associated with particular and distinct styles of life, and it is these that are important in determining people's social standing in their society. A feminine style of life, for example, may be valued less highly than a masculine one, and the way of life followed by Asians may be devalued by many whites. In these circumstances, women and Asians will be given a lower status than men and members of the ethnic majority. Type of dress and bodily adornment, type and size of house, area of residence, clothing, accent, methods of cooking and eating, and so on are taken as markers of social identities and, therefore, as symbols of status.

One of the most important writers on this idea of status is Parsons (1940, 1953, 1970). He has argued that people's social status is determined by those social positions that are most important in defining their membership of their society. Some societies define membership by birth or lineage, and a person's status reflects his or her kinship, gender, and age roles. This is the case, Parsons argues, in many tribal societies In these societies, older males generally have a high status as the elders of the society and are seen as superior in social standing to younger men and to all women. Young women may have an especially low status until they are married to a suitable man. A young woman's marriage chances may depend on whether she was born into a leading family or into one of the lesser families.

In modern societies, however, membership is no longer directly determined by birth in this way. Membership depends upon a person's public roles, and status depends on those particular roles to which people are able to achieve entry. The most important public roles for defining membership are work roles, which are organized to occupations. Into modern societies, then, status is largely determined by occupation.

Occupations differ in terms of the skills, income, and authority that they involve, and Parsons argued that they are ranked and evaluated according to how these relate to communal values. The doctor, teacher, carpenter, bishop, and housewife all differ from one another in these respects. The result of this evaluation of occupations is a scale of occupational prestige. At the bottom of the scale are manual occupations, ranked by the level of their skill. Routine non-manual occupations come in the middle of the scale, and professional and managerial occupations are at the top.

People tend to be judged on the basis of a very vague and stereotyped knowledge of their occupations and other social positions. Their houses, their cars, their clothing, and their accents, for example, may be taken as indicators of their social status. As highly valued occupations are assumed to receive a high income, a rough scale of income is often used as an alternative way of deciding a person's status. In contemporary societies, then, income and consumption become symbols of status, and people may become motivated simply to achieve a high income rather than to enter a specific occupation.

 Compare this argument about occupational prestige with our discussion of the functionalist theory of inequality in Chapter 14, pp. 565–6. You may find it useful to go over that argument before continuing with this section.

Parsons is often criticized for exaggerating the amount of consensus that exists in contemporary societies. It is certainly true that he stresses the part played by common values. He did recognize, however, that subcultures and subordinate value systems were also important. Modern societies are pluralistic in their values, and there may be competing criteria of social status.

Professional and administrative workers, for example, may follow the dominant cultural values and place their own occupations at the top of a scale of prestige, and they are likely to place manual occupations at the bottom of the scale. Manual workers, on the other hand, might agree with the high valuation of professional occupations, but they may place skilled manual occupations above routine forms of administrative and clerical work. Similarly, the dominant values may stress occupational achievement, while other value systems place greater importance on ascriptive factors such as ethnicity or gender. Sometimes these different criteria of status may come into conflict with one another. It is possible, for example, for a person to have a high status as a doctor, but a low status as black or as a woman. Such people may experience status ambiguity or status inconsistency: the way that they are seen by others will depend upon *who* those others are.

According to Weber, **status situation**, like class situation, is a major causal component in life chances. Class situations are the economic relations through which control over marketable resources is organized for the attainment of income, assets, and other life chances. Status situations are the communal relations through which the prestige that is accorded to a particular lifestyle becomes the basis of life chances.

It is because status has this effect on life chances that Weber paid particular attention to the distinct interests that people have in the preservation or enhancement of their prestige. He argued that people are motivated by their status interests as much as they are by class interests. Indeed, status interests may often be more important to people. Ethnic minority manual workers, for example, may unite with others from the same ethnic minority in a struggle for equal opportunities and rights, rather than uniting with other manual workers to raise the pay for their particular occupation.

Inequalities in life chances, then, must be seen as reflecting the effects of *both* class and status situations. A person's occupation, for example, is a position in the labour market that also has a place on a scale of prestige (Parkin 1971). Occupational prestige and position in the labour market work together to determine the life chances that people derive from their employment.

Ascribed status may also combine with market situation to shape life chances. Women and members of ethnic minorities, for example, may be prevented by discrimination from taking those jobs in the labour market for which they are properly qualified. When they are in employment they may be given lower wages for doing the same or similar work to men or members of the ethnic majority. This intrusion of status into employment prospects shows how class relations are gendered or racialized. Where age is an important consideration, class relations may also be *aged*, and the life chances of the elderly, for example, may reflect their status as much as their class situation. The task of sociological analysis is to weigh the relative importance of class and status relations in different societies and at different times.

Boundaries and social closure

The investigation of class, status, and authority situations is only the beginning of an exploration into social stratification. It helps to explain patterns of social inequality, but it does not show how boundaries come to be built and social strata formed. Social stratification exists when relatively closed social groups reproduce themselves over time and are differentiated from one another by their unequal life chances.

Social strata are demographically bounded social groups. They result from the social relations that tie together those who are in particular class, status, and command situations. Through social mobility,

Authority and authoritarian power

Weber's third dimension of power was authoritarian power. His views on this were set out in his analysis of authority and bureaucracy, and you may like to look at our discussion of these matters in Chapter 17, pp. 644–8. Authority relations result from the distribution of authority and administrative power in organizations such as modern states and large business enterprises. In all organizations, there are those who command, those with delegated powers, and those who are simply on the receiving end of commands. A person's position within a structure of authority can be called a **'command situation'**, though Weber himself did not use this specific term. Command situations create interests in the maintenance or enhancement of powers of command and they can be considered alongside class situations and status situations as the third causal component in shaping life chances.

Occupational mobility

It is important to be clear about two quite distinct ways in which occupational mobility is of interest to sociologists. In Chapter 14 we look at how rates of mobility can be used to measure the overall openness of a structure of inequality and the relative chances of changing occupational levels that are enjoyed by those in different occupations. In this chapter, on the other hand, we look at how patterns of occupational mobility are involved in the formation of social strata by defining boundaries of 'closure' around particular occupations. The study of openness cannot, of course, be completely separated from the study of closure, but it is important to keep these different concerns in mind. When you have read what we say about occupational mobility in this chapter, you might like to look at Chapter 14, pp. 574–8 and 590–3, and review our argument there.

marriage and kinship, and free-time interaction, certain social positions are linked together and are separated from others. A social stratum can be seen as a cluster of social positions among which individuals can circulate and associate freely through their own mobility and that of their children, through marital and kinship connections, and through close and intimate interactions.

In contemporary societies, these relations have most frequently been studied in relation to occupations. Occupational roles are specific combinations of class, status, and command situations—each occupation, for example, involves particular marketable skills or resources, is given a particular level of occupational prestige, and involves a specific amount of authority over others. By looking at movement and interaction among occupations, it is possible to map out the boundaries of social strata.

If it is regularly the case that, say, those who begin their working lives in lower level supervisory work end up in junior management positions, then it is sensible to view these two occupational categories as parts of the same social stratum. This view would be strengthened by any evidence that the sons of lower-level supervisors enter work as junior managers, or that the daughters of junior managers regularly marry or form domestic partnerships with the sons of lower-level supervisors. In these circumstances, career mobility, generational mobility, and marriage relations rein-

force one another to create regular and established patterns of connection within a single stratum. Similarly, if those who enter work as carpenters do not typically end their careers as doctors, if the daughters of carpenters rarely become doctors, and if the sons of carpenters rarely marry doctor's daughters, it is plausible to see these two occupations as falling into different social strata.

Particularly important in the formation of stratum boundaries are the patterns of household formation that we discuss in Chapter 10, pp. 355–7. It is through marriage or cohabitation that households are formed, and it is within households that educational and occupational opportunities are shaped. This is why occupational mobility is generally measured in relation to household membership: for example, by measuring a man's mobility in relation to the occupation of his father. Households are also central to the organization of much free-time interaction, and an investigation of stratum boundaries must look at this. It is important to know, for example, whether lawyers interact with civil servants, other than in professional consultations: do they meet in each other's homes for drinks, entertain one another for meals, or attend the same clubs with their husbands and wives? If they do, then this is evidence for considering them to be part of the same social stratum.

Figure 15.2 shows a simplified illustration of how social strata are formed from patterns of occupational mobility and interaction. In the diagram, occupations are seen as falling into the same social stratum if there

Figure 15.2. **Social stratum boundaries**

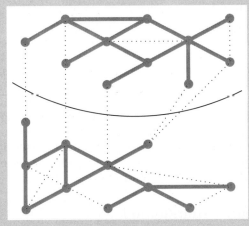

Key

- ● occupations (class, status, and command situations)
- ▬▬ mobility and interaction: high frequency
- ·········· mobility and interaction: low frequency
- ───── stratum boundary

This diagram is only a simplified and highly schematic image of social strata. It is designed to help you to understand the processes involved.

▶ Compare the diagram with those in Figure 15.1 and try to imagine how they would look if stratum boundaries were drawn as they are here. You will find it almost impossible to draw such a diagram, but thinking about it is a good intellectual exercise for grasping the nature of social stratification.

is frequent mobility or interaction between one and another. Occupations form a stratum if they are connected through chains of frequent and relatively easy connection. The occupations of different social strata, on the other hand, are connected only—if at all—through the infrequent movement and interaction of people. Boundaries between social strata can be identified wherever there is a natural break in the distribution of mobility and interaction, as this is where rates are significantly lower than they are elsewhere. If individuals are allocated to the various class, status, and command situations that make up the social positions of a society, an investigation of mobility and interaction will show how these positions are clustered together into various social strata.

Marx held, for example, that the occupants of capi-

talist class situations form a social stratum because they circulate freely from involvement with one form of capital to involvement with another, they intermarry with one another, and their children inherit their capital and the advantaged life chances that it generates. In the same way, occupants of proletarian class situations come to form a separate social stratum. They move from one type of work to another, and from work to unemployment, they marry other workers, and their children have no choice but to enter employment as soon as they are able.

> You may find these definitions very abstract, but do not worry. You will find that things fall into place as you follow through the rest of the chapter, and as we look at actual examples. For the moment, just try to understand the broad principles involved. You may find it useful to come back to this section after you have read the rest of the chapter. But first, we need some more definitions!

Consciousness and action

People have some awareness of the conditions under which they live. Where people share certain aspects of their life experiences, they are likely to develop a shared awareness of those conditions that they have in common. The members of a social stratum, then, are likely to have some common awareness of the property or market conditions that they share, the authority relations that they are involved in, their social standing in the eyes of others, and their life chances in relation to others. They may, perhaps, have an image of the boundaries of their stratum and of how it relates to the other strata of their society. These images of society are important as cognitive maps that guide them in their relations with others. In modern societies they typically take the form of class consciousness.

In the past, these images of society have developed mainly through the direct, face-to-face interactions of stratum members and from the direct personal knowledge that they have about those in other social strata. Through working together, living in the same neighbourhood, and being involved in the same leisure activities, people have forged a common outlook on life that has shaped their sense of community and solidarity. Where social strata are tightly closed, this solidarity has been particularly strong. Today, however, people's attitudes and opinions are shaped also by the media of

Class consciousness

Class consciousness is the shared consciousness of the members of a social class. It develops wherever the class situations of the members of a social stratum are the most important determinants of their life chances and of their shared experiences. Where status situations have an important effect on people's consciousness, it may be more appropriate to talk about status consciousness than class consciousness. The difference between social classes and other kinds of social strata are looked at in the next section.

mass communications. As we will show, the influence of the media and a decline in face-to-face sources of information and opinion have been the major factors responsible for reducing the strength of class consciousness and class identity in contemporary societies.

Where this common consciousness is especially well developed, it may take a political form. That is to say, the members of the stratum may have a clear understanding of what they take their shared interests to be and of the kind of political programme that is likely to further these interests. In their individual actions (for example, as voters) and in their collective action (as, say, members of trade unions or social movements) they will strive to defend and promote their interests as against those of other strata. This may lead them to advocate social change that they think will be of particular benefit to them or that accords with their political goals.

Weber stressed the part that organized groups such as trade unions, political parties, interest groups, and social movements can play in focusing the consciousness of a stratum and in making people aware of the larger, nation-wide and global interests that they share with others. These bodies and associations were all described as parties by Weber. A **party**, in this sense, is any group that is united around a particular cause or interest and that claims to represent particular strata or social categories in the political sphere. The Labour Party and the Conservative Party, the General and Municipal Workers' Union, and Friends of the Earth are all parties in Weber's sense.

The claims of parties cannot, of course, be taken at face value. Parties may claim to speak on behalf of people who actually ignore them or reject their views. Communist political parties in Europe, for example, have often claimed to represent the whole of the working class. While many of their members have been manual workers, no Communist Party in Western Europe has ever had the active support of a majority of its working class.

At the same time, the members of a social stratum can misunderstand their own situation and so act in inappropriate ways. Manual workers who are in similarly subordinate and exploited economic situations, for example, may fail to see that they have common economic interests and may also deny the relevance of these class relations to their lives. These views may be genuinely and authentically held, and they should not be rejected as mere 'false consciousness'. Sociological analysis must, nevertheless, pay particular attention to any apparent discrepancy between people's consciousness and their actual circumstances.

Systems of stratification

Life chances are shaped, then, by three aspects of power: *class situations* that result from differences of power in the economic sphere of property and the market, *status situations* that derive from differences of power in the communal sphere of prestige, and *command situations* that derive from differences of power in the sphere of authority. These operate alongside one another, but their relative importance can vary quite a lot from one society to another.

In some societies, class situations are the most important determinants of life chances, while in others the most important causal component is a command situation. It is not possible to say that any one of the three is more fundamental than the others in all circumstances. This was the point of Weber's criticism of Marx's economic determinism. The relative importance of the three components is something that can be discovered only through empirical investigation. Any investigation of social stratification must identify the various class, status, and command situations that exist in a society and assess their relative influences on life chances and the ways in which they reinforce or counteract one another.

Weber used the term **social class** to describe those social strata that are formed when class situations are the most important factor. Social classes are clusters of households whose members owe their life chances principally to their specific property ownership and market positions. A society in which all or most social strata are social classes, in this sense, can be called a **class society**. An example of a class society would be a modern capitalist society in which it might be possible to identify, for example, a working class, a middle class, and an upper class.

The term **social estates**, on the other hand, refers to

those social strata that exist when status relations are the most important factor. Social estates are clusters of households whose members owe their life chances principally to their specific social standing as superior or inferior to others. Examples of social estates include the priesthood in a traditional society based on religion. A society in which all or most of the social strata are social estates, Weber said, can be called a **status society**. Weber said far less about **command societies**, where the life chances of members of social strata are determined by their command situations. An example of such a society would be the Soviet Union, where the whole society was dominated by a ruling elite whose members occupied the top positions of authority in the state. This aspect of social stratification is considered more fully in Chapter 17.

These definitions are what Weber called 'ideal types'. They do not exist in reality in their pure form, but only ever in combination. In a status society, for example, economic power always plays an important part, and class societies will also be shaped by the distribution of prestige. The task of the sociologist is to investigate the relative importance of each factor in the particular society with which he or she is concerned.

☞ We discuss Weber's methodology in Chapter 2. Look at p. 42 to see how he defined the ideal type. Can you see what it means to talk about the concept of a class society as an ideal type?

An example of a status society in which class and authority relations, nevertheless, played an important part is the slave society of North America that existed from the sixteenth to the nineteenth century. **Slavery** is a system of stratification in which differences of status that define some people as free and others as slaves are underpinned by political and economic inequalities. These inequalities ensure that slaves carry out their assigned role of serving the free citizens of their society. Slaves lack the rights of full membership. They are objects of property relations. They can be bought and sold and have no say in their own fate.

Slavery in the Caribbean and North America grew with the forcible conquest of African tribal societies and the extension of trade with African slave-owners in the sixteenth century. Slaves and captives were transported to the Americas, where they were sold in open markets and held in their slavery by force and coercion. Slavery is an ascribed status, but one that is rooted in force. The children of slaves, for example, had no choice about their status: they were born into slavery and could do nothing to alter the situation. It was through the system of slavery that the tobacco, sugar, and cotton industries of North America were built (Paterson 1967, 1982).

American slavery was closely linked with the rise of racial ideas in Western culture. Differences of colour became markers of ethnic difference that were defined in a racialized form. Slaves were a social estate. They were the bottom stratum in a system of stratification that was headed by the white settlers and their descendants. An upper stratum of plantation-owners were at the top of the system, holding economic and political power as well as having the highest status, and the middle levels of the system comprised small independent farmers, officials, and other white groups.

Slavery was legally abolished in the United States in 1865, though the racialized status of African-Americans continued to disadvantage them. Although they were formally free, ex-slaves had few real options. Many continued to work on the plantations, often for the same master, and for them their masters simply became their employers. Many others became sharecroppers, where they were as exploited as they had been under slavery. Nevertheless, African-Americans did acquire more freedom of movement and of access to public places during the Reconstruction era at the end of the nineteenth century.

This greater freedom was felt as threatening by many whites, who had previously been able to keep a social distance from African-Americans. As a result, a number of restrictive laws were passed between 1890 and the First World War. These laws limited African-American voting rights, prevented them from using the same trains, toilets, and eating places as whites, and limited them to certain schools. This system of segregation was justified as providing 'separate-but-equal' facilities for blacks and whites, and the structure of segregation remained in place until the 1960s.

Stratification in the southern states during the era of segregation has been discussed as an example of a **caste** system. Caste has been used to describe stratification in traditional India, where status divisions defined particular ethnic groups by their 'purity' or 'pollution' in terms of the values of the dominant social strata. Weber suggested that all systems of stratification by ethnic identity tended to take a caste form. According to Warner (1936), African-Americans in the deep south were virtually an 'untouchable' caste, and the whole stratification system looked something like the second diagram in Figure 15.1.

It has also been suggested that the apartheid system of ethnic relations that existed in South Africa from 1948 to 1991 can be seen as a caste system of stratification, and that the post-apartheid state has had to grapple with the inheritance of this institutionalized racism. The American and South African situations show that caste, as a system of stratification by status, depends as much on force and law as it does on cultural values.

Britain and the United States can best be described as class societies. Ethnic segregation in the southern states of the United States was based on sharp status divisions, and ethnic divisions play an important part in the stratification of the northern states and in Britain. Nevertheless, the most important lines of social stratification are those that result from relations of economic power. The principal social strata are social classes. Ethnic and other status divisions play their part alongside and within class relations.

We will look at these class relations in the rest of this chapter, and we will try to show how class and status operate together to produce contemporary patterns of stratification.

SUMMARY POINTS

In this section we have reviewed the main concepts used in the study of social stratification. We set out a number of important theoretical points derived from the work of Weber:

▶ Social stratification must be distinguished from social inequality. It involves the formation of strata that are differentiated by their life chances.

▶ It is important to distinguish between class, status, and authority. Class involves economic power, status involves communal power, and authority involves authoritarian power.

▶ The boundaries of social strata are defined by relations of mobility and interaction.

▶ Collective action by the members of a stratum involves the formation of parties.

We showed that Weber's ideas provide a basis for understanding the relationship between stratification, sex–gender, and ethnicity. We also argued that some writers have more to say on class, while others concentrate on status.

▶ Marx is the principal theorist of stratification by class.

▶ Parsons is the principal theorist of stratification by status.

We looked, finally, at the use of these concepts in comparative studies. We highlighted:

▶ slavery as a system of social status rooted in force and coercion;

▶ caste as a particular form of ethnic stratification.

Caste

In the classical Indian caste system, five strata were defined by the Hindu religion. There were four 'varna' or pure castes, their levels of purity being reflected in their styles of life. The four varna were

▶ *Brahmins*: priestly families who controlled the sacred texts and ritual practices and were the most pure of all;

▶ *Kshatriya*: landowners and warriors;

▶ *Vaishya*: traders and farmers;

▶ *Shudra*: labourers.

The first three varna were the 'twice born', who were believed to have been through several human reincarnations. The lowest, and least pure, of the varna were not, however, at the bottom of the stratification system. The lowest stratum were the menial workers who were regarded as untouchable or as outcastes because contact with them was a source of pollution for the twice born. Contact with untouchables was possible only under closely regulated and ritually sanctioned conditions. Neither mobility nor interaction was possible across the caste lines, and each stratum was very tightly closed.

The actual pattern of caste relations in Indian villages and towns was extremely complicated, and it rarely conformed to the ideal picture. There is still much debate about how it is to be interpreted. Dumont (1966) draws on Weber, while Milner (1994) draws on Durkheim. A useful recent overview is Quigley (1993).

THE MAKING OF A CLASS SOCIETY

It was during the nineteenth century that a class society was built in Britain. From the last third of the century until well into the first half of the twentieth century this took the classic form of a division into a working class, a middle class, and an upper class. This is shown in the model in Figure 15.3, which represents the stratification system as a triangle in order to show the relative sizes of the social classes. A small upper class stands above a larger middle class and an even larger working class.

The class structure was not, of course, quite so neatly and rigidly divided into three social classes as this model suggests. The boundaries between classes were far from sharp, and each class had internal divisions into subclasses or sections. It is for this reason that the social-class classifications that we look at in Chapter 3, pp. 96–100, have divided the three basic classes into five or more social classes. Despite these qualifications, the image of British society as divided into three principal social classes gives an accurate view of the main lines of division that existed in the first half of the twentieth century. It also accords with the imagery and language employed by people themselves.

Figure 15.4 uses census data and the official socio- economic groups (SEGs) to show the distribution of men and women into various social classes. These official categories do not correspond exactly to the actual lines of social division, but they do give a general impression of the changing shape of the class structure and the composition of the various social classes.

The working class, broadly defined, amounted to over 80 per cent of the population in 1911. In 1951 it still included almost three-quarters of the population. Over this whole period, the number of semi-skilled workers in the working class was greater than the number of skilled workers, and the number of unskilled workers was much smaller. The middle classes increased from just over 12 per cent to around a quarter of the population in the same period. This was mainly a result of the increase in the number of clerical workers, though the number of professional and managerial workers also increased sharply. As we will show, the middle classes also included a number of small property-owners, who were counted along with all other property-owners in SEG 2A. This makes it difficult to estimate the number of large-scale capitalist property-owners and land-owners who occupy positions at the top of the stratification system. At the beginning of the twentieth century, this stratum was popularly known as the 'upper ten thousand', and it certainly amounted to much less than 1 per cent of the whole population.

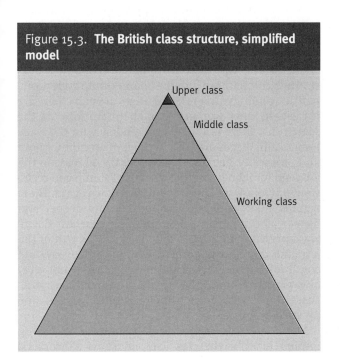

Figure 15.3. **The British class structure, simplified model**

Upper class

Middle class

Working class

CAPITALISM AND CLASS SOCIETY

The most influential attempt to understand the origins and development of the class structure in capitalist societies has been that derived from the work of Marx. According to Marx, the division between the dominant capitalist class and the subordinate working class would become ever sharper, while the middle classes would gradually disappear. Later Marxists recognized the growth in the number of clerical, managerial, and professional employees and tried to reconcile this growth of the middle class with Marx's own arguments.

Class polarization

Marx held that the growth of capitalism is marked by a drive towards economic concentration and monopoly. Driven by the need to expand the scale of production,

Figure 15.4. Stratification in England and Wales, 1911–1951

Socio-economic group		Percentage of population				Social class
		1911	1921	1931	1951	
2A	Employers and property-owners	6.71	6.82	6.70	4.97	Some upper class, some middle class
1A/1B	Professionals	4.05	4.53	4.60	6.63	
2B	Managerial and administrative	3.43	3.64	3.66	5.53	Middle class
3	Clerical	4.84	6.72	6.97	10.68	
4	Foremen, etc.	1.29	1.44	1.54	2.62	
5	Skilled manual	30.56	28.83	26.72	24.95	Working class
6	Semi-skilled manual	39.48	33.85	35.00	32.60	
7	Unskilled manual	9.63	14.17	14.81	12.03	
		100	100	100	100	

Source: adapted from Routh (1987: table 3.1).

▶ **Which particular sections of the population showed the biggest growth during the first half of the twentieth century? Which has shown the biggest fall? You might like to draw a pie chart to illustrate the social-class structure of the population in 1951.**

capitalists issue company shares on the stock exchange and so allow other capitalists to invest in their businesses. As a result, the owners and controllers of capital become more closely tied together in a structure of concentrated business power. This becomes even more marked when banks and other financial enterprises become closely and directly involved in the financing of production. As a result, small groups of *finance capitalists*, operating in both banking and industry, coordinate business activities at the national level and, increasingly, at the global level. This concentration of capital squeezes out small-scale capitalists and property-owners, leaving fewer—but wealthier—capitalists in existence.

These capitalists, he said, develop a class consciousness of their shared interests as employers and property-owners. Through their intersecting investments in business, they develop a strong awareness of their dependence on property and of the economic gulf that separates them from their employees. This also leads them to recognize the need to ensure that the state maintains a framework of property and employment law to support their position and that it pursues policies that are in the interests of business. Marx saw this occurring when capitalists actually controlled the state, becoming what he called a *ruling class*.

The growth of wealth at one end of the stratification system, Marx argued, was matched by the growth of poverty at the other end. The opposition between capitalist and proletarian, Marx believed, would become ever starker as the capitalists became richer and the proletarians became poorer. This is the inevitable result of the way that a capitalist economy works through competition and the boom–slump cycle. Competition among workers keeps wages down, as there are invariably more workers than there are jobs. At the same time, there is a long-term tendency for the wage level to fall. Wages may rise in times of economic boom and prosperity, because of a temporary increase in the demand for labour, but the periods of slump and recession that follow will push them back down again. These slumps, Marx suggested, would become deeper and deeper as capitalism developed. The constant downward pressure on wages would lead to a growth in the amount of relative poverty. Although the pay and conditions of workers might improve over time, they always improve more slowly than those of the capitalists. The gap between rich and poor gets bigger as capitalism develops.

Marx saw this economic deterioration as having implications for the class consciousness of workers. Their consciousness is rooted in the fact that they must sell their labour power on the market. They have no control over it, and they come to be seen as commodities and as mere appendages to the machines on which they work. This is a condition shared by all workers, and it is through their common experience of exploitation and alienation that workers begin to develop their class consciousness. They may initially unite around the common interests of their particular trade or occupation and form a trade union to promote their interests. As their economic position worsens, so their class consciousness is likely to deepen. This is especially likely where they work in large factories that bring together many different kinds of workers, and where they live close to each other in the same parts of the industrial towns and cities. In these circumstances, Marx said, they develop a broader awareness of their shared class interests. Occupational consciousness and solidarity gives way to true class consciousness and solidarity.

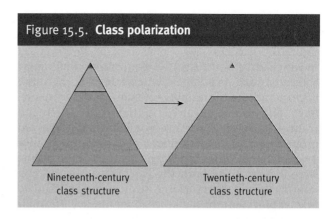

Figure 15.5. **Class polarization**

Nineteenth-century class structure

Twentieth-century class structure

☞ **You might find it useful to read our discussion of various aspects of Marx's wider views on capitalism. His view of work and the alienation of labour is covered in Chapter 13, pp. 512–15. Also in that chapter, pp. 503–4 and in Chapter 16, pp. 656–8, you will find a discussion of trade unions and of business organization. It might also be useful to review our definitions of absolute and relative poverty in Chapter 14, p. 561.**

Capitalist societies would, then, become ever more **polarized** between wealth and poverty, and the two main classes would become more sharply divided in their class consciousness. Marx went even further in some of his work and predicted the growing absolute poverty of workers. Each recession runs deeper than the one before, he argued, and so wages are constantly driven down in real terms until they reach a bare subsistence level. He sees capitalism as resulting in the *pauperization* of workers.

The growing scale of poverty—whether relative or absolute—was linked by Marx to his expectation that the development of capitalism would be marked by ever-deepening recessions. There is some evidence to support this view as a description of what happened in the first half of the nineteenth century, but matters have become more complicated since then. Capitalist production has, indeed, followed a pattern that shows successive periods of boom and slump, of expansion and recession, and recessions have often been both deep and long. However, there does not seem to be any long-term tendency for recessions to get deeper with

every downturn in the economy. It is undoubtedly the case that periodic recessions have produced high levels of relative poverty, but the level of poverty has not shown a long-term increase and there has been no straightforward increase in class consciousness with increases in poverty.

Intermediate class situations

Marx believed that the polarization of the class structure between capitalist and proletariat would be sharpened by the disappearance of all intermediate classes. In the early stages of capitalism there were a number of classes that lay between the capitalists and the proletariat. These included the peasants and small-scale property-owners, shopkeepers, and other relatively advantaged groups that formed the 'middle classes'. Marx believed that those who occupied these class situations would lose their advantages as their property was destroyed by the expansion and concentration of capitalist production. Intermediate class situations would be **proletarianized** as their occupants were forced to become wage labourers. Using the simple model that we presented in Figure 15.3, Marx's model of class polarization can be summarized as shown in Figure 15.5.

The evidence does not seem to support Marx on this. As he himself began to realize towards the end of his life, there has been a massive growth in the numbers of those in the intermediate class situations that cannot be regarded as either capitalist or proletarian in the strict sense. The huge armies of managers and professionals who hold positions of authority in the large bureaucracies of the state and the big business enterprises may be propertyless, but they enjoy vastly superior life chances to manual workers and they have close working relationships with capitalist employers. The rise of this so-called new middle class runs counter to Marx's view of class polarization.

A number of Marxist writers tried to take account of this by developing new theoretical ideas. They held that capitalism was entering a new stage of development in which large bureaucratic organizations would play a greater part. As business enterprises became more bureaucratic, so the numbers of managers, clerks, foremen, and others involved in the supervision and control of manual workers would increase. The old propertied middle class might disappear, but a new propertyless middle class was expanding. These people were distinct from both the capitalists and the proletarians: they were lacking in property and had to find employment through the labour market, but their jobs involved them in the exercise of authority over others and they enjoyed relatively advantaged life chances. The continuing expansion of this kind of work has led to successively more sophisticated attempts to understand the class situations involved (Wright 1985, 1997).

The issues raised in the debate over the claims made by Marxism can be examined in relation to the three social classes that we identified earlier. These are the working class, the middle class, and the upper class.

THE WORKING CLASS

The economic basis for a working class is the employee relationship of wage labour (technically termed their **market situation**) and the organizational setting of large-scale production (their **work situation**). Employees involved in the direct production processes of large organizations are typically, though slightly misleadingly, described as manual workers. They are involved in a complex division of labour in which each type of work is coordinated with that of other workers with a variety of skills and abilities. What unites them as proletarian workers is the fact that they have similar market and work situations. They have similar employment conditions and they are subject to the authority of employers or managers. They are, however, differentiated by the varying levels and types of skills that they possess. There are, for example, skilled or 'time-served' workers who have served an apprenticeship that trains them for their particular work and whose skill is an important marketable asset. These workers are distinct from the semi-skilled workers who have received on-the-job training in skills that are less easily transferable from one employer to another. Finally, there are unskilled workers involved in heavy labouring work and in routine manual tasks. These skill differences comprise the market capacities that give them their

varying opportunities to obtain higher wages, better conditions of work, and so on. These skill differences are the basis of internal divisions within the working class, and most social-class classifications have tried to capture them in their categories.

The making of the working class

The typical work organization for manual workers is a factory, but they also work in coal mines, shipyards, steel plants, and other settings where large numbers of workers are brought together under common management for the purposes of large-scale production. These working conditions have been the basis for the development of a distinctive working-class outlook and consciousness of class. Those who are employed in small-scale units of production, on the other hand, have been somewhat separate from the mainstream of proletarian manual workers. They have distinct work situations. Workers in small factories or workshops, farm workers, and those in domestic service, for example, all have conditions of work that involve them in a far less extensive division of labour and that tie them into closer and more personal supervision by their employer. They have less direct contact with other manual workers and they are less likely to develop a common consciousness and sense of solidarity.

For manual workers in large-scale production to form the core of a working class, there must be a high degree of mobility and interaction among them. It must be possible for workers to move from, say, unskilled to semi-skilled work, for the children of these workers to enter apprenticeships, and for skilled workers to fall into unskilled or semi-skilled work if work technology changes. This mobility among the different skill levels ties people together into a distinct social class. This will be reinforced whenever the similarities in their conditions of work, the interests that they have in relation to their employing organizations, and the proximity into which they come lead them to think, feel, and act in similar ways. In these circumstances, they will interact frequently with one another outside the workplace. This is exactly what happened to manual workers from the second half of the nineteenth century.

In the early years of the nineteenth century, manual workers were still, for the most part, employed in relatively small organizations, and they were divided from one another by trade and by geography (E. P. Thompson 1963). Although there were great similarities in their market situations, their work situations and their subjective experiences differed markedly. It was only as the scale of production was increased and the disciplinary practices of the factory were extended that they began to be forged together into something closer to what Marx called a class for itself, a class that is capable of acting consciously in its own interests (Foster 1974; see also R. J. Morris 1979; A. J. Reid 1992).

 These ideas on discipline and surveillance are taken further in our discussion of Foucault in Chapter 6, pp. 191–6. We look in more detail at what Foucault says about large-scale organizations in Chapter 16, pp. 648–9.

As the century proceeded, their work situations became more homogeneous, their life chances became less diverse, they were more likely to experience the common threat of periodic unemployment, and the level of mobility among the different kinds of manual work increased (Savage and Miles 1994). Few manual workers, and few of their children, moved into non-manual jobs, but there were relatively high rates of mobility between unskilled, semi-skilled, and skilled work. This was the case for both women and men.

Marriage relations followed a similar pattern. There were relatively few marriages across the manual/non-manual line, but marriages between the skilled and the unskilled were common. The wives of male skilled workers were often able to withdraw from the labour market and to concentrate on domestic work and family obligations. This was widely regarded as a sign of the 'respectability' of the skilled worker and his family. These women would, however, re-enter the labour market if their husbands' work became insecure. Where both partners were employed in unskilled work, which was often casual or irregular, the income of the household depended on them both remaining in employment.

Intermarriage among manual-worker households in particular localities created large and extended kinship networks that reinforced the bonds that already existed among neighbours and leisure-time associates. These dense networks of social relations were the basis for a strong sense of local class solidarity. As the industrial cities and suburbs grew in size (see Chapter 11, pp. 415–16), new migrants were drawn into these proletarian communities. The fusion of kinship and friendship around a particular locality and place of work was the basis on which a distinctive working-class culture and way of life could be built.

A number of organizations and institutions helped to forge the unity and cohesiveness of this social class. Public houses and working men's clubs, music halls, local dance halls and cinemas, and other places of leisure became important centres of shared relaxation and entertainment. Cooperative and Friendly Societies built on principles of mutual self-help and solidarity helped to counter some of the economic insecurities that manual workers faced and gave them a sense of common purpose. The trade unions and the Labour Party provided further sources of informal solidarity and cohesion, while also helping to build a shared sense of political commitment and of the need for political action in defence of common working-class interests.

These industrial and political associations were the means through which class action was taken to the national level. Trade unions had to deal with employing organizations that had become national in their scope, and the Labour Party, after its formation in 1906, represented working-class interests in the national parliament. The strength of the Labour Party in national elections grew continually until the early 1950s, and it was especially rapid after 1918. Through the trade unions and the Labour Party, manual workers acquired a broadened sense of *national* solidarity, though this was always much weaker than their local communal solidarity. For most people, the nation—and, therefore, the national working class—were abstractions with much less solidity and reality than the more local solidarities of the neighbourhood and the workplace.

The final element in the making of a working class was the explicit adoption of the language of class and the willingness of manual workers to describe themselves as 'working class'. The term was taken up with pride as a marker of social identity. It became a taken-for-granted way of defining one's position in society. It described 'us' (manual workers), and it distinguished 'us' from 'them' (the middle classes and the bosses). This shared social identity was central to the class consciousness of manual workers. They were aware of themselves as a social class with distinct interests and concerns. This made them into a class for itself, a social class characterized by the solidarity of its members and the exclusion from any kind of solidarity with those in other social classes.

The working-class world

One of the best pictures of working-class life is that given in a study carried out by Dennis and his colleagues (1956) in the West Yorkshire coal-mining town of Featherstone. The town was referred to as 'Ashton' in the book. Located just south of Leeds, close to Pontefract and Castleford, Featherstone was simply a small rural village until the first coal mine opened in 1868. A second mine was opened in 1877, and a number of additional shafts were sunk over the following thirty years.

Why did miners form strong communities?

The population grew from around 600 to almost 14,000 by the time the survey was undertaken in the early 1950s.

Most families in Featherstone depended upon mining for their livelihood. Although one of the mines had shut down in 1935, most of its employees had been able to move to others in the area. Two-thirds of all men worked in coal mining, most of them in Featherstone itself, but some were employed in a clothing factory and on the railway. Relatively few women were in paid employment, and most married women worked as housewives. However, some young and unmarried women were employed in domestic service, shop work, dress-making, teaching, or nursing. Most housing in the town had been built by the local authority or by the mining companies for their workers. Featherstone families were tenants, paying rents, not owner-occupiers. By the time of the survey, the mining industry had been nationalized, and the cottages along with the mines had become the property of the National Coal Board.

Featherstone is described by the researchers as a dirty and ugly town. It consisted of long rows of terraced houses and a few old 'back-to-backs', surrounded by the waste heaps produced by the mining industry. Despite the bleak and sombre description of its physical appearance, Featherstone is also described as a community with a real sense of solidarity. This sense of community was rooted in the work relations that the majority of the people shared and in their shared memories of the impact that the mines had had on the town and its people. Memories of the general strike of 1926, the depression of the 1930s, and the closure of one of the mines in 1935 had helped to organize their responses to contemporary events and problems.

The production of coal was a complex and hazardous task. It involved the cooperation of workers with many different kinds of skills. Underground there were the machine men, who actually worked at the coalface and cut the coal with mechanical drills, and there were the drawers-off, who salvaged the timber and steel supports from the waste, the colliers, who used pick and shovel to get the coal onto the conveyor belt, the panners, who restored the face to a state where it could be reworked, and the rippers, who maintained the tunnels through which the miners got to the coalface. There was also a whole array of surface workers.

The largest single group of workers were the colliers, who could earn between £9 and £14 a week, depending on the actual amount of coal that was cut and the number of hours of overtime that they worked. The wages of other workers varied according to the skill and danger that their work involved. These wages were far from secure, and many of the men had memories of twenty years before, when almost a half of all workers in Featherstone had been unemployed during the recession. The insecurity of their wages was a major reason for their strong commitment to trade unionism. The miners felt that they were very weak as individuals and that it was only through collective action that they could hope to redress the imbalance of power between themselves and their employer.

Featherstone households were family households, comprising husband, wife, and children. As we show in Chapter 10, pp. 366–7, working-class families were organized around a strict domestic division of labour and a separation of men's activities from those of women. In Featherstone, both men and women supported this view of the family and gender roles, women seeing it as their job to look after their husbands properly (see also E. Roberts 1984). Male manual work was such a central part of family life that gender divisions were secondary in importance to a sense of class identity. For both men and women, class was a taken-for-granted aspect of their life that was underpinned by the ideas of the male breadwinner and the female housewife. In the face of the stark and obvious divisions of class that separated them from other members of their society, there was little scope for any sense of shared gender identity that cut across class lines.

The class consciousness of the miners was concretely rooted in their shared ideas of work and masculinity—their pride in being 'real men who work hard for their living' (Dennis *et al.* 1956: 33; see also Zweig 1948). Real work was manual work, and so non-manual workers—clerks and managers—could never be seen as working class. The division between 'us' and 'them' was rooted in a strong sense of the solidarity of working men and their role in providing for their families through physically hard and demanding work.

Leisure as well as work was a means through which solidarity was developed, and men who worked together also wanted to enjoy their leisure together. Some leisure activities were directly linked to the workplace, particularly those that were organized through the Miners' Welfare Institute. The Institute provided a billiards room, a regular Saturday night dance, and meeting and theatre facilities for a dramatic society, and meeting space for various clubs and associations. Most leisure activities, however, were organized separately from the workplace. Most important were the town's six Working Men's Clubs, where men met to drink and gamble and to play cards, dominoes, and darts. The town's seven pubs played a similar role in the life of the men.

The leisure activity in which men and women participated together on a more or less equal basis was cinema-going. Individuals, couples, and families regularly watched Westerns, adventures, and comedies at the local cinema in nearby Pontefract. Some workers and their families were involved in church activities, though involvement with a church or chapel was far less than it had been in the past.

Important means through which the people of Featherstone came into contact with those from other towns and cities were music and sport. The colliery brass band played at fêtes, parades, and concerts in the town and represented it in competitions with other bands. Like the colliery cricket team, however, relatively few people were actively involved in it, and the main form of leisure was attendance at matches played by the local rugby football team. Following football did not mean simply—or even mainly—being interested in the technical side of the game. More important was its part in

Working Men's Clubs

'The Working Men's Clubs are predominantly male institutions. Only one of those in Featherstone admits women as members. The others absolutely forbid by rule the admittance of women into the club excepting for concerts on Saturday evening and Sunday midday and evening. . . . Whatever else members may do at the club, they spend a good deal of their time simply conversing over their beer. Conversation is notably free and easy and the men conversing have often been life-long acquaintances; having been at the same school and played together as children, they now, as adults, work at the same place and spend their leisure together in such places as the clubs.'

Source: Dennis *et al.* (1956: 142, 144).

expressing local solidarity through an assertion of Featherstone's superiority over other towns.

Featherstone was marked by a very strong sense of localism. This was very common in working-class communities. More than 90 per cent of the residents of Bethnal Green in 1934 had been born in east London, and even in the 1950s over a half of local residents had actually been born in the borough (Young and Willmott 1957). More than a quarter of working-class families in a national survey in 1951 had relatives living within a five-minute walk of their own home. In these circumstances, as we show in Chapter 11, pp. 414–16, extensive kinship networks tied people together and created a strong sense of community. The centrality of women in the maintenance of their family households meant that wider kinship links were also maintained through the women. 'Mum' played a key role, and visiting mum was important in sustaining bonds of social solidarity. Around these networks of kinship were circles of friendship that made themselves felt in communal support and in leisure-time activities.

These features of life in Featherstone were typical of working-class communities across the country until the 1950s. They have been documented in numerous other studies, such as those in nearby Leeds and Huddersfield (Hoggart 1957; Jackson and Marsden 1962; Jackson 1968), in Salford (R. Roberts 1973), and in many other places (McKibbin 1990).

 Look at Chapter 10, pp. 367–8, for a discussion of some further material on working-class kinship in East London and elsewhere.

THE MIDDLE CLASSES

Those who came to be called the middle classes are those employed in professional, managerial, administrative, and various technical occupations in business and public-sector organizations. This includes such occupations as personnel managers, doctors, civil servants, lawyers, and teachers. In the past, of course, many of these people would have been self-employed, and many doctors and lawyers today are partners in their practices rather than employees. However, the growth of large-scale organizations from the middle of the nineteenth century reduced the numbers in self-employment and created many new categories of employees.

Figure 15.6 shows this growth in the professions and in office work around the turn of the twentieth century. It can be seen that the old professions (the clergy, lawyers, doctors, and teachers) showed relatively modest increases between 1880 and 1911. In fact, their rate of growth was below that of manual workers in the same period. On the other hand, the number of civil service and local-government clerks was almost three times as high in 1911 as it was in 1880, the numbers of authors and journalists doubled, and the number of scientists was five times as high. By 1911

male clerks in all industries accounted for 5.7 per cent of all male employees.

In some respects, Marxist writers have been correct to treat these workers simply as a part of the proletariat. Whether they are employed in manual or in non-manual work, employees do not own or control capital. However, the educational credentials and intellectual skills of managerial and administrative workers have given them market advantages and opportunities that are far superior to those of even the best-paid manual workers. At the same time, their work situations within large bureaucracies typically involve them in the exercise of authority over other employees. These are the people that Goldthorpe (1980) has described as a **service class**—they serve the interests of large-scale organizations by exercising delegated authority on behalf of capital and the state. They fall into categories I and II of Goldthorpe's social-class classification.

During the nineteenth century, there was a growth in the number of more routine, lower-level non-manual occupations. These did not require such a high level of technical or intellectual competence and they did not, therefore, secure such advantaged life chances. They did, nevertheless, have life chances that set them apart from manual workers. These clerks, shop assistants, supervisors, commercial travellers, and technicians were often referred to as the lower middle class in order to distinguish them from the more secure and established upper middle class of professionals and managers (Crossick 1977a; Vigne and Howkins 1977). These more routine occupations fall into category III of the Goldthorpe social-class classification.

☞ You will find a full listing of the social classes in the Goldthorpe classification in Figure 3.7, p. 99.

Figure 15.6. Professional and clerical work, England and Wales, 1880–1911

Occupational category	Number of men		% increase
	1880	1911	
Clergy, ministers, priests	33,486	40,142	19.1
Barristers, solicitors	17,386	21,380	23.0
Physicians, surgeons	15,091	24,553	62.7
Dentists	3,538	7,373	108.4
Authors, journalists	5,627	12,005	113.3
Scientific	1,170	6,171	427.4
Architects	6,875	11,109	61.1
Teachers, lecturers	44,181	68,651	55.4
Civil service administration and clerks	21,353	57,475	169.2
Local government clerks	17,993	54,257	201.5

Source: Perkin (1989: table 3.1).

There are also a number of other occupations that have been seen as middle class. These are the entrepreneurs, shopkeepers, and self-employed artisans who combine small-scale property ownership with their own labour. They may be involved in productive or managerial work, working alongside their employees and in close contact with them, but their property ownership is the basis of their position as an employer. These people fall into Goldthorpe's social-class category IV and, like routine white-collar workers, have generally been seen as lower middle class in status.

This diversity of class and status situations is reflected in the use of the plural term 'middle classes', rather than the singular 'middle class'. Similarities in their life chances and lifestyles distinguish them from the working class below them, but, internally, they are highly diverse. They never had the kind of homogeneity that was found in the working class. This diversity is reflected, also, in uncertainty over where an upper boundary is to be drawn that separates them from the capital- and landowning upper class.

The making of the middle class

The terms 'middle class' and 'middle classes' came into use in the early nineteenth century to describe those in this diverse range of intermediate class situations. As a status marker, they distinguished those who had no need to work with their hands from even the most respectable member of the working class. The middle classes were 'gentlemen', though not quite such superior gentlemen as those of the upper class.

The boundaries of the middle classes, like those of all social classes, are established by patterns of mobility and interaction. The lack of clarity in their upper and lower boundaries reflects the fact that there is a small amount of short-range occupational mobility into and out of neighbouring social classes. Similarly, the internal lines of differentiation that separate the professional and managerial middle classes from the propertied middle class and all of these from routine white-collar workers reflect the tendency for mobility and social interaction to flow along the lines of economic division.

The middle classes were a predominantly urban class. Through their involvement in the public life of the urban areas in which they lived, they became the leading elements in the towns and cities. They held urban authority, though they deferred to the authority of the upper class at the national level. The cohesion of the middle classes was built through their memberships in the numerous civic bodies and voluntary associations through which they exercised this leadership.

They were members of the town council, they were magistrates, poor-law guardians, and elders of the churches and chapels, and they ran the church charities. They sat on the boards of schools and mechanics' institutes, hospitals, libraries, and savings banks, and they filled the committees of the philosophical and literary societies, sporting associations, and, above all, the political parties, clubs, and leagues (Morris 1990). These civic activities involved them in a loose network of interlocking boards and committees, around which a series of formal and informal meetings took place and in which their leisure-time interactions were forged. In a study carried out in the 1950s, Stacey (1960: ch. 5) showed how important these networks were in tying

together the middle classes of the small country town of Banbury.

It was through their participation in the public life of the towns and cities that the middle classes achieved a degree of cultural and political cohesion as a class. They were able to assert their autonomy with respect to the upper class, and they could exercise control over the working class. They were too diverse, however, to sustain any real class consciousness, and their unity weakened as the class grew in size along with the towns and cities. Where the working class developed a corporate sense of their class identity and their shared fate, the middle classes saw the world in individualistic terms. In their work they depended on their own individual efforts for their advancement, and they rejected any involvement in the collective struggles of trade unionism. Middle-class collective action was limited to the defence of particular professional privileges, regulating the behaviour of the individual members of the professions, and promoting individual opportunities and self-help.

While the diversity of the middle classes prevents any generalized account of middle-class life from being made, there are a number of common features. These can usefully be highlighted by considering the white-collar workers who filled the expanding lower levels of business bureaucracies.

The white-collar world

White-collar work has its origins in the offices, or counting houses, of the small industrial and commercial enterprises of the early Victorian period (Lockwood 1958; G. Anderson 1976). The typical firm would employ a handful of clerks to keep up to date the ledgers and account books that recorded day-to-day business transactions. All business decisions were taken by the employer, but these decisions depended on the flow of financial information that the clerks provided.

Working conditions in the Victorian office were accurately caricatured in Dickens's account of Bob Cratchit's work in Scrooge's counting house. Typically, an office would have a bookkeeper or cashier to keep the financial records and subordinate clerks to deal with the correspondence, filing, and other routine office tasks. In larger offices, a managing clerk might sit at a tall corner desk and oversee office operations, while a number of apprentice clerks might be employed to learn the trade. It was unusual for more than four clerks to be employed in any one office.

White-collar workers were propertyless, like the proletarian manual workers of the working class, but they had specific skills that gave them a superior market

White collar and blue collar

The white-collar worker is an office worker, so named because male office workers have traditionally been expected to wear a white shirt and tie. The term is often contrasted with the 'blue-collar' manual worker, whose designation comes from the colour of the cotton overalls that many manual workers wore. Lockwood (1958) describes the white-collar worker under the alternative name of 'black-coated worker', indicating that, in addition to a collar and tie, the clerk was expected to wear a dark suit.

power. In the middle of the nineteenth century, when few manual workers were earning more than £1 a week, a routine clerk might earn up to £100 a year. A qualified and specialist clerk could be on £150 (enough to be able to employ a domestic servant at home), and a managing clerk in a large office might receive up to £400 a year. Clerks were generally given holiday and sick pay, and many could look forward to a pension on retirement.

The skills that clerks had were the ability to make quick and accurate calculations and to write clearly and legibly. Those who had a broader range of general knowledge, acquired from a training in classics, arithmetic, and English literature at secondary school, could improve their chances of getting a good clerical post. Once employed, they could acquire additional skills as they learned their work, but these were generally firm-specific and gave them little opportunity to transfer from one employer to another. On the other hand, their security of employment was very good, as were their chances of promotion.

The market and work situations of clerks were highly individualized, shaped by personal recommendations and family connections (Lockwood 1958: 22, 82). Until the end of the nineteenth century, the typical clerk was recruited through the personal contacts of an employer with the would-be clerk's relatives, teachers, and friends. In fact, the whole work situation was structured by considerations of status. Chances of promotion depended on the clerk maintaining good personal relations with his employer, who expected loyalty and conformity. Pensions and fringe benefits were not a contractual matter, but depended on the personal discretion of the employer. Because of the close personal and individual relations that they had with their employer, and because of the physical separation of the office from the works, white-collar workers enjoyed higher prestige than manual workers. Unlike skilled

manual workers, they hardly had to struggle to maintain their status as respectable members of society.

The main line of division within white-collar work was that between those working in banking, insurance, and the civil service, on the one hand, and those in commercial and industrial offices, on the other. The former were, in general, better paid and lived in the better suburbs; the latter had incomes that were closer to those of skilled manual workers and they lived in the less affluent districts (Gaskell 1977). Nevertheless, even the commercial and industrial clerks differed fundamentally in their orientation, mentality, and outlook from manual workers, and they had close links through mobility and interaction with the superior clerks. Both groups had a distinctive middle-class outlook, their lifestyle and status concerns ruling out any collective solidarity or involvement with trade unions.

White-collar workers in a Victorian sorting office.

In 1851 clerks made up just 0.8 per cent of the labour force in Britain, but the growth of large-scale organizations in the second half of the century produced a massive growth in their numbers. By 1901, 4 per cent of the labour force were clerks, and by 1951 they formed 10.5 per cent (Lockwood 1958: 36). This expansion transformed their market and work situations. A growth in the average size of offices brought together larger numbers of clerks in a more extended division of labour and reduced their contacts with their employers. Indeed, their employers were likely to be corporate enterprises rather than individual entrepreneurs. Many of their distinctive conditions of work were eroded, although they continued to be employed in much smaller work groups than were manual workers.

The continuing separation of the office from the

works, and the fact that clerical workers had close and, generally, cooperative relationships with their managers, meant that manual workers tended to see clerks as a part of management. Nevertheless, major changes in their work situations were occurring. Office work was rapidly mechanized at the beginning of the twentieth century through the introduction of the typewriter, the calculating machine, and the telephone. Later in the century, the photocopier, the computer, the word-processor, and the fax machine brought about further transformations. Mechanization reduced the autonomy of clerical workers and made their skills of calculation and writing much less important. Office work became more routine in character, and white-collar workers had to learn to pace their work to the requirements of the office machines. This transformation of office work occurred not only in Britain, but also in the United States and the leading European nations (Mills 1951: ch. 9; Braverman 1974).

As a result of these changes, the earnings gap between white-collar and manual work began to close. The declining demand for basic educational skills reduced the market power of those with a good basic education. At the same time, higher level management was becoming a more technically skilled occupation, and employers required managerial recruits who had high-level educational credentials. Opportunities for the promotion of clerks into managerial grades declined, and those who entered clerical work at a young age were likely to remain there throughout their working lives.

Of fundamental importance in the first half of the twentieth century was an increase in the number of women employed in clerical work. In 1861 women comprised just over 1 per cent of commercial clerks and 4 per cent of those in public administration (Holcombe 1973). By 1911 they comprised about 20 per cent of commercial clerks and 16 per cent of public-sector clerks (G. Anderson 1976: 2). By 1951 over a half of all clerks were female. Women were largely confined to the lowest levels of clerical work and had far fewer opportunities for promotion than did their male counterparts. Nevertheless, many male clerks felt that their own loss of income and status was a result of the influx of unmarried women who were willing to do clerical work for lower rates of pay than married men could afford to take (G. Anderson 1976: 58–9). For the most part, however, women did not directly compete with men for clerical work. They entered the completely new jobs that were created by the introduction of office machinery, and they faced, to the full, the mechanization of the office. This work was so highly gendered that the word 'typewriter' originally meant the woman who operated the machine, and not the machine itself. The growth of cheap female labour and the expansion of less-skilled, machine-based office work went hand in hand with each other.

THE UPPER CLASS

It is impossible to understand the British upper class without an understanding of the importance of the values and ideas of traditional, landed society. These traditional ideas were rooted in rural and agricultural life and defined a clear status hierarchy. This hierarchy included the aristocracy that owned the land, the farmers that worked it, the old professions that serviced them, and the agricultural labourers whose work provided their incomes. In one area of life after another, traditional status considerations were weakened as modern industry expanded. At the upper levels of the stratification system, however, traditional status ideas remained important.

The very wealthiest capitalist entrepreneurs and financiers aspired to be accepted as the status equals of the landed aristocrats. If they bought land, they could begin the process of acceptance, but full acceptance might have to wait for a few generations until their new wealth had become 'old' wealth. The economically powerful, then, were forged into a single social class only because they accepted and deferred to the traditional social values associated with a landed aristocracy. They were a social estate as much as they were a social class. (This is discussed more fully in J. Scott 1991; see also F. M. L. Thompson 1963.) It was this class of landowners and wealthy capitalists that came to be described as an upper class.

The phrase upper class had come into use early in the nineteenth century to describe the aristocracy, and, as wealthy industrial and commercial capitalists began to merge with this group, they, too, came to be seen as part of the upper class. By the end of the nineteenth century, the picture of Britain as a society with an upper class, a middle class, and a working class was firmly established.

At the core of the upper class was the aristocracy, and at the heart of the aristocracy was the peerage. Peers were those with titles that gave them the right to sit in the House of Lords. Below them were the gentry who were the leading families in county 'Society' and who dominated local affairs. The peerage and the gentry were the two main status groups within the upper class, but each was internally divided to form a complex hierarchy of status levels. Each level in this hierarchy had a distinct title or honorary designation that defined its social position.

At the top of this hierarchy were the Royal Family and the great dukes. Below them were the other ranks of the hereditary peerage (the marquesses, earls, viscounts, and barons), and the more lowly baronets, knights, esquires, and gentlemen. A whole range of other status honours further differentiated these people by their relative social standing as companions, officers, and members of the various orders of knighthood, as Companions of Honour, Deputy Lieutenants, and Justices of the Peace.

The aristocratic upper class was finely divided by its gradations of status, and these status distinctions emphasized its position as the leading element in a traditional social order. Aristocratic values were deeply embedded in the state and the church, and members of other social classes regarded the upper class as their social superiors. Farmers and farm workers were directly dependent on the power of landlords, and they had little choice but to defer to them as the leaders of rural society. Throughout the middle classes and into the working class itself, attitudes of deference to the aristocracy as the natural leaders of society were strong. Class divisions, then, were reinforced by status distinctions that both stabilized and legitimized them.

The absorption of wealthy industrialists into the upper class was a slow process. The growth in the scale of industrial activity from the middle of the nineteenth century meant that many capitalist entrepreneurs could match or surpass the wealth of those in the upper class. While many continued to define themselves—and to be defined by others—as middle class, others were rapidly becoming the economic equals of the landowners. Mobility and interaction between landowners and the large industrial and commercial capitalists increased, and by the end of the nineteenth century they had come close to becoming a single social class. They had a common dependence on property and on its use as capital to generate their privileged life

Status and precedence

Social precedence was controlled by Act of Parliament and various other regulations and customs. Men and women were each graded into separate classifications of over 100 categories. These were officially listed in order of precedence for all public occasions. Extracts from the men's list (as printed in *Burke's Peerage, Baronetage, and Knightage* in the 1930s, with . . . showing categories omitted) are shown below. A version of this list is still used for determining precedence on such official occasions as the opening of parliament, royal weddings, state funerals, and official banquets.

The King
The Prince of Wales
The King's Younger Sons
The King's Grandsons
The Kings Brothers . . .
Archbishop of York
The Prime Minister
Lord Chancellor of Ireland
Lord High Treasurer
Lord President of the Privy Council . . .
Dukes of the United Kingdom and Dukes of Ireland, created since the Union
Eldest Sons of Dukes of the Blood Royal
Marquesses of England
Marquesses of Scotland . . .
Dukes' Eldest Sons
Earls of England
Earls of Scotland
Earls of Great Britain . . .

Younger Sons of Dukes of the Blood Royal
Marquesses' eldest Sons
Dukes' younger Sons
Viscounts of England
Viscounts of Scotland . . .
Serjeants at Law
Masters in Lunacy
Companions of the Bath
Companions of the Star of India . . .
Members of the Fifth Class of the Royal Victorian Order
Members of the Order of the British Empire
Baronets' younger Sons
Knights' younger Sons
Esquires
Gentlemen

chances. Aristocratic status distinctions gave this class its particular characteristics. Members of the class might take these status distinctions as the basis of their social identity and identify themselves as an upper class, but they were, in reality, a capitalist class with propertied interests in land, industry, commerce, and finance.

The making of a capitalist class

Capitalist class situations generate advantaged life chances from the ownership and control of property and from its use as capital. Capital takes the form of land, factories, or financial assets, and different capitalist class situations can be distinguished according to the particular type of capital involved. For much of the nineteenth century, ownership of land was one of the most important forms of capital. Landowners received income from the land that they rented out for commercial farming, and they earned a profit from the land that they farmed themselves. Many landowners also received an income from the commercial uses of their land for mining, railways, and housing. Land ownership was also an important basis of status and political authority.

The industrial and commercial entrepreneurs who built up large businesses during the nineteenth century had life chances that distinguished them from the middle classes and that involved them closely with landowners. They built their factories and mines on land owned by aristocrats, they invested in land on a large scale, and they invited landowners to invest in their businesses (Stone and Stone 1984). In these ways, the economic basis of a single capitalist class was established. By the turn of the twentieth century, wealthy entrepreneurs were also likely to be sending their children to the same privileged schools and to be members of the same social clubs as the aristocrats. Their sons and daughters were increasingly likely to be seen as acceptable marriage partners by the aristocrats (Davidoff and Hall 1987).

The social calendar	**Beginning of the London Season**		Henley Regatta
	May	The first garden parties, Court presentations, and balls.	Goodwood racing
		Queen Charlotte's Ball	**Close of the London Season**
		Royal Academy Summer Exhibition	August — Cowes week
			Grouse shooting begins
		Covent Garden opera season opens	Stag hunting begins
		Royal Military Tournament	September — Partridge shooting begins
		Royal Horticultural Society (Chelsea Flower Show)	Cubbing begins
			October — Pheasant shooting begins
	June	The Derby (Epsom)	November — Fox hunting begins
		Fourth of June (Eton speech day and cricket)	First county balls
		Ascot racing week (Gold Cup)	State Opening of Parliament
		Trooping the Colour and Birthday Honours List	January — New Year Honours List
			March — Cheltenham National Hunt racing (Gold Cup)
	July	Wimbledon fortnight	Grand National (Aintree)
		Polo at Hurlingham	April — Oxford and Cambridge boat race
		Oxford and Cambridge cricket match	
		Eton and Harrow crickt match	

Note: The exact dates of some sporting events alter according to the date of Easter.

Source: J. Scott (1991: 100).

In these and other ways, mobility and interaction among those in capitalist class situations grew to the point at which separate landed and industrial classes could not be distinguished as sharply as they once could. By the 1930s, industrialists, financiers, and landowners had fully merged into a single social class. This was, however, a capitalist class that continued to follow a modified form of the life style of the old upper class.

Status factors were important in solidifying the upper class. An upper circle of 'Society' families led a round of balls, parties, and sporting events that formed the upper class Social Calendar and that defined the character of the class as a whole. The country lifestyle of hunting, shooting, and fishing, the social calendar of county Society, and the system of titles and honours cast a cloak of tradition over the new forms of economic power (M. J. Weiner 1981; Rubinstein 1993).

Of great importance in tying members of the social class together were the social networks that were built around their common patterns of schooling and their similarity of social background. Boys from capitalist class families were educated privately, often at the public schools that prepared them for entry to Oxford or Cambridge, and their educational background was an important source of contacts for entry into business positions or into public life. The 'old-boy network' combined with wider networks of kinship and friendship to bind the whole class together (Davidoff 1973).

In economic terms, there were important changes to the ways in which property was held. In the nineteenth century, direct *personal* ownership of land or business was the most usual form of property ownership. As businesses expanded in size, and as land use and farming became more intensive and large scale, this direct personal form of ownership began to give way to more indirect, *corporate* forms of ownership and control. In this form of ownership, people owned companies or shares in companies, rather than owning the actual physical assets themselves.

In the large companies, financial assets rather than physical assets were the principal sources of personal wealth. Wealthy families derived their privileged life chances from the financial assets that they owned, and they were able to ensure their continuing control over the assets that generated their wealth by taking positions as directors and executives in the large companies. This was clearest in industrial and commercial businesses, but even landowners controlled their land through private companies. Wealthy capitalists diversified their sources of wealth by investing in many different companies and so acquiring business interests throughout the economy.

 We explore some of the economic aspects of these changes in ownership and control in Chapter 16, pp. 656–8. You might like to glance at that discussion before continuing with this chapter.

The capitalist social class, as it existed in the middle of the twentieth century, comprised those wealthy households who derived their privileged life chances from one of four capitalist class situations. These defined four types of capitalist that can still be distinguished:

▶ **Entrepreneurial capitalists** run the business operations of large enterprises, whose shares they own and which are, therefore, under their personal control. The businesses may operate in industry, commerce, or land. Such businesses are often family firms run by the heirs of the original founders.

▶ **Rentier capitalists** have personal investments in a large number of business enterprises and are not dependent on the success of any one particular enterprise. Their original fortunes may have come from land or from a particular business, but they diversified their investments and spread them widely.

▶ **Executive capitalists** hold top executive positions in particular enterprises. They owe their positions to their particular expertise and educational credentials and have followed a career in business.

▶ **Finance capitalists** have top positions in numerous enterprises. A finance capitalist is, typically, a part-time director in a large number of enterprises that operate in a wide range of industries. Their principal positions are often in banks, insurance companies, and other financial enterprises.

There was much mobility and overlap among these class situations. Executive capitalists, for example, could build up a large shareholding in the company that they ran and they could invest widely in other enterprises. Finance capitalists were often members of wealthy rentier families. Rentier capitalists were likely to be the sons or daughters of entrepreneurial capitalists, and so on. In all these ways, they formed parts of a single social class (J. Scott 1997: ch. 8).

SUMMARY POINTS

Stratification in Britain since the middle of the nineteenth century can best be understood as involving a division into an upper class, the middle classes, and a working class. In this section we have shown that Marx expected this structure to become ever-more polarized, and we have suggested that this has not occurred.

▶ A cohesive working class, consisting of manual workers and their families, was formed in the major industrial areas.

▶ This class had its basis in cohesive industrial communities and had a distinctive working-class culture. It did engage in the kind of political action that

Marxist theory implied, but it was not a revolutionary class.

▶ There had been a massive expansion in clerical, managerial, and professional work over the course of the century. These intermediate class situations were the basis of the expanding middle classes.

▶ The capitalist class formed an upper class, defined by its traditional social status. There was a close association between aristocratic landowners and the industrial and financial capitalists.

A FRAGMENTARY CLASS SOCIETY

We have shown how Britain came to be divided into a working class, the middle classes, and an upper class. Lines of internal division cross cut these classes, making it difficult to draw their boundaries with any precision, but their broad outlines were clear. Britain, like most other advanced societies of the time, was a class society. The social inequalities that we review in Chapter 14 and many other features of social life that we examine in other chapters were organized in relation to these class differences. It is for this reason that so much social research has taken class as one of its key variables. The class structure was not, however, polarized between capitalists and proletarians, as Marx had expected. Instead, the middle classes increased in importance. It remained, nevertheless, a class society.

In the second half of the twentieth century these lines of class division have become less clear. Class differences in economic power persist—and in many respects they have increased—but they are now less directly reflected in differences in attitude and outlook. One of the reasons for this has been the erosion of the traditional status values that, for so long, defined the particular character of class relations in Britain. The values of the traditional social order now have less of a hold on public consciousness, and so they have less of an impact on how people perceive and interpret their economic positions.

The language and imagery of class were, for much of the twentieth century, tied to quite specific ideas of status. Class divisions were perceived and defined in relation to ideas of respectability, gentility, accent, dress, and social background. The decay of these status ideas has, therefore, undermined the use of class language to describe social differences and social divisions. At the same time, many of the social conditions that, in the past, sustained a sense of class awareness have also been transformed. Working conditions and living conditions, for example, differ markedly, for many people, from those of the past. Personal and domestic consumption, encouraged by new trends in production and the mass media, have made people's productive roles less salient for their social identity. As a result, people are less likely to see their own situations in class terms. Britain remains a class society, but it has become a fragmentary class society in which people are more likely to identify themselves in terms of non-traditional status or in terms of their gender and ethnicity.

INDUSTRIALISM AND CLASS SOCIETY

The failure of Marx to foresee the full implications of the growth of the middle classes led many of his critics to reject his whole approach to class. The principal alternative to Marxism has stressed that modern societies must be seen as *industrial* societies and not as capitalist societies. These writers point to the increasingly complex industrial technology and occupational division of labour that is found in these societies. In these societies, differences in property ownership are no longer an important element in social stratification. In contemporary societies, they conclude, patterns of stratification reflect the prestige that is attached to occupations according to their functional importance in an advanced industrial economy (Kerr *et al*. 1960).

Occupational change and stratification

This argument rests on a recognition that the development of industrial technology involves what has been described as an **occupational transition**, a comprehensive shift in the occupational structure (Payne 1987*b*; see also Clark 1940). As production expands and becomes more complex, new occupations are created and the need for many older occupations disappears. An advanced technology, it is held, has a growing need for technical and specialist occupations that require high levels of education and training. The idea of the occupational transition rests on the claim that occupations can be seen as distributed into three economic sectors. In the **primary sector** are the agricultural, mining, and quarrying occupations that are involved directly with the production and extraction of raw materials and basic resources. The **secondary sector** comprises manufacturing occupations that use raw materials to produce finished consumer goods and machinery of all kinds. Finally, the **tertiary sector** contains the service and commercial occupations that distribute consumer goods and that provide banking and insurance facilities. Over time, the relative size of these three sectors alters as the scale and complexity of technology changes. The model of the occupational transition is shown in Figure 15.7.

The transition from a pre-industrial to an industrial society led to a massive growth in manufacturing capacity and, therefore, an expansion of the secondary sector. In an industrial society, the primary and the tertiary sectors are each less important than the secondary sector of manufacturing employment. This does not necessarily mean that secondary-sector occupations make up a majority of all occupations in an industrial society. Only in Britain have secondary-sector jobs ever accounted for more than a half of the total labour force. In all other industrial societies, the size of the secondary sector stabilized at around 30 per cent of the labour force. In the United States, for example, the secondary sector accounted for 38 per cent of the labour force in 1900.

The development of industrial societies in the second half of the twentieth century has led to further changes in their occupational structures. In all advanced societies there has been a continuing decline in the size of the primary sector and a corresponding increase in the number of tertiary-sector occupations. By 1967, for example, 55 per cent of all jobs in the United States were service-sector jobs, compared with 24 per cent in 1900.

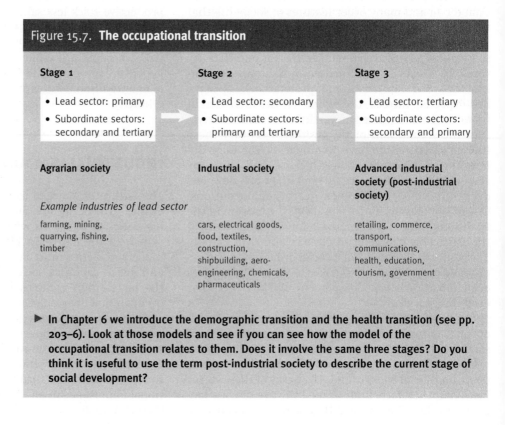

Figure 15.7. **The occupational transition**

Stage 1
- Lead sector: primary
- Subordinate sectors: secondary and tertiary

Stage 2
- Lead sector: secondary
- Subordinate sectors: primary and tertiary

Stage 3
- Lead sector: tertiary
- Subordinate sectors: secondary and primary

Agrarian society

Industrial society

Advanced industrial society (post-industrial society)

Example industries of lead sector

farming, mining, quarrying, fishing, timber

cars, electrical goods, food, textiles, construction, shipbuilding, aero-engineering, chemicals, pharmaceuticals

retailing, commerce, transport, communications, health, education, tourism, government

▶ **In Chapter 6 we introduce the demographic transition and the health transition (see pp. 203–6). Look at those models and see if you can see how the model of the occupational transition relates to them. Does it involve the same three stages? Do you think it is useful to use the term post-industrial society to describe the current stage of social development?**

By the 1970s, almost two-thirds of employment in the United States was in the service sector and only 4 per cent was in the primary sector. These trends cannot be converted directly into a shift from manual to non-manual work, but it is striking that the proportion of non-manual workers in the United States increased from 18 per cent to 59 per cent between 1900 and 1990. According to some observers, this change is so significant that they now speak of the United States as a post-industrial society, rather than simply an advanced industrial society.

This theory of industrial society, then, sees the occupational transition as having produced a massive growth in the intermediate occupations that are neither capitalist nor proletarian. The capitalist and the proletarian classes themselves have declined in size and changed in character. The decline in the primary and secondary sectors, it is argued, has led to a decline in the number of manual jobs that formed the core of the proletarian working class. The remaining manual workers are able to enjoy the income and job security that brings them closer to the middle classes. At the same time, changes in the financing of industry have made the ownership of capital far less significant than it was in the past. The small capitalist class is disappearing, to be replaced by salaried managers. It is concluded that there has been an embourgeoisement of the working class and a managerial transformation of the capitalist class.

Embourgeoisement and managerialism

Embourgeoisement is a rather awkward word that means 'becoming bourgeois' or 'becoming middle class'. It has been used as the cornerstone of a theory which suggests that the manual working class has merged with the middle classes. **Managerialism**, on the other hand, is a theory that points to the disappearance of the capitalist class. It suggests that the growth in executive and managerial occupations has reduced the power and influence of those with capital (Dahrendorf 1957).

Advocates of the theory of embourgeoisement claim that all the advanced societies experienced a greater degree of equality and of affluence from the 1940s and 1950s and that these economic changes have eroded the distinctive values and way of life of the working class. Wage levels have improved, job security is greater than ever before, and people have far higher disposable incomes than their parents and grandparents. The higher incomes of manual workers have allowed them to buy things that they could not previously afford,

and they have been able to acquire the new consumer goods that became available in the post-war period. Manual workers can afford cars, televisions, and washing machines, many own their own homes, and they can afford to furnish and decorate their homes in more comfortable and stylish ways than before. They are, embourgeoisement theorists argue, adopting middle-class values and lifestyles to match their middle-class incomes (Mayer 1963; Lipset 1964).

Advocates of managerialist theory hold that the growing scale of business enterprise has vastly increased the number of shareholders, most of whom have little or no influence over business affairs and cannot really be considered to be capitalists. At the same time, shareholding has become completely irrelevant in enterprises that can finance their own activities from their accumulated resources (Parsons 1953; Bell 1961). Managerialists see the capitalists as being replaced by salaried managers who hold the key positions in the expanding bureaucracies of the business world. Managers previously had authority delegated to them by the capitalist owners. In the second half of the twentieth century, however, they hold this authority in their own right. They owe their positions to the technical knowledge and expertise that they have acquired through their education and on which the industrial system is increasingly dependent. The growing demand for managers, it is held, has expanded the middle sections of the stratification system.

Embourgeoisement and managerialism have been seen as the bases of a fundamental change in the whole shape of the stratification system. The theory of industrial society claims that stratification in the advanced societies has changed in shape from a triangle or pyramid to a diamond. The number of those in the middle increases, while the numbers of those at the bottom and at the very top declines. This is illustrated in Figure 15.8. There is a single, large middle class that stretches from the topmost managers through to manual workers; only the marginal 'underclass' is excluded from it. For many, this middle-class society is seen as being, to all intents and purposes, classless—class as a source of social division is dead.

In summary, the theory of industrial society has suggested that contemporary systems of stratification can be characterized by three features (Goldthorpe 1964):

▶ *Reduced differentiation*: the gap between top and bottom in the stratification system declines and there is a move towards greater equality and homogeneity. This is the central theme in the idea of the shift from a pyramid to a diamond structure.

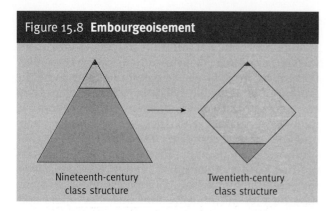

Figure 15.8 Embourgeoisement

Nineteenth-century class structure

Twentieth-century class structure

▶ *Increased consistency*: occupation becomes the primary basis of social stratification, with all other inequalities being linked closely to it. Income and prestige, for example, are closely tied to one another, and property become irrelevant.

▶ *Greater mobility*: there are high levels of occupational mobility, with many opportunities for the able and talented to rise. In this open meritocracy, there are few sharp boundaries dividing one social class from another.

What is the evidence for this? What has happened to the principal lines of class division? We will now look at these questions.

MANUAL WORKERS

Theorists of industrial society have recognized that manual work and manufacturing occupations have not completely disappeared. The life chances of many households still depend on the jobs of one or more manual workers. Nevertheless, these theorists hold that the differences in life chances between manual and non-manual workers are less marked than in the past. Economic change has increased the amount of mobility and interaction between them, and there is no longer a sharp class boundary separating a working class from a middle classes. Manual workers are no longer an inferior, exploited group in terms of their economic resources and spending power. They have undergone a process of embourgeoisement.

Affluence and the working class

The theory of embourgeoisement was an attempt to explore some of the consequences of economic growth

in the post-war period. The theory pointed to the affluence and higher levels of consumption that the mass of the population had come to enjoy. At the same time, technical change in industry was leading to the rapid disappearance of old forms of manual work. The newly affluent manual workers were employed, for the most part, in factories using automatic or continuous-flow systems of production that required them to monitor and supervise machinery rather than to engage in heavy or repetitive manual work. The new manual worker was a technician rather than an operative. Their work situations, as much as their market situations, were seen as having been fundamentally transformed.

 The technical changes in work and their implications were raised by Blauner (1964). We discuss his ideas in Chapter 13, pp. 512–15, and you might want to review what we say there.

Attention was also given to urban change in the years following the Second World War. City centres and industrial districts were redeveloped, larger numbers of people settled in the new suburbs and estates, and there was an expansion of dormitory towns set apart from the big industrial centres. Large numbers of people had moved away from the places in which traditional working-class culture had thrived. They now lived in areas that were not so closely tied to particular types and places of work. As a result, people were less likely to live close to their kin, they had fewer social contacts with their neighbours, and their leisure patterns were less bound to work and locality.

These changes, embourgeoisement theorists argued, had eroded the structural basis of the working class. Manual workers were no longer confined by the restrictive cultural outlook of working-class communal solidarity. They were no longer likely to identify themselves in class terms. At the same time, these workers and their families were becoming much more sensitive to matters of status. Their affluence allowed them to consume goods that could previously be afforded only by the middle classes, and they aspired to the status that was associated with them. Consumer lifestyles had become the means to status advancement into the middle class (Zweig 1961; Klein 1965; see also Mayer 1963; Lipset 1964).

The most sustained criticisms of the embourgeoisement thesis have come from Goldthorpe, Lockwood, and their colleagues (Goldthorpe *et al.* 1969; see also Goldthorpe and Lockwood 1963; Goldthorpe 1964; Lockwood 1960). They have shown that, while the situation of manual workers has indeed altered, the embourgeoisement thesis must be rejected. They discussed the theory's shortcomings under the three headings of the economic, relational, and normative aspects of change.

▶ *Economic aspects.* While there may have been some growth in manual worker incomes and, therefore, an increasing similarity with non-manual patterns of consumption, there are still very important differences between the work situations of manual and non-manual workers. Considered as producers, rather than as consumers, even routine non-manual workers have superior working conditions. They still enjoy greater security of employment, better pension and holiday provision, and enhanced chances of promotion.

▶ *Relational aspects.* There is little evidence that there has been any significant growth in either mobility or interaction across the manual/non-manual divide. This remains as an important social-class boundary.

▶ *Normative aspects.* Affluent manual workers have not abandoned working-class values and norms for middle-class ones. Changes in their market situation and their patterns of residence have simply led them to *adapt* their old norms to their new circumstances. There is no evidence of changing aspirations.

Not satisfied with a negative critique of the theory of embourgeoisement, Goldthorpe *et al.* undertook a study of their own. Their aim was to investigate what was really happening to manual workers. They recognized that the debate over embourgeoisement centred on what was happening to those who worked in the most advanced systems of production, and they set out

The affluent worker study

Goldthorpe and his colleagues drew a sample of 229 married men earning, in 1962, at least £17 per week. They also interviewed a small sample of 54 non-manual workers for comparison. Workers were employed in one of three factories: Vauxhall Motors, Skefco Ball Bearings, and Laporte Chemicals. Their sample was not a random one, but was chosen specifically to fit the needs of the research.

The research involved two long interviews. The first, with the worker himself, involved questions on work history, the nature of work, and trade unionism. The second interview, carried out at home, asked workers and their wives about their leisure, family relationships, education, politics, and images of society.

The results of the research were written up in three books: one on industrial attitudes and behaviour (Goldthorpe *et al.* 1968*a*), one on politics (Goldthorpe *et al.* 1968*b*), and a third one that contained the core findings in relation to class as a whole (Goldthorpe *et al.* 1969). The third volume is organized around the three central aspects of change that they identified: the economic aspects (chapter 3), relational aspects (chapter 4), and normative aspects (chapter 5).

to study this group. They sought workers in the technologically advanced industries who were geographically mobile, who were enjoying relatively high pay, and who had good living conditions in socially mixed areas. They settled on a study in Luton, a prosperous and expanding town, where they interviewed workers in the motor, engineering, and chemical industries.

Goldthorpe *et al.* found that the work situations of manual workers were, indeed, very different from those of non-manual workers. The workers reported high levels of dissatisfaction with work that they regarded as being dreary and monotonous. However, they tolerated these conditions because of the high pay that was offered. Goldthorpe *et al.* describe these workers as having an **instrumental orientation** to their work. They saw their work as a mere means to obtain income, and not as something that was, in itself, a source of meaning and satisfaction. Pay in excess of the £20 per week that was received by many of the workers was achieved only as a result of overtime working. This increased the typical working week to almost 50 hours. The clerical workers in their sample earned only slightly less than this, but they got this for a standard working week of 38.5 hours with no overtime or shift work.

Corresponding to the manual workers' instrumental view of work was their rejection of the idea of work as a source of satisfying relationships with others. They did not identify with their work, and they did not seek out work mates for friendly interaction outside the workplace. Very few manual workers were active in the sports and social clubs that were organized by their employers. These were mainly the province of the non-manual workers.

In their patterns of free-time interaction, manual workers drew less on work mates than did the clerical workers. In general, they drew their leisure-time partners from their extended family (where family members lived locally) and from their neighbours. This was particularly marked when entertaining in the home. It was very rare for anyone other than family members to be invited for a meal or party. Where interaction with non-family members did occur outside the home, this was mainly with other manual workers. There was little or no leisure-time interaction between manual and non-manual workers.

For most manual workers, however, their social relations took the form of **privatism**. They were largely confined to the private sphere of the family household. The need to work long, unsocial hours, meant that leisure-time activities were, of necessity, focused on the private, domestic world of the nuclear family. The affluent manual workers are home- and family-centred.

Although the affluent workers had broader aspirations for what they hoped to obtain and to achieve in their own lives and in those of their children, their norms and outlook were still shaped by their class situations as manual workers. They wanted greater purchasing power as consumers, and they sought higher wages to achieve this, but this was because they wanted particular consumer goods and not because they wanted a 'middle-class' status. Similarly, they wanted their children to have the kind of education that would improve their chances of entering non-manual jobs, but this was because of the greater security that these jobs offered and not because they were higher status, middle-class jobs.

Goldthorpe *et al.* give particular attention to the images of society that underpin the norms and values that the workers adopted. Very few of the affluent workers held to the two-class power model of 'us' and 'them' that characterized the traditional proletarian image of society. There was, however, no sign that support for the middle-class image of a continuous status hierarchy had grown. Images of society were not, in fact, sharply crystallized at all, and they showed much variation and flexibility.

Most typical was a *money model* of society, an image of society as organized around differences in income, assets, and material living standards. Workers saw society as consisting of one large, central social class that contained most manual and non-manual workers. Differences of income within this class were a matter of degree, and people moved up or down according to whatever income they were currently able to earn. This class was variously—and quite arbitrarily—described as working class, middle class, or even lower class. Workers contrasted this central mass with one or more small social classes with vastly superior spending power and that they called millionaires, high society, or the well-to-do. Sometimes they recognized a small impoverished class at the bottom of the class structure that they referred to simply as the poor or 'the dregs'.

When Goldthorpe *et al.* talk about the affluent workers' concern with the private or domestic sphere, they use the word 'privatization'. Since they wrote their book, however, this word has come to be used in a very different sense. Because of this change in the use of the word, commentators on social stratification now use the word 'privatism' when referring to the family-centredness of manual workers.

Privatization is now used to describe the transfer of a business from public to private ownership. In Britain, for example, the Conservative government followed a programme of privatization in which the water, gas, electricity, and other industries were sold to private shareholders. We discuss this in Chapter 16.

Goldthorpe *et al.* use what they call an action frame of reference in their study. Did you notice a similarity between their idea of the instrumental orientation to work and Weber's concept of instrumental action? See Chapter 2, p. 42, for a discussion of this.

Class and identity

The emphasis that Goldthorpe *et al.* and the original advocates of embourgeoisement placed upon affluence seems rather strange in the 1990s. The 1950s and 1960s were, indeed, periods of economic growth and prosperity for many manual workers, but there were long periods of recession during the following decades. As Marx had claimed, capitalist societies follow a cyclical pattern of booms followed by slumps. This cycle of affluence and recession has not produced the ever-deepening slumps that Marx anticipated. Indeed, absolute living standards seem to have shown a continuous improvement. Nevertheless, it is important to know whether recession has an effect on the pattern of change described by Goldthorpe and his colleagues.

Fiona Devine (1992) set out to investigate this through a restudy of Luton in the 1980s. She found that workers in Luton still shared an experience of geographical mobility, but she suggests that this did not lead them to be straightforwardly instrumental about their work. While some workers had moved to Luton in search of higher pay than they could earn elsewhere, others had been motivated simply by the search for work of any kind. The areas from which they came were often areas of high unemployment with no job prospects at all. The relatively prosperous industries of Luton offered job opportunities, where other areas could offer only the prospect of continuing unemployment.

Geographical mobility had been seen by Goldthorpe *et al.* as underpinning the family-centred lifestyles that the workers and their families had adopted in Luton. These families were recent migrants and had few members of their extended kinship networks living in the area. They had to look to their own resources for leisure and entertainment. Devine shows that the early migrants to Luton had, in fact, been followed by kin, friends, and neighbours who also sought jobs and better housing. They naturally chose to migrate to an area where friends or family were already to be found. Networks of kinship and friendship had, therefore, been rebuilt in Luton by the 1980s. People were less isolated than they had been in the 1960s, and they were less likely to be so dependent on the members of their immediate nuclear family.

Devine argues, therefore, that the Luton workers of the 1980s did not lead such privatized lifestyles as those of the 1960s. The three-generation family was an important source of informal support and sociability. While these kinship links were not on the scale of the kinship solidarity found in Featherstone and Bethnal Green, they were still very important. It was possible to rely on family members for babysitting and other forms of informal care and support, and they were important sources of leisure-time interaction. Over time, neighbours had also become more important in free-time interaction. With the expansion of local industries it was also more likely that work colleagues would be neighbours.

 You will find it useful to look at our discussion of changes in the domestic divisions of labour in Chapter 10, pp. 386–92. Perhaps you might also like to look at the discussion of the decline of community in Chapter 11, pp. 429–30.

The decline in privatism and family centredness was also manifest in work patterns. Women generally returned to the labour market after bringing up their children, and so were less exclusively concerned with domestic issues. The household division of labour remained a gendered division of labour. Husbands did not take on equal responsibility for domestic work, and neither partner saw the family household as the sole focus of their concerns. Nevertheless, household commitments did take up a large proportion of their time. By comparison with the traditional working class, there were far fewer opportunities for going to clubs and pubs or for involvement in other communal leisure activities. As in the past, however, these opportunities are gendered: opportunities for communal sociability differ between men and women. For women, childcare responsibilities are a major constraint on social activities outside the home.

A money image of society remained the most common form of class awareness. Workers judged their own income against the standards of living that they saw other working people having achieved. They compared themselves with those who were, like them, working for their living, but their knowledge of the true extent of income differences was limited. Feeling that others were not that much better off than themselves, they sought relatively modest improvements in their economic situation. They did, however, support policies of social justice and a desire for a fair system of income distribution.

For manual workers, then, class is not such an important way of describing their experiences of inequality as it was in the past. They see their situation in money terms, which they sometimes refer to in the language of class, but they do not *live* class in the way that was so common a generation ago. Class identity has weakened and other identities now rival it. This makes it difficult to use the term 'working class' to describe manual workers today (but see Roberts *et al.* 1977). The cohesive working class of the past has been transformed into a more fragmentary social class: it retains its inferior life chances and it is still identifiable as a social class through its patterns of mobility and interaction, but it no longer has any significant cultural or political cohesion. Working-class culture has dissolved, along with the working-class communities. Attitudes and values are more diverse, and they are more likely to concern issues of consumption than issues of work and production.

The 'underclass'

It is now possible to return to one issue that is left unresolved in Chapter 14. We show that the poor still exist and that they experience significantly disadvantaged life chances, but we do not say whether they should be described as forming a separate social class. Now that we have completed our discussion of stratification concepts and of the contemporary situation of manual workers, we can finally close this issue.

The poor can be said to form an underclass only if there is a social-class boundary dividing them from other manual workers. Mobility and interaction patterns would separate them from other manual workers and might, indeed, be associated with the development of a distinct culture of poverty. The evidence that we present in Chapter 14, pp. 587–8, shows that there is, in fact, a substantial turnover among those in poverty. Many obtain employment or higher pay after a period of poverty; and many unskilled workers are likely to fall into poverty whenever their labour-market situations deteriorate. There is a considerable degree of mobility across the poverty line, and the poor are linked through kinship and friendship to other manual workers.

Poverty is a condition of serious disadvantage and deprivation, but it is an ever-present possibility for any manual worker who lacks skills or whose skills are made redundant by technical advances. People fall into poverty for a number of quite different reasons. Those in irregular forms of employment are quite distinct from those in long-term unemployment. They have far better opportunities to re-enter the world of regular employment and, therefore, to escape their poverty (L. Morris 1995).

There is, then, no separate underclass. There are those who live in truly disadvantaged situations (W. J. Wilson 1987) that involve varying forms and degrees of status exclusion and that are, in much public discussion, stigmatized as an underclass of 'undeserving' second-class citizens. But they are a part of the fragmentary class of manual workers; they are not a separate and distinct social class.

PROPERTY, BUREAUCRACY, AND CLASS

One of the most striking trends in the development of contemporary societies has been a massive growth in management positions in large-scale bureaucratic organizations. This growth in the *numbers* of managers since the 1920s was seen by the supporters of the managerialist thesis as signalling a growth in their *power*. The rise to power of technically qualified managers was seen as undermining the position of the capitalist class, whose property was no longer necessary in large-scale organizations. The rise of the managers would bring about the fall of the capitalists.

The capitalist class has not disappeared, although it has been transformed in a number of very important ways. It is also the case that managers are far more diverse than the managerialist writers suggested. Most managers are involved in financial administration, but they range all the way from the top executive capitalists through senior financial managers and a whole hierarchy of levels to routine administrative and office workers at the lower levels of the corporate bureaucracies.

In Chapter 16, pp. 660–6, we discuss the trend towards debureaucratization since the 1970s. This has eroded the power and life chances of many managers, destroying what areas of common interest that they had. The middle classes have become more diverse than ever before. A capitalist class can still be distinguished from the mass of the middle classes, but the middle classes now exist as more or less completely separate entrepreneurial, professional, and administrative classes and fragments.

Management and the capitalist class

The argument in support of the managerial revolution was developed in the debate on ownership and control that we review in Chapter 16. With the growth of large-scale production, joint stock companies drew on larger pools of investment capital, and so the powers of their owners were diluted. The implications of this have been hotly debated in a series of studies (Berle and Means 1932; Florence 1961; Zeitlin 1989; J. Scott 1997), and it is now clear that ownership has remained an important factor in the control of businesses.

There are still very wealthy and powerful propertied families whose life chances are far superior to those enjoyed by most managers. These families now work alongside and through the large banks, insurance companies, and pensions funds that actually own the great

The managerial revolution

The idea of the **managerial revolution** was most forcefully stated in Burnham's (1941) book of that title. Burnham saw the managers becoming an indispensable force in business and the wider society. They would become, he said, a new ruling class, replacing the old capitalist ruling class. Later writers such as Bell (1961) have taken a rather less extreme view and have argued simply that managers, because of their technical knowledge and skills, become the single most important class in society, swelling the size of the middle class.

You might find it useful to look at our discussion of ownership and control in Chapter 16, pp. 656–8, where we set out some of the evidence that is relevant to these claims. The whole argument is reviewed in J. Scott (1997).

bulk of company shares and that provide the capital that large organizations require. There are close economic links among the executive capitalists and finance capitalists who direct the major financial and industrial enterprises, the rentier capitalists whose savings and investments feed the financial system, and the entrepreneurial capitalists who retain a substantial personal or family stake in particular enterprises. There are also strong links among them through mobility and interaction.

The close links between ownership and control in contemporary societies have been described by Mills (1956) as resulting in a 'managerial reorganization' of the capitalist class. Business enterprises have become more closely interconnected through interlocking directorships and through the intertwining shareholdings of the big financial investors. At the same time, those who hold directorships and top executive positions in these enterprises are drawn overwhelmingly from wealthy families with inherited property. A capitalist class survives because it has combined personal wealth with participation in top-level management.

Members of this class are united through similarities in their educational background. Many of them continue to follow the traditional upper class educational route of public school and ancient university. Over the period from the beginning of the Second World War to 1970, the proportion of directors in big British banks who went to a public school increased from two-thirds to over three-quarters. The proportion who went to Oxford or Cambridge university increased to almost two-thirds over the same period. Those directors with multiple directorships are especially likely to have entered business through the public school and Oxbridge route. Although larger numbers are entering business with a degree from a Business School, they are still only a minority of top executive managers. Capitalists and their families interact frequently with one another, and their membership in exclusive London social clubs is, as in the past, an important basis for their informal connections and for the building of social cohesion (Useem 1984).

While there is much continuity with upper-class cultural values and patterns of sociability, these status elements are much weaker than in the past. Traditional 'gentlemanly' norms in business were finally eroded in the 1980s, as the promotion of an enterprise culture pushed aggressive money-making values to the fore. Upper-class institutions and practices survived rather longer in the sphere of leisure, where many of the events of the Social Calendar remain as important meeting places for the wealthy. These events are now, however, dominated by the newly rich, by fashionable celebrities, and by corporate sponsorship. They have become more directly tied into business activities. The traditional lifestyle is no longer aspired to as an escape from business. It is adopted as part and parcel of the business world itself.

The extent of this change should not be overstated, but it is clear that it is no longer sensible to talk about an upper class as if it included virtually all of the capitalist class. The true upper class or aristocracy is now a minority within the capitalist class, and its distinct status no longer coincides with an overall economic superiority. It is upper class in name, but not in reality. The capitalist class stands at the top of the stratification system. Its continuing fascination with titles, honours, and traditional sporting events is a minor distraction from its real concern with the making and spending of money.

Professionals, entrepreneurs, and bureaucrats

The middle classes always had a low degree of class cohesion. They were held together by status rather than through common economic interests. The middle classes formed an open status hierarchy that stretched from the lowest clerk or shop assistant up through the ranks of management and the professions to entrepreneurs and civil servants. The rise of large-scale organization transformed clerical and managerial work. Most significantly, this raised doubts about where and how sharply to draw the boundaries that divide the middle classes from other social classes.

Large-scale organization has also transformed the

situations of small-scale entrepreneurs and those in the professions. Small businesses have come under greater pressure as the economy has become more concentrated. Many businesses have had to adapt, if they are to survive, by becoming subcontractors and suppliers to the large businesses with which they deal. At the same time, new opportunities for consultancy and service operations have been created by the growth of large-scale enterprise. Small-scale capital is particularly important in farming, building, retailing, and services, and in manufacturing industries such as engineering and textiles (Scase and Goffee 1982). In respect of their social mobility, these class situations show a relatively high level of self-recruitment. Their occupants are distinct from other sections of the middle classes. Nevertheless, a significant number of small entrepreneurs do come from a managerial background, and a much smaller number build their businesses into large-scale operations.

Professional workers have relied on their cultural capital to obtain the educational credentials that give them entry to jobs that require specialist or technical knowledge. The old professions—doctors, lawyers, the clergy, and university academics—have had their working conditions and life chances eroded as their work has become more firmly embedded in public- and private-sector bureaucracies (T. Johnson 1972). The large numbers of accountants and engineers produced from the late nineteenth century were, from the start, bureaucratic employees rather than autonomous self-employed professionals.

The growth of a whole range of newer professions that have been incorporated directly into the expanding bureaucracies has characterized the whole of the twentieth century. This has been especially rapidly since the 1950s. Teachers, social workers, medical technicians, nurses, estate agents, financial advisers, and similar occupations have grown massively in numbers. The bureaucratization of the professions destroyed traditional professional autonomy and created divisions of the kind that exist between the various levels of management.

Managers, senior and junior, owe their life chances far more to their command situations, to their authority, than to their possession of educational credentials. They have generally been promoted through the internal labour markets of the organizations for which they work, building up skills and competencies that are specific to a particular organization or industry. These skills cannot easily be transferred from one context to another and they cannot be passed directly on to sons or daughters. Savage and his colleagues (1992) follow E. O. Wright (1985) in describing these skills as 'organizational assets'.

Until recently, many managers enjoyed, in effect, lifetime employment. The fact that their organizational assets (unlike property or educational qualifications) were not transferable made little difference to them as they climbed the organizational hierarchy. Since the 1970s, however, managerial work has been transformed by the restructuring of large-scale organizations. Through debureaucratization and 'downsizing', enterprises have become less bureaucratic and hierarchies have become flatter.

Managers have lost their jobs in large numbers, and this has been especially marked where computers and information-technology equipment can be introduced. Those who have remained in employment have had to become more flexible in their working patterns. Internal labour markets have declined in importance, and much managerial work has been contracted out to self-employed consultants and service firms.

The middle classes of the first part of the century were rooted in small-scale property ownership, the exercise of authority within administrative bureaucracies, and the possession of the cultural capital required for entry to the professions. Each of these bases remains important. Small-scale property ownership did not disappear with the concentration of economic activity, and it has continued to provide opportunities for many to improve their life chances. Clerical workers, as we have shown, faced declining life chances as their

Organization and class

The organizational changes that have eroded the command situations of managers are discussed in Chapter 16. Look at pp. 665–6 and read our discussion of post-Fordism and the flexible firm. Savage and his colleagues have summarized the key points:

'Economic restructuring has involved a growing concern with product innovation, and capitalist firms which had previously relied upon organizational hierarchies increasingly look to either self-employed specialists or to professional specialists to carry out key tasks. As a result, the pyramidical organizational hierarchy is disrupted, and the power of organization assets alone to convey reward is severely questioned. Firms increasingly look to those with specific skills to perform particular jobs, rather than rely automatically on bureaucratic procedures.'
(Savage et al. 1992: 65–6)

market and work situations deteriorated with the expansion and mechanization of office work, but managerial and administrative workers continued to enjoy superior life chances and a distinct status. Similarly, the expansion of the new professions has opened up more opportunities for those with educational credentials to improve their market chances.

The cohesion that the middle classes had in the past depended on the mobility and interaction that existed among those in class situations based in property, bureaucracy, and culture. This mobility occurred when people were able to convert one kind of asset into another. Those with capital, for example, might buy private schooling for their children and so improve their chances of obtaining the educational credentials that allowed them to enter one of the professions or to join a corporate organization and achieve a senior position. Similarly, those who had a successful career in a corporate bureaucracy might be able to save enough money to set up their children in a small business.

In Britain, Savage *et al.* argue, the middle classes had a relatively low level of cohesion because the possibility of converting one type of resource into another was very limited. The professional middle class was relatively closed to those from a propertied or bureaucratic background, and very few small businesses were started by those who had been successful in management or the professions. Of particular significance, they argue, is the fact that managerial success has never depended on the achievement of a high level of technical expertise in school and university examinations.

This low level of class unity has now weakened. Using some results from the Oxford Mobility Study, Savage *et al.* show that the managerial and professional workers that are sometimes grouped together into a service class are actually very distinct from one another. They are experiencing significantly different opportunities in respect of their life chances and their lifestyles. The things that differentiate professionals from managers are more important than any similarities that there may be. Members of the professions, they argue, are much better able to pass on their class situations to their children because entry to the professions depends on cultural or educational capital.

There are particularly important differences in class interests, highlighted by the association between the professions and the state. Professional workers have an interest in a thriving public sector and are less likely to support a cut-back in the public sector or the removal of professional privileges. Managerial workers and small property-owners, on the other hand, are more likely to be committed to an expansion of the private sector and a reduction in the resources assigned to the public sector.

Many of those in these intermediate class situations do see themselves as part of a large central class, as did the affluent workers of the 1960s, but this is not an especially salient aspect of their social identity. They are more likely to see themselves in narrower occupational terms, or in terms of their gender, ethnicity, or public-service role. Neither the traditional status hierarchy nor the imagery of class is a natural or spontaneous source of social identity.

There is, then, a fragmentation of the middle classes, a division of them along the lines of propertied assets, organizational assets, and educational assets. This fragmentation has been matched by their withdrawal from involvement in the public, civic life of the towns and cities in which they live. The middle classes today no longer seek out the high degree of local participation that they had in the past. In the restudy of Banbury in the late 1960s, Stacey and her colleagues found that the much enlarged town had far less of a civic character than it had shown in the 1950s (Stacey *et al.* 1975).

SUMMARY POINTS

In this section we have looked at the fragmentation of the classic class society that existed until the middle of the twentieth century. We started out from a consideration of the ideas of industrialism and industrial society. We looked at the implications of the occupational transition for patterns of social stratification.

▶ Embourgeoisement and managerialism have fragmented all three social classes.

▶ Changes in the organization of manual work and the transformation of long-standing communities have undermined the solidarity and cohesion of the working class.

▶ Manual workers tend to be more privatized and less conscious of themselves as members of a working class.

▶ De-bureaucratization and downsizing have helped to restructure the middle classes, producing a greater separation of their entrepreneurial, professional and bureaucratic elements.

▶ The capitalist class has undergone a 'managerial reorganization' and is no longer subordinate to the status values of the aristocracy.

REVISION AND EXERCISES

Review the Summary Points in this chapter and then consider the following issues.

CONCEPTUALIZING STRATIFICATION

We looked at general concepts for understanding social stratification and at two broad interpretations of change in stratification systems. At the beginning of 'The Making of a Class Society' we looked at the theory of capitalism and class society. In 'A Fragmentary Class Society' we looked at the theory of industrialism and the fragmentation of class:

▶ **What do you understand by the following terms: stratification, stratum; interests; class situation, social class, class consciousness; status situation, social estate, style of life; party; slavery, caste; occupational transition?**

▶ **What does it mean to talk about class and status as 'causal components' in life chances?**

▶ **Make sure that you understand the principal ideas on stratification of the following writers: Weber, Marx, Parsons, Warner.**

▶ **Considering our discussion of capitalism and class society, how would you assess Marx's ideas of polarization and proletarianization?**

▶ **Turning to our discussion of industrialism and class society, what do you understand by the idea of embourgeoisement?**

SUBORDINATE SOCIAL STRATA

We looked at a number of issues in relation to the formation and fragmentation of a working class:

▶ **In what sense is it useful to see the working class as consisting of manual workers?**

▶ **What do you understand by the following: market situation, work situation, instrumental orientation, privatism; money model of society?**

▶ **What are the principal social institutions and organizations that encouraged the formation of a cohesive working class? (You will find it useful to refer to other chapters when answering this question.)**

We also returned to the debate over the idea of an underclass and considered this in relation to the theoretical ideas that we have considered:

▶ **Is the so-called underclass a true social class?**

DOMINANT AND INTERMEDIATE SOCIAL STRATA

The middle classes and the upper classes are usefully considered together, as their histories are so intertwined. We looked at the formation and fragmentation of the middle classes and at their relationship to capitalist entrepreneurs and the landowning aristocracy:

▶ **What occupations would you include in the middle classes? Try to list at least ten.**

▶ **What do you understand by the following terms: intermediate class situations, service class, white-collar worker; aristocracy, peerage.**

▶ **How would you distinguish between the following: entrepreneurial capitalist, rentier capitalist, executive capitalist, finance capitalist.**

We looked at a number of features in the organization of work that have affected class situations. Remind yourself about what we say in Chapters 13 and 16, and then consider the following:

▶ **What is meant by the idea of the managerial revolution?**
▶ **How have debureaucratization and downsizing altered the class situation of managers?**

FURTHER READING

Good general reading on the issues discussed in this chapter can be found in:

Scott, J. (1996), *Stratification and Power: Structures of Class, Status and Command* (Cambridge: Polity Press). A broad overview of the conceptual and theoretical issues considered in the first section of this chapter.

Dahrendorf, R. (1957), *Class and Class Conflict in an Industrial Society* (London: Routledge & Kegan Paul, 1959). A classic attempt to present an alternative to a Marxist view of class.

Goldthorpe, J. H., Lockwood, D., Bechhofer, F., and Platt, J. (1969), *The Affluent Worker in the Class Structure* (Cambridge: Cambridge University Press). The principal study of recent developments in working-class attitudes and organization. Also well worth reading for its account of Marxist theory and its problems.

Devine, F. (1992), *Affluent Workers Revisited: Privatism and the Working Class* (Edinburgh: Edinburgh University Press). An important reassessment of the Goldthorpe *et al.* study.

Stacey, M. (1960), *Tradition and Change: A Study of Banbury* (Oxford: Oxford University Press). Together with its companion volume (Stacey *et al.* 1975), this gives a good overview of social stratification in a 'typical' town in southern England.

——Batstone, E., Bell, C., and Murcott, A. (1975), *Power, Persistence and Change* (London: Routledge & Kegan Paul). The follow-up to the original Banbury study (Stacey 1960).

Some of the theoretical and empirical issues are taken further in:

Wright, E. O. (1985), *Classes* (London: Verso). An influential, but rather daunting theoretical exploration of class from a Marxist viewpoint. Takes issue with the argument of Dahrendorf (1957), but has some similarities with it.

Goldthorpe, J. H. (1980), *Social Mobility and Class Structure* (Oxford: Clarendon Press). The standard account of social mobility in Britain, though limited by its focus on men.

Wilson, W. J. (1987), *The Truly Disadvantaged* (Chicago: University of Chicago Press). An important study of the 'underclass' in the United States. Suggests that, treated carefully, the concept may have some value in understanding ghetto poverty.

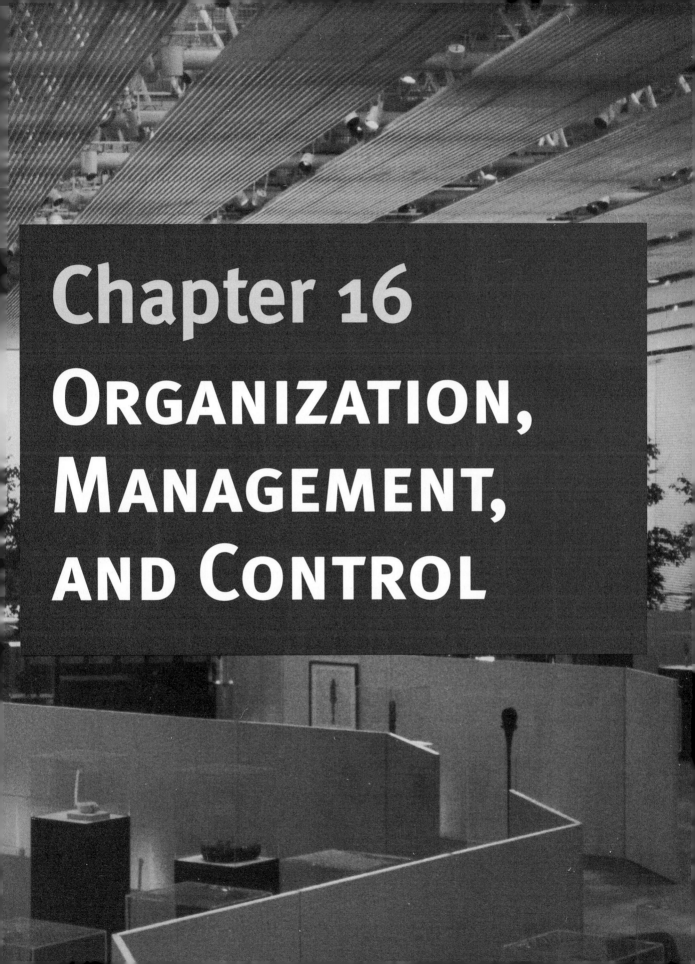

Chapter 16

ORGANIZATION, MANAGEMENT, AND CONTROL

The McDonald's operations manual

'It told operators exactly how to draw milk shakes, grill hamburgers, and fry potatoes. It specified precise cooking times for all products and temperature settings for all equipment. It fixed standard portions on every food item, down to the quarter ounce of onions placed on each hamburger patty and the thirty-two slices per pound of cheese. It specified that french fries be cut at nine thirty-seconds of an inch thick. And it defined quality controls that were unique to food service, including the disposal of meat and potato products that were held more than ten minutes in a serving bin.

'Grill men were instructed to put hamburgers down on the grill moving from left to right, creating six rows of six patties each. And because the first two rows were farthest from the heating element, they were instructed (and still are) to flip the third row first, then the fourth, fifth, and sixth before flipping the first two.'

Source: Love (1986: 141–2, quoted in Ritzer 1996: 32).

W**E** spend much of our daily lives working for organizations or trying to obtain goods or services from them. Schools, hospitals, companies, trade unions, churches, government departments, armies, prisons, and theatres are all organizations. We tend to think of them as very different in character because they carry out such different tasks, but they do all have certain basic features in common. Indeed, as you will find in this chapter, the insights obtained from the study of one organization have often been applied to apparently very different ones.

Most of the organizations that we come across are bureaucracies and we have mixed feelings about them. Bureaucratic organizations meet important needs by providing us, for example, with employment, health care, and education. On the other hand, they often seem impersonal and unconcerned with our particular requirements. Bureaucrats sometimes fuss with petty rules and regulations that appear designed to cause frustration and serve no apparent purpose. In this chapter we discuss the functions of bureaucratic rules and the way that they are used and interpreted. We also consider whether there are alternative, less bureaucratic ways of organizing activities.

An orderly society depends on discipline. Organizations can work only if their members behave in the way that they should. Hospital patients are expected to accept treatment, soldiers to obey orders, employees to do their work, and students to write essays. But why is it that people generally act in the way required by organizations? We examine in this chapter the basis of discipline and the development of methods of control. We also examine the surveillance techniques used to monitor people's behaviour.

Organizations also require management. Those who run the organization have to make sure that it achieves its goals. What is the best way to do this? One way is to divide work up into simple tasks, give workers detailed instructions, and see that they carry them out, as in the McDonald's burger bar. Is it, however, better for managers to leave it to the workers to decide the details of the way that they work and concentrate on motivating them to do their best? This raises the question of how to motivate people. Are they motivated by money or their involvement in the organization and their loyalty to it? We examine these issues too in this chapter.

We also consider who actually controls an organization. In most organizations there are many experts with a specialized knowledge of the activity concerned, but do they control what goes on? In the case of business organizations, is it the managers who are in control or those who own a company? In many industries and services there have recently been major changes in ownership with their transfer from the public to the private sector through privatization. What difference does private or public ownership make? We consider too the global corporation and the amount of control it exercises over its operations in different countries.

You will find that we discuss many different organizations, from departments of government and business corporations to mental hospitals and prisons. As you read the chapter, try and apply what you learn about organizations to any that you have personal experience or knowledge of.

UNDERSTANDING ORGANIZATIONS

We begin by considering briefly what we mean by organizations, before discussing Max Weber's analysis of bureaucracy, which has been central to the sociological study of organizations. One of the defining features of bureaucracy is discipline and we go on to examine Foucault's influential analysis of this. We also consider his concept of carceral organization and Goffman's similar notion of the total institution.

ORGANIZATIONS

The term **organization** is used in a very general way in sociology. You should not worry too much about the definition of this term, but it is worth sketching out briefly what sociologists have in mind when they refer to organizations. An organization is basically a structure for carrying out a particular social activity on a regular basis and will generally have the following features:

▶ a specific goal;

▶ a defined membership;

▶ rules of behaviour;

▶ authority relationships.

Continuity is a key characteristic of an organization. It has an existence independent of the particular individuals who make it up at any one time. There may be frequent changes of personnel, as people enter and leave it or move between its different positions, but the organization continues to exist.

The range of social groups that come into the category of organizations is not particularly well defined. It is clear that, for example, business corporations, trade unions, hospitals, schools, churches, and armies are all organizations. It is equally clear that some social groups, such as a community or a class, are not organizations. Communities and classes do not have specific goals or rules of behaviour. Other social groups, such as the family, are in an intermediate position.

A family does have some of the characteristics of an organization. It has a more or less defined membership, rules of behaviour, and authority relationships, though it cannot really be said that it has a specific goal, since it carries out many functions for its members. Child-rearing may be one goal, but satisfying the emotional needs of its members or providing mutual support are others. Textbooks on the Sociology of Organizations do not generally include the family, though some, such as that by Ahrne (1994), who adopts a broader definition of organization, do.

The term 'organization' is also used to refer to the process through which a group becomes organized. Class organization provides a good example of this. A social class consists of those who share a common economic situation (see our discussion of class in Chapter 15, pp. 604–6). As we argued above, a class is not itself an organization, but it can become organized through the creation of class organizations. If those in, say, the working class form organizations, such as trade unions or political parties, the working class becomes organized.

There is some ambiguity in the use of the terms 'organization' and 'institution'. Strictly speaking organizations are not institutions. In Chapter 1, p. 11, we defined institutions as 'established practices that regulate the various activities that make up social life'. These practices became, however, increasingly organized as society developed and the term 'institution' is often used to refer to the organizations in which these practices occur. Thus, schools, hospitals, and prisons are often described as institutions, though they should really be treated as organizations. Goffman, whose work we shall discuss shortly, uses the term 'total institution' to refer to mental hospitals and other organizations of this kind.

BUREAUCRACY

Bureaucracy is only one type of organization but one that became increasingly widespread as society developed. Most of the organizations that we come into contact with in our daily lives are bureaucratic in character, though not all. Small businesses, for example, are not usually run on bureaucratic lines. In this section we consider the meaning of bureaucracy and the issues raised by bureaucratic organization. The Sociology of Organizations has largely revolved around debates about bureaucracy and studies of the workings of bureaucratic organizations.

Weber's ideal type

Max Weber's *ideal type* of **bureaucracy** has been the starting point of the sociological study of organizations. The term 'ideal type' can be a little confusing and it is important to be clear about its meaning, which we discuss in Chapter 2, p. 42. Weber's ideal type was a statement not of what bureaucracies *ought* to be like but rather of the *key features* of bureaucratic organization.

According to Max Weber (1914) bureaucracies had the following characteristics:

▶ *Specialist expertise.* Bureaucracies contrasted with earlier forms of organization where there was no systematic specialization of tasks. Expertise depends on education and training, and bureaucracies require qualifications for entry. 'Bureaucratic administration means fundamentally the exercise of control on the basis of knowledge' (Max Weber 1920: 225).

▶ *Hierarchy.* There is a hierarchy of officials, with those in higher positions having authority over those in lower ones. The duties of the different positions are laid down in writing and behaviour is closely supervised.

▶ *Impersonal rules.* Particular cases are dealt with by reference to general rules. Bureaucrats are expected to apply rules impersonally and take no account of the individual with whom they are dealing. This applies whether they are dealing with each other or with the outside world.

▶ *Discipline.* Bureaucrats are required to obey the rules and carry out their duties in a disciplined way. The bureaucrat is expected to be self-disciplined but, if the rules are broken, the official concerned is punished.

▶ *Salaries.* Bureaucrats are paid salaries. This means that they do not have to earn their living from the performance of their duties, as officials have commonly done in the past. Their private interests and their public duties are clearly separated.

▶ *Careers.* Bureaucrats have full-time and permanent posts. Their security of employment enables them to act impartially without fear or favour. They are promoted on the basis of merit and seniority.

The interrelationships between these elements are central to the ideal type. Thus, career officials can operate impersonally because of the independence and security provided by their salaries and their permanent posts. Similarly, disciplined behaviour is bound up with the existence of a hierarchy and the application of impersonal rules in a non-emotional way.

Since Weber's time there have been numerous studies of bureaucracy that have criticized or revised the ideal type. Albrow (1970) has argued that much of the criticism of Weber has been ill-founded, because it has misunderstood or oversimplified what he wrote. His basic point is that the critics of Weber have been concerned with the *efficiency* of bureaucracy, while Weber was primarily interested in its *rationality*. Weber's writings on bureaucracy should certainly be placed in the context of his general interest in broader processes of rationalization (see Chapter 2, pp. 42–4). He did, none the less, make many statements that indicated his belief in the technical efficiency of bureaucracy:

'The decisive reason for the advance of bureaucratic organization has always been its purely *technical* superiority over any other form of organization. The fully developed bureaucratic mechanism compares with other organizations exactly as does the machine with the non-mechanical modes of production. Precision, speed, unambiguity, knowledge of the files, continuity, discretion, unity, strict subordination, reduction of friction and of material and personal costs—these are raised to the optimum point in the strictly bureaucratic administration . . .'   (Max Weber 1914: 973)

Even if it does sometimes misrepresent Weber, the post-Weberian literature has, anyway, greatly increased our understanding of the character of bureaucracy, of the ways in which bureaucratic organizations work, and the problems that they face.

The functions of rules

Much of this literature has focused on the operation of bureaucratic rules. One question it raises is whether organizations can operate effectively on the basis of obedience to the rules. It also raises more fundamental issues to do with the use and interpretation of rules by different groups.

Merton (1940) focused on the *dysfunctions* of bureaucratic rules. He argued that, instead of enabling an organization to function efficiently, obedience to the rules could prevent it achieving its goals. The problem is that obedience to the rules is such a crucial feature of bureaucracy that officials are trained to obey them to the letter. This can lead to decisions that are inappropriate to a particular situation. The application of rules can become 'an end in itself' rather than a means to the achievement of the organization's goals. Merton called this the *displacement of goals*, for it meant that the bureaucrat's goal became the correct application of the rules rather than the achievement of the goals of the organization. Bureaucrats acquired what Merton called a *trained incapacity* to work effectively.

In a similar way, Crozier's (1964) classic study of bureaucratic organization in France demonstrated how bureaucracies could be extremely rigid organizations. The impersonal application of rules prevented the development of informal and personal relationships. This made cooperation difficult, isolated the various parts of the organization from each other, and made change virtually impossible. As many studies of bureaucratic organizations have shown, organizations can work effectively only if informal relationships emerge to deal with particular issues and problems. Crozier related the extreme rigidity of the organizations that he studied to the distinctive character of French society and culture, which had resulted

in a history of periods of rigidity, when all change was resisted, followed by periods of revolutionary change.

Alvin Gouldner

Gouldner (1920–80) was born in New York and spent most of his career as a Professor of Sociology at Washington University. He also held a professorial post at the University of Amsterdam in the 1970s. His *Patterns of Industrial Bureaucracy* (1954) and the follow-up *Wildcat Strike* (1955) were path-breaking studies that explored empirically and theoretically a number of issues raised by Weber's work on bureaucracy. He is probably best known, however, for *The Coming Crisis of Western Sociology* (1970), in which he examined the historical development of sociological thinking and tried to develop a middle path between the functionalist and Marxist approaches that dominated sociology at that time. He also founded the journal *Theory and Society*. The major influences on Gouldner's thinking were Weber, the Frankfurt school (see Chapter 8, p. 280), and C. W. Mills.

In another well-known study, of an American factory, Gouldner (1954) argued that the functions and enforcement of bureaucratic rules should be understood not in terms of some notion of the needs of the organization as a whole but by reference to the interests of the various groups within it and the relationships between them. Thus, while some rules might be imposed by managers, others were imposed on management by workers, while some rules emerged in a more 'democratic' way through consultation and discussion.

Gouldner identified three patterns of bureaucracy within the factory:

▶ *Mock bureaucracy.* This consisted of rules, such as no-smoking rules, that were not enforced by management, except when the insurance inspector visited. This non-enforcement helped to create solidarity between managers and workers against the interfering outside world.

▶ *Representative bureaucracy.* This consisted of rules that were enforced but on the basis of worker consent. Thus, safety rules were applied with the active compliance of the workers, who accepted the need for them. It was representative because the workers themselves were involved, in part through union safety committees, in the process of developing and implementing these rules.

▶ *Punishment-centred bureaucracy.* This referred to the rules that one side tried to use against the other. Management tried to enforce a non-absenteeism rule on the workers. The workers tried to force management to fill vacancies according to the procedure laid down by a collective agreement, which required any new job to be offered to existing workers and restricted the managers' freedom of action.

Gouldner emphasized that in other situations a particular rule might fall into another pattern. On an oil rig the evident dangers of smoking might mean that a non-smoking rule would become an example of representative bureaucracy. Arguably the diminishing cultural acceptance of smoking has anyway tended to shift non-smoking rules into this pattern. The point is that rules do not exist in some vacuum but have to be interpreted and enforced before they become a social reality. The interests of groups and the relationships between them are crucial in shaping the way that this happens.

This important study also documented a process of bureaucratization and observed its consequences. Gouldner showed how the *succession problem* created by the arrival of a new boss led to a greater reliance on rules. The new boss lacked the informal contacts that his predecessor had developed. He was also under instructions to increase production by tightening up on worker behaviour, thereby violating what Gouldner called the *indulgency pattern* established by his predecessor. As he tried to enforce the rules, he met worker resistance, lost the workers' cooperation, and fell back even more on the formal structure of supervision and control. The workers then retaliated by 'working to rule' and insisting that management obeyed the rules laid down in the collective agreement. A vicious circle of conflict developed and led to the unofficial strike that Gouldner (1955) analysed in his follow-up study.

In another well-known study, Strauss *et al.* (1963) examined the way that rules were used and interpreted in a mental hospital. They pointed out that hardly anyone knew all the rules, which were frequently ignored or forgotten, and then reinvented when a particular crisis showed that they were needed. The rules were used only in conflicts between groups, as when nurses invoked 'the rules of the hospital' to fend off the demands that some doctors made on them. Rules also always required interpretation before they could be implemented. Did they apply to *this* person, in *this* situation and, if so, to *what* degree and for *how* long?

The various occupational groups in the hospital—psychiatrists, psychologists, nurses, students, occupational therapists, social workers—not only had different interests but had been trained in different ways and held varying and strongly held professional ideologies. Whether a rule should be implemented and how this should be done were always matters for negotiation. This went on all the time and Strauss *et al.* saw the hospital as based on what they called a *negotiated*, not an *imposed*, order.

In a similar way to Gouldner, Strauss *et al.* drew attention to the realities of rule use and rule interpretation. Rules should not be seen as fixed and objective structures that somehow exist in their own right and regulate people's behaviour. It is also important, however, to

Gouldner's patterns of industrial bureaucracy	Pattern of bureaucracy	Example of rule	Who enforces the rule?	Management–worker relationship
	Mock	No smoking	Outsiders	Solidarity
	Representative	Safety	Management *and* workers	Agreement
	Punishment-centred	Non-absenteeism	Management	Conflict
		Vacancy-filling	Workers	Conflict

be aware of differences between organizations in the way that rules are applied. Hospitals are different from factories. The *negotiated order* of the hospital reflected a distinctive occupational structure, where staff had a degree of autonomy because of their professional or semi-professional status. This autonomy gave them a greater capacity to negotiate than ordinary employees normally have.

For and against bureaucracy

It is wrong to think that Weber was an uncritical advocate of bureaucracy. He was certainly impressed by its efficiency but he was also very concerned about its implications for democracy. He was particularly interested in the character of the bureaucratic state and the relationship between bureaucrats and politicians. Bureaucrats should in principle be the servants of government but they tended to become a force in their own right. Although they were supposed to be detached and objective, like any other group they had their own interests, while their expertise and authority made it difficult for politicians to resist them. As Max Weber (1914: 991) put it, 'the political "master" always finds himself, vis-à-vis the trained official, in the position of a dilettante facing the expert'.

Weber was very aware of the dangers of bureaucratic domination under socialist regimes. He was sceptical of the socialist belief that the abolition of the private ownership of industry and the introduction of a planned economy would lead to a more equal and more productive society. He thought that the bureaucrats in charge of planning would become a secretive, selfish, and all-powerful elite. The result would be repression and inefficiency. A capitalist society based on market principles was more flexible and more responsive to people's needs.

The development of state socialist societies certainly bore out Weber's fears, but capitalist societies too became increasingly managed and controlled by bureaucratic organizations. This occurred through the nationalization of major industries and services, the growth of state welfare, and the development of the state management and state planning of the economy. Then in the 1970s and the 1980s the economic crisis of the old industrial societies led to a revival of the belief in market forces and an attempt to shift from bureaucratic control of the economy to market regulation. One form this took was privatization, which we examine later in the chapter.

Debureaucratizing tendencies have also occurred within the management of business corporations. This can be seen in both the search for new organizational forms and in changing management techniques. The rigidity of bureaucracy became increasingly serious as technological change and international competition generated pressures for greater responsiveness and flexibility. Later in the chapter, in the section on 'debureaucratization?', pp. 660–2, we examine the emergence of more flexible forms of organization.

Max Weber (1914: 975) stressed the rational and non-emotional character of bureaucracy: 'Bureaucracy develops the more perfectly, the more it is "dehumanized", the more completely it succeeds in eliminating from official business love, hatred, and all purely personal, irrational and emotional elements which escape calculation.'

A rediscovery of the importance of the emotional aspects of organizations began with the emphasis placed by the *human-relations* school of management on the emotional needs of the worker. Human resource management has taken this further with its focus on the importance of loyalty and commitment to the organization. From a different perspective, the Weberian model has been criticized by some feminists for its typically male concerns with hierarchy, formality, and impersonality rather than the female qualities of caring and sharing. We take up these issues too later in the chapter in 'Feminizing the Organization', pp. 663–5, and 'The Transformation of Management', pp. 666–70.

Bureaucracy has acquired a negative image and is commonly used as a term of abuse. When we are asked to fill in forms or find ourselves regulated by apparently unnecessary rules or wait endlessly for our case to be dealt with or feel that we are being treated in too impersonal a way, we accuse organizations of 'bureaucracy'. There is another side to bureaucracy, however. Health and safety rules protect us against accident and disease. Impersonal treatment guards against favouritism and corruption. Bureaucracies, at least in principle, treat people impartially and equally. They may work slowly but they usually also work thoroughly. When bureaucracy protects us, treats us fairly, and operates efficiently, we never sing its praises. It is important to take a balanced view of its positive and negative aspects.

DISCIPLINE, CARCERAL ORGANIZATIONS, AND TOTAL INSTITUTIONS

Discipline is central to bureaucracy. According to Foucault (1975), it is a central feature of society as a whole, for we live in what he has called a 'disciplinary society'. In this section we discuss Foucault's analysis of discipline and examine the organizations that most embody it.

Discipline

Foucault's disciplinary society is based on techniques of control that were first developed in the seventeenth and eighteenth centuries to produce what he called 'docile bodies'. These techniques attained their most developed form in the nineteenth-century prison, which became a model not only for other organizations but also for techniques of surveillance and control that have spread throughout society.

According to Foucault, discipline involved:

► control of the body;

► surveillance;

► punishment.

Discipline required a detailed *control of people's physical activities* through the systematic subdivision of *space*, *time*, and *bodily* activity. Thus, criminals were spatially confined in prisons, which were divided into blocks or wings, which were in turn subdivided into cells. *Time* was divided up through the timetable, which broke it down into short periods, and provided a means of organizing activity, and eliminating idleness. *Bodily* activity was split up through drills and exercises. The loading and firing of a gun, for example, was carried out through a specified sequence of movements. Once activity had been divided up, it could be reassembled in a coordinated and directed manner.

Discipline was dependent on *surveillance*, the continuous observation of those subject to discipline by those enforcing it. Foucault stressed the importance of visibility. People were under the gaze of those who controlled them, though the controllers themselves sought to remain invisible. The military camp, for example, was laid out in lines of tents with prescribed spaces between them, specified routes, and carefully positioned entrances and exits, so that all movement could be observed. This principle was eventually extended to many other areas of life. 'For a long time this model of the camp or at least its underlying principle was found in urban development, in the construction of working-class housing estates, hospitals, asylums, prisons, schools . . .' (Foucault 1975: 171–2).

Discipline involved new methods of *punishment* centred on the prison. In pre-industrial times relatively minor offences were punished by public execution

of the offender, who might also be tortured and suffer bodily mutilation. Rulers concerned primarily with the public demonstration of their authority applied laws in an erratic and arbitrary way, while non-observance of the law was widespread. In the late eighteenth century a much more systematic approach to the enforcement of law and the punishment of criminals emerged. This involved punishment by imprisonment, with the duration of imprisonment related to the seriousness of the crime. A wave of prison-building began. Punishment by imprisonment was concerned not with demonstrating royal power but with maintaining order.

According to Foucault, these disciplinary techniques were most developed in the nineteenth-century prison. The growth of systematic punishment through imprisonment initiated a process of **incarceration**, which basically means shutting people away from society. The regime of the nineteenth-century prison was different from that of earlier prisons because it cut off prisoners' contact with the outside world. The new prison also controlled prisoners by isolating them from each other, and keeping them under constant surveillance. He used the term **carceral organization** to refer to organizations which controlled people in these ways. We examine nineteenth-century incarceration and the new prison in 'Disciplined Organizations', pp. 650–4.

The process of incarceration extended beyond the prison, however. This was partly because the prison became the model for other carceral organizations, such as hospitals and factories, which similarly isolated people and placed them under surveillance. It was also because the techniques of control developed within prisons have been generalized *throughout* society. Thus, according to Foucault, the population at large has been increasingly controlled by dividing people up into compartments isolated from each other and keeping them under surveillance. The same principles governed the construction of the housing estate as the prison. The working class was controlled by isolating workers on estates, where they were under the surveillance of the police. This notion of the generalization of techniques of control led him to use the terms *carceral city* and *carceral society*.

Giddens has criticized Foucault for extending the idea of carceral organization too far. He argues that factories are not organizations of this sort. Some factories may well have adopted disciplinary and surveillance techniques similar to those used in prisons, but workers remain 'free wage labour', able to leave if they wish. Workers have not been isolated from the rest of society and, unlike prison inmates, can organize themselves in unions to resist the power of the employer (Giddens 1981: 172). While Foucault's notion of the generalizing of control techniques is interesting and insightful, Giddens clearly has a point.

It has also been argued by Scull (1984) that the process of incarceration was reversed by **decarceration** in the 1960s. In both Britain and the United States there was a shift from locking up 'the mad and the bad' to dealing with them through community programmes. We discuss Scull's theory of decarceration on pp. 674–5.

Total institutions

While some organizations, particularly those that employ us, may make heavy demands on our time and energy, most leave us with a separate private life. This is not the case, however, with one class of organizations, those that were labelled **total institutions** by Erving Goffman in his book *Asylums*. His study of these institutions was based on his observations of life in a mental hospital, but he was struck by the similarities between mental hospitals and other organizations, such as prisons, boarding schools, monasteries, merchant ships, and military barracks, that apparently performed very different functions.

Total institutions broadly had in common the following features, though not all would be found in every institution:

▶ *The disappearance of private life.* All daily activities were carried out within the same organization. Any sense of a separate work or private life disappeared.

Goffman and total institutions

Erving Goffman was particularly interested in people's daily rituals and face-to-face interactions, with the construction, maintenance, and change of their sense of identity, and with the way that they present themselves to others and are seen by others (see Chapter 4, pp. 133–4). His research on mental hospitals suggested the idea of the total institution, and he developed his analysis of the interactions between staff and inmates in these organizations. As we go on to show, Goffman added a whole new dimension to Weber's approach to formal organizations and bureaucracy. We also point out the similarity with Foucault's work, and you might like to look at our discussion of this in Chapter 6, pp. 191–4.

▶ *Life in common.* Each daily activity was carried out at the same time by all the inmates together. Eating, for example, became a communal activity. People were moved around in batches and treated alike.

▶ *Planned and supervised activities.* Activities were timetabled and controlled in accordance with an overall plan for the organization.

▶ *Inmate/staff division.* There was a sharp division between staff with access to the outside world and inmates separated from it. There was little contact or communication between the two groups, which held stereotyped images of each other.

▶ *The mortification of the self.* Inmates experienced the 'death' of their previous identity. They lost their roles in the wider world, at work or in the family, which were central to their sense of identity and self-esteem.

Goffman particularly emphasized the way that people were systematically stripped of their previous identity. When they entered a total institution, they were required to change their clothing and personal objects important to their sense of self were removed. Routine humiliations forced them to act in ways that were inconsistent with their previous identity. This stripping of identity involved the penetration of their private space, which protected identity from the surrounding world. Goffman called this process a *contamination of the self*:

'The model for interpersonal contamination in our society is presumably rape; although sexual molestation certainly occurs in total institutions, there are many other less dramatic examples. Upon admission, one's on-person possessions are pawed and fingered by an official as he itemizes and prepares them for storage. The inmate himself may be frisked and searched to the extent—often reported in the literature—of a rectal examination. Later in his stay he may be required to undergo searchings of his person and of his sleeping quarters, either routinely or when trouble arises. In all these cases it is the searcher as well as the search that penetrates the private reserve of the individual and violates the territories of his self.' (Goffman 1961*b*: 35–6)

Goffman was particularly interested in the changes brought about by total institutions in the inmates' sense of self, and their responses and adaptations to the situation they found themselves in. He described these organizations as 'forcing houses for changing persons' (Goffman 1961*b*: 22).

Goffman's concept of the total institution is similar to Foucault's notion of the carceral organization, though Foucault was more interested in the techniques of control developed in these organizations rather than changes in the self. The concept of total institution was also applied to a more limited range of organizations. Thus, although Goffman recognized that some of the features of the total institution could be found in other organizations, he did treat total institutions as distinctive in character, while Foucault argued that the control techniques of the carceral organization were extended throughout society.

SUMMARY POINTS

In this section we have examined a range of definitional and theoretical issues raised by the study of organization:

▶ We discussed briefly the meaning of organization and suggested that organizations generally have a specific goal, a defined membership, rules of behaviour, and authority relationships.

We went on to consider Weber's ideal type of bureaucracy and the critique of the Weberian model by later studies of organizations:

▶ According to Weber, bureaucracies are hierarchical, disciplined, and impersonal organizations of salaried, career officials.

▶ Later studies of bureaucracy showed that obedience to the rules could be dysfunctional, while rule use and interpretation varied between groups and organizations.

▶ Criticism of the rigidity and formality of bureaucracy should be balanced by an awareness of its efficiency and impartiality.

We then considered the development of disciplinary techniques of control and the character of organizations that practise these techniques:

▶ Foucault argued that discipline involved control of the body, surveillance, and punishment.

▶ Disciplinary techniques were most fully developed in the prison, which became the model for other carceral organizations, and these techniques were eventually extended throughout society.

▶ Goffman's concept of the total institution was similar to Foucault's concept of carceral organization, though Goffman was primarily concerned with the impact of the total institution on the self.

THE ADMINISTRATIVE AND MANAGERIAL REVOLUTIONS

When we consider the nineteenth-century transformation of society, we tend to think of industrialization and the technological changes associated with the production of goods. Society was also transformed by the development of a technology of social control. There was an administrative revolution as well as an industrial revolution. This was followed by the development of management and what some have considered to be a managerial revolution.

In this section we first examine the emergence of the disciplined organizations that were at the heart of the administrative revolution. We then move on to consider the growth of management, the changing relationship between managers and owners, and the rise of public ownership.

DISCIPLINED ORGANIZATIONS

Discipline was the central feature of the new organizations of the nineteenth century. These organizations controlled people much more closely, whether in the army or the factory or the prison. They were administered by officials who operated in the self-disciplined manner of the modern bureaucrat. Discipline was maintained through techniques of control, surveillance, and systematic punishment.

Bureaucratization

Bureaucratization was central to the administrative revolution, though bureaucracies of a kind had long existed. We will briefly consider these earlier forms of bureaucracy in order to highlight the distinctiveness of the new bureaucracies of the nineteenth century.

Max Weber (1914) recognized that earlier forms of bureaucracy had been created by the empires of ancient Egypt, Rome, and China to administer the huge territories they conquered. In Egypt the problem of managing waterways led to the growth of a bureaucratic administration, which then enabled the construction of the pyramids. The officials in these early bureaucracies were, however, usually paid in kind, in the form of produce from the land they governed. They were often simply given control of this land to raise as much from it as they could. They therefore became involved in its daily exploitation, did not devote themselves to the conduct of their official duties, and were largely outside the ruler's control. This kind of bureaucracy was not a disciplined bureaucracy in the modern sense of the term.

The creation of salaried bureaucrats was crucial to the rise of modern bureaucracies, and it was the rise of capitalism that made a salaried state bureaucracy possible. As we showed earlier, payment by salary was a key feature of Weber's ideal type. It meant that bureaucrats could be full-time officials devoted to their duties and under the control of their superiors. Salaries could be paid only if the state had funds at its disposal. The state could acquire such funds only if there was a money economy for it to tax. The growth in Europe of a highly commercialized capitalist economy was therefore an essential condition for the emergence of the modern career bureaucrat. At this stage of bureaucratization, capitalism and bureaucracy went together.

The development of the state in the sixteenth and seventeenth centuries was closely related to the process of bureaucratization. The concern of rulers to establish greater control over their territories led to the appointment of salaried officials to administer them. This enabled rulers to escape the dependence on the loyalty of largely independent feudal lords which had been the central problem of the medieval monarchy. Since they were paid by the ruler, salaried bureaucrats were directly under the ruler's control and subject to royal discipline.

☞ **Bureaucratization was linked to other aspects of the development of the state, which we examine in Chapter 18. See especially, pp. 728–9, and the discussion of the relationship between state welfare and bureaucratization on pp. 736–7.**

But it was not just the bureaucratization of administration that was crucial. As Dandeker (1990) has emphasized, the bureaucratization of the military played a key part in the development of the modern state. This process got under way during the military revolution of the late sixteenth and early seventeenth centuries. Rulers had previously employed independent and unreliable mercenary armies under contract. They now developed disciplined and professional military forces that were loyal to the state. While this bureaucratization of the military was a part of the process by which rulers gained control of their territories, it was also closely linked to warfare between states. The political fragmentation of Europe led to frequent wars, which drove forward the development of the state and the process of bureaucratization.

While the foundations of modern bureaucracy had been established by these earlier changes, it was during the nineteenth century that there was a general bureaucratization of society. According to Max Weber (1914), modern societies developed bureaucratic organization partly because of the problems of administering large, heavily populated territories, but the pre-industrial empires had of course faced problems of this sort. What distinguished modern societies was the multiplicity of administrative tasks found within them and the importance of expertise in carrying them out. This resulted from what Weber called 'the increasing complexity of civilization', which was due to the greater wealth, the social problems, and the growing size of organizations in industrial societies.

The bureaucracies that emerged in the nineteenth century were highly rational organizations. They operated on the basis of the expertise of their officials and the knowledge stored in their files, rather than traditional customs and beliefs. They functioned in a disciplined and unemotional manner, and their activities were calculated, systematic, and predictable. As we showed in our earlier discussion of his work, Weber considered that the sheer technical superiority of bureaucracy over other forms of organization meant that it would triumph in all fields of human activity, in the business corporation, the church, and the university, as well as the state. Later in the chapter, on pp. 656–9, we examine the bureaucratization of the business corporation.

Incarceration

The prison was as typical an organization of the nineteenth century as the factory. Imprisonment eventually became the normal method of punishment for almost all offences, apart from murder, and the prison a characteristic organization of modern society.

The prison embodied all the new techniques for instilling discipline which Foucault identified. Local jails had certainly existed earlier but prisoners had not been incarcerated. They had not been shut off from contact with the outside world, confined in cells, or subjected to silence rules, as they often were in the new prison or penitentiary, as it was called to emphasize its punitive and disciplined character. Techniques of surveillance and control were steadily tightened and culminated in the opening of Pentonville, the new model prison, in London in 1842. Prisons had become carceral organizations.

The ultimate example of discipline and surveillance was the *panopticon*, the name given to Jeremy Bentham's nineteenth-century design for a prison. This was a circular building with the cells on the periphery and guards in a central tower. The cells extended the full width of the building and had a window on each side, so that prisoners could be observed from the tower and were silhouetted by the light coming from the outer window. Venetian blinds in the tower windows would make the guards invisible to the prisoners, who would not know whether they were under observation at any particular moment.

The principles of cellular subdivision, the total visibility of those under control, and the invisibility of those in control were all exemplified by this design. It also minimized costs by enabling the supervision of a large number of prisoners by a small number of guards. If no prison was ever built exactly on these lines, these principles of surveillance and control have been commonly applied.

The growth of imprisonment was linked to the development of industrial capitalism. Imprisonment for varying lengths of time provided a more systematic means of punishing and deterring crime than the more extreme and arbitrary methods that had previously been used. A more systematic means of punishment was needed because of the rise in crime that accompanied industrial capitalism. New property laws were introduced and, therefore, a new class of crimes against property was created. These new laws reflected the importance of the principle of private property in a capitalist society. Industrial capitalism also involved the

The transformation of the prison

The eighteenth century jail

'It was common for wives to appear daily at the gates bearing meals for their jailed husbands. They were given the run of prison yards from dawn until locking up, and a judiciously placed bribe would make it possible to remain inside at night. The sexual commerce between the inside and the outside was vigorous. As far back as the seventeenth century, one prisoner had observed that whores flocked to prison like "crowes to carrion". . . . Walls often no more than eight feet high, could not stop passers by from tossing food, notes, and letters over the other side, or stop prisoners from conversing with people in the street, or on occasion splashing them with dirty water.'

Source: Ignatieff (1978: 34–5)

The new penitentiary

'At Gloucester an eighteen-foot wall was constructed around the institution. Outsiders required written permission from the magistrates to get inside. For next of kin, visits were allowed only once every six months. No food, bedding, books, or furniture were allowed in from the outside. The penitentiary enforced a new conception of the social distance between the "criminal" and the "law-abiding". Walled away inside Gloucester, "deviants" lost that precarious membership in the community implied by the free access once allowed between the old jail and the street.'

Source: Ignatieff (1978: 101–2)

▶ **In what ways did the new penitentiary embody the techniques of discipline identified by Foucault?**

widespread trading and movement of goods, which meant that property required greater protection (Ignatieff 1978).

Industrial capitalism was also linked to imprisonment in other ways. Industrialization generated disorder as craftsmen reacted against changes that threatened their livelihoods, through, for example, the Luddite machine-breaking movement. Workers challenged the authority of the employer by organizing themselves in unions and taking strike action. Economic fluctuations produced unemployment and those without any means of subsistence resorted to crime. There was, indeed, a general problem of disorder in the new industrial cities, where large masses of people were concentrated outside the traditional rural structures for maintaining order.

Prisons were a way of isolating and managing those who threatened the new social order, as was the asylum for the mentally ill, which was also established at this time. In pre-industrial society, deviants could be absorbed and managed locally within the community. In the new industrial cities they were isolated in carceral organizations.

The state was closely involved in the whole process of incarceration. Governments passed the laws which defined behaviour as criminal and in the 1820s gave new powers to magistrates to deal with minor crimes. As the courts tightened up on petty crime, new police forces were created to catch the new criminals, though the immediate effect of this seems to have been the imprisonment of large numbers of people for vagrancy and drunkenness (Ignatieff 1978: 184–5). The state also funded, directed, and inspected both prisons and asylums.

Conceptions of deviance, of both criminality and madness, were changing. Criminals had previously been considered innately wicked and the mad were treated as uncontrolled animals. In the nineteenth century it was increasingly believed that both the bad and the mad could be reformed through the application of scientific expertise. Prisons and asylums were places where deviants could be cured as well as disciplined and isolated. It was indeed at this time that the medical model of madness emerged and asylums became seen as mental hospitals where the mentally ill could be treated by psychiatry, which was establishing itself as a branch of medicine. The creation of distinct organizations for criminals and patients was, therefore, also a result of the process of occupational specialization, and the rise of new professions.

Walling criminals away: Leicester's nineteenth-century prison.

Factory discipline

The maintenance of discipline was also of great importance to the new industrialists. Discipline was crucial to profitable production. Punctuality and uninterrupted work during fixed working hours were essential, for the division of labour meant that one worker's labour was dependent on that of others, while expensive machinery had to operate continuously if owners were to get a return on their capital at a time of intense competition.

Pollard (1965) argued that the widespread employment of children presented the early British industrialists with a particular problem of discipline. In the early nineteenth-century British cotton industry, for example, some 40 per cent of those employed were under the age of 18. Child labour was not new but when

Different means used by firms to discipline children in British industry, 1833	Negative means	No.	Positive means	No.
	▶ Dismissal	353	▶ Kindness	2
	▶ Threat of dismissal	48	▶ Promotion or higher wages	9
	▶ Fines, deductions	101	▶ Reward or bonus	23
	▶ Corporal punishment	55		
	▶ Complaints to parents	13		
	▶ Confined to mill	2		
	▶ Degrading dress, badge	3		
	Total	575	*Total*	34

Source: Factory Commission Survey of 1833 (S. Pollard 1965: 222).

production had been on a small workshop or household basis children were controlled by their parents or guardians. In the industrial factory this was no longer possible, while the machine-minding typical of factory work created a problem of boredom. According to Pollard (1965: 217), 'the new mass employment removed the incentive of learning a craft, alienated the children by its monotony, and did this just at the moment when it undermined the authority of the family, and of the father in particular'.

In early nineteenth-century Britain employers relied overwhelmingly on dismissal or the threat of dismissal to maintain discipline. This was a method that could work only when alternative sources of labour were freely available, which at this time was generally the case, for there was considerable labour migration and unemployment was often high. The use of fines or deductions from pay to maintain discipline was also widespread. Corporal punishment too was widely used, particularly where children were employed.

Techniques of labour management in factories developed relatively slowly, for the early entrepreneurs were preoccupied with such matters as machinery, transport, and finance. Specialized managers to take over responsibility for these various matters, and indeed for the management of labour, did not yet exist. Some of the more advanced employers, such as Robert Owen, did invent more subtle methods of control, but these were quite exceptional. In the harsh conditions of the Industrial Revolution, the means used to maintain discipline were overwhelmingly negative and relied, as Pollard has put it (1965: 243), on 'compulsion, force and fear'. The factory may not have been a prison, but it was certainly a place of punishment.

The prison was anyway there in the background to back up the authority of the factory-owner. Behind the employer stood the magistrate and laws that made worker organization illegal and breach of the contract of employment a crime, punishing workers more harshly than employers for this. Employers (and farmers) could use the courts to discipline their workers. Thus, the prison and the state played an important part in maintaining discipline in the factory.

THE DEVELOPMENT OF MANAGEMENT

It was the growth of larger and more complex businesses that led to the emergence of specialized and pro-

Monitoring work performance in the early industrial factory

'Best known of all were the "silent monitors" of Robert Owen. He awarded four types of mark for the past day's work to each superintendent, and each of them, in turn, judged all his workers; the mark was then translated into the colours black–blue–yellow–white, in ascending order of merit, painted on the four sides of a piece of wood mounted over the machine, and turned outward according to the worker's performance. These daily marks were entered in a book as a permanent record, to be periodically inspected by Robert Owen himself.'

Source: Pollard (1965: 225)

fessional management. In this section we examine first the development of 'scientific' labour management. We go on to consider the increasing power of managers and changes in the relationship between them and owners. Lastly, we consider the growth of public ownership and its implications for management.

Scientific management

As we showed above, the techniques used to manage labour in the early factories depended largely on punishment. Later in the nineteenth century, there was a movement towards the greater use of positive incentive schemes intended to increase productivity by paying workers according to the amount they produced. This approach was most systematically developed by the school of thought known as **scientific management**, which emerged in the United States in the 1880s.

The most famous exponent of scientific management was the engineer Frederick Taylor, who published his *Principles of Scientific Management* in 1911, and scientific management is sometimes referred to as Taylorism. Its key ideas were as follows:

► *The subdivision of labour.* Work should be broken down into the smallest possible tasks requiring a minimum of skill. Workers could then be trained easily to carry out a particular task in the shortest possible time.

► *Measurement and specification of work tasks.* Work should be scientifically studied in order to establish through 'time-and-motion' study the best way of performing a task, the exact movements required, and the time that they should take.

► *Selection and training.* Workers should be selected according to their ability to carry out a particular task and then trained in the best way to carry it out.

► *Motivation and reward.* Workers are solely motivated by the wages they earn. They should be paid not by the hour but according to the amount they produce. The price per item produced should be determined by the time taken to carry out the movements involved.

► *Individualism.* Workers are motivated by individual self-interest. Social contact between workers distracts them and should be kept to a minimum. Unions are unnecessary, since rates of pay can be determined scientifically and there is therefore no basis for a conflict of interest between workers and managers.

► *Management.* Management should be completely separated from labour. Production should be planned by management, which would give workers detailed instructions, which they should follow obediently to the letter.

This method of management appeared to be scientific because it was based on experiments, and involved the careful measurement of behaviour by work study engineers trained in its techniques. It was very much an engineering approach to the management of labour, for it treated workers as machines without feelings or culture. There was no recognition that work was a meaningful activity. This indeed meant that this approach to management was not really scientific at all, for it was not based on a genuinely scientific knowledge of people. Its claim to be scientific was, however, important in legitimating it in an age when science was identified with progress. Max Weber (1914) considered it to be the ultimate example of rational factory organization but also of the dehumanizing consequences of rationalization.

Scientific management was essentially a means for exploiting labour more effectively. Its emergence in the United States towards the end of the nineteenth century is usually explained in terms of declining industrial profits at this time and the rise of labour

---

Figure 16.1. Scientific management in action. How long does it take to open a drawer?

An American corporation's unit time values for clerical tasks

Opening and closing	Minutes
File drawer, open and close, no selection	0.04
Folder, open or close flaps	0.04
Desk drawer, open side drawer of standard desk	0.014
Open centre drawer	0.026
Close side drawer	0.015
Close centre drawer	0.027
Chair activity	
Get up from chair	0.033
Sit down in chair	0.033
Turn in swivel chair	0.009
Move in chair to adjoining desk or file (4 ft. max.)	0.050

Source: Braverman (1974: 321), quoting a 1960 guide to office clerical time standards.

movements (Clegg and Dunkerley 1980: 86). Declining profits stimulated employers to develop positive means of increasing productivity through incentives, rather than simply relying on punishment or the threat of dismissal. Scientific management was also a means of responding to the growing power of unions by taking a tight managerial control over labour. It particularly attacked the power of the craft unions of skilled workers, since it deskilled labour by subdividing it into the simplest possible tasks, which could be carried out by unskilled workers.

While it developed new techniques of management, it also embodied, however, the features of industrial capitalism identified by Marx and the technology of organizational control analysed by Foucault. The division of labour, its individualization, and the reliance on monetary incentives were considered by Marx to be typical of capitalist production. The subdivision of tasks, the training of the body in specified movements, and the individualist isolation of the worker exemplify Foucault's analysis of new disciplinary techniques. Scientific management also involved the close surveillance of labour by management, for it required the constant monitoring of a worker's movements and performance.

> ☞ See 'Capitalism', in Chapter 13, p. 501, for an outline of Marx's analysis of the capitalist mode of production. In Chapter 13, p. 512–18, we discuss scientific management, deskilling, and the meaning of work.

Managerial capitalism

The growing size and complexity of organizations resulted in the rise of managers as a distinct and powerful group. Some consider that managers have taken control of industry away from the owners of capital. Others, however, have rejected this view and argue that control has passed into the hands of *finance capitalists*.

Ownership and control were originally fused in the person of the industrial entrepreneur. During the period of the Industrial Revolution the entrepreneur was a factory-owner who carried out the functions of financier, works manager, engineer, merchant, and accountant. The problems of coordinating an increasingly specialized division of labour, the rapid development of technical expertise, and the growing size of companies made it impossible, however, to carry on in this way. In the early nineteenth century the more advanced British companies began to create specialized departments to take over particular functions. Owners retained overall control, but the detailed control of a company's activities was increasingly delegated to a managerial bureaucracy.

Ownership too changed. In the first half of the nineteenth century ownership was *personal* and factories were owned by an individual, a family, or a small number of partners. Mid-century legislation then made possible the spread of *impersonal* joint-stock companies. These were owned by shareholders, who could be any members of the general public who had invested in the company through the stock exchange. The new companies were controlled by directors, who were elected by and responsible to the shareholders. These companies allowed businesses to draw on a much wider pool of capital to finance investment. The importance of apparently rather technical changes in company law was immense, for they made possible the emergence of the giant corporations that dominate the world economy today.

Ownership and management grew increasingly distinct from each other as the ownership of companies became more widely spread. As companies grew in size, it became more difficult for any one individual, or even a group of people, to own a majority of the shares. Individual share ownership increased but so also did the ownership of shares by external organizations. This initially involved the growth of share ownership by banks and insurance companies, but later on ownership by organizations such as pension funds and investment trusts, which manage and invest people's savings for them, became very important. The growing size of corporations, particularly when this resulted from mergers, resulted in the creation of huge amounts of capital owned by a range of organizations and a large number of individuals.

The growing importance of managerial coordination made managers increasingly powerful figures. Also, as management became more specialized, corporations became more dependent on management expertise and specialist managers developed a degree of professional autonomy. Thus, personnel management and marketing, for example, became distinct fields in their own right, with their own career structures, qualifications, and professional institutes.

Alfred Chandler (1977) has examined the growth of management in the United States. Professional management began in the mid-nineteenth century with the spread of railroad and telegraph companies, whose functioning required administrative coordination of their operations. The establishment of mass production was another key step, for this involved the coordination of a number of production processes, most typically in the car assembly plant. It was above all, however, the creation of corporations, such as the giant oil companies, that combined the supply of raw materials, manufacturing, and the distribution of products, that led to the creation of large managerial hierarchies to coordinate these various operations.

There have been widely differing interpretations of these changes. On the one hand, there were those, such as Berle and Means (1932) and Alfred Chandler (1962), who argued that ownership and control had actually become separated. They claimed that share ownership had become so fragmented amongst a mass of small shareholders that owners no longer had any control over corporations. Control had passed into the hands of managers and a **managerial revolution** had taken place. Some argued that the exploitative capitalist had been replaced by the socially responsible manager. Managers were not concerned with profitability so much as keeping their companies going by balancing the competing claims of all those who had a stake in industry, from shareholders to trade unions.

On the other hand, Marxists, such as Hilferding (1910) and Aaronovitch (1961), claimed that ownership was more important than ever. The spread of share ownership reduced the power of individual owners, but enabled financial organizations with large shareholdings to become the *effective* owners. Effective owners were those who were able to use their ownership of shares to exert influence over the company, even though they might not own a majority of a company's shares. Economic power became increasingly concentrated as a small number of large banks became the effective owners and gained control of the large corporations that monopolized production. The age of industrial capital had been followed by the age of **finance capital.**

These writers too argued that ownership was separated from production, in the sense that finance capital was interested only in profit and not concerned with the management of production, so long as this was profitable. It was, however, not the managers but the finance capitalists, those who controlled the big banks and other financial organizations, who had ultimate power. They could hire and fire managers at will. Indeed, their concern with profit alone made them more ruthless than traditional industrial entrepreneurs, with their deep involvement in the day-to-day running of the business, had been.

John Scott (1997) has examined this debate in the light of the accumulated research and concludes that owners still exercise control. By owners he means, however, not small individual shareholders, for he agrees that they are powerless, but those in *effective pos-*

Interpretations of changes in ownership

Issues	Managerial theorists	Marxists
Ownership	Dispersed	Concentrated
Controllers	Managers	Banks/financial corporations
Social order	Post-capitalist society	Finance capitalism

session, who are typically a 'loose grouping of major shareholders'. Scott has called these groupings *constellations of interests.* These constellations are dominated by financial institutions, such as insurance companies, banks, and pension funds, but often include other non-financial companies as well and also some executives and wealthy families with large shareholdings. They are linked together by interlocking directorates. These involve the directors of one company having seats on the boards of others (see Figure 16.2 on p. 658).

The theories of managerial revolution and finance capital have each recognized important aspects of social change, but neither approach can be accepted in its entirety. Managers do, indeed, have day-to-day power and much autonomy in their decision-making, but they are *constrained* by the interests and pressures of the leading shareholders. These shareholders are in most cases not a tightly integrated group but a looser *constellation of interests.* The insights of the two theories need to be combined if we are properly to understand how business is controlled.

Public ownership

Changes in ownership were not just a matter of changes in the private ownership of capital, for in some societies the state began to take over the ownership of certain industries and services. This led to another aspect of the managerial transformation of capitalism, the growing state management of production.

Public ownership was seen by socialists as an essential step in the transition from a capitalist to a socialist or communist society. Marx and his followers

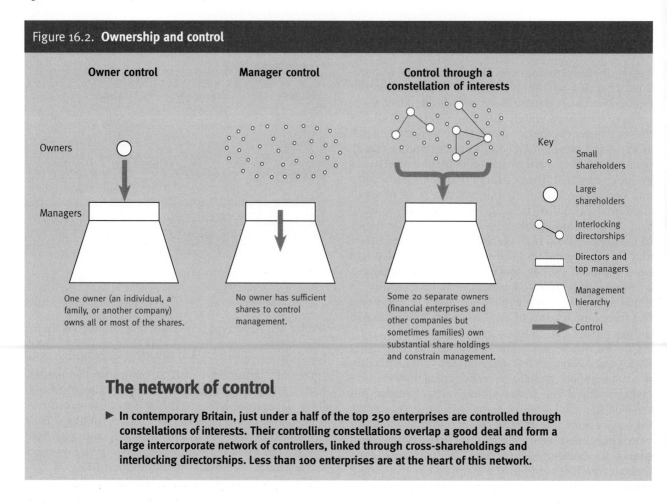

Figure 16.2. Ownership and control

Owner control

Owners

Managers

One owner (an individual, a family, or another company) owns all or most of the shares.

Manager control

No owner has sufficient shares to control management.

Control through a constellation of interests

Some 20 separate owners (financial enterprises and other companies but sometimes families) own substantial share holdings and constrain management.

Key

- Small shareholders
- Large shareholders
- Interlocking directorships
- Directors and top managers
- Management hierarchy
- Control

The network of control

▶ In contemporary Britain, just under a half of the top 250 enterprises are controlled through constellations of interests. Their controlling constellations overlap a good deal and form a large intercorporate network of controllers, linked through cross-shareholdings and interlocking directorships. Less than 100 enterprises are at the heart of this network.

considered that the private ownership of the means of production was the central feature of capitalism and the abolition of private ownership would lead to a classless society. Some Marxist writers believed that the growing concentration of ownership under finance capitalism had made it easier for the state to take control of industry, for it would only have to take over the small number of companies that were already in effective control of the economy. In the 1970s the Swedish labour movement developed a scheme for transferring the ownership of industry from private capital to worker-controlled funds (see box on p. 731).

Public ownership did develop in Britain but for rather different reasons. It began during the later nineteenth century with concerns in the cities to control the supply of water, gas, and electricity, and improve methods of urban transport. The first major expansion

of state control was driven by the imperatives of war. During the First World War the government took control of coal mining, the railways, shipping, and the munitions industry. All this was dismantled at the war's end, but there was some movement towards greater state control and public ownership during the inter-war years. This was motivated by nationalist rather than class concerns, by the problem of reorganizing Britain's more archaic industries, particularly coal mining, and the belief that new services, such as broadcasting and civil aviation, should be kept under state control.

The main extension of public ownership was carried out by the nationalizations of the Labour governments during 1945–52. This was certainly in part motivated by the labour movement's belief that key areas of the economy should be brought under public control. It

The growth of public ownership in the United Kingdom	Years	Main extensions of public ownership
	1850s–70s	Municipal ownership of water, gas, and trams
	1892–1912	Nationalization of telephone companies
	1914–18	State takes temporary control of transport, coal-mining, and munitions
	1920	Law passed to combine 120 railway companies into 4 regional groups
	1926	British Broadcasting Corporation created
	1926	Central Electricity Board created to buy and distribute electricity
	1933	London Passenger Transport Board created to control buses, trams, and underground lines
	1938	Coal Act takes coal reserves into state ownership
	1940	British Overseas Airways Corporation created
	1946	Bank of England nationalized
	1946	Coal, cable and wireless, and civil aviation nationalized
	1947	Road and rail transport nationalized
	1947	Electricity generation nationalized
	1948	British Gas created
	1948	National Health Service created
	1949	Steel industry nationalized

mainly resulted, however, from continued nationalist concerns with the backward, inefficient, and fragmented state of key industries and services. Public ownership was a means of overcoming backwardness and reorganizing these industries and services into more effective and modern units. It is significant that this extension of public ownership was described as the nationalization, not the socialization of ownership, the term used by Marxist exponents of public ownership.

What difference did nationalization make? Those who hoped for a socialist transformation of the economy were soon disappointed. Since each industry was run by its own relatively independent board, nationalization did not result in the increased planning of economic development. Although some token worker–director schemes were introduced, workers and their unions found that they had no greater influence over management than they had had before nationalization. The nationalized industries anyway had to operate within the framework of a capitalist economy and were soon themselves required to make a normal commercial profit on their operations.

This is not to say that nationalization achieved nothing, but it was more a vehicle for the state reorganization and coordination of particular industries and services than a means of controlling the economy or changing the capitalist relations of production. It led to greater state control but not to workers' control.

In state socialist societies, public ownership and state planning did become the norm. The ruling party directed economic development, planned production, and controlled the factories. Although factories were supposedly controlled by workers' councils, these actually became a means through which the ruling party controlled and disciplined labour, except in Yugoslavia. There, after a degree of independence had been established from the Soviet bloc in the later 1940s, workers' councils did acquire some real autonomy. There were no independent trade unions in state socialist countries, including Yugoslavia.

The state was in control and Weber's bureaucratic nightmare had been fully realized. As we pointed out in our discussion of Weber's view of bureaucracy, he was deeply concerned that bureaucratization would weaken democracy and result in a loss of freedom and creativity. He considered that this was particularly likely to happen under socialism, for the power of the bureaucrat would no longer be balanced by the power of the owner of private capital.

SUMMARY POINTS

In this section we have sketched out the main features of the administrative and managerial revolutions. We began by outlining the processes leading to the emergence of disciplined organizations:

▶ Bureaucratization involved the development of organizations staffed by salaried and disciplined officials under the control of their superiors.

▶ The use of industrial capitalism resulted in the systematic punishment of offenders through imprisonment and the establishment of carceral organizations to isolate and control deviants in a cost-effective way.

▶ The early industrialists maintained discipline largely through the threat of dismissal, though they also used fines, corporal punishment, and punishment through the courts.

We went on to consider the growth of labour management and the changing relationships between managers and owners.

▶ Scientific management developed new techniques for the management of labour, based on individual incentives, the subdivision of work tasks, and the detailed control of the worker's movements.

▶ The growing power of managers and the spread of ownership increasingly separated management from ownership, though the owners of capital were still in ultimate control.

▶ Increasing public ownership resulted in greater state control, particularly in state socialist societies, but not greater workers' control.

TOWARDS NEW STRUCTURES OF CONTROL

The techniques of control developed during the nineteenth and early twentieth centuries enabled a massive expansion in both the productive capacity of industrial capitalism and the apparatus of the modern state. During the twentieth century these techniques were, however, challenged, and new methods of control began to emerge that reacted against earlier tendencies.

Some debureaucratization has occurred, while management theory has moved away from the techniques of scientific management towards a more integrative style of management concerned with workers' feelings and emotions. Privatization has resulted in a shift from the bureaucratic control of industries and services to market control. There has also been a process of decarcerating the mad and the bad, though this was followed by a renewed emphasis on the imprisonment of offenders.

But have these changes reversed earlier developments or taken place within the framework established by the administrative revolution? That is the broad issue that we will be discussing in the rest of this chapter.

DEBUREAUCRATIZATION?

Although Weber was highly critical of bureaucracy, he considered that its technical superiority meant that it would become the dominant form of organization in modern societies. As we showed on p. 645, the efficiency of the bureaucratic model has, however, been questioned, and we consider here the alternative forms of organization that have emerged. We also discuss the feminist argument that bureaucracy is patriarchal in character and organizations should be feminized.

Flexible organizations

Rigidity was one of the main features of bureaucracy revealed by case studies of organizations. More flexible forms of organization that are more appropriate to situations of rapid technical change or market uncertainty have been developed. In their classic study of the Scottish electronics industry in the 1950s, Burns and Stalker (1961) showed how a more flexible form of organization, which they called *organic* organization, had emerged. They contrasted this with *mechanistic* organization, which they also found within this industry.

The *mechanistic* type had a clearly specified division of labour, coordinated by a hierarchy of managers. Everyone knew exactly what their job required and what their responsibilities were. Decisions were taken at the top of the organization, where the knowledge of business matters was concentrated. Orders came from the top down and subordinates were expected to obey instructions. This structure led to conflicts between *line* and *staff* managers.

The conflict between line and staff managers was an example of the conflict between hierarchy and expertise which is commonly found in bureaucratic organizations. Line management is concerned with production and operates in a hierarchical way, transmitting orders down to the workforce. Staff managers are specialized experts in particular fields, such as personnel, marketing, or technology. As Gouldner (1954) pointed out, there is a tension in the Weberian model of bureaucracy between authority based on expertise and authority based on hierarchical position.

The *organic* type was much more flexible. Jobs changed as the company's situation changed and relationships evolved within the organization. Roles were not clearly defined and there was little sense of particular responsibilities. Positions were still stratified by seniority but authority was exercised by those with most expertise, wherever they were located, through a network rather than a hierarchy. Communication tended to be lateral rather than vertical. The ethos of the organization was not obedience to authority but collective problem-solving. Commitment was not to the duties of the job but to the goals of the company and wider values of technical progress.

The *mechanistic* organization was clearly the more bureaucratic of the two. Although it conformed to the principles laid down by classic management teaching, its machine-like character made it inflexible and it responded poorly to the demands of change in an industry with a high rate of technical innovation. Burns and Stalker concluded that the more flexible *organic* form was much more appropriate to an environment of rapid technical change. They did not, however, argue that it was superior to the mechanistic form or that bureaucratic organization was outmoded. They recognized that the *mechanistic* form was more appropriate to situations of stable production.

A more radical and more recent departure from the classic bureaucratic organization is the network organization, which is a much more open structure based on advances in *information technology*. Computer networks can link not only those inside a company but those outside, so that a factory, its component suppliers, and retailers are all interlinked. Instead of operating on the basis of the detailed regulation of its members' behaviour, the network organization plugs them into production on a contractual basis when it requires their work. It operates on the basis of market rather than bureaucratic coordination.

Thus, the organization can subcontract work through the network to self-employed tele-workers or specialist outside organizations who provide services when required. Instead of directly employing designers or marketing specialists it can simply call them in through the network when it needs them. At the other end of its activities, instead of selling its products, it can produce according to the orders coming through the network from retailers or franchised outlets. Rapid communication and a highly flexible structure make a network organization a highly appropriate form of organization to post-Fordist production, which we discuss in Chapter 13, pp. 528–30.

It is hard to establish the boundaries of a network organization or distinguish between its internal and external activites. Benetton is one of the best-known examples of such an organization and Stewart Clegg (1990) has raised the question of how we can determine its extent. If the organization is defined by its employees, then Benetton consists of certain design and production facilities in north Italy. But are not Benetton's thousands of retail outlets, which are franchised

---

Mechanistic and organic organizations

Mechanistic	Organic
► Rigid division of labour	► Flexible tasks
► Hierarchy	► Network
► Authority based on position	► Authority based on expertise
► Obedience to authority	► Collective problem-solving
► Instructions	► Advice and consultation
► Defined duties/ responsibilities	► General commitment to goals
► Vertical communications	► Lateral
Stability	*Change*

Source: adapted from Burns and Stalker (1961: 119–22).

operations that are not staffed by Benetton employees but sell only Benetton products, part of its organization? What about the hundreds of small firms and the homeworkers who make Benetton products or carry out certain stages in production, such as the finishing-off of clothing?

The subcontracting of components production or the use of homeworkers to finish goods is nothing new, but what distinguishes Benetton is that the bulk of its production is carried out in this way. Stewart Clegg (1990: 121) suggests that Benetton should be thought of 'less as an organization *per se* and rather more as an organized network of market relations premised on complex forms of contracting made possible by advances in microelectronics technology'.

It is important to emphasize that information networks actually facilitate central control. They do enable the flow of information across the organization, so that communications are lateral and not dependent on central coordination or a managerial hierarchy. They also, however, provide those who control an organization with access to detailed information about the productivity and performance of its members.

The network organization may be a departure from the Weberian model of coordination by a hierarchy of officials but it exemplifies the tendency towards increasing surveillance identified by Foucault. The surveillance possibilities of information technology are almost limitless and many people now work in what can be called 'electronic panopticons' (see p. 652 for a description of the panopticon). The speed with which workers process data, the number of work operations they carry out, the sales they make, the frequency and length of their telephone calls, can all be monitored at any time without them being aware that they are under observation.

Cultural alternatives

Much of the early literature on organizations assumed that the principles of organization were universal, but subsequent studies showed that there were international variations in the character of organizations. Thus, it was from studying a factory in the United States that Gouldner developed the concept of *representative* bureaucracy as an alternative to the *punishment-centred* Weberian form, which was based on German experience. The more democratic culture of American society had produced a less autocratic form of bureaucracy. Crozier showed how an exceptionally rigid form of bureaucracy had developed in France.

The economic success of East Asian countries has led to a growing interest in their organizational patterns and the possibility of learning from their experience. We will consider here Stewart Clegg's (1990) account of the Japanese and Chinese patterns of organization.

Japanese industrial organization typically involves less specialized and more flexible occupations than a Western industrial organization. Workers are not seen as having particular skills but are expected to carry out any task required by management. They are moved through the various operations in a factory and acquire a knowledge of the connections between its various parts. This improves communication, which follows lateral rather than vertical paths. Research and development are less separated from production, for their personnel will have had experience of each other's work. Management is similarly unspecialized and there is a regular rotation of managers through different functions.

 To understand the wider context in which this kind of organization has developed, refer to the discussion of the integrative character of Japanese industrial relations in Chapter 13, pp. 532–3.

Chinese business organization in Taiwan is radically different in form from both the modern Western and Japanese models. Chinese businesses are organized on a family basis. The head of the family that owns the

---

A network organization

'In 1990 Lithonia Lighting, in Georgia USA, was the world's largest supplier of lighting equipment, but its competitors were catching up fast. Lithonia took a radical re-look at its organization and realized the factory was not, as they assumed, the real hub of the organization; that place belonged to their agents, who were not even employed by them, but who generated all their business. A plan emerged to create a network . . . Computers now link specifiers, agents and factories. Computer-aided design systems allow products to be tailor-made. Distributors can check stock on-line with warehouses and factories and the computers route components for each order direct to the relevant factory. . . . Lead times on orders were cut from nine days to less than one. Sales and profits doubled over six years.'

Source: The Economist, 6 Oct. 1990, quoted in Handy (1993: 272).

business controls it and the key tasks of managerial surveillance and control are kept, if possible, inside the family. Authority is related to age. Relationships are personal, familial, and based on trust—quite opposite in character to the impersonal and formalized relationships of bureaucratic organizations.

As Clegg points out, while *small* family businesses everywhere will tend to have these features, in Taiwan they are found in *large* organizations as well. Indeed, it is the need to provide an inheritance for sons, who will receive equal shares of the father's estate, that drives the expansion of Taiwan family businesses. When profits lead to the accumulation of capital, new businesses are founded, which are run by members of the family, usually by sons, who inherit them on the death of their father.

These examples show that unbureaucratic forms of organization can work well in the contemporary world. They also show that there is no such thing as a single East Asian model. Japanese and Taiwanese businesses are organized on very different principles but both have been highly successful. The success of the East Asian models also suggests that the structures promoting organizational effectiveness are culturally specific. What works in one society with one set of beliefs and practices will not work in another.

Clegg warns, however, against jumping from a universalism that ignores culture to a cultural determinism that explains everything in terms of it. Both Japan and Taiwan are Confucianist in culture, but they have developed very different organizational patterns. Clegg proposes instead an *embedded* view of organization. This accepts that organizations are based in a particular societal context but includes in this not only the culture but also the institutions, laws, and policies of the society. It also recognizes that the character of organizations is not *determined* by their context, for they are actively *constructed* out of the 'materials available' (S. R. Clegg 1990: 7).

Feminizing the organization

So far our discussion of the bureaucratic model has been concerned largely with issues of efficiency and flexibility. Another line of criticism has come from those who argue that Weber's emphasis on the formality and impersonality of bureaucracy conceals its gendered character.

Bureaucracy and patriarchy have been historically interrelated and mutually reinforcing. Nineteenth-century bureaucratization took place in a highly patriarchal society and produced male-dominated organizations. During the twentieth century these organizations increasingly employed women but in junior clerical positions, where they were excluded from promotion.

Banking provides a good example of this. Up until the 1960s sex discrimination in banking was quite explicit, with separate salary scales for men and women, and the requirement that women had to resign from their jobs when they got married, though they were usually then reappointed to non-career grades. It was not until the 1980s that this situation really changed, after the recruitment practices of Barclays Bank had been referred in 1983 to the Equal Opportunities Commission (Crompton 1997).

Patriarchy was manifest not only in the exclusion of women from bureaucratic careers, but also in the dependence of the male career on gendered domestic roles. This applied both inside and outside the office. Inside the office gendered roles took the form of the male boss–female secretary relationship, which made secretaries into 'office wives', who carried out personal caring functions and provided emotional support for the boss. Outside the office, the successful male career depended also on the housewife, whose servicing and emotional labour enabled a man to give his time and energy to his organization. The bureaucrat's self-disciplined devotion to duty, which was central to Weber's ideal type, depended on the domestic division of labour.

👉 **We discuss patriarchy, the domestic division of labour, and emotional labour in Chapter 10, pp. 366–7 and 386–90.**

If gender is important to office relationships, what about sexuality? As we pointed out earlier, the Weberian ideal type emphasized the rational and non-emotional character of bureaucratic organizations. This meant that sexuality has been largely left out of studies of organizations. Pringle argues, however, that it actually pervades the office 'in dress and self-presentation, in jokes and gossip, looks and flirtations, secret affairs and dalliances, in fantasy, and in the range of coercive behaviours that we now call sexual harassment' (1989: 90).

What is the significance of sexuality at work? Some have treated it as inappropriate behaviour that spills into the work setting but is nothing to do with work. Thus, Kanter (1977) recognized the existence of sexual behaviour in the office but treated it as a hangover of pre-bureaucratic relationships that should be

Are bureaucracies patriarchal?

eliminated. This approach maintained the Weberian view of bureaucracy as an impersonal structure in which emotional and sexual relationships should play no part. The problem with this view of sexuality as something external to organization was that it overlooked the part it played in the relationships of the organization.

Others have argued that it is an integral part of authority relationships in work organizations. According to this view, sexual harassment at work is not just a spilling-over of non-work behaviour into the work situation; it is one of the means by which male superiors establish their power over female inferiors. It is also a way of justifying the exclusion of women from occupations that involve 'serious' work and positions of power by treating women as irrational reservoirs of sexuality and emotionality.

The general treatment of sexual behaviour at work as sexual harassment also presents other problems. While Pringle accepts that sexual behaviour is a means by which women are subordinated, she points out that it can make women 'the pathetic victims of sexual harassment'. She suggests that account must also be taken of 'the power and the pleasure' that women can get from sexual interaction at work (Pringle 1989: 101–2).

One feminist response to patriarchal bureaucracies is that they should be forced to open their senior posi-

tions to women. The increased education of women and feminist pressure for equal opportunities have enabled some women to gain access to senior positions, though Savage (1992) points out that women moving into managerial and professional jobs typically move into posts that involve expertise rather than authority.

Furthermore, although the opening-up of careers to women may reduce discrimination, it does not necessarily make organizations less patriarchal in character. Women may have to act like men in order to reach and hold senior positions. Crompton and Le Feuvre reported that many of the women managers they studied 'had felt constrained to behave as "surrogate men"—even to the extent of remaining childless' (1992; 116). Women in senior posts can, none the less, make a difference. Watson (1992) has argued that 'femocrats' in the relatively open Australian state bureaucracy have been able to make some important, though limited, changes in policies, laws, services, and the bureaucracy itself that are favourable to women.

A more radical approach argues that bureaucracies cannot be feminized by women in senior positions because bureaucracies are inherently masculine in character. Their emphasis on hierarchy, formality, and impersonality is typically male. Women should instead seek to create a different kind of organization that embodies the female qualities of 'caring and sharing'.

There are two strands to this argument. It *first* involves a belief in alternative non-bureaucratic forms of organization. Activities can and should be organized in a more democratic, more participatory way, on the basis of cooperation and sharing rather than conflict and division. It *secondly* argues that women are more able than men to create this kind of organization. The organizations created by the women's movement are said to have this character.

As Witz and Savage have pointed out, the problem with this approach is that it assumes 'gender-differentiated modes of social action' (1992: 20). It presupposes that women are socialized into more participatory, cooperative, caring, and sharing patterns of behaviour. This kind of socialization is itself, however, a consequence of patriarchy, since it is male domination that pushes women into caring roles in the household. The notion of the feminine organization is, in other words, itself bound up with patriarchal assumptions.

They suggest that, instead of attaching different principles of organization to gender, we should recognize that organizations require both 'male' and 'female' activities and that both men and women can carry out both sets of activities. What matters is the relationship between these activities, and the way they are divided and distributed between men and women. Witz and

Solicitors and secretaries

'The most claustrophobic example of control through sexuality (no-one had yet labelled it "harassment") concerns a legal practice which was, for a country town, quite large. The atmosphere was one of compulsory jocularity: solicitors and secretaries gaily exchanged insults and sexual banter with each other all day, and there was a great deal of friendly fondling and patting of bottoms. They also intermarried and had a shared social life of parties and barbeques. Ex-secretaries with their babies were regular visitors, and often came back to work on a part-time or temporary basis. Beneath the enforced egalitarianism and informality there was a rigidly enforced sexual division of labour. The partners could not imagine taking on a woman lawyer or the possibility that any of the "girls" might have the capacity to do "law". . . . The women were clear that their role was to service men and were willing to put up with what was constant sexual innuendo. The overall feel of the place was not dissimilar to a brothel. While the secretaries made continuous use of mockery and parody. It seemed only to reaffirm them in "traditional" boss–secretary relationships.'

Source: Pringle (1989: 93–4).

▶ **Have you come across examples of sexual behaviour or the use of sexual language in organizations that you have worked for?**

▶ **What affect has this had on work relationships?**

Three ways of feminizing organizations

▶ **Femocracy**: increasing women's access to senior positions.
▶ **Feminine organizations**: creating alternative feminine organizations.
▶ **Degendering activities**: Redistributing activities equally between men and women.

Savage argue that work activities should be degendered. As they nicely put it, 'men can no longer go on simply organizing the world; they have to take responsibility for tidying it up too' (Witz and Savage 1992: 26).

Post-modern organizations and debureaucratization?

It has been argued that a new form of **post-modern organization** has emerged from the changes that we have been discussing. This position has been most clearly advanced by Stewart Clegg (1990), who identifies *modern* organization with the Weberian model of bureaucracy and *post-modern* organization with the alternative organizational structures that have emerged. Organic organizations, the East Asian models, and network organizations are all examples of post-modern organization and Clegg is at pains to emphasize that there is no single post-modern form.

According to Stewart Clegg, the main feature of the modern organization is **differentiation**, while the post-modern organization is characterized by **dedifferentiation** (S. R. Clegg 1990: 21, 181). By differentiation he means the division of labour into specialized roles, so that both workers and managers carry out highly specified tasks. Dedifferentiation enables organizations to become more flexible by requiring workers to be multi-skilled and managers to be generalists. While differentiated organizations are hierarchical and have central coordination, dedifferentiated ones are decentralized and take more of a network form, which, as in the Benetton case, may well dissolve the organization as a distinct and bounded entity.

Clegg's distinction between modern and post-modern organizations is very similar to that made between Fordism and post-Fordism in Chapter 13, pp. 528–30. The concept of post-modern organization helps us to make connections between organizational changes and the changes in production that have been labelled post-Fordism. Both increase the flexibility of business operations and they have both been driven by increasing competition and technological change. Neither the organic organizations studied by Burns and Stalker nor the East Asian models have, however, resulted from recent changes. It can, therefore, be a little misleading to treat them as post-modern in character. This is particularly the case with the long-established East Asian models.

Modern and post-modern organizations

Modern (Fordism)	Post-modern (post-Fordism)
▶ Differentiated	▶ Dedifferentiated
▶ Specialized roles	▶ Unspecialized
▶ Centralized	▶ Decentralized
▶ Hierarchy	▶ Network
Mass production	*Flexible production*

Has a process of **debureaucratization** taken place? It has in the sense that certain aspects of the process of bureaucratization have been challenged and reversed. On the one hand, a growing awareness of the disadvantages of bureaucracy and of the existence of alternatives that seem to work better has led to the construction of less bureaucratic forms of organization. The growth of organizational studies has contributed to this process by stimulating reflection on organizational character and structure. It has assisted with the conscious design of more appropriate organizations for particular purposes and drawn attention to structures embodying different principles and values. On the other hand, organizations have had to adapt to changes in their environment, to advances in information technology, changing markets, and feminist challenges.

These changes have occurred only in some organizations, however. Ritzer argues that the broad tendency of organizational development is towards greater rationalization and bureaucratization. He calls this the McDonaldization of society. He claims that the principles of the fast-food restaurant exemplify the ration-

alizing tendencies identified by Max Weber as characteristic of modern society. McDonald's offers efficiency, calculability, and predictability, and tightly controls its employees (see the opening extract of this chapter). It also controls the behaviour of its customers, by, for example, providing uncomfortable seats that 'lead diners to do what management wishes them to do—eat quickly and leave' (Ritzer 1996: 11).

There has been no debureaucratization of society as a whole. Bureaucratic organization remains the principle way of organizing large-scale activities and information technology has simply improved their coordination and increased central control of them. The bureaucratic model has been challenged in some businesses, where greater flexibility and higher commitment have become crucial to competitiveness. In other businesses, however, bureaucratic organization continues to be the best way of coordinating the routine production of standard goods. Bureaucratic organization also remains central to activities concerned with health, safety, equal opportunities, and protection of the environment, where objectivity, consistency, and impersonality are essential.

As we show in Chapter 18, pp. 749–50, although deregulatory government policies have diminished state regulation in some important areas of activity, the overall level of regulation has probably increased—and regulation almost always means bureaucratic organization. The term 'debureaucratization' is a useful means of drawing attention to important changes in some organizations, but these must be placed in the context of an increasingly bureaucratic society.

THE TRANSFORMATION OF MANAGEMENT

The organizational changes examined under the heading of debureaucratization were paralleled by changes in management techniques. Management thinking shifted from an emphasis on formal to informal structures, from authoritarian to integrative styles of control, from specialization to general commitment. In this section we first examine the development of the human-relations approach and then go on to consider human-resource management.

Human relations

The development of these new techniques began with the emergence of the human-relations school of management. This grew out of, but also reacted against, the *scientific-management* approach that we examined on pp. 655–6. The human-relations approach emerged from interpretations of the Hawthorne Experiments, which were conducted during the years 1924–32 at the Hawthorne factory of the Western Electric company in the United States. These experiments are important not only because of their significance for the development of management thought but also because of their methodological implications.

The first experiments were very much in the scientific-management tradition. They examined the effects of changes in lighting on the productivity of a group of workers. The experimenters found to their surprise that almost any changes they made, whether, for example, they increased or decreased the amount of light, resulted in higher productivity. They also found that productivity rose in the control group as well as the experimental group. They concluded that the conduct of the experiment had itself raised productivity. The interest shown by the investigators in the workers had changed their attitudes to their work and this had more effect on their behaviour than the experimental changes. They had discovered what has been labelled the 'Hawthorne effect'—that is, the effect of a study on the behaviour of those being studied.

This discovery led to many further experiments designed to explore the social context of work. These showed that productivity was not a matter of individual responses to monetary incentives, as assumed by scientific management. Production was regulated by the group, which established output norms and put pressure on individuals who overproduced or underproduced to conform to them.

The behaviour of work groups was in turn seen as largely the result of the style of supervision. The restriction of output was interpreted as a defensive response by workers fearing managerial interference in their work lives. Supervisors who allayed workers' anxieties, and encouraged their participation in decision-making, obtained higher levels of production.

The **human-relations** approach is generally considered to be an advance on scientific management. It rejected the individualism of scientific management and recognized the importance of group influences on the individual. It established the significance of workers' non-economic needs and argued for an essentially integrative style of management based on meeting these needs. It gave a boost to the development of personnel managers as human-relations specialists. It generally treated workers as human beings rather than machines—hence the term *human relations*.

It was claimed that the Hawthorne Experiments provided a scientific basis for the human-relations approach, but the results of the experiments have been interpreted in other ways. Carey (1967) re-examined the data and concluded that they could also support the argument that workers respond to monetary incentives. The restriction of output by the work group has also been interpreted differently. Thus, Rose (1975) has argued that it was not necessarily a response to supervisory practices, for it was quite rational to restrict output in order to make a job last as long as possible, given the high unemployment at the time. Thus, the conclusions drawn by the human-relations approach reflected a particular interpretation of the experiments' results.

The work group rules!

The rules established by one group observed during the Hawthorne Experiments.

▶ 'You should not turn out too much work. If you do, you are a "rate-buster".

▶ You should not turn out too little work. If you do, you are a "chiseler".

▶ You should not tell a supervisor anything . . . to the detriment of an associate. If you do, you are a "squealer".

▶ You should not attempt to maintain social distance or act officious. If you are an inspector, for example, you should not act like one.'

Source: Roethlisberger and Dickson (1939: 522).

The human-relations approach was, therefore, based not only on the Hawthorne Experiments but also on a particular social theory. One of the leading exponents of the approach, Elton Mayo, who directed the later stages of the experiments, believed that the integration of labour in a work community could solve tendencies in society towards excessive individualism. He was influenced by Durkheim's ideas and believed that the problem of anomie could best be solved by developing integrated industrial communities (for Durkheim's theory of anomie, see Chapter 1, pp. 8–9).

Three main lines of criticism have been advanced against the human-relations approach. First, it has been argued that it overemphasized the importance of informal social relationships. Having discovered the work group, it forgot about the significance of technology and organizational structure. Secondly, it failed to take account of the wider social context of worker behaviour. Goldthorpe *et al.* (1968a) showed that attitudes to work were at least partly shaped by orientations to work brought into the factory from the outside. Thirdly, it treated industrial conflict as irrational and assumed that it could be eliminated by more effective management. There was no sense that industrial conflict resulted from the conflict of interests between labour and capital.

☞ Refer here to our discussion of the meaning of work and its relationship to technology, of schemes to increase work satisfaction, and of the significance of orientations to work, in Chapter 13, pp. 512–18.

These criticisms were at least partially met by later developments. In the 1950s and 1960s what has been called the *neo-human-relations* approach ('neo' simply means 'new') placed less emphasis on community and took more account of organizational structure, technology, and conflict in the workplace. New techniques of work organization were developed to provide more meaningful work by rotating, enlarging, or enriching work tasks. The existence of conflict was recognized in schemes to give workers greater participation in management through various kinds of consultative arrangements, such as works councils.

The human-relations approach has been generally criticized for its managerial assumptions and it was certainly concerned with developing more effective means of managerial control. It was also limited by its focus on what went on within the confines of the work situation. Its understanding of worker behaviour was, however, an advance on that of scientific management, while in its later stages it became considerably more sophisticated in its analysis of the experience of work and work relationships. It was also based on a substantial body of research, which greatly increased our knowledge of social behaviour at work.

Human-resource management

Human-resource management (HRM) is the name given to a new emphasis in management thought since the 1980s on the central importance of a company's labour force in creating competitiveness. Like the human-relations approach, HRM seeks to integrate workers into the company but it has gone considerably further in its aims and techniques. It argues that personnel issues are too important to be left to personnel managers as human-relations specialists. They must become a central concern of *all* managers, especially top management, for a company's human resources are its most important resources. It is also more ambitious than the human-relations approach in its mission to change the whole culture and organization of the workplace.

Human relations versus scientific management	Aspects of management	Scientific management	Human relations
	Motivation of worker	Money	Social needs
	Unit of analysis	Individual	Work group
	Organizational structure	Formal	Informal
	Work tasks	Subdivided	Rotated, enlarged, enriched
	Management style	Coercive	Integrative
	Interpretation of worker behaviour	Rational, calculative	Irrational, emotional

Exponents of HRM argue that *cultural change* is crucial to competitiveness, because it is employee attitudes and beliefs that really matter. The goal of management should be to seek not a bureaucratic obedience to company rules and policies but rather the total commitment of employees to the company. Mission statements, cultural change programmes, staff development, and appraisal are typical techniques for developing this commitment. The selection of employees is also crucial, to make sure that a company recruits people who are capable of this kind of commitment.

Cultural change requires *organizational change*. Organizations should be decentralized to shift responsibility downwards in order to empower the workforce. Instead of allocating workers to specified tasks, managers should create flexible teams that can take responsibility for managing themselves and carrying out whatever work is required to meet the objectives of the company. Quality circles should be introduced to involve workers in the process of improving the quality of the product.

This highly integrative approach to the management of labour leaves little room for an independent trade unionism. Unions are based on the assumption that there is a conflict of interest between employers and employees, but HRM emphasizes the cultural unity of a company as it engages in an intensely competitive struggle with its rivals. It is, therefore, opposed to collective bargaining and seeks to individualize the relationship between the worker and the company, through individual contracts, appraisal, and performance-related pay.

HRM requires cultural and organizational changes in management as well as labour. Managers must alter their own customary ways of thinking, if they are to bring about cultural change and introduce the new programmes to achieve it. Intermediate layers of management should be stripped out, partly because they are no longer necessary if responsibility is devolved, partly because HRM calls for a closer and more direct relationship between management and labour. Thus, as Storey (1995*a*: 7) puts it, 'the panoply of HRM technology is seen in its fullest form in the management of managers'.

These ideas are linked to the growing interest in Japanese-style management that emerged during the 1980s. Japanese companies had been out-competing Western companies and one reason for their success appeared to be their much higher levels of employee commitment. Japanese workers were expected to stay with their company throughout their careers and subordinate themselves totally to it.

 HRM and the Japanese-style integration of employees into the company are closely linked to 'the "new" industrial relations', which we discuss in Chapter 13, pp. 532–3.

Thus Japanese workers have to take part in quality-circle meetings and suggest ways of improving production. They have to work long hours and sacrifice weekends and holidays to the requirements of their company. They are expected to spend much of what leisure time is left attending company social events or engaging in bonding activities with colleagues after work. It is no accident that the Japanese have a word for death through overwork—*karoshi* (see box on p. 670).

As with post-Fordism and the flexible firm, some take a sceptical view of HRM and treat it as little more than managerial rhetoric. Legge (1995) finds little to distinguish HRM from the standard prescriptions of personnel management, and argues that practice anyway falls far short of the claims made by its exponents. She sees HRM as a management fad generated by those, such as business gurus, management consultants, and publishers, who make money by riding new bandwagons. HRM has also become big business in higher education, as a justification for new posts and new degrees, for publications and research projects. Managers too use HRM qualifications to advance their careers. Personnel managers can become HRM missionaries at a time when the decline of labour organization has diminished their role as 'managers of the unions'.

Storey (1995*a*) believes, however, that HRM is distinctive and that management has been changing. He presents survey evidence that shows the growing use of HRM techniques, though he found that few companies had adopted the full HRM package. HRM is also clearly interrelated with other changes, such as the development of 'post-modern organizations', which we discussed on pp. 665–6, and post-Fordist methods of production, which we examine in Chapter 13, pp. 528–30. Similar pressures for more competitive, more flexible, more customer-oriented organizations lie behind all these innovations, and they have all been influenced by a growing interest in the advantages of non-Western alternatives.

New management styles and new methods of control have certainly developed in some companies, but this does not mean that older techniques of management have been superseded. Scientific management lives on and work-study engineers still carry out time and motion studies to establish the best way of performing a task and the time it ought to take. Legge suggests that

Work in a Japanese car factory

Inside Toyota.

'In recent years demand for the company's product has been brisk and two hours of overtime are routinely required. . . . With overtime the working day from start to finish is typically 11 hours long. . . . Even though their day is long, workers can expect little free time for rest and relaxation in the course of the working day. The scheduled meal breaks are often taken up with company business, such as Quality Circle meetings. When the norm is 32 suggestions per worker per year, membership of an 8 or 10 person Quality Circle imposes real obligations. Workers are formally entitled to 2 days off each week but, in recent years, they have been obliged to work 6 days so that the company can extract more output from existing capacity. Their one day off may not be completely free because loyal workers are expected to join in company sports and social events. Finally, the day off may be taken mid-week at the convenience of the company and the inconvenience of the worker's family. In the summer of 1987 Nippon Car chose to work Saturdays and Sundays because the local electricity utility charged a lower tariff at weekends.'

Source: Williams *et al.* (1994: 61).

HRM techniques may anyway not be appropriate in businesses where production is labour intensive, work tasks are routine, and profits depend on producing large quantities of goods at the lowest possible cost.

In such circumstances, the most effective management of human resources may be simply to force labour to work as hard as possible. In some companies the most effective management of human resources may not require HRM techniques at all!

OWNERSHIP, ORGANIZATION, AND MANAGEMENT

The literature on organizational and management change makes little reference to ownership, but in a capitalist society the control of an organization lies ultimately in the hands of its *effective* owners. We examined the concentration of effective ownership and the growth of public ownership on pp. 657–9. The concentration of ownership has continued with the rise of the global corporation, but privatization has reversed the growth of public ownership. In this section we examine the consequences of privatization and globalization for organization and management.

Privatization

We have shown that there had been a considerable extension of public ownership in Britain since the mid-nineteenth century. Since the 1980s this has been substantially reversed by privatization. Apart from the BBC, the Bank of England, and the National Health Service, all the publicly owned activities listed on p. 659, have been privatized. In this section we mainly consider the privatization of the utilities, the corporations that provide the basic services of gas, water, electricity supply, and telecommunications.

 We examine the economic and political context of privatization in 'The Crisis of the 1970s', Chapter 18, pp. 745–8. Its consequences for industrial relations are considered in Chapter 13, p. 535.

We have argued that nationalization made little difference to the capitalist character of British society. The nationalized industries had to operate within a capitalist society and therefore operated on capitalist principles. This implies that it mattered little whether businesses were privately or publicly owned, but the privatizing Conservative governments of the 1980s and 1990s clearly did believe that ownership was important. They associated public ownership with sluggish, bureaucratic, inefficient, and unresponsive organizations and claimed that privatization would make them dynamic, efficient, and responsive to consumers. We cannot here make a general assessment of the effects of privatization, but what consequences did it have for organization and management?

O'Connell Davidson (1993) has studied the consequences of privatization for the organization of

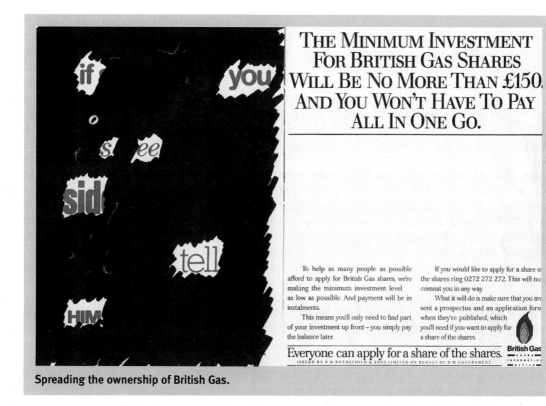

Spreading the ownership of British Gas.

water companies. Changes in their organization were designed to replace *centralized* and *bureaucratic* structures with *decentralized* and *contractual* ones. There were three main aspects to these changes:

▶ profit centres;
▶ contracting out;
▶ flexible work.

There was an internal decentralization of functions to *profit centres*. Thus, the transport and building maintenance departments became centres that were expected to make a profit on their operations. They could in theory sell their services to other parts of the organization or, indeed, to other customers outside it; similarly they could buy services from inside or outside. A centralized, vertical management structure was supposedly replaced by a devolved, horizontal pattern, in which 'managers face one another across internal markets instead of occupying positions in a hierarchy' (O'Connell Davidson 1994: 182). The profit centres were, however, in practice tightly controlled by the company's board, which did not allow them to buy in services freely.

Contracting out took different forms. Some whole functions, such as vehicle and grounds maintenance, were contracted out to other organizations. Activities such as cleaning and catering were carried out not by the water companies' own employees but by contract workers. The rationale for contracting out was that these functions could be performed more cheaply under contract, because contractors employed lower wage labour, and the water companies saved on employment costs. Furthermore, the threat of contracting out functions to lower-cost providers outside the company was used to force more work out of employees afraid of losing their jobs.

Greater *flexibility* was introduced by replacing detailed daily worksheets with weekly job plans, which specified broader sets of tasks that allowed greater discretion to workers and managers. Most of the discretion ended up, however, in the hands of management, which used it to increase workloads. The job plans allowed managers to require the completion of whole jobs in a specified time, even if this involved additional or unanticipated tasks.

The privatization of the utilities enabled senior managers to operate much more freely, for they were largely free of both owner and market control. Ownership was now spread amongst large numbers of small, passive shareholders, who had been encouraged to buy shares by the government. The monopolistic position of the utilities meant that they were also relatively free from market regulation, though vulnerable to predatory takeovers because they were such attractive prizes. Management in the privatized utilities had a high degree of independence.

The senior managers used this new freedom in many different ways. They diversified company operations into other activities both at home and abroad. They sharply increased their salaries, while also benefiting from share ownership and share options. They abandoned the industrial-relations conventions of the public sector, both increasing the exploitation of labour and cutting employment. In the water companies O'Connell Davidson studied, privatization resulted in the intensification of work, greater job insecurity, and a reduction in the size of the labour force.

The senior managers were not wholly free of external constraints, however, for they were subject to new bureaucratic controls. Because of their monopolistic position, the privatized utilities were supervised by new regulatory authorities charged with preventing them from abusing this position. The water companies were subject to the Office of Water Regulation (OFWAT) and the National Rivers Authority. Their prices, standards of service, investment programmes, and impact on the environment were all subject to regulation by these bodies.

The regulatory bodies were themselves controlled by bureaucrats with a high degree of autonomy. The effectiveness of this regulation has been a matter of considerable debate. The regulators have certainly at times intervened strongly, though they have had no control over many aspects of company operation and policy.

Thus, privatization involved both debureaucratization and bureaucratization. Debureaucratization took place internally and through some shift from state control to market control. New bureaucratic controls were, however, created to regulate some aspects of the behaviour of the privatized utilities.

Globalization

While privatization reversed nationalization, one process that has not gone into reverse has been the growing concentration of capital. The rapid growth of transnational corporations (TNCs) since the end of the Second World War has created some corporations that are indeed global in scope. Here we will consider the organizational and management issues raised by globalization, but it is first worth briefly pointing out the relationship between globalization and privatization.

Globalization has interacted with privatization in various ways. State ownership tended to keep the operations of companies within national boundaries, while privatization released them from this restriction. Equally, privatization allowed foreign companies to buy into previously nationalized activities. Globalization has promoted privatization, because the increased global mobility of capital has put pressure on governments to create an environment that will attract and retain capital. Privatization has been one of the policies adopted by governments seeking to create such an environment.

Concentration and globalization have led to decentralizing changes in organizational structure. According to the traditional *functional* model, a corporation was divided into specialized departments carrying out particular functions, such as personnel, research and development, marketing, and so on. Each department worked on the full range of products made by the company. The work of the departments was centrally coordinated and management was highly centralized.

As corporations grew larger, centralized management became unwieldy and they shifted to *divisional* structures with *product* or *area* divisions. Each division would then have a complete range of specialized departments carrying out particular functions. Coordination would be carried out at the divisional level and management was largely decentralized to this level. Area divisions were particularly appropriate for TNCs, which straddled not only large geographical areas but also countries with diverse legal, cultural, and political structures. Financial control and strategic direction have, none the less, remained centralized in the corporate headquarters, which is always firmly located in a particular country.

Some corporations have adopted more complex *matrix* structures that seek to get the best of both worlds by combining different principles of organization. Child (1984: 98) gives the example of a large transnational food corporation where 'a local manager in charge of selling breakfast cereals in Australia will report simultaneously to a world-wide breakfast cereal division and to an area division co-ordinating all the corporation's activities in Australia'. Matrix organization has been particularly adopted by companies whose operations involve large, relatively distinct projects, such as aircraft corporations or building companies.

The rise of the global corporation has created new possibilites for the transplanting of organizational structures and cultures from one country to another. As we showed on pp. 662–3, there has been a growing interest in the less bureaucratic organizational structures found in East Asia, while HRM has sought to develop Japanese-style techniques for generating greater employee commitment and loyalty. A debate has developed between those who believe that a process of Japanization has been taking place and those who

Figure 16.3. **Corporate organizational structures**

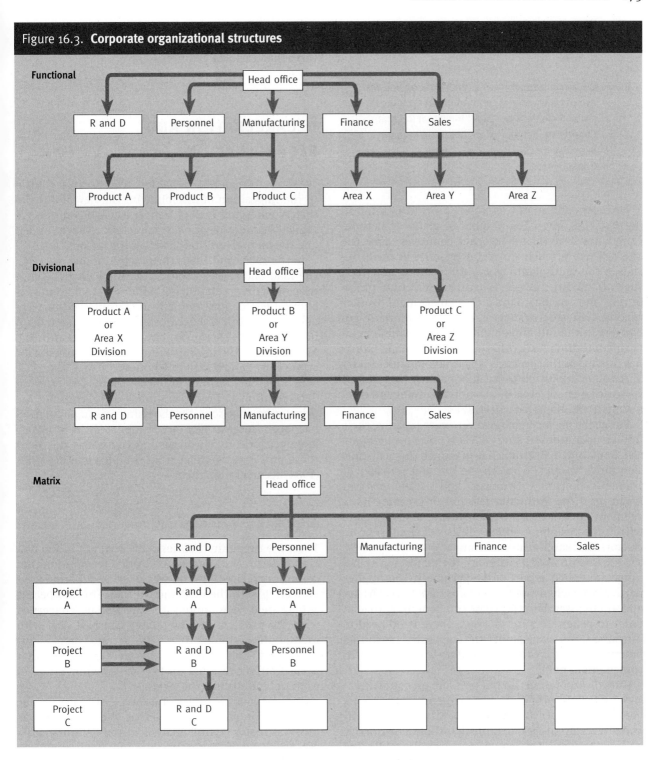

argue that Japanese organizational forms are dependent on the Japanese context and cannot travel.

 We discuss the process of globalization and the rise of transnational corporations in Chapter 12, pp. 478–80. In 'The "New" Industrial Relations', Chapter 13, pp. 532–3, we discuss whether Japanese industrial-relations practices have been transplanted.

Japanese companies themselves provide an interesting test case, given the number of plants that these companies have set up in other countries since the 1970s. There is much anecdotal evidence of the diffusion to the 'transplants' of typical Japanese practices, such as quality circles, exhaustive selection procedures, and various kinds of management–worker mixing. Case studies suggest, however, that there are barriers to the full implementation of Japanese management techniques in other countries. One such study has concluded that overseas Japanese companies find it 'difficult or impossible to Japanize because they cannot recreate Japanese levels of workforce consent and commitment' (Williams *et al.* 1994: 87).

But do Japanese companies even try to Japanize their foreign operations? A study of HRM practices in Japanese companies in Australia has suggested that a distinction must be made between the *core* and *periphery* of Japanese companies (Dedoussis and Littler: 1994). In Japan itself the distinctive features of Japanese management, such as lifetime employment, do not operate within the periphery, which consists of small subcontractors that supply the core company (see Chapter 13, p. 532). Dedoussis and Littler argue that foreign operations are treated as part of the periphery. This applies particularly when overseas plants are 'screwdriver' operations assembling Japanese components abroad in order to penetrate local markets. There is no need to introduce into such plants the expensive personnel practices used to create and maintain worker loyalty in core plants at home.

Global corporations do put pressure on countries to standardize the economic environment. Governments deregulate and privatize in order to attract investment and this results in the partial dismantling of distinctive national structures, often within particular zones (see Chapter 12, pp. 480–1). TNCs also, however, tend to adopt decentralized organizational structures, which allow for adaptation to different local contexts. Japanese TNCs have exported some Japanese management techniques to their overseas operations but they have had to adapt to the local situation. They have also sought to avoid the costs of imposing corporate cultures that are locally unnecessary.

DECARCERATION AND RECARCERATION

We showed on pp. 651–3 that incarceration was central to the imposition of discipline on the new industrial society emerging during the nineteenth century. We argued that this society was characterized by the prison and the mental hospital as well as the factory.

In the 1950s and 1960s the practice of incarcerating the mad and the bad was increasingly challenged. A process of decarceration got under way as community alternatives to imprisonment and hospitalization were developed. While the decarceration of the mentally ill has continued, there was, however, a reaction in the 1980s against the use of community punishments for crime and a return to imprisonment.

In this section we examine these processes of decarceration and recarceration. We also consider the privatizing of prisons, for the rising prison population has been increasingly accommodated in privately managed prisons. In discussing the issues raised by these processes, we refer from time to time to Scull's (1984) decarceration theory.

Alternatives to incarceration

There are two main theories of decarceration. The first is that decarceration resulted from a recognition that community-based alternatives provide superior ways of dealing with the mad and the bad. This has been a widely held view amongst professionals concerned with the problem of how society can best deal with mental illness and crime. The second theory, put forward by Scull, challenges this view and argues that decarceration resulted from the growing crisis of welfare capitalism in the 1960s.

In the 1960s there was a growing criticism of the incarceration of people in prisons and mental hospitals. Goffman's (1961*b*) analysis of the dehumanizing effects of *total institutions* on their inmates became one of the fashionable texts of the time (see 'Total Institutions', pp. 649–50). It was commonly argued that such institutions did not help either to cure or to rehabilitate those shut up inside them and, indeed, often made them worse by 'institutionalizing' them. The symptoms displayed by patients in mental hospitals were attributed to the impact of the institution itself or the adoption of an inmate role. It was argued that inmates became dependent on the institution and lost their ability to cope with the outside world when they were released. Indeed, it was said that prisons actually increased criminality, because inmates were brutalized by their prison experiences and learned new criminal skills while they were inside.

The alternatives put forward involved various forms of *community care* for the mentally ill and *community corrections* for criminals. New drugs made it easier to treat mental patients without taking them into hospitals. Crimes were punished increasingly by fines rather than imprisonment and new forms of punishment were created, such as community service, suspended sentences, attendance by day at specified centres, or residence in supervised hostels.

The incarceration of the mentally ill has certainly declined, but this has not been the case with imprisonment. The annual resident population of mental hospitals in England and Wales peaked at 148,000 in 1954 and then declined steadily to under 50,000 in 1990 (see p. 217). The prison population has risen steadily (see Figure 16.4). There is, none the less, evidence of the decreasing use of imprisonment to punish those convicted of crime, since there has been a reduction in the *rate* of imprisonment (see Figure 16.5 on p. 678). The increase in the prison population mainly reflected a rise in the crime rate and increasing numbers of untried prisoners held on remand.

Acording to Scull (1984), the emergence of superior comunity-based alternatives to the prison and the mental hospital did not explain decarceration. He put forward two main arguments against this explanation. First, he challenged the idea that comunity-based alternatives were superior. Secondly, he argued that decarceration was motivated by a concern to reduce state expenditure at a time of growing financial crisis.

Scull claimed that there was no evidence to support the notion that treatment in the community was more effective than hospital care. He argued that those who believed in community care had no idea of what it really meant:

'What has the new approach meant in practice? For thousands of the old, already suffering in varying degrees from mental confusion and deterioration, it has meant premature death. For others, it has meant that they have been left to rot and decay, physically and otherwise, in broken down welfare hostels or what are termed . . . 'personal-care' nursing homes. For thousands of younger psychotics discharged into the streets, it has meant a nightmare existence in the blighted centres of our cities, amidst neighbourhoods crowded with prostitutes, ex-felons, addicts, alcoholics, and the other human rejects now repressively tolerated by our society.' (Scull 1984: 2)

He focused mainly on the mentally ill but he also argued that community corrections were an inadequate way of controlling and rehabilitating criminals and delinquents. Those charged with supervising them were overloaded with cases and supervision became a token process involving no more than short weekly interviews. Criminals drifted into decaying inner-city areas, where they were largely left alone by the police. As both the mentally ill and the criminals congregated in these areas, there was the danger of a violent backlash against them from the local inhabitants.

According to Scull, the increasing reliance on

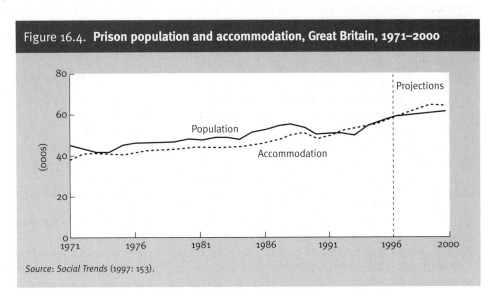

Figure 16.4. Prison population and accommodation, Great Britain, 1971–2000

Source: Social Trends (1997: 153).

community treatment and punishment resulted from the development of the welfare state and the financial crisis this had generated. This was partly because the availability of welfare meant that there was an alternative system of support for those who could not look after themselves. It was also because the expense of the welfare state had generated a financial crisis. It was cheaper to deal with deviants through community programmes and welfare payments than to lock them up in heavily staffed and expensive institutions. This was not just a matter of the running costs of these institutions, but also the need for greater capital expenditure. Most of them had been built in the nineteenth century and urgently needed replacement.

> ☞ You may find it helpful to look up our discussion of changes in welfare in other chapters. See ' "Community" care', Chapter 6, pp. 217–19, and 'Changes in State Welfare', Chapter 18, pp. 750–1.

Scull's theory of the decarceration of the mentally ill has been criticized for its economic determinism. There is evidence that the critique of the total institution together with a movement in psychiatry away from a *medical* towards a *behavioural* model of psychological problems was partly responsible for the shift from hospital to community-based treatments (Nettleton 1995: 246). Scull was, none the less, right to emphasize the importance of financial pressures.

Baggott (1994: 220) concludes that in Britain it is the 'economic argument which has been the driving force behind the development of community care policies in the 1980s'.

There has been a more fundamental attack on his theory of the decarceration of those convicted of criminal offences. Should community punishment be described as decarceration, when, as Stanley Cohen (1985) has argued, it extends surveillance and control into the society at large?

Instead of the concentration of surveillance and control in specific institutions, we now see them operating in the outside society through probation, community service, suspended sentences, and electronic tagging. More generally, there is a growing surveillance of the population at large by security cameras, cameras recording traffic offences, and surveillance cameras in city centres. This leads us back to Foucault's argument that the development of disciplinary and surveillance techniques in the carceral *organizations* of the nineteenth century was but the first step towards a disciplinary or carceral *society*.

Recarceration

There was anyway a greater use of imprisonment in the 1980s and 1990s. This involved not only rising numbers of prisoners but also a rising rate of imprisonment, as a higher proportion of offenders were punished by imprisonment and sentenced to longer terms.

Electronic tagging

'One of the three pilot schemes, in Norwich, run by a small British company called Geographix, has had 120 widely varied offenders tagged so far, criminals who would certainly have gone to prison otherwise. Only eight have been returned to court and prison for breaching their curfews—a phenomenal success. The technology works and so does the whole sentence.

'The court sets the hours of curfew to suit the crime. A man guilty of repeated violent affray on Saturday nights might be curfewed for every Thursday, Friday, and Saturday night. A persistent shoplifter might have to stay in 12 hours a day in shopping hours. If they are not home on the dot, an alarm rings at the control centre and someone phones them at home to see where they are. Within two hours someone visits them. If they clock up two hours' absence in total, they get sent a yellow card (as well as a visit). After four hours a red card, and after that it's back to court and jail. On average, most commit only two or three trivial violations.

'All those tagged have been assessed by the Probation Service as suitable cases, and given a probation order at the same time. Many officers now speak in glowing terms about tagging. They say it helps chaotic offenders to get some order into their lives, by having to keep to a timetable. It helps them to resist peer-pressure to go out committing more crimes: they can say they can't go without losing face. Many offenders themselves, grateful to escape jail, are saying it has helped them. What's more, the offenders have struck up good relationships with their taggers, whom Geographix has hand-picked as good comunicators.'

Source: Polly Toynbee, 'Tagging Along with Michael Howard', *Independent*, 10 July 1997.

▶ **Does electronic tagging amount to imprisonment at home?**

▶ **Does electronic tagging support the theory of incarceration or decarceration?**

Why did old city centres have clock towers? Why do new ones have surveillance cameras?

In the United States incarceration returned to favour as imprisonment became seen as a means of solving the problem of rising crime by taking criminals off the streets. Prison terms became longer, most notoriously with the 'three-strikes' law introduced in 1992, which meant that in some states conviction for three crimes resulted in mandatory life imprisonment. In California the size of the prison population rose from 22,600 in 1980 to 110,000 in 1993 (Cavadino and Dignan 1997: 164).

Recarceration also resulted from local reactions against decarceration. According to Dear and Wolch (1987), the decarceration of the mentally ill produced deviant ghettoes in Canadian and American cities. These ghettoes generated a reaction by property interests and neighbourhood groups that forced a return to incarceration and the opening of new carceral institutions.

British penal policy in the 1980s and the 1990s has been driven by the conflicting imperatives of a concern with costs *and* a law-and-order ideology emphasizing punishment rather than rehabilitation. The crisis of welfare capitalism had not only resulted in a financial crisis; it had also generated a crisis of order. The government's response to this was to strengthen the forces of law and order, and adopt a more punitive policy towards those who broke the law (see 'Strengthening the State', Chapter 18, pp. 754–6). Thus, Scull's crisis of welfare capitalism led to recarceration as well as decarceration.

These conflicting imperatives resulted in what has been called a *twin-track* strategy, that made greater use of both non-custodial punishments and imprisonment. In the case of minor offences, attempts have been made to keep the prison population down by the use of cautions, non-custodial punishments, and shorter sentences. The use of the fine has, however, declined since the 1970s, probably because higher levels of unemployment made it difficult to secure the payment of fines and led to more use of the conditional discharge (Cavadino and Dignan 1997). On the other hand, young offenders committing more serious crimes or reoffending have been subjected to 'short, sharp shocks' in detention centres or 'boot camps'. There has been a greater use of imprisonment and longer sentences for the more serious crimes committed by adults. The rate of imprisonment began to rise again in the 1980s and 1990s.

A rising prison population led to the building of new prisons. In 1982 the government embarked on a programme to construct twenty-one new prisons. In 1993 the Home Secretary declared that 'prison works' and announced a further programme of prison building.

Prison building could not, however, keep pace with increases in the prison population, which rose to new heights in the later 1990s (see Figure 16.4). This led to a generally acknowledged overcrowding crisis, with rising numbers of prisoners per cell and a growing pressure on educational and exercise facilities. There were also cuts in expenditure that reduced staffing levels in prisons and led to prisoners having less out-of-cell time. One expedient adopted to deal with the crisis was the purchase of a prison ship from the United States in 1997. Another was the greater use of imprisonment at home through electronic tagging.

Thus, there is evidence to support the theory of decarceration, but it must be modified to take account of rising prison populations, recent increases in rates of imprisonment, and the extension of surveillance and control techniques from the prison to the society at large.

Figure 16.5. **Changing patterns of punishment, England and Wales, 1938–1994**

Sentencing of adult offenders	Percentage of offenders		
	1938	1975	1994
Imprisonment	33.3	13.4	18.2
Probation	15.1	7.0	12.0
Community service	—	0.5	10.7
Combination order[a]	n.a.	n.a.	2.4
Fines	27.2	55.3	34.9
Suspended sentence	—	11.2	1.1
Discharge	23.4	12.0	18.2
Other	1.0	0.6	2.4
	100.0	100.0	100.0
Total no. of offenders	38,896	209,709	215,500

[a] After the 1991 Criminal Justice Act probation could be combined with other penalties.
Source: Cavadino and Dignan (1997: 207, table 8.1).

▶ What are the main changes that have taken place in methods of punishment since the 1930s and since the 1970s?

▶ Do these figures suggest that there has been a process of decarceration?

The theories of debureaucratization and decarceration are quite similar in character. In both cases, these concepts draw our attention to important changes in techniques of control, which have partially reversed previous tendencies. But just as debureaucratization has occurred in some organizations within an increasingly bureaucratic society, decarceration has taken place in some institutions within an increasingly carceral society.

Private prisons

As prison populations rose, prisons were privatized; in this section we consider the consequences of this process, drawing on a study of it by James *et al.* (1997).

In the 1980s the prison population began to grow sharply in the United States and it was there that the private prison was first revived. The American example was then followed by Australia, various European countries, including Britain, and more recently New Zealand. The international scope of privatization has, indeed, resulted in leading American companies, such as the Corrections Corporation of America, becoming transnational corporations involved in prison management in Australia and Europe. As we have pointed out, privatization and the growth of TNCs have interacted with each other.

The privatizing of prisons has taken three main forms:

▶ *Contracting out services*: the privatizing of particular services, such as catering or education, which is little different from the general tendency in both the private and public sectors to contract out the provision of specialized services;

▶ *Contracting out management*: the contracting-out of the management of the whole institution;

▶ *Privately financed prisons*: the financing of complete new institutions by private capital.

 The privatizing of prisons was linked to a more general privatizing of the enforcement of law and order, which we examine in Chapter 18, p. 756.

Privatization was closely linked to the increasing size of prison populations, for it was hoped that the private sector would be able to manage prisons more efficiently and more economically than the state. The general hostility to state management characteristic of the political and ideological climate of the 1980s clearly also lay behind it. In Britain, it was additionally motivated by the hope that private prisons would be innovative, would improve the conditions for prisoners, and would produce more orderly prisons. Overcrowding had led to deteriorating conditions and generated disorder. The Strangeways riot in 1990, and the riots that followed in some twenty-five other prisons, made prison reform urgent. Privatization was also a means of weakening union power, for the powerful Prison Officers' Association was seen as an obstacle to reform in state-managed prisons.

In Britain, the first privately managed prison was the Wolds Remand Prison, which opened in 1992. It was under the management of Group 4, which was under contract to the Home Office to manage the prison for five years on an experimental basis. Working to a contract meant that Group 4 had to achieve higher standards—for example, in prisoner education—than were required elsewhere in the prison service, but had a relatively free hand in how it achieved them. In order to

One response to prison overpopulation: the *Weare* prison ship, bought from the United States, arrives in Portland, Dorset.

make a fresh start, Wolds employed staff without previous experience of working in prisons. Unlike other British prisons, it was to have remand prisoners only, which meant that it was dealing with non-convicted prisoners who were legally 'innocent until proved guilty'.

The regime established at Wolds set out to minimize the carceral aspects of imprisonment. Its management declared that, since the prisoners were on remand only, they should have as much freedom as possible within an environment that was as normal as possible, and should make productive use of their time. Thus, they were allowed out of their cells for fifteen hours a day and were to receive six hours of education and gym each week. Maintenance of contact with their lives outside the prison was a high priority and they were

For and against the decarceration thesis	Evidence and arguments	For	Against
	Institution population	▶ Declining population of mental hospitals	▶ Increasing population of prisons
	Rates of imprisonment	▶ Long-term reduction in rate of imprisonment	▶ Increased rate of imprisonment in 1980s
	Changes in treatment and punishment	▶ Community care ▶ Non-custodial punishment	▶ Increased imprisonment ▶ Heavier sentences
	Arguments	▶ Critique of total institutions ▶ Cost of imprisonment	▶ Opposition from local communities ▶ Law and order policies

encouraged to have substantial daily visits and given access to card-phones.

The American practice of *direct supervision* was introduced. This involved prison officers having closer contact with prisoners and treating them more positively. It was based on the view that their greater involvement would make destructive prisoner behaviour less likely and enable the construction of cheaper prisons that did not have to withstand violent behaviour. In Wolds direct supervision occurred through Unit Supervisors, who took charge of living units of fifty prisoners and had a general responsibility for meeting prisoners' needs. It was believed that the isolation of the supervisor from other staff would lead to closer relationships between staff and prisoners.

The realities of prison life turned out to be somewhat different. Problems in controlling prisoners led to restrictions on their movements, while 'troublemakers' had to be segregated under a tougher regime. Supervisors complained of isolation and more staff had to be appointed to the units. While some prisoners valued the out-of-cell time, others who were used to more restricted conditions in prisons found the lack of constraint hard to manage and complained of boredom. Many services, such as education and library services, were contracted out to external providers, which had difficulty supplying them to the required level, because competition for contracts had forced them to cut costs.

In assessing the Wolds experiment, James *et al.* (1997) conclude, none the less, that it was innovatory and had achieved much. The majority of the prisoners they interviewed thought that their relationships with staff were better than those they had experienced elsewhere, while the staff too thought relationships were good. James *et al.* note that there was some evidence that the relative freedom of movement in Wolds had led to more bullying and drug use. It was the staffing problems of the Wolds that gave James *et al.* most cause for concern. They argue that in private prisons inexperienced staff face greater stress and insecurity.

The government did not wait for the five-year Wolds experiment to run its course before announcing an extension of the private sector. During 1993 it announced that six new private prisons would be built. It claimed in 1995 that private prisons were 15–25 per cent cheaper to run than state prisons, but, if this is indeed the case, it is at the expense of the staff. Private prisons seek to reduce operating costs by employing fewer staff, reducing the level of training, and paying them at lower rates. The capital intensiveness of imprisonment is increased by substituting technology for staff, as with the introduction of high-technology surveillance systems (Cavadino and Dignan 1997).

James *et al.* found it difficult to assess the significance of privatization as such. They point out that similar, possibly greater, achievements can be found in some new public-sector local prisons. Similar innovations have been made in the public sector. The achievements of Wolds seem anyway to have been partly the result of its special status as an experimental prison for remand prisoners only. They note that it has, since their study, become more integrated with the system as a whole and has received convicted prisoners, while there has been a greater emphasis on discipline and control.

Recarceration policies increased the state's financial burden at the very time when governments were trying to cut state expenditure, as part of their response to the crisis of welfare capitalism. Rising prison populations also led to overcrowding and disorder. The response of government has been to privatize prisons. As Scull had argued, the crisis of welfare capitalism played a central role in the development of penal policy but in the end the crisis led to privatization rather than decarceration.

SUMMARY POINTS

In this section we have explored the emergence of new techniques and structures of control that partially reversed the processes of bureaucratization and incarceration. We began by considering processes of debureaucratization:

▶ More flexible forms of organization have emerged, together with a growing awareness of less bureaucratic Asian models.

▶ The patriarchal character of traditional bureaucracies has been challenged by the feminizing of organizations.

▶ Debureaucratizing changes have, however, taken place within a broader context of continued bureaucratization.

We then considered related changes in the character and techniques of management:

▶ The human-relations school developed an integrative approach to the management of labour, based on a greater understanding of the social context of worker behaviour and workers' non-economic needs.

▶ HRM emphasized the importance of cultural and organizational change to generate greater worker loyalty and commitment to the company.

We went on to discuss the effects of privatization and globalization on organization and management:

► The privatization of utilities led to internal debureaucratization but also a new bureaucratic control by regulatory authorities.

► Global corporations have developed decentralized organizations based on area or product divisions within a framework of central control.

► Japanese TNCs have exported Japanese management techniques to their overseas operations only to a limited extent.

Lastly we considered decarceration and recarceration processes:

► Community-based treatments and punishments developed as an alternative to incarceration in mental hospitals and prisons.

► Decarceration was linked to a growing crisis in welfare capitalism, though this crisis also generated disorder and recarceration.

► Recarceration increased the state's financial burdens and governments responded by privatizing prisons.

REVISION AND EXERCISES

BUREAUCRATIZATION AND DEBUREAUCRATIZATION

In 'Understanding Organizations' we outlined Weber's ideal type of bureaucracy and the criticisms that have been made of it:

► **What do you understand by the following terms: bureaucracy; the dysfunctions of bureaucratic rules, the displacement of goals, and trained incapacity; mock, representative, and punishment-centred bureaucracy; negotiated order?**

► **Make sure that you are familiar with the main ideas of Weber, Merton, Crozier, Gouldner, and Strauss *et al.***

► **Why are impersonal rules central to Weber's ideal type? What features of bureaucracy enable the impersonal application of rules?**

► **How are rules actually applied in bureaucratic organizations?**

We later examined the process of bureaucratization:

► **How did modern bureaucracies differ from those of the ancient empires?**

► **How would you explain the bureaucratization of European societies?**

In 'Debureaucratization?' we considered alternative, less bureaucratic forms of organization, and in 'Privatization' we discussed its implications for bureaucracy:

► **What do you understand by the terms: mechanistic and organic organization; network organization; modern and post-modern organization?**

► **Is there an East Asian model of business organization?**

► **What are the main ways in which bureaucratic organizations can be feminized?**

► **Has privatization resulted in debureaucratization?**

► **Do you think that society is becoming less bureaucratic? Do you think that it should become less bureaucratic?**

MANAGEMENT

We examined management in 'The Development of Management' and 'The Transformation of Management':

▶ What do you understand by the terms: scientific management; the Hawthorne effect; the human-relations school, the neo-human-relations approach, HRM.

▶ What were the main methods used by early industrialists to manage labour?

▶ Did scientific management break away from these methods or develop them further? What was scientific about it?

▶ What was the significance of the Hawthorne Experiments for the development of ideas of management?

▶ Is human-resource management anything more than the latest version of the human-relations approach?

We examined the changing relationship between ownership and management in 'The Development of Management' and 'Ownership, Organization, and Management':

▶ What do you understand by the following terms: the managerial revolution and finance capital; effective ownership and constellation of interests; nationalization; contracting out; functional, divisional, and matrix organization.

▶ How would you account for the growth of management?

▶ Did the spread of ownership result in a managerial revolution or domination by finance capital?

▶ Did the extension of public ownership lead to greater worker influence over management?

▶ What effect did the privatization of the utilities have on the relationship between managers and workers and between managers and owners?

▶ Has the rise of Japanese TNCs resulted in the Japanization of management in other societies?

INCARCERATION AND DECARCERATION

We discussed the development of discipline in 'Understanding Organizations' and 'Disciplined Organizations':

▶ What do you understand by the terms: discipline and surveillance; incarceration, carceral organizations, and carceral society; total institutions, mortification of the self, and contamination of the self?

▶ Make sure that you are familiar with the main ideas of Foucault and Goffman.

▶ How did the new prison of the nineteenth century control its inmates.

▶ How would you explain the growth of imprisonment?

Later in the chapter, in 'Decarceration and Recarceration', we examined the growth of community-based methods of dealing with deviants and the later revival of imprisonment:

▶ Make sure that you are familiar with Scull's theory of decarceration.

▶ What evidence is there for a process of decarceration in Britain?

▶ Why were the mentally ill increasingly treated in the community?

▶ Does the rising prison population refute the theory of decarceration?

We then went on to consider the privatizing of prisons:

▶ What were the main forms taken by privatization?

▶ How would you explain the privatizing of prisons?

▶ What were the consequences of introducing the private management of prisons for prisoners and staff?

▶ Do you think that there are any reasons why the whole prison system should not be privatized?

FURTHER READING

Further reading on bureaucracy, organization, and management can be found in the following:

Clegg, S. R., and Dunkerley, D. (1980), *Organization, Class, and Control* (London: Routledge & Kegan Paul). A very comprehensive and clear review of the literature on organizations, which also covers scientific management and the human relations approach.

Clegg, S R (1990), *Modern Organizations: Organization Studies in the Postmodern World* (London: Sage). Travels from the Weberian model to East Asian and post-modern organizations.

Ritzer, G. (1996), *The McDonaldization of Society: An Investigation into the Changing Character of Social Life* (rev. edn., Thousand Oaks, Calif.: Pine Forge Press). A wide-ranging and highly readable application of the Weberian approach to contemporary life, which argues that it is becoming ever more rationalized and bureaucratic.

Storey, J. (1995) (ed.), *Human Resource Management* (London: Routledge). A collection of readings on HRM, which includes supporters and critics.

Further reading on punishment, imprisonment, incarceration, and decarceration can be found in the following:

Cavadino, M., and Dignan, J. (1997), *The Penal System: An Introduction* (2nd edn., London: Sage). A systematic analysis of punishment and imprisonment, which deals with privatization and discusses Scull's approach.

Goffman, E. (1961b), *Asylums: Essays on the Social Situation of Mental Patients and Other Inmates* (New York: Doubleday). A highly influential and perceptive set of essays on life in a mental hospital.

Scull, A. (1984), *Decarceration: Community Treatment and the Deviant—A Radical View* (2nd edn., Cambridge: Polity). Forcefully advances a theory of decarceration and includes an appendix which updates the original study and responds to critics.

For further reading on particular topics, see the following:

Elger, T., and Smith, C. (1994) (eds.), *Global Japanization: The Transnational Transformation of the Labour Process* (London: Routledge).

O'Connell Davidson, J. (1993), *Privatization and Employment Relations* (London: Mansell).

Scott, J. (1997), *Corporate Business and Capitalist Classes* (Oxford: Oxford University Press).

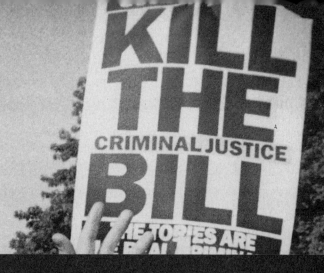

Chapter 17
POLITICS, POWER, AND PROTEST

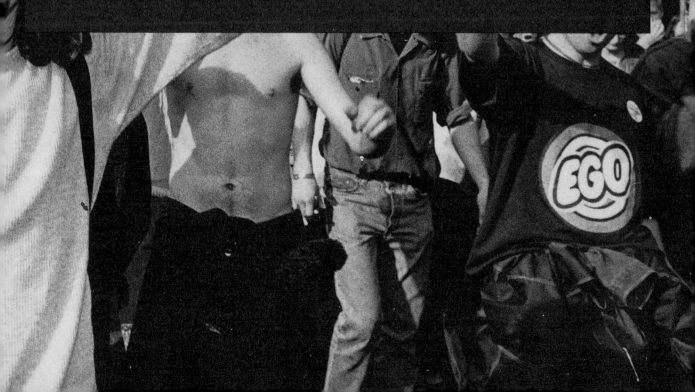

Business power

'The alcohol industry constitutes one of the most powerful concentrations of ownership in Britain today. Six companies (Bass, Grand Metropolitan, Allied Lyons, Scottish and Newcastle, Whitbread and Courage) control 74 per cent of the drinks market (beer, wine, and spirits) and own 75 per cent of the pubs. Four of the 'Big Six' are in the UK's top fifty companies, and their annual combined pre-tax profits are over £1.8 billion.

'In March 1989, the Monopolies and Mergers Commission produced a report which directly threatened their supremacy and profitability. The 500-page document concluded that the "Big Six" operated a "complex monopoly" and . . . recommended that brewers be confined to owning 2,000 public houses each and that they should be compelled to sell off the rest.

'Over at the House of Commons, Conservative back-benchers were being mustered for the counter-attack. At the time there were no fewer than forty-seven MPs with declared financial interests in the alcohol industry—either as consultants or company directors, or through family connections. . . . Ninety-three Tory MPs signed an Early Day Motion praising the brewing industry and rejecting the MMC report outright. . . . In a parallel move, the brewers brought pressure to bear through local Conservative associations. For generations the "Big Six" have had an intimate relationship with the Tory establishment. Many regional brewery chairmen and company directors are also chairman and president of constituency Conservative parties. . . . Tory back-benchers were lobbied ferociously—either directly by company directors or indirectly through constituency associations.

'The Trade and Industry Secretary [Lord Young] suggested compromises and concessions. The brewers responded by arranging for ten executive members of the 1922 Tory back-bench committee to write to the Prime Minister condemning these latest proposals. . . . After being told by the Tory Chief Whip that the troops would desert in droves, [Lord Young] surrendered. He announced that the "Big Six" could keep all their pubs and the proposal limiting brewers to 2,000 each was now dropped. . . . For the "Big Six", it was mission accomplished. On the day of Lord Young's climbdown their share value rose sharply by 26 per cent. A week later Bass, Whitbread and Courage increased the price of their beer by up to 10p a pint.'

Does the introduction of 'alcopops' give further evidence on the power of the drinks industry?

Source: Hollingsworth (1991: 65–8).

THE brewers successfully conspire to undermine government policy. How typical is this of British politics? Are governments easily manipulated by private business interests? Is this kind of influence limited to Conservative governments, or are Labour governments also pressured by private business? Some people see governments, of all parties, as the mere tools of private interests operating behind the scenes. For others, however, modern societies have democratic states that act as neutral referees and balance the interests of one section of society against another. The only way that it is possible to decide between these conflicting views is to examine the evidence. What are the realities of political power in Britain and in other societies?

To answer this question it is necessary to look at the structure and organization of the various interest groups that attempt to influence the government, at the connections between these groups and divisions of class, ethnicity, and gender, and at the factors that shape the outcomes of elections. These are the issues that we will look at in this chapter. In particular, we will look at the link between class and political action, at patterns of working-class and middle-class politics, and at the idea of a ruling class.

UNDERSTANDING POLITICS

The relationship between class and political power has been the central concern of Marxist class theory. The two main issues have been those of working-class and ruling-class politics, both of which have been long and hotly debated by Marxists and their critics. Discussion of the working class has centred on the nature of working-class consciousness and political action, while discussion of the ruling class has explored the relation of dominant classes to state power.

The working class has been seen by Marxists as developing forms of political action that challenge the established social order and, ultimately, bring about its revolutionary overthrow. The ruling class, on the other hand, has been seen as the politically organized capitalist class that has control of the state machinery. Critics of Marxism have attacked both aspects of the Marxist theory of politics. They have pointed to the failure of the working class to become the kind of revolutionary force that Marx expected, and they have rejected the idea that the state is dominated by a capitalist class. Writers in the so-called elitist tradition of social theory, for example, have replaced the Marxist concept of the ruling class with the idea of a political elite or ruling elite. They argue that those who exercise political power are drawn from a variety of classes and that political action cannot simply be reduced to class relations and class conflict.

 If you are unsure about class and Marxist class theory, you should look at our discussion of these topics in Chapter 15. Modern states and state policies are covered more fully in Chapter 18.

WORKING-CLASS AND RULING-CLASS POLITICS

Marx saw social classes as categories of people who shared certain economic interests. He believed that, when the members of a class became conscious of their shared interests, they would form or support a political party to promote their interests. Their class consciousness and their solidarity would underpin the collective action that makes them into what Marx called a **class for itself**. The members of a social class that is organized for political action are able to act for themselves, consciously and in their collective interests. They no longer form a mere class in itself, an aggregate of similar individuals. They have unity and cohesion and are organized around a shared programme of action.

As we show in Chapter 15, pp. 613–15, Marx saw capitalist societies as becoming ever more polarized. The economic division between working class and capitalist class, he held, would become more and more marked and would be reflected in a polarization of class consciousness and political action. The working class was being organized into a network of trade unions, pressure groups, and political parties that together comprised a powerful and progressive social movement. This is the **labour movement**, and Marx saw socialist and communist parties playing a leading role in it. The capitalist class, on the other hand, was directly involved in the exercise of state power. Its members held all the leading positions in parliament, government, and other state bodies. They formed a ruling class, and their political power was growing with the growth of the state. The conflict between working class and capitalist class, then, had become politically organized as a struggle between the labour movement and the ruling class.

Most sociologists now accept that Marx's view of class polarization cannot be upheld in this strong form. The development of the major capitalist societies did not confirm his expectations. Nevertheless, there is still great value in his theoretical concepts, which have proved a remarkably powerful basis for understanding some of the central trends in modern societies.

Working-class politics

With the development of modern industry and the factory system of production, workers were brought together in ever larger numbers. Marx saw this as the beginning of the development of the working class from a mere disorganized mass into a class for itself. At first, workers developed a consciousness in common with those who worked in the same trade or industry, or those who lived in the same locality. They formed trade unions to pursue their demands for higher wages and improved conditions of work, and they formed cooperatives to eliminate their dependence on profit-making retailers. As their consciousness and confidence advanced, so they developed a broader class consciousness with other workers, regardless of trade or skill. Their conflict acquired a more political character, and they became involved in political parties and parliamentary committees.

Class-conscious workers saw themselves as part of a labour movement and Marx expected them to give electoral support to political parties that voiced their demands. Wherever workers had the right to vote, he expected them to vote for parties that identified themselves with the aims of the labour movement. These

---

Social movements

A social movement is a broad alliance or network of individuals, groups, and organizations that are united by their shared goals, aspirations, and interests. A social movement may comprise trade unions, political parties, cooperatives, neighbourhood action groups, pressure groups, and any other collective organizations in so far as they share a common political purpose. Social movements may include formal organizations, but they are not themselves organizations with a formal structure of leadership and administration.

Most typically, social movements have been concerned with protest or change, rather than with defence of the existing order (A. Scott 1990). The labour movement is a social movement with its base in the working class and its organizations, and with a commitment to socialist ideals (Hobhouse 1893; Sombart 1908).

The changing face of social movements and protest: the miners and the solidarity of the Labour movement; action by Scope for people with cerebral palsy.

were Socialist, Social Democratic, Labour, and Communist parties. Through their contacts with the intellectuals who led these parties, manual workers would sharpen and crystallize the consciousness of their shared class interests.

For Marx, then, manual workers were moving towards ever-more radical forms of political action. He believed that this popular radicalism would eventually give rise to a revolution. Workers would support those organizations that aimed at the overthrow of capitalist society and looked to its replacement with a new and more humane social order. Some Marxists, interpret **revolution** to mean the violent overthrow of the social order through mass collective action. Others see it as a long-term and peaceful process of radical structural change.

Working-class consciousness and radicalism was sustained by the structures of the working-class communities. However, Marx saw numerous obstacles to its full development. The most important obstacle that Marx identified was the influence of the capitalist press, which he saw as indoctrinating the workers and giving them a **false consciousness** of their own situation. The working class might—in the short term—adopt bourgeois ideas and attitudes. They would fail to recognize their real interests. To understand working-class consciousness and action, then, it is necessary to look at the social control exercised by the ruling class (Mann 1973).

 Look at our discussion of the effects of the mass media in 'Understanding the Media', Chapter 8, p. 281. Look, in particular, at our discussion of the media-effects model. What criticisms would you make of this as an explanation of political socialization?

Ruling-class politics

Marx saw all societies as dominated by ruling classes. In capitalist societies, Marx argued, the capitalist class forms the ruling class because the owners of capital have control of the machinery of the state. The government in the modern state, he argued, is simply the executive committee of the bourgeoisie. The whole state apparatus—parliament and government, the police, the judiciary, the civil service and the military—operates as an instrument of class rule. Through their monopoly of political power, the dominant class becomes a ruling class.

The capitalist class monopolizes access to positions of political authority in the state because of the ways in which the occupants of these positions are recruited. Members of the government, top civil servants and judges, senior military officers, and holders of all other ruling positions within the state are drawn from property-owning families involved in business. Sons and, more rarely, daughters of capitalists are able to secure careers that take them into the senior levels of the state, and there is a constant circulation of personnel between positions of political authority and the business world.

Marx recognized that some members of the middle classes did hold senior positions in the state. Lawyers and managers, for example, often played an important part. However, he did not see this as undermining his position. Those from the higher levels of the middle classes were considered to be the mere servants of the bourgeoisie, who held the real power. They were a subordinate service class. Members of the working class and the lower middle class, on the other hand, were excluded even from nominal involvement in the exercise of political power.

The Marxist view is that states in capitalist societies act in the interests of business, property, and capital. This occurs, said Marx, because capitalist interests are directly represented within the state by bourgeois families and because state departments and agencies are pressured and lobbied by organized business interests. Employers' associations, trade bodies, and chambers of commerce all have the power to put pressure on these departments and agencies and to persuade them to take business interests seriously. Manipulation and pressure are not the only ways through which a state is made to act in the interests of capital. All states depend on taxation to finance their activities, and a state that wishes to retain a tax income must not threaten the profitability of the business sector that provides much of its revenue. For all these reasons, Marxists see democracy as an illusion under capitalism. The outcome of competitive elections is irrelevant to the real exercise of power. The state machinery always reflects the power of the capitalist class.

Capitalist property-owners, like the working class, can develop a class consciousness and can form themselves into a class for itself. Marx saw the state as central to the political organization of the capitalist class into a conscious ruling class. When capitalists are aware of their own economic interests, they are able to translate them into state policies. Marx holds, however, that their power extends beyond the state itself and into such areas as the churches, the mass media, and the educational system. These social institutions become organized around the power of the ruling class, and its consciousness becomes the dominant cultural force in society. The class consciousness of the dominant class becomes what later writers have called a **dominant ideology**.

The values and norms of a dominant ideology are transmitted through the mass media, the churches, and the educational system. They are the basis of socialization in families and communities. All fully socialized members of a society—capitalists and workers alike—become committed both to the underlying values of the society and to the institutions that they legitimate. The power of a capitalist class, then, is especially strong where its economic dominance is matched by a political and a cultural dominance. Where a class is dominant in all spheres of society, the Italian Marxist Gramsci described it as exercising a **hegemony**. A ruling class is a hegemonic class.

Dominant ideology

An ideology is a system of beliefs, values, and norms that expresses and legitimates the interests of a particular social group. A dominant ideology is one that expresses and legitimates the interests of a dominant social class and has become the basis of cultural socialization. Alternative ideas and forms of consciousness are difficult to establish in the face of the power behind the dominant ideology. Subordinate classes tend to accept, rather than to oppose, the existing social order. For many Marxists, this is a sign of their false consciousness: they accept the ideas of the bourgeoisie, rather than ideas that reflect their own interests.

Critics of this idea say that people are not simply socialized into a false consciousness. They have the power to develop their own ideas and values. Look at our discussion of socialization in Chapter 4 and at the critique of the Marxist view of the dominant ideology in Abercrombie *et al.* (1979). How useful do you think it is to talk about false consciousness? You might like to consider this issue in relation to our discussion of the embourgeoisement of the working class in Chapter 15, pp. 629–34.

Hegemony and class politics

Gramsci's purpose in writing about hegemony was to analyse its consequences for working-class conscious-

ness and organization. If the power of a capitalist class is so all-pervasive, it is unlikely that members of the working class will organize themselves into trade unions and parties that challenge that power. Manual workers, through their socialization, are influenced by the dominant ideology, and their attitudes and values will reflect its concerns. This does not mean, however, that the working class is completely absorbed into the system. It is typically characterized by what Gramsci called a **dual consciousness**. On the one hand, workers are subject to the hegemonic power of a dominant ideology that ties them ever more closely to the dominant bourgeois institutions. On the other hand, their practical, day-to-day experiences of exploitation and oppression lead them to develop a more autonomous and oppositional class consciousness that is rooted in the immediate day-to-day conditions of working-class life.

The politics of the working class are shaped by the tension between these two forms of consciousness. One aspect of their consciousness expresses the dominant ideology, while the other expresses their interests as an exploited class. The development of the working class into a class for itself involves a strengthening of its autonomous consciousness and, in particular, the forming of trade unions and political parties into a social movement that can exercise an effective **counter-hegemony**. That is to say, they establish forms of economic, political, and cultural consciousness and organization that allow them to challenge the hegemony of the ruling class. Through their participation in the political struggle of the labour movement, they strengthen the radical values and ideas that allow them to withstand the influence of the dominant ideology and to develop a more genuine political strategy of their own.

 Look at our discussion of Gramsci in Chapter 8, pp. 276–7, where we show how his work, like that of Lukács and the Frankfurt school, has had a major influence on studies of the mass media. Gramsci's *Prison Notebooks*, which contain his leading ideas, were written in the 1930s, but were not widely available until the 1970s. They had a major impact on the reorientation of Marxist social theory at that time.

Empirical research on the connection between class and politics has been heavily influenced by Marxist theory. While researchers have rejected many of its specific claims, and they have certainly denied that there is any inevitability about class conflict, the broad themes and concerns of Marxist theory have set the scene for their research programmes. In particular, the mainstream of empirical research has been built around the idea that political processes can be explained in terms of the dynamics of class division and class action. It has been shown, for example, that there has been a strong and enduring link between the working class and left-wing political viewpoints. This has been seen as the basis of manual worker support for trade unions (see Chapter 16, pp. 503–4) and for political parties. It has been assumed that there will be a close association between class situation and voting behaviour in any society in which all adults have the right to vote in local and national elections. Manual workers have been expected to show a strong tendency to vote for socialist and communist parties.

ELITIST THEORIES

Not all research into politics and political power has adopted this class-based point of reference. Many critics of Marxism have seen it as involving an economic determinism. Politics and culture, these critics claim, have been seen by Marxists as mere reflections of economic class relations. They are allowed no autonomy from the economic base of the society. The most notable critics of Marxism on this point were the Italian political sociologists Mosca and Pareto. They developed this criticism in their rejection of Marx's concept of the ruling class. It is wrong, they argued, to see the dominant political forces in all societies as being economically determined social classes. Positions of political authority can be held by those from a variety of backgrounds, and not only by the economically powerful.

However, Pareto and Mosca shared with Marx the idea that those in authority in society would always be a minority and that the majority would have little part to play in the running of the state. The holders of political authority were described by these writers as forming an **elite**. An elite was seen as an autonomous and independent social force that could recruit, in part, from a dominant economic class, but could also recruit from specific ethnic, religious, and other social groups. Once established, and on whatever basis, an elite can exclude the mass of the population from any effective say in political decision-making. Elections give little scope for real popular participation by the masses, and many respond to this by choosing not to vote or by accepting that their role is simply to choose between rival sections within the elite. The elite in a society is a ruling minority—an entrenched, self-perpetuating controlling group—but it is not necessarily a ruling class (Bottomore 1993).

 This might be the point at which you should turn to Chapter 15, pp. 604 and 608, and look briefly at our account of Weber. There we argue that authority is the basis of a third dimension of stratification, alongside class and status, and that elites could be understood in this way. You should be able to connect that discussion with the following discussion of Mosca and Pareto.

The ruling elite

All societies, Mosca and Pareto argued, are ruled by minorities. The idea of rule by the majority is a sham. Elections do not really determine state policies, as political leaders can manipulate the electorate and can dupe them into supporting parties that will not actually pursue their interests when in power. Parties are organized agents of sectional, minority interests, and state policies reflect these minority interests rather than majority concerns. The ruling minority—the **ruling elite**—consists of all those who occupy positions of command in the major social institutions through which power is organized in a society. The political structure of the state is one especially important cluster of social institutions, and a **political elite** lies at the heart of any ruling elite. Those who hold top positions of authority in the economy and a church, however, can also form a part of the ruling elite if these social institutions are important elements in the overall power structure of a society.

Mosca explored this by looking at the relationship between the political elite and what he called the social forces. Social forces have specific abilities, aptitudes, or skills that give them a power base in their society. For example, the military, the clergy, economic leaders, and the intelligentsia are each organized around hierarchies of authority that lie outside the sphere of the state. A political elite, then, is one element among others in the larger ruling elite. A ruling elite is a particular coalition of social forces. One particular strand of empirical research on elites has been the investigation of membership and recruitment in those top positions of authority that are seen as the basis of power in a society.

The boundaries of a ruling elite can be explored in the patterns of circulation through which social institutions are connected. Circulation—the movement of individuals from one social position to another—ties social positions together into a single structure of power. This circulation can occur within the lifetime of individuals or between one generation and another. Elite circulation is a particular form of the social mobility that we look at in Chapters 14 and 15.

Gaetano Mosca and Vilfredo Pareto

Gaetano Mosca and Vilfredo Pareto were contemporaries of Max Weber and Emile Durkheim. Mosca (1858–1941) published his major work on political sociology, translated as *The Ruling Class*, in 1896. Pareto (1848–1923) worked as an engineer and an economist before publishing his *Treatise in General Sociology* in 1916. It was Pareto who introduced the word 'elite' and who, therefore, achieved widespread recognition as an innovator. This was much to the annoyance of Mosca, who claimed to have introduced the idea of the elite, if not the word. Both writers remained intellectually active until the 1920s, though they were little known outside their native Italy. Their major works began to be translated into English only in the 1930s, after which elite studies and elitist theory became very important.

One of the leading investigators into this topic was C. Wright Mills (1956), whose study of the United States during the 1950s showed that power was centred on the political, economic, and military hierarchies and that the occupants of the top command situations in these three hierarchies overlapped to such an extent that they formed a single **power elite**. Although the relative power of the three sections of the power elite might vary over time, they were united by their common social background and interests. The power elite, according to Mills, was not solely economic in character. It was not a ruling class in the Marxist sense, despite the fact that large numbers of capitalist property-owners were members of it. The political and military hierarchies were independent of the economic hierarchy, but all three were fused together in a single power elite.

Pareto saw circulation as the means through which the skills and abilities that a state required could be brought into its political elite from outside. In many circumstances, however, circulation is limited by the *exclusion* of people from certain classes or social groups. A ruling elite might, for example, limit key positions to the male descendants of its own members and so become closed in character. Women and men from non-elite backgrounds would be unable to enter the elite,

even if they had qualities that might be useful to it. Closed elites, Pareto argued, are less able to adapt to changing circumstances. They are fixed and rigid and may face opposition from those who have superior skills and resources. They are liable to be overthrown by **counter-elites** recruited from the excluded social forces. History, then, involves a constant struggle of elites against counter-elites. There can, however, be no end to elite rule: all that can happen is the cyclical replacement of one elite by another.

Mass action and mass society

If the idea of the ruling elite can be seen as a deliberate attempt to replace the Marxist idea of the ruling class, the idea of the **mass** can be seen as an attempt to replace the Marxist concept of the proletariat or working class. Where the Marxist sees modern societies as organized around a conflict between ruling classes and working classes, elite theory sees them as organized around the relationship between elites and masses.

Pareto and Mosca were critics of equality and democracy. They and other elite theorists used such terms as the mob, the herd, and the mass to describe the newly empowered workers, whose collective actions they saw as dangerous sources of disorder. The masses were the so-called dangerous classes that were liable to be swayed by irrational ideas and that were a threat to the individualism and freedom that had slowly been achieved in modern society. More generally, equality itself was seen as a levelling process in which culture and lifestyles became homogeneous and bland, making it difficult to sustain the cultural achievements of the past. High culture was threatened by the growth of a popular mass culture and the creation of an anonymous, depersonalized, and alienated society.

☞ You might find it useful to look at our discussion of mass culture and popular culture in Chapter 8, where there is a fuller consideration of these arguments on pp. 280–1.

The masses are seen by elite theorists as incapable of critical, reflective thought. They are passive conformists, following the line of the majority and subject to manipulation by a cynical elite. Michels, a close friend and associate of Mosca, paid particular attention to the ways in which the leaders of socialist parties and trade unions could become separated from their members. Despite their radical traditions, the leaders tended to form an elite that could manipulate their passive mass membership. Because they are so easily manipulated, however, the masses are seen as susceptible to charismatic leaders who can rouse them into extremist and violent politics (Kornhauser 1959; Giner 1976).

SUMMARY POINTS

In this section we have looked at the main theoretical positions on power and politics. These are the class and the elite models. Marxist class theory looks at the organized political struggles of the working class and the capitalist class.

▶ Capitalist classes dominate all areas of the state and become ruling classes.

▶ A ruling class exercises a political and cultural hegemony.

▶ When a working class achieves consciousness as a class for itself, it is organized into a labour movement.

▶ Workers tend to develop a dual consciousness. This is a consequence of their socialization and of their own day-to-day experiences.

The elite theories of Mosca and Pareto reject economic determinism and set out an alternative to Marxism.

▶ All societies are dominated by a ruling elite that occupies the top positions of command. Its members are involved in a constant circulation from one section of the elite to another.

▶ In some circumstances a ruling elite may be opposed by a counter-elite.

▶ Elitist theories are associated with the idea of mass society and mass culture.

THE POLITICS OF CLASS

Britain and the United States are democratic political systems in which politics is organized through party competition for votes in local and national elections. A basic feature of citizenship in these and other advanced societies has been the right to vote. Until the middle of the nineteenth century, voting and party politics in both countries were largely matters for men with property. Few employees and few women had the right to vote. In the United States, the property qualification was ended in 1850, giving all adult white males the right to vote. The abolition of slavery in 1865 and a Voting Act of 1870 meant that black males, as citizens, had the right to vote. Despite these legal changes, tax requirements and literacy tests were widely used to prevent African-Americans from exercising their rights. These restrictions were not fully removed until 1966. In Britain, householders—who were mainly male—were given the right to vote in 1884, but not until 1918 was this right extended to all adult males. Only from 1920 in the United States and from 1928 in Britain did women win the right to vote in national elections.

In this section we will look at whether the formal democratic structure corresponds to the realities of political power. In particular, we will look at the extent

Elections

Parliamentary elections in Britain take place about every four or five years. The country is divided into a number of local constituencies. These constituencies are parts of counties and boroughs and are supposed to have similar numbers of people living in them. In 1900 there were 670 constituencies, and there are currently 659. Voters in each constituency elect one member of parliament from the various candidates who stand for election.

After the election, the party that has had the most MPs elected is usually able to form a government, the party leader becoming prime minister. Because Britain has a constituency system, a party with a majority of the constituency seats may not have received a majority of the votes across the whole country. Most elections give one party or another a majority of seats, but no party since 1918 has ever won a majority of the total votes.

Try to find out about the voting systems in other countries. Some of these have systems of proportional representation like that used in elections for the Northern Ireland Assembly. See if you can work out what this means and how it differs from the British constituency system.

to which politics has been structured by class during the first half of the twentieth century. We will look at patterns of working-class organization and electoral behaviour and at the background and recruitment of political elites.

ELECTIONS AND CLASS VOTING

The link between class and party has long been central to British politics. The leading study of this topic concluded that 'party allegiance has followed class lines more strongly in Britain than anywhere else in the English-speaking world' (Butler and Stokes 1969: 65). A strong link between class and politics has, nevertheless, been apparent in all European countries. The influence of class has been modified by differences in religion, ethnicity, gender, and region, but class has always been the strongest influence on voting.

The class basis of politics has usually been described in terms of the difference between parties of the left and parties of the right. Members of the working class have been seen as most likely to support left-wing parties, typically socialist or communist parties, that advocate greater equality, a redistribution of economic resources, and high levels of social welfare. Members of the middle classes and upper classes, on the other hand, have been seen as most likely to support right-wing parties that stress individual freedom and responsibility and the maintenance of the privileges and advantages of those who succeed in the market system.

Wherever class divisions are sharp, party differences tend to follow this left–right pattern (Lipset and Rokkan 1967; Korpi 1983). Communist, Socialist and Labour parties have attracted the support of manual workers across Europe, while Conservative and Liberal parties have been supported by the more advantaged classes. Class divisions have been less sharp in the United States, and left-wing parties have been weak. However, the relatively more left-wing Democratic Party has consistently gained more support from manual workers than has the more conservative Republican Party.

It was in the United States that the earliest and most influential studies of the class–party relationship were undertaken (Lazarsefeld *et al.* 1948; Cambell *et al.* 1960). These studies found that voting behaviour could be explained by differences in material interests: those with the greatest resources tended to support parties of the right, while those with fewer resources tended to vote for parties of the left. These differences were reinforced wherever social classes formed tight and rela-

tively closed social networks of interaction. In these circumstances, shared experiences produced a greater awareness of shared interests and, therefore, a strong tendency to vote for whichever party supported and promoted those interests. In Britain and continental Europe, class cohesion was especially strong, and the tendency towards class politics was particularly marked. In the United States, on the other hand, class cohesion was much weaker—social mobility was much greater—and the structural basis for a labour movement committed to socialism was never established (Sombart 1906).

Left and right

The terms left and right came into use in eighteenth-century France, where the aristocracy (who supported royal privileges) sat on the right-hand side of the parliamentary chamber. The bourgeoisie (who opposed these privileges) sat on the left-hand side. During the French Revolution, the terms came to be used more generally to describe conservative and radical opinions.

The left–right distinction implies that political parties can be arranged along a line from the most radical (at the left) to the most conservative (at the right), with 'moderate' opinion being in the centre. The terms have continued to be used as a convenient way of summarizing political differences, though there are many political parties that cannot easily be placed along such a line.

This suggests that the Marxist idea of a dominant ideology is seriously misleading. Manual workers were voting largely on the basis of class solidarity and class interests, and not on the basis of their socialization into a false consciousness. We will show, however, that these ideas can be combined through using Gramsci's idea of dual consciousness.

The labour movement and Labour politics

We show in Chapter 15 that a working class was formed in Britain by the early years of the twentieth century. The concentration of economic activity brought workers together in larger numbers, it increased their dependence on one another in a technical division of labour, and it made workers and their families completely dependent on their earnings from work. By concentrating workers' families in densely populated towns and cities, the development of industry and capitalism brought into being a social class that could be described in Marxist terms as a 'class for itself'. Skill differentials among workers diminished in importance, as did wage differentials, though a distinction between skilled and unskilled workers remained an important feature of working-class life and politics. For both sections of the working class, however, the Cooperative Societies, the trade unions, and the Labour Party were the means through which they pursued their common interests and forged a sense of class identity and class consciousness.

Working-class awareness revolved around an image of British society as divided between 'us' and 'them'. The working class—us—was seen as subordinate in terms of power to the bosses, 'gaffers', and employers—them—on whom the workers depended for their work and for their wages. 'They' were better off than 'us', and 'we' rarely saw 'them' because 'they' lived in the well-to-do districts far away from 'our' neighbourhood. This image of society saw 'them' as controlling the government, through the Conservative Party, and so having the power to determine the decisions of the state and to benefit from its policies.

Manual workers and their families were excluded from the electoral process for much of the nineteenth century. Denial of the right to organize into trade unions resulted in many urban riots and disturbances. Most notable among these was the riot at St Peter's Fields in Manchester in 1819, known to history as the

The Labour Party

The Independent Labour Party (ILP), under Keir Hardie, was formed in 1893. In 1900 the ILP joined with the Fabian Society and the Social Democratic Federation (a Marxist group led by Henry Hyndman) to form the Labour Representation Committee. The aims of the LRC, under Ramsey MacDonald, were to achieve improved working conditions through increasing the representation of manual workers in parliament. In 1906 the LRC was renamed the Labour Party. In the 1906 general election, it secured the election of 29 'Labour' MPs. Until 1913 trade unions were not allowed to use their funds for political purposes. This limited their influence over Labour Party policy, although they played a major part in shaping its policies and concerns. The first Labour government was formed at the beginning of 1924, but it lasted less than a year.

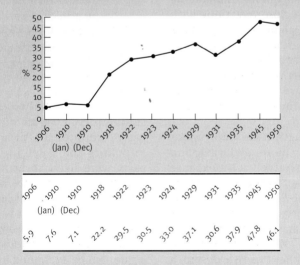

Figure 17.1. **Labour share of the vote, 1906–1950**

1906	1910 (Jan)	1910 (Dec)	1918	1922	1923	1924	1929	1931	1935	1945	1950
5.9	7.6	7.1	22.2	29.5	30.5	33.0	37.1	30.6	37.9	47.8	46.1

Source: adapted from Butler and Butler (1994: 213–16).

battle of Peterloo. The massacre of workers by the militia at Peterloo was an event that helped to change the climate of parliamentary opinion about political rights. The threat to social and political order that the dangerous classes were thought to pose led many in the upper-class and middle-class political leadership to begin to see the granting of industrial and political rights to all men—though not yet to all women—as a way of ensuring their political loyalty. If manual workers were denied these rights any longer, it was held, they would—as Marx anticipated—become ever more revolutionary. If, on the other hand, they were made full citizens of their society, they would acquire a stake in the continuance of the political system and would seek peaceful and limited changes through the electoral mechanism.

> We discuss the civil and political rights of citizenship in Chapter 14, pp. 553–4. What other set of rights did Marshall identify in his definition of citizenship?
> You might like to look at our discussion of urban riots in the 1980s in Chapter 11, pp. 435–7. Is it useful to see riots as the actions of the 'dangerous classes'?

Not until 1918 were all male manual workers able to vote in parliamentary elections. Until this time the working class had, indeed, little direct influence in national parliamentary politics. Male householders, many of whom were skilled workers, had been given the vote in 1884, and this had been a major factor in forcing the Liberal Party to enter into closer relations with the trade unions. A number of 'labour' representatives were elected to parliament as part of the Liberal block. The formation of the Labour Party in 1906 increased the parliamentary representation of the working class, and skilled workers continued to have the most important influence over Labour policy in the first two decades of the twentieth century.

The Labour Party grew in strength at the same time as the working class was becoming more solidaristic and cohesive. Its electoral growth was largely at the expense of the Liberal Party, which has not won sufficient seats to form a government since the First World War. The Labour Party received just under a tenth of the total national vote in 1910, and its share had risen to over one-third by the middle of the 1920s and to around a half by 1950. Figure 17.1 shows that this rise, despite a setback in 1931, was virtually continuous over the whole of the first half of the century. The extension of

the right to vote in 1918 increased the Labour share from 7.1 per cent to 22.2 per cent. By 1945 the Labour share had risen to 46.1 per cent. The working class had found its political voice in the Labour Party, and the Labour Party found its main electoral base in the working class.

Explaining political choice

A survey of political attitudes in the 1960s reported that only 8 per cent of electors refused to identify themselves as either working class or middle class (Butler and Stokes 1969). The vast majority of those who identified themselves as working class were manual workers or supervisors. Almost three-quarters of the people who identified themselves as working class described themselves as Labour Party supporters; and over three-quarters of those who identified themselves as middle class saw themselves as Conservatives.

Party support could be seen, in part, as involving a rational calculation of self-interest based on the perceived match between class interests and party policies. Butler and Stokes argue, however, that working-class support for the Labour Party was, more importantly, an institutionalized custom within working-class communities. Subcultural norms stressing party commitment were acquired through primary socialization in the family and were reinforced by later participation in the formal and informal social relations and activities of working-class life.

> Look at our discussion of primary and secondary socialization in Chapter 4, p. 124, and then read our account of working-class communities in Chapter 15, pp. 616–19. These sections will give you the essential background for understanding this view of voting.

Through their early socialization within the family, children developed an interest in politics and a sense of party commitment. Parents who had a strong interest in politics and a definite attachment to a particular party were likely to bring up their children with a similar interest and commitment. Children learned that their parents had a normative commitment to a particular party, and it was natural that they grew up sharing this commitment. The strength of working-class support for the Labour Party, Butler and Stokes argue, can be explained by socialization into working-class culture. Working-class culture defined British society in terms of social class and it encouraged the adoption of a class perspective in political action. Labour voting appeared to manual workers living in a working-class community as simply the normal or natural thing to do. This model of voting is shown in Figure 17.2.

The role of socialization in working-class support for the Labour Party has usefully been explored by Parkin (1967), who draws on Gramsci's ideas of hegemony and dual consciousness. Parkin begins by identifying what he calls the 'dominant institutional orders' of British society. These are the key institutions of power: the state, the Established Church, the public schools, the monarchy and the aristocracy, elites of all kinds, and the whole structure of private property and business enterprise. These institutions, he argues, have been tied into a single cohesive structure. They embodied a set of core values that correspond closely to the ideology of Conservatism. All members of society have been exposed to these values through their socialization at school and through the mass media. The values were a major influence over their attitudes and actions, and they can be considered to have been truly hegemonic.

Conservative voting can be seen as what Parkin calls a 'symbolic reaffirmation' of the hegemonic values of British society. People voted for the Conservative Party because they identified with the values with which it was associated. Labour voting, on the other hand, involved a commitment to values that ran counter to the hegemonic values. It was 'a symbolic act of deviance' from the dominant values of British society (Parkin 1967: 282). Those in the lower social strata were less influenced by the dominant values because their immediate day-to-day experiences reinforced a different view of power. However, they were unlikely to show a strong tendency towards Labour voting unless they subscribed to an alternative system of values that supported their political deviance. Labour voting was likely to occur on a significant scale only if an alternative and more radical set of values could be built and so could counter the influence of the dominant values. In the absence of such a value system, people remained subject to the overwhelming influence of the dominant values.

Labour voting is most likely to be found where it is sustained by social institutions that reinforce values of collective solidarity and—in its broadest sense—

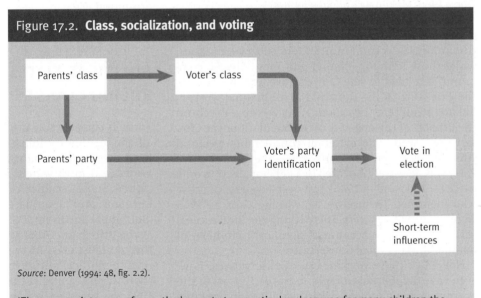

Figure 17.2. Class, socialization, and voting

Source: Denver (1994: 48, fig. 2.2).

'The appropriateness of a particular party to a particular class was for many children the main explanation as to why their parents voted as they did, especially in the working class. . . . An elector who absorbed in childhood a belief about a normative bond of class and party, and who finds this bond reinforced by many of the face-to-face associations in his adult life, may easily accept party allegiance as a natural element in his class culture, quite apart from any well-defined understanding of the benefits that his party may confer upon his class or himself' (Butler and Stokes 1969: 91).

socialism. Parkin sees the institutions of the labour movement and the working-class community as having been the basis of these radical, counter-hegemonic values. The trade unions, the cooperatives, and the Labour Party, together with nonconformist churches and Sunday schools, clubs, and pubs, and the workplace and street-corner solidarity of the traditional proletarian community were a fertile ground for the growth of alternative values. They also provided a structural barrier to the influence of the dominant values: those who lived in these communities and participated in the labour movement were relatively insulated from the hegemonic values and were better able to build on their own day-to-day experiences and to sustain the values that led them to vote for the Labour Party.

Conversely, manual workers who did not live in working-class communities were more likely to experience the full force of the hegemonic values and so were likely to vote Conservative. Workers in small towns dominated by small firms were likely to have relatively close contacts with their employers and managers, and they were unlikely to live in large occupational communities. These working and living conditions were the basis of the *deferential workers*, those who deferred to the authority of the traditional leaders of society (Lockwood 1966; McKenzie and Silver 1968).

The working class, then, has been divided in its political allegiance. Those living in cohesive and solidaristic working-class communities tended to vote Labour, while those living in smaller and more diverse communities tended to vote Conservative. For this reason, the extension of the franchise to all manual workers did not mean that the Labour Party was able to rely on the support of the majority of the population. The Conservatives were able to retain considerable electoral strength. Between 1886 and 1964, the Conservative Party was decisively defeated in a general election only twice (in 1906 and in 1945). Just over a quarter of those who identified themselves as working class in 1963 were Conservative voters. This striking electoral success was possible only because a significant number of manual workers voted Conservative.

Not all of these working-class Conservatives, however, were deferential workers. In the early years of the century, many manual workers who lived in working-class communities were supporters of the Conservative or Liberal parties. Butler and Stokes explain this in terms of their model of political socialization. People acquire their political allegiances in childhood. Those who were young in the years before the Labour Party existed, or when it was a relatively new party, were, of course, unlikely to have had parents who were already committed to the Labour Party. These people could not be socialized into an already-existing Labour-supporting subculture. It was only as the old Liberal Party collapsed during the 1920s that the Labour Party consolidated its political position and a tradition of Labour voting developed in working-class communities. Only in the post-war period have there been significant numbers of electors whose early socialization took place in families with an existing Labour Party commitment. This helps to explain the age distribution of voting preferences. Older people—socialized before the Labour Party achieved its greatest strength in working-class communities—have shown a greater tendency to vote Conservative than have younger people.

The trends in the Labour share of the vote that are shown in Figure 17.1 are the outcome of these processes. The rapidly growing share going to the Labour Party in the first three decades of the century corresponds to the period in which it was replacing the Liberal Party at the national level and was building its strength in the local working-class communities. Its slower growth in the following decades was a result of its success in retaining the support of the children of its early supporters. The trends in voting are a clear indication of the strength of the link between class and party affiliation.

POLITICAL ELITES AND RULING CLASSES

There is considerable evidence that political power in all the leading capitalist societies has been monopolized by their dominant social classes. Although this evidence is most widely available for Britain and the United States, studies of Canada, Australia, France, Germany, and Japan have all shown a similar picture (Bottomore and Brym 1989). In this section, we will look at the British and American evidence on the power of the capitalist class in the state. In a later section, we turn to political authority in the Soviet Union, where there was no capitalist class. Soviet society from 1917 to 1991 was very clearly dominated by a ruling elite that was very different in character from the political elites of capitalist societies.

Politics and power in the United States

Perhaps the most fruitful approach to the nature of class power in the United States is that of G. William

Domhoff (1967, 1971, 1979). Domhoff's work is a powerful synthesis of ideas drawn from both Marxist theory and the elitist theory of Mills. He introduces the term **governing class** to describe the particular alignment of power that exists between the capitalist social class and the exercise of political authority. Not only has the capitalist class been disproportionately advantaged in terms of its income, assets, and other life chances; it has also contributed a disproportionate number of its members to top command situations in the decision-making institutions of the state.

Domhoff substantiates this claim in relation to four processes that he holds to make up the structure of decision-making. For much of the twentieth century these processes worked together to consolidate capitalist class power in the United States. These are:

▶ *the special-interest process*: the process through which individuals and business enterprises are able to influence governments to satisfy their specific and narrow short-run interests;

▶ *the policy-formation process*: the process through which general policies of interest to the dominant class as a whole are developed and implemented;

▶ *the candidate-selection process*: the process through which dominant class members secure access to elected politicians;

▶ *the ideology process*: the process that ensures the dissemination and enforcement of the assumptions, beliefs, and attitudes that underpin the formation of policies and politicians conducive to business interests.

The *special-interest process* comprises a network of lobbyists, committees, and organizations that connect business and government. This network allows the flow of information, advice, pressure and—not infrequently—bribes. It comprises the visible world of pressure-group politics, together with the less visible behind-the-scenes world of informal pressure and power (Bachrach and Baratz 1962). Domhoff shows, for example, how lobbying organizations can undermine attempts to regulate industries and can minimize the effects of proposed legislation. Advisory committees can provide the information and guidance that departments and government agencies need for their decision-making. Hired lawyers can help companies to secure tax advantages. The special-interest process is that system of social relations through which individuals and organizations pressure, influence, and persuade governments to act in support of their interests.

The *policy-formation process* is concerned with larger, more general issues and policies. It allows the special interests of particular sectors, enterprises, and individuals to be forged into a wider class consciousness. It involves a network of foundations, research institutes, think tanks, and committees that interlock with corporate boards and government offices, and it is through these that the political dimension of a class consciousness is built (Useem 1984). Such organizations as the Council on Foreign Relations, the Committee for Economic Development, and the Business Council have been centrally involved in discussions of world trade, overseas aid, health, population, taxation, labour relations, and education. The results of these discussions have been disseminated through informal lunches and meetings and through conferences, journals, and reports. Presidential Commissions and mass-media news reports all feed into this process.

Candidate-selection involves the processes through which individuals are recruited to elected governmental posts and also the processes through which, once elected, they remain responsive to capitalist interests. Financial power is central to the selection and supervision of candidates. Elections are a costly matter, and politicians in large states and the central government depend on their personal wealth or on large-scale financial contributions to fund their campaigns. Those who have the best access to the necessary funds are likely to be selected for office or to be able to exercise a strong influence over the nomination of candidates. The biggest recipient of business donations in the United States has been the Republican Party, though large donors have often sought to maintain their influence over government by giving financial support to the Democrats as well. So long as their chosen candidates continue to support business interests, the parties can be sure of a substantial flow of funds from the business world.

These processes have ensured that politicians have been disproportionately drawn from the higher levels of the class structure, and particularly from business and professional families. Politicians are, by and large, pragmatists who seek to get along with the business interests on whom they depend. Most of them do not have strong policy preferences of their own. They have a general commitment to business and propertied interests and are responsive to their special interests and favoured policies: 'Despite the considerable efforts of organized labor and middle-income reformers, the candidate-selection process produces a predominance of politicians who sooner or later become sympathetic to the prevailing wisdom within either the moderate or ultraconservative faction of the power elite' (Domhoff 1979: 167).

The *ideology process* is a more general process that supports and reinforces the other three processes of class domination. Domhoff holds that it is through the ideology process that public opinion is moulded and that attitudes and values conducive to the dominance of the governing class are sustained. These hegemonic values are the liberal values of individualism, free enterprise, competition, equality of opportunity, and restrictions on the role of government. To be a good American is to subscribe to these values. They are central to discussions in the policy-formation process. The organizations involved in the formulation of policies disseminate them, explicitly and implicitly, through advertising and public relations, through educational strategies, and through the mass media. They create a climate of opinion that sustains the existing political arrangements. While most people may not actively and enthusiastically endorse them, they will, at the very least, adopt an attitude of resigned acquiescence. Existing arrangements are barely questioned. The ideology process minimizes the possibility that any autonomous and more radical consciousness will develop.

Local political power

Domhoff's view of the relationship between class and power at the national level has been supported by a number of studies of particular localities. Studies of Newburyport and Philadelphia in New England, Morris in the mid-west, and Muncie in Indiana have documented the existence of wealthy capitalist classes that dominate local politics. The Lynds' studies (Lynd and Lynd 1929, 1937) of Muncie during the 1920s and 1930s, for example, discovered a business class, centred around a particular dominant family, that had interests in local manufacturing and banking enterprises. This class monopolized positions of political power in the local administration and in the political parties.

Dahl (1961) studied the small city of New Haven in Connecticut, New England, during the middle and the late 1950s. His aim was to explore the question of whether the elected officials were, indeed, the holders of real decision-making power. In undertaking this research, Dahl wanted to set out a critique of the ruling elite and the ruling-class views of politics. Domhoff (1978) has shown, however, that Dahl's results are better seen as contributing to the broadening of a class perspective on political power.

Until the 1840s, New Haven, like many other New England cities and towns, was run by a patrician aristocracy of wealthy commercial and professional families. They were Congregationalists in religion, reflecting the Puritan inheritance of the founding families. The development of new industries in the nineteenth century forced them to share their power with new entrepreneurs who had interests in manufacturing, banking, and insurance. During this period, there was also much working-class migration from Ireland, Germany, Italy, and Eastern Europe, and these European migrants became actively involved in the newly established electoral system. Party leaders who sought success in the elections had to try to attract their support, and the mobilization of ethnic-minority votes became an important feature of local politics.

> ☞ If you have read Chapter 9, 'Religion, Belief, and Meaning', you will recognize some connections with Herberg's argument about ethnicity and migration in the United States. You might find it useful to go back and have another look at his argument, on p. 332. Perhaps you might also like to look back at our discussion on pp. 323–4 of what Weber said about Puritanism.

Dahl saw the 1950s as a time when there was a shift away from a concern for the sectional advantages of particular minority groups. This political shift, argues Dahl, was not unique to New Haven. It was taking place nation-wide. Mayor Lee in New Haven and President Eisenhower in Washington edged the Republicans away from the sectional matters that dominated the old 'machine politics'. The new politics was more concerned with collective benefits, and the critical area for decision-making was urban redevelopment and

Community power studies

Community power studies have often been published using false names for the towns studied. This is to highlight the fact that they are treated as general case studies rather than unique accounts. It also helps to protect the anonymity of the people studied. The most famous pseudonyms are 'Yankee City' (Newburyport), 'Jonesville' (Morris), and 'Middletown' (Muncie). Try to find these towns on a map of the United States. Can you also find New Haven, which we discuss below? Do you think it is valid to generalize from studies of these localities?

renewal. As a result of these changes, claims Dahl, the social notables (the descendants of the old patricians) and the economic notables (the entrepreneurs and people of business) lost their former dominance. Class power was counterbalanced by electoral power. Dahl recognized, however, that capitalist families remained an influential force in local politics: 'The Social and Economic Notables of today . . . are scarcely a ruling elite. . . . They are, however, frequently influential on specific decisions, particularly when these directly involve business prosperity. Moreover, politicians are wary of their potential influence and avoid policies that might unite the notables in bitter opposition' (Dahl 1961: 84).

In his critical discussion of Dahl's work, Domhoff (1978) re-examines the issue of urban redevelopment. He shows that political action by the mayor was, in fact, preceded by a long period of business lobbying and pressure, including action at the national and state level. It was only after this preparatory period, and after federal legislation had opened up new options, that local politicians saw a political opportunity and attempted to carry this through by mobilizing popular support for it. Business leaders in New Haven were organized through the Chamber of Commerce and other civic organizations, where local political policies were developed in relation to national programmes. They formed the central part of a local policy-formation and opinion-making process that connected to the national-level processes that Domhoff had identified in his other works. Dahl's study, by focusing on a relatively late phase in the whole process, ignored the earlier preparatory work in which business leaders had been heavily involved.

Domhoff has also shown that the economic and social notables can be seen as having a high level of class unity and that they must be seen in relation to the larger national capitalist class of which they are a part. American cities, he argues, are not to be seen as isolated units but as elements in a larger political economy. They are *growth machines*: engines of capital accumulation within a capitalist system that is both national and international in scope. Businesses in New Haven have been locked into this economy through links of ownership and control. Local business leaders have directorships in large multinationals, and business leaders from New York and other financial centres have connections to New Haven companies. While some small towns may be dominated by small businesses or the middle classes, Domhoff concludes that New Haven is important enough to have a significant presence of those who are indisputably members of the national capitalist class.

A British ruling class?

A series of studies have shown the ways in which political power in Britain has been linked to class advantages through structures of kinship, education and recruitment. The Conservative Party, the government, the civil service, the legal profession, and the military have all been overwhelmingly recruited from the capitalist class and have been unified through bonds of intermarriage and a common educational background (Guttsman 1963). This research showed that landed property remained a fundamental element in the structure of political power through much of the twentieth century and that the old public schools and universities (most particularly, Eton and Harrow schools and Oxford and Cambridge universities) were the means through which landed and industrial interests were tied together and through which careers in the political elite could be built. Well into the twentieth century, the upper-class institutions remained central to capitalist class power. These trends are shown for various elites in Figure 17.3.

The most systematic explorations of these processes have been undertaken by Miliband (1969) and John Scott (1991), who have drawn on similar ideas to those of Domhoff (see also Miliband 1982, 1989). Their work depends upon the identification of two distinct concepts: the capitalist class and the state elite. The capitalist class, as we showed in the last chapter, consists of those who depend upon property ownership and the use of property for their advantaged life chances. It has interests in both landed and non-landed forms of property. The **state elite**, on the other hand, comprises the leading command situations in the government, parliament, the civil service, the military and paramilitary, and the judiciary, which together make up the state system. If people from a capitalist class background disproportionately fill the leading positions in the state elite, they can be described as a ruling class.

 If you are not familiar with the idea of a capitalist class and how it developed in Britain, look at the discussion of this in Chapter 15, pp. 623–6.

However, things are rarely this straightforward. A capitalist class is small in size, and the state elite must recruit people from other class backgrounds. To deal with this issue, Scott has introduced the ideas of the **power bloc** and the power elite. A power bloc is an alignment of classes that have certain shared interests and

The top judiciary arrive for the opening of parliament. What does this tell us about power in Britain?

concerns and a common focus on the exercise of state power, although they may have many conflicting interests as well. The classes are aligned by the predominance of one class within the power bloc. A power elite exists wherever positions within the state elite are drawn overwhelmingly from a power bloc. When a capitalist class holds the paramount position within such a power bloc, it can be described as a ruling class.

To develop this argument, Scott constructed a typology of power elites to highlight the distinctive features of the British situation. This typology is shown in Figure 17.4. Power elites are classified by the extent to which they are solidaristic, with a high level of group consciousness and cohesion, and the extent to which one class within the alignment holds a paramount position. The four types of power elite are defined as follows:

▶ An *exclusive power elite* exists wherever a power bloc is drawn from a restricted and highly uniform social background and is able to achieve a high level of social solidarity and cohesion.

▶ An *inclusive power elite* exists when there is a solidaristic power bloc that is not dominated by any particular class. The power bloc draws from a limited number of classes, but these are relatively equally balanced.

▶ A *segmented power elite* exists wherever a power bloc that is dominated by a particular class is, nevertheless, divided into a number of separate and distinct fractions and so has a relatively low level of overall cohesion.

▶ A *fragmented power elite* exists wherever the constituent classes of a power bloc are relatively evenly balanced and there is very little overall solidarity and cohesion.

Wherever the structure of political recruitment is more widely drawn than in these models and no power bloc exists, there will be no power elite. In these circumstances, the distribution of power within the state cannot usefully be described in terms of the existence of a single elite.

Scott argues that political authority in Britain has, indeed, been dominated by a power bloc. An alignment of the capitalist class with those in entrepreneurial,

Figure 17.3. Elite background and recruitment, Britain, 1939–1970

	% from private school			
	1939	1950	1960	1970
Top civil servants	90.5	59.9	65.0	61.7
Ambassadors	75.5	72.6	82.6	82.5
Top army officers	63.6	71.9	83.2	86.1
Top navy officers	19.8	14.6	20.9	37.5
Top air force officers	69.7	59.1	59.5	65.0
Top judiciary	84.4	86.8	82.5	83.5

	% from Oxford or Cambridge University			
	1939	1950	1960	1970
Top civil servants	77.4	56.3	69.5	69.3
Ambassadors	49.0	66.1	84.1	80.0
Top army officers	25	8.8	12.4	24.3
Top navy officers	—	—	—	—
Top air force officers	18.2	13.6	19.1	17.5
Top judiciary	77.8	73.6	74.6	84.6

Source: Boyd (1973: tables 4–9, 13–17).

▶ **Why do you think that military officers have relatively low rates of attendance at Oxford and Cambridge? Check out the role of such specialist institutions as Sandhurst, Dartmouth, and Cranfield if you are unsure.**

Figure 17.4. Forms of power elite

professional, and managerial class situations has provided the core of those who have been recruited to top positions within the state. The capitalist class has been paramount within this alignment and it has been disproportionately represented in all the key areas of the state elite.

The solidarity of this power elite was based on the continuing significance of the old public schools and universities. Formerly the exclusive preserve of the upper class, these institutions opened up their recruitment to a wider social band during the second half of the twentieth century. The classes that make up the power bloc are precisely those that benefited from this and that have been disproportionately represented in

the various branches of the state elite. These people sat on the most important boards, commissions, councils, and committees, and they met frequently at business meetings, lunches, dinners, and ceremonies. Informal interaction in the exclusive London social clubs, involvement in the same round of social activities, and connections through marriage, tied them together into a strong structure of power. Using the categories of Figure 17.4, the British power elite can be described as an exclusive power elite within which the capitalist class has been paramount. For this reason, it can be said that Britain has had a ruling class.

TOTALITARIANISM AND COMMAND SOCIETIES

We have looked at ruling elites and their class basis in capitalist societies, but ruling elites also exist in other types of advanced industrial society. To explore this further, we will look at elite organization in Soviet Russia. This has often been described as a system of rule based on a totalitarian political system.

The concept of **totalitarianism** was introduced to describe the politics and social stratification of Nazi Germany, Fascist Italy, and the Soviet Union. In each of these three societies, it was held, a ruling elite had total control over all aspects of social life, and so totalitarian regimes differed markedly from the liberal and democratic regimes of Britain and the United States. Throughout the period of the cold war between East and West, liberal commentators on the Soviet Union stressed its totalitarian character. Their work had an ideological character, helping to legitimate and reinforce the hostility of Western governments to the Soviet Union and the states of Eastern Europe that formed the Communist bloc (Friedrich and Brzezinski 1956; Shapiro 1972; see also Lefort 1986). In their opposition to the official Marxism of the Communist systems, totalitarian theorists also contributed to the critique of Marxist ideas in the social sciences. Totalitarian theory was, in all respects, anti-Marxist.

Despite these ideological uses of totalitarianism, we will show that it has a real sociological content and that it can help us to understand modern societies with highly centralized political systems. You will find it useful to have read our discussion of command situations in Chapter 15, p. 608.

 Much of the argument about totalitarianism draws on Weber's analysis of rationality and bureaucracy. You might like to look at what we say about this in Chapter 18, pp. 728–9. In that chapter, you will also find a brief discussion of Weber's idea of charismatic authority. By this, he meant the form of authority that involves a belief in the exceptional or superhuman characteristics of the ruler.

The idea of the ecclesia is defined in Chapter 9, p. 327, where you will also find a discussion of the religious character of Soviet Communism (p. 333).

Totalitarianism defined

A totalitarian system is one in which no area of life falls outside the scope of the state. Everything is subordinate to the collective goals set by the ruling elite. There is no room for autonomous public opinion, and no proper constitutional system of decision-making. The state is a highly centralized system of command that allows its top bureaucrats to form a ruling elite. This bureaucracy operates, without restrictions, to set the agenda and to enforce all decisions. All actions of the state and its elite are justified in relation to its official ideology. The state is, in effect, organized as an *ecclesia*: an all-embracing system organized around an orthodox and tightly enforced system of beliefs. These kinds of regime tend to produce or to be produced by absolute rulers who can act as personal dictators. Such individuals may have charismatic qualities that enable them to rise to power and to mobilize mass support, but they must rely on ruthless terror and intimidation to maintain their rule.

Those who live under a totalitarian regime have little or no individual freedom. Their attitudes and opinions are shaped by the mass media and the educational system, which operate as agencies of indoctrination and propaganda in the service of the official ideology. People's movements are tightly controlled, both within the country and abroad, and they are subject to direct force and coercion, as well as more indirect surveillance by secret police.

Where Marxism sees economic forces as the most important determinants of social development, totalitarian theorists place greater emphasis on politics and

the state. For some of these theorists, however, politics must ultimately adapt to the need to develop an advanced industrial technology. Kerr *et al.* (1960), for example, hold that centralized regimes of totalitarian political control are incompatible with the requirements of an advanced industrial technology. This technology, they hold, is compatible only with the pluralistic structures of liberal democracy. According to this view, totalitarian regimes faced a critical problem. If they took steps to develop their industrial base, they

Totalitarianism

▶ *one-party rule*; absence of competitive elections; lack of restrictions on leadership;

▶ an *official ideology* as the basis of social order and centralized power;

▶ *personal dictatorship* of a pre-eminent individual;

▶ use of *terror and force*, concentration camps and political police to maintain order and conformity;

▶ *centrally planned economy*, stressing production and accumulation over consumption;

▶ *restrictions on freedom* of movement; subordination of individual and private interests to collective goals;

▶ *indoctrination and propaganda* through monopoly control over mass media, education, and all cultural institutions; attempt to maintain total conformity.

Source: adapted from Curtis (1979: 7–9).

would sow the seeds of their eventual collapse; but if they tried to maintain totalitarian control, they would be unable to achieve industrial advance and economic growth. The dilemma of totalitarianism, then, was that of industrial development and political collapse *versus* industrial stagnation and political survival. However, industrial stagnation could not be sustained in the long term. The political collapse of totalitarianism was inevitable.

The three societies seen as exemplifying the totalitarian model are the Fascist regime of 1921–43 in Italy, the Nazi regime of 1933–45 in Germany, and the Communist regime in Russia from 1917 until the 1980s. In each case, a personal dictator (Mussolini, Hitler, Stalin) seemed able to use the centralized power of a one-party state to exercise total and arbitrary power. Benito Mussolini's Fascist Party achieved power in a period of political weakness in Italy and, from the mid-1920s, established a strong and centralized system. It entered into a military alliance with Germany once Adolf Hitler had achieved similar power there. The Communist Revolution of 1917 in Russia established the Soviet Union as an important political power under Lenin, but it was as Josef Stalin rose to power in the 1920s that the system became more centralized. The system became less overtly coercive after the death of Stalin in 1953,

but most of its principal structures remained in place until the Brezhnev regime of the 1970s and 1980s.

Political command and state socialism

The most interesting society to consider in relation to the concept of totalitarianism is the Soviet Union, where centralized and autocratic political control lasted much longer. It differs from the other cases in a number of important respects. While Italy and Germany were capitalist societies and the totalitarian regimes encouraged business interests, the Soviet system grew from an explicitly anti-capitalist revolution. In both Germany and Italy, defeat in war helped to bring about the end of their totalitarian systems, while Russian totalitarianism seems to have collapsed because of its own internal problems. The Soviet Union is a useful case for assessing arguments about the incompatibility between totalitarianism and advanced industrial technology.

After the death of Lenin, Stalin used his base in the Communist Party bureaucracy to purge all actual and potential opponents to his rule. By sacking and, in later years, murdering the old revolutionaries who might have challenged him, he built a massive and centralized bureaucracy of professional administrators who

Adolf Hitler

Adolf Hitler (1889–1945) was born in Austria. He dropped out of school, intending to follow an artistic career, but he failed to gain entry to the Vienna Academy. He dodged military service and moved to Germany, where he volunteered for army service during the First World War. After the war he spied on political parties as a paid informer of the authorities, but he gradually became drawn into open political action. He joined a small party, transforming it into the National Socialist German Workers' Party and forming a paramilitary 'brown-shirt' movement.

The Nazis—as they became known—took an extreme right-wing and anti-Jewish position. Hitler was imprisoned after an attempt to overthrow the Bavarian government in 1923. After his release, he cultivated the support of big business and the established political parties and became German Chancellor (prime minister) in 1933. He immediately set up a framework of terror and abandoned constitutional restraints. Hitler built up the German army, but invaded Austria and Czechoslovakia, and found himself embroiled in war against Britain and France in 1939.

One of the principal elements in Hitler's outlook was his anti-Semitism—anti-Jewish sentiment—which he built into an ideology that justified the exclusion of Jews from most forms of employment, the confiscation of their property, and their wholesale persecution. His ideas were set out in the book that he wrote while in prison, *Mein Kampf* (1925), and they were implemented in the 'final solution'. This was a policy to remove Jews and other 'degenerates' (such as gypsies and homosexuals) from German territory to concentration and extermination camps such as Belsen, Dachau, and Auschwitz. More than six million people were murdered by the Nazis in the gas chambers at these camps.

were responsible solely to him. Those who did not conform suffered show trials, confinement in concentration camps (the infamous gulags), and extermination.

Ordinary people were subject to the same kinds of controls, their conformity being enforced by a network of police informers and a system of literary and political censorship. Deviance from political orthodoxy was regarded not only as a crime, but as a sign of mental illness. The official view was that anyone who could not see the self-evident truth of Communist ideology was, quite obviously, insane. Mental hospitals were used more as prisons than as hospitals, and the totalitarian system made use of a particularly strong form of the total institution.

> ☞ Look at our discussion of the labelling of deviant behaviour in Chapter 6, p. 153; you might also like to review what we said in 'Medicalization and the Mind', pp. 214–17. You will find a discussion of the total institution in Chapter 16, pp. 649–50.

Under Stalin's successors—Kruschev and Brezhnev were the most important—some of the more ruthless and arbitrary characteristics of the regime were dismantled. However, the tight structure of political control and censorship remained. The concentration camps and mental hospitals became, if anything, even more important in maintaining social control. Economic activity was given a greater degree of autonomy from the centralized planning system, but political, cultural, and personal life remained tightly controlled from the centre.

So, was the Soviet Union totalitarian? One organization (the Communist Party fused with the state) exercised massive power in all areas of social life. This control, however, was never 'total' in the sense implied by some of the more extreme proponents of the idea. Central control barely reached some of the more distant villages, especially in the non-Russian Republics that had been incorporated into the Soviet Union. While centralized party control was tight throughout Eastern Europe after the Second World War, the regimes of East Germany, Poland, Hungary, and Czechoslovakia were far weaker than the Stalinist system of the Soviet Union itself.

For this reason, the term cannot be used without qualification. D. Lane (1976) has made the useful suggestion that the Soviet Union should be seen as a **state socialist** system, rather than simply as totalitarian. This is an attempt to give greater attention to the relationship between economics and politics and to patterns of stratification. State socialism is a system in which the pursuit of social and economic equality is achieved through a centralized, state-directed promotion of economic development. The Soviet state, Lane argues, was concerned with mobilizing the population for industrial development. The system was a state-directed system of socialist modernization.

In state socialism, politics is related to a specific form of social stratification. The ruling elite that built the Soviet Union also built an entrenched position for itself. It eventually became the dominant force in the society. The ruling elite, sometimes described as the *nomenklatura*, came to form a self-perpetuating social stratum with privileges and life chances that were not available to the mass of the population (Matthews 1978). It is this structure of privilege for those in positions of political command that explains the persistence of the centralized structures that have been described as totalitarian. The central features of the system were geared to the maintenance of elite privileges and the suppression of all opposition to this.

The Communist regimes of Russia and Eastern Europe collapsed in a series of both peaceful and violent events from the late 1980s. This led to fundamental transformations in the whole global structure of power, some of which are discussed in Chapter 12. The collapse of Communism seemed a very sudden change, but its roots were deep within the structures of the state socialist regimes.

Under Brezhnev in the 1970s and 1980s, the Soviet economy stagnated. The industrial forces that had been developed under Stalin were held back from further development by a centralized political system that was unwilling and unable to respond to these problems. Not until Gorbachev's reforms of the mid-1980s was this problem addressed. Stagnation had made reform more acceptable to the leadership, and Gorbachev encouraged greater autonomy for market-based systems of distribution. In 1986 he launched a policy of *perestroika* or restructuring, aimed at abandoning centralized planning and administration (White 1991). This policy was rapidly extended to the political system through a policy of *glasnost* (openness or democratization). The momentum behind these changes came from the much-expanded intelligentsia of educated, professional, and non-manual employees, whose interests and consciousness differed from those of manual workers as well as from those of the *nomenklatura*, the dominant group of officials.

State socialism

'It is a society distinguished by a state-owned, more or less centrally administered economy, controlled by a dominant communist party which seeks, on the basis of Marxism-Leninism and through the agency of the state, to mobilize the population to reach a classless society' (D. Lane 1996).

Two systems compared

	Capitalism	State socialism
Public rights	'citizenship': private property and individual freedom	'comradeship': state property and equality
Means of economic coordination	market competition	planning and centralized administration
Means of political coordination	democracy and electoral competition	central control: party and bureaucracy
Means of social integration	pluralistic private associations	collectivist public associations
Basis of public order	rule of law (legal order)	politics (discretionary order)
Source of social identity	leisure and consumption	labour and production

Source: adapted from D. Lane (1996: 52).

The attempt to resolve the economic contradictions of the system weakened its totalitarian elements and allowed the emergence of, in effect, a multi-party political system. The Communist Party proved unable to hold onto its monopoly position, and the regime lost its legitimacy. However, the economic reforms did not produce a strong and growing economy. Instead, there was declining production, sharply rising price inflation, and massive unemployment. The Gorbachev reforms had failed in their economic goals, and Gorbachev himself lost control of the situation. The Soviet Union and the remnants of its totalitarian system disintegrated.

It appears, then, that Kerr and his colleagues were correct to point to the impossibility of combining a totalitarian command system with an advanced and growing industrial economy. The contradiction built into the very structure of state socialism ensured its eventual collapse.

SUMMARY POINTS

In this section we have looked at the evidence on class politics in the first half of the twentieth century. We looked, first, at the working class.

▶ Members of the working class in all industrial societies have shown a strong tendency to support parties of the left.

▶ Electoral support for Labour grew continuously through the first half of the century.

▶ Working-class support for the Labour Party in Britain developed in cohesive working-class communities that allowed the development of a strong and autonomous political consciousness.

▶ Working-class conservatism occurred mainly in smaller and more socially mixed communities where there was less class solidarity among manual workers.

We then turned to the question of whether Britain and the United States had ruling classes.

▶ The dominant class in the United States operated through the special-interest process, the policy-formation process, the candidate-selection process, and the ideology process.

▶ Local city politics was dominated by business interests linked to the national capitalist class.

▶ The ruling class in Britain is a power elite that has been highly cohesive and restricted in its social background.

Finally, we looked at politics in a non-capitalist society, the Soviet Union.

▶ The Soviet Union was a state socialist system with a totalitarian ruling elite.

PLURALISTIC POLITICS

We have shown that for the first fifty or sixty years of the twentieth century politics in capitalist societies has been organized around class. In Britain, the United States, and elsewhere, political authority, political organization, and political action have been structured around the patterns of social stratification that we describe in 'The Making of a Class Society', Chapter 15, pp. 613–27. A strong and cohesive working class was organized into trade unions and a Labour Party, and it gave much electoral support to that party. The middle classes provided the backbone of electoral support for the Conservative Party, and an upper class monopolized the exercise of political power within the state.

Our argument in Chapter 15, however, is that the clear lines of division and the contours of solidarity that characterized stratification in the first half of the twentieth century had become increasingly more fragmentary. Class divisions persisted, but they had become less visible, and social classes became less cohesive and conscious of themselves. It is now time to investigate the implications of these changes for the structure of politics. What is the nature of politics, power, and protest in a fragmentary class society?

THE END OF CLASS POLITICS?

Many researchers have identified what they believe to be a contemporary decline in the significance of class relations for political action. In place of class as a single, unitary focus for the distribution of political power, they have identified a more diverse plurality of political groups. This pluralist view of power structures is a critical development of elitist theory that turns it into a radical theory of democracy.

The classical idea of democracy—rule by the mass of the citizens—had been seen as a mere sham by Mosca and Pareto, who held that a small minority or elite would always rule. Weber held to this same point of view, but he argued that it was important to explore the electoral controls that can be imposed on elite power in modern democracies. In a democracy, he held, people can *choose* the political elite through the ballot box. Weber recognized, of course, that things were rarely as simple as this and that there were many areas in modern societies where electoral control did not exist, but his emphasis on the electoral process and party competition laid the basis for the view that later came to be called democratic elitism. According to this point of view, democracy can be seen as the competition of elites.

 You will find a more extended discussion of democracy in Chapter 18, pp. 729–30.

This position holds that the existence of elites is compatible with the idea of democracy, so long as there is more than one elite and so long as there is effective competition among them. The political sphere of a democratic society is like the economic market place. It is an arena in which party-based elites must compete for the votes of the political consumers. Just as consumer demand in the economic market is supposed to guarantee consumer sovereignty, so political demands in the electoral market are held to guarantee popular democratic sovereignty. In a competitive system, politicians will supply the policies and programmes that the electors demand.

Writers who have developed the elitist theory of democracy and the more general pluralist standpoint have often overstated their case. They have, however, identified an important dimension of contemporary politics and a fundamental area in which the exercise of political power has been transformed. In the rest of this chapter we will look at the extent to which they are correct to see class politics as having been replaced by pluralistic politics.

Pluralism, issues, and power

Pluralist theory sees a whole variety of interest groups, pressure groups, and associations as joining the older parties in the competition for power. Pluralists hold that power in contemporary industrial societies has been dispersed among a large number of individuals and organizations. Political decisions are, therefore, the outcome of shifting struggles among these groups as they each seek to pursue their particular interests or to promote their particular values. The competitive struggle for the votes of an informed and politically aware electorate occurs within this larger context, and it is no longer possible to identify monopolistic centres of political power.

Elitism and pluralism present very different images of the structure of power in modern societies. Elitists, like Marxists, see power as being concentrated in the hands of a single ruling group. Pluralists, on the other hand, see it as dispersed among a number of separate *veto groups*, each of which is able to counter the influence of others. This difference in viewpoint is also associated with a difference in methodology. Where elitists stress the circulation of individuals among social positions that carry the potential or capacity for power, pluralists stress the direct study of patterns of decision-making and the actual exercise of power. Lukes (1974) has effectively shown, however, that these should not be seen as mutually contradictory arguments. They are, rather, complementary aspects of the social distribution of power. Power exists as both a *capacity* (defined by the structural location of people and groups) and an active exercise of *agency* in individual and collective action.

Pluralist views were developed most forcefully in the 1950s and 1960s, when writers such as Robert Dahl set out their critical views on ruling-elite and ruling-class theories. In his study of New Haven, Dahl (1961) argued that elitists had merely *assumed* the existence of an all-

pervasive elite, rather than actually *demonstrating* its existence with evidence. Whether an elite exists in a particular society, he held, is an empirical question. It is a matter that is to be approached in an open-minded way and is not to be decided in advance on the basis of theoretical prejudice.

Dahl held that political power can best be investigated through the key decisions that are made in a particular society. Sociologists should examine who participates in these decisions and whose preferences actually prevail as a result of them. If a ruling elite exists, Dahl says, it will be found that the same small group of people participate in all decisions and that the outcomes of these decisions correspond to their preferences and political programmes. If this cannot be demonstrated, then there is no ruling elite.

Dahl suggests, in fact, that there is little evidence that modern societies are dominated by ruling elites. Although those who actually participate in the active exercise of power may be a minority in their society, the constitutional framework of democracy ensures that they will represent and be responsive to the majority. They are open rather than closed groups. The structure of civil and political freedom in contemporary societies requires that political parties compete for the votes of the electorate. The extension of the franchise has meant that parties are responsive to the wishes and interests of all adult citizens in their societies. In order to secure power within a democratic system, parties and candidates must try to attract the support of enough voters to give them a majority in the legislative body.

In New Haven, Dahl showed that this political participation is open to all electors, though manual workers were far less active than non-manual workers. Political issues are generally raised or organized by politically active intellectuals, experts, and reformers who are able to attract the support of other professionals and politicians. Though broader political pressure may sometimes force an issue onto the agenda, most voters limit their role to voting on the issues raised by the political activists. Political parties are coalitions of activists, and their dependence on popular votes in a democratic system means that politicians have to weigh political issues in terms of a calculation of the likely electoral support that will be given by non-activists.

A similar picture is painted of political power at the national level. A government in Britain must be drawn from a majority party or from a coalition of parties that can mobilize a majority in the House of Commons. In a presidential system, on the other hand, matters are a little more complicated. In the United States, for example, the division of powers between President and

Congress means that a presidential candidate must aim to secure a majority of the popular vote and must hope that his or her party will have or be able to attain a majority of seats in Congress. In either case, the competition for votes is seen as a guarantee that popular, majority concerns and interests will carry the day in political decision-making. The new party politics is a politics of issues rather than a politics of class.

From this point of view, the overall structure of contemporary political leadership has become more pluralistic. Each party may form a small minority in the population, but the competition among parties ensures democratic decision-making. At the same time, the political leadership itself is simply one powerful group among many. The power of the state is checked by the countervailing power of employers' associations, trade unions, and a whole variety of pressure groups and interest groups and associations. Such groups form around particular political preferences and choices, and the struggle of interest groups is a major force in the political process. This does not mean that there is no longer a ruling class. Many of the features of the old system persist, and it is certainly not the case that all political groups are equal in power. Nevertheless, there has been a greater degree of pluralism in the exercise of political power. Different sections of the population participate in different sets of decisions, and the preferences of one group may often be counterbalanced by those of others. Instead of a monolithic ruling elite, contemporary societies tend towards a greater plurality of interest groups and a fragmentation of power.

Pluralist views of the end of class, the end of ideological politics, and the decentralization of power have been taken up in the post-modernist theories of the 1980s and 1990s (G. McLennan 1989). According to these theorists, societies must be seen as resulting from the competitive struggles of a plurality of specific social groups. Foucault, for example, identified de-centred power relations that were focused in specialized organizations and agencies rather than in such overarching structures as states or social classes. Along with the pressure groups and associations identified by earlier pluralists, contemporary post-modern pluralists have identified a wider range of social groups based on consumption, lifestyle, and personal identity. Groups and group identities themselves are not fixed, but are shifting and fragmented. Individuals build up a number of identities that can vary quite significantly from one situation to another. As a result, group consciousness and large-scale collective action are abandoned for a new and radically individualized politics of difference and identity.

 If you are unsure about the points that we are making about identity, read our discussion of this whole question in Chapter 4.

Pluralist and post-modernist theories, then, claim that there is a declining significance of class and class-based politics in contemporary societies. These societies show a corresponding increase in the significance of individualistic concerns about issues and identities in the political sphere. The impact of these ideas can be seen most clearly in the debates over issue voting and over the growing significance of new social movements.

Trends in party support

We have shown that British politics in the first half of the twentieth century was marked by a very close association between social class and party preference. During the last forty years, however, this link has weakened, and the stable two-party electoral system has shifted towards a more volatile three-party system. The reasons for this political shift have been much debated, and they highlight the significance of the changing patterns of social stratification that we discussed in Chapter 15.

 If you have not yet looked at the debate about the working class in the post-war period, read our discussion of this in Chapter 15, pp. 630–4. You will find it useful background for understanding the political changes that we look at in this chapter.

The proportion of manual workers voting for the Labour Party declined from 69 per cent to 50 per cent between 1966 and 1979. After dropping even further to 38 per cent in 1983, Labour support amongst manual workers stood at 45 per cent in 1992. The proportion of non-manual workers voting for the Conservative Party remained at or above 60 per cent until 1979, and then dropped slowly but inexorably to 49 per cent by 1992. This means that about two-thirds of each class still voted for their customary or natural party in 1966, while less than a half of each did so in 1992.

As we will show later, there is also much evidence to suggest that the reasons that people have for voting one way or another have altered. People are now less likely to vote principally because of socialized class preferences. There has been a weakening of class attachment to particular political parties. The main beneficiaries of this have been the Liberal Democrats and their predecessors (the Liberals and the Social Democrats), who were supported by 14 per cent of non-manual workers and 6 per cent of manual workers in 1966, but by 25 per cent of non-manual and 20 per cent of manual workers in 1992. The main loser, until the middle of the 1980s, was the Labour Party. Figure 17.5 shows that the share of the total vote going to the Labour Party in general elections declined between 1950 and 1983. While the share of the vote going to the Labour Party recovered slightly during a trough of Conservative unpopularity after 1987, the secure core of Labour voting remained far below the level attained in 1945. Even the Labour landslide victory of 1997 was achieved with a lower share of the vote than in 1945.

A major reason for the decline in the total *share* of the vote going to the Labour Party is the decline in the number of manual workers and a corresponding increase in the number of non-manual workers. To the extent that there is still a tendency for manual workers to vote Labour, a decline in the number of manual workers will result in a fall in the Labour vote. It has been calculated that around a half of the total fall in the

Labour vote up to the 1980s can be explained in this way (Heath *et al.* 1985). Conversely, of course, about a half of the fall in the Labour vote could not be explained in these terms. Many manual workers were simply no longer willing to vote Labour in the same kind of automatic way that they had a generation earlier. The fall in the Labour vote up to the 1980s is a combined result of the declining size of the working class and a loosening of class attachments. This has led to a greater volatility in party support, and this, in turn, has created opportunities for a growth in electoral support for the Liberal Democrats.

Figure 17.5 also shows that the Labour share of the vote has increased since the middle of the 1980s. In 1983 it was 27.6 per cent, while in 1997 it reached 43.1 per cent. This was a return to the level at which it stood in 1970. This increase in the Labour share of the vote may be explained, in part, by a return of manual workers to the Labour Party, though this does not seem to involve the kind of unqualified support that the Party received in the past. However, the decline in the number of manual workers must mean that the rise in the Labour vote is a result of the increasing willingness of non-manual workers to vote Labour. The Labour Party is no longer the automatic party of choice for manual workers. It is a party that can attract both manual

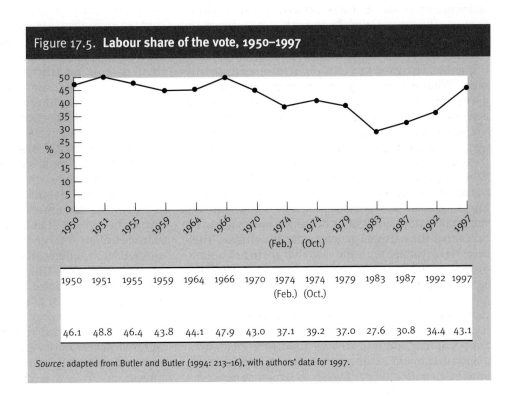

Figure 17.5. **Labour share of the vote, 1950–1997**

1950	1951	1955	1959	1964	1966	1970	1974 (Feb.)	1974 (Oct.)	1979	1983	1987	1992	1997
46.1	48.8	46.4	43.8	44.1	47.9	43.0	37.1	39.2	37.0	27.6	30.8	34.4	43.1

Source: adapted from Butler and Butler (1994: 213–16), with authors' data for 1997.

and non-manual workers, but neither of them give it unqualified long-term support.

Before we look at the reasons for this, we must examine a peculiarity of the British electoral system. As we have already shown, the governing party is the one that wins the most seats in parliament. The nature of the British constituency system is such that there is no direct relationship between the number of votes that a party receives and the number of seats that it wins. If a party's support is concentrated in particular parts of the country, it may receive a large number of votes but relatively few seats. Support for Labour, for example, was formerly very concentrated in northern working-class communities, while support for the Conservatives came from rural and more socially mixed areas. Labour could receive a large number of votes, but the concentration of these votes in particular constituencies made it difficult for them to win enough seats to win an election.

The consequences of this can be seen in Figure 17.5. In 1997 the Labour Party received 43.1 per cent of the vote and formed a government with a massive majority of 179 seats over the Conservatives, who received 31 per cent of the vote. Yet in 1970 the Labour Party had received 43.0 per cent of the vote and the Conservatives had become the governing party with a majority of 31 seats. In 1951, when its support was much more heavily concentrated in industrial constituencies, Labour received a much larger 48.8 per cent of the vote, but the Conservatives won the election with a majority of 16 seats. These figures underline the paradox that the strength of popular support for a party is not the only thing that determines its chances of forming a government. What matters is its strength relative to all other parties, and the way in which its support is spread across the country.

Class dealignment and issue voting

Why is there a greater willingness of people to vote for parties other than the traditional party of their class? This is a difficult question to answer. In fact, many researchers now hold that it no longer makes sense to talk about the natural party for a particular class. This belief is associated with the idea that there has been a process of **dealignment** between class and party. The concept of dealignment refers to the breaking of the automatic, socialized connection between class and party. Party support is no longer aligned with class background and class interests. This is still a rather controversial idea, but it provides a powerful explanation of electoral trends in the post-war period. Dealignment and the changing shape of the class structure have pro-duced a fundamental transformation in the stable two-party system that existed for the first half of the century.

This trend towards dealignment is not unique to Britain. Figure 17.6 shows that class and politics have become dealigned in all the advanced capitalist societies during the post-war period. This graph measures dealignment using the *Alford index*, a measure of association between class and party that overcomes some of the limitations of relying simply on a measure of the absolute fall in the share of the vote going to a particular party. The decline in class voting, it can be seen, has been most marked in the United States, where the process of dealignment began much earlier, but the general pattern appears in all the advanced societies.

Voter dealignment involves two interrelated processes, which can be considered in turn. These are:

▶ *partisan dealignment*: a weakening of party commitment;

▶ *class dealignment*: a breakdown in the link between class background and political behaviour.

Partisan dealignment has generally been seen as one of the main consequences of growing political awareness. Until the 1960s, only a small minority of voters had any great awareness of political issues. Most people simply did not see politics as having any relevance for them. Political attachments were a matter of taken-for-granted commitments acquired during socialization, and they were accepted largely unreflectively. People are now less likely to take over the political attitudes of their parents uncritically. They are more reflective about political matters and have a greater variety of sources of information available to them.

Traditional attachments, whether to Labour or the Conservatives, have been eroded by the expansion of formal education and the mass media, which supply information to people and encourage them to reflect upon political issues. Politics has become far more of a matter of choice. Manual workers, for example, are now as likely to be instrumental about their political behaviour as they are about their work and their involvement in trade unions. This does not mean, of course, that all normative and ideological commitments have disappeared: people do still have fundamental, ideologically grounded points of view. Nor does it mean that political issues are decided in a fully rational and critical way. The point is simply that ideological commitments are less strongly attached to particular political parties, and that people have a greater range of sources of information available to them in making their political choices.

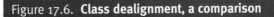

Figure 17.6. Class dealignment, a comparison

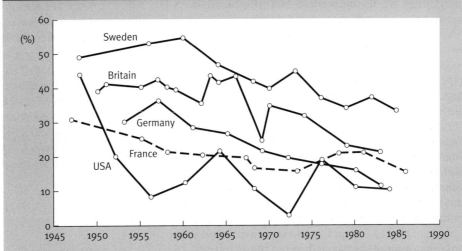

Source: Manza *et al*. (1995: fig. 1).

The Alford index

The Alford index—named after its inventor, the American sociologist Robert Alford—is the percentage of manual workers voting for left-wing parties minus the percentage of non-manual workers voting for these parties. The resulting index can vary from 0 to 100. A value of 0 occurs when voting for parties of the left is evenly spread across the population. The index rises when voting becomes more skewed. A value of 100 occurs when there is a strong association between class and party. In the unlikely event of non-manual workers showing a greater tendency than manual workers to vote for the left, the index would be negative.

This index has been criticized for using a rather crude manual/non-manual division, and alternative measures have not produced such a clear pattern. There is, however, no consensus about what a better measure should try to do. It is likely that the admittedly crude Alford index has—at the very least—shown that the class–party relationship has become less straightforward than in the past.

Increasing numbers of voters now see themselves as uncommitted to a particular political party. They are floating voters. This is why levels of party support that are recorded in political opinion polls can vary so much over time and especially during the course of an election campaign. People are pragmatic voters who make their political decisions on the basis of the perceived successes and failures of parties in relation to their policy goals. Parties are judged on their record and on their likely actions in the future.

Class dealignment is generally seen as resulting from much deeper changes. The changes in work and residential patterns among manual workers that we discuss in Chapters 11 and 15 have eroded the commu-nal bases of solidarity that previously formed manual workers into a cohesive social class. This class solidarity had been the main structural base for working-class Labour voting. With the weakening of class solidarity, the link between manual work and Labour voting was broken.

Some commentators have linked this with the idea that consumer identities are now more salient to people than class identities. The sphere of consump-tion, it is argued, is now more significant to people than their involvement in work and production. In particular, a division between publicly provided ser-vices and those provided through the market creates new bases for political action. Dunleavy and Husbands

(1985), for example, have contrasted the commodity-mode and the public-service-mode consumption of such things as housing, welfare, health, education, and transport.

In the past, these goods and services were closely associated with class divisions rooted in the sphere of production. Members of the middle classes had access to private-sector housing, health, education, and transport, consuming them as commodities. Members of the working class, on the other hand, have more typically relied on public-sector provision, consuming these under bureaucratically regulated and publicly financed conditions. Increasingly, however, manual workers have come to be divided between those who remain dependent on the public sector for these goods and those who are able to acquire them in the private sector.

The attempt to cut back state expenditure and to privatize state activities has politicized these matters, and the votes of manual workers are now likely to be split according to the *consumption sector* in which they are located. Those who remain dependent on public provision will tend to support parties that defend and promote the public sector and that seek to expand public spending. Those who have easy access to private, commodified health, transport, and housing will tend to support parties that advocate restrictions on the state and an expansion of market-based provision. Affluent manual workers, it has been argued, are more likely to vote Conservative than they are to vote Labour.

According to some writers, the various consumption sector cleavages do not coincide with one another: users of private transport may not be users of private health, and public-housing tenants may not be dependent on public-welfare benefits. People tend to occupy a number of quite distinct consumption-sector locations, each of which gives them a distinct status situation. They are subject to the cross-cutting influences of status and class. Voting choices reflect the particular pull of these contending forces as they appear to voters in a particular election. Party support is no longer an unreflective response to shared class conditions; it is a more deliberate and calculative act of political choice in relation to considerations of status and consumption.

It is not only consumer identities that have weakened the class–party relationship. Ascribed identities of gender, ethnicity, and sexuality have become less bound by tradition, and the growth of a more rational political culture has allowed people to re-examine the political implications of their personal identities. A growth in so-called post-materialist values, especially

 The *commodification* of services in the private sector has been contrasted with the *decommodified* or *juridified* provision of services in the public sector. These terms are used by Habermas (1973) and they are discussed more fully in Chapter 18, pp. 732–3, where we look at Esping-Andersen's work on welfare.

We go on to look at the growing importance of ascribed identities, such as those of gender and ethnicity. You might like to look at Chapter 4, pp. 145–7, where we discuss these and consumer identities in relation to class identity.

in the younger, post-war generation, has been seen as the basis of a concern for such issues as environmental protection, peace, citizenship rights, and the quality of life more generally (Inglehart 1990). This value shift has been linked to the growth of youth subcultures that have led many young people to abstain from voting for parties that fail to have any distinctive focus on issues relevant to them.

For all these reasons, issues have become more salient in the political sphere. Political parties have altered their policies and images, new parties have arisen, and politics has become much more a matter of issue voting than of class voting. Studies have shown that people are concerned about such issues as unemployment, European Union, prices, trade unions, the National Health Service, law and order, education. The outcomes of general elections can be explained, in large part, by the changing salience of these issues and voters' perceptions of the ability of each party to deal with them effectively (Sarlvik and Crewe 1983; M. Franklin 1985).

These judgements are not, of course, based on a detailed consideration of the small print of election manifestos. They are, rather, shaped by the presentation of issues and the arguments of party leaders in the mass media. The central point, however, is that political behaviour is motivated by conscious attitudes and opinions about broad issues, and that people act rationally in relation to the knowledge that they have about these issues (however inaccurate this knowledge might be). They are, therefore, more likely to be influenced by the discussion of issues during an election campaign and by the attempts of politicians to mobilize support around salient issues.

Rational choice and the political market

Dealignment and a growing concern for issues go a long way towards explaining the trends in Labour voting shown in Figure 17.5. During the 1980s, when Labour support was at its lowest, there was much talk about the need for the party to 'modernize' its image and abandon its association with class politics. The new and more politically aware voters, it was argued, would never be attracted to vote for the party unless it became more concerned with the issues that now mattered to people. A struggle ensued to change the party, and Tony Blair's New Labour is the result of the party's successful transformation from a class-based party to an issue-based party. The creation of New Labour was a rational response of the party leadership to the electoral situation that they faced.

This response can be understood in terms of the changing character of elections. Instead of involving the confrontation of rival ideologies, an election is now a competitive political market. The most powerful model for understanding this new kind of political system is that of Downs (1957). Any political party in a democratic system must compete for votes with other parties. This electoral competition means that the voter stands in the same position relative to political parties as the consumer does relative to the business enterprises that produce goods and services. Parties are the suppliers of policies and programmes, and they must take account of the preferences of the electors. People will vote only for those parties that are able to supply them with the policies and programmes that they think will deal with the issues that they judge to be the most important. From this model of the political market, Downs drew a number of interesting conclusions about party behaviour.

Voters choose between parties on the basis of their policies in relation to the issues with which they are concerned. It is, of course, unlikely that voters will have full information about the position of each party on every separate political issue. Even if they did have this kind of comprehensive information, they would be unlikely to find themselves in total agreement with one party and totally opposed to all others. Elections, however, require them to chose one party rather than another, and so voters must simplify their issue-based choices in some way. This can be achieved if each voter bases her or his voting decision on the overall image of a party as being, on balance, likely to act in a way that she or he will approve of. Downs argues that rational leaders of political parties will respond by putting together packages of policies that they believe will be attractive to the largest number of voters. These pack-

ages of policies define the images of the parties, and voters are able to make their political choice on the basis of them.

Downs shows that, where voters and parties act in the way that his model suggests, there will be a tendency for ideological differences to diminish and for parties to converge around particular policies (see also Przeworski and Sprague 1986). Specifically, he argues, party images will tend to converge towards the centre in any political system in which political views are evenly spread along a left–right spectrum. In such a system, each party attempts to maximize its votes by moving just far enough towards the centre to gain the support of a majority of the electorate. The optimum point for any party that seeks electoral victory is the mid-point in the spectrum of political opinions. Anywhere closer to the left or right than this mid-point would allow a rival party to win majority support. This argument is illustrated in Figure 17.7.

If a Labour Party with a left-wing image positions itself too far to the left—as shown in the top panel of the diagram—it will get the support of only, say, 30 per cent of the electorate. All those with views to the left of the party will vote for it, but those with views to its right are less likely to do so. This allows a rival party to position itself anywhere to its right and so gain up to 70 per cent of the votes. Rational party leaders, then, would try to position the Labour Party closer to the centre, so reducing the number of uncommitted voters. If the party moves to the position shown in the middle panel, for example, it would receive 40 per cent support. Even here, however, a rival centrist party could still gain up to 60 per cent of the votes and win the election. The only safe political position for a Labour Party that seeks to win elections, then, is the mid-point, as shown in the bottom panel. In this situation, a rival party may be able to secure an equal number of votes, but it cannot gain any more than this. Similar pressures, of course, operate on other parties, and a right-wing party, for example, would also be under pressure to move towards the centre. Downs concludes that, over time, democratic political systems will show a tendency for party images to become more and more similar as they gravitate towards the centre of the political spectrum.

This model—like any other model—can account for only a part of the political process in contemporary societies. Parties are not simply vote-maximizing machines that take the existing spread of public opinion as given and position themselves cynically wherever they can optimize their chances of electoral success. Parties are also driven by ideological considerations and by the expectations and interests of their core

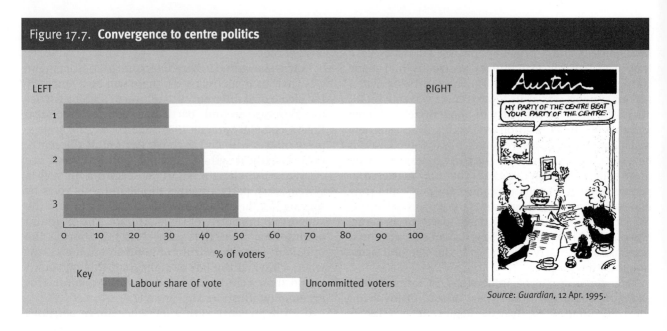

Figure 17.7. **Convergence to centre politics**

Key: Labour share of vote / Uncommitted voters

% of voters

Source: *Guardian*, 12 Apr. 1995.

of committed supporters. These commitments do persist, even in a situation of dealignment, and they are important constraints on party leaders. For this reason, parties may undertake electorally risky strategies by positioning themselves in a particular ideological position in the hope that they can shift the whole climate of public opinion in their favour. As we show in Chapter 18, the Conservative Party in Britain—like its counterparts in other capitalist societies—successfully shifted public opinion towards the right during the 1980s, reflecting a wider shift of opinion that had begun during the 1970s.

Such shifts of opinion and party practice do not mean that Downs's model loses its relevance. His model still explains the electoral constraints that are faced by parties in a competitive system, and the idea of party convergence retains its relevance. If public opinion is predominantly oriented towards the right, parties are likely to converge towards a right-of-centre position. This, it can be argued, is exactly the situation that has existed in Britain during the 1980s and 1990s. The success of 'Thatcherism' meant that a left-wing Labour Party became increasingly less likely to achieve success in general elections. Faced with the prospect of continuing defeat, there is pressure on the party leadership to relax its ideological commitments and shift towards the right. Such a strategy, of course, encounters opposition from sections within the party and from committed supporters, and the disputes that divided the Labour Party during the 1980s were focused

on exactly these considerations. The successful faction in the Labour Party—the so-called 'modernisers'—argued that public opinion was not going to swing to the left, so the party must move to the right. Any other strategy, they held, was not rational for a party that wanted to achieve electoral success.

This is, of course, a simplified model of two-party competition. Although it can explain much about politics in contemporary democratic systems (Himmelweit *et al.* 1985), Heath and his colleagues (1991) have shown that there is much continuity between the old class politics and the new issue politics. Neither theories of class politics nor theories of issue politics can be taken as full and comprehensive theories. It is necessary to combine the two.

The explanations of class politics that were proposed by Butler and Stokes and by Parkin tended to present a rather too deterministic picture. People never were simply over-socialized automatons who voted unreflectively as the bearers of deep and enduring value commitments. Working-class communities never were so custom-bound as the stronger versions of these arguments implied, and there was always a willingness to judge political issues in relation to social interests. Unless this were the case, no political change would be possible and the Labour Party could never have established itself in the first place. The dealignment thesis, on the other hand, depicts voters as purely rational calculators who respond in a conscious and deliberate way to changes in the political market place.

New Labour: a move towards the centre?

The theory ignores the continuing importance of customary and ideological commitments. People are not so cold-bloodedly rational as the stronger versions of dealignment theory imply.

Human motivation has always involved a mixture of commitment and rationality. What has changed, argue Heath and his colleagues, are the circumstances in which people find themselves and, therefore, the balance between the two types of motivation. Traditional working-class communities and patterns of work have, indeed, broken down, political awareness has increased, and the mass-media presentation of issues has become more important, but voters do still have partisan commitments that shape the pragmatic calculations that they make at election times. Labour's electoral strategy has been successful, argue Heath *et al.*, because the party has attracted voters on the centre and the left, not because they have attracted large numbers of voters from the right. It is easier to win the votes of those who have ideological commitments that lie in the same direction as those of the party leadership than it is to win the votes of ideological opponents.

The results of the 1997 general election suggest that Labour successfully attracted those with traditional working-class commitments, those to the left of centre, and also a number of uncommitted and purely pragmatic voters. The scale of the Labour victory, however, was not a result of large numbers of former Conserva-tive voters shifting their vote to the Labour Party. The Conservative vote fell by over 4 million between 1992 and 1997, and about a quarter of these people seem to have shifted to Labour. However, a quarter voted for anti-European parties of the right, and the remaining 2 million simply did not vote at all. The Labour success was made possible, in large part, by the complete collapse in support for the Conservative Party on the part of those with ideological commitments towards the right.

NEW SOCIAL MOVEMENTS

The class politics of the working class were expressed in a labour movement whose organizations and institutions translated economic considerations into electoral support for the Labour Party and into programmes for collective political action. The dealignment of class and politics that has been traced in voting behaviour is associated with wider changes in patterns of collective action that have been described as involving the rise of new social movements. By contrast with the economic and political forms of the old class-based social movements, new social movements are concerned with the promotion and change of cultural values and the construction of personal life styles. This has been seen as the basis of movements as diverse as those concerned with black power, women's liberation, peace and anti-war protest, and environmental protection, all of which grew rapidly in strength and radicalism from the 1950s. Politics has increasingly been defined by the issues raised in these new social movements. (See the critical review in A. Scott 1990, and see Byrne 1997.)

A leading theorist of the new social movements has been Alain Touraine (1971, 1981), who sees them in relation to the development of a post-industrial society. Old-style class politics, he argues, reflected the conditions of an industrial society, where the basis of economic activity lay in the ownership and control of manufacturing assets. In the new post-industrial society, on the other hand, economic activity is driven by the ownership and control of knowledge-based assets. The new social movements that dominate contemporary politics have their roots in the production and consumption of knowledge and cultural values. For some, this is particularly associated with the strengthening of so-called post-material values.

Critical theory and social movements

We outline many of the problems involved in the idea of post-industrialism in Chapter 13, but it can hardly be doubted that the production and consumption of knowledge have, indeed, acquired a much greater importance in the contemporary world. This was seen early on by the critical theorists, and was given a particularly influential expression by Herbert Marcuse (1964).

According to Marcuse, technological development had largely resolved the economic problems of capi-

talist production on which Marx had concentrated his attention. By making possible sustained economic growth, technological development had allowed advanced capitalist societies to generate levels of affluence that freed the majority of the working class from material want and motivated them to acquire more and more consumer goods. They became participants in a popular, mass culture of consumption, motivated mainly by the desire to follow the consumer lifestyles that are promoted in the mass media. Echoing earlier ideas on mass society, Marcuse held that workers had been duped by the advertising industry and the mass media into pursuing the very consumer goods whose expanded production was the basis of capitalist growth. Their pursuit of these 'false needs', he argued, leads them to identify with the capitalist system, effectively tying them into the existing social structure and destroying any motivation that they may previously have had for opposition or protest. Class consciousness and class conflict become things of the past and the proletariat can no longer be seen as an agent of revolutionary change.

Marcuse tried to identify what new agencies of revolutionary change there might be in these new circumstances. The poor and the unemployed, he held, were excluded from the benefits and advantages of consumerism. The group that some later writers would term an underclass were, therefore, a possible source of radical opposition. Their consciousness of their exploitation and oppression, he held, would lead them to appreciate the common cause that they had with the mass of exploited workers and peasants in the less developed societies of the world. Those that Franz Fanon (1967) called 'the wretched of the earth' would replace the proletariat as the principal focus of radical change in advanced capitalism.

Marcuse did, however, identify some possible sources of change from within the structure of consumer society itself. The emptiness of mass culture, he argued, led students, whose education gave them a more critical insight into the system, to reject consumerism and to espouse an alternative culture. This was a counter-culture focused around the emotional and the personal needs that are repressed by commercialized consumerism. Where the wretched of the earth would press for the material benefits of advanced capitalism to be spread more widely, the student movement of the 1960s had initiated a new politics of personal identity and of cultural and emotional emancipation.

These views have been extended by Habermas (1973). His view is that the growth of state regulation over the economy has transformed purely economic divisions into politically defined divisions. Class relations are

Herbert Marcuse

Herbert Marcuse (1898–1979) worked with Adorno and Horkheimer in Frankfurt in the 1930s, and was one of the leading proponents of critical theory. Like the other critical theorists, he advocated a reconsideration of the fundamental elements of Marxism. Marcuse stressed the importance of culture and consciousness, and he pioneered the attempt to integrate Freudian ideas with Marxism. His most influential work was *One Dimensional Man* (Marcuse 1964), which was published after he settled in the United States. This book became the key text for a whole generation of 'revolting students' in the 1960s.

latent in the social structure and are experienced only through the divisions among social categories that are defined by consumption-sector cleavages: taxpayers, the sick, schoolchildren, transport users, students, the elderly, and so on. At the same time, those who occupy these consumption categories become the basis of the new social movements that have replaced the labour movement. The students, on whom Marcuse focused, are simply one of the consumption-sector categories that are drawn into opposition to the way in which society is organized. Contemporary politics is shaped by the student movement, the women's movement, the peace movement, and a whole variety of loose social groupings concerned with transport and roads, environmental matters, health and welfare, and so on.

The rise of these new social movements reflects the wider restructuring of contemporary societies. In contemporary capitalist societies, argues Habermas, economic and political activity predominate over all other spheres of social life, and all forms of action and social relationship are shaped by technical, instrumental considerations. The social relations of the family, household, and community that sustain social identities, lifestyles and subcultures form what Habermas terms the **socio-cultural lifeworld**. They are increasingly subjected to the processes of commodification and juridification, so becoming distorted by the requirements of the economic and political systems.

An example of this would be the way in which the health and welfare needs of families are now organized. Families no longer draw solely, or even mainly, on the support of wider kinship and community networks. They must rely on the often contradictory pressures of a bureaucratic system of entitlements and commercial systems of provision. In the same way, the ancient woodlands and parklands of many communities are subject to contradictory pressures. They are subject to commodified market pressures for road building, aimed at meeting the demands of private motorists and commercial road haulage, but they are also influenced by the bureaucratic procedures of the planning and regulatory systems.

> ☞ **Do not worry if you find this argument difficult. Read our discussion of welfare and commodification in Chapter 18, pp. 732–3, and then return to Habermas's argument.**

A political culture of what Habermas calls civic privatism and familial-vocational privatism encourages political involvement only through the ballot box, not through direct participation, and it encourages an overriding orientation towards consumption, career, leisure, and status. The political issues on which people can vote in general elections are confined to a relatively narrow range. There is no real possibility of considering the fundamental social issues inherent in consumption-sector cleavages. The political system is insulated from any effective popular participation, despite the formal democratic constitutions that have been introduced. The formulation and expression of concerns generated within the socio-cultural lifeworld are suppressed. Nevertheless, this suppression cannot be complete, and alternative cultural and political forms do arise. These are the new social movements that emerge outside the framework of conventional politics.

These social movements are of two types:

▶ *defensive* social movements;
▶ *offensive* social movements.

A *defensive* movement emphasizes a romanticized, traditional way of life that is seen as being undermined by contemporary economic and political changes. This is found, Habermas argues, in conservative and fundamentalist social movements that stress the particularistic, ascriptive solidarities of gender, age, and nation. An *offensive* movement, on the other hand, aims to reassert the autonomy of the socio-cultural lifeworld by transforming it. This is found in the radical social movements that aim to liberate people from economic and political repression and to open up greater possibilities for democratic participation and the formation of autonomous identities.

For Habermas, then, the old social movements of class and interests have increasingly been replaced by new social movements. These are 'post-class' movements concerned with the politics of identity. Many of these new social movements combine both defensive and offensive responses. Feminism, for example, he sees as an offensive movement aimed at overthrowing male dominance and establishing a politics of difference. At the same time, however, it also has a defensive orientation, in so far as it roots itself in what are seen as essential female characteristics and the subordinate position of women in the nuclear family. This dual orientation, argues Habermas, underpins the many political divisions within the women's movement.

In the same way, Habermas sees the peace, anti-nuclear, and ecology movements as combining defensive and offensive orientations: they are radical movements of social change that promote greater participation in political decision-making, but they retain a concern for protecting a traditional or 'natural' environment (see A. Scott 1990: 75–8). A concern for community and environment, as we show in Chapter 12, pp. 488–90, may express a fundamentalist reaction to the central principles of economic and political rationality.

Women and the peace movement

The characteristics of a new social movement have been interestingly highlighted by Roseneil (1995) in her investigation of opposition to the United States Air Force Cruise missile base at Greenham Common, near Newbury. The defining characteristic of this opposition to the installation of nuclear weapons was that it was organized and sustained by women, who linked their anti-nuclear stance to an explicitly feminist position.

The camp began almost by chance, following a women's peace march to the airfield. The idea of a women-only camp became the focus for constructing a collective identity for the participants as they began to engage in new forms of collective action. They saw themselves as engaged in an anti-nuclear campaign, as participants in a community of women and a community of lesbians (though many participants were not lesbians), and as involved in an enjoyable, 'fun' way of life. They were tied together as participants in a way of life that was organized around autonomy, non-

violence, respect for individuality and difference, care for the environment, the pursuit of pleasure, and an emphasis on emotional and spiritual concerns.

Roseneil argues that the camp would not have been possible if there had not been a transition from private to public patriarchy (Walby 1990). The legal and economic powers of husbands that had been central to private, family-based patriarchy were reduced in the years following the Second World War as more women entered the public world of employment. In so doing, however, women entered new kinds of patriarchal relations that were integral to the institutions of the market and the state. Women did, however, gain some financial autonomy by their entry into employment and from their improved access to welfare benefits. This financial autonomy was crucial in allowing them to travel to Greenham Common and spend time at the camp. Once the peace camp had been established by its founders, participation was a realistic option for those who wished to be involved.

Experience of participation in this way of life helped women to politicize their sense of identity and, in many cases, to forge a distinctively feminist political consciousness:

'at Greenham many women experienced, often for the first time in their lives, a sense of real participation in decision-making and social life, a feeling that their opinions mattered, deserved expression and would be taken seriously. . . . For many women, reflection on this, mediated by the feminist discourses to which they became exposed at Greenham, contributed to a new consciousness of men's domination of political and social life, even within the peace movement and radical groups.' (Roseneil 1995: 145)

This raising of consciousness was achieved in the context of close interpersonal relations at the camp that led the participants to value other women's company much more highly than they had done before.

The collapse of the Soviet Union, on which the Cruise missiles had been targeted, led to the eventual decommissioning of the base and the closing of the peace camp in 1994. While the camp itself ended, the consciousness achieved and the social networks established continued to be highly valued by the participants. Involvement in the campaign had brought them into contact with groups and organizations concerned with other and related issues. Many of the women went on to become involved in anti-militarist, environmental, and animal-rights groups, in campaigns against sexual violence, and in a whole range of other political activities.

Research at Greenham Common

As a young participant in the peace camp set up at Greenham Common in 1981, Sasha Roseneil had first-hand experience on which to draw in her research. She combined this with interviews undertaken between four and ten years later, when she had trained in sociology and had decided to carry out systematic research on the topic. Contacting those whom she had known at the camp, she constructed a snowball sample of other participants to interview. These data were supplemented with documentary sources, such as diaries, newsletters, and newspapers.

Roseneil used a method of triangulation, but the core of her work drew on her own participation. Look at our discussion of participant observation in 'Ethnographic Research', Chapter 3, pp. 87–9, and consider its implications for Roseneil's work. You can find her account in Roseneil (1995).

Is personal experience of an issue or problem an advantage or a disadvantage to a researcher?

Environmental protests

Environmentalists were involved in a number of protests against the building of new roads in areas of established countryside during the 1990s. Following the Twyford Down and Solsbury Hill protests, in which many of the Greenham Common activists were involved, the most notable have been at Newbury and Fairmile (near Exeter).

The Fairmile protest camp was set up in an attempt to block the construction of a new trunk road in east Devon. It involved conventional camping arrangements (tents and prefabricated huts), together with a series of tree houses and a network of tunnels. A number of activists—most notably 'Swampy' (Daniel Hooper)—acquired new skills of tunnelling in order to establish underground defensive bunkers that would make the camp more secure. The protests ended with bailiffs, acting for the authorities, dismantling the camps and evicting activists. The tunnels and the tunnellers proved particularly difficult to remove, and the attempts drew much publicity for the campaign.

In early 1997 many of the veterans of the Newbury and Fairmile protests moved on to a new tree house and tunnel camp to protest against a proposed runway extension at Manchester airport.

Environmental protester, Swampy, at Fairmile.

SUMMARY POINTS

In this section we have looked at the end of class politics and the development of new forms of politics and protest. Party politics in Britain and the United States has become more pluralistic since the 1950s.

▶ In elections, there has been a process of dealignment: weakened party commitment and a weakened class-party link.

▶ Consumption divisions and issues of status now have a greater significance in politics.

► Electoral support for the Labour Party declined for much of the post-war period. Renewed electoral success was associated with the adoption of a new image.

► Pressures in contemporary electoral systems tend to result in party convergence towards the centre ground.

Outside the electoral system, new social movements and direct action now play a great role.

► New social movements tend to be organized around issues of consumption and personal identity, and in relation to post-material values.

REVISION AND EXERCISES

RULING ELITES AND RULING CLASSES

► Make sure that you are familiar with the main ideas of the following writers: Marx, Gramsci, Pareto, Mosca, Michels, Mills, Domhoff, Dahl, Scott, Lane.

► What do you understand by the following terms: ruling class, ruling elite; dominant ideology, hegemony; counter elite, power elite, power bloc; totalitarianism, state socialism, pluralism, democratic elitism?

► What did Domhoff mean by the following: the special-interest process, the policy-formation process, the candidate-selection process, the ideology process?

► Was Marx correct to see the modern state as the executive committee of the bourgeoisie? Look again at the case of the brewing industry given at the beginning of the chapter. Does this provide evidence in support of Marx's position?

► What forms of political power have emerged in post-Communist Russia? Can the political leadership still be described as a ruling elite? As the society moves towards capitalism, will we see the development of a ruling class?

VOTING AND ELECTIONS

► What do you understand by the following terms: franchise, left wing, right wing; dual consciousness, structural barrier; dealignment, Alford index; consumption-sector cleavages, commodification.

► Make sure that you are familiar with the main arguments of: Butler and Stokes, Parkin, Downs, Heath.

► How would you distinguish between issue politics and class politics?

► Look at Figures 17.1 and 17.5, which give data on the share of the vote going to Labour. Compile a similar graph of the share of the vote going to the Conservative Party. The results of an election are influenced by the turnout (the proportion of the total electorate who actually vote). Would you expect to find different results in a graph of the proportion of the total electorate voting for each of the parties? You will find Butler and Butler (1994) a useful source for the information that you need.

► Collect the election addresses and manifestos of the main political parties. Can their views and policies be arranged along a line from left to right? Is there any evidence for convergence in policies?

► Are the results of local elections shaped by the same factors as national elections?

SOCIAL MOVEMENTS AND SOCIAL PROTEST

▶ What do you understand by the following terms: social movement, new social movement; mass, class for itself; politics of difference, socio-cultural lifeworld?

▶ Make sure that you understand the main ideas of the following writers: Touraine, Marcuse, Habermas.

▶ Collect newspaper cuttings on environmental protests (for example, opposition to a new bypass) or on animal-welfare campaigns. What evidence do these give you on the class, age, gender, and ethnic backgrounds of participants.

▶ How useful is it to distinguish between defensive and offensive social movements?

▶ To what extent is Roseneil correct to see the Greenham camp as a distinctively feminist project?

▶ Is it correct to say that labour movements are things of the past and that all politics is now the politics of new social movements?

FURTHER READING

Good introductions to the issues of power and politics that we have looked at in this chapter can be found in the following books:

Bottomore, T. B. (1993), *Elites and Society* (2nd edn., London: Routledge & Kegan Paul). A very good summary of the main themes in elite theory. Follow this with two attempts to use elite and class concepts to explore power in the United States and Britain: Domhoff (1993) and Scott (1991).

Domhoff, G. W. (1967), *Who Rules America?* (Englewood Cliffs, NJ: Prentice Hall).

Scott, J. (1991), *Who Rules Britain?* (Cambridge: Polity Press).

Denver, D. (1994), *Elections and Voting Behaviour in Britain* (2nd edn., Hemel Hempstead: Harvester Wheatsheaf). A good, up-to-date summary of data and debates. Covers the 1992 election, but not 1997 (watch out for a third edition).

Scott, A. (1990), *Ideology and the New Social Movements* (London: Unwin Hyman). A handy summary of some of the key theoretical issues raised in studies of new social movements.

Roseneil, S. (1995), *Disarming Patriarchy: Feminism and Political Action at Greenham* (Buckingham: Open University Press). An excellent piece of ethnographic work that really gives the sense of what it means to be involved in a social movement.

For more depth on some of these issues, look at the following.

Miliband, R. (1969), *The State in Capitalist Society* (London: Weidenfeld & Nicolson). A classic early statement of the ruling-class model.

Sarlvik, B., and Crewe, I. (1983), *Decade of Dealignment* (Cambridge: Cambridge University Press). An influential statement of the dealignment thesis. Crewe was one of the first to appreciate its importance.

Heath, A., Jowell, R., and Curtice, J. (1985), *How Britain Votes* (Oxford: Pergamon). A counter-argument to Sarlvik and Crewe (1983). Also very good.

Lane, D. (1996), *The Rise and Fall of State Socialism* (Cambridge: Polity Press). A readable account by one of the leading scholars in the area.

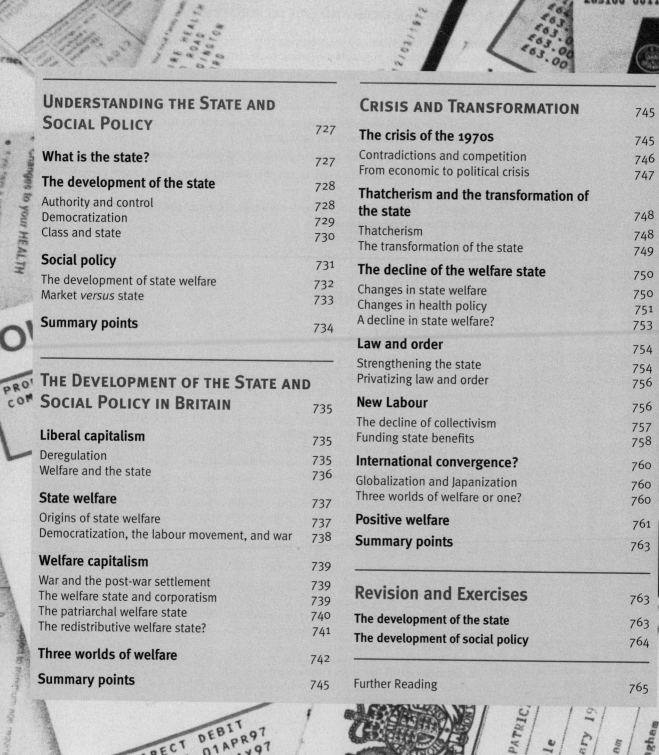

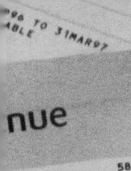

Chapter 18

THE STATE, SOCIAL POLICY, AND WELFARE

The inevitable privatization of the NHS?

'Fifty years after the National Health Service was founded, hospitals are facing privatization whichever party forms the next government, health-service managers warned yesterday. Private companies are poised to take over the running of NHS trusts, including the provision of clinical care, as a condition of investing in the new buildings that the service urgently needs, the Institute of Health Services Management said. Although care would remain free to patients it would be delivered by doctors and nurses employed by private companies.

'Fears that NHS hospitals would be privatized have been raised ever since the introduction of the NHS internal market in 1991—and constantly denied. Now managers say it is inevitable because of cuts in public funding for new hospitals—amounting to 22 per cent between 1994–99—to which both main parties are committed.'

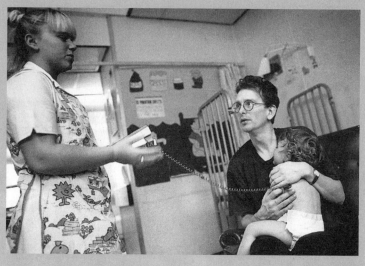

Source: Jeremy Laurance, 'No Escape from Privatization for NHS', *Independent*, 22 Apr. 1997.

'THE state' may seem a remote and vague abstraction that is something to do with distant and rather incomprehensible goings-on in the capital, but its influence is present in everything that we do. It regulates the contents and packaging of the food we eat, the television programmes we watch, the construction of the house we live in, the content of lessons in school, the way that we drive down the road, and the environment in which we work, study, or play. Indeed, the state is involved in so many activities that it is difficult to pin down what we mean by it and that is the first problem we shall address in this chapter.

We live within a framework of services provided by the state. If we go back, say, 200 years, none of these services existed. There were no state schools and there was no state medical care. There were no state pensions and no state benefits of any kind. If you fell on bad times, there would be no help from the state. Why has the state become so involved in our welfare? In this chapter we shall examine the development of social policy in Britain, the construction of a welfare state, and its consequences for welfare. We will also consider the development of state welfare in other countries, such as Sweden, Germany, and the United States.

We shall also analyse changes in the 1980s and 1990s which have transformed almost every aspect of the state's activities. We shall examine Thatcherism and the reasons for its emergence. We shall raise the question of whether New Labour will reverse the changes brought about by eighteen years of Conservative government. Is the welfare state a thing of the past or will a Labour government revive it? Is the privatizing of the NHS inevitable, as our opening piece suggests? Finally, we shall consider ideas of how welfare policy might develop in the future. Should we forget the welfare state and concentrate on the really serious problems of the environment? These will arguably have more bearing on our welfare than the problems faced by the National Health Service.

UNDERSTANDING THE STATE AND SOCIAL POLICY

In this section we begin by discussing what is meant by the state and the functions that states perform. We then examine the main aspects of the development of states, before considering the development of social policy and state welfare. While they are often treated as separate topics, the state and social policy are closely linked. On the one hand, the main expansion of the state's activities has been in the area of social policy. On the other hand, the development of social policy has been closely related to other aspects of the development of states, such as, for example, democratization and war.

WHAT IS THE STATE?

People commonly think of the government as being 'in charge of the country'. The government is, however, but a small part of what we call 'the state' and is wholly dependent upon it. The government's power depends on the existence of civil servants, law-enforcement officials, tax collectors, diplomats, and members of the armed services, to name only the more obvious people, and they are all employees of the state. When sociologists refer to 'the state', they mean both the government and the complex of organizations which enable governments to govern.

It is fairly easy to say what the government is. Even if we cannot remember all their names, we know that in Britain a group of around twenty Cabinet ministers is collectively responsible for taking key decisions on our behalf. It is much more difficult to define what we mean by the state because it is such a complex and extensive structure.

It is particularly difficult to establish the state's boundaries. Some would say that teachers, social workers, and priests are agents of the state, for they play an important role in maintaining social order, which is one of the state's main functions. Teachers and social workers are required to carry out government policy and can be closely controlled by governments. On the other hand, opposition to the state is also commonly found within these groups. It is therefore hard to 'draw a line' around the state.

The best way to approach this question is to identify the key functions that states perform. The **state** can then be said to consist of the institutions and organiza-tions involved in performing these functions. Most sociologists would agree that the state is engaged in all the following activities:

▶ the maintenance of order;
▶ policy-making and implementation;
▶ taxation;
▶ political representation;
▶ the management of external relationships.

The *maintenance of order* involves most obviously a legal system and a police force, with the military to back it up when necessary. It is not only the police and the military who maintain order, however. This also depends on a horde of inspectors, regulators, and other officials, such as air-traffic controllers, traffic wardens, auditors, health-and-safety officials, and school inspectors. As we suggested above, this function may be performed by many other, less obvious, occupations as well.

Policy-making and implementation extend into all areas of society. As the state developed and intervened increasingly in social activities, this function became ever more important. Most of the work of government departments is concerned with policy. This is also a key function of local government, for local authorities are charged with carrying out many important policies, such as those concerned with housing, education, and planning.

Taxation provides the resources that enable the state to exist. Without some form of taxation the 'unproductive' officials of the state cannot be supported. Taxation also, however, performs other functions, because it is one of the main ways through which governments implement their policies. In particular, it is largely through its tax policy that a government controls the economy and the distribution of income and wealth.

Political representation occurs through parliamentary bodies and political parties, which we examine in Chapter 17, pp. 693–8. The amount of power possessed by these bodies varies greatly. Governments may largely ignore the views of elected representatives or treat parliaments as a rubber stamp for government decisions. All contemporary state structures have such bodies, however, if only because they enable governments to legitimate their actions by presenting them as subject to 'the will of the people'.

The management of external relationships has been a key

function of the state. It was initially mainly concerned with territorial boundaries, which were the subject of diplomacy and war. Increasingly, it has become concerned with economic and environmental issues. These have become ever more regulated by supra-national institutions, such as those of the European Union (EU), which we discuss in Chapter 12, pp. 492–3. This regulation has extended into what were previously internal matters. Indeed, internal matters and external relationships can hardly now be separated in many areas of policy.

While sociologists broadly agree that the state does these things, they hold differing views on the question of who the state does these things for. Thus a *functionalist* approach to the maintenance of order would treat this as an activity performed by the state to meet one of the basic needs of society. A *Weberian* approach would see the maintenance of order in terms of the control of society by its rulers. A *Marxist* approach would argue that the maintenance of order is a means by which one class uses the state apparatus to dominate and exploit another. In societies split by ethnic or religious divisions, the maintenance of order can similarly be seen as a means by which other dominant groups control subordinate ones.

THE DEVELOPMENT OF THE STATE

In this section we draw on these approaches to examine the processes central to the development of the state and the issues that they raise. We first draw on the work of Max Weber to consider the authority of the state. We go on to discuss the notion of democracy and democratization. We then draw on the Marxist approach to set the development of the state in the context of class relationships.

Authority and control

Weber was primarily interested in the process through which rulers established control of their territories. Crucial to this was control of the use of physical force, though Weber emphasized that the state did not rule through force alone but also by establishing its authority. In *Politics as a Vocation*, Max Weber (1919: 78) declared that the state's defining feature was that it 'successfully claims the *monopoly of the legitimate use* of physical force within a territory'. There are three key notions here—*monopoly of the use of force, legitimacy, and territory*—that are central to the understanding of the development of the state. We will examine them in turn.

First, there is monopoly of the use of force. States ultimately rely on force to secure the obedience of their citizens. They must also establish a monopoly of its use. Unless the state alone is allowed to use physical force, individuals or groups can resist its commands.

The efforts made by rulers to establish a monopoly of the use of force were crucial to the early development of the state in Europe. In the feudal societies of medieval Europe the use of military force was decentralized in the hands of local lords. Rulers had no direct control over their subjects and rather little control over the local lords. These were obliged by their feudal oaths to provide military service to the ruler, but rulers frequently had great difficulty in getting them to do this and often faced military revolts by them. The beginnings of the development of the modern state can be seen in the ruler's subordination of the feudal lords to royal authority. The destruction of their castles and the creation of military forces paid to serve the ruler were crucial steps in this process.

Secondly, a monopoly of the use of force was not sufficient on its own, for control of people depended on the authority of the ruler, which itself depended on **legitimacy**. People obey rulers not simply because they are forced to do so but because they accept the authority of those they obey. When authority is accepted, it is legitimate. This notion of legitimacy becomes clearer when one considers the three types of authority identified by Weber:

▶ *Traditional.* This is found when particular individuals or groups have held a customary authority since ancient times. Tradition legitimates authority.

▶ *Charismatic.* In this case authority is held by a particular individual through personal qualities of leadership. This is the authority of great political and religious leaders who command the loyalty of their followers. It is the personal and emotional attachment of the follower to the leader which gives the leader authority.

▶ *Rational–legal.* This is the authority held by politicians and officials because they occupy certain positions in the state. Authority is here nothing to do with either tradition or personal qualities or emotion. Legitimacy derives from laws which specify that the holders of an office have certain powers.

In his customary way, Weber had created what he called *ideal types* (see Chapter 2, p. 42), in order to explore the logic of the different ways in which authority was established. These types certainly correspond to distinct and identifiable patterns of authority, but it should be emphasized that they are often found in combination. For example, political leaders whose authority is primarily based on their position as prime minister or president may well also develop a charismatic relationship with their followers.

Weber argued that there was a tendency for traditional and charismatic authority to give way to rational–legal authority as societies developed, though charismatic leaders could emerge at any time. This movement towards rational–legal authority took place through *bureaucratization*, which was central to the process through which rulers gained control of societies, for it provided them with a corps of professional administrators directly under their control. Whether these administrators have remained under the rulers' control is another matter, for bureaucrats have often taken over or tried to take over the running of the state. In the democratic state, there is always a tension between the top civil servants and elected political leaders, a tension that Weber explored at length in his work.

 We have examined important aspects of the development of states in other chapters. The bureaucratization of the state is covered in Chapter 16, pp. 650–1, the development of the nation state in Chapter 12, pp. 451–3. Authority is discussed in 'Command Situation', Chapter 15, p. 608.

Thirdly, the state's authority is exercised within a territory. The emergence of a consolidated national territory under a unified national administration was central to the construction of the nation state. This territorial aspect of the state leads us to the issue of how the state has managed its external relationships, which have greatly influenced its development.

The development of the state apparatus has been largely driven by international conflict. It was war above all that led to the centralization of the state in order to mobilize and control the population. It was indeed the demands of war that lay behind the development of taxation, which was the main function of the administrative apparatus of the early state. Through an analysis of state finances Mann has shown that state spending has been overwhelmingly on military matters. He calculated that in Britain from the twelfth to the nineteenth century between 70 and 90 per cent of state expenditure was on the military (Mann 1986: 485).

Democratization

As states developed, a process of democratization also took place. Indeed, most states nowadays seek to legitimate their authority by at least claiming to be democratic. Before discussing this process, we need to consider what democracy means and the issues that it raises.

Will market research make Britain more democratic?

'The Government is setting up a giant 5,000 strong "focus group" to test public reaction to existing and new policies and to the performance of public services. The initiative, thought to be the first of its scale in the world, will be seen as the final triumph of the market research-led techniques that helped the Labour Party to power in this year's election. . . . The "people's panel", which will cost tens of thousands of pounds, will be set up by private pollsters and paid for by the Cabinet Office. Ministers see the plan as an important way of addressing the gulf between politicians and voters, and making government more democratic. But others are likely to deride the initiative as a marketing gimmick. The pollsters will select about 5,000 people in a representative sample of the population which will sit for at least a year.'

Source: Stephen Castle, 'Blair Rules by Market Research', *Independent on Sunday*, 13 July 1997.

► In what way could a 'people's panel' of this sort make Britain more democratic?
► What effect is it likely to have on the development of government policy?
► What are its implications for the role of parliament and the significance of general elections?

Democracy means rule by the people. It comes from the Ancient Greek words *demos*, the people, and *cratia*, rule. It contrasts with *aristocracy*, rule by an elite defined by birth, and *monocracy* (more commonly called monarchy), rule by a single individual.

But how is 'the people' defined? In the so-called democracies of Ancient Greece women and slaves had no political rights, for they were not considered citizens. The definition of citizenship is crucial to democracy. Simply living in a country does not make one a citizen, for citizenship is conferred only on those considered full members of a society (see Chapter 14, pp. 553–4, for a discussion of citizenship). A large part of the population may in this way be excluded from political participation.

There is then the issue of how 'the people' can rule. A distinction is made here between *direct* and *representative* democracy. *Direct* democracy means that citizens collectively take political decisions. It is at least possible in very small societies for virtually all citizens to meet and take decisions. In social units of any size, this is clearly impossible. One possible substitute is the referendum, when all citizens vote on a particular issue, but this can only be used to decide a limited range of matters where there is a fairly simple choice. Generally, democracy has taken a *representative* form. This is where government is carried out by representatives of the people, who are selected through elections.

For elections to be meaningful, there must be choice for the voter. If only one party is allowed to put up candidates or there are restrictions on political activity, there is only the semblance of democracy. Single-party states are, therefore, not usually considered to be democracies, though they may well claim that the existence of elections and parliamentary bodies makes them democratic. Representative democracy requires a multi-party system, free competition between parties, and free political activity. This kind of political system is often labelled 'liberal democracy', because it is based on liberal ideas of the freedom (liberty) of the individual.

By **democratization** is usually meant two main processes, the emergence of representative assemblies with political power and the extension of citizenship. Parliamentary assemblies existed in medieval times, but it was only after a series of revolutions, in seventeenth-century Britain and eighteenth-century America and France, that such bodies began to acquire real power. The extension of citizenship took much longer. In most countries only men with a certain amount of wealth or income were initially allowed to vote, while colonial peoples were largely excluded from the political process until after the Second World War.

As we showed above, the existence of parliaments and elections is not, however, enough, for democracy also requires party competition and free political activity. These were not found in the totalitarian regimes of Germany, Italy, and Spain, or the state socialist countries of the Soviet bloc, which we discussed in Chapter 17, pp. 704–7. With the defeat of fascism in the 1940s and the collapse of state socialism at the end of the 1980s, the 'liberal democracies' were apparently victorious. This led Fukuyama (1989) to proclaim, in a widely publicized piece, the 'end of history'. What he meant by this rather misleading phrase was that the historical struggle between different political systems had come to an end. Liberal democracy had won.

This notion of the victory of 'liberal democracy' hardly conveys, however, the reality of world politics. Communist and state socialist ideologies may be in retreat, but this does not mean that democracy has triumphed. China with a fifth of the world's population remains a one-party state. Many countries are ruled by the military with little regard for the institutions of representative democracy. Others are controlled by nationalist or religious elites which try to suppress all opposition.

Class and state

A very different perspective on democracy has emerged from the Marxist analysis of the relationship between capitalism and the state. This places the state in the context of class relationships and treats the state as an instrument of class domination. The institutions of representative democracy are seen here not as enabling the people to rule but rather as a means through which the capitalist bourgeoisie could pursue its interests. According to this approach, the modern state was essentially a **capitalist state**. We shall see later in our discussion of 'liberal capitalism' how the early steps of democratization in Britain produced a parliament that acted very much in the interests of capital.

The domination of the state by capital was challenged by the growth of labour movements. Marx believed that, as industrial capitalism developed, class conflict would lead to the emergence of a revolutionary labour movement (see Chapter 17, pp. 687–9). Most European labour movements pursued, however, an alternative non-revolutionary strategy of gaining control of the state by parliamentary means. Before they could do this, they had to force through a democratization that would enable workers to use their weight of numbers to vote in pro-labour governments. The power of the state could then be used to reform society in order to create a fairer and more equal distribution of resources. Indeed, some argued that in this way a non-revolutionary transition could be made from a capitalist to a socialist society (see box on p. 731).

Labour governments were certainly elected, notably in Britain and Scandinavia. Did this mean that the state had become an instrument of the working class? So far as a transition to socialism was concerned, this was never really on the agenda. Labour governments accepted that the economy had to be run on capitalist lines. They did introduce welfare reforms, but, as we shall see in 'Welfare Capitalism', pp. 741–2, it was the middle class that benefited most from these.

From capitalism to socialism in Sweden?

The Swedish labour movement has been the most powerful in the world and the Social Democratic Party has dominated Swedish politics since the early 1930s. Radical Social Democrat thinkers believed that a non-revolutionary transition could be made from capitalism to socialism by using the labour movement's control of the state. The Swedish labour movement produced in the 1970s an ingenious scheme to do this. The Meidner Plan, as it was called, proposed to end the power of capital by shifting the ownership of industry from private capital to union-controlled funds, which would be created by taxing excess profits. The higher the profits made by a company, the faster it would be taken over by the workers! After intense debate a law was passed in 1983 to set up such funds, but by this time the plan had been thoroughly deradicalized and turned into a means of increasing investment in industry and supporting pension funds. The Social Democratic state remained a capitalist state.

Source: Fulcher (1991a).

Why did labour governments not introduce more radical reforms? In a study of labour government in Britain, Miliband (1969) argued that the economic power of capital inevitably limited any government's freedom of action. The greater resources of private capital enabled it to bring pressure to bear on governments, parliaments, and civil-service departments. Furthermore, while the personnel of government might change, that of the civil service did not. State officials came from elite social backgrounds and exerted a conservative influence on the development of policy. Miliband also emphasized the ideological *hegemony* of the ruling class (see Chapter 8, pp. 276–7, for a discussion of this concept). Radical alternatives were developed only weakly because the mass media and education were dominated by conservative views.

Labour governments are now arguably more than ever constrained by the economic power of capital. As we show in Chapter 12, pp. 487–8, increasing global economic integration means that capital can be moved more easily than ever from one country to another. If governments pursue policies that threaten the interests of capital, it is liable to move elsewhere, with serious consequences for the national economy. This enables large companies to blackmail governments into pursuing policies that favour them.

If we are to understand the development of the state, we must place this in the context of class relationships and the relationship between the state and the economy. There is, however, the danger then of treating the state as no more than the instrument of a class. There is also the problem of economic determinism, of explaining the development of the state solely in terms of changes in the economy.

These problems have been recognized by Marxists themselves, and Poulantzas criticized Miliband for his 'instrumentalist' view of the state. Poulantzas (1975) argued that the state could act in the interest of capital as a whole only if it had a degree of independence from it, what he called a **relative autonomy**. This enabled the state to arbitrate between the conflicting interests of different sections of capital and take a long-term rather than a short-term view of its interests. There was still, however, an underlying economic determinism in his approach, since he still saw the state's actions in terms of the interests of capital. The state's autonomy was only relative.

Skocpol (1985) argued that the state had much more autonomy than this. She returned to the Weberian tradition to emphasize the territorial character of the state. Its territorial concerns involved the state in interstate relationships. It, therefore, faced outwards as well as inwards, and its international involvements gave rulers some independence from the economic power of capital. Thus, the imperatives of war have enabled the state to take control of the economy and override the interests of private capital, at least to some degree, as during the First World War in Britain.

It is certainly correct to argue that the state must be set in the context of interstate as well as interclass relationships. The term 'autonomy' is, however, rather misleading, since it suggests that the state can somehow be an independent force. It is better to see governments as having a limited freedom of action that has to be exercised within the various constraints acting upon the state. They are constrained by both private capital and other states, by both class and interstate relationships. They are also constrained by the consequences of democratization, for, in the liberal democracies at least, rulers can rule only if they succeed in persuading the electorate to give them the power to do so.

SOCIAL POLICY

States have since earliest times been involved in the maintenance of order, the raising of taxes, and conflicts over territory. It is only since the nineteenth century that they have become drawn into the provision of welfare for their citizens through social policy. But what is 'social policy'?

Social policy is normally taken to mean government policies concerned specifically with welfare. Policies on health, housing, social security, and social services clearly fall within this category, employment and education at least partly. As Hill (1997) points out, there are, however, problems with trying to separate out social policy from other policies in this way. On the one hand, non-welfare considerations may well shape social policies. For example, economic concerns with the control of state expenditure as well as social concerns with welfare will determine the level of spending on benefits. On the other hand, other policies that are apparently nothing to do with welfare may have a considerable bearing upon it. Defence policy, for example, will shape orders for military equipment, which will affect the demand for the products of defence industries, which, in turn, will greatly affect the jobs and welfare of those that work within them.

It is, therefore, important to locate the development of social policy within the development of the state as a whole, as we do in this chapter, and not treat it in isolation from other aspects of the development of the state. Hill defines social policy as 'policy activities which influence welfare', a definition which can include any field of policy. Although we shall concern ourselves mainly with policies specifically aimed at welfare, it is important to bear these issues in mind.

While all countries have developed some form of *state welfare*, not all have developed a *welfare state*. The term **welfare state** is used by some to refer broadly to all states that provide welfare, but by others to refer only to states that have at least attempted to provide welfare for the whole population. We use it in the latter sense. As we shall see below, in some countries the state has concentrated on providing support for the poor only.

In this section we will first consider rival explanations of the extension of the state's activities into welfare provision. We will then examine the central issue of social policy—the relationship between the state and the market. In this discussion we will draw on the approaches to the state examined in 'The Development of the State'.

The development of state welfare

The functionalist approach to the development of state welfare, as taken by Wilensky (1975), explains it in terms of the 'new needs' generated by industrialization. According to this approach, industrialization destroyed self-sufficiency. People moved from the land to the city, where they became dependent on employment in paid work. Industrial economies were, however, prone to sudden slumps, when people were thrown out of work and lost the capacity to support themselves. Furthermore, traditional means of community social support were largely absent in the new industrial cities. Urbanization also created new concentrations of population, where there were severe problems of health and housing. The state stepped in to deal with the problems created by industrialization.

There can be little doubt that the development of state welfare was in some sense a response to the problems generated by industrialization. The difficulty with this approach is, however, that it assumes that needs will be met and does not account for the political process through which the welfare state was established. Nor can it explain international differences in social policy.

These issues have been addressed by those who link the development of the welfare state to class conflict. According to this approach, the welfare state developed because of the growth of a labour movement. The starting point here is not so much the needs of an industrial society but rather the class conflict generated by capitalism. Thus, Esping-Andersen and Korpi (1984) have argued that state welfare was most developed in countries like Sweden, where the working class was strongly organized and gained political power through a strong labour movement.

According to Esping-Andersen (1990), **decommodification** is central to the development of the welfare state by labour movements. In order to understand this term, we must first consider **commodification**, the term given to the process by which capitalism turned all aspects of life, including, say, health care and education, into 'things' (or commodities) that were bought and sold. Access to them then depended on people's capacity to buy them, which was in turn related to their 'market situation'—that is, their earning power or wealth. Decommodification was the opposite process through which people became independent of the market by means of the state provision of welfare as a matter of right.

State welfare as such was not enough, however, to decommodify welfare. It was only when welfare was provided on a *universal* basis—that is, made equally available to all—that it became a social right. Esping-Andersen did indeed go further than this, arguing that even universal state welfare was insufficient to produce complete decommodification. This required that 'citizens can freely, and without potential loss of job, income, or general welfare, opt out of work when they themselves consider it necessary' (Esping-

Andersen 1990: 23). If they are away from work because of illness, they must receive the same income from state benefits, and have the right to unlimited absence with minimal certification. It is only then that the constraints of the market are wholly removed from welfare provision.

Decommodification led to what Habermas (1981*a*) has called a process of **juridification**. By this he meant that welfare was provided through legal (or juridical) and administrative procedures. Rights to welfare were specified by laws, which were administered by appropriate state agencies. Although welfare became a matter of entitlement according to the law, the application of laws to particular cases always requires interpretation by administrators. This frequently leads to disputes between the agencies and their clients, and reference to the courts for resolution of the points at issue. The problems of market provision may be avoided, but state provision generates problems of its own.

According to Esping-Andersen, decommodification was crucial to the collective solidarity and therefore the strength of labour movements. If welfare was provided by the state on a universal basis, this would prevent divisive conflicts between the higher paid, who had to pay for state welfare through taxes, and the lower paid, who received it. Greater worker unity would then strengthen the collective power of workers. This was one reason why labour movements have tried to use their political power to create welfare states.

This emphasis on the role of labour movements in the development of state welfare has in turn been criticized on the grounds that it was often initially developed not by Labour or Social Democratic governments but by Liberal or even Conservative ones (Pierson 1991: 37). It can, none the less, be argued that the pressure of a labour movement generally lay in the background. This led other parties to introduce state welfare to prevent the growth of a revolutionary movement or to stop a labour party gaining power.

The development of state welfare must also be set in the context of bureaucratization and interstate relationships. The development of state welfare was in part a product of the administrative revolution, which we examine in Chapter 16, pp. 650–1. International considerations also played a part, for the military and economic effectiveness of the nation state depended on its having educated and healthy soldiers and workers. The provision of state welfare on a national basis was also a means of unifying society at a time of war. As we shall see on pp. 738–9, war and the development of state welfare have at times been closely associated with each other.

Market *versus* state

In many ways the central issue in the discussion of social policy is the relationship between the market and state provision of welfare. Two main types of social policy have emerged, one relying on the market to provide the bulk of welfare, the other relying on the state:

▶ the market model;
▶ the welfare-state model.

The *market model* is based on the principle of selective state benefits for the poor. Benefits are means-tested— that is, they are given only to those whose means (income and wealth) fall below a certain level. The rest of the population is expected to buy welfare from the market by, for example, subscribing to private welfare schemes. Thus, health care is provided mainly through insurance and private medicine, with the state funding very basic care for the poor only. Welfare is otherwise seen as the responsibility of the individual not the state. This approach to social policy is often called 'liberal' because its supporters believe in the freedom (liberty) and responsibility of the individual.

The *welfare-state* model is based on the idea that state welfare should be not selective but universal, in two senses. It should provide benefits for all, irrespective of income. It should also provide a comprehensive range of benefits, including pensions, health care, education, and employment. By providing equal access to welfare, the welfare state seeks to reduce the inequality generated by market forces. It also seeks to do this by funding state welfare through 'progressive' taxation, which requires those with higher incomes to pay more tax (as opposed to 'regressive' taxation, such as sales taxes on goods, which bears most heavily on the poor). One of its central principles is that employment should not be left to market forces. The state should manage the economy in order to maintain full employment.

 These two concepts of welfare are linked to corresponding notions of democracy and citizenship. The market model is linked to *liberal* ideologies that emphasize the importance of political democracy and see citizenship in terms of civil and political rights. The *welfare-state* model is based on a social-democratic concept of citizenship which sees it as also involving social rights to employment, education, health, and welfare. See our discussion of citizenship in Chapter 14, pp. 533–5.

The relationship between these welfare principles has been the main issue in the development of social policy. Those who support a 'market model' argue that limited state resources should be targeted on those with most need. Dependence on the state should be discouraged and people should take responsibility for their own welfare. In a society dependent on a market economy, state intervention and taxation should be kept to a minimum. This approach is usually linked to a belief in the virtues of capitalism and the importance of maintaining the free market central to the workings of a capitalist economy.

Those who advocate the welfare state argue that welfare should be taken out of the market place and made equally available to all. They argue that in a welfare state benefits should be universal because this commits the whole society to the welfare state and prevents a backlash against high taxation from those who rely on private schemes. Universal welfare also establishes high standards of state welfare, since it has to meet the needs of the middle as well as the working class. It is also argued that universal benefits avoid the problem of the 'poverty trap', which occurs in means-tested systems when claimants' incomes increase and they lose benefits, leaving them no better off and with no incentive to seek work and support themselves. In its hostility to the market principle this approach has been particularly supported by socialists seeking to transform capitalist society.

Until the 1970s it seemed as though there was a general tendency for the social policies of industrial societies to move towards welfare-state principles. The welfare state seemed to be the final stage in the development of social policy. This is why state welfare and welfare state in some usages became virtually synonymous terms. In the 1970s, however, the market model was revived by **neo-liberalism**, which simply means 'new liberalism'.

Neo-liberals sought to restore the individual's freedom and choice, which they thought had been taken away through the growth of state welfare. They called for the targeting of state welfare on those who were most in need. The rest of the population should be encouraged to enter private insurance schemes. This would not only keep state expenditure down; it would also prevent people becoming dependent on the state, and enable market forces to work. We discuss neo-liberalism further in 'Thatcherism', pp. 748–9.

Neo-liberalism is often associated with the idea that the state should be 'rolled back', to allow market forces to operate and provide individuals with greater choice. Neo-liberal policies have indeed rolled back the welfare state, but this has not meant that the state as a whole has been rolled back. Gamble (1988) has argued that neo-liberalism, like liberalism, actually implied a strong state to protect the rights and freedom of the individual. As we shall see in 'Law and Order', pp. 754–6, neo-liberalism certainly led to a strengthening of the authority of the state.

Arguments about welfare have revolved around the issue of whether the market or the state should provide it, but Giddens (1994) claims in *Beyond Left and Right* that both these positions are out of date. He calls for a programme of 'positive welfare' that would address what he considers to be the real welfare problems of the world we live in. Rather than discuss these ideas here, we will, however, address them in the context of our discussion of the future of welfare policy (see pp. 761–3).

SUMMARY POINTS

In this section we began by considering what is meant by 'the state':

▶ We defined the state in terms of its functions of maintaining order, policy-making and implementa-

Source: Independent, 22 Feb. 1995.

tion, taxation, political representation, and the management of external relationships.

We went on to examine different aspects of the development of states:

▶ Weber emphasized that the state established a monopoly of the legitimate use of physical force within a territory.

▶ As states developed they underwent a process of democratization through the emergence of representative bodies and the extension of citizenship.

▶ These were essential to democracy but not sufficient to establish it, for democracy also required free political activity and competition between parties.

▶ The development of the state must also be set in the context of class relationships, the domination of the state by capital, and the challenge to this domination from labour movements.

Finally we considered the development of social policy, which should not, we emphasized, be treated in isolation from other aspects of the development of the state:

▶ The development of social policy was a response to the problems generated by industrialization but should also be set in the context of the development of class relationships, bureaucratization, and inter-state relationships.

▶ The development of the welfare state involved a process of decommodification which made welfare independent of market situation.

▶ State welfare had developed according to two different models, the 'market model', which gave state benefits to the poor only, and the 'welfare state', which provided universal state benefits.

THE DEVELOPMENT OF THE STATE AND SOCIAL POLICY IN BRITAIN

In this section we examine the development of social policy in Britain from the early nineteenth century through to the 1970s, setting it in the context of the various aspects of the development of the state that we have just discussed. In 'Three Worlds of Welfare' we use the framework provided by Esping-Andersen to place the development of state welfare in a comparative framework.

LIBERAL CAPITALISM

Our starting point is the period of liberal capitalism during the first half of the nineteenth century. Industrial capitalism was making its breakthrough at this time and transforming British society. There was minimal state interference with the activities of the early industrialists—hence the term liberal capitalism—and state regulation initially declined, though in the 1830s new forms of bureaucratic regulation began to appear.

Deregulation

The politically dominant ideas were those of the eighteenth-century economist and philosopher Adam Smith, who believed in a society of freely competing individuals.

Smith argued that competition in a free market would be to the benefit of all. It would reduce prices but also increase wages, for employers seeking to expand production would compete for labour and wages would rise. The capitalist employer's search for profits would also make sure that industry produced only goods for which there was a demand. If this was insufficient, prices and profits would fall and industrialists would switch their investment into producing the goods that people did want to buy.

Smith believed that the state should allow market forces to operate freely, but he did recognize that it had some important duties to perform. These involved not only defence and the administration of justice, but also other tasks important to the community that could not be carried out by profit-seeking entrepreneurs. This aspect of his ideas is often forgotten by his modern-day followers.

During the first half of the nineteenth century the state deregulated key aspects of economic activity. The regulation of the wage rates for each craft and the regulation of food prices to protect the consumer had been largely removed by 1815. The freeing of international trade took longer, however. The key step in this was the ending of import duties on corn in 1846, which was followed by a general removal of import duties in the 1850s and 1860s.

The liberal state was closely linked to the interests of capitalist industrialists, who wanted to be free to develop their activities without state interference. They wanted wage rates to be set by the labour market not by the state. They also wanted free trade, in part to assist exports but also because imports of cheap food would allow them to pay lower wages. Whether liberal capitalism was in the interests of workers, as Adam Smith believed, was another matter. Skilled workers in high demand could certainly use their market power to bargain up their wages, but workers with weak bargaining power could be freely exploited. Agricultural labourers found that their bargaining position was greatly weakened by the import of food produced by cheap agricultural labour abroad.

The liberal state also had another face, however. Allowing market forces to operate freely did not mean that the state was weak. Indeed, the very reverse was in fact the case, for market forces could operate freely only within an orderly society and this meant that the state needed to be strengthened.

The transformation of society by capitalist industrialism generated much disorder. Strikes, rioting, machine-breaking, and crimes against property all grew. Trade unions and radical political movements emerged to challenge the power of the capitalist employer. There was a general tightening-up of law and order, which we outline in Chapter 16, pp. 651–4. The military were used to quell riots and demonstrations. The law was used against trade-union activity and in 1834 the 'Tolpuddle martyrs', six agricultural labourers who had joined a union, were convicted of breaking the law and transported to penal settlements in Australia.

Welfare and the state

 We refer in this section to various aspects of welfare that are discussed in other chapters. In Chapter 13, pp. 520–3, we examine the emergence of unemployment as a problem. In Chapter 6, p. 203, we consider contemporary ideas of the relationship between population increase and poverty. In Chapter 14, pp. 561–2, we discuss the distinction between the 'deserving' and 'undeserving' poor.

There was a growing awareness of social problems as Britain became an industrial society, population increased, and new industrial cities rapidly grew. It was a characteristic feature of industrial capitalism that unemployment became a recognized problem, for industrial workers were entirely dependent on paid work. The economists of the time regarded it, however, as the inevitable result of the operation of market forces. There was nothing that could be done about it. Indeed, the labour market central to a capitalist economy would work only if there was a steady supply of labour seeking employment.

The rising number of poor people, partly due to unemployment, did become a cause of concern, but not because of a concern for their condition. There was little sympathy for the 'able-bodied' poor but rather a fear that large numbers of poor people would become a burden on the local community. It was also feared that population increase was getting out of control and that support for the poor would encourage them to breed.

An industrial society anyway needed workers to labour for long hours in the unpleasant work condi-

Free trade

The apparently obscure repeal of the Corn Laws in 1846 was one of the most important events of nineteenth-century history and typical of the era of liberal capitalism. The Corn Law of 1815 had been introduced to protect the interests of British farmers and landowners by keeping out cheap foreign corn. Its repeal in 1846 marked the victory of the industrial over the agricultural interest. Cheap food imports meant that industrialists could pay lower wages to their workers. It was argued that this would make British industry more competitive and enable it to expand production. British agriculture would be forced to become more efficient and diversify its products. There was more to it than this, however. If other countries were able to export food to Britain, they would be able in return to buy industrial goods from Britain. This was a key step in the development of an international division of labour, which we discuss in Chapter 12, pp. 461–2.

tions of the early factories. The poor had to be forced to work and in 1834 the Poor Law Amendment Act introduced a new system of relief to do just that. The practice of *outdoor* relief was abolished and a system of *indoor* relief created. Only those who entered a 'workhouse' would be given support. Conditions there would be made worse than those experienced by the poorest paid worker, so that only the absolutely desperate would enter. This law generated enormous hostility amongst the poor and in practice the old system of outdoor relief largely continued. The 1834 law illustrates well, however, the attitude of the state to poverty during the period of liberal capitalism.

People who fell on hard times were otherwise dependent on the local community, charity, the pawn shop, and self-help schemes. Insecure employment and irregular wages encouraged the emergence of the pawn shop, where a loan could be obtained on the security of some item of property. In 1830 in London alone there were an estimated 500 to 600 unlicensed pawn brokers, in addition to some 342 licensed ones (Royle 1987: 186). Those with higher earnings could insure themselves against future disasters by joining 'friendly societies'. They made weekly payments and in return the societies would support them in ill health or unemployment or pay for their funeral.

In other areas of welfare the state did begin at this time to intervene. While there was little sympathy for the poor, there was a growing concern with work conditions in the factories. Reformers were concerned not just with the length of work hours but also with issues of morality, health, education, and family relationships, which were all affected by unrestricted labour in mines and factories. From 1833 a series of Factory Acts began to restrict the hours of work, though many employers resisted or circumvented them, and progress was very slow. The 1833 Act also required employers to provide two hours of education per day for child workers. In 1844 another act prohibited women and children working in the mines.

The other main area of state intervention was in public health. The first major piece of legislation was the 1848 Public Health Act, which required the establishment of local boards of health and the appointment of medical officers in places with higher than average death rates. The state had not become involved in health care as such, though in the 1840s workhouses began to provide some very basic medical care for the poor. Health care for the poor was otherwise provided through charitable foundations and public dispensaries.

Although the state's actual involvement in welfare was limited by the liberal principles dominant at the time, a new bureaucratic approach to social problems was establishing itself. This involved state investigation, the collection of information, legislation, regulation, and inspection. Inspectors' reports then fed back into the process. For example, the reports of the Factory Act inspectors shaped the development of factory legislation. There were still many barriers to effective legislation and regulation, but a state welfare machinery was coming into being. Bureaucratization played an important part in the development of state welfare.

STATE WELFARE

New attitudes towards poverty and new policies towards welfare gradually emerged during the later years of the nineteenth century. The work of Booth and Rowntree created a greater awareness of poverty and understanding of its causes (see Chapter 14, pp. 569–74). In Britain it was during the years before the First World War that the breakthough to the state provision of welfare was made, though in Germany the development of state welfare started much earlier.

Origins of state welfare

It was during the ten years or so before the First World War of 1914–18 that the British state began to take responsibility for the unemployed, the sick, the old, and the young. The initial focus was on the welfare of children. State-funded school meals were introduced in 1906 and a school medical service shortly followed. The

State welfare in Germany

State welfare developed much earlier in Germany than in Britain even though industrialization occurred there much later. In Germany legislation providing social-insurance schemes for accidents, sickness and disability, and old age was passed in the 1880s, a good twenty years earlier than in Britain. This legislation was initiated by Bismarck in an attempt to detach the German working class from the Social Democrat party, which it failed to do. The background to this early welfare legislation was the earlier extension of the vote, which was given to all adult males in 1871, and the earlier growth of a socialist political movement. This shows the significance of democratization and class organization in the development of state welfare.

1908 Children's Act made the parental neglect of children's health an offence and made the community responsible for the care of neglected children. In 1908 state pensions were brought in for the over seventies. In 1911 the National Insurance Act established unemployment benefit, sick pay, maternity and disability benefits, and free medical treatment from general practitioners.

The state welfare introduced by these measures was, however, limited in important ways. It was limited by the insurance principle, for both unemployment benefit and health benefits were introduced on this basis, which meant that they depended on weekly national-insurance contributions paid by those in employment. As Derek Fraser (1984: 166) has put it, 'the state was compelling its citizens to provide insurance for themselves rather than providing simple state medicine and sickness benefits'. Furthermore, only those who had paid contributions were entitled to benefits. Non-working wives, who had not contributed, were excluded from the benefits of the 1911 Act. The health care provided by the 1911 Act was limited to general-practice medicine. Although a Ministry of Health was established in 1919, a national hospital system had to await the creation of the National Health Service in 1947.

Some have argued that the burst of legislation before the First World War marks the beginning of the welfare state. The insurance principle meant, however, that it was a long way from the welfare-state idea that all citizens are entitled to welfare by right. None the less, its importance can hardly be exaggerated, for the state had taken a substantial responsibility for people's welfare in a quite new way.

Democratization, the labour movement, and war

To understand these reforms we must place them in the context of the changing character of class relations, going back to the mid-nineteenth century. At this time a change can be seen in the strategy of the British ruling class, which shifted from *repressing* discontent to *containing* it by incorporating the growing labour movement. By **incorporation** is meant the process of including working-class organizations in institutions of bargaining and political representation.

The process of incorporation involved democratization. The vote was gradually extended to all adult males by the Reform Acts of 1867, 1884, and 1918, which led to a growing competition for the working-class vote between the two main political parties of the time, the Conservative and Liberal parties. It also led gradually to the independent political organization of the working class, and in 1906 the unions finally created the Labour Party to represent them in parliament.

It was not, however, the Labour Party that was responsible for the welfare legislation of the years before the First World War. This was introduced by the Liberal government of 1906–14. Why would a Liberal government do this, when state-welfare provision was alien to the non-interventionist principles of the liberal state?

The growth of the labour movement and the development of socialist ideas had put pressure on the political elite to head off the threat of more radical changes. The Liberal Party, which had close links with many of the trade unions and relied on the support of organized labour, felt particularly threatened by the emergence of the Labour Party. Thus, the growth of a labour movement did lie behind the Liberal welfare legislation. It was ultimately the class conflict and class organization generated by a capitalist industrial society that led to the development of state welfare.

The development of state welfare must also be placed in the context of interstate conflict. The growing international rivalry that led towards the First World War made its own contribution to the development of state welfare. Many British politicians were keenly aware of the greater development of state welfare in Germany. The significance of a healthy population and an integrated society for national strength was well recognized. Indeed, it was the revelation of the poor physical state of British soldiers by the Boer War of 1899–1902 that gave rise to the measures to improve children's health.

The First World War itself then gave an additional momentum to the development of the state. Often described as the first 'total war', it made huge demands on the populations and resources of all the participating countries. In Britain the state intervened massively to organize production and control society. Some of its main interventions were:

▶ conscription to the armed forces in 1916;

▶ the creation of the Ministries of Food, Health (1919), Labour, Munitions, and Shipping;

▶ state control of wages and prices, food and raw materials, housing and rents;

▶ the extensive state control of industrial production and transport;

▶ the state arbitration of industrial conflict;

▶ a sixfold increase in state expenditure.

Much of the apparatus of state regulation was dismantled after the war but it none the less had a lasting effect on the development of the state and its relationship with British society (see Runciman 1993). It led to much higher levels of state expenditure and taxation, which never fell back to their pre-war levels. The wartime experience of the state control of the economy provided a model for the later extension of state control and prepared the way for a more state-managed form of capitalism. The state's wartime involvement in industrial relations stimulated both unions and employers to strengthen their organization at national level and establish relationships with the state. The 1918 extension of the vote to women over the age of 30 followed the heavy involvement of women in the war effort.

WELFARE CAPITALISM

It was during the Second World War and the years immediately after it that the *welfare state* was established. In this section we examine the creation of the welfare state and set it in the context of corporatism, for welfare depended upon the state management of the economy by corporatist means. We also consider the implications of the welfare state for social inequalities by discussing its patriarchal character and its redistributive consequences.

War and the post-war settlement

The Second World War had a far greater impact on the development of social policy than the First World War had done. It was during the Second World War that Keynesian economic policies to manage the economy in order to maintain employment gained official acceptance. The Beveridge proposals for a new system of social insurance emerged during the war years. The 1944 Education Act, which we discuss in Chapter 7, p. 242, at last established free secondary education for all. The foundations of the welfare state were laid during the war.

Why did the Second World War have such an impact? The political situation had changed considerably since the First World War. Welfare ideas and policies had developed further and the Keynesian idea of the state management of the economy had emerged in the inter-war period. The labour movement had continued to gain in strength and the Labour Party took part in the war-time coalition government. The war itself had a more general and more immediate impact on the British people through the extensive bombing of British cities, which destroyed some 200,000 houses and damaged many more. Around a quarter of British

> ## Beveridge and the welfare state
>
> William Beveridge (1879–1963) has been seen as the architect of the welfare state. He had an early career in the Civil Service before becoming Director of the London School of Economics during the years 1919–37. In 1941 he was appointed chairman of a committee of civil servants charged with inquiring into the whole field of social insurance. The Beveridge Report of 1942 emerged from the work of this committee. In 1944 he became a Liberal MP for a year and then a Liberal peer.
>
> He is best known for the Beveridge Report, which made wide-ranging proposals for welfare reform. The impact of the Report owed much to its timing, for it came out just after the first British victory of the Second World War, the battle of El Alamein. It called dramatically for a war on the 'five giant evils' of 'Want, Disease, Ignorance, Squalor, and Idleness'. Although its proposals were based on the universalist principle of equal welfare for all, they were also largely an extension of existing social-insurance schemes. It immediately became a bestseller with sales of 635,000 and generated a popular impetus for welfare reform.

housing stock was damaged in the war. It was recognized in government circles that the construction of a welfare state was the price that had to be paid for the wartime mobilization and sacrifices of the British people.

The outcome was what is generally called the 'post-war settlement'. This was a settlement in two rather different senses. First, it settled the broad framework of social policy until the 1980s. Secondly, it was a compromise between capital and labour. The labour movement accepted capitalism, while business accepted the welfare state and greater state intervention in the economy. The settlement was broadly accepted by the Conservative as well as the Labour Party.

The welfare state and corporatism

The welfare state was based on three key principles:

▶ full employment.
▶ universal welfare.
▶ free health and education.

Full employment involved the Keynesian management of the economy. *Universal welfare* was provided by the National Insurance Act of 1946, which introduced a complete range of benefits for the whole population

The Second World War generated demands for state welfare.

itiveness of British products, for employment depended on the success of British industry in meeting international competition. Governments, both Conservative and Labour, tried to involve both unions and employers in economic management through corporatism.

Corporatism involved the state developing a cooperative relationship with the organizations (or corporations) of major interest groups, such as unions and employers' organizations. It recognized the power of these organizations and tried to bring them into the state apparatus by appointing their representatives to policy-making bodies. In exchange for being given some influence over policy, they were expected to become agents of the state and implement government policy.

In particular, the government tried during the 1960s and the 1970s to persuade or indeed force them to operate prices and incomes policies. These set the rate at which prices and wages could rise in order to keep the prices of British goods down, control wage increases, and maintain Britain's economic competitiveness. This was a highly interventionist approach that involved governments in trying to regulate both wages and prices.

As we showed earlier, the British ruling class had shifted from a strategy of repressing the unions to one of incorporating them during the second half of the nineteenth century. The corporatism of the 1960s and 1970s can be considered the final stage of this process.

The patriarchal welfare state

It was widely believed that the welfare state would provide greater equality. In practice, it was, however, less egalitarian than it appeared to be. We consider here the issues raised by its patriarchal character, and then in the next section its redistributive consequences.

The British welfare state was based on patriarchal assumptions. It assumed a gendered division of labour between men in paid employment and women at home carrying out unpaid domestic and childcaring tasks. There were two main aspects of this, the social-security situation of women and their role in providing care.

The welfare state assumed that men in paid work would support women doing domestic work. Married women did not, therefore, need the same benefits as men. Until 1975 the National Insurance Act of 1946 provided lower benefits for married women, who paid contributions at a lower rate when they were in paid work. The insurance principle also meant that women in paid work who made fewer contributions, due to years off work rearing children, received lower benefits. As Pateman (1989) has argued, men were treated by the

'from the cradle to the grave'. *Free health care* was provided by the National Health Service (NHS) in 1948 and *free secondary education* by the 1944 Education Act. This involved an extensive *decommodification* of welfare, though the persistence of private medicine and private education set clear limits to this process. Superior education and superior health care could still be bought.

The central state took on a far greater role in the provision of welfare than ever before. Voluntary organizations and charities now became minor players. Health care and important parts of the economy were largely removed from the private sector. The NHS here had much in common with the series of nationalizations that took major industries and services into public ownership. The crucial maintenance of full employment involved the extensive involvement of the state in managing the economy.

The maintenance of full employment was partly a matter of managing the level of demand through Keynesian policies but also of maintaining the compet-

British welfare state as full citizens but women as wives and mothers.

Lowe (1993) recognizes the force of these arguments but points out that the 1940s changes none the less improved the position of women in important ways. Previously women not in paid employment and not paying social-insurance contributions had not been entitled to free medical care. This was now provided on a universal basis. Furthermore, the payment of pensions at age 60 to women, five years earlier than to men, and their greater longevity meant that women obtained greater benefit than men did from state pensions. The issue is not simply a matter of the amount of benefit, however, for patriarchal welfare assumptions reinforced patriarchal beliefs and therefore strengthened patriarchy generally.

The welfare state also depended on women carrying out much of the work of caring for children, the sick, and the old on an unpaid basis. In other words, the welfare state was based on the provision of welfare by the state and by women.

This was not just a matter of unpaid work but also of the absence of state childcare facilities, which led to British state childcare provision being the lowest in Europe (Phillips and Moss 1988). The assumption was that mothers looked after pre-school children. If they chose to work, they had to make their own childcare arrangements without assistance from the state.

This assumption has not been made in all industrial societies. In Sweden there has been extensive state provision of pre-school childcare. Furthermore, in Sweden either parent became entitled by law to take paid leave of up to sixty days a year to look after children (A. Gould 1993: 189).

The redistributive welfare state?

The welfare state was widely expected to create greater equality in two main ways. First, it was to provide universal benefits and equality of access to education and health. Secondly, state welfare expenditure would be redistributive. On the one hand, taxation was progressive, which meant that tax rates increased as income rose. On the other hand, the poor would benefit most from spending on social security, education, health, and other social services. Increased spending on social security and social services generally should therefore redistribute resources from those with higher to those with lower incomes.

In a number of important ways, however, the welfare state soon departed from the principles of universalism and free and equal access through:

► means-testing;

► charges;

► income-related benefits.

The *means-testing* of state benefits had become quite widespread by the 1970s (Glennerster 1995: 183). While this was an apparently reasonable way of containing costs, it created a complex poverty trap and moved away from welfare state-universalism.

Health care soon became less free as *charges* were introduced for prescriptions and for some services, such as dentistry. These charges inevitably took a higher proportion of their income from those with lower pay.

The principle of relating benefits, such as unemployment benefit and pensions, to income was introduced in the 1960s. This meant that a lower income resulted in lower benefits. These were all processes of *recommodification*, for they made welfare more dependent on market situation.

 We discussed the meaning of commodification and decommodification on pp. 732–3, and the opposed principles of means-testing and universalism. If you are unclear about any of this, return to this discussion. The issue of equality of access to education is taken up in Chapter 7, pp. 246–56.

More fundamentally, it has been demonstrated that redistribution through taxation and state spending has not occurred. On the one hand, the tax system became less progressive. On the other hand, it was the better off who benefited most from state spending. We now need to examine in more detail the arguments on both these very important points.

Lowe (1993) has summarized the changes in the tax system that have made it less progressive:

► *Declining taxation of companies and wealth.* The proportion of tax raised from taxing company profits and taxing the wealthy through death duties has fallen. A heavier burden has therefore fallen on the taxes paid by those less well off.

► *Declining progressiveness of income tax.* Changes in rates have shifted more of the tax burden on to those with lower incomes. As inflation has led to higher nominal wages, it has pushed more wage-earners over the threshold into paying taxes.

► *Expansion of allowances.* Tax does not have to be paid on income spent in certain approved ways and this has benefited the better off. For example, tax relief on loans for buying houses has benefited house-owners, and, the bigger the loan, the greater has been the benefit.

▶ *Occupational exemptions.* Many of those in middle-class occupations have enjoyed non-taxed occupational benefits. Thus, company contributions to occupational pension schemes are untaxed. Company cars and entertainment allowances have provided untaxed benefits which others have to pay for out of taxed income.

▶ *Indirect taxation.* An increasing proportion of the money raised by tax has come from indirect taxes on widely used products, such as beer, cigarettes, and petrol. There is also a general sales tax—VAT. Since these taxes are paid on consumption not on income, they cannot take account of income level. If you are too poor to pay income tax, you still pay tax on most things that you buy.

Some of these features of the tax system have been changed in recent budgets, which have reduced the benefits from allowances and created new, lower rates of tax, but the mechanisms listed all still operate.

So far as spending was concerned, Le Grand (1982) showed that public expenditure has mainly benefited the better off and this has been confirmed by later studies reviewed by Hay (1996). If we take state expenditure on health, Le Grand (1982: 26) calculated that those in the top socio-economic group (professionals, employers, and managers) received over 40 per cent more spending per ill person than those in the bottom group (semi-skilled and unskilled workers). The better off have made more use of the NHS, because of their greater knowledge of what is available from it, and their social and cultural connections with those who provide care.

He found that the same thing happened in other areas of state expenditure. His top socio-economic group received nearly 50 per cent more state education spending per person than his bottom one (Le Grand 1982: 58). The children of the better off stayed in education longer and gained higher qualifications, which, of course, improved their career prospects and earnings potential. There were similar patterns in housing expenditure and transport subsidies.

Legrand concluded that 'almost all public expenditure on the social services in Britain benefits the better off to a greater extent than the poor' (1982: 3). Note that this conclusion was reached on the basis of 1970s data, before changes in social policy increased inequality during the period of Conservative government after 1979.

Arthur Gould (1993) has argued that it is the middle class rather than the working class that has benefited from the welfare state. This was a matter not just of the middle class's capacity to exploit state welfare but also of the jobs it provided for the middle class. The welfare state has generated large numbers of salaried white-collar, professional, and semi-professional occupations in health and welfare services (including education).

THREE WORLDS OF WELFARE

So far we have been focusing on the development of state welfare in Britain. In this section we set the British experience in international context by considering different systems of state welfare and their consequences. Esping-Andersen (1990) has provided a framework for doing this and we will first outline his 'three worlds of welfare' before examining their consequences for employment and social stratification.

As we showed earlier, Esping-Andersen's central concept was the decommodification of welfare, which essentially means making people's welfare independent of the market. He carried out an international comparative study of the extent of decommodification in 1980. This study measured the degree of decommodification in the provision of pensions, and sickness and unemployment benefits. These measures were then combined into an index to capture the extent to which the 'average worker' had become independent of the market.

When countries were ranked according to their position on this index, he found that they clustered in three groups. He also examined the history of their social policies and found that these corresponded with his three clusters. This led him to identify three types of state welfare. Not all countries fitted his clusters neatly. Britain, for example, showed a relatively low level of decommodification but its social policy combined liberal and social democratic principles. Esping-Andersen pointed out that particular societies always combined different principles of social policy to some degree and therefore never fitted his types of state welfare exactly.

Two of his types correspond broadly with the two models of social policy we examined in 'Market versus State', pp. 733–4. The *liberal* type corresponded to the *market* model, providing state welfare for the poor only and expecting everyone else to take responsibility for their own welfare and buy it on the market. The *social-democratic* type was essentially based on the *welfare-state* model of providing universal state welfare.

Esping-Andersen's three types of welfare	Type of welfare	Degree of decommodification	Principles of social policy	Countries
	Liberal	Low	Individualistic self-reliance	Australia Canada United States
	Conservative	Medium	Loyalty to state and preservation of existing social order	France Germany Italy
	Social Democratic	High	Equality and social solidarity	Denmark Netherlands Norway Sweden

The third *conservative* type sought to protect traditional structures against both the individualism of the market and the egalitarian tendencies of socialism. The state provided more welfare than in the liberal model but channelled it largely through workers' entitlements to benefits and pensions. The assumption was that the male worker would provide for his family through a 'family wage' and through the benefits and pensions paid to him. Traditional gender roles were maintained and the family was expected to play a central part in welfare. State benefits could be quite generous but were related to occupation. The links between occupation and welfare meant that welfare depended on labour-market situation and was only partially decommodified.

Esping-Andersen was interested not just in the development of state welfare as such but also in its important, and often overlooked, consequences for employment and social stratification. Welfare work was a crucial source of 'post-industrial' employment, particularly for women, at a time when jobs in manufacturing industry were shrinking. Depending on the type of social policy, employment in welfare services could lead, however, to what he called 'good' or 'bad' jobs and to very different patterns of social stratification. He explored these issues by examining Sweden, the United States, and Germany as examples of each of his 'worlds of welfare'.

In Sweden the development of a universalist welfare state led to the creation of many public-sector jobs in health, education, and social services. These enabled Sweden to maintain full employment even though manufacturing industry was contracting, while a strong labour movement kept up the wages of service workers and prevented the emergence of bad jobs. A non-patriarchal welfare state enabled women to pursue full-time and relatively uninterrupted careers in service jobs. The principle of providing welfare for all also resulted in a high degree of social solidarity stretching across the working class and the middle class.

The main line of conflict in the 1980s was between rival private- and public-sector unions. This corresponded also to a gender division, between male workers concentrated in the private sector and predominantly female workers in the public sector. The gender segregation of occupations was high in Sweden, where managerial, professional, and technical occupations were dominated by men and caring occupations by women.

In the United States too health, education, and social services provided increasing employment, but the reliance on market provision led to much more expansion of private-sector services, subsidized in various ways by the state. Private-sector expansion and a weak labour movement resulted in a dual labour market with a widening gap between good and bad jobs. The good jobs were in well-paid managerial and professional occupations with plentiful 'fringe benefits' providing welfare for those employed in them. The bad jobs involved routine and menial work in low-paid services, where pay was low and workers received hardly any additional benefits.

The result was increasing inequality and social

division. Initially the good jobs were monopolized by white males and the bad ones were carried out largely by women, and by black and Hispanic workers. Esping-Andersen argues that Affirmative Action and Equal Opportunities programmes have, however, opened up routes for these groups into better jobs. He suggests that this may mean that in future social divisions will be based on class rather than ethnicity or gender.

In Germany there had been less service expansion and employment was still largely dependent on a highly productive manufacturing industry, which provided diminishing employment. The decline of employment was managed through early retirement but unemployment too was high. Lack of service jobs and the preservation of the traditional family resulted in fewer women entering the labour market than in Sweden and the United States.

The result was a large number of economically inactive people, consisting of housewives, the unemployed, and pensioners, who were supported by a relatively small and highly taxed labour force in manufacturing industry. The main line of social tension was between insiders jealously guarding their jobs and unemployed outsiders. The insiders resented the high taxes they had to pay to provide welfare for the outsiders. One form taken by this conflict was hostility to foreign workers, who were regarded as 'job thieves' or 'welfare-scroungers'.

Where does Britain come in? In 1980 Britain was probably closest to the Swedish case but moving away from it towards the American. The British welfare state had some universal features, particularly in health care, though benefits were becoming increasingly related to income. Its labour movement was not as centralized, unified, and egalitarian as the Swedish one. The British economy was less internationally competitive, public-sector employment was lower, and unemployment was much higher. Low-paid and insecure private-sector jobs in areas such as cleaning and care were expanding on American lines. The very low provision of state pre-school childcare resulted in the extensive part-time employment of women in these jobs. Britain was moving from a social-democratic welfare state towards the liberal model, as we shall see on pp. 750–4.

This is one of the problems with Esping-Andersen's typology, for there has been a general tendency, eventually even in Sweden, for all countries to move towards the liberal/market model. Some criticism has also been made of the way he identified his three clusters and grouped countries within his types (Harloe 1997). Feminists have argued that he dealt only with women's paid work and ignored their unpaid and uncommodified domestic labour (Crompton 1997).

None the less, in evaluating Esping-Andersen's work it is important to recognize its originality and the comprehensiveness of its framework. It brought statistical and historical analysis together in a fruitful and broadly convincing way. It provided a framework for studying the development of state welfare within a comparative framework. It also broadened the study of social policy by examining its consequences for employment, occupational structure, stratification, and social conflict. We will return to his typology when we place the changes of the 1980s and 1990s in comparative perspective.

Welfare worlds, employment, and social divisions	Country	World of welfare	Development of post-industrial employment	Social divisions
	United States	Liberal	'Dual' expansion of 'good' and 'bad' private-sector jobs and low unemployment	Concentration of women, blacks, and hispanics in 'bad' jobs but 'equal opportunities' programmes
	Germany	Conservative	Low expansion of service jobs and high unemployment	Tax-paying 'insiders' with jobs and unemployed 'outsiders'
	Sweden	Social democratic	Expansion of 'good' public-sector jobs and low unemployment	Private-sector male workers and public-sector female workers

SUMMARY POINTS

In this section we have examined the development of British social policy from the early nineteenth century to the 1970s. We first considered the stage of 'liberal capitalism':

▶ During the first half of the nineteenth century the state deregulated important areas of economic activity but strengthened law and order.

▶ As unemployment and urban poverty increased, the 'workhouse' was introduced to keep the costs of supporting the poor down and force them to work.

▶ The state began to intervene in welfare matters in the limited areas of factory legislation and public health.

We then considered the establishment of state welfare during the years before the First World War:

▶ Child welfare measures, old-age pensions, unemployment benefit, and sick pay were introduced.

▶ The dominance of the 'insurance principle' meant, however, that these measures were a long way from welfare-state universalism.

▶ Democratization, the growth of a labour movement, and the imperatives of international conflict lay behind these reforms.

We went on to consider the establishment of the welfare state in the 1940s:

▶ This involved universal benefits, free and equal access to health and education, and the maintenance of full employment through the Keynesian and corporatist management of the economy.

▶ The egalitarian character of the welfare state was, however, limited by its movement away from universal principles, its patriarchal assumptions, and its redistributive failure.

In 'Three Worlds of Welfare' we set the development of the British welfare state in comparative perspective.

▶ Esping-Andersen identified three types of state welfare, which were linked to different patterns of employment and social division.

CRISIS AND TRANSFORMATION

We now move on to the transformation of the state during the 1980s. This transformation was central to the development of all aspects of government policy in the 1980s and the 1990s.

We begin by considering the economic crisis of the 1970s, for it was in response to this crisis that the state was transformed. We then examine the changes in the state brought about by the Conservative governments of the 1980s and 1990s, and the changes in social policy that broke decisively away from the principles of the welfare state. From social policy we move on to law and order, for the policy changes of the 1980s had resulted in increased conflict and crime, which the government tried to contain by strengthening the forces of law and order.

Finally, we discuss state welfare at the end of the twentieth century. Will the 1997 Labour government restore the welfare state? Is there an international convergence towards the market model of welfare? Will Esping-Andersen's three worlds of welfare continue on their separate paths? We also consider whether the market and welfare-state models have become obsolete and should be replaced by a new kind of 'positive welfare' policy.

THE CRISIS OF THE 1970S

The transformation of the state was rooted in the crisis of British society in the 1970s. In order to understand contemporary policies and issues we must go back to this crisis and examine why it occurred.

The crisis of the 1970s was a profitability crisis. The profitability of British industry declined during the 1960s and 1970s to the point at which much of it was hardly making a profit at all. This is shown by the net profit rate, which measures the return on capital after

Figure 18.1. **Net profit rate of manufacturing industry, selected countries, 1960 and 1981 (%)**

Country	1960	1981
Canada	17	14
France	18	1
Germany	29	8
Japan	44	13
United Kingdom	18	2
United States	22	10

Note: figures to nearest 1%.

Source: Armstrong *et al.* (1984: 464).

allowing for the cost of replacing worn-out or out-of-date equipment. The net profit rate of British manufacturing as a whole fell from 17.5 per cent in 1960 to a low of 1.7 per cent in 1981. The crisis was particularly severe in Britain but it occurred in other countries too (see Figure 18.1).

Profit is the driving force in a capitalist economy. If profitability falls, then industry collapses, companies go bankrupt, and workers lose their jobs. Without the expectation of profit there will be no investment and no creation of new jobs. Governments find that they have to pay ever-increasing amounts of unemployment benefit at a time when their income is falling, since declining profits and rising unemployment inevitably reduce revenue from taxes. So the crisis spreads rapidly from the economy to the state.

Contradictions and competition

The crisis had internal and external causes. Its internal causes lay in the problems created by the system of welfare capitalism established by the post-war settlement. These problems became particularly severe, however, because of increasing international economic competition, which particularly threatened the economies of the old industrial societies. We first consider the internal causes.

As we showed in 'Welfare Capitalism', p. 739, the establishment of a welfare state in 1940s Britain has been interpreted as a settlement between capital and labour. Although this settlement apparently solved the problem of class conflict, welfare capitalism then gen-

erated 'vicious circles' which led to greater conflict in the 1960s and the crisis of the 1970s. These vicious circles have been seen by Marxist writers as resulting from the **contradictions of welfare capitalism** (Gough 1979). By this they mean that essential elements of welfare capitalism were in fundamental conflict with each other.

One of these vicious circles centred on state spending. The welfare state led to growing expenditure on health, education, pensions, and social services generally (see Figure 18.2). Increased state spending in capitalist societies resulted in what has been called the **fiscal crisis** of capitalism (Gough 1979: 125). Fiscal crisis essentially means taxation crisis. The higher taxation of both workers and companies in various ways diminished the profitability of industry. Workers, for example, found that their take-home pay declined as taxes rose and therefore demanded higher wages in compensation. Higher wages then diminished the profits of the companies who employed them. As the economy got into a worse state, it became more and more difficult for the government to raise from the economy the taxes it needed.

This vicious circle interacted with another one, centred on the maintenance of employment. This was one of the key principles of the welfare state, but it inevitably increased the bargaining power of workers, who could take strike action in pursuit of higher wages with little fear of losing their jobs. As we show in Chapter 13, p. 511, industrial conflict rose in the 1950s and 1960s and was at a high level in the 1970s. Full employment also meant that workers could resist attempts by employers to change work practices in order to increase productivity. Thus, the full employment of the 1960s and 1970s had consequences that weakened the competitiveness of British industry.

The economic problems generated by the contradictions of welfare capitalism were particularly serious because increasing international competition led to a general crisis of profitability, as Figure 18.1 shows. Even Japan suffered, though not as severely as the old industrial countries. Britain's crisis was one of the worst, because of economic weaknesses dating back to the nineteenth century. Three main problems are commonly identified:

▶ an archaic industrial structure;
▶ the domination of financial and trading interests;
▶ the absence of a state industrial policy.

Britain had an *archaic industrial structure* largely because Britain had industrialized first. Later indus-

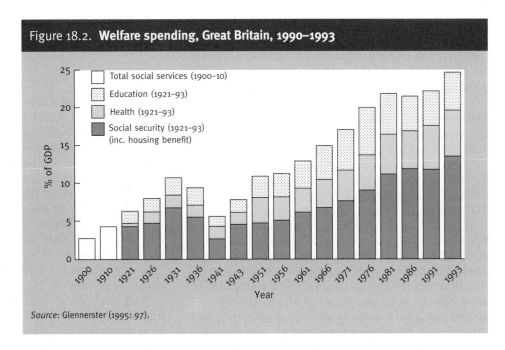

Figure 18.2. **Welfare spending, Great Britain, 1990–1993**

Source: Glennerster (1995: 97).

trializers developed industries with more advanced technology and more efficient organization. Instead of meeting foreign competition head on and modernizing its industry, Britain began to withdrew into an imperial shell in the later years of the nineteenth century. The British economy became dependent on the markets provided by the empire. By the 1960s the British empire was collapsing and British industry was exposed to the full force of international competition.

Secondly, there was the *domination of financial and trading interests* over industrial interests. The industrial supremacy of the nineteenth-century British economy provided the basis for the growth of commercial and financial interests which made money out of trade, insurance, loans, and other financial operations. These commercial and financial interests became economically dominant. Government economic policy was steered by financial rather than industrial interests (Ingham 1984).

Thirdly, there was the *absence of a state industrial policy*. In countries that industrialized later the state had become much more involved in creating industrial competitiveness. Contrasts have often been drawn with Japan, where the government had developed an industrial policy that channelled investment into new industries. In Chapter 7, pp. 243–4, we argue that in countries like Germany the state had become more

involved in developing education to meet the needs of industry.

Thus, the problems generated by the contradictions of welfare capitalism were worsened by an increasing international competition, which Britain was poorly equipped to meet because of the legacy of its nineteenth-century industrialization.

From economic to political crisis

Crises can, however, be managed and they lead to breakdown and transformation only if crisis management fails. As we showed on pp. 739–40, the governments of the 1960s and 1970s responded to Britain's growing economic problems by seeking to construct a system of corporatist cooperation between the state, the unions, and the employers. Although numerous attempts were made to achieve this, they all failed and corporatism eventually collapsed in the later 1970s.

Why did corporatism fail? It failed largely because it required the unions to control their members, but this conflicted with their basic goals, for they had been created to represent their members' interests. It failed also because of the organizational structure of both unions and employers' associations. In Britain these bodies were weakly centralized and had little control over their members. They were reluctant to act as

agencies of the state and could not deliver on the agreements that governments forced them into. In other countries like Sweden, where more centralized organizations had emerged, corporatism was more successful (Fulcher 1991a).

While the corporatist experiments of the 1960s and 1970s may now seem rather remote, their failure and the way they failed shaped the development of the British state in the 1980s. Corporatism collapsed after a series of conflicts between the unions and successive governments, and it was these conflicts which paved the way for the Conservatives' onslaught on the unions in the 1980s.

By the later 1970s the post-war settlement was becoming increasingly strained. First, the institutions of the welfare state were coming under growing criticism. On the one hand, it was becoming more apparent that the welfare state was falling short of its egalitarian goals. On the other hand, critics of the welfare state argued that public services were unresponsive to consumers and provided insufficient choice. Secondly, British governments had been unable to handle the growing economic crisis and the state's role in managing the economy was increasingly questioned. Thirdly, the political consensus on the welfare state was breaking down.

British politics polarized as alternatives emerged on the Left and the Right. Both agreed that there was a crisis and their diagnoses were remarkably similar. It was a crisis of profitability and the welfare capitalism established in the 1940s had failed. Their ways out of the crisis were, however, very different. To the Left, capitalism was collapsing and a transition should be made to a socialist society. To the Right, capitalism was collapsing and needed reinvigoration. The right-wing alternative won at the polls and after the 1979 election eighteen years of Conservative government began.

THATCHERISM AND THE TRANSFORMATION OF THE STATE

Thatcherism emerged victorious out of the polarizing of British politics in the 1970s. It was more than a new set of policies, for, as Hay (1996: 129) has argued, it sought to bring about long-term changes in the basic assumptions of British politics. It rejected the values of compromise, consensus, welfare, and equality. It tried to put in their place enterprise, market discipline, consumer choice, and freedom.

In this section we will first examine the beliefs and

principles of Thatcherism before considering the changes made to the structure of the British state.

Thatcherism

The roots of Thatcherism can be found in the thinking of the New Right, which became dominant in the Conservative Party during the 1970s. This combined two rather different strands of thought, which are labelled *neo-liberalism* and *neo-conservatism* by Hay (1996). The prefix 'neo' indicates that both were new versions of old ideas. There was at the time much talk of a return to Victorian values by those who believed that Britain could be rescued from its crisis by reviving the values and beliefs associated with its period of greatness in Victorian times.

Neo-liberalism was a restatement of the beliefs in individual freedom and market forces which had characterized the liberal ideology dominant in the early nineteenth century. Britain's economic problems were seen as the result of the growing power of the unions, increasing state intervention, and the growth of the welfare state. These all interfered with the operation of market forces and took freedom, choice, and responsibility away from the individual. Neo-liberals advocated the curbing of union power, an ending of dependence on the welfare state, and the restoration of the rights and responsibilities of the individual.

Neo-conservatism was a reassertion of the traditional values of the Conservative Party. It involved strengthening morality, reviving the traditional family, and restoring 'law and order'. The problems of Britain were seen as moral rather than economic. This strand was also strongly nationalist and concerned to defend British sovereignty against federal tendencies in Europe and to protect British identity by controlling immigration. Hall and Jacques (1983) created the much-used concept of **authoritarian populism** to describe this aspect of Thatcherism. They argued that Thatcherism combined an emphasis on the authority of the state with an appeal to popular anxieties about union militancy, permissiveness, crime, and immigration.

These two strands of Thatcherism were in some conflict with each other. The neo-liberal belief in freedom, choice, and market forces conflicted with the neo-conservative emphasis on order, morality, and tradition. Market forces are no respecters of tradition and ignore moral concerns. Neo-liberalism and neo-conservatism could unite, however, in their joint hostility to welfare dependence on the 'nanny state' and to the power of trade unions. They could also unite on the defence of property, for the protection of property rights was central to both.

The contradictions of New Right ideology	Issue	Neo-liberalism	Neo-conservatism
	Sunday trading	Favouring the free operation of the market wherever and whenever there is demand	Defending the sanctity of the Sabbath from the encroachment of the market
	Legalization of soft drugs	Favouring the freedom and autonomy of the individual to make unconstrained market choices	Seeing legalization as the last stage on the road to permissiveness and moral decay from which the paternalistic state must protect its subjects

Source: adapted from Hay (1996: 136).

▶ **Can you think of other examples of policy conflicts of this sort? What about policies towards the media or education or child labour? Are such conflicts evident in the policies of the 1997 Labour government?**

Hay (1996) argues that the populist authoritarianism of the *neo-conservative* strand was crucial in generating the political support for Thatcherism that enabled the Conservatives to win the general election of 1979. It was, however, the *neo-liberal* strand that mainly informed the policies that transformed the state.

The transformation of the state

The central objective of the Conservative transformation of the state was **marketization**. This basically meant expanding the role of market forces in British society. It is very important to grasp that, while this involved a withdrawal of the state from some of its activities, it also led to the extension of state control as well. This will become clearer as we consider particular areas of policy.

There was a shift from the corporatist management of the economy to a greater reliance on market mechanisms. Thus, the 1979 Conservative government abandoned corporatism and during the 1980s corporatist structures that involved unions and employers in policy-making were dismantled. The government neither consulted with union and employer organizations nor used them to implement its policies. Although it continued to control the wages and salaries of public-sector employees, it did not try to control wage levels in the economy as a whole through incomes policies but left the market to set them. This did not, however, mean that the state simply withdrew from the labour market.

It combined deregulation with regulation in its policies towards labour. Through deregulation the govern-ment exposed labour to market forces. The Wages Councils, which protected the low-paid workers in some industries by regulating their wages, were abolished in 1993. Unions, however, by their very nature obstructed the free operation of the labour market and this led the government to introduce a series of new laws to restrict their activities. The unions became more regulated than they had ever been before and their opposition to regulation was ruthlessly suppressed. The strategy of incorporation, which, as we showed on p. 738, had replaced repression in the nineteenth century, now gave way to a renewed repression in the 1980s.

The market sphere was more generally expanded through **privatization**, which transferred production, services, and property from the public to the private sector. Some of the main ways in which this occurred were:

▶ Publicly owned companies were sold to the private sector. British Airways or BT were examples of this kind of privatization.

▶ Local and central state services previously carried out by state employees were increasingly carried out by private companies under contract. Examples of this were the school-meals service or privately operated prisons.

▶ Public property was sold, as when councils were forced to sell council housing to tenants wishing to buy their houses.

▶ Privatization occurred in a rather different way by encouraging or forcing people to pay for services they had previously relied on the state to provide.

Thus, people began increasingly to pay privately for health, education, and the care of the old.

 We examine many of these changes in other chapters: the regulation of trade-union activity in Chapter 13, pp. 533–4; privatization in Chapter 16, pp. 670–2; the sale of council housing in Chapter 11, pp. 433–4. The introduction of market forces, the financial squeeze, and greater state regulation are all discussed in relation to education in Chapter 7, pp. 267–9.

When services could not be privatized, 'internal markets' were introduced. What this meant was that services remained in public ownership but those who provided the service were forced into competition with each other, *as though* they were operating in the private sector. This occurred in the health service (see pp. 752–3) and in education, where schools and colleges were forced to compete with each other for pupils and resources.

Privatization reduced the size of the public sector, but it also led to the extension of state regulation. It involved the heavy regulation of local authorities by the central state. They were, for example, forced to put out many of their services to competitive tendering, which meant that contracts to supply those services had to go, broadly speaking, to the cheapest provider. Privatized industries found themselves controlled by new regulatory bodies to prevent them abusing their monopolistic position. Internal markets in education and health required extensive state intervention to set them up.

The reduction of state expenditure and taxation was one of the most important goals of neo-liberalism. Attempts were certainly made to do this, but the Conservatives were unable to bring about an overall reduction, largely because social-security spending increased. The overall level of taxation was not brought down, but income-tax rates were reduced by shifting the burden of taxes from income tax to indirect taxes on goods and services. This was justified by the neo-liberal argument that individuals can choose whether or not they buy taxed products, though this argument wore a little thin in the case of taxes on 'necessities', such as the fuel used for heating or insurance.

Although attempts to reduce state expenditure ultimately failed, they did lead to the centralization of control over local-authority finances. Local-authority spending and local taxation became much more tightly controlled by central government than ever before.

The 1980s changes in the state were quite fundamental and reversed many long-term processes of change. They reversed the corporatist tendency, dating back to the First World War, to involve increasingly the unions and the employers in the management of the economy. They reversed the nationalization of important industries and services, which also went back to the First World War. They reversed the growth of local-authority services, which dated back well into the nineteenth-century. The clear distinction established in the nineteenth-century Civil Service between the public and the private began to break down as civil-service functions were privatized in various ways. On the other hand, trade unions, educational institutions, and local authorities experienced more state regulation than they had ever known before. Important changes also took place in the area of 'law and order', as we shall show on pp. 754–6.

THE DECLINE OF THE WELFARE STATE

The neo-liberal beliefs that dominated Conservative thinking on welfare matters were hostile to the principles of the welfare state and favoured a shift to market provision. The Conservatives believed that people should not be dependent on the state and should take individual responsibility for their own welfare through insurance and savings schemes provided by the private sector. State welfare should be targeted on those most in need who were unable to provide for themselves.

Conservative policy was also driven by the need to save money on public spending. This was partly because of their neo-liberal principles, which called for a reduction in state expenditure and taxation, but also because they faced a rising pressure for more state spending. Higher unemployment, the ever-rising demand for more spending on health, and increasing numbers of old people dependent on state care meant that their main problem was to prevent state spending getting completely out of control.

Changes in state welfare

Employment was central to most people's welfare and the maintenance of full employment through the Keynesian management of demand had been one of the main principles of the welfare state. This principle had already been abandoned in the 1970s by the previous Labour government. The first Thatcher government then made it clear that the aim of government eco-

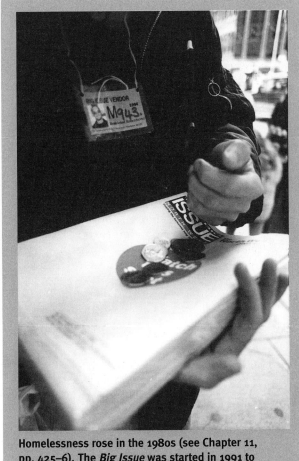

Homelessness rose in the 1980s (see Chapter 11, pp. 425–6). The *Big Issue* was started in 1991 to provide the homeless with a voice and help them to earn some money by selling it.

nomic policy was to control inflation rather than maintain employment.

Higher unemployment was considered to be in some ways beneficial, since the government wanted to create the market conditions that would attract investment from abroad. Higher unemployment helped to do this by keeping wage rates down. But it also meant increased state spending on benefits. It therefore generated pressure for the reform of the benefit system in order to keep spending under control. It also reduced the funds available for services such as health and education.

Some of the main changes in state welfare were as follows:

▶ *Linking of pensions to prices*. After 1982 pensions were increased in line with price increases not increases in average earnings. This cut the cost of the basic pension by a third during the next ten years (Glennerster 1995: 182). It also meant that, for those dependent on the state pension alone, retirement meant an ever greater drop in living standards.

▶ *Changes in unemployment benefit*. As we show in Chapter 3, p. 110, entitlement to unemployment benefit was restricted in various ways and benefits were cut, particularly for those under 18.

▶ *Increased means-testing*. The shift from universal benefits to means-tested ones did not start with Thatcherism but it certainly continued. Child benefit remained universal but its level was frozen, so inflation reduced its value and cost.

▶ *A shift from grants to loans*. The Social Fund, which provides money to meet the emergency needs of the poor, shifted from making grants to making repayable loans. The freezing of maintenance grants for students meant that they were forced to rely increasingly on loans.

▶ *Care of the old*. Social security spending on residential care rose from £10 million in 1979 to £2,072 million in 1991 (Glennerster 1995: 209). State support for the residential care of the old was then sharply cut by making local authorities responsible for it through community care and means-testing.

▶ *Child support*. The Child Support Act of 1991 was designed to transfer the financial support of single-parent families from the state to the absent parent (see Chapter 10, pp. 381–2).

As state provision declined, there was a shift towards **welfare pluralism**, the provision of welfare by a number of agencies rather than just the state. The state had earlier gradually displaced other welfare agencies to become the dominant provider of care during the 1940s. In the 1980s the role of other agencies began to increase again—yet another example of a reversal in the role of the state. This was not just because the private sector grew, though it certainly did, as in the residential care of the elderly, for example. There was also a greater reliance on voluntary organizations, charities, the family, commercial sponsors, and funding through the new state lottery.

Changes in health policy

The 1990 reform of the NHS was precipitated by the problem of funding the ever-increasing demand for health services. This growing demand resulted mainly from medical innovations producing new drugs and new treatments, and an ageing population with

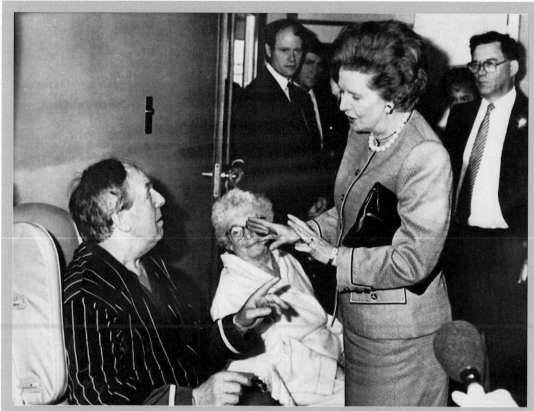

The National Health Service is safe in our hands: Margaret Thatcher visits a hospital in 1988.

growing health problems. The form taken by the changes was shaped by the government's neo-liberal ideology.

The central organizational change was to introduce an 'internal market'. The idea of an outright privatization of the NHS, to produce an American-style market system of private health care paid for by insurance, was considered but reluctantly abandoned. It would have been the neo-liberal solution of choice but, according to Glennerster (1995: 204), it was rejected because it would have actually increased spending on health. Instead an internal market was created to introduce market principles within a service that remained state funded.

The basic principle of the internal market was a separation of the purchasers from the providers of health care. Health authorities would buy services from independent hospitals, which would compete for contracts from them. Hospitals would become self-governing trusts funding themselves from these contracts. If a hospital failed to win contracts, because it provided poor services or was too expensive, it would, at least in theory, go bankrupt and close. Hospitals would therefore be under pressure to run themselves efficiently and provide improved services.

From a neo-liberal perspective, the problem with this scheme was that it did not provide the individual patient with choice. The solution to this problem was to give choice through general practitioners, who were given incentives to become 'fund-holders'. This enabled them to buy, and therefore choose, services from hospitals. Those who did not become fund-holders were reliant on the service provided through contracts made with hospital trusts by the district health authorities.

Although the NHS was preserved, the boundary between public and private health care became increasingly blurred in ways that amounted to an extensive privatization of health care. NHS hospital trusts moved increasingly into providing private care and specialized services for private hospitals. The NHS has actually become the largest provider of private care in Britain. On the other hand, health authorities and fund-holding GPs can use public funds to buy care from private hospitals.

The advantages and disadvantages of the internal market have been much debated. Its supporters claim that it has forced hospitals to become more efficient and more attentive to local needs. Contracts

Hospital managers replace nurses

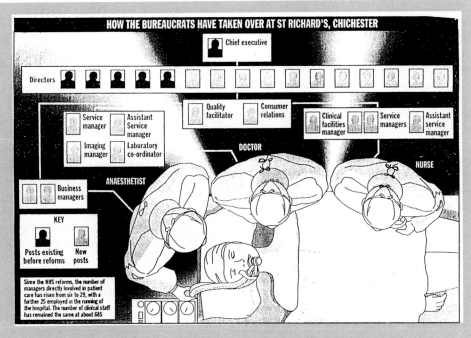

'One of the main ideas of the reforms was to improve management control in the service, which in the 1980s was likened to an out-of-control juggernaut. It was argued that the National Health Service, with 850,000 employees and a £37 million budget, was Europe's biggest employer and needed a skilled management.

'During the past four years the number of managers in the health service has increased from 4,610 to 16,690. Clerical and administrative staff has risen by 18,000 to 134,990. In contrast the number of nurses and midwifes has fallen by about 20,000, though the government says that some of that is due to reclassification.'

Source: Lois Rogers and Richard Palmer, 'NHS Reforms Spark Boom in Bureaucrats', *Sunday Times*, 28 Nov. 1993.

for specified services enable health authorities to have some control over health expenditure, which would otherwise run out of control. Its critics argue that it leads to waste as hospitals compete rather than cooperate and competition leads to the local duplication of services and equipment, which are then underused. Hospitals become management heavy as they employ managers and accountants to monitor costs and negotiate contracts. Treatment becomes dependent on financial considerations, with wards closed when the money runs out and patients denied drugs considered too expensive.

Although a basically free health service was still available to all, a three-tiered system had emerged. There was private care for those who could afford the insurance, or had it paid for them by their employers. There was superior access to public health care through

fund-holding GPs with better facilities and financial clout. There was 'ordinary care' dependent on the contract between health authorities and hospitals.

A decline in state welfare?

State welfare had moved away from the central principles of the welfare state. We identified these earlier as full employment, universal welfare, and free and equal health and education. Full employment policies had been abandoned. Welfare had become increasingly selective and benefits had been cut in various ways. Free health and education were still available, but people found themselves under a growing pressure to buy them.

In Esping-Andersen's terms, a process of *recommodification* had taken place. Welfare was increasingly a commodity provided by the market with access dependent on market situation. The level of employment depended on the competitiveness of British businesses in international markets and the attraction of foreign investment. State benefits had been restricted, reduced, and means-tested. The quality of health care and education depended more and more on purchasing power. Market mechanisms increasingly drove the operation of welfare services.

This does not, however, mean that state spending on welfare declined. Indeed, the proportion of national income spent on state welfare continued to rise (see Figure 18.2 on p. 747). The major components in this rise were spending on health and social-security benefits. Between 1979, when the Conservatives came to power, and 1994 spending on the NHS rose from 10 to 14 per cent of government spending and spending on social security from 22 per cent to 34 per cent (Timmins 1995). More and more people became dependent on state benefits, largely because of higher unemployment, the rise in non-working single parents, and higher rents, which led to the increased payment of housing benefit. The proportion of households with one or more members dependent on means-tested benefits rose from 20 per cent in 1979 to 30 per cent in 1993 (*Independent*, 9 Aug. 1995).

Nor did a movement away from *welfare state* principles necessarily mean that *state welfare* was in decline. It is important to keep in mind the distinction between the welfare state and state welfare, and the existence of diferent models of state welfare, which we discussed in 'Social Policy', pp. 733–4. Whether a movement from the welfare state to the market model means that there has been a decline in state welfare depends on one's views on the merits of these two models. It is a matter of values and beliefs, a political rather than a sociological issue.

It is also important to remember that there had been a sense in the 1970s that the welfare state was not providing good enough services. As Glennerster (1995: 192) has put it:

'What Mrs. Thatcher saw, with her populist insight, was that there was growing dissatisfaction with state services that gave little choice to their users, in which the professional view was dominant and the parent or patient in the waiting-room seemed to count for little. In a growingly sophisticated consumer society this compared poorly with the market sector.'

The 1980s *can* be seen not as a period of decline in state welfare but rather as one of reform, which addressed long-standing problems in the welfare state and injected a healthy dose of market discipline.

LAW AND ORDER

The changes in the state that we have been examining were linked to a strengthening of the law-and-order functions of the state. These are not usually considered along with social policy but arguably they are closely related to it. This is because changes in welfare policies can generate disorder. It is also because social policy and policing can be considered alternative ways of dealing with social problems. While social policy seeks to remove the causes of disorder by, for example, relieving poverty, law-and-order policies repress it.

In this section we examine the strengthening of the forces of law and order but also consider privatizing and marketizing changes that have operated here as in other areas of government policy.

Strengthening the state

Thatcherism called for a strengthening of the state to combat the growing disorder of the 1970s. There was certainly evidence of growing disorder, particularly in the rising crime rate and the major strikes of the 1970s. Crime rates had been rising for a long time but grew particularly sharply in the 1970s. Recorded offences increased by 50 per cent between 1973 and 1979 (Loveday 1996: 77), providing plentiful ammunition for the authoritarian populists in the Conservative Party during the 1979 election campaign. There were also major industrial conflicts, which openly challenged government policies (see Chapter 13, pp. 533–4).

Conservative policies themselves contributed, however, to this growing disorder in three main ways.

First, crime rates continued to rise and this rise can be plausibly linked to the higher unemployment resulting from Conservative policies. Recorded offences increased by 56 per cent between 1979 and 1990. As we show in Chapter 3, pp. 108–9, there are many problems in the definition, reporting, and recording of crimes which make it difficult to interpret changes in crime rates. Increases of this magnitude can, none the less, be taken to show that crime was rising during these years. Loveday (1996: 84–8) has summarized plentiful evidence of an association between high rates of local unemployment and crime. While government policy was not the sole cause of higher unemployment, the Conservatives' adoption of a tough anti-inflationary policy in the 1980s had clearly contributed to it, and government policy can therefore be held partly responsible for increases in crime.

Secondly, there was the relationship betwen urban deprivation and riots. Higher levels of unemployment

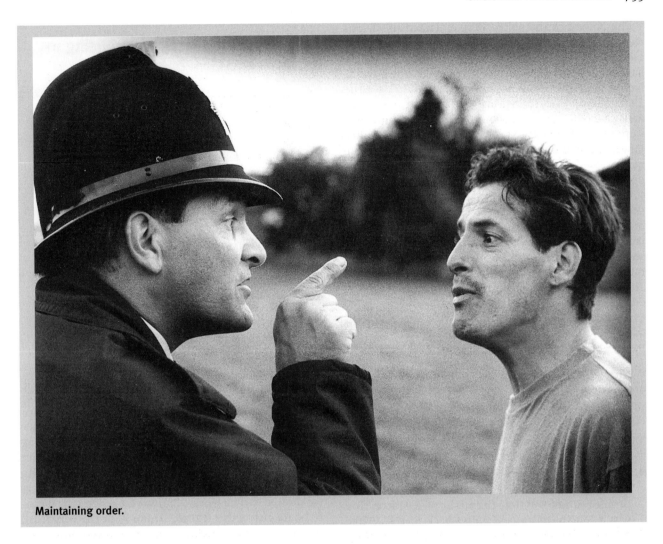

Maintaining order.

and associated deprivation were linked to the rioting that became a regular feature of city life during the 1980s and early 1990s (see Chapter 11, pp. 435–7). Changes in policing too contributed to the generation of riots.

Thirdly, there were more violent industrial conflicts. Government industrial-relation policies led to new confrontations in the 1980s and industrial disorder reached a new height in the violent battles of the 1984–5 miners' strike. The use of the police against strikers was crucial to the government's defeat of the unions in this and other 1980s strikes (see Chapter 13, p. 534).

There was also a fundamental shift in social policy during the 1980s from removing the causes of disorder through state welfare to containing and suppressing disorder through the police and the courts. The Conservatives rejected the idea that disorder resulted from social conditions and saw it in terms of individuals' moral responsibility for their actions. If they failed to act responsibly, they had to be punished and forced to obey the law.

The Conservatives strengthened the state through various changes in policing. Control of the police was centralized and largely taken out of the hands of locally controlled police authorities. The police were given new equipment and trained in new tactics for dealing with public-order situations, a process that has been described as *para-militarization*. As P. A. J. Waddington (1996: 124) has put it: 'No longer are officers deployed as a collection of individuals acting more or less at their own discretion; police now act as squads under superior command and control'. During the years 1979–83 spending on the police increased at a rate of 5 per cent a year, at a time when the government was seeking to reduce overall state spending (Brewer *et al.* 1996: 11).

The powers of the police were extended in various ways. In 1984 the police acquired the power to hold for questioning for seven days those suspected of terrorism. In 1986 the police were given greater powers to ban and control demonstrations and marches. The 1994 Criminal Justice Act ended the 'right to silence' and gave the police new powers to take non-intimate samples from suspects. It also increased police powers in dealing with such groups as football hooligans, travellers, squatters, hunt saboteurs, and road protesters.

Changes in policing were backed up by changes in the penal and judicial process. Punishments were made more severe, as we show in Chapter 16, p. 677. Legislation seeking to reduce the discretion of judges in sentencing matters brought the Conservative government into serious conflict with the judiciary in 1997. This was yet another example of the centralizing tendencies in the state.

Privatizing law and order

While the state's apparatus for maintaining law and order was being strengthened, privatizing processes were also taking place, though these reflected long-term privatizing tendencies as well as the changes in government policy during the 1980s. Four main kinds of privatization can be identified:

▶ *The expansion of private security companies.* Johnston (1996) considers that these probably employed more people by the 1990s than the public police force. This was a long-term process going back to the 1920s, which was linked to changes in industry and retailing, such as the growth of large commercial sites. The private security street patrols funded by local residents that have appeared in some areas are a much more recent phenomenon.

▶ *The privatizing of law-and-order functions.* The privatizing of prisoner escort duties and the building of private prisons are the most obvious example of this (see chapter 16, pp. 678–80). There was also a programme of identifying 'non-essential' police functions for transfer to private companies.

▶ *The introduction of market disciplines.* Measures of police performance were introduced and proposals to bring in performance-related pay, which were strongly resisted by the police.

▶ *Active citizenship.* Private citizens became more involved in police functions. There are state-sanctioned schemes, such as neighbourhood watch. There is also evidence of increasing vigilante activ-

> ## Alternative providers of policing in British cities
>
> ▶ Private security patrols of streets and residential properties
> ▶ Private security companies contracted by municipal authorities to patrol streets and protect council property
> ▶ Municipal security organizations
> ▶ Municipal constabularies: bodies of sworn constables who police parks and other public places
> ▶ 'Activated' neighbourhood watch patrols authorized by the Home Office
> ▶ Vigilantes
> ▶ Security companies set up by police organizations in order to compete locally with the private sector (proposed by several chief constables)
>
> *Source*: L. Johnston (1996: 63).

ity, which challenges police authority, though, according to Johnston, the police sometimes collude with it.

These privatizing processes may be seen as reversing the nineteenth-century development of a public police force. They raise the issue of whether the state is losing the 'monopoly of the legitimate use of force', which, as we showed earlier (see p. 728), was considered by Weber to be its distinctive feature. There is, at the very least, the possibility of police functions becoming fragmented between various competing organizations. Johnston, for example, lists seven alternative providers of policing in British cities (see box above). The movement towards a stronger state has not been a movement towards a more unified one.

NEW LABOUR

The transformation of the state in the 1980s was carried out by Conservative governments. We now move on to consider the important question of whether the 1997 Labour government is likely to reverse it (note that the time of writing is late 1997).

This raises the issue of whether the changes of the 1980s marked a long-term transformation of the relationship between state and society or were simply the result of a period of Conservative government. Runciman (1993) has argued that their significance has been exaggerated, for they were just another phase in the British political cycle. The Conservative and Labour parties have alternated in power and what one party does is periodically reversed by the other. With a return of Labour to power the changes of the 1980s could be undone. For a discussion of this issue, see Fulcher (1995, 1997) and Runciman (1995, 1997).

The decline of collectivism

The principle of collective organization was central to the British labour movement. It was the basis of the trade union, and the Labour Party was created by the unions to protect their interests in parliament. The labour movement was also committed to collective ownership, to the idea that key industries and services should be brought into public ownership, and an extensive programme of nationalization was carried out by the 1945 Labour government. The welfare-state reforms of the 1945 Labour government established the principle of collective rather than individual responsibility for welfare.

As we have seen, the neo-liberal policies of the 1980s sought to extend individual choice and were directly opposed to collective organization, collective ownership, and the universal welfare state. A Labour government might well be expected to defend the collectivist principles of the labour movement by reversing these policies.

 The decline of union membership and power is central to the decline of collectivism and you may find it helpful to refer to our examination of these issues in Chapter 13, pp. 534–6.

The Labour Party has, however, itself been moving steadily from collectivism towards individualism. Since the 1980s it has been distancing itself from the unions, and reducing their influence over the selection of MPs and at the annual party conference. It has been seeking to rebuild itself on the basis of individual members rather than collective membership through the unions, whose membership has declined steadily since 1979. The Labour Party is no longer the political wing of a labour movement. Indeed, a labour movement no longer exists in the old sense of an integrated industrial and political organization of the working class.

The Labour government has committed itself to some reversal of the 1980s industrial-relations policies,

through, in particular, minimum wage and union recognition legislation. But it seems unlikely that Labour will remove the extensive restrictions imposed on the unions' use of industrial power during the 1980s. Industrial disputes are not popular with any government and it was indeed a Labour government which in the later 1960s began the process of seeking to regulate the unions' use of the strike weapon (Peter Jenkins 1970).

So far as privatization is concerned, Labour has announced that it will bring to an end one important aspect of it, the requirement that local authorities put out services to competitive tendering. The privatization of the ownership of public industries and services will not, however, be reversed. Nor could it be, given the costs of doing this, for it would require enormous compensation payments to the owners of the companies concerned. The government has, in fact, been exploring the possibility of further privatizations. Privatization is a policy option attractive to any government, as a way of raising money by selling assets and of financing projects by using private capital instead of scarce public funds.

The maintenance of full employment was a central principle of the welfare state, but, as we showed earlier, one already abandoned by Labour in the 1970s. The government's delegation of interest-rate decisions to the Bank of England is likely to result in the control of inflation having greater priority in future. Its taxation of excess profits by privatized utility companies in order to fund schemes to get the unemployed back to work was a 'one-off' measure that indicated a different attitude but hardly marked a change of policy. Indeed, substantial continuities with Conservative ideas can be found in Labour's acceptance of the 'workfare' principle of requiring people to work for unemployment benefit.

Labour's 'Welfare to Work' programme requires those receiving benefit to accept a subsidized job, carry out voluntary work, or take up full-time education or training. As the Chancellor of the Exchequer put it when delivering his first budget: 'When the long-term unemployed sign on for benefit they will now sign up for work or training' (*Independent*, 3 July 1997). A tougher stance towards those living on benefit was also signalled by proposals to get lone parents off benefits and back to work. They would be helped back to work through state-funded childcare and assistance with finding jobs but there would also be cuts in benefit.

A National Health Service providing universal, free health care was the centrepiece of Labour's 1940s welfare state. As we show on p. 752, while the Conservatives kept the NHS in being, they introduced an internal market, created fund-holding general practices and encouraged private medicine. The Labour government has declared that it will end the internal market and abolish the distinction between fund-holding and non-fund-holding general practices. It will, however, retain some aspects of the internal market, notably the split between purchasers and providers of health care and the decentralized purchasing of health care. While previously only fund-holding practices were involved in this, all general practices will in future take part, through Primary Care Groups consisting of teams of general practitioners and community nurses.

While it claims that savings will be made by ending the internal market, the government faces, however, a worsening financial crisis in the NHS. This has led to the suggestion that more money will have to be raised through charges on patients of one kind or another. It is also argued that the involvement of private capital will have to increase (see the chapter's opening piece). Market situation and profit considerations will therefore continue to influence the provision of health care by the NHS.

 We are not dealing with education policy here because this was covered in 'Education and the State', Chapter 7, pp. 267–9. Education policy is an important part of social policy, however, and in considering the issues we discuss here you will find it helpful to refer to Chapter 7.

Labour has changed many aspects of government policy, but in key areas such as industrial relations, privatization, and social policy there are substantial continuities with the policy framework established by the previous government.

Funding state benefits

The problem of the future funding of state benefits has been dominated by a concern with the consequences of population ageing. It has been widely argued that the burden of the state pension will become insupportable as the proportion of old people in the population increases. All three main British political parties have produced proposals to shift more of the responsibility for pension funding to the individual, through compulsory savings schemes or private pension arrangements.

Underlying these concerns is the fear of the impact of a 'demographic time bomb' on the costs of care. This is

Change and continuity in policy

▶ Make a list of the main policy initiatives of the 1997 Labour government in one or more of the following areas: education, industrial relations, employment, and health. Newspapers and periodicals provide a useful source of material and your library may have back copies of newspapers on CD-ROM.

▶ What changes have been made from the policy of the previous government?

▶ What continuities are there with the policy of the previous government?

▶ Has the government significantly reversed any of the policies of the Conservatives?

▶ What conclusions would you draw on the significance of party differences for policy-making?

based on the changing proportions of elderly and working adults in the population. The number of elderly people as a proportion of the working population is known as the 'elderly dependence ratio'. It is predicted to rise from around 40 per cent in the late 1990s to nearly 60 per cent in the year 2035. The increase results both from greater longevity, which will raise the number of old people, and past declines in the birth rate, which will gradually reduce the size of the working population.

As Pilcher (1995) points out, this kind of argument is, however, based on a crude demographic determinism, which takes no account of such factors as the level of employment, working patterns, changing health needs and costs, or social policy. These all crucially affect the costs of old age and the capacity of those of working age to support the old. For example, the age at which women receive the state pension is already set to rise to 65 and there is nothing holy about this particular age as the time at which people retire. The Scandinavian countries are planning to raise the age of retirement to 67.

As it happens, the 1982 decision to link pensions to prices rather than earnings means that the cost of state pensions is predicted to fall from 4.3 per cent of gross domestic product in 1996 to 3.5 per cent in 2030 (*Independent*, 30 Oct. 1996). The pensions problem is not one of how the state pension can be funded but rather whether the state pension will provide an adequate standard of living. The link to prices rather than earnings means that, for those dependent on the state pension alone, retirement results in an ever larger drop in living standards (see Figure 18.3). If the link to earnings was restored, this would not, however, cost an unsupportable amount. It is estimated that to maintain the state pension and services to the old at their early 1990s level would require increases in taxation of only 0.5 per cent per decade (Glennerster 1995: 233).

Figure 18.3. **The declining state pension, 1981–2010**

Year	The state pension as a percentage of average male earnings
1981	23
1993	15
2010 (projected)	10

Source: Glennerster (1995: 182).

Funding issues are clearly central to the government's social policy. Its statements about health, education, and pensions all indicate that it is unwilling to take any policy initiatives that will significantly increase state expenditure. But are these funding problems due to the costs of state welfare or the political constraints on government policy?

The level of taxation is lower in the United Kingdom than in most comparable countries, as is the proportion of gross national product spent by the government on welfare (see Figure 18.4). This suggests that it is not the level of state spending on welfare that is the problem. New Labour's welfare policy, and this applies to health and education as well, is constrained by political concerns. The Labour Party believed that the main reason why it lost the 1992 election was that the Conservatives manipulated popular fears that a Labour government would increase the tax burden. It therefore committed itself before the last election not to raise income tax rates and was, initially at least, constrained by that commitment. Labour's taxation and spending policies were shaped by a perceived need to compete with a Conservative Party hostile to the principles of the welfare state.

This shows how the Thatcherite transformation has changed the political landscape of Britain. It created new institutions and new interests, and established a new political agenda, which, after eighteen years in the political wilderness, New Labour felt obliged to follow.

There are, however, not only internal political constraints; there are also international ones. It has been argued that increasing global integration reduces all governments' room for manoeuvre. This is an alternative explanation of the government's continuation of Conservative policies.

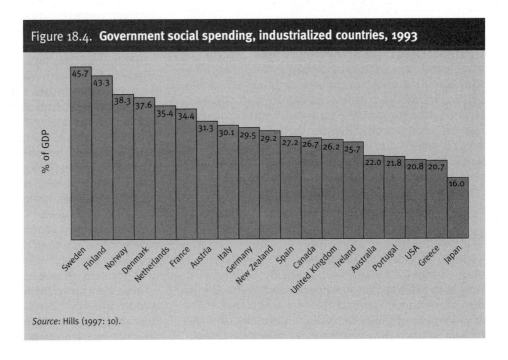

Figure 18.4. **Government social spending, industrialized countries, 1993**

Source: Hills (1997: 10).

INTERNATIONAL CONVERGENCE?

Here we consider whether global changes lie behind British changes. Is Britain merely conforming to global tendencies that are moving all countries away from the welfare-state model of state welfare?

Globalization and Japanization

It has been argued that countries can no longer afford the cost of a welfare state in a world of increasing international competition. There are three main steps in the argument:

First, international competition has put pressure on the old industrial societies, which had higher costs and found themselves out-competed by the new industrializers, to reduce the costs of state welfare.

Secondly, a growing global economic integration has made it easier for capital to move around the world. Any country whose government adopts welfare policies judged to diminish its competitiveness or likely to increase inflation will find money leaving its shores for lower cost and safer places.

Thirdly, the economically more successful countries, such as Japan and the other Asian tigers, have not developed welfare states on the European model. Lower rates of taxation have made them more competitive. Furthermore, in Japan the development of company welfare schemes has enabled companies to integrate and control their core workers. Their competitive success can be partly explained by the high commitment and high productivity of workers integrated in this way (see Chapter 13, pp. 532–3).

Arthur Gould (1993) interprets this process as leading to a 'Japanization of welfare' as European countries have been driven to cut back on state welfare and move towards the Japanese model. He also suggests, however, that the Japanese state will, in future, have to take on more responsibility for the welfare of its citizens. 'It may be that what we are now witnessing is the development of a new convergence towards a welfare pluralism in which the state continues to play an important role' (A. Gould 1993: 10).

Three worlds of welfare or one?

Gould's argument suggests that Esping-Andersen's three worlds of welfare will gradually become one. How have different societies responded to changes in the international context? Here we will consider the development of policy in Sweden, Germany, and the United States, the countries representing Esping-Andersen's three worlds of welfare (outlined earlier on pp. 742–4).

Sweden had led the way in decommodifying welfare and is generally considered to have established the most advanced welfare state. During the 1980s, however, industry became steadily less competitive and companies more transnational in character, putting pressure on the government to cut state spending and restore market disciplines. At the end of the 1980s a growing economic crisis pushed unemployment to heights unknown since the 1930s. The Social Democrats began to move in a neo-liberal direction, by, for example, cutting state benefits, privatizing state companies, and introducing market mechanisms into state services. These policy changes were speeded up by the election of a 'bourgeois' government in 1991 but broadly continued by the 1994 elected Social Democrat government.

In Germany state welfare was well developed but occupationally linked. The economy responded to increasing competition by shedding labour through early retirement and redundancy. Higher unemployment and higher pension payments put a severe strain on state finances, but only minor cost-saving changes could be made to state welfare systems. Those in work have strongly defended their entitlements and the state has been obliged to maintain them. Esping-Andersen comments that there has, none the less, been a loss of confidence in the state's capacity to deliver welfare and individuals have increasing resorted to private schemes. According to his account, Germany and other European countries are caught in a difficult situation of high unemployment and institutional rigidity, with no obvious way out (Esping-Andersen 1996: 81–4).

The United States was at the liberal extreme of state welfare policies, with market welfare provision for all but the very poor. Although state spending on welfare was low, the American response to growing economic problems in the later 1970s was to try to cut it further. The combination of means-testing and very low wages at the bottom of the job hierarchy inevitably resulted, however, in a poverty trap. There was no point in taking a job if you lost more in benefit than you gained in pay. The policy response to this problem was to cut benefits and force the unemployed into low-paid jobs. A dynamic capitalist economy had generated jobs much more successfully than the European economies have done, but these were very low-paid jobs. An unemployment problem became a poverty problem (Myles 1996).

There were clearly tendencies in all three countries to move in a neo-liberal direction, but this is not the same thing as convergence, for it appears that differences between countries persist. If three people all step

The United States exports benefit cuts and workfare

'"Think how a former welfare mother feels the first time she buys a pair of shoes for her child out of her very own pay cheque. How her chest swells with pride! Well, I want to bottle that feeling and make it Wisconsin's greatest export!"

'In his lakeside mansion, Governor Tommy Thompson is addressing a delegation of Europeans invited to hear the Wisconsin Gospel, and to take it bottled like the waters of the Jordan. Indeed, in the 12 years since he was elected on a ferocious anti-welfare campaign against benefit scroungers and layabouts, Wisconsin has exported to most of the western world some form of its workfare experiments. Our own welfare-to-work programme was born right here. Five delegations of British Labour politicians have already been through here, for this is a well-trodden welfare trail. . . .

'Does it work? That is the only question. The Governor has figures showing that Wisconsin's workfare has cut numbers on benefit by 70 per cent in 10 years. It is these figures that made the US government rush to legislate what is billed as the End of Welfare. Their draconian new law came into effect last month, unthinkably ferocious to European ears. It removes all legal entitlement to welfare from now on, leaving it up to each state. Everyone has to work for benefits, even mothers with three-month-old babies. Any babies born to welfare families get no extra money. Most alarming of all, nobody can draw welfare for more than five years over a life-time. . . .

'However, this programme is fantastically expensive—probably 60 per cent more than the simple benefit system it replaces. After all, our own very limited welfare-to-work scheme costs £3.5bn just for 18–25-year olds. First there is the child-care bill: if you force single mothers to work, you have to guarantee child-care. At even greater cost, Wisconsin has guaranteed free health care to all the low-paid, and help with transport, even buying them second-hand cars to get to a job. . . .

'The more detail was revealed, the more amazed I was by the mismatch between rhetoric and reality. The rhetoric is savage, but that's political cover for one of the most expensive attempts at lifting people out of poverty there has ever been. The curious coalition between right and left on welfare reform is because the right won the language, but the left won the money. What exactly will happen in the next recession nobody knows, but for now, the money flows as more people flow back into work. . . .'

Source: Polly Toynbee, 'Message from Wisconsin: Nirvana is a Job in a Fast Food Joint' *Independent*, 24 Nov. 1997.

▶ **How does this compare with 'welfare-to-work' in Britain?**

---

to the right, they are no closer to each other than they were before! They may have moved in the same direction but they have not converged. The three worlds of welfare identified by Esping-Andersen still seem to be there.

The international context certainly constrains government actions and, as a result of globalization, rather more now than it did in the past. It does not, however, force particular welfare policies on governments. State welfare policy in Britain must be explained primarily in terms of the dynamics of British politics and the continuities of British institutions.

POSITIVE WELFARE

In *Beyond Left and Right* Giddens (1994) rejects both the welfare-state and market models. He argues that, on the one hand, socialism is dead, while, on the other hand, the uncontrolled expansion of capitalism has come up agaist the limits of the earth's resources and popular acceptance. Neither the welfare state nor the market model is therefore viable any longer. Instead of trying to defend the welfare state against the attacks of neo-liberals, radicals should develop a new programme of 'positive welfare'.

Giddens argues that the basic assumptions of the welfare state have become problematic in the world we live in. This is not because of the cost of the welfare state. Its problems lie much deeper in its approach to 'work, solidarity, and risk management'.

The welfare state was based on the assumption that *work* meant full-time employment in paid work. Indeed, the maintenance of full employment of this sort was one of the main goals of the social democratic welfare state. Giddens argues that this model of work presumed a gendered division of labour. Full-time employment meant male employment with women remaining at home to carry out housework and childcare, but women have challenged this division of labour and increasingly taken paid work. Traditional full-time employment is anyway in decline with the rise of part-time work, self-employment, and homework.

The welfare state was associated with two forms of *solidarity* or social integration that are in decline—the nation state and class organization. Giddens argues that globalization has weakened the nation state and reduced its capacity to manage the economy and provide welfare. While class situation continues to shape people's life chances, they identify less with social classes. Class solidarity is in decline because of the decline of class communities, the greater movement of individuals across class boundaries, and the growth of an individualist consumerism.

The *risks* managed by the welfare state are anyway not the main risks nowadays. He argues that the welfare state has been centrally concerned with the *management of risk*. By this he means that the welfare state was a way of insuring against such risks as illness, unemployment, and poverty. The growth of knowledge and technology led people to believe that they could either control risks or cope with the consequences if things went wrong. Risk could be minimized through medical technology, the management of the economy, and the creation of social security through social policy.

The major risks that now threaten us are, however, what Giddens calls the 'manufactured uncertainties' resulting from the growth of knowledge and technology themselves. Environmentally caused cancers, pollution, and road accidents are major risks of this sort. These have to be addressed through preventative measures rather than technological 'fixes'. Furthermore, the state's capacity to deal with them is limited, for these risks are associated with lifestyles.

This leads Giddens to argue for what he calls 'positive welfare'. Its two key constituents are *generative* and *life* politics.

Generative politics would move away from a reliance on the bureaucratic state to self-reliance. The role of the state would be to provide the conditions in which individuals and groups could themselves take welfare initiatives. This approach to welfare would fit with the greater emphasis on local involvement in development projects in poor countries (see Chapter 12, p. 455) and debureaucratizing tendencies in organizations generally (see Chapter 16, pp. 660–6).

Life politics would focus not on issues of wealth or power but on lifestyle. Giddens argues here that happiness is not related to either wealth or power but rather to our inner lives. It depends on 'security, self-respect, and self-actualization' (Giddens 1994: 191). Indeed, the compulsive production and consumption of goods, which he sees as typical of the modern world, are the 'chief enemy' of happiness, for the lifestyles that they have created are now the main source of risk.

The welfare state's focus on the issue of equality is now out of date. Inequality is no longer the issue that it was, for rich and poor people, rich and poor countries, all face the same risks. The environmental pollution resulting from consumer lifestyles threatens everyone equally. These common risks also provide the basis for common interests, as increasing global integration makes us all more interdependent.

Giddens recognizes that there is more than a touch of utopianism in his programme but argues that it is none the less based on tendencies in the real world. He claims that there is a growing awareness that we all live on the same fragile planet. There are new globally organized social movements that put pressure on nation states to face up to global interdependence (see Chapter 12, pp. 488–90).

The problem with this argument is that international conflicts still bedevil attempts to achieve global solutions to environmental problems, as we show in 'One Earth?', Chapter 12, pp. 490–2. The nation state is not a thing of the past. So far, events suggest that a growing global interdependence has resulted not in an international consensus on environmental issues but rather in the pursuit of conflicting national interests.

Another basic problem with Giddens's analysis is the idea that the rich and the poor face the same risks. They may equally face the risk of a catastrophic global disaster, but wealth and power insulate the rich from many of the everyday risks faced by the poor. This applies both to rich and poor nations and to the rich and poor within them. The risks of illness, unemployment, and poverty, the kinds of risks from which people sought to protect themselves through the welfare state, are not equally distributed. It is difficult to argue that these inequalities no longer matter to people. Furthermore, these inequalities generate conflicts that prevent the establishment of a consensus on environmental issues.

Giddens has, however, interestingly moved the discussion of the problems faced by the welfare state away from the conflict between socialism and capitalism, between the welfare state and the market model. He has

Welfare risks

► What does welfare mean to you?

► What do you consider to be the main future risks to your welfare?

► What action can you take to protect yourself against these risks?

► How important is your financial situation to your welfare?

opened up the fundamental question of what we mean by welfare and how it can be achieved.

SUMMARY POINTS

We began this section by examining the crisis of the 1970s and its origins:

▶ In the 1970s there was an economic crisis centred on the decline of profitability.

▶ This crisis had its roots in the contradictions of welfare capitalism and increasing international competition.

Thatcherism emerged out of this crisis and responded to it by transforming the British state:

▶ There were both neo-liberal and neo-conservative strands in Thatcherism, which were in some conflict with each other.

▶ The transformation of the state involved marketizing and privatizing processes but also increased regulation and centralization.

▶ Social policy shifted from the welfare state towards the market model and the recommodification of welfare.

▶ There was a strengthening of the forces of law and order, but privatizing processes also occurred in this area of the state's activities.

The return of Labour government in 1997 raised the issue of whether the changes of the 1980s would be reversed:

▶ During the 1980s the Labour Party began to distance itself from the unions and from its traditional collectivism.

▶ While Labour has made changes to government policy, there are substantial continuities of policy.

▶ Concerns with state spending dominate social policy, but these constraints appear to be political rather than financial.

▶ Although there is an international tendency to move towards the market model of state welfare, there are still three distinct 'worlds of welfare'.

Lastly, we considered the alternative approach to welfare proposed by Giddens:

▶ Giddens argues that neither the market nor the welfare-state model is any longer appropriate to the world's real welfare problems.

▶ People can no longer be protected against risks by the welfare state, for lifestyles are the main source of danger.

▶ The role of the state should be to provide the conditions within which people can take charge of their own welfare.

REVISION AND EXERCISES

THE DEVELOPMENT OF THE STATE

In 'Understanding the State and Social Policy' we discussed different approaches to the study of the development of the state:

▶ Make sure that you are familiar with the main features of the Weberian and Marxist perspectives on the state.

▶ What do you understand by the following terms: the state; traditional, charismatic, and rational–legal authority; democracy and democratization; hegemony (see Chapter 8. p. 277); economic determinism and relative autonomy?

We went on to examine aspects of the development of the British state:

▶ What role did the state play during the period of liberal capitalism?

▶ How did the state's relationship to the labour movement change during the nineteenth century?

▶ What impact did the First World War have on the development of the state?

▶ What is meant by the 'post-war' settlement of the 1940s?

▶ What is meant by corporatism and why did it emerge during the 1960s and 1970s?

In 'Crisis and Transformation' we considered the transformation of the state during the years since 1979:

▶ Why was there a crisis of profitability in 1970s Britain and what connection did this have with the rise of Thatcherism?

▶ What is meant by neo-liberalism and neo-conservatism and what was the relationship between them?

▶ Do you think that state regulation decreased or increased during the period of Conservative government?

▶ Has the 1997 Labour government reversed the changes made by the Conservatives?

THE DEVELOPMENT OF SOCIAL POLICY

In 'Understanding the State and Social Policy' we discussed approaches to the development of social policy:

▶ Make sure that you are familiar with Esping-Andersen's ideas on the development of state welfare.

▶ What do you understand by the following terms: social policy; commodification and decommodification; the market and welfare-state models; means-testing; progressive and regressive taxation?

We went on to examine the development of state welfare in Britain:

▶ What were the main features of the welfare legislation during the years before the First World War?

▶ What was distinctive about the welfare state established in the 1940s?

▶ Did the welfare state bring about greater equality?

▶ List the main characteristics of Esping-Andersen's three 'worlds of welfare'. In which world would you place Britain?

After analysing the transformation of the state in the 1980s, we considered its implications for state welfare and social policy:

▶ In what ways did social policy move away from the welfare-state model?

▶ What is meant by an 'internal market' and what were its consequences for the NHS?

▶ What was the relationship between changes in social policy and changes in law and order?

▶ Has the 1997 Labour government reversed any of the social-policy changes of the years of Conservative rule?

▶ Has globalization resulted in the emergence of one world of welfare?

FURTHER READING

The following provide further reading on the development of the state and its transformation in recent years:

Held, D. (1992), 'The Development of the Modern State', in S. Hall and B. Gieben (eds.), *Formations of Modernity* (Cambridge: Polity). Provides a clear outline of the historical development of European states and different approaches to their study.

Miliband, R. (1969), *The State in Capitalist Society* (London: Weidenfeld & Nicolson). A classic study of the relationship between capitalism and the state, which deals not only with government but also with the civil service, the military, the judiciary, the mass media, and education.

Gamble, A. (1988), *The Free Economy and the Strong State: The Politics of Thatcherism* (London: Macmillan). Examines the crisis of the 1970s, the rise of Thatcherism, and the transformation of the state during the 1980s.

Hay, C. (1996), *Re-Stating Social and Political Change* (Buckingham: Open University Press). A sophisticated review of the literature on the state and an account of its development from the 1940s to the present, with a lot of helpful tables and diagrams.

The following all give clear and full accounts of the development of social policy in Britain:

Glennerster, H. (1995), *British Social Policy since 1945* (Oxford: Blackwell).

Hill, M. (1997), *Understanding Social Policy* (5th edn., Oxford: Blackwell).

Lowe, R. (1993), *The Welfare State in Britain since 1945* (London: Macmillan).

The following provide further reading on specific issues:

Gould, A. (1993), *Capitalist Welfare Systems: A Comparison of Japan, Britain, and Sweden* (London: Longman). A clear, thorough, and wide-ranging study of the responses of these three countries to the crisis of the welfare state.

Johnston, L. (1992), *The Rebirth of Private Policing* (London: Routledge). A wide-ranging discussion of the theory of policing, the significance of private policing, its history, and recent changes.

Pierson, C. (1991), *Beyond the Welfare State*, (Cambridge: Polity). A very useful summary and review of debates on the development and future of state welfare and discussion of the issues that they raise.

The British Sociological Association Statement of Ethical Practice

The British Sociological Association gratefully acknowledges the use made of the ethical codes produced by the American Sociological Association, the Association of Social Anthropologists of the Commonwealth and the Social Research Association.

Styles of sociological work are diverse and subject to change, not least because sociologists work within a wide variety of settings. Sociologists, in carrying out their work, inevitably face ethical, and sometimes legal, dilemmas which arise out of competing obligations and conflicts of interest. The following statement aims to alert the members of the Association to issues that raise ethical concerns and to indicate potential problems and conflicts of interest that might arise in the course of their professional activities.

While they are not exhaustive, the statement points to a set of obligations to which members should normally adhere as principles for guiding their conduct. Departures from the principles should be the result of deliberation and not ignorance. The strength of this statement and its binding force rest ultimately on active discussion, reflection, and continued use by sociologists. In addition, the statement will help to communicate the professional position of sociologists to others, especially those involved in or affected by the activities of sociologists.

The statement is meant, primarily, to inform members' ethical judgements rather than to impose on them an external set of standards. The purpose is to make members aware of the ethical issues that may arise in their work, and to encourage them to educate themselves and their colleagues to behave ethically. The statement does not, therefore, provide a set of recipes for resolving ethical choices or dilemmas, but recognizes that often it will be necessary to make such choices on the basis of principles and values, and the (often conflicting) interests of those involved.

Professional integrity

Members should strive to maintain the integrity of sociological enquiry as a discipline, the freedom to research and study, and to publish and promote the results of sociological research. Members have a responsibility both to safeguard the proper interests of those involved in or affected by their work, and to report their findings accurately and truthfully. They need to consider the effects of their involvements and the consequences of their work or its misuse for those they study and other interested parties.

While recognizing that training and skill are necessary to the conduct of social research, members should themselves recognize the boundaries of their professional competence. They should not accept work of a kind that they are not qualified to carry out. Members should satisfy themselves that the research they undertake is worthwhile and that the techniques proposed are appropriate. They should be clear about the limits of their detachment from and involvement in their areas of study.

Members should be careful not to claim an expertise in areas outside those that would be recognized academically as their true fields of expertise. Particularly in their relations with the media, members should have regard for the reputation of the discipline and refrain from offering expert commentaries in a form that would appear to give credence to material which, as researchers, they would regard as comprising inadequate or tendentious evidence.

Relations with and responsibilities towards research participants

Sociologists, when they carry out research, enter into personal and moral relationships with those they study, be they individuals, households, social groups, or corporate entities.

Although sociologists, like other researchers, are committed to the advancement of knowledge, that goal does not, of itself, provide an entitlement to override the rights of others. Members must satisfy themselves that a study is necessary for the furtherance of knowledge before embarking upon it. Members should be aware that they have some responsibility for the use to which their research may be put. Discharging that responsibility may on occasion be difficult, especially in situations of social conflict, competing social interests, or where there is unanticipated misuse of the research by third parties.

1. Relationships with research participants

Sociologists have a responsibility to ensure that the physical, social, and psychological well-being of research participants is not adversely affected by the research. They should strive to protect the rights of those they study, their interests, sensitivities, and privacy, while recognizing the difficulty of balancing potentially conflicting interests. Because sociologists study the relatively powerless as well as those more powerful than themselves, research relationships are frequently characterized by disparities of power and status. Despite this, research relationships should be characterized, whenever possible, by trust. In some cases, where the public interest dictates otherwise and particularly where power is being abused, obligations of trust and protection may weigh less heavily. Nevertheless, these obligations should not be discarded lightly.

As far as possible sociological research should be based on the freely given informed consent of those studied. This implies a responsibility on the sociologist to explain as fully as possible, and in terms meaningful to participants, what the research is about, who is undertaking and financing it, why it is being undertaken, and how it is to be promoted.

(i) Research participants should be made aware of their right to refuse participation whenever and for whatever reason they wish.

(ii) Research participants should understand how far they will be afforded anonymity and confidentiality and should be able to reject the use of data-gathering devices such as tape recorders and video cameras. Sociologists should be careful, on the one hand, not to give unrealistic guarantees of confidentiality and, on the other, not to permit communication of research films or records to audiences other than those to which the research participants have agreed.

(iii) Where there is a likelihood that data may be shared with other researchers, the potential uses to which the data might be put may need to be discussed with research participants.

(iv) When making notes, filming, or recording for research purposes, sociologists should make clear to research participants the purpose of the notes, filming, or recording, and, as precisely as possible, to whom it will be communicated.

(v) It should also be borne in mind that in some research contexts, especially those involving field research, it may be necessary for the obtaining of consent to be regarded, not as a once-and-for-all prior event, but as a process, subject to renegotiation over time. In addition, particular care may need to be taken during periods of prolonged fieldwork where it is easy for research participants to forget that they are being studied.

(vi) In some situations access to a research setting is gained via a 'gatekeeper'. In these situations members should adhere to the principle of obtaining informed consent directly from the research participants to whom access is required, while at the same time taking account of the gatekeepers' interest. Since the relationship between the research participant and the gatekeeper may continue long after the sociologist has left the research setting, care should be taken not to disturb that relationship unduly.

It is incumbent upon members to be aware of the possible consequences of their work. Wherever possible they should attempt to anticipate, and to guard against, consequences for research participants which can be predicted to be harmful. Members are not absolved from this responsibility by the consent given by research participants.

In many of its guises, social research intrudes into the lives of those studied. While some participants in sociological research may find the experience a positive and welcome one, for others, the experience may be disturbing. Even if not exposed to harm, those studied may feel wronged by aspects of the research process. This can be particularly so if they perceive apparent intrusions into their private and personal worlds, or where research gives rise to false hopes, uncalled-for self-knowledge, or unnecessary anxiety. Members should consider carefully the possibility that the research experience may be a disturbing one and, normally, should attempt to minimize disturbance to those participating in research. It should be borne in mind that decisions made on the basis of research may have effects on individuals as members of a group, even if individual research participants are protected by confidentiality and anonymity.

Special care should be taken where research participants are particularly vulnerable by virtue of factors such as age, social status, and powerlessness. Where research participants are ill or too young or too old to participate, proxies may need to be used in order to gather data. In these situations care should be taken not to intrude on the personal space of the person to whom the data ultimately refer, or to disturb the relationship between this person and the proxy. Where it can be inferred that the person about whom data are sought would object to supplying certain kinds of information, that material should not be sought from the proxy.

2. Covert research

There are serious ethical dangers in the use of covert research but covert methods may avoid certain problems. For instance, difficulties arise when research participants change their behaviour because they know they are being studied. Researchers may also face problems when access to spheres of social life is closed to social scientists by powerful or secretive interests. However, covert methods violate the principles of informed consent and may invade the privacy of those being studied. Participant or non-participant observation in non-public spaces or experimental manipulation of research participants without their knowledge should be resorted to only where it is impossible to use other methods to obtain essential data. In such studies it is important to safeguard the anonymity of research participants. Ideally, where informed consent has not been obtained prior to the research it should be obtained post-hoc.

3. Anonymity, privacy, and confidentiality

The anonymity and privacy of those who participate in the research process should be respected. Personal information concerning research participants should be kept confidential. In some cases it may be necessary to decide whether it is proper or appropriate even to record certain kinds of sensitive information.

Where possible, threats to the confidentiality and anonymity of research data should be anticipated by researchers. The identities and research records of those participating in research should be kept confidential whether or not an explicit pledge of confidentiality has been given. Appropriate measures should be taken to store research data in a secure manner. Members should have regard to their obligations under the Data Protection Act. Where appropriate and practicable, methods for preserving the privacy of data should be used. These may include the removal of identifiers, the use of pseudonyms, and other technical means for breaking the link between data and identifiable individuals such as 'broadbanding' or micro-aggregation. Members should also take care to prevent data being published or released in a form which would permit the actual or potential identification of research participants. Potential informants and research participants, especially those possessing a combination of attributes which make them readily identifiable, may need to be reminded that it can be difficult to disguise their identity without introducing an unacceptably large measure of distortion into the data.

Guarantees of confidentiality and anonymity given to research participants must be honoured, unless there are clear and overriding reasons to do otherwise. Other people, such as colleagues, research staff, or others, given access to the data must also be made aware of their obligations in this respect. By the same token, sociologists should respect the efforts taken by other researchers to maintain anonymity. Research data given in confidence do not enjoy legal privilege, that is they may be liable to subpoena by a court. Research participants may also need to be made aware that it may not be possible to avoid legal threats to the privacy of the data.

There may be less compelling grounds for extending guarantees of privacy or confidentiality to public organizations, collectivities, governments, officials, or agencies than to individuals or small groups. Nevertheless, where guarantees have been given they should be honoured, unless there are clear and compelling reasons not to do so.

4. Reputation of the discipline

During their research members should avoid, where they can, actions which may have deleterious consequences for sociologists who come after them or which might undermine the reputation of sociology as a discipline.

Relations with and responsibilities towards sponsors and/or funders

A common interest exists between sponsor, funder, and sociologist as long as the aim of the social inquiry is to advance knowledge, although such knowledge may only be of limited benefit to the sponsor and the funder. That relationship is best served if the atmosphere is conducive to high professional standards. Members should attempt to ensure that sponsors and/or funders appreciate the obligations that sociologists have not only to them, but also to society at large, research participants and professional colleagues, and the sociological community. The relationship between sponsors or funders and social researchers should be such as to enable social inquiry to be undertaken as objectively as possible. Research should be undertaken with a view to providing information or explanation rather than being constrained to reach particular conclusions or prescribe particular courses of action.

1. Clarifying obligations, roles, and rights

Members should clarify in advance the respective obligations of funders and researchers where possible in the form of a written contract. They should refer the sponsor or funder to the relevant parts of the professional code to which they adhere. Members should also be careful not to promise or imply acceptance of conditions which are contrary to their professional ethics or competing commitments. Where some or all of those involved in the research are also acting as sponsors and/or funders of research, the potential for conflict between the different roles and interests should also be made clear to them.

Members should also recognize their own general or specific obligations to the sponsors whether contractually defined or only the subject of informal and often unwritten agreements. They should be honest and candid about their qualifications and expertise, the limitations, advantages, and disadvantages of the various methods of analysis and data, and acknowledge the necessity for discretion with confidential information obtained from sponsors. They should also try not to conceal factors which are likely to affect satisfactory conditions or the completion of a proposed research project or contract.

2. Pre-empting outcomes and negotiations about research

Members should not accept contractual conditions that are contingent upon a particular outcome or set of findings from a proposed inquiry. A conflict of obligations may also occur if the funder requires particular methods to be used.

Members should try to clarify, before signing the contract, that they are entitled to be able to disclose the source of their funds, its personnel, the aims of the institution, and the purposes of the project.

Members should also try to clarify their right to publish and spread the results of their research.

Members have an obligation to ensure sponsors grasp the implications of the choice between alternative research methods.

3. Guarding privileged information and negotiating problematic sponsorship

Members are frequently furnished with information by the funder who may legitimately require it to be kept confidential. Methods and procedures that have been utilized to produce published data should not, however, be kept confidential unless otherwise agreed.

When negotiating sponsorships members should be aware of the requirements of the law with respect to the ownership of and rights of access to data.

In some political, social, and cultural contexts some sources of funding and sponsorship may be contentious. Candour and frankness about the source of funding may create problems of access or co-operation for the social researcher but concealment may have serious consequences for colleagues, the discipline and research participants. The emphasis should be on maximum openness.

Where sponsors and funders also act directly or indirectly as gatekeepers and control access to participants, researchers should not devolve their responsibility to protect the participants' interests onto the gatekeeper. Members should be wary of inadvertently disturbing the relationship between participants and gatekeepers since that will continue long after the researcher has left.

4. Obligations to sponsors and/or funders during the research process

Members have a responsibility to notify the sponsor and/or funder of any proposed departure from the terms of reference of the proposed change in the nature of the contracted research.

A research study should not be undertaken on the basis of resources known from the start to be inadequate, whether the work is of a sociological or inter-disciplinary kind.

When financial support or sponsorship has been accepted, members must make every reasonable effort to complete the proposed research on schedule, including reports to the funding source.

Members should be prepared to take comments from sponsors or funders or research participants.

Members should, wherever possible, spread their research findings.

Members should normally avoid restrictions on their freedom to publish or otherwise broadcast research findings.

At its meeting in July 1994, the BSA Executive Committee approved a set of Rules for the Conduct of Enquiries into Complaints against BSA members under the auspices of this Statement, and also under the auspices of the BSA Guidelines on Professional Conduct. If you would like more details about the Rules, you should contact the BSA Office at the address/phone number given at the end of this statement.

British Sociological Association, Unit 3F/G, Mountjoy Research Centre, Stockton Road, DURHAM, DH1 3UR [UK]. Tel.: 0191-383-0839; email: britsoc@dial.pipex.com; home page: http://dspace.dial.pipex.com/britsoc/.

The authors gratefully acknowledge the British Sociological Association for the right to reproduce this Statement.

Bibliography

Sources are cited in the text and below by the date of first publication in the original language. Where a later edition or a translation has been used, the date of the edition or translation is given after the name of the publisher.

Aaronovitch, S. (1961), *The Ruling Class* (London: Lawrence & Wishart).

Abbott, P., and Wallace, C. (1990), *An Introduction to Sociology: Feminist Perspectives* (London: Routledge).

Abercrombie, N. (1996), *Television and Society* (Cambridge: Polity).

——and Warde, A. (1992) (eds.), *Social Change in Contemporary Britain* (Cambridge: Polity).

——Turner, B. S., and Hill, S. (1979), *The Dominant Ideology Thesis* (London: George Allen & Unwin).

Aberle, D. F., Cohen, A. K., Davis, A. K., Levy, M. J., and Sutton, F. X. (1950), 'The Functional Prerequisites of a Society', *Ethics*, 60.

Abrams, P. (1978) (ed.), *Work, Urbanism, and Inequality: UK Society Today* (London: Weidenfeld & Nicolson).

Abrams, R. (1997), 'Tories Scorn Major's Nursery Revolution', *Independent*, 13 March.

Acker, J. (1989), 'The Problem with Patriarchy', *Sociology*, 23/2.

Adams, W. M. (1995), 'Sustainable Development?', in Johnston, Taylor, and Watts (1995).

Adler, A. (1928), *Understanding Human Nature* (London: George Allen & Unwin).

Adorno, T., Albert, H., Dahrendorf, R., Habermas, J., Pilot, H., and Popper, K. R. (1969), *The Positivist Dispute in German Sociology* (London: Heinemann Educational Books, 1976).

Ahrne, G. (1994), *Social Organizations: Interaction Inside, Outside, and Between Organizations* (London: Sage).

Albrow, M. C. (1970), *Bureaucracy* (London: Pall Mall).

Alexander, C. (1996), *The Art of Being Black* (Oxford: Oxford University Press).

Allan, G. (1985), *Family Life: Domestic Roles and Social Organization* (Oxford: Basil Blackwell).

Allen, J. (1995), 'Crossing Borders: Footloose Multinationals?', in Allen and Hamnett (1995).

——and Hamnett, C. (1995) (eds.), *A Shrinking World?: Global Unevenness and Inequality* (Oxford: Oxford University Press).

Althusser, L. (1965), *For Marx* (Harmondsworth: Allen Lane, The Penguin Press).

Anderson, B. (1991), *Imagined Communities* (2nd edn., London: Verso).

Anderson, G. (1976), *Victorian Clerks* (Manchester: Manchester University Press).

Anderson, M. (1971), *Family Structure in Nineteenth Century Lancashire* (Cambridge: Cambridge University Press).

——(1980a), *Approaches to the History of the Western Family* (London: Macmillan).

——(1980b) (ed.), *Sociology of the Family: Selected Readings* (Harmondsworth: Penguin).

Anderson, N. (1923), *The Hobo: The Sociology of the Homeless Man* (Chicago: University of Chicago Press).

Andreski, S. L. (1976) (ed.), *Herbert Spencer: Structure, Function, and Evolution* (London: Nelson).

Ang, I. (1985), *Watching Dallas: Soap Opera and the Melodramatic Imagination* (New York: Methuen & Co.).

Anthias, F., and Yuval-Davis, N. (1993), *Racialized Boundaries: Race, Nation, Gender, Colour and Classes and the Anti-Racist Struggle* (London: Routledge).

Arber, S., and Ginn, J. (1991), *Gender and Later Life* (London: Sage).

——Dale, A., and Gilbert, G. N. (1986), 'The Limitations of Existing Social Class Classifications for Women', in A. Jacoby (ed.), *The Measurement of Social Class* (London: Social Research Association).

Aries, P. (1972), *Centuries of Childhood: A Social History of Family Life* (New York: Alfred A. Knopf).

Armstrong, P., Glyn, A., and Harrison, J. (1984), *Capitalism since World War Two* (London: Fontana).

Ashton, D. N. (1986), *Unemployment under Capitalism: The Sociology of British and American Labour Markets* (Brighton: Harvester).

——and Lowe, G. (1991), *Making their Way: Education, Training, and the Labour Market in Canada and Britain* (Milton Keynes: Open University Press).

——and Maguire, M. (1991), 'Patterns and Experiences of Unemployment', in Brown and Scase (1991).

——and Sung, J. (1997), 'Education, Skill Formation, and Economic Development: The Singaporean Approach', in Halsey *et al.* (1997).

Atkinson, A. B. (1983), *The Economics of Inequality* (2nd edn., Oxford: Clarendon Press).

Atkinson, J. (1984), 'Manpower Strategies for Flexible Organizations', *Personnel Management*, 16.

Atkinson, J. M. (1978), *Discovering Suicide* (London: Macmillan).

Atkinson, P. (1983), 'Eating Virtue', in A. Murcott (ed.), *The Sociology of Food and Eating* (Aldershot: Gower).

Auld, J., Doorn, N., and South, N. (1986), 'Irregular Work, Irregular Pleasures: Heroin in the 1980s', in R. Matthews and J. Young (eds.), *Confronting Crime* (London: Sage).

Bachrach, P., and Baratz, M. S. (1962), 'The Two Faces of Power', *American Political Science Review*, 56.

Baggott, R. (1994), *Health and Health Care in Britain* (Basingstoke: Macmillan).

Bagguley, P., Mark-Lawson, J., Shapiro, D., Urry, J., Walby, S., and Warde, A. (1990), *Restructuring: Place, Class, and Gender* (London: Sage).

Bagilhole, B. (1994), 'Being Different is a Very Difficult Row to Hoe: Survival Strategies of Women Academics', in Davies *et al.* (1994).

Bales, R. F. (1950), *Interaction Process Analysis* (Cambridge, Mass.: Addison-Wesley).

Ball, S. (1981), *Beachside Comprehensive: A Case-Study of Secondary Schooling* (Cambridge: Cambridge University Press).

——(1990), *Politics and Policy Making in Education: Explorations in Policy Sociology* (London: Routledge).

——Bowe, R., and Gewirtz, S. (1995), 'Circuits of Schooling: A Sociological Exploration of Parental Choice of School in Social-Class Contexts', *Sociological Review*, 43.

Banks, J. (1954), *Prosperity and Parenthood* (London: Routledge & Kegan Paul).

Banton, M. (1987), *Racial Theories* (Cambridge: Cambridge University Press).

Barclay, P. (1995) (ed.), *Joseph Rowntree Foundation Inquiry into Income and Wealth*, i (York: Joseph Rowntree Foundation).

Barker, E. (1984), *The Making of a Moonie* (Oxford: Basil Blackwell).

——(1989), *New Religious Movements* (London: HMSO).

Barker, M. (1981), *The New Racism* (London: Junction Books).

——(1989), *Comics: Ideology, Power, and the Critics* (Manchester: Manchester University Press).

Barrett, M., and McIntosh, M. (1991), *The Anti-Social Family* (2nd edn., London: Verso).

Barton, L., and Walker, S. (1983) (eds.), *Race, Class, and Education* (Beckenham: Croom Helm).

Bassett, P. (1987), *Strike-Free: New Industrial Relations in Britain* (London: Macmillan).

Bates, I., Clarke, J., Cohen, P., Finn, D., Moore, R., and Willis, P. (1984), *Schooling for the Dole?* (London: Macmillan).

Batstone, E., Boraston, I., and Frenkel, S. (1978), *The Social Organization of Strikes* (Oxford: Basil Blackwell).

Baudrillard, J. (1977), *Forget Foucault* (New York: Semiotexte, 1987).

——(1981), *Simulations* (New York: Semiotexte, 1983).

Beck, U. (1992), *Risk Society: Towards a New Modernity* (London: Sage).

——and Beck-Gernsheim, P. (1995), *The Normal Chaos of Love* (Cambridge: Polity).

Becker, H. S. (1953), 'Becoming a Marihuana User', in Becker 1963.

——(1963), *Outsiders: Studies in the Sociology of Deviance* (New York: Free Press).

——(1970), *Sociological Work* (Chicago: University of Chicago Press).

——(1982), *Art Worlds* (Berkeley and Los Angeles: University of California Press).

——Greer, B., and Hughes, E. C. (1961), *Boys in White* (New York: John Wiley).

————(1968), *Making the Grade* (New York: John Wiley).

Beckford, J. A. (1989), *Religion and Advanced Industrial Society* (London: Unwin Hyman).

Beechey, V. (1987), *Unequal Work* (London: Verso).

Bell, D. (1961), *The End of Ideology* (New York: Collier-Macmillan).

——(1973), *The Coming of Post-Industrial Society: A Venture in Social Forecasting* (London: Heinemann).

——(1979), *The Cultural Contradictions of Capitalism* (London: Heinemann).

Bellah, R. N. (1967), 'Civil Religion in America', *Daedalus*, 96.

——(1970), *Beyond Belief* (New York: Harper & Row).

Benedict, R. (1934), *Patterns of Culture* (London: Routledge & Kegan Paul).

——(1946), *The Chrysanthemum and the Sword* (Tokyo: Charles E. Tuttle).

Berger, P. L. (1961*a*), *The Noise of Solemn Assemblies* (Garden City, NY: Doubleday).

——(1961*b*), *The Precarious Vision* (Garden City, NY: Doubleday).

——(1963), *Invitation to Sociology: A Humanistic Perspective* (Harmondsworth: Penguin).

——(1969), *The Social Reality of Religion [a.k.a The Sacred Canopy]* (London: Faber & Faber).

——and Luckmann, T. (1966), *The Social Construction of Reality* (Harmondsworth: Allen Lane, 1971).

Berle, A. A., and Means, G. C. (1932), *The Modern Corporation and Private Property* (London: Macmillan).

Bernardes, J. (1997), *Family Studies: An Introduction* (London: Routledge).

Bernstein, B. (1961), 'Social Class and Linguistic Development: A Theory of Social Learning', in Halsey *et al.* (1961).

——(1970), 'Education Cannot Compensate for Society', *New Society*, 387: 344–7.

——(1977), 'Social Class, Language, and Socialization', in Karabel and Halsey (1977).

——(1997), *Pedagogy, Symbolic Control, and Identity: Theory, Research, Critique* (London: Taylor & Francis).

Beynon, H., and Blackburn, R. M. (1972), *Perceptions of Work: Variations within a Factory* (Cambridge: Cambridge University Press).

Bhachu, P. (1988), '*Apni Marzi Kardhi* Home and Work: Sikh Women In Britain', in Westwood and Bhachu (1988*b*).

Bianchini, F., and Schwengel, H. (1991), 'Re-Imagining the City', in J. Corner and S. Harvey (eds.), *Enterprise and Heritage* (London: Routledge).

Black, D., *et al.* (1980), 'The Black Report', in P. Townsend and N. Davidson (eds.), *Inequalities in Health* (Harmondsworth: Penguin, 1992).

Blackburn, C. (1991), *Poverty and Health: Working with Families* (Buckingham: Open University Press).

Blau, P., and Duncan, O. D. (1967), *The American Occupational Structure* (New York: Wiley).

Blauner, R. (1964), *Alienation and Freedom: The Factory Worker and his Industry* (Chicago: University of Chicago Press).

Blaxter, M., and Paterson, E. (1982), *Mothers and Daughters: A Three Generational Study of Health Attitudes and Behaviour* (London: Heinemann Educational Books).

Blumer, H. (1966), 'Sociological Implications of the Thought of

George Herbert Mead', in H. Blumer, *Symbolic Interactionism* (Englewood Cliffs, NJ: Prentice-Hall, 1969).

Boas, F. (1911), *The Mind of Primitive Man* (New York: Macmillan).

Bocock, R. (1974), *Ritual in Industrial Society: A Sociological Analysis of Ritualism in Modern England* (London: George Allen & Unwin).

Booth, C. (1886), 'Occupations of the People of the United Kingdom', *Journal of the Royal Statistical Society* (June).

——(1901–2), *Life and Labour of the People of London* (17 vols.; London: Macmillan).

Booth, D. (1993), 'Development Research: From Impasse to a New Agenda', in Schuurman (1993).

Bordo, S. (1993), *Unbearable Weight: Feminism, Western Culture, and the Body* (Berkeley and Los Angeles: University of California Press).

Bottomore, T. B. (1993), *Elites and Society* (2nd edn., London: Routledge & Kegan Paul).

——and Brym, R. J. (1989) (eds.), *The Capitalist Class* (Hemel Hempstead: Harvester Wheatsheaf).

Bourdieu, P. (1977), *Reproduction in Education, Society, and Culture* (London: Sage).

——(1984), *Distinction: A Social Critique of the Judgment of Taste* (London: Routlege & Kegan Paul).

——(1988), *Homo Academicus* (Cambridge: Polity).

——(1997), 'The Forms of Capital', in Halsey *et al.* (1997).

Bowlby, J. (1965), *Child Care and the Growth of Love* (2nd edn., Harmondsworth: Penguin).

Bowles, S., and Gintis, H. (1976), *Schooling in Capitalist America: Educational Reform and the Contradictions of Economic Life* (London: Routledge & Kegan Paul).

Boyce, D. G. (1987), 'Crusaders without Chains: Power and the Press Barons 1896–1951', in Curran, Smith, and Wingate (1987).

Boyd, D. (1973), *Elites and their Education* (London: National Foundation for Educational Research).

Boyd-Barrett, O. (1995), 'Conceptualizing the "Public Sphere"', in Boyd-Barrett and Newbold (1995).

——and Newbold C. (1995) (eds.), *Approaches to Media: A Reader* (London: Arnold).

Bradley, H. (1989), *Men's Work, Women's Work: A Sociological History of the Sexual Division of Labour in Employment* (Cambridge: Polity).

Brah, A., and Minhas R. (1988), 'Structural Racism or Cultural Difference: Schooling for Asian Girls', in Woodhead and Mcgrath (1988).

Braverman, H. (1974), *Labor and Monopoly Capital: The Degradation of Work in the Twentieth Century* (New York: Monthly Review Press).

Brewer, J. D., Guelke, A., Hume, I., Moxon-Browne, E., and Wilford, R. (1996), *The Police, Public Order, and the State: Policing in Great Britain, Northern Ireland, the Irish Republic, the USA, Israel, South Africa, and China* (2nd. edn., London: Macmillan).

British Sociological Association (1997), *Sociology: Information and Opportunities* (Durham: British Sociological Association).

Brown, A. (1986), 'Family Circumstances of Young Children', *Population Trends*, 43.

Brown, C. (1984), *Black and White Britain* (London: Policy Studies Institute).

Brown, G., and Harris, T. (1978), *Social Origins of Depression* (London: Tavistock).

Brown, L. R. *et al.* (1996), *State of the World 1996* (London: Earthscan).

Brown, P. (1989), 'Schooling for Inequality? Ordinary Kids in School and the Labour Market', in Cosin *et al.* (1989).

——(1995), 'Cultural Capital and Social Exclusion: Some Observations on Recent Trends in Education, Employment, and the Labour Market', *Work, Employment, and Society*, 9: 29–51.

——and Scase, R. (1991), *Poor Work: Disadvantage and the Division of Labour* (Milton Keynes: Open University Press).

——Halsey, E. H., Lauder, H., and Wells, A. (1997), 'The Transformation of Education and Society: An Introduction', in Halsey *et al.* (1997).

Bruce, S. (1983), 'The Persistence of Religion: Conservative Protestantism in the United Kingdom', *Sociological Review*, 31.

——(1984), *Firm in the Faith* (Aldershot: Gower).

——(1985), 'Authority and Fission: The Protestants' Divisions', *British Journal of Sociology*, 36.

——(1986), 'Militants and the Margins. British Political Protestantism', *Sociological Review*, 34.

——(1995), *Religion in Modern Britain* (Oxford: Oxford University Press).

Bruch, H. (1973), *Eating Disorders* (New York: Basic Books).

——(1979), *The Golden Cage: The Enigma of Anorexia Nervosa* (New York: Vintage).

Bulmer, M. (1982) (ed.), *Social Research Ethics* (London: Macmillan).

Burgess, R. G. (1984), *In the Field: An Introduction to Field Research* (London: George Allen & Unwin).

——(1986) (ed.), *Key Variables in Social Research* (London: Routledge & Kegan Paul).

Burghes, L. (1994), *Lone Parenthood and Family Disruption: The Outcomes for Children* (London: Family Policy Studies Centre).

Burke, J. (1994), *Working-Class Culture in Britain, 1890–1960* (London: Routledge).

Burnham, J. (1941), *The Managerial Revolution* (New York: John Day).

Burns, T., and Stalker, G. M. (1961), *The Management of Innovation* (London: Tavistock).

Burt, C. (1946), *Intelligence and Fertility* (London: Eugenics Society).

Busfield, N. J. (1996), *Men, Women and Madness: Understanding Gender and Mental Disorder* (London: Macmillan).

Butler, D., and Butler, G. E. (1994), *British Political Facts, 1900–1994* (London: Macmillan).

Butler, D., and Stokes, D. E. (1969), *Political Change in Britain: Forces Shaping Electoral Change* (1st edn., London: Macmillan).

Butler, J. (1993), *Bodies That Matter: On the Discursive Limits of 'Sex'* (London: Routledge).

Butler, T. (1996), '"People Like Us": The Gentrification of Hackney in the 1980s', in Butler and Rustin (1996).

——and Rustin M. (1996) (eds.), *Rising in the East: The Regeneration of East London* (London: Lawrence & Wishart).

Butterworth, E., and Weir, D. (1976) (eds.), *The Sociology of Work and Leisure* (London: Allen & Unwin).

Byrne, P. (1997), *Social Movements in Britain* (London: Routledge).

Campbell, A. (1981), *Girl Delinquents* (Oxford: Basil Blackwell).

——Converse, P. S., Miller, W. E., and Stokes, D. E. (1960), *The American Voter* (New York: John Wiley).

Campbell, B. (1993), *Goliath: Britain's Dangerous Places* (London: Methuen).

Carey, A. (1967), 'The Hawthorne Studies: A Radical Criticism', *American Sociological Review*, 32: 403–16.

Castells, M. (1977), *The Urban Question* (London: Edward Arnold).

Castles, S., and Miller, M. J. (1993), *The Age of Migration: International Population Movements in the Modern World* (London: Macmillan).

Cater, E. (1995), 'Consuming Spaces: Global Tourism', in Allen and Hamnett (1995).

Cavadino, M., and Dignan, J. (1997), *The Penal System: An Introduction* (2nd edn., London: Sage).

Central Office of Information (1995), *Population* (London: HMSO).

Chamberlain, H. S. (1899), *Foundations of the Nineteenth Century* (London: John Lane, 1911).

Chanan, M. (1983), 'The Emergence of an Industry', in Curran and Porter (1983).

Chandler, A. D., Jnr. (1962), *Strategy and Structure* (Cambridge, Mass.: Belknap).

——(1977), *The Visible Hand: The Managerial Revolution in American Business* (Cambridge, Mass.: Belknap).

Chandler, J. (1993), 'Women Outside Marriage', *Sociology Review*, 2/4.

Chapman, M. (1986), *Plain Figures* (London: HMSO).

Charles, N., and Kerr, M. (1988), *Women, Food and Families* (Manchester: Manchester University Press).

Checkland, S. G. (1964), *The Rise of Industrial Society in England 1815–1885* (London: Longman).

Chernin, K. (1985), *The Hungry Self: Women, Eating and Identity* (New York: Harper & Row).

Chesney, K. (1968), *The Victorian Underworld* (Harmondsworth: Penguin).

Child, J. (1984), *Organization: A Guide to Problems and Practice* (London: Harper & Row).

Chiozza-Money, L. G. (1905), *Riches and Poverty* (London: Methuen).

Chitty, C. (1993), 'The Education System Transformed', *Sociology Review*, 2: 3.

——(1997), 'Choose . . . Education? Selection, Choice and Diversity in Secondary Education', *Sociology Review*, 6/4.

Chodorow, N. (1978), *The Reproduction of Mothering: Psychoanalysis and the Sociology of Gender* (Berkeley and Los Angeles: University of California Press).

Cicourel, A. V. (1964), *Method and Measurement in Sociology* (New York: Free Press).

Clark, C. (1940), *The Conditions of Economic Progress* (London: Macmillan & Co.).

Clarke, A. (1992), ' "You're Nicked": Television Police Series and the Fictional Representation of Law and Order', in Strinati and Wagg (1992).

Clarke, J., and Willis, P. (1984), 'Introduction', in Bates *et al.* (1984).

——Hall, S., Jefferson, J., and Roberts, B. (1976), 'Subcultures, Cultures, and Class: A Theoretical Overview', in Hall and Jefferson (1976).

Clarke, M. (1986), *Regulating the City* (Buckingham: Open University Press).

——(1990), *Business Crime: Its Nature and Control* (Cambridge: Polity Press).

Clegg, H. A. (1976), *Trade Unionism under Collective Bargaining* (Oxford: Basil Blackwell).

Clegg, S. R. (1990), *Modern Organizations: Organization Studies in the Postmodern World* (London: Sage).

——and Dunkerley, D. (1980), *Organization, Class, and Control* (London: Routledge & Kegan Paul).

Cloward, R., and Ohlin, L. (1961), *Delinquency and Opportunity* (Glencoe, Ill.: Free Press).

Coates, D. (1989), *The Crisis of Labour* (London: Philip Allan).

Coates, K., and Silburn, R. (1970), *Poverty: The Forgotten Englishmen* (Harmondsworth: Penguin).

Coffield, F. (1987), 'From the Celebration to the Marginalization of Youth', in G. Cohen (ed.), *Social Change and the Life Course* (London: Tavistock).

Cohen, A. K. (1955), *Delinquent Boys* (Glencoe, Ill.: Free Press).

Cohen, A., and Fukui, K. (1993) (eds.), *Humanizing the City: Social Contexts of Urban Life at the Turn of the Millennium* (Edinburgh: Edinburgh University Press).

Cohen, S. (1972), *Folk Devils and Moral Panics: The Creation of the Mods and Rockers* (London: Macgibbon & Kee).

——(1985), *Visions of Social Control* (Cambridge: Polity).

Cole, M. (1989) (ed.), *The Social Contexts of Schooling* (London: Falmer).

Coleman, D., and Salt, J. (1992), *The British Population: Patterns, Trends and Processes* (Oxford: Oxford University Press).

Colley, L. (1992), *Britons: Forging the Nation 1707–1837* (New Haven, Conn.: Yale University Press).

Collins, R. (1994), *Four Sociological Traditions* (Oxford: Oxford University Press).

Collison, M. (1994), 'Drug Offenders and Criminal Justice: Careers, Compulsion, Commitment and Penalty', *Crime, Law and Society*, 21.

Collison, P. (1963), *The Cutteslowe Walls: A Study in Social Class* (London: Faber & Faber).

Connell, R. W. (1995), *Masculinities* (Cambridge: Polity).

Cooke, P. (1989) (ed.), *Localities: The Changing Face of Urban Britain* (London: Unwin Hyman).

Cooley, C. H. (1902), *Human Nature and the Social Order* (New York: Scribner's).

——(1909), *Social Organization* (New Brunswick, NJ: Transaction, 1983).

Corrigan, P. (1983), 'Film Entertainment as Ideology and Pleasure: Towards a History of Audiences', in Curran and Porter (1983).

Cosin, B., Flude, M., and Hales, M. (1989) (eds.), *School, Work, and Equality* (London: Hodder & Stoughton).

Coulter, J. (1973), *Approaches to Insanity* (Oxford: Martin Robertson).

Coupland, A. (1992), 'Docklands: Dream or Disaster', in Thornley (1992).

Craib, I. (1984), *Modern Social Theory* (Brighton: Harvester Wheatsheaf).

——(1997), *Classical Social Theory* (Oxford: Oxford University Press).

CRE (1992): Commission for Racial Equality, *Set to Fail: Setting and Banding in Secondary Schools* (London: CRE).

——(1996), *Exclusion From School: The Public Cost* (London: CRE).

Creighton, S. J. (1992), *Child Abuse Trends in England and Wales 1988–1990* (London: NSPCC).

Critcher, C., Bramham, P., and Tomlinson, A. (1995), *The Sociology of Leisure* (London: Chapman & Hall).

Croal, H. (1992), *White Collar Crime* (Buckingham: Open University Press).

Crompton, R. (1997), *Women and Work in Modern Britain* (Oxford: Oxford University Press).

——and Harris, F. (1998), 'Explaining Women's Employment Patterns: "Orientations To Work" Revisited', *British Journal of Sociology*, 49/1.

——and Jones, G. (1984), *White-Collar Proletariat* (London: Macmillan).

——and Le Feuvre, N. (1992), 'Gender and Bureaucracy: Women in Finance in Britain and France', in Savage and Witz (1992).

——Gallie, D., and Purcell, K. (1996) (eds.), *Changing Forms of Employment: Organization, Skills, and Gender* (London: Routledge).

Cross, M., and Waldinger, R. (1992), 'Migrants, Minorities, and the Ethnic Division of Labour', in Fainstein, Gordon, and Harloe (1992).

Crossick, G. (1977a), 'The Emergence of the Lower Middle Class in Britain', in Crossick (1977b).

——(1977b) (ed.), *The Lower Middle Class in Britain, 1870–1914* (London: Croom Helm).

Crothers, C. (1987), *Robert Merton* (Chichester: Ellis Horwood).

Crozier, M. (1964), *The Bureaucratic Phenomenon* (London: Tavistock).

Culley, L., and Dyson, S. (1993), ' "Race", Equality and Health', *Sociology Review*, 3.

Cully, M., and Woodland, S. (1997), 'Trade Union Membership and Recognition', *Labour Market Trends*, 105/6 (June).

Cunningham, H. (1995), *Children and Childhood in Western Society since 1500* (London: Longman).

Curran, J., and Gurevitch, M. (1996) (eds.), *Mass Media and Society* (2nd edn., London: Edward Arnold).

——and Porter, V. (1983) (eds.), *British Cinema History* (London: Weidenfeld & Nicolson).

——and Seaton, J. (1991), *Power without Responsibility: The Press and Broadcasting in Britain* (4th edn., London: Routledge).

——Gurevitch, M., and Woollacott, J. (1977) (eds.), *Mass Communication and Society* (London: Edward Arnold).

——Smith, A., and Wingate, P. (1987), *Impacts and Influences: Essays on Media Power in the Twentieth Century* (London: Methuen).

Curtis, M. (1979), *Totalitarianism* (New Brunswick, NJ: Transaction Books).

Dahl, R. (1961), *Who Governs?* (New Haven, Conn.: Yale University Press).

Dahrendorf, R. (1957), *Class and Class Conflict in an Industrial Society* (London: Routledge & Kegan Paul, 1959).

Dale, R. (1989), *The State and Education Policy* (Milton Keynes: Open University Press).

——Fergusson, R., and Robinson, A. (1988) (eds.), *Frameworks for Teaching: Readings for the Intending Secondary School Teacher* (London: Hodder & Stoughton).

Dandeker, C. (1990), *Surveillance, Power and Modernity: Bureaucracy and Discipline from 1700 to the Present Day* (Cambridge: Polity).

Davidoff, L. (1973), *The Best Circles* (London: Croom Helm).

——(1990), 'The Family in Britain', in F. M. L. Thompson (1990).

——and Hall, C. (1987), *Family Fortunes* (London: Hutchinson).

Davie, G. (1990), ' "An Ordinary God": The Paradox of Religion in Contemporary Britain', *British Journal of Sociology*, 41.

——(1994), *Religion in Britain since 1945* (Oxford: Basil Blackwell).

Davies, S., Lubelska, C., and Quinn, J. (1994) (eds.), *Changing the Subject: Women in Higher Education* (London: Taylor & Francis).

Davis, Kathleen (1995), *Reshaping the Female Body: The Dilemma of Cosmetic Surgery* (New York: Routledge & Kegan Paul).

Davis, Kingsley (1945), 'The World Demographic Transition', *Annals of the American Academy of Political and Social Science*, 273.

——and Moore, W. E. (1945), 'Some Principles of Stratification', *American Sociological Review*, 10.

Davis, M. (1990), *City of Quartz: Excavating the Future in Los Angeles* (London: Vintage).

Day, G., and Murdoch, J. (1993), 'Locality and Community: Coming to Terms with Place', *Sociological Review*, 41/1.

de Vaus, G. (1991), *Surveys in Social Research* (London: UCL Press).

Dear, M., and Wolch, J. (1987), *Landscapes of Despair: From De-Institutionalization to Homelessness* (Cambridge: Polity).

Dedoussis, V., and Littler, C. (1994), 'Understanding the Transfer of Japanese Management Practices: The Australian Case', in Elger and Smith (1994).

Deem, R. (1997), 'Governing Schools in the 1990s', *Sociology Review*, 6/3.

Deem, R., Brehony, K. J., and Heath, S. (1995), *Active Citizenship and the Governing of Schools* (Buckingham: Open University Press).

Delphy, C. (1977), *The Main Enemy* (London: Women's Research and Resources Centre).

——and Leonard, D. (1992), *Familiar Exploitation* (Cambridge: Polity).

Denman, J., and McDonald, P. (1996), 'Unemployment Statistics from 1881 to the Present Day', *Labour Market Trends*, 104/1.

Dennis, N. (1993), *Rising Crime and the Dismembered Family* (London: Institute of Economic Affairs).

——and Erdos, G. (1992), *Families Without Fatherhood* (London: Institute of Economic Affairs).

——Henriques, F., and Slaughter, C. (1956), *Coal is our Life* (London: Eyre & Spottiswoode).

Denscombe, M. (1997), *Sociology Update* (Olympus Books UK).

Denver, D. (1994), *Elections and Voting Behaviour in Britain* (2nd edn., Hemel Hempstead: Harvester Wheatsheaf).

Devine, F. (1992), *Affluent Workers Revisited: Privatism and the Working Class* (Edinburgh: Edinburgh University Press).

Dicken, P. (1992), *Global Shift: The Internationalization of Economic Activity* (2nd edn., London: Paul Chapman Publishing).

Digby, A., and Searby, P. (1981), *Children, School and Society in Nineteenth-Century England* (London: Macmillan).

Dixey, R. (1988), 'A Means to Get out of the House: Working-Class Women, Leisure and Bingo', in J. Little, L. Peake, and P. Richardson (eds.), *Women in Cities* (London: Macmillan).

Dobash, R. E., and Dobash, R. P. (1980), *Violence against Wives: A Case against the Patriarchy* (London: Open Books).

————(1992), *Women, Violence, and Social Change* (London: Routledge).

Dodd, K., and Dodd, P. (1992), 'From the East End to *Eastenders*: Representations of the Working Class, 1890–1990', in Strinati and Wagg (1992).

Domhoff, G. W. (1967), *Who Rules America?* (Englewood Cliffs, NJ: Prentice Hall).

——(1971), *The Higher Circles: The Governing Class in America* (New York: Vintage Books).

——(1978), *Who Really Rules? New Haven and Community Power Reexamined* (New Brunswick, NJ: Transaction Books).

——(1979), *The Powers That Be: Processes of Ruling Class Domination in America* (New York: Vintage).

Dore, R. P. (1973), *British Factory–Japanese Factory: The Origins of National Diversity in Industrial Relations* (London: George Allen & Unwin).

Dorn, N., and South, N. (1987), *A Land Fit for Heroin* (London: Macmillan).

——Murji, K., and South, N. (1992), *Traffickers* (London: Routledge).

Douglas, J. D. (1967), *The Social Meanings of Suicide* (Princeton: Princeton University Press).

Douglas, J. W. B. (1964). *The Home and the School* (London: MacGibbon & Kee).

——Ross, J., and Simpson, H. (1968), *All Our Futures: A Longitudinal Study of Secondary Education* (London: Peter Davies).

Downes, D. (1966), *The Delinquent Solution: A Study in Subcultural Theory* (London: Routledge and Kegan Paul).

Downs, A. (1957), *An Economic Theory of Democracy* (New York: Harper & Brothers).

Drakakis-Smith, D. (1987), *The Third World City* (London: Methuen).

Dumazedier, J. (1967), *Towards a Leisure Society* (London: Collier-Macmillan).

Dumont, L. (1966), *Homo Hierarchicus*: The Caste System and its Implications (Chicago: University of Chicago Press, 1980).

Duncombe, J., and Marsden, D. (1993), 'Love and Intimacy: The Gender Division of Emotion and Emotion Work', *Sociology*, 27.

————(1995), 'Women's "Triple Shift": Paid Employment, Domestic Labour and "Emotion Work"', *Sociology Review*, 4/4.

Dunleavy, P., and Husbands, C. T. (1985), *British Democracy at the Crossroads* (London: George Allen & Unwin).

Durkheim, E. (1893), *The Division of Labour in Society* (London: Macmillan, 1984).

——(1895), *The Rules of the Sociological Method* (London: Macmillan, 1982).

——(1897), *Suicide: A Study in Sociology* (London: Routledge & Kegan Paul, 1952).

——(1912), *The Elementary Forms of the Religious Life* (London: George Allen & Unwin, 1915).

——(1925), *Moral Education: A Study in the Theory and Application of the Sociology of Education*, trans. E. Wilson and H. Schnurer (New York: Free Press of Glencoe, 1961).

——and Mauss, M. (1903), *Primitive Classification* (London: Cohen & West, 1963).

Dworkin, A. (1983), *Right-Wing Women* (New York: Pedigree Books).

Edwards, S. (1984), *Women on Trial* (Manchester: Manchester University Press).

Edwards, T. (1997), *Men in the Mirror: Men's Fashion, Masculinity, and Consumer Society* (London: Cassell).

Eldridge, J. (1993a), 'News, Truth and Power', in Eldridge (1993).

——(1993b), *Getting the Message: News, Truth, and Power* (Glasgow University Media Group, London: Routledge).

——Kitzinger, J., and Williams, K. (1997), *The Mass Media and Power in Modern Britain* (Oxford: Oxford University Press).

Elger, T., and Smith, C. (1994) (eds.), *Global Japanization: The Transnational Transformation of the Labour Process* (London: Routledge).

Ellin, N. (1996), *Postmodern Urbanism* (Oxford: Blackwell).

Elliot, J. (1997), 'What do Women Want? Women, Work, and the Hakim Debate', *Sociology Review*, 6/4: 12–18.

Elliot, F. R. (1996), *Gender, Family, and Society* (Basingstoke: Macmillan).

Elliott, B. (1978), 'Social Change in the City: Structure and Process', in P. Abrams (1978).

Emerson, J. (1970), 'Behaviour in Private Places: Sustaining Definitions of Reality in Gynecological Examinations', in H.-P. Dreitzel (ed.), *Recent Sociology, Number 2* (New York: Macmillan).

Emmer, P. C. (1993), 'Intercontinental Migration as a World Historical Process', *European Review*, 1/1: 67–74.

Engels, F. (1845), *The Condition of the Working Class in England in 1844* (Harmondsworth Penguin, 1987).

Erikson, R., and Goldthorpe, J. (1993), *The Constant Flux* (Oxford: Clarendon Press).

Esping-Andersen, G. (1990), *The Three Worlds of Welfare Capitalism* (Cambridge: Polity).

——(1996) (ed.), *Welfare States in Transition* (London: Sage).

——and Korpi, W. (1984), 'Social Policy and Class Politics in Post-War Capitalism: Scandinavia, Austria, and Germany', in Goldthorpe (1984).

Ettorre, B. (1992), *Women and Substance Use* (London: Macmillan).

Etzioni, A. (1995), *The Spirit of Community: Rights, Responsibilities, and the Communitarian Agenda* (London: Fontana).

Evans, K. (1997), 'Men's Towns: Women and the Urban Environment', *Sociology Review*, 6/3.

Evans, P., Rueschemeyer, D., and Skocpol, T. (1985), *Bringing the State Back In* (Cambridge: Cambridge University Press).

Fainstein, S. S., Gordon, I., and Harloe, M. (1992) (eds.), *Divided Cities: New York and London in the Contemporary World* (Oxford: Blackwell).

Fanon, F. (1967), *The Wretched of the Earth* (Harmondsworth: Penguin).

Farrington, D. P., and Morris, A. M. (1983), 'Sex, Sentencing and Reconviction', *British Journal of Criminology*, 23.

Featherman, D. L., Jones, R. L., and Hauser, R. M. (1975), 'Assumptions of Social Mobility Research in the United States: The Case of Occupational Status', *Social Science Research*, 4.

Featherstone, M., and Hepworth, M. (1989), 'Ageing and Old Age: Reflections on the Post-Modern Life-Course', in B. Bytheway *et al.* (eds.), *Becoming and Being Old* (London: Sage).

Febvre, L., and Martin, H.-J. (1976), *The Coming of the Book: The Impact of Printing 1450–1800* (London: New Left Books).

Felstead, A. (1996), 'Homeworking in Britain: The National Picture in the Mid-1990s', *Industrial Relations Journal*, 27/3.

—and Jewson, N. (1995), 'Working at Home: Estimates from the 1991 Census', *Employment Gazette*, 103/2.

—and Jewson, N. (1996), *Homeworkers in Britain* (London: HMSO).

Festinger, L., Riecken, H. W., and Schachter, S. (1956), *When Prophecy Fails* (New York: Harper & Row).

Fielding, N. (1981), *The National Front* (London: Routledge & Kegan Paul).

—(1982), 'Observational Research on the British Police', in M. Bulmer (ed.), *Social Research Ethics* (London: Macmillan).

Finch, J. (1989), *Family Obligations and Social Change* (Cambridge: Polity).

—and Mason, J. (1993), *Negotiating Family Responsibilities* (London: Tavistock).

Finestone, H. (1964), 'Cats, Kicks, and Color', in H. Becter (ed.), *The Other Side* (Chicago: Free Press, 1964).

Finn, D. (1984), 'Leaving School and Growing Up', in Bates *et al.* (1984).

Firestone, S. (1971), *The Dialectic of Sex* (London: Jonathan Cape).

Fischer, C. S. (1975), 'Towards a Subcultural Theory of Urbanism', *American Journal of Sociology*, 80/6.

Flanagan, W. (1993), *Contemporary Urban Sociology* (Cambridge: Cambridge University Press).

Fletcher, R. (1991), *Science, Ideology and the Media* (New Brunswick, NJ: Transaction).

Florence, P. S. (1961), *Ownership, Control, and Success of Large Companies* (London: Sweet & Maxwell).

Flynn, J. R. (1980), *Race, I.Q. and Jensen* (London: Routledge & Kegan Paul).

Foner, N. (1986), 'Sex Roles and Sensibilities: Jamaican Women in New York and London', in R. J. Simon and C. B. Brettell (eds.), *International Migration: The Female Experience* (Totowa, NJ: Rowman & Allanheld).

Forster, P. G. (1972), 'Secularization in the English Context: Some Conceptual and Empirical Problems', *Sociological Review*, 20.

Foster, J. (1974), *Class Struggle and the Industrial Revolution: Early Industrial Capitalism in Three English Towns* (London: Weidenfeld & Nicolson).

Foster-Carter, A. (1991), 'Development Sociology: Whither Now?', *Sociology Review*, 1/2.

Foucault, M. (1961), *Madness and Civilization* (New York: Vintage Books, 1973).

—(1963), *The Birth of the Clinic* (New York: Vintage Books, 1975).

—(1971), *The Archaeology of Knowledge* (New York: Pantheon, 1972).

—(1975), *Discipline and Punish* (London: Allen Lane, 1977).

—(1976), *The History of Sexuality, i. An Introduction* (New York: Vintage Books, 1980).

—(1984a), *The History of Sexuality, ii. The Use of Pleasure* (New York: Vintage Books, 1986).

—(1984b), *The History of Sexuality, iii. The Care of the Self* (New York: Vintage Books, 1988).

Frank, A. G. (1967), *Capitalism and Underdevelopment in Latin America: Historical Studies of Chile and Brazil* (New York: Monthly Review Press).

Frankenberg, R. (1966), *Communities in Britain: Social Life in Town and Country* (Harmondsworth: Penguin).

Franklin, M. (1985), *The Decline of Class Voting in Britain* (Oxford: Oxford University Press).

Fraser, D. (1984), *The Evolution of the British Welfare State: A History of Social Policy since the Industrial Revolution* (2nd edn., London: Macmillan).

Fraser, S. (1995) (ed.), *The Bell Curve Wars* (New York: Basic Books).

Frazer, E. (1987), 'Teenage Girls Reading *Jackie*', *Media, Culture, and Society*, 8.

Frazier, E. F. (1932), *The Negro Family in Chicago* (Chicago: University of Chicago Press)

Freeman, D. (1984), *Margaret Mead and the Heretic* (Harmondsworth: Penguin, 1996).

Freidson, E. (1970), *The Profession of Medicine* (New York: Dodd Mead).

Freud, S. (1900), *The Interpretation of Dreams* (London: George Allen & Unwin, 1954).

—(1901), *The Psychopathology of Everyday Life* (Harmondsworth: Penguin, 1975).

—(1905), 'Three Essays on Sexuality', in *On Sexuality*. S. Freud (Harmondsworth: Penguin, 1977).

—(1915–17), *Introductory Lectures on Psychoanalysis* (London: George Allen & Unwin, 1922).

—(1923), *The Ego and the Id* (London: Hogarth Press, 1962).

Friedan, B. (1962), *The Feminine Mystique* (New York: Dell).

Friedman, H., and Meredeen, S. (1980), *The Dynamics of Industrial Conflict* (London: Croom Helm).

Friedrich, C. J., and Brzezinski, Z. K. (1956), *Totalitarian Dictatorship and Autocracy* (New York: Praeger).

Friedrichs, R. W. (1970), *A Sociology of Sociology* (New York: Free Press).

Frith, S. (1992), 'From the Beatles to Bros: Twenty-Five Years of British Pop', in Abercrombie and Warde (1992).

Frobel, F., Heinrichs J., and Kreye O. (1980), *The New International Division of Labour* (Cambridge: Cambridge University Press).

Fromm, E. (1942), *Fear of Freedom* (London: Routledge & Kegan Paul).

Fukuyama, F. (1989), 'The End of History?', *National Interest*, 16.

Fulcher, J. (1991a), *Labour Movements, Employers, and the State: Conflict and Co-Operation in Britain and Sweden* (Oxford: Clarendon Press).

——(1991b), 'A New Stage in the Development of Capitalist Society', *Sociology Review*, 1: 2.

——(1995), 'British Capitalism in the 1980s: Old Times or New Times', *British Journal of Sociology*, 46/2.

——(1997), 'Did British Society Change Character in the 1820s or the 1980s?', *British Journal of Sociology*, 48/3.

Fuller, M. (1983), 'Qualified Criticism, Critical Qualifications', in Barton and Walker (1983).

Gabriel, Y. (1988), *Working Lives in Catering* (London: Routledge Kegan Paul).

Gallie, D. (1978), *In Search of the New Working Class* (Cambridge: Cambridge University Press).

——(1996), 'Skill, Gender, and the Quality of Employment', in Crompton *et al.* (1996).

——and Marsh, C. (1994), 'The Experience of Unemployment', in Gallie *et al.* (1994).

————and Vogler, C. (1994), *Social Change and the Experience of Unemployment* (Oxford: Oxford University Press).

——Penn, R., and Rose, M. (1996), *Trade Unionism in Recession* (Oxford: Oxford University Press).

Galton, F. (1869), *Hereditary Genius* (London: Friedmann, 1978).

Galtung, J., and Ruge, M. (1965), 'The Structure of Foreign News', *Journal of Peace Research*, 1/1.

Gamble, A. (1988), *The Free Economy and the Strong State: The Politics of Thatcherism* (London: Macmillan).

Gans, H. J. (1968), *People and Plans: Essays on Urban Problems and Solutions* (New York: Basic Books).

——(1995), 'Urbanism and Suburbanism as Ways of Life: A Reevaluation of Definitions', in Kasinitz (1995).

Garfinkel, H. (1967), *Studies in Ethnomethodology* (Englewood Cliffs, NJ: Prentice-Hall).

Garrahan, P., and Stewart, P. (1992), *The Nissan Enigma: Flexibility at Work in a Local Economy* (London: Mansell).

Gaskell, M. (1977), 'Housing and the Lower Middle Class, 1870–1914', in Crossick (1977b).

Gavron, H. (1968), *The Captive Wife* (Harmondsworth: Penguin).

Gelder, K., and Thornton, S. (1997) (eds.), *The Subculture Reader* (London: Routledge & Kegan Paul).

Gelles, R. J., and Cornell, C. P. (1987) (eds.), 'Elder Abuse: The Status of Current Knowledge', in R. J. Gelles, *Family Violence* (2nd edn., London: Sage).

Gelsthorpe, L. (1993) (ed.), *Minority Ethnic Groups in the Criminal Justice System* (Cambridge: Institute of Criminology).

Geraghty, C. (1992), 'British Soaps in the 1980s', in Strinati and Wagg (1992).

Gershuny, J. (1988), 'Time, Technology, and the Informal Economy', in R. Pahl (1988).

——(1992), 'Change in the Domestic Division of Labour in the UK, 1975–1987: Dependent Labour versus Adaptive Partnership', in Abercrombie and Warde (1992).

Giallombardo, R. (1966), *Society of Women: A Study of a Women's Prison* (New York: Wiley).

Giddens, A. (1971), *Capitalism and Modern Social Theory* (Cambridge: Cambridge University Press).

——(1976), *New Rules of the Sociological Method* (London: Hutchinson).

——(1981), *A Contemporary Critique of Historical Materialism*, i. *Power, Property, and the State* (London: Macmillan).

——(1985), *The Nation-State and Violence* (Cambridge: Polity).

——(1986), *Sociology: A Brief but Critical Introduction* (London: Macmillan).

——(1990), *The Consequences of Modernity* (Cambridge: Polity Press).

——(1991), *Modernity and Self-Identity* (Cambridge: Polity).

——(1992), *The Transformation of Intimacy* (Cambridge: Polity Press).

——(1994), *Beyond Left and Right: The Future of Radical Politics* (Cambridge: Polity).

Gillborn, D. (1992), *'Race', Ethnicity, and Education* (London: Unwin Hyman).

Gillis, J. (1974), *Youth and History* (New York: Academic Press).

Gilroy, P. (1987), *There Aint No Black in the Union Jack* (London: Hutchinson).

——(1993), *The Black Atlantic: Modernity and Double Consciousness* (London: Verso).

Giner, S. (1976), *Mass Society* (London: Martin Robertson).

Ginn J., Arber, S., Brannen, J., Dale, A., Dex, S., Elias, P., Moss, P., Pahl, J., Roberts, C., and Rubery, J. (1996), 'Feminist Fallacies: A Reply to Hakim on Women's Employment', *British Journal of Sociology*, 47/1.

Gittins, D. (1993), *The Family in Question: Changing Households and Familiar Ideologies* (2nd edn., London: Macmillan).

Glaser, B. G., and Strauss, A. L. (1965), *Awareness of Dying* (Chicago: Aldine).

————(1968), *Time for Dying* (Chicago: Aldine).

Glaser, N., and Moynihan, D. P. (1963), *Beyond the Melting Pot* (Cambridge, Mass.: MIT Press).

Glasgow University Media Group (1976), *Bad News* (London: Routledge & Kegan Paul).

Glass, D. V. (1954) (ed.), *Social Mobility in Britain* (London: Routledge & Kegan Paul).

Gleiman, H. (1995), *Psychology* (4th edn., New York: W. W. Norton).

Glennerster, H. (1985), 'The Sociology of the Media', in Haralambos (1985).

——(1995), *British Social Policy since 1945* (Oxford: Blackwell).

Glucksmann, M. A. (1995), 'Why "Work"? Gender and The "Total Social Organization of Labour"', *Gender, Work, and Organization*, 2/2: 63–75.

Gobineau, A. de. (1853–5), *Essay on the Inequality of the Human Races*.

Goffman, E. (1959), *The Presentation of Self in Everyday Life* (Harmondsworth: Penguin).

——(1961a), *Encounters: Two Studies in the Sociology of Interaction* (Indianapolis: Bobbs Merrill).

——(1961b) *Asylums: Essays on the Social Situation of Mental Patients and Other Inmates* (New York: Doubleday).

——(1963a), *Relations in Public* (New York: Free Press).

——(1963b), *Stigma* (Englewood Cliffs, NJ: Prentice-Hall).

——(1979), *Gender Advertisements* (London: Macmillan).

Gold, R. (1958), 'Roles in Sociological Field Observation', *Social Forces*, 36.

Golding, P., and Murdock, G. (1996), 'Culture, Communications, and Political Economy', in Curran and Gurevitch (1996).

Goldthorpe, J. H. (1964), 'Social Stratification in Industrial Society', *Sociological Review Monograph*, 8.

——(1980), *Social Mobility and Class Structure* (Oxford: Clarendon Press).

——(1983), 'Women and Class Analysis: In Defence of the Conventional View', *Sociology*, 17.

——(1984) (ed.), *Order and Conflict in Contemporary Capitalism* (Oxford: Oxford University Press).

——and Lockwood, D. (1963), 'Affluence and the British Class Structure', *Sociological Review*, 11.

————Bechhofer, F., and Platt, J. (1968a), *The Affluent Worker: Industrial Attitudes and Behaviour* (Cambridge: Cambridge University Press).

—————(1968b), *The Affluent Worker: Political Attitudes and Behaviour* (Cambridge: Cambridge University Press).

—————(1969), *The Affluent Worker in the Class Structure* (Cambridge: Cambridge University Press).

Gough, I. (1979), *The Political Economy of the Welfare State* (London: Macmillan).

Gould, A. (1993), *Capitalist Welfare Systems: A Comparison of Japan, Britain, and Sweden* (London: Longman).

Gould, S. J. (1981), *The Mismeasure of Man* (Harmondsworth: Penguin, 1984).

Gouldner, A. (1954), *Patterns of Industrial Bureaucracy: A Case Study of Modern Factory Administration* (New York: Free Press).

——(1965), *Wildcat Strike* (New York: Antioch Press).

——(1970), *The Coming Crisis of Western Sociology* (New York: Basic Books).

Gray, A. (1992), *Video Playtime: The Gendering of a Leisure Technology* (London: Routledge).

Gregson, N., and Lowe, M. (1994), *Servicing the Middle Classes: Class, Gender, and Waged Domestic Labour in Contemporary Britain* (London: Routledge).

Griggs, C. (1989a), 'The Rise of Mass Schooling', in Cole (1989).

——(1989b), 'The Rise, Fall, and Rise Again of Selective Secondary Schooling', in Cole (1989).

Grint, K. (1991), *The Sociology of Work: An Introduction* (Cambridge: Polity).

Gross, N., Mason, W. S., and McEachern, A. W. (1958), *Explorations in Role Analysis: Studies of the School Superintendency Role* (New York: John Wiley).

Gumplowicz, L. (1885), *Outlines of Sociology* (1st edn., Philadelphia: American Academy of Political and Social Science, 1899).

Gurevitch, M. (1996), 'The Globalization of Electronic Journalism', in Curran and Gurevitch (1996).

Guttsman, W. L. (1963), *The British Political Elite* (London: MacGibbon & Kee).

Habermas, J. (1967), *On the Logic of the Social Sciences* (Cambridge: Polity Press, 1988).

——(1968), *Knowledge and Human Interests* (London: Heinemann, 1972).

——(1968-9), *Towards a Rational Society* (London: Heinemann, 1971).

——(1973), *Legitimation Crisis* (London: Heinemann, 1976).

——(1981a), *The Theory of Communicative Action*, i. *Reason and the Rationalisation of Society* (London: Heinemann, 1984).

——(1981b), *The Theory of Communicative Action*, ii. *The Critique of Functionalist Reason* (London: Heinemann, 1987).

Hagestad, G. O. (1986), 'The Ageing Society as a Context for Family Life', *Daedalus*, 115/1.

Hakim, C. (1993), 'The Myth of Rising Female Employment', *Work, Employment, and Society*, 7/1.

——(1995), 'Five Feminist Myths about Women's Employment', *British Journal of Sociology*, 46/3.

——(1996), *Key Issues in Women's Work: Female Heterogeneity and the Polarization of Women's Employment* (London: Athlone Press).

Hall, C. (1982a), 'The Butcher, the Baker, the Candlestickmaker: The Shop and the Family in the Industrial Revolution', in Whitelegg *et al.* (1982).

——(1982b), 'The Home Turned Upside Down? The Working-Class Family in Cotton Textiles 1780-1850', in Whitelegg *et al.* (1982).

Hall, L. (1991), *Hidden Anxieties: Male Sexuality, 1900-1950* (Cambridge: Cambridge University Press).

Hall, S. (1991a), 'The Local and the Global: Globalization and Ethnicity', in King (1991).

——(1991b), 'Old and New Identities: Old and New Ethnicities', in King (1991).

——and Jacques, M. (1983) (eds.), *The Politics of Thatcherism* (London: Lawrence & Wishart).

——and Jefferson, T. (1976) (eds.), *Resistance through Rituals: Youth Subcultures in Post-War Britain* (London: Hutchinson).

——Critcher, C., Jefferson, T., Clarke, J., and Roberts, B. (1978), *Policing the Crisis: Mugging, the State, and Law and Order* (London: Macmillan).

Hallin, D. C. (1996), 'Commercialism and Professionalism in the American News Media', in Curran and Gurevitch (1996).

Halsey, A. H. (1997), 'Trends in Access and Equity in Higher Education: Britain in International Perspective', in Halsey *et al.* (1997).

——Floud, J., and Anderson, C. (1961) (eds.), *Education, Economy, and Society: A Reader in the Sociology of Education* (London: Collier-Macmillan).

——Heath, A., and Ridge, J. (1980), *Origins and Destinations: Family, Class, and Education in Modern Britain* (Oxford: Clarendon).

——Lauder, H., Brown, P., and Strait Wells, A. (1997) (eds.), *Education: Culture, Economy, and Society* (Oxford: Oxford University Press).

Hamilton, P. (1983), *Talcott Parsons* (Chichester: Ellis Horwood).

Handy, C. (1993), *Understanding Organizations* (London: Penguin).

Haralambos, M. (1985) (ed.), *Sociology: New Directions* (Ormskirk: Causeway).

Harding, S. (1986), *The Science Question in Feminism* (Milton Keynes: Open University Press).

Hargreaves, D. H. (1967), *Social Relations in a Secondary School* (London: Routledge & Kegan Paul).

——(1982), *The Challenge for the Comprehensive School: Culture, Curriculum, and Community* (London: Routledge).

Harloe, M. (1997), 'The State and Welfare', *Sociology Review*, 6/4.

Harris, N. (1986), *The End of the Third World: Newly Industrializing Countries and the Decline of an Ideology* (Harmondsworth: Penguin).

——(1995), *The New Untouchables: Immigration and the New World Worker* (London: I. B. Tauris).

Harrison, D. (1994), 'Tourism, Capitalism and Development in Less Developed Countries', in Sklair (1994).

Harrison, P. (1985), *Inside the Inner City: Life under the Cutting Edge* (London: Penguin).

Harrison, T. (1949), 'Little Kinsey: Mass Observation's Sex Survey of 1949', in Stanley (ed.), *Sex Surveyed, 1949–1994* (London: Taylor & Francis, 1995).

Hartsock, N. (1983), 'The Feminist Standpoint: Developing the Ground for a Specifically Feminist Historical Materialism', in S. Harding and M. Hintikka (eds.), *Discovering Reality: Feminist Perspectives on Epistemology, Metaphysics, Methodology and Philosophy of Science* (Dordrecht: D. D. Reidel).

Harvey, D. (1989), *The Condition of Postmodernity* (Oxford: Basil Blackwell).

Haskey, J. (1991), 'Estimated Numbers and Demographic Characteristics of One-Parent Families in Great Britain', *Population Trends*, 65.

Hay, C. (1996), *Re-Stating Social and Political Change* (Buckingham: Open University Press).

Hearnshaw, L. S. (1979), *Cyril Burt: Psychologist* (London: Hodder & Stoughton).

Heath, A. (1981), *Social Mobility* (Glasgow: Fontana).

——(1989), 'Class in the Classroom', in Cosin *et al.* (1989).

——Jowell, R., and Curtice, J. (1985), *How Britain Votes* (Oxford: Pergamon).

————Evans, G., Field, J., and Witherspoon, S. (1991), *Understanding Political Change: The British Voter, 1964–1987* (Oxford: Pergamon Press).

Heaton, T., and Lawson, T. (1996), *Education and Training* (London: Macmillan).

Hebdige, D. (1979), *Subculture: The Meaning of Style* (London: Methuen).

——(1988), *Hiding in the Light: On Images and Things* (London: Routledge).

Hegel, G. W. F. (1821), *Philosophy of Right* (Oxford: Oxford University Press, 1952).

Heidensohn, F. (1985), *Women and Crime* (London: Macmillan).

Held, D. (1980), *An Introduction to Critical Theory* (London: Hutchinson).

——(1992), 'The Development of the Modern State', in S. Hall and B. Gieben (eds.), *Formations of Modernity* (Cambridge: Polity).

Hemingway, J. (1978), *Conflict and Democracy: Studies in Trade Union Government* (Oxford: Oxford University Press).

Hendrick, H. (1994), *Child Welfare: England 1872–1989* (London: Routledge).

Herberg, W. (1955), *Protestant, Catholic, Jew* (New York: Doubleday).

Herrnstein, R. J., and Murray, C. (1994), *The Bell Curve: Intelligence and Class Structure in American Life* (New York: Free Press).

Hilferding, R. (1910), *Finance Capital* (London: Routledge & Kegan Paul, 1981).

Hill Collins, P. (1990), *Black Feminist Thought* (London: Harper Collins).

Hill, M. (1997), *Understanding Social Policy* (5th edn., Oxford: Blackwell).

Hills, J. (1995), *Joseph Rowntree Inquiry into Income and Wealth, ii* (York: Joseph Rowntree Foundation).

——(1997), *The Future of Welfare: A Guide to the Debate* (rev. edn., York: Joseph Rowntree Foundation).

Himmelweit, H., Humphreys, P., and Jaeger, M. (1985), *How Voters Decide* (Milton Keynes: Open University Press).

Hindess, B. (1973), *The Use of Official Statistics in Sociology* (London: Macmillan).

Hinton, P. R. (1995), *Statistics Explained* (London: Routledge).

Hirst, P., and Thompson, G. (1996), *Globalization in Question: The International Economy and the Possibilities of Governance* (Cambridge: Polity Press).

Hitler, A. (1925), *Mein Kampf* (London: Hurst & Blackett, 1939).

Hobbs, D. (1988), *Doing the Business* (Oxford: Oxford University Press).

——(1994), 'Professional and Organized Crime in Britain', in *The Oxford Handbook of Criminology*, ed. M. Maguire, R. Morgan, and R. Reiner (Oxford: Clarendon Press).

Hobhouse, L. J. (1893), *The Labour Movement* (London: T. Fisher Unwin).

Hobsbawm, E. J. (1969), *Bandits* (Harmondsworth: Penguin, 1972).

——(1977), *The Age of Capital 1848–1875* (London: Sphere Books).

——(1987), *The Age of Empire* (London: Weidenfeld & Nicolson).

Hochschild, A. R. (1983), *The Managed Heart: Commercialization of Human Feeling* (Berkeley and Los Angeles: University of California Press).

Hoggart, R. (1957), *The Uses of Literacy* (London: Chatto & Windus).

Holcombe, L. (1973), *Victorian Ladies at Work* (Newton Abbott: David & Charles).

Holdaway, S. (1982), '"An Inside Job": A Case Study of Covert Research on the Police', *Research Ethics* in Bulmer (1982).

——(1983), *Inside the British Police* (Oxford: Basil Blackwell).

Holdgate, M. (1996), *From Care to Action: Making a Sustainable World* (London: Earthscan).

Hollingshead, J. (1861), *Ragged London in 1861* (London: Dent).

Hollingsworth, M. (1991), *MPS for Hire* (London: Bloomsbury).

Holme, A. (1985), 'Family and Homes in East London', *New Society*, 12 July 1995.

Homan, R., and Bulmer, M. (1982), 'On the Merits of Covert Methods: A Dialogue', in Bulmer (1982).

Hopper, E. (1968), 'A Typology for the Classification of Educational Systems', *Sociology*, 2.

Horney, K. (1937), *The Neurotic Personality of our Time* (New York: W. W. Norton).

——(1946), *Our Inner Conflict* (London: Routledge & Kegan Paul).

Hornsby-Smith, M. P. (1987), *Roman Catholicism in England* (Cambridge: Cambridge University Press).

——(1991), *Roman Catholic Beliefs in England* (Cambridge: Cambridge University Press).

——Lee, R. M., and Turcan, K. A. (1982), 'A Typology of English Catholics', *Sociological Review*, 30.

Howard, E. (1898), *Tomorrow: A Peaceful Path to Real Reform* (London: Sonnenschein).

Huff, D. (1954), *How to Lie with Statistics* (London: Victor Gollancz).

Hulme, D., and Turner, M. M. (1990), *Sociology and Development: Theories, Policies, and Practices* (New York: Harvester Wheatsheaf).

Humphreys, L. (1970), *Tearoom Trade* (London: Duckworth).

Hunt, S. (1995), 'The "Race" and Health Inequalities Debate', *Sociology Review*, 5.

Hurd, G. (1973), *Human Societies: An Introduction to Sociology* (London: Routledge & Kegan Paul).

Hutchinson, J., and Smith, A. D. (1994), *Nationalism* (Oxford: Oxford University Press).

Huws, U. (1994), 'Teleworking in Britain', *Employment Gazette*, 102/2.

Hyman, R. (1972), *Strikes* (London: Fontana Collins).

Ignatieff, M. (1978), *A Just Measure of Pain: The Penitentiary in the Industrial Revolution* (New York: Columbia University Press).

Illich, I. (1973), *Deschooling Society* (Harmondsworth: Penguin).

——(1977), *Limits to Medicine: Medical Nemesis. The Expropriation of Health* (Harmondsworth: Penguin).

Ingham, G. K. (1984), *Capitalism Divided: The City and Industry in British Social Development* (London: Macmillan).

Inglehart, R. (1990), *Culture Shift in Advanced Industrial Society* (Princeton: Princeton University Press).

Jackson, B. (1968), *Working Class Community: Some General Notions Raised by a Series of Studies in Northern England* (London: Routledge & Kegan Paul).

——and Marsden, D. (1962), *Education and the Working Class* (London: Routledge & Kegan Paul).

Jacobs, J. (1961), *The Death and Life of Great American Cities* (London: Jonathan Cape).

James, A. L., Bottomley, A. K., Liebling, A., and Clare, E. (1997), *Privatizing Prisons: Rhetoric and Reality* (London: Sage).

Jameson, F. (1984), 'Postmodernism or the Cultural Logic of Late Capitalism', *New Left Review*, 146.

Jay, M. (1973), *The Dialectical Imagination* (London: Heinemann).

Jeffers, S., Hoggett, P., and Harrison, L. (1996), 'Race, Ethnicity, and Community in Three Localities', *New Community*, 22/1.

Jencks, C. (1972), *Inequality: A Reassessment of the Effects of Family and Schooling in America* (New York: Basic Books).

——Smith, M., Acland, H., Bane, M., Cohen, D., Gintis, H., Heyns, B., and Michelson, S. (1972), *Inequality: A Reassessment of the Effect of Family and Schooling in America* (New York; Basic Books).

Jenkins, P. (1970), *The Battle of Downing Street* (London: Charles Knight).

——(1987), *Mrs. Thatcher's Revolution: The Ending of the Socialist Era* (London: Jonathan Cape).

Jenkins, R. (1992), *Pierre Bourdieu* (London: Routledge).

——(1996), *Social Identities* (London: Routledge).

Jenkins, S. (1996), *Changing Places: Income Mobility and Poverty Dynamics in Britain* (Colchester: British Household Panel Study, University of Essex).

Jensen, A. (1969), 'Environment, Heredity, and Intelligence', *Harvard Educational Review*, 2.

Jewson, N. (1976), 'The Disappearance of the Sick Man from Medical Cosmologies', *Sociology*, 10.

——(1989), 'No Place Like Home: Sociological Perspectives on Housing', in *Social Studies Review*, 4/4: 128–32.

——(1990), 'Inner City Riots', *Social Studies Review*, 5/5.

——(1991), 'The Development of Cities in Capitalist Societies', *Sociology Review*, 1/2.

——(1993), 'Community', in Lawson *et al.* (1993).

——(1994), 'Family Values and Relationships', *Sociology Review*, 3/3.

——and MacGregor, S. (1997) (eds.), *Transforming Cities: Contested Governance and New Spatial Divisions* (London: Routledge).

Johnson, C. (1995), *Japan: Who Governs? The Rise of the Developmental State* (New York: W. W. Norton).

Johnson, H. M. (1961), *Sociology: A Systematic Introduction* (London: Routledge & Kegan Paul).

Johnson, T. (1972), *Professions and Power* (London: Macmillan).

Johnston, L. (1992), *The Rebirth of Private Policing* (London: Routledge).

——(1996), 'Policing Diversity: The Impact of the Public–Private Complex in Policing', in Leishman *et al.* (1996).

Johnston, R. J., Taylor, P. J., and Watts, M. J. (1995), *Geographies of Global Change: Remapping the World in the Late Twentieth Century* (Oxford: Blackwell).

Jones, M., and Jones, M. (1996), 'Techno-Primitives: British Television Science Fiction and The "Grammar Of Race"', *Sociology Review*, 5/3.

Joshi, H. (1989), *The Changing Population of Britain* (Oxford: Basil Blackwell).

Jowell, R., Brook, L., Prior, G., and Taylor, B. (1991), *British Social Attitudes* (Aldershot: Gower).

Joynson, R. B. (1989), *The Burt Affair* (London: Routledge).

Kanter, R. M. (1977), *Men and Women of the Corporation* (New York: Basic Books).

Karabel, J., and Halsey, A. (1977) (eds.), *Power and Ideology in Education* (New York: Oxford University Press).

Karn, V., Kemeny, J., and Williams, P. (1985), *Home Ownership in the Inner City* (Aldershot: Gower).

Kasinitz, P. (1995) (ed.), *Metropolis: Centre and Symbol of our Times* (London: Macmillan).

Keat, R., and Urry, J. (1975), *Social Theory as Science* (London: Routledge & Kegan Paul).

Kerr, C., and Siegel, A. J. (1954), 'The Inter-Industry Propensity to Strike', in A. Kornhauser, R. Dubin, and A. M. Ross (eds.), *Industrial Conflict* (New York: McGraw Hill).

——Dunlop, J. T., Harbison, F., and Myers, C. A. (1960), *Industrialism and Industrial Man* (Cambridge Mass.: Harvard University Press).

Kerr, M. (1958), *The People of Ship Street* (London: Routledge & Kegan Paul).

Kidd, L. (1992), 'Significant Change or Lost Opportunity', in Whiteside *et al.* (1992).

King, A. (1990), *Global Cities: Post-Imperialism and the Internationalization of London* (London: Routledge).

—(1991) (ed.), *Culture, Globalization and the World-System: Contemporary Conditions for the Representation of Identity* (London: Macmillan).

—(1996) (ed.), *Re-Presenting the City: Ethnicity, Capital, and Culture in the Twenty-First Century Metropolis* (Houndmills: Macmillan).

King, D. (1987), 'The State, Capital and Urban Change in Britain', in Smith and Feagin (1987).

King, R. (1978), *All Things Bright and Beautiful: A Sociological Study of an Infants' Classroom* (Chichester: John Wiley).

Kitzinger, J. (1997), 'Media Influence', *Sociology Review*, 6/4.

Klein, J. (1965), *Samples from English Culture* (London: Routledge & Kegan Paul).

Knox, P. L. (1995), 'World Cities in a World-System', in P. L. Knox and P. J. Taylor (eds.), *World Cities in a World-System* (Cambridge: Cambridge University Press).

—and Taylor, P. J. (1995) (eds.), *World Cities in a World-System* (Cambridge: Cambridge University Press).

Kornhauser, W. (1959), *The Politics of Mass Society* (New York: Free Press).

—(1960), *The Politics of Mass Society* (London: Routledge & Kegan Paul).

Korpi, W. (1983), *The Democratic Class Struggle* (London: Routledge & Kegan Paul).

Koss, S. (1984), *The Rise and Fall of the Political Press in Britain*, ii. *The Twentieth Century* (London: Hamish Hamilton).

Kuhn, T. S. (1962), *The Structure of Scientific Revolutions* (Chicago: University of Chicago Press).

Lacey, C. (1970), *Hightown Grammar: The School as a Social System* (Manchester: Manchester University Press).

Lane, C. (1981), *The Rites of Rulers: Ritual in Industrial Society—the Soviet Case* (Cambridge: Cambridge University Press).

Lane, D. (1976), *The Socialist Industrial State* (London: George Allen & Unwin).

—(1996), *The Rise and Fall of State Socialism* (Cambridge: Polity Press).

Lane, T., and Roberts, K. (1971), *Strike at Pilkingtons* (London: Fontana).

Lash, S., and Urry, J. (1987), *The End of Organized Capitalism* (Cambridge: Polity Press).

——(1994), *Economies of Signs and Space* (London: Sage).

Laslett, T. P. R. (1977), *Family Life and Illicit Love in Earlier Generations* (Cambridge: Cambridge University Press).

—and Wall, R. (1972) (eds.), *Household and Family in Past Time* (Cambridge: Cambridge University Press).

Lavalette, M. (1996), 'Thatcher's Working Children: Contemporary Issues of Child Labour', in Pilcher and Wagg (1996).

Lawless, P., and Brown, F. (1986), *Urban Growth and Change in Britain: An Introduction* (London: Harper & Row).

Lawson, A. (1988), *Adultery: An Analysis of Love and Betrayal* (New York: Basic Books).

Lawson, T., Scott, J., Westergaard, H., and Williams, J. (1993) (eds.), *Sociology Reviewed* (London: Collins Educational).

Layton-Henry, Z. (1984), *The Politics of Race in Britain* (London: Allen & Unwin).

Lazarsfeld, P., Berelson, B. R., and Gauzet, H. (1948), *The People's Choice* (New York: Columbia University Press).

Le Corbusier (1947), *City of Tomorrow and its Planning* (London: The Architectural Press).

Le Grand, J. (1982), *The Strategy of Equality* (London: Allen & Unwin).

Lea, J., and Young, J. (1984), *What is to be Done about Law and Order* (Harmondsworth: Penguin).

Lee, J. (1989), 'Social Class and Schooling', in Cole (1989).

Lefort, C. (1986), *The Political Forms of Modern Society* (Cambridge: Polity Press).

Legates, R. T., and Stout, F. (1996) (ed.), *The City Reader* (London: Routledge).

Legge, K. (1995), 'HRM: Rhetoric, Reality, and Hidden Agendas', in Storey (1995b).

Leishman, F., Loveday, B., and Savage, S. P. (1996), *Core Issues in Policing* (London: Longman).

Lemert, E. (1967), *Human Deviance, Social Problems and Social Control* (Englewood Cliffs, NJ: Prentice-Hall).

Levi, M. (1987), *Regulating Fraud: White Collar Crime and the Criminal Process* (London: Tavistock).

Levin, H., and Kelley, C. (1997), 'Can Education do it Alone?', in Halsey *et al.* (1997).

Lévi-Strauss, C. (1962), *Totemism* (London: Merlin Press).

Levitas, R. (1996), 'Fiddling while Britain Burns? The Measurement of Unemployment', in Levitas and Guy (1996).

—and Guy, W. (1996) (eds.), *Interpreting Official Statistics* (London: Routledge).

Levy, M. J. (1966), *Modernization and the Structure of Societies* (Princeton: Princeton University Press).

Lewis, O. (1961), *The Children of Sanchez* (New York: Random House).

—(1966), *La Vida* (New York: Random House).

Leyshon, A. (1995), 'Annihilating Space?: The Speed-Up of Communications', in Allen and Hamnett (1995).

Lincoln, C. E. (1973), *The Black Muslims in America* (Boston: Beacon Press).

Lipman, M., and Phillips, R. (1989), *You Got an Ology* (London: Robson Books).

Lipset, S. M. (1964), 'The Changing Class Structure of Contemporary European Politics', *Daedelus*, 63.

—and Bendix, R. (1959), *Social Mobility in an Industrial Society* (Berkeley and Los Angeles: University of California Press).

—and Rokkan, S. (1967) (eds.), *Party Systems and Voter Alignment* (New York: Free Press).

Lisle-Williams, M. (1984), 'Beyond the Market: The Survival of Family Capitalism in the English Merchant Banks', *British Journal of Sociology*, 35.

Living in Britain: Preliminary Results from the 1995 General Household Survey (1996) (London: HMSO).

Lockwood, D. (1958), *The Blackcoated Worker* (Oxford: Oxford University Press, 1993).

—(1960), 'The New Working Class', *European Journal of Sociology*, 1.

—(1966), 'Sources of Variation in Working Class Images of Society', *Sociological Review*, 14.

Lombroso, C., and Ferrero, W. F. (1895), *The Female Offender* (London: Fisher Unwin).

Lorimer, D. A. (1978), *Colour, Class and the Victorians: English*

Attitudes to the Negro in the Mid-Nineteenth Century (Leicester: Leicester University Press).

Love, J. F. (1986), *McDonalds behind the Arches* (Toronto: Bantam Books).

Loveday, B. (1996), 'Crime at the Core?', in Leishman, Loveday, and Savage (1996).

Lowe, R. (1993), *The Welfare State in Britain since 1945* (London: Macmillan).

Lukács, G. (1923), *History and Class Consciousness* (London: Merlin Press, 1971).

Lukes, S. (1967), 'Alienation and Anomie'. in P. Laslett and W. G. Runciman (eds.), *Politics, Philosophy and Society* (Oxford: Basil Blackwell).

——(1973), *Émile Durkheim: His Life and Work* (Harmondsworth: Allen Lane The Penguin Press).

——(1974), *Power: A Radical View* (London: Macmillan).

Lupton, D. (1996), *Food, the Body and the Self* (London: Sage).

Lutz, W. (1996) (ed.), *The Future Population of the World: What can we Assume Today?* (rev. edn., London: Earthscan).

Lynd, R. S., and Lynd, H. M. (1929), *Middletown* (New York: Harcourt Brace).

————(1937), *Middletown in Transition* (New York: Harcourt Brace).

Lyotard, J.-F. (1979), *The Postmodern Condition* (Manchester: Manchester University Press, 1984).

Mac An Ghaill, M. (1996), 'What About the Boys?: Schooling, Class and Crisis Masculinity', *Sociological Review*, 44/3: 381–97.

Macfarlane, A. (1987), *The Culture of Capitalism* (Oxford: Basil Blackwell).

McCarthy, T. (1978), *The Critical Theory of Jürgen Habermas* (London: Hutchinson).

Macgregor, S., and Pimlott, B. (1991) (ed.), *Tackling the Inner Cities: The 1980s Reviewed, Prospects for the 1990s* (Oxford: Clarendon Press).

McIntosh, M. (1968), 'The Homosexual Role', *Social Problems*, 16.

——(1975), *The Organisation of Crime* (London: Macmillan).

Mack, Joanna, and Lansley, S. (1985), *Poor Britain* (London: George Allen & Unwin).

Mack, John (1964), 'Full Time Miscreants, Delinquent Neighbourhoods and Criminal Networks', *British Journal of Sociology*, 15.

McKeganey, N., and Barnard, M. (1996), *Sex Work on the Streets: Prostitutes and their Clients* (Buckingham: Open University Press).

McKenzie, R. T., and Silver, A. (1968), *Angels in Marble* (London: Heinemann).

McKeown, T. (1979), *The Role of Medicine* (Oxford: Blackwell).

McKibbin, R. (1990), *The Ideologies of Class: Social Relations in Britain: 1880–1950* (Oxford: Oxford University Press).

Mackintosh, N. J. (1995) (ed.), *Cyril Burt: Fraud or Framed* (Oxford: Oxford University Press).

McLellan, D. (1971), *The Thought of Karl Marx* (London: Macmillan).

——(1973), *Karl Marx: His Life and Thought* (London: Macmillan).

McLennan, G. (1989), *Marxism, Pluralism and Beyond* (Cambridge: Polity Press).

McPherson, A., and Willms, J. (1989), 'Comprehensive Schooling is Better and Fairer', in Cosin *et al.* (1989).

McRobbie, A. (1991), *Feminism and Youth Culture: From Jackie to Just Seventeen* (London: Macmillan).

——and McCabe, T. (1981), *Feminism for Girls: An Adventure Story* (London: Routledge & Kegan Paul).

Maguire, Malcolm (1992), 'Training and Enterprise Councils', in Whiteside *et al.* (1992).

Maguire, Michael (1994), 'Crime Statistics, Patterns, and Trends: Changing Perceptions and their Implications', in *The Oxford Handbook of Criminology*, ed. M. Maguire, R. Morgan, and R. Reiner (Oxford: Oxford University Press, 1994).

——and Bennett, T. (1982), *Burglary in a Dwelling: The Offence, the Offender and the Victim* (London: Macmillan).

Malcolmson, R. W. (1988), 'Ways of Getting a Living in Eighteenth-Century England', in R. Pahl (1988).

Malik, K. (1996), *The Meaning of Race: Race, History, and Culture in Western Society* (London: Macmillan).

Malinowski, B. (1922), *Argonauts of the Western Pacific* (London: George Routledge).

——(1929), *The Sexual Life of Savages* (London: George Routledge).

——(1935), *Coral Gardens and their Magic* (London: Allen & Unwin).

Maltby, R., and Craven I. (1995), *Hollywood Cinema: An Introduction* (Oxford: Blackwell).

Malthus, T. R. (1798), *An Essay on the Principle of Population* (Harmondsworth: Penguin Books, 1970).

Mandel, E. (1967), *The Formation of the Economic Thought of Karl Marx* (London: New Left Books, 1971).

Mann, M. (1973), *Consciousness and Action among the Western Working Class* (London: Macmillan).

——(1986), *The Sources of Social Power* (Cambridge: Cambridge University Press).

Mannheim, H. (1940), *Social Aspects of Crime in England between the Wars* (London: Allen & Unwin).

Manza, J., Hout, M., and Brooks, C. (1995), 'Class Voting in Capitalist Democracies since World War II', *Annual Review of Sociology*, 21.

Marcuse, H. (1956), *Eros and Civilization* (London: Routledge & Kegan Paul).

——(1964), *One Dimensional Man* (London: Routledge & Kegan Paul).

Mars, G. (1982), *Cheats at Work* (London: Allen & Unwin).

Marsh, C. (1986), 'Social Class and Occupation', in R. G. Burgess (ed.) *Key Variables in Social Investigation* (London: Routledge & Kegan Paul).

Marshall, G. (1982), *In Search of the Spirit of Capitalism* (London: Hutchinson).

Marshall, T. H. (1949), *Citizenship and Social Class* (London: Pluto Press, 1992).

Martin, D. A. (1962), 'The Denomination', *British Journal of Sociology*, 13.

——(1967), *A Sociology of English Religion* (London: Heinemann Educational Books).

Marx, K. (1844), *Economic and Philosophical Manuscripts* (London: Lawrence & Wishart, 1959).

——(1845–6), *The German Ideology*, extract in *Karl Marx: Selected*

Writings in Sociology and Social Philosophy, ed. T. B. Bottomore, and M. Rubel (Harmondsworth: Penguin, 1963).

Marx, K. (1858), *Grundrisse* (Harmondsworth: Penguin, 1973).

——(1864–5), *Capital*, iii (Harmondsworth: Penguin, 1981).

——(1867), *Capital*, i (Harmondsworth: Penguin, 1976).

——and Engels, F. (1848), *The Communist Manifesto* (Harmondsworth: Penguin, 1967).

Mason, D. J. (1995), *Race and Ethnicity in Modern Britain* (Oxford: Oxford University Press).

Massey, D. (1994), *Space, Place, and Gender* (Cambridge: Polity).

——and Jess, P. (1995), *A Place in the World?: Places, Cultures, and Globalization* (Oxford: Oxford University Press).

Matthews, M. (1978), *Privilege in the Soviet Union* (London: George Allen & Unwin).

Matza, D. (1964), *Delinquency and Drift* (New York: John Wiley & Sons).

Mauss, M. (1925), *The Gift* (London: Routledge & Kegan Paul, 1966).

May, T. (1997), *Social Research: Issues, Methods and Process* (Buckingham: Open University Press).

Mayer, K.-U. (1963), 'The Changing Shape of the American Class Structure'. *Social Research*, 30.

Mayhew, H. (1861a), *London Labour and the London Poor* (London: Frank Cass).

——(1861b), *London's Underworld*, ed. P. Quennell (London: Spring Books, 1950).

Mead, G. (1927), *Mind, Self and Society* (Chicago: University of Chicago Press, 1934).

Mead, M. (1928), *Coming of Age in Samoa: A Study of Adolescence and Sex in Primitive Societies* (Harmondsworth: Penguin, 1943).

——(1930), *Growing Up in New Guinea: A Study of Adolescence and Sex in Primitive Societies* (Harmondsworth: Penguin, 1942).

——(1935), *Sex and Temperament in Three Primitive Societies* (London: George Routledge).

——(1950), *Male and Female* (Harmondsworth: Penguin, 1962).

——(1953), 'National Character', in A. L. Kroeber (ed.), *Anthropology Today* (Chicago: University of Chicago Press, 1953).

Meegan, R. (1989), 'Paradise Postponed: The Growth and Decline of Merseyside's Outer Estates', in Cooke (1989).

Mennell, S., Murcott, A., and von Otter, A. H. (1992), *The Sociology of Food: Eating, Diet and Culture* (London: Sage).

Merton, R. K. (1936), 'The Unanticipated Consequences of Purposive Social Action', *American Sociological Review*, 1.

——(1938a), *Science, Technology and Society in Seventeenth Century England* (New York: Harper & Row, 1970).

——(1938b), 'Social Structure and Anomie', *American Sociological Review*, 3.

——(1940), 'Bureaucratic Structure and Personality', *Social Forces*, 18.

——(1949), 'Manifest and Latent Function', in R. K. Merton, *Social Theory and Social Structure* (New York: Harper & Row, 1949).

——(1957), 'The Role Set: Problems in Sociological Theory', *British Journal of Sociology*, 8.

Michels, R. (1912), *Political Parties* (London: Collins Books, 1962).

Middleton, C. (1979), 'The Sexual Division of Labour in Feudal England', *New Left Review*, 113–14.

Miles, R. (1989), *Racism* (London: Routledge).

Miliband, R. (1969), *The State in Capitalist Society* (London: Weidenfeld & Nicolson).

——(1982), *Capitalist Democracy in Britain* (Oxford: Oxford University Press).

——(1989), *Divided Societies* (Oxford: Oxford University Press).

Millett, K. (1970), *Sexual Politics* (New York: Doubleday).

Mills, C. W. (1951), *White Collar* (New York: Oxford University Press).

——(1956), *The Power Elite* (New York: Oxford University Press).

——(1959), *The Sociological Imagination* (New York: Oxford University Press).

Millward, N. (1994), *The New Industrial Relations?* (London: Policy Studies Institute).

——and Stevens, M. (1986), *British Workplace Industrial Relations* (Aldershot: Gower).

——Smart, D., and Hawes, W. R. (1992), *Workplace Industrial Relations in Transition: The ED/ESRC/PSI/ACAS Surveys* (Aldershot: Dartmouth).

Milner, M. (1994), *Status and the Sacred: A General Theory of Status Relations and an Analysis of Indian Culture* (Cambridge: Cambridge University Press).

Mirza, H. (1992), *Young, Female, and Black* (London: Routledge).

Mitter, S. (1986), *Common Fate, Common Bond: Women in the Global Economy* (London: Pluto Press).

Montesquieu, Baron de Charles de Secondat (1748), *The Spirit of the Laws* (Cambridge: Cambridge University Press, 1989).

Mooney, J. (1993), *Researching Domestic Violence: The North London Domestic Violence Survey* (London: Middlesex University, Centre for Criminology).

Moore, B. (1968), *The Social Origins of Dictatorship and Democracy* (London: Allen Lane).

Morgan, D. H. J. (1996), *Family Connections: An Introduction to Family Studies* (Cambridge: Polity).

Morris, L. (1994), *Dangerous Classes* (London: Routledge).

——(1995), *Social Divisions* (London: UCL Press).

Morris, R. J. (1979), *Class and Class Consciousness in the Industrial Revolution* (London: Macmillan).

——(1990), *Class, Sect and Party: The Making of the British Middle Class, Leeds 1820–1850* (Manchester: Manchester University Press).

Morris, T. (1957), *The Criminal Area* (London: Routledge & Kegan Paul).

Mortimore, P. (1997), 'Can Effective Schools Compensate for Society', in Halsey *et al.* (1997).

Moser, C., and Kalton, G. (1979), *Survey Methods in Social Investigation* (London: Heinemann Educational Books).

Moynihan, D. P. (1965), *The Negro Family* (Washington DC: Office of Policy, Planning and Research, US Department of Labor).

Mumford, L. (1961), *The City in History: Its Origins, its Transformation, and its Projects* (London: Secker & Warburg).

Murcott, A. (1982), 'On the Social Significance of the "Cooked Dinner" in South Wales', *Social Science Information*, 21.

Murdoch, J., and Marsden, T. (1994), *Reconstituting Rurality: Class, Community, and Power in the Development Process* (London: UCL Press).

Murdock, G. (1992), 'Embedded Persuasions: The Fall and Rise of Integrated Advertising', in Strinati and Wagg (1992).

—— and Golding, P. (1977), 'Capitalism, Communication, and Class Relations', in Curran, Gurevitch, and Woollacott (1977).

Murdock, G. P. (1949), *Social Structure* (New York: Macmillan).

Murgatroyd, L., and Neuburger, H. (1997), 'A Household Satellite Account for the UK', *Economic Trends*, 527.

Murray, C. (1984), *Losing Ground: American Social Policy 1950–1980* (New York: Basic Books).

—— (1990), *The Making of the British Underclass* (London: Institute of Economic Affairs).

—— (1994), *Underclass: The Crisis Deepens* (London: Institute of Economic Affairs).

Myles, J. (1996), 'When Markets Fail: Social Welfare in Canada and the United States', in Esping-Andersen (1996).

Myrdal, G. (1944), *An American Dilemma* (New York: Harper).

National Committee of Inquiry into Higher Education (1997), *Higher Education in the Learning Society* (London: HMSO).

Naylor, K. (1994), 'Part-Time Working in Great Britain—An Historical Analysis', *Employment Gazette*, 102/12.

Neale, B., and Smart, C. (1997), 'Experiments with Parenthood', *Sociology*, 31/2.

Negrine, R. (1994), *Politics and the Mass Media in Britain* (2nd edn., London, Routledge).

Nelken, D. (1994), 'White Collar Crime', in *The Oxford Handbook of Criminology* (ed.), M. Maguire, R. Morgan, and R. Reiner (Oxford: Oxford University Press).

Nelson, G. K. (1969), *Spiritualism and Society* (London: Routledge & Kegan Paul).

Nettleton, S. (1995), *The Sociology of Health and Illness* (Cambridge: Polity).

Newburn, T., and Hagell, A. (1995), 'Violence on Screen', *Sociology Review*, 4/3.

Newby, H. (1977), *The Deferential Worker: A Study of Farm Workers in East Anglia* (London: Allen Lane).

Nichols, W. A. T. (1996), 'Social Class: Official, Sociological and Marxist', in R. Levitas and W. Guy (eds.), *Interpreting Official Statistics* (London: Routledge).

—— and Benyon, H. (1977), *Living with Capitalism* (London: Routledge & Kegan Paul).

Niebuhr, H. R. (1929), *The Social Sources of Denominationalism* (New York: Holt).

Nissel, M. (1987), *People Count: A History of the General Register Office* (London: HMSO).

Noon, M., and Blyton, P. (1997), *The Realities of Work* (London: Macmillan Business).

Oakley, A. (1972), *Sex, Gender and Society* (London: Temple Smith).

—— (1974), *The Sociology of Housework* (Oxford: Martin Robertson).

—— (1984), *The Captured Womb: A History of the Medical Care of Pregnant Women* (Oxford: Basil Blackwell).

—— Brannen, J., and Dodd, K. (1992), 'Young People, Gender and Smoking in the United Kingdom', *Health Precautions International*, 7.

O'Brien, M., and Jones, D. (1996), 'Revisiting Family and Kinship', *Sociology Review*, 5/3.

O'Connell Davidson J. (1993), *Privatization and Employment Relations* (London: Mansell).

—— (1994), 'Metamorphosis? Privatization and the Restructuring of Management and Labour', in P. M. Jackson and C. Price (eds.), *Privatization and Regulation* (London: Longman).

—— (1998), *Prostitution, Power, and Freedom* (Cambridge: Polity).

—— and Layder, D. (1994), *Methods, Sex and Madness* (London: Routledge).

O'Connor, J. (1973), *The Fiscal Crisis of the State* (London: St James Press).

O'Day, R. (1994), *The Family and Family Relationships 1500–1900: England, France and the United States of America* (Basingstoke: Macmillan).

Ohmae, K. (1990), *The Borderless World* (London: Collins).

Oppenheim, A. N. (1966), *Questionnaire Design and Attitude Measurement* (London: Heinemann Educational Books).

Oppenheim, C. (1993), *Poverty: The Facts* (rev. edn., London: Child Poverty Action Group).

Orbach, S. (1986), *Hunger Strike* (New York: W. W. Norton).

Packard, V. (1963), *The Hidden Persuaders* (Harmondsworth: Penguin).

Pahl, J. (1989), *Money and Marriage* (London: Macmillan).

—— (1993), 'Money, Marriage, and Ideology: Holding the Purse Strings?', *Sociology Review*, 3/1.

Pahl, R. (1965), 'Class and Community in English Commuter Villages', *Sociologia Ruralis*, 5.

—— (1984), *Divisions of Labour* (Oxford: Basil Blackwell).

—— (1995), *After Success* (Cambridge: Polity).

—— (1988) (ed.), *On Work: Historical, Theoretical and Comparative Approaches* (Oxford: Basil Blackwell).

Palmer, R. L. (1980), *Anorexia Nervosa* (Harmondsworth: Penguin).

Park, R. E., Burgess, E. W., and McKenzie, R. D. (1925), *The City* (Chicago: University of Chicago Press).

Parker, H., and Measham, F. (1994), 'Pick 'n' Mix: Changing Patterns of Illicit Drug Use amongst 1990s Adolescents', *Drugs*, 1.

Parker, S. (1976), 'Work and Leisure', in Butterworth and Weir (1976).

Parkin, F. (1967), 'Working Class Conservatives: A Theory of Political Deviance', *British Journal of Sociology*, 18.

—— (1971), *Class Inequality and Political Order* (London: McGibbon & Kee).

—— (1982), *Max Weber* (Chichester: Ellis Horwood).

Parsons, T. (1937), *The Structure of Social Action* (New York: McGraw-Hill).

—— (1940), 'An Analytical Approach to the Theory of Social Stratification', in Parsons (1954).

—— (1949), 'The Social Structure of the Family', in R. Anshen (ed.), *The Family, its Functions and Destiny* (New York: Harper).

—— (1951), *The Social System* (New York: Free Press).

—— (1953), 'A Revised Analytical Approach to the Theory of Social Stratification', in Parsons (1954).

—— (1954), *Essays in Sociological Theory* (rev. edn., New York: Free Press).

—— (1959), 'The School Class as a Social System: Some of its Functions in American Society', *Harvard Educational Review*, 29/4: 297–318; also in Parsons (1964).

Parsons, T. (1964), *Social Structure and Personality* (New York: Free Press of Glencoe).

——(1966), *Societies: Evolutionary and Comparative Perspectives* (Englewood Cliffs, NJ: Prentice-Hall).

——(1970), 'Equality and Inequality in Modern Society, or Social Stratification Revisited', *Sociological Inquiry*, 40.

——(1971), *The System of Modern Societies* (Englewood Cliffs, NJ: Prentice-Hall).

——and Smelser, N. J. (1956), *Economy and Society* (New York: Free Press).

——and Bales, R. F. (1956), *Family, Socialization and Interaction Process* (London: Routledge & Kegan Paul).

Parton, N. (1996), 'The New Politics of Child Protection', in Pilcher and Wagg (1996).

Pateman, C. (1989) (ed.), *The Disorder of Women* (Cambridge: Polity).

Paterson, O. (1967), *The Sociology of Slavery* (London: MacGibbon & Kee).

——(1982), 'Persistence, Continuity, and Change in the Jamaican Working-Class Family', *Journal of Family History*, 7.

——(1982), *Slavery and Social Death* (Cambridge, Mass.: Harvard University Press).

Payne, G. (1987a), *Employment and Opportunity* (London: Macmillan).

——(1987b), *Mobility and Change in Modern Society* (London: Macmillan).

Pearson, R., and Mitter, S. (1993), 'Employment and Working Conditions of Low-Skilled Information-Processing Workers in Less Developed Countries', *International Labour Review*, 132/1.

Pember-Reeves, M. (1913), *Round About a Pound a Week* (London: Virago).

Percy-Smith, J., and Hillyard, P. (1985), 'Miners in the Arms of the Law: A Statistical Analysis', *Journal of Law and Society*, 12.

Perkin, H. (1989), *The Rise of Professional Society* (London: Routledge).

Phillips, A., and Moss, P. (1988), *Who Cares for Europe's Children* (Brussels: European Commission).

Philo, G. (1990), *Seeing and Believing: The Influence of Television* (London: Routledge).

Phizacklea, A. (1990), *Unpacking the Fashion Industry: Gender, Racism, and Class in Production* (London: Routledge).

——(1995), 'Women and Migration', *Sociology Review*, 5.

——and Wolkowitz, C. (1995), *Homeworking Women: Gender, Racism and Class at Work* (London: Sage).

Pickering, W. F. S. (1984), *Durkheim on Religion* (London: Routledge & Kegan Paul).

Pierson, C. (1991), *Beyond the Welfare State* (Cambridge: Polity).

Pilcher, J. L. (1995), *Age and Generation in Modern Britain* (Oxford: Oxford University Press).

——and Wagg, S. (1996) (eds.), *Thatcher's Children: Politics, Childhood, and Society in the 1980s and the 1990s* (London: Falmer).

Pilger, J. (1997), *Breaking the Mirror: The Murdoch Effect* (Birmingham: Central Broadcasting).

Pizzey, E. (1974), *Scream Quietly or the Neighbours Will Hear* (Harmondsworth: Penguin).

Plummer, K. (1975), *Sexual Stigma: An Interactionist Account* (London: Routledge).

——(1983), *Documents of Life* (London: George Allen & Unwin).

——(1995), *Telling Sexual Stories* (London: Routledge).

Pollak, O. (1950), *The Criminality of Women* (New York: A. S. Barnes, 1961).

Pollard, S. (1965), *The Genesis of Modern Management* (Harmondsworth: Penguin).

Pollert, A. (1988), 'The "Flexible Firm": Fixation or Fact', *Work, Employment, and Society*, 2/3.

——(1996), 'Gender and Class Revisited; Or the Poverty of 'Patriarchy', *Sociology*, 30/4.

——(1991) (ed.), *Farewell to Flexibility?* (Oxford: Blackwell).

Pollock, L. (1983), *Forgotten Children: Parent–Child Relations from 1500 to 1900* (Cambridge: Cambridge University Press).

Polsby, N. (1969), *Hustlers, Beats and Others* (Harmondsworth: Penguin).

Popper, K. (1959), *The Logic of Scientific Discovery* (London: Routledge & Kegan Paul).

Potts, L. (1990), *The World Labour Market: A History of Migration* (London: Zed Books).

Poulantzas, N. (1975), *Classes in Contemporary Capitalism* (London: New Left Books).

Pratt, J., and Fearnley, R. (1996), 'Stratford City Challenge', in Butler and Rustin (1996).

Pringle, R. (1989), *Secretaries Talk: Sexuality, Power, and Work* (London: Verso).

Pryce, K. (1986), *Endless Pressure: A Study of West Indian Life Styles in Bristol* (2nd edn., Bristol: Bristol Classics).

Przeworski, A., and Sprague, J. (1986), *Paper Stones: A History of Electoral Socialism* (Chicago: Chicago University Press).

Pusey, M. (1987), *Jürgen Habermas* (Chichester: Ellis Horwood).

Quigley, D. (1993), *The Interpretation of Caste* (Oxford: Oxford University Press).

Radcliffe-Brown, A. R. (1922), *The Andaman Islanders* (Cambridge: Cambridge University Press).

——(1930), 'The Social Organisation of the Australian Tribes', *Oceana*, 1.

——(1952), *Structure and Function in Primitive Society* (London: Cohen & West).

Ransome, P. (1992), *Antonio Gramsci: A New Introduction* (New York: Harvester Wheatsheaf).

Ratcliffe, P. (1981), *Racism and Reaction* (London: Routledge).

Rattansi, A. (1988), '"Race", Education and British Society', in Dale *et al.* (1988).

Rees, T. (1992), *Women and the Labour Market* (London: Routledge).

Reid, A. J. (1992), *Social Classes and Social Relations in Britain, 1850–1914* (London: Macmillan).

Reid, I. (1977), *Social Class Differences in Britain* (London: Open Books).

——(1996), 'Education and Inequality', *Sociology Review*, 6/2.

Reiner, R. (1992), *The Politics of the Police* (Brighton: Harvester Wheatsheaf).

Revell, K. R. S. (1965), 'Changes in the Social Distribution of Property', *International Journal of Economic History*, 1.

Rex, J. A. (1961), *Key Problems of Sociological Theory* (London: Routledge & Kegan Paul).

——and Moore, R. (1967), *Race, Community, and Conflict: A Study of Sparkbrook* (London: Oxford University Press).

——and Tomlinson, S. (1979), *Colonial Immigrants in a British City: A Class Analysis* (London: Routledge & Kegan Paul).

Rich, A. (1980), 'Organising Heterosexuality and Lesbian Existence', *Signs*, 5.

Richards, M. P. M., and Elliott, B. J. (1991), 'Sex and Marriage in the 1960s and 1970s', in D. Clark (ed.), *Marriage, Domestic Life, and Social Change: Writings for Jacqueline Burgoyne (1944–88)* (London: Routledge).

Riessman, D. (1961), *The Lonely Crowd* (New Haven, Conn.: Yale University Press).

Ritzer, G. (1996), *The McDonaldization of Society: An Investigation into the Changing Character of Social Life* (rev. edn., Thousand Oaks, Calif.: Pine Forge Press).

Roberts, E. (1984), *A Woman's Place: An Oral History of Working-Class Women, 1890–1940* (Oxford: Basil Blackwell).

Roberts, H. (1985), *The Patient Patients: Women and their Doctors* (London: Pandora Press).

——(1990), *Women's Health Counts* (London: Routledge).

Roberts, K., Clark, F. G., Clark, S. C., and Semeonoff, E. (1977), *The Fragmentary Class Structure* (London: Heinemann).

——Noble, M., and Duggan, J. (1984), 'Youth Unemployment: An Old Problem or a New Life-Style' in K. Thompson (1984).

Roberts, R. (1973), *The Classic Slum: Salford in the First Quarter of the Century* (Harmondsworth: Penguin).

Robertson R. (1992), *Globalization: Social Theory and Global Culture* (London: Sage).

Robins, K. (1996), 'What is Globalization?', *Sociology Review*, 6/3.

Robinson, M., and Smith, D. (1993), *Step By Step: Focus on Stepfamilies* (Brighton: Harvester Wheatsheaf).

Robson, C. (1993), *Real World Research* (Oxford: Basil Blackwell).

Rodger, J. J. (1996), *Family Life and Social Control* (Houndmills: Macmillan).

Roethlisberger, F. J., and Dickson, W. J. (1939), *Management and the Worker* (Cambridge, Mass.: Harvard University Press).

Room, G. (1990), '*New Poverty' in the European Community* (London: Macmillan).

Rose, D., and Sullivan, O. (1993), *Introductory Data Analysis for Social Scientists* (2nd edn., Milton Keynes: Open University Press).

Rose, M. (1975), *Industrial Behaviour: Theoretical Developments since Taylor* (London: Allen Lane).

Rosen, H. (1974), *Language and Class* (3rd. edn., Bristol: Falling Wall Press).

Roseneil, S. (1995), *Disarming Patriarchy: Feminism and Political Action at Greenham* (Buckingham: Open University Press).

Rosenham, D. L. (1973), 'On Being Sane in an Insane Place', *Science*, 179.

Ross, A. M., and Hartman, P. T. (1960), *Changing Patterns of Industrial Conflict* (New York: Wiley).

Routh, G. (1987), *Occupations of the People of Great Britain, 1801–1981* (London: Macmillan).

Rowntree, S. (1901), *Poverty: A Study of Town Life* (London: Longmans Green).

——(1941), *Poverty and Progress* (London: Longmans Green).

——and Lavers, G. R. (1951), *Poverty and the Welfare State* (London: Longmans Green).

Royle, E. (1987), *Modern Britain: A Social History 1750–1985* (London: Edward Arnold).

Rubin, G. (1975), 'The Traffic in Women: Notes on the "Political Economy" of Sex', in R. Reiter (ed.), *Toward an Anthropology of Women* (New York: Monthly Review Press).

Rubinstein, W. D. (1981), *Men of Property* (London: Croom Helm).

——(1986), *Wealth and Inequality in Britain* (London: Faber & Faber).

——(1993), *Capitalism, Culture, and Decline in Britain, 1750–1990* (London: Routledge).

Ruggiero, V., and South, N. (1995), *Eurodrugs* (London: UCL Press).

Runciman, W. G. (1966), *Relative Deprivation and Social Justice* (London: Routledge & Kegan Paul).

——(1993), 'Has British Capitalism Changed since the First World War?', *British Journal of Sociology*, 44/1.

——(1995), 'New Times or Old Times? A Reply to Fulcher', *British Journal of Sociology*, 46/4.

——(1997), 'Rejoinder to Fulcher', *British Journal of Sociology*, 48/3.

Russell, D. E. H. (1986), *The Secret Trauma: Incest in the Lives of Girls and Women* (New York: Basic Books).

——(1990), *Rape in Marriage* (2nd edn., Bloomington: Indiana University Press).

Rutter, M. (1972), *Maternal Deprivation Reassessed* (Harmondsworth: Penguin).

——Maughan, B., Mortimore, P., Ouston, J., with Smith, A. (1979), *Fifteen Thousand Hours: Secondary Schools and their Effects on Children* (London: Open Books).

Sacks, H. (1965–72), *Lectures on Conversation* (Oxford: Basil Blackwell, 1992).

Salaman, G., and Thompson, K. (1973), *People and Organizations* (London: Longman).

Sarlvik, B., and Crewe, I. (1983), *Decade of Dealignment* (Cambridge: Cambridge University Press).

Sassen, S. (1991), *The Global City: New York, London, Tokyo* (Princeton NJ: Princeton University Press).

——(1996), 'Rebuilding the Global City', in A. King (1996).

Saunders, P. (1986), *Social Theory and the Urban Question* (London: Hutchinson).

——(1990), *A Nation of Home Owners* (London: Unwin Hyman).

Savage, M. (1992), 'Women's Expertise, Men's Authority: Gendered Organization and the Contemporary Middle Classes', in Savage and Witz (1992).

——and Miles, A. (1994), *The Remaking of the British Working Class, 1840–1940* (London: Routledge).

——and Warde, A. (1993), *Urban Sociology, Capitalism and Modernity* (London: Macmillan).

——and Witz, A. (1992) (eds.), *Gender and Bureaucracy* (Oxford: Blackwell).

——Barlow, J., Dickens, P., and Fielding, T. (1992), *Property, Bureaucracy and Culture: Middle Class Formation in Contemporary Britain* (London: Routledge).

Scannell, P., and Cardiff, D. (1991), *A Social History of Broadcasting*, i. *1922–1939 Serving the Nation* (Oxford: Basil Blackwell).

Scase, D., and Goffee, L. (1982), *The Entrepreneurial Middle Class* (London: Croom Helm).

Scheff, T. J. (1966), *Becoming Mentally Ill: A Sociological Theory* (New York: Aldine, 1984).

Schur, E. (1971), *Labelling Deviant Behaviour: Its Sociological Implications* (New York: Harper & Row).

Schuurman, F. J. (1993) (ed.), *Beyond the Impasse: New Directions in Development Theory* (London: Zed Books).

Schwartz, M. S., and Schwartz, C. G. (1955), 'Problems in Participant Observation', *American Journal of Sociology*, 60.

Scott, A. (1990), *Ideology and the New Social Movements* (London: Unwin Hyman).

Scott, J. (1990), *A Matter of Record: Documentary Sources in Social Research* (Cambridge: Polity Press).

——(1991), *Who Rules Britain?* (Cambridge: Polity Press).

——(1994), *Poverty and Wealth: Citizenship, Deprivation and Privilege* (Harlow: Longman).

——(1995), *Sociological Theory: Contemporary Debates* (Cheltenham: Edward Elgar).

——(1996), *Stratification and Power: Structures of Class, Status and Command* (Cambridge: Polity Press).

——(1997), *Corporate Business and Capitalist Classes* (Oxford: Oxford University Press).

Scull, A. (1979), *Museums of Madness* (London: Allen Lane).

——(1984), *Decarceration: Community Treatment and the Deviant—A Radical View* (2nd edn., Cambridge: Polity).

Seeman, M. (1959), 'On the Meaning of Alienation', *American Sociological Review*, 24.

Segalen, M. (1983), *Love and Power in the Peasant Family* (Oxford: Basil Blackwell).

Sennett, R. (1973), *The Uses of Disorder* (Harmondsworth: Penguin).

Shapiro, L. (1972), *Totalitarianism* (New York: Praeger).

Sharpe, S. (1976), *Just Like a Girl: How Girls Learn to be Women* (Harmondsworth: Penguin).

Shaw, C. (1930), *The Jack Roller: A Delinquent Boy's Own Story* (Chicago: University of Chicago Press).

Shilling, C. (1989), *Schooling for Work in Capitalist Britain* (London: Falmer).

——(1993), *The Body in Social Theory* (London: Sage).

Shils, E., and Young, M. (1953), 'The Meaning of the Coronation', *British Journal of Sociology*, 1.

Shorter, E. (1976), *The Making of the Modern Family* (London: Collins).

Sim, A. (1994), 'Did You See "Witness": The Myth of Amish Separatism', *Sociology Review*, 3.

Simmel, G. (1900), *The Philosophy of Money* (London: Routledge & Kegan Paul, 1978).

——(1908), *Soziologie: Untersuchungen über die Formen der Vergesselshaftung* (Berlin: Düncker und Humblot, 1968).

Simon, B. (1991), *Education and the Social Order 1940–1990* (London: Lawrence & Wishart).

Sivanandan, A. (1982), *A Different Hunger* (London: Pluto Press).

Skeggs, B. (1997), *Formations of Class and Gender* (London: Sage).

Skellington, R. (1992), *'Race' in Britain Today* (London: Sage).

Sklair, L. (1993), 'Competing Models of Globalization', *Sociology Review*, 3/2.

——(1994) (ed.), *Capitalism and Development* (London: Routledge).

Skocpol, T. (1985), 'Bringing the State Back In: Strategies of Analysis in Current Research', in Evans *et al.* (1985).

Sly, F. (1994), 'Mothers in the Labour Market', *Employment Gazette*, 102/11.

Smart, C. (1977), *Women, Crime and Criminology* (London: Routledge & Kegan Paul).

Smith, A. (1986), *The Ethnic Origins of Nations* (Oxford: Basil Blackwell).

——(1991), *National Identity* (Harmondsworth: Penguin).

Smith, A. D. (1994), 'The Origins of Nations', in Hutchinson and Smith (1994).

——(1976) (ed.), *Nationalist Movements* (London: Macmillan).

Smith, D., and Tomlinson, S. (1989), *The School Effect: A Study of Multi-Racial Comprehensives* (London: Policy Studies Institute).

Smith, D. E. (1987), *The Everyday World as Problematic* (Milton Keynes: Open University Press).

Smith, M. P., and Feagin, J. M. (1987) (eds.), *The Capitalist City: Global Restructuring and Community Politics* (Oxford: Basil Blackwell).

Smithers, A. (1994), 'A Quiet Revolution in Post-16 Education', *Independent*, 29 September.

Social Focus on Ethnic Minorities (1996), ed. J. Church and C. Summerfield, Office for National Statistics (London: HMSO).

Social Trends, 1992 (1992), ed. J. Church (London: HMSO).

Social Trends, 1995 (1995), ed. J. Church (London: HMSO).

Social Trends, 1996 (1996), ed. J. Church (London: HMSO).

Social Trends, 1997 (1997), ed. J. Church (London: HMSO).

Solomos, J. (1993), *Race and Racism in Britain* (London: Macmillan).

——and Back, L. (1996), *Racism and Society* (Basingstoke: Macmillan).

Sombart, W. (1906), *Why is there no Socialism in the United States*, (London: Macmillan, 1976).

——(1908), *Socialism and the Social Movement* (London: J. M. Dent, 1909).

Spearman, C. (1904), 'General Intelligence: Objectively Determined and Measured', *American Journal of Psychology*, 15.

Spender, D. (1982), *Invisible Women: The Schooling Scandal* (London: Writers and Readers Publishing Co-Operative).

Spybey, T. (1992), *Social Change, Development and Dependency: Modernity, Colonialism, and the Development of the West* (Cambridge: Polity).

——(1996), *Globalization and World Society* (Cambridge: Polity).

Sreberny-Mohammadi, A. (1996), 'The Global and Local in International Communications', in Curran and Gurevitch (1996).

Stacey, M. (1960), *Tradition and Change: A Study of Banbury* (Oxford: Oxford University Press).

——(1969), 'The Myth of Community Studies', *British Journal of Sociology*, 20/2.

——(1987), 'Health, Illness and Medicine', in P. Worsley (ed.), *The New Introductory Sociology* (Harmondsworth: Penguin, 1987).

—Batstone, E., Bell, C., and Murcott, A. (1975), *Power, Persistence and Change* (London: Routledge & Kegan Paul).

Stanley, L. (1995), *Sex Surveyed, 1949–1994* (London: Taylor & Francis).

—and Wise, S. (1983), *Breaking Out* (London: Routledge).

Stanworth, M. (1983), *Gender and Schooling: A Study of Sexual Divisions in the Classroom* (London: Hutchinson).

—(1987), 'Reproductive Technologies and the Deconstruction of Motherhood', in M. Stanworth (ed.), *Gender, Motherhood and Medicine* (Cambridge: Polity Press, 1987).

Stedman Jones, G. (1971), *Outcast London* (Oxford: Oxford University Press).

Stockman, N., Bonney, N., and Xuewen, S. (1992), 'Women's Work in China, Japan, and Great Britain', *Sociology Review*, 2/1.

Stone, L. (1977), *The Family, Sex, and Marriage in England 1500–1800* (Weidenfeld & Nicolson).

—and Stone, J. F. (1984), *An Open Elite?* (Oxford: Oxford University Press).

Storey, J. (1993), *An Introductory Guide to Cultural Theory and Popular Culture* (Hemel Hempstead: Harvester Wheatsheaf).

—(1995*a*), 'Human Resource Management; Still Marching On, or Marching Out', in Storey (1995*b*).

—(1995*b*) (ed.), *Human Resource Management* (London: Routledge).

Straus, M. A., and Gelles, R. J. (1986), 'Societal Change and Change in Family Violence from 1975 to 1985 as Revealed by Two National Surveys', *Journal of Marriage and the Family*, 48.

Strauss, A. L. (1959), *Mirrors and Masks: The Search for Identity* (London: Martin Robertson, 1977).

—Schatzman, L., Ehrlich, D., Bucher, R., and Sabshin, M. (1963), 'The Hospital and its Negotiated Order', in E. Friedson (ed.), *The Hospital in Modern Society* (New York: Free Press, 1963).

Strinati, D. (1992*a*), 'Post-Modernism: A Theory without Frontiers', *Sociology Review*, 1/4.

—(1992*b*), 'The Taste of America: Americanization and Popular Culture in Britain', in Strinati and Wagg (1992).

—(1995), *An Introduction to Theories of Popular Culture* (London: Routledge).

—and Wagg, S. (1992) (eds.), *Come on Down: Popular Media Culture* (London: Routledge).

Sullivan, H. S. (1939), *Conceptions of Modern Psychiatry* (New York: W. W. Norton, 1947).

Sullivan, O. (1997), 'Time Waits for No WoMan: An Investigation of the Gendered Experience of Domestic Time', *Sociology*, 31/2.

Sutherland, E. H. (1937), *The Professional Thief* (Chicago: University of Chicago Press).

—(1949), *White Collar Crime* (New York: Holt, Rinehart & Winston).

Sweeney, K. (1997), 'Labour Disputes in 1996', *Labour Market Trends*, 105/6 (June).

Szasz, T. (1970), *The Manufacture of Madness* (New York: Harper & Row).

Szreter, S. R. (1984), 'The Genesis of the Registrar-General's Social Classification of Occupations', *British Journal of Sociology*, 25.

Taylor, I., Evans, K., and Fraser, P. (1996), *A Tale of Two Cities: Global Change, Local Feeling, and Everyday Life in the North of England. A Study in Manchester and Sheffield* (London: Routledge).

Therborn, G. (1986), *Why Some People are More Unemployed than Others* (London: Verso).

Thomas, K. (1971), *Religion and the Decline of Magic* (London: Weidenfeld & Nicolson).

Thomas, W. I., and Znaniecki, F. (1918–19), *The Polish Peasant in Europe and America* (New York: Dover Publishing, 1958).

Thompson, E. P. (1963), *The Making of the English Working Class* (Harmondsworth: Penguin).

Thompson, F. M. L. (1963), *English Landed Society in the Nineteenth Century* (London: Routledge & Kegan Paul).

—(1990), *People and their Environment* (The Cambridge Social History of Britain 1750–1950, 2; Cambridge: Cambridge University Press).

Thompson, K. (1982), *Émile Durkheim* (Chichester: Ellis Horwood).

—(1992), 'Religion, Values and Ideology', in R. Bocock and K. Thompson (eds.), *Social and Cultural Forms of Modernity* (Cambridge: Polity Press).

—(1976) (ed.), *Auguste Comte: The Foundations of Sociology* (London: Nelson).

—(1984) (ed.), *Work, Employment and Unemployment: Perspectives on Work and Society* (Milton Keynes: Open University Press).

Thompson, P. (1978), *The Voice of the Past* (Oxford: Oxford University Press).

—(1983), *The Nature of Work: An Introduction to Debates on the Labour Process* (London: Macmillan).

—(1993), 'The Labour Process: Changing Theory, Changing Practice', *Sociology Review*, 3/2.

Thompson, W. S. (1929), 'Population', *American Journal of Sociology*, 34.

Thornley, A. (1992) (ed.), *The Crisis of London* (London: Routledge).

Thornton, S. (1997), 'The Social Logic of Subcultural Capital', in Gelder and Thornton (1997).

Thrasher, F. (1927), *The Gang* (Chicago: University of Chicago Press).

Timmins, N. (1995), 'Can We Afford the Welfare State?', *Independent on Sunday*, 24 September.

Tocqueville, A. de (1835–40), *Democracy in America* (London: Fontana Press, 1994).

Tonnies, F. (1887), *Community and Association* (London: Routledge & Kegan Paul, 1955).

Touraine, A. (1971), *The Post-Industrial Society—Tomorrow's Social History: Classes, Conflicts and Culture in the Programmed Society* (New York: Random House).

—(1981), *The Voice and the Eye: An Analysis of Social Movements* (Cambridge: Cambridge University Press).

Townsend, P. (1963), *The Family Life of Old People* (Harmondsworth: Penguin).

—(1974), 'The Concept of Poverty', in D. Wedderburn (ed.), *Poverty, Inequality and Class Structure* (Cambridge: Cambridge University Press).

—(1979), *Poverty in the United Kingdom* (Harmondsworth: Penguin).

Townsend, P. (1991), 'Living Standards and Health in the Inner Cities', in Macgregor and Pimlott (1991).

——Corrigan, P., and Kowarzik, U. (1987), *Poverty and Labour in London* (London: Low Pay Unit).

Toynbee, P. (1997), 'A New Beginning is the Way to Cure a False Start', *Independent*, 16 October.

Troeltsch, E. (1912), *The Social Teaching of the Christian Churches* (London: George Allen & Unwin, 1931).

Troyna, B., and Carrington, B. (1990), *Education, Racism, and Reform* (London: Routledge).

Tuchman, J. (1981), 'The Symbolic Annihilation of Women by the Mass Media', in S. Cohen and J. Young (eds.), *The Manufacture of News* (London: Constable).

Tunstall, J. (1971), *Journalists at Work* (London: Constable).

——(1995), 'Specialist Correspondents: Goals, Careers, Roles', in Boyd-Barrett and Newbold (1995).

——(1996), *Newspaper Power: The New National Press in Britain* (Oxford: Clarendon Press).

Turner, B. (1986), *Equality* (Chichester: Ellis Horwood).

——(1991), *Religion and Social Theory* (2nd edn., London: Routledge).

——(1996), *The Body and Society* (2nd edn., London: Sage).

Turner, H. A., Clack, G., and Roberts, G. (1967), *Labour Relations in the Motor Industry* (London: Allen & Unwin).

Turner, R. (1962), 'Role-Taking: Process versus Conformity', in A. Rose (ed.), *Human Behaviour and Social Processes* (London: Routledge & Kegan Paul).

Twigg, J. (1983), 'Vegetarianism and the Eating of Meat', in A. Murcott (ed.), *The Sociology of Food and Eating* (Aldershot: Gower).

United Nations Centre for Human Settlements (1996), *An Urbanizing World: Global Report on Human Settlements* (Oxford: Oxford University Press).

United Nations Development Programme (1996), *Human Development Report* (Oxford: Oxford University Press).

United Nations Population Fund (1996), *The State of World Population* (New York: UNFPA).

Urry, J. (1981), *The Anatomy of Capitalist Societies* (London: Macmillan).

Useem, M. (1984), *The Inner Circle* (New York: Oxford University Press).

Valentine, G. (1992), 'Women's Fear and the Design of Public Space', *Built Environment*, 16/4.

Vigne, T., and Howkins, A. (1977), 'The Small Shopkeeper in Industrial and Market Towns', in Crossick (1977).

Vincent, J. A. (1995), *Inequality and Old Age* (London: UCL Press).

Vogler, C., and Pahl, J. (1993), 'Social and Economic Change and the Organization of Money within Marriage', *Work, Employment, and Society*, 7/1.

Waddington, I. (1973), 'The Role of the Hospital in the Development of Modern Medicine', *Sociology*, 7.

Waddington, P. A. J. (1996), 'Public Order Policing: Citizenship and Moral Ambiguity', in Leishman, Loveday, and Savage (1996).

Wagg, S. (1994), 'Politics and the Media in Postwar Britain', *Sociology Review*, 4/2.

Walby, S. (1986), *Patriarchy at Work* (Cambridge: Polity Press).

——(1990), *Theorizing Patriarchy* (Oxford: Basil Blackwell).

Wallerstein, I. (1974), 'The Rise and Future Demise of the World Capitalist System: Concepts for Comparative Analysis', *Comparative Studies in Society and History*, 16.

Wallis, R. (1976), *The Road to Total Freedom* (London: Heinemann).

——(1984), *Elementary Forms of the New Religious Life* (London: Routledge & Kegan Paul).

——and Bruce, S. (1992), 'Secularization: The Orthodox Model', in S. Bruce (ed.), *Religion and Modernization: Sociologists and Historians Debate the Secularization Thesis* (Oxford: Oxford University Press).

Wallman, S. (1993), 'Reframing Context; Pointers to the Post-Industrial City', in Cohen and Fukui (1993).

Walsh, D. (1986), *Heavy Business: Commercial Burglary and Robbery* (London: Routledge & Kegan Paul).

Walvin, J. (1993), *Black Ivory: A History of British Slavery* (London: Fontana).

Warde, A. (1991), 'Gentrification as Consumption: Issues of Class and Gender', *Society and Space*, 9: 2.

——and Hetherington, K. (1993), 'A Changing Domestic Division of Labour? Issues of Measurement and Interpretation', *Work, Employment and Society*, 7/1.

Warner, W. L. (1936), 'American Class and Caste', *American Journal of Sociology* 42.

——(1953), *American Life: Dream and Reality* (Chicago: University of Chicago Press).

——and Lunt, P. S. (1941), *The Social Life of a Modern Community* (New Haven, Conn.: Yale University Press).

Warr, P. (1983), 'Job Loss, Unemployment and Psychological Well-Being', in E. Van De Vliet and V. Allen (eds.), *Role Transitions* (New York: Plenum Press).

Warren, C. A. B., and Rasmussen, P. K. (1977), 'Sex and Gender in Field Research', *Urban Life*, 6.

Waters, M. (1995), *Globalization* (London: Routledge).

Watson, S. (1992), 'Femocratic Feminisms', in Savage and Witz (1992).

——and Gibson K. (1995) (eds.), *Postmodern Cities and Spaces* (Oxford: Blackwell).

Webb, B., and Webb, S. (1932), *Methods of Social Study* (London: Longmans Green).

Weber, Marianne. (1926), *Max Weber: A Biography* (New York: 1975).

Weber, Max (1904), ' "Objectivity" in Social Science and Social Policy', in Max Weber, *The Methodology of the Social Sciences* (New York: Free Press, 1949).

——(1904–5), *The Protestant Ethic and the Spirit of Capitalism* (London: George Allen & Unwin, 1930).

——(1914), 'The Economy and the Arena of Normative and De Facto Powers', in Weber, *Economy and Society*, ed. G. Roth and C. Wittich (Berkeley and Los Angeles: University of California Press, 1968).

——(1915), *The Religion of China* (New York: Macmillan, 1951).

——(1916), *The Religion of India* (New York: Macmillan, 1958).

——(1919) 'Politics as a Vocation', in *From Max Weber: Essays in Sociology*, ed. H. H. Gerth and C. W. Mills (London: Routledge & Kegan Paul, 1948).

——(1920), 'Conceptual Exposition', in Weber, *Economy and Society* ed. G. Roth and C. Wittich (Berkeley and Los Angeles: University of California Press, 1968).

Webster, D. (1995), *Why Freud Was Wrong* (London: Fontana).

Wedderburn, D., and Crompton, R. (1972), *Workers' Attitudes and Technology* (Cambridge: Cambridge University Press).

Weeks, J. (1986), *Sexuality* (London: Tavistock).

——(1991), *Sex, Politics, and Society* (2nd edn., London: Longman).

Weiner, G. (1986), 'Feminist Education and Equal Opportunities: Unity or Discord?', *British Journal of Sociology of Education*, 7.

——Arnot, M., and David, M. (1997), 'Is the Future Female? Female Success, Male Disadvantage, and Changing Gender Patterns in Education', in Halsey *et al.* (1997).

Weiner, M. J. (1981), *English Culture and the Decline of the Entrepreneurial Spirit* (Harmondsworth: Pengion, 1985).

Wellings, K., Field, J., Johnson, A., and Wadsworth, J. (1994), *Sexual Behaviour in Britain: The National Survey of Sexual Attitudes and Lifestyles* (Harmondsworth: Penguin).

Werbner, P. (1988), 'Taking and Giving: Working Women and Female Bonds In a Pakistani Immigrant Neighbourhood', in Westwood and Bhachu (1988*b*).

Westergaard, J. H., and Resler, H. (1975), *Class in a Capitalist Society* (London: Heinemann).

Westwood, S. (1984), *All Day, Every Day: Factory and Family in the Making of Women's Lives* (London: Pluto).

——and Bhachu, P. (1988*a*) 'Images and Realities', *New Society*, 6 May.

————(1988*b*) (eds.), *Enterprising Women: Ethnicity, Economy, and Gender Relations* (London: Routledge).

——and Williams, J. (1997) (eds.), *Imagining Cities: Scripts, Signs, and Meanings* (London: Routledge).

Wheelock, J. (1990), *Husbands at Home: The Domestic Economy in a Post-Industrial Society* (London: Routledge).

White, S. (1991), *Gorbachev and After* (Cambridge: Cambridge University Press).

Whitelegg, E., Arnot, A., Bartels, E., Beechey, V., Birke, L., Himmelweit, S., Leonard, D., Ruehl, S., and Speakman, M. (1982), *The Changing Experience of Women*, (Oxford: Basil Blackwell).

Whiteside, T., Sutton, A., and Everton, T. (1992) (eds.), *16–19 Changes in Education and Training* (London: David Fulton Publishers).

Wickens, P. (1987), *The Road to Nissan* (London: Macmillan).

Wiener, M. (1980), *English Culture and the Decline of the Industrial Spirit 1850–1980* (Cambridge: Cambridge University Press).

Wilensky, H. (1975), *The Welfare State and Equality: Structural and Ideological Roots of Public Expenditure* (Berkeley and Los Angeles: University of California Press).

Williams, G. (1994), *Britain's Media: How They Are Related* (London: Campaign for Press and Broadcasting Freedom).

Williams, K., Mitsui, I., and Haslam, C. (1994), 'How far from Japan? A Case Study of Japanese Press Shop Practice and Management Calculation', in Elger and Smith (1994).

Williams, M., and May, T. (1996), *An Introduction to the Philosophy of Social Research* (London: UCL Press).

Williams, R. (1961), *The Long Revolution* (Harmondsworth: Penguin).

——(1983), 'British Film History: New Perspectives', in Curran and Porter (1983).

Willis, P. (1977), *Learning to Labour: How Working Class Kids Get Working Class Jobs* (Farnborough: Saxon House).

Willmott, P. (1986), *Social Networks, Informal Care and Public Policy* (London: Policy Studies Institute).

——(1988), 'Urban Kinship Past and Present', *Social Studies Review* 4/2.

——and Hutchison, R. (1992) (eds.), *Urban Trends 1: A Report on Britain's Deprived Urban Areas* (London: Policy Studies Institute).

——and Young, M. (1960), *Family and Class in a London Suburb* (London: Routledge & Kegan Paul).

Wilson, B. R. (1966), *Religion in Secular Society* (Harmondsworth: Penguin, 1969).

——(1976), *Contemporary Transformations of Religion* (Oxford: Oxford University Press).

Wilson, E. (1995), 'The Invisible *Flâneur*', in Watson and Gibson (1995).

Wilson, W. J. (1987), *The Truly Disadvantaged* (Chicago: University of Chicago Press).

Winnicott, D. W. (1965), *The Family and Individual Development* (London: Tavistock).

Winship, J. (1987), *Inside Women's Magazines* (London: Pandora).

Winter, K., and Connolly, P. (1996) ' "Keeping it in the Family": Thatcherism and the Children Act 1989', in Pilcher and Wagg (1996).

Wirth, L. (1938), 'Urbanism as a Way of Life', *American Journal of Sociology*, 44/1.

Witz, A. (1992), *Professions and Patriarchy* (London: Routledge).

——and Savage, M. (1992), 'The Gender of Organizations', in Savage and Witz (1992).

Wolf, N. (1991), *The Beauty Myth: How Images of Beauty are Used against Women* (New York: Wm. Morrow).

Wolff, J. (1990), 'Feminism and Modernism', in Wolff, *Feminine Sentences: Essays on Women and Culture* (Berkeley and Los Angeles: University of California Press).

Wolff, K. H. (1950), *The Sociology of Georg Simmel* (New York: Free Press).

Wood, S. (1989), 'The Transformation of Work', in S. Wood (ed.), *The Transformation of Work: Skill, Flexibility and the Labour Process* (London: Unwin Hyman).

Woodhead, M., and Mcgrath, A. (1988) (eds.), *Family, School, and Society: A Reader* (London: Hodder & Stoughton).

Wright, C. (1988), 'School Processes: An Ethnographic Study', in Dale *et al.* (1988).

Wright, E. O. (1985), *Classes* (London: Verso).

——(1997), *Class Counts* (Cambridge: Cambridge University Press).

Wrong, D. (1961), 'The Oversocialized Concept of Man in Modern Sociology', *American Sociological Review*, 26.

Yearley, S. (1991), *The Green Case: A Sociology of Environmental Issues, Arguments, and Politics* (Routledge: London).

Young, J. (1971), *The Drugtakers* (London: McGibbon & Kee).

Young, M. (1958), *The Rise of the Meritocracy 1870–2033: An Essay on Education and Equality* (London: Thames and Hudson).

Young, M., and Willmott, P. (1957), *Family and Kinship in East London* (London: Routledge & Kegan Paul).

———(1973), *The Symmetrical Family: A Study of Work and Leisure in the London Region* (London: Routledge & Kegan Paul).

Zeitlin, M. R. (1989), *The Large Corporation and the Capitalist Class* (Cambridge: Polity Press).

Zola, I. K. (1975), 'Medicine as an Institution of Social Control'. in C. Cox and A. Mead (eds.), *A Sociology of Medical Practice* (New York: Collier-Macmillan).

Zukin, S. (1995), *The Culture of Cities* (Oxford: Blackwell).

Zweig, F. (1948), *Men in the Pits* (London: Victor Gollancz).

———(1961), *The Worker in an Affluent Society* (London: Heinemann).

Index

Numbers in orange indicate the page where the main discussion of the entry can be found.

List of Figures

There is often some ambiguity about the names used for particular societies and some clarification of our usage may be helpful. We follow the usual convention in sociology by using the terms 'British society' and 'Britain' to refer to the United Kingdom as a whole. Statistics often relate, however, to one or more parts of the United Kingdom and it is important to be clear about where they refer to. 'England and Wales' form a single unit for many official statistical purposes. Some statistics relate to 'Great Britain', which means England, Wales, and Scotland but not Northern Ireland. The 'United Kingdom' refers to Great Britain and Northern Ireland. We normally use the term 'European Union' to refer to the countries formerly called the 'European Community' or the 'EEC', except where we make historical references and use the earlier terms. The United States of America is generally referred to as the 'United States'.

Acknowledgements

A great many people have helped in various ways with the production of this book. As deadlines have approached—and passed—our families have had to put up with us disappearing off to work on the latest draft, and our colleagues have had to tolerate our inattention to Departmental matters. Tim Barton at Oxford University Press has been immensely supportive, and patient, and has orchestrated the whole process with great efficiency. More recently, Angela Griffin and Hilary Walford have done their best to cope with fractious authors. A number of people have been kind enough to comment on draft materials over the years that we have been writing the book. Some of these are unknown to us, as their anonymous comments were passed on by the publishers. We are, however, grateful to them all for their comments and suggestions. We would like to acknowledge the help of those who we were able to cajole into reading chapters and providing us with the benefit of their specialist knowledge: Jane Clarke, Rosemary Crompton, Miriam Glucksmann, Geoff Hurd, Nick Jewson, Marsha Jones, Derek Layder, Jane Pilcher, Ken Plummer, Susie Scott, Nigel South, Dominic Strinati, and many others who did not, perhaps, realize quite why we were picking their brains.

James Fulcher and John Scott

Picture Credits

The authors and publishers are grateful to the following for kind permission to reproduce photographs:

Advertising Archives: p. 295, p. 671.

Karin Albinsson: p. 6, p. 126 (bottom left), p. 513, p. 539, p. 550, p. 585.

David Austin: cartoon, p. 716.

Bibliothèque Nationale, Paris: p. 36.

Bildarchiv Preussischer Kulturbesitz: p. 41, portrait of Max Weber © Bildarchive Preussischer Kulturbesitz, Berlin.

Bridgeman Art Library: p. 27, portrait of Auguste Comte by Tony Touillion, Bridgeman Art Library/Bibliothèque Nationale, Paris.

Jan Chlebik: p. 561 (right).

The Guardian: p. 347, p. 717.

Hulton Getty Picture Collection: p. 31, p. 200, p. 241, p. 288, p. 524, p. 555, p. 570, p. 618, p. 622.

Jonathan I. Murray: p. 12, p. 126 (top and bottom right), p. 155, p. 176, p. 182, p. 360, p. 453, p. 515, p. 603, p. 684 (right), p. 726, p. 755.

PA News: p. 11, p. 170, p. 224, . 253, p. 382, p. 407, p. 436, p. 450, p. 486, p. 581, p. 600, p. 679, p. 688 (left), p. 702, p. 721, p. 752.

Panos Pictures: p. 480.

Pictorial Press Ltd: p. 177, p. 274. © Polgram/Pictorial Press.

Pitt Rivers Museum, University of Oxford: p. 86.

Andrew Thompson: p. 94, p. 378, p. 439.

Geoff Thomson: cartoon, p. 734.

Tony Stone Images: p. 188, p. 316, p. 320, p. 346, p. 471, p. 476, p. 490, p. 598, p. 670.

Topham Picturepoint: p. 740.

United Colors of Benetton: p. 296.

Marshall Walker: p. 204, p. 415, p. 519, p. 525.

Sharron Wallace: p. 139.

Every effort has been made to locate the copyright owners of material used in this book, but if any have been inadvertently overlooked the publishers will be pleased to make the necessary arrangements at the first opportunity.